CC5K6 Strategies for crisis prevention and intervention.
CC5K7 Strategies for preparing individuals to live harmoniously and productively in a culturally diverse world.
CC5K8 Ways to create learning environments that allow individuals to retain and appreciate their own and each others' respective language and cultural heritage.
CC5K9 Ways specific cultures are negatively stereotyped.
CC5K10 Strategies used by diverse populations to cope with a legacy of former and continuing racism

Skills:

CC5S1 Create a safe, equitable, positive, and supportive learning environment in which diversities are valued.
CC5S2 Identify realistic expectations for personal and social behavior in various settings.
CC5S3 Identify supports needed for integration into various program placements.
CC5S4 Design learning environments that encourage active participation in individual and group activities.
CC5S5 Modify the learning environment to manage behaviors.
CC5S6 Use performance data and information from all stakeholders to make or suggest modifications in learning environments.
CC5S7 Establish and maintain rapport with individuals with and without exceptional learning needs.
CC5S8 Teach self-advocacy.
CC5S9 Create an environment that encourages self-advocacy and increased independence.
CC5S10 Use effective and varied behavior management strategies.
CC5S11 Use the least intensive behavior management strategy consistent with the needs of the individual with exceptional learning needs.
CC5S12 Design and manage daily routines.
CC5S13 Organize, develop, and sustain learning environments that support positive intracultural and intercultural experiences.
CC5S14 Mediate controversial intercultural issues among students within the learning environment in ways that enhance any culture, group, or person.
CC5S15 Structure, direct, and support the activities of paraeducators, volunteers, and tutors.
CC5S16 Use universal precautions.

Special Education Content Standard #6: Communication

Knowledge:

CC6K1 Effects of cultural and linguistic differences on growth and development.
CC6K2 Characteristics of one's own culture and use of language and the ways in which these can differ from other cultures and uses of languages.
CC6K3 Ways of behaving and communicating among cultures that can lead to misinterpretation and misunderstanding.
CC6K4 Augmentative and assistive communication strategies.

Skills:

CC6S1 Use strategies to support and enhance communication skills of individuals with exceptional learning needs.
CC6S2 Use communication strategies and resources to facilitate understanding of subject matter for students whose primary language is not the dominant language.

Special Education Content Standard #7: Instructional Planning

Knowledge:

CC7K1 Theories and research that form the basis of curriculum development and instructional practice.
CC7K2 Scope and sequences of general and special curricula.
CC7K3 National, state or provincial, and local curricula standards.
CC7K4 Technology for planning and managing the teaching and learning environment.
CC7K5 Roles and responsibilities of the paraeducator related to instruction, intervention, and direct service.

Skills:

CC7S1 Identify and prioritize areas of the general curriculum and accommodations for individuals with exceptional learning needs.
CC7S2 Develop and implement comprehensive, longitudinal individualized programs in collaboration with team members.
CC7S3 Involve the individual and family in setting instructional goals and monitoring progress.
CC7S4 Use functional assessments to develop intervention plans.
CC7S5 Use task analysis.
CC7S6 Sequence, implement, and evaluate individualized learning objectives.
CC7S7 Integrate affective, social, and life skills with academic curricula.
CC7S8 Develop and select instructional content, resources, and strategies that respond to cultural, linguistic, and gender differences.
CC7S9 Incorporate and implement instructional and assistive technology into the educational program.
CC7S10 Prepare lesson plans.
CC7S11 Prepare and organize materials to implement daily lesson plans.
CC7S12 Use instructional time effectively.
CC7S13 Make responsive adjustments to instruction based on continual observations.
CC7S14 Prepare individuals to exhibit self-enhancing behavior in response to societal attitudes and actions.

Special Education Content Standard #8: Assessment

Knowledge:

CC8K1 Basic terminology used in assessment.
CC8K2 Legal provisions and ethical principles regarding assessment of individuals.
CC8K3 Screening, pre-referral, referral, and classification procedures.
CC8K4 Use and limitations of assessment instruments.
CC8K5 National, state or provincial, and local accommodations and modifications.

Skills:

CC8S1 Gather relevant background information.

CC8S2 Administer nonbiased formal and informal assessments.

CC8S3 Use technology to conduct assessments.

CC8S4 Develop or modify individualized assessment strategies.

CC8S5 Interpret information from formal and informal assessments.

CC8S6 Use assessment information in making eligibility, program, and placement decisions for individuals with exceptional learning needs, including those from culturally and/or linguistically diverse backgrounds.

CC8S7 Report assessment results to all stakeholders using effective communication skills.

CC8S8 Evaluate instruction and monitor progress of individuals with exceptional learning needs.

CC8S9 Create and maintain records.

Special Education Content Standard #9: Professional and Ethical Practice

Knowledge:

CC9K1 Personal cultural biases and differences that affect one's teaching.

CC9K2 Importance of the teacher serving as a model for individuals with exceptional learning needs.

CC9K3 Continuum of lifelong professional development.

CC9K4 Methods to remain current regarding research-validated practice.

Skills:

CC9S1 Practice within the CEC Code of Ethics and other standards of the profession.

CC9S2 Uphold high standards of competence and integrity and exercise sound judgment in the practice of the professional.

CC9S3 Act ethically in advocating for appropriate services.

CC9S4 Conduct professional activities in compliance with applicable laws and policies.

CC9S5 Demonstrate commitment to developing the highest education and quality-of-life potential of individuals with exceptional learning needs.

CC9S6 Demonstrate sensitivity for the culture, language, religion, gender, disability, socio-economic status, and sexual orientation of individuals.

CC9S7 Practice within one's skill limit and obtain assistance as needed.

CC9S8 Use verbal, nonverbal, and written language effectively.

CC9S9 Conduct self-evaluation of instruction.

CC9S10 Access information on exceptionalities.

CC9S11 Reflect on one's practice to improve instruction and guide professional growth.

CC9S12 Engage in professional activities that benefit individuals with exceptional learning needs, their families, and one's colleagues.

Special Education Content Standard #10: Collaboration

Knowledge:

CC10K1 Models and strategies of consultation and collaboration.

CC10K2 Roles of individuals with exceptional learning needs, families, and school and community personnel in planning of an individualized program.

CC10K3 Concerns of families of individuals with exceptional learning needs and strategies to help address these concerns.

CC10K4 Culturally responsive factors that promote effective communication and collaboration with individuals with exceptional learning needs, families, school personnel, and community members.

Skills:

CC10S1 Maintain confidential communication about individuals with exceptional learning needs.

CC10S2 Collaborate with families and others in assessment of individuals with exceptional learning needs.

CC10S3 Foster respectful and beneficial relationships between families and professionals.

CC10S4 Assist individuals with exceptional learning needs and their families in becoming active participants in the educational team.

CC10S5 Plan and conduct collaborative conferences with individuals with exceptional learning needs and their families.

CC10S6 Collaborate with school personnel and community members in integrating individuals with exceptional learning needs into various settings.

CC10S7 Use group problem-solving skills to develop, implement, and evaluate collaborative activities.

CC10S8 Model techniques and coach others in the use of instructional methods and accommodations.

CC10S9 Communicate with school personnel about the characteristics and needs of individuals with exceptional learning needs.

CC10S10 Communicate effectively with families of individuals with exceptional learning needs from diverse backgrounds.

CC10S11 Observe, evaluate, and provide feedback to paraeducators.

continues on back inside cover

NINTH EDITION

EXCEPTIONAL CHILDREN

An Introduction to Special Education

WILLIAM L. HEWARD

The Ohio State University

Merrill
is an imprint of

Upper Saddle River, New Jersey
Columbus, Ohio

Library of Congress Cataloging-in-Publication Data

Heward, William L.,
   Exceptional children : an introduction to special education / William L. Heward.—9th
ed.
     p. cm.
   Includes bibliographical references and index.
   ISBN-13: 978-0-13-514436-7
   ISBN-10: 0-13-514436-1
  1. Special education—United States.   2. Exceptional children—United States.   I.
Title.
   LC3981.H49 2009
   371.90973—dc22   2007031288

Vice President and Executive Publisher: Jeffery W. Johnston
Senior Editor: Ann Castel Davis
Senior Development Editor: Heather Doyle Fraser
Senior Managing Editor: Pamela D. Bennett
Senior Project Manager: Mary M. Irvin
Senior Editorial Assistant: Penny Burleson
Design Coordinator: Diane C. Lorenzo
Cover Designer: Candace Rowley
Cover Image: Katelyn Metzger
Photo Coordinator: Lori Whitley
Operations Specialist: Laura Messerly
Director of Marketing: Quinn Perkson
Marketing Manager: Erica DeLuca
Marketing Coordinator: Brian Mounts
Photo and Text Credits: See the page following the index.

This book was set in Garamond Book by S4Carlisle Publishing Services. It was printed and bound by
Quebecor Printing Corp. The cover was printed by Phoenix Color Corp.

Pearson Education Ltd., London   Pearson Education Australia Pty, Limited
Pearson Education Singapore Pte. Ltd.   Pearson Education North Asia Ltd., Hong Kong
Pearson Education Canada, Inc.   Pearson Educación de Mexico, S.A. de C.V.
Pearson Education—Japan   Pearson Education Malaysia Pte. Ltd.
                                     Pearson Education Upper Saddle River, New Jersey

Merrill
is an imprint of

10 9 8 7 6 5 4 3 2 1
ISBN 13: 978-0-13-514436-7
ISBN 10:   0-13-514436-1

In memory of Rodney A. Cavanaugh
A truly special educator

ABOUT THE AUTHOR

WILLIAM LEE HEWARD is Emeritus Professor of Education at The Ohio State University. He majored in psychology and sociology as an undergraduate at Western Michigan University, earned his doctorate in special education at the University of Massachusetts, and joined the special education faculty at Ohio State in 1975. Bill has served as a Senior Fulbright Lecturer in Special Education in Portugal and Visiting Professor of Psychology at Keio University in Tokyo. Among the many honors he has received are Ohio State University's highest recognition of teaching excellence, the Alumni Association's Distinguished Teaching Award, and the American Psychological Association's Division 25 Fred S. Keller Behavioral Education Award for lifetime achievements in education.

Dr. Heward's current research interests include "low-tech" methods for increasing the effectiveness of group instruction and adaptations of curriculum and instruction that promote the generalization and maintenance of newly learned knowledge and skills. Bill's publications include seven other textbooks and more than 100 journal articles and book chapters. His research has appeared in the field's leading peer-reviewed journals, including *Behavioral Disorders, Education and Training in Developmental Disabilities, Exceptional Children, Learning Disabilities Research & Practice, Research in Developmental Disabilities, Teacher Education and Special Education, Teaching Exceptional Children*, and *The Journal of Special Education*.

Bill has also written for the popular market. His book *Some Are Called Clowns* (Crowell, 1974) chronicled his five summers as a pitcher for the Indianapolis Clowns, the last of the barnstorming baseball teams.

PREFACE

Special education is an ongoing story of people. It is the story of a preschool child with multiple disabilities who benefits from early intervention services. It is the story of a child with intellectual disabilities whose parents and teachers work together to ensure she participates in classroom and extracurricular activities with her peers. It is the story of a middle school student with learning disabilities who helps his parents and teachers plan an instructional program that builds on his strengths and addresses his weaknesses. It is the story of the gifted and talented child who brings new insights to old problems, the high school student with cerebral palsy who is learning English as his second language, and the young woman with visual impairments who has recently moved into her own apartment and rides a city bus to work. Special education is also the story of the parents and families of exceptional children and of the teachers and other professionals who work with them.

I hope you will find the ninth edition of *Exceptional Children* an informative, accessible, and interesting introduction to the ongoing story of special education. Whether you are an undergraduate in a preservice teacher training program or a general education teacher with years of experience, I encourage you to continue your study and involvement with children and adults with special needs.

Text Organization and Structure

My primary goals for the ninth edition remain the same as for previous editions: to present an informative and responsible introduction to the professional practices, trends, and research that define contemporary special education while also conveying the diversity and excitement of this changing field. The book begins with "A Personal View of Special Education"—ten perspectives on the purpose and responsibilities of special education—followed by fifteen chapters organized into three parts.

Part I, Foundations for Understanding Special Education, includes three chapters. Chapter 1 presents an overview of terminology, laws, policies, and practices that are consistent with the Individuals with Disabilities Education Act (IDEA) and the exceptional child's right to receive a free, appropriate education in the least restrictive environment. Chapter 2 describes regulations and best practices concerning the referral, assessment, program planning, and placement of students with special education needs. Chapter 3 discusses the important role parents and families play in the decision-making process for addressing the educational needs of their children and how special educators can form effective partnerships with parents from culturally and linguistically diverse backgrounds.

Part II, Educational Needs of Exceptional Students, contains ten categorical chapters of exceptionality. Chapters 4 through 13 describe the definitions, characteristics, prevalence, causes, historical background, assessment techniques, educational approaches, and placement alternatives, and for specific categories of special education needs, including giftedness and talent.

Part III, Special Education Across the Life Span, explains the role of special education during two critical periods in the lives of exceptional children. Chapter 14 examines early childhood special education and the important role early intervention plays in nurturing the development of young children with special needs and those who are at risk for acquiring disabilities. Chapter 15 discusses transition from secondary school and the responsibility educators and parents share in preparing students with disabilities for adulthood.

The story of special education is written every day by teachers across the country serving the needs of all children in a variety of settings. The stories of some of these exceptional teachers are included in these pages. The work of these educators is reflected in the narrative and the features of this text and shows how special and general educators can promote student achievement by using research-based instructional strategies.

Featured Teacher Essays Each chapter begins with a first-person essay by master teachers that reflects the joys, challenges, and realities of teaching exceptional children. Drawn from urban, suburban, and rural school districts across the country, the 18 featured teachers share personal experiences and wisdom gathered from years of instructing children in a variety of school settings. Nine of these teachers and their students are also featured on video clips included in the MyEducationLab course that accompanies this text.

After reading this chapter, complete the pretest for Chapter 14 on MyEducationLab to assess your initial understanding of chapter content.

MyEducationLab Access to MyEducationLab for this text allows readers to see, hear, and learn from the teachers featured in the text through video. Throughout the book, MyEducationLab icons connect key content and concepts practiced by master teachers to Homework & Exercises on MyEducationLab at www.myeducationlab.com.

Tips for Beginning Teachers Each chapter culminates with practical, quick tips for beginning teachers on how to enhance student learning and avoid common pitfalls in the classroom. These suggestions, offered by the master teacher(s) featured in the chapter, range from tips for successful co-teaching and collaboration with families, to finding a mentor, learning about students' cultures, becoming student advocates, and celebrating each student's accomplishments, no matter how small.

Teaching & Learning Features The foundation of special education, without which everything would fall apart, is good instruction provided by teachers, day in and day out. To inform you of the critical elements of good instruction and provide numerous examples of application, each chapter includes two Teaching & Learning features that describe a wide range of effective teaching interventions. From classroom management and peer support strategies for inclusion to curriculum modifications and suggestions for creating multimedia activity schedules for children, these boxes provide clear and practical guidelines for designing, implementing, and evaluating instruction for students with disabilities. All of the strategies described in the Teaching & Learning features are classroom-tested and supported by scientific research documenting their effectiveness. Furthermore, each Teaching & Learning feature includes a step-by-step "How to Get Started" section for implementing the strategy in the classroom. Here is a sampling of the topics covered across the text:

- It's Good to Go Fast! Fluency-Building Activities to Promote Student Achievement
- Guided Notes: Helping All Students Succeed in the General Education Curriculum
- "Look, I'm All Finished!" Recruiting Teacher Attention
- Let's Make Some Noise! Using Choral Responding to Improve the Effectiveness of Instruction
- Classwide Peer Tutoring: Collaborative Learning for Students with Disabilities in Inclusive Classrooms
- Using Response Cards to Increase Participation and Achievement
- The Power of Teacher Praise
- From Unwanted Obsession to Motivational Key: Using the Special Interests Areas of Children with Asperger Syndrome to Unlock the Curriculum

Go to the Homework & Exercises section in Chapter 4 of MyEducationLab and complete Homework Exercise 5. As you watch the video and answer the accompanying questions, think about how using response cards can vary from elementary to middle school level.

MyEducationLab Each of the research-based practices discussed in the Teaching & Learning features of the text are connected to Homework & Exercises and Building Teaching Skills in MyEducationLab at www.myeducationlab.com. These activities extend and further develop the strategies discussed in the text through video, artifacts, or research-based articles. Look for the MyEducationLab icon at the end of each feature on how to access this rich learning environment.

Current Issues and Future Trends Boxes Current Issues and Future Trends essays highlight the ever-changing nature of special education, with its controversial issues, triumphs, struggles, and profiles of interventions involved in special education. For example, in "Self-Determination: The Most Natural Support" (Chapter 4), Michael Wehmeyer discusses the importance of self-determination for students with intellectual disabilities. In "The Autism Wars" (Chapter 7), Catherine Maurice, author of the international best-seller *Let Me Hear Your Voice*, describes the enormous difficulties parents of children with autism face in choosing scientifically tested treatments from the many myths, fads, and miracle cures that surround autism. And in "What Happened to Functional Curriculum?" (Chapter 12), Belva Collins explains how requiring students with severe disabilities to perform well on assessments aligned with general education curriculum standards can have the unintended outcome of reducing those students' opportunities to learn needed skills for functioning in their current and future environments.

Monitoring Student Progress

Content Standards for Beginning Teachers—Common Core: Evaluate instruction and monitor progress of individuals with exceptional learning needs (CC8S8).

FUTURE PREPARATION FOR TEACHER CERTIFICATION

CEC Performance-Based Standards Although special education teacher certification and licensure requirements vary from state to state, all special educators are expected to demonstrate a common set of competencies. The Council for Exceptional Children's (CEC) Performance-Based Standards for Beginning Special Education Teachers is a comprehensive set of knowledge and skill standards organized within 10 domain areas (e.g., Foundations, Individual Learning Differences, Instructional Strategies, Assessment). The CEC Standards were developed in collaboration with the Interstate New Teacher Assessment and Support Consortium (INTASC) and serve as the basis for curriculum content of teacher preparation programs approved by the National Council for the Accreditation of Teacher Education (NCATE). Individual teachers can use the standards as a guide for assessing their own progress as professionals (Crutchfield, 2003).

The Common Core standards are printed on the inside front cover of the text. Margin notes throughout the text link critical content to specific knowledge and skill statements from CEC's Performance-Based Standards for Beginning Teachers. Look for margin notes such as the one shown here with the CEC icon.

Coverage of PRAXIS II Tests The PRAXIS II™ tests—the Subject Assessment/Specialty Area Tests of the PRAXIS Series of Professional Assessments for Beginning Teachers™—assess students' knowledge of content standards. Many states require a passing score on one or more PRAXIS II tests for licensure or certification as a special education teacher. A PRAXIS Study Grid in the Appendix shows where content areas of the PRAXIS II Test, Education of Exceptional Students, are discussed in the text. A listing of the PRAXIS Special Education Core Principles is on the inside back cover of this text.

"Teacher educators who are developing pedagogies for the analysis of teaching and learning contend that analyzing teaching artifacts has three advantages: it enables new teachers time for reflection while still using the real materials of practice; it provides new teachers with experience thinking about and approaching the complexity of the classroom; and in some cases, it can help new teachers and teacher educators develop a shared understanding and common language about teaching. . . ." [1]

As Darling-Hammond and Bransford point out, grounding teacher education in real classrooms—among real teachers and students and among actual examples of students' and teachers' work—is an important, and perhaps even an essential, part of training teachers for the complexities of teaching today's students in today's classrooms. For a number of years, we at Pearson have heard the same message from you as we have learned about the goals of your courses and the challenges you face in teaching the next generation of educators. Working with our authors and many of you, we have created a website to provide the sample classrooms and student work that research on teacher education tells us is so important. Through authentic in-class video footage, interactive simulations, rich case studies, examples of authentic teacher and student work, and more, MyEducationLab offers you and your students a uniquely valuable teacher education tool.

MyEducationLab is easy to use! In the textbook, look for the MyEducationLab logo in the margins and at the end of each Teaching & Learning feature and follow the simple link instructions to access the multimedia *Individualized Study Plan, Homework & Exercises*, and *Building Teaching Skills* assignments in MyEducationLab that correspond with the chapter content.

- **Individualized Study Plan:** You have the opportunity to take pre- and post-tests before and after reading each chapter of the text. The test results automatically generate a personalized study plan for you, identifying areas of the chapter that you should reread to fully understand chapter concepts. You are also presented with interactive multimedia exercises to help ensure your learning. The study plan is designed to help you perform well on exams and to promote deep understanding of chapter content.

- **Homework & Exercises:** These activities offer opportunities to understand content more deeply and to practice applying content. Each Homework Exercise is explicitly connected to chapter content.

- **Building Teaching Skills:** These assignments help you practice and strengthen skills that are essential to quality teaching through your critical analysis and response to student and teacher artifacts and authentic classroom videos.

The rich, authentic, and interactive elements that support the Individualized Study Plan, the Homework & Exercises and the Building Teaching Skills you will encounter throughout MyEducationLab include:

- **Video:** The authentic classroom videos in MyEducationLab show how real teachers handle actual classroom situations.

- **Simulations:** Created by the IRIS Center at Vanderbilt University, these interactive simulations give you hands-on practice at adapting instruction for a full spectrum of learners.

- **Readings:** Specially selected, topically relevant articles from ASCD's renowned *Educational Leadership* journal expand and enrich your perspectives on key issues and topics.

---

[1] Darling-Hammond, l., & Bransford, J., Eds. (2005). *Preparing Teachers for a Changing World*. San Francisco: John Wiley & Sons.

- **Student & Teacher Artifacts:** Authentic preK-12 student and teacher classroom artifacts are tied to course topics and offer you practice in working with the actual types of materials you will encounter daily as teachers.
- **Case Studies:** A diverse set of robust cases illustrate the realities of teaching and offer valuable perspectives on common issues and challenges in education.

Other Resources

- **Lesson & Portfolio Builders:** With this effective and easy-to-use tool, you can create, update, and share standards-based lesson plans and portfolios.
- **News Articles:** Looking for current issues in education? Our collection offers quick access to hundreds of relevant articles from the New York Times Educational News Feed.

Visit **www.myeducationlab.com** for a demonstration of this exciting new online teaching resource.

Instructor's Manual and Online Instructor's Manual

An expanded and improved Instructor's Manual includes numerous recommendations for presenting and extending text content. The manual consists of focus questions that cover the essential concepts addressed in each chapter; discussion questions; in-class activities such as cooperative group activities, projects, and reflection questions; and activities that build on those presented in the book and on MyEducationLab. Additional video and Internet resources are also provided for each chapter. The online version of the Instructor's Manual is available on the Instructor Resource Center at www.pearsonhighered.com. To access the manual, the online PowerPoint lecture slides, and also the test bank (see below) go to **www.pearsonhighered.com** and click on the Instructor Resource Center button. Here you will be able to login or complete a one-time registration for a user name and password.

Online PowerPoint Lecture Slides

The PowerPoint lecture slides are available on the Instructor Resource Center at www.pearsonhighered.com. These lectures highlight key concepts and summarize key content from each chapter of the text.

Test Bank and TestGen Software

A completely revised test bank of more than 750 questions also accompanies the text. These multiple-choice, short answer, and essay questions can be used to assess students' recognition, recall, and synthesis of factual content and conceptual issues from each chapter. The computerized version of the test bank (TestGen) is available in Windows and Macintosh formats, along with assessment software allowing instructors to create and customize exams and track student progress.

ACKNOWLEDGMENTS

Many people contributed ideas, insights, and suggestions that greatly enhanced the substance and quality of the ninth edition of *Exceptional Children*. A talented team of professionals at Pearson/Merrill helped transform more than 1,500 pages of manuscript into the book you are reading. Acquisitions Editor Ann Castel Davis provided appreciated support and encouragement in the ninth edition. As with the previous editions, Development Editor Heather Doyle Fraser was a source of numerous suggestions and valued constructive criticism while I worked on the manuscript. And I appreciated Heather's gentle but effective way of reminding me when (yet another) chapter was past due and what would happen to me if I did not complete it post-haste. Heather was particularly helpful in organizing the video shoots for the text.

A skillful copyeditor is an author's best friend. Luanne Dreyer Elliott improved the manuscript with a balance of technical skill and respect for an author's writing style. Thanks to Melissa Gruzs for her exquisitely careful proofreading. To be most useful as a resource to students, a comprehensive textbook must have a complete and accurate reference list and functional indexes. Bret Workman put together the "mother of all reference lists," and Wendy Allex created the name and subject indexes. I owe a special note of gratitude to Becky Savage, who obtained permissions to reprint published material. The effective and meaningful portrayal of special education requires excellent photographs. Many of the new photos in this edition are the product of the skills of photographer Katelyn Metzger and Photo Editor Lori Whitley, who accompanied me on photo shoots at local schools. And Candace Rowley's interior design and Diane Lorenzo's work on the cover are apparent in the book's attractive appearance and appealing, accessible layout.

As she has for the past five editions, Project Manager Mary Irvin used her impressive talents as a multi-tasker and capably pulled together all the parts and people and got everything between covers. It was Mary's diligent and skillful attention to detail and ability to keep countless elements of the production process going, including a sometimes confused author, that kept it on schedule.

No one author can capture the many perspectives and areas of expertise that make up a field as diverse and dynamic as special education. Many special education teachers and researchers have contributed to the currency and quality of this text. I am grateful to the 18 special and general education teachers who graciously shared their knowledge and personal experience through the Featured Teacher Essays and the Tips for Beginning Teachers in each chapter: Mary Allaire-Gifford, Carolyn Crangle, Carey Creech-Galloway, Jeanna Mora Dowse, Steven Everling, Shawn Heimlich, Douglas Jackson, Daniel Killian, Kazuko Kito, Meghan Macy, Bethany Maheady, Linda Michael, Beth Mueninghoff, Jean Michielli-Pendl, Kimberly Rich, Mary Kate Ryan-Griffith, Sandra Trask-Tyler, and Donelle Tyler.

I am especially grateful to the administrators and teachers who welcomed us into their schools and classrooms to produce 64 new video clips for the ninth edition that are integrated into the MyEducationLab Homework & Exercises and Building Teaching Skills activities. Thanks to the efforts of four of the teachers featured in the text (Shawn Heimlich, Kazuko Kito, Beth Mueninghoff, and Kim Rich), to Lynn Heward, a second grade teacher at Great Western Academy (Columbus), and to numerous teachers and staff at Colerain Elementary School (Columbus Public Schools) and the Ohio State School for the Blind, users of this text can watch teachers and students engaged in many of the research-based curriculum and instructional practices described in the book. The individual and collective talents, wisdom, and accomplishments of all of these educators provide great optimism for the future of special education. A special note of thanks to Doni Jackson (Principal, Colerain Elementary School), Theresa Tracy (Principal, Winterset Elementary School), Lou Mazolli (Superintendent, Ohio State School for the Blind), Jan Rawlins (Principal, Crestview

Elementary School, Layton, UT), and Natalie Williams (Weber State University) for their assistance with the video. Video ethnographer Carl Harris, a former professor of education, filmed all of the video clips with great skill and sensitivity.

The currency and quality of this text have been enhanced tremendously by original Teaching & Learning and Current Issues & Future Trends essays authored exclusively for this text by the following educators: Sheila Alber-Morgan (Ohio State University); Belva Collins (University of Kentucky); Jill Dardig, (Ohio Dominican University); Tom Fish (OSU), Vicki Graff (OSU), and Anke Gross (University of Cologne, Germany); Carolyn Hughes (Vanderbilt University), Erik Carter (University of Wisconsin—Madison), Marilee Dye and Corie Byers (both, Nashville Public Schools); Ed Kame'enui (University of Oregon); Jonathan Kimball (Woodfords Family Services, Portland, ME) and Robert Stromer (George Brown College, Toronto); Allison Kretlow, Sara Mackiewicz, Charles Wood, Jacklyn Mirabal, and Nancy Cooke (all, University of North Carolina at Charlotte); Moira Konrad (OSU) and David Test (UNCC); Nancy Marchand-Martella and Ronald Martella (Eastern Washington University); Catherine Maurice (Association for Science in Autism Treatment); Mary Salmon (Columbus Public Schools), Stacie McConnell (Reynoldsburg, Ohio, public schools), Diane Sainato (OSU), and Rebecca Morrison (Oakstone Academy); Barbara Schirmer (University of Detroit Mercy) and Rachel Friedman Narr (California State University Northridge); J. David Smith (The University of Virginia's College at Wise); George Sugai (University of Connecticut); Jo Webber and Brenda Scheuermann (Southwest Texas State University); Michael Wehmeyer (University of Kansas); and Natalie Williams (Weber State University).

The following professors—all of whom teach the introduction to special education course—reviewed the previous edition and provided comments and suggestions that contributed to this edition: Jim Burns (The College of St. Rose); Frances M. Butler (Weber State University); Susan L. Gibbs (University of North Carolina at Charlotte); Blanche Glimps (Tennessee State University); Ann Mungai (Adelphi University); and Sharon Piety-Nowell (Bethune-Cookman College).

Thank you to Professor Jane Piirto (Ashland University) for co-authoring Chapter 14—Giftedness and Talent. Special congratulations to Jane for receiving the Mensa Education and Research Foundation's Lifetime Achievement Award in 2007 for her research on creativity and gifted education. Sheila Alber-Morgan (Ohio State University) and David F. Bicard (University of Memphis) co-authored the Instructor's Manual. The Test Bank was prepared by Theresa Hessler (Ohio State University). This group of special educators—each of whom has taught the introduction to special education course many times—has produced a strong set of ancillary materials, and I am confident that students and instructors will appreciate and benefit from their hard work and creativity. Special thanks to Tammy Feil (Neumann College) for developing the MyEducationLab course content for this text.

Finally, I will always be grateful to Mike Orlansky, former colleague, friend, and co-author of the first four editions of *Exceptional Children*.

Most of all, I continue to benefit from the support and love of my family—wife Jill, son Lee, and daughter Lynn.

CONTENTS

PROLOGUE

A Personal View of Special Education   2

PART I

Foundations for Understanding Special Education   5

1 The Purpose and Promise of Special Education   6

Who Are Exceptional Children?   9

How Many Exceptional Children are There?   10

Why Do We Label and Classify Exceptional Children?   12
Labeling and Eligibility for Special Education   12
Possible Benefits of Labeling and Classification   12
Possible Disadvantages of Labeling and Classification   13
Alternatives to Labeling and Classification   14

Why Are Laws Governing the Education of Exceptional Children Necessary?   16
An Exclusionary Past   16
Separate Is Not Equal   17
Equal Protection   17

The Individuals with Disabilities Education Act   18
Six Major Principles of IDEA   19
Other Provisions of IDEA   22
Legal Challenges Based on IDEA   23
Related Legislation   29
No Child Left Behind Act   30

What Is Special Education?   35
Special Education as Intervention   35
Special Education as Instruction   36
Defining Features of Special Education   41

Current and Future Challenges   41
Close the Research-to-Practice Gap   41
Increase the Availability and Intensity of Early
     Intervention and Prevention Programs   43
Help Students With Disabilities Transition From
     School to Adult Life   43
Improve the Special Education–General Education
     Partnership   43

2 Planning and Providing Special Education Services   48

The Process of Special Education   51
Prereferral Process   51
Evaluation and Eligibility Determination   55
Disproportionate Representation of Students From
     Culturally Diverse Groups in Special Education   56
Program Planning   59
Placement   59
Progress Monitoring, Annual Review, and
     Reevaluation   59

Collaboration and Teaming   60
Collaboration   60
Teaming   60
Co-Teaching   62

Individualized Education Program   63
IEP Team   63
IEP Components   63
IEP Functions and Formats   65
IEP Problems and Potential Solutions   69

Least Restrictive Environment   73
A Continuum of Alternative Placements   74
Determining LRE   75

Inclusive Education   76
Promoting Inclusion With Cooperative Learning   77
Arguments For and Against Full Inclusion   77

Where Does Special Education Go From Here?   82

3 Collaborating With Parents and Families in a Culturally and Linguistically Diverse Society   88

Support for Family Involvement   91
Parents: Advocating for Needed Change   91
Educators: Seeking Greater Effectiveness   92
Legislators: Mandating Parent and Family
     Involvement   92

Understanding Families of Children With Disabilities   93
The Impact of a Child With Disabilities on the Family   93
The Many Roles of the Exceptional Parent   95
Changing Needs as Children Grow   98

Developing and Maintaining Family-Professional
Partnerships   98
  Principles of Effective Communication   *102*
  *Identifying and Breaking Down Barriers to Parent-
    Teacher Partnerships*   *104*

Working With Culturally and Linguistically Diverse
Families   106
  Understanding and Respecting Cultural Differences   *107*
  Culturally Responsive Services for Families   *108*

Home–School Communication Methods   109
  Parent-Teacher Conferences   *109*
  Written Communication   *112*
  Telephone Communications   *113*

Other Forms of Parent Involvement   116
  Parents as Tutors   *117*
  Parent Education and Support Groups   *120*
  Parent-to-Parent Groups   *120*
  Parents as Research Partners   *120*
  How Much Parent Involvement?   *122*

PART II

Educational Needs of Exceptional
Students   127

4 Intellectual Disabilities   128

Definitions and Classification Systems   132
  IDEA Definition of Mental Retardation   *132*
  AAIDD's Definition Based on Needed Supports   *133*
  *The Evolving Definition of Mental Retardation/
    Intellectual Disabilities*   *135*

Identification and Assessment   136
  Assessing Intellectual Functioning   *136*
  Assessing Adaptive Behavior   *138*

Characteristics   138
  Cognitive Functioning   *139*
  Adaptive Behavior   *141*
  Positive Attributes   *141*

Prevalence   142

Causes and Prevention   142
  Causes   *142*
  Prevention   *146*

Educational Approaches   147
  Curriculum Goals   *147*
  Instructional Methods   *152*

Educational Placement Alternatives   161
  Acceptance and Membership   *164*

5 Learning Disabilities   170

Definitions   173
  The Federal Definition   *173*
  The NJCLD Definition   *173*
  *Operationalizing the Federal Definition: IQ-Achievement
    Discrepancy*   *174*
  *Responsiveness to Intervention: A New Paradigm for
    Defining Learning Disabilities*   *175*

Characteristics   179
  Reading Problems   *179*
  Written Language Deficits   *182*
  Math Underachievement   *184*
  Social Skills Deficits   *185*
  Attention Problems and Hyperactivity   *185*
  Behavioral Problems   *185*
  Low Ratings of Self-Efficacy   *186*
  The Defining Characteristic   *186*

Prevalence   186

Causes   187
  Brain Damage or Dysfunction   *188*
  Heredity   *188*
  Biochemical Imbalance   *188*
  Environmental Factors   *189*

Identification and Assessment   189
  Intelligence and Achievement Tests   *189*
  Criterion-Referenced Tests   *190*
  Informal Reading Inventories   *190*
  Curriculum-Based Measurement   *190*
  Direct Daily Measurement   *192*

Educational Approaches   192
  Content Enhancements   *194*

Educational Placement Alternatives   203
  General Education Classroom   *203*
  Consultant Teacher   *204*
  Resource Room   *205*
  Separate Classroom   *205*
  *Should All Students With Learning Disabilities Be Educated
    in the General Education Classroom?*   *205*

6 Emotional or Behavioral Disorders   210

Definitions   213
  Federal Definition of Emotional Disturbance   *214*
  CCBD Definition of Emotional or Behavioral Disorder   *214*

Characteristics   215
  Externalizing Behaviors   *215*
  Internalizing Behaviors   *216*

Academic Achievement 219

Intelligence 220

Social Skills and Interpersonal Relationships 221

Juvenile Delinquency 221

Prevalence 221

Gender 224

Students in Juvenile Detention Facilities 224

Causes 224

Biological Factors 224

Environmental Factors 225

A Complex Pathway of Risks 227

Identification and Assessment 227

Screening Tests 229

Projective Tests 230

Direct Observation and Measurement of Behavior 230

Functional Behavioral Assessment 230

Educational Approaches 233

Curriculum Goals 233

Evidence-Based Instructional Practices 235

Fostering Strong Teacher–Student Relationships 243

Focus on Alterable Variables 243

Educational Placement Alternatives 246

Challenges, Achievements, and Advocacy 247

7 Autism Spectrum Disorders 254

Definitions 257

Definition of Autism in IDEA 258

Definition of Autism in the DSM-IV 258

Characteristics 261

Impaired Social Relationships 261

Communication and Language Deficits 261

Intellectual Functioning 262

Unusual Responsiveness to Sensory Stimuli 263

Insistence on Sameness and Perseveration 263

Ritualistic and Unusual Behavior Patterns 263

Severe Problem Behavior 264

Positive Attributes and Strengths of Students With ASD 264

Prevalence 268

Causes 268

Identification and Assessment 269

Screening 269

Diagnosis 271

Educational Approaches 271

Critical Importance of Early Intensive Behavioral Intervention 273

Applied Behavior Analysis 274

Visual Supports: Helping Students With Autism Cope With Social Situations and Increase Their Independence in the Classroom 277

Educational Placement Alternatives 282

General Education Classroom 282

Resource Room and Special Classes 283

Distinguishing Unproven Interventions from Evidence-Based Practices For Children With Autism 284

Facilitated Communication 284

Secretin Therapy 285

Why Do Fads Thrive? 285

8 Communication Disorders 294

Definitions 297

Communication 297

Language 298

Speech 299

Typical Speech and Language Development 300

Communication Disorders Defined 303

Communication Differences Are Not Disorders 305

Characteristics 306

Speech-Sound Errors 306

Fluency Disorders 307

Voice Disorders 308

Language Impairments 308

Prevalence 309

Causes 309

Causes of Speech Impairments 310

Causes of Language Disorders 310

Identification and Assessment 311

Screening and Teacher Observations 311

Evaluation Components 311

Educational Approaches 315

Treating Speech-Sound Errors 316

Treating Fluency Disorders 316

Treating Voice Disorders 317

Treating Language Disorders 319

Augmentative and Alternative Communication 321

Educational Placement Alternatives 325

Monitoring 325

Pull-Out 325

Collaborative Consultation 325

Classroom-Based 325

Separate Classroom 326

Community-Based 326

Combination 326

9 Deafness and Hearing Loss 330

Definitions 334
How We Hear 334
The Nature of Sound 335

Characteristics 336
English Literacy 336
Speaking 337
Academic Achievement 337
Social Functioning 337

Prevalence 338

Types and Causes of Hearing Loss 338
Types and Age of Onset 338
Causes of Congenital Hearing Loss 340
Causes of Acquired Hearing Loss 341

Identification and Assessment 342
Assessment of Infants 342
Pure-Tone Audiometry 342
Speech Audiometry 342
Alternative Audiometric Techniques 344
Degrees of Hearing Loss 346

Technologies and Supports 346
Technologies That Amplify or Provide Sound 346
Supports and Technologies That Supplement or Replace Sound 349

Educational Approaches 351
Oral/Aural Approaches 351
Total Communication 355
American Sign Language and the Bilingual–Bicultural Approach 359
Which Approach for Whom? 360

Educational Placement Alternatives 361
Postsecondary Education 364

10 Blindness and Low Vision 368

Definitions 371
Legal Definition of Blindness 371
Educational Definitions of Visual Impairments 373
Age at Onset 373

Characteristics 373
Cognition and Language 373
Motor Development and Mobility 374
Social Adjustment and Interaction 375

Prevalence 376

Types and Causes of Visual Impairments 376
How We See 376
Causes of Visual Impairments 377

Educational Approaches 380
Special Adaptations for Students Who Are Blind 380
Special Adaptations for Students With Low Vision 384
Expanded Curriculum Priorities 389

Educational Placement Alternatives 394
Inclusive Classroom and Itinerant Teacher Model 394
Residential Schools 395
Can a Neighborhood School Provide the Needed Specialized Services? 399
Fighting Against Discrimination and for Self-Determination 399

11 Physical Disabilities, Health Impairments, and ADHD 404

Definitions of Physical Disabilities and Health Impairments 407

Prevalence 408

Types and Causes 409
Cerebral Palsy 409
Spina Bifida 411
Muscular Dystrophy 413
Spinal Cord Injuries 414
Epilepsy 415
Diabetes 417
Asthma 418
Cystic Fibrosis 418
Human Immunodeficiency Virus and Acquired Immune Deficiency Syndrome 419

Attention-Deficit/Hyperactivity Disorder 420
Definition and Diagnosis 420
Prevalence 422
Academic Achievement and Comorbidity With Other Disabilities 422
Eligibility for Special Education 422
Causes 423
Treatment 423

Characteristics 427
Variables Affecting the Impact of Physical Disabilities and Health Impairments on Educational Performance 430

Educational Approaches 431
Teaming and Related Services 433
Environmental Modifications 435
Assistive Technology 435
Animal Assistance 437
Special Health Care Routines 437
Independence and Self-Esteem 441

Educational Placement Alternatives 443
Related Services in the Classroom 444
Inclusive Attitudes 444

12 Low-Incidence Disabilities: Severe/Multiple Disabilities, Deaf-Blindness, and Traumatic Brain Injury 450

Defining Severe, Profound, and Multiple Disabilities 453
Severe Disabilities 453
Profound Disabilities 454
Multiple Disabilities 455
Deaf-Blindness 455

Characteristics of Students With Severe and Multiple Disabilities 457

Prevalence of Severe and Multiple Disabilities 458

Causes of Severe and Multiple Disabilities 459

Traumatic Brain Injury 459
Definition 459
Prevalence of Traumatic Brain Injury 460
Types and Causes of Traumatic Brain Injury 460
Effects and Educational Implications of Traumatic Brain Injury 462

Educational Approaches 463
Curriculum: What Should Be Taught? 464
Instructional Methods: How Should Students With Severe and Multiple Disabilities Be Taught? 469
Where Should Students With Severe Disabilities Be Taught? 480
The Challenge and Rewards of Teaching Students With Severe and Multiple Disabilities 486

13 Giftedness and Talent by Jane Piirto and William L. Heward 490

Definitions 493
Federal Definitions 493
Other Contemporary and Complementary Definitions 494

Characteristics 496
Individual Differences Among Gifted and Talented Students 498
Creativity 499

Prevalence 501

Identification and Assessment 501
Multicultural Assessment and Identification 503
Gifted and Talented Girls 505
Gifted and Talented Boys 505
Gifted and Talented Students With Disabilities 505

Educational Approaches 506
Curricular Goals 506
Differentiating Curriculum: Acceleration and Enrichment 507
Lesson Differentiation in the General Education Classroom 512
Curriculum Differentiation Outside the Classroom 515
Instructional Models and Methods 518
Guidance and Counseling Needs 521

Educational Placement Alternatives and Ability Grouping 521
Special Schools 521
Self-Contained Classrooms 521
Resource Room or Pull-Out Programs 522
General Education Classroom 523
Ability Grouping 523
Advocacy 526

PART III

Special Education Across the Life Span 531

14 Early Childhood Special Education 532

The Importance of Early Intervention 536
Defining Early Intervention 536
Examining the Effectiveness of Early Intervention 536

IDEA and Early Intervention/Early Childhood Special Education 540
Early Intervention for Infants and Toddlers 540
Special Education for Preschoolers 544

Screening, Identification, and Assessment 544
Screening Tools 544
Diagnostic Tools 546
Program Planning and Evaluation Tools 547

Curriculum and Instruction in Early Childhood Special Education 547
Curriculum and Program Goals 547
Developmentally Appropriate Practice 549
Selecting IFSP/IEP Goals and Objectives 550
Instructional Adaptations and Modifications 550
Preschool Activity Schedules 555
A Supportive Physical Environment 555

Service-Delivery Alternatives for Early Intervention 557
Hospital-Based Programs 557
Home-Based Programs 557
Center-Based Programs 558
Combined Home-Center Programs 559
Families: Most Important of All 559

15 Transitioning to Adulthood 564

How Do Former Special Education Students Fare
as Adults? 567
  Completing High School 567
  Employment 568
  Postsecondary Education 568
  Overall Adjustment and Success 568

Transition Services and Models 569
  Will's Bridges Model of School-to-Work Transition 569
  Halpern's Three-Dimensional Model 570
  Definition of Transition Services in IDEA 570
  Individualized Transition Plan 570
  Transition Teaming 572
  *Beginning Transition Activities and Career Education
    Early 572*

Employment 574
  Competitive Employment 577
  Sheltered Employment 584

Postsecondary Education 585

Residential Alternatives 586
  Group Homes 587
  Foster Homes 587
  Apartment Living 588
  Supported Living 588
  Institutions 590

Recreation and Leisure 591

The Ultimate Transition Goal: A Better Life 592
  Quality of Life 592
  Misguided and Limiting Presumptions 593
  Self-Advocacy and Self-Determination 596
  Still a Long Way to Go 596

POSTSCRIPT

Developing Your Own Personal View of
Special Education 600

**Appendix: Coverage of Content Areas
for PRAXIS II Test A-1**

Glossary G-1

References R-1

Name Index I-1

Subject Index I-15

Photo Credits

Note: Every effort has been made to provide accurate and current Internet information in this book. However, the Internet and information posted on it are constantly changing, so it is inevitable that some of the Internet addresses in this textbook will change.

SPECIAL FEATURES

TEACHING & LEARNING

TITLE	STRATEGY	TEXT LOCATION
It's Good to Go Fast!	Three fluency-building tactics for building student achievement	20
Signaling for Help	An effective and quiet means for requesting teacher assistance	38
Classwide Peer Tutoring	Children with and without disabilities can be effective teachers for one another	78
A Parent Appreciation Letter	Letting parents know their efforts and contributions toward their child's achievements are valued	114
A Talking Photo Album	Helping parents with limited English proficiency teach their children English	118
Let's Make Some Noise!	Using choral responding to improve the effectiveness of group instruction	158
Using Response Cards to Increase Participation and Achievement	A simple way to provide frequent response opportunities to all children in the classroom	162
Explicit Instruction	Incorporating explicit (or direct) instruction into daily lessons	196
Guided Notes: Helping All Students Succeed in the General Education Curriculum	Teacher-prepared handouts that guide a student through a lecture with standard cues and specific space in which to write key facts, concepts, and/or relationships	200
"Look, I'm All Finished!"	Teaching students why, when, and how to seek teacher attention appropriately	222
The Power of Teacher Praise	Understanding the positive effects of teacher praise on student performance	236
Mystery Motivators	Fun and effective way to motivate students to improve social and academic performance	244
From Unwanted Obsession to Motivational Key	Using the special interests areas of children with Asperger syndrome to unlock the curriculum	266
Multimedia Activity Schedules	Computer-enhanced activity schedules promote independence by children with autism	278
Helping the Child Who Stutters	Providing a good speech model, improving the child's self-esteem, and creating a good speech environment	318
Phonemic Awareness and Phonics Instruction With Deaf and Hard-of-Hearing Students	Using hand cues and graphic symbols to show the sounds in printed words	356
Considering the Communication Needs of Students Who Are Deaf or Hard of Hearing	A matrix for addressing the communication needs of students who have hearing losses	362
Helping the Student With Low Vision	Adapting materials and helping children use low-vision aids in the classroom	390
I Made It Myself, and It's Good!	Self-operated audio prompting device helps students learn daily living skills	396
Adapting Toys for Children with Cerebral Palsy	Modifying toys to make them more accessible for students with physical disabilities	412

TITLE	STRATEGY	TEXT LOCATION
Self-Monitoring Helps Students Do More Than Just Be On-Task	Teaching students to achieve a form of self-determination by taking responsibility for their learning	428
Using Naturalistic Teaching Strategies to Build Communication Skills in Students with Severe Disabilities	Seizing "teachable moments" to promote generalization of communication skills	476
Including Students in General Education: The Peer Buddy Program	Promoting interaction and friendships among secondary students with and without disabilities	482
Using the Literary Masters to Inspire Written Expression in Gifted Students	Exposing gifted students to classic literature to inspire them to find their own voices as writers	510
Selecting Toys for Young Children with Disabilites	Choosing toys for meaningful play	538
Using Puppets in the Early Childhood Classroom	Putting puppets to instructional use in presenting activities in developmentally appropriate ways	552
Two for One: Teaching Self-Determination and Writing Together	Strategies for improving self-determination and writing skills simultaneously	576
Next Chapter Book Club	Promoting literacy learning, community inclusion, and social connectedness for adolescents and adults with intellectual disabilities	594

CURRENT ISSUES & FUTURE TRENDS

TITLE	ISSUE/TREND	TEXT LOCATION
What's in a Name? The Labels and Language of Special Education	Perspectives on the use and misuse of disability labels	14
Evidence-Based Practice: Easier Said Than Done	How teachers can judge the scientific trustworthiness of practices claiming to be "research based"	72
Self-Determination: The Most Natural Support	The importance of self-determination in ensuring a good quality of life for students with intellectual disabilities	154
Responsiveness to Intervention: A New (and Old) Idea With Great Promise	An emerging approach for early intervention and identification of learning disabilities	180
Teaching Students with Emotional and Behavioral Disorders: Then and Now	Six advances in educating children with emotional and behavioral disorders	248
The Autism Wars	The enormous difficulties parents face in choosing among conflicting claims of autism treatments	286
Deafness: The Dilemma	Deciding whether to correct deafness or cherish the right to personal diversity	348
A Paper on the Inclusion of Students with Visual Impairments	Position statement outlining an appropriate education in the least restrictive environment	400
Monkey Helpers	Personal care attendants and companions for people with disabilities	438
What Happened to Functional Curriculum?	Ensuring that involvement in the general education curriculum by students with severe disabilities does not limit their learning skills important for everyday functioning	472
Precocity as a Hallmark of Giftedness	Recognizing giftedness through predictive behaviors	500

EXCEPTIONAL
CHILDREN

Prologue

A Personal View of Special Education

My primary goal in writing this book is to describe the history, practices, advances, challenges, and opportunities that make up the complex and dynamic field of special education in as complete, clear, current, and accurate a manner as possible. This, of course, is much easier said than done: an author's descriptions of anything he holds dear are influenced by personal views. Because my personal beliefs and assumptions about special education—which are by no means unique, but neither are they held by everyone in the field—affect both the substance and the tone of this book, I believe I owe you, the reader, an explicit summary of those views. So, here are 10 assumptions that underlie and guide my efforts to understand, contribute to, and convey the field of special education.

People with disabilities have a fundamental right to live and participate in the same settings and programs—in school, at home, in the workplace, and in the community—as do people without disabilities. That is, the settings and programs in which children and adults with disabilities learn, live, work, and play should, to the greatest extent possible, be the same settings and programs in which people without disabilities participate. People with disabilities and those without have a great deal to contribute to one another and to society. We cannot do that without regular, meaningful interactions in shared environments.

People with disabilities have the right to as much self-determination as they can achieve. Special educators have no more important teaching task than that of helping students with disabilities learn how to increase their level of autonomy over their own lives. Self-determination and self-advocacy skills should be featured curriculum components for all students with disabilities.

Special education must expand and improve the effectiveness of its early identification and prevention efforts. When a disability or a condition that places a child at risk for a disability is detected early, the chance of lessening its impact (or preventing it altogether) is greater. Great strides have been made in the early detection of physical disabilities, sensory impairments, and developmental delays in infants and preschoolers. Although systematic programs of early identification and prevention of less visible disabilities, such as learning disabilities and emotional and behavioral disorders, are less well developed, the field has made a commitment to doing just that with an approach called responsiveness to intervention that you will read about in this edition.

Special education must do a better job of helping students with disabilities transition from school to adult life. Although increasing numbers of special education students are leaving high school for college or a job, a place to live on their own, and friends with whom to share recreation and leisure activities in the community, such positive outcomes still elude far too many young adults with disabilities. Special education cannot be satisfied with improving students' achievement on classroom-based measures only. We must work equally hard to ensure that the education students receive during their school years prepares them to cope with and enjoy the multifaceted demands and opportunities of adulthood.

Special education must continue to improve its cultural competence. When a student with disabilities has the additional challenge of learning in a new or different culture or language, it is critically important that her teachers provide culturally responsive curriculum and instruction. Teachers who are most effective in helping these children combine fundamentally sound instructional methods with sensitivity to and respect for their students' heritage and values.

School and family partnerships enhance both the meaningfulness and the effectiveness of special education. Professionals have too long ignored the needs of parents and families of exceptional children, often treating them as patients, clients, or even adversaries instead of realizing that they are partners with the same goals. Some special educators have given the impression (and, worse, believed it to be true) that parents are there to serve professionals, when in fact the opposite is more correct. We must recognize that parents are a child's first—and, in many ways, best—teachers. Learning to work effectively with parents is one of the most important skills the special educator can acquire.

The work of special educators is most effective when supplemented by the knowledge and services of all of the disciplines in the helping professions. It is foolish for special educators to argue over territorial rights when more can be accomplished for our students when we work together within an interdisciplinary team that includes our colleagues in psychology, medical and health services, counseling, social services, and vocational rehabilitation.

All students have the right to an effective education. An educator's primary responsibility is designing and implementing instruction that helps students with special needs learn useful academic, social, vocational, and personal skills. These skills are the same ones that influence the quality of our own lives: working effectively and efficiently at our jobs, being productive members of our communities, maintaining a comfortable lifestyle in our homes, communicating with our friends and family, and using our leisure time meaningfully and enjoyably. Instruction is ultimately effective when it helps students acquire and maintain positive lifestyle changes. To put it another way, the proof of the process is in the product. Therefore, . . .

Teachers must demand effectiveness from the curriculum materials and instructional tools they use. For many years, conventional wisdom has fostered the belief, still held by some, that teaching children with disabilities requires unending patience. I believe this notion does a great disservice to students with special needs and to the educators—both special and general education teachers—who teach them. A teacher should not wait patiently for an exceptional student to learn, attributing lack of progress to some inherent attribute or faulty process within the child, such as mental retardation, learning disability, attention-deficit disorder, or emotional disturbance. Instead, the teacher should select evidence-based practices and then use direct and frequent measures of the student's performance as the primary guide for modifying those methods as needed to improve their effectiveness. This, I believe, is the real work of the special educator. Numerous examples of instructional strategies and tactics demonstrated to be effective through rigorous scientific research are described and illustrated throughout this text. Although you will not know how to teach exceptional children after reading this or any other introductory text, you will gain an appreciation for the importance of explicit, systematic instruction and an understanding of the kinds of teaching skills a competent special educator must have. And finally, I believe that . . .

The future for people with disabilities holds great promise. We have only begun to discover the myriad ways to improve teaching, increase learning, prevent and minimize the conditions that cause and exacerbate the effects of disabilities, encourage acceptance, and use technology to compensate for disabilities. While I make no specific predictions for the future, I am certain that we have not come as far as we can in learning how to help exceptional children and adults build and enjoy fuller, more independent lives in the school, home, workplace, and community.

PART I

Foundations for Understanding Special Education

1 The Purpose and Promise of Special Education

2 Planning and Providing Special Education Services

3 Collaborating With Parents and Families in a Culturally and Linguistically Diverse Society

1

The Purpose and Promise
of Special Education

- When is special education needed? How do we know?
- If disability labels do not tell us what and how to teach, why are they used in special education?
- Why have court cases and federal legislation been required to ensure that children with disabilities receive a free, appropriate education?
- How can a special educator provide all three kinds of intervention—preventive, remedial, and compensatory—on behalf of an individual child?
- What do you think are the three most important challenges facing special education today? Why?

○ FEATURED TEACHER

SHAWN HEIMLICH
Jones Middle School • Upper Arlington, Ohio

Shawn Heimlich

Education—Teaching Credentials—Experience
- B.S., special education, The Ohio State University, 1996
- M.A., special education and applied behavior analysis, The Ohio State University, 2005
- Ohio license, intervention specialist for students with mild-to-moderate educational needs, K–12
- 12 years' experience as a special education teacher

in social studies and science for sixth, seventh, and eighth graders with mild-to-moderate disabilities. My students, ages 12 to 15, spend varying amounts of time in my cross-categorical resource room and in general education classes. Some students receive instruction in only math, reading, and language arts in the resource room, and spend the remaining six periods of the school day in general education classes. Students with moderate disabilities may spend six of the nine periods each day in the resource room (a more self-contained academic program). Paraprofessionals provide support for students in my classroom and accompany many of these students to their general education classes.

Here are some things I have learned in this classroom:

Data-Driven Instruction Does Not Allow for Complacency At the beginning of this school year, my colleagues and I began the journey of professional learning communities, a data-driven approach that focuses on instruction and assessment. We are using data collected from common assessments, benchmark assessments, and frequent informal progress monitoring for making decisions regarding curriculum, instruction, and assessment for my students. In addition to the data-driven approach of professional learning communities,

Some may call my cross-categorical resource room the Disney World® of education—the Magic Kingdom® of fun and learning. My students' parents call it a safe and supportive "home base" for their child. Student teachers call it a place to hone their teaching skills before landing in a classroom of their own. Colleagues call it a boisterous and enjoyable place to visit when they can. Some may call it loud and chaotic. Others may call it fast-paced and engaging. I just call it my classroom!

In this classroom, I provide instruction in reading and language arts and provide an alternate curriculum

I continue to use the Direct Instruction model to teach reading, math, and language arts skills. Effective implementation of these teaching techniques requires consistent data collection regarding, for example, decoding accuracy, student reading accuracy and errors, comprehension accuracy, oral reading fluency, and even daily sight vocabulary sprints. I use the data collected from daily performance of target skills to make instructional decisions for my students; continuous improvements in reading accuracy, words read per minute or sight-word fluency may direct me to continue a normal progression of lessons, or may direct me to increase the pace of a lesson or the duration of a reading session. Data gathered from observations or informal questioning during a social studies or science activity may indicate that students comprehend the concept presented and are able to answer teacher-posed questions. Or, data gathered using these same informal methods may demonstrate that students have not comprehended the concept presented. I must be willing to use the data collected to evaluate my instruction and assessment strategies in order to determine if I am an effective educator.

Value the Functional Application of Academic Skills Members of the military would certainly be less effective if skills learned in the "classroom" of basic training were not utilized in functional, real-life situations. Medical doctors would make poor professionals if they could not put "book knowledge" to the test in an exam room or operating room. Likewise, my students would be unsuccessful if they weren't able to use math skills learned in a classroom setting to determine the total purchase price of their recipe ingredients and change expected during a trip to our local grocery store. Students would be considered ill prepared for life if they weren't able to read restaurant menus or shopping ads or safety and warning signs. My students would be considered unemployable if they weren't able to complete a job application or maintain appropriate social behaviors during interactions. For these reasons, I believe it is imperative that my students apply academic skills learned in a classroom to functional, real-life tasks in community settings. Functional application of skills also improves students' generalization of skills—the extent to which they perform skills learned in one setting in other settings with various stimuli, conditions, and reinforcement.

In the Real World, Fluency Matters In my classroom, as in life, accurate performance of target skills is not sufficient for successful functioning. I would be willing to bet that, given two checkout lines at your local grocers, you'd be more inclined to pick the line with the customer and cashier who not only perform their individual skills correctly (scanning items for purchase, counting correct bills and coins to make a purchase) but who perform their respective skills more fluently. The world will not wait patiently for

you to find your bus pass or make several unsuccessful attempts at scanning your pass, or for the driver to snatch it from your hand to scan the pass for you. For these reasons, students in my classroom continually work to develop fluency of target skills. They may participate in daily sprints and 1-minute timings for increasing words read per minute, science terms defined per minute, math facts answered per minute, letters or important concepts printed per minute, map locations labeled per minute, or even body systems identified per minute. When in community settings, my students work to develop fluency of daily living skills: using a bus pass to quickly board our local public transportation system; reading a store map quickly and correctly to locate items for a given recipe; reading cleaning product labels quickly and accurately at a local Ronald McDonald House® during a monthly service learning activity; or identifying the names/photos of national monuments quickly and accurately for an upcoming eighth-grade trip to Washington, D.C. In the classroom and in the community, fluency matters for my students!

As a leader and member of our school's intervention specialist professional learning community, I work closely with all of the special education teachers in our building to identify core fluency skills in math, reading, and written expression, and to develop common assessments for tracking individual student progress. In addition to the development of common assessments to measure skill fluency, our community developed the "fluency toolkit"—a collection of fluency-building teaching strategies and activities.

High-Quality Service Learning Activities Provide Students With Meaningful Practice Throughout my teaching career, I've discovered that my students many times require higher levels of motivation to maintain engagement in an activity, or require more creative means of reinforcement for skill performance. Two years ago, I developed a service learning partnership with our local Ronald McDonald House charities and The Childhood League Center (a daycare/preschool for children with special needs and typical peer models). Through these partnerships, my students serve local agencies with volunteer time while learning important daily living and social skills. During monthly trips to the Ronald McDonald House, my students and I spend the morning cleaning public areas of the house used by families of critically ill children. This activity requires reading skills when working with various cleaning products, time management skills for completing a task within reasonable limits, the demonstration of appropriate social skills when acting as "team leader" or when interacting with Ronald McDonald staff or families, and basic organizational skills when using checklists to determine completion of a task.

In addition to House maintenance, my students shop for ingredients, complete a recipe, and package snacks for families at the Ronald McDonald House as they travel to and from local hospitals with their children. In November, my students shopped for, prepared, and served a full pancake breakfast (pancakes, hash browns, sausage links, fresh fruit, milk and orange juice) for 60 families and staff members at the Ronald McDonald House. It was a motivating, creative, and rewarding method for teaching and practicing daily living skills while serving those in our community. At The Childhood League Center, my students serve as "Middle School Buddies" for their preschool friends. My students prepare a snack, motor activity or game, and a craft activity centered on our buddies' weekly theme during our monthly trips to the Center. During these visits, my students not only practice reading, writing, and math skills, they also practice leadership skills and appropriate social behaviors as they serve as role models for their admiring preschool friends. To travel to our service learning opportunities, my students receive training from our central Ohio public transportation system on the rights, responsibilities, rules and procedures for safe travel. My students are trained to read bus signs, read basic bus maps, use bus day-passes, and role-play appropriate social behaviors expected of users of public transportation.

In my undergraduate and graduate teacher education courses, I learned the fundamentals of high-quality instruction, techniques for assessing student progress or mastery of skills, methods for promoting the generalization of skills, strategies for shaping or modifying behavior, and numerous other elements that have helped me become a successful special educator. In this classroom, I have learned that sometimes the grief over the loss of a student can make me even more loving and supportive of those I've been given the responsibility of educating. In this classroom, I have learned that a physical assault by a student and five-person restraint are demonstration of just how difficult behavior change can be once I've committed myself to a plan of action. In this classroom, I have learned that, when necessary, I must be willing to enlist the support of and collaborate with the incredible professionals that make Jones Middle School a second home. In this classroom, I have learned that my students can achieve amazing things when special educators, general education teachers, paraprofessionals, administrators, parents, agency representatives, and community members all come together to establish high expectations, rigorous programming, and support systems.

To learn more about Mr. Heimlich's classroom and the curriculum and instructional strategies he uses, go to the Homework & Exercises section in Chapter 1 on MyEducationLab and click on Homework Exercise 1.

Educating children with special needs or abilities is a difficult challenge. Teachers who have accepted that challenge—special educators—work in a dynamic and exciting field. To begin to appreciate some of the action and excitement, as well as the persistent and emerging challenges and controversies that characterize special education, it is necessary to examine some concepts and perspectives that are basic to understanding exceptional children.

WHO ARE EXCEPTIONAL CHILDREN?

All children exhibit differences from one another in terms of their physical attributes (e.g., some are shorter, some are stronger) and learning abilities (e.g., some learn quickly and use what they have learned in new situations; others need intensive repeated practice and have difficulty maintaining and generalizing new knowledge and skills). The differences among most children are relatively small, enabling these children to benefit from the general education program. The physical attributes and/or learning abilities of some children—those called **exceptional children**—differ from the norm (either below or above) to such an extent that they require an individualized program of special education and related services to fully benefit from education. The term *exceptional children* includes children who experience difficulties in learning as well as those whose performance is so superior that modifications in curriculum and instruction are necessary to help them fulfill their potential. Thus, *exceptional children* is an inclusive term that refers to children with learning and/or behavior problems, children with physical disabilities or sensory impairments, and children who are intellectually gifted or have a special talent. The term *students with disabilities* is more restrictive than *exceptional children* because it does not include gifted

As you read this text, you will notice connections to MyEducationLab at www.myeducationlab.com. Each chapter in the course contains a Pre-Test, Study Plan, Homework and Exercises, Building Skills activities, and a Post-Test. These self-assessments and study aids will help you gauge your comprehension of chapter content and also help you build a deeper, more applied understanding of the concepts discussed in each chapter.

Definition of exceptional
children

Council for
Exceptional
Children
Content
Standards for
Beginning
Teachers—Common Core:
Similarities and differences
of individuals with and
without exceptional
learning needs (CC2K5).

Definition of impairment,
disability, handicap, *and*
at-risk

Council for
Exceptional
Children
Content
Standards for
Beginning
Teachers—Common Core:
Similarities and differences
of individuals with and
without exceptional
learning needs (CC2K5).

and talented children. Learning the definitions of several related terms will help you better understand the concept of exceptionality.

Although the terms *impairment, disability,* and *handicap* are sometimes used interchangeably, they are not synonymous. **Impairment** refers to the loss or reduced function of a particular body part or organ (e.g., a missing limb). A **disability** exists when an impairment limits a person's ability to perform certain tasks (e.g., walk, see, add a row of numbers) in the same way that most persons do. A person with a disability is not *handicapped,* however, unless the disability leads to educational, personal, social, vocational, or other problems. For example, if a child who has lost a leg learns to use a prosthetic limb and functions in and out of school without problems, she is not handicapped, at least in terms of her functioning in the physical environment.

Handicap refers to a problem or a disadvantage that a person with a disability or an impairment encounters when interacting with the environment. A disability may pose a handicap in one environment but not in another. The child with a prosthetic limb may be handicapped (i.e., disadvantaged) when competing against nondisabled peers on the basketball court but experience no handicap in the classroom. People with disabilities also experience handicaps that have nothing to do with their disabilities but are the result of negative attitudes and the inappropriate behavior of others who needlessly restrict their access and ability to participate fully in school, work, or community activities.

A related term, **at-risk,** refers to children who, although not currently identified as having a disability, are considered to have a greater-than-usual chance of developing one. Educators often apply the term to infants and preschoolers who, because of biological conditions, events surrounding their births, or characteristics of their home environments, may be expected to experience developmental problems at a later time. Educators also use the term to refer to students who are experiencing significant learning or behavioral problems in the general education classroom and are therefore at risk of being identified for special education services.

Some exceptional children share certain physical characteristics and/or patterns of learning and behavior. These characteristics fall into the following categories of exceptionality:

- Intellectual disabilities (mental retardation)
- Learning disabilities
- Emotional or behavioral disorders
- Autism
- Speech or language impairments
- Hearing impairments
- Visual impairments
- Physical or health impairments
- Traumatic brain injury
- Multiple disabilities
- Giftedness and special talents

As stated previously, all children differ from one another in individual characteristics along a continuum; exceptional children differ markedly from the norm so that an individually designed program of instruction—or special education—is required if they are to benefit fully from education. However, exceptional children are more like other children than they are different. Nevertheless, an exceptional child differs in important ways from his same-age peers without disabilities. And whether and how those differences are recognized and responded to will have a major impact on the child's success in school and beyond.

HOW MANY EXCEPTIONAL CHILDREN ARE THERE?

The most complete and accurate information on how many children with disabilities live in the United States is derived from the child count data collected each year by the U.S. Department of Education. More than 6 million children and youth with disabilities, ages 3 to 21, received special education services during the 2005–2006 school year

(U.S. Department of Education, 2007). Table 1.1 shows the number of school-age students (i.e., **prevalence**) in each of the 13 disability categories used by the federal government.

Let's take a quick look at some other demographic facts about special education in the United States:

- About twice as many males as females receive special education.
- The number of children and youth who receive special education has grown every year since a national count was begun in the 1976–1977 school year.
- Early intervention programs have been major contributors to the increases since 1986. During the 2005–2006 school year, 698,938 preschoolers (ages 3 to 5) and 293,816 infants and toddlers (birth through age 2) were among those receiving special education.
- Children with disabilities in special education represent approximately 12% of the school-age population ages 6 to 17.
- The number of children who receive special education increases from age 3 through age 9. The number served decreases gradually with each successive age year after age 9 until age 17. Thereafter, the number of students receiving special education decreases sharply.
- Three out of four children ages 6 to 13 receiving special education are classified has having learning disabilities or speech/language impairments (Wagner, Marder, Blackorby, & Cardoso, 2002).
- The percentage of students receiving special education under the learning disabilities category has doubled (from 23.8% to 45.3%), whereas the percentage of students with mental retardation has decreased by well more than half (from 24.9% to 8.9%) since the federal government began collecting and reporting child count data in 1976-1977.
- The number of school-age students with autism who received special education in 2005–2006 (192,643) is 6 times the number of students classified with autism just 10 years earlier.

Although children with disabilities have special instructional needs, they are more like other children than they are different.

TABLE 1.1

Number of students ages 6–21 who received special education services under the federal government's disability categories (2005–2006 school year)

DISABILITY CATEGORY	NUMBER	PERCENT OF TOTAL
Specific learning disabilities	2,727,802	45.3
Speech or language impairments	1,143,195	19.0
Other health impairments	557,121	9.3
Mental retardation	533,426	8.9
Emotional disturbance	471,306	7.9
Autism	192,643	3.2
Multiple disabilities	132,595	2.2
Developmental delay	78,915	1.3
Hearing impairments	71,484	1.2
Orthopedic impairments	62,618	1.0
Visual impairments	25,369	0.4
Traumatic brain injury	23,449	0.4
Deaf-blindness	1,539	<0.1
All disabilities	6,021,462	100.0

Source: From U.S. Department of Education. (2007). *Individuals with Disabilities Education Act (IDEA) data* (Table 1-3). Washington, DC: Author. Available at https://www.ideadata.org/PartBReport.asp

- Although each child receiving special education is classified and reported under a primary disability category, many children are affected by more than one disability condition. In a nationwide study, the parents of more than 11,000 elementary school students in special education reported an average of 1.5 disabilities per child (Wagner & Blackorby, 2002).
- About 1 in 6 students with disabilities ages 6 to 13 are "declassified" and no longer receiving special education services 2 years later (SRI International, 2005).
- Although federal law does not mandate special education for children who are gifted and talented as it does for children with disabilities, approximately 3 million academically talented students were in pre-K to grade-12 gifted programs during the 2004–2005 school year (Council of State Directors of Programs for the Gifted, 2006).

Why Do We Label and Classify Exceptional Children?

Centuries ago, labeling and classifying people were of little consequence; survival was the main concern. Those whose disabilities prevented full participation in the activities necessary for survival were left on their own to perish and, in some instances, were even killed (Berkson, 2004). In later years, derogatory words such as "dunce," "imbecile," and "fool" were applied to people with intellectual disabilities or behavior problems, and other demeaning words were used for persons with health impairments or physical disabilities. These terms shared a common function: to exclude the person with disabilities from the facilities, activities, and privileges of everyday life.

Labeling and Eligibility for Special Education

Federal law requires labeling for students to be eligible for special education. Under the federal Individuals with Disabilities Education Act (IDEA), to receive special education and related services, a child must be identified as having a disability (i.e., labeled) and, in most cases, must be further classified into one of that state's categories, such as learning disabilities or orthopedic impairments. (IDEA allows children ages 3 to 9 to be identified as *developmentally delayed* and receive special education services without the use of a specific disability label.) In practice, therefore, a student becomes eligible for special education and related services because of membership in a given disability category.

Some educators believe that the labels used to identify and classify exceptional children stigmatize them and serve to deny them opportunities in the mainstream (e.g., Danforth & Rhodes, 1997; Harry & Klingner, 2007; Kliewer & Biklen, 1996; Reschly, 1996). Others argue that a workable system of classifying exceptional children (or their exceptional learning needs) is a prerequisite to providing needed special educational services and that using more "pleasant" terms minimizes and devalues the individual's situation and need for supports (e.g., Kauffman, 1999; Kauffman & Konold, 2007; Keogh, 2005a, 2005b).

> The stigma of cancer has not abated because people tried to cloak it with euphemisms, new terms considered more upbeat and less offensive. Imagine our reaction if someone were to say, "We no longer use the word *cancer;* now we use less unpleasant terms, such as *prolific cells* or *challenging tissue.*" The stigma of cancer has abated because people were encouraged to confront it for what it is, treat it, and prevent it. . . . We should work for a similar understanding and response to disability—a realistic, no-nonsense depiction of what it is and a loving, supportive attitude toward those who have disabilities. (Kauffman, 2003, p. 196)

Pros and cons of labeling

 Content Standards for Beginning Teachers—Common Core: Issues in definition and identification of individuals with exceptional learning needs (CC1K5).

Classification is a complex issue involving emotional, political, and ethical considerations in addition to scientific, fiscal, and educational interests (Florian et al., 2006; McLaughlin et al., 2006). As with most complex issues, valid perspectives and arguments exist on both sides of the labeling question. The reasons most often cited for and against the labeling and classification of exceptional children follow.

Possible Benefits of Labeling and Classification

- Labeling recognizes meaningful differences in learning or behavior and is a first and necessary step in responding responsibly to those differences. As Kauffman (1999) points out, "Although universal interventions that apply equally to all . . . can be implemented without labels and risk of stigma, no other interventions are possible without labels. Either all students are treated the same or some are treated differently. Any student who is treated differently is inevitably labeled. . . . When we are unwilling for whatever reason to say that a person has a problem, we are helpless to prevent it. . . . Labeling a problem clearly is the first step in dealing with it productively" (p. 452).

- A disability label can provide access to accommodations and services not available to persons without the label. For example, some middle-class parents of secondary students seek a learning disability label so their child student will receive accommodations such as additional time on college entrance exams.

- Labeling may lead to a protective response in which peers are more accepting of the atypical behavior of a child with disabilities than they would be of a child without disabilities who emitted that same behavior.

- Classification helps professionals communicate with one another and classify and evaluate research findings.

- Funding and resources for research and other programs are often based on specific categories of exceptionality.

- Labels enable disability-specific advocacy groups (e.g., parents of children with autism) to promote specific programs and spur legislative action (Association for Science in Autism Treatment, 2007).

- Labeling helps make exceptional children's special needs more visible to policy makers and the public.

Possible Disadvantages of Labeling and Classification

- Because the labels used in special education usually focus on disability, impairment, or performance deficits, some people may think only in terms of what the individual cannot do instead of what she can do or might be capable of doing (Terzi, 2005a, 2005b).

- Labels may stigmatize the child and lead peers to reject or ridicule the labeled child.

- Teachers may hold low expectations for a labeled student (Beilke & Yssel, 1999; Bianco, 2005) and treat her differentially on the basis of the label, which may result in a self-fulfilling prophecy. For example, in one study, student teachers gave a child labeled "autistic" more praise and rewards and fewer verbal corrections for incorrect responses than they gave a child labeled "normal" (Eikeseth & Lovaas, 1992). Such differential treatment could impede the rate at which a child learns new skills and contribute to a level of performance consistent with the label's prediction.

- Labels may negatively affect the child's self-esteem.

- Disability labels are often misused as explanatory constructs (e.g., "Sherry acts that way *because* she is emotionally disturbed").

- Even though membership in a given category is based on a particular characteristic (e.g., deafness), there is a tendency to assume that all children in a category share other traits as well, thereby diminishing the detection and appreciation of each child's uniqueness (Gelb, 1997; J. D. Smith & Mitchell, 2001b).

- Labels suggest that learning problems are primarily the result of something inherently wrong with the child, thereby reducing the systematic examination of and accountability for instructional variables as causes of performance deficits. This is an especially damaging outcome when a label provides a built-in excuse for ineffective instruction (e.g., "Jalen hasn't learned to read, because he has a learning disability").

- A disproportionate number of children from some minority and diverse cultural groups are included in special education programs and thus have been assigned disability labels (Harry & Klingner, 2006).

- Classifying exceptional children requires the expenditure of a great amount of money and professional and student time that might be better spent in delivering and evaluating the effects of early intervention for struggling students (L. S. Fuchs & Fuchs, 2007a).

Although the pros and cons of using disability category labels have been widely debated for several decades (Hobbs, 1975, 1976a, 1976b), neither conceptual arguments nor research

Effects of labels on behavior of others

 Content Standards for Beginning Teachers—Common Core: Teacher attitudes and behaviors that influence behavior of individuals with exceptional learning needs (CC5K4).

has produced a conclusive case for the total acceptance or absolute rejection of labeling practices. Most of the studies conducted to assess the effects of labeling have produced inconclusive, often contradictory evidence and have generally been marked by methodological weakness.

Alternatives to Labeling and Classification

Educators have proposed a number of alternative approaches to classifying exceptional children that focus on educationally relevant variables (e.g., Adelman, 1996; Hardman, McDonnell, & Welch, 1997; Iscoe & Payne, 1972; Sontag, Sailor, & Smith, 1977; Terzi, 2005a, 2005b). For example, Reynolds, Zetlin, and Heistad (1996) proposed "20/20 analysis," which would identify the lowest-achieving 20% and the highest-achieving 20% of students as eligible for broad (noncategorical) approaches to improvement of learning opportunities.

Some noted special educators have suggested that exceptional children be classified according to the curriculum and skill areas they need to learn.

> But if we shouldn't refer to these special children by using those old labels, then how should we refer to them? For openers, call them Rob, Amy, and Jose. Beyond that, refer to them on the basis of what you're trying to teach them. For example, if a teacher wants to teach Brandon to compute, read, and comprehend, he might call him a student of computation, reading, and comprehension. We do this all the time with older students. Sam, who attends Juilliard, is referred to as "the trumpet student"; Jane, who attends Harvard, is called "the law student." (T. C. Lovitt, personal communication, March 24, 2007)

For continued discussion of labeling, including the perspectives of several people with disabilities, see "Current Issues and Future Trends: What's in a Name? The Labels and Language of Special Education."

CURRENT ISSUES AND FUTURE TRENDS

WHAT'S IN A NAME? THE LABELS AND LANGUAGE OF SPECIAL EDUCATION

Some years ago at the annual convention of the Council for Exceptional Children, hundreds of attendees were wearing big yellow and black buttons that proclaimed "Label jars, not children!" Wearers of the buttons were presumably making a statement about one or more of the criticisms leveled at labeling and categorizing exceptional children, such as labeling is bad because it focuses on the child's deficits, labeling makes it more likely that others will expect poor performance or bad behavior from the child, and labels may damage the child's self-esteem.

Labels, in and of themselves, are not the problem. The relevant dictionary connotation of *label* as a noun is "a descriptive or identifying word or phrase" (*Merriam-Webster's OnLine*, 2007). Most special educators agree that a common language for referring to children who share instructional and related service needs is necessary. To suggest that services can be provided without labels is an "evasion of reality" (Kauffman, Mock, Tankersley, & Landrum, in press). As Kauffman (2002) explains, to refuse to use a meaningful label to identify a child's disability or problem is to refuse special education.

Any student who is treated differently from others is inevitably labeled. The issue is, really, whether all students should be treated the same (no labels) or some should be treated differently (which requires labeling). Some people have suggested that special treatment can be provided without labels, but that is clearly fantasy, not possibility. We cannot speak of difference or special needs without words (labels). We cannot call children nothing (i.e., we call them something). Moreover, either our labels for disabilities or special problems signify concern (something unsettling, not positive) or they are worthless for describing what needs to be changed. (p. 95)

The words that we use as labels do, however, influence the degree to which those words effectively and appropriately communicate variables relevant to the design and delivery of educational and other human services. For example, blanket labels such as *the handicapped* or *the retarded* imply that all persons in the group being labeled are alike; individuality has been lost. At the personal level, describing a child as a "physically handicapped boy" places too much emphasis on the disability, perhaps suggesting that the disability is the most important thing to know about him.

How, then, should we refer to exceptional children? At the personal level, we should follow Tom Lovitt's advice and call them by their names: Linda, Shawon, and Jackie. Referring to a child as "Mitch, a fifth-grade student with learning disabilities" helps us focus on the individual child and his primary role as a student. Such a description does not ignore or gloss over Mitch's learning problems but acknowledges that there are other things we should know about him.

It is important for everyone, not just special educators, to speak, write, and think about exceptional children and adults in ways that respect each person's individuality and to recognize strengths and abilities instead of focusing only on disabilities. Simply changing the way we talk about a person with a disability, however, will not make the problems posed by her disability go away. Some people with disabilities have spoken out against the efforts of those without disabilities to assuage their feelings with language that may be politically correct but that ignore the reality of a disability. Judy Heumann (1993), a former director of the U.S. Office of Special Education and Rehabilitation Services and a person who has used a wheelchair since she was 18 months old, explains her position:

> As our movement has evolved, we have been plagued by people, almost always not themselves disabled, attempting to change what we call ourselves. If we are "victims" of anything, it is of such terms as physically challenged, able-disabled, differently-abled, handi-capables, and people with differing abilities, to name just a few. Nondisabled people's discomfort with reality-based terms such as disabled led them to these euphemisms. I believe these euphemisms have the effect of depoliticizing our own terminology and devaluing our own view of ourselves as disabled people. . . .
>
> I have a physical disability that results in my inability to walk and perform a number of other significant tasks without the assistance of another person. This cannot be labeled away and I am not ashamed of it. I feel no need to change the word "disabled." For me, there is no stigma. I am not driven to call myself a "person with a disability." I know I am a person; I do not need to tell myself that I am. I also do not believe that being called a "person with a disability" results in my being treated any more like a human being. Maybe putting the word "disabled" first makes people stop and look at what, as a result of society's historical indifference to and/or hatred of people like me, is a critical part of my existence. . . .
>
> Let the disabled people who are politically involved and personally affected determine our own language. . . . A suggestion to those of you who do not know what to call me: ask!

Professional and advocacy organizations have taken differing views on disability labels. On the one hand, the National Federation of the Blind adopted a resolution

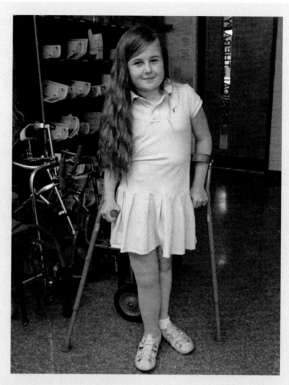

Changing the label used to identify Charlotte for special education eligibility won't lessen the impact of her disability. But referring to her as "Charlotte, a fifth grader who likes to read mysteries," helps us recognize her strengths and abilities—what she can do—instead of focusing on a disability label as if it were the most important thing to know about her.

against the use of terms such as *visually challenged* and *people with blindness*, stating that such politically correct euphemisms are "totally unacceptable and deserving only ridicule because of their strained and ludicrous attempt to avoid such straightforward, respectable words as *blindness, blind, the blind, blind person,* or *blind persons*" (Jernigan, 1993, p. 867). The American Association on Mental Retardation (AAMR) changed its name to the American Association on Intellectual and Developmental Disabilities (AAIDD) because it considered *intellectual disabilities* to be less stigmatizing than *mental retardation* (Prabhala, 2007).

Efforts to find more acceptable words and phrases to identify disabilities and the need for special education will continue as today's acceptable term becomes a pejorative in the future. As Steven Taylor, editor of the AAIDD's long-standing but newly named journal, *Intellectual and Developmental Disabilities*, noted, "Anyone who believes that we have finally arrived at the perfect terminology will be proven wrong by history. I am sure that at some future point we will find the phrase intellectual and developmental disabilities to be inadequate and demeaning" (cited in Prabhala, 2007, n.p.).

Changing the label for a disability will not lessen prejudice or stigma (real or imagined). In a discussion of the pros and cons of replacing *mental retardation* with *intellectual disabilities*, Eidelman called for a public education campaign to foster more positive attitudes towards people with disabilities: "Changing the term will make many people happy. That happiness will quickly fade when the new term is used as a pejorative. Without a long-term effort to include everyone and to educate those with negative or neutral attitudes toward our constituents, a change in terminology will become the new pejorative very quickly" (in H. R. Turnbull, Turnbull, Warren, Eidelman, & Marchand, 2002, p. 68). And a change in terminology will not reduce the effects of the condition on the person's life.

What Do You Think?

1. From the perspective of a school-aged child (or the parent or sibling of a child) who needs special education, what labels would you find most appropriate for each category of exceptionality listed earlier in this chapter?

2. What should prospective teachers learn about the types and function of labels used in special education?

3. If disability labels are necessary to identify children who need special education, how can teachers minimize the potential of labels to stigmatize and prejudice people?

WHY ARE LAWS GOVERNING THE EDUCATION OF EXCEPTIONAL CHILDREN NECESSARY?

An Exclusionary Past

It is said that a society can be judged by the way it treats those who are different. By this criterion, the U.S. educational system has a less than distinguished history. Children who are different because of race, culture, language, gender, socioeconomic status, or exceptionality have often been denied full and fair access to educational opportunities (J. A. Banks & Banks, 2007; J. D. Smith, 2004). It's important, however, to note that past practices were not entirely negative. Long before any legal requirement to do so, many children with special needs were educated by devoted teachers and parents.

In the not-so-distant past, many children with disabilities were entirely excluded from any publicly supported program of education. Before the 1970s, laws in many states permitted public schools to deny enrollment to children with disabilities (Murdick, Gartin, & Crabtree, 2006). One state law, for example, allowed schools to refuse to serve "children physically or mentally incapacitated for school work"; another state had a law stipulating that children with "bodily or mental conditions rendering attendance inadvisable" could be turned away. When these laws were contested, the nation's courts generally supported exclusion. In a 1919 case, for example, a 13-year-old student with physical disabilities (but normal intellectual ability) was excluded from his local school because he "produces a depressing and nauseating effect upon the teachers and school children" (J. D. Smith, 2004, p. 4).

When local public schools began to accept a measure of responsibility for educating certain exceptional students, a philosophy of segregation prevailed. Children with disabilities were confined to segregated classrooms, isolated from the children and teachers in the general education program. One special education teacher describes the crude facilities in which her special class operated and the sense of isolation she felt in the 1960s:

> I accepted my first teaching position, a special education class in a basement room next door to the furnace. Of the 15 "educable mentally retarded" children assigned to work with me, most were simply nonreaders from poor families. One child had been banished to my room because she posed a behavior problem to her fourth-grade teacher.
>
> My class and I were assigned a recess spot on the opposite side of the play yard, far away from the "normal" children. I was the only teacher who did not have a lunch break. I was required to eat with my "retarded" children while other teachers were permitted to leave their students.... Isolated from my colleagues, I closed my door and did my thing, oblivious to the larger educational circles in which I was immersed. Although it was the basement room, with all the negative perceptions that arrangement implies, I was secure in the knowledge that

despite the ignominy of it all I did good things for children who were previously unloved and untaught. (Aiello, 1976, p. 14)

Children with mild learning and behavioral problems usually remained in general education classrooms but received no special help. Those who did not make satisfactory academic progress were termed "slow learners" or simply "failures." If their deportment in class exceeded the teacher's tolerance for misbehavior, they were labeled "disciplinary problems" and suspended from school. Children with more severe disabilities—including many with visual, hearing, and physical or health impairments—were placed in segregated schools or institutions or kept at home. Gifted and talented children seldom received special attention in schools. It was assumed they could make it on their own without help.

Society's response to exceptional children has come a long way. As our concepts of equality, freedom, and justice have expanded, children with disabilities and their families have moved from exclusion and isolation to inclusion and participation. Society no longer regards children with disabilities as beyond the responsibility of the local public schools. No longer may a child with disabilities be turned away from school because someone believes he is unable to benefit from education. Federal legislation and court rulings have made it clear that all children with disabilities have the right to a free appropriate program of public education in the least restrictive environment.

The provision of equitable educational opportunities to exceptional children has not come about by chance. Many laws and court cases have had important effects on public education in general and on the education of children with special needs in particular. And the process of change is never finished; legal influences on special education are not fixed or static but fluid and dynamic (Yell, 2006).

Separate Is Not Equal

The history of special education is closely related to the civil rights movement. Special education was strongly influenced by social developments and court decisions in the 1950s and 1960s, especially the landmark case *Brown v. Board of Education of Topeka* (1954), which challenged the practice of segregating students according to race. In its ruling in the *Brown* case, the U.S. Supreme Court declared that education must be made available to all children on equal terms:

> Today, education is perhaps the most important function of state and local governments. Compulsory school attendance laws and the great expenditure for education both demonstrate our recognition of the importance of education to our democratic society. It is required in the performance of our most basic responsibilities. . . . In these days, it is doubtful that any child may reasonably be expected to succeed in life if he is denied the opportunity of an education. (*Brown v. Board of Education*, 1954)

The *Brown* decision began a period of intense questioning among parents of children with disabilities, who asked why the same principles of equal access to education should not apply to their children. Parents and other advocates dissatisfied with an educational system that denied equal access to children with disabilities initiated numerous court cases in the 1960s and early 1970s. Generally, the parents based their arguments on the 14th Amendment to the Constitution, which provides that no state shall deny any person within its jurisdiction the equal protection of the law and that no state shall deprive any person of life, liberty, or property without due process of law.

Equal Protection

In the past, children with disabilities usually were denied access to certain educational programs or received special education only in segregated settings. Basically, when the courts have been asked to rule on the practice of denial or segregation, judges have examined whether such differential treatment is rational and whether it is necessary. One of the most historically significant cases to examine these questions was the class-action suit *Pennsylvania Association for Retarded Children (PARC) v. Commonwealth of Pennsylvania* (1972). *PARC* challenged a state law that denied public school education to certain children considered "unable to profit from public school attendance."

The lawyers and parents supporting *PARC* argued that even though the children had intellectual disabilities, it was neither rational nor necessary to assume they were ineducable and untrainable. Because the state was unable to prove that the children were, in fact, ineducable or to demonstrate a rational need for excluding them from public school programs, the court decided that the children were entitled to receive a free, public education. In addition, the court maintained that parents had the right to be notified before any change was made in their children's educational program.

The wording of the *PARC* decision proved particularly important because of its influence on subsequent federal legislation. Not only did the court rule that all children with mental retardation were entitled to a free appropriate public education, but the ruling also stipulated that placements in general education classrooms and regular public schools were preferable to segregated settings.

> It is the Commonwealth's obligation to place each mentally retarded child in a free, public program of education and training appropriate to the child's capacity. . . . Placement in a regular public school class is preferable to placement in a special public school class and placement in a special public school is preferable to placement in any other type of program of education and training. (*PARC v. Commonwealth of Pennsylvania,* 1972)

In addition to the *Brown* and *PARC* cases, several other judicial decisions have had far-reaching effects on special education. (See Table 1.3 later in this chapter.) The rulings from some of those cases were incorporated into subsequent federal legislation, most notably the IDEA.

THE INDIVIDUALS WITH DISABILITIES EDUCATION ACT

In 1975 Congress passed Public Law 94–142, the Education for All Handicapped Children Act. This landmark piece of legislation completely changed the face of education in this country. Congress has reauthorized and amended P.L. 94–142 five times. The 1990 amendments renamed the law the Individuals with Disabilities Education Act—often referred to by its acronym, IDEA. The most recent reauthorization of IDEA, P.L. 108–466, is titled The Individuals with Disabilities Education Improvement Act of 2004. [Federal legislation is designated by a numerical system. Public Law 94–142, for example, was the 142nd bill passed by the 94th Congress. Federal statutes and regulations are published in the *United States Code.* The IDEA citation 20 U.S.C. §1400[c] refers to *United States Code,* Title 20, Section 1400, Subsection c. The regulations for IDEA, which spell out the details for meeting the law's provisions, are contained in the *Code of Federal Regulations* (CFR).]

IDEA has profoundly influenced what takes place in every school building in the country and has changed the roles and responsibilities of general and special educators, school administrators, parents, and students with disabilities in the educational process. The passage of IDEA marked the culmination of the efforts of a great many educators, parents, and legislators to bring together in one comprehensive bill this country's laws regarding the education of children with disabilities. The law reflects society's concern about treating people with disabilities as full citizens with the same rights and privileges that all other citizens enjoy.

The purposes of IDEA are

1. (A) to ensure that all children with disabilities have available to them a free appropriate public education that emphasizes special education and related services designed to meet their unique needs and prepare them for further education, employment, and independent living; (B) to ensure that the rights of children with disabilities and parents of such children are protected; and (C) to assist States, localities, educational service agencies, and Federal agencies to provide for the education of all children with disabilities;

2. to assist States in the implementation of a statewide, comprehensive, coordinated, multidisciplinary, interagency system of early intervention services for infants and toddlers with disabilities and their families;

3. to ensure that educators and parents have the necessary tools to improve educational results for children with disabilities by supporting system improvement activities;

coordinated research and personnel preparation; coordinated technical assistance, dissemination, and support; and technology development and media services; and

4. to assess, and ensure the effectiveness of, efforts to educate children with disabilities. (PL 108–466, Sec. 601 (d)).

Six Major Principles of IDEA

The majority of the many rules and regulations defining how IDEA operates fall under six major principles that have remained basically unchanged since 1975 (T. E. C. Smith, 2005; H. R. Turnbull, Stowe, & Huerta, 2007):

Zero Reject   Schools must educate *all* children with disabilities. This principle applies regardless of the nature or severity of the disability; no child with disabilities may be excluded from a free public education. The requirement to provide special education to all students with disabilities is absolute between the ages of 6 and 17. If a state provides educational services to children without disabilities between the ages of 3 to 5 and 18 to 21, it must also educate all children with disabilities in those age groups. Each state's education agency is responsible for locating, identifying, and evaluating all children, from birth to age 21, residing in the state with disabilities or who are suspected of having disabilities. This requirement of IDEA is called the *child find system*.

Nondiscriminatory Identification and Evaluation   Schools must use nonbiased, multifactored methods of evaluation to determine whether a child has a disability and, if so, whether the child needs special education. Testing and evaluation procedures must not discriminate on the basis of race, culture, or native language. All tests must be administered in the child's native language, and identification and placement decisions cannot be made on the basis of a single test score. These provisions of IDEA are known as *protection in evaluation procedures*.

Free Appropriate Public Education   All children with disabilities, regardless of the type or severity of their disability, shall receive a free appropriate public education (FAPE). This education must be provided at public expense—that is, without cost to the child's parents. An **individualized education program (IEP)** must be developed and implemented to meet the unique needs of each student with a disability. The IEP specifies the child's unique educational needs, states present levels of performance, identifies measurable annual goals, and describes the specific special education and related services that will be provided to help the child attain those goals and benefit from education. (See Chapter 2 for a detailed discussion of IEPs.) An important addition to IDEA 2004 was the stipulation that the special education and related services prescribed in a child's IEP be "based on peer-reviewed research to the extent practicable." For example, a large body of peer-reviewed research supports the use of instructional activities that build students' fluency with tool skills such as reading and math computation. See the accompanying Teaching & Learning box: "It's Good to Go Fast!"

Least Restrictive Environment   IDEA mandates that students with disabilities be educated with children without disabilities to the maximum extent appropriate and that students with disabilities be removed to separate classes or schools only when the nature or severity of their disabilities is such that they cannot receive an appropriate education in a general education classroom with supplementary aids and services. IDEA creates a presumption in favor of inclusion in the general education classroom by requiring that a student's IEP contain a justification and explanation of the extent, if any, to which the student will not participate with nondisabled peers in the general academic curriculum, extracurricular activities, and other nonacademic activities (e.g., lunch, recess, transportation, dances). To ensure that each student with disabilities is educated in the

Major principles of IDEA

Council for Exceptional Children   Content Standards for Beginning Teachers—Common Core: Rights and responsibilities of students, parents, teachers and other professionals, and schools related to exceptional learning needs (CC1K4).

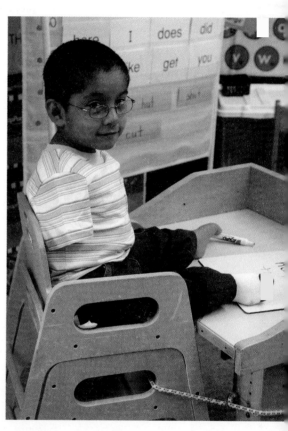

In the past, many children like Jose were denied access to education in public schools.

It's Good to Go Fast!
Fluency-Building Activities Promote Student Achievement

ere's a prediction: Ask 100 teachers, "Is practice important?" and it's virtually certain that every one will answer, *"Yes, of course"* (and many will give you a funny look for asking a question with such an obvious answer). Then ask the same 100 teachers, "What is the purpose of practice?" Their answers to this question will vary considerably, but responses such as the following will be common: practice should help students "internalize the knowledge," "attain a deep or rich understanding," and "gain confidence" with the material by remembering the knowledge or skill. These are worthy outcomes, but what does the performance of a student who has "internalized" a concept look like, and what types of practice will help students gain confidence with skill or a bit of knowledge?

Here's another purpose of practice: Practice should help students *achieve fluency* with knowledge and skills.

WHAT IS FLUENCY, AND WHY DOES IT MATTER?

Fluency is the combination of accuracy and speed that characterizes competent performance. A person who is fluent performs a skill automatically, without hesitations, as if by second nature (Binder, 1996). Accuracy, typically in the form of percent correct, is commonly used to assess student performance; fluency gives a *more complete picture of learning* than accuracy

alone. Whereas two students might each complete a page of math problems with 100% accuracy, the one who finishes in 2 minutes is more accomplished than the one who needs 7 minutes to answer the same problems. Fluency also has important *functional implications.* We must perform many of the skills we use every day in school, home, community, or the workplace at a certain rate or speed to be useful. The student who needs 5 minutes to read the directions on a worksheet that his classmates read in 1 minute may not be able to finish the task in the time allotted.

A student who is fluent with a particular skill or knowledge is likely to exhibit the following outcomes (Binder, 1996; Kubina, 2005; Kubina & Morrison, 2000; Lin & Kubina, 2005; Smyth & Keenan, 2002):

- Better *retention*—the ability to use the skill or knowledge at a later point in time, even when no opportunities to emit the behavior have occurred since prior practice.

- Greater *endurance*—the ability to stay at the task for longer periods of time and stay engaged. Fluent performers are also less likely to be distracted by minor events in the environment.

- Improved *application and generalization* of the knowledge or skill. For example, a student who has achieved fluency in component skills (e.g., multiplication facts and subtraction) may learn composite skills (e.g., long division) more quickly.

How many directional arrows can you correctly identify in 1 minute? "See-say" time trials are helping Robert attain fluency with this map-reading skill.

THREE FLUENCY-BUILDING TECHNIQUES

The three fluency-building techniques described next—repeated reading, time trials, and SAFMEDS—can be conducted as teacher-directed practice activities one-on-one in small groups or whole class. Each technique can also be used as peer-managed or independent practice activities.

Repeated Reading. Oral reading fluency is a key component of reading success (National Reading Panel, 2000). Students who can read fast can cover more material, and their comprehension is better than slower readers (Daane, Campbell, Grigg, Goodman, & Oranje, 2005). One of the most often-used interventions to improve reading fluency is repeated reading. With **repeated reading,** the student orally reads the same passage, usually three to five times during each session. With each successive reading, the student tries to increase the number of words read correctly per minute. The student first listens to the teacher, who models reading the passage; the student may read the passage silently, before beginning; and the teacher provides feedback and practice on missed words and phrases (Alber-Morgan, 2007). When the student achieves the fluency criterion on a given passage, the teacher introduces a new passage. The difficulty level of successive passages gradually increases over time. The set goal is slightly higher than the current reading rate (Bursuck & Damer, 2007). Numerous studies report that repeated reading is an effective means for improving oral reading fluency for students with and without disabilities in elementary, middle, and high school (Alber-Morgan, Ramp, Anderson, & Martin, in press; Tam, Heward, & Heng, 2006; Therrien, 2004; Yurick, Robinson, Cartledge, Lo, & Evans, 2006).

Time Trials. Giving students the opportunity to perform a skill as many times as they can in a brief period—**time trials**—can be an excellent way to build fluency. Practice in the form of 1-minute time trials helps students with and without disabilities achieve fluency with a wide range of academic, vocational, and other skills (e.g., Beck, Conrad, & Anderson, 1999; Binder, 1996; K. R. Johnson & Layng, 1994; McCuin & Cooper, 1994; A. D. Miller, Hall, & Heward, 1995; Stump et al., 1992).

SAFMEDS. *Say All Fast a Minute Each Day Shuffled* (**SAFMEDS**) consist of a deck of cards with a question, vocabulary term, or problem on one side of each card and the answer on the other side. A student answers as many items in the deck as he can during 1 minute.

The student looks at the question or problem, states the answer, flips the cards over to reveal the correct answer, and puts the card on either a "correct" or "incorrect" pile. You can find examples and guidelines for using SAFMEDS in Eshleman (2004).

HOW TO GET STARTED

Teachers should consider these guidelines when planning and conducting fluency-building activities:

- *Use fluency-building during the practice stage of learning*. During the initial acquisition stage of learning, the student should focus on learning to perform the skill correctly. A student who tries to "go fast" before she can perform the skill correctly more often than incorrectly might end up "practicing errors" instead of building fluency. (Because they reveal the correct answer to each question, SAFMEDS can help build fluency during the acquisition stage of learning.)
- *The time for each fluency-building trial should be brief*. One minute is sufficient for most academic skills. Brief *sprints* of 10 seconds, then 15 seconds, 20 seconds, and so on can help students gradually build their fluency.
- *Do fluency-building activities every day*. For example, a series of two or three 1-minute oral reading time trials could be conducted at the end of each day's lesson.
- *Make fluency building fun*. Time trials should not be presented as a test; they are a learning activity that can be approached like a game.
- *Follow fluency-building activities with a more relaxed activity*.
- *Feedback should emphasize proficiency* (total number correct), not simply accuracy (percentage correct).
- *Encourage each student to set goals and try to beat his or her own best performance*.
- *Have students keep track of their progress* by self-graphing their best performance each day.
- *Consider using a performance feedback chart* to provide both individual students and the class with feedback during a fluency-building program.

To learn more about using fluency-building strategies, go to the Building Teaching Skills section in Chapter 1 of MyEducationLab and complete the activities. As you watch the videos embedded within the activities, compare and contrast how different teachers employ these strategies in their classrooms.

least restrictive environment (LRE) appropriate for her needs, school districts must provide a continuum of placement and service alternatives. (You will find a detailed discussion of the LRE and the continuum of services in Chapter 2.)

Due Process Safeguards   Schools must provide due process safeguards to protect the rights of children with disabilities and their parents. Parental consent must be obtained for initial and all subsequent evaluations and placement decisions regarding special education. Schools must maintain the confidentiality of all records pertaining to a child with disabilities and make those records available to the parents. When parents of a child with disabilities disagree with the results of an evaluation performed by the school, they can obtain an independent evaluation at public expense. When the school and parents disagree on the identification, evaluation, placement, or provision of a FAPE and related services for the child, the parents may request a due process hearing. States also must offer parents an opportunity to resolve the matter through mediation by a third party before holding a due process hearing. Parents have the right to attorneys' fees if they prevail in due process or judicial proceedings under IDEA. The law also includes provisions that allow the court to award reasonable attorneys' fees to the prevailing school district against the attorney of a parent, or the parent who files a complaint that the court determines to be frivolous, unreasonable, without foundation, or filed for any improper purpose, such as to harass.

Although "due process hearings are a last resort to resolve conflicts or problems between school districts and parents" (Getty & Summey, 2004, p. 40), they occur with increasing frequency. The majority of due process hearings are over placement or program issues (Newcomer & Zirkel, 1999). Zirkel and D'Angelo (2002) reviewed all reported hearing decisions in the United States from 1998 to 2000 and found that schools received a favorable decision in 55% of hearings, parents prevailed in 23%, and 22% of the decisions were mixed results.

Parent and Student Participation and Shared Decision Making   Schools must collaborate with parents and students with disabilities in the planning and implementation of special education and related services. The parents' (and, whenever appropriate, the student's) input and wishes must be considered in determining IEP goals, related-service needs, and placement decisions.

Other Provisions of IDEA

Extending Special Education Services to Infants, Toddlers, and Preschoolers   Noting that states were serving at most about 70% of preschool children with disabilities and that early intervention services for infants and toddlers with disabilities from birth through age 2 were scarce or nonexistent in many states, Congress included provisions in the Education of the Handicapped Act Amendments in 1986 (P.L. 99–457) to expand services for these segments of the population. Beginning with the 1990–1991 school year, P.L. 99–457 required each state to fully serve all preschool children with disabilities ages 3 to 5—that is, to provide the same services and protections available to school-age children.

P.L. 99–457 included an incentive grant program to encourage states to provide early intervention services to infants and toddlers with disabilities and their families. The children served are those from birth through age 2 who need early intervention services because they are experiencing developmental delays or have a diagnosed biological condition likely to result in developmental delays. When Congress reauthorized IDEA in 1997 (P.L. 105–17) and again in 2004 (P.L. 108–446), it reaffirmed the nation's commitment to a system of early intervention services. Rather than mandate special services for this age group, IDEA encourages each state to develop and implement a statewide, comprehensive, coordinated, multidisciplinary, interagency program of early intervention services for infants and toddlers with disabilities and their families. The encouragement is in the form of a gradually increasing amount of federal money awarded to states that identify and serve all infants and toddlers with disabilities. Various education and human services agencies within each state work together to provide services such as medical and educational assessment, physical therapy, speech and language intervention, and parent counseling and training. These early intervention services are prescribed and implemented according to an **individualized family**

Due process safeguards

 Council for Exceptional Children

Content Standards for Beginning Teachers—Common Core: Issues, assurances, and due process rights related to assessment, eligibility, and placement within a continuum of services (CC1K6).

services plan (IFSP) written by a multidisciplinary team that includes the child's parents. (See Chapter 14 for a discussion of IFSPs.)

Related Services and Assistive Technology Children with disabilities have sometimes been prevented from attending their neighborhood schools or benefiting from educational activities by circumstances that impede their access or participation. A child who uses a wheelchair, for example, may require a specially equipped school bus. A child with special health needs may require medication several times a day. A child with an orthopedic impairment may need physical therapy to maintain sufficient strength and flexibility in her arms and legs. IDEA requires that schools provide any **related services** and **assistive technology**—devices and services such as visual aids, augmentative communication devices, specialized equipment for computer access—that a child with a disability may need to access

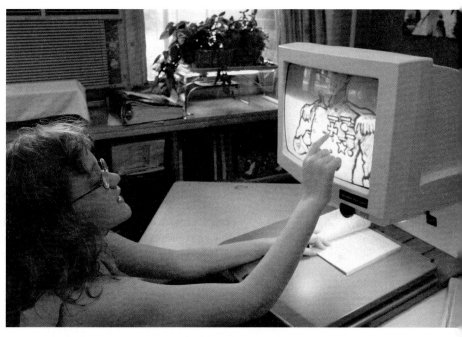

School districts must provide related services and assistive technology to students with disabilities—such as this device that enlarges printed material—so they may have access to and benefit from a public education.

and benefit from special education. Table 1.2 provides definitions of the types of related services included in the IDEA regulations. Assistive technology is defined in IDEA as follows:

> (A) IN GENERAL.—The term 'assistive technology device' means any item, piece of equipment, or product system, whether acquired commercially off the shelf, modified, or customized, that is used to increase, maintain, or improve functional capabilities of a child with a disability. (B) EXCEPTION.—The term does not include a medical device that is surgically implanted, or the replacement of such device.
>
>   (2) 'assistive technology service' means any service that directly assists a child with a disability in the selection, acquisition, or use of an assistive technology device. (P.L. 108-446, 20 USC 1401, Sec 602 (1))

Federal Funding of Special Education Laws and regulations calling for special education and related services have limited value if the schools lack the financial resources to provide them. Educating students with disabilities is very expensive. When Congress passed IDEA in 1975, it promised to provide federal funds for 40% of the "excess costs" of educating children with disabilities, based on the national average for per-student expenditures. Although federal funding for IDEA has increased in recent years, it has never reached more than about 18% of the national average (Chambers, Parrish, & Harr, 2002; Sack-Min, 2007). State and local educational administrators contend that federal financial assistance for educating students with disabilities has not been sufficient and that schools are hard pressed to meet the requirements in IDEA.

According to the Council for Exceptional Children (CEC) (2006b), "the intended federal/state/local cost-sharing partnership has not been realized because Congress never lived up to its financial obligation" (p. 1). IDEA 2004 failed to provide full funding necessary for states to meet the law's many mandates. CEC estimates that, based on funding levels approved by Congress during the past 30 years, IDEA will not reach full funding until fiscal year 2035.

Go to the Homework & Exercises section in Chapter 1 of MyEducationLab and complete Homework Exercise 2. As you complete this exercise, consider the value of assistive technology in helping students with disabilities achieve success in the classroom.

Legal Challenges Based on IDEA

Although IDEA has resulted in dramatic increases in the number of students receiving special education services and greater recognition of the legal rights of children with disabilities and their families, it has also resulted in an ever-increasing number of disputes concerning the education of students with disabilities. Parents and other advocates have

To learn more about students receiving and using related services and assistive technology go to the Homework & Exercises section in Chapter 1 on MyEducationLab and click on Homework Exercise 3.

TABLE 1.2

Types and definitions of related services that students with disabilities may need to benefit from special education

RELATED SERVICE	IDEA DEFINITION
Audiology	(1) Identification of children with hearing loss; (2) Determination of the range, nature, and degree of hearing loss, including referral for medical or other professional attention for the habilitation of hearing; (3) Provision of habilitative activities, such as auditory training, speech reading (lipreading), hearing evaluation, and speech conservation; (4) Creation and administration of programs for prevention of hearing loss; (5) Counseling and guidance of children, parents, and teachers, regarding hearing loss; and (6) Determining the child's need for group and individual amplification, selecting and fitting an appropriate hearing aid, and evaluating the effectiveness of amplification.
Counseling services	Services provided by qualified social workers, psychologists, guidance counselors, or other qualified personnel.
Early identification and assessment	Implementation of a formal plan for identifying a disability as early as possible in a child's life.
Interpreting services	(1) The following, when used with respect to children who are deaf or hard of hearing: Oral transliteration services, cued language transliteration services, sign language transliteration and interpreting services, and transcription services, such as communication access real-time translation (CART), C-Print, and TypeWell; and (2) Special interpreting services for children who are deaf-blind.
Medical services	Services provided by a licensed physician for diagnostic or evaluation purposes to determine a child's medically related disability that results in the child's need for special education and related services.
Occupational therapy	(1) Services provided by a qualified occupational therapist; and (2) includes (A) Improving, developing, or restoring functions impaired or lost through illness, injury, or deprivation; (B) Improving ability to perform tasks for independent functioning if functions are impaired or lost; and (C) Preventing, through early intervention, initial or further impairment or loss of function.
Orientation and mobility services	Services provided to blind or visually impaired children by qualified personnel to enable those students to obtain systematic orientation to and safe movement within their environments in school, home, and community.
Parent counseling and training	(1) Assisting parents in understanding the special needs of their child; (2) Providing parents with information about child development; and (3) Helping parents to acquire the necessary skills that will allow them to support the implementation of their child's IEP or IFSP.
Physical therapy	Services provided by a qualified physical therapist.
Psychological services	(1) Administering psychological and educational tests, and other assessment procedures; (2) Interpreting assessment results; (3) Obtaining, integrating, and interpreting information about child behavior and conditions relating to learning; (4) Consulting with other staff members in planning school programs to meet the special needs of children as indicated by psychological tests, interviews, and behavioral evaluations; (5) Planning and managing a program of psychological services, including psychological counseling for children and parents; and (6) Assisting in developing positive behavioral intervention strategies.
Recreation	(1) Assessment of leisure function; (2) Therapeutic recreation services; (3) Recreation programs in schools and community agencies; and (4) Leisure education.
Rehabilitative counseling services	Services provided by qualified personnel in individual or group sessions that focus specifically on career development, employment preparation, achieving independence, and integration in the workplace and community.

TABLE 1.2 (CONTINUED)

Types and definitions of related services that students with disabilities may need to benefit from special education

RELATED SERVICE	IDEA DEFINITION
School health services and school nurse services	Health services designed to enable a child with a disability to receive FAPE as described by the child's IEP. School nurse services are provided by a qualified school nurse or other qualified person. School health services are services provided by either a qualified school nurse or other qualified person.
Social work services in the schools	(1) Preparing a social or developmental history on a child with a disability; (2) Group and individual counseling with the child and family; (3) Working in partnership with parents and others on those problems in a child's living situation (home, school, and community) that affect the child's adjustment in school; (4) Mobilizing school and community resources to enable the child to learn as effectively as possible; and (5) Assisting in developing positive behavioral intervention strategies.
Speech-language pathology services	(1) Identification of children with speech or language impairments; (2) Diagnosis and appraisal of specific speech or language impairments; (3) Referral for medical or other professional attention necessary for the habilitation of speech or language impairments; (4) Provision of speech and language services for the habilitation and prevention of communicative problems; and (5) Counseling and guidance of parents, children, and teachers regarding speech and language impairments.
Transportation	(1) Travel to and from school and between schools. (2) Travel in and around school buildings. (3) Specialized equipment (such as special or adapted buses, lifts, and ramps), if required to provide special transportation for a child with a disability.
Exception—services that apply to children with surgically implanted devices, including cochlear implants	(1) Related services do not include a medical device that is surgically implanted, the optimization of that device's functioning (e.g., mapping), maintenance of that device, or the replacement of that device. (2) Nothing in paragraph (b)(1) of this section—(i) Limits the right of a child with a surgically implanted device (e.g., cochlear implant) to receive related services that are determined by the IEP Team to be necessary for the child to receive FAPE; (ii) Limits the responsibility of a public agency to appropriately monitor and maintain medical devices that are needed to maintain the health and safety of the child, including breathing, nutrition, or operation of other bodily functions, while the child is transported to and from school or is at school; or (iii) Prevents the routine checking of an external component of a surgically implanted device to make sure it is functioning properly.

Source: IDEA Regulations, 34 C.F.R. §300.34; Authority: 20 U.S.C. §1401 (26).

brought about thousands of due process hearings and hundreds of court cases. Due process hearings and court cases often place parents and schools in confrontation and are expensive and time-consuming (Getty & Summey, 2004; Lanigan, Audette, Dreier, & Kobersy, 2001).

It is difficult to generalize how courts have resolved the various legal challenges based on IDEA. Many different judicial interpretations exist for *free appropriate education* and *least restrictive environment.* The federal statute and regulations use these terms repeatedly; but in the view of many parents, educators, judges, and attorneys, they are not defined with sufficient clarity. Thus, the questions of what is appropriate and least restrictive for a particular child and whether a public school district should be compelled to provide a certain type of instructional program or service must often be decided by judges and courts on consideration of the evidence presented. Some of the key issues that courts rule on are the extended school year, related services, disciplinary procedures, and the fundamental right to an education for students with the most severe disabilities. Table 1.3 summarizes key judicial decisions that have had significant impact on special education and the lives of individuals with disabilities and their families. For detailed discussions and analyses of these and court cases, see Bartlett, Etscheidt, and Weisentstein (2007); Murdick et al. (2007); Wright and Wright (2006); and Yell (2006).

TABLE 1.3

Major court cases that have influenced special education
and the lives of individuals with disabilities

DATE	COURT CASE	EDUCATIONAL IMPLICATIONS
1954	*Brown v. Board of Education of Topeka* (Kansas)	The case established the right of all children to an equal opportunity for an education.
1967	*Hobson v. Hansen* (Washington, DC)	The court declared the tracking system, in which children were placed into either general or special classes according to their scores on intelligence tests, unconstitutional because it discriminated against African American and poor children.
1970	*Diana v. State Board of Education* (California)	A Spanish-speaking student in California had been placed in a special class for children with mental retardation based on the results of intelligence tests given in English. The court ruled that children cannot be placed in special education on the basis of culturally biased tests or tests given in other than the child's native language.
1972	*Mills v. Board of Education of the District of Columbia*	Seven children had been excluded from the public schools in Washington, DC, because of learning and behavior problems. The school district contended that it did not have enough money to provide special education programs for them. The court ruled that financial problems cannot be allowed to have a greater impact on children with disabilities than on students without disabilities and ordered the schools to readmit the children and serve them appropriately.
1972	*Pennsylvania Association for Retarded Citizens v. the Commonwealth of Pennsylvania*	This class-action suit established the right to free public education for all children with mental retardation.
1972	*Wyatt v. Stickney* (Alabama)	The decision declared that individuals in state institutions have the right to appropriate treatment within those institutions.
1979	*Larry P. v. Riles* (California)	The court ruled that IQ tests used to place African American children in special classes were inappropriate because they failed to recognize the children's cultural background and the learning that took place in their homes and communities. The court ordered that IQ tests could not be used as the sole basis for placing children into special classes.
1979	*Armstrong v. Kline* (Pennsylvania)	The case established the right of some children with severe disabilities to an extension of the 180-day public school year.
1982	*Board of Education of the Hendrick Hudson Central School District v. Rowley* (New York)	This was the first case based on P.L. 94–142 to reach the U.S. Supreme Court; while denying the plaintiff's specific request, the Court upheld for each child with disabilities the right to a personalized program of instruction and necessary supportive services.
1983	*Abrahamson v. Hershman* (Massachusetts)	The court ruled that residential placement in a private school was necessary for a child with multiple disabilities who needed around-the-clock training and required the school district to pay for the private placement.

TABLE 1.3 (CONTINUED)

**Major court cases that have influenced special education
and the lives of individuals with disabilities**

DATE	COURT CASE	EDUCATIONAL IMPLICATIONS
1984	*Department of Education v. Katherine D.* (Hawaii)	The court ruled that a homebound instructional program for a child with multiple health impairments did not meet the least restrictive environment standard and called for the child to be placed in a class with children without disabilities and provided with related medical services.
1984	*Irving Independent School District v. Tatro* (Texas)	The court ruled that catheterization was necessary for a child with physical disabilities to remain in school and that it could be performed by a nonphysician, thus obligating the school district to provide that service.
1984	*Smith v. Robinson* (Rhode Island)	The court ordered the state to pay for the placement of a child with severe disabilities in a residential program and ordered the school district to reimburse the parents' attorney fees. The U.S. Supreme Court later ruled that P.L. 94–142 did not entitle parents to recover such fees, but Congress subsequently passed an "Attorney's Fees" bill, leading to enactment of P.L. 99–372.
1985	*Cleburne v. Cleburne Living Center* (Texas)	The Supreme Court ruled unanimously that communities cannot use a discriminatory zoning ordinance to prevent establishment of group homes for persons with mental retardation.
1988	*Honig v. Doe* (California)	The court ruled that children with disabilities cannot be excluded from school for any misbehavior that is disability-related (in this case, "aggressive behavior against other students" on the part of two "emotionally handicapped" students) but that educational services could cease if the misbehavior is not related to the disability.
1989	*Timothy W. v. Rochester School District* (New Hampshire)	The U.S. Appeals Court upheld the literal interpretation that P.L. 94–142 requires that all children with disabilities be provided with a free, appropriate, public education, unconditionally and without exception. The three-judge appeals court overturned the decision of a district court judge, who had ruled that the local school district was not obligated to educate a 13-year-old boy with multiple and severe disabilities because he could not benefit from special education.
1999	*Cedar Rapids v. Garret F.*	U.S. Supreme Court ruled that a local school district must pay for the one-on-one nursing care for a medically fragile student who required continuous monitoring of his ventilator and other health-maintenance routines. The case reaffirmed and extended the Court's ruling in the 1984 Tatro case that schools must provide any and all health services needed for students with disabilities to attend school as long as performance of those services does not require a licensed physician.
2005	*Schaffer v. Weast*	In a test of the burden of proof for what constitutes an appropriate education, the Supreme Court ruled that IDEA forces parents, not schools, to prove that their children are not receiving FAPE in legal disputes.

FAPE, free appropriate public education; IDEA, Individuals With Disabilities Act; IEP, individualized education program.

Extended School Year   Most public schools operate for approximately 180 days per year. Parents and advocates have argued that, for some children with disabilities, particularly those with severe and multiple disabilities, a 180-day school year is not sufficient to meet their needs. In *Armstrong v. Kline* (1979), the parents of five students with severe disabilities claimed that their children tended to regress during the usual breaks in the school year and called on the schools to provide a period of instruction longer than 180 days. The court agreed and ordered the schools to extend the school year for these students. Several states and local districts now provide year-round educational programs for some students with disabilities, but no clear and universally accepted guidelines specify which students are entitled to free public education for a longer-than-usual school year.

Related Services   The related-services provision of IDEA has been highly controversial, creating much disagreement about what kinds of related services are necessary and reasonable for the schools to provide and what services should be the responsibility of the child's parents. The first case based on IDEA to reach the U.S. Supreme Court was *Board of Education of the Hendrick Hudson Central School District v. Rowley* (1982). Amy Rowley was a fourth grader who, because of her hearing loss, needed special education and related services. The school district had originally provided Amy with a hearing aid, speech therapy, a tutor, and a sign-language interpreter to accompany her in the general education classroom. The school withdrew the sign-language services after the interpreter reported that Amy did not make use of her services: Amy reportedly looked at the teacher to read her lips and asked the teacher to repeat instructions rather than get the information from the interpreter. Amy's parents contended that she was missing up to 50% of the ongoing instruction (her hearing loss was estimated to have left her with 50% residual hearing) and was therefore being denied an appropriate public school education. The school district's position was that Amy, with the help of the other special services she was still receiving, was passing from grade to grade without an interpreter. School personnel thought, in fact, that an interpreter might hinder Amy's interactions with her teacher and peers. It was also noted that this service would cost the school district as much as $25,000 per year. The Supreme Court ruled that Amy, who was making satisfactory progress in school without an interpreter, was receiving an adequate education and that the school district could not be compelled to hire a full-time interpreter.

Disciplining Students With Disabilities   Some cases have resulted from parents' protesting the suspension or expulsion of children with disabilities. The case of *Stuart v. Nappi* (1978), for example, concerned a high school student who spent much of her time wandering in the halls even though she was assigned to special classes. The school sought to have the student expelled on disciplinary grounds because her conduct was considered detrimental to order in the school. The court agreed with the student's mother that expulsion would deny the student a FAPE as called for in IDEA. In other cases, expulsion or suspension of students with disabilities has been upheld if the school could show that the grounds for expulsion did not relate to the student's disability. In 1988, however, the Supreme Court ruled in *Honig v. Doe* that schools could not recommend expulsion or suspend a student with disabilities for more than 10 days.

Manifestation determination

 Council for Exceptional Children   Content Standards for Beginning Teachers—Common Core: Laws, policies, and ethical principles regarding behavior management planning and implementation (CC1K2).

The IDEA amendments of 1997 (P.L. 105–17) contained provisions that enable school districts to discipline students with disabilities in the same manner as students without disabilities, with a few notable exceptions. If the school seeks a change of placement, suspension, or expulsion in excess of 10 days, the IEP team and other qualified personnel must review the relationship between the student's misconduct and her disability. This review is called a **manifestation determination** (Katsiyannis & Maag, 2001). If the team determines that the student's behavior is not related to the disability, the same disciplinary procedures used with other students may be imposed. However, the school must continue to provide educational services in the alternative placement.

IDEA 2004 revised the discipline provisions of the law such that under special circumstances (e.g., student brings to or possesses a weapon at school; possesses, uses, or sells illegal drugs at school; inflicts serious injury upon someone at school or a school function), school personnel have the authority to remove a student with disabilities to an interim alternative educational setting for up to 45 school days, whether or not the misconduct was related to the child's disability.

Right to Education   The case of *Timothy W. v. Rochester School District* (1989) threatened the zero-reject philosophy of IDEA. In July 1988, Judge Loughlin of the district court in New Hampshire ruled that a 13-year-old boy with severe disabilities and quadriplegia was ineligible for education services because he could not benefit from special education. The judge ruled in favor of the Rochester School Board, which claimed that IDEA was not intended to provide educational services to "*all* handicapped students." In his decision, the judge determined that the federal law was not explicit regarding a "rare child" with severe disabilities and declared that special evaluations and examinations should be used to determine "qualifications for education under P.L. 94–142."

In May 1989, a court of appeals overturned the lower court's decision, ruling that public schools must educate all children with disabilities regardless of how little they might benefit or the nature or severity of their disabilities. The three-judge panel concluded that "schools cannot avoid the provisions of EHA [Education of the Handicapped Amendments] by returning to the practices that were widespread prior to the Act's passage . . . of unilaterally excluding certain handicapped children from a public education on the ground that they are uneducable" (U.S. Court of Appeals, 875 F.2d 954 [1st Cir.]).

Related Legislation

Gifted and Talented Children   IDEA does not apply to children who are gifted and talented. The only federal program that addresses the needs of gifted and talented students is the Jacob K. Javits Gifted and Talented Student Education Act (P.L. 100–297), a component of the Elementary and Secondary Education Act. This moderately funded act (approximately $9.6 million in fiscal year 2007) provides federal support for demonstration programs that develop and expand models serving students who are underrepresented in gifted and talented programs, a national research center, and a position within the U.S. Department of Education with responsibility for gifted education. The Javits Act specifies that the federal funds be directed primarily to economically disadvantaged children, limited-English-proficient students, and students with disabilities who are gifted and talented.

Section 504 of the Rehabilitation Act of 1973   Another important law that extends civil rights to people with disabilities is Section 504 of the Rehabilitation Act of 1973. This regulation states, in part, that "no otherwise qualified handicapped individual shall, solely by reason of his handicap, be excluded from the participation in, be denied the benefits of, or be subjected to discrimination in any program or activity receiving federal financial assistance." This law, worded almost identically to the Civil Rights Act of 1964 (which prohibited discrimination based on race, color, or national origin), has expanded opportunities to children and adults with disabilities in education, employment, and various other settings. It requires provision of "auxiliary aids for students with impaired sensory, manual, or speaking skills"—for example, readers for students who are blind and people to assist students with physical disabilities in moving from place to place. This requirement does not mean that schools, colleges, and employers must have all such aids available at all times; it simply means that no person with disabilities may be excluded from a program because of the lack of an appropriate aid.

Section 504 is not a federal grant program; unlike IDEA, it does not provide any federal money to assist people with disabilities. Rather, it "imposes a duty on every recipient of federal funds not to discriminate against handicapped persons" (T. P. Johnson, 1986, p. 8). "Recipient," of course, includes public school districts, virtually all of which receive federal support. Most colleges and universities have also been affected; many students in private institutions receive federal financial aid. The Office of Civil Rights conducts periodic compliance reviews and acts on complaints when parents, individuals with disabilities, or others contend that a school district is violating Section 504.

Architectural accessibility for students, teachers, and others with physical and sensory impairments is an important feature of Section 504; however, the law does not call for a completely barrier-free environment. Emphasis is on accessibility to programs, not on physical modification of all existing structures. If a chemistry class is required for a premed program of study, for example, a college might make this program accessible to a student with physical disabilities by reassigning the class to an accessible location or providing assistance to the student in traveling to an otherwise inaccessible location. Not all sections of all courses need to be made accessible, but a college should not segregate students with disabilities by assigning them all to a particular section regardless of disability. Like IDEA, Section 504 calls for nondiscriminatory placement in the "most integrated setting appropriate" and has served as the basis for many court cases over alleged discrimination against individuals with disabilities, particularly in their right to employment. For a discussion of what teachers need to know about Section 504, see T. E. C. Smith (2002).

The Americans With Disabilities Act requires employers to make reasonable accommodations to allow a person with disabilities to perform essential job functions.

Americans with Disabilities Act The Americans with Disabilities Act (P.L. 101–336) was signed into law in 1990. Patterned after Section 504 of the Rehabilitation Act of 1973, the Americans with Disabilities Act (ADA) extends civil rights protection of persons with disabilities to private-sector employment, all public services, public accommodation, transportation, and telecommunications. A person with a disability is defined in ADA as a person (1) with a mental or physical impairment that substantially limits her in a major life activity (e.g., walking, talking, working, self-care); (2) with a record of such an impairment (e.g., a person who no longer has heart disease but who is discriminated against because of that history); or (3) who is regarded as having such an impairment (e.g., a person with significant facial disfiguration due to a burn who is not limited in any major life activity but is discriminated against). The major provisions of ADA follow:

- Employers with 15 or more employees may not refuse to hire or promote a person because of a disability if that person is qualified to perform the job. Also, the employer must make reasonable accommodations that will allow a person with a disability to perform essential functions of the job. The employer must make such modifications in job requirements or situation if they will not impose undue hardship on the employer.
- All new vehicles purchased by public transit authorities must be accessible to people with disabilities. All rail stations must be made accessible, and at least one car per train in existing rail systems must be made accessible.
- It is illegal for public accommodations to exclude or refuse persons with disabilities. Public accommodations are everyday businesses and services, such as hotels, restaurants, grocery stores, and parks. All new buildings must be made accessible, and existing facilities must remove barriers if the removal can be accomplished without much difficulty or expense.
- Companies offering telephone service to the general public must offer relay services to individuals who use telecommunications devices for the deaf (e.g., text telephones) 24 hours per day, 7 days per week.

No Child Left Behind Act

When Congress reauthorized the Elementary and Secondary Education Act in 2001, it renamed it the No Child Left Behind Act (NCLB). The intent of NCLB is to improve the achievement of all students, with a particular emphasis on children from low-income families (Cortiella, 2006). The ultimate goal of NCLB is that all children will be proficient in reading and math by the year 2014 and will be taught by qualified teachers highly trained in their subjects. The provisions of NCLB are based on accountability for student learning and the use of scientifically based programs of instruction.

Accountability for Student Learning   States are expected to make annual progress toward the 100% goal by 2014. NCLB requires annual assessments of at least 95% of all students in each school district in reading/language arts and math in grades 3 through 8 and at least once in grades 10–12. Test results must be disaggregated for students by poverty levels, race, ethnicities, disabilities, and limited English proficiency. Each school and children from each category must achieve state–determined pass rates, which will gradually rise. Annual school "report cards" provide comparative information on the performance of each school. By doing so, they empower parents to make more informed choices about their children's educations. These report cards are intended to show not only how well students are doing on meeting standards but also the progress that disaggregated groups are making in closing achievement gaps. Districts and schools that do not make adequate yearly progress (AYP) toward state proficiency goals for their students are initially targeted for assistance and then are subject to corrective action and ultimately restructuring. Schools that meet or exceed objectives are eligible for "academic achievement awards."

Emphasis on What Works Based on Scientific Research   NCLB puts a special emphasis on using educational programs and practices that have been clearly demonstrated to be effective through rigorous scientific research. The NCLB–funded Reading First programs are a prime example. Reading First is designed to help states, school districts, and schools ensure that every child can read at grade level or above by the end of third grade through the implementation of instructional programs and materials, assessments, and professional development grounded in scientifically based reading research. Lyon and Riccards (2007) used data from Washington State as an example of "just one of many success stories across the nation" for the Reading First program. They reported that even though the poverty rate in Reading First schools is 84% compared to the statewide average of 36%, reading achievement scores in Reading First schools increased by 22% compared to an 11% increase across the state.

Implications for Students with Disabilities   The provisions of NCLB apply to all students, including those with disabilities. When it reauthorized IDEA in 2004, Congress revised the law in order to align it with NCLB. Figure 1.1 shows how key provisions of NCLB and IDEA are related.

Although IDEA already required students with disabilities to participate in state- and district-wide assessments, the inclusion of all students' scores in a school district's report card has resulted in higher expectations for achievement by students receiving special education and increased the accountability of schools to help them attain it. Some students with mild-to-moderate disabilities are provided with accommodations (e.g., additional time, large print) when taking district- and state-wide tests. Students with severe disabilities for whom standard academic achievement tests would be inappropriate can take alternative assessments (e.g., a video portfolio demonstrating improvements in language or adaptive behavior) if their IEP team recommends them (Bolt & Thurlow, 2004). NCLB expects all students to make adequate progress, but it is not yet clear how states will define adequate progress for students with severe intellectual disabilities (Browder & Cooper-Duffy, 2003). It is too early to know how NCLB will affect students with disabilities and the quality of education they receive (Moores, 2004; Ysseldyke et al., 2004).

While recognizing that NCLB is a complex and controversial law, Yell and Drasgow (2005) state, "For the first time, education is accountable for making improvement in students' academic performance. NCLB points educators toward the tool that will allow schools to make meaningful changes in the academic achievement of their students: scientifically-based research" (p. 118). Indeed, the emphasis on scientifically proven curriculum and instruction, especially with the Reading First grants, offers the promise of effective reading instruction in the early grades, which could reduce the number of children who require special education because of reading problems.

Table 1.4 summarizes federal legislation regarding the education of exceptional children and rights of individuals with disabilities.

FIGURE 1.1

How components of No Child Left Behind (NCLB) relate to provisions of the Individuals with Disabilities Education Act (IDEA)

Source: Cortiella, C. (2006). *NCLB and IDEA: What parents of students with disabilities need to know and do* (p. 5). Minneapolis, MN: University of Minnesota, National Center on Educational Outcomes. Used by permission.

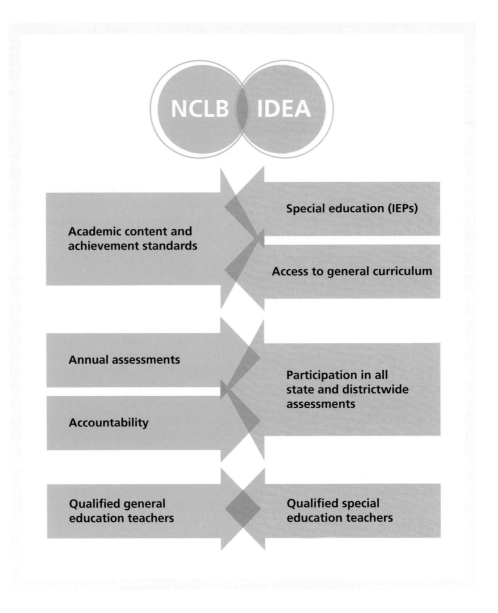

TABLE 1.4
Federal legislation concerning the education of exceptional children and rights of individuals with disabilities

DATE	LEGISLATION	EDUCATIONAL IMPLICATIONS
1958	National Defense Education Act (P.L. 85–926)	Provided funds for training professionals to train teachers of children with mental retardation
1961	Special Education Act (P.L. 87–276)	Provided funds for training professionals to train teachers of deaf children
1963	Mental Retardation Facility and Community Center Construction Act (P.L. 88–164)	Extended support given in P.L. 85–926 to training teachers of children with other disabilities
1965	Elementary and Secondary Education Act (P.L. 89–10)	Provided money to states and local districts for developing programs for economically disadvantaged and disabled children

TABLE 1.4 (CONTINUED)

Federal legislation concerning the education of exceptional children and rights of individuals with disabilities

DATE	LEGISLATION	EDUCATIONAL IMPLICATIONS
1966	Amendment to Title I of the Elementary and Secondary Education Act (P.L. 89-313)	Provided funding for state-supported programs in institutions and other settings for children with disabilities
1966	Amendments to the Elementary and Secondary Education Act (P.L. 89-750)	Created the federal Bureau of Education for the Handicapped (today's Office of Special Education)
1968	Handicapped Children's Early Assistance Act (P.L. 90-538)	Established the "first chance network" of experimental programs for preschool children with disabilities
1969	Elementary, Secondary, and Other Educational Amendments (P.L. 91-230)	Defined learning disabilities and provided funds for state-level programs for children with learning disabilities
1970	Education Amendments of 1970 (P.L. 91-230)	Mandated a study of the gifted that resulted in the *Marland Report* (1972), which many states used as a basis for building programs for gifted and talented students
1973	Section 504 of the Rehabilitation Act (P.L. 93-112)	Declared that a person cannot be excluded on the basis of disability alone from any program or activity receiving federal funds
1974	Education Amendments (P.L. 93-380)	Extended previous legislation; provided money to state and local districts for programs for gifted and talented students for the first time; protected the rights of children with disabilities and their parents in placement decisions
1975	Developmental Disabilities Assistance and Bill of Rights Act (P.L. 94-103)	Affirmed the rights of citizens with mental retardation (MR) and cited areas in which services must be provided for people with MR and other developmental disabilities
1975	Education for All Handicapped Children Act (EAHCA) (P.L. 94-142)	Mandated free appropriate public education for all children with disabilities ages 6 to 21; protected the rights of children with disabilities and their parents in educational decision making; required the development of an IEP for each child with a disability; stated that students with disabilities must receive educational services in the least restrictive environment.
1978	Gifted and Talented Children's Education Act of 1978 (P.L. 95-561)	Provided funds for in-service training programs, research, and other projects aimed at meeting the needs of gifted and talented students
1983	Amendments to the Education of the Handicapped Act (P.L. 98-199)	Required states to collect data on the number of youth with disabilities exiting their systems and to address the needs of secondary students making the transition to adulthood; gave incentives to states to provide services to infants and preschool children with disabilities
1984	Developmental Disabilities Assistance and Bill of Rights Acts (P.L. 98-527)	Mandated the development of employment-related training activities for adults with disabilities
1986	Handicapped Children's Protection Act (P.L. 99-372)	Provided authority for the reimbursement of attorney's fees to parents who prevail in a hearing or court case to secure an appropriate education for their child
1986	Education for the Handicapped Act Amendments of 1986 (P.L. 99-457)	Required states to provide free appropriate education to all 3- to 5-year-olds with disabilities who were eligible to apply for federal preschool funding; included incentive grants to encourage states to develop comprehensive interdisciplinary services for infants and toddlers (birth through age 2) and their families
1986	Rehabilitation Act Amendments (P.L. 99-506)	Set forth regulations for the development of supported employment programs for adults with disabilities

TABLE 1.4 (CONTINUED)

Federal legislation concerning the education of exceptional children and rights of individuals with disabilities

DATE	LEGISLATION	EDUCATIONAL IMPLICATIONS
1988	Jacob K. Javits Gifted and Talented Students Education Act (P.L. 100-297)	Provided federal funds in support of research, teacher training, and program development for the education of gifted and talented students
1988	Technology-Related Assistance for Individuals with Disabilities Act of 1988 (P.L. 100-407)	Created statewide programs of technology assistance for persons of all ages with disabilities
1990	Americans with Disabilities Act (P.L. 101-336)	Provided civil rights protection against discrimination to citizens with disabilities in private sector employment; provided access to all public services, public accommodations, transportation, and telecommunications
1990	Individuals with Disabilities Education Act Amendments (IDEA) of 1990 (P.L. 101-476)	Renamed the EAHCA; added autism and traumatic brain injury as new categories of disability; required all IEPs to include a statement of needed transition services no later than age 16; expanded the definition of related services to include rehabilitation counseling and social work services
1994	Goals 2000: Educate America Act (P.L. 103-227)	Provided federal funds for the development and implementation of educational reforms to help achieve eight national education goals by the year 2000
1997	Individuals with Disabilities Education Act (IDEA) of 1997 (P.L. 105-17)	Added several major provisions including: a regular education teacher must be a member of the IEP team; students with disabilities must have access to the general education curriculum; the IEP must address positive behavior support plans where appropriate; students with disabilities must be included in state- or district-wide testing programs; if a school seeks to discipline a student with disabilities resulting in change of placement, suspension, or expulsion for more than 10 days, a "manifestation determination" by the IEP team must find that the student's misconduct was not related to the disability
2001	No Child Left Behind Act of 2001 (Reauthorization of the Elementary and Secondary Education Act (P.L. 107-110)	NCLB's ultimate goal is that all children will be proficient in all subject matter by the year 2014. School districts are expected to make adequate yearly progress (AYP) toward the 100% goal, ensure that all children are taught by "highly qualified" teachers, and use curriculum and instructional methods validated by rigorous scientific research. Schools that do not make AYP are initially targeted for assistance and then subject to corrective action and ultimately restructuring
2004	Individuals with Disabilities Education Improvement Act of 2004 (P.L. 108-446)	Retained major components and principles of IDEA; key changes include: benchmarks and short-term objectives required only in IEPs for students who take alternative assessments related to alternative achievement standards; pilot program for multi-year IEPs; "response-to-instruction" may be used to identify learning disabilities; "highly qualified" special education teacher defined; under special circumstances (e.g., brings a weapon to school) a student with disabilities may be removed from school to an interim setting for up to 45 school days whether or not the misconduct was related to the child's disability

WHAT IS SPECIAL EDUCATION?

Special education is a complex enterprise that can be defined and evaluated from many perspectives. One may, for example, view special education as a legislatively governed enterprise whose practitioners are concerned with issues such as due process procedures for informing parents of their right to participate in decisions about their children's education programs and the extent to which all of the school district's IEPs include each component as required by IDEA. From a sociopolitical perspective, special education can be seen as an outgrowth of the civil rights movement, a demonstration of society's changing attitudes about people with disabilities. Each of these perspectives has some validity, and each has had and continues to play an important role in defining special education and its practice. Neither view, however, reveals the fundamental purpose of special education as *instructionally based intervention*.

Special Education as Intervention

Special education is, first of all, purposeful intervention designed to prevent, eliminate, and/or overcome the obstacles that might keep a child with disabilities from learning and from full and active participation in school and society. Special educators use three basic types of intervention: preventive, remedial, and compensatory.

Preventive Intervention   Special educators design preventive intervention to keep a potential or minor problem from becoming a disability. Preventive interventions include actions that stop an event from happening and those that reduce the negative outcomes or a disability or condition that has already been identified. Prevention can occur at three levels:

- **Primary prevention** is designed to reduce the number of new cases (**incidence**) of a disability; it consists of efforts to eliminate or counteract risk factors so that a child never acquires a disability. Educators use primary prevention efforts for all relevant persons who could be affected by the targeted problem. For example, in a schoolwide program to prevent behavior disorders, primary prevention would include building- and classroom-wide systems of positive behavior support for all students, staff, and settings (Sugai & Horner, 2005).

- **Secondary prevention** is aimed at individuals who have already been exposed to or are displaying specific risk factors and is intended to eliminate or counteract the effects of those risk factors. Secondary prevention in a schoolwide program to prevent behavior disorders would entail specialized interventions only for those students exhibiting early signs of troubled behavior.

- **Tertiary prevention** is aimed at individuals with a disability and intended to prevent the effects of a disability from worsening. For example, intensive interventions would be provided for students identified with emotional or behavioral disorders.

Preventive efforts are most promising when they begin as early as possible—even before birth, in many cases. Later chapters describe some of the promising methods for preventing and minimizing the effects of disabilities. Unfortunately, widespread primary and secondary prevention programs are rare in this country, and it is likely that it will be decades before a significant reduction in the incidence and prevalence of most disabilities is achieved. In the meantime, we must rely on remedial and compensatory efforts to help individuals with disabilities achieve fuller and more independent lives.

Remedial Intervention   Remediation attempts to eliminate specific effects of a disability. The word *remediation* is primarily an educational term; social service agencies more often use the word *rehabilitation*. Both terms have a common purpose: to teach the person with disabilities skills for independent and successful functioning. In school, those skills may be academic (reading, writing, computing), social (initiating and maintaining a conversation), self-care (eating, dressing, using the toilet without assistance), or vocational (career and job skills to prepare secondary students for the world of work). The underlying assumption of remedial intervention is that a person with disabilities needs special instruction to succeed in typical settings.

Preventive, remedial, and compensatory interventions

 Council for Exceptional Children   Content Standards for Beginning Teachers—Common Core: Models, theories, and philosophies that form the basis for special education practice (CC1K1).

Compensatory Intervention   Compensatory intervention involves teaching a substitute (i.e., compensatory) skill that enables a person to perform a task in spite of a disability. For example, although remedial instruction might help a child with cerebral palsy learn to use her hands in the same way that others do for some tasks, a headstick and a template placed over a computer keyboard may compensate for her limited fine-motor control and enable her to type instead of write lessons by hand. Compensatory interventions give the person with a disability an asset that nondisabled individuals do not need, including, for example, assistive devices or special training such as orientation and mobility instruction for a child without vision.

Special Education as Instruction

Ultimately, *teaching* is what special education is most about. But the same can be said of all of education. What, then, is *special* about special education? One way to answer that question is to examine special education in terms of the *who, what, how,* and *where* of its teaching.

Who   The most important *who* in special education has already been identified: the exceptional children whose educational needs necessitate an individually planned program of instruction. Teachers provide the instruction that is the heart of each child's individualized education program. These teachers include both general education classroom teachers and special education teachers—teachers "with a special certification who [are] specially trained to do special things with special students" (Zigmond, 2007, p. 151). Working with special educators and general education teachers are many other professionals (e.g., school psychologists, speech-language pathologists, physical therapists, counselors) and paraprofessionals (e.g., classroom aides) who help provide the educational and related services that exceptional children need. This interdisciplinary team of professionals, working together with parents and families, bears the primary responsibility for helping exceptional children learn despite their special needs.

What   Special education can sometimes be differentiated from general education by its curriculum—that is, by *what* is taught. Although every student with disabilities needs access to and support in learning as much of the general education curriculum as appropriate, the IEP goals and objectives for some special education students will not be found in state standards or the school district's curriculum guide. Some children need intensive, systematic instruction to learn skills that typically developing children acquire without instruction. Educators often use the term *functional curriculum* to describe the knowledge and skills that some students with disabilities need in order to achieve as much success and independence as they can in daily living, personal–social, school, community, and work settings. For example, self-help skills such as dressing, eating, and toileting are a critically important component of the school curriculum for many students with severe disabilities. Also, as discussed previously, some children are taught certain skills to compensate for or reduce the handicapping effects of a disability.

How   Special education also differs from general education by its use of specialized, or adapted, materials and methods. This difference is obvious when you observe a special educator use sign language with students who are deaf. When watching a special educator gradually and systematically withdraw verbal and physical prompts while helping a student learn to perform the steps of a task, you may find the differentiated nature of special education instruction less obvious; but it is no less specialized.

Where   Special education can sometimes be identified (but not defined) by *where* it takes place. Although the majority of children with disabilities spend most of the school day in general education classrooms, others are in separate classrooms or separate residential and day schools. And many of the students in general education classrooms spend a portion of each day in a resource room, where they receive individualized instruction. Table 1.5 lists the definitions of six educational placements used by the U.S. Department of Education. (To learn how students in one resource room obtain teacher assistance, see Teaching & Learning, "Signaling for Help," on p. 38)

TABLE 1.5

Federal government's definitions of educational placements for students with disabilities

EDUCATIONAL SETTING	DEFINITION
Regular classroom*	Students receive a majority of their education program in a regular classroom and receive special education and related services outside the regular classroom for less than 21% of the school day.
Resource room	Students receive special education and related services outside the regular classroom for at least 21% but no more than 60% of the school day.
Separate classroom	Students receive special education and related services outside the regular classroom for 61% to 100% of the school day.
Separate school	Students receive special education and related services in a public or private separate day school for students with disabilities, at public expense, for more than 50% of the school day.
Residential facility	Students receive special education and related services in a public or privately operated residential facility in which children receive care or services 24 hours a day.
Homebound/ hospital	Students receive special education and related services in a hospital or homebound program.

*Most educators use the term *general education classroom* instead of *regular classroom*. Note that the federal government's definition of "regular classroom" placement enables a student to leave the classroom for supplemental instruction or related services for up to one full day per week.

Source: Adapted from U.S. Department of Education. (2000). *Twenty-second annual report to Congress on the implementation of the Individuals with Disabilities Education Act* (p. II-14). Washington, DC: Author.

Special educators also teach in many settings not usually thought of as school. An early childhood special educator may spend much of his time teaching parents how to work with their infant or toddler at home. Special education teachers who work with students with severe disabilities often conduct *community-based instruction,* helping their students learn and practice functional daily living and job skills in the actual environments where those skills must be used (Owens-Johnson & Hamill, 2002).

Approximately four out of five school-age children with disabilities received at least part of their education in general education classrooms during the 2005–2006 school year (see Figure 1.2). This includes 54% who were served in a general education classroom and 25% who were served for part of each school day in a resource room, a special setting in which a special educator provides individualized instruction. About one in seven children with disabilities are educated in separate classrooms within a regular public school. About 3% of school-age students with disabilities—usually those with severe disabilities—are educated in special schools. Residential schools serve less than 1% of all children with disabilities, as do nonschool environments such as homebound or hospital programs.

The vast majority of children in the two largest groups of students with disabilities spend at least part of the school day in general education classrooms: 88% of children with learning disabilities and 95% of children with speech or language impairments (see Table 1.6). In contrast, only 43% of children with mental retardation, 49% of children with autism, 30% of children with multiple disabilities, and 38% of children with deaf-blindness

Signaling for Help

Resource rooms are busy places. Students come and go throughout the school day, each according to an individualized schedule. Each student who comes to the resource room does so because of a need for intensive individualized instruction. The IEP objectives for any given group of students in a resource room at any one time often cover a wide range of academic and social skills. Because of the varied skill levels and the ever-changing student groupings in the resource room, the special education teacher must often manage several types and levels of instruction at once. To accomplish this, teachers often assign students individualized learning activities. Resource room teachers face a difficult challenge: the need to be in several places at once. While students work at their desks, learning centers, or computers, the teacher moves about the room, providing prompts, encouragement, praise, and corrective feedback to individual students as needed.

Students in a resource room are usually working on the skills for which they need the most help—that is, difficult material they have not yet mastered. Therefore, an effective and efficient system with which students can signal the resource room teacher for assistance is needed. Hand raising, the typical attention-getting signal in the classroom, poses several problems. It is difficult to continue to work while holding one's hand in the air, a situation that results in a great deal of down time while students wait for the teacher to get to them. In addition, if several students are waving their hands in competition for the teacher's attention, it is distracting to other students and to the teacher. If unsuccessful in getting the teacher's help, students may give up trying whenever they run into difficulty. Even worse, students who are unsuccessful in obtaining the teacher's assistance may stop discriminating their need for help and simply continue to practice errors.

Students need an effective, quiet means of signaling for help that allows them to keep working with the assurance that their teacher will recognize their need for help. In Ronni Spratt's resource room for middle school students with disabilities, each student has a small flag made of colored felt, a dowel rod, and a 1 1/4-inch cube of wood. When one of Ronni's students needs assistance or wants her to check completed work, the student simply stands the flag up on his desk. While waiting for the teacher, the student can either go on to another item or work on materials in a special folder. With this simple and inexpensive system, down time is greatly reduced; and neither Ronni nor her students are distracted by hand waving or calling out.

Ronni asked her students to write down what they thought of the signal flag system after using it for about 3 months.

> This is one of the best way to work in sted of raising your hand you raise your flag and keep on working but if you raise you hand can't keep working. That is special because I get more work done. If she is working with some one els you raise it and she will get to you as fast as she can. (Brent)

> The flags in Miss Spratt's room are used for assistance from the teacher. When Miss Spratt is working you raise your flag and she will help you as soon as she has time. But you keep on working, like going on to the next problem. (Pam)

HOW TO GET STARTED

1. *Identify the classroom activities when students' use of a signaling device* to obtain teacher assistance would be appropriate and contribute to more efficient use of everyone's time and effort (e.g., independent seat work).

Signal flags are a simple and effective way for students to obtain teacher assistance and feedback.

2. *Create an inexpensive and simple-to-use signaling device* for teacher's assistance such as the flags used by Ronni Spratt's students. An effective signaling device can also be made from an empty can wrapped with red construction paper on one end and green paper on the other (Kerr & Nelson, 2006). Students set the can on one end or the other to signal "I'm working" or "I need help."

Construct a three-sided triangular signaling device by taping together strips of card stock printed with visual cues and statements (see Figure A). When the "I am working" side is turned toward the teacher, the "Keep working" prompt faces the student, and "Check my work" is face down on the student's desk. A student who has completed a portion of work, or needs teacher assistance to be able to continue working, rotates the device to reveal the "Check my work" side so the teacher can see it.

3. *Determine what students should do after activating their signal and waiting for the teacher.* It is important that a signal flag system not become an easy way for students to escape working. You don't want students to simply display their flags and then sit doing nothing. Students should continue to work productively while waiting for the teacher to arrive at their desks. One solution is to give each student a folder of alternative instructional materials to keep in his or her desk to work on while waiting for the teacher's assistance or feedback on the current assignment. The materials in each student's back-up folder should be at his or her practice stage of learning (see Chapter 4) and provide meaningful review of previously covered curriculum. The materials in students' back-up folders should not be too easy or fun or the students may put up their signal flags just to avoid working on the current material.

4. *Teach students how to use the signal device.* Instruction should be explicit (see Chapter 5) and include at minimum (a) discussing the rationale for and importance of the skill for the student and consequences; (b) modeling examples and nonexamples of when and how to use the signaling device and what students should do while waiting for the teacher (e.g., a folder of individualized instructional materials at student's practice stage of learning (see Chapter 4); and (c) role playing and guided student practice across the full range of relevant classroom situations. For more on teaching students to work independently and seek teacher assistance, see *Teaching & Learning*, "Look, I'm All Finished!" Recruiting Teacher Attention, in Chapter 6.

5. *Praise students for using the signal device and procedures properly.* It is particularly important to students who continue to work quietly and productively while waiting for the teacher to arrive at their desks. Move about the classroom in a random pattern while students are working. In addition to providing assistance and feedback to students who have raised their signal flags, from time to time stop at the desks of students who do not have their signal flags raised and show attention and interest in their work. Tell students or provide a visual cue to signal times when you cannot provide individual assistance even if their signal flags are raised. Students can also self-monitor their use of signal flags. For information on teaching students to self-monitor their work habits and productivity, see the Teaching & Learning box "Self-Monitoring Helps Students Do More Than Just Be On-Task" in Chapter 11.

Go to Homework & Exercises section in Chapter 1 of MyEducationLab and complete Homework Exercise 4. As you complete the simulation, think about how you could employ the signaling for help strategies and those presented in the simulation to create a successful learning environment for students with disabilities.

I am working.

Keep working.

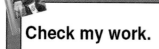

Check my work.

FIGURE A

Three-sided signal device. A three-sided signaling device can be constructed by taping together strips of card stock printed with visual cues and statements into a three-dimensional triangle. When the "Check my work." side is facing outward (i.e., signaling teacher's help or attention), the "Keep working." side faces the student (i.e., reminding the student to keep working while waiting for the teacher), and the "I am working." side is faced down on the student's desk. After the teacher assists the student, the teacher can then turn the "I am working." side outward.

Courtesy of Ya-yu Lo, University of North Carolina at Charlotte.)

FIGURE 1.2

Percentage of all students with disabilities ages 6 through 21 served in six educational placements (2005–2006 school year)

Source: From U.S. Department of Education. (2007). *Individuals With Disabilities Education Act (IDEA) data (Table AB2).* Washington, DC: Author. Available at http://www. ideadata.org/PartBdata.asp

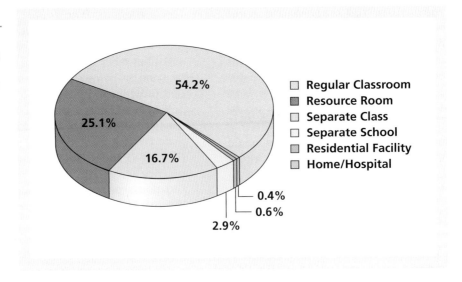

54.2%
25.1%
16.7%
2.9%
0.6%
0.4%

☐ Regular Classroom
☐ Resource Room
☐ Separate Class
☐ Separate School
☐ Residential Facility
☐ Home/Hospital

TABLE 1.6

Percentage of students ages 6 through 21 served in six educational environments (2005–2006 school year)

DISABILITY CATEGORY	REGULAR CLASSROOM	RESOURCE ROOM	SEPARATE CLASSROOM	SEPARATE SCHOOL	RESIDENTIAL SCHOOL	HOMEBOUND OR HOSPITAL
Specific learning disabilities	54.5	33.7	10.9	0.6	0.2	0.2
Speech or language impairments	88.7	6.2	4.6	0.4	<0.1	<0.1
Other health impairments	56.0	28.0	12.8	1.6	0.3	1.3
Mental retardation	14.1	29.1	51.2	4.7	0.5	0.5
Emotional disturbance	34.7	21.6	26.8	12.6	3.0	1.2
Autism	31.4	18.1	39.8	9.6	0.7	0.4
Multiple disabilities	13.3	16.9	45.1	20.1	2.2	2.3
Developmental delay	59.5	23.4	15.8	1.0	0.1	0.2
Hearing impairments	48.8	18.3	19.5	7.1	6.2	0.2
Orthopedic impairments	46.5	18.1	25.7	4.9	0.2	1.6
Visual impairments	58.2	15.2	14.2	5.7	6.1	0.6
Traumatic brain injury	40.0	27.5	24.8	5.8	0.7	1.5
Deaf-blindness	22.8	15.1	33.6	17.4	9.7	1.4
All disabilities	54.2	25.1	16.7	2.9	0.6	0.4

Source: From U.S. Office of Special Education Programs. (2007). *Individuals with Disabilities Education Act* (IDEA) data (Table 2-2c). Washington, DC: Author. Available at http://www.ideadata.org/PartBdata.asp

were educated in general education classrooms for part of each day during the 2005–2006 school year, although these figures represent increases over those of previous years.

Defining Features of Special Education

At one level, special education is an important part of society's response to the needs of exceptional children and the rights of individuals with disabilities—a response brought about by parental advocacy, litigation, legislation, and, increasingly, self-advocacy by disabled persons themselves. At another level, special education is a profession with its own history, cultural practices, tools, and research base focused on the learning needs of exceptional children and adults. But at the level where exceptional children most meaningfully and frequently contact it, *special education is individually planned, specialized, intensive, goal-directed instruction.* When practiced most effectively and ethically, special education is also characterized by the use of evidence-based teaching methods, the application of which is guided by direct and frequent measures of student performance (Greenwood & Maheady, 1997). Table 1.7 shows the fundamental dimensions and defining features of special education.

Special education is individually planned, specially designed, intensive instruction.

CURRENT AND FUTURE CHALLENGES

Professionals in special education have legitimate reason to feel good about progress in the field. Much has been accomplished in terms of making a free appropriate education available to many children with disabilities who were previously denied access to one. Educators have learned much about how to effectively teach children with severe disabilities, whom many previously had assumed were incapable of learning. Special educators and families are learning to work as partners on behalf of exceptional children. Technological advances have helped many students overcome physical impairments and communication disabilities. The remaining chapters will introduce you to many of these advances.

Although the beginnings of the field can be traced back several centuries (Safford & Safford, 1996), in many respects, special education is still in its formative years. A great deal must be done to make special education more useful to those who need it most. Following are four areas that many in the field consider critical.

Close the Research-to-Practice Gap

Special education can be nothing more, or less, than the quality of instruction (Heward & Dardig, 2001). Contrary to the contentions of some observers, special education research has produced a significant and reliable knowledge base about effective teaching practices (e.g., Coyne, Kame'enui, & Carnine, 2007; Lovitt, 2007; Vaughn, Gersten, & Chard, 2000). No knowledgeable person will argue that research has discovered everything that is important to know about teaching exceptional students. Many questions remain to be answered, the pursuit of which will no doubt lead to other questions yet to be asked.

While a significant gap remains between what is relatively well understood and what is poorly understood or not understood at all, the more distressing gap may be between research findings about teaching and learning and practices in many classrooms (Heward, 2005). For example, scientific research has revealed a great deal of knowledge about areas such as the following: features of early reading instruction that will reduce the number of children who later develop reading problems (Kame'enui, Good, & Harn, 2005; National

TABLE 1.7
Dimensions and defining features of special education instruction

DIMENSION	DEFINING FEATURES
Individually planned	• Learning goals and objectives selected for each student based on assessment results and input from parents and student • Teaching methods and instructional materials selected and/or adapted for each student • Setting(s) where instruction will occur determined relative to opportunities for student to learn and use targeted skills
Specialized	• Sometimes involves unique or adapted teaching procedures seldom used in general education (e.g., constant time delay, token reinforcement, self-monitoring) • Incorporates a variety of instructional materials and supports—both natural and contrived—to help student acquire and use targeted learning objectives • Related services (e.g., audiology, physical therapy) provided as needed • Assistive technology (e.g., adapted cup holder, head-operated switch to select communication symbols) provided as needed
Intensive	• Instruction presented with attention to detail, precision, structure, clarity, and repeated practice • "Relentless, urgent" instruction (Zigmond & Baker, 1995) • Efforts made to provide incidental, naturalistic opportunities for student to use targeted knowledge and skills
Goal-directed	• Purposeful instruction intended to help student achieve the greatest possible personal self-sufficiency and success in present and future environments • Value/goodness of instruction determined by student's attainment of learning outcomes
Research-based methods	• Recognition that not all teaching approaches are equally effective • Instructional programs and teaching procedures selected on basis of research support
Guided by student performance	• Systematic, ongoing monitoring of student progress • Results of frequent and direct measures of student learning used to inform modifications in instruction

Reading Panel, 2000); how to teach purchasing skills to students with developmental disabilities (Xin, Grasso, DiPipi-Hoy, & Jitendra, 2005); how to adapt curriculum materials and instruction in content-area classes to enhance the success of students with learning disabilities (Bulgren, 2006); and components of secondary special education programs that increase students' success in making the transition from school to work (Test, Aspel, & Everson, 2006). Unfortunately, the instruction received by many students with disabilities does not take advantage of that knowledge (e.g., Heward, 2003; Moody, Vaughn, Hughes, & Fischer,

2000; Mostert, Kavale, & Kauffman, 2008; Wehby, Symons, Canale, & Go, 1998; Zigmond, 2007).

It is critically important for special education to close the gap between the field's knowledge of evidence-based practices and the curriculum and instruction that students receive (Carnine, 1997; Deshler, 2005; Gersten, 2001; Heward & Silvestri, 2005; Odom et al., 2005; Vaughn, Klingner, & Hughes, 2000). Instructional practices supported by scientific research are featured in the Teaching & Learning boxes and described throughout this text.

Increase the Availability and Intensity of Early Intervention and Prevention Programs

It is better to intervene earlier than later. The recent increase in special education and family-focused services for infants, toddlers, and preschoolers who have disabilities or are at risk for developmental delay is a positive sign. More efforts must be made, however, to ensure that high-quality early intervention and special education preschool programs become more widely available.

Help Students With Disabilities Transition From School to Adult Life

When special education is judged by its ultimate product—the youth who leave secondary school programs—it becomes clear how much further the field must progress. Too many young adults with disabilities are unsuccessful and unhappy in their postschool adjustment (Gelb, 1997). Special education must improve the transition of youth with disabilities from school to life in their communities.

Improve the Special Education–General Education Partnership

As stated previously, most of the more than 6 million school-age students with disabilities spend the majority of the school day in general education classrooms. However, fewer than a third of the general education teachers who responded to a national survey reported they felt well prepared to teach students with special needs (U.S. Department of Education, National Center for Education Statistics, 2001).

In addition to the 12% of the school-age population receiving special education services, another 10% to 20% experience difficulties with learning or behavior problems that interfere with their ability to succeed in school. Special and general educators must develop strategies for working together and sharing their knowledge and resources to prevent these millions of at-risk and struggling students from becoming failures of our educational system.

These four areas are by no means the only important issues facing special education today. Numerous other challenges are also important:

- Increase the availability and quality of special education programs for gifted and talented students.
- Meet the chronic and increasing shortage of certified special education teachers in the United States (Boe & Cook, 2006).
- Improve the quality of pre- and in-service training programs to ensure that all special educators meet professional standards (CEC, 2003).
- Provide mentoring programs for beginning special education teachers and ongoing professional support for teachers to increase the effectiveness and retention of the teaching force.
- Develop appropriate accommodations and alternative assessments so that the participation of students with disabilities in district- and statewide tests provides fair and valid measures of their learning.
- Apply advances in technologies that reduce or eliminate the disabling effects of physical and sensory impairments.

The ultimate effectiveness of special education is measured by its ability to help secondary students with disabilities make a successful transition to adult life.

- Increase access to assistive technology that enhances the educational performance and personal independence of individuals with disabilities.
- Improve the behavior and attitudes of people without disabilities toward those with disabilities.
- Open more opportunities for individuals with disabilities to participate in the full range of residential, employment, and recreational options available to persons without disabilities.

Only time will tell how successful special education will be in meeting these challenges. And, of course, special education does not face these challenges alone. General education, adult service agencies (e.g., vocational rehabilitation and social work), the science and practice of medicine, government agencies, and society as a whole must all help find solutions.

TIPS for Beginning Teachers

SOME FUNDAMENTALS FOR SUCCESS AND SURVIVAL
by Shawn Heimlich

RECOGNIZE THE VALUE OF DATA AS AN INDICATOR OF STUDENT PROGRESS AND AS A BAROMETER OF YOUR PERFORMANCE AS A TEACHER.

- *Develop organized and efficient means for recording and tracking data.* Create data-collection sheets or binders by class period or subject area so all data collected for students are accessible and in a single location. This will give you ready access to data needed for IEP progress reports and parent conferences and for making decisions regarding instruction.
- *Involve students in the data-collection process.* Teach students how to record performance data and/or how to create graphs of performance. Use data to help students create pictures of their learning on Websites such as the NCES (National Center for Education Statistics) Kids Zone "Create a Graph" at http://nces.ed.gov/nceskids/createagraph/.
- *Supplement quantitative data with informal measures of students' performance.* Although graphs are easy to read and understand, don't forget to collect informal data in the form of observations, anecdotes, interviews, and photos. These forms of data add another dimension to the overall picture of student learning.

DON'T TRY TO "DO IT ALL."

- Especially if you are a new/beginning teacher, make a commitment to your students' learning. You don't have to be a master of all things in the building—start strong in your classroom, and volunteer for opportunities once you feel confident and comfortable in your classroom.
- *Select one building or district-level committee, and commit your time to that endeavor.* Committee participation is a wonderful way to meet others at the building level or at the district level. But, don't overcommit!
- *Select research-based, data-driven instructional programs.* You don't need to reinvent instruction when outstanding programs already exist.

BECOME A MASTER OF YOUR SCHOOL'S CURRICULUM AND STATE STANDARDS.

- *Learn the standards and benchmarks of your curriculum.* Although not an exciting one, make the reading of your school's curriculum standards and benchmarks a summer reading assignment. You will need firsthand, intimate knowledge of your standards and benchmarks if you plan to provide high-quality, effective instruction. If you don't have a copy of your subject-specific standards and benchmarks, you can find them online at your state department of education's website, or even with a teacher leader or department chair in your district.
- *Do your research.* Continually research curricular and instructional advances. Stay connected with product representatives or publishers. Read reviews of curricular programs. Look objectively at data supporting instructional programs and data that demonstrate gains in student performance. Network with colleagues who consistently use data-driven instructional techniques or curricular programs.

GET AND STAY ORGANIZED.

- *Be "ready for tomorrow at the end of today."* I make it a practice to have all lessons and instructional materials laid out for the next day before leaving my classroom at the end of each day. When each school day begins, you don't have a minute to lose. Have materials for each subject or class period ready and waiting for the next day.

- *Use "To-Do" lists.* Each day, I keep a running to-do list of items I need to copy, tasks I need to complete, student issues I need to address, people I need to contact, etc. As I complete each item, I cross it off the list or highlight it. It's very motivating to see the number of items I can complete in a given day by scanning down the list of "cross-outs" and "highlights."

- *Keep a phone log, and keep your e-mail organized.* To document parent contacts or correspondence regarding specific students, I keep a phone log. I note the date and time of the call, the nature of the call, the name of the parent contacted, the result of the call or, in some cases, the nature of the message left on the parent's voicemail. When using e-mail (my life-line to the world outside my classroom), I organize my inbox with folders and subfolders for all students, frequent contacts, various school or district issues, personal items, etc. An organized e-mail system is critical for timely and efficient communication with parents, colleagues, and administrators.

KEY TERMS AND CONCEPTS

assistive technology, p. 23
at risk, p. 10
disability, p. 10
exceptional children, p. 9
handicap, p. 10
impairment, p. 10
incidence, p. 35
individualized education program (IEP), p. 19
individualized family services plan (IFSP), p. 22

manifestation determination, p. 28
prevalence, p. 11
primary prevention, p. 35
related services, p. 23
repeated reading, p. 23
SAFMEDS, p. 21
secondary prevention, p. 35
tertiary prevention, p. 35
time trials, p. 21

SUMMARY

Who Are Exceptional Children?

- Exceptional children are those whose physical attributes and/or learning abilities differ from the norm, either above or below, to such an extent that an individualized program of special education is necessary.
- *Impairment* refers to the reduced function or loss of a particular body part or organ.
- A *disability* exists when an impairment limits a person's ability to perform certain tasks in the same way that most persons do.
- *Handicap* refers to the problems a person with a disability encounters when interacting with the environment.
- A child who is *at risk* is not currently identified as having a disability but is considered to have a greater-than-usual chance of developing one if intervention is not provided.

How Many Exceptional Children Are There?

- Children in special education represent approximately 12% of the school-age population.
- The four largest categories of children with disabilities receiving special education are learning disabilities, speech and language impairments, mental retardation, and emotional disturbance.

Why Do We Label and Classify Exceptional Children?

- Some educators believe that disability labels have negative effects on the child and on others' perceptions of her and can lead to exclusion; others believe that labeling is a necessary first step to providing needed intervention and is important for comparing and communicating about research findings.
- Alternative approaches to classifying exceptional children that do not rely on disability labels have been proposed, e.g., classifying students by the curriculum and skill areas they are learning.

Why Are Laws Governing the Education of Exceptional Children Necessary?

- Before the 1970s, many states had laws permitting public schools to deny enrollment to children with disabilities. When local public schools began to accept a measure of responsibility for educating certain exceptional students, a philosophy of segregation prevailed.
- Special education was strongly influenced by the case of *Brown v. Board of Education* in 1954, in which the U.S. Supreme Court declared that education must be made available to all children on equal terms.
- In the class-action lawsuit *PARC* (1972), the Court ruled that all children with mental retardation were entitled to a free appropriate public education and that placements in regular classrooms and regular public schools were preferable to segregated settings.
- All children with disabilities are now recognized to have the right to equal protection under the law, which has been interpreted to mean the right to a free public education in the least restrictive environment.
- All children with disabilities and their parents have the right to due process under the law, which includes the rights to be notified of any decision affecting the child's educational placement, to have a hearing and present a defense, to see a written decision, and to appeal any decision.

The Individuals with Disabilities Education Act

- The passage of IDEA by Congress in 1975 marked the culmination of the efforts of many educators, parents, and legislators to bring together in one comprehensive bill this country's laws regarding the education of children with disabilities. The law encompasses six major principles:
  - *Zero reject.* Schools must educate all children with disabilities. This principle applies regardless of the nature or severity of the disability.
  - *Nondiscriminatory identification and evaluation.* Schools must use nonbiased, multifactored methods of evaluation to determine whether a child has a disability and, if so, whether special education is needed.
  - *Free appropriate public education.* All children with disabilities shall receive a free appropriate public education at public expense. An IEP must be developed and implemented for each student with a disability that addresses the student's unique needs by providing instructional practices and services based on peer-reviewed research to the extent practicable.
  - *Least restrictive environment.* Students with disabilities must be educated with children without disabilities to the maximum extent appropriate, and they should be removed to separate classes or schools only when the nature or severity of their disabilities is such that they cannot receive an appropriate education in a general education classroom.
  - *Due process safeguards.* Schools must provide due process safeguards to protect the rights of children with disabilities and their parents.
  - *Parent and student participation and shared decision making.* Schools must collaborate with parents and with students with disabilities in the design and implementation of special education services.
- IDEA requires states to provide special education services to all preschoolers with disabilities ages 3 to 5. This law also makes federal money available to encourage states to

develop early intervention programs for disabled and at-risk infants and toddlers from birth to age 2. Early intervention services must be coordinated by an IFSP.

- IDEA requires that schools provide related services and assistive technology that a child with a disability needs to access and benefit from special education.
- Court cases have challenged the way in which particular school districts implement specific provisions of IDEA. Rulings from the various cases have established the principle that each student with disabilities is entitled to a personalized program of instruction and related services that will enable him to benefit from an education in as integrated a setting as possible.
- The Gifted and Talented Children's Education Act (P.L. 100–297) provides financial incentives to states for developing programs for gifted and talented students.
- Section 504 of the Rehabilitation Act forbids discrimination in all federally funded programs, including educational and vocational programs, on the basis of disability.
- The Americans with Disabilities Act (P.L. 101–336) extends the civil rights protections for persons with disabilities to private-sector employment, all public services, public accommodations, transportation, and telecommunications.
- NCLB requires that all children must be taught by "highly qualified" teachers, emphasizes use of evidence-based teaching methods, and requires schools to make annual progress toward the ultimate goal of all children being proficient in all subject matter by 2014.

What Is Special Education?

- Special education consists of purposeful intervention efforts at three levels: preventive, remedial, and compensatory.
- Special education is individually planned, specialized, intensive, goal-directed instruction. When practiced most effectively and ethically, special education uses research-based teaching methods and is guided by direct and frequent measures of student performance.

Current and Future Challenges

- Among the many challenges faced by special education today are the following:
  - Bridge the research-to-practice gap.
  - Make early intervention programs more widely available to infants, toddlers, and preschoolers who have disabilities or are at risk for developing them.
  - Improve the ability of young adults with disabilities to make a successful transition from school to community life.
  - Work more effectively with general education to better serve the many students who have not been identified as disabled but who are not progressing in the general education program.

 Now go to MyEducationLab at www.myeducationlab.com and take the Pretest to assess your initial comprehension of chapter content. Once you have taken the Pretest, use your individualized Study Plan for Chapter 1 to enhance your understanding of the concepts discussed in the chapter. Finally, take the Posttest to assess your comprehension of Chapter 1 content.

2

Planning and Providing
Special Education Services

- Why must the planning and provision of special education be so carefully sequenced and evaluated?
- Why do collaboration and teaming impact the effectiveness of special education?
- How should the quality of a student's individualized education program (IEP) be judged?
- Is the least restrictive environment always the general education classroom? Why?
- What elements must be in place for special education to be appropriate in inclusive classrooms?
- In what ways has special education been most successful? What are the field's greatest shortcomings and challenges?

FEATURED TEACHERS

MARY ALLAIRE-GIFFORD AND JEAN MICHIELLI-PENDL
Dunkirk Middle School • Dunkirk, New York

Mary Allaire-Gifford

Jean Michielli-Pendl

Mary Allaire-Gifford: Education—Teaching Credentials—Experience

- B.A., elementary education, Grove City College, Grove City, Pennsylvania, 1984
- M.S., special education, State University of New York, College at Buffalo, Buffalo, New York, 2003
- New York State certification in special education and elementary education
- 23 years of teaching experience: 13 years in general education, grades 4-6; 10 years as a special educator

Jean Michielli-Pendl: Education—Teaching Credentials—Experience

- B.A., elementary education, State University of New York, College at Fredonia, Fredonia, New York, 1972
- M.S., curriculum and instruction, State University of New York, College at Fredonia, Fredonia, New York, 1998
- New York State certification in elementary education
- 35 years of teaching experience: 4 years as an ESL teacher; 15 years in general education, grades 2–5; 16 years as a sixth-grade science teacher

Two Teachers Making Inclusion Work: Our Classroom, Our Students **Jean:** The greatest challenge I've faced in my career occurred when our entire school district adopted a full-inclusion model to meet the needs of our special education students. I felt quite unprepared, even after three decades in the classroom. I had never been responsible for meeting the needs of special education students and their IEPs. And this new responsibility came with another new challenge … a co-teacher!

Co-teaching is very different from teaching with the support of an instructional aide or student teacher in the classroom. Co-teaching is sharing the teaching responsibilities with another teacher to best meet the needs of students in *our* classroom.

Mary: Our school is organized by teams, two at each grade level. Generally, there are 12–16 students with disabilities on each team. I am one of two special education teachers assigned to my team. Students on my team receive special education services under the IDEA categories of learning disabilities, speech-language impairments, other health impairment, hearing impairment, and autism. Students with disabilities, for the most part, attend all general education classes with their nondisabled peers. However, there is one 40-minute self-contained math class and one 40-minute self-contained reading class at each grade level, both taught by a special education teacher.

My assignment has changed slightly each year, but the one constant has been working in the science classes with Jean. Our science classes of 18 to 27 students generally include four or five students with disabilities. I am responsible for ensuring implementation of the IEPs for all students with disabilities on my team. I provide notes, study guides, guided notes, organizational strategies, and other accommodations. Planning, making instructional materials, and co-teaching lessons with Jean are part of my day. Jean and I develop tests and quizzes together; I make sure test accommodations are being followed. I keep a record of when and how we have worked toward the successful completion of each student's IEP goals and objectives.

Creating a Successful Classroom Environment Together
Jean: Mary brings much to the co-teaching team. She began her career as a general education teacher and then studied to be a special educator. Mary is an expert in designing specialized instruction to meet IEP goals, and I am the curriculum content specialist. She is a strict taskmaster; I am a humanist. Our different qualities create a learning atmosphere in which students can grow and develop.

Mary: Many factors have contributed to the success of our co-teaching. We both take pride in what we do and strive to do our best. Jean and I make time to co-plan. That is the backbone of co-teaching. We use 40 minutes once a week for co-planning our weekly lessons. Jean and I decide which strategies we will use to convey the lessons. We plan which goals and objectives from the IEPs we will target. Each morning we post the agenda for the day. Careful, consistent planning, sequencing, and constant evaluation make our co-teaching seamless. It allows us to adjust lesson pacing and re-teach concepts as needed. When entering our science class, it is difficult to tell who is the general education teacher and who is the special education teacher.

Jean: Mary and I challenge anyone who enters our class to identify the special education students. We feel very strongly that our job is to assist *all* students. I don't teach the general education students while Mary assists the students with special needs. Both of us teach all the students. We work hard to ensure that the students see us as equals in the room. In many inclusion models, the special education teacher is relegated to the role of a consultant or assistant to the general education teacher. This was not the model we adopted. We both teach every day, sometimes the whole class and sometimes small groups.

Teaching Strategies
We've learned that most of the instructional strategies we initially incorporated to assist students with special education needs—such as guided lecture notes, colored markers, and Post-It® notes to hold their place when working on vocabulary—also help the general education students.

Most class periods include a cooperative learning activity. We realized the talents and strengths that each child could bring to a group. The students learn to respect one another as fellow classmates and contributors. Two collaborative learning strategies we use often are *numbered heads together* and *think-pair-share*.

Numbered Heads Together
When we use this strategy, we seat students in heterogeneous groups of three or four and give each student a number. We ask the class a question. Each group discusses the question and then comes up with an answer. It is important that every person in the group knows the answer to the question.

Numbered heads together has several benefits. First, students participate actively and enthusiastically. They enjoy it. Second, this strategy promotes cooperation within the group. All students must know the answer, so group members help each other understand not only the answer but also the *how* and *why* behind it. Finally, the strategy encourages individual responsibility. When a group member's number is called, that person alone has to give the final answer.

Think-Pair-Share
Many times we give one response card to a pair of students. We ask the students a question, and they engage in a practice called think-pair-share. They think quietly for 5 to 10 seconds, then pair up with their partners to discuss the answer to the question. Finally, they write their answer on the response card and flip it over. When all or most of the students are done, we ask the class to hold up their response cards. We can assess their answers and respond by re-teaching or continuing with the lesson. This technique keeps all students on task and offers them time to discuss and check their understandings with a classmate. For fun and an element of competition, the students usually keep a tally of the number of questions they answer correctly.

Jean and Mary: Although we feel the general education classroom works for most students with disabilities, it is not the most appropriate setting for everyone. For some students, the least restrictive environment is a more specialized setting. But it is better to start in the general education classroom and move toward a more restrictive setting if and as needed rather than the other way around.

To learn more about the teaching strategies discussed here, go to the Homework & Exercises section in Chapter 2 of MyEducationLab and complete Homework Exercise 1. As you watch the videos and answer the accompanying questions, think about how these strategies benefit all of the students in the classroom.

Special education is individually planned, specialized, intensive, goal-directed instruction (see Chapter 1). But how do teachers know what kinds of modifications to curriculum and instruction an individual child needs? And toward what goals should that specialized instruction be directed? In this chapter, we examine the basic process by which special education is planned, devoting particular attention to four critical aspects of educating students with disabilities: (a) the importance of teaming and collaboration among professionals, (b) the individualized education program (IEP), (c) least restrictive environment (LRE), and (d) inclusive education.

After reading this chapter, complete the Pretest for Chapter 2 on MyEducationLab to assess your initial understanding of chapter content.

THE PROCESS OF SPECIAL EDUCATION

The Individuals with Disabilities Education Act (IDEA) mandates a sequence of events that schools must follow to identify and educate children with disabilities. Although the rules and regulations that local school districts must follow are lengthy, detailed, and sometimes redundant for legal purposes, the process is designed to answer a sequence of questions that makes both educational and common sense:

- Which students might need special education?
- Does this particular child have a disability that adversely affects his educational performance? In other words, is this student eligible for special education? If the answer is yes, then. . . .
  - What specific educational needs result from the child's disability?
  - What specialized methods of instruction, accommodations, curricular modifications, related services, and/or supplementary supports are necessary to meet those needs so the student can achieve increased levels of academic achievement and functional performance and participate in the life of the school?
  - What educational setting is the least restrictive environment in which the student can receive an appropriate education?
  - Is special education helping? If not, what changes should be made in the student's program?

Figure 2.1 identifies the major steps in the sequence of planning, implementing, and evaluating special education and highlights some of the key procedures, elements, and requirements of each step.

Prereferral Process

A child who may need special education usually comes to the attention of the schools because (a) a teacher or parent reports concern about differences in learning, behavior, or development or (b) the results of a screening test suggest a possible disability. Screening tests are relatively quick, inexpensive, and easy-to-administer assessments given to large groups of children to find out who might have a disability and need further testing (Elliott, Huai, & Roach, 2007). For example, most schools administer vision screening tests to all elementary children. Before referring the child for formal testing and evaluation for special education, most schools initiate a **prereferral intervention** process.

Prereferral intervention

Council for Exceptional Children — Content Standards for Beginning Teachers—Common Core: Screening, prereferral, referral, and classification procedures (CC8K3).

FIGURE 2.1

The basic steps in planning, providing, and evaluating special education

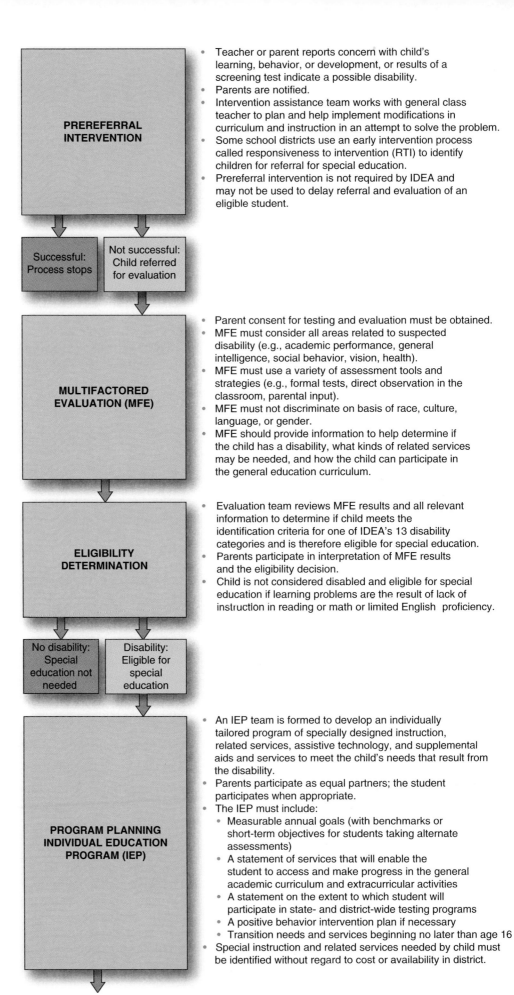

PREREFERRAL INTERVENTION

- Teacher or parent reports concern with child's learning, behavior, or development, or results of a screening test indicate a possible disability.
- Parents are notified.
- Intervention assistance team works with general class teacher to plan and help implement modifications in curriculum and instruction in an attempt to solve the problem.
- Some school districts use an early intervention process called responsiveness to intervention (RTI) to identify children for referral for special education.
- Prereferral intervention is not required by IDEA and may not be used to delay referral and evaluation of an eligible student.

Successful: Process stops

Not successful: Child referred for evaluation

MULTIFACTORED EVALUATION (MFE)

- Parent consent for testing and evaluation must be obtained.
- MFE must consider all areas related to suspected disability (e.g., academic performance, general intelligence, social behavior, vision, health).
- MFE must use a variety of assessment tools and strategies (e.g., formal tests, direct observation in the classroom, parental input).
- MFE must not discriminate on basis of race, culture, language, or gender.
- MFE should provide information to help determine if the child has a disability, what kinds of related services may be needed, and how the child can participate in the general education curriculum.

ELIGIBILITY DETERMINATION

- Evaluation team reviews MFE results and all relevant information to determine if child meets the identification criteria for one of IDEA's 13 disability categories and is therefore eligible for special education.
- Parents participate in interpretation of MFE results and the eligibility decision.
- Child is not considered disabled and eligible for special education if learning problems are the result of lack of instruction in reading or math or limited English proficiency.

No disability: Special education not needed

Disability: Eligible for special education

PROGRAM PLANNING INDIVIDUAL EDUCATION PROGRAM (IEP)

- An IEP team is formed to develop an individually tailored program of specially designed instruction, related services, assistive technology, and supplemental aids and services to meet the child's needs that result from the disability.
- Parents participate as equal partners; the student participates when appropriate.
- The IEP must include:
  - Measurable annual goals (with benchmarks or short-term objectives for students taking alternate assessments)
  - A statement of services that will enable the student to access and make progress in the general academic curriculum and extracurricular activities
  - A statement on the extent to which student will participate in state- and district-wide testing programs
  - A positive behavior intervention plan if necessary
  - Transition needs and services beginning no later than age 16
- Special instruction and related services needed by child must be identified without regard to cost or availability in district.

FIGURE 2.1

Continued

PLACEMENT IN LEAST RESTRICTIVE ENVIRONMENT (LRE)

- IEP team determines placement after the child's educational needs and the services needed to meet them have been identified.
- Placement must not be based on disability category.
- IDEA presupposes the general education classroom as the starting point for the LRE.
- IEP must explain the extent, if any, to which child will be removed from the general education classroom.
- School cannot substitute a policy of "full inclusion" for a full continuum of alternative placements.
- Parents participate in and must consent to placement decision.

IMPLEMENT SPECIAL EDUCATION (FAPE)

- The IEP is implemented in the LRE.
- The child participates in the school's general education curriculum and extracurricular activities to the maximum extent possible.
- Child participates in state- and district-wide assessments. (The IEP specifies testing accommodations or alternative assessments if necessary).
- Parents can request a change of program and placement.

PROGRESS MONITORING, ANNUAL REVIEW, AND REEVALUATION

- Parents must be provided with periodic reports on the child's progress toward meeting annual IEP goals (e.g., quarterly reports concurrent with the issuance of report cards).
- The IEP must be reviewed periodically, but not less frequently than annually.
- The IEP team revises the IEP to address any lack of expected progress in meeting annual goals or changes in the child's needs.
- At least once every 3 years, an MFE of each child with a disability must be conducted (unless the parents and school agree it is unnecessary) to determine if the child still needs special education.
- The IEP team may decide that a disability is no longer present or that the child's education is no longer adversely affected by the disability. If so, the student is declassified and special education is discontinued.

Special education discontinued	Special education continued

Go to the Homework & Exercises folder in Chapter 2 of MyEducationLab and complete Homework Exercise 2. As you watch the video and answer the accompanying questions, examine how this intervention assistance team shares ideas for helping a student who is experiencing difficulties in the general education classroom.

Although IDEA does not require prereferral intervention, local educational agencies may use up to 15% of their IDEA funds to "develop and implement coordinated, early intervening services . . . for students in kindergarten through grade 12 (with a particular emphasis on students in kindergarten through grade 3) who have not been identified as needing special education or related services but who need additional academic and behavioral support to succeed in a general education environment" (P.L. 108-466, Sec 613(f). A school district may not, however, use prereferral intervention to delay formal evaluation and assessment of a student who is eligible for special education (Yell, 2006). At any time during the prereferral process, parents have the right to request that their child receive a comprehensive evaluation for identification/eligibility for special education services.

Prereferral intervention is most often conducted by a building-based *early intervening team* (also called *intervention assistance team, student support team, teacher assistance team,* or *instructional support team*), which helps teachers devise and implement interventions for students who are experiencing academic or behavioral difficulties in the general education classroom. Early intervening teams typically consist of the school principal or designated administrator, school nurse, guidance counselor, several classroom teachers with experience across different grade levels, and one or more special education teachers, at least one of whom is skilled in designing behavior intervention plans. The classroom teacher describes the academic and/or behavior problems the student has been experiencing to the team, and together the group "brainstorms not only on the possible etiology of the problem but more importantly on possible solutions to it" (Spinelli, 2006, p. 9).

Increasingly, school districts have begun using a more formal and systematic prereferral process called **responsiveness to intervention (RTI)**. The idea of RTI is to provide early intervention in the form of scientifically validated instruction to all children in the school whose performance suggests they are at risk for school failure. Although no single model exists for RTI, the process involves universal screening and several levels or tiers of increasingly intensive instructional interventions before referral for assessment for special education eligibility (L. S. Fuchs & Fuchs, 2005, 2007a).

> The central assumption is that RTI can differentiate between two explanations for low achievement: poor instruction versus disability. If the child responds poorly to validated instruction, the assessment eliminates instructional quality as a viable explanation for poor academic growth and instead provides evidence of a disability. For children who do respond nicely, RTI serves a critical prevention function. (L. S. Fuchs, Fuchs, & Hollenbeck, 2007, p. 13)

RTI was first proposed and is most often used as an early intervening system for reading difficulties and for identifying students with learning disabilities; see Chapter 5 for further description. The logic of RTI models has been extended to mathematics (L. S. Fuchs, Fuchs, Compton, et al., 2007) and to social behavior support for students who exhibit problem behaviors in the classroom (Fairbanks, Sugai, Guardino, & Lathrop, 2007). Regardless of its form, prereferral intervention is designed to achieve the following purposes and benefits (L. S. Fuchs & Fuchs, 2005; Macy & Hoyt-Gonzales, 2007; McNamara & Hollinger, 2003; Salvia, Ysseldyke, & Bolt, 2007; Tam & Heng, 2005):

- Provide immediate instructional and/or behavior management assistance to the child and teacher.
- Reduce the frequency of identifying children for special education whose learning or behavioral problems are the result of not receiving appropriate instruction rather than a disability.
- Prevent relatively minor problems from worsening to a degree that would eventually require special education.
- Strengthen teachers' capacity to effectively intervene with a greater diversity of problems, thereby reducing the number of future referrals for special education.

- Prevent the costly and time-consuming process of assessment for special education eligibility by solving the problems that originally caused teachers or parents to be concerned about the child.
- Provide IEP teams with valuable baseline data for planning and evaluating special education and related services, for students who are referred and found eligible for special education.

Evaluation and Eligibility Determination

Teachers seldom refer children for minor or frivolous learning or behavior problems. In practice, about 90% of children who are referred are formally evaluated for special education, and about 73% of those who are tested are found eligible for special education (Ysseldyke, 2001). IDEA requires that all children suspected of having a disability receive a nondiscriminatory **multifactored evaluation (MFE).** Either the school or the parents can request that a child be evaluated for special education. Regardless of the source of the referral, the parents must be notified of the school's intent to test their child, and they must give their consent to the evaluation. Within 60 days of receiving parental consent for evaluation, the school district must complete the evaluation to determine whether the child has a disability and identify the educational needs of the child (IDEA, Sec. 614(a)(1)(C)).

Responsiveness to intervention entails several tiers of increasingly intensive instruction.

Multifactored evaluation

 Council for Exceptional Children — Content Standards for Beginning Teachers—Common Core: Legal provisions and ethical principles regarding assessment of individuals (CC8K2).

IDEA is explicit in describing some do's and don'ts that school districts must follow when evaluating a child for special education:

In conducting the evaluation, the local educational agency shall—

(A) use a variety of assessment tools and strategies to gather relevant functional, developmental, and academic information, including information provided by the parent, that may assist in determining—

   (i) whether the child is a child with a disability; and

   (ii) the content of the child's individualized education program, including information related to enabling the child to be involved in and progress in the general education curriculum, or, for preschool children, to participate in appropriate activities;

(B) not use any single measure or assessment as the sole criterion for determining whether a child is a child with a disability or determining an appropriate educational program for the child; and

(C) use technically sound instruments that may assess the relative contribution of cognitive and behavioral factors, in addition to physical or developmental factors.

Additional Requirements—Each local educational agency shall ensure that

(A) assessments and other evaluation materials used to assess a child—

   (i) are selected and administered so as not to be discriminatory on a racial or cultural basis;

   (ii) are provided and administered in the language and form most likely to yield accurate information on what the child knows and can do academically, developmentally, and functionally, unless it is not feasible to so provide or administer;

   (iii) are used for purposes for which the assessments or measures are valid and reliable;

   (iv) are administered by trained and knowledgeable personnel; and

   (v) are administered in accordance with any instructions provided by the producer of such assessments;

(B) the child is assessed in all areas of suspected disability;

(C) assessment tools and strategies that provide relevant information that directly assists persons in determining the educational needs of the child are provided; and

(D) assessments of children with disabilities who transfer from one school district to another school district in the same academic year are coordinated with such children's prior and subsequent schools, as necessary and as expeditiously as possible, to ensure prompt completion of full evaluations. (P.L. 108-446, Sec. 614(b)(2))

The MFE is conducted by a school-based *multidisciplinary evaluation team,* sometimes called a *student study team,* which includes the child's parents. The team examines the test results and all other relevant information to determine if the child has a disability that adversely affects his educational performance and is therefore entitled to special education. IDEA stipulates that a child shall not be identified as a child with a disability if the child's learning difficulties are the result of a "lack of appropriate instruction in reading . . .; lack of instruction in math; or limited English proficiency" (P.L. 108-446, Sec. 614(b)(4)) An MFE must do more than provide information on the existence of a disability for determining eligibility for special education. IDEA requires that evaluation reports also provide information about the child's educational needs and how to meet them.

Disproportionate Representation of Students From Culturally Diverse Groups in Special Education

Culturally and linguistically diverse students are both underrepresented and overrepresented in special education, depending on the group and disability category (De Valenzuela, Copeland, Huaqing Qi, & Park, 2006; Hetzner, 2007; Oswald & Coutinho, 2001; Oswald, Coutinho, Best, & Singh, 1999). Table 2.1 shows the percentage, by disability category, of students from race/ethnicity groups who received special education in the 2005–2006 school year. When all disability categories are combined, African American and Native American students were overrepresented and Asian American students were underrepresented in the special education population. Hispanic and Caucasian students were generally represented among the special education population at an overall rate close to their proportion of the resident school-age population. Some disparities are especially evident when the data are examined by disability category. For example, while African Americans account for 15.1% of the school-age population, they represent 33.7% and 28.8% of all students receiving special education for mental retardation and emotional and behavioral disorders, respectively. Even larger differences in proportional representation by race at the state and local level are sometimes apparent in data on enrollment in special education (Hetzner, 2007).

Is this disproportionate representation appropriate? Identification and classification for special education should be based entirely on the presence of a disabling condition that adversely affects the child's educational performance. The causes of disproportionate representation have been difficult to pinpoint and often controversial (Cullinan & Kauffman, 2005; Harry & Klingner, 2006, 2007; MacMillan & Reschly, 1998; Osher et al., 2004). Are students from some culturally and linguistically diverse groups more likely to have a disability than are white children? For example, a much greater proportion of students from diverse groups are born to mothers without access to maternal health care and live in poverty—factors that are associated with an increased incidence of disability. For example, half of the nation's Latino 4th graders and almost half of African American 4th graders attend public schools in which more than three-fourths of the students come from low-income families (based on federal eligibility criteria for free or reduced-price school lunch). By comparison, only 5% of white 4th graders attend schools with poverty rates this high (Center for Education Policy, 2006). Or, as some researchers have suggested, do inherent problems in the referral and placement process bias the identification of minority children (Harry & Klingner, 2006; Osher et al., 2004)? The answer to these controversial and complex questions is that probably both explanations are partly true (Serna, Forness, & Nielson, 1998).

The fact that culturally and linguistically diverse students are identified as having a disability is not, in itself, a problem. All students with disabilities that adversely affect their educational performance have the right to special education services, whatever their racial, cultural, or linguistic background. Disproportionate representation is problematic if

TABLE 2.1

Racial/ethnic composition (percentage) of students ages 6 through 21 served by disability in the 2005–2006 school year

DISABILITY	AMERICAN INDIAN/ ALASKAN	ASIAN/ PACIFIC ISLANDER	AFRICAN AMERICAN (NOT HISPANIC)	HISPANIC	WHITE (NOT HISPANIC)
Specific learning disabilities	1.8	1.7	20.1	20.5	55.8
Speech or language impairments	1.3	3.1	15.5	16.9	63.2
Other health impairments	1.2	1.5	17.1	9.4	70.8
Mental retardation	1.3	2.0	33.7	13.2	49.9
Emotional disturbance	1.5	1.1	28.8	10.8	57.8
Autism	0.7	5.3	14.8	11.0	68.2
Multiple disabilities	1.3	2.6	21.0	12.9	62.1
Developmental delay	3.7	2.6	22.2	9.3	62.2
Hearing impairments	1.3	4.9	16.3	21.9	55.6
Orthopedic impairments	0.9	3.5	15.1	20.1	60.3
Visual impairments	1.4	4.0	17.7	17.0	59.9
Traumatic brain injury	1.4	2.5	17.0	12.8	66.3
Deaf-blindness	1.6	4.5	13.0	19.4	61.5
All disabilities	1.5	2.2	20.7	16.7	59.0
Estimated percentage of resident population	1.0	4.1	15.1	18.0	61.8

Sums may not equal 100% because of rounding.

Source: Data from IDEAdata.org, U.S. Office of Special Education. *Individuals With Disabilities Education Act (IDEA) data* (Tables 1-16 and C-8). Washington, DC: Author. Available at www.ideadata.org/arc_toc7.asp#partbCC.

it means that children have been wrongly placed in special education programs that deny them appropriate educational interventions that match their full learning capacities, stigmatize them, or segregate them. For example, Skiba, Poloni-Staudinger, Galine, Simmons, and Feggins-Azziz (2006) found that African American students with disabilities were more likely to be placed in more restrictive educational settings than were white students with disabilities. In other instances, students' disabilities may be overlooked because of their membership in a racial or ethnic minority group, resulting in their being denied access to needed special education (De Valenzuela et al., 2006).

Recognizing and Combating Cultural and Racial Bias in Referral and Identification Procedures Understanding the reasons for the disproportionality phenomenon in special education is not simple. Numerous factors must be considered, and educators have identified three areas as integral to this problem: (1) incongruity between teachers and culturally and linguistically diverse students and families, which may lead to biased referrals;

(2) inaccurate assessment of culturally diverse students; and (3) ineffective curriculum and instructional practices for culturally diverse students.

Today's teachers are mostly white (90%) and female (79%) (National Education Association, 2003), and these predominately middle-class educators are teaching an increasingly diverse student population. For example, with respect to the overrepresentation of African American students in the emotional and behavior disorders category, some researchers contend that an African American behavioral style conflicts with white teachers' expectations for classroom behavior (Hale, 2001; Townsend, 2000). "When African American students 'behave' in modes affirmed and sanctioned by dimensions of African American culture (Boykin, 1983) and those modes are unfamiliar to or misinterpreted by teachers, most of whom are white, their behavior is often perceived as inappropriate" (Webb-Johnson, 2003, p. 5).

Bias in the assessment process may contribute to the disproportionate numbers of culturally diverse students in special education. The methods used to identify students for services are an inexact science; and many authors have argued that the likelihood of obtaining valid, accurate, and unbiased assessment results is lower when the student in question is from a culturally or linguistically different background (Correa et al., 1995; Langdon, Novak, & Quintanar, 2000; Ortiz, 1997; C.A. Utley & Obiakor, 2001).

Inappropriate referral to special education can occur if educators and school psychologists cannot separate the presence of unrecognized diversity or deficits from disability. Barrera (1995) notes three potential sources of learning problems in children from culturally and linguistically diverse backgrounds: (1) unrecognized cultural/linguistic

Teachers are most effective when curriculum content and instructional methods are responsive to the cultural, ethnic, and linguistic diversity among their students.

diversity, (2) deficits stemming from chronic poverty or trauma, and (3) disabilities. She contends that special education services are neither appropriate nor most efficient for learning difficulties that are not the result of inherent disabilities.

> If, for example, a child has experienced trauma that remains unaddressed, simply reducing task complexity will not be a sufficient response.... It is important, therefore, to understand the specific difficulties that may stem from unrecognized diversity or deficits. Once understood, pre-referral intervention can be directed toward eliminating their impact and assessing whether any difficulties remain. It is these difficulties, that remain after diversity and deficit have been addressed, that are the appropriate target for special education. (Barrera, 1995, p. 64)

Understanding the complex issues related to culturally diverse students in special education requires that educators understand the problems with incongruity between a teacher's interactions with students and families from diverse cultures, the assessment and referral process in special education, and ineffective instructional and discipline practices (Craig, Hall, Haggart, & Perez-Selles, 2000; B.A. Ford, 2000; Salend & Garrick Duhaney, 2005; Townsend, 2000; West, Leon-Guerrero, & Stevens, 2007). To better meet the needs of students with disabilities from diverse backgrounds, schools should address three issues. First, staff must become culturally responsive to students and families (Tam & Heng, 2005). Second, staff must implement appropriate assessment strategies for determining the educational needs of culturally diverse students. Third, educators should implement culturally responsive practices that support a multicultural approach to curriculum and instruction (J.A. Banks & Banks, 2007; Cartledge, Gardner, & Ford, 2008; J.J. Hoover, Klingner, Baca, & Patton, 2008; Obiakor, 2007).

Program Planning

If the evaluation team determines that a child has a disability that is adversely affecting his educational performance, an individualized education program (IEP) team forms, which plans an IEP. The IEP team determines the *what* (learning goals and objectives), *how* (specialized instruction and related services), *who* (teachers and related-service providers), and *when* (frequency of specialized instruction and related services) of a child's special education program. The IEP is the centerpiece of the special education process. A detailed description of the IEP follows later in this chapter.

Placement

After the IEP team determines the child's educational needs and the special education and related services necessary to meet those needs, the team then determines an educational setting in which the child can receive an appropriate education in the least restrictive environment (LRE). The placement of children with disabilities is one of the most debated and often misunderstood aspects of special education and IDEA and is discussed in depth later in this chapter and throughout the text.

Progress Monitoring, Annual Review, and Reevaluation

In addition to being specialized, intensive, and goal-directed instruction, special education is also continuously evaluated education.

Ongoing Progress Monitoring No matter how appropriate the goals on a student's IEP and well-conceived the specially designed instruction and related services identified to meet those goals, the document's usefulness is limited without ongoing monitoring of student progress. Schools are accountable for providing a free appropriate education to all children with disabilities, and accountability requires measurement (Heward, 2003; Kauffman & Konold, 2007). Direct and frequent measures of student performance provide the most meaningful information about student progress and the effectiveness of instruction (Greenwood & Maheady, 1997; McDonough et al., 2005). A variety of practical and efficient procedures for obtaining and using student performance data to monitor student progress toward IEP objectives are available (e.g., Giek, 1992; Gunter, Miller, Venn, Thomas, & House, 2002; National Center on Student Progress Monitoring, 2007).

Annual Review A child's IEP is not intended to be a permanent document. All aspects of an IEP—the annual goals and outcomes, delivery of specially designed instruction and related services, appropriateness of placement—must be thoroughly reviewed periodically, at least annually. The IEP team revises the IEP to address any lack of expected progress in meeting annual goals or changes in the child's needs.

Reevaluation For some students, the specially designed instruction and related services they receive may ameliorate a problem (e.g., speech therapy for an articulation disorder) or accommodate an impairment (e.g., a prosthesis or mobility device) such that they no longer need, or are eligible for, special education. At least once every 3 years, the school must conduct an MFE of each child with a disability (unless the parents and school agree it is unnecessary) to determine if the child still needs special education. If the IEP team decides that a disability is no longer present or that the child's education is no longer adversely affected by the disability, the student is **declassified**, and special education discontinues. Although special education is sometimes characterized as a "one-way street" down which "it's relatively easy to send children . . . but they rarely return" (Finn, Rotherham, & Hokanson, 2001, p. 339), a nationwide study of more than 11,000 students in special

Monitoring student progress

![Council for Exceptional Children logo] Content Standards for Beginning Teachers—Common Core: Evaluate instruction and monitor progress of individuals with exceptional learning needs (CC8S8).

Direct and frequent measures of student performance provide the most meaningful information about student progress and the effectiveness of instruction.

education ages 6–12 found 17% of the students were declassified after 2 years and no longer receiving special education services (SRI International, 2005).

COLLABORATION AND TEAMING

Special education is a team game. For example, let's consider a third grader, Jessica, who has disabilities. Members of a team who plan, deliver, and evaluate a program of special education and related services designed to meet the unique set of individual needs that arise from Jessica's disability might include the following: the third-grade teacher who works with Jessica in the general education classroom; the speech-language pathologist who meets with Jessica's teacher each week to co-plan language activities; the special education teacher who provides Jessica with intensive reading instruction each day in the resource room and collaborates with her general education teacher on instructional modifications for Jessica in math and science; and the adapted physical education teacher who works with Jessica in the gymnasium. Without open, honest, and frequent communication and collaboration between and among the members of Jessica's team, the quality of her education is likely to suffer. *Paraeducators*—also known as *paraprofessionals, teacher aides,* and *instructional assistants*—play important roles in delivering special education services to students with disabilities. IEP teams must be careful, however, that the paraprofessional's proximity does not have inadvertent adverse effects, such as limiting a student's independence (Giangreco, Yuan, McKenzie, Cameron, & Fialka, 2005).

Collaboration

Types of collaboration

 Content Standards for Beginning Teachers—Common Core: Models and strategies of consultation and collaboration (CC10K1).

Collaboration has become a common and necessary practice in special education (Dettmer, Thurston, & Dyck, 2005; Kochhar-Bryant, 2008; Shapiro & Sayers, 2003). Teachers are better able to diagnose and solve learning and behavior problems in the classroom when they work together (Friend & Cook, 2007; Snell & Janney, 2005). Three ways in which team members can work collaboratively are through coordination, consultation, and teaming (Bigge, Stump, Spagna, & Silberman, 1999).

Coordination is the simplest form of collaboration, requiring only ongoing communication and cooperation to ensure that services are provided in a timely and systematic fashion. Although an important and necessary element of special education, coordination does not require service providers to share information or specifics of their efforts with one another. Fortunately for Jessica, the four educators on her IEP team do much more than simply coordinate who is going to work with her when.

In *consultation,* team members provide information and expertise to one another. Consultation is traditionally considered unidirectional, with the expert providing assistance and advice to the novice. However, team members can, and often do, switch roles from consultant to consultee and back again. Jessica's third-grade teacher, for example, receives expert advice from the speech-language pathologist on strategies for evoking extended language from Jessica during cooperative learning groups but takes the consultant's role when explaining details of the science curriculum to Jessica's resource room teacher.

Teaming

Go to the Homework & Exercises section in Chapter 2 of MyEducationLab and complete Homework Exercise 3. As you watch the video, think about the importance of collaboration and teaming.

Intervention assistance *team*, child study *team*, IEP *team*: each step of the special education process involves a group of people who must work together for the benefit of a child with special needs. For special education to be most effective, these groups must become functioning and effective teams (S. G. Clark, 2000; Correa et al., 2005; Hunt, Soto, Maier, & Doering, 2003). *Teaming* is the most difficult level of collaboration to achieve; it also pays the most dividends. Teaming "bridges the two previous modes of working together and builds on their strengths while adding the component of reciprocity and sharing of information among all team members through a more equal exchange" (Bigge et al., 1999, p. 13). Teaming can occur on several levels and in several ways. Table 2.2 shows examples of coordination, consultation, and teaming activities by special educators.

Although the team approach has many variations in terms of size and structure, each member of a team generally assumes certain clearly assigned responsibilities and recognizes

TABLE 2.2

Examples of coordination, consultation, and teaming activities in special education

ACTIVITY	EXAMPLES
Coordination	• special and general education teachers working out class schedules and support schedules for students • therapists and general and special education teachers working out schedules for therapy interventions • general and special education teachers coordinating grading procedures and policies • special education teachers working with job coaches and transition teachers to set community-based experience schedules for students
Consultation	• special education teachers assisting general education teachers • vocational education teachers working with community employers • related service personnel providing support to special education and general education teachers
Teaming	• special and general education teachers, administrators, counselors, support staff, and school psychologists working together on prereferral teams to design and implement interventions in general education classrooms • special and general education teachers co-teaching in the classroom • paraprofessionals working with general education teachers • special and general education teachers serving together on curriculum-planning teams • team of professionals working together to determine whether a child is eligible for special education services • IEP teams working together to assess the current performance of a student to determine continued eligibility for special education services

Source: From *Curriculum, Assessment, and Instruction for Students with Disabilities*, 1st edition by Bigge/Stump, 1999. Reprinted with permission of Wadsworth, a division of Thomson Learning: www.thomsonrights.com <http://www.thomsonrights.com/>. Fax 800 730-2215.

the importance of learning from, contributing to, and interacting with the other members of the team. Many believe that the consensus and group decisions arising from a team's involvement provide a form of insurance against erroneous or arbitrary conclusions in the complex issues that face educators of students with disabilities. In practice, three team models have emerged (McGonigel, Woodruff, & Roszmann-Millican, 1994)—multidisciplinary, interdisciplinary, and transdisciplinary—and these are discussed next.

Multidisciplinary Teams   *Multidisciplinary teams* are composed of professionals from different disciplines who work independently of one another. Each team member conducts assessments, plans interventions, and delivers services. Teams that operate according to a multidisciplinary structure risk the danger of not providing services that recognize the child as an integrated whole; they must be careful not to "splinter" the child into segments along disciplinary lines. (An old saying described the child with disabilities as giving "his hands to the occupational therapist, his legs to the physical therapist, and his brain to the

Teaming models

 Content Standards for Beginning Teachers—Common Core: Models and strategies of consultation and collaboration (CC10K1).

teacher" [Williamson, 1978].) Another concern is the lack of communication among team members.

Interdisciplinary Teams   *Interdisciplinary teams* are characterized by formal channels of communication between members. Although each professional usually conducts discipline-specific assessments, the interdisciplinary team meets to share information and develop intervention plans. Each team member is generally responsible for implementing a portion of the service plan related to his discipline.

Transdisciplinary Teams   The highest level of team involvement, but also the most difficult to accomplish, is the *transdisciplinary team*. Members of transdisciplinary teams seek to provide services in a uniform and integrated fashion by conducting joint assessments, sharing information and expertise across discipline boundaries, and selecting goals and interventions that are discipline-free (Friend & Cook, 2007; Giangreco, Edelman, & Dennis, 1991). Members of transdisciplinary teams also share roles (often referred to as *role release*); in contrast, members of multidisciplinary and interdisciplinary teams generally operate in isolation and may not coordinate their services to achieve the integrated delivery of related services. Regardless of the team model, team members must learn to put aside professional rivalries and work collaboratively for the benefit of the student.

By teaming, these teachers are better able to diagnose and solve learning problems.

Co-Teaching

Co-teaching has become increasingly common in special education. As Mary Allaire-Gifford and Jean Michielli-Pendl described in their "Featured Teachers" essay, in co-teaching, a general education teacher and special education teacher plan and deliver instruction together in an inclusive classroom. Co-teaching takes many different forms depending on the purpose of the lesson, the individualized objectives and needed supports for students with disabilities, and the teachers' relative levels of expertise with the content (Dettmer et al., 2005; Vaughn, Schumm, & Arguelles, 1997). Salend (2008) described five different co-teaching arrangements:

- *One teaching/one helping.* One teacher instructs the whole class while the other circulates to collect information on student performance and to offer help. This arrangement takes advantage of the expertise of one teacher in a specific subject area.
- *Parallel teaching.* When it is necessary to lower the student–teacher ratio, both teachers teach the same materials to two equal-sized groups of students.
- *Station teaching.* When teaching material that is difficult but not sequential, both teachers present different content at the same time to two equal groups of students and then switch groups and repeat the lesson.
- *Alternative teaching.* When teachers need to individualize instruction, remediate skills, promote mastery, or offer enrichment, one teacher works with a smaller group or individual students while the other teacher works with the rest of the class.
- *Team teaching.* When it is desirable to blend the talents and expertise of teachers, both teachers plan and teach a lesson together. (adapted from Salend, 2008, pp. 160–162)

Suggestions for effective co-teaching can be found in Dieker (2002); Magiera, Smith, Zigmond, and Gebauer (2005); Villa, Thousand, and Nevin (2004); and Zigmond and Matta

(2005). As Mary Allaire-Gifford and Jean Michielli-Pendl emphasized, meticulous planning, open communication, and flexibility are keys to successful co-teaching. It is a mistake, however, to assume that two teachers in the classroom instead of one will automatically improve the effectiveness of a lesson. While the rationale and suggested techniques for co-teaching are logical, research on the effects of co-teaching is limited (Friend & Hurley-Chamberlain, 2006; Zigmond, 2007; Zigmond & Magiera, 2001).

INDIVIDUALIZED EDUCATION PROGRAM

The IEP is "the heart of IDEA" and "the make or break component of FAPE for every child with a disability" (Bateman & Herr, 2006, p. 10). IDEA requires that educators develop and implement an IEP for each student with disabilities between the ages of 3 and 21. (Educators develop an individualized family service plan [IFSP] for each infant and toddler [from birth through age 2] with disabilities. See Chapter 14 for a description of IFSPs.) IDEA is specific about who is to develop the IEP and what it must include.

IEP Team

Each IEP must be the product of the collaborative efforts of the members of an **IEP team**, the membership of which is specified in IDEA as the following:

> The term "individualized education program team" or "IEP Team" means a group of individuals composed of—
>
> 1. The parents of a child with a disability;
> 2. not less than 1 regular education teacher of the child (if the child is, or may be, participating in the regular education environment);
> 3. not less than 1 special education teacher, or where appropriate, at least 1 special education provider of the child;
> 4. a representative of the local education agency who—
>   i. is qualified to provide, or supervise the provision of, specially designed instruction to meet the unique needs of children with disabilities;
>   ii. is knowledgeable about the general curriculum; and
>   iii. is knowledgeable about the availability of resources of the local education agency;
> 5. an individual who can interpret the instructional implications of evaluation results, who may be a member of the team described in clauses (2) through (6);
> 6. at the discretion of the parent or the agency, other individuals who have knowledge or special expertise regarding the child, including related service personnel as appropriate; and
> 7. Whenever appropriate, the child with a disability. (P.L. 108-446, Sec. 614 (d)(1)(B))

IEP Components

Each IEP must include the following seven components:

1. A statement of the child's present levels of academic achievement and functional performance, including—
    (a) how the child's disability affects the child's involvement and progress in the general education curriculum;
    (b) for preschool children, as appropriate, how the disability affects the child's participation in appropriate activities; and
    (c) for children with disabilities who take alternate assessments aligned to alternate achievement standards, a description of benchmarks or short-term objectives;
2. A statement of measurable annual goals, including academic and functional goals, designed to—
    (a) meet the child's needs that result from the child's disability to enable the child to be involved in and make progress in the general education curriculum; and
    (b) meet each of the child's other educational needs that result from the child's disability;
3. A description of how the child's progress toward meeting the annual goals described in subclause (2) will be measured and when periodic reports on the progress the child

Go to the Homework & Exercises section in Chapter 2 of MyEducationLab and complete Homework Exercise 4. As you watch the video and answer the accompanying questions, consider the benefits of co-teaching and collaboration—both for teachers and for students.

is making toward meeting the annual goals (such as through the use of quarterly or other periodic reports, concurrent with the issuance of report cards) will be provided;

4. A statement of the special education and related services and supplementary aids and services, based on peer-reviewed research to the extent practicable, to be provided to the child, or on behalf of the child, and a statement of the program modifications or supports for school personnel that will be provided for the child—

   (a) to advance appropriately toward attaining the annual goals;

   (b) to be involved in and make progress in the general education curriculum in accordance with subclause (I) and to participate in extracurricular and other nonacademic activities; and

   (c) to be educated and participate with other children with disabilities and nondisabled children in the activities described in this subparagraph;

5. An explanation of the extent, if any, to which the child will not participate with nondisabled children in the regular class and in the activities described in subclause (4)(c);

6. (a) a statement of any individual appropriate accommodations that are necessary to measure the academic achievement and functional performance of the child on State and districtwide assessments consistent with section 612(a)(16)(A); and (b) if the IEP Team determines that the child shall take an alternate assessment on a particular State or districtwide assessment of student achievement, a statement of why—

   (aa) the child cannot participate in the regular assessment; and

   (bb) the particular alternate assessment selected is appropriate for the child;

7. The projected date for the beginning of the services and modifications described in subclause (4), and the anticipated frequency, location, and duration of those services and modifications. (P.L. 108-446, Sec. 614 (d)(1)(B))

IEPs for students age 16 and older must include information on how the child's transition from school to adult life will be supported:

8. Beginning not later than the first IEP to be in effect when the child is 16, and updated annually thereafter—

   (a) appropriate measurable postsecondary goals based upon age appropriate transition assessments related to training, education, employment, and, where appropriate, independent living skills;

   (b) the transition services (including courses of study) needed to assist the child in reaching those goals; and

   (c) beginning not later than 1 year before the child reaches the age of majority under State law, a statement that the child has been informed of the child's rights under this title, if any, that will transfer to the child on reaching the age of majority under section 615(m). (P.L. 108-446, Sec. 614 (d) (1) (A) (i))

When developing a child's IEP, the IEP team must consider the following factors:

1. *General.* The IEP Team must consider (i) the strengths of the child; (ii) the concerns of the parents for enhancing the education of their child; (iii) the results of the initial or most recent evaluation of the child; and (iv) the academic, developmental, and functional needs of the child.

2. *Consideration of special factors.* The IEP Team must—

   i. In the case of a child whose behavior impedes the child's learning or that of others, consider the use of positive behavioral interventions and supports, and other strategies, to address that behavior;

   ii. In the case of a child with limited English proficiency, consider the language needs of the child as those needs relate to the child's IEP;

   iii. In the case of a child who is blind or visually impaired, provide for instruction in Braille and the use of Braille unless the IEP Team determines, after an evaluation of the child's reading and writing skills, that instruction in Braille or the use of Braille is not appropriate for the child;

   iv. Consider the communication needs of the child, and in the case of a child who is deaf or hard of hearing, consider the child's language and communication needs; and

   v. Consider whether the child needs assistive technology devices and services. (P.L. 108-446, Sec. 614 (d) (3)(A & B))

Participation and progress in the general curriculum

 Content Standards for Beginning Teachers—Common Core: Identify and prioritize areas of the general curriculum and needed accommodations (CC7S1).

IEP Functions and Formats

The IEP is a system for spelling out where the child is, where she should be going, how she will get there, how long it will take, and how to tell if and when she has arrived. The IEP provides teachers and parents with the opportunity—and the responsibility—to first be *realistic* about the child's needs and goals and then to be *creative* about how to meet them. Being realistic does not mean taking a pessimistic or limited view of the child's current capabilities or of his potential to reach improved levels of academic achievement or functional performance. It means analyzing how specially designed, evidence-based instruction and related services can help the child get from her present levels of performance to future goals.

The IEP is also a measure of accountability for teachers and schools. Whether a particular school or educational program is effective will be judged, to some extent, by how well it is able to help children meet the goals and objectives set forth in their IEPs. Like other professionals, teachers are being called on to demonstrate effectiveness; and the IEP provides one way for them to do so. Although a child's teacher and school cannot be prosecuted in the courts if the child does not achieve his IEP goals, the school district is legally bound to provide the special education and related services identified in the IEP, and the school must be able to document that it made a conscientious and systematic effort to achieve those goals (Bartlett et al., 2007; Wright & Wright, 2006).

IEP formats vary widely across school districts, and schools may exceed the requirements of the law and include additional information. Bateman and Linden (2006) caution against overreliance on standardized forms and computers for creating IEPs. "Forms by their very nature tend to interfere with true individualization. . . . [A] proper form will contain all the required elements in the simplest way possible, allowing for the most flexibility and creativity" (pp. 82–83). Figure 2.2 shows the "non-form" for IEPs recommended by Bateman and Linden. The first page identifies the student, IEP team members, and special factors to consider as required by IDEA. The "heart of the IEP" (Bateman & Linden, 2006, p. 72) begins on the second page in a three-column sequence showing needs and present levels of performance, services that will be provided, and goals and objectives. The IEP form concludes with additional IDEA requirements and, for older students, transition components.

Figure 2.3 shows portions of the IEP for Curt, a ninth grader and low achiever seen by the school district as a poorly motivated student with a disciplinary problem and a bad attitude. Curt's parents see their son as a discouraged and frustrated student with learning disabilities, especially in written language.

One of the most difficult tasks for the IEP team is determining how inclusive the IEP document should be. It is important for educators and parents to recognize that an IEP is not the same as a curriculum. "IEP objectives are not comprehensive enough to cover the entire scope and sequence of what a student is to learn. The content taught by most special educators goes far beyond what is written in the IEP. Sometimes special educators try to incorporate an entire curriculum into the IEP, resulting in an overly long, detailed IEP" (Browder, 2001, p. 35). Strickland and Turnbull (1993) state that the definition of special education as "specially designed instruction" should be a key element in determining the content of a student's IEP.

Each area of functioning that is adversely affected by the student's disability must be represented by an annual goal on the IEP.

The determination of whether instruction is "specially designed" must be made by comparing the nature of the instruction for the student with a disability to instructional practices used with typical students at the same age and grade level. If the instructional adaptations that a student with a disability requires are (1) significantly different from adaptations normally expected or made for typical students in that setting, and if (2) the adaptations are necessary to offset or reduce the adverse effect of the disability on learning and educational performance, then

FIGURE 2.2   Example of an IEP form

Student's name _____   IEP meeting date _____

Date of birth _____   Grade _____   Case manager _____

*Copies of this IEP will circulate among staff members who are working with this student. Please observe the federal and state laws that protect the student's right to confidentiality of education records. Do **not** share with unauthorized persons, and do **not** include such sensitive information as disability category or IQ.*

Special factors to consider	Participation in statewide or other large scale assessments
For all students, consider: ☐ The student's strengths ☐ Concerns of the parent(s) for enhancing the student's education ☐ Need for assistive technology devices and services ☐ Communication needs	The following individual appropriate accommodations are necessary to measure the student's academic achievement and functional performance on state and districtwide assessments:
If behavior impedes learning of student or others, consider: ☐ Positive behavioral interventions and support strategies, including positive behavioral interventions ☐ Other strategies to address behavior	The IEP Team has determined that the student should take an alternative assessment because:
If student has limited English proficiency, consider: ☐ Language needs as they relate to student's IEP	
If student is blind or visually impaired, consider: ☐ Instruction in use of Braille (unless IEP team decides that instruction in Braille is not appropriate)	The IEP Team has determined that the student should take the following alternative assessment:
If a student is deaf or hard of hearing, consider: ☐ Opportunities for direct communication with peers and professionals in student's language and communication mode ☐ Opportunities for direct instruction in student's language and communication mode	

Additional comments about this student relevant to developing an appropriate IEP:

Unique educational needs, characteristics, and measured present levels of academic achievement and functional performance (PLOPs)	Special education, related services and supplemental aids and services (based on peer-reviewed research to the extent practicable); assistive technology and modifications or personnel support	Measurable annual goals and short-term objectives (progress markers),[1] including academic and functional goals to enable the student to be involved in and make progress in the general curriculum and to meet other needs resulting from the disability
(Including how the disability affects student's ability to participate & progress in the general curriculum)	(Including anticipated starting date, frequency, duration and location for each)	(Including progress measurement method for each goal)

[1]For students who take an alternative assessment and are assessed against other than grade level standards, the IEP **must** include short-term objectives (progress markers). For other students, the IEP **may** include short-term objectives. The IEP **must** for all students clearly articulate how the student's progress will be measured, and that progress must be reported to parents at designated intervals.

FIGURE 2.2   *Continued*

Transition services

The IEP team has developed a Transition Plan because

☐ although the student will not yet be 16 during the effective period of this IEP, the Team has determined that transition planning is appropriate at this time,

☐ the student will be 16 during the effective period of this IEP, or

☐ the student has reached the age of 16.

Transition services must address the student's individual needs, taking into account his/her strengths, preferences, and interests as described here:

Based on these factors, this IEP includes services & appropriate measurable postsecondary goals on page _____, that draw upon age-appropriate transition assessments related to training, education, employment, and, where appropriate, independent living skills.

The transition services, including the course of study needed to assist the student in reaching those goals includes:

☐ Instruction
☐ Related services
☐ Community experiences
☐ The development of employment and other post-school adult living objectives
☐ If appropriate, acquisition of daily living skills and functional vocational evaluation

The student has been informed of the IDEA rights that will transfer to him/her upon reaching the age of majority.

_____

Student's signature

Progress report

Parents will receive reports on the student's progress toward annual goals through:

☐ IEP progress report completed per the report card schedule on these dates _____ _____
_____ _____

☐ Other progress reporting system as follows:

Progress toward each annual goal must be measured through the criteria and evaluation measures established for each goal.

Participation with nondisabled students

Explanation of extent to which the student will **not** participate with nondisabled children:

(a) In regular classes:

(b) In special education services:

IEP team members

Signature	Position

Source: Reprinted from Bateman, B. D., & Linden, M. L. (2006). *Better IEPs: How to develop legally correct and educationally useful programs* (4th ed., pp. 124–126). Verona, WI: Attainment Company, Inc. Used by permission.

these adaptations should be considered "specially designed instruction" and should be included as part of the student's IEP, regardless of the instructional setting. (Strickland & Turnbull, 1993, p. 13)

Each area of functioning that is adversely affected by the student's disability must be represented by an annual goal on the IEP. Annual goals are measurable statements of what the IEP team believes the student can accomplish in 1 year if the special services provided are effective. Too often, IEP teams' hard work and best intentions for a child's progress are

FIGURE 2.3	Portions of an IEP for Curt, a ninth grader with learning disabilities and a history of disciplinary problems	

Unique educational needs, characteristics, and measured present levels of academic achievement and functional performance (PLOPs)	Special education, related services and supplemental aids and services (based on peer-reviewed research to the extent practicable); assistive technology and modifications or personnel support	Measurable annual goals and short-term objectives (progress markers),[1] including academic and functional goals to enable the student to be involved in and make progress in the general curriculum and to meet other needs resulting from the disability
(Including how the disability affects student's ability to participate & progress in the general curriculum)	(Including anticipated starting date, frequency, duration and location for each)	(Including progress measurement method for each goal)
Study skills/organizational needs: • How to read text • Note taking • How to study notes • Memory work • Be prepared for class, with materials • Lengthen and improve attention span and on-task behavior **Present level:** Curt currently lacks skills in all these areas.	1. Speech/lang. therapist, resource room teacher, and content area teachers will provide Curt with direct and specific teaching of study skills, i.e. • Note taking from lectures • Note taking while reading text • How to study notes for a test • Memorization hints • Strategies for reading text to retain information 2. Assign a "study buddy" for Curt in each content area class. 3. Prepare a motivation system for Curt to be prepared for class with all necessary materials. 4. Develop a motivational plan to encourage Curt to lengthen his attention span and time on task. 5. Provide aide to monitor on-task behaviors in first month or so of plan and teach Curt self-monitoring techniques. 6. Provide motivational system and self-recording form for completion of academic tasks in each class.	**Goal:** At the end of academic year, Curt will have better grades and, by his own report, will have learned new study skills. **Obj. 1:** Given a 20–30 min lecture/oral lesson, Curt will take appropriate notes as judged by that teacher. **Obj. 2:** Given 10–15 pgs. of text to read, Curt will employ an appropriate strategy for retaining info., i.e. mapping, webbing, outlining, notes, etc. as judged by the teacher **Obj. 3:** Given notes to study for a test, Curt will do so successfully as evidenced by his test score.
Academic needs/written language: Curt needs strong remedial help in spelling, punctuation, capitalization, and usage. **Present level:** Curt is approximately 2 grade levels behind his peers in these skills.	1. Provide direct instruction in written language skills (punctuation, capitalization, usage, spelling) by using a highly structured, well-sequenced program. *Services provided in small group of no more than four students in the resource room, 50 minutes/day.*	**Goal:** Within one academic year, Curt will improve his written language skills by 1.5 or 2 full grade levels to a 6.0 grade level as measured by a standardized test. **Obj. 1:** Given 10 sentences of dictation at his current

FIGURE 2.3   *Continued*

2. Build in continuous and cumulative review to help with short-term rote memory difficulty.

3. Develop a list of commonly used words in student writing (or use one of many published lists) for Curt's spelling program.

Adaptations to regular program:
- In all classes, Curt should sit near the front of the class.
- Curt should be called on often to keep him involved and on task.
- All teachers should help Curt with study skills as trained by spelling/ language specialist and resource room teacher.
- Teachers should monitor Curt's work closely in the beginning weeks/ months of his program.

level of instruction, Curt will punctuate and capitalize with 90% accuracy (checked at the end of each unit taught).

Obj. 2: Given 30 sentences with choices of usage, at his current instructional level, Curt will make the correct choice in 28 or more sentences.

Obj. 3: Given a list of 150 commonly used words in 6th grade writing, Curt will spell 95% of the words correctly.

[1]For students who take an alternative assessment and are assessed against other than grade level standards, the IEP **must** include short-term objectives (progress markers). For other students, the IEP **may** include short-term objectives. The IEP **must** for all students clearly articulate how the student's progress will be measured, and that progress must be reported to parents at designated intervals.

Source: Reprinted from Bateman, B. D., & Linden, M. L. (2006). *Better IEPs: How to develop legally correct and educationally useful programs* (4th ed., pp. 153–155). Verona, WI: Attainment Company, Inc. Used by permission.

muddled at best, or lost altogether, by IEP goals that are impossible to measure. Figure 2.4 presents some examples of nonmeasurable IEP goals and how IEP teams might change them into measurable goals.

IEP Problems and Potential Solutions

Since its inception, the IEP process has been problematic. J. J. Gallagher (1984) wrote that the IEP is "probably the single most unpopular aspect of the law, not only because it requires a great deal of work, but also because the essence of the plan itself seems to have been lost in the mountains of paperwork" (p. 228). More than 20 years later, Bateman and Linden (2006) expressed a similar opinion:

> Sadly, many IEPs are horrendously burdensome to teachers and nearly useless to parents and children. Far from being a creative, flexible, data-based, and individualized application of the best of educational interventions to a child with unique needs, the typical IEP is "empty," devoid of specific services to be provided, and its goals are often not measurable. It says what the IEP team hopes the student will be able to accomplish, but little about the special education interventions and the related services or the classroom modifications that will enable him or her to reach those goals. (p. 87)

Numerous studies of actual IEPs seem to support such harsh descriptions. For example, Grigal, Test, Beattie, and Wood (1997) examined IEPs for high school students and found that transition-related goals included vague outcomes (e.g., "will think about best place to live," "will explore jobs"), no evaluation procedures, and very few adaptations in activities or

FIGURE 2.4   **Turning nonmeasurable IEP goals into measurable goals**

"Measurable" is the essential characteristic of an IEP goal or objective. When a goal isn't measurable, it cannot be measured. If it cannot be measured, it violates IDEA and may result in denial of FAPE to the child. A measurable goal contains a given or condition, the learner's performance, and the desired level of performance or criteria. The learner's performance must be an observable, visible, or countable behavior.

Not Observable or Countable	**Observable and Countable**
enjoying literature	reading orally
understanding history	constructing a time line
becoming independent	dressing oneself
respecting authority	speaking to adults without vulgarities
improving, feeling, knowing	pointing, drawing, identifying, writing, etc.

Not-Measurable Goals Made Measurable

Rebecca will increase her active listening skills. This goal has no criterion to indicate the level at which Rebecca must perform to reach the goal, nor does it specify the behavior of "active listening." We could not tell if Rebecca has "improved" without knowing the previous level of her skills. Thousands and thousands of goals have used this "student will improve *X*" format. It is not measurable, not acceptable, and not useful. To improve this goal, we must ask what the writer meant by "active listening." Perhaps "following oral directions" would be an acceptable visible learner performance. If so, this measurable version is probably closer to what was intended: "Given 5 simple, two-step oral directions such as 'Fold your paper and hand it in,' Rebecca will correctly complete 4 directions."

Sara will make wise choices in her use of leisure time. Sara may, indeed, "make wise choices," but we really can't see her doing this. This goal does not describe a visible learner performance and does not include a criterion. Perhaps the writer meant something like "Sara will attend a supervised, school-sponsored extracurricular activity at least once a week."

Beth will show an appropriate level of upper body strength. This goal is easily fixed. The goal writer may well have meant, "Beth will pass the XYZ test of upper body strength at her age level."

The following two objectives appeared under the totally nonmeasurable goal of "develop functional academics" on the IEP for Alex, a highly intelligent, 16-year-old nonreader who has severe dyslexia and a high level of anger and confusion about why he can't read, write, or spell.

Given 10 words, Alex shall group letters and pronounce letter sounds in words with 80% accuracy. How do we determine whether Alex has met this progress marker? Clearly, we give 10 words to Alex (perhaps a list) and ask him to do something, but what? Is it possibly as simple as "Alex, would you read these aloud"? That's a good guess, but does the list look like "sit, bun, log, cat," or does it look like "exegesis, ophthalmology, entrepreneur"? What is 80% accuracy in reading the list? If the word "palace" were read as "place" or "tentative" as "tantative" or "when" as "where," what percentage of accuracy do we assign to each effort? Or did the writer really mean that Alex should read 80% of the words accurately? How long a time frame is Alex to be allowed to read the words? Perhaps the objective writer meant something like this: "Given 10 unfamiliar, regular CVC words, Alex will decode 9 of 10 correctly in 20 seconds."

Alex will research the history and culture of the given country with 80% accuracy. Remembering that Alex reads at a mid-first-grade level and is presently working on letter sounds and decoding, what are we to make of this objective? If Alex comes to school tomorrow morning and says, "I researched the history and culture of China without any mistakes last night," are we to check off the objective as complete? Is that what the writer intended? What about something like this: "Given a 1-hour PBS video on the history and culture of China and a tape recorder, after viewing the tape, Alex will dictate and record 10 things he learned about China, with no more than one factual error."

Source: Adapted from Bateman, B. D., & Herr, C. M. (2006). *Writing measurable IEP goals and objectives* (pp. 153–155). Verona, WI: Attainment Company, Inc. Used by permission.

materials. Other researchers have discovered that many IEPs lack necessary mandated components (S.W. Smith, 1990a, 1990b; S.W. Smith & Simpson, 1989).

Properly including all of the mandated components in an IEP is no guarantee that the document will guide the student's learning and teachers' teaching in the classroom, as intended by IDEA. Although most educators support the idealized concept of the IEP, inspection of IEPs often reveals inconsistencies between what is written on the document and the instruction that students experience in the classroom (S.W. Smith & Brownell, 1995).

Although IDEA requires parents to participate in IEP meetings and encourages student participation, research on parent and student involvement in the IEP process has produced mixed results (Test et al., in press). In a study of 109 middle school and high school IEP meetings, Martin, Van Dycke, Greene, and colleagues (2006) concluded that students' "presence can at best be viewed as tokenism because of the very low levels of student engagement and low student [expression of] opinions of their IEP meetings" (p. 197).

On the bright side, numerous studies have shown that students with widely varying disabilities can learn to be actively involved in the IEP process, even to the point of leading the meeting (e.g., Arndt, Konrad, & Test, 2006; Konrad & Test, 2004; Martin, Van Dycke, Christensen, et al., 2006; Mason, McGahee-Kovac, Johnson, & Stillerman, 2002; Test et al., 2004). Many excellent resources, curricula, and strategies for involving students in their IEPs have become available in recent years (Konrad, in press; Myers & Eisenman, 2005; Van Dycke, Martin, & Lovett, 2006). For example, Mason, McGahee-Kovac, and Johnson (2004) describe a six-session program to prepare students to lead their IEP meetings. Students progress through three levels of involvement, ultimately leading the IEP conference.

Level 1—Student presents information about or reads from his or her transition plan for the future.

Level 2—Student explains his or her disability, shares information on individual strengths and weaknesses (present levels of performance), and explains the accommodations needed.

Level 3—Student leads the IEP conference, including Level 1 and Level 2 responsibilities, introductions, and closing. (p. 19)

General education teachers also benefit from instruction in the IEP process. In a study of 393 middle school and high school IEP meetings, general education teachers rated themselves lower than all other IEP meeting participants, including students, on the extent to which they helped make decisions and knew what to do next (Martin, Huber, Marshall, & Sale, 2004). General education teachers ranked second lowest (only to students) in knowing the reason for the meetings, talking at the meetings, feeling comfortable saying what they thought, understanding what was said, and feeling good about the meeting.

Numerous resources and tools are available to help IEP teams develop IEPs that exceed compliance with the law and serve as meaningful guides for the specially designed instruction that students with disabilities need (Bateman & Herr, 2006; Courtade-Little & Browder, 2005; Gibb & Dyches, 2007; Hammer, 2004; Jung, 2007; Keyes & Owens-Johnson, 2003; Lignugaris/Kraft, Marchand-Martella, & Martella, 2001; Lytle & Bordin, 2001; Menlove et al., 2001; Wood, Karvonen, Test, Browder, & Algozzine, 2004). For example, Choosing Outcomes and Accommodations for Children (COACH) is a field-tested IEP process that guides child study teams through the assessment and planning stages of IEP development to result in annual goals and short-term objectives directly related to functional skills in integrated settings (Giangreco, Cloninger, & Iverson, 1998).

Regardless of the level of parent and student participation, the appropriateness and measurability of the goals, and the IEP team's satisfaction with the document, without instruction of the highest quality, many children with disabilities will make little progress. This reality led to the requirement in IDEA 2004 that teachers must use evidence-based practices (EBPs) to ensure their students receive the highest quality instruction. See Current Issues and Future Trends, "Evidence-Based Practice: Easier Said Than Done."

To learn more about strategies to encourage and facilitate effective student participation in their own IEPs, go to the Homework & Exercises section in Chapter 2 of MyEducationLab and complete Homework Exercise 5.

CURRENT ISSUES AND FUTURE TRENDS

EVIDENCE-BASED PRACTICE: EASIER SAID THAN DONE

Should science guide practice in special education? Most individuals would say "Yes." However, the "devil is in the details." (Odom et al., 2005, p. 137)

When Congress reauthorized IDEA in 2004, it made several changes in the law to align it with the No Child Left Behind Act (NCLB). One of the most significant changes was the stipulation that students with disabilities receive special education and related services "based on peer-reviewed research to the extent practical." Thus, Congress made a legal requirement of something many special educators had always strived to do: use the results of scientific research to ensure their students receive the highest quality instruction. It is unfortunate that a federal law is required to motivate all educators to use scientifically sound teaching practices with children whose learning is most dependent upon effective instruction. The reality, however, is that many students with disabilities have been the recipients of teaching methods that are misguided at best, and some students have been subjected to practices that research has shown repeatedly to be not only benignly ineffective but also harmful (Heward, 2003; Jacobson, Foxx, & Mulick, 2005a).

While the mandate to use evidence-based practices (EBP) may appear straightforward, it is not. Just some of the questions that the field needs to address are the following: What criteria should educators use to define EBPs? Who will apply those criteria to determine which practices teachers should use and which ones they should avoid? What are the most effective and efficient ways to disseminate information about EBPs to IEP teams and teachers? How can a teacher determine the validity and trustworthiness of an EBP for her students?

DEFINING EVIDENCE-BASED PRACTICE

No universal standards exist for defining an EBP, and the field of special education, and education in general, is working to develop criteria for determining the degree to which a practice should be considered research based. A fundamental issue is defining the type of research that should be accepted as evidence for a practice's effectiveness. The Department of Education's Institute for Education Sciences and What Works Clearinghouse have identified the **randomized experimental group design** (also called a *randomized control trial, RCT*) as the gold standard for research methodology to show evidence of an instructional technique's effectiveness. Although well-conducted RCTs provide strong experimental evidence, much of special education's research base over the past 40 years has been produced with other research methodologies, most notably nonrandomized group designs, single-subject research, and correlational studies (Odom et al., 2005). More recently, information obtained from qualitative studies has provided conceptual frameworks and support for emerging practices that can be analyzed and evaluated further with experimental studies. Examples of quality indicators for special education research using each of these four methodologies can be found in Gersten et al. (2005, p. 152); Horner et al. (2005, p. 174); B. Thompson et al. (2005, p. 191); and Brantlinger, Jimenez, Klingner, Pugach, and Richardson (2005, p. 202), respectively.

Another issue to be resolved is who will determine what practices are designated as evidence based. Traditionally, peer-reviewed literature reviews and meta-analyses (a sophisticated statistical comparison and assessment of the results produced by a group of studies that evaluated the same practice) by scholars who have examined a given topic provide one source of expert opinion (e.g., Bellini & Akullian, 2007; Lewis, Hudson, Richter, & Johnson, 2004). It is not uncommon, however, that after reviewing the existing research for a given practice, one author concludes the evidence base to be very strong while another's assessment of the same set of studies yields a much lower rating (e.g., Kavale & Forness, 1995; McIntosh, Vaughn, & Zaragoza, 1991).

Professional organizations and nonprofit groups are also contributing to the discussion of EBPs. For example, the Council for Exceptional Children (CEC) (2006a) has proposed a process and criteria by which practices would be classified at three levels:

- *Research-based practice:* Recommended for special educators' repertoire.
- *Promising practice:* May be included in special educators' repertoire with clear caveats for following the developing literature.
- *Emerging practice:* Informative, but research base does not yet lead to recommended use.

CEC's Division for Research and Division for Learning Disabilities co-produces a periodic series of *Practice Alerts* (available at www.TeachingLD.org) to inform teachers about practices at two levels of research support: "Go For It" for practices with significant amounts of consistent evidence, and "Use Caution" for practices with limited or mixed research evidence. Examples of practices that have received the "Go For It" designation are using graphic organizers (Ellis & Howard, 2007), direct instruction (Tarver, 1999), classwide peer tutoring (Maheady, Harper, & Mallette, 2003); and teaching phonological awareness (Troia, 2004).

Lists of instructional programs and practices that have met the criteria considered by various government and nonprofit organizations sufficient to be identified as evidence based can be found at these websites:

- National Center for Special Education Research http://www.ed.gov/about/offices/list/ies/ncser/index.html
- Center for Evidence-Based Practice: Young Children With Challenging Behavior http://challengingbehavior.fmhi.usf.edu/resources.htm
- NICHY Research to Practice Database http://research.nichcy.org/search.asp
- The Promising Practices Network www.promisingpractices.net/
- The Wing Institute http://winginstitute.org/
- What Works Clearinghouse www.whatworks.ed.gov/

EVIDENCE-BASED USE OF EVIDENCE-BASED PRACTICES

No matter how much scientific evidence supports a given a curriculum, program, or teaching method, a teacher should never assume effectiveness (Detrich, Keyworth, & States, 2007). When implementing any EBP, teachers should:

- *Be consistent: Treatment fidelity is paramount.* The full and intended effects of any intervention will not be realized unless the procedure is implemented as designed. Researchers use the term "with complete fidelity" when evaluating a practice.
- *Beware of eclecticism.* It is tempting to think that a combination of practices will be more effective than any single practice. Eclecticism, however, is often a recipe for failure because (1) the most important and

effective parts of each model might be rejected in favor of weaker, ineffective components; (2) some components of a given practice may not be effective when implemented without other elements of the practice; (3) elements from different practices may be incompatible with one another; (4) an eclectic mix might prevent any of the included models from being implemented with sufficient duration and intensity to obtain significant effects; and (5) teachers who use elements of multiple practices may not learn to implement any of the methods with the precision necessary for optimal results (Heward, 2003).

- *Test it yourself.* The most important and generally useful EBP of all may be direct and frequent measurement of student progress.
- *If you must modify the program, change only one variable at a time.* Modification or variation may be necessary to obtain desired levels of learning for a given student. Begin by implementing the published procedure as consistently and rigorously as possible. Then, if data show insufficient progress, change one, but only one, aspect of the program while continuing to measure student performance.

What Do You Think?

1. Why is use of EBPs a current issue in special education?

2. Identify and rank order five criteria you believe most important in determining whether an instructional program or teaching method should be designated an EBP.

3. Like television viewers who are barraged with a steady stream of commercials touting amazing results from one wonder drug after another, teachers are told by every publisher and in-service workshop presenter that the programs and methods they are pitching are "scientifically proven" to be effective. How can educators protect themselves against being taken in by false claims?

LEAST RESTRICTIVE ENVIRONMENT

IDEA requires that every student with disabilities be educated in the **least restrictive environment (LRE)**. Specifically, the law stipulates that

to the maximum extent appropriate, children with disabilities, including children in public or private institutions or other care facilities, are educated with children who are not disabled, and special classes, separate schooling, or other removal of children with disabilities from the regular educational environment occurs only when the nature or severity of the disability of a child is such that education in regular classes with the use of supplementary aids and services cannot be achieved satisfactorily. (P.L. 108-446, Sec. 612 [a][5][A])

Least restrictive environment

 Content Standards for Beginning Teachers—General Curriculum and Independence Curriculum Referenced Standards: Principles of normalization and concept of least restrictive environment (GC1K8, IC1K7).

The LRE is the setting that is most similar to a general education classroom and also meets the child's special educational needs. *Least restrictive environment* is a relative and wholly individualized concept; it is not to be determined by disability category. The LRE for one 10-year-old student who is blind might be inappropriate for another 10-year-old with the same type and degree of visual impairment. And the LRE for both students may change over time. Since the passage of IDEA, there have been many differences of opinion over which type of setting is least restrictive and most appropriate for students with disabilities. Some educators and parents consider any decision to place a student with disabilities outside the general education classroom to be overly restrictive; most, however, recognize that full-time placement in a general education classroom is restrictive and inappropriate if the child's educational needs cannot be adequately met in that environment.

The least restrictive environment is a relative concept; the LRE for one child may be inappropriate for another.

Continuum of services

Content Standards for Beginning Teachers—General Curriculum and Independence Curriculum Referenced Standards: Continuum of placement and services available for individuals with disabilities (GC1K5, IC1K4).

A Continuum of Alternative Placements

IDEA requires schools to provide a **continuum of alternative placements**—that is, a range of placement and service options to meet the individual needs of students with disabilities.

Continuum of alternative placements.

(a) Each public agency must ensure that a continuum of alternative placements is available to meet the needs of children with disabilities for special education and related services. (b) The continuum required in paragraph (a) of this section must—(1) Include the alternative placements listed in the definition of special education under §300.38 (instruction in regular classes, special classes, special schools, home instruction, and instruction in hospitals and institutions); and (2) Make provision for supplementary services (such as resource room or itinerant instruction) to be provided in conjunction with regular class placement. (Authority: 20 U.S.C. 1412 §300.115 (a) (5))

The continuum can be depicted symbolically as a pyramid, with placements ranging from the general education classroom at the bottom to special schools, residential facilities, and homebound or hospital placements at the top (see Figure 2.5). The fact that the pyramid is widest at the bottom indicates that most children with disabilities are served in *general education classrooms* and that the number of children who require more intensive and specialized placements decreases as we move up the continuum. As noted in Chapter 1, the majority of children receiving special education services have mild disabilities. As the severity of a disability increases, typically, the need for more specialized services also increases, while the number of students involved decreases. However, the fact that a larger proportion of children with severe disabilities are educated in placements outside of the general education classroom does not mean that the LRE for a student with severe disabilities is necessarily a special class or a separate school.

Five of the eight placement options depicted in Figure 2.5 are available in regular public school buildings. Children at the first three levels on the continuum have full-time placements in general education classrooms and receive various degrees and types of support by special teachers who consult or co-teach with the general education teachers. In a *resource room*, a special educator provides instruction to students with disabilities for part of the school day. Children who require full-time placement in a *separate classroom* (also called a *self-contained classroom*) are with other children with disabilities for most of the school day and participate with children without disabilities only at certain times,

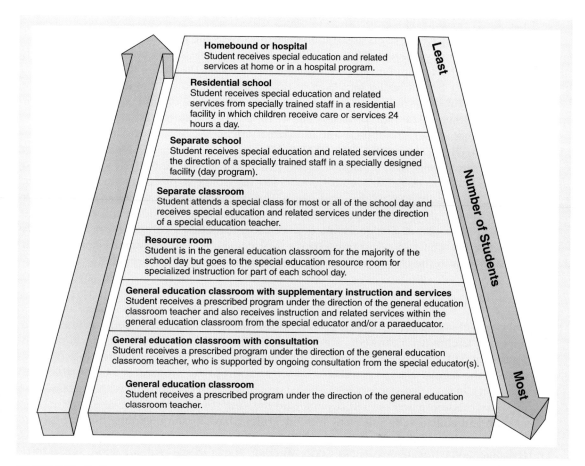

Least

Number of Students

Most

Homebound or hospital
Student receives special education and related services at home or in a hospital program.

Residential school
Student receives special education and related services from specially trained staff in a residential facility in which children receive care or services 24 hours a day.

Separate school
Student receives special education and related services under the direction of a specially trained staff in a specially designed facility (day program).

Separate classroom
Student attends a special class for most or all of the school day and receives special education and related services under the direction of a special education teacher.

Resource room
Student is in the general education classroom for the majority of the school day but goes to the special education resource room for specialized instruction for part of each school day.

General education classroom with supplementary instruction and services
Student receives a prescribed program under the direction of the general education classroom teacher and also receives instruction and related services within the general education classroom from the special educator and/or a paraeducator.

General education classroom with consultation
Student receives a prescribed program under the direction of the general education classroom teacher, who is supported by ongoing consultation from the special educator(s).

General education classroom
Student receives a prescribed program under the direction of the general education classroom teacher.

FIGURE 2.5

Continuum of alternative placements for students with disabilities

such as during lunch, recess, or perhaps art and music. Although the separate classroom provides significantly fewer opportunities for interaction with children without disabilities than does the general education classroom, it provides more integration than does placement in *separate schools* or *residential schools*, which are attended only by children with disabilities. A child in a *homebound or hospital setting* receives special education and related services on an individual basis and may have few opportunities to interact with other children.

Determining LRE

The IEP team determines the proper placement for a child after determining the child's needs that result from the disability and the special education and related services necessary to meet those needs. The legally mandated and educationally sound sequence follows: (1) The school determines whether the child has a disability and is therefore eligible for special education; (2) the IEP team determines the child's individual needs and develops an IEP that specifies the special education and related services needed to meet those needs; and (3) the child is placed in the LRE in which educators can provide an appropriate program and the child can make satisfactory educational progress.

The general education classroom is the starting point for the IEP team's discussion of placement. Before considering the provision of special instruction and related services in any setting other than the general education classroom, the IEP team must discuss if the IEP goals can be achieved in the general education classroom. Removal of a child with disabilities from the general education classroom is to occur only when the nature and severity of the child's disabilities are such that an appropriate education in that setting cannot be achieved. Placement decisions should be made by "determining whether a particular

Determining LRE

 Council for Exceptional Children

Content Standards for Beginning Teachers—Common Core: Issues, assurances, and due process rights related to assessment, eligibility, and placement within a continuum of services (CC1K6).

placement option will support the effective instructional practices that are required for a particular child to achieve his or her individual objectives and goals" (Zigmond, 2003, p. 198).

Placement of a student with disabilities should not be viewed as all or nothing at any one level on the continuum. The IEP team should consider the extent to which the student can effectively be integrated into each of three dimensions of school life: the general academic curriculum, extracurricular activities (e.g., clubs), and other school activities (e.g., recess, mealtimes). The LRE "provision allows for a 'mix and match' where total integration is appropriate under one dimension and partial integration is appropriate under another dimension" (H. R. Turnbull & Cilley, 1999, p. 41).

In addition, educators must not regard placement as permanent. The continuum concept is intended to be flexible, with students moving from one placement to another as dictated by their individual educational needs. The IEP team should periodically review the specific goals and objectives for each child—they are required to do so at least annually—and make new placement decisions if warranted. The child's parents must be informed whenever the school considers any change in placement so that the parents can either consent or object to the change and present additional information if they wish.

INCLUSIVE EDUCATION

Although often confused, the terms *inclusion* and *least restrictive environment* are not synonymous. **Inclusion** means educating students with disabilities in general education classrooms; the LRE principle requires that students with disabilities be educated in settings as close to the regular class as possible in which an appropriate program can be provided and the child can make satisfactory educational progress. For many students with disabilities, an inclusive classroom and the LRE are one and the same; but that is not always so. Much discussion and controversy and many misconceptions have arisen regarding the inclusion of students with disabilities in general education classrooms (Giangreco, 2007; Kauffman & Hallahan, 2005; Kavale & Forness, 2000; Mitchell, 2004a, 2004b; Salend, 2006; Sasso, 2001; R. L. Simpson, 2004; Zigmond, 2006).

Although many parents of children with disabilities strongly support inclusion, others have resisted it just as strongly, thinking that the general education classroom does not offer the intense, individualized education their children need (Garrick Duhaney & Salend, 2000). For example, studies of parents of children with severe disabilities have found some parents in favor of and some against inclusion (P. A. Gallagher et al., 2000; Palmer, Fuller, Arora, & Nelson, 2001). Havey (1999) reported that in 67% of the cases in which parents contested the schools' placement decision, the parents sought a more restrictive educational setting (e.g., parents wanted the child to attend a resource room for part of each day instead of full-time placement in a general education class).

As we have seen, IDEA calls for the education of each child with a disability in the LRE, removed no farther than necessary from the general education public school program. The law does not require placement of all children with disabilities in general education classes, or suggest that general education teachers should educate students with disabilities without the necessary support services, including help from special educators and other specialists. Although not all children with disabilities attend general education classes, general education classroom teachers are expected to teach a much wider range of learning, behavioral, sensory, and physical differences among their students than ever before. Thus, provision of in-service training for general educators is an important (and sometimes overlooked) requirement of IDEA. General education teachers are understandably wary of having students with disabilities placed in their classes if the school provides little or no training or support (DeSimone & Parmar, 2006). The role of teachers in general education classrooms is already a highly demanding one; they do not want their classes to become any larger, especially if they perceive exceptional children as unmanageable (Cook, Cameron, & Tankersly, 2007). General education teachers are entitled to be involved in decisions about children who are placed in their classes and to be offered continuous consultation and other support services from administrators and their special education colleagues (Kennedy & Fisher, 2001; Kochhar-Bryant, 2008).

Although some educators have expressed concern that the presence of students with disabilities impairs the academic achievement of students without disabilities, no evidence supports this. In fact, Cole, Waldron, and Majd (2004) reported that 334 students without disabilities in inclusive classrooms actually made greater gains in reading and math than did than a comparison group of 272 students without disabilities who were educated in "traditional" classrooms. When considering the results of studies such as these, it is important to consider that the most critical factor impacting student achievement is most likely to be quality of instruction and not the presence or absence of students with disabilities.

Furthermore, placement in a special education setting does not guarantee that a child will receive the specialized instruction he or she needs (e.g., P. A. Gallagher & Lambert, 2006; Moody, Vaughn, Hughes, & Fischer, 2000). We know that simply placing a child with disabilities in a general education classroom does not mean that she will learn and behave appropriately or be socially accepted by the teacher or by children without disabilities (Cook, 2004; Cook & Semmel, 1999; Freeman & Alkin, 2000; Siperstein, Parker, Norins Bardon, & Widaman, 2007). It is important for special educators to teach appropriate social skills and behavior to the child with disabilities and to educate children without disabilities about their classmates. Examples of effective inclusion programs can be found at age levels ranging from preschool (Sandall, Schwartz, & Joseph, 2000) to high school (Cobb Morocco, Clay, Parker, & Zigmond, 2006), and they include children whose disabilities range from mild (Hock, Schumaker, & Deshler, 1999) to severe (Ryndak & Fisher, 2007). Numerous strategies for successfully including students with disabilities in the general education program can be found in Friend and Bursuck (2006), Giangreco and Doyle (2007), Hughes and Carter (2006), Lewis and Doorlag (2006), Mastropieri and Scruggs (2007), Salend (2008), and J. W. Wood (2006).

Facilitating inclusion

Content Standards for Beginning Teachers—General Curriculum and Independence Curriculum Referenced Standards: Barriers to accessibility and acceptance of individuals with disabilities (GC5K1, IC5K2).

Promoting Inclusion With Cooperative Learning

As Mary Allaire-Gifford and Jean Michielli-Pendl indicated at the beginning of this chapter, cooperative learning activities provide a strategic approach for integrating students with disabilities into both the academic curriculum and the social fabric of the classroom. Cooperative learning can take many forms, but in most models all students in the class are assigned to small heterogeneous groups and help one another achieve a shared academic goal (D. W. Johnson & Johnson, 1999; Slavin, 1995). According to Slavin, two elements should be present: hold all students in the group accountable, and promote positive interdependence; that is, students are accountable for both their own achievement and the group's performance.

1. *Group goals (positive interdependence).* All members of the group work together to earn grades, rewards, or other recognition of success for the group.
2. *Individual accountability.* Each student within the group must demonstrate his or her learning and contribute in a specific way for the group to obtain success. However, the manner in which group members contribute may differ to meet individualized needs and learning objectives.

Well-designed cooperative learning activities keep students actively engaged and motivated to succeed. In addition to improved academic outcomes, cooperative learning can also promote positive social relationships, friendships, and mutual supports among students with and without disabilities in the classroom, which are vital to successful inclusion (Dion, Fuchs, & Fuchs, 2007; Maheady, Michielli-Pendl, Harper, & Mallette, 2006; Vaughn, Klingner, & Bryant, 2001).

Classwide peer tutoring is a form of cooperative learning with more than two decades of research demonstrating its effectiveness as an instructional approach for teaching reading, math, social studies, and a wide range of specialized subject areas to (and by) students with and without disabilities in inclusive classrooms (Gardner, Nobel, Hessler, Yawn, & Heron, 2007; Spencer, 2006; Van Norman & Wood, 2007). See Teaching & Learning, "Classwide Peer Tutoring."

Go to the Homework & Exercises section in Chapter 2 of MyEducationLab and complete Homework Exercise 6. As you watch the videos and answer the accompanying questions, consider how cooperative learning differs from the elementary to the middle school classroom.

Arguments For and Against Full Inclusion

Some special educators believe that the continuum of alternative placements should be dismantled and all students with disabilities placed in general education classes. For example,

TEACHING & LEARNING

Although the idea of students teaching one another is not new (Lancaster, 1806), peer tutoring has been the focus of much recent interest in special education. In traditional approaches to peer tutoring, the teacher identifies a high-achieving student to help a classmate who has not mastered a particular skill. In contrast, today's classwide peer tutoring (CWPT) models include low achievers and students with disabilities as full participants in an ongoing, whole-class activity in which all students help one another learn new curriculum content.

FOUR EVIDENCE-BASED MODELS

Four models for designing and implementing systematic peer tutoring have emerged from more than 20 years of solid empirical research as educators and researchers have successfully implemented, evaluated, and refined peer-tutoring models to varying degrees across a range of age and grade levels in general and special education classrooms (Alber Morgan, 2006; Maheady, Mallette, & Harper, 2006).

The Juniper Gardens Children's Project The Juniper Gardens Children's Project CWPT model was the brainchild of Greenwood, Delquadri, and Carta (1997). The whole class is divided into two weekly competing teams that are further broken into tutoring dyads and triads. Tutors present individual items, evaluate tutees' performance, and provide feedback and points. Daily and weekly public posting of team points serves as motivation.

A 12-year longitudinal study that compared groups of at-risk and non-risk students who had or had not received CWPT instruction found that CWPT increased students' active engagement during instruction in grades 1 to 3; improved pupil achievement at grades 2, 3, 4, and 6; reduced the need for special education services by seventh grade; and decreased the number of students who dropped out of school by the end of 11th grade (Greenwood, Maheady, & Delquadri, 2002).

The Peer-Assisted Learning Strategies The Peer-Assisted Learning Strategies (PALS) program was developed by researchers at Vanderbilt University working collaboratively with local school districts (Morgan, Young, & Fuchs, 2006). The original PALS program was designed for use in reading and math by students in grades 2–6 (D. Fuchs, Fuchs, Mathes, & Simmons, 1996). More recently, K-PALS for kindergarten (Mathes, Clancy-Menchetti, & Torgesen, 2003), First Grade PALS for beginning reading instruction (Mathes, Torgesen, Allen, & Howard-Allor, 2003), and High School PALS for content-area instruction (L. Fuchs, Fuchs, & Kazdan, 1999) have been added.

PALS tutors and tutees interact in a set of structured activities for three weekly sessions of 35 minutes. Examples of reading activities include Partner Reading with Retell, Paragraph Shrinking, and Prediction Relay. Teachers use brief scripted lessons to train all students to implement the activities independently. Nearly 15 years of research have demonstrated the effectiveness of this CWPT program in improving the reading performance of students at all performance levels, including students with disabilities, from kindergarten through high school (McMaster, Fuchs, & Fuchs, 2006).

SUNY Fredonia Classwide Student Tutoring Teams SUNY Fredonia Classwide Student Tutoring Teams (CSTT) combines elements of Slavin's (1986) Student Team Learning model with components from the Juniper Gardens CWPT model. Pupils work in four-member, heterogeneous learning teams and take turns reading and responding to items on teacher-developed study guides and/or concept cards. Tutor roles rotate clockwise on each item, and the process continues until a predetermined time limit (e.g., 20 to 30 minutes) has elapsed (Maheady, Mallette et al., 2006). One study compared CSTT instruction to conventional teacher-led instruction on the math performance of 91 low-achieving ninth- and tenth-grade pupils enrolled in a program for potential high school dropouts (Maheady, Sacca, & Harper, 1987). During CSTT instruction, students' weekly math quiz scores increased by an average of 20 percentage points

The Ohio State University Model The Ohio State University CWPT model began in the late 1970s and early 1980s with research aimed at finding a low-cost, relatively easy approach for individualizing instruction of basic reading and math skills for diverse groups of learners in the primary grades (e.g., Heron, Heward, Cooke, & Hill, 1983; Heward, Heron, & Cooke, 1982; Parson & Heward, 1979). The OSU model has been replicated and extended by hundreds of teachers in elementary, middle, and secondary classrooms across a wide range of curriculum areas such as spelling, science facts and vocabulary, algebra, geometry, reading fluency, foreign language vocabulary, and social studies (e.g., Gardner et al., 2001; Miller, Barbetta, & Heron, 1994; Wright, Cavanaugh, Sainato, & Heward, 1995). Daily sessions last about 20 minutes, with each student serving as both tutor and tutee during the session. When in the role of tutee, the child responds to questions presented by his or her partner (tutor) using a set of individualized task cards of unknown facts, problems, or items determined by a teacher-given pretest. The basic elements of the OSU model follow.

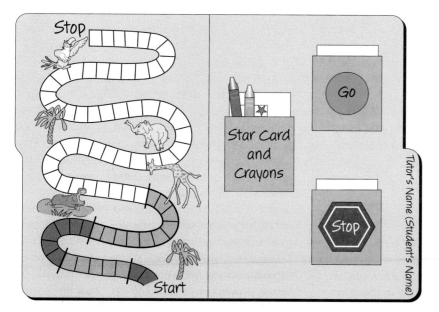

FIGURE A

Peer tutoring folder

Source: Adapted from "Total Tutoring for Special and General Educators [Instructor's Manual]" by T. E. Heron & W. L. Heward, 2000. Columbus, OH: The Ohio State University Special Education Program. Used by permission.

- When the students have learned all 10 cards, the teacher places a new set of words in the GO pocket.
- Each session ends with the partners praising and complimenting each other for their good work.

CHARACTERISTICS COMMON TO ALL FOUR MODELS

Tutoring Folders and Task Cards Each student in the class has a tutoring folder (see Figure A) containing a set of 10 task cards on specific curriculum content. Each card identifies one word, problem, concept, or fact to be taught to the child's tutoring partner. The task cards are in a GO pocket on one side of the folder. Also in the folder are a track chart to record the tutee's progress, markers to use for recording, and a STOP pocket to collect learned cards.

Practice One child begins in the role of tutor, presenting the task cards as many times as possible during a 5-minute practice period, shuffling the set of cards after each round. The teacher trains tutors to praise their partners' correct responses and to say, "Try again" when the tutee makes an error. If the tutee still does not respond correctly, the tutor says, for example, "This word is *tree;* say *tree.*" A timer signals the end of the first practice period, and the partners switch roles. While students are tutoring, the teacher walks around the room, prompting and rewarding good tutoring behaviors, answering questions, and generally supervising the activity.

Testing After the second practice period, the students reverse roles again; and the first tutor tests her partner by presenting each task card once with no prompts or cues. The teacher gives tutors about 5 minutes each to test and record their tutees' progress.

- The tutor places cards that a tutee reads or answers correctly in one pile and missed cards in another.
- The students then switch roles again, and the first tutor is now tested on the words she practiced.
- The tutors then mark the back of each card to identify if it was "correct" or "incorrect" during the test. Each tutor records his tutee's daily progress on the chart.
- When a child correctly responds to a task card on the test for three consecutive sessions, that item is considered learned, and the tutor moves it to the folder's STOP pocket.

- *Clearly defined learning tasks/ responses.* CWPT programs are based on clearly defined learning tasks and explicitly defined peer tutoring roles and teaching responsibilities. Tutoring procedures are often scripted, and each tutor is expected to use standard procedures with little variation.
- *Individualized instruction.* Frequent pre- and posttests are used to determine individualized learning tasks for each student. Additionally, because CWPT uses one-to-one instruction, each learner's performance can be observed, checked, and redirected in ways more frequent and continuous than in teacher-led group instruction.
- *High rates of active student responding (ASR).* Well-designed CWPT programs provide each student with many opportunities to respond. Depending on the curriculum content, a student may make 100 or more responses during a 10-minute peer tutoring session. Total ASR increases further in reciprocal CWPT programs because each student responds to each item in the role of tutee (initial responses to tutor's prompts, repeating missed items) and tutor (prompting responses, discriminating between correct and incorrect responses, and providing feedback).
- *Immediate feedback and praise for correct responses.* Peer tutors provide feedback and praise to their tutees, and the teacher provides feedback to the tutors as a means of promoting high-quality peer teaching and learning during CWPT sessions.
- *Systematic error correction.* Tutors immediately and systematically correct mistakes by their tutees. Materials that reveal the correct response to the tutor enable students who are themselves learning the material to detect and correct errors.
- *Continuous monitoring of student progress.* All evidence-based CWPT models incorporate direct and frequent measurement of students' progress. These data are obtained in a variety of ways, such as end-of-session assessments by tutors, regularly

scheduled, teacher-administered "check outs" of students' performances, weekly pre- and posttests, and curriculum-based measures. In some models, items missed on follow-up assessments are returned to the student's folder for additional practice and relearning.

- *Motivation.* Students have fun doing CWPT. Participation and learning are motivated by game-like formats, individual and team goals, charting their progress, and point/reward systems.

HOW TO GET STARTED

1. *Identify curriculum area and measurable learning outcome.* What should students know or be able to do as a result of CWPT?
2. *Design practice activity that will provide tutors and tutees with direct and repeated practice with this knowledge and/or skill.*
3. *Determine the sequence of activities that will make up each CWPT session.* For example: Students obtaining materials and setting up; tutoring practice trials, testing, recording performance, and clean-up/putting materials away. For each component, specify (a) materials needed, (b) what the tutors and tutees will do, (c) what the teacher (you) will do, and (d) how many minutes it should take.

4. *Create tutoring folders, task cards, and other necessary materials.* Consider having students make their CWPT materials from models you provide.
5. *Build-in a motivation component.* Specify how you will reinforce desired behavior by tutors (e.g., providing tutees with frequent response opportunities) and tutees (e.g., acquiring targeted knowledge and skills). Consider incentive systems such as "Mystery Motivators" described in Chapter 6.
6. *Teach students to carry out the CWPT procedures.* Teach peer tutoring skills as you would any other skill: be explicit, provide models, have students discriminate correct and incorrect procedures, provide guided practice, give feedback, reinforce accurate responses, and correct errors.
7. *Implement and evaluate.* Collect data to answer three questions: Are students implementing the tutoring procedures correctly? Are students acquiring and maintaining targeted knowledge and skills? Do students enjoy the CWPT program? CWPT should be fun for students and their teacher.

To learn more about using peer tutoring strategies, go to the Building Teaching Skills folder in Chapter 2 of MyEducationLab and complete the activities. As you watch the videos embedded within the activities, pay close attention to how the OSU CWPT model has been adapted to fit the needs of these students.

in a paper widely cited by advocates of full inclusion, S. J. Taylor (2005) contends that the LRE model . . .

1. *Legitimates restrictive environments.* To conceptualize services in terms of restrictiveness is to legitimize more restrictive settings. As long as services are conceptualized in this manner, some people will end up in restrictive environments.
2. *Confuses segregation and integration with intensity of services.* As represented by the continuum, LRE equates segregation with the most intensive services and integration with the least intensive services. The principle assumes that the least restrictive, most integrated settings are incapable of providing the intensive services needed by people with severe disabilities. However, segregation and integration on the one hand and intensity of services on the other are separate dimensions.
3. *Is based on a readiness model.* Implicit in LRE is the assumption that people with developmental disabilities must earn the right to move to the least restrictive environment. In other words, the person must "get ready" or "be prepared" to live, work, or go to school in integrated settings.
4. *Supports the primacy of professional decision making.* LRE invariably is framed in terms of professional judgments regarding "individual needs." The phrase "least restrictive environment" is almost always qualified with words such as "appropriate," "necessary," "feasible," and "possible" (and never with "desired" or "wanted").
5. *Sanctions infringements on people's rights.* The question imposed by LRE is not whether people with disabilities should be restricted, but to what extent.
6. *Implies that people must move as they develop and change.* As LRE is commonly conceptualized, people with disabilities are expected to move toward increasingly less restrictive environments. Even if people move smoothly through a continuum, their lives would be a series of stops between transitional placements.
7. *Directs attention to physical settings rather than to the services and supports people need.* By its name, the principle of the LRE emphasizes facilities and environments designed specifically for people with disabilities. The field has defined the mission in terms of creating "facilities," first large ones and now smaller ones, and "programs," rather than providing the services and supports to enable people with disabilities to participate in the same settings used by other people. (S. J. Taylor, 2005, pp. 222–225)

Some authors view full inclusion as a matter of social justice (e.g., Sapon-Shevin, 2007; Stainback, Stainback, & Ayres, 1996). No clear consensus exists in the field about the meaning of inclusion. To some, inclusion means full-time placement of all students with disabilities in general education classrooms; to others, the term refers to any degree of integration into the mainstream. Stainback and Stainback (1996), strong advocates and leaders of the inclusion movement, define an inclusive school as "a place where everyone belongs, is accepted, supports, and is supported by his or her peers and other members of the school community in the course of having his or her educational needs met" (p. 3). Giangreco (2006) states that inclusive education is in place only when each of the six characteristics shown in Figure 2.6 "occurs on an ongoing, daily basis" (p. 4).

Virtually all special educators support the responsible inclusion of students with disabilities in general education classrooms and the development and evaluation of new models for working more cooperatively with general educators to serve all students (Kochhar-Bryant, 2008; Schwartz, 2005; J. D. Smith & Hilton, 1997; Vaughn, Schumm, & Brick, 1998). Throughout this text, you will find descriptions of many research-based model programs and strategies for successfully and meaningfully including students with disabilities as full members in the academic and social life of general education classrooms.

Most special educators do not support eliminating the continuum of alternative placements in favor of a universal policy of full inclusion. The Council for Exceptional Children (CEC), the major professional organization in special education, supports inclusion as a "meaningful goal" to be pursued by schools but believes that the continuum of services and program options must be maintained and that IEP planning teams must make placement decisions based on the student's individual educational needs (see Figure 2. 7). The discussion of inclusion continues throughout the text.

Components of inclusive education

 Content Standards for Beginning Teachers—Common Core: Use strategies to facilitate integration into various settings (CC4S1).

Shared activities with individualized outcomes and a sense of belonging and group membership for all students are two defining features of inclusive education.

FIGURE 2.6	Characteristics of inclusive education

1. All students are welcomed in general education. The general education class in the school the student would attend if not disabled is the first placement option considered. Appropriate supports, regardless of disability type or severity, are available.
2. Students are educated in classes where the number of those with and without disabilities is proportional to the local population (e.g., 10%–12% have identified disabilities).
3. Students are educated with peers in the same age groupings available to those without disability labels.
4. Students with varying characteristics and abilities (e.g., those with and without disability labels) participate in shared educational experiences while pursuing individually appropriate learning outcomes with necessary supports and accommodations.
5. Shared educational experiences take place in settings predominantly frequented by people without disabilities (e.g., general education classes, community work sites, community recreational facilities).
6. Educational experiences are designed to enhance individually determined valued life outcomes for students and therefore seek an individualized balance between the academic-functional and social-personal aspects of schooling.

Source: From Giangreco, M. F. (2006). Foundational concepts and practices. In M. E. Snell & F. Brown (Eds.), *Instruction of students with severe disabilities* (6th ed., p. 4). Upper Saddle River, NJ: Merrill/Prentice Hall. Used by permission.

FIGURE 2.7

CEC's policy on inclusive schools

Source: Reprinted from *CEC Policy Manual, 1997 Section Three, Professional Policies, Part 1 Chapter 3, Special Education in the Schools.* Reston, VA: Council for Exceptional Children. Used by permission.

The Council for Exceptional Children (CEC) believes all children, youth, and young adults with disabilities are entitled to a free and appropriate education and/or services that lead to an adult life characterized by satisfying relations with others, independent living, productive engagement in the community, and participation in society at large. To achieve such outcomes, there must exist for all children, youth, and young adults with disabilities a rich variety of early intervention, educational, and vocational program options and experiences. Access to these programs and experiences should be based on individual educational needs and desired outcomes. Furthermore, students and their families or guardians, as members of the planning team, may recommend the placement, curriculum option, and the exit document to be pursued.

CEC believes that a continuum of services must be available for all children, youth, and young adults. CEC also believes that the concept of inclusion is a meaningful goal to be pursued in our schools and communities. In addition, CEC believes children, youth, and young adults with disabilities should be served whenever possible in general education classrooms in inclusive neighborhood schools and community settings. Such settings should be strengthened and supported by an infusion of specially trained personnel and other appropriate supportive practices according to the individual needs of the child.

Go to the Homework & Exercises section in Chapter 2 of MyEducationLab and complete Homework Exercise 7. As you read these articles and answer the accompanying questions, consider the different perspectives presented here.

Zigmond (2003, 2006) reminds us that asking what is the "best place" to educate students with disabilities misses the point of what special education is all about.

> The bedrock of special education is instruction focused on *individual* needs. The very concept of "one best place" contradicts this commitment to individualization. Furthermore, results of research on how groups of students respond to treatment settings do not help the researcher or practitioner make an individualized decision for an individual student's plan.
>
> Special educators understand about individual differences. Special educators understand that no matter how hard they try or how well they are taught, there are some students who will never be able to learn on the same schedule as most others, who will take so long to learn some things that they will have to forego learning other things, or who will need to be taught curricular content that is not ordinarily taught. Special educators understood this when they fought hard for the legal requirement of the Individualized Education Program for children with disabilities, to permit formulation of unique programs of instruction to meet unique individual needs. By continuing to ask, "What is the best place?" we are ignoring what we know....
>
> I can say with some certainty that place is not what makes special education "special" or effective. Effective teaching strategies and an individualized approach are the more critical ingredients in special education, and neither of these is associated solely with one particular environment. (Zigmond, 2003, pp. 196, 198)

WHERE DOES SPECIAL EDUCATION GO FROM HERE?

The promise of a free appropriate public education for all children with disabilities is an ambitious one. The process of bringing about this goal has been described in such lofty terms as a "new Bill of Rights" and a "Magna Carta" for children with disabilities (L. V. Goodman, 1976). Weintraub and Abeson (1974) wrote in support of IDEA before the bill's passage: "At the minimum, it will make educational opportunities a reality for all handicapped children. At the maximum, it will make our schools healthier learning environments for all our children" (p. 529). Today, most observers acknowledge that substantial progress has been made toward fulfillment of that promise.

IDEA has had far-reaching effects. In place of the once-prevalent practice of excluding children with disabilities, schools now seek the most appropriate ways of including them. As A. P. Turnbull and Turnbull (2006) observe, the student is no longer required to meet the requirements of the school, but the school is required to fit the needs of the student. Today's schools provide far more than academic instruction. Schools are committed to providing wide-ranging services to children from diverse backgrounds and with different learning needs. In effect, they have become diversified agencies offering services such as medical support, physical therapy, vocational training, parent counseling, recreation, special transportation, and in-service education for staff members.

Most people—both within and outside the field of education—have welcomed the inclusion and participation of children with disabilities in their schools and communities. Despite ample evidence of progress toward providing equal educational opportunity, it is equally true that many people—again, inside and outside the field of education—have detected significant problems and concerns with the very nature of special education (e.g., D. J. Gallagher, Heshusius, Iano, & Skrtic, 2004) or the implementation of IDEA (e.g., Finn

Regardless of where services are delivered, the most crucial variable is the quality of instruction that each student receives.

et al., 2001). Most states and local school administrators maintain that the federal government has never granted sufficient financial resources to help with the high costs of educating students with disabilities. Special education teachers express dissatisfaction about excessive paperwork, unclear guidelines, and inappropriate grouping of students with disabilities. Many are concerned that too many students from culturally diverse groups are identified for special education. General education teachers contend that they receive little or no training or support when students with disabilities are placed in their classes. There are many other problems, real and perceived, and no quick fix or easy solution can be offered.

Special education is at a crossroads. Once, access to educational opportunity was the primary issue for children with disabilities. Would they receive an education at all? Could they be served in their local community and neighborhood schools? While some access problems persist (e.g., particularly for children who live in poverty or in extremely isolated areas and for children of migrant and homeless families), the primary concern today is about the appropriateness and effectiveness of special education.

> Today, all children with disabilities receive special education and related services. Some children benefit from a special education that includes curricular elements and instructional technologies that were unavailable just a few years ago.... While special education can rightfully be proud of its accomplishments, the educational outcomes for many students with disabilities are disappointing. As a group, students with disabilities fare poorly on virtually every measure of academic achievement and social adaptation....
>
> We believe that these poor outcomes for students with disabilities reflect not so much the field's lack of knowledge about how to teach these students, as they are testament to education's collective failure to systematically implement available knowledge.... As a result, many children with disabilities are receiving a special education that is not nearly as effective as it could be. In essence, the potential effectiveness of the special education received by many of the more than 6 million children who participate in special education today is neutralized by the presence of weak approaches that are selected on the basis of ideology instead of research results. (Heward & Silvestri, 2005, p. 193)

Can we fulfill the promise of a free appropriate public education for all students with disabilities? The answer depends in part on the ability of professionals to work together; assume new roles; communicate with each other; and involve parents, families, and students with disabilities themselves. But above all, educators must realize that the most crucial variable in the effectiveness of special education is the quality of instruction that children receive.

Special education is serious business. The learning and adjustment problems faced by students with disabilities are real; and their prevention, remediation, and compensation require intensive, systematic intervention. Regardless of who does it or where it takes place, good teaching must occur. Exceptional children deserve no less.

TIPS for Beginning Teachers

MAKING CO-TEACHING WORK
By Mary Allaire-Gifford and Jean Michielli-Pendl

Collaboration between general and special education teachers is essential for effectively including students with special needs in the regular classes. Co-teaching, perhaps the highest but most difficult type of collaboration, requires continual commitment to working together for the benefit of all students in the class. Even though we taught in the same district, we knew nothing about each other when we were told that we were going to co-teach. Make an effort to get to know your partner and keep your lines of communication open from the beginning, and your transition to co-teaching will be easier.

PLAN WEEKLY AND REVIEW DAILY

- Establish and maintain a weekly time for co-planning. Mondays and Fridays tend to have more interruptions and holidays. Thursday seems to be the best day.
- Make this precious planning time sacred. Shut the door to minimize distractions and interruptions.
- With texts and supplementary materials at the ready, plan the next week's schedule of lessons.
- Before the first class period each day, write the lesson agenda on the board, and take 5 minutes to review and assign roles.

ESTABLISH CLEAR ROLES AND RESPONSIBILITIES

It is important to establish roles and responsibilities at the onset of the co-teaching experience. You are looking for equity, not equality. Co-teaching is a lot like a marriage. You never give 50/50. Sometimes you give 90%, and your co-teacher gives 10%. Sometimes you are both giving 60%. You must address the following roles and responsibilities before walking into the classroom together:

- Who creates and presents the rules and procedures?
- Who is responsible for discipline?

- Who corrects the papers?
- Who computes students' grades and enters them into the grade book?
- Who maintains the classroom, supplies, and so on, and orders more when necessary?
- Who teaches what, when, how, and whom during each lesson?
- How is each teachers' personal space handled?

BE FLEXIBLE ABOUT EVERYTHING, EXCEPT STUDENT LEARNING

Even though you've agreed upon a basic plan for who is responsible for various tasks, you must be flexible.

- You should never say, "Oh, that's not my job," or "Jason's not a special education student, I can't help him." If you react in this way, the partnership will not last long.
- Some ideas look good on paper, but don't work in practice. Continually reevaluate how things are working in the classroom.
- Give yourself the freedom to change. Be willing to try new ideas, listen to your partner, and attend professional development events, but always using student performance as your guide.
- Use direct and frequent measures of student performance as the ultimate determiner of which teaching methods work best for your students.

COMMIT TO BE COMPATIBLE

Although co-teaching does not require that both teachers use the same teaching style, it does require both teachers to respect one another and to be confident in each other's professional judgment, values, and knowledge.

KEY TERMS AND CONCEPTS

continuum of alternative placements, p. 74

declassified, p. 59

IEP team, p. 63

inclusion, p. 76

least restrictive environment (LRE), p. 73

multifactored evaluation (MFE), p. 55

prereferral intervention, p. 51

randomized experimental group design, p. 72

responsiveness to intervention (RTI), p. 54

SUMMARY

The Process of Special Education

- IDEA mandates a particular sequence of events that schools must follow in identifying and educating children with disabilities.
- Prereferral intervention is an informal, problem-solving process used to (1) provide immediate instructional and/or behavior management assistance to the child and teacher, (2) reduce the chances of identifying a child for special education who may not be disabled, and (3) identify students for evaluation.
- Any child suspected of having a disability must receive a nondiscriminatory multifactored evaluation (MFE) to determine eligibility for special education and to provide information about the child's educational needs and how to meet them.
- Culturally and linguistically diverse students are both underrepresented and overrepresented in special education, depending on the group and disability category.
- Inappropriate referral to special education can occur if educators and school psychologists cannot separate the presence of unrecognized diversity or deficits from disability.
- Schools must plan and provide an individualized education program (IEP) for each child with a disability.
- After identifying the child's educational needs and the services needed to meet them, the IEP team determines the least restrictive environment (LRE) in which the child can receive an appropriate education.
- The IEP team must review the IEP periodically, but not less frequently than annually.
- At least once every 3 years, the IEP team conducts an evaluation to determine if the child still needs special education.

Collaboration and Teaming

- Coordination, consultation, and teaming are three modes of collaboration that team members can use.
- Three models for teaming are multidisciplinary, interdisciplinary, and transdisciplinary.
- Co-teaching is two or more teachers planning and delivering instruction together. Co-teaching arrangements include one teaching/one helping, parallel teaching, station teaching, alternative teaching, and team teaching.

Individualized Education Program

- An IEP planning team must include (1) the parents of the child with a disability; (2) at least one general education teacher of the child; (3) at least one special education teacher; (4) a representative of the local education agency; (5) an individual who can interpret the instructional implications of evaluation results; (6) at the discretion of the parent or school, other individuals who have knowledge or special expertise regarding the child; and (7) whenever appropriate, the child.

- Although IEP formats vary widely, each IEP must include these seven components:
  1. A description of the child's present levels of educational performance
  2. Measurable annual goals, including benchmarks or short-term objectives for students who take alternative assessments aligned to alternative standards
  3. How the child's progress toward the annual goals will be measured and when reports on the child's progress toward meeting the annual goals will be provided
  4. The special education and related services and supplementary aids and services, based on peer-reviewed research to the extent practical, to be provided to the child
  5. An explanation of the extent, if any, to which the child will not participate with nondisabled children in the regular class
  6. Any individual accommodations that are necessary to measure the academic achievement and functional performance of the child on state- and districtwide assessments (or alternative assessment selected if appropriate)
  7. The projected date for the beginning of the services and modifications described in number 4 and the anticipated frequency, location, and duration of those services and modifications
- Beginning when the student reaches age 16, IEPs must also include information on how the educational program will support the child's transition from school to adult life.
- Without direct and ongoing monitoring of student progress toward IEP goals and objectives, the document's usefulness is limited.
- The IEP provides teachers and presented with the opportunity—and the responsibility—to first be *realistic* about the child's needs and goals and then to be *creative* about how to meet them.
- IEP formats vary widely across school districts, and schools may exceed the requirement of the law and include additional information.
- Each area of functioning that is adversely affected by the student's disability must be represented by an annual goal on the IEP.

Least Restrictive Environment

- The LRE is the setting closest to the general education classroom that also meets the child's special educational needs.
- The LRE is a relative concept; the LRE for one child might be inappropriate for another child with the same disability.
- The continuum of services is a range of placement and service options to meet the individual needs of students with disabilities.
- The IEP team must determine the LRE after it has designed a program of special education and related services to meet the child's unique needs.

Inclusive Education

- Inclusion is the process of integrating children with disabilities into the academic and social activities of regular schools and general education classes.
- Well-planned, carefully conducted inclusion can be generally effective with students of all ages, types, and degrees of disability.
- A few special educators believe that the continuum of alternative placements LRE principle should be replaced with a policy of full inclusion, in which all students with disabilities are placed full-time in general education classrooms.
- Cooperative learning activities in which students work in small heterogeneous groups to help one another achieve a common academic goal or product can be an effective strategy for integrating students with disabilities into the academic and social fabric of the classroom.
- Most special educators and professional organizations, such as the Council for Exceptional Children (CEC), support inclusion as a goal but believe that the continuum of alternative placements and program options must be maintained and that placement decisions must be based on the student's individual educational needs.

Where Does Special Education Go From Here?

- The field of special education has made substantial progress toward fulfilling the promise of a free appropriate public education for all children with disabilities.
- Implementation of IDEA has brought problems of funding, inadequate training and support for teachers, and opposition by some to including children with disabilities in general education classes.
- Regardless of where special education services are delivered, the most crucial variable is the quality of instruction that each child receives.

 Now go to MyEducationLab at www.myeducationlab.com and take the Pretest to assess your initial comprehension of chapter content. Once you have taken the Pretest, use your individualized Study Plan for Chapter 2 to enhance your understanding of the concepts discussed in the chapter. Finally, take the Posttest to assess your comprehension of Chapter 2 content.

3

Collaborating With Parents and Families in a Culturally and Linguistically Diverse Society

- What can a teacher learn from the family of a child with disabilities?
- In what ways is a child's disability likely to affect the family system and roles of parents?
- How can a teacher who is not the parent of a child with a disability communicate effectively and meaningfully with parents of exceptional children?
- How can a teacher communicate effectively and meaningfully with families from diverse cultures?
- What forms of home–school communication are likely to be most effective?
- How much parent and family involvement is enough?

FEATURED TEACHERS

CAROLYN CRANGLE AND BETHANY MAHEADY
Dunkirk City School District • Dunkirk, New York

Carolyn Crangle

Bethany Maheady

Ms. Crangle's Education—Teaching Credentials—Experience

- B.S., special studies, SUNY Fredonia, Fredonia, New York, 1988; M.Ed., special education, State University College at Buffalo, Buffalo, New York, 1992
- New York State permanent certification in special education, K–12
- 19 years of experience as an elementary-level special educator

Ms. Maheady's Education—Teaching Credentials—Experience

- B.A., Spanish, SUNY Fredonia, Fredonia, New York, 1975; M.S., education/developmental reading, SUNY Fredonia, Fredonia, New York, 1977

- New York State permanent certification in education, K–6; Spanish certification, 7–12
- 33 years of teaching experience as a general educator working with bilingual, limited-English-proficient (LEP), and special-needs students in a general education classroom setting

Current Teaching Positions and Duties We have taught together at Dunkirk Elementary School Number 3 for the past 16 years. School Number 3 is a small urban school (300 pupils) with a high proportion of culturally and linguistically diverse students, most of whom come from home environments with very limited resources. Historically, our school has had a reputation as a tough setting because so many of our children have significant learning and behavioral challenges. Initially, we worked together to mainstream children with special needs into general education classes, primarily in their areas of strength. We subsequently created a full-inclusion program in which instructional services are planned and provided collaboratively by general and special educators, and all support services are "pushed in." We share responsibility for lesson planning, instruction, and evaluation. We use a combination of whole-class instruction and small heterogeneous learning groups within a proactive and positive classroom-management system to create a safe and productive learning environment. One of our priorities is maintaining a comprehensive parent-involvement program that emphasizes frequent and ongoing communication and parental empowerment.

 Go to the Homework & Exercises section in Chapter 3 of MyEducationLab and complete Homework Exercise 1. As you watch the video and answer the accompanying questions, think about how a positive classroom environment can enhance instruction.

Collaborating With Parents and Families: Respecting Difference and Diversity Given the extensive needs of our students, it is critical that we work collaboratively with their parents and caregivers. At times, this is easier said than done. Many of our students' parents face extreme challenges in their daily lives. Moreover, cultural and linguistic factors (e.g., non-native-English-speaking ability, different cultural expectations related to the roles of teachers and parents/caregivers) occasionally impede effective communication and collaboration. However, we feel privileged to work in such a culturally and linguistically rich community. At School Number 3, we recognize and celebrate diversity regularly and publicly. For example, we often enlist parent volunteers to prepare ethnic foods and participate in multicultural programs. Occasionally, this brings a previously uninvolved parent into the classroom in a nonthreatening manner. We also never forget to send thank-you notes and timely reminders about upcoming parent–teacher conferences. After eating rice and beans and dancing merengue together, parents and caregivers often feel more comfortable and welcome at school and are more inclined to participate again in the future.

At School Number 3, we teach respect for and acceptance of difference and diversity. We have created an inviting classroom environment with an open-door policy. We encourage parents to observe or volunteer in the classroom, attend individualized education program (IEP) meetings and annual reviews, and participate in our ongoing school–home communication systems. We're fortunate because many teachers and staff members at our school are bilingual in Spanish and English. This allows us to communicate orally and in writing in most parents' native language. We also model good working relationships by collaborating with all related-services personnel and including parents as significant members of our instructional team.

Strategies for Specific Students and Families

Some parents are well informed and highly involved in their children's educational programs. For instance, we met Nicole's parents at the beginning of the school year. They were initially concerned about her transition from a local private school to School Number 3. Nicole is a shy and sensitive girl with special needs. By communicating frequently and openly, we developed a partnership with her parents; and Nicole has had a positive and productive school year. She developed self-confidence, new friendships, and a wide range of knowledge and skills. At her annual review meeting, Nicole's mom stated that this was the most rewarding meeting about her daughter she had ever experienced. She thanked everyone on the team for caring so much and working so hard to ensure her daughter's success in school. She is a concerned and supportive parent, and we acknowledged this often in our ongoing interactions.

It is also critical to recognize that parents can play a powerful advocacy role in their children's educational program. Johnny, a bilingual student with special needs, for example, had a long history of academic failure in literacy despite intensive, ongoing remedial instruction. For quite a while, we had sought a laptop computer and keyboard training to enhance Johnny's literacy and content-area skills. However, it was not until his mother became actively involved by specifically requesting such adaptive equipment that he actually gained access to the technology. Ongoing collaboration among Johnny's personal aide, mother, and teachers allowed us to provide the much-needed instructional assistance both within and out of school.

Finally, we have refined our Instructional Support Team concept by inviting parents to participate more actively in their children's educational programs. We ask for their input in setting academic and behavioral goals and offer suggestions for intervention strategies that can be used at home. We also continually monitor parents' satisfaction with the educational services being provided. Ultimately, our success as educators depends on the extent to which we can engage parents and families in their children's lifelong learning.

Go to the Homework & Exercises section in Chapter 3 of MyEducationLab and complete Homework Exercise 2 to see Nicole's IEP meeting.

The family is the most powerful and pervasive influence in a young child's life. A child has learned literally hundreds of skills from parents and family members long before a professional with the job title "teacher" arrives. A parent is a child's first teacher, the person who gives encouragement, prompts, praise, and feedback. With rare exceptions, no one ever knows or cares about a child as much as a parent does. Yet only recently have special educators begun to fully appreciate these fundamental truths.

Too often in the past, educators viewed parents as either troublesome (if they asked too many questions or, worse, offered suggestions about their child's education) or uncaring (if they did not jump to attention whenever the professional determined the parent needed something—usually advice from the professional). Parents, too, have often seen professionals as adversaries. But today, parent involvement and family support are understood as essential elements of special education. Special educators now realize that parents and families are powerful and necessary allies.

 After reading this chapter, complete the Pretest for Chapter 3 on MyEducationLab to assess your initial understanding of chapter content.

SUPPORT FOR FAMILY INVOLVEMENT

A number of forces have combined to focus attention on the importance of a strong parent/family–teacher partnership based on mutual respect and participation. Although many factors have contributed to the increased emphasis on collaboration between parents and teachers in the education of exceptional children, three issues are clear: (1) parents want to be involved, (2) educational effectiveness is enhanced when parents and families are involved, and (3) federal law requires collaboration between schools and families.

Parents: Advocating for Needed Change

For decades, parents of exceptional children have advocated for equal access to educational opportunities for their children, and they have done so with impressive effectiveness. As you learned in Chapters 1 and 2, parents played the primary role in bringing about litigation and legislation establishing the right to a free and appropriate public education for all children with disabilities.

The first parent group on behalf of children with disabilities was the National Society for Crippled Children, organized in 1921. The United Cerebral Palsy Association, organized in 1948, and the National Association for Retarded Citizens (now called The Arc), organized in 1950, are two national parent organizations largely responsible for making the public aware of the special needs of children with disabilities. The Learning Disabilities Association of America (LDA), formed in 1963, also organized by and consisting mostly of parents, has been instrumental in bringing about educational reform. Parent members of The Association for Persons with Severe Handicaps (TASH), founded in 1975, have been forceful and effective advocates for family-focused educational services and the inclusion of students with severe and multiple disabilities in neighborhood schools and general education classrooms. The mission of the Association for Science in Autism Treatment (ASAT), founded in 1998 by parents and professionals, is to disseminate accurate, scientifically sound information about autism and treatments for autism and to improve access to effective, science-based treatments for all people with autism. Many other parent-led organizations continue today to advocate for effective education, community acceptance, needed services, and the rights of individuals with disabilities.

A parent is a child's first teacher.

Family involvement as cornerstone for planning

Council for Exceptional Children   Content Standards for Beginning Teachers—Common Core: Family systems and the role of families in supporting development (CC2K4).

The developers of a highly regarded program for planning and implementing inclusive educational programs for students with disabilities present four powerful arguments for viewing active family involvement as the cornerstone of relevant and longitudinal educational planning:

- *Families know certain aspects of their children better than anyone else does.* As educators, we must remind ourselves that we spend only about half the days of the year with our students, seeing them less than a third of each of those days. Nonschool time may provide key information that has educational implications, such as the nature of a student's interests, motivations, habits, fears, routines, pressures, needs, and health.
- *Families have the greatest vested interest in seeing their children learn.* In our professional eagerness to help children learn, we sometimes convey the message to parents that teachers care more about children than parents do. Of course, this is rarely the case.
- *The family is likely to be the only group of adults involved with a child's educational program throughout her entire school career.* Over the course of a school

career, a student with special educational needs will encounter so many professionals that it will be difficult for the family to remember all of their names. Some of these professionals will work with the child for a number of years, others for a year or less. Professionals are encouraged to build on an ever-evolving, family-centered vision for the child rather than reinventing a student's educational program each year as team membership changes.

- *Families must live with the outcomes of decisions made by education teams all day, every day.* People rarely appreciate having someone else make decisions that will affect their lives without being included in the decision making. As professionals making decisions, we must constantly remind ourselves that these decisions are likely to affect other people besides the child and have an effect outside of school. (Giangreco, Cloninger, & Iverson, 1998, pp. 19–22)

Educators: Seeking Greater Effectiveness

To meet the special needs of children with disabilities, educators must expand the traditional role of the classroom teacher. This expanded role demands that we view teaching as more than instructing academic skills in the classroom. Today's special educator attaches high priority to designing and implementing instructional programs that enable students with disabilities to use and maintain academic, language, social, self-help, recreation, and other skills in school, at home, and in the community. As part of their home and community life, children may participate in some 150 different kinds of social and physical settings (Dunst, 2001). The large number of nonschool settings in which children live, play, and learn illustrates two important points. First, the many different settings and situations exemplify the extent of the challenge teachers face in helping children use newly learned skills throughout their daily lives. Second, the many different settings and social situations children experience in home and community provide extended opportunities for learning and practicing important skills. It is clear that to be maximally effective, teachers must look beyond the classroom for assistance and support, and parents and families are natural and necessary allies.

Extensive evidence shows that the effectiveness of educational programs for children with disabilities is increased when parents and families are actively involved (e.g., Guralnick, 1997; Keith et al., 1998; L. Newman, 2004; Raimondo & Henderson, 2001; Resetar, Noell, & Pellegrin, 2006; Senechal & LeFevre, 2002; M. Wagner, Newman, Cameto, Garza, & Levine, 2005). At the very least, teachers and students benefit when parents provide information about their children's use of specific skills outside the classroom. But parents can do much more than just report on behavior change. They can provide extra skill practice and teach their children new skills in the home and community. When parents are involved in identifying what skills their children need to learn (and, just as important, what they do *not* need to learn), the hard work expended by teachers is more likely to produce outcomes with real significance in the lives of children and their families.

Legislators: Mandating Parent and Family Involvement

IDEA and parent participation

 Council for Exceptional Children

Content Standards for Beginning Teachers—Common Core: Rights and responsibilities of students, parents, teachers, other professionals, and schools related to exceptional learning needs (CC1K4).

Congress made parent involvement a key component of the Education of All Handicapped Children Act (P. L. 94–142), the original federal special education law. Each reauthorization of the law has strengthened and extended parent and family participation in the education of children with disabilities. For example, Congress reaffirmed and made clear its belief in the importance of parent and family involvement in the introduction to Individuals with Disabilities Education Act (IDEA) 1997: "Over 20 years of research and experience has demonstrated that the education of children with disabilities can be made more effective by . . . strengthening the role of parents and ensuring that families of such children have meaningful opportunities to participate in the education of their children at school and at home" (U.S.C. 601[c][5][B]).

Parent participation in the form of shared decision making is one of six basic principles of IDEA that provide the general framework for carrying out national policies for the education of children with disabilities. IDEA provides statutory guidelines that schools must follow with parents of children with disabilities with regard to referral, testing, program planning, placement, and evaluation. In addition, the law mandates due process procedures if parents believe that their child's needs are not being met.

Three factors are responsible for increased parent and family involvement in the education of children with disabilities: parents want it, educators know it's a good idea, and the law requires it. But the most important reasons why families and educators should strive to develop collaborative partnerships are the benefits to the child with disabilities:

- Increased likelihood of targeting meaningful IEP goals
- Greater consistency and support in the child's two most important environments: home and school
- Increased opportunities for learning and development
- Access to expanded resources and services

UNDERSTANDING FAMILIES OF CHILDREN WITH DISABILITIES

When parents and teachers work together for the mutual benefit of a child with disabilities, they make a powerful team. To work together, they must communicate with one another. Effective communication is more likely when each party understands and respects the responsibilities and challenges faced by the other. For educators, an important initial step in developing a partnership with families is to strive for an understanding of how a child with disabilities might influence the family system and the many interrelated roles of parenthood.

The Impact of a Child With Disabilities on the Family

The birth of a baby with disabilities or the discovery that a child has a disability is an intense and traumatic event. Many studies have been conducted on the emotional responses and adjustments of parents of children with disabilities (e.g., Blacher, 2001; Eden-Piercy, Blacher, & Eyman, 1986; P. M. Ferguson, 2003; Frey, Fewell, & Vadasy, 1989; H. L. Johnson, 1993). This research has shown that most parents go through an adjustment process, trying to work through their feelings. For example, widely cited research by Blacher (1984) found three consistent stages of adjustment. First, parents experience a period of emotional crisis characterized by shock, denial, and disbelief. This initial reaction is followed by a period of alternating feelings of anger, guilt, depression, shame, lowered self-esteem, rejection of the child, and overprotectiveness. Eventually, parents reach a third stage in which they accept their child. Based on their observations of 130 participants in two parent support groups over a period of several years, Anderegg, Vergason, and Smith (1992) developed a revised model of Blacher's work they call the grief cycle, which consists of three stages: confronting, adjusting, and adapting. Numerous firsthand reports by parents describe a similar sequence of experiences (e.g., Boushey, 2001; Fleischmann, 2004; Holland, 2006).

Poyadue (1993) suggests a stage beyond acceptance or adapting that involves appreciation of the positive aspects of family life with a child with a disability. Growing evidence supports this concept. For example, J. M. Patterson and Leonard (1994) interviewed couples whose children required intensive home care routines because of chronic and complex health care needs and found roughly equal numbers of positive and negative responses. Positive responses included increased closeness among couples and stronger family bonds. In another study, the majority of 1,262 parents of children with disabilities agreed with the following statements: "The presence of my child is very uplifting. Because of my child, I have many unexpected pleasures. My child is the reason I am a more responsible person" (Behr, Murphy, & Summers, 1992, p. 26). D. Skinner, Bailey, Correa, and Rodriguez (1999) found that many of the 150 Latina mothers in their study believed that having a child with disabilities made them better mothers. And parents in several studies reported not only coping successfully with the challenges posed by a child with disabilities but also benefits to the family (Blacher & Baker, 2007; Fleischmann, 2004; Hastings, Beck, & Hill, 2005; Naseef, 2001; Taunt & Hastings, 2002).

Figure 3.1 shows a five-stage "resilience model" that identifies experiences and tasks for parents as they move from identification of their child's disability through acceptance and enlightenment. Kochhar-Bryant (2008) developed this model based on the following:

Go to the Homework & Exercises section in Chapter 3 of MyEducationLab and complete Homework Exercise 3. As you read the article and answer the accompanying questions, think about how this parent–teacher partnership—one that is built on communication and mutual respect— benefits the student, his family, and his teacher.

Parental responses to disability

Content Standards for Beginning Teachers—Common Core: Concerns of families of individuals with exceptional learning needs and strategies to help address these concerns (CC10K3).

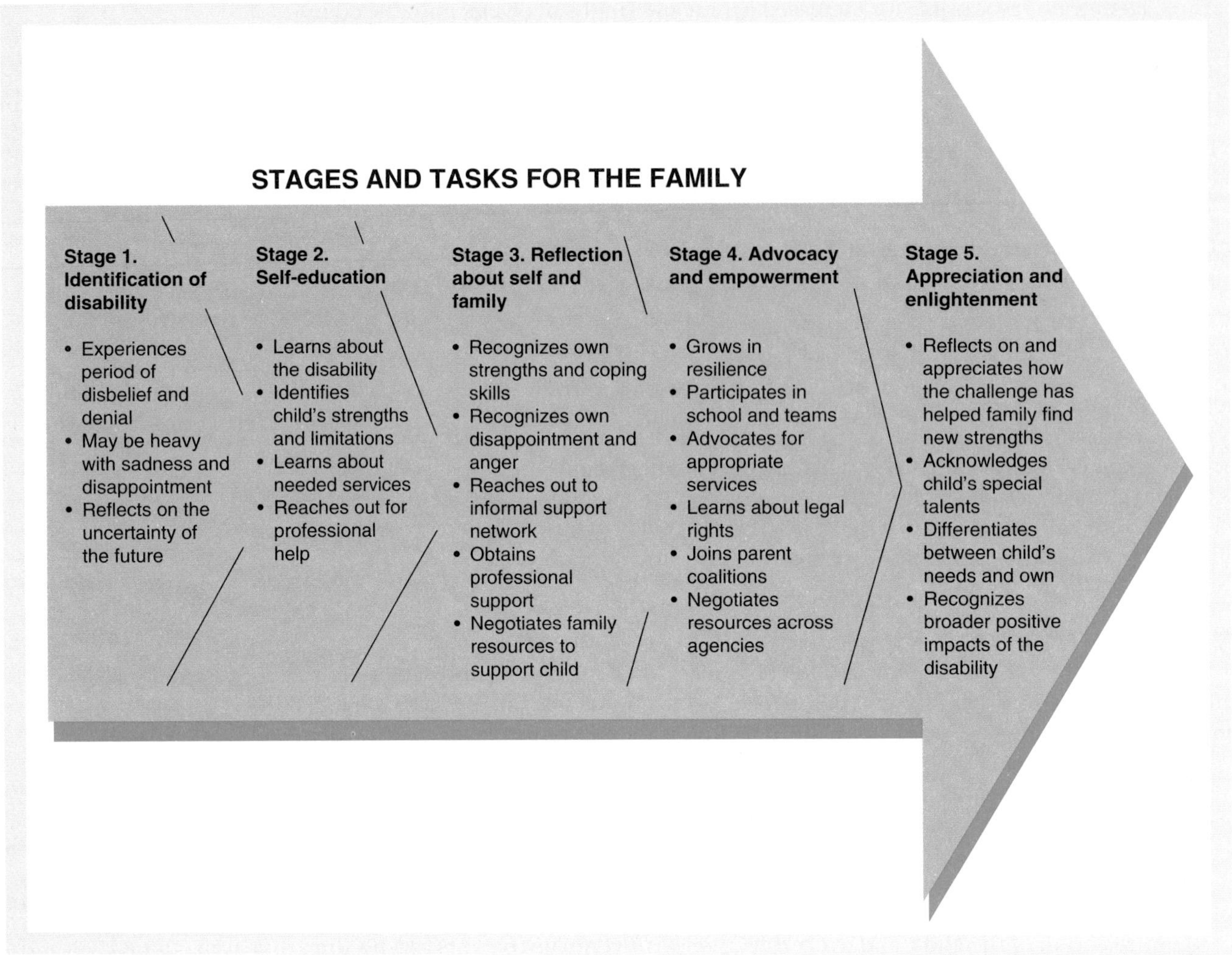

STAGES AND TASKS FOR THE FAMILY

Stage 1. Identification of disability

- Experiences period of disbelief and denial
- May be heavy with sadness and disappointment
- Reflects on the uncertainty of the future

Stage 2. Self-education

- Learns about the disability
- Identifies child's strengths and limitations
- Learns about needed services
- Reaches out for professional help

Stage 3. Reflection about self and family

- Recognizes own strengths and coping skills
- Recognizes own disappointment and anger
- Reaches out to informal support network
- Obtains professional support
- Negotiates family resources to support child

Stage 4. Advocacy and empowerment

- Grows in resilience
- Participates in school and teams
- Advocates for appropriate services
- Learns about legal rights
- Joins parent coalitions
- Negotiates resources across agencies

Stage 5. Appreciation and enlightenment

- Reflects on and appreciates how the challenge has helped family find new strengths
- Acknowledges child's special talents
- Differentiates between child's needs and own
- Recognizes broader positive impacts of the disability

FIGURE 3.1

A resilience model toward family strength

Source: From Kochhar-Bryant, C. A. (2008). *Collaboration and system coordination for students with special needs: From early childhood to the postsecondary years* (p. 213). Upper Saddle River, NJ: Merrill/Prentice Hall. Used by permission of Pearson Education, Inc.

1. Parents and family members are the best sources of knowledge about the child and their own strengths and needs in coping.
2. Parents are under stress and need to be included in the service delivery and support process.
3. Parents possess resilience that may not be immediately appreciable but should be identified and built upon.
4. Parents are engaged in a continuous adjustment process that can be facilitated if recognized by professionals. (p. 212)

Educators should refrain from expecting parents of children with disabilities to exhibit typical reactions. Relying on any stages-of-adjustment theory or model as the basis for planning or delivering family services poses three potential problems. First, it is easy to assume that all parents must pass through a similar sequence of stages and that time is the most important variable in adjustment. In fact, parents react to the birth or diagnosis of a child with disabilities in many ways (V. Florian & Findler, 2001; Hutton & Caron, 2005; S. Lin, 2000; Ulrich & Bauer, 2003). For some parents, years may pass, and they still are not comfortable with their child. Yet other parents, as we have just discussed, report that having a child with disabilities has strengthened their life or marriage (Flaherty & Glidden, 2000; Scorgie & Sobsey, 2000).

The sequence and time needed for adjustment differ for every parent. The one common thread is that almost all parents and families can be helped during their adjustment by sensitive and supportive friends and professionals (L. Fox, Vaughn, Wyatte, & Dunlap, 2002).

A second concern is that many parents view explanations of stages of mourning and adjustment as patronizing and condescending, which hinders meaningful communication (Snow, 2001). And third, some stages-of-adjustment theories have a distinct psychiatric flavor, which may lead professionals to mistakenly assume that parents must be maladjusted in some way and in need of counseling.

The Many Roles of the Exceptional Parent

Parenthood is an awesome responsibility, and parenting any child requires tremendous physical and emotional energy. All parents have a great deal in common. Hart and Risley (1995), who conducted a longitudinal study of 42 families with young typically developing children, noted: "Raising children made all the families look alike. All the babies had to be fed, changed, and amused. As we went from one home to another we saw the same activities and lives centered on caregiving. . . . Most impressive of all that the parents had in common was the continual and incredible challenge a growing child presents" (pp. 53, 55).

Parents of children with disabilities, however, experience added physical, emotional, and financial stress (Chiasson & Reilly, 2008). Educators who are not parents of a child with disabilities, chronic illness, or severe problem behavior cannot possibly know the 24-hour, 7-day reality of being the parent of such a child (Fox et al., 2002; Hutton & Caron, 2005). Nonetheless, educators should strive to understand as much as possible how a child with special needs affects (and is affected by) the family system.

In addition to providing love and affection, parents of children with disabilities fulfill at least nine other varied and demanding roles, as described next.

Caregiver Taking care of any young child is a demanding task. But the additional caregiving requirements of children with disabilities can be tremendous and cause added stress (Carpenter, 2000; T. B. Smith, Oliver, & Innocenti, 2001). And the level of care needed by some children with severe disabilities or chronic health conditions can be nonstop:

> Mike sleeps when he wants to, mostly during the day. He sleeps with a heart monitor on which alarms several times per night, because he stops breathing frequently. Usually I'm up by 8:00 and often cannot go to bed until 12:00 or 1:00 because of Mike's feedings, medication. It's hard to fit all of this into a day and still have time for sleep. (Bradley et al., 1992)

Although many parents receive help from extended family members and friends in caring for a child with disabilities, the amount and level of help are often insufficient. **Respite care** can reduce the mental and physical stress on parents and families created by the day-to-day responsibilities of caring for a child with disabilities (see Figure 3.2).

Provider Food, clothing, shelter, music lessons, sports, hobbies: it costs a lot of money to raise a typically developing child from birth to adulthood. Providing for a child with disabilities, however, usually means additional expenses, sometimes in the tens of thousands of dollars. For example, consider the economic impact on this family of a child with physical disabilities and chronic health problems:

> We had to find another place to live with first floor bedroom, widened doorways, enlarged front porch, central air, ramp, van. House renovation: $10,000. Van: $18,500. Air: $1,450. Porch: $1,400. Ramp: $1,000. Furnishings to accommodate supplies: $800. We've got the following equipment: Suction machine, portable suction machine, generator for emergency power, hospital bed, air pressure mattress, wheelchair, room monitor, humidifier, bath chair, oxygen, air cleaner, gastronomy tube pump, breathing treatment machine. And all the following expenses have gone up: formula, diapers, appliances, utility bills, medications. (Bradley et al., 1992)

It is not just families of children with physical disabilities or health conditions who face financial burdens. Many parents of children with learning and behavioral problems pay thousands of dollars for specific treatments, behavioral intervention programs, and in-home therapy. While some families receive financial assistance from federal, state, and/or local agencies (Frisk, 2006), those sources seldom cover the costs (S. J. Taylor, 2005). On top of the

Roles of exceptional parents

Content Standards for Beginning Teachers—Common Core: Concerns of families of individuals with exceptional learning needs and strategies to help address these concerns (CC10K3) (also CC2K4).

Respite care

Content Standards for Beginning Teachers—Common Core: Concerns of families of individuals with exceptional learning needs and strategies to help address these concerns (CC10K3).

FIGURE 3.2	Respite: Support for families

Parents of nondisabled children frequently hire others to care temporarily for their children. For parents of children with disabilities, however, the range of child care options is severely limited. Many parents of children with severe disabilities identify the availability of reliable, high-quality child care as their single most pressing need (Warfield & Hauser-Cram, 1996). In response to this need, many communities have developed respite care programs. **Respite care** is the short-term care of a family member with disabilities to provide relief for parents from caretaking duties.

Quality respite care can reduce the mental and physical stress on parents and families created by the day-to-day (in some cases, moment-to-moment) responsibilities of caring for a child with disabilities. The most frequently requested support service by families, "respite can make difference between a struggling or thriving family" (Solomon, 2007, p. 39). The mother of a son born with a neurological condition that produces frequent seizures and extreme hyperactivity describes her family's experience with respite care:

> During the first 4 years of Ben's life, we averaged 4 hours of sleep a night. We were wearing ourselves out; I have no doubt we would have completely fallen apart. My husband, Roger, used his vacations for sleeping in. The respite program came along just in time for us. It was hard at first. There's an overwhelming guilt that you shouldn't leave your child. We didn't feel like anyone else could understand Ben's problems. But we had to get away. Our church gave us some money, with orders to take a vacation. It was the first time Roger and I and our 12-year-old daughter, Stacy, had really been together since Ben was born.

Families and their advocates can locate respite service providers in their communities through the National Respite Locator Service at www.respitelocator.org/.

additional expenses, families of children with disabilities often have reduced income because one parent works part-time instead of full-time or must withdraw from the workforce altogether to care for the child (Solomon, 2007; Waldman & Perlman, 2006).

Teacher   Most children learn many skills without anyone teaching them. Children with disabilities, however, often do not acquire new skills as naturally or independently as their typically developing peers do. In addition to learning systematic teaching techniques (J. B. Stoner & Angell, 2006), some parents must learn to use and/or teach their children to use special equipment and assistive devices such as hearing aids, braces, wheelchairs, and adapted eating utensils (Parette & Brotherson, 1996).

Counselor   All parents are counselors in the sense that they deal with their children's changing emotions, feelings, and attitudes. But in addition to all of the normal joys and pains of raising a child, parents of a child with disabilities must deal with their child's feelings that result from his particular disability: "Will I still be deaf when I grow up?" "I'm not playing outside anymore; they always tease me." "Why can't I go swimming like the other kids?" Parents play an important role in how the child with disabilities comes to feel about himself. Their interactions can help develop an active, outgoing child who confidently tries new experiences or a withdrawn child with negative attitudes toward himself and others.

Behavior Support Specialist   All children act out occasionally, and all parents are challenged and frustrated from time to time by their children's noncompliance and misbehavior. But the frequency and severity of challenging behaviors exhibited by some children with disabilities can make it nearly impossible for some families to experience and enjoy normal routines of daily life (L. Fox et al., 2002). A. P. Turnbull and Ruef (1996) interviewed 14 families with children with mental retardation who frequently exhibited problem behavior. The parents reported that their children frequently engaged in at least one of four categories of problem behavior: aggression toward others, property destruction, self-injurious behavior, or pica (eating inedible objects). The children's problem behavior fell into one of two domains, according to the behavior's impact on the child and the family: dangerous behavior (e.g., "He punches his face a lot on the jaw line—his cheek bone, his mouth, occasionally his forehead.... He will eventually bleed from his mouth") and difficult behavior (e.g., "When I am around him it is constant noise. He talks or squawks. By afternoon I am frazzled") (A. P. Turnbull & Ruef, 1996, p. 283). Such behavior demands specialized and consistent treatment, and some parents of exceptional children must become skilled in behavior-support techniques to achieve a semblance of normal family life (e.g., Becker-Cottrill, McFarland, & Anderson, 2003; Boulware, Schwartz, & McBride, 1999; Delaney & Kaiser, 2001; Luchshyn, Dunlap, & Albin, 2002).

Parent of Siblings Without Disabilities As with studies investigating parental reactions to a child with disabilities, research on the effects of such children on their siblings has yielded varied findings. Clearly, children are deeply influenced by having a brother or a sister with special needs (McHugh, 2003); the nature of that influence, however, is varied. Some studies have found negative effects, such as a higher incidence of emotional or behavioral problems (Orsillo, McCaffrey, & Fisher, 1993), lower self-esteem (McHale & Gamble, 1989), or resentment or jealousy (Hutton & Caron, 2005) in siblings of children with disabilities. But researchers have also reported many instances of siblings displaying nurturing and affection toward their brother or sister with disabilities (Hannah & Midlarsky, 2005; Stoneman, 1998). The positive relationships between a sibling and his or her brother or sister with disabilities often last well into adulthood (Orsmond & Seltzer, 2000).

Brothers and sisters of a child with disabilities often have concerns about their sibling's disability: uncertainty regarding the cause of the disability and its effect on them, uneasiness about the reactions of friends, and a feeling of being left out or being required to do too much for the child with disabilities (Hutton & Caron, 2005). Parents play key roles in determining the nature of the relationship between their children and the extent to which their children without disabilities develop into happy, well-adjusted adolescents and adults.

Marriage Partner Having a child with disabilities can put stress on a marriage. Specific stressors can be as diverse as arguing over who is to blame for the child's disability; disagreeing about expectations for the child's behavior; and spending so much time, money, and energy on the child with disabilities that little is left for each other (V. Florian & Findler, 2001). It is a mistake, however, to assume that the presence of a child with disabilities has a negative effect on marital relationships. Most families of children with disabilities experience average to above-average levels of marriage adjustment (e.g., Flaherty & Glidden, 2000; Stoneman & Gavidia-Payne, 2006), and studies have found that a child with disabilities can strengthen a marriage in part because of a couple's shared commitment to the child (Flaherty & Glidden, 2000; Scorgie & Sobsey, 2000).

Information Specialist/Trainer of Significant Others Grandparents, aunts and uncles, neighbors, the school bus driver: all of these people can be important influences on a child's development. While parents of children without disabilities can reasonably expect them to receive certain kinds of treatment from significant others, parents of children with disabilities know they cannot necessarily depend on appropriate actions and reactions from others. These parents must try to ensure that other people interact with their child in ways

Go to the Homework & Exercises section in Chapter 3 of MyEducationLab and complete Homework Exercise 4. As you read the article and answer the accompanying questions, consider the impact of the parent–professional partnership on the student's positive behavioral support plan.

Brothers and sisters without disabilities often have special needs and concerns because of their sibling's disability.

that support their child's dignity, acceptance, opportunities for learning, and maintenance of adaptive behaviors. One mother of a child with Down syndrome describes her response to anyone who stares at her son: she looks the person squarely in the eye and says, "You seem interested in my son. Would you like to meet him?" (Schulz, 1985, p. 6). This usually ends the staring and often creates an opportunity to provide information or begin a friendship.

Advocate IDEA not only defines the rights of parents of children with disabilities but also requires specific efforts and responsibilities. Although involvement in their child's educational process is expected and desirable for all parents, participation is a must for parents of exceptional children. They must acquire special knowledge (e.g., about different kinds of related services), learn special skills (e.g., how to participate effectively in individualized family services plan [IFSP]/IEP meetings), and be consistent and firm in presenting their concerns and wishes regarding learning goals, placement options, and career development opportunities for their children (Lindstrom, Doren, Metheny, Johnson, & Zane, 2007; Luker & Lucker, 2007; J. B. Stoner & Angell, 2006; P. W. D. Wright & Wright, 2006). In addition, many parents of children with disabilities have concerns over and above those of most parents; they must often advocate for effective educational services and opportunities for their children in a society that devalues persons with disabilities (McCabe, 2007; Yell & Drasgow, 2000).

Changing Needs as Children Grow

Family life-cycle stages

Council for Exceptional Children

Content Standards for Beginning Teachers—Common Core: Concerns of families of individuals with exceptional learning needs and strategies to help address these concerns (CC10K3).

Another way to increase our understanding of how a child with disabilities might affect his or her family and vice versa is to examine the likely impact of the child's and family's changing needs at various ages (Lindstrom et al., 2007; A. Turnbull, Turnbull, Erwin, & Soodak, 2006). Table 3.1 identifies some of the major issues and concerns that parents and siblings face during four life-cycle stages and suggests strategies for supporting families as they pass through those stages. And the demands of parenting a child with disabilities often do not end when the child reaches adulthood. Many parents in their 70s and 80s continue to care for their adult children with disabilities (Llewellyn, Gething, Kendig, & Cant, 2004).

DEVELOPING AND MAINTAINING FAMILY–PROFESSIONAL PARTNERSHIPS

A. P. Turnbull and colleagues (2006) define a family–professional partnership as a collaborative relationship in which families (not just parents) and professionals capitalize on and defer to each other's judgments and expertise as appropriate to secure and increase the benefits of education for students, other family members, and professionals. To better understand the characteristics of effective family–professional partnerships, Blue-Banning, Summers, Frankland, Nelson, and Beegle (2004) conducted in-depth focus groups and interviews with 137 adult family members of children with and without disabilities and 53 professionals. The participants represented a wide range of ethnic groups and socioeconomic levels and resided in Kansas, North Carolina, and Louisiana. The results suggested that collaborative partnerships are facilitated by professional behaviors clustered around these six dimensions: communication, commitment, equality, skills, trust, and respect (see Table 3.2).

The study by Blue-Banning and colleagues (2004) gives empirical support to something that educators have known for a long time but practiced too seldom: Effective home-school partnerships are characterized by family members and professionals jointly pursuing shared goals in a climate of mutual respect and trust (Kashara & Turnbull, 2005; J. B. Stoner & Angell, 2006; A. P. Turnbull et al., 2006). Families receive supports in the form of the knowledge and resources that empower them to participate as full partners, and professionals receive input from families that helps them be more effective teachers.

Professionals can use the Family–Professional Partnership Scale to obtain parents' ratings of the relative importance and their satisfaction with various aspects of their partnership with their child's special education service providers (Summers et al., 2005). Parents use a 5-point scale, ranging from 1 (a little important/very dissatisfied) to 5 (critically

TABLE 3.1

Issues faced by family members and ways that professionals can help during four life-cycle stages of a person with disabilities

LIFE-CYCLE STAGES

	BIRTH AND EARLY CHILDHOOD	CHILDHOOD
Issues for Parents	• Discovering and coming to terms with exceptionality • Obtaining an accurate diagnosis • Informing siblings and relatives • Locating early intervention services • Participating in IFSP meetings • Seeking to find meaning in the exceptionality • Clarifying a personal ideology to guide decisions • Addressing issues of stigma • Identifying positive contributions of exceptionality • Setting great expectations	• Establishing routines to carry out family functions • Adjusting emotionally to educational implications • Clarifying issues of mainstreaming versus special class placement • Advocating for inclusive experiences • Participating in IEP conferences • Locating community resources • Arranging for extracurricular activities • Developing a vision for the future
Issues for Siblings	• Less parental time and energy for sibling needs • Feelings of jealousy because of less attention • Fears associated with misunderstandings about exceptionality	• Division of responsibility for any physical care needs • Oldest female sibling may be at risk • Limited family resources for recreation and leisure • Informing friends and teachers • Possible concern about younger sibling surpassing older • Issues of mainstreaming into same school • Need for basic information on exceptionality
Enhancing Successful Transitions	• Advise parents to prepare for the separation of preschool children by periodically leaving the child with others. • Gather information and visit preschools in the community. • Encourage participation in Parent-to-Parent programs. (Veteran parents are matched in one-to-one relationships with parents who are just beginning the transition process.) • Familiarize parents with possible school (elementary and secondary) programs, career options, or adult programs so they have an idea of future opportunities.	• Provide parents with an overview of curricular options. • Ensure that IEP meetings provide an empowering context for family collaboration. • Encourage participation in Parent-to-Parent matches, workshops, or family support groups to discuss transitions with others.

continues

TABLE 3.1 (CONTINUED)

Issues faced by family members and ways that professionals can
help during four life-cycle stages of a person with disabilities

LIFE-CYCLE STAGES

	ADOLESCENCE	**ADULTHOOD**
Issues for Parents	• Adjusting emotionally to possible chronicity of exceptionality • Identifying issues of emerging sexuality • Dealing with physical and emotional changes of puberty • Addressing possible peer isolation and rejection • Planning for career/vocational development • Arranging for leisure activities • Expanding child's self-determination skills • Planning for postsecondary education	• Addressing supported employment and living options • Adjusting emotionally to any adult implications of dependency • Addressing the need for socialization opportunities outside the family • Initiating career choice or vocational program • Planning for possible need for guardianship
Issues for Siblings	• Overidentification with sibling • Greater understanding of differences in people • Influence of exceptionality on career choice • Dealing with possible stigma and embarrassment • Participation in sibling training programs • Opportunity for sibling support groups	• Possible issues of responsibility for financial support • Addressing concerns regarding genetic implications • Introducing new in-laws to exceptionality • Need for information on career/living options • Clarify role of sibling advocacy • Possible issues of guardianship
Enhancing Successful Transitions	• Assist families and adolescents to identify community leisure activities. • Incorporate into the IEP skills that will be needed in future career and vocational programs. • Visit or become familiar with a variety of career and living options. • Develop a mentor relationship with an adult with a similar exceptionality and an individual who has a career that matches the student's strengths and preferences.	• Provide preferred information to families about guardianship, estate planning, wills, and trusts. • Assist family members in transferring responsibilities to the individual with an exceptionality, other family members, or service providers as appropriate. • Assist the young adult or family members with career or vocational choices. • Address the issues and responsibilities of marriage and family for the young adult.

Source: Adapted from Turnbull, A. P., & Turnbull, H. R. (1990, 1997, 2001). *Families, professionals, and exceptionality: Collaborating for empowerment* (2nd ed., pp. 134–135; 3rd ed., p. 149; 4th ed., p. 173), and Turnbull, A., Turnbull, H., Erwin, E., & Soodak, L. (2006). *Families, professionals, and exceptionality: Positive outcomes through partnership and trust* (5th ed., p. 93). Upper Saddle River, NJ: Merrill/Prentice Hall. Used by permission.

TABLE 3.2

Six dimensions of high-quality family-professional partnerships and professional behaviors that facilitate them

COLLABORATIVE PARTNERSHIP THEME	INDICATORS
Communication: The quality of communication is positive, understandable, and respectful among all members at all levels of the partnership. The quantity of communication is also at a level to enable efficient and effective coordination and understanding among all members.	Sharing resources Being clear Being honest Communicating positively Being tactful Being open Listening Communicating frequently Coordinating information
Commitment: The members of the partnership share a sense of assurance about (a) each other's devotion and loyalty to the child and family, and (b) each other's belief in the importance of the goals being pursued on behalf of the child and family.	Demonstrating commitment Being flexible Regarding work as "more than a job" Regarding child and family as "more than a case" Encouraging the child and family Being accessible to the child and family Being consistent Being sensitive to emotions
Equality: The members of the partnership feel a sense of equity in decision making and service implementation, and actively work to ensure that all other members of the partnership feel equally powerful in their ability to influence outcomes for children and families.	Avoiding use of "clout" Empowering partners Validating others Advocating for child or family with other professionals Allowing reciprocity among members Being willing to explore all options Fostering harmony among all partners Coming to the table/avoiding "turfism" Acting "equal"
Skills: Members of the partnership perceive that others on the team demonstrate competence, including service providers' ability to fulfill their roles and to demonstrate "recommended practice" approaches to working with children and families.	Taking action Having expectations for child's progress Meeting individual special needs Considering the whole child or family Being willing to learn
Trust: The members of the partnership share a sense of assurance about the reliability or dependability of the character, ability, strength, or truth of the other members of the partnership.	Being reliable Keeping the child safe Being discreet
Respect: The members of the partnership regard each other with esteem and demonstrate that esteem through actions and communications.	Valuing the child Being nonjudgmental Being courteous Exercising nondiscrimination Avoiding intrusion

Source: From Blue-Banning, M., Summers, J. A., Frankland, H. C., Nelson, L. L., & Beegle, G. (2004). Dimensions of family and professional partnerships: Constructive guidelines for collaboration. *Exceptional Children, 70,* p. 174. Copyright 2004 by the Council for Exceptional Children. Reprinted with permission.

important/very satisfied), to rate 18 statements describing child-focused and family-focused aspects of the partnership. For example:

Your child's service providers
- Have the skills to help your child succeed.
- Speak up for your child's best interests.
- Treat your child with dignity.
- Are honest, even when they have bad news.
- Protect your family's privacy.
- Pay attention to what you have to say. (pp. 75–76)

Principles of Effective Communication

Regular two-way communication with parents is the key operational element of the family–professional partnership. Without open, honest communication between teacher and parent, many of the positive outcomes we have examined cannot be achieved. The family members in the study by Blue-Banning and colleagues (2004) said they needed frequent communication, but they also highlighted the importance of the quality of communication. "Family members stressed that communication should be honest and open, with no hidden information and no 'candy-coating' of bad news" (p. 173). Family members and professionals emphasized the need for two-way communication, stating that both professionals and parents should listen carefully and nonjudgmentally to what each has to say. One father stated it like this:

> The first thing is to listen to us . . . because we know our kids better than anybody. . . . I think some of these people have preconceived notions about everything. . . . So if I tried to say to them [professionals] something, it'd be LISTEN TO ME. (p. 175)

The authors of a study on the perspectives of parents of children with autism on their interactions with education professionals concluded that

> parents wanted communication on a daily basis with their son's teacher, but they wanted quality communication. Parents wanted to be informed of achievements, but they also wanted to know of any problems that the teachers had encountered. . . . The parent participants in this study also emphasized their need for frequent, honest, and open communication between home and school. (J. B. Stoner et al., 2005, pp. 46, 47)

C. L. Wilson (1995) recommends five principles for effective communication between educators and parents.

Accept Parents' Statements   Accepting parents' statements means conveying through verbal and nonverbal means that parents' input is valued. Parents are more likely to speak freely and openly when they believe that what they say is respected. Acceptance means conveying, "I understand and appreciate your point of view." It does not mean the teacher must agree with everything that a parent says.

Listen Actively   Good listeners attend and respond to a conversation partner in a sincere and genuine manner. A good listener pays attention to content, noting who said it and how. For example, in an IFSP/IEP conference attended by extended family members, an educator should notice if a grandparent seems to be speaking for the child's parents or if the mother and father express different opinions about an issue through tones of voice or body language. An active listener not only interprets, sorts, and analyzes what the speaker says but also responds to the speaker's message with animation and interest (V. F. Howard, Williams, & Lepper, 2005). Figure 3.3 illustrates the skill of active listening.

Question Effectively   To the extent possible, educators should use open-ended questions when communicating with parents, especially during conferences. For example, an open-ended question such as "What did Sharena do with her homework project last week?" is more likely to evoke a descriptive and informative reply from parents than is the closed-ended question "Is Sharena having trouble with her homework?" which might result in a yes or no response. Questions to parents should not focus solely on problems or deficits, and teachers must respect families' desire to keep some things private and "in the family" (A. Turnbull et al., 2006).

Encourage   It is important for parents to hear good news about their son or daughter. Describing or showing parents specific instances of their child's good behavior or improved performance encourages parental involvement.

Principles of effective communication

Content Standards for Beginning Teachers—Common Core: Foster respectful and beneficial relationships between families and professionals (CC10S3).

Active listening

Content Standards for Beginning Teachers—Common Core: Foster respectful and beneficial relationships between families and professionals (CC10S3).

FIGURE 3.3   **Active listening**

The following excerpts contrast the communication styles of two early childhood teachers, a passive listener and an active listener, while discussing IEP goals with a parent.

Passive Listening

Parent: I would very much like to have my child use his communication board on a more regular basis. Currently, he becomes very frustrated because he can't tell us what he needs. [The parent frowns and looks sad.]

Passively listening teacher: All the students in my class are able to speak. We will have the speech language pathologist work with Andy so that he can speak as well. [The teacher is fiddling with papers she needs for her next parent conference.]

Parent: Perhaps you didn't read Andy's file carefully. His cerebral palsy is so involved that he isn't able to make any understandable speech sounds. We have already had him evaluated by a speech therapist, and he created the communication board for Andy so he could develop his language skills.

Passively listening teacher: [Still looking at her other papers.] We have an excellent speech language pathologist. She will have Andy talking in no time. Andy can work with her during circle time since that is oral and Andy wouldn't be able to participate.

Parent: We don't want Andy to miss out on circle time. He loves to be a part of the group. We can choose appropriate pictures to put on his communication board so he can respond with the rest of the children. He gets very frustrated when he is not allowed to be with the rest of the students.

Passively listening teacher: Oh, we don't let the children bring toys to the circle. He has to be able to speak up like everyone else. Also, I've been meaning to talk to you about his behavior. He has been refusing to cooperate with our group activities. I'd like to send him to time out when this happens.

Parent: [She gives a big sigh.] As I've said, Andy gets very frustrated when he isn't able to communicate and when he isn't a part of the group. I don't think time out would be the right answer for this problem.

Passively listening teacher: Well, if you don't allow us to control his behavior, I don't know how Andy is ever going to be able to be a part of this class. [She looks at her watch, ready to end the meeting.]

Active Listening

Actively listening teacher: We didn't address this in our last IEP meeting, but I think Cherise has matured in her language and self-help skills enough that she is ready to start toilet training. What do you think about this? [Teacher leans forward and looks parent in the eye.]

Parent: Do you really think she could learn to go by herself? If would be such a relief not to have her in diapers, now that we are expecting another child. [The parent smiles.]

Actively listening teacher: [Nods enthusiastically.] I just want to explain what this would involve and make sure we can work on this at both home and school. I'd like to check her every 15 minutes to see if there is a pattern to when she is wet and then start putting her on the potty at those most likely times each day. Can you do the same thing when she is at home with you in the afternoon and evening? [The teacher watches the parent's face and notices that her mouth falls a little.]

Parent: I don't think I could check every 15 minutes. We have the two older ones, so I'm always driving them to activities; and Cherise's therapy sessions usually run at least 45 minutes and I don't like to disturb her once she's started a session. [The parent sits back in her chair, pushing away from the table.]

Actively listening teacher: Of course, you are probably on the go so much there isn't a lot of down-time when you could stop and do this every 15 minutes. Is there any period of time, like maybe the hour just before bed that you could work on this? I find kids learn toilet-training so much faster when we work on it at school and at home. [The teacher raises her eyebrows in a hopeful gesture.]

Parent: Maybe I could ask my husband to watch Cherise when I take her older sister to her dance lessons. That way she'd be home for the two hours before bed. Would that be enough to make a difference?

Actively listening teacher: I appreciate you rearranging your hectic schedule. I think that could make a big difference, and once Cherise is out of diapers, you'll have a little more free time with the new baby.

Parent: I'm so glad you think we can do this. It would make a big difference not to have two in diapers, and Cherise will be happier if she can be like the big girls. [She hesitates.] But what if I can't carry through at home? What if she doesn't learn?

Actively listening teacher: I know it's hard to do these things at home when your hands are full. We'll keep working on it at school. Cherise might not learn right away, but I've got some ways to motivate her. You just let me know if you don't think it's going well at home and we'll go back to the drawing board.

Parent: Thank you for being so understanding. I'll give it my best shot. I'm so glad you thought to work on this. It's like you read my mind.

Source: Adapted from Howard, V. F., Williams, B. F., & Lepper, C. (2005). *Very young children with special needs: A formative approach for today's children* (3rd ed., pp. 121–122). Upper Saddle River, NJ: Merrill/Prentice Hall. Used by permission.

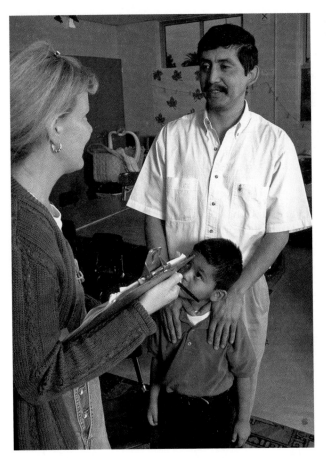

Parent–teacher communication is enhanced when teachers actively listen to what parents say.

Roadblocks to communication

 Council for Exceptional Children **Content Standards for Beginning Teachers—Common Core:** Foster respectful and beneficial relationships between families and professionals (CC10S3).

Stay Focused Although greetings and some small talk are desirable before getting down to business, conversations between parents and teachers should focus on the child's educational program and progress. Educators must be sensitive to cultural differences and the idiosyncratic conversational styles of individual families (Gonzalez-Mena, 2006; Lynch & Hanson, 2004). But teachers must also learn to distinguish when extended small talk is drifting too far from the purpose at hand so that they can refocus the conversation.

Identifying and Breaking Down Barriers to Parent–Teacher Partnerships

Let's face it: parents and teachers do not always communicate effectively and cooperate with one another. They may sometimes even seem to be on opposite sides, battling over what each thinks is best for the child. The child, unfortunately, never wins that battle. She needs to have the people responsible for the two places where she spends most of her life—home and school—work together to make those environments consistent with and supportive of her job of learning. Teachers should work to increase the likelihood that their interactions with parents and families are characterized by cooperation. They must be responsive to the practices and beliefs of families from diverse cultural backgrounds and identify and eliminate attitudes and behaviors that block family involvement.

Professional Roadblocks to Communication Parents' and teachers' assumptions about and attitudes toward one another are sometimes counterproductive. Teachers sometimes complain that parents are uninterested, uncooperative, or hostile. Parents may complain that educators are negative, unavailable, or patronizing. We should examine factors that cause friction between parents and teachers, not to assign fault but to identify what we can change and improve. Professionals who recognize that some of their own behaviors may diminish the potential for productive partnerships with parents are in a better position to change their actions and obtain the benefits that such relationships can provide (Hanhan, 2008; Matuszny, Banda, & Coleman, 2007).

Although educators cannot directly change the attitudes of parents, they can—and, as professionals, must—identify and eliminate personal behaviors that may serve as barriers to communication with families. Some professionals hold stereotypes and false assumptions about what parents of children with disabilities must be feeling and what they must need (Dyson, 1996; Voltz, 1994). Such attitudes often lead to poor relationships between families and professionals. We should not be surprised if parents feel intimidated, confused, angry, hostile—or just terminate their involvement altogether—when professionals interact with them in any of the following ways:

- *Treating parents as vulnerable clients instead of equal partners.* Professionals who see parents only as persons who need their help make a grave mistake. Teachers need parents and what they have to offer as much as parents need teachers.
- *Keeping professional distance.* Most professionals in human services develop some degree of distance to avoid getting too involved with a client—supposedly to maintain objectivity and credibility. But aloofness or coldness in the name of professionalism has hindered or terminated many parent–teacher relationships. Parents must believe that the educators working with their children really care about them (L. G. L. Nelson, Summers, & Turnbull, 2004).
- *Treating parents as if they need counseling.* Some professionals make the faulty assumption that having a child with disabilities causes a parent to need therapy or parent education. A mother of a child who attended a preschool for students with developmental delays described her frustration: "Everybody who came here was aimed at me. Everybody

is telling me 'You need parent counseling.' I mean I have lived for 30 years. I never needed help and all of a sudden I need help on how to do this and help on how to do that. I feel like they are saying John is not the problem, I am the problem" (S. S. Rao, 2000, p. 481).

- *Blaming parents for their child's condition.* Some parents do feel responsible for their child's disability and, with a little encouragement from a professional, can be made to feel completely guilty. A productive parent–professional relationship focuses on collaborative problem solving, not blame.

- *Disrespecting parents as less intelligent.* Teachers sometimes give too little recognition to parents' information and suggestions. Parents are considered too biased, too involved, or too unskilled to make useful observations (Lake & Billingsley, 2000). Some professionals concede that parents have access to needed information but contend that parents cannot, or should not, make any decisions based on what they know. "They treat me like I'm uneducated. They break down things into real small pieces and then ask me to repeat things. I have gone to nursing school. I can read. Maybe they met other people who cannot read but they can ask me 'Rose, can you read?' They treat you like you are a child" (S. S. Rao, 2000, p. 481).

- *Treating parents as adversaries.* Some teachers expect the worst whenever they interact with parents. Even when that attitude can be partially explained by previous unpleasant encounters with unreasonable parents, it usually becomes a self-fulfilling prophecy and is at best a negative influence on new relationships.

- *Labeling parents.* Some educators seem eager to label parents (Sonnenschein, 1981). If parents disagree with a diagnosis or seek another opinion, they are *denying;* if parents refuse a suggested treatment, they are *resistant;* and if parents insist that something is wrong with their child despite test evidence to the contrary, they are *anxious.*

Conflict Resolution Through Dialoguing   Not all ineffective parent–teacher relationships are caused by professional mishandling. Some parents are genuinely difficult to work with or unreasonable. Parents sometimes fight long and hard for services for their child. But after finding services and when the child is receiving an appropriate education, the parents continue their intense advocacy until minor issues with professionals become major confrontations. One mother stated, "For years I have scrapped and fought for services. Now I come on like gangbusters over issues that are really not that important. I don't like what has happened to me. I've ended up to be an aggressive, angry person" (Bronicki & Turnbull, 1987, p. 10).

Although some teachers voice concern that parents of children with disabilities are unrealistic and make too many demands of schools (e.g., Chesley & Calaluce, 1997), most recognize that these parents, like all parents, are simply advocating for the best possible educational services and outcomes for their children. When someone sees things differently from us and we both have vested interests in the outcome, we often resort to argument in an attempt to resolve our differences. Although a teacher may "win" an argument with parents—if one defines winning as forcing the parents to agree verbally or simply give up their perspective—arguing is rarely a useful tool in a partnership. *Dialoguing* is an approach to conflict resolution in which both parties try to see each other's point of view. Gonzalez-Mena (2006) points out differences between a dialogue and an argument:

- The object of an argument is to win; the object of a dialogue is to gather information.
- The arguer tells; the dialoguer asks.
- The arguer tries to persuade; the dialoguer seeks to learn.
- The arguer tries to convince; the dialoguer wants to discover.
- The arguer sees two opposing views and considers hers the valid or best one; the dialoguer is willing to understand multiple viewpoints. (p. 117)

Most of us are better at arguing than we are at dialoguing. That's probably because we have had much more practice with the former. We tend to argue first and think rationally (if we do at all) later. But later might be too late if in "winning" the argument, we have damaged the parent–teacher relationship. Gonzalez-Mena (2006) recommends using the RERUN approach—reflect, explain, reason, understand, and negotiate:

Dialoguing to resolve conflicts

 Content Standards for Beginning Teachers—Common Core: Foster respectful and beneficial relationships between families and professionals (CC10S3).

- *Reflect.* Acknowledge what you perceive the other person is thinking or feeling. If you understand what the person is feeling, you might say, "I think you're looking at it this way." If you perceive that the other person is very emotional, acknowledge your perception: "You sound really upset." These two openers are invitations for the person to talk more. People who know that their feelings and thoughts are received and accepted are more likely to be open to listening—if not right away, eventually.
- *Explain.* Explain your perspective concisely. But do not lecture. Remember, we have two ears and only one mouth—a reminder that we should listen twice as much as we talk.
- *Reason.* The explanation of your perspective should include the reason you believe or feel the way that you do.
- *Understand.* Next comes the hardest part. Tune in to both your own and the parent's thoughts and feelings, and try to understand the situation from both points of view. You don't have to say anything out loud at this point; just be sure you have clarity. You may have to talk inwardly to yourself to get it. Self-reflection is an important part of the process. When you think you understand, you're ready for the next step.
- *Negotiate.* Try brainstorming together until you can find a mutually satisfying solution. Don't give up. Refuse to take an either–or attitude. If you don't get stuck in a dualistic frame of mind, you can probably find a third or fourth solution that differs from or combines both of your stances on the matter. Creative negotiators can open up new avenues of action that no one has ever thought of before. (adapted from Gonzalez-Mena, 2006, p. 119)

You will find additional suggestions for resolving conflicts and disagreements with parents in Fiedler, Simpson, and Clark (2007), Heron and Harris (2001), Montgomery (2005), and T. C. Smith, Gartin, Murdick, and Hilton (2006).

WORKING WITH CULTURALLY AND LINGUISTICALLY DIVERSE FAMILIES

Differences in the cultural beliefs and linguistic practices of professionals and families can serve as barriers to family involvement (Greenen, Powers, & Lopez-Vasquez, 2001; Matuszny et al., 2007; Tam & Heng, 2005). Teachers who fail to recognize and respect differences between their own cultural perspectives and the values and beliefs of families are prone to biased and faulty judgments about parents that weaken the parent–teacher partnership.

Antunez (2000) outlined several potential barriers in working with parents and families from culturally diverse backgrounds.

- *Language skills.* Inability to understand the language of the school is a major deterrent to parents who have not achieved full English proficiency. In these cases, interactions with the schools are difficult, and, therefore, practically nonexistent.
- *Home-school partnerships.* In some cultures, such as many Hispanic ones, teaming with the school is not a tradition. Education has been historically perceived as the responsibility of the schools, and parent intervention is viewed as interference with what trained professionals are supposed to do.
- *Work interference.* Work is a major reason stated by parents for noninvolvement in school activities. Conflicts between parent and school schedules may mean parents cannot attend school events, help their children with homework, or in other ways become active participants in their children's education.
- *Knowledge of the school system.* A great number of low-income parents view schools as an incomprehensible and purposefully exclusionary system. Lack of trust is often the result of misunderstanding the perceived intentions of each party. Sending home communications in English only and scheduling meetings at times when parents cannot attend serve to reinforce parent apprehension. Schools often misperceive the lack of involvement that results from mistrust and apprehension as a lack of concern for the children's education.
- *Self-confidence.* Many parents of English language learner (ELL) students believe that their participation does not help schools perform their jobs as educational institutions; as a result, they

separate themselves from the process. Parents who feel uncomfortable in the school setting are less likely to be involved than those who have developed a sense of equal partnership are.

- *Past experiences.* Many non–English-speaking parents have had negative education experiences of their own, and these memories linger through adulthood. In some cases, these parents have fallen victim to racial and linguistic discrimination by the schools. Negative feelings toward home–school interaction are often reinforced when schools communicate with parents only to share bad news about their children. (Antunez, 2000, pp. 4–5)

Understanding and Respecting Cultural Differences

The demands and challenges faced by families who may be less educated, poor, or isolated from the dominant American culture may prevent them from becoming actively involved in school partnerships. The literature on culturally diverse families supports the following notions about these families (Banks, 2007; Cartledge, Kea, & Ida, 2000; Correa, Jones, Thomas, & Morsink, 2005; Gollnick & Chinn, 2006; Kochhar-Bryant & Price, 2008; Lian & Fontánez-Phelan, 2001; Lynch & Hanson, 2004):

Many families are English-language learners (ELL). In the year 2000, one in five people in America 5 years old and older spoke a language other than English at home. Researchers estimate that by 2030, students whose first language is other than English will make up 40% of the school-age population (National Symposium on Learning Disabilities in English Language Learners, 2004). Although students nationwide speak more than 400 languages, 77% of ELL students speak Spanish as their native language. Schools should provide materials in both the native and English language and preferably communicate with the family directly through home visits or by telephone.

Many families live in low-income and poverty. Approximately 38 percent of America's school-aged children live below or near the poverty line (Fuller, 2008). Two thirds of children of ELL parents come from low-income families (Comacho, 2007).

Practitioners should understand that although the parents may not have finished school or cannot read, they are "life educated" and know their child better than anyone else does. In Spanish, the term *educado* (educated) does not mean "formal schooling" but means that a child is skilled in human relations, well mannered, respectful of adults, and well behaved.

If families are undocumented immigrants, they are naturally fearful of interaction with anyone representing authority. Building families' trust and cooperation, even if they are undocumented immigrants, is important. The special educator's role is not to engage in the activities of the Office of Immigration and Naturalization Services. The school's focus is on educating children, who by law are not a suspect class (Correa, Gollery, & Fradd, 1988).

Families from culturally diverse backgrounds tend to be family-oriented. Extended family members—*compadres* or *padrinos* (godparents) in the Hispanic culture—may play important roles in child rearing and family decisions. A child's disability or even a mild language problem may be an extremely personal subject for discussion with outsiders, and families may seek solutions for problems within the family structure. It is important for educators to respect this informal kinship system of support and to understand that schooling may represent a much more formal and impersonal support service for some families. The close, insular aspect of a family is a strength that helps the family function and cope with the stresses sometimes associated with raising a child with a disability (D. Bailey, Skinner, Correa, Arcia, et al., 1999; Rueda, Monzo, Shapiro, Gomez, & Blacher, 2005).

Culturally diverse families may have different experiences with and views about disability, and some may hold idiosyncratic ideologies and practices about the cause and treatment of disability. For example, in some Hispanic cultures, parents may believe that God sent the child with disabilities to them as a gift or blessing, while others may believe the child was sent as a test or a punishment for previous sins. In studies on Latino families, parents acknowledged transforming their lives since the birth of their child by becoming better parents (D. Bailey, Skinner, Correa, Arcia, et al., 1999; D. Bailey, Skinner, Correa, Blanes, et al., 1999). Many

Cultural and linguistic differences

 Content Standards for Beginning Teachers—General Curriculum and Independence Curriculum Referenced Standards: Potential impact of differences in values, languages, and customs that can exist between the home and school (CC1K10) (also CC3K4, CC6K3, CC10K4).

Native American cultural/tribal groups do not consider the birth of a child with a disability to be a negative or tragic event. Health and physical characteristics that might be defined as disabilities in mainstream culture may be framed as special strengths rather than deficiencies. "Native American societies have an uncanny gift for tolerance" (Boyd-Ball, 2007, n.p.).

Although previous studies have reported the existence of folk beliefs and alternative treatments for disabilities in some cultural groups, more recent research finds that for Puerto Rican and Mexican families such beliefs are not prevalent (D. Bailey, Skinner, Correa, Blanes, et al., 1999; D. Skinner, Correa, Skinner, & Bailey, 2001). Families did report knowing about *el mal ojo* (the evil eye) or *el susto* (a scare or fright experienced by the pregnant mother) as explanations given for disabilities but did not believe them to be true of their own children. They reported that some family members (usually the elders) might believe that, to cure the child, the family must make *mandas* (offerings to God or a Catholic saint) or seek the help of a *curandero* (a local healer). However, almost all families interviewed used traditional Western medicine to treat the child with disabilities.

The educational system—in particular, the special education system—may be intimidating to the family. Although this may be true for any family, regardless of cultural or linguistic background, for a non–English-speaking family or one that is less well educated and poor, a professional's use of educational jargon may be especially intimidating. Some families may even put the professional on a pedestal and, believing the professional is the expert, not question or comment on their own wishes for their child's education.

Although it is important that professionals understand the cultural and linguistic practices of the community and families they serve, an important caveat must be stated: Just as professionals should refrain making assumptions about how the parents of a child with a disability feel based on a model or theory of adjustment, educators must also avoid the error of assuming that all members of a cultural or ethnic group necessarily share the same experience, values, or beliefs.

Culturally Responsive Services for Families

Educators can increase the involvement of families from culturally and linguistically diverse backgrounds by using strategies such as the following (Al-Hassan & Gardner, 2002; Matuszny et al., 2007; Tam & Heng, 2005):

- Have native-speaking staff members make initial contacts.
- Provide trained, culturally sensitive interpreters during parent–teacher conferences and IEP/IFSP meetings.
- When a language interpreter is not available, use a **cultural interpreter** whenever possible for conferences and family interviews. A cultural interpreter is a person

    who can create bridges of understanding between school and home culture. These individuals do not necessarily have to speak the home language of an immigrant family, but they must have enough of a basic understanding of the home culture to help the school understand that home culture and to help the family understand school culture, policies, and practices. (Gabel, 2004, p. 23)

- Conduct meetings in family-friendly settings.
- Identify and defer to key decision makers in the family.
- Recognize that families from diverse cultures may view time differently from the way professionals do, and schedule meetings accordingly.
- Provide transportation and child care to make it easier for families to attend school-based activities.

A culturally responsive educator strives to develop awareness of and respect for the beliefs and values held by parents and family members from diverse cultural groups.

Cultural Reciprocity Educators should also work toward **cultural reciprocity,** understanding how differing values and belief systems may influence families' perspectives, wishes, and decisions. For example, a special educator who views disability as a physical phenomenon that can be assessed and treated objectively may have difficulty developing an effective partnership with parents who view disability as a blessing or a punishment that is

---

FIGURE 3.4   Building cultural reciprocity

Professionals who seek to make a difference for children must be willing to take the initiative in building a bridge between the cultures of diverse families and the culture of schools. To build this bridge, Beth Harry recommends that professionals initiate a two-way process of information sharing and understanding called *cultural reciprocity*. The process is recursive, meaning that each step informs the others.

- **Step 1.** Identify the cultural values embedded in your interpretation of a student's difficulties or in a recommendation for service. Ask yourself which values underlie your recommendation. Next, analyze experiences that have contributed to your holding of these values. Consider the roles of nationality, culture, socioeconomic status, and professional education in shaping your values.
- **Step 2.** Find out whether the family being served recognizes and values your assumptions and, if not, how family members' views differ from yours.
- **Step 3.** Acknowledge and give explicit respect to any cultural differences identified, and fully explain the cultural basis of your assumptions.
- **Step 4.** Through discussion and collaboration, determine the most effective way of adapting your professional interpretations or recommendations to the value system of this family.

Harry points out that "by developing your own cultural self-awareness, you are able to recognize the cultural underpinnings of your professional practice. This, in turn, enables you to facilitate conversations with the families." Through the process, families also acquire knowledge about the special education system, which supports them in making informed decisions about services. "With cultural reciprocity, we find not only better relationships, but more reasonable goals that are implemented."

Source: Adapted from ERIC/OSEP Special Project. (2001). *Family involvement in special education* (Research Connections in Special Education, no. 9, pp. 4–5). Arlington, VA: ERIC Clearinghouse on Disabilities and Gifted Education.

---

to be treated with a spiritual perspective (Harry, Rueda, & Kalyanpur, 1999; D. Bailey, Skinner, Correa, Arcia, et al., 1999).

Understanding differences between our own perspectives and those of people from other cultures and ethnic groups requires careful examination of our own cultural background and belief system. "Understanding that our own beliefs and practices are but one cultural variation should make it easier to respect, and therefore to serve, the wide diversity of families whose children are served by special education programs" (Harry, 2003, p. 138). See Figure 3.4, "Building Cultural Reciprocity."

HOME–SCHOOL COMMUNICATION METHODS

Although no single method of communication will be effective or even appropriate with every parent and family, teachers can increase the number of families they reach and the frequency and quality of communications by making a variety of communication avenues available to families. Some families prefer face-to-face meetings; others appreciate receiving written messages or phone calls; still others feel more comfortable communicating with teachers through e-mail messages (S. K. Stuart, Flis, & Rinaldi, 2006). Teachers should ask parents which methods of communication they prefer.

Parent–Teacher Conferences

Parent–teacher conferences are a universal method of home–school communication. In a face-to-face meeting, teachers and parents can exchange information and coordinate their efforts to assist the child with disabilities in school and at home. Unfortunately, parent–teacher conferences are often stiff, formal affairs with anxious teachers and worried

Cultural reciprocity

 Content Standards for Beginning Teachers—General Curriculum and Independence Curriculum Referenced Standards: Culturally responsive factors that promote effective communication and collaboration with individuals with exceptional learning needs, families, school personnel, and community members (CC10K4) (also CC3K4, CC6K3).

parents wondering what bad news they will hear this time. With some thoughtful planning and a systematic approach to conducting parent–teacher conferences, however, teachers can improve the productivity and comfort for all participants.

Preparing for the Conference   Preparation is the key to effective parent–teacher conferences. It entails establishing specific objectives for the conference, obtaining and reviewing a printout or record of the student's recent grades, selecting examples of the student's work, perhaps a graph or chart showing his cumulative progress, and preparing an agenda for the meeting (Dardig, 2008; Kroth & Edge, 2007). Figure 3.5 shows an outline that teachers can use to prepare an agenda and record notes of a parent–teacher conference.

FIGURE 3.5   Outline for a parent–teacher conference

Conference Outline

Date _____ 2-10-09 _____   Time _____ 4:30 – 5:00 _____

Student's Name _____ Jeremy Wright _____
Parents' Name(s) _____ Barbara and Tom Wright _____
Teacher's Name _____ Tim G. _____
Other Staff Present _____ None _____

Objectives for Conference: (1) Show graph of J's reading progress, (2) find out about spelling program, (3) get parents' ideas: intervention for difficulties on playground/in gym, (4) share list of books for leisure reading

Student's Strengths
• good worker academically, wants to learn
• excited about progress in reading fluency

Area(s) Where Improvement Is Needed:
• continue w/spelling @ home
• arguments & fighting w/other kids

Questions to Ask Parents:
• Interactions w/friends while playing in neighborhood?
• How would they feel about f'dback from classmate re: playground/gym behavior?
• Consequences?

Parents' Responses/Comments:
• very pleased w/reading – want to build on it.
• wondering how long w/in-home spelling?
• willing to give rewards @ home: playground/gym

Examples of Student's Work/Interactions:
• graph of corrects/errors per min.: reading
• weekly pre- & post-test scores: spelling.

Current Programs and Strategies Used by Teacher:
• reading: silent read, two 1-min. time trials, self-charting comprehension practice
• spelling: practice w/tape recorder, self-checking

Suggestions for Parents:
• continue spelling games (invite friends)
• Show interest in/play fantasy games (Dung. & Dragons) w/J

Suggestions from Parents:
• Try using some high-interest spelling words (e.g., joust, castle)
• Matt & Amin could help with playground/gym program

Follow-up Activities: (Agreed to in conf)

Parents:
• Continue to play spelling game 2 nights per week
• Take J to library for adventure books

Teacher:
• Ask J for high-interest words & use 3-4 in his weekly list.
• Develop peer intervention strategy w/Matt, Amin & J (group contingency?)

Date to Call for Follow-up:
Feb. 24 (Tuesday) _____ (check when called)

Conducting the Conference   The child's classroom is an appropriate setting for most parent–teacher conferences because it provides ready access to student records and curriculum materials and reminds the teacher and parents that the purpose of the conference is to work together to improve the child's education. Wherever parent conferences are held, the area should be arranged so that it is conducive to partnership interactions. Teachers should not sit behind their desks, creating a barrier between themselves and the parents, or have parents sit in undersized children's chairs.

A four-step sequence for conducting parent–teacher conferences recommended by Stephens and Wolf (1989) 20 years ago remains sound advice today:

1. *Build rapport.* Establishing mutual trust and the belief that the teacher really cares about the student is important to a good parent–teacher conference. A minute or two devoted to relevant small talk helps build rapport. Instead of beginning with a superficial statement about the weather or traffic, the teacher might begin by commenting on some recent news or community or national event that is likely to be of interest to the family or their child.

2. *Obtain information.* Parents can provide teachers with important information for improving instruction. As suggested earlier, teachers should use open-ended questions that cannot be answered with a simple yes or no. For example, "Which school activities has Felix mentioned lately?" is better than "Has Felix told you what we've been doing in school?" The first question encourages parents to provide more information; the teacher is trying to build a conversation, not preside over a question-and-answer session. Throughout the conference, the teacher should show genuine interest in listening to parents' concerns, avoid dominating the conversation, and stay focused on the purpose of the meeting. Teachers should refrain from making gestures, facial expressions, and other forms of "body language" that suggest frustration, suspicion, confrontation, or defensiveness. Above all, professionals should not make comments that lecture ("Do you realize . . ."), criticize or judge ("That was a mistake . . ."), or threaten ("Unless you take my advice . . .") (Fiedler et al., 2007; Hanhan, 2008).

3. *Provide information.* The teacher should give parents concrete information about their child in jargon-free language. The teacher should share examples of schoolwork and data on student performance—what the student has already learned and what he needs to learn next. If the student has made insufficient progress, the teacher and parents should discuss together ways to improve it.

4. *Summarize and follow up.* The conference should end with a concise summary of the discussion and any decisions that were made. The teacher should review strategies agreed on during the conference and indicate the activities that either party has agreed to do to help carry out those strategies. Some teachers record notes on a laptop computer during the conference and at the conclusion of the meeting print a copy so that parents will also have a record of what was said or agreed to.

These strategies are relevant for all types of parent–teacher meetings. However, IEP and IFSP planning and evaluation meetings, which are discussed in Chapters 2 and 14, respectively, entail additional procedural requirements. You can find detailed suggestions for planning and conducting parent–teacher conferences in Dardig (2008); Hanhan (2008); Jordan, Reyes-Blane, Peel, Peel,

Planning and conducting parent–teacher conferences

Council for Exceptional Children

Content Standards for Beginning Teachers—Common Core: Plan and conduct collaborative conferences with individuals with exceptional learning needs and their families (CC10S5) (also CC7S3).

Go to the Homework & Exercises section in Chapter 3 of MyEducationLab and complete Homework Exercise 5 to see Ms. Crangle and Ms. Maheady conduct a parent–teacher conference. As you watch the video and answer the accompanying questions, consider the interaction between the teachers and the parent.

Showing parents examples of their children's progress sets the occasion for parental praise and approval of student effort.

and Lane (1998); and Kroth and Edge (2007). For some families, holding a conference in the home might be appropriate and appreciated (T. C. Smith et al., 2006).

Written Communication

Home–school written communications

Council for Exceptional Children

Content Standards for Beginning Teachers—Common Core: Involve the individual and family in setting instructional goals and monitoring progress (CC7S3).

Although much can be accomplished in a face-to-face meeting, parent-teacher conferences should not be the sole means of home–school communication. Written messages, especially when part of a systematic program of ongoing information exchange, can be an effective way to maintain home–school communication.

Teachers should never rely on written messages, regardless of their form, as the sole method of communicating with parents. Educators must also be sensitive to the cultural and linguistic backgrounds and educational levels of parents (Al-Hassan & Gardner, 2002). A study of parents' rights documents published by state departments of education found that only 4% to 8% of the materials were written at the recommended reading level for parents (Fitzgerald & Watkins, 2006). Up to 50% of the documents were written at the college reading level or higher and "nearly all lacked additional organizational and textual features that would make them more readable" (p. 507). If parents must spend a great deal of time trying to understand the written messages from their child's school, they may view those messages as a nuisance and be discouraged from active involvement in their child's education.

Happy Grams and Special Accomplishment Letters The simplest type of home-school written message is a brief note informing parents of something positive their child has accomplished at school. Many teachers regularly send students home with such "happy grams," giving parents an opportunity to praise the child at home and stay abreast of activities in the classroom. A book by M. L. Kelly (1990) includes tear-out masters of school-home notes that teachers can duplicate and use for a variety of communication purposes.

A letter to parents detailing the accomplishment of an important milestone or special achievement by their child is an excellent way to build a partnership. You will find an example of such a letter and suggestions for how teachers can develop a system for writing them in Teaching & Learning, "A Parent Appreciation Letter."

Go to the Homework & Exercises section in Chapter 3 of MyEducationLab and complete Homework Exercise 6. As you watch the video and answer the accompanying questions, consider the pros and possible cons of using a home–school journal.

Two-Way Home–School Reporting Forms and Dialogue Notebooks Teachers can build a two-way, parent-teacher communication system around a reporting form or a notebook that the child carries between home and school. Teachers can develop and use a standard form or checklist to inform parents about their child's homework assignments and behavior in the classroom (Olympia, Andrews, Valum, & Jensen, 1993; Sicley, 1993). Parents sign the form to indicate they have received it and can use the form themselves to provide information or request assistance from the teacher(s). To be most effective, home–school communication forms should be simple to use, with spaces for teachers and parents to circle or check responses and to write short notes to one another.

Home-school dialogue notebooks offer another form of written communication between parents and teachers (Davern, 2004; Hall, Wolfe, & Bollig, 2003). V. L. Williams and Cartledge (1997) describe a notebook system that a teacher used to communicate regularly with the parents of children with emotional and behavioral disorders. Williams and Cartledge emphasize the importance of being organized, persistent, and flexible in expectations for parent participation.

> I placed a basket near the door. . . . [S]tudents . . . were to put their notebook in the basket before going to breakfast. I would read the parent notes while the students were eating breakfast, and I also used [other] periods. . . . I usually wrote to the parents during the afternoon recess. . . .
>
> [N]ot all parents immediately embraced this communication system. This is where persistence became important. . . . I always tried to respond positively to every parent, and I worked to help them gradually increase their levels of participation. Some parents were comfortable with just signing their names on the notebook to let me know that they had read

my message; some [wrote] . . . about their child's activities during the previous night; and some [shared] . . . special or personal events that they felt would be of significance to their child's schooling. (V. L. Williams & Cartledge, 1997, p. 32)

Home–School Contracts   A home–school contract specifies parent-delivered rewards for the child contingent on her behavior or academic performance in the classroom. For example, M. M. Kerr and Nelson (2006) describe a home–school contract developed by the teacher and parents of a child who interrupted the teacher and disrupted other students during math and social studies classes. The student received a checkmark for each class period that he participated in class discussions instead of disrupting others; when he earned 50 checkmarks, his parents agreed to buy him a gerbil. Home–school contracts use parent-controlled rewards, build in parent recognition and praise of the child's accomplishments, and involve the teacher and parents together in a positive program to support the child's learning.

Class Newsletters and Websites   Class newsletters and websites are additional methods of fostering home–school communication. Although producing a newsletter or designing a website requires a lot of work, it can be worth the effort. Most teachers today have access to a computer and word-processing software. A one- or two-page monthly newsletter can give parents—especially those who do not attend meetings or open houses—information that is too long or detailed to give over the telephone. A newsletter is also an excellent way to recognize parents who participate in various activities. Featuring student-produced stories, photos, and news items in a class newsletter or website transforms a teacher task into an enjoyable and meaningful learning activity for the entire class.

Telephone Communication

Phone Calls to Parents   Regular telephone calls can be an effective and efficient way to maintain home–school communication and parent involvement. A brief conversation that focuses on a child's positive accomplishments lets parents and teachers share the child's success and recognize each other's contributions. Short, positive calls from the teacher also reduce parents' fear that calls from school always indicate a problem. Teachers should set aside time on a regular basis so that each child's parent receives a call at least once every 2 or 3 weeks. Teachers should ask parents what times they prefer to receive calls. Keeping a log helps to maintain the schedule and reminds teachers of any necessary follow-up.

Voice Mail Messages for Parents   Telephone answering machines are a convenient, low-cost technology for home–school communication. By recording daily messages on an answering machine, teachers can give parents a great deal of information for relatively little cost. Parents can call and listen at their convenience, literally 24 hours a day. Recorded telephone messages can provide schoolwide and classroom-by-classroom information, good news (e.g., citizen of the month), serve as a homework hotline (Dardig, 2008), and provide parents with suggestions for working with their children at home (Heward, Heron, Gardner, & Prayzer, 1991). Parent callers can also leave messages on the machine, pose a question, offer an idea or suggestion for the teacher, and so on.

Teachers have developed other strategies for home–school communication in addition to the methods described here (e.g., classroom bulletin board that informs parents and families of upcoming events and curriculum foci [Dardig, 2005, 2008]). Whatever system of home–school communication a school or teacher uses, it should not be "one size fits all families" but tailored to meet each family's needs and preferences (S. K. Stuart et al., 2006, p. 48).

Regardless of the mode of parent–teacher communication or differences in cultural experiences and language backgrounds of the participants, educators should follow the suggestions shown in Figure 3.6 in their interactions with parents and families. Contrast these 10 guidelines with the professional roadblocks to communication described earlier.

Go to the Homework & Exercises section in Chapter 3 of MyEducationLab and complete Homework Exercise 7. As you examine these artifacts, think about the benefits (for both families and teachers) of creating a class newsletter.

A Parent Appreciation Letter

JILL C. DARDIG

Once in a while I receive a thank you note from a student. Sometimes these notes are hand-written; nowadays most are e-mailed. No matter what the mode of transmission, getting one of these letters really makes my day—a little positive recognition goes a long way!

A student's note might thank me for doing a small thing such as writing a reference letter, for taking the time to listen about a problem or challenge with which they are dealing, for teaching a class they really enjoyed, or for helping with something more substantial such as helping them obtain a summer job, teaching position, or another significant matter over the course of their college experience.

Like teaching, parenting can be a challenging and exhausting enterprise, especially when parenting a child whose special needs require extended energy and intensive support. In addition, many parents of children with disabilities have a history of receiving negative or problem-oriented letters and phone calls from school concerning their child. And when they do, these parents may feel that their children's difficulties reflect poorly on them, making their jobs as parents even more stressful.

What can a teacher do to recognize and show appreciation for the efforts, endurance, and successes of parents of children with special needs? A Parent Appreciation Letter, which celebrates their child's achievement, whether big or small, is a wonderful way to tell parents that you share in their joy when their child takes a step forward, and to congratulate them on their contribution to this happy event.

HOW TO GET STARTED

Make a "Special Accomplishments Chart" Set up a "Special Accomplishments Chart" to record special achievements of all of the students in your class on an ongoing basis. Keep the chart on a clipboard or in a notebook in a handy place in your classroom. The chart shown here includes examples of entries by teachers across a range of grade levels.

Student	Accomplishment and Significance	Date	Letter Sent to Parents?
Laura—preschool	Put her coat on without help and quickly while in her wheelchair before recess; this may seem like a small thing, but it's a big step towards her achieving independence and fitting in with her peers.	10/6	Yes, 10/6
Martha—2nd grade	Inserted and kept her hearing aid in and turned on to proper volume every day without reminders; this enables her to comprehend instructions and lesson content; she's on top of everything this week!	10/6	Yes, 10/6
Akeelah—4th grade	Spelling test improvement—earned 100% on advanced grade-level tests 3 weeks in a row in a subject she had been struggling with; she showed motivation and commitment to study every day at school and at home— her regular class teacher noted this progress.	10/6	Not yet
Carlo—7th grade	Orientation & mobility—using his cane, Carlo successfully traveled from resource room to inclusion class on a different floor of the school building by himself; I know he's working on independent travel at home and out in the community; he expressed pride in his accomplishment and has mentioned that he may not need a buddy to accompany him to the restroom and lunchroom anymore!	10/9	Not yet
Lee—8th grade	Social behavior—on several occasions, chose appropriate option (calmly moved on to the next section, came back later to work on difficult problem) when frustrated with written work, then tried again and was successful;	10/15	Yes, 10/15

	politely asked teacher for help on another occasion; also helped a classmate make an appropriate choice; these behaviors will serve him well next year in high school.		
Branden—sophomore in high school	Vocational—at nursing home work-study placement, increased speed and accuracy of serving lunches to residents; served entire floor in a half hour and still had time for some very nice conversations with the residents (they love and appreciate Branden and his nice sense of humor); got a rave review from his supervisor, possible future career?	10/16	Yes, 10/19
Jordan—senior in high school	Excelled in our math unit on handling checking and savings accounts; these skills will be so useful for her in the near future; she expressed an interest in having an actual bank account and learning more about budgeting.	10/16	Not yet

Transform Notes on Chart to Letters Each week or two, select one or more students whose parents will receive a Parent Appreciation Letter. Each letter should state its purpose, identify and provide some interesting detail about the student's achievement, explain the importance of the achievement, thank the parents for helping their child succeed in school, and provide a link between the current accomplishment and future successes. (See the letter, following.)

If you send a Parent Appreciation Letter by surface mail or with the student (rather than by e-mail), don't be surprised if your student tells you that the letter is on the refrigerator door at home for the entire family to enjoy.

To learn more about home–school communication strategies, go to the Building Teaching Skills section in Chapter 3 of MyEducationLab and complete the activities.

Mrs. Stacy Walker
School
Address
Phone and E-mail

Dear Mr. and Mrs. Gonzales,

I want to let you know that Martha has responded so well to our program that teaches her to insert her hearing aid and keep it in place and turned to the correct volume all day.

After several weeks of practice both at school and at home, Martha is now completely independent on this task and does not have to be reminded to do so. The checklist Martha uses every morning and after lunch has allowed her to successfully monitor her own behavior, and I think the reminder should not even be necessary after she is successful for a few more weeks.

For the past few weeks, I have noticed that Martha responds to my instructions immediately, is following oral directions about her schoolwork correctly the first time they are given, and is interacting more with her classmates during small group work and during specials. To a great extent, her progress seems to have eliminated most of her confusion and frustration about what she needs to do while in class and what her classmates are saying to her that she previously misunderstood or missed entirely.

Please keep me informed after Martha's next visit to the audiologist so that I can make any necessary modifications to the use and care of her hearing aid.

Martha is a lovely girl and a delight to have in my class. Thanks for all you have done to work with Martha and me on her "Aid-In" program.

Sincerely,
Mrs. Stacy Walker

Guidelines for communicating with parents

 Council for Exceptional Children Content Standards for Beginning Teachers—Common Core: Foster respectful and beneficial relationships between families and professionals (CC10S3) (also CC1K7 & CC9S7).

FIGURE 3.6	Ten guidelines for communicating with parents and families

1. *Don't assume that you know more about the child, his needs, and how those needs should be met than his parents do.* If you make this assumption, you will usually be wrong and, worse, miss opportunities to obtain and provide meaningful information.

2. *Junk the jargon.* Educators whose speech is laced with technical terminology will have difficulty communicating effectively with parents (or with anyone else, for that matter). Speak in clear, everyday language and avoid the "alphabet soup" of special education (e.g., FAPE, IFSP, MFE).

3. *Don't let assumptions and generalizations about parents and families guide your efforts.* Do not assume a parent is in the *x, y,* or *z* stage of adjustment and therefore needs *a, b,* or *c* type of support or program. If you are genuinely interested in what a father or mother feels and wants, and you should be, ask.

4. *Be sensitive and responsive to the cultural and linguistic backgrounds of parents and families.* The information and support services desired by families from diverse cultural and ethnic groups vary, and majority educators must work to be sensitive to those differences.

5. *Don't be defensive or intimidated.* Unless you are one, you cannot ever really know what being the parent of a child with disabilities is like. But as a trained teacher, you do know something about helping children with disabilities learn. That's your job; it's what you do every day. Offer families the knowledge and skills you have without apology, and welcome their input.

6. *Refer families to other professionals when needed.* As a teacher, you interact with parents and families in an effort to improve the child's educational progress. You are not a marriage counselor, therapist, or financial advisor. If a parent or a family member indicates the need for non–special education services, offer to refer him to professionals and agencies qualified to provide them.

7. *Help parents strive for a realistic optimism.* Children with disabilities and their families benefit little from professionals who are doom-and-gloom types or who minimize the significance of a disability. Help parents analyze, plan, and prepare for their child's future.

8. *Start with something parents can be successful with.* When parents show an interest in helping their child at home, don't set them up to fail by giving them complicated materials, complex instructions, and a heavy schedule of nightly tutoring. Begin with something simple that is likely to be rewarding to the parent and the child.

9. *Respect a parent's right to say no.* Most educators are eager to share what they know and to help families plan and carry out shared teaching goals. But professionals sometimes "fail to recognize the more basic needs of families, one of which is to not need a professional support person! . . . there comes a time when parents and other members of the family wish to be left alone" (J. S. Howard et al., 2005, p. 124).

10. *Don't be afraid to say, "I don't know."* Sometimes parents will ask questions that you cannot answer or request services you cannot provide. The mark of a true professional is knowing the limits of your expertise and when you need help. It is okay to say, "I don't know." Parents will think more highly of you.

OTHER FORMS OF PARENT INVOLVEMENT

Lim's (2008) definition of parent involvement as "any activities that are provided and encouraged by the school and that encourage parents in working on behalf of their children's learning and development" (p. 128) is a good one because it recognizes the wide variety of forms and levels at which parent involvement can occur and focuses on benefits for the child. Parents as tutors, parent education and support groups, and parents as research partners represent three very different types of parent involvement with a common purpose of educational benefits for children.

Parents as Tutors

Typically developing children acquire many skills that children with disabilities do not learn without systematic instruction. For children with disabilities, the casual routines of everyday life at home and in the community may not provide enough practice and feedback to teach them important skills. Many parents of exceptional children have responded to this challenge by systematically teaching their children self-help and daily living skills (e.g., Carothers & Taylor, 2004; Cavkaytar, 2007), assisting their children with homework (J. R. Patton, Jayanthi, & Polloway, 2001), or providing home-based academic tutoring to supplement classroom instruction (Fiedler et al., 2007; Resetar, Noell, & Pellegrin, 2006).

The majority of parents who participate in systematic home tutoring programs organized by their child's teacher or school describe it as a positive experience for them and their children. A mother and father wrote: "We really enjoyed teaching M. to tell time, and he enjoyed working with us. He learned so quickly and we were so happy and proud to see the progress he was making. We have two other children. Doing this program allowed us to spend time alone with M." (Donley & Williams, 1997, p. 50).

Properly conducted home-based parent tutoring can enhance a child's educational progress and give enjoyment to both child and parent. Guidelines for home-based parent tutoring include the following:

- *Keep sessions short.* Aim for 15- to 20-minute sessions 3 or 4 days per week.
- *Make the experience positive.* Parents should praise the child's attempts.
- *Provide frequent opportunities for the child to respond.* Tutoring materials and activities should evoke numerous responses from the child rather than require the child to passively attend to a great deal of explanation and demonstration by the parent.
- *Keep parent responses to the child consistent.* By praising the child's correct responses (materials and activities at the child's appropriate instructional level are a must) and providing a consistent, unemotional response to errors (e.g., "Let's read that word again, together"), parents can prevent the frustration and negative results that can occur when home tutoring is mishandled.
- *Use tutoring to practice and extend skills already learned in school.* For example, parents can use spelling or vocabulary words from school as the questions or items for an adapted board game (Wesson, Wilson, & Higbee Mandelbaum, 1988), and parents can read storybooks to promote literacy skills (e.g., Tardáguila-Harth & Correa, 2007).
- *Keep a record.* Parents, like classroom teachers, can never know the exact effects of their teaching unless they keep records. A daily record enables both parents and child to see gradual progress that might be overlooked if subjective opinion is the only basis for evaluation. Most children do make progress under guided instruction, and a record documents that progress, perhaps providing the parent with an opportunity to see the child in a new and positive light. To read about a home-based parent-tutoring program that illustrates these recommendations, see Teaching & Learning, "A Talking Photo Album Helps Parents With Limited English Proficiency Teach Their Children English."

If parents wish to tutor their children at home, they should be helped to do so. Teachers should recognize, however, that not all parents want to teach their children at home or have the time to learn and use the necessary teaching skills—and professionals must not interpret that situation as an indication that parents do not care enough about their children.

Parents as tutors

Content Standards for Beginning Teachers—Common Core: Assist individuals with exceptional learning needs and their families in becoming active participants in the educational team (CC10S4) (also CC1K7).

Properly conducted, home-based parent tutoring sessions strengthen the child's educational programs and are enjoyable for the child and the parent.

A Talking Photo Album Helps Parents With Limited English Proficiency Teach Their Children English

BY ALLISON G. KRETLOW, SARA M. MACKIEWICZ, CHARLES L. WOOD, JACKLYN V. MIRABAL, AND NANCY L. COOKE

A CHALLENGE FOR TEACHERS AND PARENTS

Ms. Reed, a school psychologist in an elementary school with a growing population of students with limited English proficiency (LEP), faced a great challenge. Several new teachers asked her for guidance in teaching students with LEP. Some of their students had recently moved to the United States and were still learning common English vocabulary words. Ms. Reed knew that increasing students' common English vocabulary would immediately impact their success in the classroom. Typically, teachers ask parents to practice at home the concepts taught at school; however, this approach was not an option because these students' parents were also just beginning to learn English.

Ms. Reed felt frustrated because she knew the parents with LEP were interested in helping their children learn and succeed in school. These parents regularly attended parent–teacher conferences and participated in after school workshops. Ms. Reed needed to find a way for parents to help their children learn without requiring them to be proficient English speakers.

The challenges the parents at Ms. Reed's school faced are not unique, unfortunately. Many parents of students who are not proficient English speakers face similar challenges to providing home support to their children. In particular, studies have demonstrated that Hispanic parents, just like the parents in Ms. Reed's school, face many barriers to helping their children learn English and academics in the home (Klimes-Dougan, Lopez, Nelson, & Adelman, 1992).

Researchers have documented several reasons why these parents have difficulty helping their children learn (C. E. Johnson & Viramontez Anguiano, 2004; Ramirez, 2003). First, many parents of students with LEP are not proficient English speakers themselves, which makes it very difficult for them to interact with their children's teachers, to get involved in school activities, and to help their children develop English vocabulary at home. For example, parents may not be able to read the directions on their children's homework, read or write notes about academic progress, or speak with their children's teachers about ways to help them at home.

Second, many parents with LEP have limited formal education, which, when combined with limited English, increases the parents' difficulty in providing academic support in the home. Though research has shown that parent tutoring can be highly effective (e.g., Resetar et al., 2006), many parents with LEP and limited formal education may not read well in Spanish or English, which limits their adeptness to tutor their children using the typical tutoring materials a teacher might send home (e.g., workbooks, teacher-created materials in English).

Third, parents with LEP may not have access to appropriate materials to help their children learn English (e.g., tutoring programs in Spanish and English, technology). Not only do families with LEP face the difficulty of learning English, they also often face poverty. Though some commercial materials for tutoring exist, many parents do not know they exist, do not know where to get them, or cannot afford to purchase them.

One afternoon while observing a classroom including students with and without special needs, Ms. Reed noticed a student using an assistive technology device called a Talking Photo Album™ (TPA) (Attainment Company, 2007) to communicate with his teacher and peers. Suddenly the idea came to her. "I bet parents could use these at home to tutor their children in English vocabulary."

PARENT TUTORING WITH A TALKING PHOTO ALBUM™

A TPA is a battery-operated recording and playback device that looks like a small picture album. The

Mother and daughter use a Talking Photo Album™ to learn English vocabulary together.

TEACHING & LEARNING

book has 24 pages, and each page contains a recording device that can record up to 10 seconds of audio material. Pushing a button embedded on the edge of each page plays the recorded information. Teachers place pictures into each page by sliding a card into a clear pocket. The parent shows the child a picture, the child says the name of the picture (e.g., "umbrella"), the parent presses the button to hear the recording in English, and the parent provides appropriate feedback (e.g., "yes, umbrella" or "try again").

SUCCESS WITH PARENT TUTORING

Ms. Reed and the teachers were thrilled. Some students learned almost 100 new English vocabulary words in just a few months of parent tutoring with a TPA. But that's not all: The parents acquired many new English words, too. Ms. Reed also learned that her students' siblings, eager to participate, sometimes "chimed in" during home tutoring sessions or played "tutor and tutee" with the materials. This was a great success.

HOW TO GET STARTED

Educators interested in offering a TPA for home-based parent tutoring in English vocabulary will need to prepare the materials, teach parents how to use the materials, and evaluate the success of the program.

1. *Prepare the TPA.* Make a list of vocabulary words commonly found in the classroom, home, and/or community. Target 10 to 12 words at a time to use in the album. Place pictures of targeted vocabulary on each page and match the same pictures on the opposite sides. Make a clear audio recording of the corresponding English and Spanish words on each page. For more details, see Wood, Mackiewicz, Van Norman, and Cooke (2007).

2. *Teach parents how to tutor with a TPA.* Teach parents to use effective tutoring behaviors such as brisk pacing and corrective feedback. Send the prepared TPA home with students. Ask parents to tutor their children at least five times a week. Ask parents to send the TPA back to school at the end of each week.

3. *Evaluate the tutoring program.* Assess each student's mastery of new vocabulary frequently. This can be done using accuracy (i.e., the number of pictures named correctly) or fluency (i.e., the number of pictures named correctly in a preset number of minutes). Measure students' generalization of learned words by testing students to see if they can name the "real thing" (e.g., a refrigerator, a window) represented in the pictures they have learned. Replace cards with new pictures when students demonstrate that they have learned the words. For example, after checking students' progress weekly, replace learned cards with new cards and send any "not yet mastered" cards back home for more practice.

Go to the Homework & Exercises section in Chapter 3 of MyEducationLab and complete Homework Exercise 8. As you watch the video and answer the accompanying questions, compare and contrast the tutoring technique depicted in the video with the TPA tutoring technique discussed here.

Some parents may choose not to do home tutoring because they feel it may compete with other activities in the home and negatively affect their family's overall quality of life (Parette & Petch-Hogan, 2000).

Parent Education and Support Groups

Parent education and parent support groups

 Council for Exceptional Children   Content Standards for Beginning Teachers—Common Core: Concerns of families of individuals with exceptional learning needs and strategies to help address these concerns (CC10K3).

Education for parenting is not new; such programs date back to the early 1800s. Parent education programs can serve a variety of purposes and occur in different formats: from one-time-only events that inform parents of a new school policy, to make-it-and-take-it workshops in which parents make instructional materials to use at home (e.g., a math facts practice game), to multiple-session programs on IEP/IFSP planning or behavior support strategies.

The parent education literature consistently agrees that parents should be involved in planning and conducting parent groups as much as possible (Kroth & Edge, 2007; A. Turnbull et al., 2006). Educators can use both open and closed needs-assessment procedures to determine what parents want from a parent program. An *open needs assessment* consists of questions such as these:

The best family time for my child is when we _____ .
I will never forget the time that my child and I _____ .
When I take my child to the store, I am concerned that she will   .
The hardest thing about having a special child is _____ .
I wish I knew more about   .

A *closed needs assessment* asks parents to select from a list of topics they would like to learn more about. For example, educators can give parents a list of topics (e.g., bedtime behavior, interactions with siblings, homework, making friends, planning for the future) and ask them to check any item that is something of a problem and circle any topic that is a major concern or interest. Figure 3.7 shows a parents' and families' needs and preferences survey that combines open and closed assessment items (Matuszny et al., 2007).

When helping families assess their strengths and needs, professionals should not overlook the importance of leisure time.

Parent-to-Parent Groups

Parent-to-Parent (P2P) programs help parents of children with special needs become reliable allies for one another (Santelli, Poyadue, & Young, 2001). The programs give parents of children with disabilities the opportunity to receive support from a parent who has experienced similar circumstances and challenges. It carefully matches trained and experienced parents in a one-to-one relationship with parents who have been newly referred to the program. "Because the two parents share so many common disability and family experiences, an immediacy of understanding is typically present in the match. This makes the informational and emotional support from the veteran parents all the more meaningful" (Santelli et al., 1997, p. 74). The first Parent-to-Parent program, called Pilot Parents, was formed in 1971 by the parent of a young child with Down syndrome in Omaha, Nebraska. Parent to Parent—USA, a national nonprofit organization committed to ensuring access and quality in Parent-to-Parent support across the country, supports the activities of hundreds of local Parent-to-Parent groups and 36 statewide programs (www.p2pusa.org).

Parents as Research Partners

Researchers in special education are concerned about the social validity of their studies (Carnine, 1997; Horner, Carr, et al., 2005). Are they investigating socially significant variables? Are the methods used to change student performance acceptable? Did the changes observed make any real difference in the child's life? Who better than parents can identify meaningful outcomes, observe and measure performance in the home and community, and let researchers know if their ideas and findings have any real validity?

| FIGURE 3.7 | Sample needs assessment for determining parents'/families' needs and preferences |

Parents'/Family's Needs and Preferences Information Sheet

Parent of _____   Date: _____

Directions: Welcome to *(Name of school)* and *(child's name)* classroom. To help me ensure that your experience this year is a positive one, please fill in the information requested below. Your input will help me understand your preferences for receiving information and attending meetings, and will inform me about how I can better help you understand your child's educational program and progress.

1. **I would like to receive the following information (please check all that apply):**

    _____   How to participate in individual education program (IEP) meetings

    _____   Parents' rights as they pertain to parents of children with disabilities

    _____   How to access community services for children with disabilities

    _____   How to work with my child

    _____   Materials that I can borrow for working with my child

    _____   Information about parent/family support groups

    _____   Information about transition from school to work

    _____   Other: _____

2. ***I hope to receive information about my child (circle *one* choice):**

    Daily   Twice a week   Weekly   Monthly   As needed

    ****Note from the teacher:* I will do my best to meet your needs; however, we may need to discuss our schedules before a commitment is made regarding the frequency for receiving information.**

3. **Other needs that should be considered in planning meetings (please check all that apply):**

    _____   Transportation to IEP meetings that are held at the school

    _____   Meetings held closer to my home

    _____   Child care at the meeting location while I attend meetings held about my child

    _____   Professionals who use understandable language during meetings

    _____   Training on how to work with my child who has disabilities

    _____   A person of the same ethnic background who is trained to provide information about my child who has disabilities

    _____   School staff members who participate in my community (example: showing interest by attending community events, school sports events, etc)

    _____   Other: _____

4. **How would you prefer to receive information from the school about your child? Please number your *top three preferences* in order from most preferred to least preferred, using the numbers 1, 2, and 3; (1 = *most preferred* method and 3 = *least preferred* of your top three choices):**

    _____   Telephone call (Two best times for you to receive a call? _____)

    _____   Please provide your e-mail address: _____

    _____   Written note/letter (*Circle one*: sent in the mail; sent home with child; either)

    _____   Home–school journal (small notebook that is passed on daily, from home to school and school to home)

    _____   Other: _____

continues

FIGURE 3.7 **CONTINUED**

5. **Please answer the following about attending and participating in meetings about your child:**

_____ I will always attend meetings as long as I receive enough notice

_____ I am not comfortable attending meetings at school, but would attend if they are held closer to my home (e.g., at a nearby coffee shop, in your home)

_____ I can always be part of the meeting if a conference call is held

_____ I am unable to attend most/all weekday daytime meetings due to my work schedule, but could attend on the following days/times: _____

6. **In which of the following types of events might you like to participate? (please check all that apply):**

_____ Classroom celebrations

_____ School carnivals

_____ Field trips

_____ Committee member

_____ Sharing information with students (e.g., about your culture, your job, your birthplace)

_____ Other: please list _____

7. **Do you have cultural beliefs and/or concerns that may affect your child's needs or participation in class that you wish us to be aware of? (If yes, please explain):**

Note: This information sheet can be filled out by the parent/family, or with minor adjustments to a few sentences, it can be used as a guide for conducting a telephone interview or face-to-face interview.

Source: Reprinted from Matuszny, R. M., Banda, D. R., & Coleman, T. J. (2007). A progressive plan for building collaborative relations with parents from diverse backgrounds. *Teaching Exceptional Children, 39*(4), pp. 28–29. Used by permission of the Council for Exceptional Children, Reston, VA.

A model research-partnership program conducted at the Fred S. Keller School in New York embraces parents as full partners in conducting action research with their children. "The parents are the scientists, and they conduct empirical studies under the supervision of the schools' parent educators" (Donley & Williams, 1997, p. 46). Parents are assisted in the development of their research projects by their child's teachers, other parents, and a paid parent educator. The experience culminates with a poster session presentation at the end of the school year during which the parent-scientists display the academic, social, and affective gains that their children achieved. Donley and Williams recognize that some school programs do not have the resources to hire a parent educator. They provide several suggestions for schools with more limited resources to approximate their model.

How Much Parent Involvement?

It is easy to get carried away with a good concept, especially one like parent and family involvement, which has so much promise for positive outcomes. But teachers and other professionals who provide special education services to children with disabilities must not take a one-sided, unidirectional view of parent involvement. Sometimes the time and energy required for parents to participate in home-based tutoring programs or parent education groups cause stress among family members or guilt if the parents cannot

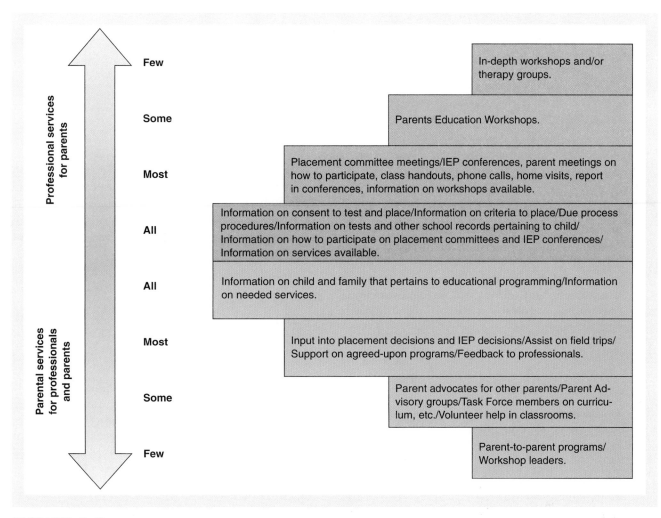

FIGURE 3.8

Mirror model for parent involvement

Source: From Kroth, R. L., & Edge, D. (2007). *Communicating with parents and families of exceptional children* (4th ed.). Denver: Love. Reprinted by permission.

fulfill teachers' expectations (Callahan, Rademacher, & Hildreth, 1998; A. Turnbull et al., 2006). The time required to provide additional help to a child with disabilities may take too much time and attention away from other family members (Parette & Petch-Hogan, 2000).

Kroth and Edge (2007) describe the mirror model for parent involvement (see Figure 3.8), which recognizes that parents have a great deal to offer as well as a need to receive services from special educators. The model attempts to give parents an equal part in deciding what services they need and what services they might provide to professionals or other parents. The top half of the model assumes that professionals have certain information, knowledge, and skills that they should share with parents to help them with their children. The bottom half of the model assumes that parents have information, knowledge, and skills that can help professionals be more effective in assisting children. The model assumes that not all parents need everything that professionals have to offer and that no parent should be expected to provide everything. All parents should be expected to provide and obtain information, most will be active participants in IEP planning, and fewer will participate in or contribute to workshops and extended parent education groups.

Parents and family are the most important people in a child's life. Skilled and caring teachers should be next in importance. Working together, teachers, parents, and families can and do make a difference in the lives of exceptional children.

Mirror model for parent involvement

 Council for Exceptional Children — Content Standards for Beginning Teachers—Common Core: Models and strategies of consultation and collaboration (CC10K1).

TIPS for Beginning Teachers

COLLABORATING WITH PARENTS AND FAMILIES

by Carolyn Crangle and Bethany Maheady

BE AWARE OF AND APPRECIATE YOUR OWN CULTURE

- Educate yourself about your own ethnic background, perceptions, and attitudes.
- Awareness and appreciation of diversity can be acquired by reading, attending classes and/or professional development activities, community involvement, and seeking out direct instructional opportunities with students from diverse backgrounds.

LEARN ABOUT YOUR STUDENTS' CULTURE, LANGUAGE, AND THEIR HOME LIVING ARRANGEMENTS

- Try to create a mutual feeling of trust, open-mindedness, and concern.
- Learn about your students' lives by making home visits.
- Participate in community events that your students' families attend.

LISTEN TO YOUR STUDENTS' PARENTS AND CAREGIVERS—THEY KNOW THEIR CHILDREN WELL AND WANT WHAT IS BEST FOR THEM

- Let parents/caregivers know that you share a common goal—to do what's best for their children—and that if everyone works together, the goal is more likely to be reached.
- Validate the information, feelings, and concerns parents share with you by letting their ideas influence your instructional decision making.

EMPOWER PARENTS AND CAREGIVERS TO BECOME LIFELONG ADVOCATES AND EDUCATIONAL SUPPORTERS FOR THEIR CHILDREN

- Make parents and caregivers aware of their legal rights and responsibilities.

- Provide parents with instructional materials with which they can help their children succeed in school.
- Foster awareness of relevant support services such as translators, school social workers, and relevant advocacy groups.

COMMUNICATE EFFECTIVELY, FREQUENTLY, AND POSITIVELY WITH THE PARENTS

- Verbal and written interactions should be clear, concise, and informative.
- Whenever possible, communicate in the family's native language.
- Use parent-friendly language to communicate early and often: parent–teacher and/or IEP conferences, home–school journals, home notes, Happy Grams, student progress reports, daily/weekly assignment sheets, and report card conferences are all useful tools for effective communication.

COLLABORATION AMONG PARENTS/ CAREGIVERS AND PROFESSIONAL EDUCATORS IS ESSENTIAL

- Instructional roles and responsibilities must be clearly defined.
- All participants must be open-minded and flexible to change.
- Discussions must remain focused on the improvement of pupil outcomes.

KEY TERMS AND CONCEPTS

cultural interpreter, p. 108
cultural reciprocity, p. 108
respite care, p. 95

SUMMARY

Support for Family Involvement

- Three factors are responsible for the increased emphasis on parent and family involvement in the education of children with disabilities: parent advocacy, educators' desire to increase their effectiveness, and legislative mandates.
- A successful parent–teacher partnership provides benefits for the professional, the parents, and, most important, the child.

Understanding Families of Children With Disabilities

- Many parents have reported experiencing similar sequences of emotions and challenges as they reacted and adjusted to the birth or diagnosis of a child with a disability (e.g., shock, denial, grief, reflection, advocacy, appreciation). However, educators should not use any stages of adjustment theory or model as the basis for assuming that an individual parent feels a certain way or has specific needs.
- Parents of children with disabilities fulfill at least nine roles and responsibilities: caregiver, provider, teacher, counselor, behavior support specialist, parent of siblings without disabilities, marriage partner, information specialist/trainer for significant others, and advocate for school and community services.
- A child's disability affects parents and siblings without disabilities in different ways during the different life-cycle stages.
- Respite care—the temporary care of an individual with disabilities by nonfamily members—is a critical support for many families of children with severe disabilities.

Developing and Maintaining Family–Professional Partnerships

- Five principles of effective communication between educators and parents are accepting what is being said, active listening, questioning appropriately, encouraging, and staying focused.
- Attitudes of and behaviors by professionals that serve as barriers to communication with parents and families include making assumptions about the services and information that parents need, treating parents as clients or adversaries instead of partners, keeping professional distance, acting as if parents need counseling, blaming parents for their child's disability or performance, disrespecting parents' suggestions, and labeling parents who don't act the way the professional believes they should.
- Dialoguing is an approach to conflict resolution in which both parties try to see each other's point of view.

Working With Culturally and Linguistically Diverse Families

- Differences in the cultural beliefs and linguistic practices of professionals and families often serve as barriers to parent involvement.
- Cultural interpreters help school personnel understand the home culture and help the family understand school culture, policies, and practices.
- Understanding differences between our own perspectives and those of people from other cultures and ethnic groups requires careful examination of our own cultural background and belief system.

Home–School Communication Methods

- The most common modes of home–school communication are parent-teacher conferences, written messages, and telephone calls. Teachers are using class newsletters, websites, and e-mail to communicate with families with increasing frequency and effectiveness.
- Ten guidelines for communicating with parents of children with disabilities:
  - Don't assume you know more about a child than the parents do.
  - Junk the jargon, and speak in plain, everyday language.
  - Don't let assumptions or generalizations guide your efforts.
  - Be sensitive and responsive to cultural and linguistic differences.
  - Don't be defensive toward or intimidated by parents.
  - Refer families to other professionals when needed.
  - Help parents strive for a realistic optimism.
  - Start with something that parents can be successful with.
  - Allow and respect parents' right to say no.
  - Don't be afraid to say, "I don't know."

Other Forms of Parent Involvement

- Many parents can help teach their child with disabilities.
- Parents and professionals should work together in planning and conducting parent education groups.
- Parent-to-Parent groups provide new parents of children with disabilities support from parents who have experienced similar circumstances and challenges.
- Parents who serve as research partners help brainstorm research questions, collect performance data on their children, and share those data with other parents and teachers.
- The mirror model of parent involvement assumes that not all parents need everything that professionals have to offer and that no parent should be expected to participate in every form of school involvement.

 Now go to MyEducationLab at www.myeducationlab.com, and take the Pretest to assess your initial comprehension of chapter content. Once you have taken the Pretest, use your individualized Study Plan for Chapter 3 to enhance your understanding of the concepts discussed in the chapter. Finally, take the Posttest to assess your comprehension of Chapter 3 content.

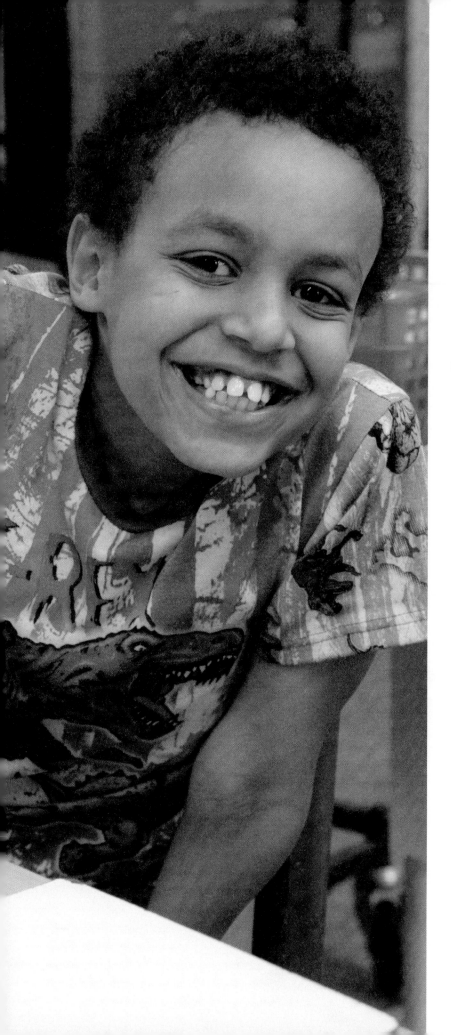

PART II
Educational Needs of Exceptional Students

4 Intellectual Disabilities

5 Learning Disabilities

6 Emotional or Behavioral Disorders

7 Autism-Spectrum Disorders

8 Communication Disorders

9 Deafness and Hearing Loss

10 Blindness and Low Vision

11 Physical Disabilities, Health Impairments, and ADHD

12 Low-Incidence Disabilities: Severe/Multiple Disabilities, Deaf-Blindness, and Traumatic Brain Injury

13 Giftedness and Talent

4

Intellectual Disabilities

- What can be gained by classifying a child with intellectual disabilities by the intensities of supports she needs to access and benefit from education?
- What is most important in determining a person's level of adaptive functioning: intellectual capability or a supportive environment?
- How are the characteristics of students with intellectual disabilities relevant to planning and delivering instruction?
- What factors might account for the wide differences in the prevalence of mental retardation within the school-age population reported by the states?
- Why has the prevention of mental retardation proven so difficult?
- What should curriculum goals for students with intellectual disabilities emphasize?
- What are the most important features of effective instruction for students with intellectual disabilities?
- What is needed to make education for a student with intellectual disabilities appropriate in a general education classroom?

FEATURED TEACHER

SANDIE TRASK-TYLER
Blendon Middle School • Westerville, Ohio

Sandie Trask-Tyler

Education—Teaching Credentials—Experience
- B.S., special education, Ohio Dominican University, 1983
- M.A., special education and applied behavior analysis, The Ohio State University, 1989
- Ohio developmental handicaps, K–12; multiple handicaps, K–12
- 23 years of teaching: first 6 years at the Ohio State School for the Blind teaching secondary students with visual impairments and mental retardation

Current Teaching Position and Students The eight sixth, seventh, and eighth graders in my self-contained classroom have a wide range of abilities and educational needs associated with mild to-severe mental retardation. Most have additional disabilities, such as communication disorders or physical and motor problems, and usually remain with me in my classroom throughout their middle school years. Each student receives individualized instruction and supports in self-help and daily-living skills, social and communication skills, and functional academics.

Classroom Support The students spend most of the school day in my classroom working on both individualized lessons and group activities. Two aides help me with instructional activities and accompany students when they attend general education classes such as art, physical education, and music. The aides implement behavior interventions, provide student instruction, and collect data. A speech-language therapist, an occupational therapist, and a physical therapist team with me on classroom activities and contribute their expertise to promote student success and independence. This year I am collaborating with seventh-grade science and social studies teachers to include my students in hands-on activities in their classrooms and complete a service-learning project together. I also modified course material to cover topic areas that my students would be able to work on independently. Each student spends about 15 minutes a day with a reading buddy, an eighth grader without disabilities who shares activities such as reading flash cards or curriculum content and/or completing reading worksheets. This is a wonderful social and learning opportunity for all participants.

Functional Curriculum My job is to prepare students for life in their community and eventual transition into the real world. All of my students have individualized daily schedule checklists on their desks that list various activities to be completed. The students' individualized education program (IEP) goals provide the foundation for all of the instruction that occurs in the classroom. To evaluate student performance, I keep a notebook for each student indexed by subject area that includes a data collection sheet for each IEP goal and objective. To track lesson implementation, I check off the dates we work on each student objective in the class attendance book. This helps me quickly identify which IEP goals we have or have not worked on each day.

Go to the Homework & Exercises section in Chapter 4 of MyEducationLab and complete Homework Exercise 1. As you watch the video and answer the accompanying questions, think about how a well-organized classroom can enhance classroom instruction.

Within each curricular area, I target functional activities and skills that will facilitate each student's independence. Math skills include recognizing coin values, counting money, purchasing skills, calculator skills, telling time, interpreting charts and calendars, and measurement skills using rulers, yardsticks, and measuring cups and spoons. Students work on various reading and writing activities in language arts. For reading, I usually select the Edmark Functional Sight Word Series, which includes four 100-word sets of fast food/restaurant words, grocery words, community signs, and job/work-related words. Some students also use the Edmark Reading Milestones Series, which allows them to read stories at their own reading level and complete workbook pages. Writing activities include completing a note to go home, creating shopping lists, writing their home address, filling out various forms, and completing modified book reports.

Science lessons focus on concepts that will increase students' understanding, enjoyment, and everyday functioning of the physical world in which we live. I do lessons on weather and temperature, plant identification and growth, equipment use and safety, and animal care. The students conduct hands-on experiments, which they can apply to everyday life such as substituting ingredients in recipes. Skills in social studies include reading maps and understanding directions; recognizing different cultures; and identifying government figures, facts, and symbols. To develop vocational skills and work-related experience, each student is responsible for at least one classroom job every day. The students deliver mail, fill the pop machine, recycle paper and pop cans, water plants, answer the telephone, collate and staple papers, sort and wrap coins, and shred paper. I emphasize the importance of starting and completing real-work activities independently. These jobs integrate a variety of skills such as counting, independent travel around the school building, getting and putting away supplies, using appropriate social greetings, and other interpersonal skills.

During group lessons, I always make sure each student has his own materials so everyone can respond and practice together. Repetition with feedback is my primary teaching strategy. We practice skills over and over and work on generalizing across settings, staff, materials, and situations. I plan classroom activities that integrate many curricular areas so students can practice their skills in a more natural context. One of their favorite activities is food preparation. I create recipes that use various sight words, kitchen vocabulary, equipment, and measurements. Students must use their safety skills and their social skills to communicate with one another when sharing ingredients. Food preparation is a wonderful way to work on fine-motor skills, the use of both hands, and/or midline crossing in a functional activity. Before the cooking activity, students write out their shopping lists, look through a grocery circular to find needed items, and shop for the items. At the store, students work on reading their shopping lists, writing down prices, unloading carts, and paying for their groceries.

Our class auction is another activity that provides a fun and meaningful opportunity to practice a variety of skills. I videotaped an actual auction and then had the auctioneer visit our classroom to talk about his job. We then practiced bidding as we would at an auction. I developed a classroom reinforcement program using the auction concept. Students earn classroom money for completing homework, completing jobs, and getting "caught being good." At the end of each week, we hold an auction where students can bid on items of interest. The skills that students work on during this activity include withdrawing and depositing money into their savings accounts. Students who have difficulty writing can use deposit, withdrawal, date, and number stamps. Students also work on calculator skills, writing skills, money-management skills (e.g., "Do I have enough money to bid?"), and group-interaction skills. It's very exciting to watch the students learn about handling money.

Our service-learning project this year included working with other seventh-grade students to learn about growing plants and sharing them with residents of a local nursing home. We learned about different types of flowers and vegetables and conducted a science experiment growing seeds in different types of soil.

Each student picked a seed they wanted to follow as it sprouted and grew and was responsible for planting, watering, measuring and recording data on their plant's growth. Students entered their data into the computer and graphed growth of their flowers, vegetables, and herbs. As the plants were growing, students created and decorated clay pots. They also designed gift tags using their writing and word-processing skills. When the plants were mature, we walked to a nearby nursing home and gave the residents plants in our handmade pots. We also planted the vegetable and herb plants in a separate garden area so the residents could enjoy fresh tomatoes and cucumbers. This was an awesome activity that integrated community service, student cooperation and teamwork, science activities, language arts skills, creativity, and math skills.

Communicating With Parents   Parents know they can call or e-mail me anytime at school or home. We are fortunate to have a phone in our classroom so students can practice their telephone skills. They get excited when they answer the phone and a parent is on the other end. We have a weekly class newsletter to which every student contributes at least one article per week. Each issue includes digital photos of the students at work in the classroom and a description of activities for the upcoming week. All students take home and receive an e-mail copy of the newsletter, and I e-mail it to other teachers and related-service specialists. I also organize a monthly family-out-to-eat night at local restaurants so students and families can socialize.

What I Like Best About Being a Special Education Teacher   The best part of my job is having the ability to create fun activities that provide meaningful practice of learned skills and develop new ones. A class necklace business has been a wonderful activity to incorporate many students' IEP goals and objectives into a functional outcome. We live in "Buckeye Country," where a lot of people are avid fans of The Ohio State University Buckeyes. As a class activity several years ago, my students made Buckeye necklaces to wear during the football season. When other teachers started asking us to make necklaces for them and their friends, a class business was born! This project allows students at all ability levels to participate. It is exciting to watch the students build skills and self-esteem through making and selling their product. The students take turns performing different jobs such as production manager, marketing manager, and quality-control manager. As a result, they learn about the process of buying the materials needed, producing the product, and selling the product. The students manage the money for expenses and decide how to use the profits.

A consultant colleague says he never knows what he'll see next in my classroom. He mentions the "campsite," a tent one student uses as a quiet retreat from the busy classroom; the "vending machine," where students can buy a treat with classroom money they've earned; the claw-foot "bathtub" where students can relax and read or complete independent work; and the "Barnes and Noble area," a student-created nook where they can sit in soft chairs with a drink and read and/or listen to books on tape, CDs, or vintage Elvis records. His praise challenges me to think of other ways to enhance my classroom environment to better support the needs and interests of my students.

The 200-year history of special education as a field is deeply rooted in the education and treatment of people with mental retardation. In the United States, the first public school special education classes were for children with intellectual disabilities. And the first federal legislation in support of special education provided funds for training professionals to prepare teachers for children with mental retardation.

When they hear the words "special education," many people think of children with mental retardation—a disability increasingly being referred to with the term *intellectual disabilities.* In 2007, the American Association on Mental Retardation, the leading professional organization concerned with the study, treatment, and prevention of mental retardation, changed its name to the American Association on Intellectual and Developmental Disabilities (AAIDD). Consistent with the practice of most special educators today, this text uses the terms *mental retardation* and *intellectual disabilities* interchangeably, except for instances where the terminology itself is being discussed.

Most people have a notion of what mental retardation is and what people with mental retardation are like. Unfortunately, much of that awareness consists of misconceptions, oversimplifications, and fear. For example, undergraduate special education majors recorded everyday remarks about mental retardation made by people outside the university; following is a typical statement:

> After telling a fellow waitress about her career plans to teach children labeled as having mental retardation, . . . her co-worker's response was, "Why would you want to teach children who cannot learn?" (Danforth & Navarro, 1998, p. 36)

In spite of misguided and negative perceptions held by some, persons with intellectual disabilities are increasingly enjoying the benefits and responsibilities of participating in the educational and societal mainstream. This chapter presents some key factors in understanding

 After reading this chapter, complete the Pretest for Chapter 4 on MyEducationLab to assess your initial understanding for chapter content.

the complex concept of mental retardation. It also looks at some contemporary instructional practices that have improved educational outcomes for students with mental retardation.

DEFINITIONS AND CLASSIFICATION SYSTEMS

Various terms for and definitions of mental retardation have been proposed, adopted, and debated over the years (Goodey, 2005; Trent, 1994). First, we will look at the traditional and still most commonly used approach to defining and classifying mental retardation, one based primarily on the assessment of intellectual functioning. Then we will examine the most recent conception of intellectual disabilities, which is based on the level of supports person needs to function effectively.

Definitions of MR

 Council for Exceptional Children

Content Standards for Beginning Teachers of Students with MR/DD: Definitions and issues related to the identification of individuals with MR/DD (MR1K1).

IDEA Definition of Mental Retardation

In 1973, the American Association on Mental Retardation (AAMR) published a definition that, with minor rewording, was incorporated into the Individuals with Disabilities Education Act (IDEA) and continues to serve today as the basis by which most states identify children for special education services under the disability category of mental retardation. In IDEA, **mental retardation** is defined as "significantly subaverage general intellectual functioning existing concurrently with deficits in adaptive behavior and manifested during the developmental period that adversely affects a child's educational performance" (34 C.F.R., Sec. 3000. 7[b][5]).

The definition specifies three criteria for a diagnosis of mental retardation. First, "significant subaverage intellectual functioning" must be demonstrated. The word *significant* refers to a score of ≥2 standard deviations below the mean on a standardized intelligence test (a score of approximately 70 or less; IQ testing is discussed later in the chapter). Second, an individual must be well below average in both intellectual functioning and adaptive behavior; that is, intellectual functioning is not the sole defining criterion. Third, the deficits in intellectual functioning and adaptive behavior must occur during the developmental period to help distinguish mental retardation from other disabilities (e.g., impaired intellectual performance due to traumatic brain injury). The requirement "that adversely affects a child's educational performance" is automatically met when a child exhibits substantial limitations in intellectual functioning and adaptive behavior.

Which student has intellectual disabilities? The terms *mental retardation* and *intellectual disabilities* identify substantial limitations in functioning: not something inherent within the individual.

Persons with mental retardation have traditionally been classified by the degree or level of intellectual impairment as measured by an IQ test. The most widely used classification system consists of four levels of mental retardation according to the range of IQ scores shown in Table 4.1. The range of scores at the low and high ends of each level represents

TABLE 4.1

Classification of mental retardation by IQ score

LEVEL	INTELLIGENCE TEST SCORE
Mild	50–55 to approximately 70
Moderate	35–40 to 50–55
Severe	20–25 to 35–40
Profound	Below 20–25

Source: Based on the *AAMR's Classification of Mental Retardation* (Grossman, 1983) and the *Diagnostic and Statistical Manual of Mental Disorders (DSM-IV-TR)* (American Psychiatric Association, 2000).

the inexactness of intelligence testing and highlights the importance of clinical judgment in diagnosis and classification.

For many years, students with mental retardation in the public schools were classified as either *educable mentally retarded (EMR)* or *trainable mentally retarded (TMR).* These terms referred to mild and moderate levels of disability, respectively. This two-level classification system did not include children with severe and profound mental retardation, because they were often denied a public education and were likely to reside in a state-operated institution. Most special educators consider the terms EMR and TMR to be archaic and inappropriate because they suggest predetermined achievement limits (Beirne-Smith, Patton, & Kim, 2006).

AAIDD's Definition Based on Needed Supports

In 1992, the AAMR published a system for diagnosing and classifying mental retardation that represented a conceptual shift from viewing mental retardation as an inherent trait or permanent condition to a description of an individual's functioning in the context of his present environment and the supports needed to improve it. That definition was revised slightly in 2002 and, with replacement of the term *mental retardation* with *intellectual disability,* reads as follows:

> Intellectual disability is a disability characterized by significant limitations in both intellectual functioning and in adaptive behavior as expressed in conceptual, social, and practical adaptive skills. This disability originates before age 18. (Luckasson et al., 2002, p. 1)

The AAIDD's Committee on Terminology and Classification has identified the following five assumptions as essential to understanding and appropriately applying the definition:

1. Limitations in present functioning must be considered within the context of community environments typical of the individual's age peers and culture.
2. Valid assessment considers cultural and linguistic diversity as well as differences in communication, sensory, motor, and behavioral factors.
3. Within the individual, limitations often coexist with strengths.
4. The purpose of describing limitations is to develop a profile of needed supports.
5. With appropriate personalized supports over a sustained period, the life functioning of the person with intellectual disability generally will improve. (Luckasson et al., 2002, p. 1)

The definition is based on the theoretical model shown in Figure 4.1. Five factors that influence human functioning are listed in the left column. The center and right side of the figure "depict the essential mediational role that supports play between the multidimensional aspects of MR/ID and individual functioning" (Schalock, Buntinx, et al., 2007, p. 7). The AAIDD defines supports as "resources and strategies that aim to promote the development, education, interests, and personal well-being of a person and that enhance individual functioning" (Luckasson et al., 2002, p. 15).

AAIDD

Council for Exceptional Children — Content Standards for Beginning Teachers of Students With MR/DD: Organizations and publications in the field of MR/DD (MR9K1).

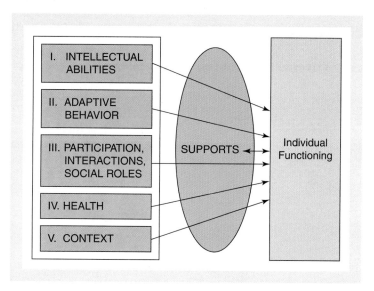

FIGURE 4.1

Theoretical model for the AAIDD's definition of mental retardation/ intellectual disabilities

Source: Mental Retardation: Definition, Classification, and Systems of Supports by Ruth A. Luckasson. Copyright 2002 by American Association on Intellectual Developmental Disabilities. Reproduced with permission of American Association on Intellectual Developmental Disabilities in the formats Textbook and Other Book via Copyright Clearance Center.

Supports needed by a student with intellectual disabilities are identified as part of the IEP process. For adults, an interdisciplinary team can use the AAIDD's Supports Intensity Scale to develop a profile of the types and intensity of needed supports within each of five dimensions: intellectual abilities; adaptive behavior (conceptual, practical, social skills); participation, interactions, and social roles; health (physical health, mental health, etiologic factors); and context (environments, culture, and opportunities) (J. R. Thompson et al., 2004).

The AAIDD definition, called the "2002 System," provides conceptual and procedural recommendations for functionally classifying mental retardation according to an individual's profile of needed supports. This approach represents a change from classifying mental retardation on the basis of estimates of an individual's intellectual deficiencies to estimating the intensities of supports needed to improve functioning in her school, home, community, and work environments. The AAIDD classifies needed supports at four levels of intensities: intermittent, limited, extensive, and pervasive (ILEP) (see Table 4.2).

The AAIDD's System 2002 definition has been the subject of considerable debate and criticism by a number of well-respected professionals in the field of mental retardation (e.g., Greenspan, 2006; J. W. Jacobson, Mulick, & Rojahn, 2007; MacMillan, Siperstein, & Leffert, 2006). Among the concerns expressed by these authors are the following:

- IQ testing will remain a primary (and in practice perhaps the only) means of diagnosis.
- Adaptive skills cannot be reliably measured with current assessment methods.
- The levels of needed supports are too subjective.

ILEP classification system

Council for Exceptional Children: Content Standards for Beginning Teachers of Students With MR/DD: Relate levels of support to the needs of the individual (MR3S1) (also CC2K2).

TABLE 4.2

Definitions of intensities of supports for individuals with intellectual disabilities

Intermittent	Supports on an "as needed basis." Characterized by episodic nature, person not always needing the support(s), or short-term supports needed during life-span transitions (e.g., job loss or an acute medical crisis). Intermittent supports may be high or low intensity when provided.
Limited	An intensity of supports characterized by consistency over time, time-limited but not of an intermittent nature, may require fewer staff members and less cost than more intense levels of support (e.g., time-limited employment training or transitional supports provided during the school to adult period).
Extensive	Supports characterized by regular involvement (e.g., daily) in at least some environments (such as work or home) and not time-limited (e.g., long-term support and long-term home living support).
Pervasive	Supports characterized by their constancy and high intensity; provided across environments; potential life-sustaining nature. Pervasive supports typically involve more staff members and intrusiveness than do extensive or time-limited supports.

Source: Mental Retardation: Definition, Classification, and Systems of Supports by Ruth A. Luckasson. Copyright 2002 by American Association on Intellectual Developmental Disabilities. Reproduced with permission of American Association on Intellectual Developmental Disabilities in the formats Textbook and Other Book via Copyright Clearance Center.

- Classification will remain essentially unchanged in practice because the four intensities of supports—intermittent, limited, extensive, and pervasive—will simply replace the four levels of retardation based on IQ scores—mild, moderate, severe, and profound.

The Evolving Definition of Mental Retardation/Intellectual Disabilities

Over the past four decades, the conception of mental retardation has undergone numerous changes in terminology, IQ score cutoffs, and the relative role of adaptive functioning (see Schalock, Luckasson, & Shogren, 2007, for a review). Each of the changes has reflected an ongoing attempt to better understand mental retardation/intellectual disabilities (MR/ID), and to achieve more effective and reliable methods of identification, classification, research, and habilitation.

In an article explaining the AAIDD's shift to the term **intellectual disabilities,** Schalock, Luckasson, and Shogren (2007) noted that:

> This term [intellectual disabilities] covers the same population of individuals who were diagnosed previously with mental retardation in number, kind, level, type, and duration of the disability and the need of people with this disability for individualized services and supports. Furthermore, every individual who is or was eligible for a diagnosis of mental retardation is eligible for a diagnosis of intellectual disability. (p. 116)

If the two terms refer to the same disability and group of people, one might reasonably ask what purpose changing the name serves. According to Schalock, Luckasson, and colleagues (2007), the term *intellectual disability* (a) reflects current professional practices that focus on functional behaviors and contextual factors; (b) provides a logical basis for providing individualized supports due to its social-ecological framework; (c) is less offensive to persons with disabilities; and (d) is more consistent with international terminology.

In an essay arguing that the term *mental retardation* has outlived its usefulness and is an inappropriate, misleading, and often harmful term that has been used to refer to a very heterogeneous group of people who have greater differences among them than similarities, J. D. Smith (2006) argued that

> The term has been used to describe a vast aggregation of diverse human circumstances. The only rationale for this aggregation appears to be the reasoning that the category contains people with intellectual, social, and developmental traits that make them more alike than different. This is simply not the case. Many persons called mentally retarded are more different than they are alike. A person who is described as having a need for *intermittent* support will almost certainly be more similar to a person without mental retardation than to a person who is described as having mental retardation and a *pervasive* need for support. (p. 172)

Haywood (2006) has argued that a diagnosis of mental retardation be applied only to "those persons who now are regarded as severely and profoundly mentally retarded, and perhaps some portion of the moderate category" (p. xvii). Indeed, some children are so clearly and consistently behind their peers in academic, social, language, and self-care skills that it is obvious to anyone who interacts with them that they require special education and related services. How MR/ID is defined is not much of an issue for these children; they experience pervasive and substantial limitations in all or most areas of development and functioning. But this group is only a small portion of the total population of persons with mental retardation. The largest segment consists of school-age children with mild intellectual disabilities. How MR/ID is defined determines what special educational services many thousands of children are eligible (or ineligible) to receive.

Thus, disagreements among professionals over what constitutes mental retardation are much more than academic exercises or philosophical debates. A subtle difference between

Although Emily needs extensive supports in some areas of life functioning, she needs only limited supports in other areas.

Continuing debate and evolution of definition of MR

Content Standards for Beginning Teachers of Students With MR/DD: Trends and practices within the field of MR/DD (MR1K5) (also CC1K5).

two definitions can determine whether the diagnosis of mental retardation or intellectual disabilities is associated with a particular person and whether or not schools provide appropriate educational supports (Gross & Hahn, 2004; Perske, 2005; Scullin, 2006; Stowe, Turnbull, & Sublet, 2006).

The debate over the definition and terminology will surely continue. But regardless of the term used to identify the combination of intellectual and adaptive behavior limitations currently known as mental retardation—or even if society decides not to identify and name it—substantial challenges in learning and independence constitute a real disability for the children and adults who experience them. And helping individuals with disabilities achieve to their fullest potential is what special education is all about.

IDENTIFICATION AND ASSESSMENT

Assessing Intellectual Functioning

When educators assess a child's intellectual functioning as part of a multifactored evaluation, a school psychologist or other trained professional administers an intelligence (IQ) test. An IQ test consists of a series of questions (e.g., vocabulary, similarities), problem solving (e.g., mazes, block designs), memory, and other tasks assumed to require certain degrees of intelligence to answer or solve correctly (Venn, 2007). Educators use the child's performance on those items to derive a score representing her intelligence.

IQ tests are standardized tests; that is, the same questions and tasks are always presented in a certain, specified way with the same scoring procedures used each time the test is administered. IQ tests are also norm-referenced tests. During its development, a **norm-referenced test** is administered to a large sample of people selected at random from the population for whom the test is intended. Developers then use test scores of persons in the norming sample to represent how scores on the test are generally distributed throughout that population.

IQ scores seem to be distributed throughout the population according to a phenomenon called the *bell-shaped curve,* or **normal curve,** shown in Figure 4.2. A mathematical concept called the **standard deviation** describes how a particular score varies from the mean, or average score, of all the scores in the norm sample. Test developers apply an algebraic formula to the scores achieved by the norm sample on a test to determine what

Standardized tests, norm-referenced tests, the normal curve, and standard deviation

Content Standards for Beginning Teachers of Students With MR/DD: Specialized terminology used in the assessment of individuals with MR/DD (MR8K1) (also CC8K1).

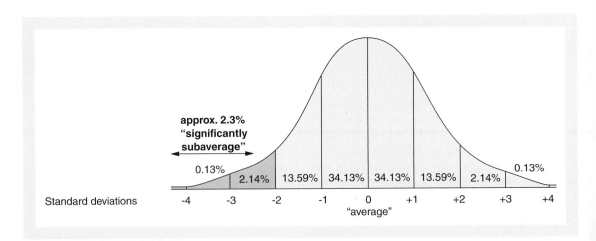

FIGURE 4.2

Theoretical distribution of IQ scores on the normal curve

value equals 1 standard deviation for that test. A child's IQ test score can then be described in terms of how many standard deviations above or below the mean it is. Theoretically, an equal number of people score above and below the mean, and about 2.3% of the population falls ≥2 standard deviations below the mean, which the AAIDD calls "significantly subaverage."

According to the AAIDD, a diagnosis of MR/ID requires an IQ score approximately 2 standard deviations below the mean, which is approximately 70 or below on the two most widely used intelligence tests, the Wechsler Intelligence Scale for Children (WISC-IV) (Wechsler, 2003) and the Stanford-Binet Intelligence Scales (Roid, 2003). The IQ cutoff score of 70 is intended only as a guideline and should not be interpreted as a hard-and-fast requirement (Luckasson et al., 2002; Schalock, Buntinx, et al., 2007). A higher IQ score of 75 or more may also be associated with mental retardation if, according to a clinician's judgment, the child exhibits deficits in adaptive behavior thought to be caused by impaired intellectual functioning.

Although IQ tests have been widely criticized, they can provide useful information. IQ scores are particularly useful for objectively identifying an overall performance deficit and have proven to be a strong predictor of school achievement. Because IQ tests are composed largely of verbal and academic tasks—the same things a child must master to succeed in school—they correlate highly with school achievement.

Even though the major intelligence tests are among the most carefully constructed and researched psychological assessment instruments available, they are still far from perfect and have both advantages and disadvantages. Following are several additional important considerations (Overton, 2006; Salvia, Ysseldyke, & Bolt, 2007; Venn, 2007):

- *The concept of intelligence is a hypothetical construct.* No one has ever seen a thing called intelligence; it is not a precise entity but something we infer from observed performance. We assume it takes more intelligence to perform some tasks at a given age than it does to perform others.

- *An IQ test measures only how a child performs at one point in time on the items included on the test.* An IQ test samples only a small portion of an individual's skills and abilities; we infer from that performance how a child might perform in other situations.

- *A person's IQ score can change significantly.* IQ scores can change, particularly in the 70–85 range that formerly constituted borderline retardation. Hence, observers are hesitant to give a diagnosis of mental retardation on the basis of an IQ score that might increase after a period of intensive, systematic intervention.

- *Intelligence testing is not an exact science.* Among the many variables that can affect a person's IQ score are motivation, the time and location of the test, inconsistency or bias by the test administrator in scoring responses that are not precisely covered by the test manual, which IQ test was selected, and which edition of that test was used. Because each of the widely used IQ tests measures a child's performance on a different set of tasks, when "an IQ score appears in isolation we must ask the question, 'IQ as measured by which test?'" (Venn, 2007, p. 145). IQ scores on the Wechsler series of intelligence tests increased steadily during the 20th century at a rate of about .3 IQ points per year (Flynn, 1987, 1998; Kanaya, Scullin, & Ceci, 2003). This rise, known at the "Flynn effect," has been masked by the periodic renorming of IQ tests to reset the mean at 100 (Flynn, 2000; Scullin, 2006).

- *Intelligence tests can be culturally biased.* The Binet and Wechsler IQ tests tend to favor children from the population on which they were normed—primarily white, middle-class children. Some of the questions may tap learning that only a middle-class child is likely to have experienced. Both the Binet and Wechsler, which are highly verbal, are especially inappropriate for children for whom English is a second language (Venn, 2007).

- *An IQ score should never be used as the sole basis for making a decision on the provision or denial of special education services.* An IQ score contributes just one component of a multifactored, nondiscriminatory assessment.

IQ scores and diagnosis of MR

 Council for Exceptional Children   Content Standards for Beginning Teachers of Students With MR/DD: Definitions and issues related to the identification of individuals with MR/DD (MR1K1).

Issues to consider with IQ tests/scores

 Council for Exceptional Children   Content Standards for Beginning Teachers—Common Core: Uses and limitations of assessment instruments (CC8K4).

- *An IQ score should not be used to determine educational objectives or design instruction.* Results of teacher-administered, criterion-referenced assessments of a student's performance of curriculum-specific skills are generally more useful for planning what to teach.

Assessing Adaptive Behavior

Adaptive behavior is "the collection of conceptual, social, and practical skills that have been learned by people in order to function in their everyday lives" (Luckasson et al., 2002, p. 73). The systematic assessment of adaptive behavior is important for reasons beyond the diagnosis of mental retardation. The adaptive skills exhibited by a person with intellectual disabilities—as well as the nature and severity of maladaptive behaviors—are critical factors in determining the supports a student requires for success in school, work, community, and home environments (Schalock, 1999; J. R. Thompson et al., 2004). A number of instruments for assessing adaptive behavior have been developed. Most consist of a series of questions that a person familiar with the individual, such as a teacher, parent, or caregiver, answers.

AAMR Adaptive Behavior Scale   A frequently used instrument for assessing adaptive behavior by school-age children is the AAMR Adaptive Behavior Scale—School (ABS-S:2) (Lambert, Nihira, & Leland, 1993). The ABS-S:2 consists of two parts. Part 1 contains 10 domains related to independent functioning and daily living skills (e.g., eating, toilet use, money handling, numbers, time); Part 2 assesses the individual's level of maladaptive (inappropriate) behavior in seven areas (e.g., trustworthiness, self-abusive behavior, social engagement). Another form, the ABS-RC:2, assesses adaptive behavior in residential and community settings (Nihira, Leland, & Lambert, 1993).

Vineland Adaptive Behavior Scales   The Vineland Adaptive Behavior Scales are available in three versions. The Interview Editions in Survey Form or Expanded Form are administered by an individual who is very familiar with the person being assessed, such as a parent, teacher, or a direct caregiver (Sparrow, Balla, & Cicchetti, 2005).

Scales of Independent Behavior—Revised   Educators can use the Scales of Independent Behavior—Revised (SIB-R) (Bruninks, Woodcock, Weatherman, & Hill, 1996) to measure adaptive behavior of individuals ranging in age from infancy to 80+ years. The SIB-R's 14 subscales (e.g., social interaction, eating and meal preparation, money and value) take 45 to 60 minutes to administer in a structured interview or checklist format. The SIB-R also includes eight optional problem behavior subscales.

Measurement of adaptive behavior has proven difficult in large part because of the relative nature of social adjustment and competence: Actions that may be considered appropriate in one situation or by one group may not be in another situation or by another group (Schalock, 1999). No universal agreement exists concerning exactly which adaptive behaviors all of us should exhibit. As with IQ tests, cultural bias can be a problem in adaptive behavior scales; for instance, one item on some scales requires a child to tie a laced shoe, but some children have never had a shoe with laces. Ongoing research on the measurement of adaptive behavior may help resolve these problems.

CHARACTERISTICS

Mental retardation is seldom a time-limited condition. Although some children with mental retardation make tremendous advancements in adaptive skills (some to the point of functioning independently and no longer being considered under any disability category), most are affected throughout their life span (Beadle-Brown, Murphy, & Wing, 2005; Bernheimer, Keogh, & Guthrie, 2006; Hawkins, Eklund, James, & Foose, 2003).

Many children with mild intellectual disabilities are not identified until they enter school, and some not until they reach the second or third grade, when more difficult academic work is required. Most students with mild mental retardation master academic skills up to about the sixth-grade level and can learn job skills well enough to support themselves independently or semi-independently.

Children with moderate intellectual disabilities show significant delays in development during their preschool years. As they grow older, discrepancies in overall intellectual development and adaptive functioning generally grow wider between these children and age-matched peers without disabilities. People with moderate mental retardation are more likely to have health and behavior problems than are individuals with mild retardation.

Individuals with severe and profound intellectual disabilities are almost always identified at birth or shortly afterward. Most of these infants have significant central nervous system damage, and many have additional disabilities and/or health conditions (Heikua et al., 2005). Although IQ scores can serve as the basis for differentiating severe and profound retardation from one another, the difference is primarily one of functional impairment. Chapter 12 is devoted to the characteristics and education of students with severe disabilities.

Cognitive Functioning

Deficits in cognitive functioning and learning characteristics of individuals with mental retardation include poor memory, slow learning rates, attention problems, difficulty generalizing what they have learned, and lack of motivation.

Memory   Students with mental retardation have difficulty remembering information (Carlin et al., 2003; Cherry, Njardvok, & Dawson, 2000). As would be expected, the more severe the cognitive impairment, the greater the deficits in memory. In particular, research has found that students with mental retardation have trouble retaining information in short-term memory (Bray, Fletcher, & Turner, 1997). *Short-term memory,* or working memory, is the ability to recall and use information that was encountered just a few seconds to a couple of hours earlier—for example, remembering a specific sequence of job tasks an employer stated just a few minutes earlier. Children with mental retardation require more time than chronological age-matched peers without disabilities to automatically recall information and therefore have more difficulty handling larger amounts of cognitive information at one time (Bergeron & Floyd, 2006). Early researchers suggested that once persons with mental retardation learned a specific item of information sufficiently to commit it to *long-term memory*—information recalled after a period of days or weeks—they retained that information about as well as persons without retardation (Belmont, 1966; N. R. Ellis, 1963).

More recent research on memory abilities of persons with mental retardation has focused on teaching metacognitive or executive control strategies, such as rehearsing and organizing information into related sets, which many children without disabilities learn to do naturally (Bebko & Luhaorg, 1998; Carlin, Soraci, & Strawbridge, 2005). Students with mental retardation do not tend to use such strategies spontaneously but can be taught to do so with improved performance on memory-related and problem-solving tasks as an outcome of such strategy instruction (Merrill, 1990, 2005).

Learning Rate   The rate at which children with intellectual disabilities acquire new knowledge and skills is well below that of typically developing children (Beirne-Smith et al., 2006). A frequently used measure of learning rate is *trials to criterion*—the number of practice or instructional trials needed before a student can respond correctly without prompts or assistance. For example, while just 2 or 3 trials with feedback may be required for a typically developing child to learn to discriminate between two geometric forms, a child with mental retardation may need 20 to 30 or more trials to learn the same discrimination.

Because students with intellectual disabilities learn more slowly, some educators have assumed that instruction should be slowed down to match their lower rate of learning.

Students with severe intellectual disabilities often have additional disabilities or health conditions.

Cognitive functioning of students with MR

 Council for Exceptional Children   Content Standards for Beginning Teachers of Students With MR/DD: Psychological, social/emotional, and motor characteristics of individuals with MR/DD (MR2K3) (also CC2K2, CC3K5).

Research has shown, however, that students with intellectual disabilities, like all learners, benefit from opportunities to learn to "go fast" (A. D. Miller, Hall, & Heward, 1995; Jolivette, Lingo, Houchins, Barton-Arwood, & Shippen, 2006). (To learn about two strategies for building students' fluency, see Teaching & Learning, "It's Good To Go Fast!" in Chapter 1.)

Attention The ability to attend to critical features of a task (e.g., to the outline of geometric shapes instead of dimensions such as their color or position on the page) is a characteristic of efficient learners. Students with mental retardation are often slower to attend to relevant features of a learning task than are same-age students without disabilities (Merrill, 2005) and instead may focus on distracting irrelevant stimuli (Atwell, Conners, & Merrill, 2003; Carlin, Chrysler, & Sullivan, 2007; Dickson, Deutsch, Wang, & Dube, 2006). In addition, individuals with mental retardation often have difficulty sustaining attention to learning tasks (Tomporowski & Hagler, 1992). These attention problems compound and contribute to a student's difficulties in acquiring, remembering, and generalizing new knowledge and skills.

Effective instructional design for students with mental retardation must systematically control for the presence and saliency of critical stimulus dimensions as well as the presence and effects of distracting stimuli. After initially directing a student's attention to the most relevant feature of a simplified task and reinforcing correct responses, the teacher can gradually increase the complexity and difficulty of the task. A student's selective and sustained attention to relevant stimuli will improve as she succeeds (Huguenin, 2000).

Generalization and Maintenance of Learned Skills Many students with disabilities, especially those with intellectual disabilities, have trouble using their new knowledge and skills in settings or situations that differ from the context in which they first learned those skills. Such transfer, or generalization, of learning occurs without explicit programming for many children without disabilities but may not be evident in students with mental retardation without specific programming to facilitate it. Researchers and educators are no longer satisfied by demonstrations that individuals with mental retardation can initially acquire new knowledge or skills. One of the most important and challenging areas of contemporary research in special education is the search for strategies and tactics for promoting the generalization and maintenance of learning by individuals with mental retardation (Cooper, Heron, & Heward, 2007).

Learned helplessness and outer-directedness

 Council for Exceptional Children Content Standards for Beginning Teachers of Students With MR/DD: Psychological, social/emotional, and motor characteristics of individuals with MR/DD (MR2K3) (also CC2K2).

Motivation Some students with mental retardation exhibit an apparent lack of interest in learning or in problem-solving tasks (Switzky, 1997). Some individuals with intellectual disabilities develop *learned helplessness,* which describes an individual's expectation of failure, regardless of his efforts, based on experiences of repeated failure. In an attempt to minimize or offset failure, the person may set extremely low expectations for himself and not appear to try very hard. When faced with a difficult task or problem, some individuals with mental retardation may quickly give up and turn to or wait for others to help them (Fidler, Hepburn, Mankin, & Rogers, 2005). Some acquire a problem-solving approach called *outer-directedness,* which describes an individual's distrust of her own responses to situations and reliance on others for assistance and solutions (Fidler, Philofsky, Hepburn, & Rogers, 2005; Zigler, 1999).

Rather than an inherent characteristic of mental retardation, the apparent lack of motivation may be the product of frequent failure and prompt dependency acquired as the result of others' caretaking. After experiencing success, individuals with mental retardation do not differ from persons without mental retardation on measures of outer-directedness (Bybee & Zigler, 1998). The current emphasis on teaching self-determination skills to students with intellectual disabilities is helping more and more of these students become self-reliant problem solvers who act upon their world rather than passively wait to be acted upon (C. H. Fowler, Konrad, Walker, Test, & Wood, 2007; Wehmeyer et al., 2007). (See Current Issues and Future Trends, "Self-Determination: The *Most* Natural Support," later in this chapter.)

Adaptive Behavior

By definition, children with mental retardation have substantial deficits in adaptive behavior. These limitations can take many forms and tend to occur across domains of functioning. Limitations in self-care skills and social relationships as well as behavioral excesses are common characteristics of individuals with mental retardation.

Self-Care and Daily Living Skills   Individuals with mental retardation who require extensive supports must often be taught basic self-care skills such as dressing, eating, and hygiene. Direct instruction and environmental supports such as added prompts and simplified routines are necessary to ensure that deficits in these adaptive areas do not seriously limit one's quality of life. Most persons with mild intellectual disabilities learn how to take care of their basic needs, but they often require training in self-management skills to achieve the levels of performance necessary for independent living and successful employment (e.g., Grossi & Heward, 1998).

Social Development   Making and sustaining friendships and personal relationships present significant challenges for many children with mental retardation (Guralnick, Connor, Neville, & Hammond, 2006). Poor communication skills, inability to recognize the emotional state of others, and unusual or inappropriate behaviors when interacting with others can lead to social isolation (Matheson & Jahoda, 2005; Williams, Wishart, Pitcarin, & Willis, 2005). It is difficult at best for someone who is not a professional educator or paid caretaker to want to spend the time necessary to get to know a person who stands too close, interrupts frequently, does not maintain eye contact, and strays from the conversational topic. Teaching appropriate social and interpersonal skills to students with intellectual disabilities is one of the most important functions of special education (Carter, Hughes, Guth, & Copeland, 2005).

Behavioral Excesses and Challenging Behavior   Students with intellectual disabilities are more likely to exhibit behavior problems than are children without disabilities (Dekker, Koot, van der Ende, & Verhulst, 2002; Douma, Dekker, de Ruiter, Tick, & Koot, 2007; Emerson, 2003). Difficulty accepting criticism, limited self-control, and bizarre and inappropriate behaviors such as aggression or self-injury are observed more often in children with mental retardation than in children without disabilities. Some genetic syndromes associated with mental retardation tend to include abnormal behavior. For example, children with Prader-Willi syndrome (described in Table 4.3, later in the chapter) often engage in self-injurious or obsessive-compulsive behavior (Holsen & Thompson, 2004; Dimitropoulos, Feurer, Butler, & Thompson, 2001). In general, the more severe the intellectual impairment, the higher the incidence of problem behavior. Individuals with mental retardation and psychiatric conditions requiring mental health supports are considered as dual-diagnosis cases. Data from one report showed that approximately 10% of all persons with mental retardation had mental health problems. The incidence of mental illness and behavior disorders in children and adults with mental retardation is about two to three times higher than that of the general population (Dosen & Day, 2001). Although comprehensive guidelines are available for treating psychiatric and behavioral problems of persons with mental retardation (Rush & Francis, 2000), much more research is needed on how best to support this population (Didden, Korzilius, van Oorsouw, & Sturmey, 2006).

Positive Attributes

Descriptions of the learning characteristics and adaptive behavior of individuals with intellectual disabilities focus on limitations and deficits and paint a picture of a monolithic group of people whose most important characteristics revolve around the absence of desirable

Adaptive behavior of individuals with MR/DD

 Council for Exceptional Children   Content Standards for Beginning Teachers of Students With MR/DD: Psychological, social/emotional, and motor characteristics of individuals with MR/DD (MR2K3) (also CC2K2).

Although challenged by significant limitations in learning and adaptive behavior, people with intellectual disabilities also possess many positive attributes.

traits. But individuals with mental retardation are a huge and disparate group composed of people with highly individual personalities (Haywood, 2006; J. D. Smith & Mitchell, 2001b). Many children and adults with mental retardation display tenacity and curiosity in learning, get along well with others, and are positive influences on those around them (Reiss & Reiss, 2004; J. D. Smith, 2000).

Prevalence

Many factors contribute to the difficulty of estimating the number of people with mental retardation. Some of these factors include changing definitions of mental retardation/intellectual disabilities, the schools' reluctance to label children with mild intellectual impairment, and the changing status of schoolchildren with mild mental retardation (some are declassified during their school careers, others are no longer identified after leaving school) (Drew & Hardman, 2007). Historically, the federal government estimated the prevalence at 3% of the general population, although recent analyses find little objective support for this figure. If prevalence figures were based solely on IQ scores, 2.3% of the population theoretically would have mental retardation (see Figure 4.2).

Basing prevalence estimates on IQ scores only, however, ignores the other necessary criterion for mental retardation—deficits in adaptive functioning and the need for supports. Some professionals believe that if adaptive behavior is included with intellectual ability when estimating prevalence, the figure drops to about 1%. In fact, two national studies estimated the prevalence of mental retardation at 0.78% (Larson et al., 2001) and 1.27% of the U.S. population (Fujiura, 2003).

The 1% estimate is consistent with data reported by the U.S. Office of Special Education Programs (2007a) on the number of children receiving special education. During the 2005–2006 school year, 533,426 students ages 6 through 21 received special education under the disability category of mental retardation. These students represented 9.6% of all school-age children in special education, or 0.81% of the total school-age population. Mental retardation is the fourth-largest disability category after learning disabilities, speech or language impairments, and other health impairments.

Prevalence rates vary greatly from state to state. For example, the prevalence of mental retardation as a percentage of total school enrollment in 2005–2006 ranged from a low of 0.31% (Maine) to a high of 2.41% (West Virginia) (U.S. Office of Special Education Programs, 2007a). Such differences in prevalence are in large part a function of the widely differing criteria for identifying students with mental retardation (Denning, Chamberlain, & Polloway, 2000; Scullin, 2006). Prevalence figures also vary considerably among districts within a given state (Hetzner, 2007).

Causes and Prevention

Causes

Causes of MR

Content Standards for Beginning Teachers of Students With MR/DD: Causes and theories of intellectual disabilities and implications for prevention (MR2K1).

Researchers have identified more than 350 causes of mental retardation (Dykens, Hodapp, & Finucane, 2000; Luckasson et al., 2002). Figure 4.3 lists etiologic factors associated with mental retardation that the AAIDD categorizes as **prenatal** (occurring before birth), **perinatal** (occurring during or shortly after birth), or **postnatal** (occurring after birth). Each of these etiologic factors can be classified further as biomedical or environmental (social, behavioral, educational). However, a combination of biological and environmental factors are often involved in individual cases of mental retardation, making specific determination extremely difficult (Heikua et al., 2005; van Karnebeek et al., 2005).

Approximately 35% of cases have a genetic cause, another third involve external trauma or toxins, and etiology remains unknown for another third of cases (Heikua et al., 2005; Szymanski & King, 1999). Nevertheless, knowledge of etiology is critical to efforts designed to lower the incidence of mental retardation (Moser, 2000) and may have implications for some educational interventions (Hodapp & Dykens, in press; Powell, Houghton, & Douglas, 1997).

Timing	Biomedical	Social	Behavioral	Educational
Prenatal	1. Chromosomal disorders 2. Single-gene disorders 3. Syndromes 4. Metabolic disorders 5. Cerebral dysgenesis 6. Maternal illnesses 7. Parental age	1. Poverty 2. Maternal malnutrition 3. Domestic violence 4. Lack of access to prenatal care	1. Parental drug use 2. Parental alcohol use 3. Parental smoking 4. Parental immaturity	1. Parental cognitive disability without supports 2. Lack of preparation for parenthood
Perinatal	1. Prematurity 2. Birth injury 3. Neonatal disorders	1. Lack of access to birth care	1. Parental rejection of caretaking 2. Parental abandonment of child	1. Lack of medical referral for intervention services at discharge
Postnatal	1. Traumatic brain injury 2. Malnutrition 3. Meningoencephalitis 4. Seizure disorders 5. Degenerative disorders	1. Impaired child caregiver 2. Lack of adequate stimulation 3. Family poverty 4. Chronic illness in the family 5. Institutionalization	1. Child abuse and neglect 2. Domestic violence 3. Inadequate safety measures 4. Social deprivation 5. Difficult child behaviors	1. Impaired parenting 2. Delayed diagnosis 3. Inadequate early intervention services 4. Inadequate special-educational services 5. Inadequate family support

FIGURE 4.3

Etiologic risk factors for mental retardation

Source: Mental Retardation: Definition, Classification, and Systems of Supports by Ruth A. Luckasson. Copyright 2002 by American Association on Intellectual Developmental Disabilities. Reproduced with permission of American Association on Intellectual Developmental Disabilities in the formats Textbook and Other Book via Copyright Clearance Center.

Biomedical Causes   Researchers have identified specific biomedical causes for about two thirds of individuals with more severe levels of mental retardation (Batshaw, Pellegrino, & Roizen, 2007). Table 4.3 describes some of the more common prenatal conditions that often result in mental retardation. The term *syndrome* refers to a number of symptoms or characteristics that occur together and provide the defining features of a given disease or condition. **Down syndrome** and **fragile X syndrome** are the two most common genetic causes of mental retardation (J. E. Roberts et al., 2005).

It is important to understand that none of the etiologic factors shown in Figure 4.3 and Table 4.3 *is* mental retardation. These conditions, diseases, and syndromes are commonly associated with mental retardation; but they may or may not result in the deficits of intellectual and adaptive functioning that define mental retardation. "The cause of mental retardation is whatever causes this impairment in functioning. A biomedical risk factor may be present, but by itself it does not cause mental retardation" (Luckasson et al., 2002, p. 126). Any risk factor, such as low birth weight or Trisomy 21 (Down syndrome), causes mental retardation only when it results in impaired intellectual and adaptive functioning sufficient to meet the criteria for diagnosis.

Some of the health conditions and disorders shown in Table 4.3 require special education and related services as disabilities in their own right and/or are causes of other disabilities whether or not mental retardation is also involved. A number of these conditions are discussed in Chapter 9 (cytomegalovirus, meningitis, rubella) and Chapter 11 (diabetes, epilepsy, head injuries, hydrocephalus, muscular dystrophy, spina bifida).

TABLE 4.3

Some prenatal conditions associated with mental retardation

SYNDROME	DEFINITION/CAUSE	REMARKS/CHARACTERISTICS
Down syndrome	Caused by chromosomal abnormality; most common of three major types is trisomy 21, in which the 21st set of chromosomes is a triplet rather than a pair. Most often results in moderate level of mental retardation, although some individuals function in mild or severe range. Affects about 1 in 1,000 live births; probability of having a baby with Down syndrome increases to approximately 1 in 30 for women at age 45.	Best-known and well-researched biological condition associated with mental retardation; estimated to account for 5–6% of all cases. Characteristic physical features: short stature; flat, broad face with small ears and nose; upward slanting eyes; small mouth with short roof, protruding tongue may cause articulation problems; hypotonia (floppy muscles); heart defects common; susceptibility to ear and respiratory infections. Older persons at high risk for Alzheimer's disease.
Fetal alcohol spectrum disorder (FASD)	FASD incorporates fetal alcohol syndrome (FAS), fetal alcohol effect (FAE), and alcohol-related neurodevelopmental disorder (ARND). Mother's excessive alcohol use during pregnancy has toxic effects on fetus, including physical defects and developmental delays. FAS is diagnosed when the child has two or more craniofacial malformations and growth is below the 10th percentile for height and weight. Children who have some but not all of the diagnostic criteria for FAS and a history of prenatal alcohol exposure are diagnosed with FAE, a condition associated with hyperactivity and learning problems.	One of the leading causes of mental retardation, FAS has an incidence higher than Down syndrome and cerebral palsy. In addition to cognitive impairments, some children experience sleep disturbances, motor dysfunctions, hyperirritability, aggression, and conduct problems. Although risk of FASD is highest during first trimester of pregnancy, pregnant women should avoid drinking alcohol at any time.
Fragile X syndrome	A triplet, repeat mutation on the X chromosome interferes with production of FMR-1 protein, which is essential for normal brain functioning; majority of males experience mild-to-moderate mental retardation in childhood and moderate-to-severe deficits in adulthood; females may carry and transmit the mutation to their children but tend to have fewer disabilities than affected males.	Affects approximately 1 in 4,000 males; the most common inherited cause of mental retardation and the most common clinical type of mental retardation after Down syndrome. Characterized by social anxiety and avoidance (avoiding eye contact, tactile defensiveness, turning the body away during face-to-face interactions, and stylized, ritualistic forms of greeting); preservative speech often includes repetition of words and phrases.
Klinefelter syndrome (XXY males)	Males receive an extra X chromosome. Sterility, underdevelopment of male sex organs, acquisition of female secondary sex characteristics are common; sometimes includes mild levels of cognitive retardation.	XXY males often have problems with social skills, auditory perception, language, sometimes mild levels of cognitive retardation; more often associated with learning disabilities than with mental retardation.
Phenylketonuria (PKU)	Genetically inherited condition in which a child is born without an important enzyme needed to break down an amino acid, phenylalanine, found in many common foods; failure to break down this amino acid causes brain damage that often results in aggressiveness, hyperactivity, and severe mental retardation.	Mental retardation resulting from PKU has been virtually eliminated in the United States through widespread screening. By analyzing the concentration of phenylalanine in a newborn's blood plasma, doctors can diagnose PKU and treat it with a special diet. Most children with PKU who receive a phenylalanine-restricted diet early enough have normal intellectual development.

TABLE 4.3 (CONTINUED)

Some prenatal conditions associated with mental retardation

SYNDROME	DEFINITION/CAUSE	REMARKS/CHARACTERISTICS
Prader-Willi syndrome	Caused by deletion of a portion of chromosome 15. Initially, infants have hypotonia (floppy muscles) and may have to be tube fed. Initial phase is followed by development of insatiable appetite; constant preoccupation with food can lead to life-threatening obesity if food seeking is not monitored. Affects 1 in 10,000 to 25,000 live births.	Associated with mild retardation and learning disabilities; behavior problems common: impulsivity, aggressiveness, temper tantrums, obsessive-compulsive behavior; some forms of self-injurious behavior, such as skin picking; delayed motor skills, short stature, small hands and feet, underdeveloped genitalia.
Williams syndrome	Caused by deletion of material on the seventh chromosome; cognitive functioning ranges from normal to mild and moderate levels of mental retardation.	Characteristic elfin-like facial features; physical features and manner of expression exudes cheerfulness and happiness; described as "overly friendly," lack of reserve toward strangers; often have uneven profiles of skills, with strengths in vocabulary and story-telling skills and weaknesses in visual-spatial skills; often hyperactive, may have difficulty staying on task and low tolerance for frustration or teasing.

Sources: Astley & Clarren (2000); Beirne-Smith, Patton, & Kim (2006); Belser & Sudhalter (2001); Dimitropoulos et al. (2001); Dykens (2000); Dykens & Rosner (1999); Fidler, Hepburn, Most, Philofsky, & Rogers (2007); Hagerman & Cronsiter (1996); Levine & Wharton (2000); Luckasson et al. (2002); Mervis, Klein-Tasman, & Mastin (2001); J. E. Roberts et al. (2005); S. Ryan & Ferguson (2006); Stratton, Howe, & Battaglia (1996); Sudhalter & Belser (2001); Symons, Butler, Sanders, Feurer, & Thompson (1999); Symons, Clark, Roberts, & Bailey (2001); L. A. Thomas (2001).

Environmental Causes   Individuals with mild intellectual disabilities, those who require less intensive supports, make up about 90% of all persons with MR/ID (Drew & Hardman, 2007). The vast majority of those cases exhibit no demonstrable evidence of organic pathology—no brain damage or other biological problem. When no biological factor is evident in an individual with mental retardation, the cause is presumed to be *psychosocial disadvantage*, the combination of a poor social environment early in the child's life. Professionals sometimes use the term *developmental retardation* to refer to intellectual disability thought to be caused primarily by environmental influences such as minimal opportunities to develop early language, child abuse and neglect, and/or chronic social or sensory deprivation (MacLean, 2003). Although no direct evidence proves that social and environmental deprivation cause mental retardation, researchers generally believe that these influences cause many cases of mild intellectual disabilities.

Research conducted at the Juniper Gardens Children's Project has led to a hypothesis of developmental retardation as an intergenerational progression in which the cumulative experiential deficits in social and academic stimulation are transmitted to children from low socioeconomic status (SES) environments (Greenwood et al., 1992; Greenwood, Hart, Walker, & Risley, 1994). Several key contributors to this cycle of environmentally caused retardation follow (Greenwood et al., 1994):

1. Limited parenting practices that produce low rates of vocabulary growth in early childhood
2. Instructional practices in middle childhood and adolescence that produce low rates of academic engagement during the school years
3. Lower rates of academic achievement and early school failure and early school dropout
4. Parenthood and continuance of the progression into the next generation (p. 216)

Psychosocial disadvantage and developmental retardation

 Content Standards for Beginning Teachers of Students With MR/DD: Causes and theories of intellectual disabilities and implications for prevention (MR2K1) (also CC2K3).

McDermott (1994) provides additional support for the hypothesis of developmental retardation, finding that SES explains much of the variability in prevalence rates of mental retardation reported by different school districts. Her findings are "consistent with the notion that a large percentage of mental retardation is based on environmental causes, most notably, deprivation in the early years of life" (p. 182). Children who live in poverty have a higher than normal chance of being identified as mentally retarded (Fujiura & Yamaki, 2000).

Prevention

Prevention of MR

Content Standards for Beginning Teachers of Students With MR/DD: Causes and theories of intellectual disabilities and implications for prevention (MR2K1).

Probably the biggest single preventive strike against mental retardation (and many other disabling conditions, including blindness and deafness) was the development of an effective rubella vaccine in 1962. When **rubella** (German measles) is contracted by mothers during the first 3 months of pregnancy, it causes severe damage in 10% to 40% of unborn children. Fortunately, this cause of mental retardation can be eliminated if women are vaccinated for rubella before becoming pregnant.

Advances in medical science have enabled doctors to identify certain genetic influences associated with mental retardation. Genetic disorders are detected during pregnancy by two types of tests: screening procedures and diagnostic tests. Obstetricians routinely provide noninvasive screening procedures, such as ultrasound and maternal serum alpha-fetoprotein (AFP), to women whose pregnancy is considered at risk for a congenital disability. Maternal serum screening measures the amount of AFP and other biochemical markers in the mother's bloodstream and can identify pregnancies at risk for disabilities such as Down syndrome and spina bifida.

Invasive diagnostic tests, such as amniocentesis and chorionic villi sampling, can confirm the presence of various disorders. **Amniocentesis** requires withdrawing a sample of fluid from the amniotic sac surrounding the fetus during the second trimester of pregnancy (usually the 14th to 17th week). Fetal cells are removed from the amniotic fluid and grown in a cell culture for about 2 weeks. At that time, a chromosome and enzyme analysis is performed to identify the presence of about 80 specific genetic disorders before birth. Many of these disorders, such as Down syndrome, are associated with mental retardation.

A prenatal diagnostic test that may eventually replace amniocentesis is **chorionic villi sampling (CVS).** A small amount of chorionic tissue (a fetal component of the developing placenta) is removed and tested. An advantage of CVS is that it can be performed earlier than amniocentesis (during the 8th to 10th week of pregnancy). Because fetal cells exist in relatively large numbers in the chorion, they can be analyzed immediately without waiting 2 to 3 weeks for them to grow. Although CVS is being used more often, it has been associated with a miscarriage rate of about 10 in 1,000 (compared with 2.5 in 1,000 for amniocentesis) and is still considered experimental.

In the United States, women who are at risk for giving birth to a baby with a disabilities on the basis of the parents' genetic backgrounds are commonly referred to **genetic counseling** (Roberts, Stough, & Parrish, 2002). Genetic counseling consists of a discussion between a specially trained medical counselor and the prospective parents about the possibility that they may give birth to a child with disabilities. For discussions of ethical considerations of genetic testing for disabilities, see Beirne-Smith and colleagues (2006), Drew and Hardman (2007), Kuna (2001), J. D. Smith and Mitchell (2001a), and Zucker (2004).

Newborn screening tests for inherited conditions and biomedical risk factors are now mandatory in every state. A procedure called *tandem mass spectrometry* developed in the late 1980s measures various components of blood, urine, or plasma in about 2 minutes for 20 to 30 different metabolic disorders (Nehring, 2003). A simple blood test administered to virtually every baby born in the United States has drastically reduced the incidence of mental retardation caused by **phenylketonuria (PKU).** By analyzing the concentration of phenylalanine in a newborn's blood plasma, doctors can diagnose PKU and treat it with a phenylalanine-restricted diet. Most children with PKU who receive treatment have normal intellectual development (Beirne-Smith et al., 2006).

Toxic exposure through maternal substance abuse such as alcohol (Ryan & Ferguson, 2006) and environmental pollutants (e.g., lead poisoning) are two major causes of preventable intellectual disabilities that can be combated with education and training (Howard, Williams, & McLaughlin, 1994).

Medical advances have noticeably reduced the incidence of mental retardation caused by some of the known biological factors. Huge advances in research, however, are needed to approach a reduction in the incidence of biomedical mental retardation by 50%, which the President's Committee on Mental Retardation set as a goal in 1976 to be reached by the year 2000.

EDUCATIONAL APPROACHES

The search for effective methods for educating students with intellectual disabilities began more than 200 years ago, when Jean Marc Gaspard Itard kept a detailed diary of his efforts to teach a young boy who was found in the woods and thought to be a feral child. Itard, whom many consider to be the father of special education, showed that intensive, systematic intervention could produce significant gains with a child thought to be incapable of learning (Itard, 1806/1962).

Since Itard's time, researchers working in mental retardation have developed numerous methods of specialized instruction, some of which have contributed to improved practice in all areas of education. Similarly, efforts by early advocates on behalf of children and adults with mental retardation blazed trails for advocacy groups representing individuals with other disabilities. Table 4.4 highlights some key historical events and their implications for the education and treatment of children and adults with mental retardation.

Curriculum Goals

What do students with intellectual disabilities need to learn? Too often in the past, children with mild intellectual disabilities were presented with a slowed- and/or watered-down version of the general education curriculum that focused largely on traditional academic subjects. For example, a group of children with mild mental retardation might spend several weeks on a geography unit learning the 50 states and their capitals. Students with more severe intellectual impairments often spent hours putting pegs into pegboards and sorting plastic sticks by color because educators believed that these isolated skills were developmental prerequisites for more meaningful activities. Unfortunately, knowing that Boise is the capital of Idaho or being able to sort by color did not help these students become more independent.

Improved instructional techniques and supports are enabling many students with mild-to-moderate intellectual disabilities to participate meaningfully in the general education curriculum (Soukup, Wehmeyer, Bashinski, & Bovaird, 2007; Wehmeyer, 2006).

Academic Curriculum   Programs for all students with intellectual disabilities should include the basic skills of reading, writing, and math (Al Otaiba & Hosp, 2004; Bradford, Shippen, Alberto, Houchins, & Flores, 2006; Jolivette et al., 2006; Joseph & Seery, 2004). Browder and Snell (2000) define functional academics as "the most useful parts of the 'three R's'—reading, writing, and arithmetic" (p. 497). Choosing functional academic targets is not as simple as it might seem. The most useful part of writing for one student (e.g., making a grocery list) may not be a functional writing skill for another student (e.g., writing the number of items packaged on the job). Educators must carefully assess each student's current routines to find those skills that the student requires and/or could use often. Educators should also consider skills that future environments are likely to require.

Teachers must be on guard against the faulty assumption that a traditional academic skill cannot be functional because it is not a typical activity or learning outcome for students with mental retardation. For example, while *crystal* and *limestone* might not seem to be functional sight words, such words might be extremely functional for a student with a rock collection (Browder, 2000).

History of MR

Content Standards for Beginning Teachers of Students With MR/DD: Historical foundations and classic studies of MR/DD (MR1K4).

TABLE 4.4

A history of the education of children with mental retardation: Key events and implications

DATE	HISTORICAL EVENT	EDUCATIONAL IMPLICATION
1799	Jean Marc Gaspard Itard published an account of his work with Victor, the Wild Boy of Aveyron.	Itard showed that intensive treatment could produce significant learning. Many consider Itard to be the father of special education.
1848	Edouard Seguin helped establish the Pennsylvania Training School.	This was the first educational facility for persons with mental retardation in the United States.
1850	Samuel Gridley Howe began the School for Idiotic and Feeble Minded Youth.	This was the first publicly funded residential school in the United States.
1896	The first public school class for children with mental retardation began in Providence, RI.	This began the special class movement, which grew to 1.3 million children in 1974, the year before IDEA.
1905	Alfred Binet and Theodore Simon developed a test in France to screen those students not benefiting from the general education classroom.	The test enabled empirical identification of students with mental retardation and contributed to the growth of the special class movement.
1916	Lewis Terman of Stanford University published the Stanford-Binet Intelligence Scale in the United States.	Many schools adopted IQ testing as a means of identifying children with below-average general intelligence.
1935	Edgar Doll published the Vineland Social Maturity Scale.	It provided a standardized method for assessing a person's adaptive behavior, which later became part of the definition of mental retardation.
1950	Parents formed the National Association for Retarded Children (known today as The Arc).	The Arc remains a powerful and important advocacy organization for persons of all ages with mental retardation.
1958	National Defense Education Act (P.L. 85–926)	Provided funds for training professionals to train teachers of children with mental retardation.
1959	AAMR published its first manual on the definition and classification of mental retardation, with diagnosis based on an IQ score of one standard deviation below the mean (approximately 85) (Heber, 1959).	Many students were identified in the borderline category of mental retardation and served in special classes for "slow learners" or EMR students.
1961	John F. Kennedy established the first President's Panel on Mental Retardation.	The panel's first report (Mayo, 1962) made recommendations that helped guide national policy with respect to mental retardation (e.g., citizenship, education, prevention).
1969	Bengt Nirje published a key paper defining normalization. Wolf Wolfensberger championed normalization in the United States.	Normalization became a leading philosophy guiding the development and delivery of educational, community, vocational, and residential services for persons with mental retardation.
1973	AAMR published a revised definition that required a score on IQ tests of 2 standard deviations below the mean (approximately 70 or less) and concurrent deficits in adaptive behavior.	This eliminated the category of borderline mental retardation.
1992	AAMR published "System '92," a radically different definition of mental retardation with a classification system based on intensities of supports.	New definition and classification system generated cautious support by some and concern by others; few states used the '92 system for identifying and planning services for students with mental retardation.

TABLE 4.4 (CONTINUED)

A history of the education of children with mental retardation: Key events and implications

DATE	HISTORICAL EVENT	EDUCATIONAL IMPLICATION
2002	AAMR published a revision of the 1992 definition; retains classification by intensities of supports; returns to IQ of approximately 2 standard deviations below mean; adds social participation and interactions as fifth dimension of functioning.	Impact of AAMR's "System 2002" on special education not yet known.
2007	AAMR changed its name to American Association on Intellectual and Developmental Disabilities (AAIDD) and replaced the term *mental retardation* with *intellectual disabilities*.	According to AAIDD, the term *intellectual disability* (a) reflects current practices that focus on functional behaviors and contextual factors; (b) provides a logical basis for providing individualized supports due to its social-ecological framework; (c) is less offensive to persons with disabilities; and (d) is more consistent with international terminology.

Complete immersion in the academic curriculum, however, can be a restrictive and ineffective education for a student with mental retardation. Care must be taken that a student's involvement in the academic portions of the general education curriculum does not limit opportunities to learn the skills that will help him function independently and successfully in current and future environments.

> Seventeen-year-old Corey Bohn doesn't know his phone number and can't make change for a dollar.
>
> His Down syndrome makes it a struggle to talk, recognize letters, cross a street, or even let someone know when he's in pain.
>
> Nevertheless, Corey, who attends Doss High School in Jefferson County, now is expected to learn versions of grade-level academics such as the Pythagorean theorem, the periodic table of elements, principles of cell division and the parts of a novel—all before he leaves high school.
>
> "I just don't think learning that is important for him," said Debbie Bohn, Corey's mother, who is a special-education teacher. "He's not practicing money skills like he used to." (Kenning, 2007)

The challenge facing general and special educators who teach students with intellectual disabilities is aligning the academic and functional curricula in ways that allow each student to benefit as much as possible from access to the general education curriculum while learning from a personalized curriculum of functional skills across life domains (Browder, Ahlgrim-Delzell, Courtade-Little, & Snell, 2006; Browder et al., 2004)

Functional Curriculum   Educators choose learning activities in a functional curriculum because they will maximize a student's independence, self-direction, health and fitness, and enjoyment in everyday school, home, community, and work environments. Examples of practical skills include purchasing (Ayres, Langone, Boon, & Norman, 2006; Xin, Grasso, Dipipi-Hoy, & Jitenda, 2005), shopping, ordering in a restaurant (Mechling, Pridgen, & Cronin, 2005), cooking (Graves, Collins, Shuster, & Kleinert, 2005), telling time (Horn, Shuster, & Collins, 2006), and nutrition and fitness (Simpson, Swicegood, & Gaus, 2006).

G. M. Clark (1994) suggests that teachers determine functional knowledge or skills by seeking answers to these questions:

- Does the content focus on necessary knowledge and skills . . . [so that the student can] function as independently as possible in the home, school, or community?
- Does the content provide a scope and sequence for meeting future needs?

Functional curriculum goals

Council for Exceptional Children Content Standards for Beginning Teachers of Students With MR/DD: Plan instruction for independent functional life skills relevant to the community, personal living, sexuality, and employment (MR7S3).

Serving as salesclerk for the Buckeye Necklaces business that she and her classmates created helps Sarah learn functional skills.

Integrating life skills into curriculum

 Council for Exceptional Children

Content Standards for Beginning Teachers—Common Core: Integrate affective, social, and life skills with academic curricula (CC7S7).

Self-determination

 Council for Exceptional Children

Content Standards for Beginning Teachers—Common Core: Use procedures to increase the individual's self-awareness, self-management, self-control, self-reliance, and self-esteem (CC4S5) (also CC7S14).

- Do the student's parents think the content is important for both current and future needs?
- Does the student think the content is important for both current and future needs?
- Is the content appropriate for the student's chronological age and current intellectual, academic, or behavioral performance level(s)?
- What are the consequences to the student of not learning the concepts and skills? (p. 37)

An even simpler approach to determining whether any given skill represents functional curriculum is to contemplate this question from the student's perspective: "Will I need it when I'm 21?" (Beck, Broers, Hogue, Shipstead, & Knowlton, 1994). The answer to this question is critical, because when educators fail to relate curriculum for a student with mental retardation to outcomes with direct relevance to that student's eventual independence and quality of life, "years of valuable opportunities for meaningful learning can be wasted" (Knowlton, 1998, p. 96).

As students with intellectual disabilities reach middle and secondary school, the emphasis on learning functional skills that will help them transition to adult life in the community becomes especially critical. Several models and taxonomies of adult functioning provide frameworks from which to build functional curriculum activities (e.g., Brolin, 2004; Cronin, Patton, & Wood, 2005). For example, Life Skills Instruction includes 147 major life demands that are associated with a variety of specific life skills and organized around six domains of adult functioning (Cronin et al., 2005). Table 4.5 shows examples of how academic and social-skills instruction can be related to some of these life skills.

Self-Determination   Self-determined learners set goals, plan and implement a course of action, evaluate their performance, and make adjustments in what they are doing to reach their goals. **Self-determination** has been defined as follows:

> a combination of skills, knowledge, and beliefs that enable a person to engage in goal directed, self-regulated, autonomous behavior. An understanding of one's strengths and limitations together with a belief in oneself as capable and effective are essential to self-determination. When acting on the basis of these skills and attitudes, individuals have greater ability to take control of their lives and assume the role of successful adults. (Field, Martin, Miller, Ward, & Wehmeyer, 1998, p. 2)

Realizing the concept of self-determination in the classroom means teaching skills and attitudes to enable skills such as choice/decision making, goal setting, problem solving, self-evaluation, self-management, self-advocacy, and self-awareness. Learning self-determination skills can serve as both a curriculum goal in its own right as well as a means to help students achieve other learning outcomes (Wehmeyer et al., 2007). For example, Agran, Blanchard, Wehmeyer, and Hughes (2002) taught four middle school students with mental retardation a four-step problem-solving sequence to achieve self-set goals related to their participation and success in the general education classroom:

> First, the student was taught to verbalize, "What is the problem?" and to say out loud what it was. Second, the student was taught to ask, "What can I do about it?" and to verbalize the proposed solution. Third, the student was taught to implement the proposed solution. Last, the student was taught to ask, "Did that fix the problem?" For example, Natalie was taught to ask herself, "What is the problem?" and to respond by saying, "I need to say at least one sentence during class." After responding to teacher or student questions, she would ask, "Did that fix the problem?" Following class she would count the number of verbal comments she had made. Next, she would ask, "Did I meet my goal?" (p. 283)

Teaching students to take responsibility for their learning is an important component of self-determination. Students should be taught to take an active role in their learning at an early age. Teaching students with disabilities to recruit assistance from the classroom teacher is one strategy for helping them succeed in general education classrooms and to take an active role in their education. For example, Craft, Alber, and Heward (1998) taught four

TABLE 4.5

Relationship of scholastic/social skills to adult life skills

	EMPLOYMENT EDUCATION	HOME AND FAMILY	LEISURE PURSUITS	COMMUNITY INVOLVEMENT	EMOTIONAL–PHYSICAL HEALTH	PERSONAL RESPONSIBILITY RELATIONSHIPS
Reading	Reading classified ads for jobs	Interpreting bills	Locating and understanding movie information in a newspaper	Following directions on tax forms	Comprehending directions on medication	Reading letters from friends
Writing	Writing a letter of application for a job	Writing checks	Writing for information on a city to visit	Filling in a voter registration form	Filling in your medical history on forms	Sending thank you notes
Listening	Understanding oral directions of a procedure change	Comprehending directions	Listening to a weather forecast to plan an outdoor activity	Understanding campaign ads	Attending lectures on stress	Taking turns in a conversation
Speaking	Asking your boss for a raise	Discussing morning routines with family	Inquiring about tickets for a concert	Stating your opinion at the school board meeting	Describing symptoms to a doctor	Giving feedback to a friend
Math applications	Understanding difference between net and gross pay	Computing the cost of doing laundry in a laundromat versus home	Calculating the cost of a dinner out versus eating at home	Obtaining information for a building permit	Using a thermometer	Planning the costs of a date
Problem-solving	Settling a dispute with a co-worker	Deciding how much to budget for rent	Role-playing appropriate behaviors for various places	Knowing what to do if you are the victim of fraud	Selecting a doctor	Deciding how to ask someone for a date
Survival skills	Using a prepared career-planning packet	Listing emergency phone numbers	Using a shopping-center directory	Marking a calendar for important dates (e.g., recycling, garbage collection)	Using a system to remember to take vitamins	Developing a system to remember birthdays
Personal-social	Applying appropriate interview skills	Helping a child with homework	Knowing the rules of a neighborhood pool	Locating self-improvement classes	Getting a yearly physical exam	Discussing how to negotiate a price at the flea market

Source: From *Life Skills Instruction: A Practical Guide for Integrating Real Life Content into the Curriculum at the Elementary and Secondary Levels for Students with Special Needs or Who Are Placed at Risk,* 2nd ed. by M. E. Cronin, J. R. Patton, & S. J. Wood, 2007, Austin, TX: PRO-ED. Copyright 2007 by PRO-ED. Reprinted by permission.

fourth graders with mental retardation to recruit teacher attention while they worked on spelling assignments in a general education classroom. The students learned to show their work to the teacher two to three times per session and to make statements such as "How am I doing?" or "Look, I'm all finished!" Recruitment training, which was conducted in the special education classroom, increased the frequency of each student's recruiting, the frequency of teacher praise, the percentage of worksheet items completed, and the accuracy with which the students completed the assignments. After the study, the general education teacher stated, "They fit in better, they were more a part of the group, and they weren't being disruptive because they were working." (To learn more about this strategy for teaching students to take an active role in their learning, see Teaching & Learning, "'Look, I'm All Finished!' "Recruiting Teacher Attention" in Chapter 6.)

Self-determination requires a complex set of skills and is a lofty goal for any student. However, students with intellectual disabilities can learn self-determination skills, and those who do are more likely to achieve IEP goals and make a successful transition from school to adult life (Agran et al., 2005; Ganz & Sigafoos, 2005; German, Martin, Huber Marshall, & Sale, 2000; C. H. Fowler et al., in press; S. H. Lee et al., in press; Test, Fowler, Brewer, & Wood, 2005). You can find information on research-validated curriculum models and instructional materials for teaching self-determination to students with disabilities as well as specific lesson plans online from the National Self-Determination Synthesis Project (www.uncc.edu/sdsp/sd_lesson_plans.asp).

Instructional Methods

Students with intellectual disabilities learn best when instructional methods are explicit, systematic, and derived from empirical research, such as the following practices (Heward, 2003):

- Assess each student's present levels of performance to help identify and prioritize the most important instructional targets.
- Define and task-analyze the new knowledge or skills to be learned.
- Design instructional materials and activities so the student has frequent opportunities for active student response in the form of guided and independent practice.
- Use **mediated scaffolding** (i.e., provide and then fade prompts and cues so student can respond to naturally occurring stimuli).
- Provide systematic consequences for student performance in the form of contingent reinforcement, instructional feedback, and error correction.
- Incorporate fluency-building activities into lessons.
- Incorporate strategies for promoting the generalization and maintenance of newly learned skills.
- Conduct direct and frequent measurements of student performance, and use those data to inform instructional decisions. (p. 197)

Some of these components of effective instruction are described here; others are discussed in subsequent chapters.

Task analysis

Council for Exceptional Children **Content Standards for Beginning Teachers—Common Core:** Use task analysis (CC7S5).

Task Analysis **Task analysis** means breaking down complex or multistep skills into smaller, easier-to-learn subtasks. The subskills or subtasks are then sequenced, either in the natural order in which they are typically performed or from easiest to most difficult. Assessing a student's performance on a sequence of task-analyzed subskills helps pinpoint where instruction should begin. Figure 4.4 shows a task analysis and data collection form developed for teaching a preschooler with disabilities a routine for arriving at his classroom each morning (Snell & Brown, 2006a).

During the task-analysis stage of instructional planning, it is important to consider the extent to which the natural environment requires performance of the target skill for a given duration or at a minimum rate. For example, Test, Spooner, Keul, and Grossi (1990) included specific time limits for each of the 17 steps in a task analysis used to teach two secondary students with severe mental retardation to use the public telephone to call home. The

FIGURE 4.4 — Example of a task analysis and data collection form for child's arrival routine at preschool

Teachers: Carlene Johnson, Ted Grayson, Jo Milano   **Instructional Cue:** Arrival at preschool in family car; parent/sitter: "Let's go to school"
Student: Timothy   **Settings:** Bus/car arrival area, sidewalk, hallway, classroom   **Target:** Morning arrival routine
Day(s): Daily at arrival   **Stage of Learning:** Acquisition   **Teaching Method:** Constant time delay (0, 4 seconds)
Probe Schedule: First Tuesday each month   **Baseline/Probe Method:** Multiple opportunity task analytic assessment (4-second latency)

Task Steps → Dates	9/21	9/22	9/23	9/24	9/27	9/28	9/30	10/1	10/4	10/5							
Delayed prompt ↓	−	−	0	0	4	4	4	4	4	−							
1. Unbuckle your seat belt (assist buckle and straps)	−	−	✔	✔	✔	✔	✔	✔	+	+							
2. Open your door (assist from outside car)	−	−	✔	✔	✔	✔	✔	✔	✔	−							
3. Get out of car and close the door (assist one hand)	+	−	✔	✔	✔	✔	✔	✔	✔	−							
4. Walk to preschool (on sidewalk)	−	−	✔	✔	✔	✔	✔	✔	✔	−							
5. Open the door (assist pulling)	−	−	✔	✔	✔	✔	✔	+	+	+							
6. Walk to your room	+	−	✔	✔	+	+	+	+	+	+							
7. Open the door and go in	−	−	✔	✔	✔	✔	✔	✔	✔	+							
8. Look at teacher, or peer, wave hello	−	−	✔	✔	✔	✔	✔	✔	✔	−							
9. Find your cubby	+	+	✔	✔	✔	+	+	+	+	+							
10. Take off your coat	−	−	✔	✔	✔	✔	✔	✔	✔	−							
11. Grab it (by the collar)	−	−	✔	✔	✔	✔	✔	✔	✔	−							
12. Hang it up (on hook)	−	+	✔	✔	✔	✔	+	+	+	+							
13. Get your picture (from table)	−	−	✔	✔	✔	✔	✔	✔	✔	+							
14. Put your picture (on board) where you want to play	−	−	✔	✔	✔	✔	✔	✔	✔	−							
15. Go play (goes to selected activity)	−	−	✔	✔	✔	✔	✔	+	+	+							
Total independent	3	2	0	0	1	2	3	5	6	8							
Baseline/Teach/Probe	B	B	T	T	T	T	T	T	T	P							

Task analysis: Arrival routine
Student: Timothy

Date	Teacher	Anecdotal Comments
9/23	Carlene	Waited for help on most steps
9/25	Ted	Seemed sleepy, ear infection meds
10/4	Ted	He's more sure
10/5	Jo	Great probe!

[Located on back of task analysis]

Materials: Activity picture chart, garment or backpack
Criterion: 10 of 15 steps correct (67%)
Recording Key: Test: + correct, − incorrect; Teach: + unprompted correct, ✔ prompted correct (gestural/partial physical prompt); − unprompted/prompted error; NR no response
Latency Period: 0 seconds, 4 seconds for 3 of 5 teaching days

Source: From Snell, M. E., & Brown, F. (2006). Designing and implementing instructional programs. In M. E. Snell & F. Brown (Eds.), *Instruction of students with severe disabilities* (6th ed., p. 120). Reproduced by permission of Pearson Education, Inc., Upper Saddle River, NJ.

authors determined the specific sequence of steps and the time limit for each step by having two adults without disabilities use the telephone.

Active Student Response   For several decades, research in general and special education has been unequivocal in its support of the positive relationship between students' active engagement with academic tasks and their achievement (Brophy, 1986; Ellis, Worthington, & Larkin, 2002; Fisher et al., 1980; Greenwood, Delquadri, & Hall, 1984; Heward, 1994; Rosenshine & Berliner, 1978; Swanson & Hoskyn, 2001). Providing instruction with high levels of active student participation is important for all learners, but it is particularly important for students with disabilities: "The pedagogical clock continues to tick mercilessly, and the opportunities for these students to advance or catch up diminish over time" (Kame'enui, 1993, p. 379).

Researchers have used terms such as *academic learning time, opportunity to respond,* and *active student response* to refer to this important variable. Heward (1994) defined **active student response (ASR)** as

> an observable response made to an instructional antecedent….ASR occurs when a student emits a detectable response to ongoing instruction. The kinds of responses that qualify as

CURRENT ISSUES AND FUTURE TRENDS

SELF-DETERMINATION: THE *MOST* NATURAL SUPPORT

BY MICHAEL L. WEHMEYER

If you listed what you think students with intellectual disability need most to transition successfully from high school to their adult life, what would be on that list? It would, most likely, look something like this:

✓ Job skills and workplace supports
✓ Independent living and community inclusion skills
✓ Post-secondary education and training
✓ Transportation
✓ Health care
✓ Friends, family, and supports

Those (and other items) are all, obviously, important to enable students with intellectual disability to become independent, self-sufficient young adults. Another item that should be on the list may not be as obvious. Research has shown that students with disabilities, including students with intellectual disability, who are more self-determined when they leave high school, achieve more positive employment, independent living, and quality of life outcomes than do their peers with disabilities who are less self-determined.

Self-determination may be the most important factor in ensuring a good quality of life for students with intellectual disabilities as they transition to adulthood.

What does "being self-determined" mean? Have you met people who you just knew would make it in life? These people had goals and plans to achieve them. They could identify barriers to success and solve problems to remove them. They knew what they were good at and capitalized on their strengths. They take charge of their own learning, work toward self-set goals, and are ready when opportunities become available. Perhaps these qualities even describe you. These people are self-determined.

As you will learn from this text, people who are self-determined *act* in ways that enable them to solve problems in their lives, set and attain goals, make decisions, advocate on their own behalf, and generally improve the quality of their lives. In our own work, we have defined self-determination as "volitional actions that enable one to act as the primary causal agent in one's life and to maintain or improve one's quality of life" (M. L. Wehmeyer, 2006, p. 117). The ideas of "volitional action" and "causal agent" are central to understanding what is meant by being self-determined. By acting volitionally, we mean that people who are self-determined act based on their preferences and interests and not based on coercion or someone else's preferences and interests. There's more to being self-determined, though, than simply doing what you want rather than what someone else wants. The word *volition* is defined as the exercise of the capability of a person to make a *conscious* choice or decision with *intention*. Acting volitionally implies that one does so consciously and with intention. Self-determined behavior is not just acting to gratify instant needs or acting recklessly for short-term pleasure; it is acting consciously and with intention based on one's preferences and interests to choose, make decisions, advocate, and, generally, self-govern and self-regulate one's behavior in pursuit of one's goals.

The second part of this definition implies that self-determined people are causal agents in their lives. The noun *determination* in the term *self-determination* originates from the philosophical doctrine of *determinism*, which proposes that all events—including human behavior—are in some way *caused* (i.e., determined). Obviously, causes of human behavior are varied, from genes to environment; the meaning of *self-determination* (or *self-determinism*) is that one's actions are *caused* by oneself as opposed to something or someone else (i.e., other-determination). Self-determination refers to self-caused action.

People who are self-determined are causal agents in their lives. The adjective *causal* means expressive of or indicative of cause—showing the interaction of cause and effect. The term *agent* is a noun that refers to one who acts or has the authority to act. Self-determined people act "with authority" to make or cause something to happen in their lives. Causal agency implies more, however, than just causing action; it implies that the individual who makes or causes things to happen in his or her life does so with an eye toward *causing* an effect to accomplish a specific end or to cause or create change; in other words, they act volitionally and intentionally.

Does all this fussing about terms and definitions matter? Well, it does to people with intellectual disability. People too often equate self-determination with physically acting independently, without help, and with "controlling" one's own life. People with intellectual disability have limitations to their capacity to solve difficult problems or make complex decisions and in many meaningful ways, to "control" their lives. The important point to understand, though, is that being self-determined is *not* about doing things independently; it is about making things happen in one's life by acting volitionally and being a causal agent. Even if a student cannot independently make a decision, for example, she can be actively supported to engage in the decision-making process; and if the student needs others' support to make that decision, he can still be "self-determined" as long as the ultimate decision takes into account, to the maximum degree practicable, the student's preferences, interest, beliefs, values, skills, abilities, and long-term goals.

In too many cases, the way others understand self-determination limits the degree to which educators work to promote the self-determination of students with intellectual disability. This is in spite of the fact that research has shown that students with intellectual disability can acquire the knowledge and skills to make more effective decisions, solve problems, set and attain goals, self-advocate, and so forth (Chambers et al., 2007). In fact, a host of evidence-based practices have been shown to enhance the knowledge and skills that enable students to become more self-determined (Lee, Amos, et al., 2006). My research with my colleagues has focused on developing and establishing an evidence base for a model of teaching to enable teachers to, in essence, teach students to teach themselves! This model, the Self-Determined Learning Model of Instruction, teaches students to self-direct the learning process and engage in a self-regulated problem-solving process to enable them to set goals, create plans to address those goals, and to self-monitor and self-evaluate their progress toward those goals (see M. L. Wehmeyer et al., 2007 for more information). Relatedly, a substantial literature base shows that students with intellectual disability can learn to self-regulate behavior or self-direct learning when taught skills such as self-instruction, self-monitoring, antecedent cue regulation, self-evaluation, and self-reinforcement (e.g., Fowler et al., 2007). For tips on promoting student-directed learning in inclusive settings, see Agran, King-Sears, Wehmeyer, and Copeland (2003).

Also, a visible component of many school districts' emerging efforts to promote student self-determination involves promoting student involvement in educational planning and decision making. These activities range from teaching students to use presentation software, such as Microsoft's PowerPoint®, to present information about themselves during an IEP meeting to the implementation of more systematic, curricular efforts that promote self-determination by teaching students skills to run their IEP meeting (see M. L. Wehmeyer et al., 2007 for a discussion of such programmatic efforts).

Promoting self-determination has become a critical issue in the education of students with intellectual disability, and there is every reason to believe that this will be the case in the future. So, I suggest that if you haven't done so already, add one more item to your list of items you "must teach" to students with intellectual disability:

✓ Self-determination

What Do You Think?

1. What is the relationship between self-determined learning goals and the motivation to achieve them? Think of your own life.

2. Should the components and purposes of self-determination for students with intellectual disabilities differ from those for students with other types of disabilities? For students without disabilities?

3. What should a teacher do if she believes that a self-determined learning goal expressed by a student with intellectual disabilities is inappropriate or maladaptive?

Source: "Self-Determination: The Most Natural Support": Michael L. Wehmeyer, Ph.D. Michael Wehmeyer is Professor in the Department of Special Education and Director of the Beach Center for Disability at the University of Kansas. His research interests include access to the general education curriculum by students with intellectual disabilities, self-determination, and technology use by people with disabilities.

Effective instruction for all students, with or without disabilities, is characterized by frequent opportunities for active student response and systematic feedback.

To learn more about how a general education teacher can use choral responding in reading mastery, math, and spelling, go to the Homework & Exercises section in Chapter 4 of MyEducationLab and complete Homework Exercise 2.

To learn more about using instructive feedback in the classroom, go to the Homework & Exercises section in Chapter 4 of MyEducationLab and complete Homework Exercise 3.

ASR are as varied as the kinds of lessons that are taught. Depending upon the instructional objective, examples of ASR include words read, problems answered, boards cut, test tubes measured, praise and supportive comments spoken, notes or scales played, stitches sewn, sentences written, workbook questions answered, and fastballs pitched. The basic measure of how much ASR a student receives is a frequency count of the number of responses emitted within a given period of instruction. (p. 286)

When all variables are held constant (e.g., quality of curriculum materials, students' prerequisite skills, motivational variables), an ASR-rich lesson will generally result in more learning than will a lesson in which students make few or no responses. To read about the simplest and quickest way to increase ASR for all students during group instruction, see Teaching & Learning, "Let's Make Some Noise!"

Systematic Feedback Instructional feedback—information provided to students about their performance—falls into two broad categories: (a) praise and/or other forms of confirmation or **positive reinforcement** for correct responses, and (b) error correction for incorrect responses. Feedback is generally most effective when it is specific, immediate, positive, frequent, and differential (comparing the student's present performance with past performance; e.g., "You read 110 words today, Jermon. That's five more than yesterday.").

Several studies have found that providing a type of feedback that Werts and colleagues call *instructive feedback* can increase the efficiency of instruction for students with mental retardation and other disabilities (Gursel, Tekin-Iftar, & Boxkurt, 2006; Werts, Caldwell, & Wolery, 2003). When giving feedback to students on their responses to targeted items, the teacher intentionally and methodically presents "extra information." For example, when praising a student's correct response when reading the word *corn,* the teacher might say, "Right, this word is *corn;* it is a vegetable." The instructive feedback is the statement "it is a vegetable."

Using feedback effectively is one of the most important skills for teachers (Konold, Miller, & Konold, 2004). Effective teachers change the focus and timing of the feedback they provide as a student progresses from initial attempts at learning a new skill through practicing a newly acquired skill. When a student is first learning a new skill or content knowledge, feedback should follow each response (see Figure 4.5). Feedback during this **acquisition stage of learning** should focus on the accuracy and form of the student's response (e.g., "Very good, Kathy. Two quarters equal fifty cents."). By providing feedback after each response, the teacher reduces the likelihood that the student will practice errors.

When a student can accurately perform a new skill with some degree of consistency, she should begin making a series of responses before the teacher provides feedback. Feedback during this **practice stage of learning** should emphasize the correct rate at which the student performs the target skill (e.g., "Dominique, you correctly answered 28 problems in 1 minute. Way to go!"). Providing feedback after each response during the practice stage may have a detrimental effect on learning because it blocks the student's opportunity to develop fluency.

Transfer of Stimulus Control Trial-and-error learning is inefficient and frustrating for students without disabilities. For students with mental retardation and other learning problems, it is likely to be a complete waste of time. Instead of waiting to see whether the student will make a correct response, the effective teacher provides a prompt (e.g., physical guidance, verbal directions, pictures, prerecorded auditory prompts) that makes a correct

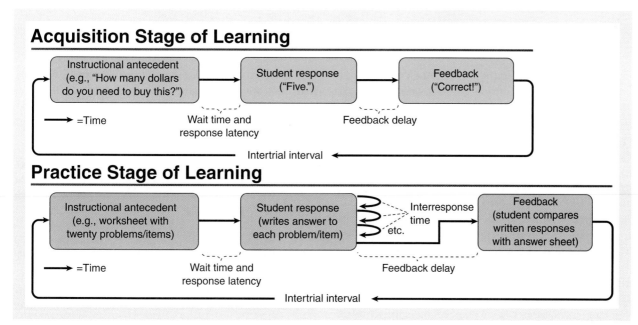

FIGURE 4.5

Feedback within a series of instructional trials during the acquisition and practice stages of learning

Source: Reprinted from Heward, W. L. (1994). Three "low-tech" strategies for increasing the frequency of active student response during group instruction. In R. Gardner, III, D. M. Sainato, J. O. Cooper, T. E. Heron, W. L. Heward, J. W. Eshleman, & T. A. Grossi (Eds.), *Behavior analysis in education: Focus on measurably superior instruction* (p. 284). Reprinted with permission of Wadsworth, a division of Thomson Learning: www.thomsonrights.com <http://www.thomsonrights.com/>. Fax 800 730-2215.

response very probable (West & Billingsley, 2005). For example, Wood, Frank, and Hamre-Nietupski (1996) provided picture prompts for students to help them correctly perform each step in a task analysis for opening a combination lock found on student lockers. The correct response is reinforced, the prompt is repeated, and another correct student response is reinforced. The response prompts are then gradually and systematically withdrawn so that the student's performance comes under the stimulus control of natural cues: "persons, objects, or events that should act as 'signals' for learned behavior to occur outside of instruction situations" (Billingsley, 1998, p. 157).

Generalization and Maintenance   **Generalization** and **maintenance** refer to the extent to which students use what they have learned across settings and over time. Although much remains to be learned about helping students with mental retardation and other disabilities get the most out of what they learn, researchers have developed the promising beginnings of a reliable "technology of generalization" (J. O. Cooper et al., 2007). Three of many evidence-based strategies for promoting generalization and maintenance are described here:

- *Aim for naturally occurring reinforcement contingencies.* The most basic strategy for promoting generalization and maintenance is to increase the probability that a student's performance of a newly learned skill will be reinforced in the natural environment (e.g., the general education classroom, the playground, the community, recreational and work settings) (Baer, 1999). Teachers can accomplish this by (a) teaching functional skills that students need and that the people in the student's natural environment are likely to value and (b) teaching students to perform new skills with the accuracy and fluency necessary to produce reinforcement in the natural environment.

- *Program common stimuli.* If the generalization setting differs greatly from the setting where teaching takes place, the student may not perform the new behavior. Teachers can program common stimuli in two basic ways: (a) incorporate into the teaching situation as many typical features of the generalization setting as possible and (b) create a new common stimulus that the student learns to use in the teaching setting and can

Promoting generalization and maintenance

 Council for Exceptional Children — Content Standards for Beginning Teachers—Common Core: Use strategies to facilitate maintenance and generalization of skills across learning environments (CC4S4).

Let's Make Some Noise!

Using Choral Responding to Improve the Effectiveness of Group Instruction

BY WILLIAM L. HEWARD AND CHARLES L. WOOD

Teachers recognize the importance of actively engaging students during group instruction. Posing a question or problem to the entire class and then calling on one student to answer is the most common strategy teachers use to obtain student participation during group instruction. This provides an active learning opportunity for only the student who is called on and often results in more frequent responses by high-achieving students and few or no responses by low-achieving students. An alternative to one-student-at-a-time participation is **choral responding (CR)**—all students in the group responding orally in unison to a question or item presented by the teacher. Choral responding has been around since the days of the one-room schoolhouse and has always been a widely used teaching technique in foreign language classes. Choral responding is the simplest, fastest way to increase ASR in group instruction.

BENEFITS AND USES OF CHORAL RESPONDING

Choral responding has several advantages over calling on one student at a time to respond. First, with CR the teacher asks every student in the class to actively participate. Second, it gives the teacher immediate feedback on whether or not the students are "getting it" and if review is needed. Third, CR is an effective strategy for including students with special learning needs in general education classrooms. Fourth, CR builds confidence in low achieving students by allowing them to perform well in front of their peers. Finally, when students are engaged in CR, off-task and disruptive behaviors are reduced.

Choral responding has been the response mode in numerous studies demonstrating a strong relationship between frequent student response during instruction and improved learning outcomes (e.g., Cihak, Alberto, Taber-Doughty, & Gama, 2006; Maheady, Michielli-Pendl, Mallette, & Harper, 2002; Sainato, Strain, & Lyon, 1987; Sterling, Barbetta, Heward, & Heron, 1997).

Choral responding can be used to review or to check students' maintenance of previously learned concepts. For example, a high school history teacher could use CR to review the day's Civil War lesson. "Okay, class. I'm going to ask a series of questions about what we've covered in today's lesson. Your response will be 'Confederate' or 'Union.'"

Teachers can also use CR to teach new knowledge and skills. Whether a lesson primarily reviews or teaches new material is determined by the type and sequence of CR questions. Choral responding is a primary means for student participation in the highly effective Direct Instruction model programs to teach language, reading, math, and spelling (Carnine, Silbert, Kame'enui, Tarver, & Jongjohann, 2006; Engelmann & Colvin, 2006).

HOW TO GET STARTED

Select curriculum/lesson content. Choral responding is most effective with curriculum content that meets three criteria. Each question, problem, or item presented for CR . . .

- Has only one correct answer
- Can be answered with brief responses (1 to 5 words)
- Is suitable for a fast-paced presentation

Prepare questions and instructional materials. By preparing the CR questions or problems in advance, the teacher can provide more response opportunities for students, maintain an energetic pace, attend to her students' responses, and provide effective feedback. The teacher will not lose time and visual contact with students when using prepared Powerpoint® slides or overhead transparencies for questions or problems that require a visual display (e.g., math problems, words, geometric shapes), rather than writing items on a chalkboard during the lesson.

Schedule a 5- to 10-minute CR session. Use brief CR lessons for different subjects throughout the school day. Three mini-lessons are better than one extended session of massed practice.

Conduct choral responding. We recommend the following procedures for CR:

- *Give clear directions.* Tell students the type of response(s) desired, and model one or two trials. For example, "I'm going to ask some questions about yesterday's science lesson. If I hold up this paper clip and ask, 'What will a magnet do to this object?' On my signal, you say, 'attract' or 'not attract'." To make your expectations clear, demonstrate several examples and nonexamples of correct responding.

- *Provide a "thinking pause" if needed.* Let the complexity of the question/problem and students' relative level of mastery determine the length of the pause. For difficult questions, use a longer pause between your question and your signal to respond.

- *Give a clear signal for students to respond.* Signals such as a finger snap, a clap, a hand or arm movement, or saying, "Everyone," "How many?" helps students respond in unison and makes it easier to detect correct and incorrect responses. If the thinking pause is longer than a few seconds, say, "Get ready" just before the signal.

- *Provide feedback on the group response:*
  - *You hear only correct answers.* (a) Confirm and praise correct responses (e.g., "Yes!/All right!" "You got it." "Great!"), and (b) immediately present the next question, item, or problem.
  - *One or two incorrect answers.* (a) State the correct answer (e.g., "Yes, there are 12 hydrogen atoms in a molecule of glucose."), and (b) present the same item again a few trials later.
  - *More than a few incorrect responses.* (a) State the correct answer and give brief explanation (with demonstration and/or illustration if relevant), (b) immediately repeat the same question for CR, and (c) return to the same question a few trials later. Avoid long explanations when correcting errors. Succinct questions maintain students' attention to the lesson content.
- *Randomly call on individual students throughout the lesson:*
  - Ask the question first, then call an individual student's name instead of giving the usual signal for everyone to respond. This helps all students maintain attention and not "drop out" when it is not their turn.
  - This is an excellent tactic for giving low-achieving students opportunities to succeed in front of their peers. If low performers answer correctly, you can be confident that other students are also correct. Use this as an opportunity to reinforce a student's accuracy, not to single out a student for his mistakes.
- *Maintain a lively pace.* Present the next question immediately after you have given feedback on the previous response. Fast pacing promotes students' participation and accuracy, and decreases off-task behavior (Tincani, Ernsbarger, Harrison, & Heward, 2005).
- *Praise students' participation and correct responding.* For example, say, "You're so smart!" and give "high fives" throughout the lesson. Your praise and approval can increase students' motivation and make the CR lesson more fun.
- *Combine CR with other ASR techniques.* Integrate CR into lessons with other techniques for generating high rates of ASR such as response cards and guided notes. (See Teaching & Learning, "Using Response Cards to Increase Participation and Achievement," later in this chapter. Also see Teaching & Learning, "Guided Notes: Helping All Children Succeed in the General Education Curriculum," in Chapter 5.)

Have fun with choral responding. CR games add variety to a typical school day. Using CR games is a good way to end a difficult lesson or a long period of independent seatwork (Wood & Heward, 2007):

- *CR Simon Says.* Play this game as you would normally play Simon Says, but add a CR requirement.

For example, the teacher says, "Simon says, 'Name the closest planet to the sun,' then touch your head." Students respond, "Mercury," and touch their heads. Teacher says, "Spell October and hop on one foot." Several students do not respond, but a few do. Teacher says, "Remember, I didn't say Simon says!"

- *Back and Forth Counting.* This CR game gives students a lot of practice counting forward, backward, and in multiples. The game can be played as teacher vs. students, between two groups of students, or one on one. One team says a number, and the other team has to quickly respond by saying the next number in sequence. Each team responds "back and forth" (e.g., Team one, "3." Team two, "6," team one, "9" and so forth) until a team makes a mistake.
- *CR Hot Potato.* Have students stand and form a large circle. Present fast-paced CR on content that does not require much thinking time (e.g., basic facts). While students respond in unison, have them pass the "hot potato" (i.e., a bean bag or small ball) around the circle. Continue CR and say, "Stop" when the class makes an error. The student holding the bean bag or ball gets "caught holding the hot potato."
- *Student as Teacher.* You can easily teach students to lead CR review sessions. With experience using CR, many students can imitate the teaching procedures, including signals, error correction, and pacing. Model the teaching procedures, let a student present CR questions from a script or poster, and give the student feedback on his or her presentation. Students enjoy leading CR review sessions. The opportunity to lead a CR session often serves as an effective reward for students who are not motivated to participate in large-group activities. Consider using student CR teachers during morning drills or transitions throughout the school day.
- *Quiet CR.* When it is necessary to have a quiet classroom (e.g., the class next door is taking a test), replace CR with other easy-to-see hand or finger responses. Wear two-colored work gloves (yellow and blue cotton work gloves). Students can hold up fingers to match a multiple-choice answer (Pratton & Hales, 1986) or show "thumbs up" or "thumbs down" to indicate "yes" or "no" responses. Younger students can be instructed to "Touch your ears if the answer is true, touch your nose if the answer is false."

To learn more about choral responding strategies, go to the Building Teaching Skills section in Chapter 4 of MyEducationLab and complete the activities. As you watch the videos and complete the activities, compare the similarities and differences in the teachers' techniques.

To learn more about strategies of generalization and maintenance, go to the Homework & Exercises section of Chapter 4 of MyEducationLab and complete Homework Exercise 4.

transport to the generalization setting, where it prompts or assists performance of the target skill.

- *Community-based instruction.* Teaching in the actual setting where students are ultimately to use their new skills increases the probability of generalization and maintenance. Community-based instruction is a widely used practice in special education with a good research base to support it (Owens-Johnson & Hamill, 2002). However, simply conducting instruction in the community is no guarantee of generalization and maintenance. A poorly designed lesson will be ineffective regardless of where it is conducted. And community-based instruction can be expensive and typically is not available on a daily basis. Morse and Schuster (2000) found that 2 days per week of community-based instruction supplemented by simulation training in the classroom were effective in teaching students with mental retardation to shop for groceries.

Direct and frequent measurement

Council for Exceptional Children **Content Standards for Beginning Teachers—Common Core:** Evaluate instruction and monitor progress of individuals with exceptional educational needs (CC8S8) (also CC7S13).

Direct and Frequent Measurement   Teachers should verify the effects of their instruction by measuring student performance directly and frequently. Measurement is *direct* when it objectively records the learner's performance of the behavior of interest in the natural environment for that skill. Measurement is *frequent* when it occurs on a regular basis; ideally, measurement should take place as often as instruction occurs. Figure 4.4 shows how teachers recorded daily measures of student's performance of each step of morning routine, including the degree of independence and whether an adult provided a prompt or assistance.

When teachers do not collect direct and frequent measurements of students' performance to verify the effects of instruction, they are prone to two mistakes: (1) continuing ineffective instruction when no real learning has occurred (e.g., perhaps a teacher believes a certain type of instruction is effective) and (2) discontinuing an effective program of instruction

Community-based instruction provides these students an opportunity to acquire vocational skills in a real work setting.

because subjective judgment finds no improvement (e.g., without object measures it is difficult to discern that a student's reading rate has increased from 70 words per minute to 80 words per minute. (Heward, 2005, p. 321)

EDUCATIONAL PLACEMENT ALTERNATIVES

Children with mild intellectual disabilities were traditionally educated in self-contained classrooms in the public schools, and students with moderate and severe mental retardation were routinely placed in special schools. Today many children with mental retardation are educated in general education classrooms.

During the 2005–2006 school year, 14.1% of students with mental retardation were educated in the general education classroom, with 29.1% being served in resource room programs and 50.2% in separate classes (U.S. Office of Special Education Programs, 2007a). About 6.7% of students with mental retardation are educated in separate schools, residential facilities, or home/hospital environments. Sometimes a number of small neighboring school districts pool their resources to offer a special school program for students with moderate, severe, and profound mental retardation. However, many special educators today believe that separate schools prohibit students from obtaining an education in the least restrictive environment and that all children should attend their local neighborhood schools regardless of the type or severity of their disability (e.g., Baumgart & Giangreco, 1996; Stainback & Stainback, 1996; Taylor, 2005).

As you learned in Chapter 2, simply putting a child with disabilities into a general education classroom does not mean that he will be accepted socially or receive the most appropriate and needed instructional programming (Siperstein, Parker, Norins Bardon, & Widamon, 2007). Many special and general educators, however, are developing programs and methods for teaching students with mental retardation alongside their classmates without disabilities. Systematically planning for the student's inclusion in the classroom through team games and collaborative learning and group investigation projects and directly training all students in specific skills for interacting with one another are just some of the methods for increasing the chances of a successful general education class placement (Agran, King-Sears, Wehmeyer, & Copeland, 2003; Bauer & Brown, 2001; Giangreco & Doyle, 2007; Grenot-Scheyer, Fisher, & Staub, 2001; Janney & Snell, 1996, 1997; Kennedy & Fisher, 2001; Krajewski & Flaherty, 2000; Ryndak & Fisher, 2007; Salend, 2008; Schwartz, 2005). Peer tutoring and peer buddy programs can also promote the instructional and social inclusion of students with mental retardation into general education classrooms (Campbell Miller, Cooke, Test, & White, 2003; Copeland et al., 2002, 2004; Hughes & Carter, 2006; Mortweet et al., 1999).

Students with intellectual disabilities often benefit from similar programs for students who are not disabled. During the early elementary grades, students with mental retardation as well as their chronological-age peers need instruction in basic academic skills. Reading, math, and writing are core curricular areas that should be included in programs for all students (Al Otaiba & Hosp, 2004; Bradford et al., 2006; Jolivette et al., 2006; Joseph & Seery, 2004). During this period, most students with intellectual disabilities benefit from full or partial inclusion in general education classroom settings.

One of the best ways to provide meaningful access to academic and social life of the classroom is to adapt instruction so that every student can participate frequently and successfully with the curriculum (S. H. Lee et al., 2006). Like choral responding described earlier, using response cards is another evidence-based strategy for providing high rates of successful engagement with the curriculum for all students (Heward et al., 1996; Randolph, 2007). See Teaching & Learning, "Using Response Cards to Increase Participation and Achievement."

The relative appropriateness of spending the entire school day in a general education classroom may change for some students as they move from the elementary grades to high school, when opportunities for community-based instruction in vocational and life skills are critical.

Placement alternatives for students with MR Content

 Council for Exceptional Children Standards for Beginning Teachers of Students With MR/DD: Continuum of placement services available for individuals with MR/DD (MR1K3).

Facilitating inclusion for students with MR

Council for Exceptional Children Content Standards for Beginning Teachers of Students With MR/DD: Approaches to creating positive learning environments for individuals with MR/DD (MR5K1) (also CC4S1).

Most students with intellectual disabilities benefit from instruction in basic academic and social skills in inclusive classrooms.

Rashawn raised his hand for the last time. He wanted to answer several of his teacher's questions, especially when she asked whether anyone could name the clouds that look like wispy cotton. But it wasn't his day to get called on. He tried to follow along but soon lost interest and laid his head on his desk.

Dean did get called on once, but he didn't raise his hand too often. It was easier just to sit there. If he were quiet and still like Rashawn, then he wouldn't have to think about learning all this weather stuff. But it got too hard for Dean to just sit, so he started acting out. This got his teacher's attention.

"Dean, please pay attention!"

"Stop that, Dean!"

"Dean, how do you expect to learn this material for tomorrow's test if you're not part of the group?"

The next day, Rashawn and Dean did poorly on the test of meteorology concepts. Each boy had a history of poor school achievement; and teachers sometimes used terms such as *intellectual disabilities, learning disabilities*, and *attention deficit disorder* as explanations for their lack of success. But perhaps their poor scores, as well as their chronic underachievement, were directly influenced by the quality of instruction they received.

Neither boy had actively participated during the previous day's lesson. Instead of being active learners who responded frequently to the lesson's content, both boys were at best passive observers. Educational research has shown that students who respond actively and often learn more than do students who passively attend to instruction (E. S. Ellis et al., 2002). Although most teachers recognize the importance of active student participation, it is difficult to implement during group instruction. Teachers commonly pose a question to the entire class and then call on one student. This technique often results in frequent responses by high-achieving students and few or no responses by low-achieving students such as Rashawn and Dean (Maheady et al., 2002). Like choral responding described earlier in this chapter, response cards (RC) are one alternative to the traditional hand-raising (HR) and one-student-participating-at-a-time method of group instruction.

WHAT ARE RESPONSE CARDS?

Response cards are cards, signs, or items that all students simultaneously hold up to display their responses to a question or problem. Teachers use two basic types of RCs: preprinted and write-on. When using preprinted RCs, each student selects from a personal set of cards the one with the answer she wishes to display. Examples include yes/true and no/false cards, numbers, colors, traffic signs, molecular structures, and parts of speech. Instead of using a set of different cards, teachers can distribute a single preprinted RC with multiple answers to each student (e.g., a card with clearly marked sections identified as proteins, fat, carbohydrates, vitamins, and minerals for use in a lesson on healthful eating habits). In its humblest version, the preprinted RC with multiple responses is a "pinch

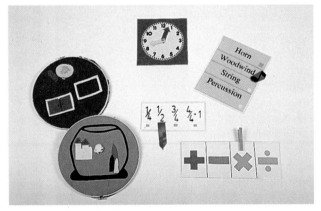

Response cards, which are easily created for any curriculum area, enable each student in the class to answer every question or problem presented by the teacher.

card": the student responds by holding up the card with her fingers pinching the part displaying her answer. Colored clothespins also make good pinching tools. Preprinted RCs may also have built-in devices for displaying answers, such as a cardboard clock with movable hour and minute hands.

When using write-on RCs, students mark their answers on blank cards that they erase between learning trials. Teachers can make a set of 40 durable write-on RCs from a 4-by-8-foot sheet of white laminated bathroom board (available from builders' supply stores). The cost is generally less than $20, including the charge for cutting the sheet into 9-by-12-inch RCs. Dry-erase markers are available at most office supply stores, and paper towels or tissues will easily wipe the RCs clean.

Students can also use small chalkboards as write-on RCs, but responses may be difficult for the teacher to see in a full-size classroom. Write-on RCs can be custom-made to provide background or organizing structure for responses. For example, music students might mark notes on an RC that has permanent treble and bass clef scales; students in a driver's education class could draw where their car should go on RCs with permanent street intersections.

RESEARCH

Numerous studies have evaluated the effects of RCs on student participation and learning in general and special education classrooms at the elementary, middle, and secondary levels (e.g., Cavanaugh, Heward, & Donelson, 1996; Christle & Schuster, 2003; Davis & O'Neill, 2004; C. Horn et al., 2006; Marmolejo, Wilder, & Bradley, 2004; Randolph, 2007). For example, a study by Gardner, Heward, and Grossi (1994) comparing write-on RCs with HR during whole-class science lessons in an inner-city fifth-grade classroom produced three major findings.

First, when using RCs, each student responded to teacher-posed questions an average of 21.8 times per 30-minute lesson, compared to a mean of 1.5 academic responses when the teacher called on individuals. The higher participation rate takes on additional significance when its cumulative effect is calculated over the course of a 180-day school year. By using RCs instead of HR for just 30 minutes per day, each student in the class would make an additional 3,700 academic responses during the school year. Second, all 22 students scored higher on next-day quizzes and 2-week review tests that followed lessons with RCs than they did on quizzes and tests that followed lessons with HR. Third, all but one student preferred RCs over hand raising.

In addition to increased participation and learning outcomes for students, several studies have found improved on-task behavior and/or decreases in the frequency of disruptions and inappropriate behavior when student used RCs (e.g., Armendariz & Umbreit, 1999; Christle & Schuster, 2003; Davis & O'Neill, 2004; Godfrey et al., 2003; Lambert, Cartledge, Lo, & Heward, 2006).

HOW TO GET STARTED

Suggestions for All Types of RCs

- Model several question-and-answer trials, and give students practice on how to use RCs.
- Maintain a lively pace throughout the lesson; keep intervals between trials short.
- Give clear cues when students are to hold up and put down their cards.
- Students can learn from watching others; do not let them think it is cheating to look at classmates' RCs.

Suggestions for Using Preprinted RCs

- Design the cards to be as easy to see as possible (e.g., consider size, print type, color codes).
- Make the cards easy for students to manipulate and display (e.g., put answers on both sides of the cards; attach a group of related cards to a ring).
- Begin instruction on new content with a small set of fact/concept cards (perhaps only two), gradually adding additional cards as students' skills improve.

Suggestions for Using Write-On RCs

- Limit language-based responses to one to three words.
- Keep a few extra markers on hand.
- Be sure students do not hesitate to respond because they are concerned about making spelling mistakes: (a) provide several practice trials with new terms before the lesson begins; (b) write new terms on the chalkboard, and tell students to refer to them during the lesson; and/or (c) use the "don't worry" technique, telling students to try their best but that misspellings will not count against them.
- Students enjoy doodling on their response cards. After a good lesson, let students draw on the cards for a few minutes.

Go to the Homework & Exercises section in Chapter 4 of MyEducationLab and complete Homework Exercise 5. As you watch the video and answer the accompanying questions, think about how using response cards can vary from elementary to middle school level.

As students get older, their needs begin to differ and thus curricular differentiation becomes an important consideration.... Rather than being integrated into a world history class, many students with mental retardation may be better served by learning the necessary functional skills for independent living. Skills such as job readiness, how to use leisure time, how to budget and shop, how to cook and how to maintain a household are important. While all individuals must learn these skills in order to be independent, most students learn them on their own, without specific instructional activities that focus on these areas. Students with mental retardation, on the other hand, often need structured learning experiences in order to learn these skills. (Smith & Hilton, 1997, pp. 6–7)

The extent to which a general education classroom is an appropriate placement for a student with mental retardation, as with any student with disabilities, should be determined by the student's individual needs. "School inclusion can then be seen as a means (as opposed to just a goal unto itself) toward the ultimate objective of community inclusion and empowerment" (Polloway, Smith, Patton, & Smith, 1996, p. 11).

Acceptance and Membership

Normalization and social role valorization

Council for Exceptional Children — Content Standards for Beginning Teachers of Students With MR/DD: Trends and practices within the field of MR/DD (MR1K5) (also CC4S5).

Since the early 1970s, the principle of **normalization** has provided a conceptual foundation and touchstone for improving the life experiences of persons with intellectual disabilities. The concept, which originated in Scandinavia, was first described in an American publication by Nirje (1969) in a book published by the President's Committee on Mental Retardation. Recently, Perske (2004) reexamined Nirje's original "eight planks of normalization" such as a normal rhythm of the day, a normal routine of life (e.g., living in one place and working in another), a normal rhythm of the year (e.g., observing holidays, personal religious days, and relaxation days), a normal developmental experience of the life cycle (e.g., experiencing the settings and atmospheres enjoyed by typical peers), valuing individual choices (e.g., allowing the dignity and freedom to fail), and so forth.

Wolfensberger (1972), one of the first and best-known champions of normalization in the United States, wrote that the principle refers to the use of progressively more normal settings and procedures "to establish and/or maintain personal behaviors which are as culturally normal as possible" (p. 28). Normalization is not a single technique or set of procedures but an overriding philosophy. It says that persons with mental retardation should, to the greatest extent possible, be both physically and socially integrated into everyday society regardless of their degree or type of disability.

While the principle of normalization has helped individuals with mental retardation who are physically present in many school, community, and work settings today, it has not gained them acceptance and true membership (Lemay, 2006). Wolfensberger (1983) proposed the concept of *social role valorization (SRV)* as a necessary and natural extension of the normalization principle. He writes, "The most explicit and highest goal of normalization must be the creation, support, and defense of valued social roles for people who are at risk of social devaluation" (p. 234).

The key premise of SRV is that people's welfare depends extensively on the social roles they occupy: People who fill roles that are positively valued by others will generally be afforded by the latter the good things of life, but people who fill roles that are devalued by others will typically be badly treated by them. This implies that in the case of people whose life situations are very bad, and whose bad situations are bound up with occupancy of devalued roles, then if the social roles they are seen as occupying can somehow be upgraded in the eyes of perceivers, their life conditions will usually improve, and often dramatically so. (Wolfensberger, 2000, p. 105)

Perhaps the greatest current expression and extension of the normalization/SRV concept in special education can be found in the growing movement toward teaching self-determination skills to individuals with intellectual disabilities. In his presidential address to the AAMR, Wagner (2000) offered this example of the relationship between self-determination and social role valorization:

How do we . . . implement this dream of highly valued roles in society? One thing we need to do is . . . celebrate the people who, in fact, currently have highly valued roles. . . . [For example] . . . there is Christina. She has big dreams. . . . About 6 years ago, she was mainstreamed into a large high school. In central Louisiana. . . . [S]he went out for the cheerleading squad and became a cheerleader. Then, a few years later when she was a senior, Christina decided that she wanted to be Homecoming Queen. She saw no problem at all with the fact that she has Down syndrome. . . . [S]he ran for Homecoming Queen and won. Christina is my heroine of big dreams. She did not let her handicaps stand in the way of realizing her dreams. I think it is also a testament to that high school that they did not let her handicaps stand in the way either. (p. 442)

One of the most important things that special educators can do is to help students like Christina identify their goals and provide the instruction and supports that will enable them to pursue those goals. As support for self-determination and social role valorization grows among both educators and the public, the time draws nearer when all persons with intellectual disabilities will experience the benefits of valued membership in integrated school, community, and employment settings.

TIPS for Beginning Teachers

ORGANIZATION IS KEY
by Sandie Trask-Tyler

GET TO KNOW YOUR STUDENTS BEFORE THE SCHOOL YEAR STARTS

- Send a welcome note to all of your students in the middle of the summer and include a picture of yourself. Highlight something they can look forward to when school starts.
- Organize a class get-together for your students and their families before the start of school. This is a great opportunity for everyone to meet each other and a wonderful way for parents to network.

BE PREPARED TO BUY EXTRA CLASSROOM SUPPLIES

- Stock up on classroom supplies during the back-to-school sales in the summer.
- Save your personal spending receipts for classroom purchases. You may be able to use these expenditures on your taxes.
- Shop at yard sales and auctions for all types of items you can use in your classroom at a great price.

CREATE A SYSTEM OF ORGANIZATION THAT WORKS FOR YOU

- Label boxes, shelves, and cabinets with words and/or pictures of what belongs there to assist staff and students in locating and replacing items.

- Create a spreadsheet of student and staff information such as phone numbers, addresses, parents' names, etc., and keep a copy at home and school for easy access.
- Create a spreadsheet with students' school information, including date of birth, multifactored evaluation due date, IEP due date, related services, and so on.
- Set up a notebook or clipboard for each student with his corresponding IEP data sheets. You can group them into the different curricular areas and even insert student work samples so all of their learning information is in one location.
- Set up a teacher binder that includes general substitute teacher information, overall class schedule, student transportation information, copies of emergency information, drill procedures, each student's IEP, and other classroom information (such as the previously mentioned spreadsheets).

KEY TERMS AND CONCEPTS

acquisition stage of learning, p. 156

active student response (ASR), p. 153

adaptive behavior, p. 138

amniocentesis, p. 146

choral responding, p. 158

chorionic villi sampling, p. 146

Down syndrome, p. 143

fetal alcohol spectrum disorder, p. 144

fragile X syndrome, p. 143

generalization, p. 157

genetic counseling, p. 146

intellectual disabilities, p. 135

maintenance, p. 157

mediated scaffolding, p. 152

mental retardation, p. 132

normal curve, p. 136

normalization, p. 164

norm-referenced test, p. 136

perinatal, p. 142

phenylketonuria (PKU), p. 146

positive reinforcement, p. 156

postnatal, p. 142

practice stage of learning, p. 156

prenatal, p. 142

response cards, p. 162

rubella, p. 146

self-determination, p. 150

standard deviation, p. 136

task analysis, p. 152

SUMMARY

Definitions and Classification Systems

- IDEA defines mental retardation as "significantly subaverage general intellectual functioning existing concurrently with deficits in adaptive behavior and manifested during the developmental period that adversely affects a child's educational performance."

- Four degrees of mental retardation are classified by IQ score: mild, moderate, severe, and profound.

- AAIDD's 2002 definition of intellectual disabilities represents a shift away from conceptualizations of mental retardation as an inherent trait or permanent state to a description of the individual's present functioning and the environmental supports needed to improve it.

- The AAIDD's 2002 system classifies intellectual disabilities by four levels and intensities of supports needed to improve functioning in the environments in which the individual lives: intermittent, limited, extensive, and pervasive.

- Changes in terminology and definitions reflect professionals' desire to refer to people with mental retardation/intellectual disabilities with dignity and to achieve more effective and reliable methods of identification, classification, research, and education.

Identification and Assessment

- An IQ test consists of a series of questions (e.g., vocabulary, similarities), problem solving (e.g., mazes, block designs), memory, and other tasks assumed to require certain amounts of intelligence to answer or solve correctly.

- IQ scores seem to be distributed throughout the population according to a phenomenon called the *normal curve*. Theoretically, about 2.3% of the population falls ≥ 2 standard deviations below the mean, which the AAMR calls "significantly subaverage."

- The IQ cutoff score of 70 is intended only as a guideline and should not be interpreted as a hard-and-fast requirement. An IQ score of 75 or higher may be associated with mental retardation if, according to a clinician's judgment, the child exhibits deficits in adaptive behavior thought to be caused by impaired intellectual functioning.

- Because IQ tests are composed largely of verbal and academic tasks—the same things a child must master to succeed in school—they correlate highly with school achievement.

- Adaptive behavior consists of the conceptual, social, and practical skills that people need to function in their everyday lives.

- Systematic assessment of adaptive behavior is important because the exhibited adaptive skills—as well as the nature and severity of maladaptive behaviors—of a person with mental retardation are critical factors in determining the nature and degree of supports she requires for success in school, work, community, and home environments.

- Most instruments for assessing adaptive behavior consist of a series of questions answered by someone familiar with the individual.
- Measurement of adaptive behavior has proven difficult, in large part because of the relative nature of social adjustment and competence: behavior that is considered appropriate in one situation or by one group may not be in or by another.

Characteristics

- Children with mild intellectual disabilities may experience substantial performance deficits only in school. Their social and communication skills may be normal or nearly so. They are likely to become independent or semi-independent adults.
- Most children with moderate intellectual disabilities show significant developmental delays during their preschool years.
- Research has found that students with intellectual disabilities have trouble retaining information in short-term memory.
- Students with intellectual disabilities do not tend to use metacognitive or executive control strategies such as rehearsing and organizing information. When taught to use such strategies, their performance on memory-related and problem-solving tasks is likely to improve.
- Students with intellectual disabilities learn at a slower rate than do their typically developing age-mates.
- Students with intellectual disabilities often have trouble attending to relevant features of a learning task, may focus instead on distracting irrelevant stimuli, and often have difficulty sustaining attention.
- Students with intellectual disabilities often have difficulty generalizing and maintaining newly learned knowledge and skills.
- Some individuals with mental retardation develop learned helplessness, a condition in which a person expects failure regardless of his efforts.
- Some students with intellectual disabilities exhibit outer-directedness; they seem to distrust their own responses to situations and rely on others for assistance and solutions.
- Children with mental retardation have substantial deficits in adaptive behavior that take many forms and tend to occur across domains of functioning. Limitations in self-care skills and social relationships as well as behavioral excesses are common characteristics of individuals with mental retardation.
- Many children and adults with intellectual disabilities display positive attributes such as tenacity and curiosity in learning, getting along well with others, and being a positive influence on those around them.

Prevalence

- Theoretically, 2.3% of the population would score 2 standard deviations below the norm on IQ tests; but this does not account for adaptive behavior, the other criterion for diagnosis of mental retardation. Many experts now cite an incidence figure of approximately 1% of the total population.
- During the 2005–2006 school year, approximately 0.8% of the total school enrollment received special education services under the disability category of mental retardation.

Causes and Prevention

- More than 350 causes of mental retardation have been identified.
- Each causal variable is classified by when it occurs (i.e., prenatal, perinatal, or postnatal) and whether its influence is biomedical or environmental (social, behavioral, educational).
- Biomedical causes are identified for about two thirds of individuals with severe and profound levels of mental retardation.
- Although etiology is unknown for most individuals with mild mental retardation, psychosocial disadvantage in early childhood is suspected as causal factor in many cases.
- Virus vaccines, amniocentesis, CVS, genetic counseling, and early screening tests have reduced the incidence of mental retardation caused by some genetic disorders.

Educational Approaches

- Students with intellectual disabilities need instruction in basic academic skills that are required and/or could be used often in their current and future environments.
- Curriculum should focus on functional skills that will help the student succeed in self-care, vocational, domestic, community, and leisure domains.
- Major components of explicit systematic instruction are task analysis, active student response, systematic feedback, transfer of stimulus control from teacher-provided cues and prompts to natural stimuli, programming for generalization and maintenance, and direct and frequent measurement of student performance.

Educational Placement Alternatives

- During the 2005–2006 school year, approximately 14% of students with mental retardation were educated in general education classrooms; 29% in resource rooms; 50% in separate classrooms; and about 7% in separate schools, residential facilities, or home/hospital environments.
- During the early elementary grades, many students with intellectual disabilities benefit from full or partial inclusion in general education classroom settings.
- Strategies for facilitating successful placement in a general education class include planning for the student's inclusion through team games, collaborative learning, and group investigation projects and by directly training all students in specific skills for interacting with one another.
- The relative appropriateness of inclusion in the general education classroom may change for some students with intellectual disabilities as they move from the elementary grades to the secondary level, when opportunities for community-based instruction in vocational and life skills are critical.
- Teachers should determine the extent to which a general education classroom is an appropriate placement for a student with intellectual disabilities based on the student's individual needs.
- The principles of normalization, social role valorization, and self-determination are important in helping people with intellectual disabilities achieve acceptance and membership in society.

Now go to MyEducationLab at www.myeducationlab.com, and take the Pretest to assess your initial comprehension of chapter content. Once you have taken the Pretest, use your individualized Study Plan for Chapter 4 to enhance your understanding of the concepts discussed in the chapter. Finally, take the Posttest to assess your comprehension of Chapter 4 content.

5

Learning Disabilities

FEATURED TEACHERS

MEGHAN L. MACY
Cornelius Elementary School • Cornelius, North Carolina

Meghan Macy

Education—Teaching Credentials—Experience

- B.A., Special Education, University of North Carolina at Charlotte, 2004
- M.Ed., Special Education, University of North Carolina at Charlotte, 2007
- 4 years of teaching special education

My Students and Classroom I have the best job! I am a resource and inclusion teacher for students who receive special education services in general education classrooms for some portion of the school day. Most of my students are served under the specific learning disability category. I also teach students with behavioral or emotional disorders, autism, other health impairments, and developmental delay. Most of my day is spent in the resource room, but I co-teach language arts in general education classrooms several times a day.

Instructional Strategies My district uses a research-based reading program that covers critical components in beginning reading such as phonemic awareness, phonics, and comprehension, but my students often need instructional strategies that are more explicit and interactive to help them master these skills. Three teaching strategies I use on a daily basis are choral responding, response cards, and repeated reading. I also design instructional activities that provide mediated scaffolding to support students when they learn a new skill and judicious review to promote mastery. Here are some examples.

Mediated scaffolding refers to a variety of temporary supports that enable students to respond correctly while learning new curriculum content. The teacher gradually withdraws the "scaffolds," and the students become independent performers. I use mediated scaffolding in reading, writing, and math. For example, when teaching students to sound out CVCe words (e.g., *cake, ride*), I draw bars over the long vowels to prompt accurate decoding. After students respond correctly to a series of words with this scaffold in place, I begin fading out the bars. I also use picture symbols, written directions, graphic organizers, and audiotaped prompts that students can use to plan, draft, edit, and revise written compositions. As their writing skills improve, students' dependence on these scaffolds decreases. When I introduce students to math word problems, mediated scaffolding takes the form of reducing the complexity of instructional examples. Students first practice solving short word problems that require only a single step. Over time, I fade in "distracter words" and additional steps to make the problems more challenging.

Judicious review provides students with varied and distributed practice of newly learned skills. For example, I use brief choral responding sessions to review high-frequency letter–sound correspondences, vocabulary word meanings, and basic math facts. I use response cards to review identifying parts of speech, discriminating between concrete and abstract nouns, telling time, and basic geometry. I also give students review exercises to help them apply and integrate mastered skills (e.g., complex story problems, content-area reading passages). Repeated reading is another strategy I use to strengthen students' oral reading fluency. After our reading lessons, my students do timed oral readings from a program called *Read Naturally.* This kind of judicious review helps students build fluency with connected text, and they really enjoy setting new reading goals and charting their progress.

Collaboration   This year I became actively involved in our school's responsiveness to intervention (RTI) team. The RTI team also includes one school psychologist, an administrator, an exceptional children's specialist, our school guidance counselor, and five general education teachers. Our team helps classroom teachers design interventions to address the needs of students who are struggling. RTI entails a sequence of tiered interventions, with each tier providing more intensive intervention and support. We brainstorm research-based interventions for students who are beginning to struggle before the child falls so far behind that referral for special education is necessary. We basically design a special education-type program without the confines of a label and the hoops of eligibility. As team members, we contribute our different skills in a productive way.

Working with parents   Establishing a strong parent–teacher partnership is critical to successful teaching. The earlier you can build trust with families, the better the outcome for your students. I love that I get to work with some families for 4 years. I contact the parents of each new student and chat informally about expectations. I also ask them about their hopes and dreams for their children. As a college student, I provided respite care for a young man with Asperger syndrome and worked very closely with his family during a difficult transition to middle school. I witnessed firsthand the parents' continuing struggles and frustrations with the school system. This experience gave me an inside glimpse into the family life of students with special needs that I will never forget. I strongly recommend that anyone going into special education get to know the family of a student with a disability.

The input from a student's family is important, so I also make accommodations for families to be involved in the process, even if this means having meetings at their home, before or after school hours.

Personal Experience   I love watching my students progress from not knowing letter names to reading third-grade materials with confidence and enjoyment! I also enjoy celebrating students' success. We always have something to celebrate—passing an end-of-grade test, reaching a reading fluency goal, or exiting the special education program altogether.

I hold high expectations for my students. I find that as long as I remain energetic, maintain a positive attitude, and have integrity when providing quality instruction, I can help my students overcome obstacles. There are difficult days to be sure, just like any other profession, but it is a rare joy to join a child in his struggle to learn a new skill and then to watch him use it successfully.

I remember Grayson, whose father told me, "My kid will be the kid that does not pass the third-grade test." This shook me, but I remember thinking, "Oh, yes he will!" Grayson and I worked hard together all year. I began my day a couple minutes early to do extra repeated readings with Grayson. Before the bell rang in the afternoon, we found some extra time to review early phonics patterns. We designed a special home reading program complete with incentives and communication logs. Grayson's general education classroom teacher provided opportunities for him to read text aloud on his instructional level, and she also incorporated many direct instruction tactics in her classroom. Grayson knew he was far behind his peers and worked hard every single day. The morning of the test, his mother told me he had thrown up because he was so nervous. I remember the pit in my stomach and choking back my own tears trying to get him focused and calm before the test. Not only did Grayson pass that test, he knocked it out of the park! I will never forget the look of pride on his face. That pride is his, he earned it and he deserves it.

By the late 1950s most public schools had established special education programs (or at least offered some type of special service) for children with mental retardation, students with physical disabilities, children with sensory impairments, and those with emotional or behavioral disorders. But there remained a group of children with serious learning problems who did not fit into the existing categories of exceptionality. The children seemed physically intact, yet they seemed unable to learn certain basic skills and subjects at school. Because the schools at that time had no programs for these children, parents searching for help for their children turned to physicians and psychologists. Understandably, these professionals viewed the children from the vantage points of their respective disciplines and used terms such as *brain damage, minimal brain dysfunction, neurological impairment, perceptual handicap, dyslexia,* and *aphasia* to describe or account for the children's learning problems. Some of these terms are still used today because a variety of disciplines continue to influence the field of learning disabilities.

The term *learning disabilities* was coined by Samuel Kirk in a 1963 address to a group of parents whose children were experiencing serious difficulties in learning to read, write, spell, or solve math problems. The parents liked the term and that very evening voted to form the Association for Children with Learning Disabilities. Today, the organization's name is Learning Disabilities Association of America (LDA), and it is a powerful advocacy group for persons with learning disabilities. In 1975 *learning disabilities* was included as a special education category in IDEA.

The number of children identified as learning disabled has nearly tripled since the passage of Individuals with Disabilities Education Act (IDEA), making it the largest category in special education and fueling an ongoing debate on the nature of the learning disability concept. Some believe the increase in the number of children identified as learning disabled indicates the true extent of the disability. Others contend that too many low achievers—children without a disability who are doing poorly in school because they have not received a sufficient amount or intensity of effective instruction—have been improperly diagnosed as learning disabled, placing a severe strain on the limited resources available to serve those students challenged by a true disability.

Considerable confusion and disagreement exist among professionals and parents on even the most basic question: What is a learning disability? In some ways, learning disabilities has brought out both the worst and the best that special education has to offer. Learning disabilities has served as a breeding ground for fads and miracle treatments ("New Diet Regimen Cures Learning Disabilities!"). At the same time, some of the most innovative and productive researchers in special education have devoted their careers to the study and treatment of learning disabilities. Many instructional strategies that were developed for students with learning disabilities have influenced and benefited the entire field of education.

DEFINITIONS

Numerous definitions for learning disabilities have been proposed, but none has been universally accepted. The two definitions that have had the most influence are the federal definition in IDEA and a definition proposed by the National Joint Committee on Learning Disabilities (NJCLD).

The Federal Definition

Learning disability is defined in IDEA as follows:

> *In General*—The term "specific learning disability" means a disorder in 1 or more of the basic psychological processes involved in understanding or in using language, spoken or written, which disorder may manifest itself in an imperfect ability to listen, think, speak, read, write, spell, or to do mathematical calculations.
>
> *Disorders Included*—Such term includes such conditions as perceptual disabilities, brain injury, minimal brain dysfunction, dyslexia, and developmental aphasia.
>
> *Disorders Not Included*—Such term does not include a learning problem that is primarily the result of visual, hearing, or motor disabilities, of mental retardation, of emotional disturbance, or of environmental, cultural, or economic disadvantage. (P.L. 108-466, Sec. 602[30])

The NJCLD Definition

The NJCLD is a group composed of representatives from 13 professional organizations concerned with the education, treatment, and rights of children and adults with learning

After reading this chapter, complete the pretest for Chapter 5 on MyEducationLab to assess your initial understanding of chapter content.

LDA

 Content Standards for Beginning Teachers of Students with LD: Professional organizations and sources of information relevant to the field of LD (LD9K2).

IDEA definition of LD

 Content Standards for Beginning Teachers—Common Core: Issues in definition and identification of individuals with exceptional learning needs (CC1K5).

Students with learning disabilities have significant learning problems that cannot be explained as primarily the result of another recognized disability or lack of opportunity to learn due to environmental, cultural, or economic conditions.

disabilities. The NJCLD (1990/2001) believes that the federal definition of learning disabilities contains several inherent weaknesses:

1. *Exclusion of adults.* Learning disabilities can occur at all ages, but the IDEA definition refers only to school-age children.
2. *Reference* to *"basic psychological processes."* Use of this phrase has led to debate on how to teach students with learning disabilities, which is a curricular issue, not a definitional one.
3. *Inclusion of spelling as a learning disability.* Spelling can be subsumed under "written expression" and should be eliminated from the definition.
4. *Inclusion of obsolete terms.* Including terms such as *dyslexia, minimal brain dysfunction, perceptual impairments,* and *developmental aphasia,* which historically have proven difficult to define, only adds confusion to the definition.
5. *Wording of the exclusion clause.* The IDEA definition suggests that learning disabilities cannot occur along with other disabilities. However, a person may have a learning disability along with another disability but not *because of* another disability.

In response to these problems with the federal definition, the NJCLD (1990/2001) developed the following definition:

> Learning disabilities is a general term that refers to a heterogeneous group of disorders manifested by significant difficulties in the acquisition and use of listening, speaking, reading, writing, reasoning, or mathematical abilities.
>
> These disorders are intrinsic to the individual and presumed to be due to central nervous system dysfunction, and may appear across the life span. Problems in self-regulatory behaviors, social perception, and social interaction may exist with learning disabilities but do not themselves constitute a learning disability.
>
> Although learning disabilities may occur concomitantly with other handicapping conditions (for example, sensory impairment, mental retardation, serious emotional disturbance) or with extrinsic influences (such as cultural differences, insufficient or inappropriate instruction), they are not the result of those conditions or influences. (p. 1)

Operationalizing the Federal Definition: IQ–Achievement Discrepancy

When operationalizing the federal definition for the purpose of identifying students with learning disabilities, most states and school districts require that three criteria be met for a diagnosis of learning disabilities:

1. A severe discrepancy between the student's intellectual ability and academic achievement
2. An exclusion criterion: the student's difficulties are not the result of another known condition that can cause learning problems
3. A need for special education services

Ability–achievement discrepancy

 Council for Exceptional Children Content Standards for Beginning Teachers of Students with LD: Philosophies, theories, models, and issues related to individuals with LD (LD1K2).

IQ–Achievement Discrepancy   Children with learning disabilities exhibit an unexpected difference between general ability and achievement—a discrepancy that would not be predicted by the student's general intellectual ability (Kavale & Forness, 2000). Children who are having minor or temporary difficulties in learning should not be identified as learning disabled. According to federal guidelines that accompanied the original IDEA, only children with a "severe discrepancy between achievement and intellectual ability" were to be identified as learning disabled (U.S. Office of Education, 1977b, p. 65083).

The most common practice for identifying children with learning disabilities is to determine if a severe discrepancy exists between their expected and actual achievement. This involves comparing a student's score on an IQ test with her score on a standardized achievement test. While such a comparison seems simple on the surface, in practice it is fraught with problems (Fletcher et al., 2002; Fuchs, Fuchs, Mathes, Lipsey, & Roberts, 2002; Gresham, 2002; Kavale, 2002). The federal government proposed several mathematical formulas for determining a severe discrepancy. All of the proposed formulas were eventually rejected, and the final rules and regulations for IDEA did not contain a specific definition of and formula for determining a severe discrepancy. This confusion and disagreement about exactly how a severe discrepancy should be determined led to widely differing procedures for identifying and classifying students as learning disabled (Fuchs & Young, 2006; Kavale, 2002; Ysseldyke, 2001).

Exclusion The IDEA definition of learning disabilities identifies students with significant learning problems that are not "primarily the result" of other conditions that can impede learning, such as another recognized disability or lack of opportunity to learn due to environmental, cultural, or economic conditions. The word *primarily* in the definition recognizes that learning disabilities can coexist with other disabilities; in that case, the student typically receives services under category of the other disability.

Need for Special Education Students with learning disabilities show specific and severe learning problems despite standard educational efforts and therefore need specially designed instruction to meet their unique needs. This criterion is meant to avoid the overidentification of children who have not had the opportunity to learn. Such children should progress satisfactorily as soon as they receive effective instruction at a curricular level appropriate to their current skills.

Responsiveness to Intervention: A New Paradigm for Defining Learning Disabilities

Recognizing the problems inherent in the discrepancy approach to determining eligibility for special education and with concern for the large and growing number of children being identified under the learning disabilities category, Congress significantly changed the way that schools could determine a child's eligibility for special education under the specific learning disabilities category when reauthorizing IDEA in 2004:

> When determining whether a child has a specific learning disability . . . a local educational agency shall not be required to take into consideration whether a child has a severe discrepancy between achievement and intellectual ability. . . . [And] a local educational agency may use a process that determines if the child responds to scientific, research-based intervention as a part of the evaluation procedures." (P.L. 108-466, Sec. 614[b][6][A-B])

Researchers who have implemented intensive programs of remedial instruction for struggling readers in the early grades report that a small percentage of those students (5% to 7%) fail to make adequate progress (e.g., O'Conner, 2000; Torgesen, 2001). "It is reasonable to think that these students, whose response to treatment is significantly lower than expected, could be identified with reading/learning disabilities" (Vaughn et al., 2003, p. 393).

The ability–achievement discrepancy approach for diagnosing learning disabilities, excluding factors such as the quality of instruction the child has received, requires a student to fall far enough behind for a discrepancy to exist and precludes early identification and prevention. By contrast, a **responsiveness to intervention (RTI)** approach shifts the identification of learning disabilities from a "wait-to-fail" model to one of early identification and prevention (Vaughn & Fuchs, 2003b).

An RTI Model and Example Cases The value and trustworthiness of RTI depend on two factors: (a) the consistent, rigorous implementation of research-based interventions and (b) a system of accurate, reliable, easy-to-use measures of student progress in the presence of each level of intervention. Curriculum-based measurement (CBM) is the primary method of progress monitoring in RTI. CBM, which is discussed in more detail later in this chapter, uses multiple, ongoing measures of child performance rather than limiting determination to a single point in time. Although no single method exists for conducting RTI, the three-tiered model depicted in Figure 5.1 has gained a great deal of support (Division for Learning Disabilities, 2007; L. S. Fuchs & Fuchs, 2007a, 2007b; E. Johnson, Mallard, Fuchs, & McKnight, 2006). A student who moves through each tier of the model experiences all three levels of preventive intervention introduced in Chapter 1. Teachers use the RTI model described next to prevent reading problems and identify children who need special education for reading disabilities.

Difficulty defining and identifying LD

 Content Standards for Beginning Teachers of Students with LD: Philosophies, theories, models, and issues related to individuals with LD (LD1K2).

Responsiveness to intervention

 Content Standards for Beginning Teachers—Common Core: Models, theories, and philosophies that form the basis for special education practice (CC1K1) (also CC1K3).

FIGURE 5.1

Responsiveness to intervention model: Tier 1, Tier 2, and Tier 3 (special education)

Source: National Research Center on Learning Disabilities (2007). Responsiveness to intervention in the SLD determination process. [Brochure]. Lawrence, KS: Author. Retrieved October 17, 2007, from the National Research Center on Learning Disabilities Web site: http://www.nrcld.org <http://www.nrcld.org/>.

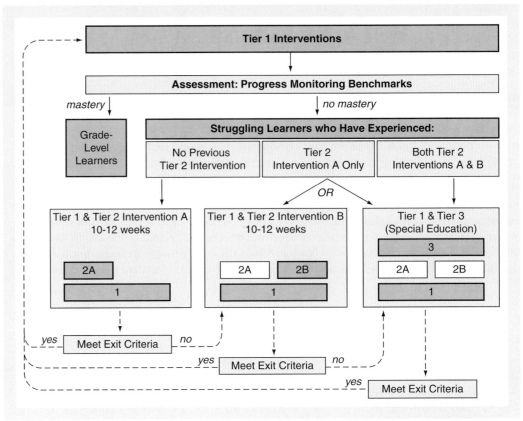

Adapted from Vaughn (2003)

Tier 1: Primary Intervention in the General Education Classroom Primary prevention is provided to all students in the form of evidence-based curriculum and instruction in the general education classroom (Foorman, 2007). Frequent progress monitoring assesses the performance of students whose scores on a screening test fall below benchmarks for critical reading skills. Students are considered at risk if both their level of performance and rate of growth on the CBM are well below those of their classmates. At-risk students who continue to struggle during Tier-1 instruction are moved to Tier 2 (see Figure 5.2).

Tier 2: Secondary Intervention Students who are struggling in the general education program receive an intensive fixed-duration trial (e.g., 10 to 12 weeks) of small-group supplemental tutoring using a research-validated program (Vaughn & Roberts, 2007). A student who makes satisfactory progress during this intensive prevention trial, such as Jordan in Figure 5.2, "is deemed disability-free (and remediated); he or she then is returned to the original classroom environment" (Vaughn & Fuchs, 2003b, p. 139).

L. S. Fuchs and Fuchs (2007a, 2007b) recommend using a **dual discrepancy** criterion and designate a student as nonresponsive only when the student (a) fails to make adequate growth in the presence of instruction and (b) completes Tier-2 intervention(s) below the benchmark criteria. A student who is not responsive to Tier-2 intervention may receive a second Tier-2 intervention trial (with some modifications to the intervention based on observations of the student during the first trial) or move directly to Tier 3 (as with the case example of Taylor in Figure 5.3).

Tier 3: Tertiary Intervention (Special Education) Tier 3 is special education (Stecker, 2007). The school conducts a multifactored evaluation to determine disability classification and special education eligibility.

> If the child fails to respond to a program with which the vast majority of children learn, then the inference is that the child's deficits render learning uniquely challenging and require a special education. The failure to respond verifies that the deficit resides in the individual, not the instructional program. (Vaughn & Fuchs, 2003b, p. 142)

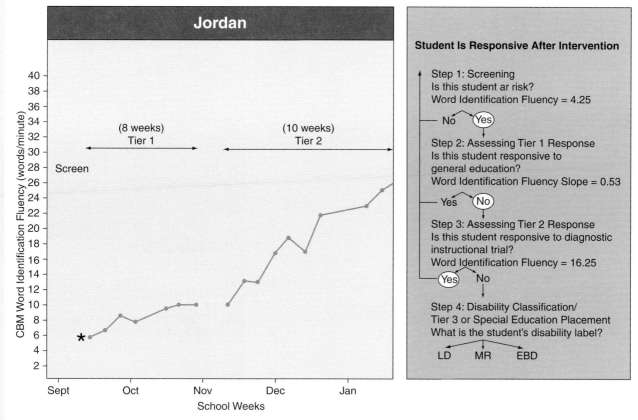

Jordan's case represents an assessment made during Tier 1 with indication of non-responsiveness and advancement to Tier 2 instruction with assessment made and no indication of continued non-responsiveness. Jordan began with an oral reading fluency of five words per minute, which flagged Jordan as being at risk. As Jordan progressed through Tier 1 instruction, Jordan failed to make adequate progress, which suggests that Jordan requires more intensive intervention than can be offered through the school's Tier 1 instructional program. Continued progress monitoring during Tier 2 intervention shows that Jordan is responding to the diagnostic instructional trial and that no further level of intervention is warranted. Jordan's progress will continue to be monitored with the following possible outcomes:

1. Student will reach the targeted goal for oral reading fluency (ORF) and return to Tier 1 instruction.
2. Student will continue with Tier 2 instruction as long as he/she makes adequate progress.

FIGURE 5.2

Example profile of a student who is nonresponsive to Tier-1 intervention and responsive after Tier-2 intervention

Source: National Research Center on Learning Disabilities (2007). Responsiveness to intervention in the SLD determination process. [Brochure]. Lawrence, KS: Author. Retrieved October 17, 2007, from the National Research Center on Learning Disabilities Web site: http://www.nrcld.org<http://www.nrcld.org/>.

Advantages and Benefits of RTI   Educators have articulated numerous potential benefits and goals of RTI (Bradley, Danielson, & Doolittle, 2007; E. Johnson et al., 2006; NJCLD, 2005; L. S. Fuchs & Fuchs, 2007a, 2007b), including the following:

- Earlier identification of students using a problem-solving approach, instead of a "wait-to-fail" approach
- Reduction in the number of students referred for special education
- Reduction in the overidentification of minority students
- Provision of more instructionally useful data than those provided by traditional methods of assessment and identification
- Increased likelihood that students are exposed to high-quality instruction in the general education classroom by stipulating that schools use evidence-based instructional practices and routinely monitor the progress of all students

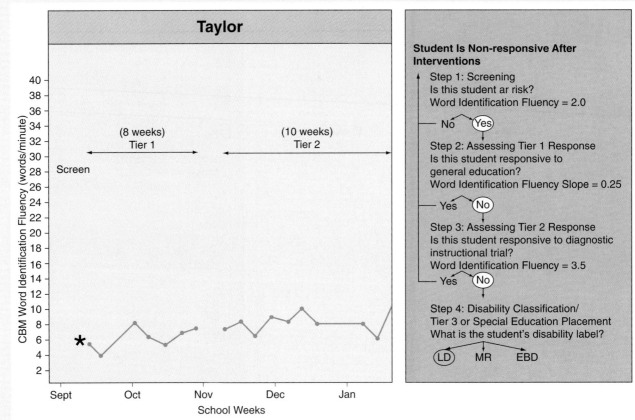

Taylor's case represents an assessment made during Tier 1 with indication of non-responsiveness and advancement to Tier 2 instruction with assessment made and indication of continued non-responsiveness resulting in a learning disability classification. Taylor began with an ORF of five words per minute, which identified Taylor as at risk for reading failure. As Taylor continued in the general class (Tier 1), Taylor failed to make adequate progress and was referred for Tier 2 intervention. The initial assessment in Tier Two showed Taylor had an ORF of seven words per minute. As Taylor continued with Tier Two instruction, Taylor failed to make adequate progress. This suggests the need for a student-centered, comprehensive evaluation and problem-solving approach that ensures individualized instruction to address Taylor's specific learning disability (i.e., Tier 3 or special education).

FIGURE 5.3

Example profile of a student who is nonresponsive to Tier-1 intervention and nonresponsive after Tier-2 intervention

Source: National Research Center on Learning Disabilities (2007). Responsiveness to intervention in the SLD determination process. [Brochure]. Lawrence, KS: Author. Retrieved October 17, 2007, from the National Research Center on Learning Disabilities Web site: http://www.nrcld.org<http://www.nrcld.org/>.

- Encouraged access to early intervention because, with the regular monitoring of progress, at-risk students are identified early, and an infrastructure for the appropriate delivery of services is already established
- Service to all students with achievement problems, so that only those students who fail to respond to multiple levels of intervention efforts receive the label learning disabled.

Many leading special educators, including some who have helped develop the RTI concept and methodology, have expressed concerns with RTI (e.g., Fuchs & Deshler, 2007; Kavale et al., 2006). Practitioners are also cautious. One survey found that although 75% of school psychologists endorsed using RTI and phonemic awareness as components of diagnosis of learning disabilities, 62% also endorsed the IQ–achievement discrepancy criterion (Machek & Nelson, 2007). Noting the reality that the consistent use of effective, evidence-based instruction does not occur in many classrooms, Ysseldyke (2005) warns that

[With RTI] we will probably identify more students as LD and those students will be more variable than those identified using the discrepancy model. "RTI resistance" is here now, and will get serious when too many students are identified as LD using RTI approaches. And, then we will do what we always have done and what government agencies like welfare agencies and departments of natural resources always have done: We will put upper limits and/or "slot limits" on conditions to control eligibility. Departments of natural resources use "slot limits" (e.g., one may keep only fish between 16–24 inches) to define "keepers." When the harvest gets too high they modify the slot (say from 16–24 to 20–24) and redefine "keepers." As in the classification decisions we make, definitions and numbers are more politically than scientifically determined. (p. 127)

In spite of legitimate concerns and questions that have been raised about RTI, it holds great promise. Kame'enui (2007) stated that "Arguably, RTI, at least the essence of it as a concept, is thoroughly consistent with the statutory intent and practice of special education" (2007, p. 7). However, educators have much to learn, and we should move cautiously. See Current Issues and Future Trends, "RTI: A New (Old) Idea With Great Promise."

CHARACTERISTICS

To describe the various categories of exceptionality, observers typically list the physical and psychological characteristics often exhibited by individuals who make up that group. For example, early in the field's history, a task force commissioned to identify the characteristics of children with learning disabilities found that 99 separate characteristics were reported in the literature (Clements, 1966). An inherent danger in such lists is the tendency to assume, or to look for, each of those characteristics in all children in the category. This danger is especially troublesome with learning disabilities because the category includes children who exhibit a wide range of learning, social, and emotional problems. In fact, Mercer and Pullen (2008) suggest that it is theoretically possible for an individual with learning disabilities to exhibit one of more than 500,000 combinations of cognitive or socioemotional problems.

Learning disabilities are associated with problems in listening, reasoning, memory, attention, selecting and focusing on relevant stimuli, and the perception and processing of visual and/or auditory information. These perceptual and cognitive processing difficulties are assumed to be the underlying causes of the following characteristics that students with learning disabilities experience, either individually or in combination: reading problems, deficits in written language, underachievement in math, poor social skills, attention deficits and hyperactivity, behavior problems, and low self-esteem/self-efficacy.

Reading Problems

Difficulty with reading is by far the most common characteristic of students with learning disabilities. Researchers estimate that 90% of all children identified as learning disabled are referred for special education services because of reading problems (Kavale & Forness, 2000). Children who fail to learn to read by the first grade tend to fall farther and farther behind their peers, not only in reading but in general academic achievement as well (Kame'enui, Good, & Harn, 2005). For example, longitudinal studies have found that 74% of children diagnosed with learning disabilities are still receiving special education for reading problems in the ninth grade (Fletcher et al., 1994; Stanovich & Siegel, 1994).

Evidence suggests that specific reading disability, sometimes called dyslexia, is a persistent deficit, not simply a developmental lag in linguistic or basic reading skills (Lyon, 1995). The International Dyslexia Association defines **dyslexia** as

> a specific learning disability that is neurobiological in origin. It is characterized by difficulties with accurate and/or fluent word recognition and by poor spelling and decoding abilities. These difficulties typically result from a deficit in the phonological component of language that is often unexpected in relation to other cognitive abilities and the provision of effective classroom instruction. (Lyon, Shaywitz, & Shaywitz, 2003, p. 2)

Torgesen and Wagner (1998) state that (a) the "most severe reading problems of children with learning disabilities lie at the word, rather than the text, level of processing" (i.e., inability to accurately and fluently decode single words), and (b) the most common cognitive limitation of these children involves a dysfunction in the awareness of the phonological

Responsiveness to intervention begins with primary prevention for all students in the form of evidence-based curriculum and instruction in the general education classroom.

Dyslexia/reading disabilities

Council for Exceptional Children — Content Standards for Beginning Teachers—Common Core: Educational implications of characteristics of various exceptionalities (CC2K2).

CURRENT ISSUES AND FUTURE TRENDS

RESPONSIVENESS TO INTERVENTION: A NEW (AND OLD) IDEA WITH GREAT PROMISE

BY EDWARD J. KAME'ENUI

Education as a discipline of study and practice is forever introducing new ideas and practices. Some would argue that it's a sign, and perhaps an expected result, of an immature and emerging discipline (Kuhn, 1996). Furthermore, sometimes the new idea characterized as a model, approach, process, construct, strategy or initiative is—if you dig deep enough—actually a variation of "old" ideas, constructs, approaches, and models. In many ways, responsiveness to intervention (RTI) is one of those ideas, constructs, models, approaches, or processes that is both new and old. RTI represents both hopeful promise and serious doubt and will invariably mean different things to different people. In truth, that is the nature of many, if not most, concepts or constructs we use in education and special education (e.g., consider the various meanings of the concepts or constructs *learning, disability, teaching, assessment, intelligence,* and *reading*). As an ambiguous construct, RTI ostensibly invokes a focus on both the particular (e.g., What does RTI mean for a specific child who is struggling with reading, mathematics, writing, social studies or science?) and the general (e.g., What does RTI mean for all children, those who are struggling and those who aren't?).

In an idealized state, RTI could represent the essence of special education, which is defined in federal legislation as "specially designed instruction to meet the unique needs" of an individual child (PL 108-446, IDEA, 2004). This "specially designed instruction" means that the architecture of the instruction or intervention is carefully considered, "designed," and tailored specifically to meet the unique needs of a particular child so that educators meet the specified instructional goals and objectives for that child. The "architecture" of the instruction or intervention encompasses what is taught; how it is taught and delivered, including the amount of teacher guidance and scaffolding provided; the explicitness of the teacher direction; the timing, pacing, and daily schedule of when instruction is delivered; and the conditions under which instruction is delivered and assessed.

In the idealized world, the essence of RTI resides in the critical details of the intervention, including, for example, the following: (a) the scientific evidence for the architecture and delivery of the intervention with a particular child under specific conditions taught to specific criterion levels of performance relevant to that individual child; (b) a child's response to the intervention; (c) the implementation of the intervention with high fidelity;

and (d) the technical adequacy of the measures used to evaluate the efficacy of the intervention. For readers new to special education, RTI is new, and at first glance, appears complex to implement in real classrooms with real students. And the same is true for readers already marinated in the special education community and for veterans familiar with both the old and new terms.

As a new term and construct, RTI requires clarification and historical perspective, particularly its currency, purpose, application, and reach. RTI is an abridged rendering of language found in IDEA 2004 (Section 614 (b)(6)(B)): "In determining whether a child has a specific learning disability, a local educational agency may use a process that determines if the child *responds to scientific, research-based intervention* as a part of the evaluation procedures" (emphasis added). Importantly, the statutory deference to RTI or to determining "if the child *responds to scientific, research-based intervention*" is a direct and explicit response to language in the previous paragraph (i.e., Paragraph (A) in Section 614 (b)(6)) of the law that presumably rejects a term and construct introduced almost 50 years ago (Kirk & Bateman, 1962) and considered fundamental and instrumental to the identification of learning disabilities—the determination of a *severe discrepancy.* The statute states: "a local educational agency shall *not be required to take into consideration whether a child has a severe discrepancy between achievement and intellectual ability* in oral expression, listening comprehension, written expression, basic reading skill, reading comprehension, mathematical calculation, or mathematical reasoning" (emphasis added). Thus, the potential elimination of *severe discrepancy* as a component of learning disabilities and the simultaneous introduction and use of RTI as a potential substitute component of learning disability in federal law require our serious examination both as ideas and as practices.

As a new term, RTI is now conspicuously and actively invoked in the current discourse of the special education and general education communities. It will naturally and incrementally become defined or redefined in theory, research, and practice, and not surprisingly reified in its various forms as truth, not unlike its predecessor, *severe discrepancy.* Thus, the introduction of RTI offers the field of special education an opportunity to take stock of its thinking about this construct and what it means for the research and practice of special education. Classification systems, like scientific facts (Popper, 1959), represent tentative conclusions that require continuous testing, retesting, and validation. Sound science requires our unending attention and care, and for RTI to gain appropriate validation, it must be put to careful and unending rigorous research.

The RTI construct has its origins in public health, where Caplan and Grunebaum first introduced the idea and principles in 1967 (Simeonsson, 1994). Arguably, the concept of RTI is thoroughly consistent with the statutory intent and practice of special education, which requires a process of continuously evaluating and determining how a child responds as an individual to "specially designed" instruction or interventions. The important difference in the language of the statute and our current practice is the now clear and important stipulation that the interventions implemented in the practice of RTI are "scientific, research-based" interventions, and that measures used are "reliable and valid for the purpose of assessment" and "implemented with fidelity."

As a new construct in federal law, RTI will require careful federal guidance and direction that is still forthcoming, particularly in the due process procedures invoked in identifying (or failing to identify) students who may have a learning disability. Moreover, because RTI is ripe in the current discourse and practice of the profession, the implementation of RTI at the child, classroom, school, and district levels will be decidedly varied in form, process, and technical substance. Additionally and not surprisingly, although RTI holds significant promise for the practice of special education, it is seriously underdetermined empirically, particularly the use of interventions that are yoked to the use of "technically

sound" assessment instruments as required by the federal law. Although it would be easy to view RTI as singular in its focus on interventions and a child's responses to those interventions, what the law makes transparent is that RTI is essentially an assessment and instructional process that is dynamic, recursive, and based on rigorous scientific research. Clearly, much work remains to be done, and the field should ensure that the most rigorous research on RTI is supported and that it yields important and useful results for practice.

What Do You Think?

1. How does the identification of a child as having a learning disability through RTI depend on the school's selection and implementation of "scientific, research-based" interventions?

2. How do RTI and determining a severe discrepancy between achievement and intellectual ability as approaches to identifying children with learning disabilities differ along a continuum of static and dynamic?

3. How might RTI improve the education received by all students in a school?

Edward J. Kame'ennui is Dean-Knight Professor of Education at the University of Oregon. From 2005–2007, he served as the U.S. Department of Education's first Commissioner of the National Center for Special Education Research. Dr. Kame'enui's research interests include beginning reading instruction, vocabulary curriculum design, and learning disabilities.

---

structure of words in oral language (p. 226). **Phonological awareness** refers to the "conscious understanding and knowledge that language is made up of sounds" (Simmons, Kame'enui, Coyne, & Chard, 2007, p. 49). The most important aspect of phonological awareness for learning to read is **phonemic awareness,** the knowledge that words consist of separate sounds, or **phonemes,** and the ability to manipulate these individual sound units. A child with phonemic awareness can do these things (Simmons et al., 2007):

1. Orally blend sounds to make a word (e.g., "what word do you have if you put these sounds together: /c/, /aaaa/, /t/?"—*cat*)

2. Isolate beginning, middle, and ending sounds (e.g., "What is the first sound in *rose*?"—/rrrr/)

3. Segment a word into sounds (e.g., "Say the sounds in the word *sat*"—/ssss/—/aaaa/—/t/)

4. Manipulate sounds within a word (e.g., "What word do you have if you change the /ssss/ in *sat* to /mmmm/?—*mat*) (p. 50)

Recent research suggests that children with severe reading disabilities, particularly those who are resistant to interventions effective for the majority of struggling readers, may share a second processing problem in addition to deficits in phonological awareness. Many children and adults with dyslexia show a significant deficit in *visual naming speed* (the ability to rapidly name visually presented stimuli) compared to a typical reader

Phonological awareness

 Content Standards for Beginning Teachers of Students with LD: Effects of phonological awareness on the reading abilities of individuals with LD (LD3K2).

(Lovett, Steinbach, & Frijters, 2000; Wolf, Bowers, & Biddle, 2000). When asked to state the names of visually presented material such as letters, many individuals with reading disabilities have difficulty rapidly retrieving and stating the names of the letters, even though they know the letter names. The term *double-deficit hypothesis* is used to describe children who exhibit underlying deficits in phonological awareness and rapid naming speed (Wolf & Bowers, 2000).

Of course, comprehension is the goal of reading. And comprehension lies at the phrase, sentence, paragraph, and story level, not in identifying single words. But the inability to rapidly identify words impairs comprehension in at least two ways. First, faster readers encounter more words and idea units, thereby having the opportunity to comprehend more. Second, assuming that both word recognition and comprehension consume finite cognitive processing resources, a struggling reader who devotes more processing resources to identify words has "fewer cognitive processing resources … available for comprehension. The less efficient word reading of students with reading disabilities overloads working memory and undermines reading comprehension" (Jenkins & O'Conner, 2001, pp. 1–2).

Extensive research over the past 35 years has produced more than 2,000 peer-reviewed journal articles about early reading acquisition and reading difficulties. This research has revealed a great deal about the fundamental nature of children's reading disabilities and the type of instruction most likely to prevent and remediate reading problems (Bursuck & Damer, 2007; Foorman, 2007; Jenkins & O'Conner, 2002; Kame'enui et al., 2005; Vaughn & Roberts, 2007). Figure 5.4 describes key principles of effective beginning reading instruction consistent with recommendations based on a review of that research by the National Reading Panel (2000).

Written Language Deficits

Many students with learning disabilities have problems writing and spelling. Students with learning disabilities perform significantly lower than their age-matched peers without disabilities on all written expression tasks, especially vocabulary, grammar, punctuation, and spelling (Graham & Harris, 2003; P. L. Newcomer & Barenbaum, 1991). Some students with learning disabilities are competent readers but struggle mightily with written language. For example, Figure 5.5 shows the story written by a 10-year-old student when shown an illustration of prehistoric cavemen. Sean's oral reading of his story reveals a huge disparity between his written and oral language abilities.

Compounding the weak language base that many students with learning disabilities bring to the writing task is an approach to the writing process that involves minimal planning, effort, and metacognitive control (Englert, Wu, & Zhao, 2005; Graham & Harris, 2005). Many of these students use a "retrieve-and-write" approach in which they retrieve from immediate memory "whatever seems appropriate and write it down" (De La Paz & Graham, 1997, p. 295). They seldom use the self-regulation and self-assessment strategies of competent writers: setting a goal or plan to guide their writing, organizing their ideas, drafting, self-assessing, and rewriting. As a result, they produce poorly organized compositions containing a few poorly developed ideas (Sexton, Harris, & Graham, 1998).

Fortunately, teachers can help most students with learning disabilities to improve their writing and spelling skills by explicit instruction on specific writing skills and strategic approaches to writing and giving frequent opportunities to practice with systematic feedback and motivation (e.g., Alber & Walshe, 2004; Bui, Schumaker, & Deshler,

Comprehension and beginning reading instruction

 Content Standards for Beginning Teachers of Students with LD: Relationships among reading instruction methods and LD (LD7K1) (also LD3K3).

Written language deficits

 Content Standards for Beginning Teachers—Common Core: Educational implications of characteristics of various exceptionalities (CC2K2) (also LD3K3).

Explicit instruction of letter–phoneme relationships prevents reading problems better than encouraging children to figure out the sounds for the letters by giving clues.

FIGURE 5.4 **Research-based principles of early reading instruction**

1. *Begin teaching phonemic awareness directly in kindergarten.* Many children and adults who cannot read are not aware of phonemes. If phonemic awareness does not develop by age 5 or 6, it is unlikely to develop later without instruction. Activities such as the following help develop children's phonemic awareness:

   - *Phoneme deletion.* What word would be left if the /k/ sound were taken away from *cat*?
   - *Word-to-word matching.* Do *pen* and *pipe* begin with the same sound?
   - *Phoneme counting.* How many sounds do you hear in the word *cake*?
   - *Odd word out.* What word starts with a different sound: *bag, nine, beach, bike*?

   Teachers should start teaching phonemic awareness before beginning instruction in letter–phoneme relationships and continue phonemic awareness activities while teaching the letter–phoneme relationships.

2. *Teach each letter–phoneme relationship explicitly.* Only about 40 to 50 letter–sound relationships are necessary to read. Telling children explicitly what single sound a given letter or letter combination makes will prevent reading problems better than encouraging children to figure out the sounds for the letters by giving clues. Many children have difficulty figuring out the individual letter–phoneme correspondences if they hear them only in the context of words and word parts. Therefore, teachers should separate phonemes from words for instruction. For example, the teacher shows the children the letter *m* and says, "This letter says /mmm/."

   A new phoneme and other phonemes the children have learned should be practiced for about 5 minutes each day in isolation. The rest of the lesson should use these phonemes in words and stories composed of only the letter–phoneme relationships the children have learned in isolation up to that point.

3. *Teach frequent, highly regular letter–sound relationships systematically.* To teach systematically means coordinating the introduction of the letter–phoneme relationships with the material the children are asked to read. The words and stories should be composed of only the letter–phoneme relationships the children have learned. The order of the introduction of letter– phoneme relationships should be planned to allow reading material composed of meaningful words and stories as soon as possible. For example, if the first three letter–phoneme relationships the children learn are /a/, /b/, /c/, the only real word the children can read is *cab*. But if the first three letter–phoneme relationships are /m/, /a/, /s/, the children can read *am, Sam, mass, ma'am*.

4. *Show children exactly how to sound out words.* After children have learned two or three letter–phoneme relationships, teach them how to blend the sounds into words. Show them how to move sequentially from left to right through spellings as they sound out each word. Every day practice blending words composed of only the letter–phoneme relationships the children have learned.

5. *Give children connected, decodable text to practice the letter–phoneme relationships.* Children need extensive practice in applying their knowledge of letter–sound relationships to reading. The most effective integration of **phonics** and reading occurs with *decodable text*—text composed of words that use the letter–phoneme relationships the children have learned to that point and a limited number of sight words that have been systematically taught. As the children learn more letter–phoneme relationships, the texts become more sophisticated.

   Texts that are less decodable do not integrate phonological knowledge with actual reading. For example, *"The dog is up"* is the first sentence children read in one meaning-based program with an unintegrated phonics component. The sound–letter relationships the children had learned up to this point were /d/, /m/, /s/, /r/, /t/. By applying their phonics knowledge, the children could read only "_____ d_____ _____ _____." But if children have learned /a/, /s/, /m/, /b/, /t/, /h/, /f/, /g/, /i/, they can read "Sam has a big fist." The sentence is 100% decodable because the phonics component has been integrated properly into the child's real reading.

   Text that is less decodable requires children to use prediction or context to figure out words. Although prediction is valuable in comprehension for predicting the next event or predicting an outcome, it is not useful in word recognition. The use of pre-dictable text rather than decodable text might allow children to use prediction to figure out a passage. However, the strategy would not transfer to real reading. Predictable text gives children false success. While such success may motivate many children, ultimately they will not be successful readers if they rely on text predictability to read.

6. *Use interesting stories to develop language comprehension.* Research does not rule out the use of interesting, authentic stories to develop language comprehension. But it does recommend not using these stories as reading material for nonreaders. Teacher-read stories play an important role in building children's oral language comprehension, which ultimately affects their reading comprehension. Story-based activities should be structured to build comprehension skills, not decoding skills.

   During the early stages of reading acquisition, children's oral language comprehension level is much higher than their reading comprehension level. The stories teachers read to children to build their comprehension should be geared to their oral language comprehension level. The material used to build children's decoding should be geared to their decoding skills, with attention to meaning. Teachers should teach comprehension strategies and new vocabulary using orally presented stories and texts that are more sophisticated than the early decodable text the children read. The teacher should read these stories to the children and dis-cuss the meaning with them. After the children become fluent decoders, they can apply these comprehension strategies to their own reading.

Source: Adapted from Grossen, B. (2006). Six principles for early reading instruction. In W. L. Heward, *Exceptional children: An introduction to special education* (8th ed., pp. 186–188). Upper Saddle River, NJ: Merrill/Prentice Hall.

FIGURE 5.5

Written language sample from a 10-year-old student with learning disabilities

Source: Courtesy of Timothy E. Heron, The Ohio State University.

Sean's Written Story	Sean's Oral Reading of His Story
A loge tine ago they atene a cosnen they head to geatthere on fesee o One day tere were sane evesedbeats all gaseraned tesene in cladesn they hard a fest for 2 meanes.	A long time ago there were ancient cave men. They had to get their own food. One day there were some wildebeests. They all gathered them and killed them. They had a feast for two months.

FIGURE 5.6

Journal entries written by a seventh-grade student with learning disabilities, before and after instruction and practice with software programs with speech feedback and word-prediction components

Source: From Williams, S. C. (2002). How speech-feedback and word-prediction software can help students write. *Teaching Exceptional Children, 34*(3), 76. Used by permission.

November 21
Prompt: Describe your idea of the "ideal" thanksgiving dinner

MY FAVORITE FOOD IS A GRILL HOG IN A PUMPKIN IN A ROAST HAM IN A MAYBE A TURKEY my favorite DESSERT food strawberry pie THE END

February 27
Prompt: Describe your favorite clock

The clock that I have it is very old it was the first clock that my grandpa had it run off of current and it might go to the time it will go off in a little bird will comes at of the box. The box look like a house in it has a to pendulums on the bottom of the house inside of the house it has people in it. On the otside it has to door on it in it has to windows the color is color is brown on the top of the clock it is black.

Darnell's daily session in the "writing room" is spent practicing, self-evaluating, and self-editing the specific writing skills identified on his IEP.

2006; K. R. Harris, Graham, & Mason, 2006; Konrad & Trela, 2007; Lienemann, Graham, Leader-Janssen, & Reid, 2006; Marchisan & Alber, 2001; Patel & Laud, 2007; Walker, Shippen, Alberto, Houchins, & Cihak, 2005). For example, Figure 5.6 shows the improvements in the writing of a seventh grader with learning disabilities after instruction and practice with software programs with speech feedback and word prediction components.

Math Underachievement

Numerical reasoning and calculation pose major problems for many students with learning disabilities. Students with learning disabilities perform lower than typically achieving children on every type of arithmetic problem at every grade level (Cawley, Parmar, Foley, Salmon, & Roy, 2001). Deficits in retrieving number facts and solving story problems are particularly evident (Geary, 2004; N. C. Jordan & Hanich, 2000). The math competence of students with learning disabilities progresses about 1 year for every 2 years in school, and the skills of many children plateau by age 10 or 12 (Cawley, Parmar, Yan, & Miller, 1998).

Given these difficulties, it is not surprising that more than 50% of students with learning disabilities have IEP goals in math (Kavale & Reese, 1992). As with reading and writing, explicit, systematic instruction that provides guided, meaningful practice with feedback can improve the math performance of students with learning disabilities (e.g., Fahsl, 2007; L. S. Fuchs & Fuchs, 2003; Maccini, Mulcahy, & Wilson, 2007; Owen & Fuchs, 2002; Witzel, Mercer, & Miller, 2003).

Social Skills Deficits

Students with learning disabilities are prone to social problems (Baum, Duffelmeyer, & Greenlan, 2001). After reviewing 152 studies, Kavale and Forness (1996) concluded that about 75% of students with learning disabilities exhibit deficits in social skills. Poor social skills often lead to rejection, low social status, fewer positive interactions with teachers, difficulty making friends, and loneliness—all of which are experienced by many students with learning disabilities regardless of classroom placement (Lane, Pierson, & Givner, 2004; Ochoa & Palmer, 1995; Pavri & Monda-Amaya, 2000; Wiener, 2004). The poor social skills of students with learning disabilities may be due to the ways they interpret social situations relative to their own experiences and inability to perceive the nonverbal affective expressions of others (Meadan & Halle, 2004; Most & Greenbank, 2000).

Although researchers who studied messages by children on an Internet site for people with learning disabilities found "rare instances" when children described positive social relationships (e.g., "I have lots of friends."), the group as a whole overwhelmingly expressed social difficulties.

Some students with learning disabilities, however, experience no problems getting along with their peers and teachers. For example, Sabornie and Kauffman (1986) reported no significant difference in the sociometric standing of 46 high school students with learning disabilities and 46 peers without disabilities. Moreover, they discovered that some of the students with learning disabilities enjoyed socially rewarding experiences in inclusive classrooms.

One interpretation of these contradictory findings is that social competence and peer acceptance are not characteristics of learning disabilities but are outcomes of the different social climates created by teachers, peers, parents, and others with whom students with learning disabilities interact (Vaughn, McIntosh, Schumm, Haager, & Callwood, 1993). Researchers have begun to identify the types of problems experienced by children with learning disabilities who are ranked low in social acceptance and to discover instructional arrangements that promote the social status of students with learning disabilities in the general education classroom (Bryan, 2005; Court & Givon, 2003; Vaughn, Elbaum, & Schumm, 1996).

Attention Problems and Hyperactivity

Some students with learning disabilities have difficulty attending to a task and/or display high rates of hyperactivity. Children who consistently exhibit these problems may be diagnosed with attention-deficit/hyperactivity disorder (ADHD). A high degree of **comorbidity** (two conditions occurring in the same individual) between learning disabilities and ADHD has frequently been reported (T. J. Smith & Adams, 2006). A national study examining the demographics of elementary and middle school students with disabilities found that of 28% of parents whose children were receiving special education under the category of learning disabilities reported their children as also having ADHD (M. Wagner & Blackorby, 2002). ADHD is described in detail in Chapter 11.

Behavioral Problems

Researchers have consistently found a higher-than-usual incidence of behavioral problems among students with learning disabilities (Cullinan, 2007). In a study of 790 students enrolled in K–12 learning disabilities programs in Indiana, the percentage of students with behavioral problems (15%) remained consistent across grade levels (McLeskey, 1992). Although these data definitely show increased behavioral problems among children with learning disabilities, the relationships between the students' behavior problems and academic difficulties are not known. In other words, we do not know whether the academic deficits or the behavioral problems cause the other difficulty, or whether both are products of other causal factors. And it is important to note that many children with learning disabilities exhibit no behavioral problems.

Regardless of the interrelationships of these characteristics, teachers and other caregivers responsible for planning educational programs for students with learning disabilities need skills for dealing with social and behavioral difficulties as well as academic deficits. Some of these important teaching skills are described in Chapter 6.

Social, attention, and behavioral problems

 Content Standards for Beginning Teachers of Students with LD: Psychological, social, and emotional characteristics of individuals with LD (LD2K3) (also CC2K2).

Low Ratings of Self-Efficacy

Students with learning disabilities are more likely to report lower levels of self-efficacy, mood, effort, and hope than are their peers without learning disabilities. It is not known whether a tendency for negative self-perceptions is an inherent characteristic of learning disabilities or the result of a painful history of frustration and disappointment with academic and social situations (Cosden, Brown, & Elliott, 2002), "day-to-day struggles, and/or future worries" (Lackaye, Margalit, Ziv, & Ziman, 2007, p. 111).

The Defining Characteristic

Academic achievement of students with LD

Content Standards for Beginning Teachers—Common Core: Educational implications of characteristics of various exceptionalities (CC2K2) (also LD3K3).

Although students with learning disabilities are an extremely heterogeneous group, it is important to remember that the fundamental, defining characteristic of students with learning disabilities is the presence of specific and significant achievement deficits seemingly in spite of adequate overall intelligence. The difference between what students with learning disabilities "are expected to do and what they can do . . . grows larger and larger" over time (Deshler, Schumaker, Lenz, et al., 2001, p. 97). The performance gap becomes especially noticeable and handicapping in the middle and secondary grades, when the academic growth of many students with disabilities plateaus. By the time they reach high school, students with learning disabilities are the lowest of the low achievers, performing below the 10th percentile in reading, written language, and math (Hock, Schumaker, & Deshler, 1999).

The difficulties experienced by children with learning disabilities—especially for those who cannot read at grade level—are substantial and pervasive and usually last across the life span (Price, Field, & Patton, 2003). The tendency to think of learning disabilities as a "mild" disability erroneously supports "the notion that a learning disability is little more than a minor inconvenience rather than the serious, life-long condition it often is [and] detracts from the real needs of these students" (Hallahan, 1998, p. 4).

It is important for teachers to remember that children with disabilities have useful skills and interests and to maintain a positive outlook and not be entirely focused on a student's deficits (see Figure 5.7).

PREVALENCE

Learning disabilities make up by far the largest of all special education categories. During the 2005–2006 school year, more than 2.7 million students ages 6 to 21 received special education under the specific learning disabilities category (U.S. Office of Special Education, 2007a). This figure represents 45.3% of all school-age children with disabilities and about 4% of the school-age population. As a result of different methods employed by the states for diagnosing learning disabilities, the percentage of children served in this special education category ranges widely from a low of 1.7% of the school-age population in Kentucky to a high of 6.0% in Oklahoma (U.S. Department of Education, 2007a). Across grade levels, males with learning disabilities outnumber females by a 3:1 ratio.

The number of students identified with learning disabilities has grown tremendously since the passage of IDEA. The current number is triple the number of students with learning disabilities who received special education in 1976–1977, the first year the federal government reported such data. Swanson (2000) notes that the rising incidence of children with learning disabilities might be considered an epidemic. "These increases are unparalleled and unwarranted, especially when viewed in relation to other high-incidence mild disabilities (i.e., mental retardation and emotional disturbance)" (Kavale, Holdnack, & Mostert, 2006, p. 113).

Many educators and administrators have expressed alarm over the rising prevalence figures for learning disabilities. They believe the ever-increasing numbers of students classified as learning disabled are the result of overidentification and misdiagnosis of low-achieving students, which reduces the resources available to serve students who have a true disability. Lyon (1999), of the National Institute of Child and Human Development, suggested that learning disabilities has become "a sociological sponge to wipe up the spills of general education" (p. A1).

FIGURE 5.7   The importance of maintaining a positive focus

Tom Lovitt is a pioneer in the education of children's learning disabilities and one of the field's more productive teachers and scholars. His carefully conducted research and thoughtful writing have spanned five decades and dealt with virtually every aspect of special education. In one of his classic books on teaching children with learning problems, *In Spite of My Resistance . . . I've Learned from Children*, Lovitt (1977) wrote that, all things being equal, a teacher who imparts many skills to many children is good, and one who does not is not. After all, teaching is helping children learn new things.

Although Lovitt consistently declares that the development of children's academic and social skills is the primary purpose for teachers and students to come together, he also warns us to not become so concerned with fixing everything we believe is wrong with the student that we forget about recognizing and building upon all that is positive.

We teachers, in all good faith, set out to remediate as many of the "shortfalls" as possible so that youth with learning disabilities will be as normal and wonderful as we are. We should reconsider this total remedial approach to learning disabilities. One reason for considering an alternative should be obvious if we thought of a day in the life of a student with learning disabilities. First, the teacher sets out to remediate his reading, then his math, and then his language, social skills, and soccer playing. Toward the end of the day, she attempts to remediate his metacognitive deficits. That lad is in a remediation mode throughout the day. Is it any wonder that some of these youngsters have self-concepts, self-images, self-esteems, and attributions that are out of whack?

We should spend some time concentrating on these youngsters' positive qualities. If a girl is inclined toward mechanics, or a boy to being a chef, we should nurture those skills. And if a child doesn't have a negotiable behavior, we should locate one and promote it. I can't help but think that if every youngster, LD or otherwise, had at least one trade, skill, or technique about which he or she was fairly competent, that would do more for that youngster's adjustment than would the many hours of remediation to which the child is subjected. Perhaps that accent on the positive would go a long way toward actually helping the remediation process. If children knew they could excel in something, that might help them become competent in other areas as well.

(T. C. Lovitt, March 24, 2007, personal communication)

Some authorities contend that the concept of learning disabilities is poorly defined and functions as a catchall category for any student who is experiencing learning problems and does not meet eligibility requirements for other disability categories (Kavale et al., 2006).

> [The definition of specific learning disabilities] has always been too broad to be wrong and too vague to be complete. . . . The meaning of SLD has been diluted by a conventional wisdom suggesting that "there are many types of learning disabilities," thereby extending its boundaries to the point the SLD is no longer a distinct classification. . . . The logical relation shift from *All students with SLD have learning problems* to *All students with learning problems have SLD,* which is patently not true if SLD is properly viewed as a categorical designation. (p. 115)

CAUSES

In most cases, the cause (etiology) of a child's learning disability is unknown. Many causes have been proposed, which probably reflects the diverse characteristics of students with learning disabilities. Just as there are different types of learning disabilities (e.g., language disabilities, math disabilities, reading disabilities), there are likely to be different causes. Four classes of suspected causes are brain damage, heredity, biochemical imbalance, and environmental factors.

Causes of LD

 Content Standards for Beginning Teachers of Students with LD: Etiologies of LD (LD2K1).

Neurological bases of LD

 Council for Exceptional Children

Content Standards for Beginning Teachers of Students with LD: Neurobiological and medical factors that may impact the learning of individuals with LD (LD2K2).

Brain Damage or Dysfunction

Some professionals believe that all children with learning disabilities suffer from some type of neurological injury or dysfunction. This belief is inherent in the NJCLD (1990/2001) definition of learning disabilities, which states that learning disorders are "presumed to be due to central nervous system dysfunction." When evidence of brain damage is not found (which is the case for the majority of children with learning disabilities), the term *minimal brain dysfunction* is sometimes used, especially by physicians. This wording implies brain damage by asserting that the child's brain does not function properly.

Recent advances in magnetic resonance imaging (MRI) technology have enabled researchers to discover that specific regions of the brains of some individuals with reading and language disabilities show activation patterns during phonological processing tasks that differ from the patterns found in the brains of people without disabilities (e.g., C. J. Miller, Sanchez, & Hynd, 2003; Richards, 2001; Simos, Breier, Fletcher, Bergman, & Papanicolaou, 2000). The brain structure of some children with reading disabilities differs slightly from that of children without disabilities (D. W. Collins & Rourke, 2003; Leonard, 2001).

This research holds promise for understanding the biological bases of dyslexia and other specific learning disabilities. As Leonard (2001) points out, however, we do not yet know how and to what extent the brain's neural networks are affected by the child's experiences (i.e., learning) and vice versa. Thus, we do not know whether neurobiological factors associated with learning disabilities contribute to the learning problems of children, are the product of an unstimulating environment, or a combination. However, growing evidence indicates that intensive remedial reading instruction reduces differences in the ways that the brains of children with reading disabilities and those of children without reading problems are activated (Rourke, 2005). For example, Shaywitz and colleagues (2004) reported that an average of 105 hours of individual tutoring that focused on teaching the **alphabetic principle** (how letters and combinations of letters represent the small segments of speech called phonemes) and oral reading fluency practice not only improved children's reading fluency but "facilitated the development of the neural systems that underlie skilled reading" (p. 933).

Special educators should refrain from placing too much emphasis on theories linking learning disabilities to brain damage or brain dysfunction. There are three major reasons for such caution. First, not all children with learning disabilities display clinical (medical) evidence of brain damage, and not all children with brain damage have learning disabilities. Second, assuming a child's learning problems are caused by a dysfunctioning brain may serve as a built-in excuse for continuing to provide ineffective instruction. When a student with suspected brain damage fails to learn, his teachers may be quick to presume that the brain injury prevents him from learning and may be slow to analyze and change instructional variables. Third, whether "learning disabilities in an individual case are symptoms that result from brain injury or developmental delay will not essentially alter the methods of teaching the student" (Myers & Hammill, 1990, p. 22).

Heredity

Siblings and children of persons with reading disabilities have a slightly greater than normal likelihood of having reading problems. Growing evidence indicates that genetics may account for at least some family links with dyslexia (Galaburda, 2005; Grigorenko, 2003; Raskind, 2001). Research has located possible chromosomal loci for the genetic transmission of phonological deficits that may predispose a child for reading problems later (Cardon et al., 1994; Kaplan et al., 2002).

Biochemical Imbalance

Several popular theories in the 1970s, which continue to find traction from time to time in the popular media, held that biochemical disturbances within a child's body caused learning disabilities. For example, Feingold (1975, 1976) claimed that artificial colorings and flavorings in many of the foods children eat can cause learning disabilities and hyperactivity. He recommended a treatment for learning disabilities that consisted of a diet with no foods containing synthetic colors or flavors. In a comprehensive review of research studies that tested the special diet, Spring and Sandoval (1976) concluded that very little scientific evidence supported Feingold's theory.

Research also has suggested that learning disabilities can be caused by the inability of a child's bloodstream to synthesize a normal amount of vitamins (Cott, 1972). Some physicians began *megavitamin therapy* with children with learning disabilities, which consisted of massive daily doses of vitamins in an effort to overcome the child's suspected vitamin deficiencies. Two studies designed to test the effects of megavitamin treatment on children with learning disabilities and hyperactivity found that huge doses of vitamins did not improve the children's performance (Arnold, Christopher, Huestis, & Smeltzer, 1978; Kershner, Hawks, & Grekin, 1977). Most professionals today give little credence to biochemical imbalance as a significant cause of or treatment for learning disabilities. (However, some professionals advocate specialized diets and vitamin therapies as treatments for autism. See Chapter 7 and Schreibman, 2005, for a discussion.)

Environmental Factors

Although virtually impossible to document as primary causes of learning disabilities, environmental factors—particularly impoverished living conditions early in a child's life and limited exposure to highly effective instruction in school—probably contribute to the achievement deficits experienced by many children who receive special education. The tendency for learning disabilities to run in families suggests a correlation between environmental influences on children's early development and subsequent achievement in school. Evidence for this relationship can be found in longitudinal research such as that conducted by Hart and Risley (1995), who found that infants and toddlers who received infrequent communication exchanges with their parents were more likely to show deficits in vocabulary, language use, and intellectual development before entering school.

Another environmental variable that is likely to contribute to children's learning problems is the quality of instruction they receive. Many special educators today believe that Engelmann (1977) was correct when he claimed more than 30 years ago that the vast majority of "children who are labeled 'learning disabled' exhibit a disability not because of anything wrong with their perception, synapses, or memory, but because they have been seriously mistaught" (pp. 46–47).

Although the relationship between poor instruction and learning disabilities is not clear, a great deal of evidence shows that many students' learning problems can be remediated by direct, intensive, and systematic instruction. It would be naive, however, to think that the achievement problems of all children with learning disabilities are caused entirely by inadequate instruction. Nevertheless, from an educational perspective, intensive, systematic instruction should be the intervention of first choice for all students with learning disabilities.

IDENTIFICATION AND ASSESSMENT

Educators frequently use five forms of assessment with students with learning disabilities: standardized intelligence and achievement tests, criterion-referenced tests, informal reading inventories, curriculum-based measurement, and direct daily measurement.

Intelligence and Achievement Tests

Standardized intelligence and achievement tests are widely used with children with learning disabilities because a discrepancy between intellectual ability and achievement remains a primary factor in determining eligibility for special education services (Kavale et al., 2006; Machek & Nelson, 2007). These norm-referenced tests are constructed so that one student's score can be compared with the scores of other students of the same age who have taken the test. (See Chapter 4 for a discussion of intelligence tests.) Widely used standardized tests for assessing a student's overall academic achievement include the Iowa Tests of Basic Skills (Hoover, Heironymus, & Frisbie, 2007), the Peabody Individual Achievement Test (Markwardt, 1998b), the Woodcock-Johnson III Tests of Achievement (Woodcock, McGrew,

Standardized achievement tests

 Council for Exceptional Children

Content Standards for Beginning Teachers of Students with LD: Terminology and procedures used in the assessment of individuals with LD (LD8K1).

& Mather, 2001), and the Wide Range Achievement Test—4 (WRAT-4) (Wilkinson & Robertson, 2005). Scores on these tests and similar tests are commonly reported by grade level; a score of 3.5, for example, means that the student's score equals the average score of the students in the norm group who were halfway through the third grade.

Some norm-referenced tests are designed to measure achievement in certain academic areas. Frequently administered reading achievement tests include the Gates-MacGinitie Reading Tests (MacGinitie, MacGinitie, Maria, & Dreyer, 2000), the Gray Oral Reading Tests (Wiederholt & Bryant, 2001), the Test of Reading Comprehension (V. L. Brown, Hammill, & Wiederholt, 1995), and the Woodcock Reading Mastery Test (Woodcock, 1998). Norm-referenced tests used to assess mathematics achievement include KeyMath—3: A Diagnostic Inventory of Essential Skills (Connolly, 2007), the Stanford Diagnostic Mathematics Test (Beatty, Madden, Gardner, & Karlsen, 1995), and the Test of Mathematical Abilities (Brown, Cronin, & McEntire, 1994).

Criterion-Referenced Tests

Criterion-referenced tests differ from norm-referenced tests in that a child's score on a criterion-referenced test is compared with a predetermined criterion, or mastery level, rather than with normed scores of other students. The value of criterion-referenced tests is that they identify the specific skills the child has already learned and the skills that require instruction. One criterion-referenced test widely used by special educators is the Brigance Diagnostic Comprehensive Inventory of Basic Skills (Brigance, 1999), which includes 140 skill sequences in four subscales: readiness, reading, language arts, and math. Some commercially distributed curricula now include criterion-referenced test items for use as both a pretest and a posttest. The pretest assesses the student's entry level to determine which aspects of the program she is ready to learn; the posttest evaluates the effectiveness of the program. Criterion-referenced tests can be, and often are, informally developed by classroom teachers.

Informal Reading Inventories

Teachers' growing awareness of the inability of formal achievement tests to provide useful information for planning instruction has led to greater use of teacher-developed and -administered tests, particularly in the area of reading. An informal reading inventory usually consists of a series of progressively more difficult sentences and paragraphs that a student reads aloud. By directly observing and recording aspects of the student's reading skills (e.g., mispronounced vowels or consonants, omissions, reversals, substitutions, and comprehension), the teacher can determine the level of reading material that is most suitable for the child and the specific reading skills that require remediation (Carnine, Silbert, Kame'enui, Tarver, & Jongjohann, 2006).

Curriculum-Based Measurement

Any measurement system must be valid and reliable. Repeatedly putting a ruler in a pot of water might yield a reliable measure of 3 inches, but it would not produce a valid measure of the water's temperature. As silly as that example might seem, too often, measures used in education fail to provide a meaningful index of children's progress in the curriculum. **Curriculum-based measurement (CBM)** involves frequent assessment of a student's progress in learning the objectives that make up the curriculum in which the student is participating (Deno, 1985; L. S. Fuchs & Fuchs, 1996; Howell & Nolet, 2000). CBM is a **formative evaluation** method in that it provides information on student learning as instruction takes place over time. By contrast, the results of a **summative evaluation** cannot be used to inform instruction, because it is conducted after instruction has been completed (e.g., at the end of a grading period or school year).

One study found that teachers who used CBM made an average of 2.5 changes in students' instructional plans over the course of 20 weeks, compared to an average of just 0.27 changes by teachers who were not using CBM (Fuchs, Fuchs, Hamlett, & Stecker, 1991). Other studies have reported that students whose teachers tailor instruction plans on CBM data perform and achieve better academically than do students whose teachers do not use CBM (Stecker & Fuchs, 2000; Wesson, 1991).

Go to the Homework & Exercises section in Chapter 5 of MyEducationLab and complete Homework Exercise 1. As you watch the video and answer the accompanying questions, think about how using technology is enhancing this curriculum-based measure.

In addition to being valid and reliable, CBMs should be easy to administer; cost- and time-efficient; and, perhaps most important, sensitive to small, incremental changes in student performance over time (Kame'enui et al., 2005). One set of CBMs with these attributes is the Dynamic Indicators of Basic Early Literacy Skills (DIBELS) (Good & Kaminski, 2003). DIBELS was developed to be an efficient indicator of key reading skills for early identification of children at risk for reading difficulties and to assess the effects of interventions designed to prevent such failure. DIBELS consists of a set of 1-minute fluency measures used to regularly monitor the development of prereading and early reading skills. Research has demonstrated that children who meet the benchmark goal for each measure are likely (odds greater than 80%) to become proficient readers (Good, Simmons, & Kame'enui, 2001). The DIBELS measures are free and can be downloaded in English and Spanish at http://dibels.uoregon.edu. Also available on this website are video clips showing an examiner administering each of the DIBELS measures to a student.

The DIBELS measures and their respective benchmarks are as follows:

- *Initial sounds fluency.* This measure assesses a child's skill to identify and produce the initial sound of a given word. The examiner shows four pictures to the child, names each picture, and then asks the child to identify the picture that begins with the sound the examiner produces orally (e.g., "This is *sink, cat, gloves,* and *hat.* Which picture begins with /s/?" and the student points to the correct picture). Benchmark: 25 or more initial sounds per minute by the middle of kindergarten.

- *Letter-naming fluency.* Students are presented with a page of upper- and lowercase letters arranged in a random order and are asked to name as many letters as they can in 1 minute. Students are told if they do not know a letter they will be told the letter. Benchmark: Students are considered at risk for difficulty achieving early literacy benchmark goals if they perform in the lowest 20% of students in their district. Students are considered at some risk if they perform between the 20th and 40th percentile using local norms. Fall, winter, and spring of kindergarten, and fall of first grade.

- *Phonemic segmentation fluency.* This assesses a child's ability to segment three- and four-phoneme words into their individual phonemes fluently. For example, the examiner says, "sat," and the student says, "/s/-/a/-/t/" to receive three possible points for the word. After the student responds, the examiner presents the next word. Benchmark: 35 or more phonemes per minute by the end of kindergarten.

- *Nonsense word fluency.* This test of the alphabetic principle assesses a child's letter–sound correspondence and ability to blend letters together to form unfamiliar "words." For example, if the stimulus word is "vaj," the student could say, "/v/-/a/-/j/" or say the word /vaj/ to obtain a total of three letter-sounds correct. Benchmark: 50 or more letter sounds per minute by the middle of first grade.

- *Oral reading fluency.* This assesses a child's skill in reading connected text. Students read an unfamiliar passage of grade-level material for 1 minute. Omissions, substitutions, and hesitations of more than 3 seconds are scored as errors. Self-corrections within 3 seconds are scored as correct. The number of correct words per minute is the oral reading fluency rate. Benchmark: 40, 90, and 110 or more words read correctly per minute by the end of first, second, and third grade, respectively.

- *Retell fluency.* Provides a comprehension check for the oral reading assessment, prevents child from speed-reading without attending to meaning, identifies children whose comprehension is not consistent with their fluency, and provides explicit linkage with core component of National Reading Panel (2000) recommended practices. Examiner says, Please tell me all about what you just read. Try to tell me everything you can. Begin." Score is the number of words the child retells that illustrate understanding of the passage. For children whose retell fluency is about 50% of their oral reading fluency score, their oral reading fluency score provides a good overall indication of their reading proficiency, including comprehension.

Adapted from the official DIBELS home page, http://dibels.uoregon.edu, retrieved June 21, 2007.

Self-recording direct and daily measures of academic performance is an excellent way to involve students in their own learning.

Go to the Homework & Exercises section in Chapter 5 of MyEducationLab and complete Homework Exercise 2. As you read the article and answer the accompanying questions, consider the benefits of precision teaching for this student who has learning disabilities and struggles with reading.

History of LD

Content Standards for Beginning Teachers of Students with LD: Historical foundations, classical studies, and major contributors in the field of LD (LD1K1).

Council for Exceptional Children

Detailed accounts of how DIBELS measures can provide an index of early identification and assessment of children at risk for reading failure and evaluate a school's core can be found in Good et al. (2003, p. 221–222) and Kame'enui and colleagues (2005).

Direct Daily Measurement

Direct daily measurement, the cornerstone of the behavioral approach to education introduced in Chapter 4, means observing and recording a measure of the student's performance each time a specific skill is taught. In a program teaching multiplication facts, for example, the student's performance of multiplication facts would be assessed each day that multiplication was taught. Measures such as correct rate (e.g., number of multiplication facts stated or written correctly per minute), error rate, and percentage correct are often recorded. Direct daily measurement provides information about student learning on a continuous basis, enabling the teacher to modify instruction in accordance with changing (or unchanging) performance, not because of intuition, guesswork, or the results of a test that measures something else (Heward, 2003).

Some teachers of students with learning disabilities use a special system of direct daily measurement called **precision teaching** (Lindsley, 1996). Precision teachers make instructional decisions based on changes in the frequency of a student's performance (e.g., number of words read correctly per minute) as plotted on a standard graphic display called the **standard celeration chart**. Precision teaching is neither a specific method of teaching nor a curriculum; it is a way of evaluating the effects of instruction and making instructional decisions. Additional information about precision teaching and the standard celeration chart can be found in J. O. Cooper, Kubina, and Malanga (1998); Graf and Lindsley (2002); and Kubina and Cooper (2001). Detailed descriptions and examples of precision teaching can be found on the Standard Celeration Society's website http://celeration.org/.

EDUCATIONAL APPROACHES

Not long ago, instruction of students with learning disabilities emphasized the remediation of basic skill deficits, often at the expense of providing opportunities for students to express themselves, learn problem-solving skills, or access the general education curriculum in meaningful ways. "The overemphasis on the 'basics' with the exclusion of any creative or cognitively complex activities provides many students with LD an unappealing intellectual diet" (Gersten, 1998, p. 163). Table 5.1 describes some key historical events and their implications for the education of students with learning disabilities. More detailed accounts of the history of the learning disabilities field can be found in Bateman (2005); Hallahan and Mock (2003); Healey (2005); Keogh (2005b); Lerner and Kline (2006); McNamara (2007); and Mercer and Pullen (2008).

In recent years, however, the field has shifted its instructional focus from a remediation-only mode to an approach designed to give students with learning disabilities meaningful access to and success with the core curriculum. By incorporating the six principles of effective instructional design shown in Figure 5.8, general class teachers and special educators can make curriculum and instruction more effective for students with and without disabilities (Coyne, Kame'enui, & Carnine, 2007).

Many students with learning disabilities (a) have difficulty organizing information on their own, (b) bring limited stores of background knowledge to many academic activities, and (c) often do not approach learning tasks in effective and efficient ways. Thus, contemporary best practice in educating students with learning disabilities is characterized by explicit instruction (see Teaching & Learning, "Explicit Instruction"), the use of content enhancements, and teaching learning strategies to students (Bulgren, 2006; Gersten, 1998; Hock et al., 1999; Swanson, 2001).

TABLE 5.1

A history of the education of children with learning disabilities:
Key events and implications

DATE	HISTORICAL EVENT	EDUCATIONAL IMPLICATIONS
1920s–1940s	Research by Alfred Strauss and others (Cruick-shank, Doll, Kephart, Kirk, Lehtinen, Werner) with children with mental retardation and brain injury at the Wayne County Training School in Michigan found relationships between brain injury and disorders that interfered with learning: perceptual disorders, perseveration, disorders of conceptual thinking, and behavioral problems such as hyperactivity and impulsivity.	In the book *Psychopathology and Education of the Brain-Injured Child,* Strauss and Lara Lehtinen (1947) recommended strategies for relieving perceptual and conceptual disturbances of children with brain injury and thus reducing their symptomatic learning problems.
1950s–1960s	By the early 1950s, most public schools had established special education programs for children with mental retardation, sensory impairments, physical disabilities, and behavioral disorders. But there remained a group of children who were having serious learning problems at school, yet did not fit into any of the existing categories of exceptionality. They did not "look" disabled; the children seemed physically intact, yet they were unable to learn certain basic skills and subjects at school.	In searching for help with their children's problems, parents turned to other professionals—notably doctors, psychologists, and speech and language specialists. Understandably, these professionals viewed the children from the perspectives of their respective disciplines. As a result, terms such as *brain damage, minimal brain dysfunction, neurological impairment, perceptual handicap, dyslexia,* and *aphasia* were often used to describe and to account for the children's learning and behavior problems.
1963	The term *learning disabilities* was coined by Samuel Kirk in an address to a group of parents whose children were experiencing serious difficulties in learning to read, were hyperactive, or could not solve math problems.	The parents liked the term and, that very evening, voted to form the Association for Children With Learning Disabilities (ACLD).
1966	A national task force identified 99 different characteristics of children with *minimal brain dysfunction* (the term used at the time) reported in the literature (Clements, 1966).	The inherent danger in such lists is a tendency to assume that each of those characteristics is exhibited by *all* of the children considered to be in the category. This danger is especially troublesome with learning disabilities, because the children who make up the category are an extremely heterogeneous group.
mid-1960s–1970s	The concept of process, or ability, testing grew out of the belief that learning disabilities are caused by a basic underlying difficulty of the child to process, or use, environmental stimuli in the same way that children without disabilities do. Two of the most widely used process tests for diagnosing and assessing learning disabilities were developed during this time: the Illinois Test of Psycholinguistic Abilities (ITPA) (Kirk, McCarthy, & Kirk, 1968) and the Marianne Frostig Developmental Test of Visual Perception (Frostig, Lefever, & Whittlesey, 1964).	The ability training approach dominated special education for children with learning disabilities, from the field's inception through the 1970s. The three most widely known ability training approaches were psycholinguistic training, based on the ITPA; the visual-perceptual approach (Frostig & Horne, 1973); and the perceptual-motor approach (Kephart, 1971).
1968	The National Advisory Committee on Handicapped Children drafted and presented to Congress a definition of learning disabilities.	This definition was later incorporated into IDEA and used to govern the disbursement of federal funds for support of services to children with learning disabilities.

(continues)

TABLE 5.1 CONTINUED

A history of the education of children with learning disabilities: Key events and implications

DATE	HISTORICAL EVENT	EDUCATIONAL IMPLICATIONS
1968	The Division for Children with Learning Disabilities (DCLD) was established within the Council for Exceptional Children (CEC).	DCLD has become the largest division of CEC.
1969	The Children with Learning Disabilities Act (part of P.L. 91–230) was passed by Congress.	This legislation authorized a 5-year program of federal funds for teacher training and the establishment of model demonstration programs for students with learning disabilities.
late 1970s–early 1980s	Reviews of research showing the ineffectiveness of psycholinguistic training (Hammill & Larsen, 1978), the visual-perceptual approach (Myers & Hammill, 1976), and perceptual-motor approaches (Kavale & Mattson, 1983) were published.	Process testing and ability training gradually gave way to increased use of a skill training approach. If a student has not learned a complex skill and has had sufficient opportunity and wants to succeed, a skill trainer would conclude that the student has not learned the necessary prerequisite skills and provides direct instruction and practice on those prerequisite skills.
1975	Congress passed the Individuals with Disabilities Education Act (P.L. 94–142).	Learning disabilities was included as one of the disability categories in IDEA.
1980s and 1990s	Research on instructional design, content enhancements, and learning strategies provides additional knowledge on effective teaching methods for students with learning disabilities.	Skill training approach supplemented with increased emphasis on helping students with learning disabilities have meaningful contact with the general curriculum.
2001	In response to concerns about the large number of children identified as learning disabled, the U.S. Office of Special Education sponsored a Learning Disabilities Summit in Washington, DC.	Nine white papers were developed on topics such as diagnostic decision making, classification models, early identification, and the nature and legitimacy of learning disabilities as a disability. Recommendations included in these papers play influential role in how learning disabilities are treated in the reauthorization of IDEA in 2004.
2004	IDEA Improvement Act of 2004 changed the rules for determining whether a child has a specific learning disability. Schools are no longer required to document that a severe discrepancy between achievement and intellectual ability exists and may instead use an identification process based on a child's responsiveness to research-based intervention.	Schools using a responsiveness to intervention (RTI) model provide systematic help for all students struggling with basic skills (usually reading) in the early grades. Referral for special education evaluation and possible diagnosis of a learning disability is reserved for students who fail to make satisfactory progress after one or two 10- to 12-week trials of intensive small-group intervention using research-based instructional programs.

Content Enhancements

Educating students with learning disabilities at the middle and secondary levels is particularly difficult. Most are "ill-prepared for high school" and have reading and language skills at the fourth- to fifth-grade level (Deshler, Schumaker, Lenz, et al., 2001). Lectures and assigned readings in textbooks are widely used in middle and high school classrooms to present academic content to students. The teacher talks and assigns a portion of a high-vocabulary, content-dense text; and students are held responsible for obtaining, remembering, and using the information later (usually on a quiz or a test). A combination of poor reading, listening,

Big Ideas
Highly selected concepts, principles, rules, strategies, or heuristics that facilitate the most efficient and broadest acquisition of knowledge.

Conspicuous Strategies
Sequence of teaching events and teacher actions that make explicit the steps in learning. They are made conspicuous by the use of visual maps or models, verbal directions, full and clear explanations, and so forth.

Mediated Scaffolding
Temporary support for students to learn new material. Scaffolding is faded over time.

Strategic Integration
Planful consideration and sequencing of instruction in ways that show the commonalities and differences between old and new knowledge.

Primed Background Knowledge
Related knowledge, placed effectively in sequence, that students must already possess in order to learn new knowledge.

Judicious Review
Sequence and schedule of opportunities learners have to apply and develop facility with new knowledge. The review must be adequate, distributed, cumulative, and varied.

FIGURE 5.8

Six major principles of effective instructional design

Source: From Kame'enui, E. J., Carnine, D. W., & Dixon, R. C. (2007). Introduction. In M. D. Coyne, E. J. Kame'enui, & D. W. Carnine (Eds.), *Effective teaching strategies that accommodate diverse learners* (3rd ed., p. 10). © 2007. Reproduced by permission of Pearson Education, Inc., Upper Saddle River, NJ.

note-taking, and study skills, compounded by a limited store of background knowledge, makes obtaining needed information from reading, lectures, and homework assignments a daunting task for students with learning disabilities.

Content enhancement is the general term for a wide range of techniques teachers use to enhance the organization and delivery of curriculum content so that students can better access, interact with, comprehend, and retain that information (Hock et al., 1999; Lenz & Bulgren, 1995). To most effectively use a content-enhancement approach, teachers must

> think critically about the content they cover, determine what approaches to learning need to be in operation for students to be successful....The teacher, in effect, teaches content and learning processes simultaneously.... [S]tressing what the students should learn as well as how. (S. Baker, Gersten, & Scanlon, 2002, p. 67)

Four types of content enhancements often helpful to students with learning disabilities are graphic organizers, note-taking strategies, mnemonics, and learning strategies.

Graphic Organizers Graphic organizers are visual-spatial arrangements of information containing words or concepts connected graphically that can help students see meaningful hierarchical, comparative, and sequential relationships (Dye, 2000; Horton, Lovitt, & Bergerud, 1990; Ives, 2007). Bulgren, Deshler, Schumaker, and Lenz (2000) have developed a graphic device and teaching routine called the *concept-anchoring table/routine* that helps students relate a new concept to a concept and information with which they are already familiar (see Figure 5.9). Students complete the anchoring table as part of a seven-step, teacher-guided instructional routine that enables students to use their background experiences and knowledge (e.g., *roof*) to understand the new concept (e.g., layers of atmosphere). Research has shown that the concept-anchoring routine helps students learn abstract or complex information such as "federalism" or "commensalism" (Bulgren et al., 2000; Deshler, Schumaker, Bulgren, et al., 2001).

Note-taking Strategies Traditional lecture is widely used in middle and high school classes to present curriculum content to students. The teacher talks, and students are held responsible for obtaining, remembering, and using the information at a later time (usually on a quiz or test). Students who take good notes and study them later consistently receive

Go to the Homework & Exercises section in Chapter 5 of MyEducationLab and complete Homework Exercise 3. The highly effective Direct Instruction curricula authored by Engelmann and colleagues are based on a thoroughly developed model of explicit instruction (G. Adams & Carnine, 2003; Engelmann & Colvin, 2006; Marchand-Martella, Slocum, & Martella, 2004).

Content enhancements: Graphic organizers, note-taking strategies, and mnemonics

 Council for Exceptional Children

Content Standards for Beginning Teachers of Students with LD: Methods for guiding individuals in identifying and organizing critical content (LD4K5).

Explicit Instruction

BY NANCY E. MARCHAND-MARTELLA AND RONALD C. MARTELLA

Although most teachers have read or heard about the importance of explicit instruction, many are unsure about how to include the fundamental principles and practices of explicit instruction into their daily lessons.

EXPLICIT INSTRUCTION DEFINED

Explicit, or direct, instruction is "a systematic method of teaching with emphasis on proceeding in small steps, checking for student understanding, and achieving active and successful participation by all students" (Rosenshine, 1987, p. 34). This type of instruction is also referred to as "demonstration-prompt-practice" (Stevens & Rosenshine, 1981). Rosenshine (1986) provides highlights of research on explicit instruction of well-defined knowledge and skills such as math procedures, grammatical rules, and vocabulary. These highlights include the following:

- Start every lesson by correcting the previous day's homework and reviewing what students have recently been taught.
- Describe the goals of today's lesson.
- Present new material in small steps, giving clear and detailed explanations of the skill(s) to be learned (modeling), checking often for student understanding through strategic questioning.
- Provide repeated opportunities for students to practice in an active manner and to obtain feedback on their performance (guided practice).
- Monitor student learning through varied exercises (e.g., seatwork).
- Continue providing practice opportunities until students are performing skills independently and with ease (independent practice).
- Review previous week's lesson at the beginning of each week; review what students have learned over the past 4 weeks at the end of each month.

Thus, explicit instruction can be summarized as unambiguous, clear, and *direct* teaching (Arrasmith, 2003): Teachers show students what to do, give them opportunities to practice with teacher feedback, and then provide opportunities for students to apply these skills on their own over time. It is not trial-and-error learning, discovery, exploration, facilitated learning, or some other approach where teachers *assist* performance rather than *directly provide* knowledge/information to students (K. R. Harris & Graham, 1996).

WHY EXPLICIT INSTRUCTION IS IMPORTANT

Students qualify for special education because they are significantly behind their peers in one or more academic areas. These students must be accelerated in their learning to catch up, so teachers must do *more* in *less* time. The most effective way of shortening the learning time for these students is through the direct teaching of skills.

"Instructional approaches that have yielded significant outcomes for students with LD are characterized as being well specified, explicit, carefully designed, and closely related to the area of instructional need (reading, spelling, math)" (Vaughn & Fuchs, 2003b, p. 140). For example, instruction found to be most effective in teaching students to read involves systematic and explicit techniques (i.e., instruction includes a carefully selected set of skills organized into a logical sequence) (Armbruster, Lehr, & Osborn, 2003; National Institute of Child Health and Human Development, 2000). Additionally, explicit instructional techniques are fundamental for students who are acquiring math skills. "The teacher reveals or makes transparent the connections between knowledge acquisition and knowledge application, rather than leaving the student to discover those connections more incidentally" (L. S. Fuchs & Fuchs, 2001, p. 93). Therefore, in explicit instruction, teachers initially take full responsibility for student learning but gradually relinquish responsibility to students as they become successful. "This progression can be seen as a continuum that moves from teacher modeling, through guided practice using prompts and cues, to independent and fluent performance by the learner" (Rosenshine, 1986, p. 69).

EXAMPLES OF EXPLICIT INSTRUCTION IN PUBLISHED CURRICULA

Several curricular programs feature explicit instruction. Perhaps the most well-known is Direct Instruction in reading, math, and language published by Science Research Associates. Figure A shows Exercise 5 from Lesson 4 of *Reading Mastery Signature Edition, Grade K* (Englemann & Bruner, 2008). In this lesson, the sound for the letter *m* (/m/) is introduced by the teacher (modeling) and practiced by the students (guided practice). The /m/ is reviewed in the same lesson and over subsequent lessons during independent practice activities.

Figure B shows a phonemic awareness activity from *Voyager Passport, Level A,* "Lesson 7" (Voyager Expanded Learning, 2008). As you can see, final sound discrimination is introduced by the teacher (modeling); it is practiced by the students with the teacher assisting (guided practice), and then done independently during the lesson and in subsequent lessons for review.

SOUNDS
EXERCISE 5

Introducing the new sound mmm as in mat

a. (Touch the first ball of the arrow.) Here's a new sound. My turn to say it. When I move under the sound, I'll say it. I'll keep on saying it as long as I touch under it. Get ready. (Move quickly to the second ball of the arrow. Hold for two seconds.) **mmm.**

b. (Touch the first ball of the arrow.) My turn again. Get ready. (Move quickly to the second ball of the arrow. Hold for two seconds.) **mmm.**

c. (Touch the first ball of the arrow.) My turn again. Get ready. (Move quickly to the second ball of the arrow. Hold for two seconds.) **mmm.**

d. (Touch the first ball of the arrow.) Your turn. When I move under the sound, you say it. Keep on saying it as long as I touch under it. Get ready. (Move quickly to the second ball of the arrow. Hold for two seconds.) *mmm.* Yes, **mmm.**

To Correct
(If the children do not say *mmm:*)
1. **mmm.**
2. (Touch the first ball of the arrow.) Say it with me. Get ready. Move quickly to the second ball of the arrow. Hold for two seconds. Say mmm with the children.) *mmm.*
3. (Touch the first ball of the arrow.) Your turn. Get ready. (Move quickly to the second ball of the arrow. Hold for two seconds.) *mmm.*

e. (Touch the first ball of the arrow.) Again. Get ready. (Move quickly to the second ball of the arrow. Hold for two seconds.) *mmm.* Yes, **mmm.**
f. (Repeat *e* until firm.)
g. (Call on individual children to do *d.*)
h. Good saying **mmm.**

FIGURE A

Script from a Direct Instruction lesson using explicit instruction to introduce a new letter–sound correspondence

Source: From *Reading Mastery —Reading Presentation Book A—Grade K, 6e* © 2008 (Exercise 5 from Lesson 4). Used by permission from The McGraw-Hill Companies, Inc.

FIGURE B

Example of lesson using explicit instruction for phonemic awareness skills

Source: From Adventure 3 Phonemic Awareness *Voyager Passport,* Level A (Lesson 7, p. 118). Copyright 2008 by Voyager Expanded Learning. Used by permission from Voyager Expanded Learning.

Phonemic Awareness (10 min.)
Final Sound Discrimination

Materials: letter squares *d*, *n*, *p*, *t*; Individual Reading Mat A (1 per student and teacher)

HOW TO GET STARTED

Following are guidelines and suggestions for teachers who want to incorporate principles of explicit instruction into nonexplicit lessons:

1. *Determine whether or not a lesson is explicit.* Teachers can recognize if a lesson is explicit or not by considering the directedness of the information provided to the students. For example, if students are expected to find answers on their own without previous instruction, the lesson is not likely to be explicit. Phrases such as "encourage children to identify," "challenge children to say," "help children focus," "work with children to build," "help them discover," and "facilitate learning by" are used in nonexplicit programs.

   Explicit programs are more likely to use phrases such as "My turn to say it," "I'm going to show you," "Watch me," "This is _____," and "Let's say it together." In explicit programs and instruction, teachers model or show students how to do something, provide students with practice and teacher feedback, and include independent activities for students to practice on their own.

2. *Once you identify nonexplicit instructional formats, make them more explicit.* For example, the following sample illustrates nonexplicit instruction from *Rigby Literacy*, Grade 1, Level 4, Day 1, "The animal walk" (Rigby, 2004).

Initial and final consonant sounds Find the words *like* and *little* in the book. What is the same about these words? Let's say the words aloud. What sound do you hear at the beginning of each word? Find the words *slug* and *bug*. What is the same about these words? Let's say the words aloud. What sound do you hear at the end of each word? (p. 94).

Teachers can make this lesson more explicit by

a. *Modeling* what is the same about these words (e.g., "Find the words *like* and *little* in the book. Both of these words begin with the sound /l/.)

b. *Providing guided practice* (e.g., "What sound is the same in both of these words?" "Yes, /l/.")

c. Including *independent* practice activities (e.g., students complete independent assignments focused on /l/)

Nancy E. Marchand-Martella and Ronald C. Martella are professors of special education at Eastern Washington University.

To learn more about explicit instruction strategies, go to the Building Teaching Skills section in Chapter 5 of MyEducationLab. As you watch the videos and complete the activities, compare the similarities and differences in the teachers' techniques.

FIGURE 5.9

A concept-anchoring table for "layers of the atmosphere"

Source: Bulgren, J. A. (2006). Integrated content enhancement routines: Responding to the needs of adolescents with disabilities in rigorous inclusive secondary content classes. *Teaching Exceptional Children, 38*(6), 57. Used by permission.

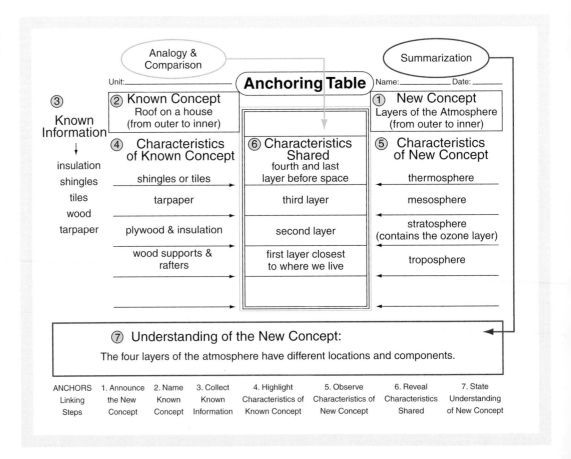

higher test scores than do students who only listen to the lecture and read the text (Kiewra, 2002). The listening, language, and, in some cases, motor skill deficits of many students with learning disabilities make it difficult for them to identify what is important during a lecture and write it down correctly and quickly enough to keep up. While trying to choose and write one concept in a notebook, the student with learning disabilities might miss the next two points.

Because content classes at the middle and secondary level tend to be delivered in traditional lecture format, an emphasis on note taking qualifies as a "signature practice" for engaging and supporting all students in challenging content learning (Morocco, Brigham, & Aguilar, 2006). Many secondary teachers consider the ability to take notes a key ingredient for success in high school and beyond. Students learn to organize information, focus on important content, and create a database from which to study as they prepare for tests (Brigham, Parker, Morocco, & Zigmond, 2006).

Strategic note taking and guided notes are two methods by which teachers can organize and enhance lecture content so that students with disabilities and their general education peers can take good notes. *Strategic note taking* involves specially designed note paper containing cues such as "What do you already know about this topic?" or "List new vocabulary and terms" that help students organize information and combine new knowledge with prior knowledge (Boyle, 2001). Boyle and Weishaar (2001) examined the effects of strategic note taking on the recall and comprehension of content from a videotaped science lecture by high school students with learning disabilities or mild intellectual disabilities. Students in the experimental group were taught to use strategic note taking while viewing the lecture, and students in the control group used their own notes during the videotaped lecture. The students who used strategic note taking recorded a greater number of notes and scored higher on measures of immediate free recall and long-term free recall (i.e., 2 days later) than did the students who took their own notes.

Guided notes are teacher-prepared handouts that provide an outline of the lecture content, which students complete during class by writing in key facts, concepts, and/or relations (Heward, 2001; Lazarus, 1996). For suggestions on creating and using guided notes, see Teaching & Learning, "Guided Notes." A variation of guided lecture notes, *structured reading worksheets* are teacher-prepared supplements that help students study and comprehend assigned reading from content-rich textbooks by prompting them to find points and write key points (Alber, Nelson, & Brennan, 2002).

Mnemonics Research has demonstrated that memory-enhancing strategies called mnemonics can help students with learning disabilities recall specific academic content (Brigham & Brigham, 2001; Swanson, 1999). **Mnemonic strategies** combine special presentation of information with explicit strategies for recall and are most often used to help students remember large amounts of unfamiliar information or make connections between two or more facts or concepts. Three of the most commonly used mnemonic strategies by special education teachers are letter strategies, keyword method, and pegword method.

Letter strategies are acronyms and acrostics. Common examples of acronym mnemonics are HOMES to remember the names of the Great Lakes (Huron, Ontario, Michigan, Erie, and Superior) and FACE to remember the four notes in the spaces between the lines on a music staff. Acrostics are sentences in which the first letter of each word stands for a different word. For example, "Kids playing croquet on freeways get smashed" can help students remember the life sciences classification system: kingdom, phylum, class, order, family, genus, and species (Kleinheksel & Summy, 2003); and "Every good boy deserves fudge" reminds them of the notes on the five lines of the music staff.

The *keyword method* is used to link a new, unfamiliar word with familiar information. Mastropieri and Scruggs (2007) give the following example of how a teacher could use a keyword mnemonic to help a student remember that the Italian word *strada* means "road." First, identify a keyword for *strada* that sounds like the new word but is familiar and easy to picture. In this case, "straw" would be a good keyword because it sounds like *strada* and is easy to picture. Next, draw (or ask students to imagine) a picture of the keyword and its

Traditional lecture is widely used in middle and high school classes. Most successful students take notes during lectures and study them later. Note taking serves two functions: a *process function* (the note taker interacts with the curriculum content during the lecture by listening, looking, thinking, and writing) and a *product function* (the note taker produces a summary/list of key points for later study) (Boyle, 2001; Katayama & Robinson, 2000).

Many students with learning disabilities lack the complex set of skills necessary for effective note taking. Effective note taking requires the ability to discriminate between relevant and irrelevant content and facts, attend to teachers' "verbal signposts," organize information, and record information accurately and fluently (C. A. Hughes & Suritsky, 1994; Kiewra, 2002). These skills are noticeably lacking in the repertoires of many students without disabilities as well.

WHAT ARE GUIDED NOTES?

Guided notes (GN) are teacher-prepared handouts that "guide" a student through a lecture with standard cues and specific space in which to write key facts, concepts, and/or relationships. Guided notes help students succeed with both functions of note taking. With regard to the process function, guided notes take advantage of one of the most consistent and important findings in recent educational research: *Students who make frequent, relevant responses during a lesson learn more than students who are passive observers.* To complete their GNs, students must respond throughout the lecture by listening, looking, thinking, and writing about the lesson's content. Guided notes assist students with the product function of note taking because they are designed so that all students can produce a standard and accurate set of lecture notes for study and review. Guided notes can be designed so that students create a set of study cards for subsequent review and practice (see figure).

Numerous studies have found that students at all achievement levels in elementary through postsecondary classrooms perform better on tests of retention of lecture content when they used GNs than on tests based on lectures when they took their own notes (e.g., Austin, Lee, Thibeault, Carr, & Bailey, 2002; Beckley, Al-Attrash, Heward, & Morrison, 2008; Hamilton, Seibert, Gardner, & Talbert-Johnson, 2000; Heimlich, 2005; Itoi, 2004; Lazarus, 1993; Neef, McCord, & Ferreri, 2006; Sweeney et al., 1999; Wood, Heward, Heimlich, & Itoi, 2006).

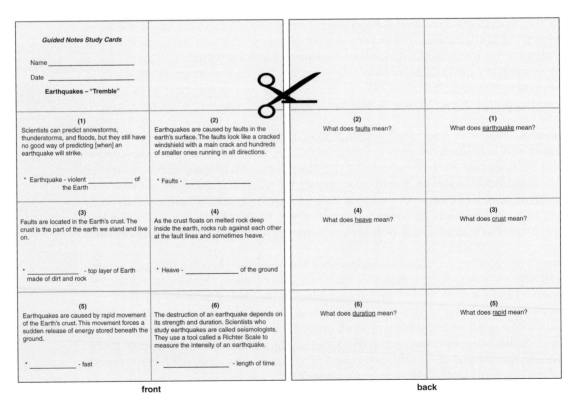

front

back

FIGURE D

Guided notes study cards for a lesson on science vocabulary

Source: From C. L. Wood (2005). *Effects of random study checks and guided notes study cards on middle school special education students' notetaking accuracy and science vocabulary quiz scores* (p. 182–183). Unpublished doctoral dissertation, The Ohio State University. Reprinted by permission.

Other Advantages of Guided Notes In addition to requiring students to actively respond to curriculum, helping them produce an accurate set of notes, and improved retention of course content, other advantages of GNs include the following (Heward, 2001):

- *Students can easily identify the most important information.* Because GNs cue the location and number of key concepts, facts, and/or relationships, students can better determine if they are "getting it" and are more likely to ask the teacher to clarify. Teachers often report that students ask more content-specific questions during lectures when GNs are used.
- *Teachers must prepare the lesson or lecture carefully.*
- *Teachers are more likely to stay on-task with the lecture's content and sequence.* Teachers, especially those who are most knowledgeable and interested in their subject matter, get side-tracked from main points students need to know. While these tangential points may be interesting, they make it difficult for even skilled note takers to determine what's most important in a lecture/demonstration.
- *GNs can improve students' independent note-taking skills.* Gradually fading the use of GNs can help students learn to take notes in classes in which GNs are not used (D. M. White, 1991). For example, after several weeks of providing students with GNs for the entire lecture, the teacher might give GNs for only three quarters of the lecture, then one half of the lecture, and so on.

How to Get Started

Here are steps and suggestions for creating and using GNs (Heward, 2001):

1. *Examine existing lecture outlines to identify the most important course content* that students must learn and retain via lectures. Remember: less can be more. Student learning is enhanced by lectures with fewer points supported by additional examples and opportunities for students to respond to questions or scenarios.
2. *Include all facts, concepts, and relationships* students are expected to learn on guided notes.
3. *Include background information* so that students' note taking focuses on the important facts, concepts, and relationships they need to learn.
4. *Delete the key facts, concepts, and relationships from the lecture outline,* leaving the remaining information to provide structure and context for students' note taking.
5. *Insert cues such as asterisks, bullets, and blank lines to show students where, when, and how many facts or concepts to write* and provide students with a legend that explains each symbol, such as the example at the bottom of the page.
6. *Leave ample space for students to write.* Providing three to four times the space needed to type the content will generally leave enough room for students' handwriting.
7. *Don't require students to write too much.* Using GNs should not unduly slow down the pace of the lesson.
8. *Enhance GNs with supporting information, resources, and additional opportunities to respond.* Insert diagrams, illustrations, photos, highlighted statements, or concepts that are particularly important, and resources such as websites into GNs. Interspersing sets of questions or practice problems within the GN gives students additional opportunities to respond and receive teacher feedback during the lesson.
9. *Use PowerPoint slides, overhead transparencies, or other visuals to project key content.* Visually projecting the key facts, definitions, concepts, and

---

~ Explanation of Symbols in Guided Notes ~

●,✳,★,❶, Write a definition, concept, key point, or procedure next to each bullet, asterisk, star, or numbered circle.

_____ Fill in blank lines with a word or phrase to complete a definition, concept, key point, or procedure during lecture/class.

☛ The pointing finger comes into play when you review and study your notes after class. It is a prompt to think of and write your own examples of a concept or ideas for applying a particular strategy.

📖 *Big idea* 📖 Big ideas are statements or concepts with wide-ranging implications for understanding and/or applying course content.

relationships helps ensure that all students access the most critical content and improves the pace of the lecture.

10. *Intersperse opportunities for other forms of active student response during lesson.* Stop lecturing from time to time, and ask a series of questions, to which the students respond chorally or with response cards (see Chapter 4), referring to their GNs for answers as needed.

11. *Consider gradually fading the use of guided notes* to help students learn to take notes in classes in which they are not used.

12. *Provide follow-up activities* to ensure that students study and review their notes such as daily quizzes, collaborative review activity, and random study checks (C. L. Wood et al., 2006).

 Go to the Homework & Exercises section in Chapter 5 of MyEducationLab and complete Homework Exercise 4. As you watch the video and answer the accompanying questions, think about the benefits of using guided notes with both general and special education students.

referent doing something together. In this case, the interactive picture could show straw lying beside a road (see Figure 5.10). Finally, the teacher instructs the student to look at the picture and begins the following dialogue to help the student acquire the keyword strategy:

> The Italian word *strada* means road. The keyword for *strada* is *straw* [show picture]. Remember this picture of straw lying on a road? Remember this picture of what? Good, straw lying on a road. Now, when I ask you for the meaning of *strada*, think first of the keyword, *straw*. Then think back to the picture with the straw in it, remember that the straw was on a road, and then retrieve the answer, *strada* means road. Now what does *strada* mean? Good, *strada* means road. And how did you remember that? Good, you thought of the key word, *straw*, and remembered the picture of *straw* on the road. (Mastropieri & Scruggs, 2007, p. 232)

The *pegword method* employs rhyming words for numbers (1 is "bun," 2 is "shoe," 3 is "tree," etc.) when information to be remembered is numbered or ordered. For example, to remember that Newton's first (or number 1) law of motion is that objects at rest tend to stay at rest, show a picture of a *bun* (1) resting. To remember that insects have six legs, create a picture of insects on *sticks* (6).

Learning Strategies Proficient learners approach tasks and problems systematically. They identify what needs to be done, make a plan, and evaluate their progress. An accomplished writer knows how to identify and organize the content of a paper to enhance its persuasiveness. When adding a series of unlike fractions, a skilled math student immediately looks to see if all of the denominators are even numbers. Unless they are explicitly taught, however, many students with learning disabilities are unaware

FIGURE 5.10

Mnemonic picture for remembering that the Italian word *strada* means "road"

Source: Mastropieri, M. A., & Scruggs, T. E. (2007). *The inclusive classroom: Strategies for effective instruction* (3rd ed., p. 232). © 2007. Reproduced by permission of Pearson Education, Inc., Upper Saddle River, NJ.

Strada (Straw)   Road

Straw

of the strategies, or "tricks of the trade," that proficient learners use (Deshler & Schumaker, 1993).

A learning strategy can be defined as "an individual's approach to a learning task. A strategy includes how a person thinks and acts when planning, executing, and evaluating performance on a task and its outcomes" (Deshler & Lenz, 1989, p. 205). Donald Deshler and Jean Schumaker and their colleagues at the University of Kansas (Schumaker & Deshler, 1992) have conducted extensive research on how to help students with learning disabilities acquire and use effective learning strategies. They have developed, field-tested, and validated a learning strategies curriculum for adolescents with learning disabilities (Bui, Schumaker, & Deshler, 2006; Deshler & Schumaker, 2006; Ellis, Deshler, Lenz, Schumaker, & Clark, 1991).

Students use task-specific strategies to guide themselves successfully through a learning task or problem. A mnemonic device might be used to help students remember the steps of the strategy. For example, Maccini and Hughes (2000) taught secondary students with learning disabilities to recite the letters in *star* as cues for the steps in systematically solving algebra word problems: search the problem, translate the words into an equation, answer the problem, and review the solution.

EDUCATIONAL PLACEMENT ALTERNATIVES

General Education Classroom

IDEA requires that students with disabilities be educated with students without disabilities and have access to the core curriculum to the maximum extent possible, and that they be removed from the general education classroom only to the extent that their disability necessitates. During the 2005–2006 school year, 54% of students with learning disabilities were educated in general education classrooms (U.S. Office of Special Education, 2007).

Research on the academic achievement of students with learning disabilities in inclusive classrooms is mixed. Some studies have reported better learning outcomes for students with learning disabilities in inclusive general education classrooms than in pull-out programs (e.g., E. Baker, Wang, & Walberg, 1995; Rea, McLaughlin, & Walther-Thomas, 2002). Other studies of students with learning disabilities in the general education classroom have reported disappointing achievement results (e.g., Schumm, Moody, & Vaughn, 2000), concerns about inadequate instruction (e.g., Chard & Kame'enui, 2000), teachers' limited understanding of learning needs of students with LD (DeSimone & Parmar, 2006), and poor acceptance by teachers and/or peers (e.g., B. G. Cook, 2001; B. G. Cook, Tankersley, Cook, & Landrum, 2000).

Many studies have compared the social functioning and self-concepts of students with learning disabilities in different educational placements. The contention of advocates of full inclusion for students with learning disabilities is that pull-out services such as resource room and special class placement stigmatize students, thus damaging self-concept and limiting opportunities to develop relationships with typical peers. For example, Wiener and Tardif (2004) studied 117 children with learning disabilities in different educational placements and found a "slight superiority of the more inclusive programs" (p. 30) with respect to peer acceptance, number of friends, self-perceptions of mathematics competence, and behavior problems. The authors noted, however, that the differences between groups were not large and were "especially small" when compared to the differences between children with and without learning disabilities." Wiener and Tardif warned, "It would be inappropriate to conclude that the major variable influencing the social and emotional adjustment of children with LD is the special education placement" (p. 30).

Elbaum (2002) conducted a **meta-analysis** of 36 studies examining the self-concept of students with learning disabilities in different placements and concluded that, "contrary to the stigmatization perspective, students with LD placed in general education classrooms did not, overall, have higher self-concepts than students placed in either part-time or full-time special education classrooms" (p. 222). But Elbaum properly noted that, while no one placement is preferable in terms of self-concept for all students with learning disabilities, individual students may be "profoundly affected by a placement that jeopardized their self-esteem" and that, when making placement decisions for a child, individualized education program

Learning strategies

Content Standards for Beginning Teachers of Students with LD: Methods for teaching individuals to independently use cognitive processing to solve problems (LD4K4).

Placement alternatives

Content Standards for Beginning Teachers—Common Core: Demands of learning environments (CC5K1).

TABLE 5.2

The 10 most important skills and behaviors for a student with learning disabilities to achieve success in a general education classroom

STUDENT SKILL/BEHAVIOR	MEAN RATING*
Follows directions in class	3.72
Comes to class prepared with materials	3.48
Uses class time wisely	3.48
Makes up assignments and tests	3.43
Treats teachers and peers with courtesy	3.40
Completes and turns in homework on time	3.37
Works cooperatively in student groups	3.19
Completes tests with a passing grade	3.19
Appears interested in subject	2.90
Takes notes in class	2.88

*Skills are ordered from most to least important as ranked by teachers; 4 is the highest possible score.

Source: Reprinted from "Instructional Practices in Mainstreamed Secondary Classrooms" by L. Ellet, 1993, *Journal of Learning Disabilities, 26,* 57–64. © 1993 by Hammill Institute on Disability. Used by permission.

(IEP) teams "should guard against a priori assumptions about the benefit or detriment of specific placements to students' self-concept. Each student's social and emotional needs, as well as the student's own preference with regard to placement options, ought to be taken into account" (pp. 222, 223).

All of the methods described in the previous section for enhancing the general education curriculum help promote the success of students with learning disabilities in general education classrooms. Special educators can facilitate the success of these students in general education classrooms by teaching them behaviors that are valued by general education teachers. For example, when asked to rate which of 30 different social skills were critical for success in the classroom, the majority of 366 teachers in grades K–12 rated self-control (controlling temper in conflict situations) and cooperation (complying with teacher's directions) as the most essential (Lane, Pierson, & Givner, 2003). Table 5.2 lists the 10 student skills and behaviors that 89 general education high school teachers in another study identified as most important for success in the general education classroom (Ellet, 1993). Another strategy for increasing the likelihood of successful inclusion is to interview successful students to find out their secrets for success in a particular teacher's classroom (Monda-Amaya, Dieker, & Reed, 1998).

Consultant Teacher

A consultant teacher provides support to general education classroom teachers and other staff members who work directly with students with learning disabilities. The consultant teacher helps the general education teacher select assessment devices, curriculum materials, and instructional activities. The consultant may even demonstrate teaching methods or behavior management strategies. A major advantage of this model is that the consultant teacher can work with several teachers and thus indirectly provide special education services to many children. A major drawback is that the consultant has little or no direct contact with the children. Heron and Harris (2001) describe procedures that consultant teachers can use to increase their effectiveness in supporting children in the general education classroom.

Resource Room

A resource room is a specially staffed and equipped classroom where students with learning disabilities come for one or several periods during the school day to receive individualized instruction. A resource room teacher serves an average of 20 students with disabilities. During the 2005–2006 school year, 34% of students with learning disabilities were served in resource rooms (U.S. Office of Special Education, 2007a).

The resource teacher is a certified special educator whose primary role is to teach needed academic skills, social skills, and learning strategies to the students who are referred to the resource room. Students typically attend their general education classrooms for most of the school day and come to the resource room for one or more periods of specialized instruction in the academic and/or social skill areas in which they need the most help. In addition to teaching students with learning disabilities, the resource teacher also works closely with each student's general education teacher(s) to suggest and help plan each student's program in the general education classroom.

In a resource room, students with learning disabilities can receive intensive, specialized instruction on the academic and social skills in which they need the most help.

Some advantages of the resource room model are that (a) students do not lose their identity with their general education class peer group; (b) students can receive the intensive, individualized instruction they need every day, which may not be possible in the general education classroom; and (c) flexible scheduling allows the resource room to serve a fairly large number of students. Some disadvantages of resource rooms are that they (a) require students to spend time traveling between classrooms, (b) may result in inconsistent instructional approaches between settings, and (c) make it difficult to determine whether students should be held accountable for what they missed while out of the general education classroom.

Separate Classroom

During the 2005–2006 school year, 11% of students with learning disabilities were served in separate classrooms (U.S. Office of Special Education, 2007a). In a separate classroom, a special education teacher is responsible for all educational programming for 8 to 12 students with learning disabilities. The academic achievement deficiencies of some children with learning disabilities are so severe that they need full-time placement in a setting with a specially trained teacher. In addition, poor work habits and inappropriate social behaviors make some students with learning disabilities candidates for the separate classroom, where distractions can be minimized and individual attention stressed. As noted in Chapter 2, IEP teams are not to view a student's placement in a separate classroom (or any other educational setting) as permanent. A student should be placed in a separate classroom only after legitimate and supported attempts to serve her effectively in less-restrictive environments have proven unsuccessful.

Should All Students With Learning Disabilities Be Educated in the General Education Classroom?

For the majority of students with learning disabilities, the least restrictive environment for all or most of the school day is the general education classroom attended by their same-age peers. The movement toward full inclusion of all students with disabilities in general education classrooms, however, has many leading researchers and advocates for students with learning disabilities worried. They think that although the full-inclusion movement is based on strong beliefs and has the best intentions at heart, little research supports it ("Award-Winning Researchers Raise Questions About 'Inclusion,'" 2001; D. Fuchs & Fuchs, 1994; Kauffman & Hallahan, 2005; Mock & Kauffman, 2005; Swanson, 2000; Zigmond, 2003). They fear that the special education services for students with learning disabilities guaranteed by IDEA—particularly the meaningful development and implementation of IEPs and the identification of the least restrictive environment for each

Perspectives on full inclusion

 Content Standards for Beginning Teachers of Students with LD: Philosophies, theories, models, and issues related to individuals with LD (LD1K2) (also CC5K1).

TIPS for Beginning Teachers

WORKING WITH STUDENTS WITH LEARNING DISABILITIES
by Meghan L. Macy

We worry what a child will be tomorrow, yet we forget he is someone today.

MAINTAIN HIGH EXPECTATIONS

This is difficult for some teachers. I have seen my students make great accomplishments when their parents, other teachers, and I encouraged them to achieve higher goals.

- Teach students the organizational, self-management, and social skills they need to succeed in school, community, and work. Don't just expect your students to be "good students" naturally. Teach them to be good students.
- Raise the bar for your students, and tell them they will have to work harder to get the same gains their peers get easily.
- Aim for each of your students to achieve success in the general education classroom. Communicate agreed-upon expectations with your students, their general education teachers, and their parents.
- Celebrate students' success as they reach their goals. Do something extra fun or different as a reward when your students accomplish a major goal such as completing an entire level of their reading program.

PROVIDE SYSTEMATIC AND EXPLICIT INSTRUCTION

Unison response techniques such as choral responding and response cards give students many opportunities to actively participate. Students don't like to "sit and listen" for very long. They'll learn more and have more fun when they're actively engaged.

- Skip the fluff. Go right to the big idea at the root of the concept or skill you are teaching. Minimize extra "teacher talk." Students don't need long-winded explanations; just be clear and get to the point.
- Use model–lead–test ("I do, we do, you do") when introducing a new skill. This technique supports students when they are learning something new.
- Teach easy-to-follow rules (e.g., "When a word ends in a consonant and *y*, change the *y* to *i* and add *es*)

or strategies (e.g., PEMDAS: **P**arentheses first, **E**xponents, **M**ultiplication and **D**ivision left to right, **A**ddition and **S**ubtraction left to right) students can remember. The simpler you make it, the easier it is to teach and the easier it will be for the students to apply it.

- Correct students' mistakes. Don't let them practice errors. Use model–lead–test or model–test to get firm on new skills.
- Evaluate students' progress frequently. Use progress-monitoring tools such as DIBELS (dibels. uoregon.edu) or AIMSweb (www.aimsweb.com) to evaluate each student's progress and to determine if you need to reteach the skill or modify your instruction.

PROVIDE SUFFICIENT PRACTICE

My own experience practicing as a swimmer informs my work with my students. When I first began competitive swimming, I watched the champion swimmers with envy. Our team practiced for 3 hours every day. After many years and thousands of hours of practice, I was able to qualify for state, regional, and national meets. I never won at that level, but I was in the race and enjoyed participating. When I teach, I never lose that memory. Our students with learning disabilities may not be first in the class, but they need the practice just to compete. They need hours and hours of drill and hard work.

- Conduct brief 2- to 5-minute reviews of content at the beginning, middle, and end of each lesson.
- Build fluency with the tool skills students need for higher-level problems. Use 1-minute timings for repeated reading and math drills. Let students chart or graph their progress, and help them set increasingly higher goals.
- Create frequent opportunities for students to practice new skills in varied contexts (e.g., other writing assignments, application exercises in different content areas, more challenging math problems that require use of previously mastered skills).
- Review, review, and review, and when you think you do not need to review, review again.

student along a continuum of placement options—will be lost if full inclusion becomes reality. They wonder, for example, how a high school student with learning disabilities who reads at the fourth-grade level and spends the entire school day in general education subject-matter classes will receive the individualized, intensive reading instruction that she needs.

All of the major professional and advocacy associations concerned with the education of children with learning disabilities have published position papers against full inclusion (Council for Learning Disabilities [CLD], 1993; Division for Learning Disabilities [DLD], 1993; Learning Disabilities Association of America [LDA], 1993; National Joint Committee on Learning Disabilities [NJCLD], 1993). Each group supports the placement of students with learning disabilities in general education classrooms to the maximum extent possible, given that the instructional and related services required to meet each student's individualized educational needs are provided; but they strongly oppose any policy that mandates the same placement and instruction for all students with learning disabilities. Each group believes that special education for students with learning disabilities requires a continuum of placement options that includes the possibility of some or even all instruction taking place outside the general education classroom.

For some students with learning disabilities, the general education classroom may actually be more restrictive than a resource room or special class placement when the instructional needs of the student are considered—and remember that academic deficit is the primary characteristic and remedial need of students with learning disabilities. However, placing a student with learning disabilities in a resource room or special class does not guarantee that he will receive the intensive, specialized instruction he needs. For example, Moody, Vaughn, Hughes, and Fischer (2000) found that only three of the six resource room teachers they observed provided differentiated reading materials and instruction to match the individual needs of their students.

The collective message of research on outcomes for students with learning disabilities in inclusive classrooms and other settings is consistent with the findings for students with other disabilities: Where a student is taught is not as important as the quality of instruction that student receives.

CLD, DLD, LDA, and NJCLD

Content Standards for Beginning Teachers of Students with LD: Professional organizations and sources of information relevant to the field of LD (LD9K2).

KEY TERMS AND CONCEPTS

alphabetic principle, p. 188
comorbidity, p. 185
criterion-referenced tests, p. 190
curriculum-based measurement (CBM), p. 190
dual discrepancy, p. 176
dyslexia, p. 179
formative evaluation, p. 190
graphic organizers, p. 195
guided notes, p. 199
learning disabilities, p. 173

meta-analysis, p. 203
mnemonic strategies, p. 199
phonemes, p. 181
phonemic awareness, p. 181
phonics, p. 183
phonological awareness, p. 181
precision teaching, p. 192
responsiveness to intervention (RTI), p. 175
standard celeration chart, p. 192
summative evaluation, p. 190

SUMMARY

Definitions

- The federal definition of *specific learning disability* is a disorder in one or more of the basic psychological processes involved in understanding or in using language, spoken or written, which may manifest in an imperfect ability to listen, think, speak, read, write, spell, or perform mathematical calculations.

- The National Joint Committee on Learning Disabilities (NJCLD) has defined learning disabilities as a heterogeneous group of disorders manifested by significant difficulties in the acquisition and use of listening, speaking, reading, writing, reasoning, or mathematical abilities. These disorders are intrinsic to the individual and presumed to be due to central nervous system dysfunction.
- There is no universally agreed-on definition of learning disabilities. Most states require that three criteria be met: (a) a severe discrepancy between potential or ability and actual achievement, (b) learning problems that cannot be attributed to other disabilities, and (c) special educational services needed to succeed in school.
- Responsiveness to intervention (RTI), a promising approach to the prevention and early identification of learning disabilities, uses curriculum-based measurement of at-risk children's progress during one or two 10- to 12-week trials of intensive individual or small-group instruction with scientifically validated instruction. Failure to respond to this treatment suggests a learning disability.

Characteristics

- Difficulty reading is the most common characteristic of students with learning disabilities. It is estimated that 90% of all children identified as learning disabled are referred for special education services because of reading problems.
- Many students with learning disabilities show one or more of the following characteristics: deficits in written language, underachievement in math, poor social skills, attention deficits and hyperactivity, behavior problems, and low self-esteem/self-efficacy.
- The fundamental, defining characteristic of students with learning disabilities is specific and significant achievement deficits in the presence of adequate overall intelligence.
- In addition to their academic and social-skills deficits, students with learning disabilities possess positive attributes and interests that teachers should identify and try to strengthen.

Prevalence

- Learning disabilities make up the largest category in special education. Students with learning disabilities represent almost one half of all students receiving special education.
- About three times as many boys as girls are identified as learning disabled.
- Some educators believe the ever-increasing number of students classified as learning disabled is the result of overidentification and misdiagnosis of low-achieving students.

Causes

- Although the actual cause of a specific learning disability is seldom known, four suspected causal factors are brain damage, heredity, biochemical imbalance, and environmental factors.
- Specific regions of the brains of some individuals with reading and language disabilities show abnormal activation patterns during phonological processing tasks.
- Genetics may account for at least some family links with dyslexia. Research has located possible chromosomal loci for the genetic transmission of phonological deficits that may predispose a child for reading problems later.
- Biochemical imbalance due to artificial colorings and flavorings in a child's diet or vitamin deficiencies have been suggested as causes of learning disabilities. Most professionals today give little credence to these causes.
- Environmental factors—particularly impoverished living conditions early in a child's life and poor instruction—are likely contributors to the achievement deficits of many children with learning disabilities.

Identification and Assessment

- Five forms of assessment are frequently used with students with learning disabilities:
  - Norm-referenced tests compare a child's score with the scores of age mates who have taken the same test.
  - Criterion-referenced tests, which compare a child's score with a predetermined mastery level, are useful in identifying specific skills the child has learned as well as skills that require instruction.

- Teachers use informal reading inventories to observe directly and record a child's reading skills.
- Curriculum-based measurement (CBM) is a formative evaluation method that measures a student's progress in the actual curriculum in which she is participating. CMB is the primary means of assessment in RTI models.
- Direct and daily measurement involves assessing a student's performance on a specific skill each time it is taught.
- Precision teaching is a special type of direct and daily measurement system in which teachers use the standard celeration chart to guide instructional decisions based on changes in a student's frequency of performance.

Educational Approaches

- Contemporary best practice in educating students with learning disabilities is characterized by explicit instruction, the use of content enhancements, and teaching learning strategies to students.
- Explicit instruction is unambiguous, clear, direct teaching of targeted knowledge or skills: Students are shown what to do, given frequent opportunities to practice with teacher feedback, and opportunities to later apply what they have learned.
- Content enhancements such as graphic organizers, note-taking strategies, and mnemonics help make curriculum content more accessible to students with learning disabilities.
- Learning strategies help students guide themselves successfully through specific tasks or general problems.

Educational Placement Alternatives

- About one half of students with learning disabilities are educated in general education classrooms.
- In some schools, a consultant teacher helps regular classroom teachers work with children with learning disabilities.
- In the resource room, a special educator provides specialized instruction to students for one or more periods in the academic and/or social skill areas in which they need the most help.
- Approximately 1 in 10 students with learning disabilities are educated in separate classrooms.
- Many researchers and advocates for students with learning disabilities do not support full inclusion, which would eliminate the continuum of service-delivery options.
- Where a student is taught is not as important as the quality of instruction that student receives.

 Now go to MyEducationLab at www.myeducationlab.com, and take the pretest to assess your initial comprehension of chapter content. Once you have taken the pretest, use your individualized Study Plan for Chapter 5 to enhance your understanding of the concepts discussed in the chapter. Finally, take the posttest to assess your comprehension of Chapter 5 content.

6

Emotional or Behavioral Disorders

FOCUS QUESTIONS

- What are the points of agreement and disagreement between the definition of emotional disturbance in the Individuals with Disabilities Education Act (IDEA) and the definition of emotional or behavioral disorders by the Council for Children with Behavior Disorders?
- Whose disability is more severe: the acting-out, antisocial child or the withdrawn child?
- What factors might account for the disparity between the number of children receiving special education under the emotional disturbance category and researchers' estimates of the prevalence of emotional or behavioral disorders?
- How can research findings about the cumulative interplay of risk factors for behavioral problems in adolescence and adulthood guide the development and implementation of prevention programs?
- Although screening and assessment tools for emotional or behavioral disorders are becoming increasingly sophisticated and efficient, schools seldom use them. Why?
- What are the most important skills for teachers of students with emotional or behavioral disorders?
- Why might the inclusion of children with emotional or behavioral disorders in general education classrooms be more (or less) intensely debated than the inclusion of children with other disabilities?
- What are the largest current impediments to children with emotional or behavioral disorders receiving the most effective education possible?

FEATURED TEACHER

KIMBERLY RICH
Crestview Elementary School • Davis School District, Layton, Utah

Kimberly Rich

Education—Teaching Credentials—Experience
- Para-Education Certificate, Salt Lake Community College, 1999
- B.S. in Elementary and Special Education, Weber State University, 2003
- Utah Level-2 Professional Educator License in Elementary Education grades 1–8 and Special Education Mild/Moderate Disabilities grades K–12

- 5 years teaching students with emotional or behavior disorders; 3 years staff at a group home for youth in state custody

Current Position and Students My room is the only self-contained special education classroom at Crestview Elementary, an urban school with an enrollment of approximately 350 students. This year I have a very a diverse class of 13 African American, Mexican American, Bolivian American, and Caucasian third and fourth graders from low- to middle-income families. My students receive special education services under the disability categories of emotional disturbance, autism, learning disabilities, and other health impairment. Their academic skills span a tremendous range: in reading, from beginning reader to seventh-grade level; in math, from simple addition and subtraction skill to long division skills. In addition to their academic needs, many of my students also receive speech and language services, psychological services, and occupational therapy.

Each morning I teach reading, writing, and math in the special education classroom. In the afternoon our students receive science and social studies instruction in general education classrooms. They also attend physical education, computer, art, and library with their general education classes. A para-educator from the self-contained classroom accompanies and supports the students as needed in the general education classes.

All of my students participate in district and statewide assessments with accommodations as determined appropriate by their IEP teams, such as flexible scheduling, small-group settings, having math and science tests read to them, and a reduction in distractions.

Curriculum and Instruction The curriculum in our classroom consists of grade-level core academic skills, social skills, and the goals on each student's individualized education program (IEP). For reading we use SRA's *Reading Mastery* and Houghton Mifflin's *A Legacy of Literacy,* the basic reading series used in our school's general education curriculum. For written language instruction, I use Sopris West's *Step Up to Writing* program. For math I use a combination of Edge Enterprises' *Strategic Math Series* and a series of lesson plans created by our school's teachers to meet state curriculum standards.

To ensure that our students' needs are being met and addressed, we continually monitor each student's progress toward meeting his IEP goals. Each student's IEP includes both academic and behavioral goals. Here's one of the IEP goals for Katie, an 8-year-old girl who has difficulty following directions: In all school settings, Katie will follow directions in 5 seconds with no more than 2 incidents of noncompliance per week for 4 consecutive school weeks.

The teaching approach I have found most effective is direct instruction, which allows for students to have a high rate of response and be engaged for longer periods of time. Direct instruction is often delivered based on student need and ability. Small-group or one-to-one instruction is a typical delivery pattern.

Classroom Management For classroom management I use a point system with five color-coded levels. Blue is the highest level, followed by green, orange, red, with yellow as the lowest level. The higher levels entail greater privileges, and students gain or lose the privileges as they move up or drop down the system based on their daily behavior at school. Each student has a daily level sheet that lists our classroom responsibilities (rules) on the positive side and the opposite behavior of our classroom responsibilities on the negative side. Throughout the school day, students earn positive points each time they demonstrate a classroom responsibility. When students exhibit negative behaviors, they receive negative points. My aides and I use tally marks to record these points on the students' daily level sheets.

A student who receives 10 negative marks drops one level. Students can receive an automatic level drop for a single occurrence of certain behaviors such as excessive verbal aggression, physical aggression, stealing, not returning their daily home note, or not completing daily reading or homework. When a student receives a level drop, I note the time on his daily level sheet. The student will then stay on that level for 1 day, after which he can buy his way back up to level blue at a cost of 10 points per level. A bulletin board shows students' current levels, providing a visual reminder of their privileges.

At the end of each week, students can purchase a dice roll with points they have earned during the week. We have a menu with six rewards, numbered from 1 to 6. Students roll a single die and then receive the reward on the menu that matches the number rolled. When students on the blue level arrive at school each morning, one student is selected to spin the spinner to earn bonus points for the group and a chance at a Mystery Motivator. (For a complete description of Mystery Motivators, see Teaching & Learning, "Mystery Motivators," later in this chapter.)

To ensure that the items on the reward menu are of high interest to the students, the class chooses the rewards at the beginning of the year. Their favorite things are mechanical pencils, popcorn, no-homework coupons, extra recess coupons, computer game time, eating lunch in the classroom with their teachers (!), and a free book. We change the items on the reward menu every few weeks.

Daily, my students take home a note that goes to parents informing them exactly the number of times their student demonstrated both positive and negative behaviors at school that day. The note has a place for the parent/guardian's signature and space for parents to write a comment or question for me. When students return their note the next day signed by a parent, they receive points. The daily home notes build a trusting relationship with parents and reduces miscommunication between student, family, and school staff.

School- and District-Wide Collaboration I am a member of the Case Management Team and coordinator of Positive Behavior Interventions Support (PBIS)/Utah Behavior Initiatives team (UBI) at our school. Our PBIS/UBI team developed and evaluates school-wide systems of positive behavioral support for our students such as our tardy tracker, Principal's 200 Club, and school-wide social skills instruction. In addition the school Multi-Disciplinary Special Education Team meets weekly to discuss special education students' assessments and progress.

Other professionals I work with are the school psychologist, speech and language pathologist, and occasionally an adapted physical education specialist. The school psychologist services may include weekly sessions for social skills or anger management. The speech and language pathologist services may include weekly sessions for articulation or understanding of language skills. The adapted physical education specialist works with students on basic physical education skills such as throwing a ball, skipping, jumping rope, bouncing a ball, and so on, as decided upon by assessments and included as a goal on the IEP.

My classroom serves as a training site for teachers and administrators in our district to learn strategies for effective social skills instruction. Teachers observe social skills instruction in my classroom. I then observe these teachers conducting social skills instruction in their classrooms and offer suggestions and support.

Why I Enjoy Being a Special Education Teacher I have the privilege of seeing my students make noticeably great progress, usually in a short time frame. My students usually come into my classroom having experienced no success in school. As we address their diverse academic and behavior needs, they feel success and begin to enjoy attending school. The following experience with Chad illustrates what success can do to change a student's attitude. Chad had a long history of physical aggression toward students and teachers that was trigged by frustrations with schoolwork and combative interactions with peers on the playground. Chad was completing a writing assignment that asked the question, "*What was the best thing that happened this school year?*" Chad's response was "*Coming to a new school and being put in Ms. Rich's class. I actually like going to school now.*" Students like Chad give me the motivation to continue to strive to help other students feel successful and recognize their potential.

To learn more about these classroom management and motivation strategies, go to the Homework & Exercises section in Chapter 6 on MyEducationLab and complete Homework Exercise 1.

Childhood should be a happy time: a time to play, make friends, and learn—and for most children it is. But some children's lives are in constant turmoil. Some children strike out at others, sometimes with disastrous consequences. Others are so shy and withdrawn that they seem to be in their own worlds. In either case, playing with others, making friends, and learning all the things a child must learn are extremely difficult for these children. These are children with emotional or behavioral disorders. They are referred to by a variety of terms: emotionally disturbed, socially maladjusted, psychologically disordered, emotionally handicapped, or even psychotic if their behavior is extremely abnormal or bizarre.

After reading this chapter, complete the pretest for Chapter 6 on MyEducationLab to assess your initial understanding of chapter content.

Many children with emotional or behavioral disorders are disliked by their classmates and teachers; even their siblings and parents may reject them. Sadder still, they often do not even like themselves. The child with behavioral disorders is difficult to be around, and attempts to befriend him (most are boys) may lead to rejection, verbal abuse, or even physical attack. Although most children with emotional or behavioral disorders are of sound mind and body, their noxious or withdrawn behavior is as serious an impediment to their functioning as are the intellectual, learning, sensory, and physical disabilities that challenge other children. Children with emotional or behavioral disorders make up a significant proportion of students who need special education.

DEFINITIONS

Like their colleagues in intellectual disabilities and learning disabilities, special educators who work with students with emotional or behavioral disorders have been struggling to reach consensus on a definition. A clear definition of emotional or behavioral disorders is lacking for numerous reasons. First, disordered behavior is a social construct; no clear agreement exists about what constitutes good mental health. All children behave inappropriately at times. How often, with how much intensity, and for how long must a student exhibit problem behavior before he is considered disabled because of the behavior? Second, different theories of emotional disturbance use concepts and terminology that do little to promote meaning from one definition to another. Third, expectations and norms for appropriate behavior are often quite different across ethnic and cultural groups. Finally, emotional or behavioral disorders sometimes occur in conjunction with other disabilities (most notably learning disabilities), making it difficult to determine whether one condition is an outcome or the cause of the other.

Of the many definitions of emotional or behavioral disorders that have been proposed, the two that have had the most influence are the definition in the Individuals with Disabilities Education Act (IDEA) and one proposed by a coalition of professional associations concerned with children with behavior problems.

Federal Definition of Emotional Disturbance

IDEA definition of E/BD

 Content Standards for Beginning Teachers of Students with E/BD: Educational terminology and definitions of individuals with E/BD (BD1K1).

Emotional disturbance is one of the disability categories in the IDEA under which a child is eligible to receive special education services. The IDEA defines **emotional disturbance** as:

(i)   [a] condition exhibiting one or more of the following characteristics over a long period of time and to a marked degree that adversely affects educational performance:

(A)   An inability to learn which cannot be explained by intellectual, sensory, and health factors;

(B)   An inability to build or maintain satisfactory interpersonal relationships with peers and teachers;

(C)   Inappropriate types of behavior or feelings under normal circumstances;

(D)   A general pervasive mood of unhappiness or depression; or

(E)   A tendency to develop physical symptoms or fears associated with personal or school problems.

(ii)   Emotional disturbance includes schizophrenia. The term docs not apply to children who are socially maladjusted, unless it is determined that they have an emotional disturbance under paragraph (i) of this section. (P.L. 108-446, 20 C.F.R. §300.8[c][4])

At first glance, this definition may seem straightforward enough. It identifies three conditions that must be met: *chronicity* ("over a long period of time"), *severity* ("to a marked degree"), and *difficulty in school* ("adversely affects educational performance"); and it lists five types of problems that qualify. But in fact, this definition is extremely vague and leaves much to the subjective opinion of the authorities who surround the child. What do terms such as *satisfactory* and *inappropriate* really mean? Differing degrees of teacher tolerance for student behavior (Walker, Ramsey, & Gresham, 2005), differences between teachers' and parents' expectations for student behavior (Konold, Walthall, & Pianta, 2004), and the fact that expectations for behavior vary across ethnic and cultural groups (Cullinan & Kauffman, 2005; Taylor, Gunter, & Slate, 2001) make the referral and identification of students with emotional or behavioral disorders a difficult and subjective process.

And how does one determine that some behavior problems represent "social maladjustment," whereas others indicate true "emotional disturbance"? Many children experiencing significant difficulties in school because of their behavior are ineligible for special education under IDEA because their problems are considered to be "merely" conduct disorders or discipline problems (Forness & Kavale, 2000). The federal definition was derived from a single study conducted by Eli Bower (1960) in the Los Angeles county schools nearly 50 years ago. Bower himself never intended to make a distinction between emotional disturbance and social maladjustment. Indeed, he stated that the five components of the definition were, in fact, meant to be indicators of social maladjustment (Bower, 1982).

It is difficult to conceive of a child who is sufficiently socially maladjusted to have received that label but who does not display one or more of the five characteristics (especially "B") included in the federal definition. As written, the definition seemingly excludes children on the very basis for which they are included. This illogical criterion for ineligibility, the dated and arbitrary list of the five characteristics, and the subjective wording that enables school districts to not serve many children with behavioral problems have produced strongly voiced criticism of the federal definition (e.g., Forness & Kavale, 2000; Kauffman, 2005; F. H. Wood et al., 1997).

CCBD Definition of Emotional or Behavioral Disorder

In response to the problems many saw with the federal definition, the Council for Children with Behavioral Disorders (CCBD, 1989, 2000) drafted a new definition using the term *emotional or behavioral disorder*. The CCBD definition was later adopted by the National Mental Health and Special Education Coalition (a group of 30 education, mental health, and child advocacy organizations) and subsequently submitted to the U.S. Congress as a proposed replacement for the IDEA definition. The CCBD definition of **emotional or behavioral disorder** reads as follows:

1. The term "emotional or behavioral disorder" means a disability that is characterized by emotional or behavioral responses in school programs so different from appropriate age, cultural, or ethnic norms that the responses adversely affect educational performance, including academic, social, vocational or personal skills; more than a temporary, expected response to stressful events in the environment; consistently exhibited in two different settings, at least one of which is school-related; and unresponsive to direct intervention in general education, or the condition of the child is such that general education interventions would be insufficient.

2. The term includes such a disability that co-exists with other disabilities.

3. The term includes a schizophrenic disorder, affective disorder, anxiety disorder, or other sustained disorder of conduct or adjustment, affecting a child if the disorder affects educational performance as described in paragraph (1). (*Federal Register,* February 10, 1993, p. 7938)

Advantages of this definition according to the CCBD (2000) are that it clarifies the educational dimensions of the disability; focuses directly on the child's behavior in school settings; places behavior in the context of appropriate age, ethnic, and cultural norms; and increases the possibility of early identification and intervention. Perhaps most important, the revised terminology and definition do not require "meaningless distinctions between social and emotional maladjustment, distinctions that often waste diagnostic resources when it is already clear that serious problems exist" (p. 7).

CHARACTERISTICS

Children with emotional or behavioral disorders are characterized primarily by behavior that falls significantly beyond the norms of their cultural and age group on two dimensions: externalizing and internalizing. Either pattern of abnormal behavior has adverse effects on a child's academic achievement and social relationships.

Externalizing Behaviors

The most common behavior pattern of children with emotional or behavioral disorders consists of antisocial, or externalizing, behaviors. In the classroom, children with **externalizing behaviors** frequently do the following (adapted from H. M. Walker, 1997, p. 13):

- Get out of their seats
- Yell, talk out, and curse
- Disturb peers
- Hit or fight
- Ignore the teacher
- Complain
- Argue excessively
- Steal
- Lie
- Destroy property
- Do not comply with directions
- Have temper tantrums

Rhode, Jensen, and Reavis (1998) describe noncompliance as the "king-pin behavior" around which other behavioral excesses revolve. "Noncompliance is simply defined as not following a direction within a reasonable amount of time. Most of the arguing, tantrums, fighting, or rule breaking is secondary to avoiding requests or required tasks" (p. 4). An ongoing pattern of such behavior presents a major challenge for teachers. Antisocial, noncompliant children "can make our teaching lives miserable and single-handedly disrupt a classroom" (Rhode et al., 1998, p. 3).

Council for Children with Behavior Disorders (CCBD)

 Council for Exceptional Children — Content Standards for Beginning Teachers of Students with E/BD: Professional and ethical practice, organizations and publications relevant to the field of E/BD (BD9K1).

Externalizing behaviors and noncompliance

 Council for Exceptional Children — Content Standards for Beginning Teachers of Students with E/BD: Social characteristics of individuals with E/BD (BD2K3).

All children sometimes cry, disrupt others, and refuse to comply with requests of parents and teachers; but children with emotional or behavioral disorders do so frequently. Also, the antisocial behavior of children with emotional or behavioral disorders often occurs with little or no apparent provocation. Aggression takes many forms—verbal abuse toward adults and other children, destructiveness and vandalism, and physical attacks on others. These children seem to be in continuous conflict with those around them. Their own aggressive outbursts often cause others to strike back. It is no wonder that children with emotional or behavioral disorders are seldom liked by others and find it difficult to establish friendships.

Many believe that most children who exhibit deviant behavioral patterns will grow out of them with time and become normally functioning adults. Although this optimistic outcome holds true for some children who exhibit problems such as withdrawal, fears, and speech impairments (Rutter, 1976), research indicates that it is not so for children who display consistent patterns of aggressive, coercive, antisocial, and/or delinquent behavior (J. R. Nelson, Stage, Duppong-Hurley, Synhorst, & Epstein, 2007; Trembley, 2000). A pattern of antisocial behavior early in a child's development is the best single predictor of delinquency in adolescence.

> Preschoolers who show the early signs of antisocial behavior patterns do not grow out of them. Rather, as they move throughout their school careers, they grow into these unfortunate patterns with disastrous results to themselves and others. This myth that preschoolers will outgrow antisocial behavior is pervasive among many teachers and early educators and is very dangerous because it leads professionals to do nothing early on when the problem can be effectively addressed. (H. M. Walker et al., 2005, p. 44)

Children who enter adolescence with a history of aggressive behavior stand a very good chance of dropping out of school, being arrested, abusing drugs and alcohol, having marginalized adult lives, and dying young (Lipsey & Derzon, 1998; H. M. Walker et al., 2005).

Internalizing Behaviors

Some children with emotional or behavioral disorders are anything but aggressive. Their problem is the opposite—too little social interaction with others. They are said to exhibit **internalizing behaviors.** Although children who consistently act immaturely and withdrawn do not present the threat to others that antisocial children do, their behavior creates a serious impediment to their development. These children seldom play with others their own age. They usually do not have the social skills needed to make friends and have fun, and they often retreat into daydreams and fantasies. Some are extremely fearful of certain things without reason (i.e., phobia), frequently complain of being sick or hurt, and go into deep bouts of depression (King, Heyne, & Ollendick, 2005; Maag & Swearer, 2005). Obviously, such behavior limits a child's chances to take part in and learn from the typical school and leisure activities that children participate in and enjoy. Table 6.1 describes the most common types of anxiety disorders and mood disorders seen in school-age children.

Because children who exhibit the internalizing behaviors characteristic of some types of anxiety and mood disorders may be less disturbing to classroom teachers than are antisocial children, they are in danger of not being identified (Lane & Menzies, 2005). Happily, the outlook is fairly good for the child with mild or moderate degrees of withdrawn and immature behavior who is fortunate enough to have competent teachers and other school professionals responsible for his development. Carefully targeting the social and self-determination skills the child should learn and systematically arranging opportunities for and reinforcing those behaviors often prove successful (T. L. Morris, 2004).

Early pattern of antisocial behavior

 Council for Exceptional Children Content Standards for Beginning Teachers—Common Core: Effects an exceptional condition can have on an individual's life (CC3K1) (also BD2K3).

Internalizing behaviors

 Council for Exceptional Children Content Standards for Beginning Teachers of Students with E/BD: Social characteristics of individuals with E/BD (BD2K3).

Internalizing behaviors limit a child's chances to take part in the school and leisure activities in which most children participate.

TABLE 6.1

Types of anxiety, mood, and other emotional disorders in children

CONDITION	CHARACTERISTICS/SYMPTOMS	REMARKS
ANXIETY DISORDERS	Maladaptive emotional state or behaviors caused by excessive and often irrational fears and worries.	
Generalized anxiety disorder	Excessive, unrealistic worries, fears, tension that lasts 6 months or more; in addition to chronic anxiety, symptoms include restlessness, fatigue, difficulty concentrating, muscular aches, insomnia, nausea, excessive heart rate, dizziness, and irritability.	Excessive worrying interferes with normal activities. Children tend to be very hard on themselves, striving for perfection, sometimes redoing tasks repeatedly; they may also seek constant approval or reassurance from others. Usually affects children between the ages of 6 and 11.
Phobias	Intense fear reaction to a specific object or situation (e.g., snakes, dogs, or heights); level of fear is inappropriate to the situation and is recognized by the person as being irrational; can lead to the avoidance of common, everyday situations.	Most phobias can be treated successfully with behavior therapy techniques such as systematic desensitization (gradual and repeated exposure to feared object or situation while relaxing) and self-monitoring.
Obsessive/compulsive disorder (OCD)	Persistent, recurring thoughts (obsessions) that reflect exaggerated anxiety or fears; typical obsessions include worry about being contaminated, behaving improperly, or acting violently. The obsessions may lead an individual to perform a ritual or routine (compulsions)—such as washing hands, repeating phrases, or hoarding—to relieve the anxiety caused by the obsession.	OCD most often begins in adolescence or early adulthood. Most individuals recognize their obsessions are irrational and that the compulsions are excessive or unreasonable. Behavioral therapy is effective in treating most cases of OCD; medications are often effective.
Anorexia nervosa	Refusal to maintain body weight at or above a minimally normal weight for age and height. Obsessive concern with body weight or shape. Intense anxiety about gaining weight or becoming fat, even though severely underweight. Two subtypes: restricting food intake by starving oneself down to an abnormal weight and binge-eating/purging.	Anorexia and bulimia (see below) are primarily disorders of females, particularly adolescent girls. Early in the course of anorexia, the person often denies the disorder. Depression, anxiety, compulsive exercise, social withdrawal, obsessive/compulsive symptoms, and substance abuse are often associated with eating disorders.
Bulimia nervosa	Recurrent episodes of (a) binge eating (eating in a discrete period of time an amount of food much larger than most people would eat under similar circumstances while feeling that one cannot stop eating) and (b) inappropriate compensatory behavior in order to prevent weight gain (e.g., self-induced vomiting, misuse of laxatives or other medications, fasting, excessive exercise).	Preoccupation with weight and shape and excessive self-evaluation are primary symptoms of both anorexia and bulimia. Many patients demonstrate a mixture of both anorexic and bulimic behaviors.

(Continues)

TABLE 6.1 CONTINUED

Types of anxiety, mood, and other emotional disorders in children

CONDITION	CHARACTERISTICS/SYMPTOMS	REMARKS
Post-traumatic stress disorder (PTSD)	Prolonged and recurrent emotional reactions after exposure to a traumatic event (e.g., sexual or physical assault, unexpected death of a loved one, natural disaster, witnessing or being a victim of acts of war or terrorism). Symptoms: flashbacks and nightmares of the traumatic event; avoiding places or things related to the trauma; emotional detachment from others; and difficulty sleeping, irritability, or poor concentration.	Increased recognition of PTSD in children has occurred in the U.S. since the terrorist attacks of September 11, 2001. Individual and group counseling and support activities can be helpful. Teachers can help by providing an environment in which the child with PTSD feels safe and positive social attention for the child's involvement with normal activities.
Selective mutism (also called elective mutism, speech phobia)	Child speaks normally to specific person or group (e.g., family members) but refuses to talk to others. May be a response to trauma, more often caused by anxiety or fear of speaking in certain settings or to certain individuals or groups.	Treatment uses positive approach, no attention or punishment for not speaking, reinforcement for approximations of speaking (e.g., participation in class activities, nonspeech vocalizations).
MOOD DISORDERS	Characterized by impaired functioning due to episodes of abnormally depressed or elevated emotional state.	
Depression	Marked by pervasive sad mood and sense of hopelessness. Symptoms include social withdrawal; irritability; feelings of guilt or worthlessness; inability to concentrate; loss of interest in normal activities; drastic change in weight, appetite, or sleeping pattern; prolonged crying bouts; recurring thoughts of suicide. Several symptoms must be exhibited over a period of time and not be temporary, reasonable responses to life circumstances (e.g., grief over death of a family member).	Researchers estimate that 15% to 20% of adolescents experience depression at one time or another; adolescent girls are twice as likely as boys to be depressed. Depression is often overlooked in children, especially when symptoms are overshadowed by externalizing behavioral disorders. Teachers should be attentive for signs of possible depression and refer students for evaluation.
Bipolar disorder (formerly called manic-depressive disorder)	Alternative episodes of depressive and manic states. During manic episodes, person is in an elevated mood of euphoria—a feeling of extraordinary elation, excitement—and exhibits three or more of the following symptoms: excessive egotism; very little sleep needed; incessant talkativeness; rapidly changing thoughts and ideas in uncontrolled order; easily distracted; agitated, "driven" activities; and participation in personally risky activities. The peak age at onset of first symptoms falls between the ages of 15 and 19. Five years or more may elapse between the first and second episodes, but the time periods between subsequent episodes usually narrow.	Some patients are reluctant to participate in treatment because they find the experience of mania very enjoyable. Patients often recall this experience and minimize or deny entirely the devastating features of full-blown mania or the demoralization of a depressive episode. Regular patterns of daily activities, including sleeping, eating, physical activity, and social and/or emotional stimulation may help. Medications are often effective in treating acute episodes, preventing future episodes, and providing stabilizing moods between episodes.

TABLE 6.1 CONTINUED

Types of anxiety, mood, and other emotional disorders in children

CONDITION	CHARACTERISTICS/SYMPTOMS	REMARKS
OTHER DISORDERS		
Schizophrenia	A severe psychotic disorder characterized by delusions, hallucinations (hearing voices), unfounded fears of persecution, disorganized speech, catatonic behavior (stupor and muscular rigidity), restricted range and intensity of emotional expression (affective flattening), reduced thought and speech productivity, and decreased initiation of goal-directed behavior. Affects males and females with equal frequency. Onset typically occurs during adolescence or early adulthood. Most persons with schizophrenia alternate between acute psychotic episodes and stable phases with few or no symptoms.	Although no cure exists, most children with schizophrenia benefit from a variety of treatments, including antipsychotic medication, behavioral therapy, and educational interventions such as social skills training. The general goals of treatment are to decrease the frequency, severity, and psychosocial consequences of psychotic episodes and to maximize functioning between episodes.
Tourette syndrome	An inherited neurological disorder characterized by motor and vocal tics (repeated and involuntary movements) such as eye blinking, facial grimacing, throat clearing or sniffing, arm thrusting, kicking, or jumping. About 15% of cases include *coprolalia* (repeated cursing, obscene language, and ethnic slurs). Symptoms typically appear before age 18; males affected 3 to 4 times more often than females. Many students also have attentional problems, impulsiveness, compulsions, ritualistic behaviors, and learning disabilities.	Tics are experienced as irresistible; student may seek a secluded spot to release symptoms after delaying them. Tics are more likely during periods of tension or stress, and decrease with relaxation or when focusing on an absorbing task. Tolerance and understanding of symptoms are of paramount importance to students; untimed exams (in a private room if vocal tics are a problem), and permission to leave the classroom when tics become overwhelming are often helpful.

Sources: American Psychiatric Association (2000b, 2000c, 2002, 2004, 2007); Anderson Downing (2007); Anxiety Disorders Association of America (2007); Cullinan (2007); Kauffman (2005); Maag and Swearer (2005); March and Morris (2004); Rutherford, Quinn, and Sathur (2004); Schum (2002); Tourette Syndrome Association (2007); von Hahn (2004a).

It is a grave mistake, however, to believe that children with emotional disorders characterized primarily by internalizing behaviors have only mild and temporary problems. The severe anxiety and mood disorders that some children experience not only cause pervasive impairments in their educational performance—they also threaten their very existence. Indeed, without identification and effective treatment, the extreme emotional disorders of some children can lead to self-inflicted injury or even death from substance abuse, starvation, or suicidal behavior (Webber & Plotts, 2008).

Academic Achievement

Most students with emotional or behavioral disorders perform one or more years below grade level academically (Cullinan, 2007). Many of these students exhibit significant deficiencies in reading and math achievement as well as deficits in study skills (Anderson, Kutash, & Duchnowski, 2001). Numerous studies of the academic achievement of students with emotional or behavioral disorders have consistently reported dismal outcomes such as the following (Cullinan & Sabornie, 2004; Landrum, Katsiyannis, & Archwamety, 2004; K. L. Lane, Carter, Pierson, & Glaeser, 2006; Nelson, Benner, Lane, & Smith, 2004; R. Reid, Gonzalez,

Academic achievement of students with E/BD

 Content Standards for Beginning Teachers—Common Core: Educational implications of characteristics of various exceptionalities (CC2K2).

Nordness, Trout, & Epstein, 2004; Trout, Nordness, Pierce, & Epstein, 2003; U.S. Department of Education, 2004; Wagner & Cameto, 2004; Wagner, Kutash, Duchnowski, Epstein, & Sumi, 2005):

- Two thirds cannot pass competency exams for their grade level.
- They are more likely to receive grades of "Ds" and "Fs" than are students with other disabilities.
- Achievement deficits remain stable or get worse as students grow older.
- They have the highest absenteeism rate of any group of students.
- Only one in three leave high school with a diploma or certificate of completion, compared to 50% of all students with disabilities and 76% of all youth in the general population.
- More than 60% drop out of high school.

The strong correlation between behavior problems and low academic achievement is a reciprocal relationship (Landrum, Tankersley, & Kauffman, 2003). Disruptive and defiant behavior interrupts instruction and limits participation in classroom activities and assignment completion. As a result of this lack of engagement with the curriculum, students with emotional or behavioral disorders may fail to learn. As L. Payne, Marks, and Bogan (2007) point out, the problem is further exacerbated when students achieving below grade level or with splintered skills receive ineffective instruction from teachers who are unaware of the students' academic skills deficits or who cannot address the deficits.

> In such a scenario, instruction is provided at an inappropriate level and the student with EBD becomes frustrated, leading to a rise in misbehavior. This describes the behavior-academic link for problems in the school setting. The cycle continues: The student receives few opportunities for positive reinforcement of academic behaviors, the student views school and related academic activities (or perhaps a particular subject area) as aversive stimuli, and the student engages in avoidance or escape behaviors that cause him or her to get even further behind academically. (p. 3)

In addition to the challenges to learning caused by their behavioral excesses and deficits, many students with emotional or behavioral disorders also have learning disabilities and/or language delays, which compound their difficulties in mastering academic skills and content (Glassberg, Hooper, & Mattison, 1999; J. R. Nelson, Benner, & Cheney, 2005).

Intelligence

Many more children with emotional or behavioral disorders score in the slow learner or mild intellectual disabilities range on IQ tests than do children without disabilities. Two research groups who reviewed a total of 25 studies on performance of students with emotional and behavioral disorders on IQ tests published between 1991 and 2000 reported a mean score of 96 across the studies (R. Reid et al., 2004; Trout et al., 2003). No studies have found an average IQ of 100 or higher. On the basis of his review of research related to the intelligence of children with emotional and behavioral disorders, Kauffman (2005) concluded that "although the majority fall only slightly below average in IQ, a disproportionate number, compared to the normal distribution, score in the dull normal and mildly retarded range, and relatively few fall in the upper ranges" (p. 207).

Whether children with emotional or behavioral disorders actually have any less real intelligence than do children without disabilities is difficult to say. An IQ test measures how well a child performs certain tasks at the time and place the test is administered. It is almost certain that the disruptive behavior exhibited by a child with emotional or behavior disorders has interfered with past opportunities to learn many of the tasks included on the test. Rhode and colleagues (1998) estimate that the average student actively attends to the teacher and to assigned work approximately 85% of the time, but that students with behavior disorders are on task only about 60% or less of the time. This difference in on-task behavior can have a dramatic impact on learning. Off-task and disruptive behavior frequently produces teacher attention, which can have the unintended effect of reinforcing the undesired behavior. Teaching students to obtain teacher attention when they have completed some work is one strategy for breaking this pattern. See Teaching & Learning, "'Look, I'm All Finished!' Recruiting Teacher Attention."

Social Skills and Interpersonal Relationships

The ability to develop and maintain interpersonal relationships during childhood and adolescence is an important predictor of present and future adjustment. As might be expected, students with emotional or behavioral disorders are often rejected by peers and experience great difficulty in making and keeping friends (Bierman, 2005; Gresham, Lane, MacMillan, & Bocian, 1999). The findings of a study comparing the social relationships of secondary students with behavioral disorders with those of same-age peers without disabilities is typical of much of the published literature on social skills of students with emotional or behavioral disorders. The students with behavioral disorders reported lower levels of empathy toward others, participation in fewer curricular activities, less frequent contacts with friends, and lower-quality relationships than were reported by their peers without disabilities (Schonert-Reichl, 1993).

Juvenile Delinquency

Students with emotional or behavioral disorders are 13.3 times more likely to be arrested during their school careers than are students without disabilities (Doren, Bullis, & Benz, 1996a). More than one third of students with emotional or behavioral disorders are arrested during their school years (K. Henderson & Bradley, 2004). In 2005, U.S. law enforcement agencies made about 2.1 million arrests of persons under the age of 18 (Snyder & Sickmund, 2007). As staggering as this number may seem, it represents a 25% decline in juvenile arrests since 1996. Although males are generally arrested for crimes involving aggression (e.g., assault, burglary) and females have been associated with sex-related offenses (e.g., prostitution), females accounted for 29% of all juvenile arrests and 18% of juvenile violent crime arrests in 2005 (Snyder & Sickmund, 2006).

Arrest rates for juveniles increase sharply during the junior high years. This pattern probably reflects both the greater harm adolescents can cause to society as a result of their inappropriate behavior and the fact that younger children are often not arrested (and therefore do not show up on the records) for committing the same acts that lead to the arrest of an older child. Younger children, however, are being arrested, and they are committing serious crimes. On average, juveniles were involved in one quarter of serious violent victimizations annually over the last 25 years (Office of Juvenile Justice and Delinquency Prevention, 2007). Youth under the age 15, for example, accounted for one third of all violent and property crime arrests in 2005.

About half of all juvenile delinquents are *recidivists* (repeat offenders). Recidivists are more likely to begin their criminal careers at an early age (usually by age 12), commit more serious crimes, and continue a pattern of repeated antisocial behavior as adults (Farrington, 1995; Tolan & Thomas, 1995). One study in Oregon found that 20% of juvenile offenders committed 87% of all crimes by juveniles (L. Wagner & Lane, 1998).

Prevalence

Estimates of how many children have emotional or behavioral disorders vary tremendously. A review of 50 epidemiological studies of mental health problems in children found an average prevalence of 8.3% (R. E. Roberts, Attkisson, & Rosenblatt, 1998). A review of 30 studies of behavior problems of preschoolers from low-income families found a mean prevalence of 30% (Qi & Kaiser, 2003). Such wide-ranging estimates suggest that different criteria are being used to decide what constitutes emotional or behavioral disorders (Feil et al., 2005). Differences in prevalence figures, however, stem as much from how the data are collected as they do from the use of different definitions and instruments (Cullinan, 2007). Most surveys ask teachers to identify students in their classes who display behavior problems at that point in time. Many children exhibit inappropriate behavior for short periods, and such one-shot screening procedures will identify them.

Credible studies indicate that between 3% and 10% of children have emotional or behavioral problems that are sufficiently serious and persistent to warrant intervention (Kauffman, 2005). Annual reports from the federal government, however, show that far

"Look, I'm All Finished!"
Recruiting Teacher Attention

BY SHEILA R. ALBER-MORGAN AND WILLIAM L. HEWARD

Preparing any student with disabilities for inclusion in a general education classroom should include explicit instruction in classroom survival skills such as staying on task during a lesson, following teachers' directions, and completing assigned seat work. These skills are likely to enhance any student's acceptance and success in the classroom. Because teachers value such "good student" behaviors, students are also likely to receive teacher praise and attention for exhibiting them (K. L. Lane, Givner, & Pierson, 2004; Lane, Wehby, & Cooley, 2006).

Students with emotional or behavioral disorders are very good at getting their teachers' attention. Unfortunately, that attention is often for the wrong behaviors. A penchant for disruptive behavior and academic skill deficits make students with emotional or behavioral disorders especially prone to negative interactions with teachers and poor achievement in general education classrooms. Teaching students to politely recruit positive teacher attention for academic efforts can reverse this pattern of negativity. Teachers may be willing to spend more time with students who politely seek assistance and are receptive to feedback, and they will have more time to devote to instruction.

But classrooms are busy places, and teachers can easily overlook students' important academic and social behaviors. It is hard for teachers to be aware of students who need help, especially low-achieving ones who are less likely to ask; a disruptive student is more likely to get his teacher's attention than is the student who is working quietly and productively (Wehby, Symons, Canale, & Go, 1998).

Although teachers in general education classrooms are expected to adapt instruction to serve students with disabilities, this is not always the case. For example, the secondary teachers interviewed in one study believed that students with disabilities should take responsibility for obtaining the help they need (Schumm et al., 1995). Thus, politely recruiting teacher attention and assistance can help students with disabilities function more independently and actively influence the quality of instruction they receive.

Students with emotional or behavior disorders (Alber, Anderson, Martin, & Moore, 2004; Lo & Cartledge, 2006; B. W. Smith & Sugai, 2000; Todd, Horner, & Sugai, 1999), learning disabilities (Alber, Heward, & Hippler, 1999; Wolford, Alber, & Heward, 2001), and intellectual disabilities (Craft, Alber, & Heward, 1998) have learned to recruit teacher and peer attention for performing academic tasks in general education classrooms.

Politely recruiting teacher attention and assistance is one way that students can influence the quality of instruction they receive.

WHO SHOULD BE TAUGHT TO RECRUIT?

While politely obtaining teacher assistance is a valuable skill for any student, it is particularly important for students such as the following:

Withdrawn Willamena Willamena seldom asks a teacher anything. Because she is so quiet and well behaved, her teachers sometimes forget she's in the room. Withdrawn Willamenas are prime candidates for recruitment training.

In-a-Hurry Harry Harry is usually half-done with a task before his teacher finishes explaining it. Racing through his work allows him to be the first to turn it in. But his work is often incomplete and error-filled, so he doesn't hear much praise from his teacher. Harry would benefit from recruitment training that includes self-checking and self-correction.

Shouting Shelly Shelly has just finished her work, and she wants her teacher to look at it—right now! But Shelly doesn't raise her hand. She gets her teacher's attention—and disrupts most of her classmates—by shouting across the room. Students like Shelly should be taught appropriate ways to solicit teacher attention.

Pestering Pete Pete always raises his hand, waits quietly for his teacher to come to his desk, and then politely asks, "Have I done this right?" But sometimes he repeats this routine a dozen times in a 20-minute period, and his teachers find it annoying. Positive

TEACHING & LEARNING

teacher attention often turns into reprimands. Recruitment training for Pete, and for all students, will teach him to limit the number of times he cues his teachers for attention.

HOW TO GET STARTED

1. *Identify target skills.* Students should recruit attention for behaviors that are valued by teachers and therefore likely to be reinforced—for example, writing neatly and legibly, working accurately, completing assigned work, cleaning up at transitions, and making contributions when working in a cooperative group.

2. *Teach self-assessment.* Students should self-assess their work before recruiting teacher attention (e.g., Harry asks himself, "Is my work complete?"). After the student can reliably distinguish between complete and incomplete work samples, she can learn how to check the accuracy of her work with answer keys or checklists of the steps or components of the academic skill. Or she can spot-check two or three items before asking the teacher to look at it.

3. *Teach appropriate recruiting.* Teach students when, how, and how often to recruit and how to respond to the teacher after receiving attention.

   - *When?* Students should signal for teacher attention after they have completed and self-checked a substantial part of their work. Students should also be taught when not to try to get their teacher's attention (e.g., when the teacher is working with another student, talking to another adult, taking the lunch count).

   - *How?* The traditional hand raise should be part of every student's recruiting repertoire. Depending on teacher preferences and the routines in the general education classroom, students should be taught other methods of gaining attention (e.g., signaling the need for help or feedback by standing up a small flag on their desks or bringing their work to the teacher's desk).

   - *How often?* While helping Withdrawn Willamena learn to seek teacher attention, don't turn her into a Pestering Pete. How often a student should recruit varies across teachers and activities (e.g., independent seat work, cooperative learning groups, whole-class instruction). Direct observation in the classroom can establish a desired rate of recruiting. It is also a good idea to ask the general education classroom teacher when, how, and with what frequency she prefers students to ask for help.

   - *What to say?* Students should be taught several statements that are likely to evoke positive feedback from the teacher (e.g., "Please look at my work." "Did I do a good job?" "How am I doing?"). Keep it simple, but teach the student

to vary her verbal cues so she will not sound like a parrot.

   - *How to respond?* Students should respond to their teacher's feedback by establishing eye contact, smiling, and saying, "Thank you." Polite appreciation is very reinforcing to teachers and will increase the likelihood of more positive attention the next time.

4. *Model and role play the complete recruiting sequence.* Begin by providing students with a rationale for recruiting (e.g., the teacher will be happy you did a good job, you will get more work done, your grades might improve). Thinking aloud while modeling is good way to show the recruiting sequence. While performing each step, say, "Okay, I've finished my work. Now I'm going to check it. Did I put my name on my paper? Yes. Did I do all the problems? Yes. Did I follow all the steps? Yes. Okay, my teacher doesn't look busy right now. I'll raise my hand and wait quietly until she comes to my desk." Have another student pretend to be the general education classroom teacher and come over to you when you have your hand up. Say, "Mr. Patterson, please look at my work." The helper says, "Oh, you did a very nice job." Then smile and say, "Thank you, teacher." Role play with praise and offer corrective feedback until the student correctly performs the entire sequence on several consecutive trials.

5. *Prepare students for alternate responses.* Not every recruiting response by a student will result in teacher praise; some efforts may even be followed by criticism (e.g., "This is all wrong. You need to pay better attention."). Use role playing to prepare students for these possibilities and have them practice polite responses (e.g., "Thank you for helping me with this.").

Politely recruiting teacher attention and assistance is one way students can actively influence the quality of instruction they receive. For more information on teaching students to recruit teacher attention, see Alber and Heward (2000).

Sheila Alber-Morgan is a faculty member in the special education program at The Ohio State University.

Source: From Alber, S. R., & Heward, W. L. (1997). Recruit it or lose it! Training students to recruit contingent teacher attention. *Intervention in School and Clinic, 5,* 275–282. Copyright 1997 by the Hammill Institute on Disability. Used with permission.

Go to the Homework & Exercises section in Chapter 6 of MyEducationLab and complete Homework Exercise 2. As you watch the video and answer the accompanying questions, think about how Ms. Rich could use these strategies with her students.

fewer children are being served than the most conservative prevalence estimates. The 471,306 children ages 6 to 21 who received special education under the IDEA category of emotional disturbance during the 2005–2006 school year represented only about 0.9% of the school-age population (U.S. Department of Education, 2007). Although this figure marked the greatest number of children with emotional or behavioral disorders ever served and ranked emotional disturbance as the fourth-largest disability category in special education (8.1% of all students ages 6 through 21 served under IDEA), most children with emotional or behavioral disorders are not receiving special education.

The number of children being served represents less than half of the 2% estimate the federal government used previously in its estimates of funding and personnel needs for students with emotional and behavioral disorders. Kauffman (2005) believes that social policy and economic factors caused the government to first reduce its estimate of the prevalence of behavioral disorders (from 2% to 1.2%) and then to stop publishing an estimate altogether. "The government obviously prefers not to allow wide discrepancies between prevalence estimates and the actual number of children served. It is easier to cut prevalence estimates than to serve more students" (p. 50).

Regardless of what prevalence study or estimate one turns to, the evidence shows that many thousands of schoolchildren have emotional or behavior problems that are adversely affecting their educational progress, but these students are not presently receiving the special education they need. Although IDEA mandates that all children with disabilities receive an individualized program of special education and related services, in practice, determination of whether a child is disabled under the category of emotional disturbance is often more a function of a school district's available resources to provide needed services than a function of the child's actual needs for such services.

Gender

More than three fourths of children identified for special education because of emotional or behavioral disorders are boys (M. Wagner et al., 2005). Boys identified as emotionally or behaviorally disordered are likely to have externalizing disorders in the form of antisocial, aggressive behaviors (Furlong, Morrison, & Jimerson, 2004). Although girls with emotional or behavioral disorders are more likely to show internalizing disorders such as anxiety and social withdrawal, research shows that girls have problems with aggression and antisocial behavior as well (Talbott & Thiede, 1999).

Students in Juvenile Detention Facilities

In 2003, 96,655 juveniles were in residential detention facilities (Sickmund, Sladky, Kang, & Puzzanchera, 2007). A national survey found that one third of all of youth in juvenile corrections facilities were eligible for special education and related services under IDEA and that nearly one half (47.7%) of those students were classified with emotional disturbance (Quinn, Rutherford, Leone, Osher, & Poirier, 2005).

Causes

Causes of E/BD

Council for Exceptional Children Content Standards for Beginning Teachers of Students with E/BD: Etiology and diagnosis related to various theoretical approaches in the field of E/BD (BD2K1).

The behavior of some children with emotional or behavioral disorders is so self-destructive and apparently illogical that it is difficult to imagine how they got that way. We shake our heads in bewilderment and ask, "Where did that behavior come from?" Numerous theories and conceptual models have been proposed to explain abnormal behavior (see Bigby, 2007; Cullinan, 2007; Kauffman, 2005; Webber & Plotts, 2008). Regardless of the conceptual model used to view emotional or behavioral disorders, the suspected causes can be grouped into two major categories: biological and environmental.

Biological Factors

Brain Disorders   Many individuals who have brain disorders experience problems with emotion and behavior. Brain disorders are the result of either *brain dysgenesis* (abnormal brain development) or *brain injury* (caused by influences such as disease or trauma that alter the structure or function of a brain that had been developing normally up to that point). (Traumatic brain injury is discussed in Chapter 12.) For the vast majority of children with emotional or behavioral disorders, however, there is no evidence of brain disorder or injury (Kauffman, 2005).

Genetics   Evidence indicates the presence of genetic links to some forms of emotional or behavioral disorders (McGuffin & Rutter, 2002; Rhee & Waldman, 2002). The disorder with the strongest research support for a genetic risk factor is *schizophrenia,* a severe and debilitating form of mental illness characterized by auditory hallucinations (hearing voices), delusions, unfounded fears of persecution, and disordered speech. Relatives of schizophrenics have an increased risk of acquiring schizophrenia that cannot be explained by environmental factors alone; and the closer the relation, the higher the probability of acquiring the condition (Pennington, 2002). However, genetics alone has not been found to cause schizophrenia. A person in either of the two highest risk groups (a child of two parents with schizophrenia or an identical twin of a sibling with the condition) still has a less than 50% chance of developing schizophrenia (Plomin, 1995).

Temperament   No agreed-upon definition of **temperament** exists, but it is generally conceived to be a person's behavioral style or typical way of responding to situations. Because physiological differences or markers are associated with differences in infants' temperament, it is considered an inborn biological influence (Kagan & Snidman, 2004). An infant who seldom cries but smiles and coos when passed from one person to another might be said to have an easygoing temperament. In contrast, an infant who is distractible, frequently fusses, and withdraws from new situations might show signs of a difficult temperament.

Some research shows that an easy or positive temperament is correlated with resilience to stress (J. D. Smith & Prior, 1995) and that a difficult temperament at an early age increases the likelihood of behavior problems in adolescence (Caspi, Henry, McGee, Moffitt, & Silva, 1995). Children with an inhibited temperament style characterized by withdrawing from novel situations, playing alone, and spending time on the periphery of social action in the second year of life were more likely to develop social phobias and symptoms of anxiety by age 13 (Schwartz, Snidman, & Kagan, 1999).

Although a child's temperament may not in itself cause emotional or behavior problems, it may predispose the child to problems by interacting with environmental factors, such as making parenting interactions more difficult (J. R. Nelson et al., 2007). Thus, certain events that might not produce problem behavior in a child with an easygoing temperament might result in disordered behavior by the child with a difficult temperament (Rimm-Kaufman & Kagan, 2005; Teglasi, 2006).

Environmental Factors

Three primary environmental factors contribute to the development of conduct disorder and antisocial behavior: (a) an adverse early rearing environment, (b) an aggressive pattern of behavior displayed when entering school, and (c) social rejection by peers. Considerable evidence shows that these causal factors occur in sequence (Dodge, 1993; Pennington, 2002; Sprague & Walker, 2000; H. M. Walker et al., 2005). The settings in which these events occur are home, school, and the community.

Home   The relationship children have with their parents, particularly during the early years, is critical to the way they learn to behave. Observation and analysis of parent–child interaction patterns show that parents who treat their children with love, are sensitive to their children's needs, and provide praise and attention for desired behaviors tend to have children with positive behavioral characteristics. Decades of research show clearly that children with emotional or behavior problems are more likely to come from homes in which parents are inconsistent disciplinarians, use harsh and excessive punishment to manage behavior problems, spend little time engaged in prosocial activities with their children, do not monitor the whereabouts and activities of their children, and show little love and affection for good behavior (A. Biglan, 1995; McEvoy & Welker, 2000; Patterson, Reid, & Dishion, 1992; Watson & Gross, 2000). When such conditions are present in the

Influence of home and community

Content Standards for Beginning Teachers—Common Core: Characteristics and effects of the environmental milieu of the individual with exceptional learning needs and the family (CC2K3) (also CC2K4).

home, a young child may be "literally trained to be aggressive during episodes of conflict with family members" (Forgatch & Paterson, 1998, p. 86).

Because of the research on the correlation between parental child-rearing practices and behavior problems, some mental health professionals have been quick to pin the blame for children's behavior problems on parents. But the relationship between parent and child is dynamic and reciprocal; in other words, the behavior of the child affects the behavior of the parents just as much as the parents' actions affect the child's actions (Cullinan, 2007). Therefore, at best it is not practical and at worst it is wrong to blame parents for the emotional or behavior problems of their children. Instead, professionals must work with parents to help them systematically change certain aspects of the parent–child relationship in an effort to prevent and modify those problems (Beard & Sugai, 2004; Dunlap et al., 2006; Landy, 2002; Lien-Thorne & Kamps, 2005).

School   School is where children spend the largest portion of their time outside the home. Therefore, it makes sense to observe carefully what occurs in schools in an effort to identify factors that may contribute to problem behavior. Also, because most children with emotional or behavioral disorders are not identified until they are in school, it seems reasonable to question whether school contributes to the incidence of behavioral disorders. Educational practices that contribute to the development of emotional or behavioral problems in children include ineffective instruction that results in academic failure, unclear rules and expectations for appropriate behavior, inconsistent and punitive discipline practices, infrequent teacher praise and approval for academic and social behavior, and failure to individualize instruction to accommodate diverse learners (Furlong et al., 2004; Lago-Delello, 1998; Kauffman, 2005; Sprague & Walker, 2000).

A teacher's actions can maintain and actually strengthen deviant behavioral patterns even though the teacher is trying to help the child. Consider the all too common interaction between teacher and student illustrated in Figure 6.1 (Rhode et al., 1998). It begins with

FIGURE 6.1

Coercive pain control

Source: Reprinted from Rhode, G., Jensen, W. R., & Reavis, H. K. (1998). *The tough kid book: Practical classroom management strategies* (p. 5). Longmont, CO: Sopris West. Used with permission.

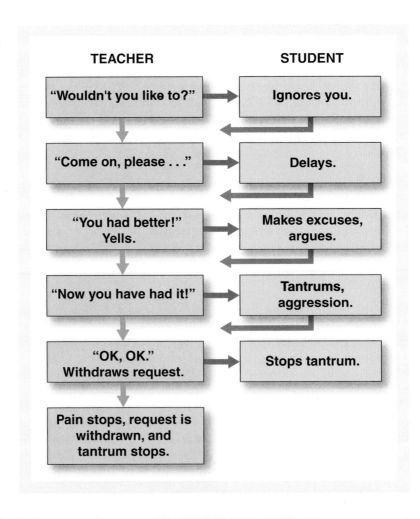

a teacher request that the student ignores and follows a predictable and escalating sequence of teacher pleas and threats that the student counters with excuses, arguments, and eventually a full-blown tantrum. The escalating aggression and tantruming become so aversive to the teacher that she withdraws the task demand (thereby reinforcing and strengthening the student's disruptive behavior) so the student will stop tantruming (thereby reinforcing the teacher's withdrawing the request) (Gunter, Denny, Jack, Shores, & Nelson, 1993; Maag, 2001). This process has been called *coercive pain control* because the child learns to use painful behavior (e.g., arguing, making excuses, tantruming, property destruction, even physical aggression) to get what he wants (Patterson, 1982).

Community   When students associate with peers who exhibit antisocial behavior, they are more likely to experience additional trouble in the community and at school. Gang membership, drug and alcohol abuse, and deviant sexual behavior are community factors that contribute to the development and maintenance of an antisocial lifestyle (Harland, 1997; Karnick, 2004; H. M. Walker et al., 2005).

A Complex Pathway of Risks

It is impossible to identify a single factor or isolated event as the definite cause of a child's emotional or behavioral disorder. Most chronic behavior problems are the accumulated effect of exposure to a variety of family, neighborhood, school, and societal risk factors. And research into genetics and brain-related factors has not advanced to the point where the presence and contribution of a genetic predisposition for greater susceptibility or resilience to a given risk factor can be identified. The greater the number of risk factors and the longer a child's exposure to them, the greater the probability that the child will experience negative outcomes (Sprague & Walker, 2000). Figure 6.2 illustrates this pattern of antisocial behavior development as originally conceived by Patterson and his colleagues (Patterson, 1982; Patterson et al. 1992). Although the interplay of these risk factors is complex, and the specific contribution of any given risk factor cannot be determined, the outcome is highly predictable.

Although knowledge of these risk factors provides information necessary for planning and implementing prevention programs (M. A. Conroy & Brown, 2006; Dwyer, Osher, & Hoffman, 2000), teachers should know that effective intervention and treatment of children's existing behavior problems do not require precise knowledge of etiology. Attempting to determine the extent to which various factors in a child's past are responsible for his current behavior problems is "an impossible and quite unnecessary task. Disruptive child behavior can be changed very effectively without knowing the specific, original causes for its acquisition and development" (Walker, 1997, p. 20).

IDENTIFICATION AND ASSESSMENT

Assessment of emotional or behavioral disorders, as with all disabilities, should answer four basic questions concerning special education services:

1. Who might need help?
2. Who really does need help (who is eligible)?
3. What kind of help is needed?
4. Is the help benefiting the student?

In practice, however, many school districts do not use any systematic method for identifying children with emotional or behavioral disorders. This is because most children with emotional or behavioral disorders identify themselves. Antisocial children seldom go unnoticed: "To have one in your classroom is to recognize one" (Rhode et al., 1998, p. 3). This does

Even though the teacher is trying to help, a child's problem behavior can be maintained and actually strengthened by what takes place in the classroom.

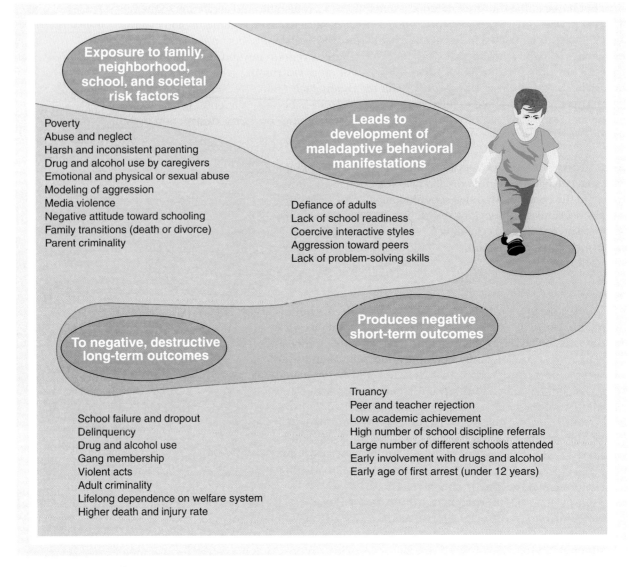

Exposure to family, neighborhood, school, and societal risk factors

Poverty
Abuse and neglect
Harsh and inconsistent parenting
Drug and alcohol use by caregivers
Emotional and physical or sexual abuse
Modeling of aggression
Media violence
Negative attitude toward schooling
Family transitions (death or divorce)
Parent criminality

Leads to development of maladaptive behavioral manifestations

Defiance of adults
Lack of school readiness
Coercive interactive styles
Aggression toward peers
Lack of problem-solving skills

Produces negative short-term outcomes

Truancy
Peer and teacher rejection
Low academic achievement
High number of school discipline referrals
Large number of different schools attended
Early involvement with drugs and alcohol
Early age of first arrest (under 12 years)

To negative, destructive long-term outcomes

School failure and dropout
Delinquency
Drug and alcohol use
Gang membership
Violent acts
Adult criminality
Lifelong dependence on welfare system
Higher death and injury rate

FIGURE 6.2

The path to long-term negative outcomes for children and youth who are at risk for school failure, delinquency, and violence

Source: Reprinted from Walker, H. M., & Sprague, J. R. (1999). The path to school failure, delinquency, and violence: Causal factors and some potential solutions. *Intervention in School and Clinic, 35,* 67–73. Copyright 1999 by the Hammill Institute on Disability. Reprinted with permission.

not mean, however, that identification is a sure thing. Identification is always more difficult with younger children because the behavior of all young children changes quickly and often. Also, there is danger that some children with internalizing behaviors go undetected because their problems do not draw the attention of parents and teachers (Lane & Menzies, 2005; R. J. Morris, Shah, & Morris, 2002).

Children who display patterns of antisocial behavior when entering school run the risk of developing more serious and long-standing behavior problems as they progress through school and life. Unfortunately, many students with emotional or behavioral disorders experience delay between the onset of the disability and beginning of special education services (M. Wagner et al., 2005), which only serves to make it more difficult to reverse this all-too-common trajectory of behavior problems early in life, leading to tragic outcomes during adolescence and adulthood. M. A. Conroy and Brown (2006) state that it is "imperative that current policies and practices be changed from a *reactive* to a *proactive* mode by identifying young children who are either chronically exposed to established risk factors or demonstrate problematic behavior patterns at an early age" (p. 225).

The responsiveness to intervention (RTI) approach described in Chapter 5 holds promise for early identification and intervention of children who exhibit problem behaviors in the classroom (Fairbanks, Sugai, Guardino, & Lathrop, 2007; Gresham, 2005).

Screening Tests

Screening is the process of differentiating between children who are not likely to be disabled and those who either show signs of behavioral disturbance or seem to be at risk for developing behavior problems. Children identified through a screening process then undergo more thorough assessment to determine their eligibility for special education and their specific educational needs.

Most screening devices consist of behavior rating scales or checklists that are completed by teachers, parents, peers, and/or children themselves, such as the Behavior Assessment System for Children (BASC) (Reynolds & Kamphaus, 2002), the Social Skills Rating System for Children (SSRS) (Gresham & Elliott, 1990), and the Behavior Rating Profile (BRP-2) (Brown & Hammill, 1990). Teachers' ratings of child behavior tend to be consistent over time, and teachers' ratings of young children's behavior are good predictors of behavior at an older age (Montague, Enders, & Castro, 2005). Brief descriptions of three widely used screening tests for emotional or behavioral disorders follow.

Child Behavior Checklist (CBCL)   The CBCL is one of several assessment tools included in the Achenbach System of Empirically Based Assessment (ASEBA) (Achenbach & McConaughy, 2003), a widely used and researched collection of checklists and assessment devices (Bérubé & Achenbach, 2007; Konold, Walthall, & Pianta, 2004). This school-age version comes in teacher report, parent report, and self-report forms and can be used with children ages 6 through 18 (Achenbach & Rescorla, 2001). The teacher's report form (CBCL TRF 6/18) includes 112 behaviors (e.g., "sudden changes in mood or feelings," "not liked by other pupils") that are rated on a 3-point scale: "not true," "somewhat or sometimes true," or "very true or often true." The CBCL also includes items representing social competencies and adaptive functioning such as getting along with others and acting happy.

Behavioral and Emotional Rating Scale (BERS)   The BERS assesses a student's strengths in 52 items across five areas of functioning: interpersonal strengths (e.g., reacts to disappointment in a calm manner); family involvement (e.g., participates in family activities); intrapersonal strengths (e.g., demonstrates a sense of humor); school functioning (e.g., pays attention in class); and affective strengths (e.g., acknowledges painful feelings of others) (Epstein, 2004). Data from a strength-based assessment such as the BERS may be used to present positive attributes of students in individualized education program (IEP) meetings, as an aid in writing IEP goals and objectives, and as an outcome measure to document a student's progress on strength-related IEP goals and objectives (Epstein, Hertzog, & Reid, 2001).

Systematic Screening for Behavioral Disorders (SSBD)   The SSBD employs a 3-step **multiple gating screening** process for progressively narrowing down the number of children suspected of having serious behavior problems (Walker & Severson, 1992). In Gate I, classroom teachers rank order every student in their classrooms according to behavioral profiles on two dimensions: externalizing problems and internalizing problems. The top three students on each teacher's list progress to Gate II, the Critical Events Index.

Critical events are behaviors of high salience and concern even if their frequency is low. Any occurrence of these target behaviors is an indicator of major disruption of social-behavioral adjustment processes in school. The 33 items that make up the Critical Events Index include externalizing behaviors such as "is physically aggressive with other students" and "makes lewd or obscene gestures" and internalizing behaviors such as "vomits after eating" and "has auditory or visual hallucinations." Students who exceed normative criteria on the Critical Events Index advance to Gate III of the SSBD, which consists of direct and repeated observations during independent seat-work periods in the classroom and on the playground during recess. Children who meet or exceed cutoff criteria for either or both

Screening tools for E/BD

 Content Standards for Beginning Teachers of Students With E/BD: Characteristics of behavioral rating scales (BD8K1) (also CC8K3).

observational measures are referred to child study teams for further evaluation to determine their eligibility for special education.

Projective Tests

A **projective test** consists of ambiguous stimuli (e.g., "What does this inkblot look like to you?") or open-ended tasks (e.g., "Complete this sentence for me: 'Most girls like to . . .'"). It is assumed that responses to items that have no right or wrong answer will reveal a person's true personality characteristics. The most famous projective test is the Rorschach Test (Rorschach, 1942), which consists of a set of 10 cards, each containing an inkblot; the left and right halves being mirror images of each other. The subject is shown one card at a time and told, "Tell me what you see, what it might be for you. There are no right or wrong answers."

Another well-known projective test is the Thematic Apperception Test (TAT) (Morgan & Murray, 1935). A person taking the TAT is shown a series of pictures and asked to make up a story about each picture, telling who the people are; what they are doing, thinking, and feeling; and how the situation will turn out.

Although the results of projective tests may be interesting, they are of little or no value in planning or evaluating special education. Projective tests assess an indirect and extremely limited sample of a child's behavioral repertoire and, just as important, they do not assess how the child typically acts over a period of time. One-time measures—whether direct or indirect—are not a sufficient basis for identifying the presence of an emotional or behavioral disorder or planning education and treatment.

Direct Observation and Measurement of Behavior

Measurable dimensions of behavior

Content Standards for Beginning Teachers—Common Core: Basic terminology used in assessment (CC8K1).

In assessment by direct observation and measurement, the actual behaviors that cause concern about a child are clearly specified and observed in the settings in which they normally occur (e.g., in the classroom, on the playground). Behavior can be measured objectively along several dimensions: frequency, duration, latency, topography, and magnitude (see Figure 6.3).

The advantage of assessing and describing emotional or behavioral disorders in terms of these dimensions is that identification, design of intervention strategies, and evaluation of treatment effects can all revolve around direct and objective measurement. This approach leads to a direct focus on the child's problem—the behavior that is adversely affecting his life—and ways of dealing with it such as strengthening a desired alternative behavior as opposed to concentrating on some presumed (and unreachable) problem within the child (Cullinan, 2007). Detailed procedures for various techniques for observing and measuring behavior can be found in J. O. Cooper, Heron, and Heward (2007).

Functional Behavioral Assessment

Functional behavioral assessment

Content Standards for Beginning Teachers—Common Core: Use functional assessments to develop intervention plans (CC7S4).

Functional behavioral assessment (FBA) is a systematic process for gathering information to understand why a student may be engaging in challenging behavior. School psychologists, special educators, and behavior analysts use this information to generate hypotheses about what the behavior's function, or purpose, is for the student. Two major types of behavioral functions of problem behaviors are (a) to get something the student wants (positive reinforcement) (e.g., hitting other students produces attention from the teacher) and (b) to avoid or escape something the student doesn't want (negative reinforcement) (e.g., disruptive behavior when the teacher presents academic tasks results in removal of the task).

Knowledge of a behavior's function can point to the design of an appropriate and effective **behavioral intervention plan (BIP),** a required IEP component for all students with disabilities whose school performance is adversely affected by behavioral issues (Etscheidt, 2006). For example, knowing that a student's tantrums are maintained by teacher attention suggests a different intervention than one indicated for misbehavior that is maintained by escape from challenging academic tasks. Recent research literature contains numerous examples of using FBA to guide the successful intervention for extremely challenging and disruptive behavior (e.g., Heckaman, Conroy, Fox, & Chait, 2000; Kamps, Wendland, & Culpepper, 2006; Liaupsin, Umbreit, Ferro, Urso, & Upreti, 2006;

FIGURE 6.3 | Five measurable dimensions of behavior

FREQUENCY OR RATE: how often a particular behavior occurs, usually expressed as a count per standard unit of time (e.g., 6 talkouts per minute). All children cry, get into fights with other children, and sulk from time to time; yet we are not apt to think of them as emotionally disturbed. The primary difference between children with behavioral disorders and other children is the frequency with which these behaviors occur. Although disturbed children may not do anything their nondisabled peers do not do, they do certain undesirable things too often (e.g., crying, hitting others) and/or engage in adaptive behaviors too infrequently (e.g., playing with others).

DURATION: how long a child engages in a given activity (e.g., worked on math problems for 12 minutes). The amount of time children with behavioral disorders engage in certain activities is often markedly different—either longer or shorter—from that of other children. For example, most young children have temper tantrums, but the tantrums generally last no more than a few minutes. A child with emotional or behavioral disorders may tantrum for more than an hour at a time. The problem may also be one of too short a duration. For example, a child who cannot stick to an academic task for more than a few seconds at a time.

LATENCY: the time that elapses between the opportunity to respond and the beginning of the behavior. The latency of a child's behavior may be too long (e.g., several minutes elapse before he begins to comply with the teacher's request) or too short (e.g., the child immediately begins screaming and tantruming at the slightest provocation or frustration, thus having no time to consider more appropriate alternative behaviors).

TOPOGRAPHY: the physical shape or form of behavior. Printing your name in block letters and signing your name in cursive have different topographies. Some children with emotional or behavioral disorders emit behaviors that are seldom, if ever, seen in typical children (e.g., setting fires, cruelty to animals). These behaviors may be maladaptive, bizarre, or dangerous to the child or others.

MAGNITUDE: the force or intensity with which behavior is emitted. The magnitude of a child's responses may be too little (e.g., talking in a volume so low that she cannot be heard) or too much (e.g., slamming the door).

Lo & Cartledge, 2006; Wright-Gallo, Higbee, Reagon, & Davey, 2006). FBA entails one or more of three basic assessment methods: indirect assessment, direct assessment, and functional analysis (Horner & Carr, 1997; Neef & Peterson, 2007).

Indirect Functional Behavior Assessment The easiest and quickest form of FBA involves asking teachers, parents, and others who know the child well about the circumstances that typically surround the occurrence and nonoccurrence of the problem behavior and the reactions the behavior usually evokes from others. "Such procedures are referred to as 'indirect' because they do not involve observing the behavior, but rather soliciting information based on others' recollections of the behavior" (Neef & Peterson, 2007, p. 509). A number of instruments for conducting indirect FBA via structured interview, questionnaire, or checklist have been published (e.g., the Motivation Assessment Scale [Durand & Crimmins, 1992]; Questions About Behavioral Function [Matson & Vollmer, 1995]; and Stimulus Control Checklist [Rolider & Van Houten, 1993]). One widely used empirically validated tool for indirect FBA, the Functional Assessment Interview, includes a student-assisted form so students can serve as their own informants (Kern, Dunlap, Clarke, & Childs, 1995; O'Neill et al., 1997). The interview questions the informant to identify behavior(s) that cause trouble for the student at school, describe the student's class schedule and its relation to problem behavior, rate the intensity of behaviors across class periods and times of day, describe the situation in which the problem behavior

FIGURE 6.4	Hypothesized functions of aggression, property destruction, and tantrums by a 13-year-old student diagnosed with oppositional defiant disorder and attention-deficit/hyperactivity disorder		

Antecedent	Behavior	Consequence	Function
When adult or peer attention is diverted from Brian . . .	he engages in a variety of problem behaviors, which result in . . .	attention from adults and peers.	Gain attention from adults and peers
When Brian's access to preferred toys and activities is restricted . . .	he engages in a variety of problem behaviors, which result in . . .	gaining access to preferred toys and activities.	Gain access to preferred toys and activities
When Brian is required to perform difficult or undesirable tasks . . .	he engages in a variety of problem behaviors, which result in . . .	The tasks being removed.	Escape from difficult and/or nonpreferred tasks

Source: From N. A. Neef and S. M. Peterson (2007). Functional behavior assessment. In J. O. Cooper, T. E. Heron, & W. L. Heward, *Applied behavior analysis* (2nd ed., pp. 515). Upper Saddle River, NJ: Pearson Education, Inc. Used by permission.

typically occurs (e.g., difficult, boring, or unclear material; peer teasing; teacher reprimands), and describe the events that often follow the behavior and may function to maintain it.

Descriptive Functional Behavior Assessment   Descriptive FBA entails direct observation of the problem behavior under naturally occurring conditions. Using a technique called **ABC recording,** an observer records a temporally sequenced account of each occurrence of the problem behavior(s) in context of the antecedent conditions and events and consequences for those behaviors as those events unfold in the student's natural environment (J. O. Cooper et al., 2007). This assessment technique is so named because it obtains information on (a) the antecedent events that occasion or trigger problem behavior (e.g., transitions from one classroom or activity to another, task difficulty), (b) the nature of the behavior itself (e.g., duration, topography, intensity), and (c) the consequences that may function to maintain the behavior (e.g., teacher attention, withdrawal of task demands).

IEP teams often combine the results of indirect and direct FBAs to obtain a picture of function. Figure 6.4 shows the hypothesized functions of aggression, property destruction, and tantrums by Brian, a 13-year-old student diagnosed with oppositional defiant disorder and attention-deficit/hyperactivity disorder as determined by the results of a Functional Assessment Interview and ABC recording. In some cases, the results of an indirect and/or descriptive FBA lead to an effective treatment plan. To reveal the controlling variables for many chronic problem behaviors, however, a functional analysis is required (Thompson & Iwata, 2007).

Functional Analysis   Functional behavioral assessment might also include a **functional analysis,** the experimental manipulation of several antecedent or consequent events surrounding the target behavior in an attempt to verify the hypothesized functions of the behavior (e.g., systematically varying the difficulty of academic tasks to test if the child's oppositional behavior is triggered by difficult tasks) (Iwata, Dorsey, Slifer, Bauman, & Richman, 1994). The same or similar antecedent conditions and consequences identified through indirect and descriptive FBA are used in a functional analysis, but those variables are manipulated in a controlled or *analog* setting rather than the natural environment. This allows better control of the variables, and the safety of child and others can be ensured. Functional analysis purposely results in occurrences of the problem behavior; therefore, only highly trained personnel who have attained appropriate consents from parents/guardians and have ensured that adequate safeguards are in place to protect the student and others from any harm should conduct it.

FIGURE 6.5	Interventions for attention and escape functions of aggression, property destruction, and tantrums by a 13-year-old student diagnosed with oppositional defiant disorder and attention-deficit/hyperactivity disorder

ATTENTION FUNCTION

Intervention	Antecedent	Behavior	Consequence
Teach a new behavior	When adult or peer attention is diverted from Brian . . .	he will raise his hand and say, "Excuse me . . ."	and adults and peers will provide attention to Brian.
Teach a new behavior	When adult or peer attention is diverted from Brian . . .	he will self-monitor his appropriate independent work and match teacher recordings . . .	and the teachers will provide him with one-on-one time if he meets a specific criterion.
Change the antecedent	During independent work times, adults will provide attention to Brian every 5 minutes . . .	to increase the probability that Brian will appropriately work independently . . .	which will increase adult opportunities to praise and attend to appropriate behavior.
Change the antecedent	Allow Brian to play with peers during leisure times . . .	to increase the probability that Brian will play appropriately . . .	which will increase adult opportunities to praise appropriate behavior and for peers to respond positively.

ESCAPE FUNCTION

Intervention	Antecedent	Behavior	Consequence
Teach a new behavior	When Brian is required to perform a difficult or undesirable task . . .	he will say, "May I take a break now?" . . .	And the teacher will allow Brian to take a break from the task.
Change the reinforcement contingency	When Brian is required to perform difficult or undesirable tasks . . .	and he engages in a variety of problem behaviors . . .	he will be required to continue working on the task and the time out intervention will be discontinued.

Source: From N. A. Neef and S. M. Peterson (2007). Functional behavior assessment. In J. O. Cooper, T. E. Heron, & W. L. Heward, *Applied behavior analysis* (2nd ed., p. 517). Upper Saddle River, NJ: Pearson Education, Inc. Used by permission.

A functional analysis with Brian confirmed and clarified the hypothesized functions of his problem behaviors and led to the design of a successful multicomponent intervention shown in Figure 6.5. Detailed descriptions of how to conduct FBAs can be found in Neef and Peterson (2007) and Umbreit, Ferro, Liaupsin, and Lane (2007).

EDUCATIONAL APPROACHES

Curriculum Goals

What should students with emotional or behavioral disorders be taught? An obvious but only partially correct answer is that students with externalizing problems should learn to control their antisocial behavior and that those with internalizing problems should learn to have fun and make friends. However, if programs serving children with emotional or behavioral disorders treat maladaptive behavior at the expense of academic instruction, students who already possess deficient academic skills fall even further behind their peers. Special education for students with emotional or behavioral disorders must include effective instruction in the personal, social, and academic skills required for success in school, community, and vocational settings.

Academic Skills Although students with emotional or behavioral disorders require special education to work on their specific behavior problems and social skills deficits, systematic instruction in reading, writing, and arithmetic are as important to students with emotional or behavioral disorders as they are to any student who hopes to function successfully in school and society (Hodge, Riccomini, Buford, & Herbst, 2006; Wehby, Lane, & Falk, 2003). With the emphasis of No Child Left Behind on academic achievement of all students, the academic course schedules of nearly all secondary students with emotional or behavior disorders closely resemble those of students in the general population. Nearly all secondary school youth with emotional or behavior disorders take language arts, math, and social studies in a given semester, and 84% take science (Wagner & Cameto, 2004). Only foreign language is taken at a markedly lower rate by youth with emotional or behavior disorders than by youth in the general population.

Until recently, however, very few studies on academic interventions with students with emotional or behavioral disorders appeared in the peer-reviewed research literature (Hodge et al., 2006; Pierce, Reid, & Epstein, 2004). The authors of one review found only 55 teacher-mediated academic interventions published over a period of 30 years (Mooney, Epstein, Reid, & Nelson, 2003).

Fortunately, most students with emotional or behavioral disorders make excellent progress when provided with explicit, systematic instruction (Benner, 2007; Lingo, Bott Slaton, & Jolivette, 2006; Mooney et al., 2003).

Effective instruction is the foundation for effective behavior management in the classroom. Teachers must guard against the tendency to avoid noncompliance and disruptive outbursts by providing students with behavior problems with limited academic instruction in the form of easier tasks, fewer opportunities to respond, and lowered expectations (Gunter et al., 1993; Sutherland, Alder, & Gunter, 2003; Wehby et al., 1998).

Social Skills Social skills instruction is an important curriculum component for students with emotional or behavioral disorders. Many of these students have difficulty holding a conversation, expressing their feelings, participating in group activities, and responding to failure or criticism in positive and constructive ways. They often get into fights and altercations because they lack the social skills needed to handle or defuse provocative incidents. The slightest snub, bump, or misunderstood request—which would be laughed off or ignored by most children—can precipitate an aggressive attack by some students.

Learning the social and nonacademic skills that match teacher expectations for student behavior is especially important for children with emotional or behavioral disorders (Meier, DiPerna, & Oster, 2006). A survey of 717 teachers across grade levels identified the following five skills as critical to success in general education classrooms:

- Controls temper in conflict situations with peers
- Controls temper in conflict situations with adults
- Follows/complies with directions
- Attends to teacher's instructions
- Easily makes transitions from one classroom activity to another (K. L. Lane, Wehby, et al., 2006, p. 161)

Many studies on teaching social skills to students with emotional or behavioral disorders have been published. Based on his review of 13 reviews of published research on teaching skills, Maag (2006) concluded that the state of social skills training (SST) for students with emotional or behavioral disorders "seems to range from dismal to guarded optimism" and that researchers too often ignore long-standing recommendations for enhancing the efficacy of SST and the potential for generalization. "Schools need to create and nurture a culture in which SST would be an important and ongoing component of the curriculum that benefits not only target students but also their peers" (p. 14). A review by Gresham, Cook, Crews, and Kern (2004) concluded that social skills training is generally effective and is an essential component of a comprehensive program for students with emotional and behavior disorders.

Go to the Homework & Exercises section in Chapter 6 of MyEducationLab and complete Homework Exercise 3. As you watch the video and answer the accompanying questions, examine how Ms. Rich uses explicit instruction with her students.

Social skills instruction and curricula

Content Standards for Beginning Teachers of Students with E/BD: Sources of specialized materials for individuals with E/BD (BD4K1).

Numerous social skills curricula and training programs have been published, such as the following:

- *Taking Part: Introducing Social Skills to Children* (Cartledge & Kleefeld, 1991) helps students in preschool classrooms through third grade learn social skills in six units: making conversation, communicating feelings, expressing oneself, cooperating with peers, playing with peers, and responding to aggression and conflict.
- *The Prepare Curriculum: Teaching Prosocial Competencies* (Goldstein, 2000) is designed for students who are aggressive, withdrawn, or otherwise deficient in social competencies. Activities and materials for middle and high school students are provided in 10 areas, such as problem solving, anger control, stress management, and cooperation.
- *The Walker Social Skills Curriculum* includes ACCEPTS: A Curriculum for Children's Effective Peer and Teacher Skills (Walker, McConnell, et al., 1988), for children grades K–6, and ACCESS: Adolescent Curriculum for Communication and Effective Social Skills (Walker, Todis, Holmes, & Horton, 1988) for students at the middle and high school levels.

Television programs (T. Bryan & Ryan, 2001) and children's books are sometimes used to provide examples and content for social skills instruction for students with emotional and behavioral disorders (Brame, 2000; Sridhar & Vaughn, 2000). Regardless of the social skills targeted, instruction should be explicit, with appropriate behaviors modeled, opportunities for role playing, guided practice with feedback, and strategies to promote the maintenance and generalization of learned skills (Elksnin & Elksnin, 2006; K. L. Lane, Menzies, Barton-Arwood, Doukas, & Munton, 2005; Maag, 2006; Meadows & Stevens, 2004).

Evidence-Based Instructional Practices

A four-phase review process to identify scientific, research-based teaching methods for students with emotional or behavioral disorders revealed these four strategic approaches:

(a) teacher praise (reinforcement);

(b) high rates of opportunities to respond during instruction;

(c) clear instructional strategies, including direct instruction; and

(d) positive behavior support, including school-wide, functional assessment-based individual plans and self-management. (T. J. Lewis, Hudson, Richter, & Johnson, 2004, p. 250)

Two of these practices, providing high rates of active student responding—with choral responding and response cards—and explicit, direct instruction were described in Chapters 4 and 5, respectively. Functional behavior assessment was explained earlier in this chapter. School-wide positive behavioral support and self-management are described in the remainder of this section. Proactive, positive classroom management and the use of peer mediation and support are also described. To read about the importance of teacher praise as reinforcement, see Teaching & Learning, "The Power of Teacher Praise."

School-wide Systems of Positive Behavioral Support   Traditionally, discipline in the schools has focused on the use of punishment in an effort to control the misbehavior of specific students. Not only are such strategies generally ineffective in achieving long-term reductions in problem behavior or increases in overall school safety (Morrison & D'Incau, 2000; Skiba, 2002), they also do not teach students desired, prosocial behaviors. Among the most important advances in student discipline procedures over the past decade is the development of school-wide behavior support systems that promote and foster positive behaviors by all students. The goals of school-wide systems are to define, teach, and support appropriate behaviors in a way that enhances the academic and social behavior success of all students (Lewis & Sugai, 1999).

Schools that implement school-wide systems of positive behavior support use a team-based approach to teach appropriate behavior to all students in the school. All teachers and school staff participate in teaching and rewarding desired student behavior, consequences

Go to the Homework & Exercises section in Chapter 6 of MyEducationLab and complete Homework Exercise 4. As you watch the video and answer the accompanying questions, consider how Ms. Rich incorporates her social skills curriculum into her teaching.

Contingent teacher praise and positive reinforcement

 Content Standards for Beginning Teachers of Students with E/BD: Theory of reinforcement techniques in serving individuals with E/BD (BD1K5).

Research has repeatedly shown that the systematic use of praise and attention and other forms of positive reinforcement for desired behaviors is a powerful classroom management and instructional tool.

The Power of Teacher Praise

Social approval, often conveyed through verbal praise, is a powerful reinforcer for most people. The original experimental demonstrations of the power of adults' social attention as reinforcement for children's behavior took place in a series of four studies designed by Montrose Wolf and carried out by the preschool teachers at the University of Washington's Institute of Child Development in the early 1960s (K. E. Allen, Hart, Buell, Harris, & Wolf, 1964; F. R. Harris, Johnston, Kelly, & Wolf, 1964; Hart, Allen, Buell, Harris, & Wolf, 1964; M. K. Johnston, Kelly, Harris, & Wolf, 1966). Describing those early studies, Risley (2005) wrote:

> We had never seen such power! The speed and magnitude of the effects on children's behavior in the real world of simple adjustments of something so ubiquitous as adult attention was astounding. Forty years later, social reinforcement (positive attention, praise, "catching them being good") has become the core of most American advice and training for parents and teachers—making this arguably the most influential discovery of modern psychology. (p. 280)

Numerous studies since have shown repeatedly the positive effects of contingent praise on the behavior of infants (e.g., Poulson & Kymissis, 1988), preschoolers (e.g., Connell, Randall, Wilson, Lutz, & Lamb, 1993; Wolery, 2000), and school-age students with and without disabilities (e.g., Kratochwill & Stoiber, 2000; Martella, Marchand-Martella, Young, & MacFarlane, 1995; Sutherland, Wehby, & Copeland, 2000). Yet many educators do not appreciate that the systematic use of contingent praise and attention may be the most powerful motivational and classroom management tool they have (Flora, 2004). Teacher praise and attention are especially important for students with learning and behavior problems.

MISGUIDED ADVICE

Some argue against the use of praise and rewards for student performance (Deci, Koestner, & Ryan, 1999; Lepper, Keavney, & Drake, 1996). Alfie Kohn (1993a, 1993b), in particular, has gained considerable attention for claiming that extrinsic motivators such as incentive plans, grades, and verbal praise damage the intrinsic motivation of students and employees to perform and learn. Using faulty interpretations of research of questionable validity, Kohn argues that praise is not only ineffective but actually harmful to children. In an article titled "Five Reasons to Stop Saying 'Good Job!'" Kohn (2001) warned early childhood teachers that praising and rewarding students for their accomplishments manipulates children, creates praise junkies, steals their pleasure, causes children to lose interest, and reduces achievement. Not only does this stand in stark contrast to an extensive research literature showing the positive benefits of such practices, the "planned use of positive reinforcement is antithetical to [Kohn's pejorative description of the practice as] blurted-out judgments, slathered-on praise, knee-jerk tendencies, and evaluative eruptions" (Strain & Joseph, 2004, p. 58).

Research conducted in classrooms and laboratories does not support Kohn's contention that students are "punished by rewards" (Cameron, 2005). Cameron, Banko, and Pierce (2001) conducted a meta-analysis of 145 experimental studies and concluded that no scientific evidence indicated any detrimental effects of reward on intrinsic motivation.

LOW RATES OF TEACHER PRAISE

Kohn and others concerned that teachers are praising their students too frequently need not worry. In spite of its documented effectiveness in increasing academic performance and desired student behaviors, studies over the past three decades have consistently found very low rates of teacher praise. In a study of 104 teachers in grades 1 through 12, M. A. White (1975) found that rates of teacher praise dropped with each grade level; and in every grade after second, the rate at which teachers delivered statements of disapproval to students exceeded the rate of teacher approval. Numerous studies have reported similar low rates of teacher praise in regular classrooms and special education classrooms (e.g., Baker & Zigmond, 1990; Deno, Maruyama, Espin, & Cohen, 1990; Harrop & Swinson, 2000; Nowacek, McKinney, & Hallahan, 1990). Especially discouraging are several studies in classrooms for students with emotional or behavioral disorders that found teachers' rates of praise as low as 1 per hour or less (Shores et al., 1993; Van Acker, Grant, & Henry, 1996; Wehby, Symons, & Shores, 1995).

FOUR POSSIBLE REASONS FOR INFREQUENT TEACHER PRAISE

Some teachers worry that students will come to expect to be praised or rewarded. They believe students should want to learn for intrinsic reasons. It would be wonderful if all students came to school prepared to work hard and to learn for "intrinsic" reasons. The ultimate intrinsic motivator is success itself (Skinner, 1989)—using new knowledge and skills effectively enough to enjoy control over one's environment, be it solving a new algebra problem or reading a mystery with sufficient fluency and endurance to find out who did it. But it is naïve and irresponsible for educators to expect students with few skills and a history of failure to work hard without positive consequences. Contingent teacher praise and other extrinsic motivators such as points toward a grade or slips of paper as entries in the classroom lottery are proven to help students attain the performance levels necessary to meet the naturally existing reinforcement contingencies of success.

Some teachers believe that praising takes too much time away from teaching. Detecting and praising performance improvements, particularly by low-achieving students who have experienced little academic success, is one of the most effective forms of teaching. It is unfortunate that some educators believe they are not teaching when they are praising student accomplishments.

Some teachers feel it is unnatural to praise. Teachers who think it is unnatural to praise students' good behavior are, in some respects, correct. The natural contingencies of the classroom undermine the use of praise and strengthen reprimanding behavior. Teacher reprimands typically produce an immediate change in student behavior (e.g., the child stops disrupting class), which negatively reinforces reprimanding (Maag, 2001). By contrast, when a teacher praises a student for behavior, such as working quietly in class, usually no immediate consequence reinforces the teacher's praising behavior (e.g., the student just continues working as before). The pervasiveness of these naturally occurring contingencies is supported by the fact that while few teachers must be taught to identify misbehavior and issue reprimands, many teachers need help learning to catch students being good.

Classrooms are busy, and many student behaviors worthy of praise and attention go unnoticed. Teachers may not notice many desirable behaviors if students do not call attention to themselves. Teachers are more likely to notice and pay attention to a disruptive student than to a student who is working quietly and productively.

HOW TO GET STARTED

1. *Always be on the lookout for student behavior worthy of praise.* Even the most unskilled and unruly student is correct or obedient sometimes. Don't miss these critical teaching moments.

2. *Arrange opportunities for students to do something well just so you can give approval.* For example, an easy way to provide a low-achieving student with an opportunity to succeed in front of his classmates is to ask a question he is likely to know and then call on him to answer.

3. *Don't worry about sounding wooden and unnatural at first.* Teachers are often concerned their students will think they are not being genuine. Practice four or five praise statements you can say when you observe specific behaviors or performance improvements by your students. Providing specific praise and approval is like any other skill; you'll get better with practice.

4. *Use self-management to increase your praise rate.* Set a goal to give a certain number of praise statements in a class period (Keller, Brady, & Taylor, 2005; Keller & Duffy, 2005; Silvestri & Heward, 2005). Prompt yourself to praise desired student behavior by marking reminders in your lesson plan or by playing a cassette tape with randomly spaced beeps. Self-record your praising behavior by marking a card or moving pennies from one pocket to another. Reward yourself with a treat after school for meeting your goal. Start small, and gradually increase your daily goal as your praising skills improve.

5. *Don't worry about overpraising.* Of all the mistakes a teacher might make, providing too much praise and approval for students' good academic and social behaviors is not likely to be one of them.

Go to the Homework & Exercises section in Chapter 6 of MyEducationLab and complete Homework Exercise 5. As you watch the video and answer the accompanying questions, consider how teacher praise is affecting the students in this classroom.

for rule violations are clearly defined and consistently applied, and objective data are used to evaluate and continually improve the system (Netzel & Eber, 2003; Peterson & Lacy-Rismiller, 2005; Sugai & Horner, 2005). Successful school-wide systems of behavior support are characterized by the following (Center on Positive Behavioral Interventions & Supports, 2007):

1. *Behavioral expectations are stated.* A small number of behavioral expectations are clearly defined. These often are simple, positively framed rules such as "Be respectful, be responsible, and be safe" or "Respect yourself, respect others, and respect property" (e.g., Netzel & Eber, 2003).

2. *Behavioral expectations are defined and taught.* The behavioral expectations are taught to all students in the building. Specific examples are provided for behavioral expectations (e.g., "Being respectful in class means raising your hand when you want to speak or get help. During lunch or in the hall, being respectful means using a person's name when you talk to him or her."). Behavioral expectations are taught directly with a systematic format: the general rule is presented, the rationale for the rule is discussed, positive examples ("right way") are described and rehearsed, negative examples ("wrong way") are described and modeled, and students practice the "right way" until they demonstrate fluent performance.

3. *Appropriate behaviors are acknowledged.* Appropriate behaviors are acknowledged on a regular basis. Some schools do this through formal systems (tickets, rewards); others do it through social events. Schools strive to establish a ratio of four positive adult interactions with students for every one that is negative.

4. *Behavioral errors are corrected proactively.* When students violate behavioral expectations, clear procedures are needed for showing them that their behavior was unacceptable and preventing unacceptable behavior from resulting in inadvertent rewards.

5. *Program evaluations and adaptations are data driven and made by a team.* Successful schools establish a simple, efficient strategy for continually assessing if they are succeeding, and they establish a decision-making process that allows adaptation to behavioral challenges. At the school-wide level, general measures of the school climate include behavior incident reports, attendance rates, tardies, detention, and suspension rates.

6. *Individual student support systems are integrated with school-wide discipline systems.* School-wide behavior support does not replace the need for a comprehensive set of more intensive interventions for the 1% to 7% of students in most schools who require more individualized and ongoing behavioral support (see Figure 6.6).

FIGURE 6.6

Continuum of school-wide positive behavioral supports

Source: Adapted from OSEP Technical Assistance Center on Positive Behavioral Interventions & Supports. (2007). U.S. Department of Education. http://www.pbis.org/schoolwide.htm

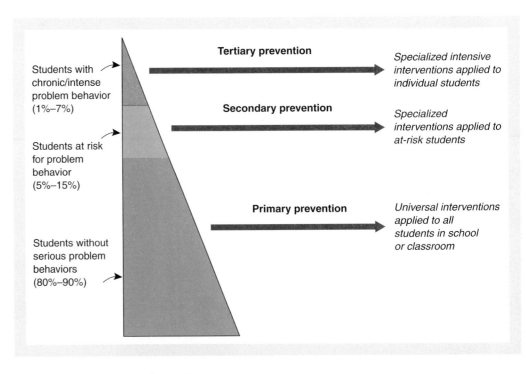

Self-Management Many children with emotional or behavioral disorders believe they have little control over their lives. Things just seem to happen to them, and being disruptive is their means of reacting to an inconsistent and frustrating world. These students can learn responsibility and achieve self-determination through **self-management**—making responses to increase or decrease the future frequency of a target behavior one wishes to change (Wehmeyer & Schalock, 2001). Self-management is also an important tool for promoting the generalization and maintenance of treatment gains from one setting to another.

Of the many forms of self-management, self-monitoring and self-evaluation are the most widely used and most researched. **Self-monitoring** is a relatively simple procedure in which a person observes his own behavior and records the occurrence or nonoccurrence of a specific target behavior. A person using **self-evaluation** compares his performance against a predetermined standard or goal.

Sometimes the student may match his self-recorded data with the teacher's rating of the same behavior and earn points for matching the teacher's assessment. Figure 6.7 shows an example of a self-monitoring form for a student who is verbally and physically aggressive and bullies other children during transitions between classes. At the end of each transition, the student marks whether or not he performed each of five different behaviors that are

Self-monitoring and self-evaluation

Council for Exceptional Children Content Standards for Beginning Teachers—Common Core: Use procedures to promote individual's self-awareness, self-management, self-control, self-reliance, and self-esteem (CC4S5) (also CC4S2, CC4S4).

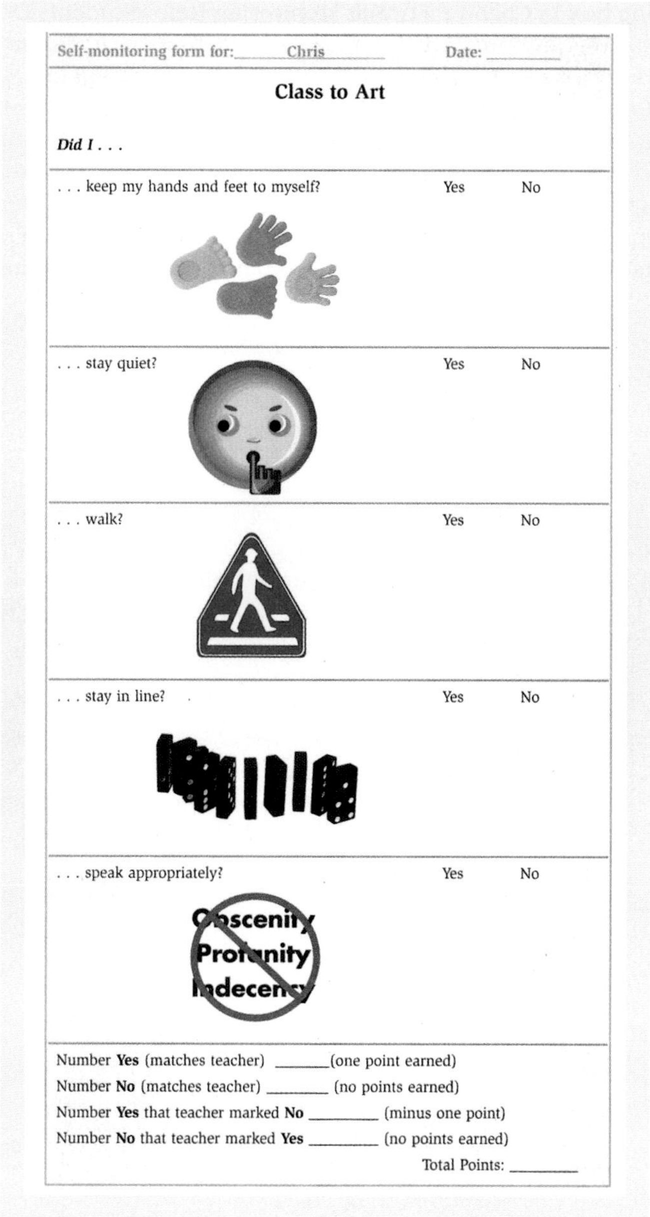
Self-monitoring form for: Chris   Date: ______

Class to Art

Did I . . .

. . . keep my hands and feet to myself? Yes No

. . . stay quiet? Yes No

. . . walk? Yes No

. . . stay in line? Yes No

. . . speak appropriately? Yes No

Number **Yes** (matches teacher) ______(one point earned)
Number **No** (matches teacher) ______ (no points earned)
Number **Yes** that teacher marked **No** ______ (minus one point)
Number **No** that teacher marked **Yes** ______ (no points earned)
Total Points: ______

FIGURE 6.7

Form used by elementary student to self-monitor behavior during transitions in hallway between classes

Source: From Patton, B., Jolivette, K., & Ramsey, M. (2006). Students with emotional and behavioral disorders *can* manage their own behavior. *Teaching Exceptional Children, 39*(2), p. 18. Used by permission.

Go to the Homework & Exercises section in Chapter 6 of MyEducationLab and complete Homework Exercise 7. As you watch the videos and answer the accompanying questions, compare and contrast the self-monitoring techniques used in Ms. Rich's and Ms. Heward's classrooms.

Go to the Homework & Exercises section in Chapter 6 of MyEducationLab and complete Homework Exercise 8. As you watch the video consider how his student uses these self-management tools in his independent seat work.

incompatible with the problem behaviors. He then compares his self-assessment with his teacher's rating of his behavior and earns or loses points accordingly. If this student earns four points, he can select from a list of reinforcers he has agreed to (e.g., being line leader, using special paint in art).

Numerous studies have demonstrated that students with various disabilities can use self-monitoring and self-evaluation to regulate their behavior (e.g., D. H. Anderson, Fisher, Marchant, Young, & Smith, 2006; Gumpel & Shlomit, 2000; Levendoski & Cartledge, 2000; Moxley, 1998; Patton, Jolivette, & Ramsey, 2006; L. D. Peterson, Young, West, & Hill Peterson, 1999; Smith & Sugai, 2000; Wood, Murdock, Cronin, Dawson, & Kirby, 1998).

Although the self-monitoring form itself provides a visual reminder to self-monitor, audio prompts in the form of prerecorded beeps or tones are often used (e.g., Todd et al., 1999). Tactile prompts can also be used to signal self-recording moments. For example, the MotivAider (http://www.habitchange.com) is a small, battery-operated device that can be programmed to vibrate at fixed or variable time intervals. The MotivAider is excellent for signaling students to self-monitor or perform other self-management tasks. It can also remind teachers to attend to the behavior of students. Flaute, Peterson, Van Norman, Riffle, and Eakins (2005) describe 20 ways for using a MotivAider to improve behavior and productivity in the classroom. For more information about self-monitoring, see the Teaching & Learning box in Chapter 11, "Self-Monitoring Helps Students Do More Than Just Be On-Task."

"Countoons" are self-management tools that remind young children not only what behavior to record but also what consequences will follow if they meet predetermined performance criteria. Daly and Ranalli (2003) created six-frame countoons that enable students to self-record an inappropriate behavior and an incompatible appropriate behavior. In the countoon shown in Figure 6.8, Frames 1 and 4 show the student doing her math work, appropriate behavior that is counted in Frame 5. The criterion number of math problems to meet the contingency, in this case 10, is also indicated in Frame 5. Frame 2 shows the student talking with a friend, the inappropriate behavior to be counted in Frame 3. The student must

FIGURE 6.8

Example of a countoon that can be taped to a student's desk as a reminder of target behaviors, the need to self-record, and the consequence for meeting the contingency.

Source: From "Using Countoons to Teach Self-Monitoring Skills" by P. M. Daly and P. Ranalli, 2003, *Teaching Exceptional Children, 35*(5), p. 32. Copyright 2003 by the Council for Exceptional Children. Reprinted by Permission.

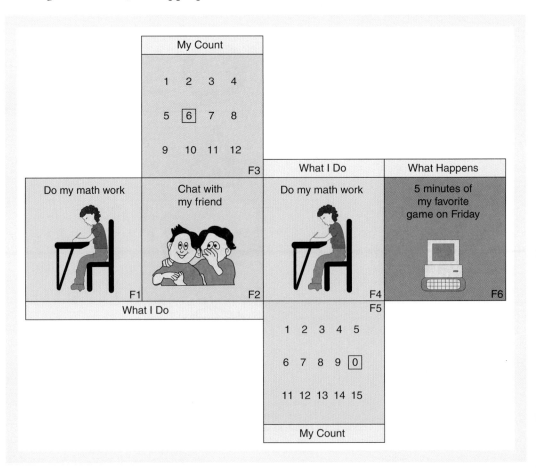

not chat more than six times to meet the contingency. The "What Happens" frame (F6) depicts the reward the student will earn by meeting both parts of the contingency.

For a review of principles and strategies for self-management, see J. O. Cooper and colleagues (2007). Detailed procedures and materials for teaching self-monitoring and other self-management skills to students can be found in Daly and Ranalli (2003), Joseph and Konrad (in press), McConnell (1999), and Patton, Jolivette, and Ramsey (2006). "KidTools" and "KidSkills" are free software programs that children can use to create self-management tools and can be downloaded in Windows or Macintosh versions at http://kidtools.missouri.edu. Training modules for teachers with video demonstrations and practice materials can also be downloaded at this site.

Proactive, Positive Classroom Management   Teachers of students with emotional or behavior disorders must design and manage classroom environments that are effective in decreasing antisocial behavior and increasing the frequency of positive teacher–student interactions as a basis for building positive behavior and academic success. This is a very tall order. Fortunately, teachers can turn to a strong base of clearly defined, evidence-based practices for guidance on effective classroom management (e.g., Cipani, 2008; Kerr & Nelson, 2006; Lane, Falk, & Wehby, 2006; Rhode, Jensen, & Morgan, 2003; Zirpoli, 2008).

The majority of classroom behavior problems can be prevented by the use of proactive behavior management. *Proactive strategies* are preplanned interventions that anticipate behavior problems and stop them before they occur. "It is much more difficult to remediate the problems caused by a Tough Kid than to prevent them. Once a teacher has lost the management tempo in a classroom and things are out of control, it is far more difficult to reestablish control" (Rhode et al., 1998, p. 19).

Proactive strategies include the following: Structure the physical environment of the classroom (e.g., have the most difficult students sit nearest the teacher); establish clear rules and expectations for appropriate behavior (Barbetta, Leong-Norona, & Bicard, 2002); schedule and sequence lesson activities to minimize downtime; present instructions to students in ways that increase the probability of compliance (Walker & Sylvester, 1998); keep students actively engaged during instruction (Godfrey et al., 2003; Gunter, Hummel, & Conroy, 1998; Lambert, Cartledge, Lo, & Heward, 2006; Sutherland & Wehby, 2001); use praise and positive reinforcement to motivate desired behavior (Maag, 2001; Sutherland, Wehby, & Yoder, 2002; Webber & Scheuermann, 1991; Witzer & Mercer, 2003); and anticipate and address problem behaviors before they occur (Crosby, Jolivette, & Patterson, 2006; T. Lewis, Colvin, & Sugai, 2000).

Managing the classroom environment for students with emotional or behavior disorders requires a great deal of knowledge and skill. In addition to the strategies already mentioned, teachers must know when and how to use a large set of behavior change tactics and tools such as *shaping, contingency contracting, extinction* (ignoring disruptive behavior), *differential reinforcement of alternative or incompatible behavior, response cost* (a loss of reinforcers as a consequence for misbehavior, like a fine), *time out* (restricting a student's access to reinforcement for a brief time following an inappropriate behavior [Ryan, Saunders, Katsiyannis, & Yell, 2007]), and *overcorrection* (requiring restitution beyond the damaging effects of the antisocial behavior, e.g., when a child who takes another child's cookie must return it plus one of her own Cooper et al., 2007). These techniques should not be implemented as isolated events but incorporated into an overall instructional and classroom management plan that includes the previously mentioned proactive strategies and perhaps a **token economy** or **level system** in which students access greater independence and more privileges as they demonstrate increased behavioral control (Anderson & Katsiyannis, 1997; Cruz & Cullinan, 2001; Lyon & Lagarde, 1997).

When designing and implementing classroom management strategies, teachers of students with emotional or behavioral disorders must be careful not to create an environment in which coercion is the primary means by which students are motivated to participate and follow rules. In addition to promoting escape and avoidance behavior by those being

Proactive classroom management

 Content Standards for Beginning Teachers—Common Core: Basic classroom management strategies for individuals with exceptional learning needs (CC5K2) (also BD4S2, BD5S1).

coerced, coercive environments do not teach what to do as much as they focus on what not to do (Sidman, 1989).

Peer-mediated support and interventions

Council for Exceptional Children Content Standards for Beginning Teachers of Students with E/BD: Functional classroom designs for individuals with E/BD (BD5K2).

Peer Mediation and Support   The power of the peer group can be an effective means of producing positive changes in students with behavioral disorders. Strategies for teaching peers to help one another decrease inappropriate behavior include the following:

- *Peer monitoring.* A student is taught to observe and record a peer's behavior and provide the peer with feedback (Anderson et al., 2006; Christensen, Young, & Marchant, 2004).
- *Positive peer reporting.* Students are taught, encouraged, and reinforced for reporting each other's positive behaviors (Bowers, McGinnis, Ervin, & Friman, 1999).
  - *Peer tutoring.* In serving as academic or social skills tutors for one another, students with emotional or behavioral disorders may also learn better social skills (Blake, Wang, Cartledge, & Gardner, 2000; Dion, Fuchs, & Fuchs, 2005; Spencer, 2006).
  - *Peer support and confrontation.* Peers are trained to acknowledge one another's positive behaviors, and when inappropriate behavior occurs or is about to occur, peers are trained to explain why the behavior is a problem and to suggest or model an appropriate alternative response (Bullock & Foegen, 2002; Nelson, Martella, & Marchand-Martella, 2002).

Peer tutoring can be an excellent way for children to learn valuable social skills.

Implementing a peer support, or group process, model is much more complicated than bringing together a group of children and hoping they will benefit from positive peer influence. Most children with serious emotional or behavioral disorders have not been members of successfully functioning peer groups in which appropriate behavior is modeled and valued (Hallenbeck & Kauffman, 1995), nor have many such children learned to accept responsibility for their actions (Rockwell & Guetzloe, 1996). The teacher's first and most formidable challenge is helping promote group cohesiveness.

Although group process treatment programs take many forms, most incorporate group meetings and group-oriented contingencies. Two types of group meetings are usually held daily. A planning meeting is held each morning in which the group reviews the daily schedule, each group member states a behavioral goal for the day, peers provide support and suggestions to one another for meeting their goals, and a group goal for the day is agreed on. An evaluation meeting is held at the end of each day to discuss how well the individual and group goals were met, and each group member must give and receive positive peer comments. Problem-solving meetings are held whenever any group member, including the teacher, feels the need to discuss a problem. The group identifies the problem, generates several solutions, discusses the likely consequences of each solution, develops a plan for the best solution, and makes verbal commitments to carry out the plan.

To learn more about teaching students with emotional or behavioral disorders with a group process approach, go to the Homework & Exercises section in Chapter 6 of MyEducationLab and complete Homework Exercise 9.

Group contingencies specify certain rewards and privileges that are enjoyed by the group if their behavior meets certain criteria (Hansen & Lignugaris/Kraft, 2005; Heering & Wilder, 2006; Lannie & McCurdy, 2007). Popkin and Skinner (2003) conducted an interesting application of a group contingency with students with emotional or behavioral disorders. The researchers wrote *spelling* and a performance criterion on each of a set of 30 index cards (e.g., five cards with 75%, eight cards with 80%, and five cards with 95%). At the end of the school day, the teacher randomly selected one of the cards. If the students' average performance as a class exceeded the criterion shown on the card, the entire group received a reward. The students who had been doing well in spelling improved (e.g., *B* students became *A* students), and the students who had done poorly showed large increases in their performance (e.g., failing students earned *A*s and *B*s). After several weeks, similar sets of cards with *mathematics* and *grammar* were added to the deck. Students contributed ideas for the rewards. The students helped determine the rewards and the criteria for earning the them. See Teaching & Learning, "Mystery Motivators" on p. 244.

Fostering Strong Teacher–Student Relationships

In addition to academic and behavior management skills, the teacher of children with emotional or behavioral disorders must establish healthy and positive child–teacher relationships. William Morse (1976, 1985), one of the pioneers in the education of children with emotional or behavioral disorders, identified two important affective characteristics necessary for teachers to relate effectively and positively to students with behavior problems. Morse called these traits differential acceptance and empathetic relationship.

Differential acceptance means the teacher can receive and witness frequent and often extreme acts of anger, hate, and aggression from children without responding similarly. Of course, this is much easier said than done. But the teacher of students with emotional or behavioral disorders must view disruptive behavior for what it is—behavior that reflects the student's past frustrations and conflicts with himself and those around him—and try to help the child learn better ways of behaving. Acceptance should not be confused with approving or condoning antisocial behavior; the child must learn that he is responding inappropriately. Instead, this concept calls for understanding without condemning.

Having an *empathetic relationship* with a child refers to a teacher's ability to recognize and understand the many nonverbal cues that often are the keys to understanding the individual needs of children with emotional or behavioral disorders. Teachers should communicate directly and honestly with behaviorally troubled children. Many of these children have already had experience with supposedly helpful adults who have not been completely honest with them. Children with emotional or behavioral disorders can quickly detect someone who is not genuinely interested in their welfare.

The teacher of children with emotional or behavioral disorders must also realize that his actions serve as a powerful model. Therefore, it is critical that the teacher's actions and attitudes be mature and demonstrate self-control. At the same time, teachers who take themselves too seriously risk overreacting to emotionally charged situations with students and risk burnout (Abrams, 2005). Richardson and Shupe (2003) suggest that teachers use an appropriate sense of humor to build relationships with students, diffuse conflict, engage learners, and help manage their own stress levels.

Differential acceptance and empathetic relationship

 Content Standards for Beginning Teachers—Common Core: Teacher attitudes and behaviors that influence behavior of individuals with exceptional learning needs (CC5K4).

Focus on Alterable Variables

The twofold task of the teacher of children with emotional or behavioral disorders is helping students (a) replace antisocial and maladaptive behaviors with more socially appropriate behaviors and (b) acquire academic knowledge and skills. The frequent displays of antisocial behavior, the absence of appropriate social skills, and the academic deficits exhibited by many students with emotional or behavioral disorders make this a staggering challenge. The challenge is all the more difficult because the teacher seldom, if ever, can control (or even know) all of the factors affecting a student's behavior. Typically, a host of contributing factors exists over which the teacher can exert little or no influence (e.g., the delinquent friends with whom the student associates before and after school). But it does little good to bemoan the student's past (which no one can alter) or to use all of the negative factors in the student's current life that cannot be changed as an excuse for failing to help the student in the classroom.

Special educators should focus their attention and efforts on those aspects of a student's life that they can effectively control. Bloom (1980) uses the term *alterable variables* to refer to things that both make a difference in student learning and can be affected by teaching practices. Alterable variables include key dimensions of curriculum and instruction such as the amount of time allocated for instruction; the sequence of activities within the overall lesson; the pacing of instruction; the frequency with which students actively respond during instruction; how and when students receive praise or other forms of reinforcement for their efforts; and the manner in which errors are corrected. The teachers who focus on the identification and systematic management of alterable variables are those most likely to make a difference in the lives of children with emotional or behavioral disorders.

Alterable variables

 Content Standards for Beginning Teachers—Common Core: Effective management of teaching and learning (CC5K3).

Mystery Motivators Can Improve Students' Social and Academic Behavior

BY NATALIE ALLEN WILLIAMS

There are three important things to remember about education. The first one is motivation, the second is motivation, and the third is motivation. (Terrell Bell, former U.S. Secretary of Education)

All of us, children and adults alike, learn and perform better when we are motivated. While some educators believe that students must be "intrinsically motivated" to learn and that efforts to motivate students with praise, recognition, and other forms of "extrinsic" rewards are unnecessary, "it is naive and irresponsible for educators to expect students with limited skills and a history of academic failure to work diligently and happily without positive consequences" (Heward, 2005, p. 330). The ability to motivate students is important for all teachers; it is an essential skill for teachers who work with children with emotional or behavioral disorders. Mystery Motivators are a fun and effective way to motivate students to learn difficult curriculum content and achieve new levels of performance.

WHAT ARE MYSTERY MOTIVATORS?

Mystery Motivators are special rewards for appropriate student behavior presented in a game-like format. Students know that when they meet the performance criteria for specific academic or social behaviors they will have an opportunity to receive a Mystery Motivator, but they do not know what the Mystery Motivator is or when the game will make it available. The suspense surrounding the identity and availability of the Mystery Motivator builds students' anticipation and incentive to perform well (Rhode, Jenson, & Reavis, 1998). Mystery Motivator incentive systems take a wide variety of forms and can be used with individual students, small groups or teams within a class, or the whole class to improve academic and social behaviors.

DO THEY WORK?

Teachers have conducted Mystery Motivator incentive systems with students from preschool to secondary classrooms. Teachers have used Mystery Motivators to decrease a wide range of disruptive behaviors (e.g., De Martini-Scully, Bray, & Kehle, 2000; Kehle, Bray, Theodore, Jenson, & Clark, 2000; Murphy, Theodore, Aloiso, Alric-Edwards, & Hughes, 2006), to improve in-school academic performance (Skinner, Williams, & Neddenriep, 2004), and to increase the completion and accuracy of homework (Madaus, Kehle, Madaus, & Bray, 2003). Parents also have used Mystery Motivators to reduce disruptive behavior and noncompliance at bedtime (Mottram & Berger-Gross, 2004; Robinson & Sheridan, 2000). Mystery Motivators are sometimes so effective that "remarkable reductions of disruptive behavior" occur (Murphy et al., 2006, p. 53).

HOW TO GET STARTED

Use the following steps to prepare, implement, and evaluate a Mystery Motivator incentive system:

1. *Define target behaviors and performance criteria.* Identify the academic and/or social behaviors you want to motivate students to change (e.g., arriving on time to class, completing homework, participating in class discussions, following class rules, exhibiting positive behaviors on the playground or in the cafeteria), and define them in observable and measurable terms. Specify the performance levels students must achieve to be eligible for the Mystery Motivator (e.g., all students in class complete assigned academic work during the school day and have no rule infractions). Do not make the initial performance criteria too high.

2. *Create a pool of rewards.* Observe what students do in their free time, listen to the things they talk about, and ask the students to suggest rewards that they would like to work for. Have the students check or rank their preferences from a list of activities, privileges, and tangible items (e.g., free homework pass, pencils, trading cards, computer time, 10 minutes' free time, bubble gum party.) Rhode and colleagues (1998) provide many ideas and examples of possible rewards that can serve as Mystery Motivators.

3. *Select rewards that will serve as Mystery Motivators.* Unknown to the students, write the names of the most-preferred rewards on index cards. Create a few additional Mystery Motivators that will be complete surprises to the students—include some fun and silly things, such as the teacher will sing a song chosen by the students, do 25 sit-ups, or wear a wig and funny glasses while teaching a lesson!

4. *Print a big "?" on the outside of an envelope, and seal one of the Mystery Motivator cards inside.* Display the envelope in a conspicuous place in your classroom, for example, taped to the middle of the chalkboard or hung from the ceiling by a string. When students see the envelope, their interest and anticipation for what's inside will build.

5. *Create a device and procedure by which students will reveal the availability of Mystery Motivator.* Spinners and charts with "invisible ink" markers are two effective and motivating ways for students to find out if they will receive a Mystery Motivator.

   a. *Spinners.* Students who meet the criteria for the target behavior gain access to a spinner and a corresponding reward menu (see photo). Each item on the reward menu has a corresponding numbered section on the spinner based on

Students enjoy using the spinner to reveal what reward they or the class will receive.

its relative value to the students. Landing on the larger-sized sections of the spinner gains access to the less-valuable rewards on the menu. When the spinner lands on the smallest slice, which is marked with the "?", the student immediately receives the Mystery Motivator. (Instead of using a spinner, students can roll dice to determine which reward on the menu they will receive.)

b. *Chart and invisible markers.* The method uses a special set of colorful markers that contains a pen that writes in invisible ink and several colorful "developer pens" in different colors that "magically" reveal the invisible writing when rubbed over it. (Crayola® Changeables is a widely available brand of these markers.) Create a simple chart of squares labeled with the days of the week and a bonus square. Using the "ghost writer" pen, mark a "?" in several randomly selected squares. Each day the student meets the performance criteria, he is allowed to select one

of the developer pens and color in that day's square on chart. If a "?" appears, the student receives the Mystery Motivators. Students who meet the performance criteria each day of the week could be allowed to color in a "bonus square" for a chance at another Mystery Motivator as shown here or they could gain access to a spinner and reward menu.

6. *Introduce the program to students.* On the first day of the program, point to the envelope and say, "You're probably wondering what this envelope with the big question mark is all about." Then explain that the students can earn rewards for good behavior including the possibility of the Mystery Motivator. Demonstrate how the spinner or chart works. Describe and model examples and nonexamples of the target behavior and performance criteria. It may be helpful to have students role play the target behaviors.

A key to the success of the program is teacher hype (Rhode et al., 1998). Refer to the Mystery Motivator often ("It's squiggly and really cool!"), but keep its identity a secret. Tell students the Mystery Motivator is something they really want, something you have heard them talking about, something they have told you they would be willing to work for, and so on.

7. *Evaluate the program, and use the data to revise and improve it.* While Mystery Motivator incentive systems are fun for students and teachers alike, they have a serious purpose and should be evaluated in terms of their effects on student behavior and learning. As you would when implementing any new curriculum or instructional method, take data on the students' performance of the target behaviors during the Mystery Motivator program and compare it to their performance levels before the program. Ask students for their opinions and perceptions of the program. Do they like it? Would they like to see changes in the program? Use all of this information to continually evaluate and make improvements in the program's effectiveness.

Get Wild for a Mystery Motivator

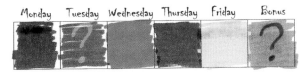

If coloring in a square with the "magic" pen reveals a "?" the student (or group) receives the Mystery Motivator.

Natalie Allen-Williams is a faculty member in the teacher education department at Weber State University. A former teacher of students with emotional and behavioral disorders and program consultant, her research interests include proactive classroom management strategies, functional behavior assessment, and reading strategies for students with EBD. Dr. Allen-Williams appears on the video "Including Students with EBD in General Education" on the Exceptional Teachers DVD.

Go to the Building Teaching Skills section in Chapter 6 of MyEducationLab and complete the activities. As you watch the video and answer the accompanying questions, consider how the Mystery Motivators technique is applied in the classroom.

EDUCATIONAL PLACEMENT ALTERNATIVES

Placement alternatives

Council for Exceptional Children   Content Standards for Beginning Teachers of Students with E/BD: Advantages and disadvantages of placement options and the continuum of services for individuals with E/BD (BD5K1).

Students with emotional or behavioral disorders are served across the continuum of educational placements. During the 2005–2006 school year, approximately 35% of school-age children with emotional or behavioral disorders were educated in general education classrooms, 22% in resource rooms, 27% in separate classrooms, 12% in special schools, and 4% in residential or homebound placements (U.S. Department of Education, 2007). Although the trend in recent years has been for increased placement of students with emotional and behavior disorders in general education classrooms, slightly more than half of all students in this disability category receive their education in separate classrooms, special schools, and residential facilities.

Improving special education services for school-age youths with disabilities in correctional institutions is another important challenge. About 450,000 school-age youths are placed in detention centers or training schools each year in the United States, with another 300,000 sent to adult jails (Leone, Rutherford, & Nelson, 1991). The educational outlook is bleak for juveniles with disabilities who find themselves in jails and detention centers. Although it can be argued that adjudicated delinquents are, by virtue of the behaviors that precipitated their arrest, behaviorally disordered, most juvenile offenders receive few or no special education services (McIntyre, 1993a). Those incarcerated youths who do receive special education services typically receive substandard services (Leone & Meisel, 1997).

The relatively high proportion of students with emotional or behavior disorders who are served in more restrictive settings compared to students in most other disability categories probably reflects the fact that only students with the most severe behavioral problems are identified and served. As a result, most students receiving special education because of emotional or behavioral disorders have serious, long-standing problems that require intensive interventions in highly structured environments (Landrum, Katsiyannis, & Archwamety, 2004). Consistent implementation of the specialized supports and programming needed by these students can be very difficult in the regular classroom (Simpson, 2004).

A major challenge of educating students with emotional or behavioral disorders is arranging an environment in which academic and social skills can be learned at acceptable rates and the safety of all students is protected. Supporters of full inclusion believe that the general education classroom can be made into such an environment for all students with disabilities. Some positive outcomes have been reported for students with emotional or behavioral disorders in general education classrooms. For example, a study comparing middle school students who spent the entire school day in separate classrooms with students who participated in various classes in general education classrooms for at least 1 hour per day found that the students who spent part of the day in regular classrooms had better academic records and better work habits than did the students who spent the entire day in special classes (Meadows, Neel, Scott, & Parker, 1994). Although these results seem to support the contention that students with emotional or behavioral disorders should be educated in general education classrooms, the authors point out that the students included in the general education classrooms did not exhibit the extreme aggression, lack of self-control, or degree of withdrawal that the students who stayed in the separate classrooms did. They also noted that placement in general education classrooms typically represents "a major reduction, . . . if not a complete cessation, of differential programming" (p. 178). That is, the general education teachers did not make instructional or management accommodations to meet the needs of the students with behavior problems. Without specialized instruction or accommodations, it is hard to imagine how students with severe emotional or behavioral disorders would receive an appropriate education in the general education classroom.

While supporting the education of students with emotional or behavioral disorders in the general education classroom when their individual needs can be met, the CCBD does

A major challenge of educating students with emotional or behavioral disorders is arranging an environment in which academic and social skills can be learned at acceptable rates.

not believe that the general education classroom is the most appropriate placement for all students with emotional and behavioral disorders.

> CCBD supports a full continuum of mental health and special education services for children and youth with emotional or behavioral disorders. We believe that educational decisions depend on individual student needs. Consequently, . . . CCBD does not support the notion that all . . . students with emotional or behavioral disorders are always best served in general education classrooms. (CCBD, 1993, p. 1)

Meticulous planning, coordination, and support needed are often unavailable to make inclusion effective. When an IEP team makes the decision to place a student with emotional or behavioral disorders in a general education classroom or to transition a student from a more restrictive setting to the general education classroom, it is imperative that the student and the general education teacher be prepared before and supported after the placement. Preparation includes identifying the social and academic expectations in the general education classroom, assessing the student's current social and academic skills against those expectations, teaching the student additional skills needed to meet those expectations, and in-service training for the teacher on special techniques of behavior management (Meier, DiPerna, & Oster, 2006; Nelson, 2000). Support following the general class placement should include a crisis intervention support plan and ongoing consultation and in-class modeling and intervention by a special educator trained to work with students with behavioral disorders (Shapiro, Miller, Swaka, Gardill, & Handler, 1999; Simpson, 2006; Walker et al., 2005).

CHALLENGES, ACHIEVEMENTS, AND ADVOCACY

Special education for students with emotional or behavioral disorders faces a number of critical and ongoing issues. A continuing concern of many advocates for children with emotional or behavioral disorders is revising the federal definition of this disability so that all children with emotional and behavioral problems that adversely affect their educational performance are eligible for special education.

Despite public concern over school safety and youth violence and widespread recognition that antisocial behavior is a chronic disabling condition that exacts tremendous social and financial costs for society, we do little to prevent it. Instead of intervening early when problems are small and more likely to respond to intervention, we wait until children are older and their antisocial behavior is well established and much more difficult to change (Kauffman, 1999). The knowledge and tools for early detection and prevention are available (e.g., Sprague & Walker, 2000; Strain & Timm, 2001). What is needed is the national resolve and commitment of resources sufficient for a large-scale program of early detection and prevention.

The issues presented here are not new. Most have been recognized, discussed, and debated for decades. And each will likely remain problems well into the future. Many other issues and problems could be added to the list (Katsiyannis & Yell, 2004; Polsgrove & Ochoa, 2004). Although the challenges faced by those who work with and advocate for students with emotional or behavioral disorders appear daunting and unrelenting, the field has experienced significant advances and successes to help guide the future.

For example, the field has identified specific program components and instructional practices that, when used in combination, are likely to result in successful outcomes for students with emotional or behavioral disorders (Dunlap et al., 2006; Lewis et al., 2004). Many of those achievements and best practices have been described in this chapter. We must now work diligently to close the gap between what is known about effective special education for students with emotional or behavioral disorders and what those students experience each day in the classroom.

For a review of some achievements in the field by George Sugai, one of our leading researchers and contributors to the education of children with emotional or behavioral disorders, see Current Issues and Future Trends, "Teaching Students with Emotional and Behavioral Disorders: Then and Now."

To learn more about how general and special education teachers work together to support the inclusion of students with emotional and behavioral disorders, go to the Homework & Exercises section in Chapter 6 on MyEducationLab and complete Homework Exercise 10.

CURRENT ISSUES AND FUTURE TRENDS

TEACHING STUDENTS WITH EMOTIONAL AND BEHAVIORAL DISORDERS: THEN AND NOW

BY GEORGE SUGAI

When I began teaching students with emotional and behavioral disorders (EBD) in the 1970s, I relied on a relatively small set of behavioral tools: (a) token economies, (b) precision teaching, (c) behavioral contracting, (d) social skills instruction, (e) continuous progress monitoring, and (f) direct instruction. Since then the basic tools have not changed dramatically, except for some important empirical and application tweaks to make them workable in different contexts. These enhancements included, for example, functional behavioral assessment, explicit social skills instruction, precorrections, curriculum-based measurement, and comprehensive person-centered planning.

So, although I believe that the behavioral and academic interventions that we consider trustworthy and effective today have not changed significantly since the 1970s, I believe that how we educate students with EBD is noticeably different from and better than my early teaching experiences (Kauffman, 2005). These advances are more systemic than they are intervention- or practice-related, and I describe them in six general ways:

1. Public Law 94-142 and IDEA significantly increased the level of *accountability* for doing the "right things" for kids with EBD and their families (Yell, Shriner, & Katsiyannis, 2006). All of the following advances have increased the likelihood that students with EBD get what they need when and where then need it: the use of data to guide decision making (e.g., functional behavioral assessments); the selection of interventions based on these data (e.g., behavioral intervention plans and supports); high priority for targeting educationally important, immediate and long-term student needs (e.g., short- and long-term objectives); regular progress monitoring and reviews; and institutionalized due process safeguards.

2. Rather than reacting to problem behavior, educators today are giving higher priority to *preventing* the development and triggering of problem behavior (Greenberg et al., 2003). It is no longer acceptable or effective to develop a plan that is limited to excluding or punishing students who engage in problem behaviors. In fact, the research evidence suggests that a "get tough" only approach actually exacerbates the problem and has negative side effects (e.g., reduced academic achievement, negative interpersonal relationships, increases in antisocial behavior) (Mayer, 1996; Walker et al., 2005). Prevention is about redesigning teaching and learning environments to remove triggers for antisocial behavior, to add prompts for desirable behavior, to eliminate consequences that maintain problem behavior, and to increase consequences that support or strengthen the occurrence of prosocial behavior (Crone & Horner, 2003).

3. The recent introduction of the school-wide positive behavior support (PBS) logic has helped schools be more effective and efficient in how they organize and use behavioral interventions (Safran & Oswald, 2003). Using a continuum of behavior support as the basic template, interventions are organized into three basic interrelated tiers (Horner, Sugai, & Lewis-Palmer, 2005). Primary-tier interventions are implemented by all staff across all school settings with all students. Secondary-tier interventions are established for those students who do not respond to or benefit from the primary-tier interventions, and who benefit from smaller instructional grouping where greater attention and engagement can be provided. Tertiary-tier interventions are intensive supports specially designed for those students who do not benefit from primary- and secondary-tier interventions. These interventions are usually intensive and implemented individually.

4. Although a *data-based problem-solving approach* has been available for many years, its emphasis and applications have increased dramatically through the logic of the *responsiveness-to-intervention (RTI)* process (Kame'enui, 2007). RTI has enhanced the three-tiered continuum of support by emphasizing the use of (a) empirically supported instruction and interventions, (b) direct measures of student performance as indicators of student performance, (c) regular and early universal screening to identify

students who are not responding to instruction or interventions, (d) calibrated data-decision rules for guiding decisions about responsiveness, and (e) a continuum of increasingly more specialized interventions to support students who are not responsive to a given instruction or intervention (Gresham, 2005). RTI has the potential to further refine the effectiveness, efficiency, and relevance of our instructional and intervention decisions, and to screen better for those students whose behaviors might be characterized as EBD.

5. Educating students with EBD is no longer a single-system or -discipline endeavor, and the participation of relevant and valued supports from multiple entities is considered more effective and comprehensive. These *systems, or communities, of care* are often school-based and involve the family and student in a wraparound process in which relevant others (e.g., extended family members, public and mental health workers, community outreach advocates, physicians) work together to develop the most comprehensive person-centered plan possible that addresses the wide range of immediate and long-term needs and objectives of the child and family (Scott & Eber, 2003).

6. A final advancement is the increased emphasis on the *systemic supports* necessary to maximize the accurate and sustainable implementation of an effective intervention and the durability of student outcomes (Sugai, Horner, & McIntosh, in press). This systems perspective focuses on intervention selection and implementation by school leadership teams, the role of administrators in leading and guiding the implementation effort, the use of information or data to guide intervention decision making, and organizational supports (e.g., prompts, reinforcers, professional development) that educators need to accurately use a particular intervention or instructional strategy. At the district level, the interactive roles of policy, visibility, funding, coaching/facilitation, coordination, and evaluation are also important for supporting sustained school-level implementation of effective interventions and instruction (Sugai & Horner, 2006).

In conclusion, the work I now do in personnel preparation and research for students with EBD looks remarkably similar to my early teaching experiences in that effective instructional and behavioral tools are essentially the same in form and function. However, what differs remarkably is the increased attention toward systems-level effectiveness and efficiency. In particular, prevention has become a much more important emphasis, notably along a continuum of behavioral support that organizes effective interventions into primary-, secondary-, and tertiary-tier interventions. The use of this continuum is enhanced through the RTI approach, which defines and operationalizes how to examine student behavior in the context of a given intervention and make timely and informed instructional decisions. Finally, the effectiveness of a given intervention is only as good as the fidelity with which that intervention is implemented. As a result, attention to classroom, school and district structures has increased to support implementers. Although onerous at times, federal and state policies are setting the expectations and levels of accountability for doing the best and right thing for students with EBD and their families.

Teaching students with EBD in the 1970s was an exciting and important time in my life, and we had excellent tools for the job. Since then, I have learned that good tools are necessary but not sufficient. To obtain optimal results, we have to be smart about what we use, how we organize what we do, how we use information to make good decisions about what we need to do, and what supports we can put in place to support those who are doing the work. It is a good time to be an educator of students with EBD. And tomorrow will be even better.

What Do You Think?

1. Which of the six advances identified by the author do you think has had the most significant effect on the education of students with EBD? Why?

2. In what ways are the rationale, basic structures, and operations of PBS and RTI similar?

3. What do you think will be the most important advance in educating students with emotional and behavioral disorders in the next 10 or 20 years?

George Sugai is the Carole J. Neag Endowed Chair in Behavior Disorders at the University of Connecticut and Co-Director of the National Center on Positive Behavioral Interventions & Supports, funded by the U.S. Office of Special Education. Dr. Sugai's research interests include effective applications of applied behavior analysis principles, function-based support of problem behavior, and school-wide PBS.

TIPS for Beginning Teachers

WORKING WITH STUDENTS WITH EMOTIONAL AND BEHAVIORAL DISORDERS
by Kimberly Rich

BE CONSISTENT

Students learn to trust you as you are consistent with them.

- *Set up class procedures and expectations clearly right from the beginning.* Have students repeat these at the beginning of each day, reminding them what you expect from them.
- *If students earn a privilege, make sure they get it.*
- *If students lose a privilege, make sure they lose it.*

USE YOUR SENSE OF HUMOR

It is very difficult to work with students who have many academic and behavior needs.

- *Laugh at yourself from time to time.* Your students need to see you enjoying yourself.
- *Create a Sunshine folder.* Collect great thoughts or things students have given to you that put a smile on your face. When you've had a rough day, pull the folder out.

STAY IN CONTROL

When in control in stressful situations, you are providing a positive role model for your students.

- *Never take personally anything students do or say when they are escalated.* Know they are lashing out at you because you are there.
- *When you make a mistake with a student, and you will, apologize.* For example, yesterday, another staff member gave James permission to go to the bathroom. I stopped James as he was walking out of the door and told him he was not allowed to leave the classroom without permission. Then my staff member told me James had asked for and received permission from her. I immediately apologized to James for stopping him and then praised him for asking permission the correct way.

EACH DAY SPEND TIME WITH YOUR STUDENTS IN A NONACADEMIC SITUATION

Spending time with your students in nonacademic settings and situations will strengthen your relationship with them.

- *Join your students on the playground.* You will learn many things about your students from the way they interact with others and their conversations. You will also be much more approachable to your students.
- *Eat lunch with your students.* The conversations that you will have will teach you about their likes and dislikes, how their night before went, what their morning was like, and what things they hope for themselves.

PURCHASE A DIGITAL TIMER

Using a digital timer throughout the day requires you to be honest about "time," especially as it relates to monitoring task completion and transitions. A timer frees you from having to guess how much time has passed since you directed students to begin or change tasks.

- *You can use a timer to measure academic progress such as repeated readings or math timings.*
- *Use it to implement behavior expectations.* Give students a specific time frame to complete a task or assignment.
- *Use it to decrease transition time.* For example, give 1 minute for all students to have their desk cleaned off.

KEY TERMS AND CONCEPTS

ABC recording, p. 232
behavioral intervention plan (BIP), p. 230
duration (of behavior), p. 231
emotional disturbance, p. 214
emotional or behavioral disorders, p. 215
externalizing behaviors, p. 215
frequency (or rate) (of behavior), p. 231
functional analysis, p. 232
functional behavioral assessment, p. 230
group contingencies, p. 242
internalizing behaviors, p. 216

latency (of behavior), p. 231
level system, p. 241
magnitude (of behavior), p. 231
multiple gating screening, p. 229
projective test, p. 230
self-evaluation, p. 239
self-management, p. 239
self-monitoring, p. 239
temperament, p. 225
token economy, p. 241
topography (of behavior), p. 231

SUMMARY

Definitions

- No single, widely used definition of emotional and behavioral disorders exists. Most definitions require a child's behavior to differ markedly (extremely) and chronically (over time) from current social or cultural norms.
- Many leaders in the field do not like the definition of "emotional disturbance" in IDEA because students who are "socially maladjusted" are not eligible for special education services.
- The CCBD proposed a definition of emotional or behavioral disorders as a disability characterized by "behavioral or emotional responses in school programs so different from appropriate age, cultural, or ethnic norms that they adversely affect educational performance" (*Federal Register*, February 10, 1993, p. 7938).

Characteristics

- Children with externalizing problems frequently exhibit antisocial behavior; many become delinquents as adolescents.
- Children with internalizing problems are overly withdrawn and lack social skills needed to interact effectively with others.
- As a group, students with emotional or behavioral disorders perform academically 1 or more years below grade level.
- A large number of students with emotional or behavioral disorders also have learning disabilities and/or language delays.
- On the average, students with emotional or behavioral disorders score slightly below average on IQ tests.
- Many students with emotional or behavioral disorders have difficulty developing and maintaining interpersonal relationships.
- About one third of students with emotional or behavioral disorders are arrested during their school years.

Prevalence

- Estimates of the prevalence of behavioral disorders vary tremendously. Credible studies indicate that 3% to 10% have emotional and behavioral problems that warrant intervention.
- Far fewer children with emotional or behavioral disorders are receiving special education than the most conservative prevalence estimates.

Causes

- Biological factors related to development of behavioral disorders include brain disorders, genetics, and temperament.

- Environmental etiologic factors occur in the home, school, and community.
- Although knowledge of causes is necessary for planning and implementing prevention programs, effective intervention and treatment of children's existing behavior problems do not require precise knowledge of etiology.

Identification and Assessment

- Systematic screening should be conducted as early as possible to identify children who are at risk for developing serious patterns of antisocial behavior.
- Most screening instruments consist of behavior rating scales or checklists that are completed by teachers, parents, peers, and/or children themselves.
- Projective tests may yield interesting results, but they are rarely useful in planning and implementing interventions.
- Direct observation and measurement of specific problem behaviors within the classroom can indicate whether and for which behaviors intervention is needed. Five measurable dimensions of behavior are rate, duration, latency, topography, and magnitude.
- Functional behavioral assessment (FBA) is a systematic process for gathering information to discover a problem behavior's function, or purpose, for the student. Two major types of behavioral functions of problem behaviors are (a) to get something the student wants (positive reinforcement), and (b) to avoid or escape something the student doesn't want (negative reinforcement).
- Results of FBA can point to the design of an appropriate and effective behavior intervention plan (BIP).

Educational Approaches

- Students with emotional or behavioral disorders require systematic instruction in social skills and academics.
- School-wide systems of positive behavior support teach appropriate behavior to all students in the school.
- A good classroom management system uses proactive strategies to create a positive, supportive, and noncoercive environment that promotes prosocial behavior and academic achievement.
- Self-management skills can help students develop control over their environment, responsibility for their actions, and self-direction.
- Group process approaches use the influence of the peer group to help students with emotional or behavioral disorders learn to behave appropriately.
- Two important affective traits for teachers of students with emotional or behavioral disorders are differential acceptance and empathetic relationship.
- Teachers should concentrate their resources and energies on alterable variables—those things in a student's environment that the teacher can influence that make a difference in student learning and behavior.

Educational Placement Alternatives

- About one in three students with emotional or behavioral disorders is educated in general education classrooms.
- Although the trend in recent years has been for increased placement of students with emotional and behavior disorders in general education classrooms, 43% of all students in this disability category receive their education in separate classrooms, special schools, and residential facilities.
- Comparing the behavioral and academic progress of students with emotional or behavioral disorders in different educational placements in an effort to determine which setting is the best is difficult because students with milder disabilities are included first and more often, whereas those students who exhibit more severe behavioral disturbances tend to remain in more restrictive placements.
- When a student with emotional or behavioral disorders is placed in a general education classroom, it is imperative that the student and the general education teacher be prepared before and supported after the placement.

Challenges, Achievements, and Advocacy

- Two of the most pressing challenges for the field of emotional or behavioral disorders are (a) ensuring that all students with emotional or behavioral problems that adversely affect their educational performance receive special education services, and (b) developing large-scale programs of early detection and prevention.

- Although the basic behavioral and academic interventions for students with emotional or behavioral disorders have been available for several decades, advances in how educators apply those tools at the systems level are improving success rates. (See Current Issues and Future Trends, "Teaching Students With Emotional and Behavioral Disorders: Then and Now" in this chapter.)

 Now go to MyEducationLab at www.myeducationlab.com, and take the pretest to assess your initial comprehension of chapter content. Once you have taken the pretest, use your individualized Study Plan for Chapter 6 to enhance your understanding of the concepts discussed in the chapter. Finally, take the posttest to assess your comprehension of Chapter 6 content.

Autism Spectrum Disorders

FOCUS QUESTIONS

- How are the two major subtypes of autism spectrum disorders—autistic disorder and Asperger syndrome—defined and differentiated from one another?
- How might some of the behaviors characteristic of autism spectrum disorders become assets for the child as a learner?
- What factors might account for the enormous increase in the prevalence of autism spectrum disorders in recent years?
- How have etiologic theories and the search for causes of autism changed from the first reports of the disability to today?
- Why are research and development of tools for early screening and diagnosis of autism spectrum disorders so critical?
- What skills are most important for teachers of children with autism spectrum disorders?
- What features of an educational environment (a general education classroom, resource room, or special class) will enable a child with autism spectrum disorders to benefit optimally from placement in that setting?
- Why are fads and unproven interventions so prevalent in the education and treatment of children with autism?

FEATURED TEACHERS

KAZUKO KITO AND BETH MUENINGHOFF
Winterset Elementary School, Columbus, Ohio

Kazuko Kito

Beth Mueninghoff

Education—Teaching Credentials—Experience
Kazuko Kito

- B.S. and M.A., special education, The Ohio State University, 1995 and 1998
- Ohio certificates in Education of Developmentally Handicapped (K–12), Multiply Handicapped (K–12), and Early Education of the Handicapped
- 5 years as a primary-grade resource room teacher for students with high-incidence disabilities and 4 years teaching in a special needs preschool

Education—Teaching Credentials—Experience
Beth Mueninghoff

- B.A., psychology, Western Kentucky University, 1988
- Special education certification program in multiple/severe disabilities, Ohio Dominican University, 2000
- Ohio certificates in Education of Developmentally Handicapped (K–12) and Multiply Handicapped (K–12)
- 7 years as special education teacher; 13 years teaching self-help skills to adults with disabilities in residential settings

Our School, Classrooms, and Students Winterset Elementary is an urban, public school with an enrollment of about 280 culturally and socioeconomically diverse children in grades K–5.

Kazuko: My special needs preschool classroom is a full-day unit for 4- and 5-year-olds with multiple disabilities. This year, five of my seven students have a diagnosis of autism spectrum disorders. Two students come from families whose native language is Somali and who have significant communication delays in English and in their first language.

Beth: I teach one of our school's two primary special education classes. My students are 6 to 9 years old in grades K–2. Three students come from homes in which Arabic, Spanish, or Somali, is spoken. The socioeconomic level of my students ranges from poverty level to middle class. Seven of my eight students this year have a diagnosis of autism. All of my students have communication/speech needs and receive support services from a speech pathologist. Some of my students talk; others are nonverbal. There are many different skill levels in the room. For example, MaryAnn is a kindergartener with severe communication delays and is taught in my classroom for the entire day. She works on social skills such as following directions, and she also works on academic skills such as letter and number identification and counting. Javan, who has the most advanced social and communication skills among my students, attends general education kindergarten classes for reading, music, library, and physical education. One of my teaching assistants accompanies Javan in his general education classes to help him with appropriate social skills, such as following directions. Javan's academic performance is nearly at grade level, but he needs assistance to learn to function socially with typically developing peers.

Teaching Strategies   I have found that several teaching strategies or methods are consistently effective with our the students, as described here:

Visual Supports   Many children with autism have difficulties comprehending spoken language but respond well to visual stimuli. Picture cards are one way to make words and abstract concepts more concrete. We place picture cards all around our classrooms to help the children learn vocabulary (e.g., "shelf"), directions (e.g., "first-then"), and classroom expectations (e.g., "quiet").

Picture cards can provide an alternative method of communication for a nonverbal child or reluctant speaker. In some instances, systematic pairing of picture cards with spoken language eventually evokes speech from a nonverbal or reluctant child.

Picture cards can also be incorporated into interventions for problem behavior. Sometimes the more you speak to a child who is having a tantrum, the more the child's behavior escalates into a real meltdown. Using the picture cards seems to help the child deescalate, reminding him of the appropriate behaviors. Kazuko calmly holds up "quiet" and "stop" picture cards in front of a tantruming child and models those behaviors. She consistently, from the first day of school in the fall, reinforces the children's exhibits of self-control.

Picture activity schedules are another effective instructional tool. Many children with autism function more independently and successfully when visual supports provide some predictabilities in their environment. Having a visual schedule seems to give them a sense of security and control. It also lets them know what comes next so that transitions from one activity to another are not so difficult.

Modeling, Frequent Opportunities to Respond, and Reinforcement   Our children have difficulty acquiring and generalizing new skills to the extent in which those skills become meaningful and useful to them. The children need to be provided with multiple and repeated opportunities to practice whatever they are learning.

Telling a student with autism what to do is often ineffective. Instead of saying, "Javan, stop bothering MaryAnn and wait for your turn" and expecting him to understand and comply, we demonstrate exactly what the desired behavior looks like, by sitting up straight, putting our hands together, being quiet, watching the child whose turn it is, and so forth. Immediately after modeling the skill, we have the student imitate it. Then we follow up with numerous opportunities to practice the skill in meaningful contexts across sessions. We "catch them being good," stop, and reinforce, reinforce, reinforce. It may seem like common sense, but we continually remind ourselves of these basic but important strategies.

Functional Analysis and Problem Solving   Some children with autism sometimes present challenging behaviors such as self-stimulating behaviors, extreme and long-lasting temper tantrums, aggression toward others, and even self-injury. One of our most important roles as special education teachers is to be problem solvers. We work as a team, and with the help of our instructional assistants, we assess the environment and identify what antecedent conditions or events may be triggering the problem behavior and what consequence may be sustaining it. We are fortunate to have three other special education teachers in our school. We often brainstorm as a group to create effective interventions for a child's problem behavior. It is also important to teach the child an alternative appropriate behavior and reinforce it while trying to decrease the inappropriate behavior.

Teaching Philosophies Kazuko: "It is better to light candles than to curse the darkness." I don't know who said this, but it has been my guiding philosophy since the day I heard it. Teaching a child with autism is no easy task, and one can be easily overwhelmed by the enormity of a child's skills deficits and behavioral excesses. Every child has a set of skills, or strengths, and it is our job is to find those strengths and build on them. I constantly ask myself three questions: "What can this child do now?" "What is the next step?" and "Where do I want to see this child at the end of the school year?" Continually asking and answering these questions helps me develop purposeful, goal-oriented lesson plans and activities that meet each child's current skills.

Beth: I begin with having high expectations for my students. I believe all students can learn and that we just need to tap into what motivates each student to achieve his highest level of performance. We need to teach the students the power of choice, no matter how simple the choice. I give my students many opportunities to make choices throughout the day. I observe their choices, and then I use those choices to motivate them to learn.

Although we both have much more to learn about teaching children with special needs, we each feel good about where we are in our careers as special education teachers. There are some difficult days when I feel like quitting, and yet, I honestly think this is one of the most rewarding jobs we could have. When we step back and see how far our students have come, we know that what we are doing is making a real difference in their lives.

To learn more about the strategies Ms. Kito and Ms. Meuninghoff use in their classrooms, go to the Homework and Exercises section in Chapter 7 of MyEducationLab and complete Homework Exercise 1.

Autism is an intriguing, fascinating, and "baffling" childhood disorder (Simpson, 2001, p. 68). It can also be one of the most frightening, exhausting, and heartbreaking experiences for the parents and families of children affected with the condition. Until recently, the prognosis for children with autism was extremely poor, with problems of daily living persisting into adulthood and requiring intensive supervision and supports for more than 90% of individuals (Bristol et al., 1996; Matson, 1994). On the brighter side, however, a great deal of exciting and promising research is producing better futures for many children and young adults with autism and their families.

The field of autism has undergone enormous changes in recent years; and the condition has moved from being a relatively unrecognized disability, even within the field of special education, to one of widespread interest in education and society in general. Still, much remains unknown about the disability. Richard Simpson (2004), who, like most people, was "both fascinated and spellbound" (p. 137) by children with autism when he first began working with them more than 30 years ago, has written:

> In spite of the extraordinary recent media coverage and other attention that autism has received, it continues to have the same mystique that it had when I first entered the field. That is, in spite of significant advancements in treating and understanding individuals with autism spectrum disorders, the disability remains a mystery. Even when viewed through a disability lens, individuals with ASD are a particularly challenging and enigmatic group. (p. 138)

After reading this chapter, complete the pretest for Chapter 7 on MyEducationLab to assess your initial understanding of chapter content.

DEFINITIONS

Autism is a neurobehavioral syndrome marked by qualitative impairments of social interaction and communication, and by restricted, repetitive, and stereotyped patterns of behavior. Leo Kanner, a psychiatrist at Johns Hopkins Hospital in Baltimore, was the first to describe and name the condition when he published case reports on a group of 11 children in 1943. He wrote that the children displayed behaviors that differed "so markedly and uniquely from anything reported so far, that each case merits . . . a detailed consideration of its fascinating peculiarities" (Kanner, 1943/1985, p. 11). The children he described shared the following characteristics:

- Difficulty relating to others in a typical manner
- Extreme aloneness that seemed to isolate the child from the outside world
- Resistance to being picked up or held by parents
- Significant speech deficits, including mutism and echolalia
- In some cases, very good rote memory
- Early specific food preferences
- Obsessive desire for repetition and sameness
- Bizarre, repetitive behavior such as rocking back and forth
- Lack of imagination, few spontaneous behaviors such as typical play
- Normal physical appearance

Kanner called this condition *early infantile autism.*

Definition of Autism in IDEA

When Congress reauthorized IDEA in 1990 (P.L. 101–476), autism was added as a disability category under which children were entitled to special education. IDEA defines the disability as follows:

(i) *Autism* means a developmental disability affecting verbal and nonverbal communication and social interaction, generally evident before age three, that adversely affects a child's educational performance. Other characteristics often associated with autism are engagement in repetitive activities and stereotyped movements, resistance to environmental change or change in daily routines, and unusual responses to sensory experiences.

(ii) Autism does not apply if a child's educational performance is adversely affected primarily because the child has a serious emotional disturbance as defined in paragraph (c)(4) of this section.

(iii) A child who manifests the characteristics of autism after age three could be identified as having autism if the criteria in paragraph (c)(1)(i) of this section are satisfied. (34 C.F.R., Part 300 §300.8[c][1][i–iii] [August 14, 2006])

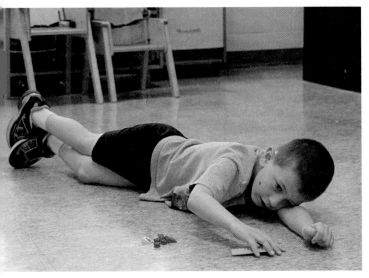

A child with autism spectrum disorders might focus his attention on one object or activity for hours.

Definition of Autism in the DSM-IV

Most children receiving special education and related services under the IDEA disability category of autism have received a diagnosis of one of five disorders of childhood subsumed under the umbrella term *pervasive developmental disorder (PDD)* in the *Diagnostic and Statistical Manual of Mental Disorders, Fourth Edition (DSM-IV)* published by the American Psychiatric Association (2000a). Instead of PDD, most professionals now use the term **autism spectrum disorders (ASD)** to refer to this related group of conditions (Volkmar & Pauls, 2003). The five subtypes of ASD are autistic disorder; Asperger syndrome; Rett syndrome; childhood disintegrative disorder; and pervasive developmental disorder—not otherwise specified (PDD-NOS). These related disorders are differentiated from one another primarily by the age of onset and the severity of various symptoms.

Autistic Disorder   **Autistic disorder** is marked by three defining features with onset before age 3: (1) qualitative impairment of social interaction (e.g., lack of social or emotional reciprocity); (2) qualitative impairment of communication (e.g., delay or total absence of spoken language); and (3) restricted, repetitive, and stereotyped patterns of behavior, interests, and activities (e.g., persistent preoccupation with parts of objects). The combination of behavioral deficits (e.g., inability to relate to others, lack of functional language) and behavioral excesses (e.g., self-stimulation, bizarre and challenging behaviors) makes children with "classic autism" stand out as strikingly different from most children. Figure 7.1 shows the DSM-IV diagnostic criteria for autistic disorder.

The parents of 21 children diagnosed with autism reported that the average age of their child when the parents first recognized something was wrong was 15 months (Hutton & Caron, 2005). The changes in behavior associated with autism may be gradual or quite sudden, as shown in the following parent's account reported by Fleischmann (2004):

It wasn't a gradual change that happened. It was an Invasion of the Body Snatchers experience. One day he looked the same and that's the only way I recognized him. He no longer made eye contact, spoke, sang, interacted. . . . He screamed and cried and stayed awake and stomped and hid under mattresses and pillows and ate dirt. (p. 39)

Asperger Syndrome   At the mild end of the autism spectrum is **Asperger syndrome.** Although recognized descriptions of Asperger syndrome vary somewhat, the most distinctive feature is impairments in all social areas, particularly an inability to understand how to interact socially. Children with Asperger syndrome do not have general language

FIGURE 7.1

A. A total of six (or more) items from (1), (2), and (3), with at least two from (1), and one each from (2) and (3):

1. Qualitative impairment in social interaction, as manifested by at least two of the following:
   a. Marked impairment in the use of multiple nonverbal behaviors such as eye-to-eye gaze, facial expression, body postures, and gestures to regulate social interaction.
   b. Failure to develop peer relationships appropriate to developmental level.
   c. A lack of spontaneous seeking to share enjoyment, interests, or achievements with other people (e.g., by a lack of showing, bringing, or pointing out objects of interest).
   d. Lack of social or emotional reciprocity.

2. Qualitative impairments in communication as manifested by at least one of the following:
   a. Delay in, or total lack of, the development of spoken language (not accompanied by an attempt to compensate through alternative modes of communication such as gestures or mime).
   b. In individuals with adequate speech, marked impairments in the ability to initiate or sustain a conversation with others.
   c. Stereotyped and repetitive use of language or idiosyncratic language.
   d. Lack of varied, spontaneous make-believe play or social imitative play appropriate to developmental level.

3. Restricted repetitive and stereotyped patterns of behavior, interests, and activities, as manifested by at least one of the following:
   a. Encompassing preoccupation with one or more stereotypic and restricted patterns of interest that is abnormal either in intensity or focus.
   b. Apparently inflexible adherence to specific, nonfunctional routines or rituals.
   c. Stereotypic and repetitive motor mannerisms (e.g., hand or finger flapping or twisting, or complex whole-body movements).
   d. Persistent preoccupation with parts of objects.

B. Delays or abnormal functioning in at least one of the following areas, with onset prior to age 3 years: (1) social interaction, (2) language as used in social communication, or (3) symbolic or imaginative play.

C. The disturbance is not better accounted for by Rett's Disorder or Childhood Disintegrative Disorder.

FIGURE 7.1

DSM-IV diagnostic criteria for autistic disorder

Source: Reprinted from American Psychiatric Association. (2000). *Diagnostic and statistical manual of mental disorders* (4th ed., text rev., p. 75). Washington, DC: Author.

delay, and most have average or above-average intelligence. Figure 7.2 shows the DSM-IV diagnostic criteria for Asperger syndrome.

Following are other characteristics exhibited by many individuals with Asperger syndrome (Attwood, 2006; Barnhill, 2007; Myles & Simpson, 2001; Ritvo, 2006; Safran, 2001; Simpson, 2007; Winter-Messiers et al., 2007):

- Repetitive and stereotyped behaviors, perseveration
- Intense interest in a particular subject, often atypical things or parts of things (e.g., tractors or washing-machine motors), to the exclusion of everything else
- Preoccupation with one's own interests
- Clumsiness, difficulty with fine- and/or gross-motor activities
- Impaired use of nonverbal behaviors related to social interaction such as eye gaze, facial expression, body posture, and gestures
- Inflexible adherence to routines
- Fascination with maps, globes, and routes

FIGURE 7.2

DSM-IV diagnostic criteria for Asperger syndrome

Source: Reprinted from American Psychiatric Association. (2000). *Diagnostic and statistical manual of mental disorders* (4th ed., text rev., p. 84). Washington, DC: Author.

A. Qualitative impairment in social interaction, as manifested by at least two of the following:
  (1) Marked impairments in the use of multiple nonverbal behaviors such as eye-to-eye gaze, facial expression, body postures, and gestures to regulate social interaction
  (2) Failure to develop peer relationships appropriate to developmental level
  (3) A lack of spontaneous seeking to share enjoyment, interests, or achievements with other people (e.g., by a lack of showing, bringing, or pointing out objects of interest to other people)
  (4) Lack of social or emotional reciprocity

B. Restricted repetitive and stereotyped patterns of behavior, interests, and activities, as manifested by at least one of the following:
  (1) Encompassing preoccupation with one or more stereotyped and restricted patterns of interest that is abnormal either in intensity or focus
  (2) Apparently inflexible adherence to specific, nonfunctional routines or rituals
  (3) Stereotyped and repetitive motor mannerisms (e.g., hand or finger flapping or twisting, or complex whole-body movements)
  (4) Persistent preoccupation with parts of objects

C. The disturbance causes clinically significant impairment in social, occupational, or other important areas of functioning.

D. There is no clinically significant general delay in language (e.g., single words used by age 2 years, communicative phrases used by age 3 years).

E. There is no clinically significant delay in cognitive development or in the development of age-appropriate self-help skills, adaptive behavior (other than social interaction), and curiosity about the environment in childhood.

F. Criteria are not met for another specific pervasive developmental disorder or schizophrenia.

- Superior rote memory, tendency to amass many related facts
- Difficulty judging personal space
- Speech and language impairments in the areas of semantics, pragmatics, and prosody (volume, intonation, inflection, and rhythm); pedantic, odd speech patterns; formal style of speaking
- Difficulty understanding others' feelings
- Extensive vocabulary, reading commences at an early age (*hyperlexia*)
- Perfectionist, frustrated when asked to submit work one feels is below standard

Their peculiarities and social skills deficits make it difficult for children with Asperger syndrome to develop and maintain friendships. Because they have average or above-average intelligence and often are highly verbal, students with Asperger syndrome are sometimes misdiagnosed or considered slackers by teachers and peers.

Rett Syndrome **Rett syndrome** is a distinct neurological condition that begins between 5 and 30 months of age following an apparently normal early infancy. The baby's head growth slows, purposeful use of the hands is replaced with stereotypic hand movements (e.g., wringing and mouthing); a gradual onset of unsteadiness and awkward gait occurs, and severe impairments in language and cognitive abilities ensue. Seizures are common. Rett syndrome primarily affects girls. Although it is on the ASD continuum, Rett syndrome is considered to be a distinct neurological condition.

Childhood Disintegrative Disorder **Childhood disintegrative disorder** shares behavioral characteristics with autistic disorder, but the condition does not begin until after age 2 and sometimes not until the child has reached age 10. Medical complications are common, and the prognosis for significant improvement is usually very poor.

Pervasive Developmental Disorder—Not Otherwise Specified (PDD-NOS) Children who meet some, but not all, of the qualitative or quantitative criteria for autistic disorder are often diagnosed as having **pervasive developmental disorder—not otherwise specified (PDD-NOS).** All children with PDD-NOS have significant impairments in socialization with difficulties in either communication or restricted interests. The boundaries for PDD-NOS are not well defined, and children with socialization problems as the result of other conditions may be misdiagnosed.

Several studies have found that the majority of children diagnosed with Asperger syndrome also meet the diagnostic criteria for autism (Howlin, 2003; Tryon, Mayes, Rhodes, & Waldo, 2006); a finding that supports Wing's (1998) contention that "Asperger syndrome and high-functioning autism are not distinct conditions" (p. 23). The term *autism spectrum disorders* reflects a consensus in the field that the social and communication impairments fall on a spectrum, or continuum, of severity, with autistic disorder representing the most severe form and Asperger disorder representing the mildest form. And as Wing (1992), noted, the social and communication impairments at the mildest end of the spectrum "shade into the eccentric end of the wide range of normal behavior" (p. 138).

CHARACTERISTICS

As we look at the most commonly observed characteristics of children with autism spectrum disorders, remember these important points: Some children on the spectrum are very severely affected in most or all domains of functioning, while others are only mildly affected. Considerable overlap of the conditions along the spectrum occurs, meaning that children with different diagnoses may share many characteristics. On the other hand, two children with the same diagnosis may be affected in markedly different ways. "There is no single behavior that is always typical of autism and no behavior that would automatically exclude an individual child from a diagnosis of autism" (National Research Council, 2001, p. 11).

Characteristics of autism

 Content Standards for Beginning Teachers—INDEP CURR: Psychological and social-emotional characteristics of individuals with disabilities (IC2K4) (also, CC2K2).

Impaired Social Relationships

Many children with ASD have difficulty perceiving the emotional state of others, expressing emotions, and forming attachments and relationships. Parents often report that their attempts to cuddle and show affection to the child are met with a profound lack of interest on the child's part. The child seems not to know or care whether he is alone or in the company of others.

Many children with ASD fail to exhibit social gestures such as showing and pointing things out to others or waving and nodding their head at others. Although some children with ASD "demonstrate basic gestures such as pulling, pushing, or leading others by the hand to get things they want, the use of these gestures typically lacks any social component; the child seems to be using the adult just as a means to an end" (Professional Development in Autism Center, 2004, n.p.).

Young children with ASD often show deficits in **joint attention,** an "early-developing social communication skill in which two people (usually a young child and an adult) use gestures and gaze to share attention with respect to interesting objects or events" (Jones & Carr, 2004, p. 13). A typically developing child looks where someone else is looking, as when a child notices that his mother has turned her head to look at something and does the same, or when a child turns his head or eyes in the direction someone is pointing. Joint attention allows the young child and another person to interact with their shared environment in the same frame of reference, an important factor in the development of language and social skills.

Communication and Language Deficits

About half of children with autistic disorder are mute; they do not speak, but they may hum or occasionally utter simple sounds. The speech of those who do talk may consist largely of **echolalia**—verbatim repetitions of what people around them have said—and

Mustafa's token board reminds him to use his developing speech and social skills when interacting with others.

noncontextual speech phrases without any apparent communicative purpose. Echolalia may be immediate or delayed. For example, Murphy (2003) reported that throughout the day a 7-year-old boy with autism repeated phrases he had heard from movies, cartoons, television shows, announcers of sporting events, and teachers during math instruction, such as the following:

"Hermione, we need to go find Harry!"

"Hi Squidward!"

"Angelica, help me!"

"Today's Noggin show was brought to you by your good friends at McDonald's."

"Jeff Gordon rounds the far outside turn!"

"Add five carry the one." (p. 22)

Some children with ASD have an impressive vocabulary but do not use it in appropriate or useful ways. A common characteristic of children with autism is the concrete or literal processing of verbal information. They understand straightforward cause-and-effect relationships and questions that have a definite answer more easily than they do abstract concepts, idiomatic expressions, or humor. For example, "the concept of using an umbrella to stay dry in the rain is very concrete and easy for a child with autism to understand, whereas an idiomatic figure of speech such as 'it's raining cats and dogs' may prove incomprehensible to a child with autism" (Professional Development in Autism Center, 2004, n.p.).

Many children with ASD can learn to request and label items, but understanding the subtleties of humor is often something that remains confusing into adulthood. That's why we were so excited one day when Sammy came up with a new response to an old question. Sammy had been taught to answer the question "What is your mommy's name?" Then one day in December he surprised us all when instead of answering "Chris Hall," he looked right at us with a serious face and responded, "Chris—mis." Three seconds later he started cracking up and saying, "Mommy is Christmas!" "Mommy is Christmas!" We all laughed along; and since then, Sammy has come up with many more jokes to delight everyone around him. (Michelle Anderson, personal communication, 2004)

Intellectual Functioning

A diagnosis of autism can be made in a child with severe or profound intellectual disabilities (mental retardation) as well as in a child who is intellectually gifted. Although autism spectrum disorders occur across the full range of intellectual abilities, epidemiological surveys show that between 40% and 80% of individuals with autistic disorder also meet the diagnostic criteria for mental retardation (Chakrabarti & Fombonne, 2001; Romanczyk, Weinter, Lockshin, & Ekdahl, 1999). Some professionals use the terms *low-functioning autism* and *high-functioning autism* to differentiate individuals with and without mental retardation.

Uneven skill development is a common characteristic of autism, and about 10% to 15% of children exhibit "splinter skills"—areas of relatively superior performance that are unexpected compared to other domains of functioning. For example, a child may draw very well or remember things that were said a week before but have no functional language and refrain from eye contact with others.

A very few persons are **autistic savants,** people with extraordinary ability in an area such as memorization, mathematical calculations, or musical ability while functioning at the mental retardation level in all other areas (Kelly, Macaruso, & Sokol, 1997; Treffert, 1988, 1989). The betting calculations by Raymond in the movie *Rain Man* are illustrative of savant syndrome.

Many children with autism exhibit *overselectivity,* the tendency to focus on a minute feature of an object or a person rather than the whole. For example, if shown a guitar for the first time, a child might focus on the sound hole and not consider anything else about the instrument, such as its size, shape, other parts, or even the sound that it makes. This overselectivity interferes with the child's understanding of what a guitar is—the totality of its parts and function. The tendency to overselect hinders learning new concepts and interferes with the child's ability to interpret relevant meaning from the environment. The tendency to attend to individual details rather than integrate them into a Gestalt or "big picture" is a key element of a neuropsychological theory in autism called *weak central coherence* (Noens & van Berckelaer-Onnes, 2005).

Obsessive attention on a specific object or activity is another characteristic often seen in individuals with autism spectrum disorder. This focused attention may last for a long time and can be very difficult to break. For instance, if a child with autism has focused his attention on trains, he may continually choose to play with trains and resist playing with other toys. Focused attention may impede his ability to shift attention to other people or activities, such as a parent who is entering the room or another child who is attempting to join his play.

Some children with autism possess a strong aptitude for rote memory for certain things. For example, a child with autism may be able to name all of the Cy Young Award winners in the major leagues and repeat the script of an entire movie verbatim. Yet the same child may have difficulty recalling what he did during recess or remembering the sound that the letter *k* makes.

Unusual Responsiveness to Sensory Stimuli

Many children with autism react to sensory stimulation in atypical ways. This takes the form of over- and underresponsiveness to sensory stimulation. An *overresponsive* (hypersensitive) individual may not be able to stand certain sounds, may dislike being touched or the feel of certain textures, and may refuse to eat foods with certain smells or tastes. For example, Temple Grandin, an adult with autism who has a Ph.D. in animal science and designs environments and equipment to improve the humane and healthful handling of livestock, describes in her autobiography (*Thinking in Pictures and Other Reports of My Life with Autism*) how overly sensitive skin and certain sounds bothered her as a child:

> Washing my hair and dressing to go to church were two things I hated as a child. . . . Scratchy petticoats were like sandpaper scraping away at raw nerve endings. . . . loud noises were also a problem, often feeling like a dentist's drill hitting a nerve. They actually caused pain. I was scared to death of balloons popping because the sound was like an explosion in my ear. Minor noises that most people can tune out drove me to distraction. . . . My ears are like microphones picking up all sounds with equal intensity. (1995, pp. 66–68)

An *underresponsive* (hyposensitive) child appears oblivious to sensory stimulation to which most people react. Some children with autism do not seem to feel pain in a normal way. Some underresponsive children will spin round and round, rock back and forth, or rub and push things hard into their skin to create additional forms or higher intensities of stimulation. It is not uncommon for an individual with autism to display a combination of both over- and underresponsiveness—for example, being hypersensitive to tactile stimulation but unresponsive to many sounds.

Insistence on Sameness and Perseveration

Children with autism often have issues about routines or repetitive behaviors. Some children demonstrate an obsessive need for sameness and may throw huge tantrums when routines at home or in the classroom are changed. They may insist on having everything in the same place all the time and get very upset if anything is moved. Sometimes a verbal child with autism may show this desire for sameness in a preoccupation with a certain subject or area of interest to the exclusion of all others. This child may talk incessantly about one topic, regardless of how bored his listeners are with it, and show no interest in anything else. He may ask the same question over and over, regardless of the reply.

Ritualistic and Unusual Behavior Patterns

Some children with autism engage in ritualistic routines and repetitive behaviors. They may exhibit **stereotypy,** a pattern of persistent and repetitive behaviors such as rocking their bodies when in a sitting position, twirling around, flapping their hands at the wrists, or humming a set of three or four notes over and over again. A child may spend hours at a time gazing at his cupped hands, staring at lights, spinning objects, clicking a ballpoint pen, and so on.

Severe Problem Behavior

Many students with autism exhibit behavior problems in the form of property destruction, aggression toward others, and even self-injury.

> Often the parents report that the child sometimes bites himself so severely that he bleeds, or that he beats his head against walls or sharp pieces of furniture so forcefully that large lumps rise and his skin turns black and blue. He may beat his face with his fists....Sometimes the child's aggression will be directed outward against his parents or teachers in the most primitive form of biting, scratching, and kicking. Some of these children absolutely tyrannize their parents by staying awake and making noises all night, tearing curtains off the window, spilling flour in the kitchen, etc. (Lovaas & Newsom, 1976, p. 309)

Problem behaviors may be situation-specific. For example, Lovaas, Freitag, Gold, and Kassorla (1965) described a child with autism whose self-injury occurred during the song "Wheels on the Bus" but not during "Michael, Row Your Boat."

Many individuals with autism experience a variety of sleep problems, such as delayed onset of sleep, brief sleep duration, and night walking (Hoffman, Sweeney, Gilliam, & Lopez-Wagner, 2006). Food and eating problems are also common in children with autism spectrum disorders. Some children have extremely narrow food preferences, often sensory based (e.g., rcfusing foods with greater texture), some refuse to eat altogether, or choke, gag, and spit out food (Ledford & Gast, 2006; Williams & Foxx, 2007). Some children with autistic disorder engage in **pica,** the compulsive, recurrent consumption of nonfood items (e.g., paper, dirt, pebbles, feces, hair). Stiegler (2005) cited the following account of one parent's experience with his child's pica:

> Over the last couple years we have pulled out of [our son's] throat: a set of keys, large bull-dog clips, sticks, rocks, wads of paper, opened safety pins, wire (from the screen). Plus add the stuff that he gets down before we can get it out: magnets from the fridge, Barbie parts, paper, money, paper clips, etc. (Menard, 1999, n.p.)

Positive Attributes and Strengths of Students With ASD

After reading graphic descriptions of the social and communication impairments, skill deficits, and behavioral excesses exhibited by individuals with ASD, it is easy to overlook their strengths and positive attributes. Not all individuals with ASD are always unattached to those around them or behave in a stilted manner. As Greenspan and Weider (1997) remind us, many children with autism are "quite loving and caring, thoughtful and creative" (p. 88).

As we might expect, a noticeable difference exists between descriptions of autism and Asperger syndrome by people with and without the conditions (Grandin, 1995; Kluth, 2004; Willey, 2003). While people without disabilities tend to focus on the social, communication, and cognitive differences compared to typical functioning, a number of people with autism and Asperger syndrome have described positive features associated with their disability. For example, Temple Grandin (2006), describes some of the positive features associated with her disability:

I think in pictures and sounds. I don't have the ability to process abstract thought the way that you do. Here's how my brain works: It's like the search engine Google for images. If you say the word "love" to me, I'll surf the Internet inside my brain. Then, a series of images pops into my head. What I'll see, for example, is a picture of a mother horse with a foal, or I think of "Herbie the Lovebug," scenes from the movie *Love Story* or the Beatles song, "Love, love, all you need is love ..."

[O]ne of the features of being autistic is that I'm good at synthesizing lots of information and creating systems out of it.

Some people might think if I could snap my fingers I'd choose to be "normal." But I wouldn't want to give up my ability to see in beautiful, precise pictures. I believe in them. (n.p.)

It is important not to overlook the many positive attributes and strengths of children with autism.

Lianne Willey (2001), a woman with Asperger syndrome, writes:

We can describe a situation like no one else. We can tell you what intangibles feel like and secret flavors taste like. We can describe for you, in unbelievable depth, the intricate details of our favorite obsessions. (p. 29)

The intense interest and preoccupation exhibited by students with Asperger syndrome toward their favorite obsessions is viewed by most educators as an eccentric foible at best and as an impediment to the development of social relationships and to engagement with the academic curriculum at worst. However, encouraging students' involvement with their special interest areas (SIAs) can lead to positive outcomes and strengths in other areas of functioning, as suggested in Figure 7.3. "School, home, and community environments of individuals with AS must be infused with opportunities for them to demonstrate their strengths through engagement in their SIAs" (Winter-Messiers et al., 2007, p. 78).

To learn about one strategy that teachers can use as a means to develop an apparent eccentricity or needless obsession into a student's strengths in academic, social, and other areas, see Teaching & Learning, "From Unwanted Obsession to Motivational Key."

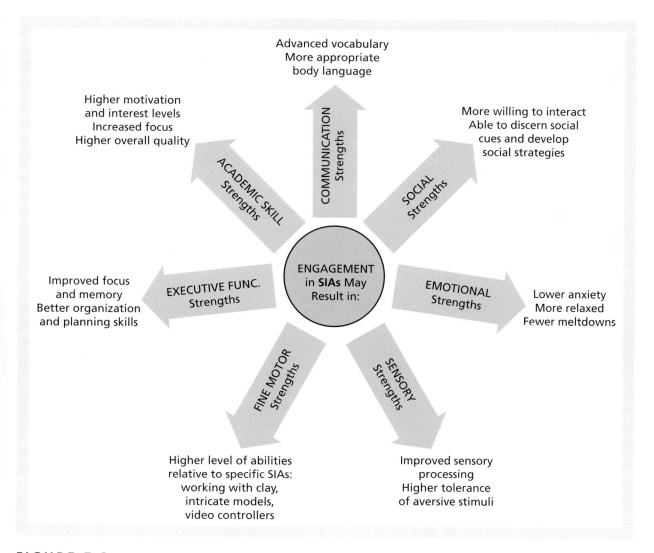

FIGURE 7.3

Potential positive effects in a variety of domains as result of providing a student with Asperger syndrome frequent opportunities to engage in special interest areas (SIAs)

Source: From Winter-Messiers, M. A., Herr, C. M., Wood, C. E., Brooks, A. P., Gates, M. A. M., Houston, T. L., & Tingstad, K. I. (2007). How far can Brian ride the Daylight 4449 Express? A strength-based model of Asperger syndrome based on special interest areas. *Focus on Autism and Other Developmental Disabilities, 22,* 67–79. Copyright 2007 by the Hammill Institute on Disability. Reprinted with permission.

From Unwanted Obsession to Motivational Key:
Using the Special Interests Areas of Children With Asperger Syndrome to Unlock the Curriculum

Many students with Asperger syndrome are enthralled with particular subjects or things. According to Atwood (2003), such special interest areas (SIAs) are "a dominant characteristic of over 90% of children and adults with Asperger syndrome" (p. 127). Because the child spends so much time talking about or fiddling with the object of his interest, these SIAs are often viewed as a deficit. However, teachers can take advantage of students' obsessions, be it toilet brushes or tarantulas, and can turn a perceived deficit into a strength (Winter-Messiers, in press).

CAUGHT IN A BEHAVIOR TRAP

Some contingencies of reinforcement are especially powerful, producing substantial and long-lasting behavior changes. Baer and Wolf (1970) called such contingencies **behavior traps.** Behavior trapping is a fairly common phenomenon, experienced by everyone from time to time. Behavior traps are particularly evident in the activities we just cannot get (or do) enough of. Alber and Heward (1996) describe an elementary teacher's creation of a behavior trap that took advantage of a fifth grader's obsession with baseball cards:

> Carlos experiences school as tedious and unrewarding. With few friends of his own, Carlos finds that even recess offers little reprieve. But he does find solace in his baseball cards, often studying, sorting and playing with them in class. His teacher, Ms. Greene, long ago lost count of the number of times she had to stop an instructional activity to separate Carlos and his beloved baseball cards. Then one day, when she approached Carlos' desk to confiscate his cards in the middle of a lesson on alphabetization, Ms. Greene discovered that Carlos had already alphabetized all the left-handed pitchers in the National League! Ms. Greene realized she'd found the secret to sparking Carlos' academic development.
>
> Carlos was both astonished and thrilled to learn that Ms. Greene not only let him keep his baseball cards at his desk, but also encouraged him to "play with them" during class. Before long, Ms. Greene had incorporated baseball cards into learning activities across the curriculum. In math, Carlos calculated batting averages; in geography, he located the hometown of every major leaguer born in his state; and in language arts, he wrote letters to his favorite players requesting an autographed photo. Carlos began to make significant gains academically and an improvement in his attitude about school was also apparent.
>
> But school became really fun for Carlos when some of his classmates began to take an interest in his knowledge of baseball cards and all the wonderful things you could do with them. Ms. Greene helped Carlos form a classroom Baseball Card Club, giving him and his new friends opportunities to develop and practice new social skills as they responded to their teacher's challenge to think of new ways to integrate the cards into the curriculum. (p. 285)

The most effective behavior traps share four essential features: (a) they are "baited" with virtually irresistible reinforcers that "lure" the student to the trap; (b) only a low-effort response already in the student's repertoire is necessary to enter the trap; (c) interrelated contingencies of reinforcement inside the trap motivate the student to acquire, extend, and maintain targeted academic and/or social skills; and (d) they can remain effective for a long time because the student shows few, if any, satiation effects.

The fetish trap is one of four types of behavior traps described by Alber and Heward (1997). Because fetish traps are baited with the most powerful motivators, they have the potential to be the most effective behavior trap. SIAs can function as the irresistible bait to help students with Asperger syndrome develop positive, constructive knowledge and skills.

HOW TO GET STARTED

1. *Identify the child's SIAs.* This is the easiest assessment a teacher will ever conduct. The objects, events, people, or things that qualify as SIAs are known to anyone who has spent any time with the child.

2. *Determine how to incorporate the SIAs into academic curriculum and social activities.* For example, a student's endless fascination with dinosaurs could be integrated across academic areas, as shown in Figure A.

3. *Make entering the trap easy.* A student does not have to earn his way into a behavior trap. Making access to an SIA contingent on completing a task or engaging in behaviors that do not involve the SIA can be an effective motivator. Using an SIA as a contingent reinforcer in this way, however, is not behavior trapping. In a behavior trap, the student has free access to the SIA. Provide materials that may be required to engage in the SIA, and prompt the student to use them in ways that will incorporate the targeted skills (e.g.,. "Tyler, would you show me how many different types of structures are identified on this map?").

4. *Start small, and use the trap bait judiciously.* Use the SIA to help the student build on skills with which he has experienced some success, then gradually build on those skills. For example, even

Academic areas	Dinosaurs-integrated assignments
Reading	Read *The Complete Guide to Prehistoric Life* (Haines & Chambers, 2006).
Writing	Research and write a paper on *Tyrannosaurus rex*.
Spelling	Learn to spell names of dinosaurs.
History	Research the Precambrian period.
Speech	Present life history of paleontologist George Gaylord Simpson.
Math	Write story problems about tons of leaf consumption by *Triceratops*.
Science	Research the asteroid theory of the Cretaceous extinction.
Art	Design and build a clay or papier mâché model of the *Stegosaurus*.
Internet skills	Research the paleontology wing of the Smithsonian Institution (Washington, DC) and the American Museum of Natural History (New York). Consult with paleontologists online.

FIGURE A

Examples of how a student's interest in dinosaurs could be integrated across curriculum areas

Source: From Winter-Messiers, M. A., Herr, C. M., Wood, C. E., Brooks, A. P., Gates, M. A. M., Houston, T. L., & Tingstad, K. I. (2007). How far can Brian ride the Daylight 4449 Express? A strength-based model of Asperger syndrome based on special interest areas. *Focus on Autism and Other Developmental Disabilities, 22,* 67–97. Copyright 2007 by the Hammill Institute on Disability. Reprinted with permission.

though Tyler is crazy about maps, requiring him to write a 10-page research report on the topic (especially if his writing skills are poor) could destroy the effectiveness of maps as behavior trap bait. Better to begin by asking Tyler to label and classify his favorite map components, then write brief descriptions about them, then compare and contrast the functions of the components, and so on. In this way, Tyler may in time write reports with all the detail of an experienced cartographer.

5. *Don't be in a hurry to eliminate the SIA.* Remember that you're not trying to eliminate the student's interest in his SIA, but use it to learn new academic and social skills, which may eventually lead to the student developing other interests.

6. *Involve the target student's peers.* Encourage peers to participate in SIA-related curriculum activities. Peer involvement increases opportunities for the target student to practice social and language skills. A bonus may be that peers acquire interest in and useful knowledge about their classmate's SIA.

7. *Periodically change the curriculum areas and activities associated with the SIA.* Although a student may not tire of his SIA outside of the trap (that is possible, however, and something to watch for), an SIA may lose its effectiveness as bait if a trap focuses solely on a specific curriculum area or activity.

8. *Evaluate the effects.* Look for observable changes in the student's use of skills and knowledge the behavior trap was designed to "catch." Collect data on the amount of time the student actively engaged with the SIA-related curriculum, the completion and accuracy of academic products, and the student's comments. The student's behavior will suggest ways that an ineffective trap can be revised. Over time, the student's competence and interest in the curriculum area targeted by the trap may grow to the point where the trap is no longer necessary.

Go to the Homework & Exercises section in Chapter 7 of MyEducationLab and complete Homework Exercise 2. As you watch the video and answer the accompanying questions, consider how Tyler's general education teacher could tap into his special interests.

PREVALENCE

Not long ago, autism was considered a rare disorder, with an estimated incidence of about 6.5 in 10,000 children (Gillberg, 1995). More recent population studies have reported much higher incidence rates, ranging from 30 to 121 cases per 10,000 people (California Department of Developmental Services, 1999; Kadesjo, Gillberg, & Hagberg, 1999; Yergin-Allsopp et al., 2003). The incidence of autism is so high that some states have reported it to be an epidemic (Feinberg & Vacca, 2000). The most recent prevalence estimate from the U.S. Centers for Disease Control and Prevention (2007) is that 1 in 150 children have autism. This would make autism far more common than childhood cancer, Down syndrome, or diabetes. Boys are affected about four times more often than girls are (Fombonne, 1999).

Autism is the fastest-growing disability category in special education. In the 2005–2006 school year, 192,643 students ages 6 to 21 received special education services under the IDEA category of autism (U.S. Department of Education, 2007). This figure represents an astounding increase of nearly 16 times the 12,238 students with autism served in 1991–1992.

In a study of the number of children aged 6 to 11 years served by special education services in Minnesota under the primary disability category of autism, Gurney and colleagues (2003) found that diagnoses of ASD increased from 3 per 10,000 in 1991–1992 to 52 per 10,000 in 2001–2002, and that the increasing "trends show no sign of abatement" (p. 622). The factors responsible for the dramatic increase in the number of students being served under this disability category are unclear. The huge increase may be due to greater awareness of ASD, changes in federal and state policy and law favoring better identification and reporting of autism, more widespread screening and better assessment procedures, greater availability of services for the diagnostic category, and/or an actual increase in the true incidence of ASD (Fombonne, 2003; Gillberg & Wing, 1999; Gurney et al., 2003). Regardless of causes, the increased number of children being identified with ASD clearly presents a "daunting challenge" for the schools and communities that must develop the infrastructure and expertise needed to serve them (Simpson, 2004, p. 138).

CAUSES

Causes of autism

 Content Standards for Beginning Teachers—INDEP CURR: Etiologies and medical aspects of conditions affecting individuals with disabilities (IC2K3).

As Schreibman (2005) noted, "When a definite etiology for a disorder is unknown, theories of etiology proliferate. Nowhere is that more apparent than in the field of autism" (p. 75). So many causes of autism have been proposed over the years that "it's a dull month without a new cause for autism" (Rutter, 2005).

From the 1950s to the mid-1970s, many professionals believed that parents who were indifferent to the emotional needs of their children caused autism. This notion may have had its beginnings in Kanner's (1943/1985) observations that many of the parents of his original "autistic" group were preoccupied and that "there were very few really warmhearted fathers and mothers" (p. 50).

During the 1950s and 1960s, Bruno Bettelheim perpetuated the notion that autism could be attributed to the psychopathology of parents. Bettelheim's (1967) theory of *psychogenesis* claimed that autism was an outcome of uninterested, cold parents who were unable to develop an emotional bond with their children. Sadly, mothers of children with autism were called "refrigerator mothers" and led to believe they were the cause of their children's disability. For parents, the idea that they are to blame creates a great deal of guilt on top of the grief already experienced when they find their toddler exhibiting the disturbing behavioral markers of autism.

No causal link between parental personality and autism has ever been discovered and, in 1977, the National Society for Autistic Children (today, the Autism Society of America) stated, "No known factors in the psychological environment of a child have been shown to cause autism." Nevertheless, many parents "are still trying to overcome the guilt and the professional bullying associated with that initial blame" (Scheuermann & Weber, 2002, p. 2).

Recent research shows a clear biological origin for autism in the form of abnormal brain development, structure, and/or neurochemistry (Akshoomoff, 2000; Hyman & Towbin, 2007).

Numerous genetic links to autism have been identified, but we still do not completely understand their causal relationships (Autism Research Institute, 1998; Mueller & Courchesne, 2000; NIH, 2007). The cause of Rett syndrome, for example, has been identified as an abnormality in the MECP2 gene on the X chromosome. Autism might best be viewed as a behavioral syndrome that may be produced by multiple biological causes (Berney, 2000; Mueller & Courchesne, 2000). An excellent source of reliable, science-based information about causes and proposed biological treatments for autism is the Autism Speaks website: http://www.autismspeaks.org.

Although the cause of autism is unknown, research continues to bring us closer to answering that question. The disorder clearly has a genetic component; having one child with autism greatly increases the chances of having another child with autism. However, a genetic factor is not the single cause, because if one identical twin has autism, the other twin may not. Because identical twins share the same genes, some other factor must be contributing to the presence of autism. The current theory among autism genetics researchers supports the idea of complex inheritance. This means that multiple genetic factors are likely to be involved, which in combination may predispose an individual to developing autism. In addition to the presence of a necessary, but currently still-unknown, combination of autism- related genes, exposure to certain environmental factors might lead to the development of autism in some individuals (Interactive Autism Network, 2007). What these environmental factors are is still unknown.

Although the precise neurobiological mechanisms that cause autism have not yet been discovered, "it is clear that autism reflects the operation of factors in the developing brain" (National Research Council, 2001, p. 11). As Lord (2007) noted,

> New technology in studies of brain function draw our attention not just to differences in processing in different regions of the brain, but to possible differences in connectivity. However, credible neurobiological hypotheses of the origins or risks for autism still remain few. (p. 4)

Although questions have been raised about whether vaccinations (specifically, the measles-mumps-rubella [MMR] vaccine and vaccines containing thimerosal used for protection against diphtheria, tetanus, pertussis, and hepatitis B) could be a factor involved in autism, no evidence of this relationship has been found (Institute of Medicine, 2004).

IDENTIFICATION AND ASSESSMENT

Because the specific neurobiological causes of autism are not known, no medical test is available for ASDs. Determining whether a child has an ASD is based on an assessment of behavioral characteristics. Diagnosis is most often made according to criteria described in the DSM-IV (see Figures 7.1 and 7.2) (American Psychiatric Association, 2000a).

Autism can be reliably diagnosed at 18 months, and researchers are actively pursuing reliable methods for detecting warning signs in children as young as 14 months (Goin & Myers, 2004; Landa, 2007). For no other disability is early identification more critical. Early diagnosis enables early intervention, which is highly correlated with dramatically better outcomes than intervention that begins later in the child's life.

> There is enormous excitement about finding children with ASD at very young ages and being able to minimize some of the likely secondary deficits produced, but not necessary, in autism, including lack of social engagement and experience. (Lord, 2007, p. 1).

Unfortunately, many children are not formally diagnosed with autistic disorder until the age of 5 or older (Sivberg, 2003; Wiggins, Baio, & Rice, 2006). Children with Asperger syndrome are on average 5.5 years older when diagnosed than are children with autistic disorder (Goin-Kochel, Mackintosh, & Myers, 2006).

Screening

Many parents of children with autism report that their baby developed in typical fashion for the first year or more, acquiring some meaningful communication skills and enjoying cuddling and hugging. But then between 12 and 15 months of age, the child began showing an oversensitivity to certain sounds or touch; no longer seemed to understand even simple words or gestures; and became increasingly withdrawn, aimless, and perseverative

(Greenspan, 1992). Sometimes the early warning signs appear well before the baby's first birthday. When they do appear during the first year of life, they usually are not in the form of delays in major motor milestones (Landa, 2003, 2007). Many babies who are later diagnosed with autism often sit, crawl, and start to walk on time but show delayed or unusual development in social and communication domains.

Signs that warrant concern during the first year and a half of life include lack of pointing or gestures, infrequent or poor-quality imitation of the caregiver's facial expression, no single words by 16 months, lack of smiling, not responding to name being called, lack of joint attention (e.g., not looking at what parent looks at or points to), and loss of previously acquired language or social skills at any age (Filipek et al., 2000; Landa, 2004, 2007; Professional Development in Autism Center, 2004). In addition to these early markers, very young children with ASD may engage in repetitive and stereotyped patterns of specific behaviors by, for example, repeating certain behaviors over and over; saying scripted verses from familiar videos or TV shows again and again; or showing obsessive interest in certain objects, activities, or parts of objects. First Signs, Inc., is a national nonprofit organization dedicated to educating parents and physicians about the early warning signs of autism and other developmental disorders (http://www.firstsigns.org).

Brief descriptions of three widely used screening instruments for ASD follow.

Checklist for Autism in Toddlers (CHAT)   The CHAT identifies children at age 18 months who are at risk for social-communication disorders (Baron-Cohen, Allen, & Gillberg, 1992). It is a short questionnaire with nine items filled out by the parents and five items by a primary health care worker. The CHAT looks at (a) joint attention, including pointing to show and gaze monitoring (e.g., looking to where a parent is pointing) and (b) pretend play (e.g., pretending to pour tea from a toy teapot). Any child who fails the CHAT should be rescreened approximately 1 month later. If he fails the CHAT for a second time, the child should be referred to a specialist for a diagnostic evaluation.

If a child passes the CHAT on the first administration, no further action needs to be taken. However, passing the CHAT does not guarantee that a child will not go on to develop a social-communication problem of some form. If parents are worried, they should seek referral.

Modified Checklist for Autism in Toddlers (M-CHAT)   The M-CHAT (Robins, Fein, Barton, & Green, 2001) is an expanded American version of the original CHAT, which was developed in the UK. Its goal is to improve the sensitivity of the CHAT for an American audience. Of the M-CHAT's 23 questions, those found to best discriminate between children diagnosed with and without ASDs were 9 items pertaining to social relatedness and communication, such as the following:

- "Does your child ever use his/her index finger to point, to indicate interest in something?"
- "Does your child ever bring objects over to you (parent) to show you something?"
- "Does your child imitate you? (e.g., if you make a face, will your child imitate it?)"
- "If you point at a toy across the room, does your child look at it?" (Robins, et al., 2001)

A child fails the M-CHAT when she fails two or more of the critical items or any three items. A child who fails the M-CHAT should be evaluated in more depth by the physician or referred for a developmental evaluation with a specialist. Not all children who fail the M-CHAT will meet criteria for a diagnosis on the autism spectrum.

Social Communication Questionnaire (SCQ)   The SCQ is a 40-item screening tool completed by a parent or other primary caregiver in less than 10 minutes (Rutter, Bailey, & Lord, 2003). Although the SCQ was developed for screening children age 4 years and up, a recent study found that it correctly identified 89% of children ranging in age from 17–45 months and made no false-positives (an incorrect diagnosis of a person who does not have the disability) if a cut-off score of 11 was used (Wiggins, Bakeman, Adamson, & Robins, 2007).

Autism Spectrum Screening Questionnaire (ASSQ)   The ASSQ is a 27-item checklist that is completed by parents and teacher when screening symptoms characteristic of Asperger syndrome and other high-functioning ASDs in children (Ehlers, Gillberg, & Wing, 1999).

Diagnosis

Children who fail screening tests or whose parents or professionals have reason for concern undergo a complete diagnostic evaluation. A diagnosis of autism should be given by a professional with expertise in autism. That professional could be a developmental pediatrician, a psychologist, a psychiatrist, or a neurologist. In addition to administering an autism diagnostic tool with proven validity and reliability, it is vital that the clinician directly observe the child.

Following are brief descriptions of several of the growing number of rating scales, observation checklists, and diagnostic interviews that have been developed to aid the examiner's evaluation of a child suspected of having ASD. Professionals and parents should remember, however, that no single test or assessment device is fail-proof, especially when diagnosing a disability with such a wide range of expression. Gupta (2003) notes that although the idea that autism disorders fall on a spectrum is popular, "it is vague with no clear-cut endpoints that state clearly when normal variation ends and disorder begins, and it does not address the issue of discordance among the three key domains of autistic symptoms in which a vast range of permutations and combinations are possible" (p. 62). Gupta suggests that including different shades of the disorder under one rubric increases the likelihood of both *false-positives* and *false-negatives* (failing to diagnose a disability in an individual who has it), which in turn leads to disagreements and conflicts over obtaining and paying for needed services.

Childhood Autism Rating Scale (CARS)   The CARS is one of the most widely used instruments for diagnosing autism. It consists of 15 items rated on a 1 to 4 scale based on information from a parent report, records, and direct observation of the child (Schopler, Reichler, & Renner, 1988).

Autism Diagnostic Interview—Revised (ADI-R) and Autism Diagnostic Observation Scale—Generic (ADOS-G)   The ADI-R is a semistructured interview of the primary caregivers of a child or adult suspected of having autism (Lord, Rutter, & Le Couteur, 1994). A trained examiner conducts a detailed interview with the child's primary caregiver, typically requiring at least 2 hours to complete. Questions cover communication, social development and play, repetitive and restrictive behaviors, behavior problems, and family characteristics. The ADI-R has been called the "gold standard" for diagnosis of autism for research purposes (Filipek et al., 2000).

Results from the ADI-R ideally are supplemented by the ADOS-G, which consists of a trained examiner working with the child in a prescribed set of interactions designed to evoke behaviors characteristic of autism (Lord et al., 2000).

Asperger Syndrome Diagnostic Scale (ASDS)   The ASDS is designed to identify Asperger syndrome in children ages 5 through 18 (Myles, Bock, & Simpson, 2001). It consists of 50 yes–no items that can be answered by parents, family members, teachers, speech and language pathologists, psychologists, and other professionals familiar with the child. The ASDS yields a quotient that predicts the likelihood that the individual assessed has Asperger syndrome.

Mikinley's academic and social skills have begun to flourish in a structured and consistent learning environment.

EDUCATIONAL APPROACHES

Children with autism are among the most difficult students to teach. They may often focus on irrelevant stimuli while seeming oblivious to instructional stimuli, show little or no apparent interest in peers or teachers, and with little or no warning may have an angry outburst of aggression or self-injury. Such children require instruction that is carefully planned, meticulously delivered, and continually evaluated and analyzed. Seldom does a child with autism progress without an education that is truly special.

This reality, combined with "the myriad ways in which persons with autism spectrum disorders manifest their disability," has made the area "fertile ground" for the advancement of countless strategies (Simpson, 2001, p. 68). Table 7.1 summarizes some key events in the history of understanding and treating autism and their educational implications. More detailed treatments of the history of autism can be found in Gupta (2003), Firth (2003), Heflin and Alaimo (2007), and Rimland (1994).

A great deal of exciting research in recent years has contributed to improved educational outcomes for children with autism and promises a better future for these children and their families (e.g., Dawson & Osterling, 1997; Green, 2001; Maurice & Taylor, 2005; Schwartz, Sandall, Garfinkle, & Bauer; 1998; Schreibman, 2005; Simpson, 2005). This

TABLE 7.1

A history of the education of children with autism: Key events and implications

DATE	HISTORICAL EVENT	EDUCATIONAL IMPLICATIONS
1911	Eugen Bluer, a Swiss psychiatrist, coins the term *autism*—from the Greek word, *autos* (self)—to describe patients with schizophrenia who actively withdrew from social contact.	When used later to name a condition in children who displayed behaviors similar to Bluer's patients, the term *autism* implied that children purposively withdrew from those around them.
1943	Leo Kanner, a child psychiatrist at Johns Hopkins University, describes the characteristics of a childhood disorder he calls *early infantile autism.*	Kanner's observation that "there were very few really warmhearted fathers and mothers" may have caused some to speculate that indifferent, nonresponsive parents were responsible for the disorder.
1944	Hans Asperger, an Austrian pediatrician with a special interest in "psychically abnormal" children, publishes a paper describing a pattern of behavior based on his work with more than 400 children with "autistic psychopathy."	The combination of behaviors and abilities he described later came to be known as Asperger syndrome.
1965	Autism Society of America (ASA) is founded (originally National Society for Autistic Children).	ASA's mission is to promote lifelong access and opportunity for all individuals within the autism spectrum and their families to be fully participating, included members of their community.
1967	Bruno Bettleheim's book, *An Empty Fortress,* advances the notion that children actively or purposively withdrew into their own worlds because of cold and uncaring parents.	Bettleheim's theory that autism was caused by "refrigerator mothers" led to much professional blaming and mistreatment of parents and devastating guilt.
1981	Lorna Wing publishes an article in Great Britain in which the term *Asperger syndrome* is used for the first time.	Wing's seminal paper generated renewed interest in Asperger syndrome, especially in Europe.
1987	Ivar Lovaas publishes results of the Young Autism Project, in which children with autism participated in an intensive early intervention program of one-to-one behavioral treatment for more than 40 hours per week for 2 years or more before age 4.	This was the first study to show that early, intensive, behavioral intervention could enable some children with autism to achieve normal functioning. It gave hope to parents and provided other researchers and practitioners with principles on which to build.
1990	Individuals with Disabilities Education Act (IDEA) Amendments of 1990 (P.L. 101-476) are made law.	Autism was added as a new disability category under which children were entitled to special education.

TABLE 7.1 Continued

A history of the education of children with autism: Key events and implications

DATE	HISTORICAL EVENT	EDUCATIONAL IMPLICATIONS
1993	Catherine Maurice's *Let Me Hear Your Voice: A Family's Triumph Over Autism* is published.	This powerful account of a mother's efforts to find help for her two children brought attention to the importance of science-based treatment for autism.
1994	Asperger syndrome is officially recognized in the *Diagnostic and Statistical Manual of Mental Disorders (DSM-IV)* as a pervasive developmental disability within the autism spectrum.	This created increased awareness of Asperger syndrome among clinicians, researchers, and educators.
1994	The National Alliance for Autism Research (NAAR) is founded, the first organization in the United States dedicated to promoting research seeking to identify causes and potential biomedical cures for autism.	NAAR-funded research has been leveraged into more than $48 million in autism research awards by the National Institute of Health and other funding sources and has led to advances in the neurosciences and other scientific fields.
1998	The Association for Science in Autism Treatment (ASAT) is founded with the twin goals of disseminating accurate, science-based information about autism and promoting access to effective, science-based evaluation and treatment for all people with autism.	ASAT's website (www.asatonline.org) provides valuable information to families, professionals, and policymakers.
2002	CEC's Division on Developmental Disabilities (DDD) includes ASD within its purview and journal, *Focus on Autism and Other Disabilities.*	Special educators with interests in ASD have a centralized source of information and a voice within CEC.
2006	Combating Autism Act of 2006 (P.L. 109-416)	Authorized nearly $1 billion over 5 years to combat autism through research, screening, early detection and early intervention, increasing federal spending on autism by at least 50%. It includes provisions relating to the diagnosis and treatment of persons with ASD, and expands biomedical research on autism, including a focus on possible environmental causes.
2007	National Autism Center initiates The National Standards Project with the goal of ratifying a set of evidence-based treatment approaches for autism.	Phase I entails developing a model for critically examining scientific evidence for educational and behavioral interventions. In Phase II panelists will use the model to review existing literature to generate a handbook for educators and parents outlining specific evidence-based program components, procedures, and implementation strategies.

section examines the importance of early intervention, introduces applied behavior analysis, and describes several specific tactics for teaching children with autism.

Critical Importance of Early Intensive Behavioral Intervention

Intensive, behaviorally based early intervention has helped some children with autism learn communication, language, and social skills so that they have been able to succeed in general education classrooms. One of the earliest and most powerful examples of the potential of systematic early intervention on the lives of children with autism is the work of Ivar Lovaas and his colleagues at the University of California at Los Angeles (Lovaas, 1987;

Smith, Eikeseth, Klevstrand, & Lovaas, 1997; Smith & Lovaas, 1998). In 1987 Lovaas reported the results of a study that provided a group of 19 children with autism with an intensive early intervention program of one-to-one behavioral treatment for more than 40 hours per week for 2 years or more before they reached age 4. Intervention also included parent training and inclusion in a preschool setting with typically developing children. When compared with a group of 19 similar children at age 7, the children in the early intervention group had gained an average of 20 IQ points and made major advances in educational achievement. Nine of the children had moved from first to second grade in general education classrooms and were considered by their teachers to be well adjusted.

Follow-up evaluations of the same group of 19 children several years later at the average age of 11.5 years showed that the children had maintained their gains (McEachin, Smith, & Lovaas, 1993). In particular, 8 of the 9 "best-outcome" children were considered "indistinguishable from average children on tests of intelligence and adaptive behavior" (p. 359). In discussing the outcomes of this research, Lovaas (1994) states:

> After 1 year of intensive intervention, fifty percent of the children can be integrated into regular kindergarten classrooms. Then, we have them repeat kindergarten to get a head start on first grade. Successful passing of first grade is the key. Those that pass first grade are likely to obtain normal IQ scores and normal functioning. The children who don't make it into first grade are likely to need intensive supports for their entire life. (n.p.)

Although some have raised important questions about the validity and generality of this research (e.g., Gresham & MacMillan, 1997a, 1997b), several replications of the "UCLA model," including a study in which children were randomly assigned to early intensive behavioral intervention or an alternate intervention, have produced similar results (Cohen, Amerine-Dickens, & Smith, 2006; Smith, Groen, & Wynn, 2000).

The work of Lovaas and colleagues represents a landmark accomplishment in the education of children with autism (Baer, 2005). First, they discovered and validated at least some of the factors that can be controlled to help children with autism achieve normal functioning in a general education classroom. Second, the dramatic improvements that were previously considered unattainable in the children's social, communication, and cognitive functioning helped spur wide-ranging interest and research funding for a disorder for which custodial care was thought to be the only option (National Institute of Mental Health, 2004). Third, the successful outcomes offer a legitimate basis for hope and encouragement for parents and teachers desperate to learn how to help children with autism.

Applied Behavior Analysis

ABA

Council for Exceptional Children

Content Standards for Beginning Teachers—INDEP CURR: Prevention and intervention strategies for individuals with disabilities (IC4K2) (also, IC1K7).

The teaching methods used in the Lovaas early intervention project were derived from **applied behavior analysis (ABA).** ABA is a scientific approach to designing, conducting, and evaluating instruction based on empirically verified principles describing functional relations between events in the environment and learning (Cooper, Heron, & Heward, 2007). Teaching methods derived from ABA are used effectively not only with learners with autism and other disabilities but also with students in general education (Alberto & Troutman, 2006; Heward et al., 2005).

From the perspective of ABA, "autism is a syndrome of behavioral deficits and excesses that have a biological basis but are nonetheless amenable to change through carefully orchestrated, constructive interactions with the physical and social environment" (Green, 2001, p. 73). ABA uses behavioral principles such as positive reinforcement to teach children skills in a planned, systematic manner. Children receive repeated opportunities across the day, settings, people, and materials to practice their new skills.

Treatments based on other models can yield beneficial outcomes for children with autism. For example, an intervention derived from developmental psychology and designed to improve joint attention and symbolic play enhanced mother–child interactions and raised children's scores on standardized tests of IQ and language (Kasari, Freeman, & Paparella, 2006). However, no other form of treatment for children with autism has the amount or quality of scientific evidence attesting to its effectiveness as does early intensive behavioral intervention (*Clinical Practice Guideline,* 1999; Jacobson, Mulick, & Green, 1998; Professional Development in Autism Center, 2004; Smith, 2007). Intervention programs consisting of an eclectic mix of components from different treatment models are not as effective as early intensive behavioral intervention based on ABA (e.g., Eikeseth, Smith, Jahr, & Eldevik, 2002; Howard, Sparkman, Cohen, Green, & Stanislaw, 2005).

Because of the documented accomplishments of some children with autism after receiving intensive ABA therapy, many parents and practitioners have advocated for ABA programs and services for children with autism (e.g., Yell & Drasgow, 2000). However, misunderstandings about ABA are widespread, and many teachers and parents have a narrow or incorrect view of what ABA is and is not. (See Figure 7.4, "What is ABA?")

> In many respects, it is a misnomer to refer to "the ABA approach." Although ABA offers educators a collection of teaching techniques whose effectiveness has been empirically validated, it does not prescribe any particular instructional method. ABA includes a philosophy, a set of principles from which situation-specific educational interventions with a high probability of success can be derived, and—most important—a data-driven method for continuously evaluating the effectiveness of those interventions. (Heward, 2005, p. 321)

One of the most common misconceptions is the belief that ABA consists only of **discrete trial training (DTT),** one-on-one sessions during which a routinized sequence of contrived learning trials is presented as teacher and child sit at a table. For example, an item or instruction is presented (e.g., "Touch the spoon."), the child responds, and reinforcement is provided for a correct response. Each sequence of antecedent stimulus, child response, and consequence (or feedback) is a trial (as illustrated in the top half of Figure 4.5 on page 157).

As Baer (2005) points out,

> The discrete trial method of teaching, or DTT, is as old as teaching and much older than education. It can be described as follows:
>
> 1. The teacher prepares a set of problems to present to a student one at a time.
> 2. This sequence is usually in an optimum order for teaching and learning, to the best of the teacher's ability.
> 3. The student responds or fails to respond to each problem.
> 4. The teacher responds to each of the student's responses or nonresponses, rewarding or acknowledging correct responses; ignoring, correcting, or reproving incorrect responses; and either ignoring or prompting responses after nonresponses.
> 5. The cumulative effect of this teaching is to impart a new set of integrated facts, a concept, or a skill.
>
> The discrete trial method is the method whereby children learn games and parents teach children language. It is commonly used in school classrooms for teaching any subject matter. DTT is the method of Socratic dialogue, it is often how law students are taught their most useful skills, and it is often how medical interns are taught clinical and diagnostic skills. (p. 10)
>
> [DTT] is used in countless variations. Whether DTT is drudgery or sublimely informative depends not on its format, but on how skillfully the teacher has prepared what the student will encounter and how skillfully the teacher can answer whatever response to the encounters the student may make. (p. 24)

DTT is not ABA, and ABA can be done without DTT. However, DTT plays an important role in ABA-based programming for children with autism, and it is a teaching method that special educators should know how to use with a high degree of skill (Dib & Sturmey, 2007; Grindle & Remington, 2002). It is also important to know that using DTT is just one type of teaching arrangement, and ABA programming uses a variety of procedures to help individuals with autism acquire and generalize new skills (Anderson & Romanczyk, 1999; Green, 2001; Sundberg & Partington, 1998). Following is a partial list of systematic strategies based on ABA for teaching students with autism:

- Strategies for shifting control over a student's responses from contrived stimuli used in training to naturally occurring stimuli and novel events he encounters in his environment (Green, 2001; Reeve, Reeve, Townsend, & Poulson, 2007)

Discrete trial training

Content Standards for Beginning Teachers—INDEP CURR: Prevention and intervention strategies for individuals with disabilities (IC4K2) (also, IC1K7).

Council for Exceptional Children

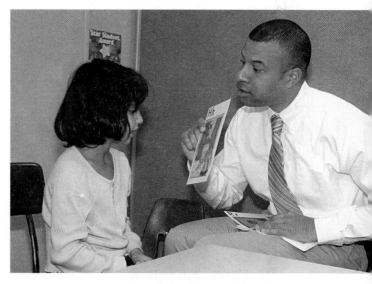

Instructional sessions featuring discrete trial training are an important part of Ayah's school day.

FIGURE 7.4   What is ABA?

ABA stands for *applied behavior analysis,* a science devoted to improving and understanding human behavior. ABA focuses on objectively defined, observable behaviors that are important to the daily lives of the participants, and it seeks to improve those behaviors while demonstrating reliable relationships between the procedures employed and the improvements in behavior.

What ABA Is

ABA is individualized. (This is the *applied* of ABA.) Teaching goals are determined by a careful assessment of the current skills and behavioral deficits of the individual in the context of his environment. Skills to be taught are not selected from a predetermined list, but are selected on an individual basis. Behaviors that are most likely to produce beneficial outcomes for the child and his family are the primary focus of ABA-based teaching.

ABA is data-based evaluation and decision making. (This is the *behavior* of ABA.) Direct and frequent measurement is the foundation of ABA. Measurement is direct when a learner's performance of the target behavior is observed and recorded as it occurs in the natural environment for that skill. Frequent measurement is better than infrequent measurement. Ideally, measurement should occur as often as instruction occurs.

ABA is designed to be effective. (This is the *analysis* of ABA.) Because data are collected directly and frequently during instruction, assessment of learning is continuous. By examining the data, teachers, therapists, and parents can determine whether or not the instruction is working. If the child is not making reasonable progress, instruction is modified.

ABA is doable. Although ABA requires far more than learning to administer a few simple procedures, it is not so complicated as to be prohibitive. Parents can learn the basic principles of ABA and can incorporate teaching strategies based on those principles into daily interactions with their children. For example, a parent can work on her child's greeting behavior throughout the day. Whenever the child encounters a new person or a parent or sibling greets the child, she can prompt the child to wave and make eye contact and then praise and reinforce that behavior.

ABA is, in the words of one mother of a young child with autism, "Good old-fashioned hard work." ABA is not a magic bullet or a miracle cure. It requires diligent, continuous analysis of the relationship between behavior and the environment in which behavior occurs. Because behavior is always happening, teaching is always happening. ABA is certainly intensive; but when used correctly as the basis for designing and evaluating treatment for young children with autism, ABA can produce meaningful, life-changing results.

What ABA Is Not

ABA does not prescribe instructional settings, teaching formats, or materials. ABA can be used to guide discrete trial instruction for reading skills delivered by a teacher while sitting at a table with a child. ABA can also guide a parent's provision of incidental learning trials for language acquisition while giving her child a bath. ABA does not require that certain items be used as rewards or consequences for behavior. The items and activities to be used as rewards (technically called *reinforcers*) are determined by the child's preferences and by the effects those items and activities have when provided as consequences for the child's behavior.

Because ABA does not dictate any specific type of instructional method or format, the phrase "ABA method" is a misnomer. ABA is broader than any "brand name" method of behaviorally based instruction or therapy (e.g., Lovaas method, PECS, the verbal behavior method). Many service providers and parents mistakenly believe that ABA is one of these ABA-based brand names. However, training in a brand name is no substitute for in-depth training in the science of applied behavior analysis.

ABA is not bribery. Every effort is made to increase children's motivation and make learning fun. Naturally occurring consequences are used as reinforcers whenever possible. For example, instead of using just teacher praise or edible items when teaching play and social skills to children, naturally occurring consequences, such as access to favorite toys and interacting with other children, are provided as reinforcers for appropriate play and socialization behaviors.

ABA is not punitive. Positive strategies are used until they are exhausted, and reinforcers are delivered systematically to increase appropriate behavior. The goal of ABA is not to decrease maladaptive behavior but to increase the strength and frequency of appropriate behavior. An important element of ABA is to determine the function of behavior. For example, does a child tantrum and hit himself or others because he wants attention? Does he throw things because he needs help? Knowing why a child exhibits challenging behaviors allows parents and teachers to teach appropriate replacement behaviors, such as tapping a person on the shoulder to get attention or using spoken words or a communication device to say, "I need help."

Source: Adapted from Silvestri, S. M., Wood, C. L., Allen, N. J., Anderson, M. A., Murphy, C. M., & Heward, W. L. (2006). What is ABA? In E. A. Boutot & M. Tincani (Eds.), *Autism articles: What parents need to know* (pp. 43–45). Austin, TX: PRO-ED.

- Alternative forms of communication such as the Picture Exchange Communication System (Bondy & Frost, 2002; Charlop-Christy, Carpenter, Le, LeBlanc, & Kellet, 2002; Marckel, Neef, & Ferreri, 2006; Schwartz, Garfinkle, & Bauer, 1998)
- Functional analyses of verbal behavior have led to some effective teaching practices for spoken and written language (Barbera, 2007; Greer & Ross, 2008; Sundberg & Partington, 1998)
- Peer-mediated interventions for social relationships (McConnell, 2002; Petursdottir, McComas, McMaster, & Horner, 2007; Strain & Schwartz, 2001)
- Strategies to increase students' active responding during academic instruction (Whalen & Schreibman, 2003)
- Self-management tactics (Lee, Simpson, & Shogren, 2007; Newman, Reinecke, & Meinberg, 2000)
- Methods of errorless discrimination learning (Jerome, Frantino, & Sturmey, 2007; Sidman, 1994)
- Functional assessment of challenging behavior (Neef & Peterson, 2007)
- Functional communication training (Mancil, 2006)
- Naturalistic strategies for teaching language and social skills (Goldstein, 2002; Koegel & Koegel, 2006; McGee, Morrier, & Daly, 1999). (See Teaching & Learning, "Using Naturalistic Teaching Strategies to Build Communication Skills for Students With Severe Disabilities," in Chapter 12.)

ABA is not a panacea; it is the most effective intervention we have at the current time. ABA does not offer answers as to why autism happens; it offers a practical means of helping children who are autistic. ABA is not a biological intervention, although it may have concrete impact on a developing nervous system. ABA will not recover all kids from autism, but it will recover some. ABA does not solve all of our problems, and I hope that something easier to administer and cheaper will come along sometime soon—but for the moment, ABA offers all children with autism, every one of them, a real opportunity to learn. (Maurice & Taylor, 2005, p. 35)

Excellent descriptions of a variety of teaching methods based on ABA for children with autism can be found in Harris and Handleman (2000); Keenan, Kerr, and Dillenberger (2000); Maurice, Green, and Foxx (2001); Scheuermann and Webber (2002); Sturmey and Fitzer (2007); and Sulzer-Azaroff and Associates (2008). The Autism Special Interest Group of the Association for Behavior Analysis International (2008) has published a set of consumer guidelines for identifying, selecting, and evaluating behavior analysts working with individuals with ASDs.

Visual Supports: Helping Students With Autism Cope With Social Situations and Increase Their Independence in the Classroom

Visual supports encompass a wide variety of interventions that involve visual cues and prompts that help students to perform skills with greater independence and accuracy (Cohen & Sloan, 2007; Rao & Gagie, 2006). Picture activity schedules and social stories are two strategies for students with ASD that entail visual supports.

Picture Activity Schedules   Some level of independent performance is needed for success in inclusive classrooms. For preschoolers with autism, a lack of play skills "might prevent opportunities for learning and successful participation in inclusive classrooms. The impending isolation might serve to perpetuate the children's deficits in socialization and communication" (Morrison, Sainato, BenChaaban, & Endo, 2002, p. 58). Numerous studies have shown that children with autism can be taught to use picture activity schedules to increase their independence in selecting and carrying out a sequence of activities in the classroom (e.g., Bevill, Gast, MaGuire, & Vail, 2001; Bryan & Gast, 2000; Goodman & Williams, 2007; Massey & Wheeler, 2000; McClannahan & Krantz, 1999; Morrison et al., 2002; Spriggs, Gast, & Ayres, 2007). Teachers can also incorporate video into activity schedules (Kimball, Kinney, Taylor, & Stromer, 2004; Stromer, Kimball, Kinney, & Taylor, 2006). To learn how to create video modeling into activity schedules, see Teaching & Learning, "Multimedia Activity Schedules."

Visual supports and picture activity schedules

 Content Standards for Beginning Teachers—INDEP CURR: Prevention and intervention strategies for individuals with disabilities (IC4K2) (also, IC1K7).

Multimedia Activity Schedules:
Promoting Independence Among Children With Autism

BY JONATHAN W. KIMBALL AND ROBERT STROMER

Devon and two friends are playing with the train set in their preschool classroom. A timer suddenly beeps from across the room, and Devon scurries from the play center toward the sound. The beeping comes from a computer, and the monitor displays a photograph of Devon playing with a locomotive. Devon uses the mouse to click a large button in the corner of the screen and watches as a new photo appears, depicting the classroom's sand table. This photo also has a button. When he clicks it, Devon sees a 10-second video clip of one child inviting another to play at the sand table. A new photo appears showing Devon at the sand table with other children. Devon leaves the computer, approaches a peer, and says, "Come play." Together, the two children head toward the sand table.

In this vignette, Devon, a 4-year-old with autism, is using an activity schedule presented on a computer. Before learning to follow such a schedule, Devon had received intensive teacher instruction in a number of play skills: playing with trains and sand, building with blocks, playing a picture-matching memory game, and "cooking" on the toy stove.

1. Click on Activity Photo

2. Look at Video

3. Look at Cue to Play

4. Initiate Activity

5. Do Activity

6. Put Materials Away

Devon's independence and social interactions with classmates have increased dramatically since he learned to use multimedia activity schedules.

Before learning to use an activity schedule, Devon, like many children with autism, would not spontaneously demonstrate even the skills he had mastered during guided practice. Instead, during free time he remained alone and engaged in repetitive, nonfunctional rituals known as stereotypy—for instance, rapidly flapping his hands or stacking Legos in a particular pattern—until an adult asked him to participate in one of the centers. In the vignette, however, adults are conspicuously absent.

ACTIVITY SCHEDULES AND ACTIVE KIDS

Part of a larger class of assistive technology known as visual supports, an activity schedule traditionally is a series of separate images—photos, icons, or words depicting activities a child can perform—presented in sequence in a notebook or on cards. Once a child such as Devon can complete three or four activities in isolation, he may be ready to learn how to follow an activity schedule to perform these activities in a sequence. Activity schedules (not unlike low-tech pocket calendars or high-tech PDAs used by adults) have an excellent track record in helping children with autism remain engaged in a sequence of activities, for extended periods of time, without adult prompting. Students with disabilities have successfully employed activity schedules:

- for work tasks and leisure
- at school or at home
- for finite (a worksheet or a puzzle) or open-ended (reading or ball play) skills
- in a group or alone

Once children become competent with a schedule, they often can follow it when the images are rearranged or when new ones are substituted or added.

An activity schedule essentially exchanges one form of prompting for another. But this is a distinction with a real difference: The child who has learned to employ a portable visual schedule no longer requires a teacher or a parent to tell her when to initiate one activity and when to move on to the next. Thus, a child who previously relied on adults for direction may become a self-directed child. Beyond being a mere mechanism for prompting, then, an activity schedule can be a major tool for promoting independence and self-determination.

Multimedia Activity Schedules Children with autism have difficulty understanding or responding appropriately to complex stimuli such as spoken words or the human face. Research has shown, however, that these children attend very well to two-dimensional images such as what appears on television or computer monitors; in fact, Devon, like many children with autism, often watches videos and plays on computers to the exclusion of most other activities. If visual prompts such as those in activity schedules must be attended to in order to be effective, and if children with autism are naturally motivated to attend to computers, then it is sensible to conclude that children with autism may readily learn to follow activity schedules presented via computer. Having brought activity schedules to the computer, it is a short step to bringing the audio-visual capabilities of computers to activity schedules.

The marriage of these two technologies is greater than the sum of their parts. More than an expensive toy, the computer becomes a means of delivering instruction; more than a prompting system, the activity schedule becomes a context for embedding auditory and visual instructional material. In other words, once a child has acquired the skill of schedule following, she may then learn additional skills while following a multimedia schedule. The computer integrates two forms of instructional and assistive technology that have usually been researched and developed separately: activity schedules and video modeling (Bellini & Akullian, 2007; Nikopoulos & Keenan, 2004). Children with autism not only have learned to independently follow computer schedules but in doing so also have learned skills such as the following (Kimball, Kinney, Taylor, & Stromer, 2004):

- Sight-word reading
- Spelling
- Daily living skills
- Functional play routines
- Social-communication skills such as asking for help or, like Devon, seeking a playmate

Because lack of social skills is a defining feature of autism, Devon's accomplishment is truly significant. Importantly, once children have learned new skills while following computer activity schedules, they have retained those skills when the same pictures are presented in portable notebooks.

How to Get Started

1. *Notebook schedules.* Lynn McClannahan and Patricia Krantz (1999) provide an excellent guide for developing and using notebook activity schedules. The closest thing to a manual for this type of technology, their book discusses prerequisite skills, preparing a first schedule, proceeding from teaching a child to follow a schedule to using schedules to foster social skills, and troubleshooting.

2. *Multimedia schedules.* Teaching with multimedia schedules requires a few more steps for teachers. Teachers should be comfortable with Microsoft PowerPoint and with handling digital cameras and images. Step-by-step procedures for developing schedules in PowerPoint that include sounds, videos, and even built-in beeping timers like Devon's are detailed in Rehfeldt, Kinney, Root, and Stromer (2004). While multimedia schedules have the potential to capitalize on the naturally motivating properties of computers and video, children with autism also should be able to imitate actions from videos and use a computer mouse or touch-screen. Devon's teacher, using the steps outlined by McClannahan and Krantz, taught him his first activity schedule on a computer before he then learned to complete the same activities following a notebook schedule. Now when Devon moves from one activity to the next in his schedule, a stranger might have difficulty distinguishing him from his typically developing playmates.

Jonathan W. Kimball is Senior Behavior Analyst at Woodfords Family Services in Portland, Maine. Robert Stromer teaches at the Centre for Community Services and Health Sciences, George Brown College, Toronto, Canada. They gratefully acknowledge the contributions of Elizabeth M. Kinney and Bridget A. Taylor to the development of multimedia activity schedules.

Go to the Building Teaching Skills section in Chapter 7 of MyEducationLab and complete the activities. As you watch the video and answer the accompanying questions, compare how different types of multimedia and instructional software can enhance instruction for students who have autism.

TEACHING & LEARNING

Social stories

 Council for Exceptional Children

Content Standards for Beginning Teachers—INDEP CURR: Prevention and intervention strategies for individuals with disabilities (IC4K2) (also, IC1K7).

Social Stories Learning to tolerate change and how and when to use communication and social interaction skills within the typical rules and conventions that govern social situations is a major challenge for many students with autism (Charlop-Christy, 2007). **Social stories** explain social situations and concepts, including expected behaviors of the persons involved, in a format understandable to an individual with ASD. Social stories can answer a child's questions about concepts and provide information about social behavior that she is not likely to ask for or obtain in other ways (Gray, 1995, 2000). According to Gray and Garand (1993), teachers can use social stories to describe a situation and expected behaviors, explain simple steps for achieving certain goals or outcomes, and teach new routines and anticipated actions. Providing social stories before an event or activity can decrease a child's anxiety, improve his behavior, and help him understand the event from the perspective of others.

Social stories are written at the student's level of comprehension and usually contain four basic types of sentences (Santosti, Powell-Smith, & Kincaid, 2004) (see Figure 7.5):

- Descriptive sentences identify the contextual variables of the target situation.
- Directive sentences describe the desired behavior with respect to a specific social cue or situation.
- Perspective sentences describe the reactions and feelings of others about the situation.
- Affirmative sentences express shared beliefs or reference a rule or law about the situation to reassure the individual.

Social stories are usually constructed with one sentence per page. Photographs or line drawings depicting key information and important aspects of the events are sometimes added to illustrate the sentence on each page (see Figure 7.6). Comic book conversation is a modification of social story that uses pictures, simple figures, and comic strip components such as speech bubbles instead of text (Glaeser, Pierson, & Fritschman, 2003; Rogers & Myles, 2001).

Several studies have reported improvements in children's behavior after systematic exposure to social stories (Adams, Gouvousis, VanLue, & Waldron, 2004; Kuoch & Mirenda, 2003; Lorimer, Simpson, Myles, & Ganz, 2002; Scattone, Wilczynski, Edwards, & Rabian, 2002; Soenksen & Alper, 2006). For example, Ivey, Heflin, and Alberto (2004) found that three 5- to 7-year-old boys with autism increased their independent and appropriate participation in novel activities when parents read social stories to the children once a day for 5 days before

---

FIGURE 7.5 **Social story on sportsmanship illustrating four major types of sentences used to construct social stories**

Text	Sentence Type
Sometimes, recess is on the playground.	Descriptive
When I go to the playground, I like to play football.	Descriptive
There are other kids who like to play football with me, too.	Perspective
When I play football, others like me to be a good sport.	Perspective
This is a good idea.	Affirmative
A good sport is someone who says "good job" or "awesome" during a good play or for winning the game, no matter whose team they are on.	Descriptive
A good sport would never yell at anybody while playing football during recess.	Descriptive
That hurts others' feelings.	Perspective
I will try to practice my sportsmanship skills when I play football during recess.	Directive
I will try to say things like "good job," "nice pass," or "awesome."	Directive
If I show all of these sportsmanship skills, my friends will want to play with me more often.	Perspective

Source: From Santosti, F. J., Powell-Smith, K. A., & Kincaid, D. (2004). A research synthesis of social story interventions for children with autism spectrum disorders. *Focus on Autism and Other Developmental Disabilities, 19,* 194–204, by the Hammill Institute on Disability. Reprinted with permission.

At my school, students eat lunch in the cafeteria.

p. 1

The cafeteria can be very crowded at lunch.

p. 2

When I go to the cafeteria, I get my tray and stand at the end of the line. I stay in line and wait with everyone else to get my lunch.

p. 3

When I have to wait I can think of other things. I can think of a song or my favorite book.

p. 4

Soon it will be my turn and I can choose my lunch.

p. 5

Waiting in line is hard but I try my best to wait calmly. Everyone feels good when people wait their turn.

p. 6

FIGURE 7.6

Sample social story about waiting in the lunch line at the school cafeteria with pictures illustrating the text

Source: From Crozier, S., & Sileo, N. M. (2005). Encouraging positive behavior with social stories: An intervention for children with autism spectrum disorders. *Teaching Exceptional Children, 37*(6), p. 30. Used by permission.

the events. However, the research base for social stories is limited, and the mechanisms for how social stories affect behavior are not fully understood.

Sufficient positive outcomes have been attained with social story interventions to date, however, that the method should be considered a promising practice (Santosti et al., 2004; Simpson, 2005, 2007). Social stories may be most effective when part of a multicomponent intervention that includes other elements such as response prompts, feedback, reinforcement, and self-recording of desired behaviors (Scattone, Wilczynski, Edwards, & Rabian, 2002; Thiemann & Goldstein, 2001). For example, Crozier and Tincani (2005) found that a social story supplemented by occasional verbal prompts (e.g., "Remember to raise your hand when you want to talk to a teacher," p. 153) was more effective than the social story alone. Numerous examples of social stories and detailed suggestions for how to write and use them can be found in Crozier and Sileo (2005) and Gray (2000).

EDUCATIONAL PLACEMENT ALTERNATIVES

During the 2005–2006 school year, approximately 31% of students with autism were educated in the general education classrooms, with 18% served in resource room programs and 40% in separate classes (U.S. Department of Education, 2007). About 10% of students with autism attended special schools or residential facilities.

Javan's improving ability to participate in group activities is helping him benefit from the increasing amount of time he spends in the general education classroom.

General Education Classroom

Students with autism are increasingly placed in general education classrooms for the purpose of improved social integration. Under the right conditions, students with autism become "accepted, visible members" of peer groups (Boutot & Bryant, 2005). A strong argument for educating children with autism in inclusive settings is that socially competent children are an essential ingredient for peer-mediated interventions, one of the best-researched and most effective types of interventions for young children with autism. As McConnell (2002) notes, however, "the data suggest strongly that inclusion is a necessary, but not likely sufficient, condition for social interaction interventions for young children with autism" (p. 367).

Schwartz, Billingsley, and McBride (1998) described five strategies essential to providing effective education for young children with autism in inclusive classrooms:

Teach Communication and Social Competence   Without communication and social interactions among children, an inclusive program may provide little more than parallel instruction.

- *Provide systematic instruction in imitation skills.* Imitation is critical to learning from and relating to others. Embed imitation training throughout the day—in small groups, opening circle, gym, and outdoor play.
- *Plan opportunities for students with disabilities to interact directly with typically developing peers.* For example, at opening circle, begin with a desirable toy such as a jar of bubbles and then help all children share the toy directly with other children instead of passing the toy from child to teacher to child.

Use Instructional Strategies That Maintain the Class's Natural Flow   Instead of isolating children with disabilities to provide individualized instruction, teach within the context of developmentally appropriate activities and routines.

- *Use naturalistic teaching procedures.* Instruction should involve activities that are interesting to students, take advantage of child-initiated interactions, and use naturally occurring consequences.
- *Use different cues and prompts to ensure that each child receives adequate support.* Provide only what help is required so the children do not become dependent on teacher assistance.

Teach and Provide Opportunities for Independence   While interdependence is appropriate and normal in human relationships, we expect children to become increasingly independent as they grow.

- *Give children choices whenever possible, and teach choice making when necessary.*
- *Picture schedules can help some children learn to follow the sequence and duration of daily activities.*

- *Because it is easy to overlook nonverbal children, give them frequent chances to respond to teacher initiations.*
- *Maintain high expectations for all children.* Celebrate small victories, and immediately "up the ante," all the while believing that the child has the ability to reach the next objective.

Build a Classroom Community That Includes All Children   Classrooms should be learning communities where everyone makes a valuable contribution and has something to learn.

- *Use activities that will engage children with a large range of abilities.* Plan open-ended activities that use preferred materials, support many responses, and address strengths of children with disabilities.
- *Allow every child to have a turn and play a role.* For example, every child, including children with autism, can take a turn being in charge of handing out materials. This puts the children with disabilities on an equal footing with others in the group and requires them to be communicative partners with peers.

Promote Generalization and Maintenance of Skills   Unless children demonstrate skills across a variety of situations and maintain them over time, they will have limited ability to participate meaningfully in inclusive environments.

- *Target skills that will be useful in each child's life.* Skills a child needs in many situations and those typically enjoyed by same-age children are likely to be generalized and maintained because they are frequently practiced and produce naturally reinforcing outcomes.
- *Use instructional prompts judiciously, and fade them rapidly.* To keep children from depending on adult assistance and direction, use the least directive and intrusive prompt that ensures successful skill performance. Fade the prompt as quickly as possible without disrupting performance.
- *Distribute learning trials naturally.* Capitalize on teaching opportunities that occur within natural school routines and activities.
- *Use common materials for instruction.* Teach with materials frequently found in preschools, child-care settings, and the homes of young children. Arrange for children to practice with these materials across many settings in the classroom. (Adapted from Schwartz, Billingsley, & McBride, 1998, pp. 19–26)

Resource Room and Special Classes

The general education classroom will not be the least restrictive environment for all students with ASD.

> Most children with severe and pervasive disabilities need a classroom that will start at their unique skill levels. The children need to learn numerous and diverse behavior changes, probably different in each of their cases, that, cumulatively, would enable each child to enter and benefit from the general curriculum. To assign children with autism who do not possess those skills to the usual public school classroom is to assign them to regression. (Baer, 2005, p. 9)

Because instructional time is such a precious commodity for students with disabilities, it must be used wisely. For no group of children is this more true than it is for students with autism. Because the potential is high for significant improvements in functioning by children with autism who receive early intensive behaviorally based education and treatment, the phrase "make every minute count" is more than just a slogan. In addition to using words such as *intensive, specialized,* and *focused,* we do not exaggerate by invoking the term *urgent* when describing the special education these children receive. Many students with autism spend a portion of each school day in the general education classroom with same-age peers and part of the day in a resource room where they receive intensive, specialized instruction focused on their individualized education program (IEP) goals and objectives.

Go to the Homework & Exercises section in Chapter 7 of MyEducationLab and complete Homework Exercise 3. As you watch the video and answer the accompanying questions, notice the interactions between the preschool children who have autism and their typically developing peers in this inclusive classroom.

To learn more about inclusive practices, go to the Homework & Exercises section in Chapter 7 and complete Homework Exercise 4.

To learn more about academic instruction in reading and language for children with autism in a resource room, go to the Homework & Exercises section in Chapter 7 of MyEducationLab and complete Homework Exercise 5.

To learn more about social skills instruction for a child with autism and her typically developing peers in a resource room, go to the Homework & Exercises section in Chapter 7 of MyEducationLab and complete Homework Exercise 6.

To learn more about parent–teacher involvement and collaboration, go to the Homework & Exercises section in Chapter 7 of MyEducationLab and complete Homework Exercise 7.

Instruction in a special class or resource room typically features a high frequency of instructional trials per minute; careful specification of and planning for transferring the control of students' responses from teacher-contrived antecedent and consequent stimuli to naturally occurring events; specific strategies for promoting the generalization of newly learned skills to the regular classroom, the community, and the home; continuous recording of data on each child's performance of targeted skills; and the daily review of those data as the basis for making curricular and instructional decisions.

Providing supplemental or booster lessons in the resource room using the same curriculum materials the students encounter in the general education classroom can enhance students' success with those materials in the regular classroom. A resource room can provide an effective setting in which to conduct small-group learning activities with typically developing peers from the regular classroom. The presence of general classroom peers while practicing and learning new skills, especially social and language skills, can make generalization to the regular classroom more natural and likely.

Whatever the setting, involvement with parents and consistency between home and school are critical (Boutot & Tincani, 2006).

DISTINGUISHING UNPROVEN INTERVENTIONS FROM EVIDENCE-BASED PRACTICES FOR CHILDREN WITH AUTISM

A long-standing problem in the field of autism is the popularity of unproven educational interventions and other forms of treatment and therapy for children with autism. Swimming with dolphins, megadoses of vitamins, strange diets, weighted vests, hormone injections, and holding therapy are just some of the treatments for which fantastic claims have been made. Because educators need to understand this issue, we look at two examples of unproven treatments that promised great outcomes and were used widely, identify several factors that contribute to the continued appearance and popularity of dubious interventions, and then suggest several resources that special educators and parents can consult for objective information.

Although special education has always been fertile ground for fads and exaggerated claims (Jacobson, Foxx, & Mulick, 2005a), the field of autism "is particularly well known for its willingness to embrace and/or maintain a liberal tolerance toward unproven and controversial interventions and treatments" (Simpson, 2004, p. 139). Many controversial treatments and cures for autism have been promoted, most without scientific evidence of their effects and benefits (Heflin & Simpson, 2002; Metz, Mulick, & Butter, 2005; Romanczyk et al., 1999; Schreibman, 2005). Two examples are facilitated communication and secretin therapy.

Facilitated Communication

Facilitated communication (FC) is a process by which a communication partner, called a facilitator (most often a teacher; sometimes a friend or parent), provides physical support to assist an individual who cannot speak or whose speech is limited to typing on a keyboard or pointing at pictures, words, or other symbols on a communication board. Facilitated communication was developed in Australia for use with persons with cerebral palsy (Crossley, 1988; Crossley & Remington-Guerney, 1992). It was brought to the United States and used primarily with persons with autism and mental retardation by Biklen, who claimed that individuals with autism and other severe disabilities can carry on typed conversations on complex topics such as current events and economics after training with FC.

Advocates reported that FC has produced dramatically more sophisticated language than the user can produce by speech, signing, or gestures (Biklen, 1990, 1992; Crossley, 1988), which led to speculations of an "undisclosed literacy" consistent with "normal intellectual functioning" by individuals previously thought to have severe or profound intellectual disabilities.

Facilitated communication produced tremendous interest and controversy, both in the professional literature and in the popular media. Claims of meaningful and extensive communication and vocabulary use by individuals with autism or mental retardation whose use of language had previously been nonexistent or extremely limited generated understandable excitement that a powerful and widely effective new treatment might have been discovered. Even though little or no scientific evidence supported these claims, FC was soon being widely implemented in special education and adult human services programs serving individuals with disabilities. During the 1990s, many state education and mental retardation agencies and school districts hired FC experts and sent their teachers to be trained in the new technique. Many children and adults with disabilities were "facilitated" on a daily basis. All of this was done in the absence of any rigorous, scientific evaluation of FC.

Although some educators and many parents raised questions from the beginning about the efficacy and appropriateness of FC, asking for data supporting its use, many more were too excited about the promises of this new wonder therapy to ask many questions. But as the uniformly negative results of carefully controlled empirical studies on FC accumulated (e.g., Oswald, 1994; Simpson & Myles, 1995; Wheeler, Jacobson, Paglieri, & Schwartz, 1993), more began to question its use. Research designed to validate FC has repeatedly demonstrated either facilitator influence (correct or meaningful language is produced only when the facilitator "knows" what should be communicated) or no unexpected language competence compared with the participants' measured IQ or a standard language assessment (for a review, see Jacobson, Foxx, & Mulick, 2005b).

In the light of the overwhelming scientific evidence showing that the communication attributed to individuals with severe disabilities during FC was influenced by the facilitator (Rimland, 1993), several prominent professional organizations passed resolutions or position statements cautioning that FC is unproven and that no important decisions should be made regarding a student's or client's life that are based on the process unless authorship can be confirmed (e.g., AAMR, 1994; APA, 1994). Nevertheless, advocates still promote the use of FC, and it is used in various schools and programs serving children with autism and other developmental disabilities (e.g., Biklen, 2005; Biklen & Cardinal, 1997).

Secretin Therapy

Secretin therapy is a good example of how a systematic line of carefully controlled experiments can help separate fact from fiction and hype from legitimate hope. Secretin is an amino acid hormone released within the proximal duodenum in response to gastric acid secretion. Horvath and colleagues (1998) reported improvements in function in three children with autism who were experiencing gastrointestinal problems and had received intravenous infusions of purified porcine secretin to assess their pancreatic functioning. This report was followed by an explosion of interest in secretin as a treatment for autism, with multiple Internet sites devoted to its use and availability. However, numerous highly controlled studies employing **double-blind, placebo-controlled** studies have found no significant differences on any measure of language, behavior, or autism symptom severity after treatment with secretin compared to treatment with a placebo (Coniglio et al., 2001; Coplan et al., 2003; Dunn-Geier et al., 2000; Molloy et al., 2002; Sandler et al., 1999).

Another study reported that children with autism/PDD with chronic, active diarrhea exhibited a reduction in aberrant behavior when treated with secretin but that problem behaviors of children with autism/PDD who did not have gastrointestinal problems were unaffected by the treatment (Kern, Miller, Evans, & Trivedi, 2002). If discomfort from gastrointestinal problems is a causal factor for some of a child's problem behaviors and secretin relieves that discomfort, it is possible that secretin therapy is correlated with a reduction in problem behavior in such children—but not because it is related to autism. "The bottom line is that secretin does not seem to have any significant effect on the behaviors of children with autism" (Schreibman, 2005, p. 191).

Why Do Fads Thrive?

Parents and teachers of children with a devastating disability such as autism are easy targets for interventions that promise cures. As many authors and families have noted, who among us, parent or teacher, wouldn't look for anything that might help (Maurice & Taylor, 2005)?

CURRENT ISSUES AND FUTURE TRENDS

THE AUTISM WARS

BY CATHERINE MAURICE

Many parents I know, as well as many researchers and clinicians, routinely use the phrase "the autism wars." We know what we're talking about, but people unfamiliar with the politics of autism diagnosis and treatment might not. Briefly, "the autism wars" refers to the fierce infighting and conflicting claims of individuals or groups, each of whom claims to know how best to treat children with autism and derides the theories and methods of the other camps. In an environment where funding is scarce, fear and passion run high, and children's futures are at stake, the autism wars can generate much rancor, to say nothing of confusion.

On Monday, for example, a parent may consult one doctor and be told to place her child in a therapeutic nursery. The doctor will tell the parent to avoid at all costs any program based on behavior analysis because such programs are manipulative, damaging, and tantamount to dog training. On Tuesday, the parent might be told that therapeutic nurseries have little impact on autistic behaviors and often reinforce such behaviors in spite of their warm and fuzzy talk about "nurturing the whole child" and "finding the hidden child within the autistic shell." On Wednesday, the parent is informed by another parent writing on the Internet that massive doses of vitamin B6 can produce meaningful language in the child or that an injection of secretin can have a positive effect on the symptoms of autism.

In the course of hearing or reading these recommendations, the parent learns that professionals are "not to be trusted" and that parents should always "trust their own instincts" and "follow their hearts" when it comes to selecting autism treatments. On Thursday, the same parent is advised to try "an eclectic approach: a little of this and a little of that." Finally, on Friday, the parent is told that there is not a whole lot that anyone can do for autism anyway, so why not come to a weekly support group to discuss "coping" and "feelings" with a coping facilitator?

For a parent of a newly diagnosed child or for a young person intending to teach students with autism, the barrage of conflicting messages can produce frustration, fear, and even despair. It is nothing short of outrageous that the organizations and individuals to whom parents and caregivers have turned for help have by and large failed to produce a set of clear, strong, discriminatory guidelines based on sound scientific principles as well as humanitarian concerns to lead people through the morass of so-called options for autism treatments.

Instead, many experts have tolerated, even encouraged, this time-consuming and expensive experimentation on our children—perhaps to remain popular with parents, who love anyone who gives them hope. But if my child is diagnosed with cancer, I could presumably go to a reputable cancer center and find out which treatments have solid empirical research behind them, which are still experimental, which are "alternative" (an unfortunate euphemism for "there are no scientific data supporting this treatment"), and which are known to cause harm. A reputable cancer treatment center would give me the objective information I needed to make a truly informed choice about my child's well-being. But with autism, bogus therapies have been allowed free rein. The situation is perhaps now beginning to change; but for far too long, too much money, time, and energy have been wasted on fads and "breakthroughs." Colleagues have estimated that more than 100 such miracle cures and "exciting new interventions" currently are being marketed to an extremely vulnerable population (Lockshin, Gillis, & Romanczyk, in press).

I have had two children diagnosed with autism. The sudden loss of language, the increasingly odd and stereotypical behaviors, the avoidance of eye contact, the tantrums, the toe-walking, the crying, the withdrawal into absence and staring—only a parent who has been through this can understand what it means to watch your child slip away into some foreign world, where she herself seems increasingly frustrated and frightened by her inability to communicate her most basic needs. When my daughter and then later my son received this terrifying diagnosis, many people, both professionals and parents, told me how "expert" they were in autism. I was told about their degrees, their far-flung reputations, and their personal experience. But few people had ever bothered to read, much less refer me to, published data in peer-reviewed, science-based journals. All was opinion; all was anecdote; all was theory.

Through the grace of God, I managed to stumble my way through many deviations, mistakes, and wrong turns until I found the program and the people who could truly help my children. Although I was told that applied behavior analysis was cold and harmful, that autism was lifelong, severe, and incurable, I managed somehow to hold onto a little flame of reason in the face of opinion and ideology. The research was there. The data were there. None of the other saviors and experts had anywhere close to the 30-year history of empirical evidence that the field of behavior analysis has accrued.

In 1995, both my daughter and my son were reevaluated (by the same people who first diagnosed them) and were found to have "no significant residua of autism." Throughout their school years, they have been enrolled in general education, without the need for any special services. My daughter, 18 years old, has just graduated from high school and will be attending a 4-year, selective liberal arts college. My son, age 16, has completed his sophomore year in high school, earning high honors for the year. And yes, they have friends; they have their own personalities and opinions about everything; and they know what it means to empathize with another, to feel another's joy or pain or fear.

No, recovery does not happen to all families who choose intensive behavioral intervention, and that truth cannot be stated often enough. There is still so much work to do in order to understand clearly what causes autism and how to prevent it, cure it, or help children recover from it. So far, only a minority of children who receive intensive early intervention are reaching a level of functioning where they are no longer considered autistic. I am glad that the National Alliance for Autism Research (NAAR) was founded to advance the search for a biological understanding of autism. I am glad that other groups, organizations, and research centers around the country are focusing more money and time on the biomedical side of autism. We need serious scholarship and research if we are ever to alleviate the symptoms of autism in every child who receives this diagnosis. One day, I know, such efforts will lead to treatments that may be more effective, less costly, and less labor-intensive than applied behavior analysis (ABA).

However, as such research is going forward, let us not abandon the children who are alive today or leave them floundering in a sea of controversial alternative therapies. At the moment, it appears that ABA offers the best hope for progress. No, not all children will recover under intensive ABA, but virtually all children seem to make appreciable progress. Most develop some level of meaningful language, even if problems remain. Today, I know many families who delight in their children's ever-growing capacity to communicate verbally, to learn, and to love; and even as their children grow older, the learning never ceases.

Does that mean that I believe that ABA is the only current worthwhile treatment for autism? It is not a question of what I or anyone else believes. It is a question of what objective data exist to back up any treatment claim. The education and treatment of children with autism should be based on scientific research, on logic, on common sense, on ethics—not on belief. "Belief" is what has produced those scores of "*exciting new breakthrough treatments*" that you can find on the Internet. Today, more than ever, it is incumbent on all of us to turn to science—the hard science, not the pseudo-science that abounds in popular books, newsletters, and Internet chat rooms—for

guidance on how to help children with autism. And for the sake of all our children, we should never just accept at face value what anyone tells us about research. We need to ask for that research, read it, and find out where it was published. Find out about relevant peer review, control groups, intake evaluations, outcome data, and independent confirmation of findings. Beware of self-published research or research that relies heavily on parent surveys.

One of the hallmarks of good research is finding every possible way to eliminate observer bias. A survey that parents fill out and submit over the Internet about what they think works or not, when so many families are combining three or more treatments at once, is not considered an objective piece of data; and it is irresponsible for anyone to publish the results of such surveys as research. In the history of autism, many bogus treatments have been rushed to market before demonstrating anywhere near enough evidence of their safety and effectiveness. The profiteers are not going to voluntarily curb their behavior. As long as parents are willing to pay thousands of dollars for snake oil, people will sell them snake oil. Only consumers can decide whether or not to keep the purveyors of such marginal treatments in business. It is up to all of us to bring the same kind critical thinking to autism treatments as we would, at the very least, to the purchase of a used car.

Reason and tenderness can walk hand in hand. Judgment, intelligence, compassion, and mercy all have their place in autism treatment. We parents love our children. That's a given. We owe it to them to separate profiteering from progress, sense from nonsense, hope from hype.

What Do You Think?

1. If a child or family member of yours was diagnosed with autism, how would you find the most effective treatment and support?

2. What reasons might account for strong opinions held by some educators against the use of intensive behavioral intervention for educating children with autism?

3. Do you think parents of children with autism may be more vulnerable or inclined to use unproven treatments than parents of children with other disabilities? Why or why not?

RECOMMENDED READINGS ABOUT SCIENCE, PSEUDOSCIENCE, AND DISCRIMINATORY THINKING

Sagan, C. (1995). *The demon-haunted world: Science as a candle in the dark.* New York: Random House.
Singer, M.T., & Lalich, J. (1996). *Crazy therapies: What are they? Do they work?* San Francisco: Jossey-Bass.

RECOMMENDED ORGANIZATIONS, WEBSITES, AND PUBLICATIONS

Autism Biomedical Information Network. www.autism-biomed.org

Maurice, C., Green, G., & Luce, S. C. (Eds.). (1996). *Behavioral intervention for young children with autism: A manual for parents and professionals.* Austin, TX: PRO-ED.

National Alliance for Autism Research. www.NAAR.org

Report of the autism task force. (1999). Augusta: Maine Administrators of Services for Children with Disabilities. www.madsec.org

The Association for Science in Autism Treatment. http://www.asatonline.org

_____

Catherine Maurice holds a Ph.D. in French literature and literary criticism from New York University. She is the author of *Let Me Hear Your Voice; A Family's Triumph Over Autism* (Knopf, 1993), published in multiple languages throughout the world, and the principal editor of two books on research-based interventions for autism: *Behavioral Intervention for Young Children with Autism: A Manual for Parents and Professionals* (Maurice, Green, & Luce, 1996) and *Making a Difference: Behavioral Intervention for Autism* (Maurice, Green, & Foxx, 2001). She was a founding member of the Association for Science in Autism Treatment and continues to serve on its advisory board. In 2001, *Psychology Today* named her the recipient of its Mental Health Award. She lectures widely about the importance of bringing more accountability and scientific rigor into the education and treatment of children with autism.

Children with autism need and deserve an education derived from scientific research, not unproven treatments and fads.

On the Internet, and in huge conferences, parents are encouraged to mix up chemical cocktails for their children, to put them on radical diets, to subject them to hours of brushing and stroking, even to inject them with unproven substances. Often, the promoters of these fads encourage parents to submit testimonials, and these testimonials are then published as "research." One colleague estimates that there are now over 100 proposed treatments—each one has its web site, its passionate advocates, and its claim to copious research. (Maurice, 2004, n.p.)

Unproven treatment fads for children with autism thrive . . .

- When the available treatments are not producing cures for the majority of those treated.
- When the underlying cause of a disorder is unknown or mysterious.
- Because hope and need are far stronger motivators than reason or skepticism.
- When we lean too much on the authority, fame, or niceness of those promoting the fads.
- Because often, neither parents nor the professionals they consult understand what constitutes credible evidence. (adapted from Maurice, 2004)

Programs for children with ASDs that have adopted unproven methods have slowed students' progress and fostered the creation of unrealistic expectations. Such "overreliance on undocumented interventions and treatments has complicated the process of discriminating innovative interventions that have promise for effective professional application from those whose primary strength is hyperbole and exaggeration" (Simpson, 2004, p. 140).

Fortunately, parents and professionals can turn to systematic evaluations of autism treatments and objective reports such as the National Research Council's (2001) report *Educating Children with Autism,* the State of Maine's *Report of the Autism Task Force* (1999), and *Clinical Practice Guidelines: Report of the Recommendations* (1999), published by the New York State Department of Health. The National Autism Center's (2007)

National Standards Project will develop a handbook of evidence-based practices and implementation guidelines for schools.

To read one parent's perspectives on the anguish of trying to separate unsubstantiated claims from scientifically validated treatments for her two children, see Current Issues and Future Trends, "The Autism Wars."

TIPS for Beginning Teachers

WORKING WITH STUDENTS WITH AUTISM SPECTRUM DISORDERS
by Kito Kazuko and Beth Mueninghoff

INDIVIDUALIZE TO THE MAX

All special education involves developing instructional programs designed to meet the individual needs of each child. For students with autism, the need to individualize cannot be overstated.

- Each student will have many more learning needs than you can meet. Most will exhibit communication, self-help, academic, and social skills that are far behind those of typical children. You will not be able to teach everything at once, or even everything—ever. Observe each child during academic, social, and other routines during the school day, and ask yourself which skills will be immediately useful for each student and have a greatest positive impact on her daily life.
- Carefully observing a child's autistic nature often helps identify effective reinforcers. Many children with autism develop their own unique special interests, and often they seem content in their own world as long as they have what they want. Some autistic children appear to lack a desire to reach out to the world outside. We often use their autism to work for us in teaching important skills to our children. For example, if John has a fixation for wheels, we can use cars and other toys with wheels to teach him to make a request using a sign or a picture card.

FOCUS ON TEACHING SKILLS, NOT DECREASING BEHAVIORS

Some students with autism have frequent tantrums, are aggressive toward others, make stereotypic movements, or engage in self-injurious behaviors. Children with autism, like all children, may engage in challenging and harmful behaviors because they have not learned appropriate ways in which to meet their needs.

- *Instead of telling a student what not to do, suggest what to do.* For example, if a student grabs a book from another student, explain that the student should ask for the book, model the appropriate behavior and then have the student imitate it.
- *Create and use interventions that offer children alternative behaviors.* Interventions that focus solely on reducing the frequency of negative behaviors are often ineffective and shortsighted because they do not teach the children alternative, appropriate ways to control their world.
- *Try to determine what function a negative behavior has for a student.* For example, when James throws a tantrum, is he usually involved in a difficult task or an undesirable activity? After you have discovered this function, then teach an appropriate replacement behavior (e.g., teach James how to signal or ask for a break from a task).

TAKE ADVANTAGE OF TEACHABLE MOMENTS

Teachable moments are naturally occurring situations or events that provide the opportunity to teach a lesson on the spot. A child spilling his milk during snack time, for example, provides his teacher with a wonderful chance to provide prompts and instruction for a variety of language, emotional, communication, and social skills—in addition to the real-world practice of motor, self-help, and vocational skills involved in cleaning up the mess!

- *Always be on the lookout for teachable moments.* Actions that occur at any time throughout the day can provide wonderful learning opportunities, particularly during transitions. Use naturally occurring situations throughout the day for students to practice their language and social skills.
- *Don't just wait for teachable moments to occur; contrive them.* For example, during a snack or play activity, hide the juice or part of a toy so that the child has to communicate to obtain the desired item.

COMMUNICATE AND CELEBRATE WITH PARENTS

Kazuko uses home-school communication journals as well as a daily activity sheet. Beth uses only home-school communication journals. In a journal, we write to inform parents of how their children did at school. Kazuko sends home a daily activity sheet to encourage socialization as well as communication between parent and child.

- *Home-school dialogue journal.* This notebook goes back and forth between home and school. At the beginning of a school year, make a daily entry to inform parents about their child's school day. The parents also write in the journal whenever they have a concern, question, or something they wish to share with the teacher. As the school year progresses, make an entry on an as needed basis. The parents also write in the journal to bring whatever they feel is important to the teacher's attention. It is also a good way to celebrate together even the tiniest progress a child makes at home or school.

- *Daily home-school report with picture symbols.* This communication sheet with picture symbols shows activities the students have enjoyed at school. A daily activity sheet consists of numerous picture symbols. Circle the activities the students enjoyed at school such as speech, cooking, and art. Also write a word or two to give parents more details for each activity, for example, circle "cooking" and write "we made red Jell-O" next to it. Ask the parents to go over the sheet and talk about what happened at school with their child. At the beginning of a school year, ask parents to go over this report with their child at home. The pictures help the children "talk about" what they did at school with their parent. It is also informative for the parents, because the report includes information such as their child's behavior, activities, and supplies that need to be sent to school.

- *Celebrate accomplishments.* Each time a student moves another step toward reaching your high expectations for success, celebrate that achievement with the student and his family.

KEY TERMS AND CONCEPTS

applied behavior analysis (ABA), p. 274
Asperger syndrome, p. 258
autism p. 257
autism spectrum disorders (ASD), p. 258
autistic disorder, p. 258
autistic savants, p. 262
behavior trap, p. 266
childhood disintegrative disorder, p. 260
discrete trial training (DTT), p. 275
double-blind, placebo-controlled study, p. 285

echolalia, p. 261
facilitated communication, p. 284
joint attention, p. 261
pervasive developmental disorders—not otherwise specified (PDD-NOS), p. 261
pica, p. 264
Rett syndrome, p. 260
social stories, p. 280
stereotypy, p. 263

SUMMARY

Definitions

- Autism spectrum disorders (ASD) include five developmental disabilities of childhood: autistic disorder; Asperger syndrome; Rett syndrome; childhood disintegrative disorder; and pervasive developmental disorder—not otherwise specified (PDD-NOS).

- Autistic disorder is marked by three defining features, with onset before age 3 years: (a) qualitative impairment of social interaction; (b) qualitative impairment of communication; and (c) restricted, repetitive, and stereotyped patterns of behavior, interests, and activities.

- Asperger syndrome is marked by impairments in all social areas, particularly an inability to understand how to interact socially. Other defining characteristics include repetitive and stereotyped behaviors, preoccupation with atypical things, pedantic speech patterns, and difficulties with motor activities. Children with Asperger syndrome do not have general language delay, and most have average or above-average intelligence.

- Rett syndrome, a distinct neurological condition that begins between 5 and 30 months of age, is marked by a slowing of head growth, stereotypic hand movements, a gradual onset of unsteadiness and awkward gait, and severe impairments in language and cognitive abilities.
- Childhood disintegrative disorder shares characteristics with autistic disorder, but the condition does not begin until after age 2 and sometimes not until age 10.
- Pervasive developmental disorder—not otherwise specified (PDD-NOS) is the diagnosis given to children who meet some, but not all, of the criteria for autistic disorder. PDD-NOS is marked by significant impairments in socialization with difficulties in either communication or restricted interests.

Characteristics

- Some children with ASD are severely affected in most or all domains of functioning, while others are only mildly affected. Children with different diagnoses along the spectrum may share many characteristics.
- Impaired social relationships include difficulty in perceiving the emotional state of others, expressing emotions, and forming attachments and relationships, as well as deficits in joint attention (e.g., not looking at what a parent points to).
- Many children with ASD do not speak. Echolalia is common among those who do talk.
- Children with ASD tend to exhibit concrete or literal processing of verbal information and have difficulty understanding the social meanings of language.
- A diagnosis of ASD can be made for a child with severe or profound mental retardation as well as for one who is intellectually gifted.
- Many children with ASD exhibit the following cognitive and learning characteristics:
  - Overselectivity—the tendency to focus on a minute feature of an object or a person rather than the whole
  - Obsessive attention on a specific object or activity for long periods of time
  - Strong aptitude for rote memory for certain things but difficulty recalling recent events
  - Uneven skill development—areas of relatively superior performance that are unexpected compared to other domains of functioning
- Very rarely, autism savant syndrome—an extraordinary ability in a specific area or skill while functioning at the mental retardation level in all other areas
- Children with ASD may show unusual responsiveness to sensory stimuli: overresponsiveness (hypersensitivity)—for example, intense dislike of certain sounds, being touched, or the feel of certain textures—and/or underresponsiveness (hyposensitivity)—for example, no reaction to stimuli that are painful to most people.
- Children may obsess about having everything in their environment stay the same and become very upset when items are moved or when routines change.
- Children may exhibit stereotypic and self-stimulatory behaviors, such as rocking their bodies when in a sitting position, twirling around, flapping hands, flicking fingers, or spinning things.
- Children may exhibit aggressive and self-injurious behavior.
- Some people with autism spectrum disorders have described positive features associated with their disability, such as sensitivity to detail and intense interest in topics, which can be assets to functioning in some environments.

Prevalence

- Historically considered a rare disorder, recent estimates show autism occurs in as many as 1 in 150 people.
- Boys are affected about 4 times more often than are girls.
- Autism is the fastest-growing category in special education.
- Reasons for the huge increase in the number of children with ASD receiving special education are not clear but may include more awareness of the disability, more widespread screening and better assessment procedures, greater availability of services via the disability category, and an actual increase in the true incidence of the disability.

Causes

- For many years, it was widely thought that parents who were indifferent to the emotional needs of their children caused autism. However, no causal link between parental personality and autism was ever discovered.
- Recent research shows a clear biological origin for autism in the form of abnormal brain development, structure, and/or neurochemistry.
- Some experts believe that certain genes may make a child more susceptible to autism but that exposure to certain environmental factors may lead to the development of the disorder in some individuals.

Identification and Assessment

- No medical test for autism spectrum disorders is available; a diagnosis is most often made according to DSM-IV criteria.
- Autism can be reliably diagnosed at 18 months of age with research currently developing methods for diagnosis by the child's first birthday.
- Screening of babies for early warning signs is critical because early diagnosis is correlated with dramatically better outcomes.
- Signs that warrant concern during the first 18 months of life include lack of pointing or gestures, infrequent or poor imitation, no single words by 16 months, lack of smiling, not responding to name, lack of joint attention, and loss of previously acquired language or social skills.

Educational Approaches

- Children with autism are among the most difficult to teach of all students; they require carefully planned, meticulously delivered, and continually evaluated and analyzed instruction.
- Although the prognosis for children with autistic disorder was traditionally extremely poor, early intensive behaviorally based education and treatment has helped some children achieve communication, language, and social skills so they can succeed in general education classrooms.
- Among the many treatments and therapies available for helping children with autism, interventions based on applied behavior analysis (ABA) have the clearest and most consistent research evidence supporting their effectiveness.
- Discrete trial training (DTT) is an important part of ABA-based programming for children with autism. However, DTT alone does not constitute ABA, and ABA can be done without DTT.
- ABA programming uses a variety of procedures to help individuals with autism acquire and generalize new skills, such as strategies for shifting stimulus control, the Picture Exchange Communication System, peer-mediated interventions, functional assessment, and naturalistic teaching strategies, to name a few.
- Picture activity schedules—a series of images, photos, icons, or video clips depicting activities a child can perform, presented in sequence—can help children with autism independently select and carry out a sequence of activities in the classroom.
- Social stories, which explain social situations and expected behaviors of the persons involved in a format understandable to a student with ASD, can decrease a child's anxiety about an event, improve his behavior, and help him understand events from the perspective of others.

Educational Placement Alternatives

- Approximately 3 in 10 students with ASD are educated in general education classrooms. About 18% of students with ASD are served in resource rooms, 40% in separate classrooms, and 10% in separate schools or residential facilities.
- Strategies for providing effective education for young children with autism in inclusive classrooms include (Schwartz et al., 1998) the following:
  - Teach communication and social competence.
  - Use instructional strategies that maintain the class's natural flow.
  - Teach and provide opportunities for independence.

- Build a classroom community that includes all children.
- Promote the generalization and maintenance of skills.

- Instruction in the resource room or other specialized setting should feature a high frequency of instructional trials, procedures for transferring control of student responses from teacher-contrived events to naturally occurring events, strategies for promoting the generalization of newly learned skills, and daily review of data on each child's performance for making curricular and instructional decisions.

- Regardless of the setting in which a child with autism is served, the presence of socially competent children is helpful because peer-mediated interventions are among the most effective types of interventions for teaching communication and social skills to children with ASD.

- Whatever the child's educational placement, parent involvement and consistency between home and school are critical components for optimal learning.

Distinguishing Unproven Interventions From Evidence-Based Practices for Children With Autism

- A serious problem in the field of autism is the popularity of unproven interventions and therapies.

- Parents and professionals should select autism treatments on the basis of careful and systematic evaluations of the scientific evidence of their effects and benefits.

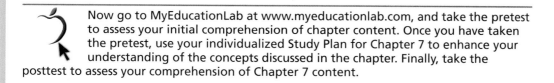

Now go to MyEducationLab at www.myeducationlab.com, and take the pretest to assess your initial comprehension of chapter content. Once you have taken the pretest, use your individualized Study Plan for Chapter 7 to enhance your understanding of the concepts discussed in the chapter. Finally, take the posttest to assess your comprehension of Chapter 7 content.

8

Communication Disorders

- How do definitions of speech and language impairments relate to one another and to typical language development?
- What basic types of communication disorders might statements such as "The dogs runned home" and "That foop is dood" signal?
- What is the relative prevalence of speech and language impairments by gender and age groups?
- How are causes of speech and language impairments classified?
- What are the major components of a comprehensive evaluation to detect the presence and extent of a communication disorder?
- What are the basic goals and common elements of effective interventions for speech-sound errors? for language disorders?
- How does the role of the speech-language pathologist change as a function of the educational setting in which a child with communication disorders is served?

FEATURED TEACHER

STEVEN EVERLING
Northwest Elementary School • Pinellas County School District, Largo, Florida

Steven Everling

Education—Teaching Credentials—Experience

- B.A., communication sciences and disorders, University of South Florida, 1995
- M.S., speech-language pathology, University of South Florida, 2000
- Florida, speech and language impaired, K–12; Florida, exceptional student education, K–12; Florida, licensure as a speech-language pathologist; certificate of clinical competence in speech-language pathology from the American Speech-Language-Hearing Association
- 11 years of experience as a speech-language pathologist

Current Teaching Position and Students I've been a speech-language pathologist in the Pinellas County Schools for 11 years. My first 4 years were in a middle school. For 3 years I taught the entire academic curriculum—language arts, reading, math, science, and social studies—in a self-contained classroom for students with severe language impairments. The emphasis was on promoting language development across the curriculum. The next year, I taught language arts to students who were in the language-impaired resource program and provided pull-out speech therapy services to students with impairments of articulation, voice, and fluency. For the past 7 years, I have delivered speech and language services in both a resource room and an inclusion setting at Northwest Elementary, a K–5 building with about 700 students.

The 50 students I'm serving this year are between the ages of 3 and 12 and are classified as speech and/or language impaired. Students range among grades PK–5. Some of my students also receive services because of developmental delay, learning disability, or emotional disturbance.

IEP Goals Here are examples of IEP goals and objectives for some of my students this year:

Annual goal. Brian will complete story-related activities on four out of five opportunities over five consecutive sessions.

Short-term objective 1. Brian will sequence story events.

Short-term objective 2. Brian will identify and discuss the conflict and resolution of a story, with or without prompts.

Annual goal. Sarena will increase speech intelligibility by decreasing the use of a consonant deletion pattern at the appropriate developmental level on 8 of 10 opportunities over five consecutive sessions.

Short-term objective 1. Sarena will be able to decrease her rate of speech.

Short-term objective 2. Sarena will more closely approximate consonant sounds within utterances in the speech therapy room.

Annual goal. Lee will increase fluent speech on four out of five opportunities over five consecutive sessions.

Short-term objective 1. Lee will identify fluent and nonfluent speech in himself.

Short-term objective 2. Lee will identify struggle behaviors in himself.

Short-term objective 3. Lee will produce sentences fluently using an easy onset strategy.

Curriculum Materials and Teaching Strategies I try to create functional communication situations that best support my students' individual speech and language needs. For students with language-related impairments, this includes making connections to reading and spelling wherever appropriate. I help students develop meaningful strategies they can implement as active learners to construct their own meanings through both interpersonal interactions and interactions with print. Examples of thematic materials that I have found useful include *Literature-Based Reading Activities* (Yopp & Yopp, 2001) and *The Magic of Stories: Literature-Based Language Intervention* (Strong & North, 1996), among others.

For children with language needs, strategies must be specific to the individual child. In general, I have found that many children with language disabilities have significant problems making inferences in both the oral and print domains. For example, Brian, an 11-year-old with specific learning disabilities and language impairments, could not organize the structure of a storybook. Brian's special education teacher and I collaborated on teaching him several ways to organize text-based information. These strategies included story search procedures to find important information and story maps and other graphic organizers to arrange key information so that he could make reasonable inferences. I help students with articulation, voice, or fluency problems develop techniques and strategies that enable them to be more effective communicators in their everyday school and home environments.

Collaboration and Teaming I work and interact with several different professionals daily. I collaborate with general education and special education teachers to help them become aware of the unique communication needs of students with speech and/or language impairments. I also explain and demonstrate techniques they can use to facilitate language learning and assist in the generalization of skills and strategies the students have learned in speech and language therapy. I talk frequently with the school psychologist because the speech and language assessments I administer are often a component of the multifactored evaluations conducted whenever a student is referred for special education. On occasion, I interact with the occupational and physical therapists on ways we can assist each other with skill carryover for students.

What I Like Most About Being a Special Educator There are two things I like most about being a special educator. First, I enjoy working with a variety of students, each of whom presents a unique set of speech and/or language needs. From the student who stutters, to the student who exhibits speech-sound errors, to the student who has difficulties with language-based concepts, finding effective strategies for communicative success is always rewarding. Second, I appreciate collaborating with other educators and school personnel who share a similar desire to help students achieve their potential.

Advice to Someone Considering a Career in Special Education My main advice for anyone considering a career in special education is first and foremost to set high, yet realistic, expectations for students in both academics and behavior. In my experience, students generally strive to reach the standards expected of them. Second, it is important to be flexible, because each day you'll be confronted with new situations and challenges. Third, open communication with parents can make all the difference. Involving parents in their child's education encourages appropriate student behavior and increases the likelihood that the skills you are teaching in the classroom will be practiced and reinforced at home.

The Most Difficult Thing About Being a Special Educator The most difficult thing about this job is finding enough time to get everything accomplished: student instruction, lesson planning, individualized education programs (IEPs) and related paperwork, parent contacts, school-wide faculty duties and responsibilities, just to name a few. However, I have found that the longer I work in the school system, the more efficiently and effectively I can manage the multiple responsibilities of a special educator's typical school day.

Most Meaningful Accomplishments as a Special Educator My most meaningful accomplishments occur when my students improve in their ability to be effective communicators. For example, a first-grade student, John, who was receiving services for both specific learning disabilities and speech impairments, presented with such a severe phonological impairment that his speech was nearly impossible to understand. John produced most speech sounds in the front of his mouth while omitting sounds at the end of words, which made his speech unintelligible to most listeners. For example, toward the end of our first therapy session, when John said, "Ti to toe," I had to ask him to repeat himself a couple of times before I realized he was trying to say, "Time to go." All of John's utterances exhibited similar speech patterns. Over the course of his first- and second-grade years, I saw John 2 hours per week for speech therapy. At the beginning of his first-grade year, his reluctance to speak was a clear effect of his not being understood by his parents, teachers, and friends. One can imagine John's frustration: always being asked to repeat himself and then still not being understood. By the end of his second-grade year, John's speech, while still noticeably in error, was for the vast majority of utterances intelligible to those with whom he most commonly interacted. By that time, John had become a much more verbal and assertive child, a result, at least partially, of his now being able to more effectively communicate with others. Students like John make my responsibilities as a speech-language pathologist real and meaningful.

Communication—the sending and receiving of information—is such a fundamental part of the human experience that we cannot stop communicating even when we want to. You may decide to say nothing, but sometimes saying nothing communicates a great deal. Still, imagine trying to go through an entire day without speaking. How would you make contact with other people? You would be frustrated when others did not understand your needs and feelings. By the end of the day, besides feeling exhausted from trying to make yourself understood, you might even start to question your ability to function adequately in the world.

Although relatively few people with communication disorders are completely unable to express themselves, an exercise such as the one just described would increase your awareness of some of the problems and frustrations faced every day by children and adults who cannot communicate effectively. Children who cannot absorb information through listening and reading and/or cannot express their desires, thoughts, and feelings in spoken words are virtually certain to encounter difficulties in their schools and communities. When communication disorders persist, it may be hard for children to learn and develop and to form satisfying relationships with other people.

After reading this chapter, complete the pretest for Chapter 8 on MyEducationLab to assess your initial understanding of chapter content.

DEFINITIONS

Before we define communication disorders, a discussion of some basic terms is necessary.

Communication

Communication is the interactive exchange of information, ideas, feelings, needs, and desires. It involves encoding, transmitting, and decoding messages. Each communication interaction includes three elements: (a) a message, (b) a sender who expresses the message, and (c) a receiver who responds to the message. Although intra-individual communication occurs when the same person is both sender and receiver of the same message (e.g., when we talk to ourselves or write a note to remind ourselves to do something when we read it later), communication most often involves at least two participants, each playing the dual roles of sender and receiver.

In addition to enabling some degree of control in a social environment, communication serves several important functions, particularly between teachers and children (Lindfoors, 1987; Owens, 2008).

Narrating   Children need to be able to tell (and follow the telling of) a story—that is, a sequence of related events connected in an orderly, clear, and interesting manner. Five-year-old Cindy tells her teacher, "I had a birthday party. I wore a funny hat. Daddy made a cake, and Mommy took pictures." Fourteen-year-old Ian tells the class about the events leading up to Christopher Columbus's first voyage to America.

Explaining/Informing   Teachers expect children to interpret the explanations of others in speech and writing and to put what they understand into words so that their listeners or readers will be able to understand it, too. In a typical classroom, children must respond frequently to teachers' questions: "Which number is larger?" "How do you suppose the story will end?" "Why do you think George Washington was a great president?"

Requesting   Children are expected to communicate their wishes and desires to others in socially appropriate ways. A child who has learned to state requests clearly and politely is more likely to get what she wants and less likely to engage in inappropriate behavior as a way to communicate her needs.

Expressing   It is important for children to express their personal feelings and opinions and to respond to the feelings of others. Speech and language can convey joy, fear, frustration, humor, sympathy, anger. A child writes, "I have just moved. And it is hard to find a friend because I am shy." Another tells her classmates, "Guess what? I have a new baby brother!" Through such communicative interactions, children gradually develop a sense of self and an awareness of other people.

Although speech and language form the message system most often used in human communication, spoken or written words are not necessary for communication to occur. In fact, researchers estimate that between 50% and 90% of the information in some face-to-face interactions may be communicated by nonspeech means (Lue, 2001; Owens, 2008). Both paralinguistic behaviors and nonlinguistic cues play major roles in human communication. *Paralinguistic behaviors* include speech modifications (e.g., variations in pitch, intonation, rate of delivery, pauses) and nonlanguage sounds (e.g., "oohh," laughter) that change the form and meaning of the message. *Nonlinguistic cues* include body posture, facial expressions, gestures, eye contact, head and body movement, and physical proximity.

Language

Language is a formalized code used by a group of people to communicate with one another. All languages consist of a set of abstract symbols—sounds, letters, numbers, elements of sign language—and a system of rules for combining those symbols into larger units (Hulit & Howard, 2006; Owens, 2008). Languages are not static; they grow and develop as tools for communication as the cultures and communities of which they are part change (Pence & Justice, 2008). Nearly 7,000 living languages are spoken in the world (Gordon, 2005). It is estimated that 60%–75% of the world's population speak more than one language (Baker, 2000).

The symbols and rules governing language are essentially arbitrary no matter what language is spoken. The arbitrariness of language means there is usually no logical, natural, or required relationship between a set of sounds and the object, concept, or action it represents. The word *whale,* for example, brings to mind a large mammal that lives in the sea; but the sound of the word has no apparent connection with the creature. *Whale* is merely a symbol we use for this particular mammal. A small number of *onomatopoeic words*—such as "tinkle," "buzz," and "hiss"—are considered to sound like what they represent, but most words have no such relationship. Likewise, some hand positions or movements in sign language, called *iconic signs,* look like the object or event they represent (e.g., tipping an imaginary cup to one's lips is the manual sign for "drink"). Remember, language is used to express descriptions of and relations between objects and events; it does not reproduce those objects and events.

Five Dimensions of Language   Language is often described along five dimensions that define its *form* (phonology, morphology, syntax), *content* (semantics), and *use* (pragmatics). **Phonology** refers to the linguistic rules governing a language's sound system. Phonological rules describe how sounds can be sequenced and combined. The English language uses approximately 45 different sound elements, called **phonemes.** Only the initial phoneme prevents the words *pear* and *bear* from being identical, for example; yet in one case we think of a fruit, in the other a large animal.

The **morphology** of a language is concerned with the basic units of meaning and how those units are combined into words. **Morphemes,** the smallest elements of language that carry meaning, can be sounds, syllables, or whole words. *Free morphemes* can stand alone (e.g., *fit, slow*). *Bound morphemes* do not carry meaning by themselves; they are grammatical markers that change the meaning of words when attached to free morphemes (e.g., *unfit, slowly*). The word *baseballs* consists of two free morphemes (*base* and *ball*) and one bound morpheme (*s*).

Syntax is the system of rules governing the meaningful arrangement of words into sentences. If morphemes could be strung together in any order, language would be an unintelligible tangle of words. Syntactical rules are language-specific (e.g., Japanese and English have different rules); and they specify the acceptable (i.e., grammatical) relationships among the subject, verb, object, and other sentence elements. The meaning of a sentence cannot be derived from the congregate meanings of the individual words; it is found in the interactive meanings of those words as the result of their grammatical and sequential relationships with one another. For example, "Help my chicken eat," conveys a meaning much different from "Help eat my chicken."

Semantics has to do with the meaning of words and combinations of words. A competent language user possesses semantic knowledge that includes vocabulary and concept development, connotative meanings by context (*hot* refers to air temperature when discussing the weather but means something else when talking about an athlete's recent performance), categories (*collies* and *beagles* are *dogs*), and relationships between words such as antonyms and synonyms.

Pragmatics is a set of rules governing how spoken language is used to communicate. There are three kinds of pragmatic skills (American Speech-Language-Hearing Association, 2007a): (a) using language to achieve various communicative functions and goals (e.g., greeting, informing, demanding, promising, requesting); (b) changing language according to the conversational context (e.g., talking differently to a baby than to an adult, giving background information to an unfamiliar listener, speaking differently in a classroom than on a playground); and (c) following rules for conversations and storytelling (e.g., taking turns, staying on topic, rephrasing when misunderstood, how close to stand when someone is talking, facial expressions and eye contact). Rules vary across languages and cultures.

Good communicators use nonlinguistic cues such as body posture and gestures and pragmatic conversational skills such as turn taking.

Speech

Speech is the oral production of language. Although it is not the only vehicle for expressing language (e.g., gestures, manual signing, pictures, and written symbols are also used), speech is the fastest, most efficient method of communication by language. Speech sounds are the product of four separate but related processes (Hulit & Howard, 2006): *respiration* (breathing provides the power supply for speech); *phonation* (the production of sound when the vocal folds of the larynx are drawn together by the contraction of specific muscles, causing the air to vibrate); *resonation* (the sound quality of the vibrating air, shaped as it passes through the throat, mouth, and sometimes nasal cavities); and *articulation* (the formation of specific, recognizable speech sounds by the tongue, lips, teeth, and mouth). Figure 8.1 shows the organs used to produce speech sounds.

Speech is one of the most complex and difficult human endeavors. Hulit and Howard (2006) describe just some of what happens in speaking a single word, *statistics.*

The tip of the tongue is lifted from a resting position to an area on the roof of the mouth just behind the upper teeth called the alveolar ridge to produce the "s" sound. The tongue is pressed against the alveolar ridge hard enough to produce constriction, but not so hard as to stop the airflow altogether. As the speaker slowly contracts the muscles of exhalation under

FIGURE 8.1

Speech organs

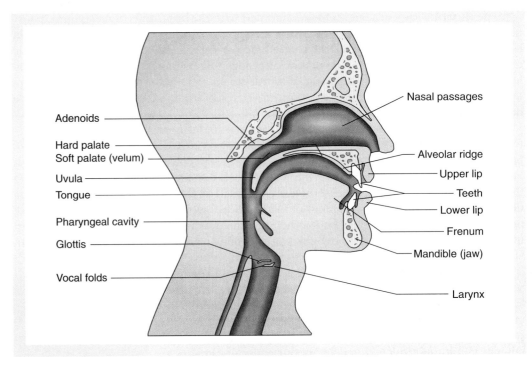

precise control, air is forced between the tip of the tongue and the alveolar ridge. Leaving the tongue in the same area, the speaker now presses a little harder to stop the airflow and then quickly releases the contact for the production of the "t" sound. The tongue drops to a neutral position and the vocal folds in the larynx vibrate to produce the vowel "a." The speaker turns off the larynx and lifts the tongue to the alveolar ridge for the next "t," then vibrates the vocal folds for the vowel "i" while the tongue stays in a forward but slightly lowered position. The speaker turns the larynx off again and moves the tongue to the alveolar ridge yet again to produce the controlled constriction for the next "s," followed by increased pressure to stop the air flow and release it for the "t." The larynx is turned on one more time and the tongue lowered to a neutral position for the "i," and then turned off as the tongue arches to the back of the mouth where it contacts the velum, or fleshy part of the roof of the mouth, for the "k." Finally, the tongue tip darts to the alveolar ridge for the production of the final "s" sound.

All of this occurs in the production of *one* word! (p. 5)

Most languages begin in oral form, developed by people speaking with each other. Reading and writing are secondary language forms that use graphic symbols to represent the oral form. There is no one-to-one correspondence, however, between **graphemes** (print symbols or letters) and phonemes.

Typical Speech and Language Development

Despite the complexity of speech and language, most children, without any formal instruction, learn to talk during the first few years of life. The process of learning language is a remarkable one that is not fully understood. For centuries parents, teachers, and scholars have been fascinated by the phenomenon of language acquisition in children.

Understanding how young, typically developing children acquire language is helpful to the teacher or specialist working with children who have delayed or disordered communication. Knowledge of typical language development can help the specialist determine whether a particular child is simply developing language at a slower-than-usual rate or whether the child shows an atypical pattern of language development. Figure 8.2 identifies some of the key features of speech and language development of a typically developing child. As we consider typical language development, remember that the ages at which children acquire certain speech and language skills are not rigid and inflexible. Children's abilities and early environments vary widely, and all of these factors affect language development. Nevertheless, most children follow a predictable sequence in their acquisition of speech and language.

Typical language development

Content Standards for Beginning Teachers—Common Core: Educational implications of characteristics of exceptionalities (CC2K1).

FIGURE 8.2	Overview of typical language development

Birth to 6 months
- Infant first communicates by crying, which produces a reliable consequence in the form of parental attention.
- Different types of crying develop—a parent can often tell from the baby's cry whether she is wet, tired, or hungry.
- Comfort sounds—coos, gurgles, and sighs—contain some vowels and consonants.
- Comfort sounds develop into babbling, sounds that in the beginning are apparently made for the enjoyment of feeling and hearing them.
- Vowel sounds, such as /i/ (pronounced "ee") and /e/ (pronounced "uh"), are produced earlier than consonants, such as /m/, /b/, and /p/.
- Infant does not attach meaning to words she hears from others but may react differently to loud and soft voices.
- Infant turns eyes and head in the direction of a sound.

7 to 12 months
- Babbling becomes differentiated before the end of the first year and contains some of the same phonetic elements as the meaningful speech of 2-year-olds.
- Baby develops inflection—her voice rises and falls.
- She may respond appropriately to "no," "bye-bye," or her own name and may perform an action, such as clapping her hands, when told to.
- She will repeat simple sounds and words, such as "mama."

12 to 18 months
- By 18 months, most children have learned to say several words with appropriate meaning.
- Pronunciation is far from perfect; baby may say "tup" when you point to a cup or "goggie" when she sees a dog.
- She communicates by pointing and perhaps saying a word or two.
- She responds to simple commands such as "Give me the cup" and "Open your mouth."

18 to 24 months
- Most children go through a stage of echolalia, in which they repeat, or echo, the speech they hear. Echolalia is a normal phase of language development, and most children outgrow it by about the age of 2½.
- There is a great spurt in acquisition and use of speech; baby begins to combine words into short sentences, such as "Daddy bye-bye" and "Want cookie."
- Receptive vocabulary grows even more rapidly; at 2 years of age she may understand more than 1,000 words.
- Understands such concepts as "soon" and "later" and makes more subtle distinctions between objects such as cats and dogs and knives, forks, and spoons.

2 to 3 years
- The 2-year-old child talks, saying sentences such as "I won't tell you" and asking questions such as "Where my daddy go?"
- She participates in conversations.
- She identifies colors, uses plurals, and tells simple stories about her experiences.
- She can follow compound commands such as "Pick up the doll and bring it to me."
- She uses most vowel sounds and some consonant sounds correctly.

(Continues)

| FIGURE 8.2 | Overview of typical language development (Continued) |

3 to 4 years
- The normal 3-year-old has lots to say, speaks rapidly, and asks many questions.
- She may have an expressive vocabulary of 900–1,000 different words, using sentences of three to four words.
- Sentences are longer and more varied: "Cindy's playing in water"; "Mommy went to work"; "The cat is hungry."
- She uses speech to request, protest, agree, and make jokes.
- She understands children's stories; grasps such concepts as funny, bigger, and secret; and can complete simple analogies such as "In the daytime it is light; at night it is . . . "
- She substitutes certain sounds, perhaps saying "baf" for "bath" or "yike" for "like."
- Many 3-year-olds repeat sounds or words ("b-b-ball," "l-l-little"). These repetitions and hesitations are normal and do not indicate that the child will develop a habit of stuttering.

4 to 5 years
- The child has a vocabulary of more than 1,500–2,000 words and uses sentences averaging five words in length.
- She begins to modify her speech for the listener; for example, she uses longer and more complex sentences when talking to her mother than when addressing a baby or a doll.
- She can define words such as "hat," "stove," and "policeman" and can ask questions such as "How did you do that?" or "Who made this?"
- She uses conjunctions such as "if," "when," and "because."
- She recites poems and sings songs from memory.
- She may still have difficulty with consonant sounds such as /r/, /s/, /z/ and /j/ and with blends such as "tr," "gl," "sk," and "str."

After 5 years
- Language continues to develop steadily, although less dramatically, after age 5.
- A typical 6-year-old uses most of the complex forms of adult English and has an expressive vocabulary of 2,600 words and a receptive understanding of more than 20,000 words.
- Most children achieve adult speech sound production by age 7.
- Grammar and speech patterns of a child in first grade usually match those of her family, neighborhood, and region.

Source: Adapted from ASHA (2001d); Hart & Risley (1999); Hodson (1994); Hulit & Howard (2006); Owens (2008); Porter & Hodson (2001); Shames & Anderson (2002).

As the descriptions in Figure 8.2 indicate, children's words and sentences often differ from adult forms while children are learning language. Children who use structures such as "All gone sticky" and "Where he is going?"; pronunciations such as "cwackers" and "twuck"; or word forms such as "comed," "goed," or "sheeps" gradually learn to replace them with acceptable adult forms. These early developmental forms drop out as the child matures, usually without any special drilling or direct instruction (Hulit & Howard, 2006; Owens, 2008). It is also worth noting that children often produce speech sounds inconsistently. The clarity of a sound may vary according to factors such as where the sound occurs in a word and how familiar the word is to the child. Children whose expressive vocabularies consist of fewer than 50 words and/or produce limited word combinations at 24 months of age are considered late talkers. Kelly (1998) reviews the late talker literature and makes recommendations for serving this population of children.

A major longitudinal study has provided a great deal of information about the social and linguistic environment in which typical children learn to talk. Hart and Risley (1995, 1999) conducted monthly hour-long observations over a period of $2\frac{1}{2}$ years of children from 42 diverse families. The researchers recorded everything said by, to, and around each of the children during unstructured activities in their daily lives at home. Of the many interesting results of this landmark study, two findings are especially notable. First, children between the ages of 11 and 36 months of age are exposed to a tremendous amount of spoken language. "Perhaps most striking of all our findings . . . was the sheer amount of children's exposure to talk and interaction among the people around them. Over the years of observation, we regularly recorded an average of 700–800 utterances per hour within the children's hearing" (Hart & Risley, 1999, p. 34).

Second, children who are learning to talk practice their new skill relentlessly, actively participating in literally thousands of learning trials every day. They say words again and again, they repeat what they hear, they describe things, they talk to themselves while playing, they say what they want, they ask questions, and they respond to questions. After the children in the Hart and Risley study said their first word at an average age of 11 months, their number of utterances per hour increased steadily. On average, at 19 months of age the children became talkers: their frequency of utterances containing recognizable words had grown to exceed the frequency of nonword utterances (see Figure 8.3). At 28 months, the children became speakers: their frequency of talking matched their parents'. At age 3, the children said an average of 1,400 words per hour, using an average of 232 different words per hour and almost 20,000 total words in a 14-hour waking day.

Most children learn patterns of speech and language appropriate to their families and neighborhoods before they enter school.

Communication Disorders Defined

The American Speech-Language-Hearing Association (ASHA) (1993) defines a **communication disorder** as "an impairment in the ability to receive, send, process, and comprehend concepts or verbal, nonverbal and graphic symbols systems. A communication disorder may be evident in the processes of hearing, language, and/or speech" (p. 40).

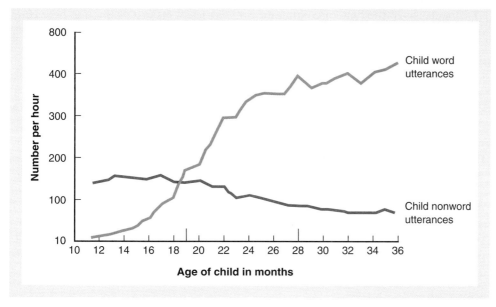

FIGURE 8.3

Typical pattern of growth in talking

Source: Hart, B., & Risley, T. R. (1999). *The social world of children learning to talk* (p. 280). Baltimore: Brookes. Used with permission.

By how much must a child's communication abilities differ from those of others for the difference to be considered an impairment? As previously noted, the development of speech and language is a highly individual process. No child conforms exactly to precise developmental norms; some are advanced, some are delayed, and some acquire language in an unusual sequence. The range of social acceptability and functionality of any dimension of speech or language is tremendous. As Hulit and Howard (2006) observe:

> We have no exact standards for how much language a normal speaker has or even for how well he uses the language he has. We have vague ideas about acceptable male and female voices, but most of us have a tolerance for voices that go beyond even our own standards. We may notice that well-known television journalists such as Tom Brokaw and Barbara Walters have some problems with "r" and "l," but few of us would consider these individuals speech-defective. There are people we would all agree are normal speakers who are more nonfluent than other people we would all agree are stutterers. So how do we determine what a communication defect is? (pp. 405–406)

When does a communication difference become a communication disorder? In making such judgments, Haynes and Pindzola (2004) emphasize the impact that a communication pattern has on one's life. A communication difference would be considered a disability, they note, when any one of these criteria is met:

- The transmission and/or perception of messages are faulty.
- The person is placed at an economic disadvantage.
- The person is placed at a learning disadvantage.
- The person is placed at a social disadvantage.
- The person's self-esteem or emotional growth is negatively affected.
- The problem causes physical damage or endangers the health of the person.

To be eligible for special education services, a child's communication disorders must have an adverse effect on learning. The Individuals with Disabilities Education Act (IDEA) defines *speech or language impairment* as "a communication disorder, such as stuttering, impaired articulation, a language impairment, or a voice impairment that adversely affects a child's educational performance" (34 C.F.R., Part 300 §300.8[c][11].

Like all disabilities, communication disorders vary widely by degree of severity. The speech and language of some children deviate from that of most children to such an extent that they have serious difficulties in learning and interpersonal relations. Children who cannot make themselves understood or who cannot comprehend ideas that are spoken to them by others are likely to experience a severe handicap in virtually all aspects of education and personal adjustment. A severe communication disorder may lead others—teachers, classmates, people in the community—to erroneously believe the child does not care about the world around him or simply has nothing to say (Downing, 1999).

Specialists in the field of communication disorders make a distinction between speech impairments and language impairments. A child may have a speech impairment, a language impairment, or both.

Definition of speech and language impairments

 Council for Exceptional Children Content Standards for Beginning Teachers—Common Core: Issues in definition and identification of individuals with exceptional learning needs (CC1K5).

Speech Impairments A widely used definition considers speech to be impaired "when it deviates so far from the speech of other people that it (1) calls attention to itself, (2) interferes with communication, or (3) provokes distress in the speaker or the listener" (Van Riper & Erickson, 1996, p. 110). The three basic types of **speech impairments** are articulation disorders (errors in the production of speech sounds), fluency disorders (difficulties with the flow or rhythm of speech), and voice disorders (problems with the quality or use of one's voice). Each is discussed later in the chapter.

It is always important to keep the speaker's age, education, and cultural background in mind when determining whether speech is impaired. A 4-year-old girl who says, "Pwease weave the woom" would not be considered to have a speech impairment, but a 40-year-old woman would surely draw attention to herself with that pronunciation because it differs markedly from the speech of most adults. A traveler unable to articulate the /l/ sound would not be clearly understood when he tries to buy a bus ticket to Lake Charles, Louisiana. A male high school student with an extremely high-pitched voice might be reluctant to speak in class for fear of being mimicked and ridiculed by his classmates.

Many children have mild-to-moderate speech disorders. Usually, their speech can be understood, but they may mispronounce certain sounds or use immature speech, like that of younger children. These problems often disappear as a child matures. If a mild or moderate articulation problem does not improve over an extended period or if it appears to have an adverse effect on the child's interaction with others, referral to a speech-language pathologist is indicated (Owens, 2008).

Language Impairments   ASHA (1993) defines a **language disorder** as "impaired comprehension and/or use of spoken, written, and/or other symbol systems. The disorder may involve (1) the form of language (phonology, morphology, and syntax), (2) the content of language (semantics), and/or (3) the function of language in communication (pragmatics) in any combination" (p. 40).

Some children have serious difficulties in understanding language or expressing themselves through language. A child with a **receptive language disorder** may be unable to learn the days of the week in proper order or may find it impossible to follow a sequence of commands such as "Pick up the paint brushes, wash them in the sink, and then put them on a paper towel to dry." A child with an **expressive language disorder** may have a limited vocabulary for her age, be confused about the order of sounds or words (e.g., "hostipal," "aminal," "wipe shield winders"), and use tenses and plurals incorrectly (e.g., "Them throwed a balls"). Children with difficulty in expressive language may or may not also have difficulty in receptive language. For instance, a child may be able to count out six pennies when asked and shown the symbol 6, but she may not be able to say the word "six" when shown the symbol. In that case, the child has an expressive difficulty, but her receptive language is adequate. She may or may not have other disorders of speech or hearing.

Communication Differences Are Not Disorders

Before entering school, most children have learned patterns of speech and language appropriate to their families and communities. The way each of us speaks is the result of a complex mix of influences, including race and ethnicity, socioeconomic class, education, occupation, geographical region, and peer group identification (Salend & Salinas, 2003). Every language contains a variety of forms, called **dialects,** that result from historical, linguistic, geographical, and sociocultural factors. Each dialect shares a common set of rules with the standard language. Standard American English (as used by most teachers, in textbooks, and on newscasts) is an idealized form seldom used in everyday conversation. As it is spoken in North America, English includes at least 10 regional dialects (e.g., Appalachian English, Southern English, New York dialect, Central Midland) and several sociocultural dialects (e.g., Black English, Latino English) (Wolfram & Ward, 2006).

The dialect of any group of people is neither inferior nor superior to the dialect spoken by another group. "There are dialects of English spoken by many people and dialects spoken by fewer people, but number of speakers does not indicate superiority or correctness. Every dialect of English is linguistically correct within the rules that govern it, and every dialect of English is as valid as any other" (Hulit & Howard, 2006, p. 336). A child who uses a dialect different from the dominant culture of the school should not be treated as having a communication disorder (Battle, 1998; Seymour, Bland-Stewart, & Green, 1998; Van Keulen, Weddington, & DeBose, 1998).

If the teacher does not accept natural communication differences among children and mistakenly assumes that a speech or language impairment is present, problems may arise in the classroom and in parent–teacher communication (Reed, 2005). On the other hand, some children with communication differences have communication disorders within their dialects, and such impairments must not be overlooked (Payne & Taylor, 2006; Van Keulen et al., 1998).

Dialects and communication differences

 Content Standards for Beginning Teachers—Common Core: Issues in definition and identification of individuals with exceptional learning needs (CC1K5) (also CC2K5 and CC6K1).

Although Joshua's physical disabilities make it difficult for him to articulate speech sounds well enough to be understood, his communication board has opened up social interaction for him.

CHARACTERISTICS

Speech-Sound Errors

Four basic kinds of speech-sound errors occur:

- *Distortions.* A speech sound is distorted when it sounds more like the intended phoneme than another speech sound but is conspicuously wrong. The /s/ sound, for example, is relatively difficult to produce; children may produce the word "sleep" as "schleep," "zleep," or "thleep." Some speakers have a lisp; others a whistling /s/. Distortions can cause misunderstanding, although parents and teachers often become accustomed to them.
- *Substitutions.* Children sometimes substitute one sound for another, as in saying "train" for "crane" or "doze" for "those." Children with this problem are often certain they have said the correct word and may resist correction. Substitution of sounds can cause considerable confusion for the listener.
- *Omissions.* Children may omit certain sounds, as in saying "cool" for "school." They may drop consonants from the ends of words, as in "pos" for "post." Most of us leave out sounds at times, but an extensive omission problem can make speech unintelligible.
- *Additions.* The addition of extra sounds makes comprehension difficult. For example, a child might say "buhrown" for "brown" or "hamber" for "hammer."

Traditionally, all speech-sound errors by children were identified as articulation problems and thought to be relatively simple to treat (McReynolds, 1990). Articulation refers to the movement of muscles and speech organs necessary to produce various speech sounds. Research during the past two decades, however, has revealed that many speech-sound errors are not simply a function of faulty mechanical operation of the speech apparatus but are directly related to problems in recognizing or processing the sound components of language (phonology).

Articulation Disorders   An **articulation disorder** means that a child is at present not able to produce a given sound physically; the sound is not in his repertoire of sounds. A severe articulation disorder is present when a child pronounces many sounds so poorly that his speech is unintelligible most of the time; even the child's parents, teachers, and peers cannot easily understand him. The child with a severe articulation disorder may say, "Yeh me yuh a da wido," instead of "Let me look out the window," or perhaps, "Do foop is dood" for "That soup is good." The fact that articulation disorders are prevalent does not mean that teachers, parents, and specialists should regard them as simple or unimportant. On the contrary, as Haynes and Pindzola (2004) observe, an articulation disorder severe enough to interfere significantly with intelligibility is a debilitating communication problem; and articulation disorders are not necessarily easy to diagnose and treat effectively.

Phonological Disorders   A child is said to have a **phonological disorder** if she has the ability to produce a given sound and does so correctly in some instances but does not produce the sound correctly at other times. Children with expressive phonological disorders are apt to experience problems in academic areas, and they are especially at risk for difficulties in reading (Bishop & Snowling, 2004; Catts, Fey, Tomblin, & Zhang, 2002) and writing (Dockrell, Lindsay, Connelly, & Mackie, 2007).

Determining whether a speech sound error is primarily an articulation or a phonological disorder is important because the treatment goals and procedures differ. General indicators used by clinicians for differentiating between articulation disorders and phonological disorders are shown in Figure 8.4.

Articulation and phonological disorders

 Council for Exceptional Children

Content Standards for Beginning Teachers—Common Core: Educational implications of characteristics of various exceptionalities (CC2K2).

FIGURE 8.4	Distinguishing articulation and phonological disorders	

Articulation Disorder	Phonological Disorder
• Difficulty with only a few sounds, with limited effect on intelligibility • Consistent misarticulation of specific sounds • Sound errors are motoric • Co-existing communication disorders possible but not as likely as with phonological disorders	• Multiple sound errors with obvious impairment of intelligibility • Inconsistent misarticulation of sounds • Can motorically produce sound but not in appropriate places • Errors consistent with a phonological process (e.g., final consonant deletion, making an error on a sound in one position but producing that sound correctly in another position, as in omitting "t" in "post" but producing "t" in "time") • Other language delays likely (because phonology is a component of language)

Source: Hall, Oyer, and Haas (2001); Sunderland (2004).

Fluency Disorders

Typical speech makes use of rhythm and timing. Words and phrases flow easily, with certain variations in speed, stress, and appropriate pauses. ASHA (1993) defines a **fluency disorder** as an "interruption in the flow of speaking characterized by atypical rate, rhythm, and repetitions in sounds, syllables, words, and phrases. This may be accompanied by excessive tension, struggle behavior, and secondary mannerisms" (p. 40).

Stuttering The best-known (and probably least understood) fluency disorder is **stuttering,** a condition marked by rapid-fire repetitions of consonant or vowel sounds, especially at the beginnings of words, prolongations, hesitations, interjections, and complete verbal blocks (Ramig & Shames, 2006). Developmental stuttering is considered a disorder of childhood. It usually begins between the ages of 2 and 5, and 98% of cases begin before the age of 10 (Mahr & Leith, 1992). It is believed that 4% of children stutter for 6 months or more and that 70% to 80% of children 2 to 5 years old who stutter recover spontaneously, some taking until age 8 to do so (Yairi & Ambrose, 1999). Stuttering is far more common among males than females, and it occurs more frequently among twins. It is believed that approximately 3 million people in the United States stutter (Stuttering Foundation of America, 2007). The incidence of stuttering is about the same in all Western countries: regardless of what language is spoken, about 1% of the general population has a stuttering problem at any given time. The causes of stuttering remain unknown, although the condition has been studied extensively with some interesting results (Bloodstein, 1995). Stuttering tends to run in families (Buck, Lees, & Cook, 2002); but it is not known whether this is the result of a genetic connection or an environment conducive to the development of the disorder, or a combination of hereditary and environmental factors (Yairi, 1998, 2004).

Stuttering is situational; that is, it appears to be related to the setting or circumstances of speech. A child may be likely to stutter when talking with people whose opinions matter most to him, such as parents and teachers, and in situations such as being called on to speak in front of the class. Most people who stutter are fluent about 95% of the time; a child

Fluency disorders

Council for Exceptional Children — Content Standards for Beginning Teachers—Common Core: Educational implications of characteristics of various exceptionalities (CC2K2).

with a fluency disorder may not stutter at all when singing, talking to a pet dog, or reciting a poem in unison with others. Reactions and expectations of parents, teachers, and peers clearly have an important effect on any child's personal and communicative development.

Cluttering   One type of fluency disorder is known as **cluttering,** a condition in which speech is very rapid, with extra sounds or mispronounced sounds. The clutterer's speech is garbled to the point of unintelligibility. Hulit and Howard (2006) point out two differences between stuttering and cluttering: (a) the stutterer is usually acutely aware of his fluency problems, while the clutterer may be oblivious to his disorder; (b) when a stutterer is asked to pay more attention to his speech, he is likely to stutter more; but the clutterer can often improve his fluency by monitoring his speech.

Voice Disorders

Voice disorders

Content Standards for Beginning Teachers—Common Core: Educational implications of characteristics of various exceptionalities (CC2K2).

Voice is the sound produced by the larynx. A **voice disorder** is characterized by "the abnormal production and/or absences of vocal quality, pitch, loudness, resonance, and/or duration, which is inappropriate for an individual's age and/or sex" (ASHA, 1993, p. 40). A voice is considered normal when its pitch, loudness, and quality are adequate for communication and it suits a particular person. A voice—whether good, poor, or in between—is closely identified with the person who uses it.

Voice disorders are more common in adults than in children. Considering how often some children shout and yell without any apparent harm to their voices, it is evident that the vocal cords can withstand heavy use. In some cases, however, a child's voice may be difficult to understand or may be considered unpleasant (Sapienza & Hicks, 2006). *Dysphonia* describes any condition of poor or unpleasant voice quality.

The two basic types of voice disorders involve phonation and resonance. A *phonation disorder* causes the voice to sound breathy, hoarse, husky, or strained most of the time. In severe cases, there is no voice at all. Phonation disorders can have organic causes, such as growths or irritations on the vocal cords; but hoarseness most frequently comes from chronic vocal abuse, such as yelling, imitating noises, or habitually talking while under tension. Misuse of the voice causes swelling of the vocal folds, which in turn can lead to growths known as vocal nodules, nodes, or polyps. A breathy voice is unpleasant because it is low in volume and fails to make adequate use of the vocal cords.

A voice with a *resonance disorder* is characterized by either too many sounds coming out through the air passages of the nose (*hypernasality*) or, conversely, not enough resonance of the nasal passages (*hyponasality*). The hypernasal speaker may be perceived as talking through her nose or having an unpleasant twang. A child with hypernasality has speech that is excessively nasal, neutral, or central-sounding rather than oral, clear, and forward-sounding (Hall et al., 2001). A child with hyponasality (sometimes called *denasality*) may sound as though he constantly has a cold or a stuffed nose, even when he does not. As with other voice disorders, the causes of nasality may be either organic (e.g., cleft palate, swollen nasal tissues, hearing impairment) or functional (perhaps resulting from learned speech patterns or behavior problems).

Language Impairments

Receptive and expressive language impairments

Content Standards for Beginning Teachers—Common Core: Educational implications of characteristics of various exceptionalities (CC2K2).

Language impairments can involve problems in one or more of the five dimensions of language: phonology, morphology, syntax, semantics, and/or pragmatics. Language impairments are usually classified as either receptive or expressive. As described previously, *receptive* language impairment interferes with the understanding of language. A child may, for example, be unable to comprehend spoken sentences or follow a sequence of directions. An *expressive* language impairment interferes with the production of language. The child may have a very limited vocabulary, may use incorrect words and phrases, or may not even speak at all, communicating only through gestures. A child may have good receptive language when an expressive disorder is present or may have both expressive and receptive disorders in combination. Educators sometimes use the term *language-learning disability (LLD)* to refer to children with significant receptive and/or expressive language disorders.

To say that a child has a language delay does not necessarily mean that the child has a language disorder. As Reed (2005) explains, a *language delay* implies that a child is slow to develop linguistic skills but acquires them in the same sequence as typically developing children do. Generally, all features of language are delayed at about the same rate. A *language disorder,* however, suggests a disruption in the usual rate and sequence of specific emerging language skills. For example, a child who consistently has difficulty in responding to who, what, and where questions but who otherwise displays language skills appropriate for her age would likely be considered to have language impairment.

Children with serious language disorders are almost certain to have problems in school and with social development. They frequently play a passive role in communication. Children with impaired language are less likely to initiate conversations than are their peers. When language-disordered children are asked questions, their replies rarely provide new information related to the topic. It is often difficult to detect children with language disorders; their performance may lead people to mistakenly classify them with disability labels such as mental retardation, hearing impairment, or emotional disturbance, when in fact these descriptions are neither accurate nor appropriate.

Young children with oral language problems are likely to have reading and writing disabilities (Catts et al., 2002; Snowling, Bishop, & Stothard, 2000). For example, Catts (1993) reported that 83% of kindergarteners with speech-language delays eventually qualified for remedial reading services. The problem is compounded because children with speech-language delays are more likely than their typically developing peers to be "treatment-resistors" to generally effective early literacy interventions (Al Otaiba, 2001).

PREVALENCE

Estimates of the prevalence of communication disorders in children vary widely. Reliable figures are hard to come by because investigators often employ different definitions of speech and language disorders and sample different populations. In the 2005–2006 school year, 1,143,195 children ages 6 to 21 received special education services under the IDEA category of "speech or language impairments" (U.S. Department of Education, 2007). This number represents about 2.5% of the school-age population and 19% of all students receiving special education services, making speech or language impairments the second-largest category after learning disabilities.

The actual number of children with speech and language impairments is much higher. Approximately 50% of children who receive special education services because of another primary disability (e.g., mental retardation, learning disabilities, hearing impairments) also have communication disorders (Hall et al., 2001).

According to a national survey by ASHA (2006), school-based speech-language pathologists (SLPs) work with a median caseload of 50 students each month. Approximately half of all elementary students who are served by SLPs have speech and language production problems (see Table 8.1). Fewer than 1 in 10 children with speech and language impairments have fluency disorders.

Speech and language impairments are more prevalent among males than females and are about the same in each of the major geographical regions of the United States. Approximately two thirds of school-age children served by SLPs are boys (Hall et al., 2001). The percentage of children with speech and language disorders decreases significantly from the earlier to the later school grades.

CAUSES

Many types of communication disorders and numerous possible causes are recognized. A speech or language impairment may be *organic*; that is, attributable to damage, dysfunction, or malformation of a specific organ or part of the body. Most communication disorders, however, are not considered organic but are classified as functional. A *functional communication disorder* cannot be ascribed to a specific physical condition, and its origin is not clearly known. A child's surroundings provide many opportunities to learn appropriate and

Language delays

 Content Standards for Beginning Teachers—Common Core: Educational implications of characteristics of exceptionalities (CC2K1).

TABLE 8.1

Percentage of elementary children served by speech-language pathologists (SLPs), by type of communication disorder

AREA OF INTERVENTION	% OF SLPs WHO REGULARLY SERVE STUDENTS IN THIS AREA	MEAN NUMBER OF CHILDREN SERVED
Articulation/phonological disorders	91%	23
Pragmatics/social communication	77%	8
Fluency	69%	3
Specific language impairment	61%	18
Auditory processing	61%	9
Verbal apraxia	56%	3
Augmentative/alternative communication (AAC)	50%	5
English language learners (ELL)	35%	8
Voice/resonance	29%	2
Dysphagia (swallowing)	10%	4
Communication effectiveness (e.g., accent modification)	2%	6

Source: American Speech-Language-Hearing Association (2006).

inappropriate communication skills, and some specialists believe that functional communication disorders derive mainly from environmental influences.

Causes of Speech Impairments

Examples of physical factors that frequently result in speech impairments are **cleft palate,** paralysis of the speech muscles, absence of teeth, craniofacial abnormalities, enlarged adenoids, and traumatic brain injury. **Dysarthria** refers to a group of speech disorders caused by neuromuscular impairments in respiration, phonation, resonation, and articulation. Lack of precise motor control needed to produce and sequence sounds causes distorted and repeated sounds. An organic speech impairment may be a child's primary disability, or it may be secondary to other disabilities, such as mental retardation or cerebral palsy.

Causes of Language Disorders

Factors that can contribute to language disorders in children include cognitive limitations or mental retardation, hearing impairments, behavioral disorders, structural abnormalities of the speech mechanism, and environmental deprivation (Bacon & Wilcox, 2006). Language is so important to academic performance that it can be impossible to differentiate a learning disability from a language disorder (Silliman & Diehl, 2002).

Some severe disorders in expressive and receptive language result from injury to the brain. **Aphasia** describes a loss of the ability to process and use language. Aphasia is one of the most prevalent causes of language disorders in adults, most often occurring suddenly after a cardiovascular event (stroke). Head injury is a significant cause of aphasia in children. Aphasia may be either expressive or, less commonly, receptive. Children with mild aphasia have language patterns very similar to those of typically developing children but may have difficulty retrieving certain words and tend to need more time than usual to communicate. Children with severe aphasia, however, are likely to have a markedly reduced storehouse of words and language forms.

Research indicates that genetics may contribute to communication disorders. Scientists in Britain have discovered a gene area that affects speech (Porterfield, 1998), and other researchers have reported genetic links to phonological disorders (Uffen, 1997) and stuttering (Yairi, 1998).

Environmental influences also play an important part in delayed, disordered, or absent language. The communication efforts of some children are reinforced; other children, unfortunately, are punished for talking, gesturing, or otherwise attempting to communicate. A child who has little stimulation at home and few chances to speak, listen, explore, and interact with others will probably have little motivation for communication and may well experience delays in language development (Ratner, 2004).

IDENTIFICATION AND ASSESSMENT

"Don't worry; she'll grow out of it."
"Speech therapists can't help a child who doesn't talk."
"He'll be all right once he starts school."

These are common examples of misguided, inaccurate, yet widely held attitudes toward communication disorders. Although some children who experience mild speech impairments or language delays do get better, many do not improve and deteriorate without intervention. To avoid the consequences of unrecognized or untreated speech and language impairments, it is especially important for children to receive professional assessment and evaluation services (Hall et al., 2001).

Screening and Teacher Observations

In some school districts, SLPs screen the spoken language abilities of all kindergarten children. These screenings might involve norm-referenced tests, informal assessments developed by the SLP, and questionnaires or checklists for parents and teachers (Justice, 2006; Owens, Metz, & Haas, 2007). Classroom teachers also play an important role in identifying children who may have speech and language impairments. Teachers can use a checklist such as the one in Figure 8.5 to identify children with whom the SLP can conduct individualized screening for possible communication disorders. Children who fail a speech and language screening test are candidates for a systematic, in-depth evaluation.

Evaluation Components

Testing procedures vary according to the suspected type of disorder. Often the specialist conducts broad screenings to detect areas of concern and then moves to more detailed testing in those areas. There is no perfect test or method of assessing children's speech and language (Silliman & Diehl, 2002). Most examiners will use a variety of assessment devices and approaches in an effort to obtain as much relevant information as possible to inform diagnostic decisions and treatment plans. A comprehensive evaluation to detect the presence and extent of a communication disorder would likely include the following components:

- *Case history and physical examination.* Most professional speech and language assessments begin with the creation of a case history about the child. This typically involves completing a biographical form that includes information such as the child's birth and developmental history, health record, scores on achievement and intelligence tests, and adjustment to school. The parents may be asked when the child first crawled, walked,

Screening for communication disorders

 Content Standards for Beginning Teachers—Common Core: Screening, prereferral, referral, and classification procedures (CC8K3).

Assessment and diagnosis of communication disorders

 Content Standards for Beginning Teachers—Common Core: Screening, prereferral, referral, and classification procedures (CC8K3) (also CC8K1).

FIGURE 8.5	A checklist for identifying speech and language problems in the classroom

Directions: The following behaviors may indicate that a child in your classroom has a language impairment that is in need of language intervention. Please check the appropriate items.

_____ Child mispronounces sounds and words.

_____ Child omits word endings, such as plural -s and past tense -ed.

_____ Child omits small, unemphasized words, such as auxiliary verbs or prepositions.

_____ Child uses an immature vocabulary, overuses empty words, such as "one" and "thing," or seems to have difficulty recalling or finding the right word.

_____ Child has difficulty comprehending new words and concepts.

_____ Child's sentence structure seems immature or overreliant on forms, such as subject-verb-object. It's unoriginal, dull.

_____ Child has difficulty with one of the following:

    _____ Verb tensing   _____ Articles   _____ Auxiliary verbs

    _____ Pronouns   _____ Irreg. verbs   _____ Prepositions

    _____ Word order   _____ Irreg. plurals

_____ Child has difficulty relating sequential events.

_____ Child has difficulty following directions.

_____ Child's questions are often poorly formed.

_____ Child has difficulty answering questions.

_____ Child's comments are often off topic or inappropriate for the conversation.

_____ There are long pauses between a remark and the child's reply or between successive remarks by the child. It's as if the child is searching for a response or is confused.

_____ Child appears to be attending to communication but remembers little of what is said.

Source: Robert E. Owens, Jr. *Language Disorders: A Functional Approach to Assessment and Intervention,* 4/e. Published by Allyn and Bacon, Boston, MA. Copyright © 2004 by Pearson Education. Reprinted by permission of the publisher.

and uttered words. Social skills, such as playing readily with other children, may also be considered. The specialist carefully examines the child's mouth, noting any irregularities in the tongue, lips, teeth, palate, or other structures that may affect speech production. If the child has an organic speech problem, the child is referred for possible medical intervention.

- *Articulation test.* Speech errors by the child are assessed. A record is kept of the sounds that are defective, how they are being mispronounced, and the number of errors. Examples of articulation tests include the Photo Articulation Test (Lippke, Dickey, Selmar, & Soder, 1997) and the Goldman-Fristoe Test of Articulation (Goldman & Fristoe, 2000).

- *Hearing test.* Hearing is usually tested to determine whether a hearing problem is causing the suspected communication disorder. Audiometry, a formal procedure for testing hearing, is discussed in Chapter 9.

- *Auditory discrimination test.* This test is given to determine whether the child is hearing sounds correctly. If unable to recognize the specific characteristics of a given sound, the child will not have a good model to imitate. The Test of Auditory Discrimination (Goldman, Fristoe, & Woodcock, 1990) is frequently used.

- *Phonological awareness and processing.* Included in the many phonological skills of children who are competent speakers and users of language is the ability to distinguish the presence and absence of speech sounds, differences between and among sounds, and when individual sounds begin and end. They can remember language sounds and reproduce them at a later time. Children without phonological awareness and processing skills not only have problems with receptive and expressive oral language but also have great difficulties in learning to read. Phonological processing measures include the Test of Phonological Awareness (Torgeson & Bryant, 1994) and the Comprehensive Test of Phonological Processing (Wagner, Torgeson, & Rahsotte, 1999).

A comprehensive assessment of communication disorders includes articulation, auditory discrimination, vocabulary tests, and a language sample.

- *Vocabulary and overall language development test.* The amount of vocabulary a child has acquired is generally a good indicator of language competence. Frequently used tests of vocabulary include the Peabody Picture Vocabulary Test—III (Dunn & Dunn, 1997) and the Comprehensive Receptive and Expressive Vocabulary Test (Wallace & Hammill, 2002). An overall language test, such as the Test of Language Development (Hammill & Newcomer, 1997) or the Clinical Evaluation of Language Fundamentals (Semel, Wiig, & Secord, 2003), assesses the child's understanding and production of language structures (e.g., important syntactical elements such as the concept that conjunctions show relations between the sentence elements they connect).

- *Language samples.* An important part of any evaluation for communication disorders is obtaining accurate samples of the child's expressive speech and language. The examiner considers factors such as intelligibility and fluency of speech, voice quality, and use of vocabulary and grammar. Some SLPs use structured tasks to evoke language samples. They may, for example, ask a child to describe a picture, tell a story, or answer a list of questions. Most specialists, however, use informal conversation to obtain language samples, believing that the child's language sample will be more representative if the examiner uses natural conversation rather than highly structured tasks (Hadley, 1998). Open-ended questions such as "Tell me about your family" are suggested rather than yes–no questions or questions that can be answered with one word, such as "What color is your car?" To ensure a complete and accurate record of the talk and reduce distractions for the child caused by note taking, examiners usually create an audio record of the child's language samples.

- *Observation in natural settings.* Objective observation and measurement of children's language use in social contexts is an important element of assessment for communication disorders. It is imperative that the observer sample the child's communication behavior across various settings rather than limit it to a clinic or an examining room. A parent–child observation is frequently arranged for young children. The specialist provides appropriate toys and activities and requests the parent to interact with the child in typical fashion.

After all the data from the multifactored evaluation have been gathered, the SLP reviews the results of the case. Because there is often so much assessment information, some SLPs use computer programs to help organize and analyze the results (Hall et al., 2001). The SLP then develops a treatment plan in cooperation with the child's parents and teachers to set up realistic communication objectives and determine the methods that will be used.

Assessment of Communication Disorders in Children Whose First Language Is Not English or Who Use Nonstandard English   It is often difficult to distinguish between a student whose learning and communication problems result from a disability and a student whose primary need is systematic, culturally responsive instruction that values and builds on the skills he already possesses in his first language (L1) to enable him to improve his English communicative and literacy skills (Roseberry-McKibbin, 2007). While all educators must be careful not to confuse communication differences with delayed or disordered speech and language, proper assessment of the speech-language skills of children from diverse cultural, linguistic, and socioeconomic backgrounds poses a difficult challenge for language-majority educators (Salend & Salinas, 2003).

IDEA requires that assessment for the purpose of identifying children with disabilities be conducted in the child's native language. Although a few standardized language-proficiency tests are available in languages other than English (see McLaughlin & Lewis [2008] for a review), translation or adaptation of tests into other languages poses certain problems (Díaz-Rico & Weed, 2005; Rhodes, Ochoa, & Ortiz, 2005). For example, DeAvila (1976) pointed out the great variety in language within Hispanic populations and notes that when Mexican American children were given a test in Spanish that was developed with a population of Puerto Rican children, they performed even more poorly than on an admittedly unfair English test. To illustrate the confusion that may result from inappropriate translations, DeAvila observed that a Spanish-speaking child may use any one of five distinct words to describe a kite, depending on the family's country of origin: *cometa, huila, volantin, papalote,* or *chiringa.* Thus, although translation of tests and other materials into a child's native language may be helpful in many instances, educators must take care to avoid an improper translation that may actually do a disservice to the culturally and linguistically different child.

Culturally and linguistically diverse students should not be diagnosed with a speech-language impairment (SLI) if "problems" are observed only in English and not in their first language. "Exposure to two languages is *not* a cause of a disability. If a student has a genuine SLI, difficulties will be observed in both L1 and in English" (Roseberry-McKibbin, 2007, p. 175).

It should not be surprising that students who are English language learners and students whose first language is English but who speak a nonstandard dialect often perform poorly on formal tests of English speech and language skills. It is important that the results of formal language tests not be the sole basis for diagnosing a speech or language impairment. Results of formal speech and language tests administered by a competent SLP should be supplemented with direct observations of a student's communicative behaviors in natural settings where he can use whichever language he is most comfortable with.

Carefully testing the child's language proficiency in both first and second language (L1 and L2) combined with an analysis of authentic conversational behavior provide the opportunity to better evaluate a student's true communicative competence.

Best practices in assessing speech and language competence of children who do not speak standard English as their first language include assessments of basic interpersonal communication skills (BICS) and cognitive academic language proficiency (CALP). BICS are a set of language skills required in everyday face-to-face communication situations (e.g., conversing about the weather). CALP refers to language proficiency specific to academic learning situations (e.g., "Compare formal and functional properties of sand and granite."). A typical English language learner needs about 2 years under ideal conditions to develop BICS to a level similar to native speakers, and achieving a similar level of performance with CALP requires 5 to 7 years (Cummins, 2002).

Students who demonstrate an adequate level of BICS but inadequate CALP are often misdiagnosed as having an SLI (see Figure 8.6). Roseberry-McKibbin (2007) points out:

> It is important to keep in mind that skills in BICS is acquired in about two years, but CALP takes much longer. Thus, a student may have good English conversational skills, and perform well in context embedded and cognitively undemanding situations, but continue to face challenges in subjects such as social studies and science.
>
> It is important to not make the error of assessing a student for an SLI using tests that are context reduced and cognitively demanding when the student has only been exposed to English for one or two years. The student's adequate conversation skills do not mean that

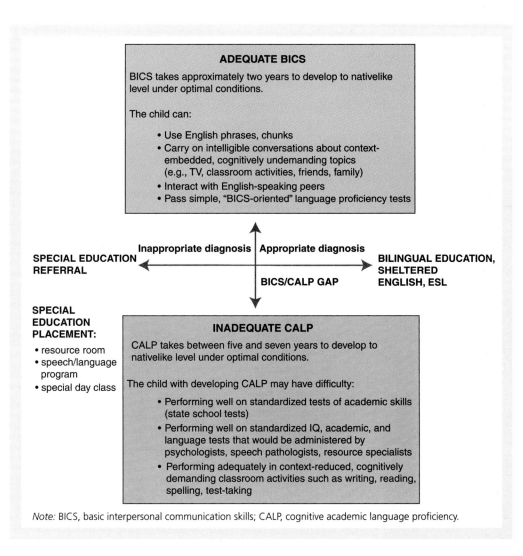

FIGURE 8.6

Language proficiency
misdiagnosis model

Source: From Roseberry-McKibbin,
C. (2008). *Multicultural students
with special language needs:
Practical strategies for assessment
and intervention* (3rd ed.).
Oceanside, CA: Academic
Communication Associates, Inc.
Used with permission.

she can succeed with tasks such as answering questions after hearing a complicated story
only one time with no accompanying visual cues. (p. 85)

EDUCATIONAL APPROACHES

Various approaches are employed in the treatment of children with communication disorders.
Speech-language pathologist (SLP) is the preferred term for the school-based professional with
primary responsibility for identifying, evaluating, and providing therapeutic services to children
with communication disorders (ASHA, 2001e). But terms such as *speech therapist, speech clinician,* and *speech teacher* are still used in some schools. As a key member of a child's IEP team,
the SLP's goal is to correct the child's speech and/or language problems or to help the child
achieve the maximum communicative potential, which may involve compensatory techniques
and/or augmentative and alternative means of communication (Hall et al., 2001). Speech-
language pathology addresses both organic and functional causes and encompasses practitioners with numerous points of view who use a wide range of accepted intervention techniques.

Some SLPs employ structured exercises and drills to correct speech sounds; others
emphasize speech production in natural language contexts. Some prefer to work with children in individual therapy sessions; others believe that group sessions are advantageous for
language modeling and peer support. Some encourage children to imitate the therapist's
speech; others have the child listen to recordings of his own speech. Some specialists follow
a structured, teacher-directed approach in which targeted speech and language behaviors
are precisely prompted, recorded, and reinforced; others use less-structured methods. Some
SLPs focus on a child's expressive and receptive communication; others devote attention to
other aspects of the child's behavior and environment, such as developing self-confidence

and improving interactions with parents and classmates. Clearly, educators can explore many possible options in devising effective, individualized treatment plans for students with communication disorders.

Treating Speech-Sound Errors

A general goal of specialists in communication disorders is to help the child speak as clearly and pleasantly as possible so that a listener's attention will focus on the child's message rather than how he says it.

Articulation Errors   The goals of therapy for articulation problems are acquisition of the correct speech sound(s), generalization of the sound(s) to all speaking settings and contexts (especially the classroom), and maintenance of the correct sound(s) after therapy has ended. Traditional articulation therapy involves discrimination and production activities.

Discrimination activities are designed to improve the child's ability to listen carefully and detect the differences between similar sounds (e.g., the /t/ in *take,* the /c/ in *cake*) and to differentiate between correct and distorted speech sounds. The child learns to match his speech to that of a standard model by using auditory, visual, and tactile feedback. A generally consistent relationship exists between children's ability to recognize sounds and their ability to articulate them correctly.

The SLP uses audition, visual, and tactile feedback to help children match their speech to that of the standard model.

Production is the ability to produce a given speech sound alone and in various contexts. Therapy emphasizes the repetitive production of sounds in various contexts, with special attention to the motor skills involved in articulation. Exercises are employed to produce sounds with differing stress patterns. The SLP may have the child carefully watch how sounds are produced and then use a mirror to monitor his own speech production. Children are expected to accurately produce problematic sounds in syllables, words, sentences, and stories. They may record their own speech and listen carefully for errors. Therapy progresses from having the child articulate simple sounds in isolation; then in syllables, words, phrases, sentences, and structured conversation; and finally in unstructured conversation. As in all communication training, it is important for the teacher, parent, and specialist to provide a good language model, reinforce the child's improving performance, and encourage the child to talk.

Phonological Errors   When a child's spoken language problem includes one or more phonological errors, the goal of therapy is to help the child identify the error pattern(s) and gradually produce more linguistically appropriate sound patterns (Barlow, 2001). For example, a child who frequently omits final consonants might be taught to recognize the difference between minimally contrastive words—perhaps using a set of cards with the words *sea, seed, seal, seam,* and *seat* (Hall et al., 2001). Therapeutic tasks are constructed so that the child is rewarded for following directions (e.g., "Pick up the *seal* card") and speaking clearly enough for the therapist to follow his or her directions (e.g., the child directs the SLP to give him the *seat* card). To respond correctly, the child must attend to and use the information in the final consonant sound.

Sounds are not taught in isolation. Children with phonological problems can often articulate specific sounds but are not using those sounds in proper linguistic context.

Although the distinction between articulation errors and phonological errors is important, many children with communication disorders have problems with both. The therapeutic approaches for articulation and phonological disorders are not incompatible and can be used in conjunction for some children.

Treating Fluency Disorders

Throughout history, people who stutter have been subjected to countless treatments—some of them unusual, to say the least. Past treatments included holding pebbles in the mouth, sticking fingers into a light socket, talking out of one side of the mouth, eating raw oysters, speaking with the teeth clenched, taking alternating hot and cold baths, and speaking on inhaled rather than exhaled air (Ham, 1986; Hulit & Howard, 2006). For many years, it was widely thought that a tongue that was unable to function properly in the mouth caused stuttering. As a result, it was common for early physicians to prescribe ointments to blister or numb the tongue or even to remove portions of the tongue through surgery!

Application of behavioral principles has strongly influenced recent practices in the treatment of fluency disorders (Inghram, 2003). A therapist using this methodology regards stuttering as learned behavior and seeks to replace it by establishing and encouraging fluent speech. For example, one stuttering treatment program called the Lidcombe Program trains parents to positively reinforce their child's fluent utterances in the home. Onslow, Packman, and Harrison (2003) report that studies evaluating the effectiveness of the Lidcombe Program with over 750 children worldwide have reported a 95% success rate.

Children may learn to manage their stuttering by deliberately prolonging certain sounds or by speaking slowly to get through a "block." They may increase their confidence and fluency by speaking in groups, where pressure is minimized and successful speech is positively reinforced. They may learn to monitor their own speech and to reward themselves for periods of fluency (Ryan, 2004). They may learn to speak to a rhythmic beat or with the aid of devices that mask or delay their ability to hear their own speech. Audio recorders are often used for drills, simulating conversations, and documenting progress.

Children often learn to control their stuttering and produce increasingly fluent speech as they mature. No single method of treatment has been recognized as most effective. Stuttering frequently decreases when children enter adolescence, regardless of which treatment method was used. Often, the problem disappears with no treatment at all. Results from studies of the phenomenon of spontaneous recovery from stuttering have reported that 65% to 80% of children diagnosed as stutterers apparently outgrow or get over their dysfluencies without formal intervention (Yairi & Ambrose, 1999). Nevertheless, an SLP should be contacted when a child exhibits signs of stuttering or when the parents are concerned about speech fluency. Although some children who stutter improve without help, many do not. Early intervention may prevent the child from developing a severe stutter. In its initial stages, stuttering can almost always be treated successfully by teachers, parents, and a speech-language pathologist working together. When interacting with a child who stutters, a teacher should pay primary attention to what the child is saying rather than to his difficulties in saying it. When the child experiences a verbal block, the teacher should be patient and calm, say nothing, and maintain eye contact with the child until he finishes speaking. For specific suggestions for how classroom teachers can help children with speech dysfluencies, see Teaching & Learning, "Helping the Child Who Stutters."

Interacting with a child who stutters

 Content Standards for Beginning Teachers—Common Core: Teacher attitudes and behaviors that influence behavior of individuals with exceptional learning needs (CC5K4).

Treating Voice Disorders

A thorough medical examination should always be sought for a child with a voice disorder. Surgery or other medical interventions can often treat organic causes. In addition, SLPs sometimes recommend environmental modifications; a person who is consistently required to speak in a noisy setting, for example, may benefit from the use of a small microphone to reduce vocal straining and shouting (Sapienza & Hicks, 2006). Most remedial techniques, however, offer direct vocal rehabilitation, which helps the child with a voice disorder gradually learn to produce more acceptable and efficient speech. Voice therapy often begins with teaching the child to listen to his own voice and learn to identify those aspects that need to be changed. Depending on the type of voice disorder and the child's overall circumstances, vocal rehabilitation may include activities such as exercises to increase breathing capacity, relaxation techniques to reduce tension, or procedures to increase or decrease the loudness of speech (Harris & Harris, 1997; Johnston & Umberger, 1996).

Because many voice problems are directly attributable to vocal abuse, behavioral principles can be used to help children and adults break habitual patterns of vocal misuse. For example, a child might self-monitor the number of abuses he commits in the classroom or at home, receiving reinforcement for gradually lowering the number of abuses over time. Computer technology has also been successfully applied in the treatment of voice disorders.

Helping the Child Who Stutters

There is no single treatment for stuttering because the causation, type, and severity of nonfluencies vary from child to child. Despite this variability, teachers can significantly help a child who stutters by providing a good speech model, improving the child's self-esteem, and creating a good speech environment.

HOW TO GET STARTED

Provide a Good Speech Model

- *Reduce your rate of speech.* Young children often imitate the speech rate of their parents and other significant adults. This rate may be inappropriately fast for the child's motoric and linguistic competencies. Slower speech provides the child the time needed to organize thoughts, choose vocabulary and grammatical form, and plan the speech act motorically.

- *Create silences in your interactions.* Pauses placed at appropriate places in conversation help create a relaxed communication environment, slower rate of speech, and a more natural speech cadence. Pause for 2 to 3 seconds before responding to a child's questions and statements.

- *Model simple vocabulary and grammatical forms.* Stuttering is more likely to occur in longer words, words that are used less frequently, and more grammatically complex sentences.

- *Model normal nonfluencies.* You may need to make a conscious effort to use normal nonfluencies, such as interjections ("um" or "ah") or an occasional whole-word repetition, phrase repetition, or pause. Knowing that even fluent speech contains nonfluencies will help children accept nonfluencies and reduce the fear of speaking.

Improve the Child's Self-Esteem

- *Disregard moments of nonfluency.* Reinforce occurrences of fluency and ignore nonfluencies. Do not give instructions such as "Slow down," "Take a deep breath," or "Stop and start over," which imply that the child is not doing enough. This might increase guilt and diminish self-confidence.

- *Show acceptance of what the child expresses rather than how it is said.* Ask the child to repeat only the parts of the utterance that were not understood rather than those that were nonfluent. This request indicates that you did listen and that the message is important.

- *Treat the child who stutters like any other child in the class.* Do not reduce your expectations because of the nonfluencies.

- *Acknowledge nonfluencies without labeling them.* Do not refer to the problem of stuttering. Instead, use words that the child uses to describe her speech, such as "bumpy" or "hard." Assure the child that it is okay to have dysfluencies; everyone does.

- *Help the child feel in control of speech.* Follow the child's lead in conversation. Speech will more likely be fluent if the child can talk about areas of interest.

- *Accept nonfluencies.* Try not to be overly concerned about normal nonfluencies because you see the child as a stutterer. Maintain eye contact and remain patient.

Create a Good Speech Environment

- *Establish good conversational rules.* Interruptions may distract the child and increase nonfluencies. Ensure that no one interrupts and that everyone gets a chance to talk.

- *Listen attentively.* Active listening lets the child know that content is important. Use naturalistic comments (e.g., "Yes, Johnny, that is a large blue truck.") in place of absentminded "uh-huhs" and generic statements (e.g., "Good talking!").

- *Suggest that the child cease other activities while speaking.* It is sometimes difficult to perform two different motoric acts, such as coloring and talking, simultaneously. Asking the child to stop other activities while speaking may improve fluency.

- *Prepare the child for upcoming events.* The emotionality of birthdays, holidays, field trips, and changes in the daily schedule may cause apprehension and increase stuttering. Discussing upcoming events can reduce fear associated with the unknown and should enhance the child's fluency.

Source: From LaBlance, G. R., Steckol, K. F., & Smith, V. L. (1994). Stuttering: The role of the classroom teacher. *Teaching Exceptional Children, 26*(2), 10–12. Adapted by permission.

To learn more about students with communication disorders and the instructional strategies that can be beneficial for them, go to the Homework & Exercises section in Chapter 8 of MyEducationLab and complete Homework Exercise 1.

Some instruments enable speakers to see visual representations of their voice patterns on a screen or a printout; speakers thus can monitor their own vocalizations visually as well as auditorily and develop new patterns of using their voices more naturally and efficiently (Bull & Rushakoff, 1987).

Treating Language Disorders

Treatments for language disorders are also extremely varied. Some programs focus on pre-communication activities that encourage the child to explore and that make the environment conducive to the development of receptive and expressive language. Clearly, children must have something they want to communicate. And because children learn through imitation, it is important for the teacher or specialist to speak clearly, use correct inflections, and provide a rich variety of words and sentences.

The changing and expanding role of school-based SLPs today includes connecting children's oral language to literacy components of the curriculum as much as possible (ASHA, 2001d; Culatta & Wiig, 2006). SLPs work with classroom teachers to create language-rich classroom environments that expose children to high-quality language input characterized by diverse content (vocabulary), form (the ways that words and sentence structure are organized), and use (pragmatics; how language is used in social contexts) (Justice, 2004). Figure 8.7 shows examples of content, form, and use experiences and objectives for 3- and 4-year-old children.

Children with very limited oral language might be taught how to orally "read" pictures as a language-enhancement activity (Alberto & Fredrick, 2000). Teachers can use story boards and song boards with pictures illustrating language: The teacher places and removes pictures from the board as she tells the story or points to the appropriate picture while singing a line (Skau & Cascella, 2006). Children with language impairments might develop written language skills by exchanging e-mail letters with pen pals (Harmston, Strong, & Evans, 2001).

Vocabulary Building   Children with language disorders have a limited store of words to call upon. Vocabulary has been called the building block of language (Dockrell & Messer, 2004). Speech-language pathologists and classroom teachers use a wide variety of techniques to build students' vocabulary, including graphic organizers, mnemonics, and learning strategies introduced in Chapter 5 (Foil & Alber, 2002; Jitendra, Edwards, Sacks, & Jacobson, 2004). Various types of drama activities can also be effective in teaching vocabulary (e.g., students take turns acting out the meaning of target words while the rest of the class tries to identify the word) (Alber & Foil, 2003).

Alber and Foil (2003) recommend that teachers use the following sequence to help students learn new vocabulary:

1. Display each new word, pronounce it, give the meaning of the word, and have students repeat it.
2. Provide and have students repeat multiple examples of the word used in context.
3. Connect the word and its meaning to students' current knowledge, and prompt students to describe their experiences related to the word.
4. Provide multiple opportunities for students to use the word in context during guided practice, and provide feedback on their responses.
5. Help students discriminate between words with similar meanings but subtle differences (e.g., *separate* and *segregate*).
6. Assign independent practice activities; challenge students to select new vocabulary words to learn independently.
7. Promote generalization and maintenance by prompting students to use their new vocabulary, providing praise and other forms of reinforcement when students' speech and writing contain new vocabulary, and having students self-record how often they use new vocabulary.

Naturalistic Strategies   Speech-language pathologists are increasingly employing naturalistic interventions to help children develop and use language skills. Naturalistic

FIGURE 8.7	Examples of content, form, and use experiences and objectives in language-rich preschool classrooms

	Experiences	**Objectives**
Content	Children experience many different word types, including adjectives, nouns, verbs, prepositions, and adverbs. Children are exposed to the ways that important societal concepts are expressed, such as kinship (*brother, uncle, aunt*), time (*tomorrow, yesterday*), and shelter (*house, apartment*). Children are exposed to gradations of precision in using vocabulary (*old, stale, musty*), learn the multiple meanings of words (*run*), learn to organize concepts (*farmer, nurse, pharmacist*), and learn how to play with words (*a grasshopper man is a man who collects grasshoppers*). Children are exposed to diverse ways to express similar things (*that towel, that white towel, the towel he has*).	1. To understand and use words of time (*yesterday, tomorrow, year, month*) 2. To understand and use words of emotion (*sad, happy, angry, excited*) 3. To understand and use words of transportation (*car, tractor, airplane*) 4. To understand and use words of emotion as noun descriptions (*the happy boy, the sad bunny*) 5. To categorize words (*bear, cat, and dog are animals*)
Form	Children experience many different grammatical constructions, including elaborated noun phrases (*the old dark house*), various verb constructions (*walks, is walking, will walk, walked*), and prepositional phrases (*under the table*). Children hear sentences that are simple, complex, and compound; and they are exposed to diverse ways to link ideas syntactically (e.g., *If you want a slicker, you need to come and get one*). Children experience question types of many different constructions, including auxiliary inverted (*Is he going?*), tag (*He is going, isn't he?*), and the *who, what, when, why, where* forms of questions.	1. To add -er to words to make "worker" words (*a person who farms is a farmer*) 2. To understand and use personal pronouns (*I, we, he, she, it*) 3. To understand and use plural forms (*shoe/shoes*) 4. To elaborate nouns with articles and adjectives (*the fast, green car*) 5. To use future-tense verbs to discuss future events (*we will go*)
Use	Children are exposed to the many ways that language is used for social and functional purposes. Children are exposed to diverse speech acts (*label, repeat, answer, request, greet, protest*) and learn conversational moves (*initiating a topic, maintaining a topic, closing a topic*). They listen to and produce stories that are organized temporally and causally, and they are exposed to strategies for solving communication breakdowns. They are encouraged to initiate with their peers, to take turns, and to negotiate for objects. They learn how to talk to different people (*friends, teachers, librarians*) in different settings (*schools, stores, homes*).	1. To initiate to peers when needing help or wanting something 2. To maintain a topic for two or more turns in a conversation 3. To follow or give directions with two or more steps 4. To tell a personal event as a story to a peer 5. To use language for many different purposes (e.g., question, comment, request action, request information, reply, greet, and leave)

Source: From Justice, L. M. (2004). Creating language-rich preschool classroom environments. *Teaching Exceptional Children, 37*(2), pp. 40 & 42. Used by permission.

approaches were developed as an alternative to didactic language interventions because children often experienced difficulties in generalizing new skills from structured teaching settings to everyday contexts. In contrast to didactic teaching approaches, which use contrived materials and activities (e.g., pictures, puppets) and massed trials to teach specific skills, naturalistic interventions are characterized by dispersed learning trials carried out in the natural environment as opportunities occur for teaching functional communication (Hancock & Kaiser, 2006). Naturalistic approaches occur in the context of typical conversational interchanges that follow the child's "attentional lead" (Goldstein, Kaczmarek, & Hepting, 1994).

Kaiser and Grim (2006) make the following recommendations about naturalistic interventions, which are also known as *milieu teaching strategies*:

- Teach when the child is interested.
- Teach what is functional for the student at the moment.
- Stop while both the student and the teacher are still enjoying the interaction. (pp. 455–456)

Naturalistic interventions involve structuring the environment to create numerous opportunities for desired child responses (e.g., holding up a toy and asking, "What do you want?") and structuring adult responses to a child's communication (e.g., the child points outside and says, "Go wifth me," and the teacher says, "Okay, I'll go with you."). Effective milieu teaching more closely resembles a conversation than a structured instructional episode (Kaiser & Grim, 2006). However, good naturalistic teaching does not mean the teacher should wait patiently to see whether and when opportunities for meaningful and interesting language use by children occur. Environments in which language teaching takes place should be designed to catch students' interest and increase the likelihood of communicative interactions that can be used for teaching purposes. Six strategies for arranging environments that create naturally occurring language teaching opportunities are described in Figure 8.8.

No matter what the approach to treatment, children with language disorders need to be around children and adults with something interesting to talk about. As Reed (2005) points out, educators assumed for many years that a one-to-one setting was the most effective format for language intervention. Emphasis was on eliminating distracting stimuli and focusing a child's attention on the desired communication task. Today, however, it is generally recognized that language is an interactive, interpersonal process and that educators should use naturally occurring intervention formats to expose children with language disorders to a wide range of stimuli, experiences, contexts, and people that cannot be replicated in one-to-one therapy.

Whatever intervention methods they use, effective SLPs establish specific goals and objectives, keep precise records of their students' performance, and arrange the learning environment so that each child's efforts at communication will be rewarded and enjoyable.

Augmentative and Alternative Communication

Augmentative and alternative communication (AAC) refers to a diverse set of strategies and methods to assist individuals who cannot meet their communication needs through speech or writing. AAC entails three components (Kangas & Lloyd, 2006):

1. A representational symbol set or vocabulary
2. A means for selecting the symbols
3. A means for transmitting the symbols

Each of the three components of AAC may be unaided or aided. *Unaided AAC techniques* do not require a physical aid or device. They include oral speech, gestures, facial expressions, general body posture, and manual signs. Of course, individuals without disabilities use a wide range of unaided augmentative communication techniques. *Aided AAC techniques* of communication involve an external device or piece of equipment. AAC devices range from no-tech (e.g., paper and pencil) to low-tech (e.g., the child pushes a switch to transmit a single word or phrase) to high-tech electronic equipment (e.g., computerized voice-output device) (Piché, 2007).

Individuals who do not speak so that others can understand must have access to vocabulary that matches as nearly as possible the language they would use in various situations if they could speak. Beukelman and Miranda (1998) suggest that decisions about what items to include in a student's augmentative vocabulary should take into account the following:

- Vocabulary that peers in similar situations and settings use
- What communication partners (e.g., teachers, parents) think will be needed
- Vocabulary the student is already using in all modalities
- Contextual demands of specific situations

Naturalistic interventions/milieu teaching strategies

 Council for Exceptional Children — Content Standards for Beginning Teachers—Common Core: Design learning environments that encourage active participation in individual and group activities (CC5S4) (also CC4S3).

Augmentative and alternative communication

 Council for Exceptional Children — Content Standards for Beginning Teachers—Common Core: Augmentative and assistive communication strategies (CC6K4).

FIGURE 8.8	Six strategies for increasing naturalistic opportunities for language teaching

1. **Interesting materials.**   Students are likely to communicate when things or activities in the environment interest them. *Example:* James lay quietly on the rug, with his head resting on his arms. Ms. Davis sat at one end of the rug and rolled a big yellow ball right past James. James lifted his head and looked around for the ball.

2. **Out of reach.**   Students are likely to communicate when they want something that they cannot reach. *Example:* Mr. Norris lifted a drum off the shelf and placed it on the floor between Judy and Annette, who were both in wheelchairs. Mr. Norris hit the drum three times and then waited, looking at his two students. Judy watched and clapped her hands together. Then, she reached for the drum with both arms outstretched.

3. **Inadequate portions.**   Students are likely to communicate when they do not have the necessary materials to carry out an instruction. *Example:* Mr. Robinson gave every student except Mary a ticket to get into the auditorium for the high school play. He told his students to give their tickets to the attendant. Mr. Robinson walked beside Mary toward the entrance. When Mary reached the attendant, Mr. Robinson paused and looked at Mary. She pointed to the tickets in his hand and signed "give me." Mr. Robinson gave her a ticket and she handed it to the attendant who said "Thank you. Enjoy the play."

4. **Choice-making.**   Students are likely to communicate when they are given a choice. *Example:* Peggy's favorite pastime is listening to tapes on her tape recorder. On Saturday morning, Peggy's father said to her, "We could listen to your tapes" (pointing to the picture of the tape recorder on Peggy's communication board) "or we could go for a ride in the car" (pointing to the picture of the car). "What would you like to do?" Peggy pointed to the picture of the tape recorder. "OK, let's listen to this new tape you like," her father said as he put the tape in and turned on the machine.

5. **Assistance.**   Students are likely to communicate when they need assistance in operating or manipulating materials. *Example:* Tammy's mother always places three clear plastic containers with snacks (cookies, crackers, popcorn) on the kitchen table before Tammy returns from school. When Tammy arrives home and is ready for a snack, she goes to the table and chooses what she wants. The containers are hard to open, so Tammy usually brings the container with her chosen snack to her mother. Her mother responds to this nonverbal request by modeling a request form that specifies Tammy's choice (e.g., "Open popcorn.").

6. **Unexpected situations.**   Students are likely to communicate when something happens that they do not expect. *Example:* Ms. Esser was helping Kathy put on her socks and shoes after rest time. After assisting with the socks, Ms. Esser put one of the shoes on her own foot. Kathy stared at the shoe for a moment and then looked up at her teacher, who was smiling. "No," laughed Kathy, "my shoe."

Source: From Kaiser, A. P., & Grim, J. C. (2006). Teaching functional communication skills. In M. E. Snell & F. Brown (Eds.), *Instruction of students with severe disabilities* (6th ed.) (p. 464). Upper Saddle River, NJ: Pearson Education, Inc. Reprinted by permission.

Symbol Sets and Symbol Systems   After selecting the vocabulary for an AAC system, the educator must choose or develop a collection of symbols to represent the vocabulary. Numerous *symbol sets* are commercially available (e.g., the Oakland Picture Dictionary [Kirsten, 1981], Picture Communication Symbols [Mayer-Johnson, 1986], and the Pictogram Ideogram Communication symbols [Johnson, 1985]). These sets are a collection of pictures or

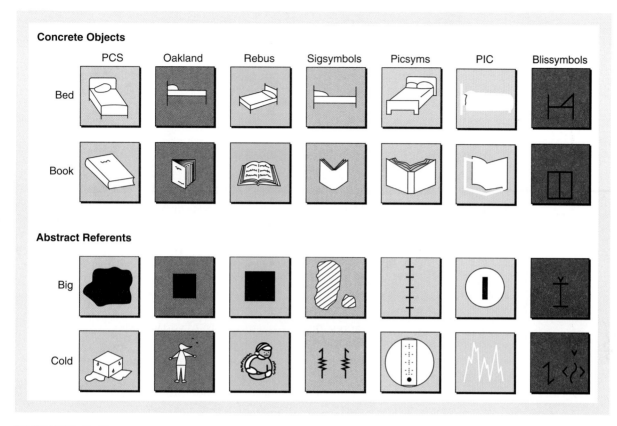

FIGURE 8.9

Examples from widely used graphic symbol sets (PCS = Picture Communication Symbols; PIC = Pictogram Ideogram Communication)

Source: From Vanderheiden, G. C., & Lloyd, L. L. (1986). Non-speech modes and systems. In S. W. Blackstone (Ed.), *Augmentative communication* (ff. 49–161). Rockville, MD: American Speech-Language-Hearing Association. Reprinted by permission.

drawings in which each symbol has one or more specified meanings, from which a person's AAC vocabulary might be constructed. Symbol sets are graphic, which means that the symbols look like the object or concept they represent as much as possible. Mayer-Johnson has an electronic version of its symbols that can be incorporated into picture overlays. Symbol sets may also be homemade, consisting of photos, pictures, and perhaps words and the alphabet.

In contrast to symbol sets, *symbol systems* are structured around an internal set of rules that govern how new symbols are added to the system. One of the best-known symbol systems is Blissymbolics, which represents concepts through a combination of geometric shapes. The user of Blissymbolics combines multiple symbols to create new meanings (e.g., "school" is communicated by selecting the symbols "house-gives-knowledge"). Because many of the Blissymbolics are abstract, however, and do not look like the concept they represent, some individuals have difficulty learning the system. Figure 8.9 shows how common concrete and abstract vocabulary are represented by Blissymbols and six other symbol sets.

Selecting the Symbols   Students select symbols in augmentative communication by direct selection, scanning, or encoding responses (Kangas & Lloyd, 2006). *Direct selection* involves pointing to the symbol one wishes to express with a finger or fist or sometimes with a wand attached to the head or chin. With a limited number of selections widely spaced from one another, the user can select symbols by "eye pointing." *Scanning* techniques present choices to the user one at a time, and the user makes a response at the proper time to indicate which item or group of selections she wants to communicate. Scanning can be machine or listener assisted (e.g., the listener may point to symbols one at a time while watching for the user's eye blink, which signals selection). *Encoding* involves giving multiple signals to indicate the location of the symbol or the item to be selected. Usually, the user makes a pair of responses that directs the listener to a specific printed message on

---

FIGURE 8.10 How to talk with a person who uses AAC

Communicating with someone who does not speak can be a challenging, even unnerving, experience for many natural speakers. Here are 10 suggestions for those who use speech to communicate that will help improve the quality of their conversations with people who use AAC:

- Introduce yourself.
- Ask the person to show you how the communication system works.
- Pause to let the person construct a message. Be patient; it might take a while.
- Relax and give yourself a chance to get used to a slower rhythm of communication. Don't feel like you have to fill all the silent spaces by talking all the time.
- Be sure to give your new friend a chance to ask you questions or to make comments.
- Even though you might guess what's coming next from context, don't finish the person's sentences unless given permission or prompted to do so.
- Interact at eye-to-eye level if you can. If the person's in a wheelchair, you might grab a chair and sit across from her.
- Pay attention to facial expressions and gestures, just as you would with someone who communicates by speech.
- Don't be afraid to say you don't understand something and to ask to have it repeated.
- Talk directly to the person; don't communicate with her through someone else.

Source: Adapted from Blackstone, S. W. (1991). Beyond public awareness: The road to involvement! *Augmentative Communication News, 4*(2), 6. Used by permission of Augmentative Communication, Inc., Monterey, CA.

This communication device enables the user to select and transmit synthesized speech via a wand attached to the head.

a reference list. In a display in which symbols are organized by color and number, for example, a student can first touch one card (to select the red group of messages) and then make a second pointing response to indicate which number message in the red group is intended. Figure 8.10 provides suggestions on how to communicate with a person who uses AAC.

Transmitting the Symbols After the educator has selected vocabulary and a symbol set, she must determine a method of transmitting the symbols. The most common tool for augmentative communication display and transmission is the *communication board,* a flat area (often a tray or a table attached to a wheelchair) on which the symbols are arranged for the user to select. A student may have a basic communication board of common words, phrases, numbers, and so forth for use across many situations. He may also have various situational boards, or miniboards, with specific vocabulary for certain situations (e.g., at a restaurant, in science class). Students can also transport and display symbols in a wallet or a photo album.

A variety of electronic devices offer a wide range of alternatives for transmitting communication symbols. Dedicated communication aids—such as the Prentke Romich Intro Talker, the Prentke Romich Liberator, DECtalk by Digital Equipment Company, and Sentient System's Dynavok—offer computerized speech selection and transmission. To learn how the Dynavok and other assistive technology were used to help an 11-year-old boy who was unable to speak and participate in a general education classroom, see Erickson and Koppenhaver (1998).

A student might need more than one AAC device. Anna, a second grader with severe disabilities, uses her BIGmack, with its voice output to respond "I'm here" when her teacher takes the attendance every morning. She also uses another voice-output communication aid with 8 messages (Message Mate) to request specific things she wants or needs throughout the day (e.g., water, a break, time on the computer). Although she makes good use of facial expressions and vocalizations, Anna also relies on an adapted photo album that contains pictures from magazines, postcards, and photographs with different comments written underneath them to serve as a conversation book during social times with her classmates. (Downing, 2000, p. 35)

EDUCATIONAL PLACEMENT ALTERNATIVES

During the 2005–2006 school year, approximately 89% of children with speech or language impairments were served in the general education classroom—6% in resource rooms and 4.6% in separate classes (U.S. Department of Education, 2007). A wide variety of service delivery models for students with communication disorders are used within and across these three educational placement options. ASHA recognizes the following seven service delivery models (ASHA Ad Hoc Committee on the Roles and Responsibilities of the School-Based Speech-Language Pathologist, 2000).

Monitoring

The SLP monitors or checks on the student's speech and language performance in the general education classroom. This option is often used just before a student is dismissed from therapy.

Pull-Out

The traditional and still most prevalent model of service delivery is the pull-out approach, sometimes called *intermittent direct service*. The child may be seen individually or in small groups of up to three children. Depending on the needs of the individual child, pull-out may involve sessions of up to 1 hour 5 days per week.

According to ASHA (2001e), most of the students receiving services from school-based SLPs during the 1999–2000 school year met with the SLP at least two times a week, most often for 21- to 30-minute sessions. The classroom teacher and the SLP collaborate so that curriculum materials used in the classroom can be incorporated into the child's speech and language therapy sessions.

Many SLPs believe it is impossible to adequately serve a child with speech or language impairments with an isolated, pull-out approach (two or three 30-minute sessions each week with a specialist) (Harn, Bradshaw, & Ogletree, 1999). Because communication is seen as occurring most appropriately in the natural environment, remedial procedures are increasingly carried out in the general education classroom during ongoing routines rather than in a special speech room.

Collaborative Consultation

Increasingly communication disorders specialists serve as consultants for regular and special education teachers (and parents) rather than spending most of their time providing direct services to individual children (Dohan & Schulz, 1998). SLPs who work in school settings more often function as team members concerned with children's overall education and development. The SLP often provides training and consultation for the general education classroom teacher, who may do much of the direct work with a child with communication disorders. The specialist concentrates on assessing communication disorders, evaluating progress, and providing materials and techniques. Teachers and parents are encouraged to follow the specialist's guidelines.

Classroom-Based

Increasingly, SLPs are working as educational partners in the classroom, mediating between students' communication needs and the communication demands of the academic curriculum. Teachers can integrate language and speech goals into daily curriculum activities when

Placement alternatives

Content Standards for Beginning Teachers—Common Core: Issues, assurances, and due process right related to assessment, eligibility, and placement with a continuum of services (CC1K6).

Collaboration with SLPs

Content Standards for Beginning Teachers—Common Core: Models and strategies of consultation and collaboration (CC10K1).

To learn more about how SLPs can use instructional discourse in the classroom to increase children's language competence, go to the Homework & Exercises section in Chapter 8 of MyEducationLab and complete Homework Exercise 2.

SLPs become classroom collaborators. The advantage is that services are brought to the child and the teacher, and communication connections with the curriculum are made more directly. Hall and colleagues (2001) and Lue (2001) offer numerous suggestions for how teachers can help children with communication disorders in the classroom.

Training classroom teachers and parents to promote children's speech and language development has become an increasingly important aspect of the SLP's responsibilities (Al Otaiba & Smartt, 2003). A growing controversy among some members of the SLP profession is the extent to which services for students with speech and language impairments provided in general education classrooms should take "a therapeutic focus" versus an "educational focus" (Prelock, 2000a, 2000b). Although SLPs in the schools are being encouraged to provide services within inclusive models, they often express concern that they are becoming more like classroom teachers and that the therapy they should be providing to students on their caseloads is becoming watered down as a result. Ehren (2000) discusses these concerns and offers solutions to the role confusion and dissatisfaction of many SLPs who provide in-classroom speech-language services. Ehren suggests that SLPs can preserve their role identity and the integrity of services provided by maintaining a therapeutic focus and sharing the responsibility for student success with classroom teachers.

Separate Classroom

Students with the most severe communication disorders are served in special classrooms for children with speech or language impairments. During the 2005–2006 school year, approximately 1 in 20 children with speech or language impairments were served in separate classes (U.S. Department of Education, 2007).

Community-Based

In community-based models, speech and language therapy is provided outside of the school, usually in the home. This model is most often used with preschoolers and sometimes for students with severe disabilities, with an emphasis on teaching functional communication skills in the community.

Combination

Variations of all these models exist, and many schools and SLPs serve children using combinations of two or more models (Culatta & Wiig, 2006).

To learn more about the strategies discussed in this chapter, go to the Building Teaching Skills section in Chapter 8 of MyEducationLab and complete the activities.

TIPS for Beginning Teachers

SUPPORTING STUDENTS WITH LANGUAGE DISORDERS

by Steve Everling

LANGUAGE IMPAIRMENTS

Although each student with a language impairment presents a unique profile, teachers can implement some general strategies when working with these students.

- *Thoroughly explain new vocabulary.* Students with language impairments often have problems learning and retaining new words, so explaining new vocabulary is essential. To create an environment for success for these students, present the new vocabulary orally and in writing with a definition, and then provide visual cues (pictures) and examples. After presenting and explaining these words, post the visual cues in the classroom so that students can refer to them as needed.

- *Embed new vocabulary across the curriculum.* Students will need a lot of practice and repetition with new vocabulary. The best way to provide this practice is to create opportunities for the students to use new vocabulary across content areas and in different contexts. For example, if you are teaching farm animal vocabulary, have students read books about farm animals during reading, design a farm animal habitat during science, and graph animal characteristics (e.g., which animals eat hay) as part of their math lesson.

- *Provide longer wait time.* Students with language impairments sometimes need a little longer to formulate and express responses to questions. Wait 3 or 4 seconds longer than you normally would to give the student a chance to answer, and don't interrupt or hurry the student with her answer.

- *Break multistep directions into smaller components.* Complying with a teacher's complex, multistep direction, "Put your paper in your desk and push in your chair before you go to the bathroom," may be overwhelming for a student with a language impairment. To lessen frustration and create more opportunities for compliance, break up your directions into smaller tasks, such as:

  Step 1: "Put your paper in your desk."
  Step 2: "Stand up and push in your chair."
  Step 3: "Now you may go to the bathroom."

  Do not move onto a new direction until the student completes each task successfully. Once the student consistently follows shorter directions, you can start to give longer directions.

ARTICULATION ERRORS

Although students in the primary grades exhibit variability in speech-sound development, most typically developing children consistently make most speech sounds by the time they begin kindergarten.

- *Do not confuse typical speech-sound development with serious articulation errors.* Even typically developing children sometimes have difficulty with the /r/ and /l/ sounds and complex consonant blends, like the /str/ in *street*, which may not fully develop until first or second grade. However, a kindergarten child who is difficult to understand may be at risk for communication and literacy learning problems, so be sure to monitor his progress.

- *Consult with your school's SLP if you have a hard time understanding a child's speech.* Whenever you are uncertain whether a student's speech-sound development is where it should be, consult with your school's SLP. The SLP will be able to answer your questions and, if need be, begin a formal evaluation and intervention process with the student.

STUTTERING

Many teachers are unsure of what to do with a student who stutters. Here are a few general guidelines:

- *Don't anticipate what the student wants to say and finish the utterance for her.* Instead, try to listen attentively, letting the student work through the stuttering moment on her own.

- *Consistently model a relaxed and unhurried speaking style.* Your calm and steady speech will have a more positive effect on the student than telling him to "slow down" or "relax."

- *Ask the student what strategies she uses to speak more fluently.* It is okay to speak openly and individually with the student about her stuttering. Implementing these strategies in the classroom can make the educational process more effective and enjoyable for the student and give her a sense of empowerment.

KEY TERMS AND CONCEPTS

aphasia, p. 311
articulation disorder, p. 306
augmentative and alternative communication (AAC), p. 321
cleft palate, p. 310
cluttering, p. 308
communication, p. 297
communication disorder, p. 303
dialect, p. 305
dysarthria, p. 310
expressive language disorder, p. 305
fluency disorder, p. 307
grapheme, p. 300
language, p. 298

language disorder, p. 305
morpheme, p. 299
morphology, p. 299
phoneme, p. 298
phonological disorder, p. 306
phonology, p. 298
pragmatics, p. 299
receptive language disorder, p. 305
semantics, p. 299
speech, p. 299
speech impairment, p. 304
stuttering, p. 307
syntax, p. 299
voice disorder, p. 308

SUMMARY

Definitions

- Communication is any interaction that transmits information. Narrating, explaining, informing, requesting, and expressing are major communicative functions.
- A language is an arbitrary symbol system that enables a group of people to communicate. Each language has rules of phonology, morphology, syntax, semantics, and pragmatics that describe how users put sounds and ideas together to convey meaning.
- Speech is the oral production of language; it is the fastest and most efficient method of communication by language.
- Typical language development follows a relatively predictable sequence. Most children learn to talk and use language without any formal instruction; by the time they enter first grade, their grammar and speech patterns match those of the adults around them.
- A communication disorder is "an impairment in the ability to receive, send, process, and comprehend concepts or verbal, nonverbal and graphic symbol systems" (ASHA, 1993, p. 40).
- A child has a speech impairment if his speech draws unfavorable attention to itself, interferes with the ability to communicate, or causes social or interpersonal problems.
- The three basic types of speech impairments are articulation disorders (errors in the production of speech sounds), fluency disorders (difficulties with the flow or rhythm of speech), and voice disorders (problems with the quality or use of one's voice).
- Some children have trouble understanding language (receptive language disorders); others have trouble using language to communicate (expressive language disorders); still others have language delays.
- Speech or language differences based on cultural or regional dialects are not communication disorders. However, children who use a different dialect may also have speech or language disorders.

Characteristics

- Four basic kinds of speech-sound errors exist: distortions, substitutions, omissions, and additions.
- A child with an articulation disorder cannot produce a given sound physically.
- A child with a phonological disorder can produce a given sound and does so correctly in some instances but not at other times.
- Stuttering, the most common fluency disorder, is marked by rapid-fire repetitions of consonant or vowel sounds, especially at the beginnings of words, prolongations, hesitations, interjections, and complete verbal blocks.
- A voice disorder is characterized by abnormal vocal quality, pitch, loudness, resonance, and/or duration for the speaker's age and sex.
- Language impairments involve problems in phonology, morphology, syntax, semantics, and/or pragmatics; they are usually classified as either receptive or expressive.

Prevalence

- About 2.5% of school-age children receive special education for speech and language impairments, the second-largest disability category under IDEA.
- Nearly twice as many boys as girls have speech impairments.
- Children with articulation and spoken language problems represent the largest category of speech-language impairments.

Causes

- Although some speech and language impairments have physical (organic) causes, most are functional disorders that cannot be directly attributed to physical conditions.

Identification and Assessment

- Assessment of a suspected communication disorder may include some or all of the following components: (a) case history and physical examination, (b) articulation test, (c) hearing test, (d) auditory discrimination test, (e) phonological awareness and processing, (f) vocabulary and overall language development test, (g) language samples, and (h) observation in natural settings.

Educational Approaches

- Speech-language pathologists (SLPs) employ a wide range of techniques for identifying, evaluating, and providing therapeutic services to children. These include structured exercises and drills as well as individual and group therapy sessions.
- A general goal of treating speech-sound errors is to help the child speak as clearly as possible. Addressing articulation and phonological errors involves discrimination and production activities. Fluency disorders can be treated with the application of behavioral principles and self-monitoring, although many children recover spontaneously.
- Voice disorders can be treated surgically or medically if the cause is organic. Most remedial techniques offer direct vocal rehabilitation. Behavioral principles help break habitual patterns of misuse.
- Language disorder treatments vary widely. Precommunication activities encourage exploration of expressive language. SLPs connect oral language to literacy components of the curriculum. Naturalistic interventions disperse learning trials throughout the natural environment and normal conversation.
- Augmentative and alternative communication may be aided or unaided and consists of three components: a representational symbol set or vocabulary, a means for selecting the symbols, and a means for transmitting the symbols.

Educational Placement Alternatives

- Most children with speech and language problems (89%) attend general education classes.
- ASHA recognizes seven service-delivery models: monitoring, pull-out, collaborative consultation, classroom-based, separate classroom, community-based, and combination.

 Now go to MyEducationLab at www.myeducationlab.com and take the pretest to assess your initial comprehension of chapter content. Once you have taken the pretest, use your individualized Study Plan for Chapter 8 to enhance your understanding of the concepts discussed in the chapter. Finally, take the post-test to assess your comprehension of Chapter 8 content.

9

Deafness and Hearing Loss

- What distinguishes a child who is deaf from a child who is hard of hearing in terms of the primary sensory modes used for learning and communication?
- How might deafness affect a child's acquisition and use of speech and language, overall academic achievement, and social functioning?
- How does the prevalence of hearing loss in school-age children compare to that of older segments of the population?
- What implications for a child's education result from the type of hearing loss and age of onset?
- What advantages does the precise assessment of a child's hearing loss hold for intervention?
- In what ways do students who are deaf and hard of hearing use technologies and supports that amplify, supplement, or replace sound?
- How do oral/aural, total communication, and bilingual–bicultural approaches to teaching children who are deaf and hard of hearing differ in their philosophies and methods?
- How might a student's and his family's perspectives and wishes regarding educational placement be influenced by their membership in the Deaf culture?

FEATURED TEACHER

DOUGLAS JACKSON
El Paso Regional Day School Program for the Deaf • Hillside Elementary School, El Paso, Texas

Douglas Jackson

Education—Teaching Credentials—Experience

- B.A., social studies education, University of Northern Colorado, 1978
- M.S., education of the deaf, University of Rochester/National Technical Institute for the Deaf, New York, 1982
- Texas and Florida certifications in hearing impaired, K–12; social studies (secondary); and gifted, K–12
- 23 years of experience teaching students with special needs

Current Teaching Position For the past 13 years, I have taught science, social studies, math, and art to elementary-age deaf students at Hillside Elementary. Texas is divided into regional day school programs for deaf education. At Hillside Elementary, a neighborhood school of about 700 students, nine deaf-education teachers, two speech therapists, and interpreters serve 70 deaf students. We serve the students of 13 school districts in our region. Some students travel as much as an hour each way to come to school. This is not unusual. Hearing impairment is a low-incidence disability and a very cost-intensive one. We are a total communication program, which means we stress the simultaneous use of speech and sign.

Students I have five students in my fifth-grade homeroom, all of whom receive special education and related services under the Individuals with Disabilities Education Act (IDEA) categories of hearing or speech or language impairments. Almost all of our students are Hispanic, and some come from homes in which Spanish is the primary or only language. A couple of our students have deaf parents who were born in Mexico.

Socioeconomically, we run the gamut. Some of our students come from middle-class families, and some come from poor families—sometimes desperately so. We get to know our students very well, and our students get to know each other better than their own siblings sometimes.

Curriculum Materials and Teaching Strategies

We try to parallel the materials and the units covered in the general education curriculum, adapting a lot of the language in the texts. I often turn textbook content into plays that incorporate the students' personalities and interests and take advantage of the great resources provided by local culture. Sometimes students draw backgrounds and create props, and we videotape these plays. I use participatory theater as a teaching tool for several reasons: (a) Plays help the students understand the material better; (b) active learning is always better than passive attending; (c) plays personalize the material, helping the students understand that the events and concepts they're learning about are central to the history and current life of their world; (d) plays bring out the students' natural creativity; and (e) plays help the students feel less daunted by the textbook. Our greatest role-playing academic exercise is our annual mock trial in the 243rd District Courtroom of Judge David Guaderrama. With the assistance of Assistant District Attorney Lori Hughes and Federal Public Defender Bruce Weathers, our students are defendants, witnesses, attorneys, bailiffs, and jurors. Over the years we have brought Goldilocks, Snow White's stepmother, the third Little Pig, Hansel and Gretel, and others to justice, and along the way we have taught our students about our system of justice and the services (especially interpreters) they require to ensure their constitutional rights. Besides, with all of the costumes and preparation, a mock trial is the coolest school play imaginable.

I cannot overstate the impact technology has had on my classroom and my students. My students are visual learners, and I feel blessed to be working at a time when there are so many tools that allow my students to use that strength. My Smart Board™, for example, has become a window through which my students can manipulate digital images, streaming video, websites, Powerpoints, and even their teacher's written scrawl to understand the relationships in everything from the rock cycle and animal adaptations to fractions and decimals to the causes and effects of the Civil War. The only problem is that my Smart Board is also my blank canvas on which I can create literally anything. There are so many possibilities, but you must choose the ones that you are actually going to invest your time, energy, and passion in. We use technology in many ways—video letters with deaf students in other places, distance-learning sessions with the Texas School for the Deaf, and structured Internet research assignments.

In the past 5 years I have been doing much more inclusion with fifth- and fourth-grade general education classes, with a great deal of success both educationally and socially. Working with these combined groups has certainly taught me a lot. The faculty members and students at our school have been wonderful to our students, and many have made an effort to learn to communicate with them.

In the past few years my students have also done many PowerPoint® presentations for classmates, faculty members, and civic groups. These began in 2003 with a presentation on effective mainstreaming to faculty members at our elementary, middle, and high school campuses. It has continued with presentations on the rights and responsibilities of deaf people in our system of justice (for El Paso Bar Association members in 2004), in medical situations (for Texas Tech medical students in 2005) and in the workplace (for business people in a civic group in 2006). It is amazing to see how much more powerful these messages are when they are delivered by smart, funny, charming, and dynamic young people than when they are offered by a middle-aged bald man such as myself. It is rewarding watching students master the tools that can help them overcome their own problems.

Personal Qualities Important for Special Educators

Being a great teacher is like being a great lawyer, doctor, chef, or artist. At some point it stops being a role you "play" and becomes a role you "are." I mean, look at Van Gogh or Picasso or Renoir. They were always themselves—every brushstroke a fingerprint of the artist. You can't tell where the self ends and the profession begins. Great teachers do that. They don't just look at the state standards and try to decide how they will cover them. They're always seeing the world through the eyes of a teacher; and when something new and interesting happens to them, they think about how they can share that experience with their students. I would be lying if I said that I had this skill from day 1. Many of my early efforts as a teacher were 10 steps forward and 9 steps back, sometimes 9 steps forward and 10 steps back. It is something that I am still working on now—I am very much a work in progress.

Lately I have been thinking a lot about the technological revolution that has taken place in my field. Earlier waves of technology led to the creation of the telephone, radio, and television, and made deaf people feel even more isolated. My students can use e-mail, Sidekicks, videophones, and telephone relay services to communicate instantly with friends and family members who are next door or on the other side of the world. Having this enormous array of tools at our disposal should make us aware of the great strides made by pioneers in this field who didn't have all of these cool toys. My fellow teachers and I are walking in the footsteps of giants—in truth, giants who frequently and sometimes heatedly disagreed with each other, but giants who paved the way for generations of teachers and students to come. A great teacher honors those giant footsteps and makes the best effort he can when the footsteps end, and he must expand the trail in his size $10^1/_2$ Nikes.

To learn more about students with hearing impairments and how Smart Boards can be beneficial in instruction, go to the Homework & Exercises section in Chapter 9 of the MyEducationLab for this text, and complete Homework Exercise 1.

As Lou Ann Walker, the child of deaf parents, observes in her autobiography, people who have normal hearing usually find it difficult to fully appreciate the enormous importance of the auditory sense in human development and learning: "Nature attaches an overwhelming importance to hearing. As unborns we hear before we can see. Even in deep comas, people often hear what is going on around them. For most of us, when we die, the sense of hearing is the last to leave the body" (Walker, 1986, p. 165).

A sighted person can simulate blindness by closing her eyes or donning a blindfold, but it is virtually impossible for a hearing person to turn off his ears. The basic structure of the inner ear is present in the fetus at 6 months, and hearing begins before birth (Brownell, 1999). Throughout life, all hearing animals obtain information about the world around them, from all directions, 24 hours a day. When a twig snaps behind us, we don't have to be looking to know that we are not alone.

In addition to its tremendous survival advantage, hearing plays the lead role in the natural, almost effortless manner by which most children acquire speech and language. Newborns respond to sounds by startling or blinking. At a few weeks of age, infants with normal hearing can listen to quiet sounds, recognize their parents' voices, and pay attention to their own gurgling and cooing sounds. Hearing infants as young as 1 month can discriminate speech sounds (Hulit & Howard, 2006). By the time they are 1 year old, hearing children can produce many of the sounds of their language and are speaking their first words. Children develop language by constantly hearing people talk and associating these sounds with innumerable activities and events. Sound acquires meaning, and children quickly learn that people convey information and communicate their thoughts and feelings by speaking and hearing.

In contrast, for children who cannot hear speech sounds, learning a spoken language is anything but natural or effortless. Children who are deaf simply do not have access to an auditorally based language. As we will see, however, when children who are deaf are exposed to a visual, grammatically complete, sign-based language as their first language, they acquire language and communication skills in a manner quite similar to the acquisition of speech by hearing children. For children who can hear enough speech with hearing aids or other technologies, techniques such as speech training and speechreading can provide access to spoken English and enable them to acquire developmentally appropriate language to communicate effectively. Whether a child's hearing loss is mild or profound, early identification and assessment are keys to providing needed special education services.

After reading this chapter, complete the pretest for Chapter 9 on MyEducationLab to assess your initial understanding of chapter content.

It may be impossible for a person with typical hearing to comprehend fully the difficulties prelingual deafness imposes on learning to comprehend and produce spoken language.

Definitions

Definitions: hearing impairment, deaf, residual hearing, hard of hearing

 Content Standards for Beginning Teachers—D/HH: Educational definitions and identification criteria for individuals who are D/HH (DH1K1).

Like other disabilities, hearing loss can be defined and classified from different perspectives and for different purposes. A medical definition describes the degree of hearing loss on a continuum from mild to profound. Educational definitions of hearing loss focus on the child's ability to use his hearing to understand speech and learn language and the effects on educational performance. For example, under the disability category of hearing impairment, IDEA defines **deafness** and **hearing impairment** as follows:

> Deafness means a hearing impairment that is so severe that the child is impaired in processing linguistic information through hearing, with or without amplification, [and] that adversely affects a child's educational performance. (P.L. 108-446, 20 U.S.C. §1401 [2004], 20 C.F.R. §300.8[c][3])
>
> Hearing impairment means an impairment in hearing, whether permanent or fluctuating, that adversely affects a child's education performance but that is not included under the definition of deafness in this section. (P.L. 108-446, 20 U.S.C. §1401 [2004], 20 C.F.R. §300.8[c][5])

Most special educators distinguish between children who are deaf and those who are hard of hearing. *Normal hearing* generally means that a person has sufficient hearing to understand speech. Under adequate listening conditions, a person with normal hearing can interpret speech in everyday situations without using any special device or technique. A child who is deaf cannot use hearing to understand speech. Even with a hearing aid, the hearing loss is too great to allow a deaf child to understand speech through the ears alone. Although a deaf person may perceive some sounds through **residual hearing**, she uses vision as the primary modality for learning and communication.

A child who is **hard of hearing** has a significant hearing loss that makes some special adaptations necessary. Children who are hard of hearing can use their hearing to understand speech, generally with the help of a hearing aid. Though they may be delayed or deficient, the speech and language skills of a child who is hard of hearing are developed mainly through the auditory channel.

Many persons who are deaf do not view their hearing loss as a disability and consider the term **hearing impairment** inappropriate and demeaning because it suggests a deficiency or pathology. Like other cultural groups, members of the Deaf community share a common language and social practices (Woll & Ladd, 2005). When the cultural definition of hearing loss is used, *Deaf* is spelled with a capital *D*, just as an uppercase letter is used to refer to a person who is French, Japanese, or Jewish. While person-first language is considered the appropriate way to refer to individuals with disabilities, persons who identify with the **Deaf culture** prefer terms such as teacher of the Deaf, school for the Deaf, and Deaf person.

Deaf culture and community

 Content Standards for Beginning Teachers—D/HH: Cultural dimensions of hearing loss that may affect the individual (DH3K2) (also DH1K2).

How We Hear

Audition, the sense of hearing, is a complex and not completely understood process. The function of the ear is to gather sounds (acoustical energy) from the environment and to transform that energy into a form (neural energy) that can be interpreted by the brain. Figure 9.1 shows the major parts of the human ear. The *outer ear* consists of the external ear and the auditory canal. The part of the ear we see, the **auricle** (or *pinna*), funnels sound waves into the **auditory canal (external acoustic meatus)** and helps distinguish the direction of sound.

When sound waves enter the external ear, they are slightly amplified as they move toward the **tympanic membrane** (eardrum). Variations in sound pressure cause the eardrum to move in and out. These movements of the eardrum change the acoustical energy into mechanical energy, which is transferred to the three tiny bones of the *middle ear* (the *hammer, anvil,* and *stirrup*). The base (called the *footplate*) of the third bone in the sequence, the stirrup, rests in an opening called the *oval window*, the path through which sound energy enters the inner ear. The vibrations of the three bones (together called the **ossicles**) transmit energy from the middle ear to the inner ear with little loss.

The most critical and complex part of the entire hearing apparatus is the *inner ear*, which is covered by the *temporal bone*, the hardest bone in the entire body. The inner ear contains the **cochlea**, the main receptor organ for hearing, and the *semicircular canals*, which control the sense of balance. The cochlea, named for its resemblance to a coiled snail

To learn more about Deaf culture, go to the Homework & Exercises section in Chapter 9 of MyEducationLab and complete Homework Exercise 2.

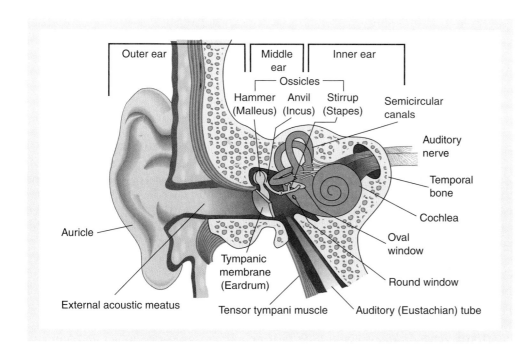

FIGURE 9.1

Basic anatomy of the
human ear

shell, consists of two fluid-filled cavities that contain 30,000 tiny hair cells arranged in four rows. Energy transmitted by the ossicles moves the fluid in the cochlea, which in turn stimulates the hair cells. Each hair cell has approximately a hundred tiny spines, called *cilia*, at the top. When the hair cells are stimulated, they displace the fluid around them, which produces minute electrochemical signals that are transmitted along the auditory nerve to the brain. High tones are picked up by the hair cells at the basal, or lowest turn of the cochlea, and low tones stimulate hair cells at the apex, or top, of the cochlea. When hair cells move, they also produce low-level sounds, called *otoacoustic emissions (OAEs)*. Deafness in newborns may be diagnosed by the detection of OAEs (Ross & Levitt, 2000).

The Nature of Sound

Sound is measured in units that describe its intensity and frequency. Both dimensions of sound are important in considering the needs of a child with a hearing loss. The intensity or loudness of sound is measured in **decibels (dB)**. Zero dB represents the smallest sound a person with normal hearing can perceive, which is called the *zero hearing-threshold level (HTL)*, or **audiometric zero**.

Larger-decibel numbers represent increasingly louder sounds on a ratio scale in which each increment of 10 dB is a tenfold increase in intensity. A low whisper 5 feet away registers about 10 dB; conversational speech 10 to 20 feet away ranges from approximately 20 to 55 dB. Traffic on a city street produces sound at about 70 dB, and a lawnmower about 100 dB. Sound of about 125 dB or louder will cause pain to most persons.

The frequency, or pitch, of sound is measured in cycles per second, or **hertz (Hz)**; 1 Hz equals 1 cycle per second. Pure tones consist of one frequency only. Speech and most environmental sounds are complex tones made up of a variety of frequencies. The lowest note on a piano has a frequency of about 30 Hz, middle C about 250 Hz, and the highest note about 4,000 Hz. Human hearing is limited to a range of approximately 20 to 20,000 Hz, but many audible sounds are outside the speech range, the frequency range of ordinary conversation. Although a person who cannot hear very low sounds (e.g., a foghorn) or very high sounds (e.g., a piccolo) may suffer some inconvenience, she will encounter no significant problems in the classroom or everyday life. A person with a severe hearing loss in the speech range, however, is at a great disadvantage in acquiring and communicating in a spoken language.

The frequency range generally considered most important for hearing spoken language is 500 to 2,000 Hz, but some speech sounds have frequencies below or above that range.

Degree and frequency range of hearing loss

Council for Exceptional Children

Content Standards for Beginning Teachers—D/HH: Effects of sensory input on the development of language and cognition (DH6K3) (also, CC2K2).

For example, the /s/ phoneme (as in the word *sat*) is a high-frequency sound, typically occurring between 4,000 and 8,000 Hz (Northern & Downs, 2002). A student whose hearing loss is more severe at the higher frequencies will thus have particular difficulty in discriminating the /s/ sound. Conversely, phonemes such as /dj/ (the sound of the *j* in *jump*) and /m/ occur at low frequencies and will be more problematic for a student with a low-frequency hearing loss. As you might expect, a student with a high-frequency hearing loss tends to hear men's voices more easily than women's voices.

CHARACTERISTICS

Any discussion of characteristics of students who are deaf or hard of hearing should include three qualifications. First, students who receive special education because of hearing loss comprise an extremely heterogeneous group (Karchmer & Mitchell, 2005). It is a mistake to assume that a commonly observed behavioral characteristic or average level of academic achievement is representative of all children with hearing loss.

Second, the effects of hearing loss on a child's communication and language skills, academic achievement, and social and emotional functioning are influenced by many factors, including the type and degree of hearing loss, the age at onset, the attitudes of the child's parents and siblings, opportunities to acquire a first language (whether through speech or sign), and the presence or absence of other disabilities (Schirmer, 2004).

Third, generalizations about how deaf people are supposed to act and feel must be viewed with extreme caution (Andrews, Leigh, & Weiner, 2004). Lane (1988), for example, makes a strong case against the existence of the so-called psychology of the deaf. He shows the similarity of the traits attributed to deaf people in the professional literature to traits attributed to African people in the literature of colonialism and suggests that those traits do not "reflect the characteristics of deaf people but the paternalistic posture of the hearing experts making these attributions" (p. 8). In addition, he argues that the scientific literature on the psychology of the deaf is flawed in terms of test administration, test language, test scoring, test content and norms, and its description of subject populations, arguments that have been noted by other researchers as well (Komesaroff, 2007; Moores, 2001; Paul & Quigley, 1990).

English Literacy

English literacy skills

Council for Exceptional Children

Content Standards for Beginning Teachers—D/HH: Effects of sensory input on the development of language and cognition (DH6K3) (also, CC2K1, CC2K2, DH3K4).

A child with a hearing loss—especially a prelingual loss of 90 dB or greater—is at a great disadvantage in acquiring English language skills. Hearing children typically acquire a large vocabulary and a knowledge of grammar, word order, idiomatic expressions, fine shades of meaning, and many other aspects of verbal expression by listening to others and to themselves from early infancy. A child who, from birth or soon after, cannot hear the speech of other people will not learn speech and language spontaneously, as do children with normal hearing. Because reading and writing involve graphic representations of a phonologically based language, the deaf child who has not benefited from exposure to a rich grammatical model of spoken English must strive to decode, comprehend, and produce text based on a language for which she may have little understanding.

Students with hearing loss have smaller vocabularies when compared to peers with normal hearing, and the gap widens with age (American Speech-Language-Hearing Association [ASHA], 2007a). Children with hearing loss learn concrete words such as *tree*, *run*, *book*, and *red* more easily than abstract words such as *before*, *after*, *equal to*, and *jealous*. They also have difficulty with function words such as *the*, *an*, *are*, and *a*.

They may omit endings of words, such as the plural *-s*, *-ed*, or *-ing*. Because the grammar and structure of English often do not follow logical rules, a person with prelingual hearing loss must exert a great deal of effort to read and write with acceptable form and meaning. For example, if the past tense of "talk" is "talked," then why doesn't "go" become "goed"? If the plural of "man" is "men," then shouldn't the plural of "pan" be "pen"? Learning words with multiple meanings is difficult. It is not easy to explain the difference between the expressions "He's beat" (tired) and "He was beaten" to a person who has never had normal hearing.

Deaf students often have difficulty differentiating questions from statements. Most have difficulty understanding and writing sentences with passive voice ("The assignment was given yesterday.") and relative clauses ("The gloves I left at home are made of leather."). Many students who are deaf write sentences that are short, incomplete, or improperly arranged. The following sentences taken from stories written by elementary deaf students illustrate some of the English literacy problems attributable to not hearing spoken language:

Bobby is walked.

The boy sees a brown football on the hold hand.

The trees is falling a leaves.

The happy children is friending.

Speaking

Atypical speech is common in many children who are deaf or hard of hearing. Of all of the challenges that hearing loss poses to learning the vocabulary, grammar, and syntax of English aside, not being able to hear one's own speech makes it difficult to assess and monitor it. As a result, children with hearing loss may speak too loudly or not loudly enough. They may speak in an abnormally high pitch or sound as though they are mumbling because of poor stress, poor inflection, or poor rate of speaking. The speech of children with hearing loss may be difficult to understand because they omit quiet speech sounds such as /s/, /sh/, /f/, /t/, and /k/, which they cannot hear.

Academic Achievement

Most children with hearing loss have difficulty with all areas of academic achievement, especially reading and math. Studies assessing the academic achievement of students with hearing loss have routinely found them to lag far behind their hearing peers, and the gap in achievement between children with normal hearing and those with hearing loss usually widens as they get older (ASHA, 2007a). The average deaf student who leaves high school at age 18 or 19 is reading at about the fourth-grade level (Kuntze, 1998; Traxler, 2000), and their mathematics performance is in the range of fifth to sixth grade (Traxler, 2000). Approximately 30% of deaf students are functionally illiterate when they leave school, compared to less than 1% of hearing students (Paul & Jackson, 1993).

It is important not to equate academic performance with intelligence. Deafness itself imposes no limitations on the cognitive capabilities of individuals, and some deaf students read very well and excel academically (Karchmer & Mitchell, 2005; Williams & Finnegan, 2003). The problems that deaf students often experience in education and adjustment are largely attributable to inadequate development of a first language as well as the mismatch between the demands of spoken and written English and the students' ability to understand and communicate in English.

Social Functioning

Hearing loss can influence a child's behavior and socioemotional development. Children with severe-to-profound hearing losses often report feeling isolated, without friends, and unhappy in school, particularly when their socialization with other children with hearing loss is limited. These social problems appear to be more frequent in children with mild or moderate hearing losses than in those with severe-to-profound losses (ASHA, 2007a). Children with hearing loss were more likely to have behavioral difficulties in school and social situations than were children with normal hearing. A study of more than 1,000 deaf adolescents who were considered disruptive in the classroom (Kluwin, 1985) found that the most frequently related factor was reading ability; that is, students who were poorer readers were more likely to exhibit problem behaviors in school. Even a slight hearing loss can cause a child to miss important auditory information, such as the tone of a teacher's voice while telling the class to get out their spelling workbooks, which can lead to the child's being considered inattentive, distractible, or immature (Easterbrooks, 1999).

To learn more about teaching writing to students who are deaf, go to the Building Teaching Skills section in Chapter 9 of MyEducationLab and complete the activities.

Speech skills

Council for Exceptional Children Content Standards for Beginning Teachers—D/HH: Effects of sensory input on the development of language and cognition (DH6K3) (also, CC2K2, DH3K4).

Academic achievement

Council for Exceptional Children Content Standards for Beginning Teachers—D/HH: Effects of sensory input on the development of language and cognition (DH3K4) (also, CC2K2, DH2K2).

Social functioning

Council for Exceptional Children Content Standards for Beginning Teachers—D/HH: Impact of educational placement options with regard to cultural identity and linguistic, academic, and social-emotional development (DH3K1) (also DH3K2, CC2K5, CC2K6).

Children and adults with hearing loss frequently express feelings of depression, withdrawal, and isolation, particularly those who experience adventitious loss of hearing (Connolly, Rose, & Austen, 2006; Sheetz, 2004). Research has not provided clear insights into the effects of hearing loss on behavior; however, it appears that the extent to which a child with hearing loss successfully interacts with family members, friends, and people in the community depends largely on others' attitudes and the child's ability to communicate in some mutually acceptable way (Ita & Friedman, 1999; Marschark & Clark, 1998). Children who are deaf with deaf parents are thought to have higher levels of social maturity and behavioral self-control than do deaf children of hearing parents, largely because of the early use of manual communication between parent and child that is typical in homes with deaf parents.

Many individuals who are deaf choose to work, live, and socialize primarily with other deaf people; members of hearing society may mistakenly view this as clannishness. Certainly, communication plays a major role in anyone's adjustment. People with hearing loss are fully capable of developing positive relationships with their hearing peers when a satisfactory method of communication can be used. Figure 9.2 lists some tips for making your speech more accessible to an individual who is speechreading.

PREVALENCE

Approximately 28 million Americans, or 10% of the population, have hearing loss difficulty in receiving and processing spoken communication (ASHA, 2007b; National Institute on Deafness and Other Communication Disorders, 2007a). Hearing loss affects males more than females. More than half of all persons with hearing loss are 65 years or older, and less than 4% are under 18 years of age (Mitchell, 2006). Profound hearing loss occurs in about 1 of every 1,000 births.

During the 2005–2006 school year, 71,484 students ages 6 to 21 received special education services under the disability category of hearing impairments (U.S. Department of Education, 2007). This represents 1.2% of all school-age students who received special education services and about 0.1% of the resident student population. The actual number of school-age children with hearing loss in special education programs is somewhat higher because some children with hearing impairments are counted under another primary disability category (e.g., mental retardation, cerebral palsy, deaf-blind). It is not known precisely the percentage of these students who are deaf or hard of hearing. A national survey of students with hearing impairments found that 45% of students had severe or profound hearing loss (Gallaudet Research Institute, 2005). About one third to as many as one half of students who are deaf or hard of hearing have another disabling condition (Blackorby & Knokey, 2006; Knoors & Vervloed, 2005).

TYPES AND CAUSES OF HEARING LOSS

Types and Age of Onset

Types of hearing loss

 Content Standards for Beginning Teachers—D/HH: Effects of sensory input on the development of language and cognition (DH1K3).

The two main types of hearing loss are conductive and sensorineural. **Conductive hearing loss** results from abnormalities or complications of the outer or middle ear. A buildup of excessive wax in the auditory canal can cause a conductive hearing loss, as can a disease that leaves fluid or debris. Some children are born with incomplete or malformed auditory canals. A hearing loss can also be caused if the eardrum or ossicles do not move properly. As its name implies, a conductive hearing loss involves a problem with conducting, or transmitting, sound vibrations to the inner ear. If the rest of the auditory system is intact, conductive hearing losses can often be corrected through surgical or medical treatment. Hearing aids are usually beneficial to persons with conductive impairments.

Sensorineural hearing loss refers to damage to the auditory nerve fibers or other sensitive mechanisms in the inner ear. The cochlea converts the physical characteristics of sound into corresponding neural information that the brain can process and interpret; impairment of the cochlea may mean that sound is delivered to the brain in a distorted fashion or not delivered at all. Amplification (making the source of sound louder) may not help the person with a sensorineural hearing loss. Surgery or medication cannot correct most

FIGURE 9.2 **Tips for communicating with someone who is deaf**

When presented with an opportunity to communicate with a person who is deaf, many people with normal hearing are unsure of themselves. As a result, they may avoid deaf people altogether or use ineffective and frustrating strategies when they do attempt to communicate. The following tips for facilitating communication were suggested by the Community Services for the Deaf program in Akron, Ohio. These tips provide basic information about three common ways that deaf persons communicate: through speechreading, with sign language or the assistance of an interpreter, and by written communication. Usually, the person will indicate the approach with which he is most comfortable.

If the person relies mainly on speechreading, here are things you can do to help:

- Face the person and stand or sit no more than four feet away.
- The room should have adequate illumination, but don't seat yourself in front of a strong or glaring light.
- Try to keep your whole face visible.
- Speak clearly and naturally and not too fast.
- Don't exaggerate your mouth movements.
- Don't raise the level of your voice.
- Some words are more easily read on the lips than others are. If you are having a problem being understood, try substituting different words.
- It may take a while to become used to the deaf person's speech. If at first you can't understand what she is saying, don't give up.
- Don't hesitate to write down any important words that are missed.

If the deaf person communicates best through sign language (and you do not), it will probably be necessary to use an interpreter. Here are some considerations to keep in mind:

- The role of the interpreter is to facilitate communication between you and the person who is deaf. The interpreter should not be asked to give opinions, advice, or personal feelings.
- Maintain eye contact with the deaf person and speak directly to him. The deaf person should not be made to take a back seat in the conversation. For example, say, "How are you today?" instead of "Ask him how he is today."
- Remain face-to-face with the deaf person. The best place for the interpreter is behind you and a little to your side. Again, avoid strong or glaring light.
- Remember, it is the interpreter's job to communicate everything that you and the deaf person say. Don't say anything that you don't want to be interpreted.

Written messages can be helpful in exchanging information. Consider the following:

- Avoid the temptation to abbreviate your communication.
- Write in simple, direct language.
- The deaf person's written English may not be grammatically correct, but you will probably be able to understand it. One deaf person, for example, wrote, "Pay off yesterday, finish me," to convey the message, "I paid that loan off yesterday."
- Use visual aids, such as pictures, diagrams, and business cards.
- Don't be afraid to supplement your written messages with gestures and facial expressions.
- Written communication has limitations, but it is often more effective than no communication at all.

sensorineural hearing loss. The combination of both conductive and sensorineural impairments is called a *mixed hearing loss*.

Hearing loss is also described in terms of being *unilateral* (present in one ear only) or *bilateral* (present in both ears). Most students who receive special education for hearing loss have bilateral losses, although the degree of impairment may not be the same in both ears. Children with unilateral hearing loss generally learn speech and language without major difficulties, although they tend to have problems localizing sounds and listening in noisy or distracting settings.

Age of onset

Council for Exceptional Children

Content Standards for Beginning Teachers—D/HH: Impact of the onset of hearing loss, age of identification, and provisions of services on the development of the individual who is D/HH (DH2K2).

It is important to consider the age of onset—whether a hearing loss is **congenital** (present at birth) or **acquired** (appears after birth). The terms **prelingual hearing loss** and **postlingual hearing loss** identify whether a hearing loss occurred before or after the development of spoken language. A child who cannot hear the speech of other people from birth or soon after will not learn speech and language spontaneously, as do children with normal hearing. To approximate the experience of a child who is deaf from birth or early childhood, watch a television program in which a foreign language is being spoken—with the sound on the TV set turned off. You would face the double problem of being unable to read lips and understand an unfamiliar language.

A child who acquires a hearing loss after speech and language are well established, usually after age 2, has educational needs very different from the prelingually deaf child. The educational program for a child who is prelingually deaf usually focuses on acquisition of language and communication, whereas the program for a child who is postlingually deaf usually emphasizes the maintenance of intelligible speech and appropriate language patterns.

Causes of Congenital Hearing Loss

Causes of hearing loss

Council for Exceptional Children

Content Standards for Beginning Teachers—D/HH: Etiologies of hearing loss that can result in additional sensory, motor, and/or learning differences (DH1K3).

Although more than 400 causes of hearing loss have been identified, a national survey of more than 37,000 students found that the cause could not be determined in 53% of cases (Gallaudet Research Institute, 2005).

Genetic Factors   About one half of all congenital deafness is caused by genetic abnormalities (Tran & Grunfast, 1999). Genetic hearing loss may be autosomal dominant, autosomal recessive, or X-linked (related to the sex chromosome). *Autosomal dominant hearing loss* exists when one parent, who carries the dominant gene for hearing loss and typically has a hearing loss, passes the gene on to the child. In this case there is at least a 50% probability that the child will also have a hearing loss. The probability is higher if both parents have the dominant gene or if both grandparents on one side of the family have hearing loss due to genetic causes.

Approximately 80% to 90% of inherited hearing loss is caused by *autosomal recessive hearing loss*, in which both parents typically have normal hearing and carry a recessive gene (Tran & Grunfast, 1999). In this case there is a 25% probability that the child will have a hearing loss. Because both parents usually have normal hearing, and because no other family members have hearing loss, there is no prior expectation that the child may have a hearing loss.

In *X-linked hearing loss*, the mother carries the recessive trait for hearing loss on the sex chromosome and passes it on to male offspring but not to females. This kind of hearing loss is rare, accounting for only about 1% to 2% of hereditary hearing loss.

Even though 90% of children who are deaf are born to hearing parents, about 30% of the school-age population of students who are deaf have relatives with hearing loss (Moores, 2001). Because most hereditary deafness is the result of recessive genetic traits, the marriage of two deaf persons results in only a slightly increased risk of deafness in their children because there is a small chance that both parents' deafness was affected by the same exact genetic syndrome (Northern & Downs, 2002).

Hearing loss is one of the known characteristics of more than 200 genetic syndromes, such as Down syndrome, Usher syndrome, Treacher Collins syndrome, and fetal alcohol syndrome.

Maternal Rubella   Although rubella (also known as German measles) has relatively mild symptoms, it can cause deafness, visual impairment, heart disorders, and a variety of other serious disabilities in the developing child when contracted by a pregnant woman, particularly during the first trimester. A major epidemic of rubella in the United States and Canada between 1963 and 1965 accounted for more than 50% of the students with hearing loss in special education programs in the 1970s and 1980s. Since an effective vaccine was introduced in 1969, the incidence of hearing loss caused by rubella has decreased significantly.

Congenital Cytomegalovirus   Both rubella and **cytomegalovirus (CMV)** are members of a group of infectious agents known as TORCHES (toxoplasmosis, rubella, cytomegalovirus, herpes simplex, and syphilis). CMV is a common viral infection, and most people who are infected with it experience minor symptoms such as respiratory infections that soon disappear. Approximately 1% of infants have CMV on their saliva; and 10% of those may later develop various conditions including mental retardation, visual impairment, and, most often, hearing impairment. It is estimated that 4,000 children are born in the United States each year with significant hearing impairments caused by CMV infection (Strauss, 1999). At present, no prevention or treatment for CMV exists. However, a blood test can determine if a woman of childbearing age is at risk for developing an initial CMV infection during pregnancy.

Prematurity   It is difficult to precisely evaluate the effects of prematurity on hearing loss, but early delivery and low birth weight are more common among children who are deaf than among the general population.

Causes of Acquired Hearing Loss

Otitis Media   A temporary, recurrent infection of the middle ear, **otitis media** is the most common medical diagnosis for children. Nearly 90% of all children will experience otitis media at least once, and about one third of children under age 5 have recurrent episodes (Bluestone & Klein, 2007). Antibiotics usually are an effective treatment; but if untreated, otitis media can result in a buildup of fluid and a ruptured eardrum, which causes permanent conductive hearing loss.

Meningitis   The leading cause of postlingual hearing loss is meningitis, a bacterial or viral infection of the central nervous system that can, among its other effects, destroy the sensitive acoustic apparatus of the inner ear. Children whose deafness is caused by meningitis generally have profound hearing losses. Difficulties in balance and other disabilities may also be present.

Ménière's Disease   A fairly rare disorder of the inner ear, Ménière's disease is characterized by sudden and unpredictable attacks of vertigo (dizziness), fluctuations in hearing, and *tinnitus* (the perception of sound in the head when no outside sound is present). In its severest form, Ménière's disease can be incapacitating. Little is understood about the mechanisms underlying the condition, and at present no reliable treatment or cure exists (Schessel, 1999). Ménière's disease most often appears in people between the ages of 40 and 60, but it can affect children under the age of 10.

Noise-Induced Hearing Loss   Noise pollution—repeated exposure to loud sounds, such as industrial noise, jet aircraft, guns, and amplified music—is increasingly recognized as a cause of hearing loss. Exposure to "toxic noise is the main culprit" for approximately one third of the 28 million Americans with permanent hearing loss (Kulman, 1999, p. 2). Noise-induced hearing loss is the most common occupational disease and the second most frequently self-reported occupational injury (ASHA, 2007c).

Noise-induced hearing loss (NIHL) caused by chronic exposure to recreational and occupational noise often occurs gradually, and the person may not realize his hearing is being damaged until it is too late (Haller & Montgomery, 2004). Sources of noise that can cause NIHL include motorcycles, leafblowers, and target shooting, all emitting sounds from 120 to 150 decibels. Prolonged or repeated exposure to noise above 85 dB can cause gradual hearing loss. Regular exposure of more than 1 minute to noise at 110 dB risks permanent hearing loss (NIDCD, 2007b).

Herer, Knightly, and Steinberg (2007) identified the following warning signs for excessive noise: being within 3 feet of someone and having to shout to be understood, experiencing ringing in the ears (tinnitus) after leaving the area, and hearing only muffled or soft sounds 1 to 2 hours later. For more information about noise-induced hearing loss and how to prevent it, visit the Wise Ears website, www.nidcd.nih.gov/health/wise.

IDENTIFICATION AND ASSESSMENT

Assessment of Infants

Early identification of hearing loss

Council for Exceptional Children Content Standards for Beginning Teachers—D/HH: Specialized terminology used in assessing individuals who are D/HH (DH8K1) (also DH2K2).

Typical development of behaviors related to sound

 Council for Exceptional Children Content Standards for Beginning Teachers—D/HH: Effects of sensory input on the development of language and cognition (DH3K4) (also CC2K5).

The earlier a hearing loss is identified, the better a child's chances are for receiving early intervention and treatment and for developing good language and communication skills (Calderon & Naidu, 2000). Unfortunately, hearing loss goes undetected in many children, and detection does not always lead quickly to intervention. A national survey of parents of preschool children with hearing loss found that parents suspected their baby had a hearing loss at an average age of 17 months and had the diagnosis confirmed at a mean age of 22 months (Meadow-Orlans et al., 1997). Half of the children who were hard of hearing in this study did not have their hearing loss diagnosed until they were 2.5 years old. More discouraging are the data on the lag time between diagnosis and intervention: Children waited an average of 8 months for a hearing aid, 10 months for speech and auditory services, and 11 months to begin sign language.

All infants, hearing and deaf alike, babble, coo, and smile. Later on, children who are deaf tend to stop babbling and vocalizing because they cannot hear themselves or their parents, but the baby's increasing silence may go unnoticed for a while and then be mistakenly attributed to other causes. Figure 9.3 lists some common auditory behaviors emitted by infants with normal hearing. Failure to demonstrate these responses may mean that an infant has a hearing loss, and an audiological exam is recommended.

Universal newborn and infant hearing screening is mandated in 42 states and the District of Columbia, and legislation is pending in two other states (ASHA, 2007d). The two most widely used methods of screening for hearing loss in infants measure physiological reactions to sound. With *auditory brain stem response*, sensors placed on the scalp measure electrical activity as the infant responds to auditory stimuli. In *otoacoustic emission* screening, a tiny microphone placed in the baby's ear detects the "echoes" of hair cells in the cochlea as they vibrate to sound (Ross & Levitt, 2000).

Pure-Tone Audiometry

Audiometry and audiograms

Council for Exceptional Children Content Standards for Beginning Teachers—D/HH: Specialized terminology used in assessing individuals who are D/HH (DH8K1) (also DH8K2).

A procedure called *pure-tone audiometry* is used to assess the hearing of older children and adults. The examiner uses an **audiometer**, an electronic device that generates sounds at different levels of intensity and frequency. The child, who receives the sound either through earphones (air conduction) or through a bone vibrator (bone conduction), is instructed to hold up a finger when he hears a sound and to lower it when he hears no sound. The test seeks to determine how loud sounds at various frequencies must be before the child can hear them. Most audiometers deliver tones in 5-dB increments from 0 to 120 dB, with each decibel level presented in various frequencies, usually starting at 125 Hz and increasing in octave intervals (doubling in frequency) to 8,000 Hz. The results of the test are plotted on a chart called an **audiogram** (see Figure 9.4).

To obtain a hearing level on an audiogram, the child must be able to detect a sound at that level at least 50% of the time. For example, a child who has a 60-dB hearing loss cannot detect a sound until it is at least 60 dB loud, in contrast to a child with normal hearing, who would detect that same sound at a level between 0 and 10 dB.

Speech Audiometry

Speech audiometry tests a person's detection and understanding of speech. A list of one- and two-syllable words is presented at different decibel levels. The **speech reception threshold (SRT)**, the decibel level at which the individual can understand half of the words, is measured and recorded for each ear. It is important to recognize that while a child might identify single words 50% of the time

An audiometer generates tones of precise intensity and frequency.

when spoken at a given volume and frequency, that does not always translate into ability to follow conversational speech (Woolsey, 2001).

FIGURE 9.3 | **Expected auditory behaviors**

1 Month
- Jumps or startles in response to loud noises
- Begins making gurgling sounds
- Responds to voice

3 Months
- Coos, babbles
- Turns to voices
- May quiet down to familiar voices close to ear
- Stirs or awakens from sleep when there is a loud sound relatively close by

6 Months
- Makes vocal sounds when alone; engages in vocal play
- Turns head toward sounds or when name is called and speaker is not visible
- Vocalizes when spoken to directly
- Imitates sounds

9 Months
- Responds differently to a cheerful versus angry voice
- Tries to copy the speech sounds of others
- Babbling acquires inflection

12 Months
- Locates a sound source by turning head (whether the sound is at the side, above, or below level)
- Ceases activity when parent's voice is heard
- Responds to own name
- Uses single words such as *mama* or *dada* correctly
- Vocalizes emotions
- Laughs spontaneously
- Disturbed by nearby noise when sleeping
- Imitates sounds and words
- Understands some familiar phrases or words
- Responds to music or singing
- Increases type and amount of babbling

18 Months
- Comes when called
- Responds to *no*
- Follows simple commands
- Uses 4–10 words in addition to *mama* or *dada*

24 Months
- Has vocabulary of more than 50 words
- Uses two words together
- Follows simple directions
- Responds to rhythm of music
- Uses voice for a specific purpose
- Shows understanding of many phrases used daily in life
- Plays with sound-making objects
- Uses well-inflected vocalization
- Refers to himself/herself by name
- Names a picture or object

Source: Adapted from American Speech-Language-Hearing Association (2007d) and Northern and Downs (2002).

Mild Loss (41 to 55 dB)

Vicki:

- Is able to understand face-to-face conversation with little difficulty

- Misses much of the discussion that goes on in her classroom—particularly if several children are speaking at once or if she cannot see the speaker clearly

- Has some classmates who are unaware she has a hearing loss

- Benefits from wearing a hearing aid

- Receives occasional speech and language assistance from a speech-language pathologist

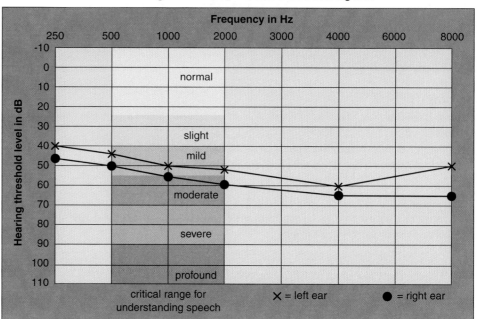

Audiogram for Vicki, who has a mild hearing loss

Moderate Loss (56 to 70 dB)

Antoine:

- Without a hearing aid can hear conversation only if it is loud and clear

- Can hear male voices more easily than female voices (loss is less pronounced in the lower frequencies)

- Finds it impossible to follow most class discussions, even though his teacher arranges favorable seating for him

- Has impaired but intelligible speech

- Attends a part-time special class for children with hearing loss and is in a regular classroom for part of the day

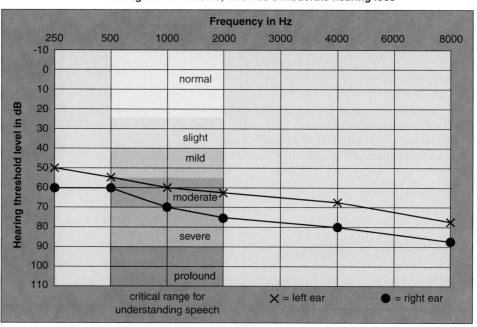

Audiogram for Antoine, who has a moderate hearing loss

FIGURE 9.4

Audiograms for students with mild, moderate, severe, and profound degrees of hearing loss and the effects of different degrees of hearing loss on speech and language and probable educational needs

Alternative Audiometric Techniques

Several alternative techniques have been developed for testing the hearing of children and individuals with severe disabilities who cannot understand and follow conventional audiometry procedures. In **play audiometry**, the child is taught to perform simple but distinct activities, such as picking up a toy or putting a ball into a cup, whenever she hears

Severe Loss (71 to 90 dB)

Brante:

- Can hear voices only if they are very loud and 1 foot or less from her ear
- Wears a hearing aid, but it is unclear how much she gains from it
- Can distinguish most vowel sounds but hears only a few consonants
- Can hear a door slamming, a vacuum cleaner, and an airplane flying overhead
- Communicates by speech and signs
- Must always pay close visual attention to a person speaking with her
- Splits her school day between a special class and a regular classroom with an educational interpreter

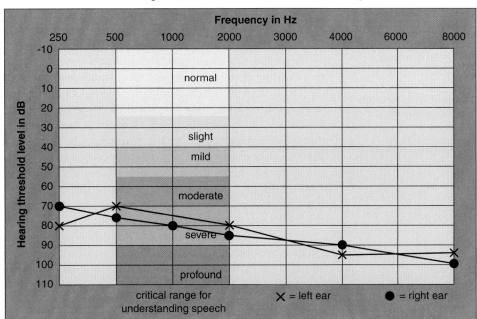

Audiogram for Brante, who has a severe hearing loss

Profound Loss (91 dB or more)

Steve:

- Cannot hear conversational speech at all
- Has a hearing aid that helps him be aware of certain loud sounds, such as a fire alarm or a bass drum
- Uses vision as his primary modality for learning
- Uses American Sign Language as his first language and principal means of communication
- Has not developed intelligible speech
- Attends a residential school for the deaf

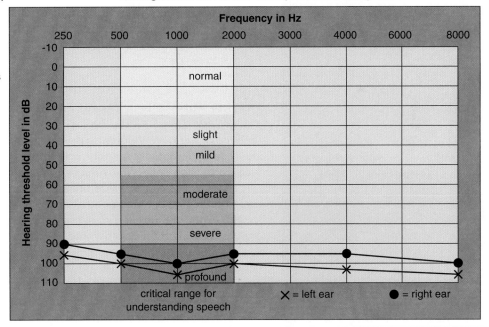

Audiogram for Steve, who has a profound hearing loss

FIGURE 9.4 Continued

the signal, either pure tones or speech. A similar procedure is **operant conditioning audiometry**, in which the child receives a token or a small candy when he pushes a lever in the presence of a light paired with a sound. No reinforcer is given for pushing the lever when the light and sound are off. Next, the sound is presented without the light. If the child pushes the lever in response to the sound alone, the examiner knows the child can hear that sound. **Behavior observation audiometry** is a passive assessment procedure in which the child's reactions to sounds are observed. A sound is presented at an increasing level of intensity until a response, such as head turning, eye blinking, or cessation of play, is reliably observed.

Degrees of Hearing Loss

Hearing loss is usually described by the terms *slight, mild, moderate, severe,* and *profound,* depending on the average hearing level, in decibels, throughout the frequencies most important for understanding speech (500 to 2,000 Hz). It is important to recognize, however, that no two children have exactly the same pattern of hearing, even if their responses on a hearing test are similar. Just as a single intelligence test cannot provide sufficient information to plan a child's educational program, the special education needs of a child with hearing loss cannot be determined from an audiometric test alone. Children hear sounds with differing degrees of clarity, and the same child's hearing ability may vary from day to day. Some children with very low levels of measurable hearing can benefit from hearing aids and can learn to speak. On the other hand, some children with less apparent hearing loss cannot function well through the auditory channel and must rely on vision as their primary means of communication.

Figure 9.4 shows the audiograms of four children with mild, moderate, severe, and profound hearing loss and describes some of the effects. Although no audiogram depicting a slight hearing loss is shown, children who cannot hear or discriminate speech sounds at less than 25 dB may experience major obstacles to learning (Schirmer, 2004). Even a minimal hearing loss of 15 dB that "may not be problematic for a linguistically sophisticated person who has disciplined attending skills . . . can sabotage the overall development of an infant or child who is in the process of learning language and acquiring knowlcdgc" (Pakulski & Kaderavek, 2002, p. 97).

TECHNOLOGIES AND SUPPORTS

In years past, it was assumed that people who were deaf simply did not hear at all. But hearing loss occurs in many degrees and patterns, and nearly all deaf children have some amount of residual hearing. Modern methods of testing hearing and improved technology for the amplification of sound enable many children with even severe and profound hearing loss to use their residual hearing productively.

Technologies That Amplify or Provide Sound

Hearing Aids   A **hearing aid** is an amplification device; it makes sounds louder. Early versions indiscriminately amplified all sounds, which made them ineffective for most children with sensorineural hearing loss. Modern hearing aids can differentially amplify selected frequencies, and therefore can be tailored to each child's individual pattern of hearing loss.

Hearing aids can be worn behind the ear, in the ear, completely in the ear canal, on the body, or incorporated into eyeglass frames. Children can wear hearing aids in one or both ears (monaural or binaural aids). Whatever its shape, power, or size, a hearing aid picks up sound, magnifies its energy, and delivers this louder sound to the user's middle ear. In many ways, a hearing aid is like a miniature public address system, with a microphone, an amplifier, and controls to adjust volume and tone. Digital hearing aids first became available in 1987 but with little success due to their large size and short battery life; they have become much improved and enable enhanced sound processing and noise reduction (Ricketts, 2007).

The earlier in life a child can be fitted with an appropriate hearing aid, the more effectively he will learn to use hearing for communication and awareness. Today, it is not at all unusual to see infants and preschool children wearing hearing aids; the improved listening conditions become an important part of the young child's speech and language development. To derive the maximum benefit from a hearing aid, a child should wear it throughout the day. Residual hearing cannot be effectively developed if the aid is removed or turned off outside the classroom.

To derive maximum benefit from a hearing aid, a child should wear it throughout the day.

It is difficult for any child to learn in a noisy classroom, but children who are deaf or hard of hearing are especially reliant on good classroom acoustics in order to hear and comprehend spoken language. Hearing aids offer minimal benefit in noisy and reverberant classrooms (Nelson, 2001). A signal-to-noise ratio (SNR) of at least +15 dB is considered necessary for students to achieve maximum benefit of a personal amplification device and their residual hearing (ASHA, 1995). An ambient noise level of 35 dB or less generally will allow all speakers' voices to reach all students at the desired +15 dB SNR. However, classrooms today are inherently noisy. When Knecht, Whitelaw, and Nelson (2000) recorded noise levels in 32 unoccupied elementary classrooms, they found only four with background noise levels within the recommended limit. The average ambient noise in most of the other classrooms was 10 to 15 dB above the ASHA guideline.

Group Assistive Listening Devices   Group assistive listening devices can solve the problems caused by distance, noise, and reverberation in the classroom. In most systems, a radio link is established between the teacher and the children with hearing loss, with the teacher wearing a small microphone transmitter (often on the lapel, near the lips) and each child wearing a receiver that doubles as a personal hearing aid (Crandell & Smaldino, 2001a). An FM radio frequency is usually employed, and wires are not required, so teacher and students can move freely around the classroom. The FM device creates a listening situation comparable to the teacher's "being only 6 inches away from the child's ear at all times" (Ireland, Wray, & Flexer, 1988, p. 17).

Cochlear Implants   Unlike hearing aids, which deliver amplified sound to the ear, a **cochlear implant** bypasses damaged hair cells and stimulates the auditory nerve directly. The implant is surgically placed under the skin behind the ear. An implant has four basic parts: an external *microphone*, which picks up sound from the environment; an external *speech processor*, which selects and arranges sounds picked up by the microphone; a *transmitter;* and a *receiver/stimulator*, which receives signals from the speech processor and converts them into electric impulses. *Electrodes* collect the impulses from the stimulator and send them directly to the brain via the auditory nerve (see Figure 9.5).

Hearing aids

Council for Exceptional Children — **Content Standards for Beginning Teachers—D/HH: Strategies for stimulating and using residual hearing (DH6K8).**

Group listening devices

Council for Exceptional Children — **Content Standards for Beginning Teachers—D/HH: Strategies for stimulating and using residual hearing (DH6K8).**

Cochlear implants

Council for Exceptional Children — **Content Standards for Beginning Teachers—D/HH: Issues and trends in the field of education of individuals who are D/HH (DH1K4) (also DH3K2).**

FIGURE 9.5

Internal and external components of the cochlear implant

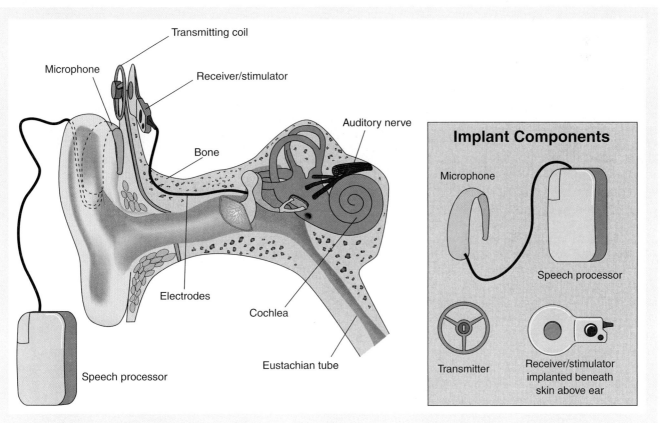

Transmitting coil

Microphone

Receiver/stimulator

Auditory nerve

Bone

Electrodes

Cochlea

Eustachian tube

Speech processor

Implant Components

Microphone

Speech processor

Transmitter

Receiver/stimulator implanted beneath skin above ear

Cochlear implant surgery usually takes 2 to 3 hours, and the child stays overnight in the hospital. About 4 weeks later, the child returns to the implant center for initial stimulation of the device and tune-up sessions over 2 to 3 days. An implant does not restore or create normal hearing. It can, however, give a deaf person a useful auditory understanding of the environment and help him or her to understand speech. The National Association for the Deaf (2007) estimates that about 60,000 people worldwide have received cochlear implants since their approval by the Food and Drug Administration in 1989 (NIDCD, 2001), and that some 13,000 adults and 10,000 children in the United States have received cochlear implants. A national survey found that 11% of deaf and hard-of-hearing students had cochlear implants (Gallaudet Research Institute, 2005).

When coupled with intensive postimplantation therapy, cochlear implants can help young children acquire speech, language, developmental, and social skills. While many questions about cochlear implants remain to be answered, initial research reports have described significant improvements in speech perceptions, speech production, and language skills compared to peers without cochlear implants (Edwards, 2007; Marschark, Rhoten, & Fabich, 2007; Vermeulen, van Bon, Schreuder, Knoors, & Snik, 2007). It is not yet known if there is an optimal age for implantation, but earlier implantation seems to yield better outcomes.

Tremendous controversy surrounds cochlear implants (National Association for the Deaf, 2000). Some members of the Deaf community are vehemently opposed to cochlear

CURRENT ISSUES AND FUTURE TRENDS

DEAFNESS: THE DILEMMA

BY BONNIE TUCKER

During the last twenty years, technological advances to assist people with hearing loss surpassed the expectation of many. Hearing aids improved tremendously, both with respect to quality and aesthetics. The newer aids block out background noise and emphasize sound in the speech range, which has enabled some severely hearing-impaired people to benefit from aids for the first time.... Cochlear implants have enabled some profoundly deaf people, both children and adults, to understand speech without having to rely on speechreading or interpreters; some cochlear implantees are able to converse on the voice telephone with strangers.

Twenty years ago I, for one, did not foresee these almost Orwellian transformations. Today, however, my vision for the future is unlimited. Given the rapidly advancing state of technology in this area, it is not unrealistic to assume that twenty years hence the technological advances of the past two decades will seem outmoded, even ancient. It is not unrealistic to assume that in twenty years cochlear implants will enable profoundly deaf people to understand speech in most circumstances, including on the telephone. We are not there yet, but we are on our way.

Many members of the Deaf community, including leaders of the National Association of the Deaf (NAD), ...

do not want cochlear implants. They do not want to hear. They want their children to be Deaf, and to be a part of the Deaf world. "We like being Deaf," they state. "We are proud of our Deafness. . . ." They claim the right to their own "ethnicity, with our own language and culture, the same way that Native Americans or Italians bond together"; they claim the right to "personal diversity," which is "something to be cherished rather than fixed and erased." And they strongly protest the practice of placing cochlear implants in children.... These same individuals, however, are among the strongest advocates for laws and special programs to protect and assist people with hearing loss. They argue fiercely for the need for interpreters, TTYs, telephone relay services, specially funded educational programs, and close-captioning, at no cost to themselves. On the one hand, therefore, they claim that deafness is not a disability, but a state of being, a "right" that should not be altered. On the other hand, they claim that deafness is a disability that society should compensate for by providing and paying for services to allow deaf people to function in society....

Do Deaf people have the right to refuse to accept new technology, to refuse to "fix" their Deafness if such repair becomes possible? Yes, absolutely. They do have the right, if they wish to exercise that right, to cherish implants and consider the procedure to be a form of genocide of the Deaf culture (e.g., Hyde & Power, 2006; Komesaroff, 2007; Lane & Bahan, 1998). Luterman (1999) offers the following explanation of a position that is difficult for most hearing people to understand:

> People who have never heard do not experience hearing impairment as a loss. This is why they can believe, much to the consternation of the normally hearing population, that deafness is a cultural difference rather than a deficit. It would be analogous, for example, to those who had ESP thinking that the rest of us were terribly handicapped in our communication abilities, while we who do not possess ESP and have never had it do not feel the least handicapped. The only way we would is if those with ESP constantly reminded us of our deficiency and tried to "fix" us. (p. 75)

To read more about the contrasting views of deafness as a cultural difference or as a sensory impairment to be remedied, see Current Issues and Future Trends, "Deafness: The Dilemma."

Supports and Technologies That Supplement or Replace Sound

Interpreters *Interpreting*—signing the speech of a teacher or other speaker for a person who is deaf—began as a profession in 1964 with the establishment of a professional organization called the Registry of Interpreters for the Deaf (RID). Many states have programs for training interpreters, who must meet certain standards of competence to be certified by the RID. The organization was initially composed primarily of freelance interpreters, who interpret primarily for deaf adults in situations such as legal or medical interactions.

Interpreters

Council for Exceptional Children — Content Standards for Beginning Teachers—D/HH: Communication modes used by and with individuals who are hearing and those who are D/HH (DH6K5) (also DH4K3, DH6K1).

---

their Deaf culture, their Deaf ethnicity, their "visually oriented" personal diversity. They have every right to choose not to fix their Deafness. . . . Do Deaf people have the right to demand that society pay for the resulting cost of that choice, however? No, I do not believe they do.

By way of analogy, suppose that blindness and quadriplegia were "curable" due to advanced technology. Blind people could be made to "see" via artificial means such as surgical implantation or three-dimensional eyeglasses; quadriplegic individuals could be made to "walk" and use their arms via artificial means such as surgical nerve implantation or specially built devices. Oh, the blind people might not see as perfectly as sighted people—they might still miss some of the fine print. And the quadriplegic individuals might walk with a limp or move their arms in a jerky fashion. But, for the most part, they would require little special assistance.

Suppose that 10 blind people chose not to make use of available technology for the reason that blindness is not a "disability," not something to be fixed, but that blind people are simply "auditory oriented," and 20 quadriplegic people chose not to make use of available technology for the reason that quadriplegics are simply "out-of-body oriented." How long will society agree to pay for readers, attendants, and other services and devices to assist those blind and quadriplegic individuals who have exercised their right to be diverse? More important, how long should society be asked to pay for such services and devices?

When technology advances to the extent that profoundly deaf people could choose to "hear"—which, eventually, it surely will—Deaf people will have to resolve the dilemma, both for reasons of practicality and

morality. . . . Deaf people will have to decide whether to accept hearing or to remain Deaf. They have every right to choose the latter course. If they do so, however, they must assume responsibility for that choice and bear the resultant cost, rather than thrust that responsibility upon society. . . . As our grandparents used to say, "You can't have your cake and eat it too."

What Do You Think?

1. If your newborn was diagnosed with profound deafness, would you consider cochlear implants? Why or why not?

2. Do you think there are interventions or treatments for people with other disabilities that should be discussed and debated as cochlear implants have for Deaf children? Why or why not?

3. Does society have the right or responsibility to deny supports and services to a person who has chosen not to use an available technology that would make those supports and services unnecessary?

Bonnie Tucker is a professor of law at Arizona State University. Deaf since infancy, and unable to wear hearing aids, Dr. Tucker had cochlear implant surgery at the age of 52. She is the editor and part author of *Cochlear Implants: A Handbook* (McFarland, 1998).

Source: From Tucker, B. (1993). Deafness: 1993–2013—The dilemma. *The Volta Review, 95,* 105–108. Reprinted with permission from the Alexander Graham Bell Association for the Deaf and Hard of Hearing. www.agbell.org.

The role of the *educational interpreter* (sometimes referred to as an *educational transliterator*) has made it possible for many students with hearing loss to enroll in and successfully complete postsecondary programs. The use of educational interpreters in elementary and secondary classrooms has also increased (Chafin Seal, 2004; Monikowski & Winston, 2005). Duties of interpreters vary across schools; they are likely to perform tasks such as tutoring, assisting general and special education teachers, keeping records, and supervising students with hearing loss (Cawthon, 2001).

Speech-to-Text Translation   Computer-aided speech-to-text translation increases access by deaf students to live presentations, such as public or classroom lectures. A leading example of this technology is the C-Print speech-to-text service developed at the National Technical Institute for the Deaf at the University of Rochester (Elliot, Stinson, Francis, Coyne, & Easton, 2003). A trained captionist types the teacher's lecture and students' comments into a laptop computer using a shorthand code. Special software translates the code (e.g., typing "kfe" produces "coffee"), and the text appears on a screen or a student's personal laptop computer monitor about 3 seconds after the words are spoken. The text display remains on the screen for approximately 1 minute, which provides students with much more time to consider the words than using an interpreter or speechreading would.

The system does not provide a verbatim translation of the lecture, which would be impossible at speech rates of 150 words per minute. Captionists are trained to eliminate redundancies, identify key points, and condense information on the fly, keeping as close as possible to the original (see Figure 9.6). Text files can be saved, edited, and printed after class. Students find the condensed C-Print notes easier to study than stenographers' transcripts (Elliot, Foster, & Stinson, 2002).

Television Captioning   Today, most programming on commercial and public network television, as well as many live newscasts and sporting events, is captioned (printed text appears at the bottom of the screen, similar to watching a film with subtitles), providing access to televised news and entertainment for deaf people. Since 1993, a federal law has required that all new television sets sold in the United States be equipped with an internal device that allows the user to position captions anywhere on the screen.

Speech-to-text translation and TV captioning

Council for Exceptional Children

Content Standards for Beginning Teachers—D/HH: Communication modes used by and with individuals who are hearing and those who are D/HH (DH6K5) (also DH4K3, DH6K1).

FIGURE 9.6   Sample from a lecture and corresponding C-Print notes

Original Lecture

If you want to sell me the car, you are going to have to understand that process. You are out there with a car, and I am sitting here with some dollar amount that I am quite prepared to swap for the right car, but if you do not understand what my desires and concerns are, you don't have much chance of selling me the car. That is true whether you are a car dealer or car manufacturer or somebody trying to sell a car. We are looking at the process. The way the process worked in my case, I'll be completely open with you, I picked up the telephone and called an individual who was selling cars.

C-Print Text

If you want to sell me the car, you are going to have to understand that process. If you do not understand what my desires and concerns are, you don't have much chance of selling me the car. That is true whether you are a car dealer or car manufacturer or an individual selling a car. We are looking at the process. The way it worked in my case is I telephoned an individual selling cars.

Source: From "C-Print: A Computerized Speech-to-Print Transcription System" by B. G. McKee, P. G. Giles, V. S. Everhart, M. S. Stinson, & J. B. Henderson, 1998, *Captionist Training Manual*, p. 43. Copyright 1998 by Rochester Institute of Technology. Reprinted with permission.

Lewis and Jackson (2001) found that deaf students comprehended more from scripts that were accompanied by video than they did by reading the scripts alone. This finding suggests that visual stimuli provide essential information that deaf viewers can use to improve their comprehension. Lewis and Jackson suggest that acquiring "television literacy" (through the use of captioned videos in the classroom) might advance the reading skills of deaf students by exposing them to English vocabulary and syntax.

Text Telephones   The telephone served as a barrier to deaf people in employment and social interaction for many years, but acoustic couplers now make it possible to send immediate messages over conventional telephone lines in typed or digital form. Text telephones (TT) (originally called TTY or TDD systems) enable the user to send a typed message over telephone lines to anyone else who has a TT. As a result of the Americans With Disabilities Act, TTs are now available in most public places such as airports and libraries, and every state has a relay service that enables TT users to communicate with a person on a conventional telephone via an operator who relays the messages. Relay numbers are published in every phone directory.

Alerting Devices   Some individuals who are deaf or hard of hearing use special devices to alert them to certain sounds or events. For example, to signal the doorbell, a fire alarm, or an alarm clock, a sound- or vibration-sensitive switch can be connected to a flashing light or to a vibrator. Hearing-ear dogs are trained to alert a deaf person to important sounds in the environment (Guest, Collis, & McNicholas, 2006).

Hearing dogs are trained to alert a deaf person to important sounds such as a ringing telephone.

EDUCATIONAL APPROACHES

Over the years, many philosophies, theories, and specialized methods and materials have been developed for teaching children who are deaf and hard of hearing. Most of these approaches have been enthusiastically promoted by their advocates and critically denounced by others. Indeed, for more than 100 years people have waged an impassioned debate over how best to teach children who do not hear (Drasgow, 1998). Table 9.1 highlights some key historical events and implications for the education of students with hearing loss. Histories of deaf education can be found in Carroll (1996), Lang (2005), Padden and Humphries (2006), and Van Cleve (2007).

The many practices for teaching students who are deaf and hard of hearing (Easterbrooks, 2006) are conducted within one of three major approaches: the **oral/aural approach**, total communication, and bilingual–bicultural approach.

Oral/Aural Approaches

Educational programs with an oral/aural emphasis view speech as essential if students who are deaf are to function in the hearing world. Training in producing and understanding speech and language is incorporated into virtually all aspects of the child's education. A purely oral approach without any manual communication was used widely in the United States before the 1970s. Today, only about one fourth of educational programs for students with hearing loss identify themselves as as solely oral/aural programs, though, with increasing numbers of deaf and hard-of-hearing children educated in general education classrooms, the actual proportion educated orally appears to be increasing (Foster & Cue, 2007).

A child who attends a program with an oral emphasis typically uses several means to develop residual hearing and the ability to speak as intelligibly as possible (P. Stone, 1997). Auditory, visual, and tactile methods of input are frequently used. Much attention is given to amplification, auditory training, speechreading, the use of technological aids, and, above all, talking. A few schools and classes maintain a purely oral environment and may even prohibit

History of education of students who are D/HH

Council for Exceptional Children   Content Standards for Beginning Teachers—VI: Major contributors to the field of education of individuals who are D/HH (DH1K5) (also DH7K1).

Oral/aural approach

Council for Exceptional Children   Content Standards for Beginning Teachers—D/HH: Models, theories, and philosophies that provide the basis for education practice for individuals who are D/HH (DH1K2) (also DH4K2, DH4K3, DH6K5).

TABLE 9.1

A history of the education of students who are deaf or hard of hearing: Key events and implications

DATE	HISTORICAL EVENT	EDUCATIONAL IMPLICATIONS
Late 16th century	Pedro Ponce de Leon (1520–1584), an Augustinian monk and scholar, established in Spain a school for the deaf children of noble families.	This was the first educational program for exceptional children of any kind.
18th century	Schools for children who were deaf were set up in England, France, Germany, Holland, and Scotland.	Both oral and manual methods of instruction were used.
1817	The American Asylum for the Education of the Deaf and Dumb (renamed the American School for the Deaf) opened in Hartford, CT, under the leadership of Thomas Gallaudet and Laurent Clerc, a deaf French educator.	Children with hearing loss were among the first in the United States to receive special education. Gallaudet and Clerc used sign language as their method of instruction at the school. Some consider Clerc to be the father of deaf education in the United States.
Early 19th century	Students who were deaf were considered to be most appropriately served in asylums or special sanctuaries and removed from normal society.	The prevailing philosophy of the early 19th century was that persons who were deaf were incapable of benefiting from oral instruction.
1864	Gallaudet University (then called the National Deaf-Mute College) was founded.	Deaf students now had opportunity to pursue a postsecondary education in a setting that held high expectations for achievement.
Mid- to late 19th century	Instruction in speech and speechreading became widely available to students who were deaf throughout the United States. Several day schools were established for deaf children. Alexander Graham Bell criticized residential schools and the use of sign language, which he believed contributed to the segregation of deaf people.	Oral approaches dominated to such a great degree that the use of sign language in schools was officially prohibited at an international conference in 1880. It was not until many years later that schools relaxed their restrictions against the use of sign language. This era marked the beginning of what some have called "the Hundred Years War" over what methods of communication are best for deaf children.
Mid- to late 20th century	The majority of students whose deafness was caused by the rubella epidemics of the mid-1960s departed from the school-age population.	Enrollments in public residential schools for children with hearing impairments in the United States declined sharply as public school programs became more widely available.
1960s	Research by linguist William Stokoe at Gallaudet showed that sign language used by the deaf community was a legitimate language in its own right.	What had been called "the Sign Language" was given a new name, American Sign Language (ASL).
1968	Congress funded the National Technical Institute for the Deaf (NTID) at the Rochester Institute for Technology.	NTID offers technical and vocational degree programs for deaf students.

TABLE 9.1 CONTINUED

A history of the education of students who are deaf or hard of hearing: Key events and implications

DATE	HISTORICAL EVENT	EDUCATIONAL IMPLICATIONS
1970s	Total communication (TC) was adopted as the method of communication and instruction by the majority of deaf education programs.	TC attempts to present instructional content via simultaneous use of speech and sign language. While TC is still used frequently today, it has not raised the academic achievement of deaf students.
1986	In response to concerns about the academic and employment outcomes of deaf students, Congress established the Commission on Education of the Deaf (CED) with the Education of the Deaf Act of 1986.	CED began its 1988 report to Congress: "The present state of education for persons who are deaf in the United States is unsatisfactory. Unacceptably so" (p. viii). The report included 52 recommendations for improving the education of students with hearing loss.
1988	Students at Gallaudet University protested the hiring of a hearing president at their college in the Deaf President Now movement.	The movement led to the hiring of I. King Jordan as the first deaf president of Gallaudet, galvanized the deaf community, and increased the awareness of many in hearing society of the concerns and issues facing the Deaf culture.
1989	FDA approves use of cochlear implant surgery as means of bypassing the inner ear and providing a sense of sound directly through the auditory nerve for those with sensorineural hearing loss.	Educators have to find the most effective methods for helping deaf children receive maximum benefit from cochlear implants. There has been much controversy; many in the Deaf community view cochlear implants as a threat to the existence of their language and culture.
1990s	The Deaf community increased its activism and self-advocacy, especially with regard to ASL as a Deaf child's first language.	There is increased interest in and use of a bilingual/bicultural (bi–bi) approach, in which ASL is the language of instruction and English is taught as a second language.

children from pointing, using gestures, or spelling out words to communicate. Children in these programs must express themselves and learn to understand others through speech alone. Other oral/aural programs also emphasize speech and listening skills but are more flexible and may use and encourage a variety of approaches to help students produce and understand spoken language.

Educators who use an oral approach acknowledge that teaching speech to children who are deaf is difficult, demanding, and time-consuming for the teacher, the parents, and—most of all—the student. Speech comes hard to the deaf child. The rewards of successful oral communication, however, are thought to be worth the effort. And indeed, most students with hearing losses no worse than severe can learn speech well enough to communicate effectively with hearing people. The best results are obtained with students who are enrolled in indisputably comprehensive oral programs or who are integrated most of the school day into general education programs (Paul & Quigley, 1990).

Auditory training/learning

Content Standards for Beginning Teachers—D/HH: Strategies to facilitate cognitive and communicative development in individuals who are D/HH (DH6K7) (also DH4K3).

A combination of amplification and auditory training can help a child make the most of his residual hearing.

Speechreading

Content Standards for Beginning Teachers—D/HH: Strategies to facilitate cognitive and communicative development in individuals who are D/HH (DH6K7) (also DH4K2).

Auditory Learning Listening comprises 45% of daily communication for adults, and children spend up to 60% of the school day in situations where they are expected to be listening effectively (Crandell & Smaldino, 2001b). Many children with hearing loss have much more auditory potential than they actually use, and their residual hearing can be improved in the context of actual communication and daily experiences. All children with hearing loss, regardless of whether their preferred method of communication is oral (speech) or manual (signs), should receive training and practice with improving their listening skills.

Auditory training for young children with hearing loss begins by teaching awareness of sound. Parents might direct their child's attention to sounds such as a doorbell ringing or water running. They might then focus on localization of sound—for example, by hiding a radio somewhere in the room and encouraging the child to look for it. Discrimination of sounds is another important part of auditory training; a child might learn to notice the differences between a man's voice and a woman's voice, between a fast song and a slow song, or between the words *rack* and *rug*. Identification of sounds comes when a child can recognize a sound, word, or sentence through listening.

The focus today is on *auditory learning*—that is, teaching the child to learn to listen and to learn by listening instead of simply learning to hear (Ling, 1986, 2002). Advocates of auditory learning contend that the first three levels of auditory training—detecting, discriminating, and identifying sounds—are important but insufficient for developing the student's residual hearing. Auditory learning emphasizes a fourth and highest level of listening skills—the comprehension of meaningful sounds.

Some teachers find it helpful to conduct formal auditory training/learning sessions in which a child is required to use only hearing: he would have to recognize sounds and words without looking at the speaker. In actual practice, however, the student gains useful information from vision and the other senses to supplement the information received from hearing. Consequently, all senses should be effectively developed and constantly used.

Speechreading **Speechreading** is the process of understanding a spoken message by observing the speaker's face. All children with hearing loss, whether they have a significant amount of or very little residual hearing and whether they communicate primarily through oral or manual means, use their vision to help them understand speech. Some sounds are readily distinguished by watching the speaker's lips. For example, the word *pail* begins with the lips in a shut position, whereas the lips are somewhat drawn together and puckered at the corners for the word *rail*. Paying careful attention to a speaker's lips may help an individual with hearing loss derive important clues—particularly if she also can gain additional information through residual hearing, signs or gestures, facial expressions, and the context or situation.

Speechreading, however, is extremely difficult and has many limitations. About half of all English words have some other word(s) that appear the same in pronunciation; that is, although they sound quite different, they look alike on the lips. Words such as *bat*, *mat*, and *pat*, for example, look exactly alike and simply cannot be discriminated by watching the speaker's lips. To complicate matters, visual clues may be blocked by a hand or a pencil, chewing gum, or a mustache. Many speakers are virtually unintelligible through speechreading; they may seem not to move their lips at all. In addition, it is extremely tiring to watch lips for a long time, and it may be impossible to do so at a distance, such as during a lecture.

Walker (1986) estimates that even the best speechreaders detect only about 25% of what is said through visual clues alone; "the rest is contextual piecing together of ideas and expected constructions" (p. 19). Shanny Mow (1989), a deaf playwright, graphically described the frustrations of speechreading:

> Like the whorls on his fingertips, each person's lips are different and move in a peculiar way of their own. When young, you build confidence as you guess correctly "ball," "fish," and "shoe" on your teacher's lips. This confidence doesn't last. As soon as you discover there are

more than four words in the dictionary, it evaporates. Seventy percent of the words when appearing on the lips are no more than blurs. Lipreading is a precarious and cruel art which rewards a few who have mastered it and tortures the many that have tried and failed.

Despite the problems inherent in speechreading, it can be a valuable tool in a deaf or hard-of-hearing person's communication repertoire. Research shows that speechreading skills can improve when deaf persons practice speechreading their own speech and others via computer-assisted video instruction (DeFilippo, Sims, & Gottermeier, 1995; Sims & Gottermeier, 1995). Initial evaluations of a computer-based, interactive videodisc program developed at Bloomsburg (Pennsylvania) University show promise in helping people with hearing loss make better use of their vision to decode speech (Slike, Thornton, Hobbis, Kokoska, & Job, 1995; Slike & Hobbis, 1998).

Cued Speech **Cued speech** supplements oral communication with a visual representation of spoken language in the form of hand signals that represent the 45 phonemes of spoken English. Cued speech helps students identify syllabic and phonetic features of speech that cannot be distinguished through speechreading. The hand signals must be used in conjunction with speech; they are neither signs nor manual alphabet letters and cannot be read alone. Eight hand shapes identify consonant sounds, and four locations around the chin identify vowel sounds. A hand shape coupled with a location gives a visual indication of a syllable. According to Orin Cornett, who developed the system in 1964, cued speech can give intensive language input to young children because it clarifies the patterns of spoken English and does not disrupt the natural rhythm of speech (Cornett & Daisey, 2001). Some research shows that students taught with cued speech develop reading and spelling at levels comparable to hearing children (Hage & Leybaert, 2006; Leybaert & Alegria, 2005).

Visual Phonics The purpose of **visual phonics** is "to clarify the sound–symbol relationship between spoken English and print" (Waddy-Smith & Wilson, 2003, p. 15). Unlike instructional strategies that teach phonics to hearing children, letter–sound correspondence, visual phonics is not a sound system but is a visual system that consists of 45 hand shapes and grapheme cues.

> The hand cues provide visual and kinesthetic information that can be associated with the way a sound is produced verbally. For example, the /p/ sound is represented with a hand cue that simulates the "plosiveness" of /p/—the air being released from the lips. The grapheme cues are unique symbols that when paired with letters provide students with a visual correlate for the sound a letter might "make" in a particular word. (Friedman Narr, 2006, p. 55)

Although visual phonics was developed several decades ago, until recently, support was based largely on anecdotal reports and the logic underlying the approach (Woolsey, Satterfield, & Roberson, 2006). In the past several years, however, research on the approach has provided increasing evidence about its effectiveness (e.g., Trezek & Malmgren, 2005; Trezek & Wang, 2006; Trezek, Wang, Woods, Gampp, & Paul, 2007). To learn more about using visual phonics and the research demonstrating its effectiveness in teaching deaf and hard-of-hearing students to learn to read, see Teaching & Learning, "Phonemic Awareness and Phonics Instruction."

Total Communication

Educational programs with an emphasis on **total communication** (also called *simultaneous communication*, or *simcom*) advocate the use of a variety of forms of communication to teach English to students with hearing loss. Practitioners of total communication maintain that the simultaneous presentation of English language by speech and manual communication (signing and fingerspelling) makes it possible for children to use either one or both types of communication (Hawkins & Brawner, 1997). Since its introduction as a teaching philosophy in the 1960s, total communication has become the most widely used method of instruction in schools for the deaf. A survey of 137 early intervention programs for deaf and hard-of-hearing students in 39 states found that 66% of the programs used total communication (Meadow-Orlans et al., 1997).

Cued speech

Council for Exceptional Children Content Standards for Beginning Teachers—D/HH: Strategies to facilitate cognitive and communicative development in individuals who are D/HH (DH6K7) (also DH4K2).

Total communication

Council for Exceptional Children Content Standards for Beginning Teachers—D/HH: Models, theories, and philosophies that provide the basis for education practice for individuals who are D/HH (DH1K2) (also DH4K2, DH4K3, DH6K5).

Phonemic Awareness and Phonics Instruction With Deaf and Hard-of-Hearing Students

BY BARBARA R. SCHIRMER AND RACHEL A. FRIEDMAN NARR

Teaching phonemic awareness and phonics to deaf and hard-of-hearing students has seemed illogical and a poor use of valuable instruction time to many teachers. Yet phonemic awareness and phonics not only *can* be taught to children who do not fully hear the sounds of English but *should* be taught so that these children have more tools to use as they navigate learning to read.

Phonological awareness and phonics instruction have been found to be so important in reading development that children without these skills are at a great disadvantage in learning to read English (e.g., Ehri, 2005; Eldredge, 2005; National Reading Panel, 2000). As in all alphabetic languages, the basic unit of writing in English reflects a correspondence (though not a perfect match) between phonemes and graphemes, or sounds and letters. If the reader is aware of the phonemes that make up spoken words, then she can map these sounds to English letters, letter combinations, syllables, and words.

These findings suggest that phonemic awareness may well be related to the reading performance of deaf children, given that research has shown considerably greater similarities than differences between the reading processes of deaf and hearing readers (Schirmer & McGough, 2005). And, indeed, results have shown that deaf readers, particularly more skilled readers, can access phonological information (e.g., Dyer, MacSweeney, Szcerbinski, Green, & Campbell, 2003; Harris & Moreno, 2004).

Furthermore, recent findings are very promising in demonstrating that deaf children can be taught to access phonological information and apply it effectively in reading (Colin, Magnan, & Ecalle, 2007; Trezek & Malmgren, 2005; Trezek & Wang, 2006; Trezek, Wang, Wood, Gampp, & Paul, 2007). The key has been finding a medium through which deaf children can become aware of the sounds of spoken language and teaching them explicitly and systematically how to link these sounds to decoding written words within the child's

vocabulary. (This is important because if the child's vocabulary does not include the written word, then the ability to link sounds and letters will not help the child identify the word's meaning.)

HOW TO GET STARTED WITH STUDENTS WHO SIGN

When young children develop phonemic awareness, they internalize rules and patterns associated with the sound-based properties of words. For children who are deaf and hard of hearing, the concept of the *phoneme* can be a mental representation. While deaf and hard-of-hearing students may choose to vocalize or talk during these activities, voicing is not *necessary* to demonstrate comprehension of phonemes.

Students who are deaf and hard of hearing and students who are deaf in oral/aural programs may benefit from the strategies for beginning reading instruction described in Figure 5.4. Students who rely on sign-based communication, either through simultaneous communication or American Sign Language, need the phonological properties of words to be represented through visual, tactile, and kinesthetic stimuli, as the following suggestions demonstrate:

- *Use a variety of sensory stimuli to teach phonemic awareness and phonics to promote well-developed mental representations.* Teach phonemes through a systematic multimodal method that capitalizes on the student's intact senses (vision, tactile, kinesthetic). Visual phonics and cued speech are systems that use hand cues to represent the 44 to 46 phonemes in spoken English visually. These are two distinct systems that are not used interchangeably. (For a comparison of Visual Phonics and Cued Speech, see Friedman Narr, 2006.)

- *Teach speechreading cues directly to show how sounds and words look when other people say them.* For example, when students know that only three sounds are made with both lips together

Visual phonics hand cues for /b/, /ae/, and /g/ sounds.

(/m/, /b/, /p/), they can make reasonable choices about decoding and spelling options. Instruction in speechreading can be paired with phonemic awareness and phonics lessons. In the *sandwich technique*, you sign and say (or mouth) the whole word, then fingerspell or write the word but leave out the target phoneme, then say (or mouth) that phoneme (not the letter name), and finally sign and say (or mouth) the whole word again.

- *Teach students how to analyze words and decode in chunks.* One technique is to directly teach spelling patterns and regularities (e.g., b*oat*; l*ight*), onsets and rimes (e.g., b-ook, th-ink), and prefixes and suffixes (e.g., re-play, walk-ing). Another technique is to fingerspell words in chunks, such as syllable-by-syllable (e.g., el-e-phant) instead of letter-by-letter.

- *Teach phonics in context to support skills taught in isolation.* Students will be more engaged and motivated, and they will realize that the point of phonics is to identify words during reading, not simply to learn lists of letter–sound correspondences. For example, when reading, point out the similarities between new words in the material and previously learned words with the same number of syllables, words that have a particular spelling pattern, or words that begin with a certain sound, letter, or lip-shape.

Learning Visual Phonics The International Communication Learning Institute (ICLI) is the parent organization that regulates training in See the Sound–Visual Phonics. Groups or individuals who want to use it can receive training from licensed ICLI trainers. Trainings range from 8 to 14+ hours, depending on the amount of time desired for guided practice. Learning visual phonics is generally quick and easy. Like most newly acquired skills, the more you use it, the more fluent you will become.

Teachers can use visual phonics in conjunction with any reading curriculum. When teaching phonemic awareness and phonics instruction, the teacher uses the visual phonics hand cues and grapheme symbols (see photos) to *show* sounds in words, which makes the *concept of the phoneme* completely accessible, even if the acoustic properties are not. Visual phonics is not used for communication; instead, it is used at the phoneme and word level only. Trezek and her colleagues have demonstrated efficacy with visual phonics when teachers use it in conjunction with established reading instructional curricula (Trezek & Malmgren, 2005; Trezek & Wang, 2006; Trezek et al., 2007). (You can find contact information for finding a trainer at www.icli.org.)

Barbara R. Schirmer is Vice President for academic affairs and professor of education at the University of Detroit. She is the co-author of *What Is Special About Special Education: Examining the Role of Evidence-Based Practices* (PRO-ED, 2006). Rachel A. Friedman Narr is Assistant Professor of Special Education at California State University Northridge.

To learn more about teaching phonemic awareness and phonics to students with hearing impairments, go to the Homework & Exercises section in Chapter 9 of MyEducationLab and complete Homework Exercise 3.

Examples of grapheme cues used in visual phonics.

Manually coded English and fingerspelling

Council for Exceptional Children

Content Standards for Beginning Teachers—D/HH: Strategies to facilitate cognitive and communicative development in individuals who are D/HH (DH6K7) (also DH4K2).

Manually Coded English   Teachers who practice total communication generally speak as they sign and make a special effort to follow the form and structure of spoken English as closely as possible. Several English-based sign systems have been designed for educational purposes, with the intention of facilitating the development of reading, writing, and other language skills in students with hearing loss. Manually coded English refers to several educationally oriented sign systems, such as Signing Essential English (commonly known as SEE I) (Anthony, 1971), Signing Exact English (SEE II) (Gustason, Pfetzing, & Zawolkow, 1980), and Signed English (Bornstein, 1974). While manually coded English borrows many signs and incorporates some of the features of American Sign Language (to be discussed), it follows correct English usage and word order. Unfortunately, deaf students must often learn and use two or more sign language systems, depending on the person with whom they are communicating.

Fingerspelling   Fingerspelling, the manual alphabet, is used to spell out proper names for which no signs exist and to clarify meanings. Fingerspelling is an integral part of American Sign Language (ASL) and an important aspect of becoming bilingual in English and ASL (Haptonstall-Nykaza & Schick, 2007). It consists of 26 distinct hand positions, one for each English letter. A one-hand manual alphabet is used in the United States and Canada (see Figure 9.7). Some manual letters—such as "C," "L," and "W"—resemble the shape of printed English letters, whereas others—such as "A," "E," and "S"—have no apparent similarity. As in typewriting, each word is spelled out letter by letter.

FIGURE 9.7

The manual alphabet used to fingerspell English in North America

American Sign Language and the Bilingual–Bicultural Approach

American Sign Language (ASL) is the language of the Deaf culture in the United States and Canada. Although the sign languages used by native deaf speakers were once thought to be nonlanguages (alinguistic), work by the linguist William Stokoe (Stokoe, 1960; Stokoe, Armstrong, & Wilcox, 1995) showed that ASL is a legitimate language in its own right rather than an imperfect variation of spoken English. ASL is a visual-spatial language in which the shape, location, and movement pattern of the hands; the intensity of motions; and the signer's facial expressions all communicate meaning and content. Because ASL has its own rules of phonology, morphology, syntax, semantics, and pragmatics, it does not correspond to spoken or written English (Valli, Lucas, & Mulrooney, 2005). Articles, prepositions, tenses, plurals, and word order are expressed differently from English. It is as difficult to make precise word-for-word translations between ASL and English as it is to translate many foreign languages into English word for word.

Some ASL signs are *iconic*; that is, they convey meaning through hand shapes or motions that look like or appear to imitate or act out their message. In making the sign for "cat," for example, the signer seems to be stroking feline whiskers on her face; in the sign for "eat," the hand moves back and forth into an open mouth. Most signs, however, have little or no iconicity; they do not resemble the objects or actions they represent. If sign language were simply a form of pantomime, then most nonsigners would be able to understand it with relative ease. But the vast majority of signs cannot be guessed by people who are unfamiliar with sign language.

Several researchers have found that deaf infants and toddlers achieve language development milestones in sign and at about the same rate as hearing children do with spoken language (Emmorey, 2002; Goldin-Meadow, 2003; Masataka, 1996). "When deaf children have full visual access to a natural signed language, they acquire it in the same effortless manner as hearing children acquire a spoken language" (Drasgow, 1998, p. 334).

During the 1990s the Deaf community as well as a growing number of both hearing and deaf special educators began calling for the use of ASL as the language of instruction (Baker & Baker, 1997; Drasgow, 1998; Mahshie, 1995; Pittman & Huefner, 2001; Strong, 1995). They

ASL

Council for Exceptional Children

Content Standards for Beginning Teachers—D/HH: Communication modes used by and with individuals who are hearing and those who are D/HH (DH6K5) (also DH4K3, DH6K1).

Although some signs, such as "cat" and "eat," are iconic—they look like the objects or actions they represent—most are not.

Bilingual–bicultural approach

 Content Standards for Beginning Teachers—D/HH: Models, theories, and philosophies that provide the basis for education practice for individuals who are D/HH (DH1K2) (also DH4K2, DH4K3, DH6K5).

believe that ASL provides a natural pathway to linguistic competence and that English is better learned in the context of a **bilingual–bicultural (bi–bi) approach** after the child has mastered his native or first language (ASL). Proponents of this model view deafness as a cultural and linguistic difference, not a disability, and recognize ASL as the deaf child's natural language. The goal of the bilingual–bicultural education approach is to help deaf students become bilingual adults who are competent in their first language, ASL, and can read and write with competence in their second language, English.

The basic theoretical argument for bilingual education is that students who have a solid foundation in their native language (L1) will be able to use their literacy-related L1 skills as a springboard for learning the majority second language (L2) (Musselman, 2000). Ewolt (1996) suggests that a top-down bilingual-bicultural approach that encourages deaf students to pursue "the construction of meaning through relevant, enjoyable, natural communication" (p. 294) will overcome their lack of knowledge of sentence form and print characteristics.

Some related support for the bilingual-bicultural approach can be found in research demonstrating a correlation between early exposure to and development of fluency in ASL and increased competence and English literacy (Prinz et al., 1996; Strong & Prinz, 1997). Mayer and Akamatsu (1999), however, question the extent of L1–L2 interdependence when the two languages under consideration are a native sign language and the written form of an oral language. They also point out the logical inconsistency and danger of not providing deaf students with direct instruction and practice in the bottom-up literacy skills such as English language principles and phonics just because those are the skills with which they have the most difficulty. To date, although the rhetoric advocating for bilingual–bicultural is high and many programs have been implemented, there is little objective data evaluating program outcomes and effectiveness (DeLana, Gentry, & Andrews, 2007; Schirmer, 2001).

Which Approach for Whom?

Educators, scientists, philosophers, and parents—both hearing and deaf—have for many years debated the most appropriate instructional methods for children who are deaf. The controversy continues today. In the past, however, fundamental disagreement focused on the extent to which deaf children should express language through speech and perceive the communication of others through speechreading and residual hearing. Today, the focal point has switched to which language modality—auditory or visual—best suits a child's acquisition of an initial language. Research has yet to provide (and perhaps never will provide) a definitive answer to the question of which communication method is best.

American Sign Language (ASL) is a complete language with its own vocabulary, syntax, and grammatical rules.

Different children communicate in different ways. Some children with hearing loss, unfortunately, have experienced deep frustration and failure because of rigid adherence to an oral-only program. They have left oral programs without having developed a usable avenue of communication. Equally unfortunate is the fact that other children with hearing loss have not been given an adequate opportunity to develop their auditory and oral skills because they were placed in educational programs that did not provide good oral instruction. In both cases, children have been unfairly penalized. Every child who is deaf should have access to an educational program that uses a communication method best suited to her unique abilities and needs (Marschark, 2007). Mahshie (1995) recommends letting the child choose her first language:

Choosing auditory or visual language modality

 Content Standards for Beginning Teachers—D/HH: Issues and trends in the field of education of individuals who are D/HH (DH1K4) (also DH6K1, DH6K5).

> In environments where the Deaf child encounters both spoken and signed language separately—as whole languages—during the course of natural interactions, it has become apparent to both parents and professionals that the child will be the guide regarding his or her predisposition toward a more oral or more visual language. In this win–win situation, the choice of a first language is clearly the child's. (p. 73)

Early and continued access to language and the communication modality best suited to their individual needs and preferences, effective instruction with meaningful curriculum, and self-determination are the keys to increasing the number of deaf or hard-of-hearing people who can access and enjoy the full spectrum of educational, social, vocational, and recreational opportunities society has to offer.

One important task for individualized education program (IEP) teams for students who are deaf or hard of hearing is careful consideration and documentation of the individual communication needs of each student. To learn about one systematic way of doing so, see Teaching & Learning, "Considering the Communication Needs of Students Who Are Deaf or Hard of Hearing."

EDUCATIONAL PLACEMENT ALTERNATIVES

In most areas of the United States, parents and students now have the option of choosing between local public school programs and residential school placement. Today, approximately 86% of children who are deaf or hard of hearing attend local public schools: 49% receive most of their education in general education classrooms, 18% attend resource rooms for part of the school day, 19% are served in separate classrooms, and 7% attend special schools (U.S. Department of Education, 2007). Most students with hearing loss who are included in general education classrooms are hard of hearing and have hearing losses of less than 90 dB.

Of the 6% of students with hearing loss who attend residential schools, about one third live at home with their families and commute to the school. More than 90% of the students currently enrolled in residential schools have severe and profound prelingual hearing loss. Nearly one third of the students with hearing loss served in residential schools have additional disabilities.

Examining the question of where students who are deaf should be educated yields some research evidence—and much strong opinion—to support both inclusive and segregated settings (Cerney, 2007). As Bat-Chava (2000) notes, where a child who is deaf is educated also influences the likelihood of his or her cultural identity. In schools in which oral English is the language of instruction, supplemented by fingerspelling and English-based sign systems, students are more likely to view hearing loss as a disability. Schools in which ASL is the language of instruction foster the perspective of Deaf culture.

In a study of the effects of inclusion on the academic achievement of high school students who are deaf, Kluwin (1993) reported that although those students who were included in general education classrooms for academic content fared better on achievement measures than did students who spent all or most of the day in a separate class, the difference may have been the result of curriculum programming and class selection, not the actual place where instruction took place. After assessing the self-concepts of 90 deaf secondary students across different educational placements, Van Gurp (2001) concluded there were academic advantages to more integrated, resource room–type placements and social advantages in attending segregated schools.

Cawthon (2001) found that elementary teachers in inclusive classrooms directed about half as many utterances to deaf students as they did to hearing students and that educational interpreters were critical factors in how well the deaf students understood and participated in classroom discourse and learning activities. The skill level of an educational interpreter plays a critical role in the success and appropriateness of a general education classroom placement for students who are deaf. An educational interpreter must provide the deaf or hard-of-hearing student with all speech and other auditory information in the classroom, a formidable task for the most highly skilled interpreter. In a report of a study that approximately 60% of 2,100 educational interpreters from across the United States had inadequate skills, Schick, Williams, and Kupermintz (2006) concluded that "many deaf and hard-of-hearing students receive interpreting services that will seriously hinder reasonable access to the classroom curriculum and social interaction" (p. 3).

A skilled interpreter in the classroom is no guarantee that students with hearing loss will receive and participate in accurate communication. Garay (2003) recommends that deaf

Placement options

Council for Exceptional Children — Content Standards for Beginning Teachers—Common Core: Demands of learning environments (CC5K1) (also DH1K4, DH5K2).

Inclusion

Council for Exceptional Children — Content Standards for Beginning Teachers—D/HH: Impact of educational placement options with regard to cultural identity and linguistic, academic, and social-emotional development (DH3K1) (also DH1K4, DH5K1).

Considering the Communication Needs of Students Who Are Deaf or Hard of Hearing

BY SUSAN R. EASTERBROOKS & SHARON K. BAKER

According to IDEA, students' IEPs must contain a written statement of how the IEP team considered the communication needs of each student who is deaf or hard of hearing. This requirement for appropriately serving students with hearing losses brings important questions to the attention of those unfamiliar with the field. Unless done well, however, such a statement will miss the mark of its intention. This seemingly simple question is actually complex and challenges schools and districts to broaden their perspectives.

Students who are deaf or hard of hearing form a heterogeneous group whose needs vary greatly. Some have cochlear implants and communicate orally. Some use an English-based sign system or ASL. Others have additional disabilities or come from homes where the spoken language is not English. Educators need to use many approaches and philosophies to meet all variations within the population (e.g., Baker & Baker, 1997; Goldberg, 1997; Gustason, 1997; Stone, 1997). IEP teams need to address several questions when considering the communication needs of students who have hearing losses. Team members should ask these questions at each IEP meeting, and answers should lead to decisions regarding placement, language mode, use of technology, and access to appropriate language models.

COMMUNICATION NEEDS MATRIX

We developed the matrix shown in Figure A to help IEP teams consider pertinent information relevant to the communication needs of students who are deaf or hard of hearing. In schools for the deaf, such a matrix may not be needed, given the expertise available on site. Local school systems, however, especially those with few students with hearing losses and, consequently, few teachers of the deaf, may benefit from such guidance.

HOW TO GET STARTED

1. Begin by answering each question and placing an X in the column corresponding to the evidence gathered by observing the student's behavior or noting his family history. For example, if a child has deaf parents, then his early experiences are likely to be with ASL. If a child received a cochlear implant and sufficient auditory instruction as a preschooler, then his early experiences were more auditory than visual. If the child shows evidence of further neurological impairment, he may be at risk for poor auditory processing or for poor development of an auditory-based communication system. Each of these situations will have had a significant effect on the child's present communication needs.

2. Tally the Xs at the bottom of each column to get a sense of where the school's, family's, and child's relative strengths lie.

3. Use this information to engage in a discussion of the student's communication needs. Be sure to have at least two people with training and experience in deaf education participate in this discussion.

4. After discussing the information gathered to complete the form, include decisions on the IEP. Retain the matrix in the student's file as a means of documenting that you have met the IDEA requirement to consider the communication needs of a student who is deaf or hard of hearing.

Source: Adapted from S. R. Easterbrooks & S. K. Baker, (2001), Considering the Communication Needs of Students Who Are Deaf or Hard of Hearing. *Teaching Exceptional Children, 33*(3), 70–76. Used with permission.

To learn more about the communication needs of students with hearing impairments, go to the Homework & Exercises section in Chapter 9 of MyEducationLab and complete Homework Exercise 4.

Place an X in the most appropriate column corresponding to the question. Provide descriptive evidence to document your consideration. Tally the number of Xs in each column to suggest a response to communication needs.

Name: CH   Date: 11-11-08

Question	Listens: Oral A-V Cues	Looks: English Orientation (word order) E.g. English Signs/Cued Speech	Looks: American Sign Language Orientation (spatial)	Tactile:	Other:
What is the Child's Current Style/Mode of Understanding the World?	Understands less than 1/2 of auditory message.	Watches others. Lipreads. Comprehends signs well. Understand >75%. X			
What is the Child's Current Style/Mode of Responding to the World?	Speech is understandable approx. 75% of the time. X	Supports speech with signs. Speaks to parents Signs to friends. X			
In Which Mode/Style Does the Child Show Best Autonomy?		Most comfortable when he can support his speech with signs. X			
What is the Parents' Present Communication Mode/Style?	Most of their interactions are spoken X	Are learning to sign X			
What Mode/Style Do the Parents State They Prefer or Support?	X	Parents are learning to sign. Very committed to English word order & reading. X	Do not support ASL		
What Were the Child's Earliest Communication Experiences?	Heard until age 2 yrs. 4 mos. (CA = 9-4) X				
What Resources are Available for Family/School/ Community Development?	No oral program nearby	Community college has sign classes X			
What Information Is Available from a Psychological Evaluation?		WISC-III Pic Arr = 13 Coding = 10 X	WISC-III Pic Compl = 7 Obj Assemb = 8		
What Skills in Languages/ Modes Do the Teachers in This System Have?		X	X		
In Which Mode/Style Is There the Highest Degree of Likelihood of Consistency from School to Home to Community?		Mom reports neighbors and church members are learning to sign X	No deaf family members. Rural Community. No ASL users in community.		
TALLY	4	9	1	0	0

Needs Relative to Mode/Style:

Uses total communication receptively and expressively. In group situations, needs sign. One-on-one can communicate in oral mode. Continue interaction with other deaf students.

Needs Relative to Family Development:

Family is working hard to help him learn to read. Reads at beginning 2nd grade level. Oriented to English syntax. Family needs access to sign instruction.

Classroom Modifications:

Needs classroom buddy system to help him keep up with printed work. Teacher needs to check comprehension of instruction and directions frequently. One-on-one reading support. Interpreter situationally.

Technology Related to Communication:

Assistive listening device.

FIGURE A

Matrix for considering the communication needs of students who are deaf or hard of hearing

Source: Adapted from S. R. Easterbrooks & S. K. Baker. (2001). Considering the communication needs of students who are deaf or hard of hearing. *Teaching Exceptional Children, 33*(3), 70–76. Reprinted with permission.

TEACHING & LEARNING

students be taught how to effectively use interpreters: for example, how to let interpreters know when they do not understand something, and how to appropriately and effectively indicate that they have something to ask the teacher or contribute to the class discussion.

In an effort to identify strategies to overcome barriers to meaningful participation by students with hearing loss in general education classrooms, Stinson and Liu (1999) conducted observations and focus groups with elementary general education teachers, teachers of the deaf, interpreters, notetakers, deaf and hard-of-hearing students, and their hearing classmates. The authors organized their findings into a list of 16 specific strategies to make placement in the general education classroom educationally beneficial. They suggested several strategies for each type of individual in the classroom (e.g., teacher, interpreter, hearing peers). Stinson and Liu made the following recommendations for students with hearing loss:

- Be responsible for taking the initiative in the classroom and believe the outcome will be at least somewhat successful.
- Have and use communication skills for participating in the general education classroom (e.g., repairing miscommunications, taking turns).
- When participating in small-group learning activities, carry out a specific task and share the information with the group.

While full inclusion has benefited some deaf students, all of the professional and parent organizations involved with educating students who are deaf have issued position statements strongly in favor of maintaining a continuum of placement options (e.g., Commission on Education of the Deaf, 1988; National Association of the Deaf, 2002). Moores (1993), a respected leader in the field of deaf education, voiced the perspective of many deaf educators and parents:

> For many deaf children the concept of total inclusion, as currently promulgated, could in reality be exclusionary in practice. Placing a deaf child in a classroom in physical contiguity to hearing children does not automatically provide equal access to information. In fact, it can be isolating, both academically and socially. (p. 251)

As with all learners, we should never overlook the most fundamental factor in determining how successful a student will be in a general education classroom (or any other placement): quality of instruction. After studying the math achievement of 215 secondary students with hearing loss who were either in self-contained classrooms or mainstreamed into general education classes with or without an interpreter, Kluwin and Moores (1989) concluded, "Quality of instruction is the prime determinant of achievement, regardless of placement" (p. 327).

Postsecondary Education

Gallaudet University and NTID

 Content Standards for Beginning Teachers—D/HH: Model programs, including career/vocational and transition, for individuals who are D/HH (DH7K1) (also DH10K2).

The percentage of students with hearing loss who attend postsecondary educational programs has risen dramatically since the 1980s. About 40% of all students with hearing loss go on to college education (Gallaudet Research Institute, 2005). A growing number of educational opportunities are available to students with hearing loss after completion of high school. The oldest and best known is Gallaudet University in Washington, DC, which offers a wide range of undergraduate and graduate programs in the liberal arts, sciences, education, business, and other fields. The National Technical Institute for the Deaf (NTID), located at the Rochester Institute of Technology, provides wide-ranging programs in technical, vocational, and business-related fields such as computer science, hotel management, photography, and medical technology. Both Gallaudet and NTID are supported by the federal government, and each enrolls approximately 1,500 students who are deaf or hard of hearing.

More than 100 other institutions of higher education have developed accredited programs specifically for students with hearing loss (King, DeCaro, Karchmer, & Cole, 2001). Among these are four regional postsecondary programs that enroll substantial numbers of students with hearing loss: St. Paul (Minnesota) Technical-Vocational Institute, Seattle (Washington) Central Community College, the Postsecondary Education Consortium at the University of Tennessee, and California State University at Northridge.

It is hoped that the increase in postsecondary programs will expand vocational and professional opportunities for deaf adults.

TIPS for Beginning Teachers

TAKING ADVANTAGE OF RESOURCES IN SCHOOL AND COMMUNITY
by Douglas Jackson

VISUALIZE, INTERNALIZE, REFLECT

As teachers, we are responsible for covering a variety of academic courses using spoken and signed language; for addressing the auditory, speech, and other needs of our students; and for documenting our efforts on IEPs thicker than some metropolitan phone books. With all of this in mind, our task becomes how to do all of this effectively and successfully.

- Visualize what you want to accomplish and how you want to accomplish it. Imagine the obstacles in your way (time and resource limitations, red tape, etc.) and how you can overcome them (collaboration, grants, activities).
- When you learn new skills or information, whether they are new signs or Visual Phonics or the Fairview Reading Program, internalize the new skills and information so that they are entwined with your personality, sensibilities, and particular gifts as an educator.
- Take time to reflect. Think about what worked, what didn't, what you could do differently in the future, and what's next.

KNOCK DOWN THE CLASSROOM WALLS

We are never more powerful than when we realize not only our strengths but also our weaknesses.

- Use your resources. There are dozens of people in your school who can do things that you can't do and who know things that you don't know. Their skills and knowledge can benefit both you and your students.
- Communicate and collaborate with your peers. You can begin to foster this communication and collaboration by sharing your ideas and materials. Everyone has a different perspective that can be helpful in difficult situations in the classroom with students or outside the classroom with parents.

KNOCK DOWN THE SCHOOL'S WALLS

Beyond your school walls are doctors, lawyers, artists, business owners, police officers, and civic and government leaders. These professionals can teach your students things they cannot always learn in a classroom.

- Create partnerships. Identify professionals who are willing to become potential partners with your class by sharing their time, skills, and knowledge— or those who are interested in mentoring specific students. In this way you can become an educational bridge between your students and these professionals.
- Design activities (simulations, presentations, art, drama, etc.) to maximize the impact of these work-world opportunities. Try asking your professional partners if they have any feedback or input for you.

PICK YOUR BATTLES

As educators we are surrounded by situations crying out for change, challenges we feel compelled to take on but battles we can't always fight simultaneously. Pick the battles that are most important, and devote your energy, creativity, and passion to them.

- Choose initiatives that make your school a better place for your students. Hold off (for now) on those that don't seem to have a clear outcome or impact.
- Create opportunities in your class to infuse the curriculum with hands-on, meaningful lessons that connect with your students.
- Develop a list of the goals, behaviors, and values that are important to you as an educator. This will ultimately help you decide which battles to pick when they all seem worth fighting.

ENJOY THE RIDE

Sometimes I find myself walking down the hall of my school, obsessing about this meeting or that bit of paperwork or whatever the slings and arrows of outrageous bureaucracy happen to be that day. I will look up and see a small child walking down the hall, wide-eyed with the many possibilities of educational discovery in front of her, a voyage that she might feel is as important as those of Columbus, Isaac Newton, and Neil Armstrong. And, of course, she is absolutely right. When I see this look of wonder, I realize that we teachers have the coolest job in the world. We are eyewitnesses for many amazing voyages of discovery.

KEY TERMS AND CONCEPTS

acquired, p. 340
American Sign Language (ASL), p. 359
audiogram, p. 342
audiometer, p. 342
audiometric zero, p. 335
audition, p. 334
auditory canal (external acoustic meatus), p. 334
auditory training, p. 354
auricle, p. 334
behavior observation audiometry, p. 345
bilingual–bicultural (bi–bi) approach, p. 360
cochlea, p. 334
cochlear implant, p. 347
conductive hearing loss, p. 338
congenital, p. 340
cued speech, p. 355
cytomegalovirus, p. 341
Deaf culture, p. 334
deafness, p. 334
decibel (dB), p. 335

fingerspelling, p. 358
hard of hearing, p. 334
hearing aid, p. 346
hearing impairment, p. 334
hertz (Hz), p. 335
operant conditioning audiometry, p. 344
oral-aural approach, p. 351
ossicles, p. 334
otitis media, p. 341
play audiometry, p. 344
postlingual hearing loss, p. 340
prelingual hearing loss, p. 340
residual hearing, p. 334
sensorineural hearing loss, p. 338
speech audiometry, p. 342
speech reception threshold (SRT), p. 342
speechreading, p. 354
total communication, p. 355
tympanic membrane, p. 334
visual phonics, p. 355

SUMMARY

Definitions

- Hearing loss exists on a continuum from mild to profound, and most special educators distinguish between children who are deaf and those who are hard of hearing. A deaf child cannot understand speech through the ears alone. A hard-of-hearing child can use hearing to understand speech, generally with the help of a hearing aid.
- Many Deaf persons do not view hearing loss as a disability. Like other cultural groups, members of the Deaf community share a common language (ASL) and social practices.
- Sound is measured by its intensity (decibels [dB]) and frequency (Hertz [Hz]); both dimensions are important in considering the special education needs of a child with a hearing loss. The frequencies most important for understanding speech are 500 to 2,000 Hz.

Characteristics

- Deaf children—especially those with a prelinguistic loss of 90 dB or greater—are at a great disadvantage in acquiring English literacy skills, especially reading and writing.
- The speech of many children with hearing loss may be difficult to understand because they omit speech sounds they cannot hear, speak too loudly or softly, speak in an abnormally high pitch, speak with poor inflection, and/or speak at an improper rate.
- As a group, students who are deaf and hard of hearing lag far behind their hearing peers in academic achievement, and the achievement gap usually widens as they get older.
- Children with severe-to-profound hearing losses often report feeling isolated and unhappy in school, particularly when their socialization with other children with hearing loss is limited.
- Many deaf individuals choose membership in the Deaf community and culture.

Prevalence

- Students with hearing loss represent about 1.2% of all school-age students receiving special education.

Types and Causes of Hearing Loss

- Hearing loss is described as conductive (outer or middle ear) or sensorineural (inner ear) and unilateral (in one ear) or bilateral (in both ears).
- A prelingual hearing loss occurs before the child has developed speech and language; a postlingual hearing loss occurs after that time.
- Causes of congenital hearing loss include genetic factors, maternal rubella, heredity, congenital cytomegalovirus (CMV), and prematurity.
- Causes of acquired hearing loss include otitis media, meningitis, Ménière's disease, and noise exposure.

Identification and Assessment

- Auditory brain-stem response and otoacoustic emission are two methods of screening for hearing loss in infants.
- A formal hearing test generates an audiogram, which graphically shows the intensity of the faintest sound an individual can hear 50% of the time at various frequencies.
- Hearing loss is classified as slight, mild, moderate, severe, or profound, depending on the degree of hearing loss.

Technologies and Supports

- Technologies that amplify or provide sound include hearing aids, assistive listening devices, and cochlear implants.
- Technologies and supports that supplement or replace sound include educational interpreters, speech-to-text translation, television captioning, text telephones, and alerting devices.

Educational Approaches

- The oral/aural approach views speech as essential if students are to function in the hearing world; much emphasis is given to amplification, auditory training, speechreading, the use of technological aids, and, above all, talking.
- Total communication uses speech and simultaneous manual communication via signs and fingerspelling in English word order.
- In the bilingual–bicultural approach, deafness is viewed as a cultural and linguistic difference, not a disability, and American Sign Language (ASL) is used as the language of instruction.

Educational Placement Alternatives

- Eighty-six percent of children who are deaf or hard of hearing attend local public schools: 49% attend general education classrooms, 18% attend resource rooms for part of the school day, 19% are served in separate classrooms, and 7% go to residential schools.
- All of the professional and parent organizations involved in deaf education have issued position statements strongly in favor of maintaining a continuum of placement options.
- Access to the language and communication modality best suited to their individual needs and preferences, effective instruction with meaningful curriculum, and self-advocacy are the keys to improving the future for people who are deaf or hard of hearing.

Now go to MyEducationLab at www.myeducationlab.com and take the pretest to assess your initial comprehension of chapter content. Once you have taken the pretest, use your individualized Study Plan for Chapter 9 to enhance your understanding of the concepts discussed in the chapter. Finally, take the posttest to assess your comprehension of Chapter 9 content.

10

Blindness and Low Vision

FEATURED TEACHER

JEANNA MORA DOWSE
Piñon and Ganado Unified School Districts • Apache County, Arizona

Jeanna Mora Dowse

Education—Teaching Credentials—Experience
- A.A., nursing, New Mexico State University, 1986
- B.S., elementary education, Texas Tech University, 1991
- M.A., visual impairment, University of Arizona, 1997

- Arizona standard elementary education, K–8; Arizona English as a second language, K–12; Arizona standard visually impaired, K–12
- 10 years as a teacher of students with visual impairments

Current Teaching Position and Students I am an itinerant teacher of children with visual impairments (VI) in two rural school districts in Apache County. I have a caseload of nine students in the Piñon Unified School District and eight students in Ganado. My students range in age from 4 to 17 years old and are in preschool through ninth grade. All of my students are members of the Navajo tribe. Many are from families that receive welfare. Some of my students speak both Navajo and English, some have been identified as limited English proficient, and some are not fluent in either language.

IEP Goals The Arizona State Department of Education requires that 75% of a student's IEP goals be based on the Arizona State Curriculum Standards. Most of my students can access the general curriculum with adaptations or modifications. It is very important for me to consult with the classroom teachers to identify individualized education program (IEP) goals and objectives that will accomplish this. Most of my students need help with literacy skills, understanding their visual impairment, and learning how to self-advocate for needed accommodations. Here are some examples of IEP goals and objectives for several of my students this year:

Annual goal. The student will complete the braille program "Patterns: Reading-Readiness Level" (red) with 90% accuracy as documented by program guidelines and recorded by a certified VI teacher.

Short-term objective 1. The student will tactually identify and then verbalize the letters *a–m* in braille as documented by mastery tests.

Short-term objective 2. The student will tactually identify and then verbalize the letters *n–z* in braille as documented by mastery tests.

Annual goal. The student will identify characters in a story and retell the story in sequence with 90% accuracy when five different stories are read aloud on five different occasions.

Short-term objective 1. The student will listen to a variety of story boxes and verbally and tactually identify the main characters in the story with 90% accuracy.

Short-term objective 2. The student will listen to a variety of story boxes and will verbally retell a story in sequence with 90% accuracy.

Annual goal. The student will use interpersonal skills to express to teachers and coaches the need for adaptations or modifications for his visual impairment.

Short-term objective 1. The student will research his visual impairment on the Internet and document in writing four details regarding his visual impairment.

Short-term objective 2. The student will interview at least two individuals with the same type of visual impairment and write a short essay documenting information obtained from the interviews.

Curriculum Materials and Teaching Strategies

My students need hands-on activities. I have found that students enjoy story boxes with objects from the stories inside a box. They can feel the objects and act out the story. My students need many opportunities to listen to language and books. I encourage parents and teachers to expose my students to as many real-life experiences as possible. They learn the importance of writing when they can write or dictate their own books and letters to family and friends. My students who are emergent readers/writers make books from objects they have collected on a walk or from things they bring from home.

Collaboration and Teaming

We are required by the state of Arizona to write multidisciplinary team reports. That is, service providers no longer write individual reports but must collaborate to write one assessment report. We also consult with each other when we are providing services to the same student. I am lucky to work with some very good school psychologists, physical therapists (PTs), occupational therapists (OTs), and speech-language pathologists (SLPs). We often work with the same student at one time and explain what each person can do to enhance the student's success. For example, the PT and the OT have given me ideas about positioning, and the SLP has suggested how I can elicit spontaneous speech. When a student is having difficulty in a particular area, we brainstorm about how we can help. For example, the PT was working to help a student use her walker to travel independently from one classroom to another. The student had the ability to move faster, but she seemed to purposely take more time than was necessary. We created a special "telephone book" for her with pictures of her teachers and their 4-digit phone numbers. Each time she reached a classroom, she was to use her book to call her teacher to let that person know she had made it. There were no more problems with her arriving late to class. She loved using the phone, and her teachers would praise her for walking so independently and promptly.

The Most Difficult Thing About Being a Special Educator

The most difficult thing for me is ensuring that classroom teachers and special education teachers follow through with my recommendations. I frequently have to remind the teachers to adhere to the modifications and adaptations needed for my students. I also have to ensure that teaching assistants understand why they are doing certain things that I have recommended. It takes a lot of patience and instruction to make sure that school personnel follow through.

Advice for Someone Considering a Career in Special Education

Special education is a very challenging and worthwhile endeavor. Treat every student as an individual, and search for a key to unlock his unique way of learning and interpreting the world. Parents and administrators are not the enemy, and you should make every effort to include them in meeting the special needs of your students. Remember that you are part of a team; you should not feel as though you are alone. A positive attitude takes less energy than a negative one.

Meaningful Accomplishments

During my first year, I worked with a 3-year-old boy who was congenitally blind. His parents were extremely protective of him, and it took a lot of instruction to educate the parents about their child's capabilities and that it was okay to let him explore and discover the world. This student is now in the fourth grade and flourishing.

Sixteen-year-old Maria is a bright, college-bound student who has been totally blind since birth. She took a series of intellectual and psychological tests and performed well, scoring at about her expected age and grade level. Something unusual happened, however, on one of the test items. The examiner handed Maria an unpeeled banana and asked, "What is this?" Maria held the banana and took several guesses but could not answer correctly. The examiner was astonished, as were Maria's teachers and parents. After all, this section of the test was intended for young children. Even though Maria had eaten bananas many times, she had missed out on one important aspect of the banana experience: she had never held and peeled a banana by herself.

This true story illustrates the tremendous importance of vision in obtaining information about our world. Many concepts that children with normal vision seem to acquire effortlessly may not be learned at all by children with visual impairments—or may be learned incorrectly—unless someone deliberately teaches them. Teachers who work with children with visual impairments find it necessary to plan and present a great many firsthand experiences, enabling children with visual impairments to learn by doing things for themselves. Good teachers understand, however, that even when a concept is deliberately presented to children with visual impairments, they may not learn it in exactly the same way that children with normal vision would.

This is true because although students with visual impairments may learn to make good use of their other senses (hearing, touch, smell, and taste) as channels for contacting the environment, they do not totally compensate for loss of vision. Touch and taste cannot tell a child much about things that are far away or even just beyond her arms' reach. And while hearing can provide a good deal of information about the near and distant environment, it seldom provides information that is as complete, continuous, or exact as the information people obtain from seeing their surroundings.

Vision plays a critical role in learning in the classroom. For example, normally sighted students are routinely expected to exercise several important visual skills. They must be able to focus on different objects and shift their vision from near to far as needed. They must have good hand-to-eye coordination, maintain visual concentration, discriminate among colors and letters, see and interpret many things simultaneously, and remember what they have seen. Children with visual impairments, however, have deficits in one or more of these abilities. As a result, they need special equipment and/or adaptations in instructional materials or procedures to function effectively in school.

DEFINITIONS

Unlike other disabilities covered by the Individuals with Disabilities Education Act (IDEA), visual impairment has both legal and educational definitions.

Legal Definition of Blindness

The legal definition of blindness is based on visual acuity and field of vision. **Visual acuity**—the ability to clearly distinguish forms or discriminate among details—is most often measured by reading letters, numbers, or other symbols from the Snellen Eye Chart. The familiar phrase "20/20 vision" does not, as some people think, mean perfect vision; it simply indicates that at a distance of 20 feet, the eye can see what a normally seeing eye sees at that distance. As the bottom number increases, visual acuity decreases.

A person whose visual acuity is 20/200 or less in the better eye after the best possible correction with glasses or contact lenses is considered **legally blind** by the federal government (Social Security Administration, 2000). If Jane has 20/200 vision while wearing her glasses, she needs to stand at a distance of 20 feet to see what a normally sighted person can see from 200 feet. In other words, Jane must get much closer than normal to see things clearly. Her legal blindness means that she will likely find it difficult to use her vision in many everyday situations. But many children with 20/200, or even 20/400, visual acuity succeed in the classroom with special help. Some students' visual acuity is so poor they cannot perceive fine details at any distance, even while wearing glasses or contact lenses. An individual with visual

Importance of visual experience

Content Standards for Beginning Teachers—VI: Impact of visual impairment on learning and experience (VI3K1).

After reading this chapter, complete the pretest for Chapter 10 on MyEducationLab to assess your initial understanding of chapter content.

Visual acuity, field of vision, tunnel vision

Content Standards for Beginning Teachers—VI: Specialized terminology used in assessing individuals with VI (VI8K1) (also VI1K5).

FIGURE 10.1

A street scene as it might be viewed by persons with 20/20 vision, 20/200 visual acuity, and restricted fields of vision

(a) Normal vision

(b) cataracts

(c) glaucoma

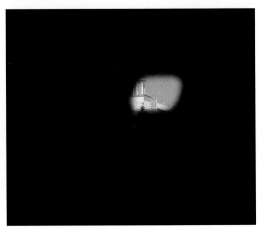

(d) advanced glaucoma

acuity of no better than 20/70 in the better eye after correction is considered **partially sighted** for legal and governmental purposes.

A person may also be considered legally blind if his **field of vision** is extremely restricted. When gazing straight ahead, a normal eye can see objects within a range of approximately 160 to 170 degrees. A person whose vision is restricted to an area of 20 degrees or less is considered legally blind. Some people with **tunnel vision** describe their perception as viewing the world through a narrow tube; they may have good central vision but poor peripheral vision at the outer ranges of the visual field. Conversely, some eye conditions make it impossible for people to see things clearly in the center of the visual field but allow relatively good peripheral vision. Because a person's visual field often deteriorates gradually over a period of years without notice, a thorough visual examination should always include measurement of the visual field as well as visual acuity. Figure 10.1 shows what a person might see with normal or poor visual acuity or a limited field of vision.

Children who are legally blind are eligible to receive a wide variety of educational services, materials, and benefits from governmental agencies. They may, for example, obtain Talking Books and playback devices from the Library of Congress. Their schools may be able to buy books and educational materials from the American Printing House for the Blind because the federal government allots states and local school districts a certain financial allowance for each legally blind student. A person who is legally blind is also entitled to vocational training, free U.S. mail service, and an income-tax exemption. To learn about services available to persons with visual impairments, go to websites of the American Printing House for the Blind (www.aph.org) and the American Federation of the Blind (www.afb.org).

Even though these services and benefits are important to know about, the legal definition of blindness is not especially useful for teachers. Some children who do not meet the

Federal entitlements for children who are legally blind

 Council for Exceptional Children

Content Standards for Beginning Teachers—VI: Federal entitlements that provide specialized equipment and materials for individuals with VI (VI1K1).

criteria for legal blindness have visual impairments severe enough to require special education. Other students whose visual impairments qualify them as legally blind have little or no need for special education services.

Educational Definitions of Visual Impairments

The definition of *visual impairment* in the Individuals with Disabilities Education Act (IDEA) emphasizes the relationship between vision and learning:

> *Visual impairment including blindness* means an impairment in vision that, even with correction, adversely affects a child's educational performance. The term includes both partial sight and blindness. (20 U.S.C. §1401 [2004], 20 C.F.R. §300.8[c][13])

Students with visual impairments display a wide range of visual abilities—from total blindness to relatively good vision. The precise clinical measurements of visual acuity and visual field used to determine legal blindness have limited relevance for educators. Instead, educators classify students with visual impairments based on the extent to which they use vision and/or auditory/tactile means for learning.

- A student who is *totally blind* receives no useful information through the sense of vision and must use tactile and auditory senses for all learning.
- A child who is *functionally blind* has so little vision that she learns primarily through the auditory and tactile senses; however, she may be able to use her limited vision to supplement the information received from the other senses and to assist with certain tasks (e.g., moving about the classroom).
- A child with **low vision** uses vision as a primary means of learning but may supplement visual information with tactile and auditory input.

Age at Onset

Like other disabilities, visual impairment can be congenital (present at birth) or adventitious (acquired). Most visual impairments of school-age children are congenital. It is useful for a teacher to know the age at which a student acquired a visual impairment. A child who has been blind since birth has quite a different perception of the world than does a child who lost his vision at age 12. The first child has a background of learning through hearing, touch, and the other nonvisual senses, whereas the second child also has a large background of visual experiences on which to draw. Most people who are adventitiously blind retain a visual memory of things they saw. This memory can be helpful in a child's education; an adventitiously blind child may, for instance, remember the appearance of colors, maps, and printed letters. At the same time, however, the need for emotional support and acceptance may be greater than it might be for a congenitally blind child, who does not have to make a sudden adjustment to the loss of vision (Wahl et al., 2006).

CHARACTERISTICS

Cognition and Language

This chapter began with a story about a bright teenage girl without sight who could not identify the object she was holding as a banana. Maria had eaten bananas many times, she could spell and read the word *banana*, and she could explain the best climate for growing bananas. But because she'd never held an unpeeled banana, Maria was not able to identify it.

Consider what two children, one with normal vision and one with limited or absent vision, might learn from their everyday experiences with a family pet.

> Children with normal vision see a cat's mouth open when it meows or spits, so they can connect the sound to the cat. When they pet the kitty, they feel the soft fur and see the cat's entire

Definitions of visual impairment

Council for Exceptional Children — Content Standards for Beginning Teachers—VI: Educational definitions, identification criteria, labeling issues, and incidence and prevalence figures for individuals with VI (VI1K3).

Age of onset

Council for Exceptional Children — Content Standards for Beginning Teachers—VI: Development of secondary senses when vision is impaired (VI2K2) (also VI2K5).

Children who have been blind since birth have a background of learning through hearing, touch, and other nonvisual senses.

body simultaneously. When Dad tells the cat to stop scratching the couch, they look at Dad, see that he is looking at the cat, and follow his gaze over to where the cat is pawing at the couch.

The experience is different for children with visual impairments. They have no way of knowing what the meow, growl, or purr is. They can pinpoint where the sound is coming from, but they cannot see what it is coming from. When the cat remains still long enough, they can feel its soft fur, but they can feel only part of the cat at a time. They can't see that the cat has a head with ears, a body, four legs, four paws with claws, and a tail. . . . And if they get scratched, the paw comes out of and returns to nowhere. Children with visual impairments can still learn the concept of cat, but if they rely on incidental learning, it will take quite a while to put this jumble of isolated experiences together. (Ferrell, 1996, pp. 79–80)

Sighted children without other disabilities are constantly learning from their experiences and interactions with their environment. As they move about, the sense of sight provides a steady stream of detailed information about their environment and about relationships between things in that environment. Without any effort on their part or on the part of others, children with normal sight produce great stores of useful knowledge from everyday experiences. Visual impairments, however, preclude most such incidental learning.

The sense of vision gives children the ability to organize and make connections between different experiences, connections that help the child make the most of those experiences. Children who are blind perform more poorly than sighted children do on cognitive tasks requiring comprehension or relating different items of information. Impaired or absent vision makes it difficult to see (literally, of course, but also cognitively) the connections between experiences. "It is as though all the educational experiences of the blind child are kept in separate compartments" (Kingsley, 1997, p. 27).

This makes learning even simple language concepts such as "cats have tails" and "bananas are smooth" difficult. Abstract concepts, analogies, and idiomatic expressions can be particularly difficult for children who cannot see. Featured teacher Jeanna Mora Dowse shared this experience:

> One morning, the OT was working with a 4-year-old student who was blind. This student was taking his time walking to the therapy room, so the OT told him to "Shake a leg!" The student stopped, shook his right leg, and then continued walking as slowly as before. The OT had to explain to him that "Shake a leg!" was just an expression for "Hurry up."

There is no evidence that these challenges to learning restrict the potential of children with visual impairments. They do, however, magnify the importance of repeated, direct contact with concepts through nonvisual senses (Chen & Downing, 2006a).

Direct, repeated contact through nonvisual senses is critical for learning by children with visual impairments. Morgan is learning the concept of cause and effect by hitting the switch that turns the fan on and off.

Motor Development and Mobility

Blindness or severe visual impairment often leads to delays or deficits in motor development (Brambring, 2006, 2007). Stone (1997) explains two reasons for this. First, a significant portion of the purposeful movements of fully sighted babies involves reaching for things they see. The child's efforts to grasp objects, especially those that are just out of reach, strengthen muscles and improve coordination, which in turn enable more effective movement. The absence of sight or clear vision, however, reduces the baby's motivation to move. For the child who is blind, the world is no more interesting when sitting up and turning her head from side to side than it is when she is lying on the floor. Second, a child without clear vision may move less often because movements in the past have resulted in painful contact with the environment. Parents' concern for their children's safety may also contribute to reduced opportunities for physical exploration and activity (Stuart, Lieberman, & Hand, 2006).

In addition to limiting a child's opportunities to learn through contact and experience with the physical environment, decreased motor development and movement can lead to physical and social detachment. Children who are blind "may put their natural energy, which would otherwise have found purposeful outlets, into rocking, poking or flapping, all of which can affect their learning and social acceptability" (Stone, 1997, p. 89).

Even limited vision can have negative effects on motor development. Children with low vision have poorer motor skills than do children who are sighted. Their gross motor skills, especially balance, are weak. They frequently cannot perform motor activities through imitation, and they are usually more careful of space (Bouchard & Tétreault, 2000).

Social Adjustment and Interaction

Compared with typically sighted children, children with visual impairments play and interact less during free time and are often delayed in the development of social skills (Celeste, 2006; Erin, Dignan, & Brown, 1991; Skellenger, Hill, & Hill, 1992). Some young children with sensory impairments experience difficulty in receiving and expressing affection, behaviors that have been shown to facilitate future development in other areas of social competence (Compton & Niemeyer, 1994). Although many adolescents with visual impairments have best friends, many also struggle with social isolation and must work harder than their sighted peers to make and maintain friendships (Leigh & Barclay, 2000; Lifshitz, Irit, & Weisse, 2007; Rosenblum, 1998, 2000; Sacks & Wolffe, 2006).

Students with visual impairments are often not invited to participate in group activities such as going to a ball game or a movie because sighted peers just assume they are not interested. Over time students with visual impairments and their sighted age mates have fewer and fewer shared experiences and common interests as bases for conversation, social interactions, and friendships.

Rosenblum (2000) identifies several issues influencing the limited social involvement of many adolescents with visual impairments. Because of the low incidence of the disability, many children with visual impairments cannot benefit from peers or adult role models who are experiencing the same challenges because of visual impairments. Social isolation becomes particularly pronounced for many teenagers with visual impairments when sighted peers obtain drivers' licenses.

Another factor contributing to social difficulties is that the inability to see and respond to the social signals of others reduces opportunities for reciprocal interactions (Campbell, 2007; Frame, 2000). During a conversation, for example, a student who is blind cannot see the gestures, facial expressions, and changes in body posture used by her conversation partner. This inability to see important components of communication hampers the blind student's understanding of the conversation partner's message. And her failure to respond with socially appropriate eye contact, facial expressions, and gestures suggests lack of interest in her partner's communicative efforts and makes it less likely that the individual will seek out her company in the future.

Some individuals with visual impairments engage in repetitive body movements or other behaviors such as body rocking, eye rubbing, hand flapping, and head weaving. These behaviors were traditionally referred to in the visual impairment literature as "blindisms" or "blind mannerisms" (Kingsley, 1997). *Stereotypic behavior* (stereotypy) is a more clearly defined term that subsumes blindisms and mannerisms. It is also a more appropriate term: some sighted children exhibit such behaviors, and they do not occur among all children who are blind (Gense & Gense, 1994).

Although not usually harmful, stereotypic behavior can place a person with visual impairments at a great social disadvantage because these actions are conspicuous and may call negative attention to the person. It is not known why many children with visual impairments engage in stereotypic behaviors (Bak, 1999). However, behavioral interventions such as differential reinforcement of incompatible behaviors and self-monitoring have helped individuals with visual impairments reduce stereotypic behaviors such as repetitive body rocking or head drooping during conversation (McAdam, O'Cleirigh, & Cuvo, 1993; Woods & Miltenberger, 2006).

Social and emotional development

 Content Standards for Beginning Teachers—VI: Effects of visual impairment on development (VI2K3) (also CC2K2).

Stereotypic behavior

 Content Standards for Beginning Teachers—VI: Effects of visual impairment on development (VI2K3) (also CC2K2).

Many persons who have lost their sight report that the biggest difficulty socially is dealing with the attitudes and behavior of those around them. The beliefs, superstitions, and mythology that form "the folklore of blindness" no doubt influence some of those attitudes and behaviors.

> The influence of the folklore of blindness generally is expressed in attitudes towards (and by) blind people that sound absurd but are genuinely felt.... One finds that folk beliefs are divided into two groups. On the negative side of this dichotomy are the beliefs that blind people are either helpless and pathetic or evil and contagious and probably deserve their fate. On the more positive side are the beliefs that blind people have special or even magical abilities, special powers of perception, and deserve special attention. (Wagner-Lampl & Oliver, 1994, pp. 267–268)

PREVALENCE

Prevalence of visual impairments

 Content Standards for Beginning Teachers—VI: Educational definitions, identification criteria, labeling issues, and incidence and prevalence figures for individuals with VI (VI1K3).

Children with visual impairments constitute a very small percentage of the school-age population—fewer than 2 children in 1,000. During the 2005–2006 school year, 25,369 children ages 6 to 21 received special education services under IDEA within the category of visual impairments (U.S. Office of Special Education, 2007). According to Sacks and Silberman (1998), almost one half of the school-age population of students with visual impairments has at least one additional disability. Thus, the total number of students with visual impairments is higher than the data reported for IDEA because some students with visual impairments are served and counted under other disability categories such as deaf-blindness and multiple disabilities. The American Printing House for the Blind (2006) reported that 49,270 children from birth to age 21 were eligible for services for visual impairment. The American Foundation for the Blind estimated that 93,600 children under the age of 18 had "serious difficulty seeing" (Ferrell, 2007). Still, visual impairment is a low-incidence disability.

Even when viewed as a percentage of the population of students who receive special education services, the prevalence of visual impairments is very small: only about 0.4%, or 1 in 200 to 250, of all school-age children with IEPs are served under the disability category of visual impairments (U.S. Office of Special Education, 2007). Educators and parents of children with visual impairments frequently express concern about this low prevalence because they fear that when financial resources are limited, students with visual impairments may not receive adequate services from specially trained teachers. It can be particularly difficult for a local public school to provide the comprehensive services needed by a child with visual impairment who resides in a rural area. Small school districts often cooperate with each other in employing special teachers for students with visual impairments.

TYPES AND CAUSES OF VISUAL IMPAIRMENTS

How We See

Anatomy and function of the eye

 Content Standards for Beginning Teachers—VI: Basic terminology related to the structure and function of the human eye (VI1K4).

Effective vision requires proper functioning of three anatomical systems of the eye: the optical system, the muscular system, and the nervous system. A simplified diagram of the eye appears in Figure 10.2. The eye's optical system collects and focuses light energy reflected from objects in the visual field. As light passes through the eye, several structures bend, or refract, the light to produce a clear image. The light first hits the *cornea*, the curved transparent membrane that protects the eye (much as an outer crystal protects a watch face). It then passes through the *aqueous humor*, a watery liquid that fills the front chamber of the eye. Next the light passes through the *pupil*, a circular hole in the center of the colored *iris*; the pupil contracts or expands to regulate the amount of light entering the eye. The light then passes through the *lens*, a transparent, elastic structure. After the light passes through the *vitreous humor*, a jellylike substance that fills most of the eye's interior, it reaches the innermost layer of the eye, the *retina*. This multilayered sheet of nerve tissue at the back of the eye has been likened to the film in a camera: for a clear image to be seen, the light rays must come to a precise focus on the retina.

The eye's muscular system enables **ocular motility**, the eye's ability to move. Six muscles attached to the outside of each eye enable it to search, track, converge, and fixate on images. These muscles also play a significant part in depth perception (**binocular vision**),

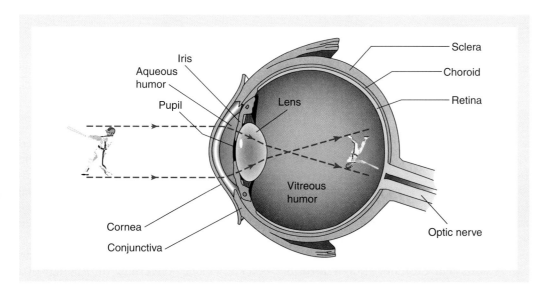

FIGURE 10.2

Basic anatomy of the human eye

the ability to fuse the separate images from each eye into a single, three-dimensional image. Inside the eye, tiny muscles adjust the shape of the lens, making it thicker or thinner, so the eye can bring objects at different distances into sharp focus (**accommodation**).

The eye's nervous system converts light energy into electrical impulses and transmits that information to the brain, where it is processed into visual images. The retina consists of millions of light receptors called *cones* and *rods*. The cones enable detection of color and detail necessary for tasks such as reading and are located in the center of the retina and function best in good light. The rods, which are responsible for peripheral vision, detection of movement, and vision in dim light, are distributed around the periphery of the retina. The *optic nerve* carries the electrical messages from the cones and rods directly to the *visual cortex* at the base of the brain.

Causes of Visual Impairments

Damage or disturbances to any part of the eye's optical, muscular, or nervous systems can result in impaired vision. Causes of visual impairments are grouped into three broad categories: refractive errors, structural impairments, and cortical visual impairments.

Refractive Errors   **Refraction** is the process of bending light rays when they pass from one transparent structure into another. As just described, the normal eye refracts, or bends, light rays so that a clear image falls directly on the retina. However, for many people— perhaps half the general population—the size and shape of the eye prevent the light rays from focusing clearly on the retina. In **myopia**, or *nearsightedness*, the eye is longer than normal from front to back, causing the image to fall in front of the retina instead of exactly on it. A child with myopia can see near objects clearly; but more distant objects, such as a chalkboard or a movie, are blurred or not seen at all (see Figure 10.1). The opposite of myopia is **hyperopia**, commonly called *farsightedness*. The hyperopic eye is shorter than normal, preventing the light rays from converging on the retina. A child with hyperopia has difficulty seeing near objects clearly but can focus well on more distant objects. Glasses or contact lenses can compensate for many refractive errors by changing the course of light rays to produce as clear a focus as possible.

Structural Impairments   Visual impairments can be caused by poor development of, damage to, or malfunction of one or more parts of the eye's optical or muscular systems. Cataracts and glaucoma are two of the numerous causes of visual impairment due to damage or disintegration of the eye itself. A **cataract** is a cloudiness in the lens of the eye that blocks the light necessary for seeing clearly. **Glaucoma** is abnormally high pressure within the eye caused by disturbances or blockages of the fluids that normally circulate within the eye. Central and peripheral vision are impaired or lost entirely when the increased pressure damages the optic nerve (see Figure 10.1).

Types and causes of visual impairment

Content Standards for Beginning Teachers—VI: Basic terminology related to diseases and disorders of the human visual system (VI1K5).

Dysfunction of the muscles that control and move the eyes can make it difficult or impossible for a child to see effectively. **Nystagmus**, a rapid, involuntary, back-and-forth movement of the eyes in a lateral, vertical, or rotary direction, can cause problems in focusing and reading. **Strabismus** is an inability to focus on the same object with both eyes because imbalance of the eye muscles creates an inward or outward deviation of one or both eyes. If left untreated, strabismus and other disorders of ocular motility can lead to permanent loss of vision.

Cortical Visual Impairments   Some children with visual impairments have nothing wrong with their eyes. The term **cortical visual impairments (CVI)** refers to decreased vision or blindness due to known or suspected damage to or malfunction of the parts of the brain that interpret visual information. Causes of CVI include insufficient oxygen at birth (anoxia), head injury, hydrocephalus, and infections of the central nervous system. Visual functioning may fluctuate depending on environment, lighting conditions, and activities. Some children with CVI use their peripheral vision, some are photophobic, some are attracted to bright light, and some will gaze at the sun.

Table 10.1 summarizes some of the most common types and causes of visual impairments. Although a teacher seldom needs detailed knowledge concerning the etiology of a

TABLE 10.1

Types and causes of visual impairments

CONDITION	DEFINITION/CAUSE	REMARKS/EDUCATIONAL IMPLICATIONS
Albinism	Lack of pigmentation in the eyes, skin, and hair; results in moderate-to-severe visual impairment by reducing visual acuity and causing nystagmus; heredity.	Children with albinism almost always have photophobia, a condition in which the eyes are extremely sensitive to light; eye fatigue may occur during close work.
Amblyopia	Reduction in or loss of vision in the weaker eye from lack of use; caused by strabismus, unequal refractive errors, or opacities of the lens or cornea.	Close work may result in eye fatigue, loss of place, poor concentration; seating should favor functional eye.
Astigmatism	Distorted or blurred vision caused by irregularities in the cornea or other surfaces of the eye that produce images on retina not in equal focus (refractive error).	Loss of accommodation when object brought close to face; avoid long periods of reading or close tasks that cause discomfort; child may complain of headaches and fluctuating vision.
Cataract	Blurred, distorted, or incomplete vision caused by cloudiness in the lens; caused by injury, malnutrition, or rubella during pregnancy, glaucoma, retinitis pigmentosa, heredity, aging.	Avoid glare of any kind; light source behind child; good contrast between print and paper; variation in near and distant tasks can prevent tiring.
Color deficiency or color blindness	Difficulty distinguishing certain colors; red-green confusion is most common; caused by cone malformation or absence, macular deficiency, heredity.	Usually not an educationally significant visual impairment; teach alternative ways to discriminate objects usually identified by color (e.g., tags for clothing colors, position of red and green on traffic lights).
Cortical visual impairment (CVI)	Impaired vision due to damage to or malfunction of the visual cortex and/or optic nerve; causes include anoxia, head injury, and infections of the central nervous system; many children with CVI have additional disabilities, such as cerebral palsy, seizure disorders, mental retardation.	Visual functioning may fluctuate depending on lighting conditions and attention; vision usually does not deteriorate; improvement sometimes occurs over a period of time; some children with CVI use their peripheral vision; some are photophobic; some are attracted to bright light and will gaze at the sun; visual images should be simple and presented singly.
Diabetic retinopathy	Impaired vision as a result of hemorrhages and the growth of new blood vessels in the area of the retina due to diabetes; leading cause of blindness for people ages 20 to 64.	Provide good lighting and contrast; magnification; pressure to perform can affect blood glucose.

TABLE 10.1 CONTINUED

Types and causes of visual impairments

CONDITION	DEFINITION/CAUSE	REMARKS/EDUCATIONAL IMPLICATIONS
Glaucoma	Abnormally high pressure within the eye due to disturbances or blockages of the fluids that normally circulate within the eye; vision is impaired or lost entirely when the increased pressure damages the retina and optic nerve.	Fluctuations in visual performance may frustrate child; be alert to symptoms of pain; eye drops administered on schedule; child may be subjected to teasing because of bulging eyes.
Hyperopia (farsightedness)	Difficulty seeing near objects clearly but able to focus well on distant objects; caused by a shorter-than-normal eye that prevents light rays from converging on the retina (refractive error).	Loss of accommodation when object brought close to face; avoid long periods of reading or close tasks that cause discomfort.
Macular degeneration	Central area of the retina gradually deteriorates, causing loss of clear vision in the center of the visual field; common in older adults but fairly rare in children.	Tasks such as reading and writing difficult; prescribed low-vision aid or closed-circuit TV; good illumination; avoid glare.
Myopia (nearsightedness)	Distant objects are blurred or not seen at all but can see near objects clearly; caused by an elongated eye that focuses images in front of the retina (refractive error).	Encourage child to wear prescribed glasses or contact lens; for near tasks child may be more comfortable working without glasses and bringing work close to face.
Nystagmus	Rapid, involuntary, back-and-forth movement of the eyes, which makes it difficult to focus on objects; when the two eyes cannot focus simultaneously, the brain avoids a double image by suppressing the visual input from one eye; the weaker eye (usually the one that turns inward or outward) can actually lose its ability to see; can occur on its own but is usually associated with other visual impairments.	Close tasks for extended period can lead to fatigue; some children turn or tilt head to obtain the best focus; do not criticize this.
Retinitis pigmentosa (RP)	The most common genetic disease of the eye; causes gradual degeneration of the retina; first symptom is usually difficulty seeing at night, followed by loss of peripheral vision; heredity.	High illumination with no glare; contracting visual field causes difficulties with scanning and tracking skills necessary for tasks such as reading; teach student to locate visual objects with systematic search grid; as RP is progressive, curriculum should include mobility training, especially at night, and braille training if prognosis is loss of sight.
Retinopathy of prematurity (ROP)	Caused by administering high levels of oxygen to at-risk infants; when the infants are later removed from the oxygen-rich incubators, the change in oxygen levels can produce an abnormally dense growth of blood vessels and scar tissue in the eyes, leading to visual impairment and often total blindness.	High illumination, magnifiers for close work; telescopes for distance viewing; students may have brain damage resulting in mental retardation and/or behavior problems.
Strabismus	Inability to focus on the same object with both eyes due to an inward or outward deviation of one or both eyes; caused by muscle imbalance; secondary to other visual impairments.	Classroom seating should favor student's stronger eye; some students may use one eye for distance tasks, the other eye for near tasks; frequent rest periods may be needed during close work; may need more time to adjust to unfamiliar visual tasks.

Sources: From American Foundation for the Blind (2007); Mason (1997); Lighthouse International (2007); Miller and Menacker (2007); Sacks and Silberman (1998); Steinweg, Griffin, Griffin, and Gingras (2005).

child's visual impairment, understanding how a student's visual impairment affects classroom performance is important. It is useful to know, for example, that Traci's cataracts make it difficult for her to read under strong lights, that Derek has only a small amount of central vision in his right eye, or that Naoko will need to administer eye drops to relieve the pressure caused by her glaucoma before leaving on a class field trip.

EDUCATIONAL APPROACHES

Educators have developed numerous specialized teaching methods and curriculum materials in an effort to overcome the obstacles to learning presented by blindness and low vision. Advances in instructional methodology and, in particular, technology have greatly increased access to the general education curriculum and academic success among students with visual impairments. As one high school student who is blind remarked, "By taking advantage of technology around me, I am able to have an education equal to my sighted peers" (Leigh & Barclay, 2000, p. 129). However, the education of students with visual impairments is a field with a history of more than 150 years, and today's developments were made possible by the contributions of many teachers and researchers who came before (Geruschat & Corn, 2006; Koenig & Holbrook, 2000; Moore, 2006). Table 10.2 highlights some key historical events and their implications for the education of students with visual impairments.

History of education of students with VI

 Content Standards for Beginning Teachers—VI: Historical foundations of education of individuals with VI (VI1K2).

Special Adaptations for Students Who Are Blind

Because they must frequently teach skills and concepts that most children acquire through vision, teachers of students who are blind must plan and carry out activities that will help their students gain as much information as possible through the nonvisual senses and by participation in active, practical experiences (Chen & Downing, 2006a, 2006b; Levack, 1997). For example, a blind child may hear a bird singing but get no concrete idea of the bird itself from the sound alone. A teacher interested in teaching such a student about birds might plan a series of activities that has the student touch birds of various species and manipulate related objects such as eggs, nests, and feathers. The student might assume the responsibility for feeding a pet bird at home or in the classroom. Through such experiences, the child

TABLE 10.2

A history of the education of children with visual impairments:
Key events and implications

DATE	HISTORICAL EVENT	EDUCATIONAL IMPLICATIONS
1784	Shocked at seeing people who were blind performing as jesters or begging on the streets of Paris, Victor Hauy resolved to teach them more dignified ways of earning a living. He started the first school for children who were blind. Hauy's curriculum included reading and writing (using embossed print), music, and vocational skills.	The competence of Hauy's students influenced the establishment of other residential schools in Europe and Russia in the early 19th century.
1821	Samuel Gridley Howe founded the Perkins School for the Blind, the oldest and best-known residential school for students who are blind.	Many methods and materials for teaching students with visual impairments were developed at Perkins. Anne Sullivan and her famous pupil, Helen Keller, spent several years at Perkins.
1829	The first draft of a tactile method of reading created by Louis Braille was published. He was a student at a Paris school for children who were blind.	Braille's system of embossed six-dot cells proved the most efficient of several methods of reading by touch and is the primary means of literacy for the blind today.

TABLE 10.2 CONTINUED

A history of the education of children with visual impairments:
Key events and implications

DATE	HISTORICAL EVENT	EDUCATIONAL IMPLICATIONS
1862	The Snellen chart was developed by a Dutch ophthalmologist.	The chart provided a fast, standardized test of visual acuity; it is still used today as a visual screening tool for schoolchildren.
1900; 1909/1913	The first public school class for children who were blind opened in Chicago; the first classes for children with low vision began in Cleveland and Boston.	Students with visual impairments were educated in public schools; children with low vision were educated in special "sight-saving classes" in which all instruction was conducted orally.
1932	The Library of Congress made Talking Books available to any person who is legally blind.	Availability of recorded books and other print materials enhanced the range of curriculum content accessible to students with visual impairments.
1938	The first itinerant teaching program for children with visual impairments attending general education classrooms began in Oakland, California.	This marked the beginning of the long and relatively successful history of including children with visual impairments in general education classrooms.
1940s–1950s	Thousands of children became blind or severely visually impaired by retinopathy of prematurity (ROP) caused by the increased use of oxygen with premature infants.	Residential schools were not able to accommodate the large influx of visually impaired children; thus, special education programs and services for students with visual impairments became much more widely available in the public schools in the 1950s and 1960s.
1944	Richard Hoover developed a system for teaching orientation and mobility (O&M) skills to persons with visual impairments. It featured a long white cane.	This system of O&M and the "Hoover cane" became standard parts of the curriculum for students with visual impairments.
1951	The Perkins brailler was invented.	The first fast and easy method for writing braille improved access to and participation in education.
Mid-1960s	Natalie Barraga published research showing that children with low vision do not lose their remaining sight by using it and that visual functioning can be improved by use.	Barraga's (1964, 1970) work was instrumental in ending the sight-saving classes attended by children with low vision for more than 50 years.
1970s	Development of the Kurzweil Reading Machine, the world's first text-to-speech optical scanning machine, provided access to print materials not available in braille, large-print, or recorded formats.	Though large, slow, and very expensive compared to the lightweight, portable technologies available today, the Kurzweil set the stage for a continuing explosion of technological advancements that have benefited the lives of many people with visual impairments.
1997	The Individuals with Disabilities Education Act (IDEA '97) mandated that orientation and mobility (O&M) services be provided to any student with a disability who needs them.	This expanded the role of O&M specialists in schools to include training in the use of wheelchairs, electronic travel devices, and public transportation for students with disabilities other than visual impairments.
1996/2004	American Federation for the Blind (AFB) publishes/revises "expanded core curriculum" of nonacademic skill needs that affect blind and visually impaired students' overall success in life (Hatlen, 1996; 2004a).	Provides rationale and template for assessing IEPs, curriculum and instruction, and related services provided to students with visual impairments.

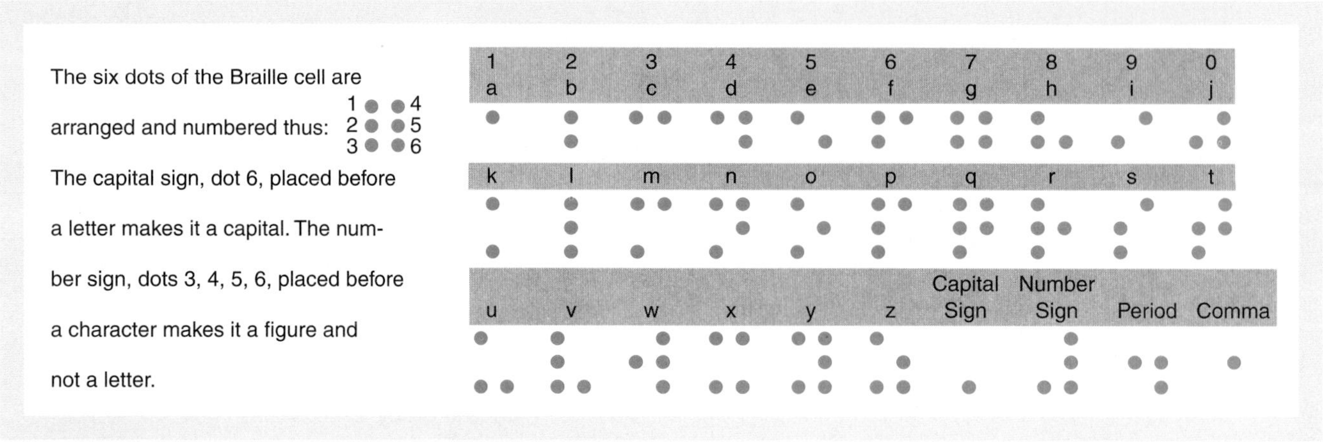
The six dots of the Braille cell are arranged and numbered thus:
1 4
2 5
3 6
The capital sign, dot 6, placed before a letter makes it a capital. The number sign, dots 3, 4, 5, 6, placed before a character makes it a figure and not a letter.
1 2 3 4 5 6 7 8 9 0
a b c d e f g h i j
k l m n o p q r s t
u v w x y z
Capital Sign
Number Sign
Period
Comma

FIGURE 10.3

The braille system for representing numbers and letters

Source: From the Division for the Blind and Physically Handicapped, Library of Congress, Washington, DC.

with visual impairments can gradually obtain a more thorough and accurate knowledge of birds than she could if her education were limited to reading books about birds, memorizing vocabulary, or feeling plastic models.

Braille, brailler, slate and stylus

Council for Exceptional Children Content Standards for Beginning Teachers—VI: Strategies for teaching braille reading and writing (VI4K1).

Braille Braille is the primary means of literacy for people who are blind. **Braille** is a tactile system of reading and writing in which letters, words, numbers, and other systems are made from arrangements of raised dots (see Figure 10.3).

In some ways, braille is like the shorthand that secretaries use. A set of 189 abbreviations, called *contractions*, helps save space and permits faster reading and writing. For example, when the letter *r* stands by itself, it means *rather*. The word *myself* in braille is written *myf*. Frequently used words, such as *the*, *and*, *with*, and *for*, have their own special contractions. For example, the *and* symbol appears four times in the following sentence:

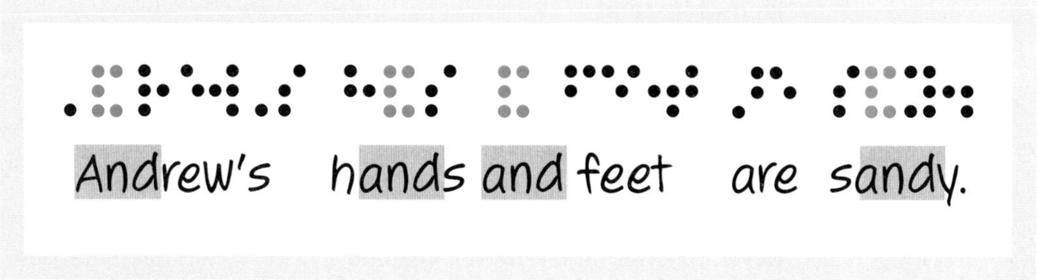
Andrew's hands and feet are sandy.

Go to the Homework & Exercises section in Chapter 10 on MyEducationLab and complete Homework Exercise 1.

Students who are blind can read braille much more rapidly than they can read the raised letters of the standard alphabet. The speed of braille reading varies a great deal from student to student; however, it is almost always much slower (about 100 words per minute for good braille readers) than the speed of print reading (Wetzel & Knowlton, 2006a). Most children who are blind are introduced to braille in the first grade. Rex, Koenig, Wormsley, and Baker (1994) recommend that children receive 1 to 2 hours of instruction in reading and writing braille each day, because this is the same amount of time typically devoted to literacy skills for sighted children in the primary grades. Rather than have the child learn to write out every word, letter by letter, and later unlearn this approach, teachers introduce contractions early in the program (Wormsley, 2004). Of course, it is important for the child to eventually know the full and correct spelling of words, even if every letter does not appear separately in braille.

Although it usually takes several years for children to become thoroughly familiar with braille, it is no more difficult than learning to read print for sighted children.

> True, some people claim that the braille code is more *complex* than the print code because more symbols are used. But if a child receives good reading instruction and has a rich

variety of background experiences, learning to read braille should not be "difficult." If a child says that braille is difficult to read, it is probably because she has heard an adult say so. (Koenig, 1996, pp. 233–234)

Young children generally learn to write braille by using a *brailler*, a six-keyed mechanical device that somewhat resembles a typewriter. Older students are usually introduced to the *slate and stylus*, in which the braille dots are punched out one at a time by hand, from right to left. The slate-and-stylus method has certain advantages in note taking; for example, it is much smaller and quieter than the brailler.

Braille Technological Aids   Most braille books are large, expensive, and cumbersome. It can be difficult for students to retrieve information quickly when they must tactilely review many pages of braille books or notes. Technological developments have made braille more efficient, thus enabling many students who are blind to function more independently in general education classrooms, universities, and employment settings.

Braille 'n Speak is a battery-powered, pocket-sized device for note taking with a keyboard for braille entry and voice output. It can translate braille into synthesized speech or print.

The Mountbatten Pro Brailler is an electronic brailler that is easier to use than the manual, mechanical brailler (Cooper & Nichols, 2007). Braille embossers print braille from digital text; and some printers produce pages with both braille and print formats, enabling blind and sighted readers to use the same copy.

Tactile Aids and Manipulatives   Manipulatives are generally recognized as effective tools in teaching beginning mathematics skills to elementary students. When using most manipulatives, such as Cuisenaire rods, however, sighted students use length and color to distinguish the various numerical values of the rods. Belcastro (1993) has developed a set of rods that enables students who are blind to quickly identify different values by feeling the lengths and tactile markings associated with each number.

Tactile-experience books created by gluing, stapling, or otherwise attaching artifacts from actual events experienced by the child to the pages of a simple and sturdy book can help young children who are blind or have severe visual impairments acquire book concepts and early literacy skills (Lewis & Tolla, 2003). Each page of a tactile experience book includes braille or print related to the artifacts on the page.

Another mathematical aid for students who are blind is the Cranmer abacus. Long used in Japan, the abacus has been adapted to assist students who are blind in learning number concepts and making calculations. Manipulation of the abacus beads is particularly useful in counting, adding, and subtracting.

For more advanced mathematical functions, the student is likely to use the Speech-Plus talking calculator, a small electronic instrument that performs most of the operations of any standard calculator. It "talks" by voicing entries and results aloud and also presents them visually in digital form. This is only one of many instances in which the development of synthetic speech technology has helped people who are blind. Talking clocks and spelling aids are also available.

In the sciences and social studies, several adaptations encourage students who are blind to use their tactile and auditory senses for firsthand manipulation and discovery (Chen & Downing, 2006b). Examples are embossed relief maps and diagrams, three-dimensional models, and electronic probes that give an audible signal in response to light. Curriculum modification projects, such as MAVIS (Materials Adaptation for Students With Visual Impairments in the Social Studies) and SAVI (Science Activities for the Visually Impaired), emphasize how students with visual impairments can, with some modifications, participate in learning activities along with normally sighted students.

Technological Aids for Reading Print   The Optacon (optical-to-tactile converter) is a small, handheld electronic device that converts regular print into a readable vibrating form.

The brailler is a six-keyed device that punches the raised braille dots in special paper.

Braille technological aids

 Council for Exceptional Children   Content Standards for Beginning Teachers—VI: Strategies for teaching braille reading and writing (VI4K1).

Tactile aids and manipulatives

 Council for Exceptional Children   Content Standards for Beginning Teachers—VI: Strategies for teaching use of the abacus, talking calculator, tactile graphics, and adapted science equipment (VI4K7).

The Optacon does not convert print into braille but into a configuration of raised pins representing the letter the camera is viewing. When the tiny camera of the Optacon is held over a printed *E*, for example, the user feels on the tip of one finger a vertical line and three horizontal lines. Although extensive training and practice are required, many children and adults who are blind are able to read regular print effectively with the aid of the Optacon. The Optacon II enables the user to scan print on computer screens.

The Kurzweil 1000 is a sophisticated computer-based reading system that uses an optical-character-recognition system to scan and read printed or electronic text with synthetic speech. The user can regulate the speed, have the machine spell out words letter by letter if desired, and even choose from a variety of natural-sounding voices. The "intelligence" of the Kurzweil reading machines is constantly being improved; and the machines are currently in use at most residential schools and also in many public school programs, public libraries, rehabilitation centers, and colleges and universities. The first Kurzweil Reading Machine weighed more than 300 pounds and cost $50,000. But the costs of reading machines have decreased greatly, and machines manufactured by Kurzweil, IBM, and Arenstone with computer accessories can be purchased for about $1,000.

Computer access and keyboarding

Content Standards for Beginning Teachers—VI: Strategies for teaching technology skills to individuals with VI (VI4K6) (also VI4K5).

Computer Access   Assistive technology that provides access to personal computers offers tremendous opportunities for the education, employment, communication, and leisure enjoyment of individuals with visual impairments. These technologies include (a) hardware and software that magnify screen images, (b) speech-recognition software that enables the user to tell the computer what to do, and (c) software that converts text files to synthesized speech.

Keyboarding is an important means of communication between children who are blind and their sighted classmates and teachers and is also a useful skill for further education and employment. Instruction in keyboarding should begin as early as feasible in the child's school program. Today, handwriting is seldom taught to students who are totally blind, with the noteworthy exception of learning to sign one's name in order to assume responsibilities such as maintaining a bank account, registering to vote, and applying for a job.

Special Adaptations for Students With Low Vision

Between 75% and 80% of school-age children enrolled in educational programs for visually impaired students have some potentially useful vision. Learning by students with low vision need not be restricted to the nonvisual senses, and they generally learn to read print (Corn & Koenig, 1996).

Visual efficiency/visual functioning

Content Standards for Beginning Teachers—VI: Strategies for teaching visual efficiency skills and use of print adaptations, optical devices, and nonoptical devices (VI4K9).

Functional Vision   *Visual efficiency* and **functional vision** are related terms denoting how well a person uses whatever vision he has (Barraga & Erin, 2001; Corn, 1989). A child's functional vision cannot be determined or predicted by measurements of visual acuity or visual field. Some children with severe visual impairments use the limited vision they have very capably. Other children with relatively minor visual impairments cannot function as visual learners; they may even behave as though they were blind.

Utley, Roman, and Nelson (1998) suggest that vision is functional when one or more visual–motor skills (e.g., fixation or localization, scanning, tracking, gaze shift; see Table 10.3) achieve the following: (a) is an essential step that the individual uses to accurately and efficiently perform a task; (b) promotes more independent performance in home, school, vocational, or community environments; or (c) enhances the degree of choice and autonomy of an individual, thereby enhancing her quality of life. The fundamental premises underlying the development of functional vision is that children learn to see, that functional vision is teachable behavior, and that children must be actively involved in using their own vision (Utley et al., 1998).

Merely furnishing a classroom with attractive things for children to see is not sufficient. Without training, a child with low vision may be unable to derive much meaningful information through vision. Forms may be perceived as vague masses and shapeless, indistinct blobs. Children with low vision need systematic training in visual recognition and

TABLE 10.3

Definitions and examples of four visual and visual–motor skills

VISUAL AND VISUAL–MOTOR SKILLS	DEFINITIONS AND EXAMPLES
Fixation	*Definition:* Active alignment of the line of sight (i.e., visual axis) in one or both eyes on a stationary object or person. *Example:* Looking at a tube of toothpaste while reaching to pick it up and apply it to the toothbrush.
Scanning	*Definition:* Visually searching for an object or person among a display of visual stimuli. *Example:* Visually locating the appropriate bus or van at dismissal time.
Tracking	*Definition:* Visually following a moving stimulus. *Example:* Watching the trajectory of coins as they are sorted into the appropriate locations in the cash drawer.
Gaze shift	*Definition:* Shifting fixation in space from one location to another. *Example:* Fixating on one type of cutlery and then others (i.e., first soup spoons; then forks, knives, and teaspoons) as the appropriate silverware for a particular meal is selected.

Source: From Utley, B. L., Roman, C., & Nelson, G. L. (1998). Functional vision. In S. Z. Sacks & R. K. Silberman (Eds.), *Educating students who have visual impairments with other disabilities* (p. 399). Baltimore: Paul H. Brookes Publishing Co., adapted with permission.

discrimination to learn to use their visual impressions intelligently and effectively, to make sense out of what they see (Li, 2004; Lueck, 2004). Teachers should not limit instruction in use of vision skills to isolated "visual stimulation sessions" but should incorporate the instruction throughout the student's daily schedule (Ferrell & Muir, 1996; Li, 2003) and teach it within the context of meaningful activities (see Figure 10.4).

Optical Devices   Many ophthalmologists and optometrists specialize in the assessment and treatment of low vision. A professional examination can help determine which types of optical aids, if any, can benefit a particular child with low vision. These special devices might include glasses and contact lenses, small handheld telescopes, and magnifiers placed on top of printed pages. Such aids cannot give normal vision to children with visual impairments but may help them perform better at certain tasks, such as reading small print or seeing distant objects.

Optical aids are usually specialized rather than all-purpose, and children whose vision is extremely limited are more likely to use monocular (one-eye) than binocular (two-eye) aids, especially for seeing things at a distance. Juanita might, for example, use her glasses for reading large print, a magnifier stand for reading smaller print, and a monocular telescope for viewing the chalkboard. A usual disadvantage of corrective lenses and magnifiers is that

Optical devices

 Council for Exceptional Children

Content Standards for Beginning Teachers—VI: Strategies for teaching visual efficiency skills and use of print adaptations, optical devices, and nonoptical devices (VI4K9).

	Example of embedding opportunities to use and develop functional visual skills throughout the daily schedule for Paula, a 15-year-old girl with cerebral palsy who demonstrates visual skills about 50% of the time
FIGURE 10.4	

Place and time	Activity and visual skills needed
At home 7:30–8:30 A.M. Getting ready for school	Have Paula choose what she wants to wear. Her mother puts 2 sets of clothes in front of her but does not describe them. She asks Paula what she wants to wear either by naming the color or pointing to the clothing. *Visual skills needed to choose:* Localization and shift attention.
At school, First period class: Daily living skills—Grooming	After brushing and arranging Paula's hair have her look in a magnifying mirror and ask her how she likes her hair. Once in a while change her hairstyle to see if she notices the difference. *Visual skills needed to examine hair:* Visual attending, localization, and scanning.
At school, Second period class: Home economics—Laundry	While sorting clothes into a light and a dark pile, ask Paula to decide into which pile each piece of clothing should go. *Visual skills involved:* Visual attending, localization, shifting attention, and scanning.
At school, lunch	Present Paula with 2 types of food with which she is familiar without telling her what they are. Have her choose what she wants to eat. If she has difficulty identifying the food, allow her to smell it. *Visual skills she will need:* Visual attending, localization, and shift attention.
Afternoon community outing	While grocery shopping, encourage Paula to identify items that are easily recognizable or that she frequently uses. Encourage her to say what the item is and where it is. For example, place her between the bananas and the apples or near just one item. *Visual skills involved:* Visual attending, localization, and scanning.
	While outdoors, encourage Paula to tell you what she sees or ask her to point to specific items (e.g., cars, flowers, green grass, fire hydrants). *Visual skills involved:* Visual attending, localization, tracking, and scanning.

Source: From Li, A. (2003). A model for developing programs to improve the use of vision in students who are visually impaired with multiple disabilities. *RE:view, 35*(1), p. 38. Reprinted with permission of the Helen Dwight Reid Educational Foundation. Published by Heldref Publications, 1319 Eighteenth St., NW, Washington, DC 20036-1802. Copyright © 2003.

To learn more about using a monocular device, go to the Homework & Exercises section in Chapter 10 on MyEducationLab and complete Homework Exercise 2.

the more powerful they are, the more they tend to distort or restrict the peripheral field of vision. Some field-widening lenses and devices are now available for students with limited visual fields. These include prisms and fish-eye lenses designed to make objects appear smaller so that a greater area can be perceived on the unimpaired portions of a student's visual field. It is usually a good idea to furnish optical aids on a trial or loan basis so that the student can gradually learn to use and evaluate them in natural settings. A follow-up session should then be scheduled.

Closed-circuit television systems are used in some classrooms to enable students with low vision to read regular-sized printed materials. These systems usually include a sliding table on which a book is placed, a television camera with a zoom lens mounted above the book, and a television monitor nearby. The student can adjust the size, brightness, and contrast of the material and can select either an ordinary black-on-white image or a negative white-on-black image, which many students prefer. The teacher may also have a television monitor that lets him see the student's work without making repeated trips to the student's desk. A disadvantage of closed-circuit television systems is that they are usually not portable, so the student who uses television as a primary reading medium is largely restricted to the specially equipped classroom or library. Many students with low vision use ZoomText, a computer program that enlarges and enhances images and text on their computer screens.

Recent advances in computer and optical technologies have led to the development of a number of low-vision devices called *augmented reality systems*. These lightweight, head-mounted devices track the position of the user's head and project the desired images onto beam-splitting optics that allow the user to see an overlay or superimposed image on the environment (Feiner, 2002). One augmented-reality system for people with low vision, called Nomad, uses a high-resolution laser to project an image directly onto the user's retina. Studies have shown that Nomad can function as a substitute computer monitor (Kleweno, Seibel, Viirre, Kelly, & Furness, 2001) and that users can read print with the device (Goodrich, Kirby, Wagstaff, Oros, & McDevitt, 2004).

Reading Print Students with low vision use three basic approaches for reading print: (a) *approach magnification* (reducing the distance between the eye and the page of print from 40 cm to 5 cm results in 8× magnification), (b) *lenses* (optical devices), and (c) *large print*. Many books and other materials are available in large print for children with low vision. The American Printing House for the Blind produces books in 18-point type. Some states and other organizations produce large-type materials; but the size and style of the print fonts, spacing, paper, and quality of production vary widely. The sentence you are reading now is set in 10-point type. Here are four examples of different large-print type sizes:

Most optical aides are designed for special purposes. Brennan uses his monocular telescope to focus on distance targets for independent travel.

This is 14-point type.

This is 18-point type.

This is 20-point type.

This is 24-point type.

Although print size is an important variable, other equally important factors to consider are the quality of the printed material, the font or typeface, the contrast between print and page, the spacing between lines, and the illumination of the setting in which the child reads (Griffin, Williams, Davis, & Engelman, 2002; Russell-Minda et al., 2007). Educators generally agree that a child with visual impairments should use the smallest print size that she can read comfortably. A child may be able to transfer from large print to smaller print as reading efficiency increases, just as most normally sighted children do. Table 10.4 compares the advantages and disadvantages of large-print materials and optical devices.

Most children with low vision can learn to read regular-sized print with or without the use of optical aids. This makes a much wider variety of materials available to the students and eliminates the added cost of obtaining large-print books or enlarging texts with special duplicating machines. Additionally, regular-sized print books are easier to store and carry around than are large-print books (Barraga & Erin, 2001). Some children with visual impairments are dual-media learners, who learn to use both print and braille simultaneously (Lusk & Corn, 2006a, 2006b).

This student with low vision is using ZoomText, a software program that enables her to produce and read large print.

Based on their research on reading by children with low vision, Gompel, van Bon, and Schreuder (2004) recommend that teachers accommodate the slower reading rates of most children with low vision by doing the following:

- Provide 1½ to 2 times as much time as sighted children for reading.
- Ensure sufficient time to study, and use auditory reading aids such as talking books or text-to-speech computer software if time is not available.
- Allow extra time on tests.

TABLE 10.4

Advantages and disadvantages of large-print materials and optical devices for readers with low vision

LARGE-PRINT MATERIALS	OPTICAL DEVICES
Advantages	**Advantages**
• Little or no instruction is needed to use a large-print book or other materials.	• Users have access to materials of various sizes, such as regular texts, newspapers, menus, and maps.
• A low vision clinical evaluation is not needed.	• Optical devices have a lower cost per child than large-print materials do.
• Students carry large-print books like other students carry books in their classes.	• Devices are lighter weight and more portable than large-print materials are.
• Funds for large-print books come from school districts that may require parental or other funding for optical devices.	• There is no ordering or waiting time for production or availability.
	• Users have access to distant print and objects, such as chalkboards, signs, and people.
Disadvantages	**Disadvantages**
• Fewer words can be seen at once; large-print materials are more difficult to read smoothly with a natural sweep of eye movements.	• A low vision clinical evaluation must be obtained for the prescription of optical devices.
• Enlarging print by photocopy emphasizes imperfect letters.	• Funding for clinical evaluation and optical devices must be obtained.
• Pictures are in black, white, and shades of gray.	• Instruction in the use of the optical devices is needed.
• Fractions, labels on diagrams, maps, and so forth are enlarged to a print size smaller than 18-point type.	• The cosmetics of optical devices may cause self-consciousness.
• The size and weight of large-print texts make them difficult to handle.	• Optical problems associated with the optics of devices need to be tolerated.
• Large-print materials are not readily available after the school years, and students may be nonfunctional readers with regular-size type.	

Source: A. Corn & G. Ryser, (1989) "Access to Print for Students with Low Vision." *Journal of Visual Impairment & Blindness, 83,* 340–349. Reprinted with permission from American Foundation for the Blind, 15 West 16th St., New York, NY 10011.

Classroom Adaptations Minor classroom adaptations can be very important for students with low vision. As Bennett (1997) points out, the most effective low-vision device is proper light. Although most classrooms have adequate lighting, adjustable lamps may be helpful for some children. Rosenthal and Williams (2000) recommend that additional lighting should come from the side of the eye with the greatest usable vision. Many students benefit from desks with adjustable or tilting tops so that they can read and write at close range without constantly bending over and casting a shadow. Writing paper should have a dull finish to reduce glare; an off-white color such as buff or ivory is generally better than white. Worksheets photocopied on colored paper can be difficult for students with low vision to use; if needed, an aide or a classmate can first go over the worksheet with a dark pen or marker. Some teachers have found it helpful to give students with low vision chairs with wheels so that they can easily move around the chalkboard area or other places in the classroom where instruction is taking place without constantly getting up and down. A teacher can make many other modifications using common sense and considering the needs of the individual student with low vision. For suggestions on helping students with low vision in the classroom, see Teaching & Learning, "Helping the Student With Low Vision."

Expanded Curriculum Priorities

In addition to learning to use braille, functional vision skills, and low-vision aids, students with visual impairments receive an "expanded core curriculum" (Hatlen, 2004a), which includes orientation and mobility, listening skills, and functional life skills.

Orientation and Mobility   **Orientation** is knowing where you are, where you are going, and how to get there by interpreting information from the environment. **Mobility** involves moving safely and efficiently from one point to another. Although the two sets of skills are complementary, orientation and mobility are not the same thing (Wall Emerson & Corn, 2006). A person can know where he is but not be able to move safely in that environment, and a person may be mobile but become disoriented or lost.

Orientation and mobility (O&M) instruction is considered a related service by IDEA and is included in the IEP of virtually all children with significant visual impairments. O&M specialists have developed many specific techniques (e.g., trailing, squaring off, using arms as bumpers) and mobility devices (e.g., a shopping cart, a suitcase on wheels) to teach students with visual impairments to understand their environment and maneuver through it safely and effectively (Perla & Ducret, 1999; Tellefson, 2000; Tolla, 2000).

For most students, more time and effort are spent on orientation training than on learning specific mobility techniques. It is extremely important that from an early age, children with visual impairments be taught basic concepts that will familiarize them with their own bodies and their surroundings. For example, they must be taught that the place where the leg bends is called a "knee" and that rooms have walls, doors, windows, corners, and ceilings. Perla and O'Donnell (2004) stress the importance of systematically teaching students to respond to orientation and mobility obstacles and puzzles as problem-solving opportunities so that they will not have to depend on others each time they find themselves in a novel environment.

Cane Skills   The long cane is the most widely used device for adults with severe visual impairments who travel independently. The traveler does not tap the cane but sweeps it lightly in an arc while walking to gain information about the path ahead. Properly used, the cane serves as both a bumper and a probe. It acts as a bumper by protecting the body from obstacles such as parking meters and doors; it is also a probe to detect in advance things such as drop-offs or changes in travel surface (e.g., from grass to concrete or from a rug to a wooden floor).

Even though mastery of cane skills can do much to increase a person's independence and self-esteem, cane use exacts physical effort and poses certain disadvantages (Gitlin, Mount, Lucas, Weirich, & Gramberg, 1997). The cane cannot detect overhanging obstacles such as tree branches and provides only fragmentary information about the environment, particularly if the person who is blind is in new or unfamiliar surroundings.

Until recently, formal O&M instruction, especially for cane use, was seldom given to children younger than about 12 years of age. However, the importance of early development of travel skills and related concepts is now generally recognized. Today, it is not at all unusual for preschool children to benefit from the services of an O&M specialist; but there is

Under the watchful eyes of an orientation and mobility specialist, Creighton is learning how to gain information about the path ahead by sweeping his cane in an arc.

TEACHING & LEARNING

What does a child with low vision actually see? It is difficult for us to know. We can obtain some idea of total blindness by wearing a blindfold, but the majority of children with visual impairments are not totally blind. Even when two children share the same cause of visual impairment, it is unlikely that they see things in exactly the same way. And each child may see things differently at different times.

Corn believes that curriculum development and instructional planning for children with low vision should be guided by the following basic premises about low vision and its effects on a person (Corn, Erin, et al., 2004; Corn & Koenig, 1996):

- *Children with congenital low vision view themselves as whole.* Although it may be proper to speak of residual vision in reference to those who experience adventitious low vision, those with congenital low vision do not have a normal vision reference. They view the world with all of the vision they have ever had.

- *Children with low vision generally view the environment as stationary and clear.* Although there are exceptions, it is a misconception that people with low vision live in an impressionistic world in which they are continuously wanting to clear the image.

- *Low vision offers a different aesthetic experience.* Low vision may alter an aesthetic experience, but it does not necessarily produce a lesser one.

- *The use of low vision is not always the most efficient or preferred method of functioning.* For some tasks, the use of vision alone or in combination with other senses may reduce one's ability to perform. For example, using vision may not be the most efficient method for determining how much salt has been poured on one's food.

- *Those who have low vision may develop a sense of visual beauty, enjoy their visual abilities, and use vision to learn.*

HOW TO GET STARTED

The following suggestions for teachers of students with low vision are from the Vision Team, a group of specialists in visual impairment who work with general education classroom teachers in 13 school districts in Hennepin County, Minnesota.

- Using the eyes does not harm them. The more children use their eyes, the greater their efficiency will be.

- Holding printed material close to the eyes may be the best way for the child with low vision to see. It will not harm the eyes.

- Although eyes cannot be strained from use, the eyes of a child with low vision may tire more quickly. A change of focus or activity helps.

- Copying is often a problem for children with low vision. The child may need a shortened assignment or more time to do classwork.

- It is helpful if the teacher verbalizes as much as possible while writing on the chalkboard or using the overhead projector.

- The term *legally blind* does not mean educationally blind. Most children who are legally blind function educationally as sighted children.

- Contrast, print style, and spacing can be more important than the size of the print.

- One of the most important things a child with low vision learns in school is to accept the responsibility of seeking help when necessary rather than waiting for someone to offer help.

- In evaluating quality of work and applying discipline, the teacher best helps the child with low vision by using the same standards that he uses with other children.

Using Low-Vision Aids Children who have low-vision aids, such as special eyeglasses, magnifiers, and telescopes, may need instruction and assistance in learning how to use them most effectively. Here are some tips for teachers to share with children to help them become accustomed to low-vision aids:

- *Low-vision aids take time to get used to.* At first, it seems like just a lot more things to take care of and carry around, but each aid you have will help you with a special job of seeing. You will get better with practice. In time, reaching for your telescope to read the chalkboard will seem as natural as picking up a pencil or pen to write. It's all a matter of practice.

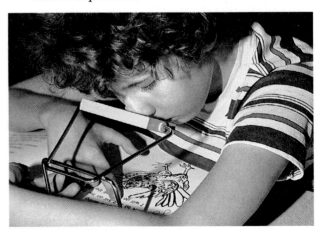

Low-vision aids should be portable and easy to use.

- *Lighting is very important*. Always work with the most effective light for you. It makes a big difference in how clear things will look. Some magnifiers come with a built-in light, but most times you will have to use another light. A desk lamp is best. (The overhead light casts a shadow on your book or paper as you get close enough to see it.) Be sure the light is along your side, coming over your shoulder.

- *Be sure to keep your aids clean*. Dust, dirt, and fingerprints are hard to see through. Clean the lenses with a clean, soft cloth (never paper). Always be sure your hands are clean to begin with.

- *Keep your aids in their cases when you are not using them*. They will be more protected and always ready for you to take with you wherever you go.

- *Carry your low-vision aids with you*. Most of them are small and lightweight. In that way, you will have them when you need them. If you have aids you use only at school, you may want to ask your teacher to keep them in a safe place for you.

- *Experiment in new situations*. Can you see the menu at McDonald's? watch the football game? see prices on toys? find your friend's house number? The more often you use your low-vision aid, the better you will get at using it.

- *Try out different combinations of aids with and without your glasses or contact lenses*. In this way, you will find the combination that works best for you.

Sources: Allman & Lewis (2000); Bennett (1997); Brilliant (1999); Corn, Lidoff, & Massof (2000); Tips for using low-vision aids, from Dean, M. *A Closer Look at Low Vision Aids.* Connecticut State Board of Education and Services for the Blind, Division of Children's Services, 184 Windsor Ave., Windsor, CT 06095. Reprinted by permission.

 To learn more about assistive devices for students with visual impairments, go to the Homework & Exercises section in Chapter 10 of MyEducationLab and complete Homework Exercise 5.

Children may need help from teachers and others to learn how to use and become accustomed to low-vision aids. An O&M specialist helps Brennan with his monocular.

To learn more about using a cane for orientation and mobility, go to the Homework & Exercises section in Chapter 10 of MyEducationLab and complete Homework Exercise 4.

disagreement over which, if any, mobility device is most suitable for initial use by very young children (Dykes, 1992). Professionals recognize the long cane's benefits of increased protection and confidence while traveling but question whether preschoolers can handle the motor and conceptual demands of long cane use. These concerns have led to the development of a variety of alternative mobility devices, including modified and smaller canes such as the Connecticut precane (Foy, Von Scheden, & Waiculonis, 1992) and the kiddy cane (Pogrund, Fazzi, & Schreier, 1993).

Guide Dogs   Fewer than 2% of people with visual impairments travel with the aid of guide dogs (Hill & Snook-Hill, 1996). Like the cane traveler, the guide dog user must have good O&M skills to select a route and to be aware of the environment. The dog wears a special harness and has been trained to follow several basic verbal commands, to provide protection against obstacles, and to ensure the traveler's safety. Guide dogs are especially helpful when a person must travel over complicated or unpredictable routes, as in large cities. Several weeks of intensive training at special guide dog agencies are required before the person and the dog can work together effectively. Guide dogs are not usually available to children under 16 years of age or to people with multiple disabilities. Young children, however, should have exposure to and positive experiences with dogs so they are comfortable with them and can make informed choices later about the possibilities of working with a guide dog (Young, 1997).

Although owning a guide dog is a major responsibility and sometimes inconvenient, many owners report increased confidence and independence in traveling and say that their dogs often serve as icebreakers for interactions with sighted people (Hill & Snook-Hill, 1996; Minor, 2001). However, guide dogs are not pets but working companions for their owners, and sighted people should abide by the following guidelines (Ulrey, 1994):

- Do not pet a guide dog without first seeking the owner's permission.
- Do not take hold of the dog's harness, as this might confuse the dog and the owner.
- If a person with a guide dog appears to need assistance, approach on his or her right side (guide dogs are usually on the left side) and ask if he or she needs help.

Sighted Guides   Most people who are blind find it necessary to rely occasionally on the assistance of others. The **sighted-guide technique** is a simple method of helping a person with visual impairments to travel:

- When offering assistance to a person who is blind, speak in a normal tone of voice and ask directly, "May I help you?" This helps the person locate you.
- Do not grab the arm or body of the person who is blind. Permit him to take your arm.
- The person with visual impairment should lightly grasp the sighted person's arm just above the elbow and walk half a step behind in a natural manner. Young children might hold on to the index finger or pinky of an adult sighted guide.
- The sighted person should walk at a normal pace, describing curbs or other obstacles and hesitating slightly before going up or down. Never pull or push a person who is blind when you are serving as a sighted guide.
- Do not try to push a person who is blind into a chair. Simply place his hand on the back of the chair, and the person will seat himself.

When students with visual impairments attend general education classes, it may be a good idea for one of the students and the O&M specialist to demonstrate the sighted guide technique to classmates. To promote independent travel, however, overreliance on the sighted guide technique should be discouraged once the student has learned to get around the classroom and the school.

Electronic Travel Aids   A variety of electronic travel aids facilitate the orientation and mobility of individuals with visual impairments. The laser beam cane converts infrared light into sound as the light beam strikes objects in the traveler's path. Different levels of vibration in the cane signal relative proximity to an obstacle. Other electronic travel aids are designed for use in conjunction with a standard cane or guide dog. The Mowat Sensor is a flashlight-sized device that bounces ultrasound off objects and gives the traveler information about the distance and location of obstacles through changes in vibration. The SonicGuide, which is worn on the head, converts reflections of ultrasound into sounds of varied pitch, amplitude, and tone that enable the traveler to determine distance, direction, and characteristics of objects in the environment.

Recent research has developed accessible and affordable global positioning system (GPS) technologies and other way-finding products for people with visual impairments that can announce present location, provide audible or tactile cues for the location of pay phones and restrooms, interpret traffic signals, read street signs, give distance and direction information, and more (Marston, Loomis, Klatzky, & Golledge, 2007; Ponchillia et al., 2007; Ponchillia, Rak, Freeland, & LaGrow, 2007).

Whatever the preferred method of travel, most students with visual impairments learn to negotiate familiar places, such as school and home, on their own. Many students with visual impairments can benefit from learning to use a systematic method for obtaining travel information and assistance with street crossing. Good orientation and mobility skills have many positive effects. A child with visual impairments who can travel independently is likely to develop more physical and social skills and more self-confidence than will a child who must continually depend on other people to get around. Good travel skills also expand a student's opportunities for employment and independent living.

Listening Skills   Children with visual impairments, especially those who are blind, must obtain an enormous amount of information by listening. Vision is thought to be the coordinating sense, and it has been estimated that 80% of information received by a normally sighted person comes through the visual channel (Arter, 1997; Best, 1992). Children who are blind must use other senses, predominately touch and hearing, to contact and comprehend their environment. A widely held misconception is that persons who are blind automatically develop a better sense of hearing to compensate for their loss of sight. Children with visual impairments do not have a super sense of hearing, nor do they necessarily listen better than their normally sighted peers do. It is more accurate to say that, through proper instruction and experiences, children with visual impairments learn to use their hearing more efficiently (Koenig, 1996; Tuba Tuncer & Altunay, 2006).

The systematic development of listening skills is an important component of the educational program of every child with visual impairments. Listening is not the same thing as hearing; it is possible to hear a sound without understanding it. Listening involves being aware of sounds, discriminating differences in sounds, identifying the source of sounds, and attaching meaning to sounds (Heinze, 1986).

Learning-to-listen activities can take an almost unlimited variety of forms. Young children, for example, might learn to discriminate between sounds that are near and far, loud and soft, high-pitched and low-pitched. A teacher might introduce a new word into a sentence and ask the child to identify it or ask children to clap each time a key word is repeated. In the "shopping game," a child begins by saying, "I went to the store and I bought _____." Each player repeats the whole list of items purchased by previous students and then adds his or her own item to the list (Arter, 1997). It is important to arrange the rules of such games so that children who fail to remember the list are not eliminated, which would result in fewer opportunities to practice for the children with the weakest listening and auditory memory skills. Older students might practice higher-order listening skills such as identifying important details with distracting background noises, differentiating between fact and opinion, or responding to verbal analogies.

Students with visual impairments, particularly in high school, make frequent use of recorded materials. In addition to using recordings of texts, lectures, and class discussions, students with visual impairments and their teachers can obtain on a free-loan basis thousands of recorded books and magazines and playback equipment through the Library of Congress, the American Printing House for the Blind (APH), the Canadian National Institute for the Blind, Recordings for the Blind, and various other organizations. But a listener can process auditory information at more than twice the speed of the average oral reading rate of about 120 words per minute (Aldrich & Parkin, 1989). Variable-speed cassette tape

Listening skills

Council for Exceptional Children
Content Standards for Beginning Teachers—VI: Strategies for teaching listening and compensatory auditory skills (VI4K4).

recorders available from the American Printing House for the Blind accelerate the playback rate of recorded text without significantly distorting the quality of the speech. In addition to tactile markings on the controls and a window that allows users to feel with their fingertip if the tape is playing, the APH Handicassette has built-in pitch control and a speech-compression feature that electronically shortens the length of selected words. With practice, students can listen to accelerated and compressed speech at speeds of up to 275 words per minute without affecting comprehension (Arter, 1997).

Functional Life Skills   Some special educators have expressed concern that efforts to help students with visual impairments match the academic achievement of their sighted age mates have too often come at the expense of sufficient opportunities to learn daily living and career skills (Lohmeier, 2005; Sacks et al., 1998). Specific instruction and ongoing supports should be provided to ensure that students with visual impairments learn skills such as cooking, personal hygiene and grooming, shopping, financial management, transportation, and recreational activities that are requisites for an independent and enjoyable adulthood (Corn, 2000; Kaufman, 2000; Rosenblum, 2000). To find out how three secondary students who are blind were taught to prepare some of their favorite snack foods, see Teaching & Learning, "I Made It Myself, and It's Good!"

Some students with visual impairments will also benefit from direct instruction on how to deal with strangers, how to interpret and explain their visual impairments to other people, and how to make socially acceptable gestures in conversation.

EDUCATIONAL PLACEMENT ALTERNATIVES

In the past, most children with severe visual impairments were educated in residential schools. Today, however, 88% of children with visual impairments are educated in public schools, and two of three receive at least some of their education in general education school classrooms: 58% of all school-age students with visual impairments are members of general education classes, and 17% attend resource rooms for part of each day (U.S. Department of Education, 2007b). Separate classrooms in public schools serve another 14% of the school-age population of children with visual impairments.

Inclusive Classroom and Itinerant Teacher Model

Inclusive education for students with visual impairments has had advocates for many years. Cruickshank (1986), for example, suggested that "the blind child is perhaps the easiest exceptional child to integrate into a regular grade in the public schools" (p. 104). To make inclusion successful, however, a full program of appropriate educational and related services must be provided (Erin & Spungin, 2004; Pugh & Erin, 1999).

Most students with visual impairments in general education classrooms receive support from itinerant teacher-consultants, sometimes called vision specialists. These specially trained teachers may be employed by the school district; a nearby residential school; or a regional, state, or provincial education agency. Although their roles and caseloads vary widely from program to program, most itinerant teacher-consultants are expected to assume some or all of the following responsibilities (Flener, 1993; Olmstead, 2005):

- Collaboratively develop with the general education classroom teacher curricular and instructional modifications according to the child's individual needs.
- Provide direct instruction on compensatory skills to the student with visual impairments (e.g., listening, typing skills).
- Obtain or prepare specialized learning materials.
- Adapt reading assignments and other materials into braille, large-print, or tape-recorded form or arrange for readers.
- Make referrals for low-vision aids services; train students in the use and care of low-vision aids.

Functional life skills

Content Standards for Beginning Teachers—VI: Strategies for teaching social, daily living, and functional life skills to individuals with VI (VI4K15).

To learn more about functional life skills and students with visual impairments, go to the Homework & Exercises section in Chapter 10 of MyEducationLab and complete Homework Exercise 6.

Placement alternatives

Content Standards for Beginning Teachers—Common Core: Issues, assurances, and due process right related to assessment, eligibility, and placement with a continuum of services (CC1K6).

- Interpret information about the child's visual impairment and visual functioning for other educators and parents.
- Help plan the child's educational goals, initiate and maintain contact with various agencies, and keep records of services provided.
- Consult with the child's parents and other teachers.

The itinerant teacher-consultant may or may not provide instruction in O&M. Some schools, particularly in rural areas, employ dually certified teachers who are also O&M specialists. Other schools employ one teacher for educational support and another for O&M training. Students on an itinerant teacher's caseload may range from infants to young adults and may include children who are blind, those with low vision, and students with multiple disabilities.

Some large public school programs have O&M instructors in special resource rooms for students with visual impairments. In contrast with the itinerant teacher-consultant who travels from school to school, the resource room teacher remains in one specially equipped location and serves students with visual impairments for part of the school day.

The amount of time the itinerant teacher-consultant or resource room teacher spends with a visually impaired student who attends general education classes varies considerably. Some students may be seen every day because they require a great deal of specialized assistance. Others may be seen weekly, monthly, or even less frequently because they can function well in the general education class with less support.

For inclusion to succeed, a child with visual impairments needs a skilled and supportive general education classroom teacher. This was underscored by a study that asked adolescents to assess the impact of visual impairments on their lives (Rosenblum, 2000). All 10 students in the study attended public school general education classrooms for at least 50% of the school day. Several students reported that a general education teacher made it difficult for them to use disability-specific skills such as braille or computerized speech output in the classroom. ("It took him about a quarter to get the stuff [tests and worksheets] to the braillist in the first place" [p. 439].) Other participants reported that insensitive teachers caused them to feel humiliation and frustration about having a visual impairment. ("The science teacher wanted me to identify rocks by a visual method and I told her I can't. She goes, 'Well, you're going to have to if you want to get a good grade'" [p. 439].) Several other participants reported that general education teachers treated them like younger children. ("The teachers talk to me differently like I'm more of a 6 year old rather than a 13 year old" [p. 43].)

Patrick is getting along fine in the general education classroom—thanks to the instructional adaptations jointly planned by his itinerant vision specialist and his classroom teacher.

Importance of general education classroom teacher

Council for Exceptional Children

Content Standards for Beginning Teachers—VI: Attitudes and actions of teachers that affect the behaviors of individuals with VI (VI3K3).

Residential Schools

About 6% of school-age children with visual impairments attend residential schools (U.S. Department of Education, 2007). Residential schools continue to meet the needs of a sizable number of children with visual impairments. The current population of residential schools consists largely of children with visual impairments with additional disabilities, such as mental retardation, hearing impairment, behavioral disorders, and cerebral palsy. (See Chapter 12 for information on children with multiple disabilities, including those who are deaf-blind.) Some parents cannot care for their children adequately at home; others prefer the greater concentration of specialized personnel, facilities, and services that a residential school usually offers.

Parents and educators who support residential schools for children with visual impairments frequently point to the leadership that such schools have provided over a long period and their range of services. These supporters argue that a residential school can be

Residential schools

Council for Exceptional Children

Content Standards for Beginning Teachers—VI: Historical foundations of education of individuals with VI (VI1K2) (also VI1K6).

I Made It Myself, and It's Good!

For special education to contribute to meaningful lifestyle changes for students, it must help them gain functional skills for postschool environments. Being able to prepare one's own food is a critical skill for independent living. Steve, Lisa, and Carl were 17 to 21 years old and enrolled in a class for students with multiple disabilities at a residential school for the blind. They were living in an on-campus apartment used to teach daily living skills. Teachers had made several unsuccessful attempts to teach basic cooking skills to the three. None possessed any functional vision or braille skills, and their IQ scores ranged from 64 to 72 on the Perkins Binet Test of Intelligence for the Blind.

To learn new skills, especially those involving long chains of responses such as following the steps of a recipe, students like Steve, Lisa, and Carl require intensive instruction over many trials. And once they have learned a new skill, it may not generalize to other settings and situations or be maintained over time. The challenge was to discover a method for teaching cooking skills that would be effective initially but also would enable the students to prepare recipes for which they had not received instruction and that resulted in long-term maintenance of their new skills.

A "WALKMAN COOKBOOK"

Because Steve, Lisa, and Carl were blind, it was not possible to use picture cookbooks or color-coded recipes, which have been used successfully with learners with intellectual and other disabilities (e.g., Book, Paul, Gwalla-Ogisi, & Test, 1990). Instead, the students used tape-recorded recipes. Each student wore a cooking apron with two pockets. One pocket at the waist held a small tape recorder; the second pocket, located at the chest, held a switch that the students pushed to turn the tape player on and off. Each step from the task-analyzed recipes was prerecorded in sequence on a cassette tape (e.g., "Open the bag of cake mix by tearing it at the tab."). A beep signaled the end of each direction.

PERFORMANCE MEASURES

The number of recipe steps each student independently completed was measured during preinstruction (baseline), instruction, and maintenance phases. To assess generalization, the instructors conducted probes on two classes of recipes on which the students received no training. Simple generalization recipes could be prepared with the same set of cooking skills learned in a related trained item. Complex generalization recipes required a combination of skills learned in two different trained recipes. Figure A shows the relationship

A cook who cannot see may learn to pour and measure the ingredients by placing her fingers in the bowl.

between the trained recipes and the two types of recipes used to assess generalization. As a measure of social validity, each trial was also scored as to whether the food prepared was edible.

BASELINE

To objectively assess whether learning has occurred, student performance must be measured before instruction begins. The first baseline trial was conducted without the tape-recorded recipes to determine which food preparation steps, if any, each student could already perform without any assistance or adaptive equipment. It was then necessary to find out whether the students could successfully prepare any of the recipes if they were simply given the tape-recorded instructions. After being shown how to operate the tape recorder to play back the instructions, each student was asked to prepare each recipe but was given no other prompts, assistance, or feedback.

FIGURE A

Relationships between trained recipes and two classes of untrained recipes used to assess generalization of learning

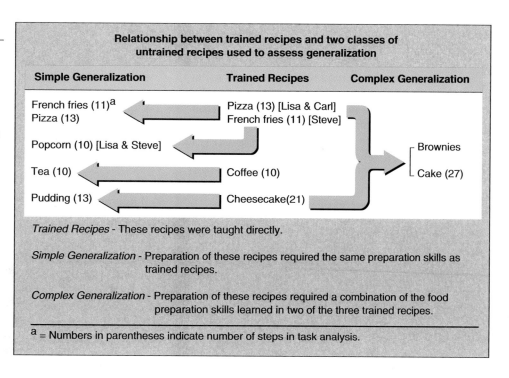

Relationship between trained recipes and two classes of untrained recipes used to assess generalization

Simple Generalization	Trained Recipes	Complex Generalization
French fries (11)[a] Pizza (13)	Pizza (13) [Lisa & Carl] French fries (11) [Steve]	
Popcorn (10) [Lisa & Steve]		Brownies
Tea (10)	Coffee (10)	Cake (27)
Pudding (13)	Cheesecake(21)	

Trained Recipes - These recipes were taught directly.

Simple Generalization - Preparation of these recipes required the same preparation skills as trained recipes.

Complex Generalization - Preparation of these recipes required a combination of the food preparation skills learned in two of the three trained recipes.

[a] = Numbers in parentheses indicate number of steps in task analysis.

INSTRUCTION

Students were told that the taped recipes explained exactly what to do and where to find the food items and utensils. They practiced using the remote switch to control the rate of instructions by stopping the tape each time they heard a beep. Training for each step of the task analysis consisted of a three-component least-to-most prompt hierarchy (verbal, physical, and hand-over-hand guidance) following errors and verbal praise for correct responses. Training on a recipe continued until a student correctly performed all steps on two consecutive trials over two sessions.

RESULTS

Lisa, Carl, and Steve needed a total of 12, 19, and 35 instructional trials, respectively, to learn the three different recipes. (Steve required a greater number of trials to master the coffee and cheesecake recipes due to repeated spills when pouring liquids. Ms. Trask-Tyler solved this problem by teaching Steve to use his fingers to feel where and how much liquid he was pouring.) Additionally, after mastering the trained recipes, each student was able to prepare both the simple and the complex generalization recipes with the tape recorder, even though they had not received any instruction on those recipes.

The ultimate evaluation of cooking skills instruction is whether or not the food can be eaten: Does it taste good? A mistake on any one of several crucial steps in the 27-step task analysis for making microwave cake (e.g., not stirring the egg into the batter) would result in a cake no one would want to eat. Before training, none of Steve's 13 attempts to make any of the trained recipes could be eaten, whereas all 6 of his posttraining attempts were edible. Before training, Steve was unsuccessful in all 20 of his attempts to

make the simple generalization recipes and on each of 4 attempts to prepare the complex generalization recipes. After learning how to make the related recipes, he was able to follow tape-recorded recipes to successfully prepare the recipes for which he had received no direct training: on 82% of the trials (9 of 11) with the simple generalization recipes and on all 3 trials with the complex generalization recipes. In two follow-up probes conducted 6 weeks and 4 months after the study ended, Steve was still able to prepare all of the recipes successfully. Lisa and Carl showed similar gains in their ability to prepare food for themselves.

INDIVIDUALIZED, NORMALIZED, AND SELF-DETERMINED

Self-operated audio prompting systems (SOAPS), such as the one used by Steve, Lisa, and Carl, offer several advantages (also see Davis, Brady, Williams, & Burta, 1992; Grossi, 1998; Lancioni, O'Reilly, & Oliva, 2001; Mechling, 2007; Post, Storey, & Karabin, 2002). First, the prerecorded instructions or prompts can be individualized. For example:

- Tape-recorded instructions can be as precise or general as necessary, depending on known or probable tasks and environments.
- Vocabulary can be modified, pacing of instructions speeded up or slowed down, and instructions for particularly difficult steps repeated or given in more detail.
- Students might use their own voice to record special prompts or reminders relevant to certain steps of the task (e.g., "Have I checked for spills?").
- Verbal praise and encouragement from teachers, parents, friends, or the student himself could also be included in the instructions.

Second, individuals with disabilities are currently using a variety of assistive devices to increase their independence in domestic, community, and employment settings. The learner in natural settings, however, may not use some assistive devices. A student in a crowded restaurant, for example, may hesitate to remove a laminated ordering card from her pocket or purse because it marks her as different. By contrast, the popularity of Walkman-like personal stereos and iPods enables the wearer of audio headphones to listen to self-delivered prompts in a private, unobtrusive, and normalized manner that does not impose on or bother others.

Third, the self-operated feature of the system puts the student in control of the environment, thereby increasing the probability of independent functioning and level of self-determination. As Carl remarked when sharing with his girlfriend the microwave cake he had just made, "I made it myself, and it's good!"

How to Get Started

If the SOAPS will be used to help a student complete multistep activities (e.g., making macaroni and cheese):

1. Create a task analysis of the activity.
2. Write a script of instructions for each step of the task analysis using language that the student understands.
3. Record the script, embedding a standard phrase or distinct tone between instructions to cue the student when to stop and start the playback device.

If the SOAPS will be used to help a student stay on task and be productive during an ongoing activity (e.g., washing dishes):

1. Write a variety of simple statements that are likely to function for the student as prompts to keep working, encouragement and praise, and/or cues to self-evaluate her performance.
2. Record the prompts, praise statement, and/or cues to self-evaluate in a random sequence at irregular intervals.
3. If listening to music would be appropriate for the student while doing the activity, consider embedding the instructions or prompts within a recording of the student's favorite singer or band.

For all SOAPS:

1. If necessary, teach the student how to operate the portable audio device before introducing the prerecorded instructions or prompts.
2. Observe and monitor the student's initial use of the SOAPS to determine if the length and complexity of the steps/instructions are appropriate and efficient.
3. Ask the student if any changes in the instructions or prompts would make the system more effective or enjoyable to use.

Source: Description of the teaching program from Springer and the *Journal of Behavioral Education, 4*(3), 2005, pp. 283–311, "Teaching young adults with developmental disabilities and visual impairments to use tape-recorded recipes: Acquisition, generalization, and maintenance of cooking skills" by Sandra A. Trask-Tyler, T. A. Grossi, & W. L. Heward. Copyright © 2005. Reprinted with kind permission from Springer Science and Business Media.

 To learn more about the functional skills discussed here, go to the Building Teaching Skills section in Chapter 10 of MyEducationLab and complete the activities.

the least restrictive environment for some students with visual impairments and multiple disabilities. Among the advantages cited were specialized curriculum and equipment, participation in extracurricular activities, individualized instruction, small classes, and improved self-esteem.

Like placement at any other point in the continuum of educational settings, placement in a residential school should not be regarded as permanent. Many children with visual impairments move from residential schools into public schools (or vice versa) as their needs change. Some students in residential schools attend nearby public schools for part of the school day. Most residential schools encourage parent involvement and have recreational programs that bring students with visual impairments into contact with sighted peers. Independent living skills and vocational training are important parts of the program at virtually all residential schools.

In several states, public schools cooperate closely with residential school programs that serve children with visual impairments. A residential school for students who are blind has an opportunity to work closely with consumers, parents, professionals, and funding agencies in developing a wide array of community-based services. Cooperative working relationships and creative short- and long-term planning efforts have the potential to generate positive and reality-based services that respond to present-day needs within the context of community integration. Residential schools—primarily because of the expertise of their staff but also because of their location, centralization of resources, and availability of facilities—have the potential to become responsive resource centers on regional and state levels.

Residential schools have long played an important role in training teachers of children with visual impairments on both a preservice and in-service basis. The residential school is usually well equipped to serve as a resource center for instructional materials and as a place where students with visual impairments can receive specialized evaluation services. An increasing number of residential schools now offer short-term training to students with visual impairments who attend regular public schools. One example is a summer workshop emphasizing braille, mobility, and vocational training.

Can a Neighborhood School Provide the Needed Specialized Services?

Some vision professionals resist noncategorical special education programs for students with visual impairments. It is unrealistic, they argue, to expect general education teachers or teachers trained in other areas of special education to be competent in specialized techniques such as braille, O&M, and visual efficiency. The Council for Exceptional Children's Division of Visual Impairments (DVI) recognizes that a student's need for instruction in the expanded core curriculum may require different educational placements at various times during his or her school years (Huebner, Garber, & Wormsley, 2006). (See Current Issues and Future Trends, "A Paper on the Inclusion of Students With Visual Impairments," by the American Foundation for the Blind, following.)

Although financial restrictions may require some public school and residential school programs for children with visual impairments to close down or consolidate with programs for children with other disabilities, strong support exists for the continuation of highly specialized services. It is likely that both public school and state-run residential programs for children with visual impairments will continue to operate well into the future, occasionally challenging each other for the privilege of serving the relatively small number of available students. The results of this competition may well prove favorable if both types of programs are encouraged to improve the quality of their educational services.

Inclusion

 Content Standards for Beginning Teachers—VI: Issues and trends in special education and the field of VI (VI1K6).

Fighting Against Discrimination and for Self-Determination

Like other groups of individuals with disabilities, people with visual impairments are becoming increasingly aware of their rights as citizens and consumers. They are fighting discrimination based on their disabilities (Koestler, 2004; Lunsford, 2006) and experiencing the benefits of self-determination (Agran, Hong, & Blankenship, 2007). Many people—even some special educators who work with students with visual impairments—underestimate their students' capacities and deny them a full range of occupational and personal choices. The future should bring a shift away from some of the vocations and settings in which people with visual impairments have traditionally worked (e.g., piano tuning, rehabilitation counseling) in favor of a more varied and rewarding range of employment opportunities.

> Some years ago, a reporter asked a prominent blind woman, "What is it that blind people would want from society?" The woman replied, "The opportunity to be equal and the right to be different."
>
> What did this woman mean by two remarks that seem diametrically opposite? Perhaps she meant that print and braille are equal, but very different; that the need for independent travel is similar for sighted and blind persons, but the skills are learned very differently by blind people; and that concepts and learning that occur for sighted people in a natural, spontaneous manner require different learning experiences for blind persons. Perhaps she was emphasizing that blind persons should have the opportunity to learn the same knowledge and skills as sighted people, but that their manner of learning will be different. (Hatlen, 1996)

CURRENT ISSUES AND FUTURE TRENDS

A PAPER ON THE INCLUSION OF STUDENTS WITH VISUAL IMPAIRMENTS

AMERICAN FOUNDATION FOR THE BLIND

"Inclusion," "full inclusion" and "inclusive education" are terms which recently have been narrowly defined by some (primarily educators of students with severe disabilities) to espouse the philosophy that ALL students with disabilities, regardless of the nature or the severity of their disability, receive their TOTAL education within the general education environment. This philosophy is based on the relatively recent placement of a limited number of students with severe disabilities in general education classrooms. Research conducted by proponents of this philosophy lacks empirical evidence that this practice results in programs which are better able to prepare ALL students with visual impairments to be more fully included in society than the current practice, required by federal law, of providing a full range of program options.

Educators and parents of students with visual impairments have pioneered special education and inclusive program options for over 164 years. It is significant that the field of education of visually impaired students was the first to develop a range of special education program options, beginning with specialized schools in 1829 and extending to inclusive (including "full inclusion") public school program options since 1900.

Experience and research clearly support the following three position statements outlining the essential elements which must be in place in order to provide an appropriate education in the least restrictive environment for students with visual impairments.

I. Students with visual impairments have unique educational needs which are most effectively met using a team approach of professionals, parents and students. In order to meet their unique needs, students must have specialized services, books and materials in appropriate media (including braille), as well as specialized equipment and technology to assure equal access to the core and specialized curricula, and to enable them to most effectively compete with their peers in school and ultimately in society.

The unique educational needs of all students with visual impairments cannot be met in a single environment, even with unlimited funding. It is critical that a team approach be used in identifying and meeting these needs and that the team must include staff who have specific expertise in educating students with visual impairments. The proposal that ALL of the needs of ALL students can be met in one environment, the regular classroom, violates the spirit as well as the letter of the law—IDEA.

II. There must be a full range of program options and support services so that the Individualized Education Program (IEP) team can select the most appropriate placement in the least restrictive environment for each individual student with a visual impairment. The right of every student with a visual impairment to an appropriate placement in the least restrictive environment, selected by the IEP team from a full range of program options and based upon each student's needs, is nothing more or less than is mandated by federal law.

III. There must be adequate personnel preparation programs to train staff to provide specialized services that address the unique academic and non-academic curriculum needs of students with visual impairments. There must also be ongoing specialized personnel development opportunities for all staff working with these students as well as specialized parent education.

Students with visual impairments have the right to an appropriate education that is guided by knowledgeable specialists who work collaboratively with parents, the student and other education team members. Access to training on an ongoing basis is essential for all team members, especially parents who provide the necessary continuity and support in their child's education.

PLACEMENT DOES NOT NECESSARILY PROVIDE ACCESS

Providing equal access to all individuals with disabilities is the key element of the Rehabilitation Act of 1973 and the Americans with Disabilities Act of 1992. Access involves much more than providing ramps. Access is also the key element of inclusion, which involves much more than placement in a particular setting. The relationship of access and inclusion may not be obvious to individuals who are not familiar with the educational and social impact of a vision loss. Placing a student with a visual impairment in a regular classroom does not, necessarily, provide access and the student is not, necessarily, included. A student with a visual impairment, who does not have access to social and physical information because of the visual impairment, is not included, regardless of the physical setting. Students with visual impairments will not be included unless their unique educational needs for access are addressed by specially trained personnel in appropriate environments and unless these students are provided with equal access to core and specialized curricula through appropriate specialized books, materials and equipment.

Conclusion: Students with visual impairments need an educational system that meets the individual needs of ALL students, fosters independence, and is measured by the success of each individual in the school and community. Vision is fundamental to the learning process and is the primary basis upon which most traditional education strategies are based. Students who are visually impaired are most likely to succeed in educational systems where appropriate instruction and services are provided in a full array of program options by qualified staff to address each student's unique educational needs, as required by Public Law 101-476, The Individuals with Disabilities Education Act (IDEA).

What Do You Think?

1. Should the least restrictive environment (LRE) for students with visual impairments be defined differently from the LRE for students with other disabilities? Why or why not?

2. Can a residential school be the LRE for a student who has been blind from birth? for a child who lost her sight in elementary school? Why or why not?

3. Do you think any single educational setting can serve as an LRE for a student with visual impairment? Why or why not?

TIPS for Beginning Teachers

SUPPORTING STUDENTS WITH VISUAL IMPAIRMENTS IN THE GENERAL EDUCATION CLASSROOM
by Jeanna Mora Dowse

Although each student with a visual impairment is unique and requires a specially designed set of accommodations and modifications to meet her own academic and social goals, teachers should follow some fundamental guidelines when working with any student who relies on nonvisual senses for communication and learning. Using the following tips and techniques will increase the effectiveness of your communication with students who have visual impairments and encourage and promote their confidence and independence.

COMMUNICATE WITH CLARITY AND RESPECT

- Always state the name of the student you are speaking to in the classroom. The student with a visual impairment will not notice eye contact.

- Indefinite pronouns such as "this," "that," and "there" can be confusing to students with visual impairments. It is better to name specific items, events, or people.

- Individuals with visual impairments frequently make idiomatic references to sight, and it is okay for their teachers and peers to do so also: e.g., "Do you see what I mean?" or "Let's take a look at this next sentence."

- Always give a verbal warning when you are about to hand something to a student with visual impairments. This avoids unnecessary surprises and helps the student respond efficiently.

- Include specific spatial references when giving your student directions. For example, telling the student, "The book is on your left," or "The desk is 10 feet in front of you," is better than saying, "It's over there," or "It's near the table."

- When writing or drawing on the board, describe your actions verbally in a manner useful for all students in the class. Be sure not to talk down to the student with a visual impairment.

- Introduce yourself by name when meeting your student outside the classroom. Do not assume that he will recognize your voice, and do not ask, "Guess who this is?"

- When you are about to leave the student's vicinity, tell him that you are going.

- When you need to physically show your student how to do something, use the *hand-under-hand* technique. Have the student place her hands on top of yours so she can feel the movement of your hands. This is usually more effective than placing your hands over the student's hands.

EXPECT AND ENABLE INDEPENDENCE

- If students are expected to perform jobs or responsibilities in your classroom, be sure also to assign a meaningful job to your students with visual impairments.

- Allow students with visual impairments time to obtain and put away materials. If a student had to use glue and scissors for an activity, make sure she returns those items to their proper places. Although it is often much easier to get and put away materials for students with visual impairments, it is critical that they learn to become self-sufficient and pick up after themselves.
- Peers are often the most effective and efficient teachers of social skills. Cooperative groups are a great way for students with visual impairments to learn important social skills.
- Always make safety a priority, but do not overprotect students with visual impairments. Hands-on experiences are the best way for a student to learn new concepts.
- Provide real-life experiences whenever possible. When on a school field trip, give the student with a visual impairment sufficient time to explore her environment.

KEY TERMS AND CONCEPTS

accommodation, p. 377
binocular vision, p. 376
braille, p. 382
cataract, p. 377
cortical visual impairment (CVI), p. 378
field of vision, p. 372
functional vision, p. 384
glaucoma, p. 377
hyperopia, p. 377
legally blind, p. 371
low vision, p. 373
mobility, p. 389

myopia, p. 377
nystagmus, p. 378
ocular motility, p. 376
orientation, p. 389
orientation and mobility (O&M), p. 389
partially sighted, p. 372
refraction, p. 377
sighted-guide technique, p. 392
strabismus, p. 378
tunnel vision, p. 372
visual acuity, p. 371

SUMMARY

Definitions

- Legal blindness is defined as visual acuity of 20/200 or less in the better eye after correction with glasses or contact lenses or a restricted field of vision of 20 degrees or less.
- An educational definition classifies students with visual impairments based on the extent to which they use vision and/or auditory/tactile means for learning.
- A student who is totally blind receives no useful information through the sense of vision and must use tactile, auditory, and other nonvisual senses for all learning.
- A child who is functionally blind has so little vision that she learns primarily through the auditory and tactile senses; however, she may be able to use her limited vision to supplement the information received from the other senses.
- A child with low vision uses vision as a primary means of learning.
- The age at onset of a visual impairment affects a child's educational and emotional needs.

Characteristics

- Children with severe visual impairments do not benefit from incidental learning that normally sighted children obtain in everyday experiences and interactions with the environment.
- Visual impairment often leads to delays or deficits in motor development.
- Some students with visual impairments experience social isolation and difficulties in social interactions due to limited common experiences with sighted peers; inability to see

and use eye contact, facial expressions, and gestures during conversations; and/or stereotypic behaviors.

- The behavior and attitudes of sighted persons can be unnecessary barriers to the social participation of individuals with visual impairments.

Prevalence

- Visual impairment is a low-incidence disability affecting fewer than 2 of every 1,000 children in the school-age population. About one half of all students with visual impairments have additional disabilities.

Types and Causes of Visual Impairment

- The eye collects light reflected from objects and focuses the objects' image on the retina. The optic nerve transmits the image to the visual cortex of the brain. Difficulty with any part of this process can cause vision problems.
- Refractive errors mean that the size and shape of the eye prevent the light rays from focusing clearly on the retina.
- Structural impairments are visual impairments caused by poor development of, damage to, or malfunction of one or more parts of the eye's optical or muscular systems.
- Cortical visual impairment (CVI) refers to decreased vision or blindness due to damage to or malfunction of the parts of the brain that interpret visual information.

Educational Approaches

- Braille—a tactile system of reading and writing in which letters, words, numbers, and other systems are made from arrangements of embossed six-dot cells—is the primary means of literacy for students who are blind.
- Students who are blind may also use special equipment to access standard print through touch, reading machines, and prerecorded materials.
- Children with low vision should be taught to use visual efficiency or functioning.
- Students with low vision use three basic methods for reading print: magnification, optical devices, and large print.
- Students who are blind or have severe visual impairments need instruction in orientation (knowing where they are, where they are going, and how to get there) and mobility (moving safely and efficiently from one point to another).
- Systematic development of listening skills is an important component of the educational program of every child with visual impairments.
- The curriculum for students with visual impairments should also include systematic instruction in functional living skills such as cooking, personal hygiene and grooming, shopping, financial management, transportation, and recreational activities.

Educational Placement Alternatives

- Two of three children with visual impairments spend at least part of each school day in general education classes with sighted peers.
- In many districts, a specially trained itinerant vision specialist provides support for students with visual impairments and their general education classroom teachers.
- Some large school districts have resource room programs for students with visual impairments.
- About 6% of children with visual impairments, especially those with other disabilities, attend residential schools.
- Career opportunities will likely expand as individuals with visual impairments become more self-determined.

Now go to MyEducationLab at www.myeducationlab.com and take the pretest to assess your initial comprehension of chapter content. Once you have taken the pretest, use your individualized Study Plan for Chapter 10 to enhance your understanding of the concepts discussed in the chapter. Finally, take the posttest to assess your comprehension of Chapter 10 content.

11

Physical Disabilities, Health Impairments, and ADHD

- How might the effects of an acute health condition on a student's classroom participation and educational progress differ from those of a chronic condition?
- Why is the prevalence of chronic medical conditions in children much higher than the number of students receiving special education under the disability categories in the Individuals with Disabilities Education Act (IDEA) of orthopedic impairments and other health impairments?
- What does a classroom teacher need to know about physical disabilities and health impairments in children?
- Why do you think attention-deficit/hyperactivity disorder (ADHD) is not included as a separate disability category in IDEA?
- How might the visibility of a physical disability or health impairment affect a child's self-perception, social development, and level of independence across different environments?
- What are some of the problems that members of transdisciplinary teams for students with physical disabilities and multiple health needs must guard against?
- Of the many ways that the physical environment, social environment, and instruction can be modified to support the inclusion of students with physical disabilities, health impairments, and ADHD, which are most important?

FEATURED TEACHER

MARY KATE RYAN-GRIFFITH
A. Mario Loiederman Middle School • Silver Spring, Maryland

Mary Kate Ryan-Griffith

Education—Teaching Credentials—Experience

- B.S., special education/ elementary education, Peabody College for Teachers, Vanderbilt University, 1980
- M.A., education of the hearing impaired, Gallaudet University, 1984
- Maryland professional certificates: special education, K–12; hearing impaired, K–12; and elementary education, K–6
- 4 years as a fourth-grade teacher; 16 years as a special educator

Current Teaching Position and Students For the first 6 years of my special education career, I was the resource teacher for the entire elementary school, with a caseload of up to 50 students. Our model for service delivery of special education has changed dramatically in the past several years. We have moved from the traditional model of separate programs with pull-out resource services to a departmentalized approach, assigning each special educator in the building to a grade level. The special educator serves all children with special needs on her grade level in an inclusion model, with minimal pull-out for specialized groups or differentiation. I am currently assigned to the fourth grade. I co-teach in three classrooms and have two pull-out reading groups. I currently work with 16 students with a wide range of disabilities: physical challenges

405

caused by cerebral palsy and bone defects, learning disabilities, attention-deficit/hyperactivity disorder (ADHD), emotionally disabled, and one child who is hard of hearing.

Adaptations and Teaching Strategies These children can function in the general education classroom, but they require support. These supports range from academic to physical. Some children in wheelchairs require desks with a cut-out that they can get in and under. Tables and desks may need to be raised, and special seats in bathrooms are sometimes necessary. Walkers, standards, and leg braces are everyday pieces of equipment. If children's hands are not fully functional, special pencil grips and eating utensils are a great help.

The computer has been the greatest advance for improving academic abilities. For example, Bridget's cerebral palsy causes spasticity in her hands, which makes writing or standard keyboarding very difficult. I work therefore with the occupational therapist to create *overlays*—pages fitted to a special type of keyboard that run on a special software program. Each overlay is created with specific types of information about a subject, such as different kinds of maps or generic sentence parts relating to a book we are reading. By touching the keyboard, Bridget can independently create sentences related to the subject. She really enjoys her schoolwork because she is relieved of the drudgery of writing or typing and creates it herself. My students use a variety of typing/voice programs. Tim has learning disabilities and severe motoric impact in his hands. His writing is basically illegible; so he types on a program that gives him choices for words, then voices his paragraph back to him. In this way he can work independently and monitor his own spelling and grammar. We also use programs that create graphic organizers for children. This helps to improve comprehension, especially when students are writing a report. I also use low-tech devices and strategies to aid reading and writing such as raised-line paper and multicolored paper; a ruler, index cards, or paper to maintain students' place; or, for the extremely distracted, a cut-out window in a long page so they see only one line at a time.

In the classroom I may read to children from books and tests and have them dictate their responses. Some children use this as a crutch, so I create transitions: First, I write everything, then the student writes a line, then a paragraph, and then she writes it all herself with support for spelling and mechanics. Sometimes children need me to write for them because they lack confidence, so building a positive attitude is paramount to success.

Advice to Someone Considering a Career in Special Education Attitude is everything. I broke my neck in a car accident one week after completing student teaching for my master's degree from Gallaudet University. Clinically, I am an *incomplete quadriplegic* because I only traumatized my spinal cord, not severed it. I am paralyzed from the chest down and have some slight impairment of the arms and hands. I am very independent. I drive myself to work using hand controls, and my van has a special seat and a lift. My husband and I adapted our house with a ramp, a larger bathroom, and a tub seat for showers. I frequently use a reacher (a long metal rod with a clamp at the end) to get things that are out of my reach; but otherwise, I don't require much special equipment. I tend to use things in the environment to help me. Anything that can extend my reach is subject to use, whether a spatula in the kitchen or a ruler in school. I am relatively healthy, though I do take daily medication for spasticity. I can punch out any bully when my legs go into spasm.

I have used a wheelchair for 23 years. For years after my accident I went through all the stages of grief, from denial to acceptance. Much like the death of a loved one, I grieved over the loss of my abilities to dance, run, and do other ambulatory activities; and that loss still pains me occasionally, even now. However, I have always believed that where a door closes, someone opens a window and that human beings are the most adaptable creatures on earth. I have learned to perform cherished activities from my chair. I get a kick out of surprised looks when I take to the dance floor.

I have always taught from a chair. In my job I work with both parents and children who are dealing with challenges. Some parents have children who were born with challenges and medically diagnosed at birth. Others have children who qualified for special education after encountering academic difficulties. At some point, all of these parents must go through the grief process. They need to grieve the loss of the "perfect child," get through the guilt that they did something that made their child that way, and in some cases get past denying that there is a problem. It is a process in which I can relate with parents and help them understand their child on another level. For example, even though I'm in a wheelchair and their child is learning disabled, the need to do things differently and the understanding that it is a lifelong process are the same. It is something that special education teachers need to be sensitive to. This is an enormous realization for the parents, who have to deal with not only the disability but also the meetings, the paperwork, the everyday needs of the child, and the question "where do we go from here?"

Children experience the same grief process, but more on a level of "I can't do what others are doing." I try to relate my experience of having to do things differently to whatever my students are concerned with at the time. I explain that having to do things differently doesn't mean they are stupid. Everyone has his own special way of learning, and my job is to find out how children learn so I can teach them better. For older kids I explain their test scores and what an individualized education program (IEP) means. I bring them into their challenges so that they own them. Getting vested in and feeling positive about their progress is extremely important. Another important way I get through to kids is by talking about myself. When I encounter a new group of students, I always begin by telling about myself, bringing them into my challenges, explaining why I'm in a wheelchair, and letting them ask questions. This way they also start to talk about themselves, and we can relate our experiences with doing things differently and feelings about our challenges. I also talk to the general education classes so they can become more sensitive to the challenges of others. In this way they can start to see people, not chairs. Then we all go out and take a ride on my lift.

Children with physical disabilities and health impairments are an extremely varied population. Describing them with a single set of characteristics would be impossible, even if we used very general terms. Their physical disabilities may be mild, moderate, or severe. Some children with special health care needs are extremely restricted in their activities and intellectual functioning; others have no major limitations on what they can do and learn. Some appear no different than the typical child; others have highly visible impairments or health conditions. Children may have a single impairment or a combination of disabilities. They may have lived with the physical disability or health impairment since birth or have acquired it recently. Some children must use special assistive devices that call attention to their disability; others display behaviors they cannot control. Some disabilities are always present; others occur only from time to time. Over an extended period, the degree of disability may increase, decrease, or remain about the same.

As you can see, the students whose special education needs we consider in this chapter have a great many individual differences. Natalie, for example, has undergone long periods of hospitalization and finds it difficult to keep up with her academic work. Gary takes medication that controls his seizures most of the time, but it also tends to make him drowsy in class. Brian, who uses a wheelchair for mobility, is disappointed that he cannot compete with his classmates in football, baseball, and track. Yet he participates fully in all other aspects of his high school program with no special modifications other than the addition of a few ramps in the building and a newly accessible washroom. Most of Bryan's teachers and friends, in fact, do not think of him as needing special education at all. Janella becomes tired easily and attends school for only 3 hours per day. Ken does his schoolwork in a specially designed chair that helps him sit more comfortably in the classroom.

An appropriate education for a child with physical or health impairments may require modifications of the classroom environment; assistive technology for communication, access, mobility; related services such as physical or occupational therapy; and special health care services in the classroom. It is important for teachers (and often for other students as well) to understand how a particular condition may affect a child's learning, development, and behavior. Because some physical impairments and health conditions may result in occasional complications or emergencies in the classroom, it is also important for teachers to know how to manage such situations effectively and when and how to seek help. Although general statements about some physical disabilities and health conditions are appropriate, a host of variables determine the effects on the child and his educational needs. These variables include the degree and severity of the impairment, age of onset, and environmental context. Thus, basic information and suggested guidelines shape the basic approach in this chapter.

After reading this chapter, complete the pretest for Chapter 11 on MyEducationLab to assess your initial understanding of chapter content.

DEFINITIONS OF PHYSICAL DISABILITIES AND HEALTH IMPAIRMENTS

Children with physical disabilities and health conditions who require special education are served under two of the Individuals with Disabilities Education Act (IDEA) disability categories: orthopedic impairments and other health impairments. According to IDEA, a *severe orthopedic impairment*

Definitions of orthopedic impairments and other health impairments

Council for Exceptional Children
Content Standards for Beginning Teachers—P&HD: Issues and educational definitions of individuals with P&HD (PH1K1).

> adversely affects a child's educational performance. The term includes impairments caused by a congenital anomaly (e.g., clubfoot, absence of some member, etc.), impairments caused by disease (e.g., poliomyelitis, bone tuberculosis), and impairments from other causes (e.g., cerebral palsy, amputations, and fractures or burns that cause contractures). (20 U.S.C. §1401 [2004], 20 C.F.R. §300.8[c][8])

Although IDEA uses the term *orthopedic impairments,* children with physical disabilities may have orthopedic impairments or neuromotor impairments. An **orthopedic impairment** involves the skeletal system—bones, joints, limbs, and associated muscles. A **neuromotor impairment** involves the central nervous system, affecting the ability to move, use, feel, or control certain parts of the body. Although orthopedic and neurological impairments are two distinct and separate types of disabilities, they may cause similar limitations in movement. Many of the same educational, therapeutic, and recreational activities are likely to be appropriate for students with orthopedic and neurological impairments (Best, Heller, & Bigge, 2005). And a close relationship exists between the two types: for example, a child who cannot move his legs because of damage to the central nervous system (neuromotor impairment) may also develop disorders in the bones and muscles of the legs (orthopedic impairment), especially if he does not receive proper therapy and equipment.

> **Other health impairment** means having limited strength, vitality, or alertness, including a heightened alertness to environmental stimuli, that results in limited alertness with respect to the educational environment, that—
>
> (i) Is due to chronic or acute health problems such as asthma, attention deficit disorder or attention deficit hyperactivity disorder, diabetes, epilepsy, a heart condition, hemophilia, lead poisoning, leukemia, nephritis, rheumatic fever, sickle cell anemia, and Tourette syndrome; and
>
> (ii) Adversely affects academic performance. (20 U.S.C. §1401 [2004], 20 C.F.R. §300.8[c][9])

Health impairments include diseases and special health conditions that affect a child's educational activities and performance such as cancer, diabetes, and cystic fibrosis. Children with attention-deficit/hyperactivity disorder (ADHD) are served under the other health impairments category of IDEA, with the reasoning that their condition results in a heightened alertness that adversely affects their educational performance. However, many children with ADHD who meet eligibility requirements for special education are served under other disability categories, most often emotional disturbance or learning disabilities. ADHD is discussed in detail later in this chapter.

Note the common clause in each definition: *that adversely affects a child's educational performance.* According to IDEA, a child is entitled to special education services if her educational performance is adversely affected by a physical disability or a health-related condition. Physical disabilities and health conditions may be congenital (a child is born with a missing limb) or acquired (a child without disabilities sustains a spinal cord injury at age 15). Not all students with physical disabilities and health conditions need special education. Most physical disabilities and health impairments that result in special education are **chronic conditions**—that is, they are long-lasting, most often permanent conditions (e.g., cerebral palsy is a permanent disability that will affect a child throughout his life). By contrast, an **acute condition,** while it may produce severe and debilitating symptoms, is of limited duration (e.g., a child who acquires pneumonia will experience symptoms, but the disease itself is not permanent). Some chronic physical disabilities and health conditions have flare-ups or episodes of acute symptoms (e.g., a child with cystic fibrosis may experience periods of acute respiratory difficulties).

Chronic and acute conditions

 Council for Exceptional Children

Content Standards for Beginning Teachers—P&HD: Medical terminology related to P&HD (PH2K1).

PREVALENCE

Studies of the number of children who have physical disabilities and health impairments have produced hugely diverse findings. A recent review of prevalence studies found estimates of chronic health conditions in childhood ranging from as low as 0.22% to as high as 44%, depending on the researchers' concepts and operationalizations (van der Lee, Mokkink, Grootenhuis, Heymans, & Offringa, 2007). In the middle of that range is Sexson and Dingle's (2001) estimate that chronic medical conditions affect up to 20% (approximately 12 million) school-age children in the United States. Whatever the actual number, researchers widely accept that the incidence of chronic health conditions has increased considerably in recent decades. In 1960, data showed that just 1.8% of American children and adolescents had a chronic health condition that limited their activities, compared to 7% in 2004 (Perrin, Bloom, & Gortmaker, 2007).

Clearly, a great many children's lives are affected by physical disabilities and health impairments. During the 2005–2006 school year, however, only 62,618 children between the ages of 6 and 21 received special education services under the disability category of orthopedic impairment compared with 557,121 children served under the category of other health impairments (U.S. Department of Education, 2007a). Together, these two disability categories represent 1% and 9.3% of all school-age children receiving special education services, respectively.

Two factors make the actual number of children with physical disabilities and health conditions much higher than the number of children receiving special education services under these two IDEA categories. First, numerous children have chronic health conditions or physical impairments that do not adversely affect their educational performance sufficiently to warrant special education (Hill, 1999). Second, because physical and health impairments often occur in combination with other disabilities, children may be counted under other categories, such as multiple disabilities, speech impairment, or mental retardation. For example, for the purpose of special education eligibility, a diagnosis of mental retardation usually takes precedence over a diagnosis of physical impairment.

TYPES AND CAUSES

Literally hundreds of physical impairments and health conditions can adversely affect children's educational performance. Here we address only those that are encountered most frequently in school-age children. For a more extensive discussion of the many physical impairments and chronic health conditions that may result in special education, see Batshaw, Pellegrino, and Roizen (2007); Best, Heller, and Bigge (2005); or Hill (1999).

Cerebral Palsy

Cerebral palsy—a disorder of voluntary movement and posture—is the most prevalent physical disability in school-age children. In some programs, half or more of the students considered to have physical or health impairments have cerebral palsy. Cerebral palsy is a permanent condition resulting from a lesion to the brain or an abnormality of brain growth. Many diseases can affect the developing brain and lead to cerebral palsy (Batshaw et al., 2007). Children with cerebral palsy experience disturbances of voluntary motor functions that may include paralysis, extreme weakness, lack of coordination, involuntary convulsions, and other motor disorders. They may have little or no control over their arms, legs, or speech, depending on the type and degree of impairment. The more severe forms of cerebral palsy are often diagnosed in the first few months of life. In many other cases, however, cerebral palsy is not detected until the child is 2 to 3 years old, when parents notice that their child is having difficulty crawling, balancing, or standing. The motor dysfunction usually does not get progressively worse as a child ages. Cerebral palsy can be treated but not cured; it is not a disease, not fatal, not contagious, and, in the great majority of cases, not inherited.

Between 23% and 44% of children with cerebral palsy have cognitive impairments, ranging from mild-to-severe intellectual disabilities (Odding, Roebroeck, & Stam, 2006). Sensory impairments are also common in children with cerebral palsy; 5% to 15% have hearing loss (Nechring & Steele, 1996), and 60% to 70% have impaired vision, particularly strabismus (Odding et al., 2006). It is important to note that no clear relationship exists between the degree of motor impairment and the degree of intellectual impairment (if any) in children with cerebral palsy (or other physical disabilities). A student with only mild motor impairment may experience severe developmental delays, whereas a student with severe motor impairments may be intellectually gifted (Willard-Holt, 1998).

The causes of cerebral palsy are varied and not clearly known (Pellegrino, 2007). It has most often been attributed to the occurrence of injuries, accidents, or illnesses that are *prenatal* (before birth), *perinatal* (at or near the time of birth), or *postnatal* (soon after birth) and that result in decreased oxygen to low-birth-weight newborns. Recent improvements in obstetrical delivery and neonatal care, however, have not decreased the incidence of cerebral palsy, which has remained steady during the past 20 years or so at about 2 to 2.5

Types and causes of physical disabilities and health impairments

 Content Standards for Beginning Teachers—P&HD: Etiology and characteristics of P&HD across the life span (PH2K2) (also PH2K1).

in every 1,000 live births (Odding et al., 2006). An additional 1,500 preschool children acquire cerebral palsy through illness or accidents (NICHCY, 2004). Factors most often associated with cerebral palsy are mental retardation of the mother, premature birth (gestational age of 32 weeks or less), low birth weight, and a delay of 5 minutes or more before the baby's first cry.

Because the location and extent of brain damage are so variable in individuals with cerebral palsy, a diagnosis of the condition is not descriptive of its effects. Cerebral palsy is classified in terms of the affected parts of the body and by the nature of its effects on muscle tone and movement (Best & Bigge, 2005). The term *plegia* (from the Greek "to strike") is often used in combination with a prefix indicating the location of limb involvement:

- *Monoplegia.* Only one limb (upper or lower) is affected.
- *Hemiplegia.* Two limbs on same side of the body are involved.
- *Triplegia.* Three limbs are affected.
- *Quadriplegia.* All four limbs (both arms and legs) are involved; movement of the trunk and face may also be impaired.
- *Paraplegia.* Only legs are impaired.
- *Diplegia.* Impairment primarily involves the legs, with less severe involvement of the arms.
- *Double hemiplegia.* Impairment primarily involves the arms, with less severe involvement of the legs.

Cerebral palsy is defined according to its effects on muscle tone (hypertonia or hypotonia) and quality of movement (athetosis or ataxia) (Pellegrino, 2007). Approximately 50% to 60% of all individuals with cerebral palsy have *spastic cerebral palsy,* which is characterized by tense, contracted muscles (**hypertonia**). Their movements may be jerky, exaggerated, and poorly coordinated. They may be unable to grasp objects with their fingers. When they try to control their movements, they may become even jerkier. If they can walk, they may use a scissors gait, standing on the toes with knees bent and pointed inward. Deformities of the spine, hip dislocation, and contractures of the hand, elbow, foot, and knee are common.

Athetosis occurs in about 20% of all cases of cerebral palsy. Children with *athetoid cerebral palsy* make large, irregular, twisting movements they cannot control. When they are at rest or asleep, little or no abnormal motion occurs. An effort to pick up a pencil, however, may result in wildly waving arms, facial grimaces, and extension of the tongue. These children may not be able to control the muscles of their lips, tongue, and throat and may drool. They may also seem to stumble and lurch awkwardly as they walk. At times their muscles may be tense and rigid; at other times, they may be loose and flaccid. Extreme difficulty in expressive oral language, mobility, and activities of daily living often accompanies this form of cerebral palsy.

Ataxia is noted as the primary type of involvement in only 1% to 10% of cases of cerebral palsy (Hill, 1999). Children with *ataxic cerebral palsy* have a poor sense of balance and hand use. They may appear to be dizzy while walking and may fall easily if not supported. Their movements tend to be jumpy and unsteady, with exaggerated motion patterns that often overshoot the intended objects. They seem to be constantly attempting to overcome the effect of gravity and stabilize their bodies.

Rigidity and *tremor* are additional but much less common types of cerebral palsy. Children with the rare rigidity type of cerebral palsy display extreme stiffness in the affected limbs; they may be fixed and immobile for long periods. Rhythmic, uncontrollable movements mark tremor cerebral palsy; the tremors may actually increase when the children attempt to control their actions.

Most infants born with cerebral palsy have **hypotonia,** or weak, floppy muscles, particularly in the neck and trunk. When hypotonia persists throughout the child's first year without being replaced with spasticity or athetoid involvement, the condition is called generalized hypotonia. Hypotonic children typically have low levels of motor activity, are slow to make balancing responses, and may not walk until 30 months of age (Bleck, 1987). Severely

Limbs affected by cerebral palsy

Content Standards for Beginning Teachers—P&HD: Medical terminology related to P&HD (PH2K1).

Hypertonia, athetosis, ataxia, and hypotonia

Content Standards for Beginning Teachers—P&HD: Medical terminology related to P&HD (PH2K1) (also PH2K2, PH3K1, CC2K1).

hypotonic children must use external support to achieve and maintain an upright position.

Because most children with cerebral palsy have diffuse brain damage, pure types of cerebral palsy are rare. Children may also be described as having *mixed cerebral palsy,* consisting of more than one of these types, particularly if their impairments are severe.

Because cerebral palsy is such a complex condition, it is most effectively managed through the cooperative involvement of physicians, teachers, physical therapists, occupational therapists, communication specialists, counselors, and others who work directly with children and families. Dormans and Pellegrino (1998) have compiled a detailed handbook to guide the education of children with cerebral palsy by interdisciplinary teams. Regular exercise and careful positioning in school settings help the child with cerebral palsy move as fully and comfortably as possible and prevent or minimize progressive damage to muscles and limbs. Most children with cerebral palsy can learn to walk, although many need to use wheelchairs, braces, and other assistive devices, particularly for moving around outside the home. Orthopedic surgery may increase a child's range of motion or obviate complications such as hip dislocations and permanent muscle contractions.

The Mobility Opportunities Via Education (MOVE) Curriculum is a systematic program for teaching walking and functional mobility skills to students with cerebral palsy and other severe physical disabilities. Some research demonstrates evidence of its effectiveness (Barnes & Whinnery, 2002; Whinnery & Barnes, 2002). The MOVE curriculum is a top-down, activity-based program in which a transdisciplinary team consisting of therapists, teachers, and parents assesses the child's current skills and designs an individualized program of systematic practice of mobility skills within the natural context of the child's typical daily activities. Physical supports are gradually faded: Children move from the Rifton Gait Trainer (Community Playthings, 1999), which provides total support for individuals just beginning to bear their weight and learning to take reciprocal steps, to adult assistance, to independent movement as their accomplishments increase. The motor impairment of children with cerebral palsy can make it frustrating, if not impossible, for them to play with toys. See Teaching & Learning, "Adapting Toys for Children With Cerebral Palsy."

Although cerebral palsy affects Joey's control over his movements, it has not dampened his enthusiasm and determination for learning.

Spina Bifida

Congenital malformations of the brain, spinal cord, or vertebrae are known as *neural tube defects.* The most common neural tube defect is **spina bifida,** a condition in which the vertebrae do not enclose the spinal cord. As a result, a portion of the spinal cord and the nerves that normally control muscles and feeling in the lower part of the body fail to develop normally. Of the three types of spina bifida, the mildest form is **spina bifida occulta,** in which only a few vertebrae are malformed, usually in the lower spine. The defect is usually not visible externally. It is estimated that up to 10% of the general population may have spina bifida occulta (Liptak, 2007). If the flexible casing (meninges) that surrounds the spinal cord bulges through an opening in the infant's back at birth, the condition is called **meningocele.** These two forms do not usually cause any loss of function for the child.

In **myelomeningocele**—the most common and most serious form of spina bifida—the spinal lining, spinal cord, and nerve roots all protrude. The protruding spinal cord and nerves are usually tucked back into the spinal column shortly after birth. This condition carries a high risk of paralysis and infection. In general, the higher the location of the lesion on the spine, the greater the effect on the body and its functioning. About 6 in 10,000 live births in the United States result in myelomeningocele; and it affects girls at a much higher rate than boys (Liptak, 2007).

Spina bifida and related terms

 Council for Exceptional Children — Content Standards for Beginning Teachers—P&HD: Medical terminology related to P&HD (PH2K1) (also PH2K2, PH3K1).

Clean intermittent catherization (CIC)

 Council for Exceptional Children — Content Standards for Beginning Teachers—P&HD: Specialized health care interventions for individuals with P&HD (PH5K2).

Adapting Toys for Children With Cerebral Palsy

Spontaneous and independent use of commercially available toys is not possible for many children with cerebral palsy. The toys often require more coordination or strength than these youngsters have. Continuous inability to engage in physical activity and gain mastery over the environment may cause the child to lose motivation and become passive. Because playing is an integral part of intellectual, social, perceptual, and physical development, growth in these areas may be limited when the child cannot actively play.

HOW TO GET STARTED

Fortunately, toys can be adapted to make them more accessible to children with physical disabilities. Six types of modifications are most effective in promoting active, independent use of play materials.

Stabilize the toy. Stabilizing a toy enhances its function in two ways. First, it prevents the child's uncontrolled movements and difficulty directing the hand to desired locations from moving objects out of reach or knocking them over. Second, many children with cerebral palsy have difficulty performing tasks that require holding an object with one hand while manipulating it in some way with the other hand. Toys with a base can be clamped to a table. Masking tape is an inexpensive and effective way to secure many toys. Velcro is another. The hook side of Velcro can be placed on the toy, while the loop side is mounted on a clean surface. Suction cups can also stabilize a toy for a short time on a clean, nonwood surface.

Create boundaries. Restricting the movement of toys such as cars or trains makes it easier for some children to use and retrieve them and prevents the toy from being involuntarily pushed out of reach. Boundaries can be created in various ways, depending on how the object is to be moved. For example, push toys can be placed in the top of a cardboard box or on a tray with edges to create a restricted area. Pull toys can be placed on a track, and items that require a banging motion, such as a tambourine, can be held in a wooden frame with springs.

Add a grasping aid. The ability to hold objects independently can be facilitated in a variety of ways. A Velcro strap can be placed around the child's hand, with Velcro also placed on the materials to be held, thus creating a bond between the hand and the object. A universal cuff can be used for holding sticklike objects such as crayons or pointers. Simply enlarging an item by wrapping foam or tape around it may make it easier to hold.

Make the toy easier to manipulate. Some toys require isolated finger movements, use of a pincer grasp, and controlled movements of the wrist, which are

An adapted switch makes battery-operated toys accessible and fun for Madelyn.

too difficult for a child with physical disabilities. Various adaptations can help compensate for deficits in these movements. Extending and widening pieces of the toy will make swiping and pushing easier. Flat extensions, knobs, or dowels can be used to increase the surface area. A crossbar or a dowel, placed appropriately, can compensate for an inability to rotate the wrist.

Add a special activation switch. Some children have such limited hand function that they can operate only those toys that are activated by a switch. Commercially available, battery-operated toys can be modified to operate by adapted switches. Teachers and parents can make and adapt their own switches and toys (Grass, 2001; Plaxen, 2005) or purchase them from a number of firms that serve persons with disabilities (e.g., www.ablenetinc.com). After determining some physical action that the child can perform consistently and with minimum effort (e.g., moving a knee laterally, lifting a shoulder, or making a sound), select the type of switch best suited to that movement. The switch is always positioned in the same place, which facilitates automatic switch activation and allows the child to give full attention to the play activity rather than concentrating on using the switch.

Consider the child's positioning needs. An occupational or physical therapist should determine the special positioning needs of each child. Good positioning will maximize freedom of movement, improve the ability to look at a toy, and facilitate controlled, relaxed movement. Placement of the toy is crucial. It should be within easy reach and require a minimum of effort to manipulate. The child should not become easily fatigued or have to struggle. The child must be able to look at the toy while playing.

Other considerations. Activities should be interesting and facilitate cognitive growth yet not be beyond the child's conceptual capabilities. Toys should be sturdy and durable. Avoid toys with sharp edges or small pieces that can be swallowed.

These principles for adapting toys can be applied to other devices, such as communication aids, computers, environmental controls, and household items, to make them easier to use. Making an educational environment more accessible gives children with physical disabilities greater control of their surroundings and the opportunity to expand the scope of their learning experiences.

Source: Adapted from Schaeffler, C. (1988, Spring). Making toys accessible for children with cerebral palsy. *Teaching Exceptional Children, 20,* 26–28. Used by permission.

As stated here, these principles for adapting toys can also be applied to other devices. To learn more about this concept, go to the Homework & Exercises section in Chapter 11 of MyEducationLab and complete Homework Exercise 1.

About 80% to 90% of children born with myelomeningocele develop **hydrocephalus,** the accumulation of cerebrospinal fluid in tissues surrounding the brain (Hill, 1999). Left untreated, this condition can lead to head enlargement and severe brain damage. Hydrocephalus is treated by the surgical insertion of a **shunt,** a one-way valve that diverts the cerebrospinal fluid away from the brain and into the bloodstream. Replacements of the shunt are usually necessary as a child grows older. Teachers who work with children who have shunts should be aware that blockage, disconnection, or infection of the shunt may result in increased intracranial pressure. Warning signs such as drowsiness, vomiting, headache, irritability, seizures, and change in personality should be heeded because a blocked shunt could be life-threatening (Dias, 2003). Shunts can be removed in many school-age children when the production and absorption of cerebrospinal fluid are brought into balance.

Usually children with spina bifida have some degree of paralysis of the lower limbs and lack full control of bladder and bowel functions. In most cases, these children have good use of their arms and upper body (although some children experience fine-motor problems). Children with spina bifida usually walk with braces, crutches, or walkers; they may use wheelchairs for longer distances. Some children need special help in dressing and toileting; others can manage these tasks on their own.

Because the spinal defect usually occurs above where nerves that control the bladder emerge from the spinal cord, most children with spina bifida have urinary incontinence and need to use a *catheter* (tube) or bag to collect their urine. Medical personnel teach **clean intermittent catheterization (CIC)** to children with urinary complications so that they can empty their bladders at convenient times (Rues, Graff, Ault, & Holvoet, 2006). CIC is effective with both boys and girls, works best if used every 2 to 4 hours, and does not require an absolutely sterile environment (McLone & Ito, 1998).

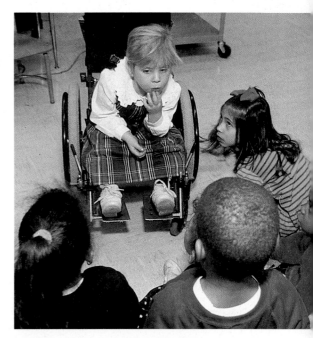

"I think the best part of the story was when . . ." Learning self-catheterization has given Kristine more control over her classroom schedule and increased her participation.

Muscular Dystrophy

Muscular dystrophy refers to a group of about 40 inherited diseases marked by progressive *atrophy* (wasting away) of the body's muscles. **Duchenne muscular dystrophy (DMD)** is the most common and most severe type. DMD affects only boys (1 in 3,500 male births), but about one third of cases are the result of genetic mutation in families with no history of the disease (Best, 2005a). Muscle weakness is usually evident between the ages of 2 and 6, when the child begins to experience difficulty in running or climbing stairs. The child may walk with an unusual gait, showing a protruding stomach and hollow back. The calf muscles of a child with muscular dystrophy may appear unusually large because the degenerated muscle has been replaced by fatty tissue.

Go to the Homework & Exercises section in Chapter 11 of MyEducationLab and complete Homework Exercise 2. As you read the article and answer the accompanying questions, think about how beneficial this skill would be for students with spina bifida.

Children with muscular dystrophy often have difficulty getting to their feet after lying down or playing on the floor. They may fall easily. By age 10 to 14, the child loses the ability to walk; the small muscles of the hands and fingers are usually the last to be affected. Some doctors and therapists recommend the early use of electrically powered wheelchairs; others suggest employing special braces and other devices to prolong walking as long as possible.

Treatment focuses on maintaining function of unaffected muscles for as long as possible, facilitating ambulation, helping the child and the family cope with limitations imposed by the disease, and providing emotional support and counseling to the child and the family (Hill, 1999). Regular physical therapy, exercise, and the use of appropriate aids and appliances can maintain a good deal of independence. The child should be encouraged to be as active as possible. However, a teacher should be careful not to lift a child with muscular dystrophy by the arms: even a gentle pull may dislocate the child's limbs.

At this time, no known treatment or cure exists for any form of muscular dystrophy. Although some cases may be mild and progress very slowly, enabling the person to live into adulthood with only moderate disability, muscular dystrophy is often fatal in adolescence or young adulthood (National Institutes of Health, 2007). Death is often caused by heart failure or respiratory failure due to atrophied chest muscles.

Schools need improved programs of education and counseling for students with terminal illnesses. These programs should give realistic support to the child and family in dealing with death and in making the best possible use of the time available (Kreicbergs et al., 2004; Rues et al., 2006). When a child dies, teachers and classmates are seriously affected, and their needs should be considered and talked about. For a discussion of ways in which classroom teachers can help themselves, classmates, and parents deal with the death of a student, see Munson and Hunt (2005), Peckham (1993), Thornton and Krajewski (1993), Spinelli (2004), and Wrenn (1994).

Spinal Cord Injuries

Location and effects of spinal cord injuries

Content Standards for Beginning Teachers—P&HD: Medical terminology related to P&HD (PH2K1).

Spinal cord injuries are usually the result of a lesion to the spinal cord caused by a penetrating injury (e.g., a gunshot wound), stretching of the vertebral column (e.g., whiplash during an auto accident), fracture of the vertebrae, or compression of the spinal cord (e.g., a diving accident). Motor vehicle accidents (38.5%), acts of violence (24.5%), falls (21.8%), and sports (7.2%) are the most common causes of spinal cord injuries (National Spinal Cord Injury Statistical Center, 2006a). Injury to the spinal column is generally described by letters and numbers indicating the site of the damage; for example, a C5–6 injury means the damage has occurred at the level of the fifth and sixth cervical vertebrae, a flexible area of the neck susceptible to injury from whiplash and diving or trampoline accidents. A T12 injury refers to the 12th thoracic (chest) vertebra and an L3 to the 3rd lumbar (lower back) area. In general, paralysis and loss of sensation occur below the level of the injury. The higher the injury on the spine and the more the injury (lesion) cuts through the entire cord, the greater the paralysis (Hill, 1999).

Males represent 78% of the approximately 11,000 persons in the United States who are victims of traumatic spinal cord injuries each year, and most are between 16 and 30 years old (National Spinal Cord Injury Statistical Center, 2006b). Students who have sustained spinal cord injuries usually use wheelchairs for mobility. Motorized wheelchairs, though expensive, are recommended for those with **quadriplegia** (also called *tetraplegia*), whereas children with **paraplegia** can use self-propelled wheelchairs. Children with quadriplegia may have severe breathing problems because the muscles of the chest, which normally govern respiration, are affected. In most cases, children with spinal cord injuries lack bladder and bowel control and need to follow a careful management program to maintain personal hygiene and avoid infection and skin irritation.

Rehabilitation programs for children and adolescents who have sustained spinal cord injuries usually involve physical therapy, the use of adaptive devices for mobility and independent living, and psychological support to help them adjust to a sudden disability. Personal care attendants (PCAs) assist many individuals with spinal cord injury, particularly those with quadriplegia, with activities of daily living. Adolescents and adults are often particularly concerned about sexual function. Even though most spinal cord injuries do affect sexuality, with understanding partners and positive attitudes toward themselves, many people with spinal cord injuries enjoy satisfying sexual relationships (Byzek, 2001).

Epilepsy

Whether we are awake or asleep, electrical activity continually occurs in the brain. A *seizure* is a disturbance of movement, sensation, behavior, and/or consciousness caused by abnormal electrical discharges in the brain. "Some have likened the event, known as a seizure, to an engine misfiring or to a power surge in a computer" (Hill, 1999, p. 231). Anyone can have a seizure. It is common for a seizure to occur when someone has a high fever, drinks excessive alcohol, or experiences a blow to the head.

When seizures occur chronically and repeatedly, however, the condition is known as a *seizure disorder* or, more commonly, **epilepsy.** Epilepsy is not a disease, and it constitutes a disorder only while a seizure is actually in progress. Researchers estimate that 3% of the population is prone to seizures and that 1% of the general population has epilepsy (Brumback, Mathews, & Shenoy, 2001; Goldman, 2006).

The cause of epilepsy for approximately 30% of cases is identified from among at least 50 different conditions known to result in seizure activity, such as cerebral palsy; infections of the brain or central nervous system; metabolic disorders such as hypoglycemia, genetics, and alcohol or lead poisoning; an underlying lesion caused by scar tissue from a head injury; high fever; an interruption in blood supply to the brain; or rough handling of a baby (shaken-baby syndrome) (Lowenthal, 2001; Weinstein & Gaillard, 2007). Epilepsy can occur at any stage of life but most frequently begins in childhood. A wide variety of psychological, physical, and sensory factors are thought to trigger seizures in susceptible persons—for example, fatigue, excitement, anger, surprise, hyperventilation, hormonal changes (as in menstruation or pregnancy), withdrawal from drugs or alcohol, and exposure to certain patterns of light, sound, or touch.

Many misconceptions about epilepsy have circulated in the past, and some remain prevalent even today (Bishop & Boag, 2006; Kanner & Schafer, 2006). Negative public attitudes, in fact, have probably been more harmful to people with epilepsy than has the condition itself. During a seizure, a dysfunction in the electrochemical activity of the brain causes a person to lose control of the muscles temporarily. Between seizures (i.e., most of the time), the brain functions normally. Teachers, school health care personnel, and perhaps classmates need to be aware that a child is affected by a seizure disorder so that they can be prepared to deal with a seizure if one should occur in school. Several types of seizures occur.

The **generalized tonic-clonic seizure** (formerly called *grand mal*) is the most conspicuous and serious type of seizure. A generalized tonic-clonic seizure can be disturbing and frightening to someone who has never seen one. The affected child has little or no warning that a seizure is about to occur; the muscles become stiff, and the child loses consciousness and falls to the floor. Then the entire body shakes violently as the muscles alternately contract and relax. Saliva may be forced from the mouth, legs and arms may jerk, and the bladder and bowels may be emptied. In most cases, the contractions diminish in 2 to 3 minutes, and the child either goes to sleep or regains consciousness in a confused or drowsy state. Generalized tonic-clonic seizures may occur as often as several times a day or as seldom as once a year. They are more likely to occur during the day than at night. A tonic-clonic seizure, although very frightening to someone who has never before witnessed such an episode, is not a medical emergency unless it lasts a very long time or unless the seizures occur frequently without a return to consciousness between seizures (Dean, 2006). Figure 11.1 describes first aid for convulsive seizures in the classroom.

The **absence seizure** (previously called *petit mal*) is far less severe than the generalized tonic-clonic seizure but may occur much more frequently—as often as 100 times per day in some children. Usually a brief loss of consciousness occurs, lasting anywhere from a few seconds to half a minute or so. The child may stare blankly, flutter or blink her eyes, grow pale, or drop whatever she is holding. She may be mistakenly viewed as daydreaming or not listening. The child may or may not be aware that she has had a seizure, and no special first aid is necessary. The teacher should keep the child's parents advised of seizure activity and may also find it helpful to explain it to the child's classmates.

Epilepsy and types of seizures

 Council for Exceptional Children

Content Standards for Beginning Teachers—P&HD: Medical terminology related to P&HD (PH2K1) (also PH2K2, PH3K1).

FIGURE 11.1   **First aid for generalized tonic-clonic seizures**

During a generalized tonic-clonic seizure, the body stiffens and/or jerks; the child may cry out, fall unconscious and then continue massive jerking movements. Bladder and bowel control may be lost. Seizures usually last a minute or two. Breathing is shallow or even stops briefly—renews as jerking movements end. The child may be confused, weary, or belligerent as consciousness returns.

First aid for a convulsive seizure protects the child from injury while the seizure runs its course. The seizure itself triggers mechanisms in the brain to bring it safely to an end. There are no other first aid steps that can hasten that process. When this type of seizure happens, the teacher should:

- Keep calm. Reassure the other children that the child will be fine in a minute.
- Ease the child gently to the floor and clear the area around him of anything that could hurt him.
- Put something flat and soft (like a folded jacket) under his head so it will not bang against the floor as his body jerks.
- Turn him gently onto his side. This keeps his airway clear and allows any fluid in his mouth to drain harmlessly away.
  DON'T try to force his mouth open.
  DON'T try to hold on to his tongue.
  DON'T put anything in his mouth.
  DON'T restrain his movements.
- When the jerking movements stop, let the child rest until full consciousness returns.
- Breathing may have been shallow during the seizure, and may even have stopped briefly. This can give the child's lips or skin a bluish tinge, which corrects naturally as the seizure ends. In the unlikely event that breathing does not begin again, check the child's airway for any obstruction. It is rarely necessary to give artificial respiration.

Some children recover quickly after this type of seizure; others need more time. A short period of rest, depending on the child's alertness following the seizure, is usually advised.

If the child is able to remain in the classroom afterwards, he or she should be encouraged to do so. Staying in the classroom (or returning to it as soon as possible) allows for continued participation in classroom activity and is psychologically less difficult for the child. Of course, if he has lost bladder or bowel control, he should be allowed to go to the rest room first. A change of clothes kept in the health room or the principal's office will reduce embarrassment when this happens.

If a child has frequent seizures, handling them can become routine once teacher and classmates learn what to expect. One or two of the children can be assigned to help while the others get on with their work.

Source: Epilepsy Foundation. (2007). *Managing seizures at school.* Landover, MD. Available online: http://www.epilepsyfoundation.org/living/children/education/managing.cfm

---

Procedures for handling seizures

 Content Standards for Beginning Teachers—P&HD: Specialized health care interventions for individuals with P&HD (PH5K2).

A **complex partial seizure** (also called *psychomotor*) may appear as a brief period of inappropriate or purposeless activity. The child may smack her lips, walk around aimlessly, or shout. She may appear to be conscious but is not actually aware of her unusual behavior. Complex partial seizures usually last from 2 to 5 minutes, after which the child has amnesia about the entire episode. Some children may respond to spoken directions during a complex partial seizure.

Sudden jerking motions with no loss of consciousness characterize a **simple partial seizure.** Partial seizures may occur weekly, monthly, or only once or twice a year. The teacher should keep dangerous objects out of the child's way and, except in emergencies, should not try to physically restrain him.

Many children experience a warning sensation, known as an *aura*, a short time before a seizure. The aura takes different forms; affected individuals describe distinctive feelings, sights, sounds, tastes, and even smells. The aura can be a useful safety valve enabling the child to leave the class or the group before the seizure actually occurs. Some children report that the warning provided by the aura helps them feel more secure and comfortable.

In some children, absence and partial seizures can go undetected for long periods. An observant teacher can be instrumental in detecting the presence of a seizure disorder and in referring the child for appropriate medical help. The teacher can also assist parents and physicians by noting both the effectiveness and the side effects of any medication. With proper medical treatment and the support of parents, teachers, and peers, most students with seizure disorders lead full and normal lives. Antiepileptic drugs provide complete control in more than 50% of children and reduce the frequency of seizures in another 20% to 30% (Epilepsy Foundation, 2007). Some children require such heavy doses of medication, however, that their learning and behavior are adversely affected; and some medications have undesirable side effects, such as excessive fatigue, nausea, slurred speech, lack of appetite, and thickening of the gums. All children with seizure disorders benefit from a realistic understanding of their condition and accepting attitudes on the part of teachers and classmates (Kanner & Schafer, 2006; Shafer & DiLorio, 2006). Although the student with seizure disorders may be uncomfortable about letting friends know about the condition, classmates should be aware, so that they will know how to respond—and how not to respond—in the event of a seizure (Hill, 1999).

Diabetes

Diabetes is a chronic disorder of metabolism that affects an estimated 20.8 million children and adults in the U.S., or 7% of the population (American Diabetes Association, 2007). About one third of those affected, 6.2 million people, are unaware that they have the disease. Most teachers will encounter students with diabetes at one time or another in their career.

Without proper medical management, the diabetic child's system cannot obtain and retain adequate energy from food. Not only does the child lack energy but also many important parts of the body (particularly the eyes and the kidneys) can be affected by untreated diabetes. Early symptoms of diabetes include thirst, headaches, weight loss (despite a good appetite), frequent urination, and cuts that are slow to heal.

Children with **Type 1 diabetes** (formerly called *juvenile diabetes* or *early-onset diabetes*) have insufficient insulin, a hormone normally produced by the pancreas and necessary for the metabolism of glucose, a form of sugar produced when food is digested. To regulate the condition, the patient must receive daily injections of insulin under the skin. Most children with diabetes learn to inject their own insulin—in some cases as frequently as four times per day—and to determine the amount of insulin they need by testing the level of sugar and other substances in their urine. Children with diabetes must follow a specific and regular diet prescribed by a physician or a nutrition specialist. Physicians also usually suggest a regular exercise program.

Type 2 diabetes, the most common form of diabetes, results from insulin resistance (the body failing to properly use insulin), combined with relative insulin deficiency. Type 2 diabetes occurs most often in adults who are overweight, but the recent increase in childhood obesity has led to a dramatic rise in the incidence of Type 2 diabetes in children (Hannon, Rao, & Arslanian, 2005).

Teachers who have a child with diabetes in their classrooms should learn how to recognize the symptoms of both too little sugar and too much sugar in the child's bloodstream and the kind of treatment indicated by each condition (Getch, Bhukhanwala, & Neuharth-Pritchett, 2007).

Hypoglycemia (low blood sugar), also called *insulin reaction* or *diabetic shock,* can result from taking too much insulin, unusually strenuous exercise, or a missed or delayed meal (the blood sugar level is lowered by insulin and exercise and raised by food). Symptoms of hypoglycemia include faintness, dizziness, blurred vision, drowsiness, and nausea. The child may appear irritable or have a marked personality change. In most cases, giving the child some form of concentrated sugar (e.g., a sugar cube, a glass of fruit juice, a candy bar) ends the insulin reaction within a few minutes. The child's doctor or parents should inform the teacher and school health personnel of the appropriate foods to give in case of insulin reaction.

Hyperglycemia (high blood sugar) is more serious; it indicates that too little insulin is present and the diabetes is not under control. Its onset is gradual rather than sudden. The symptoms of hyperglycemia, sometimes called *diabetic coma,* include fatigue; thirst; dry, hot skin; deep, labored breathing; excessive urination; and fruity-smelling breath. A doctor or nurse should be contacted immediately if a child displays such symptoms.

Diabetes and related terms

Content Standards for Beginning Teachers—P&HD: Medical terminology related to P&HD (PH2K1) (also PH2K2, PH3K1).

Asthma

Causes, characteristics, and effects of asthma

Council for Exceptional Children — Content Standards for Beginning Teachers—P&HD: Impact of P&HD on individuals, families, society (PH3K1) (also PH2K2, PH3K1, CC2K2).

Asthma is a chronic lung disease characterized by episodic bouts of wheezing, coughing, and difficulty breathing. An asthmatic attack is usually triggered by allergens (e.g., pollen, certain foods, pets); irritants (e.g., cigarette smoke, smog); exercise; or emotional stress. The result is a narrowing of the airways in the lungs. This reaction increases the resistance to the airflow in and out of the lungs, making it harder for the individual to breathe. The severity of asthma varies greatly, from a period of mild coughing to extreme difficulty in breathing that requires emergency treatment. Many asthmatic children experience normal lung functioning between episodes.

Asthma is the most common lung disease of children; estimates of its prevalence range from 7% to as high as 10% of school-age children (Asthma and Allergy Foundation of America, 2007). The causes of asthma are not completely known, though most consider it the result of an interaction of heredity and environment. Symptoms generally begin in early childhood, but sometimes do not develop until late childhood or adolescence. Asthma tends to run in families, which suggests that an allergic intolerance to some stimulus may be inherited. Symptoms of asthma might also first appear following a viral infection of the respiratory system.

Primary treatment for asthma begins with a systematic effort to identify the stimuli and environmental situations that provoke attacks. The number of potential allergens and irritants is virtually limitless, and in some cases it can be extremely difficult to determine the combination of factors that results in an asthmatic episode. Changes in temperature, humidity, and season (attacks are especially common in autumn) are also related to the frequency of asthmatic symptoms. Rigorous physical exercise produces asthmatic episodes in some children.

Asthma can be controlled effectively in most children with a combination of medications and limiting exposure to known allergens. Most children whose breathing attacks are induced by physical exercise can still enjoy physical exercise and sports through careful selection of activities (e.g., swimming generally provokes less exercise-induced asthma than running) and/or taking certain medications before rigorous exercise. Although asthma is biochemical in origin, an interrelationship exists between emotional stress and asthma. Periods of psychological stress or higher emotional responses increase the likelihood of asthmatic attacks, and asthmatic episodes produce more stress. Treatment often involves counseling or an asthma teaching program (Hill, 1999), in which children and their families are taught ways to reduce and cope with emotional stress.

Asthma is the leading cause of absenteeism in school. It is estimated that 14 million school days are lost each year because of asthma (approximately 8 days for each student with asthma) (Asthma and Allergy Foundation of America, 2007). Chronic absenteeism makes it difficult for the child with asthma to maintain performance at grade level, and homebound instructional services may be necessary. The majority of children with asthma who receive medical and psychological support, however, successfully complete school and lead normal lives. By working cooperatively with parents and medical personnel to minimize the child's contact with provoking factors and constructing a plan to assist the child during attacks, the classroom teacher can play an important role in reducing the impact of asthma (Getch & Neuharth-Pritchett, 1999).

Cystic Fibrosis

Cystic fibrosis

Council for Exceptional Children — Content Standards for Beginning Teachers—P&HD: Impact of P&HD on individuals, families, society (PH3K1) (also PH2K2, PH3K1, CC2K2).

Cystic fibrosis is a genetic disease of children and adolescents in which the body's exocrine glands excrete thick mucus that can block the lungs and parts of the digestive system. Cystic fibrosis occurs predominantly in Caucasians, but it can affect all races. Children with cystic fibrosis often have difficulty breathing and are susceptible to pulmonary disease (lung infections). Malnutrition and poor growth are common characteristics of children with cystic fibrosis because of pancreatic insufficiency that causes inadequate digestion and malabsorption of nutrients, especially fats. Affected children often have large and frequent bowel movements because food passes through the system only partially digested. Getting children with cystic fibrosis to consume enough calories is critical to their health and development.

The disease may result from a missing chemical or substance in the body. Medical research has not determined exactly how cystic fibrosis functions, and no reliable cure has yet been found. Medications prescribed for children with cystic fibrosis include enzymes to facilitate digestion and solutions to thin and loosen the mucus in the lungs. Children with cystic fibrosis undergo daily physiotherapy in which the chest is vigorously thumped and vibrated to dislodge mucus, followed by positioning the body to drain loosened secretions.

Many children and young adults with cystic fibrosis can lead active lives. During vigorous physical exercises, some children may need help from teachers, aides, or classmates to clear their lungs and air passages. Although the life expectancy of people with cystic fibrosis used to be very short—in the 1950s, few children with cystic fibrosis lived to attend elementary school—the prognosis for affected children continues to improve. In 2006 the predicted median age of survival was 37 years; more than 40% of the cystic fibrosis population is age 18 and older, and many people with cystic fibrosis live into their 30s, 40s, and beyond (Cystic Fibrosis Foundation, 2007).

Human Immunodeficiency Virus and Acquired Immune Deficiency Syndrome

Persons with **acquired immune deficiency syndrome (AIDS)** cannot resist and fight off infections because of a breakdown in the immune system. Opportunistic infections such as tuberculosis, pneumonia, and cancerous skin lesions attack the person's body, grow in severity, and ultimately result in death. At present, no known cure or vaccine exists for AIDS, although recent drug therapy advances include AZT.

AIDS is caused by the **human immunodeficiency virus (HIV),** which is found in the bodily fluids of an infected person (blood, semen, vaginal secretions, and breast milk). HIV is transmitted from one person to another through sexual contact and blood-to-blood contact (e.g., intravenous drug use with shared needles, transfusions of unscreened contaminated blood). Pregnant women can also transmit HIV to their unborn children. Most people who become infected with HIV show no symptoms of AIDS for 8 to 12 years, and not all persons who are infected with HIV develop AIDS (Centers for Disease Control and Prevention [CDC], 2007a).

The number of people worldwide who have contracted HIV/AIDS is staggering. Researchers estimate that 40 million people worldwide carry the HIV virus, with as many as 4.3 million new cases per year, resulting in 2.9 million deaths (Joint UN Programme on HIV/AIDS, 2006). Although the overall incidence rate for new cases of AIDS in the United States has decreased in recent years, the disease is still of epidemic proportions. At the end of 2003, an estimated 1,039,000 to 1,185,000 persons in the United States were living with HIV/AIDS (CDC, 2007b). Approximately 40,000 persons in the United States become infected with HIV each year. Since 1999, the estimated annual incidence of AIDS among women has increased 15%. Most of these women are of childbearing age, and many more have HIV infection but have not yet developed AIDS. Of the more than 984,000 cumulative cases of AIDS diagnoses reported in the United States through 2005, approximately 9,100 have involved children under the age of 13 (CDC, 2007c). The CDC reports 550,394 cumulative deaths in the United States due to AIDS (2007c).

In addition to health problems and significant weight loss, children with HIV/AIDS demonstrate significant neurological complications and developmental delays, particularly in expressive language, attention, memory, and motor functioning. Researchers are unsure of the extent to which these complications are caused by the HIV virus's direct effect on the brain, the opportunistic infections that arise because of the weakened immune system, the powerful regimen of medications taken to combat the spread of HIV, or a combination of these factors (Sexson & Dingle, 2001).

Because of fear generated by misconceptions about the spread of the disease, some school districts have barred children with HIV/AIDS from attending school in defiance of the IDEA principle of zero reject (Turnbull, Stowe, & Huerta, 2007). However, saliva, nasal secretions, sweat, tears, urine, and vomit do not transmit HIV unless blood is visible; and the presence of a child with HIV/AIDS in the classroom presents no undue health risks to other

HIV/AIDS

Content Standards for Beginning Teachers—P&HD: Types and transmission routes of infectious and communicable diseases (PH2K4) (also PH2K1, PH3K1).

children (CDC, 2007d). Children with HIV/AIDS cannot legally be excluded from attending school unless they are deemed a direct health risk to other children (e.g., exhibit biting behavior, have open lesions).

Because children with HIV/AIDS and their families often face discrimination, prejudice, and isolation, teachers and school personnel should actively facilitate school/peer acceptance and the social adjustment of a child with HIV/AIDS (Hill, 1999). Parents are not required to inform the school that their child has HIV (or any other medical or health condition), and a particular student or staff member may have HIV without knowing it.

Additionally, all teachers and school personnel must be trained in **universal precautions,** a set of standard safety techniques that interrupt the chain of infection spread by potential biohazards such as blood and bodily fluids from any child. Universal precautions include safe administration of first aid for a cut, nose bleed, or vomiting. For an excellent overview of the importance of universal precautions, including step-by-step guidelines for proper methods of putting on and removing protective gloves, cleaning up potentially contaminated areas in the classroom, and proper handwashing, see Edens, Murdick, and Gartin (2003).

To prevent the disease from spreading further among the preadolescent and adolescent populations, schools must include HIV/AIDS prevention in the curriculum. Students receiving special education services may be more prone to contracting HIV because of a lack of knowledge about the disease. For recommendations on developing and implementing an HIV/AIDS prevention and education curriculum for students with disabilities, see Kelker, Hecimovic, and LeRoy (1994) and Sileo (2005).

ATTENTION-DEFICIT/HYPERACTIVITY DISORDER

Everyone has difficulty attending at times (attention deficit), and we all sometimes engage in high rates of purposeless or inappropriate movement (hyperactivity). A child who consistently exhibits this combination of behavioral traits may be diagnosed with **attention-deficit/hyperactivity disorder (ADHD).** In many respects, ADHD reflects "either too much (e.g., fidgeting) or not enough (e.g., lack of impulse control or attention) of what adults expect in certain settings" (Goldstein & Goldstein, 1998, pp. 4–5). Children with ADHD present a difficult challenge to their families, teachers, and classmates. Their inability to stay on task, impulsive behavior, and fidgeting impair their ability to learn and increase the likelihood of unsatisfactory interactions with others.

Wolraich's (1999) contention that ADHD "has the distinction of being both the most extensively studied mental disorder and the most controversial" (p. 163) suggests that the condition is both well known and little understood (Bicard, 2002). Although the last decade of the 20th century witnessed an explosion of interest in ADHD, historical references to the symptoms that are diagnosed as ADHD today suggest that such children have been with us for centuries (Barkley, 2005; Conners, 2000; Goldstein & Goldstein, 1998).

The first published account of the disorder in the medical or scientific literature appeared in 1902, when British physician George Still described Still's disease. Still believed that children who were restless and exhibited problems maintaining attention suffered from a "defect of moral control" that he presumed to be the result of brain injury or dysfunction. Over the years, researchers have used a variety of terms to refer to this combination of behavioral symptoms: *postencephalitic disorder* in the 1920s, *brain damage syndrome* in the 1940s, *minimal brain dysfunction* in the 1960s, and *hyperkinetic impulse disorder of children* in the 1970s (Mather & Goldstein, 2001). Because medical science has found no clear-cut evidence of brain damage, emphasis in defining and diagnosing the condition has focused and relied on the description and identification of a combination of behavioral symptoms.

Definition and Diagnosis

The symptoms of ADHD occur in two broad dimensions: those indicative of faulty attention and those related to hyperactivity and impulsivity. Symptoms of hyperactivity and impulsivity tend to occur together with high frequency. With regard to predicting future functioning, however, "the greater the degree of reported impulsive behavior, the more problems in the classroom and later life. Thus, it has been increasingly hypothesized that the core impairment in ADHD represents faulty inhibition or self-control, leading to a constellation of related symptoms" (Mather & Goldstein, 2001, p. 49).

Children are diagnosed as having ADHD according to criteria found in the *Diagnostic and Statistical Manual of Mental Disorders* (DSM-IV-TR) (American Psychiatric Association, 2000a). "The essential feature of attention-deficit/hyperactivity disorder is a persistent pattern of inattention and/or hyperactivity-impulsivity that is more frequent and severe than is typically observed in individuals at a comparable level of development" (p. 85). To diagnose ADHD, a physician must determine that a child has consistently displayed six or more symptoms of either inattention or hyperactivity–impulsivity for a period of at least 6 months, with the onset of symptoms before the age of 7 (see Figure 11.2).

FIGURE 11.2   Diagnostic criteria for ADHD

A. Either (1) or (2):
1. Six (or more) of the following symptoms of *inattention* have persisted for at least 6 months to a degree that is maladaptive and inconsistent with developmental level:

   Inattention
   a. Often fails to give close attention to details or makes careless mistakes in schoolwork, work, or other activities.
   b. Often has difficulty sustaining attention in tasks or play activities.
   c. Often does not seem to listen when spoken to directly.
   d. Often does not follow through on instructions and fails to finish schoolwork, chores, or duties in the workplace (not due to oppositional behavior or failure to understand instructions).
   e. Often has difficulty organizing tasks and activities.
   f. Often avoids, dislikes, or is reluctant to engage in tasks that require sustained mental effort (such as schoolwork or homework).
   g. Often loses things necessary for tasks or activities (e.g., toys, school assignments, pencils, books, or tools).
   h. Is often easily distracted by extraneous stimuli.
   i. Is often forgetful in daily activities.

2. Six (or more) of the following symptoms of *hyperactivity–impulsivity* have persisted for at least 6 months to a degree that is maladaptive and inconsistent with developmental level:

   Hyperactivity
   a. Often fidgets with hands or feet or squirms in seat.
   b. Often leaves seat in classroom or in other situations in which remaining seated is expected.
   c. Often runs about or climbs excessively in situations in which it is inappropriate (in adolescents or adults, may be limited to subjective feelings of restlessness).
   d. Often has difficulty playing or engaging in leisure activities quietly.
   e. Is often "on the go" or often acts as if "driven by a motor."
   f. Often talks excessively.

   Impulsivity
   g. Often blurts out answers before questions have been completed.
   h. Often has difficulty awaiting turn.
   i. Often interrupts or intrudes on others (e.g., butts into conversations or games).

B. Some hyperactive–impulsive or inattentive symptoms that caused impairment were presented before age 7 years.
C. Some impairment from the symptoms is present in two or more settings (e.g., at school [or work] and at home).
D. There must be clear evidence of clinically significant impairment in social, academic, or occupational functioning.
E. The symptoms do not occur exclusively during the course of pervasive developmental disorder, schizophrenia, or other psychotic disorder and are not better accounted for by another mental disorder (e.g., mood disorder, anxiety disorder, dissociative disorder, or a personality disorder).

Code based on type:
Attention-Deficit/Hyperactivity Disorder, Combined Type: if both Criteria A1 and A2 are met for the past 6 months.
Attention-Deficit/Hyperactivity Disorder, Predominantly Inattentive Type: if Criterion A1 is met but Criterion A2 is not met for the past 6 months.
Attention-Deficit/Hyperactivity Disorder, Predominantly Hyperactive–Impulsive Type: if Criterion A2 is met but Criterion A1 is not met for the past 6 months.
Coding note: For individuals (especially adolescents and adults) who currently have symptoms that no longer meet full criteria, "In Partial Remission" should be specified.

Source: Reprinted from *Diagnostic and Statistical Manual of Mental Disorders*, 4th ed., Text Revision, pp. 92–93. (Copyright 2000). American Psychiatric Association.

The diagnosing physician assigns one of three subtypes of ADHD, depending on a child's constellation of symptoms: ADHD, combined type; ADHD, predominantly inattentive type; and ADHD, predominantly hyperactive-impulsive type. Within the population of children with ADHD, approximately 55% have been diagnosed with the combined type, 27% with the predominantly inattentive subtype, and 18% the hyperactive–impulsive subtype (Wilens, Biederman, & Spencer, 2002).

The diagnostic criteria for ADHD are extremely subjective. For example, what is the basis for deciding whether a child is "often 'on the go'"? And how can one determine that a child who avoids or dislikes schoolwork or homework does so because of an attention deficit as opposed to one of many other possible reasons? A child who is diagnosed by one physician as not having ADHD may very well be diagnosed by another as having it.

Because no valid, independent test for ADHD exists, teacher referrals and parents' descriptions of their children's behavior play a significant role in whether or not a child is diagnosed. One study found that "Teachers were the most likely [46% of the time] to be the first to suggest the diagnosis of ADHD, followed by parents [30%]" (Sax & Kautz, 2003, p. 17). Parents have been known to engage in "physician shopping," taking their child from one doctor to another until a diagnosis of ADHD is made (Reid, Maag, & Vasa, 1994). Although the DSM-IV diagnostic criteria state that a child must demonstrate symptoms before the age of 7, in practice many children are not diagnosed until they are well into elementary school or even high school (Zentall, 2006).

Prevalence

The most frequently cited estimate of the prevalence of ADHD is 3% to 5% of all school-age children (American Psychiatric Association, 2000a). A random national sample of family pediatricians found that 5.3% of all elementary students screened received a diagnosis of ADHD (Wolraich et al., 1990). These figures suggest that the typical classroom will have one or two children either diagnosed as ADHD or presenting the problems typically associated with ADHD.

Child count data reported by the states reveal a large increase in the numbers of students served under IDEA's other health impairments category, because the federal government stipulated that students with ADHD were eligible under that disability category. Some states reported increases of 20% in the number of children served under the other health impairments category between the 1997–1998 and 1998–1999 school years (U.S. Department of Education, 2000). Nationwide, the number of children served in the other health impairments category increased from 63,982 in 1992–1993 to 557,121 in 2005–2006, by far the biggest proportional increase of any disability category (U.S. Department of Education, 2007b).

Boys are about four times more likely to be diagnosed with ADHD than are girls, with the ratio being higher at younger ages (Barkley, 2005; Schnoes et al., 2006).

Academic Achievement and Comorbidity With Other Disabilities

Achievement of students with ADHD and comorbidity with other disabling conditions

 Council for Exceptional Children

Content Standards for Beginning Teachers—Common Core: Educational implications of characteristics of various exceptionalities (CC2K2) (also LD3K1).

Most children with ADHD struggle in the classroom. They score lower than do their age mates on IQ and achievement tests; more than half require remedial tutoring for basic skills; and about 30% repeat one or more grades (Barkley, 2005). A national study of more than 1,400 students found that 58% of those students receiving special education services under the disability category of emotional disturbance had ADHD and that 20% of those students receiving special education in the mental retardation and learning disability categories had ADHD (Schnoes, Reid, Wagner, & Marder, 2006). Many children with Asperger syndrome and Tourette syndrome are identified as having ADHD (Kube et al., 2002; Prestia, 2003).

Eligibility for Special Education

Researchers estimate that between 40% and 50% of students with ADHD qualify for special education services, the majority being served under the disability categories of behavioral disorders and learning disabilities (Reid & Maag, 1998; Zentall, 2006). As already noted, many students with ADHD are served under the emotional disturbance and learning disability categories. Students with ADHD can be served under the other health impairment category if the outcome of the disorder is a "heightened alertness to environmental stimuli that results in limited alertness with respect to the educational environment that adversely affects academic performance" (20 U.S.C. §1401 [2004], 20 C.F.R. §300.8[c][9]).

Many children with ADHD who are not served under IDEA are eligible for services under Section 504 of the Rehabilitation Act. As discussed in Chapter 1, Section 504 is a civil rights law that provides certain protections for persons with disabilities. Under Section 504, schools may be required to develop and implement accommodation plans designed to help students with ADHD succeed in the general education classroom. Accommodation plans often include such adaptations and adjustments as extended time on tests, preferred seating, additional teacher monitoring, reduced or modified class or homework assignments and worksheets, and monitoring the effects of medication on the child's behavior in school.

Causes

In most cases, the specific causes of the inattention and hyperactivity–impulsivity that lead to a child's diagnosis of ADHD are not known. Although many consider ADHD to be a neurologically based disorder, no clear and consistent causal evidence links brain damage or dysfunction to the behavioral symptoms of ADHD (National Institute of Health Consensus Statement, 1998). However, significant evidence indicates that genetic factors may place individuals at a greater-than-normal risk of an ADHD diagnosis (Willcutt, Pennington, & DeFries, 2000). Genetics may provide certain risk or resilience factors, and environmental influences (i.e., life experiences) then determine whether an individual receives a diagnosis of ADHD (Goldstein & Goldstein, 1998).

ADHD is associated with a wide range of genetic disorders and diseases (Levy, Hay, & Bennett, 2006). For example, individuals with fragile X syndrome, Turner syndrome, and Williams syndrome (see Chapter 4) frequently have attention and impulsivity problems. Symptoms of ADHD are also associated with conditions such as fetal alcohol syndrome, prenatal exposure to cocaine, and lead poisoning.

Research using neuroimaging technologies has shown that some individuals with ADHD have structural or biochemical differences in their brains (e.g., Berquin et al., 1998; Castellnos, 2001; Filipek et al., 1997). Not all individuals diagnosed with ADHD, however, have brains that appear different from those of individuals without ADHD. And some people without ADHD have brain structures similar to those with ADHD.

The causes of ADHD are not well understood. Similar patterns of behavior leading to the diagnoses of ADHD in two different children likely, if not certainly, will be caused by completely different factors or sets of factors (Goldstein & Goldstein, 1998; Gresham, 2002; Maag & Reid, 1994). And different causal factors may influence a child's inattention and/or impulsivity in different situations or environments. A full understanding of those causal factors may be necessary in order to develop optimal interventions with long-lasting effects.

Treatment

Drug therapy and behaviorally based interventions are the two most widely used treatment approaches for children with ADHD.

Drug Therapy Prescription stimulant medication is the most common intervention for children with ADHD. Methylphenidate, sold under the trade name Ritalin, is the most frequently prescribed medication for ADHD. Other stimulants such as dextroamphetamine (Dexedrine), dextroamphetamine sulfate (Adderall), methamphetamine hydrochloride (Desoxyn), and pemoline (Cylert) are also widely prescribed. The U.S. Drug Enforcement Agency classifies the medications prescribed to treat ADHD as Schedule II drugs (a group that includes barbiturates, codeine, and morphine), meaning they have some therapeutic value but also some potential for abuse.

The number of children on stimulant medication has increased tremendously since the early 1990s. An estimated 700,000 children received medication for ADHD in the late 1980s. By 1995 the number had more than doubled to 1.6 million children (Safer, Zito, & Fine, 1996). In 2000 researchers estimated that more than 3 million U.S. schoolchildren were receiving drug treatment for ADHD (Jensen, 2000). Diller (1998) reports that sales of Ritalin for children in the United States account for 90% of the worldwide consumption of the drug. According to the U.S. Drug Enforcement Agency (2002), the production of Ritalin increased by 900% from 1990 to 2001, and the production of amphetatmines (Dexedrine and Adderall) increased by 5,767% from 1993 to 2001. Klein (2007) reported that children in the United States are 10 times more likely to take a stimulant medication for ADHD than are kids in Europe, and that the United States consumes about 85% of the stimulants manufactured for ADHD.

> Direct-to-parent marketing of ADHD drugs—most of which are stimulants—has grown pervasive over the last few years.... Homemaker-targeted magazines, such as *Family Circle, Woman's Day* and *Redbook,* feature advertising spreads for Vyvanse, Shire US Inc.'s new entry in the growing stable of ADHD medications. The ads show "Consistent Kevin through the day, even through homework," picturing a well-groomed boy smiling as he wields his pencil through a work sheet, and "Consistent Sarah," who even at 6 p.m. contentedly pecks away at the piano keys.
>
> *ADDitude* magazine, published for people with ADHD, has ads for four medications. One ad touts a flavored, chewable form of methylphenidate with the slogan, "Give me the grape."
>
> Doctors and therapists increasingly see parents seeking to change their child's medication or coming in with their own diagnosis of ADHD and suggestions for medications they have seen advertised. Many of the companies offer coupons for a free trial supply. (Klein, 2007)

Why are stimulant medications prescribed so frequently for children with ADHD? Undoubtedly, there are many reasons, but two factors seem certain. First, many children demonstrate hyperactivity and impulsivity that are troublesome to their parents and teachers. Second, many children with ADHD show improvements in behavior when taking stimulant medication.

When prescribed and monitored by a competent physician, Ritalin has proven to be a safe and often effective intervention (Multimodal Treatment Study Group, 1999). Reviews of controlled studies show that 70% to 80% of school-aged children diagnosed with ADHD respond positively to Ritalin, at least in the short term (Barkley, 2005; Swanson, McBurnett, Christain, & Wigal, 1995). Only 50% of preschoolers with ADHD are positive responders to medications (Sonuga-Barke, 2001). A positive response typically includes a reduction in hyperactivity, increased attention and time on task, increased academic productivity, and improvements in general conduct. No clear evidence indicates that stimulant medications lead to improved academic achievement (e.g., better grades and scores on achievement tests) (Flora, 2007; Pelham, 1999; Pelham, Wheeler, & Chronis, 1998). A longitudinal study that followed children with ADHD who had taken Ritalin for 4 years found the children did not make gains in either specific or general areas of academic achievement from the first through the fifth grade (Frankenberger & Cannon, 1999).

Although teachers and parents generally report favorable outcomes for children who are taking stimulant medication, common side effects include insomnia, decreased appetite, headaches, weight loss, decrease of positive affect, and irritability. These side effects are usually of short duration and can often be controlled with a reduction in dosage (Goldstein & Goldstein, 1998). Additional problems have been reported with children not taking their medication as prescribed, trying to catch up on missed pills by taking too many pills at once, and trading or even selling their medications (Hancock, 1996; Wood & Zabel, 2001).

Mather and Goldstein (2001) believe that "the immediate short-term benefits of stimulant medications far outweigh the liabilities and thus appear to justify the continued use of these medications in the treatment of ADHD" (p. 63). Based on their assessment of two meta-analyses of medication studies, Forness, Kavale, Crenshaw, and Sweeney (2000) suggest that it is unwise and could be considered malpractice not to include drug therapy as part of a comprehensive treatment program for children with ADHD.

Some professionals, however, have voiced concerns that the drugs may have little or no long-term benefits on academic achievement and that educators and parents rely too much on medical interventions (Flora, 2007; Maag & Reid, 1994; Northup, Galley, Edwards, & Fountain, 2001). They view drug treatment as an inappropriate, easy way out that might produce short-term improvements in behavior but result in long-term harm. "When stimulants work in the short-term, pharmacological intervention may be used as a crutch and may postpone or prevent the use of non-pharmacological interventions, which may be more effective in the long run" (Swanson et al., 1993, p. 158).

The effects of stimulant medication on an individual child are difficult to predict. Although the majority of children respond positively to stimulants, 20% to 30% show either no response or a negative response (i.e., their symptoms get worse) (Gresham, 2002). Physicians cannot use a child's response or lack of response to stimulant medication as a basis for confirming the ADHD diagnosis (DuPaul & Stoner, 2003). And physicians cannot use a child's age, size, or weight to determine the optimum dosage in terms of the desired effects on hyperactivity and safety. Direct and daily measurement of a student's performance on academic tasks during alternating drug and placebo conditions is a promising technique for evaluating the effects of the drug and determining appropriate dosage levels (e.g., Northup, Fusilier, Swanson, Roane, & Borrero, 1997; Stoner, Carey, Ikeda, & Shinn, 1994).

The American Academy of Pediatrics (2001) has published a set of practice guidelines for the safe use of stimulant medication in treating school-aged children with ADHD. Gadow and Nolan (1993), DuPaul and Stoner (2003), and Goldstein and Goldstein (1998) are excellent sources of information for educators on this important topic.

Because the diagnosis of ADHD often leads to the prescription of stimulant medication, it is important that teachers have valid knowledge of the condition and its treatment. Unfortunately, educators hold many misconceptions about ADHD and its treatment by stimulant medication. Snider, Busch, and Arrowood (2003) asked 145 teachers to rate how much they agreed or disagreed with 13 statements about ADHD and its treatment by stimulant medication. All of the questions were either true or false on the basis of scientific research, and more than half of the teachers answered only 5 of the 13 questions correctly (see Table 11.1). In discussing these results, Snider and colleagues wrote,

> The teachers who responded to this survey had less knowledge about ADHD and the use of stimulant medication than one would expect considering their pivotal role in the recognition and treatment of ADHD. . . .
>
> A diagnosis of ADHD is thought to explain a cause when in fact it does nothing more than describe a set of symptoms that include inattention, hyperactivity, impulsivity (e.g., Why is Johnny inattentive? Because he has ADHD. Why does he have ADHD? Because he is inattentive.) When the explanation is circular, the presumed cause is sometimes called an "explanatory fiction" (Michael, 1993, p. 53). This often happens when a cause cannot be observed independent of the effect that it is supposed to explain.
>
> Unnecessary referrals could be avoided if more teachers understood this important concept. ADHD has no known cause or cure, so there is no valid independent way of diagnosing it. Teachers must be especially sensitive to ambiguities in the diagnosis of ADHD because the treatment often involves powerful stimulant drugs. (pp. 50, 53–54)

Behavioral Intervention The principles and methods of applied behavior analysis provide teachers and parents with practical strategies for teaching and living with children with ADHD (Flick, 2000; Goldstein & Brooks, 2007). These methods include positive reinforcement for on-task behavior, modifying assignments and instructional activities to promote success, and systematically gradually teaching self-control. Teacher-administered interventions for children with ADHD include restructuring the environment (e.g., seating the child close to the teacher and breaking assignments into small, manageable chunks); providing frequent opportunities to actively respond within ongoing instruction; and providing differential consequences for child behavior (e.g., positive reinforcement such as praise and tokens for appropriate behavior, ignoring inappropriate behavior, and time out or response cost for inappropriate behavior) (Garrick Duhaney, 2003; Harlacher, Roberts, & Merrell, 2006; Salend, Elhoweris, & van Garderen, 2003). Interventions based on functional assessment of off-task, disruptive, and distracting behavior by students with ADHD have also proven effective (e.g., Lo & Cartledge, 2006; Stahr, Cushing, Lane, & Fox, 2006).

An important line of research with major implications for treating children with ADHD is exploring how to teach self-control to children whose learning is adversely affected by impulsivity. A deficit of *executive function*, or the ability to verbally think through and control one's actions, has been hypothesized as being a primary characteristic of children diagnosed with ADHD (Barkley, 2005; Sonuga-Bourke, Dalen, Daley, & Remington, 2002).

Behavioral interventions for ADHD

 Content Standards for Beginning Teachers—Common Core: Teach individuals to use self-assessment, problem solving, and other cognitive strategies to meet their needs (CC4S2) (also CC5K2).

TABLE 11.1

Percentage of classroom teachers who correctly rated statements about ADHD and its treatment by stimulant medication

ITEM	PERCENTAGE CORRECT
ADHD is the most commonly diagnosed psychiatric disorder of childhood. (True)	58
There are data to indicate that ADHD is caused by a brain malfunction. (False)	10
ADHD symptoms (e.g., fidgets, does not follow through on instruction, easily distracted) may be caused by academic deficits. (True)	63
Stress and conflict in the student's home life can cause ADHD symptoms. (True)	71
Diagnosis of ADHD can be confirmed if stimulant medication improves the child's attention. (False)	33
Stimulant medication use may decrease the physical growth rate (i.e., height) of students. (True)	38
Stimulant medication use may produce tics in students. (True)	45
Adderall, Ritalin, and Dexedrine have abuse potential similar to Demerol, cocaine, and morphine. (True)	46
The long-term side effects of stimulant medications are well understood. (False)	67
Over time, stimulant medication loses its effectiveness. (True)	46
While on stimulant medication, students exhibit similar amounts of problem behaviors as their normally developing peers. (False)	27
Short-term studies show that stimulant medication improves the behaviors associated with ADHD. (True)	86
Studies show that stimulant medication has a positive effect on academic achievement in the long run. (False)	6

Note. Statements were rated using a 5-point Likert-type scale (1 = *strongly disagree* to 5 = *strongly agree*). Percentage correct indicates percentage of respondents who answered 4 or 5 to an item that was true and 1 or 2 to an item that was false.

Source: From "Teacher knowledge of stimulant medication and ADHD" by V.E. Snider, T. Busch, and L. Arrowood, 2003, *Remedial and Special Education, 24,* p. 50. Copyright 2003 by the Hammill Institute of Disability. Reprinted with permission.

Since learning to self-monitor his behavior, Brandon's impulsiveness has decreased.

According to this hypothesis, children with ADHD would be unlikely candidates for, and perhaps incapable of, learning self-control (Abikoff, 1991). Recent research has demonstrated, however, that children with ADHD can learn to self-regulate their behavior to reduce impulsiveness (Reid, Trout, & Schartz, 2005)

Neef, Bicard, and Endo (2002) demonstrated that children with ADHD can learn self-control when treatment regimens are directly tied to assessment. Results of a subsequent study demonstrated that children with ADHD can learn to follow rules and describe their own behavior, provided they receive clear instructions and consistent reinforcement (Bicard & Neef, 2002). Results of these studies and research on self-monitoring (e.g., Huff & DuPaul, 1998) and correspondence training show promise for treating children who have ADHD. Correspondence training is a procedure in which children are reinforced for "do–say" verbal statements about what they had done previously and "say–do" statements describing what they plan to do (e.g., Paniagua, 1992; Shapiro, DuPaul, & Bradley-King, 1998). See Teaching & Learning, "Self-Monitoring Helps Students Do More Than Just Be On Task."

CHARACTERISTICS

The characteristics of children with physical disabilities and health impairments are so varied that attempting to describe them is nearly impossible. Knowing the underlying cause of a student's physical impairment or health condition provides limited guidance in planning needed special education and related services. One student with cerebral palsy may require few special modifications in curriculum, instruction, or environment, while the severe limitations in movement and intellectual functioning experienced by another student with cerebral palsy require a wide array of curricular and instructional modifications, adaptive equipment, and related services. Some children with health conditions have chronic but relatively mild health conditions; others have extremely limited endurance and vitality, requiring sophisticated medical technology and around-the-clock support to maintain their very existence. And a given physical or health condition may take markedly different *trajectories* in the same child (Best, 2005a). For example, treatment of cancer may prolong and enhance the life of a child, lead to complete remission of the disease, or have little or no positive effects on a child's life. The treatment itself (e.g., the extent to which hospitalization is required, the immediate effects of chemotherapy on the child's physical and emotional condition) and its outcome will both have significant impact on when and what type of special education and related services the child needs.

The combined effects of all of these variables render lists of learning and behavioral characteristics of children with physical disabilities and health impairments highly suspect at best. Nevertheless, two cautiously qualified statements can be made concerning the academic and socioemotional characteristics of children with physical disabilities and health impairments. First, although many students with physical disabilities or health impairments achieve well above grade level—indeed, some are intellectually gifted—as a group, these students function below grade level academically. In addition to the neurological motor and orthopedic impairments that hamper their academic performance, the daily health care routines and medications that some children must endure have negative side effects on academic achievement. For example, Frueh (2007) described how the mother of a 15-year-old with epilepsy helps teachers understand the effects of seizures and medication on a student's school performance.

> I tell them, "Imagine you have the flu. Plus, you've taken a nighttime cold medicine. You head off to school and must perform on par all day, feeling awful, and do all of your work. In addition to that, the teacher pats you on the back and speaks to you the whole time to encourage you along. Now, write the alphabet backwards with your non-dominant hand, while swinging your opposite foot backwards in a circle." Kids with epilepsy take medication every day that makes them feel that way. That helps teachers really identify with what their students are going through.

The educational progress of some children is also hampered by frequent and sometimes prolonged absences from school for medical treatment when flare-ups or relapses require hospitalization (Kline, Silver, & Russell, 2001).

Second, as a group, students with physical disabilities and health impairments perform below average on measures of social-behavioral skills. Coster and Haltiwanger (2004) reported that classroom teachers and other school professionals, such as physical and occupational therapists, rated more than 40% of the 62 elementary students with physical disabilities below mean on six of seven social-behavioral tasks considered necessary for optimal functioning and learning in school (e.g., following social conventions, compliance with adult directives, positive interaction with peers and adults, constructive responses to feedback, and personal care awareness).

Coping emotionally with a physical disability or a chronic health impairment presents a major problem for some children (Antle, 2004; Boekaerts & Roeder, 1999; Kanner & Schafer, 2006). Maintaining peer relationships and a sense of belonging to the group can be difficult for a child who must frequently leave the instructional activity or the classroom to participate in therapeutic or health care routines. Anxiety about fitting in at school may be created by prolonged absences from school (Olsen & Sutton, 1998). Students with physical disabilities and health impairments frequently identify concerns about physical appearance as reasons for emotional difficulties and feelings of depression (Sexson & Dingle, 2001).

Self-Monitoring Helps Students Do More Than Just Be On Task

Self-monitoring is a relatively simple procedure in which a person observes his behavior systematically and records the occurrence or nonoccurrence of a specific target behavior. Self-monitoring not only often changes the behavior observed and recorded, it also typically changes the behavior in the desired direction.

Self-monitoring has helped students with and without disabilities be on task more often in the classroom (Wood, Murdock, Cronin, Dawson, & Kirby, 1998), decrease talk-outs and aggression (Martella, Leonard, Marchand-Martella, & Agran, 1993; Gumpel & Shlomit, 2000), improve their performance in a variety of academic subject areas (Maag, Reid, & DiGangi, 1993; Wolfe, Heron, & Goddard, 2000), and complete homework assignments (Trammel, Schloss, & Alper, 1994). In addition to improving the target behavior, self-monitoring enables students to achieve a form of self-determination by taking responsibility for their learning (Wehmeyer et al., 2000; Wehmeyer & Schalock, 2001).

CAN STUDENTS WITH ADHD SELF-MONITOR THEIR OWN BEHAVIOR?

How can a teacher expect a student who seldom sits still, pays little attention to instruction, and frequently disrupts the class to carefully observe his own behavior and accurately self-record whether he is on task and productive? Asking a child with ADHD to self-monitor his behavior may seem at first like asking the fox to guard the hen house. How can a student with ADHD pay attention to his own paying attention? Isn't he likely to forget? And if he does remember, what will keep him from recording that he was on task even if he wasn't? Although these are understandable and legitimate questions and concerns, research has shown self-monitoring to be an effective intervention for students diagnosed with ADHD (e.g., Barry & Messer, 2003; Harris, Friedlancer, Saddler, Frizzelle, & Graham, 2005; Lo & Cartledge, 2006).

HOW TO GET STARTED

Following are suggestions based on more than 30 years of research on self-monitoring. For a review of principles and strategies for self-monitoring, see Cooper, Heron, and Heward (2007). You can find detailed procedures and materials for teaching self-monitoring and other self-management skills to students in Daly and Ranalli (2003); Joseph and Konrad (in press); McConnell (1999); and Patton, Jolivette, and Ramsey (2006).

1. Specify the target behavior and performance goals. In general, students should self-monitor their performance of academic or social tasks (e.g., number of math problems answered, participating in class discussions, transitioning between activities, having materials ready for class) instead of an on-task behavior such as "paying attention." On-task behavior does not necessarily result in a collateral increase in productivity (Maag, Reid, & DiGangi, 1993). By contract, when productivity is increased, improvements in on-task behavior almost always occur as well. However, a student whose persistent off-task and disruptive behaviors create problems for him or others in the classroom may benefit more from self-monitoring on-task behavior, at least initially.

Encourage students' participation in selecting and defining the behaviors to be self-monitored and in setting performance goals. Some students will work harder to achieve self-selected goals than teacher-determined goals (Olympia, Sheridan, Jenson, & Andrews, 1994).

2. Select or create materials that make self-monitoring easy. Simple paper-and-pencil recording forms, wrist counters, hand-tally counters, and countdown timers can make self-monitoring easy and efficient. Self-recording forms consisting of nothing more than a series of boxes or squares are often effective. At various intervals, the student might write a + or −, circle yes or no, or mark an × through a smiling face or sad face; or record tally marks for the number of target responses made during a just-completed interval.

For example, elementary students with ADHD used the form shown on the next page to self-monitor whether they worked quietly, evaluated their work, and followed a prescribed sequence for obtaining teacher assistance during independent seat-work activities (Lo & Cartledge, 2006). The form served the dual purpose of reminding the students of the expected behaviors and as a device on which they self-recorded those behaviors. Countoons are self-monitoring forms that illustrate the target behaviors to be self-monitored and the consequences for meeting the performance contingency (see Figure 6.8) (Daly & Ranalli, 2003).

KidTools and KidSkills are software programs children can use to create charts and tools for self-monitoring and other self-management tasks. You can download both programs at no cost in Windows or Macintosh versions at http://kidtools.missouri.edu. You can also download training modules for teachers with video demonstrations and practice materials at this site.

3. Provide supplementary cues to self-monitor. Although the self-monitoring device or form itself provides a visual reminder to self-monitor, additional prompts or cues to self-monitor are often helpful. As a general rule, teachers should provide frequent prompts at the beginning of a self-monitoring intervention and gradually reduce their number as the student becomes accustomed to self-monitoring. Teachers can use auditory prompts in the form of prerecorded beeps or tones to cue self-monitoring. For example, Todd, Horner, and Sugai (1999) had a student place a check mark next to *Yes* or *No* under the heading

suddenly loses the use of her legs in an accident has likely had a normal range of experiences throughout childhood but may need considerable support from parents, teachers, specialists, and peers in adapting to life with this newly acquired disability.

Visibility   Physical impairments and health conditions range from highly visible and conspicuous to not visible. How children think about themselves and the degree to which others accept them often are affected by the visibility of a condition. Some children use a variety of special orthopedic appliances, such as wheelchairs, braces, crutches, and adaptive tables. They may ride to school on a specially equipped bus or van. In school they may need assistance using the toilet or may wear helmets. Although such special devices and adaptations help children meet important needs, they often have the unfortunate side effect of making the physical impairment more visible, thus making the child look even more different from her classmates without disabilities.

The visibility of some physical disabilities may cause other children and adults to underestimate the child's abilities and limit opportunities for participation. By contrast, many health conditions such as asthma or epilepsy are not visible, and others may not perceive that the child needs or deserves accommodations. This misperception is supported by the fact that the child functions normally most of the time (Best, 2005a).

EDUCATIONAL APPROACHES

Special education of children with physical disabilities and health impairments in the United States has a history of more than 100 years (see Table 11.2). While some students with physical and health impairments can fully access and benefit from education with minimal accommodations or environmental modifications, the intensive health and learning needs of other students require a complex and coordinated array of specialized instruction, therapy, and related services. In addition to progressing in the general education curriculum to the maximum extent possible, many students with physical disabilities or health impairments also need intensive instruction in a "parallel curriculum" on ways of "coping with their disabilities" (Bowe, 2000, p. 75). Similar in function to the "expanded core curriculum"

Effects of P&HD on academic achievement and social/emotional development

 Content Standards for Beginning Teachers—Common Core: Educational implications of various exceptionalities (CC2K2) (also PH3K1).

History of education of students with P&HD

 Content Standards for Beginning Teachers—P&HD: Historical foundations related to knowledge and practices in P&HD (PH1K2).

TABLE 11.2

A history of the education of children with physical disabilities and health impairments: Key events and implications

DATE	HISTORICAL EVENT	EDUCATIONAL IMPLICATIONS
1893	Industrial School for Crippled and Deformed Children was established in Boston.	This was the first special institution for children with physical disabilities in the United States (Eberle, 1922).
Circa 1900	The first special classes for children with physical impairments began in Chicago.	This was the first time children with physical disabilities were educated in public schools (La Vor, 1976).
Early 1900s	Serious outbreaks of tuberculosis and polio occurred in the United States.	This led to increasing numbers of children with physical impairments being educated by local schools in special classes for the "crippled" or "delicate" (Walker & Jacobs, 1985).
Early 20th century	Winthrop Phelps demonstrated that children could be helped through physical therapy and the effective use of braces. Earl Carlson (who himself had cerebral palsy) was a strong advocate of developing the intellectual potential of children with physical disabilities through appropriate education.	The efforts of these two American physicians contributed to increased understanding and acceptance of children with physical disabilities and to recognition that physical impairment did not preclude potential for educational achievement and self-sufficiency.

(Continues)

TABLE 11.2 CONTINUED

A history of the education of children with physical disabilities
and health impairments: Key events and implications

DATE	HISTORICAL EVENT	EDUCATIONAL IMPLICATIONS
Early 20th century to 1970s	Decisions to "ignore, isolate, and institutionalize these children were often based on mental incompetence presumed because of physical disabilities, especially those involving communication and use of upper extremities" (Conner, Scandary, & Tullock, 1988, p. 6).	Increasing numbers of children with mild physical disabilities and health conditions were educated in public schools. Most children with severe physical disabilities were educated in special schools or community agencies (e.g., the United Cerebral Palsy Association).
1975	P.L. 94-142 mandated a free appropriate public education for all children with disabilities and required schools to provide related services (e.g., transportation services, physical therapy, school health services) necessary for students to be educated in the least restrictive environment.	No longer could a child be denied the right to attend the local public school because there was a flight of stairs at the entrance, bathrooms were not accessible, or school buses were not equipped to transport wheelchairs. The related services provision of IDEA transformed schools from "solely scholastic institutions into therapeutic agencies" (Palfrey, 1995, p. 265).
1984	The Supreme Court ruled in *Independent School District v. Tatro* that schools must provide intermittent catheterization as a supportive or related service if necessary to enable a student with disabilities to receive a public education.	The *Tatro* ruling expanded the range of related services that schools are required to provide and clarified the differences between school health services, which can be performed by a nonphysician, and medical services, which are provided by physicians for diagnostic or eligibility purposes.
1984	The World Institute on Disability was co-founded by Ed Roberts, an inspirational leader for self-advocacy by persons with disabilities.	This was a major milestone in the civil rights and self-advocacy movement by people with disabilities.
1990	Americans with Disabilities Act (P.L. 101-336) was passed.	ADA provided civil rights protections to all persons with disabilities in private sector employment and mandated access to all public services, accommodations, transportation, and telecommunications.
1990	Traumatic brain injury was added as a new disability category in the reauthorization of IDEA (P.L. 101-476).	Increased awareness, services, research, and resources for teachers developed concerning the educational needs of children with TBI.
1999	The U.S. Supreme Court ruled in *Cedar Rapids v. Garret F.* that a local school district must pay for the one-on-one nursing care for a medically fragile student who required continuous monitoring of his ventilator and other health-maintenance routines.	The decision reaffirmed and extended the Court's ruling in the 1984 *Tatro* case that schools must provide any and all health services needed for students with disabilities to attend school, as long as performance of those services does not require a licensed physician.
2004	Improving Access to Assistive Technology Act of 2004 (P.L. 108-364); third time Congress amended and extended provisions of the Technology-Related Assistance for Individuals with Disabilities Act of 1988.	Congress funds an Assistive Technology Act Project (ATAP) in each state to assist persons with disabilities to obtain AT services throughout their entire life span. ATAP activities include product demonstrations, AT device loan programs, financing assistance, and public awareness regarding the availability, benefits, and costs of AT. For more info, go to www.resna.org/taproject.

for students with visual impairments, the "parallel curriculum" for students with physical and health impairments includes using adaptive methods and assistive technologies for mobility, communication, and daily-living tasks; increasing independence by self-administering special health care routines; and learning self-determination and self-advocacy skills.

Teaming and Related Services

The transdisciplinary team approach has special relevance for students with physical disabilities and health impairments. No other group of exceptional children comes into contact, both in and out of school, with as many different teachers, physicians, therapists, and other specialists. Because the medical, educational, therapeutic, vocational, and social needs of these students are often complex and frequently affect each other, educational and health care personnel must openly communicate and cooperate with one another (Shafer & DiLorio, 2006; Thies & McAllister, 2001). Two particularly important members of the team for many children with physical disabilities and health impairments are the physical therapist and the occupational therapist. Each is a licensed health professional who must complete a specialized training program and meet rigorous standards.

Physical therapists (PTs) are involved in the development and maintenance of motor skills, movement, and posture. They may prescribe specific exercises to help a child increase control of muscles and use specialized equipment, such as braces, effectively. Massage and prescriptive exercises are perhaps the most frequently applied procedures; but physical therapy can also include swimming, heat treatment, special positioning for feeding and toileting, and other techniques. PTs encourage children to be as motorically independent as possible; help develop muscular function; and reduce pain, discomfort, or long-term physical damage. They may also suggest do's and don'ts for sitting positions and activities in the classroom and may devise exercise or play programs that children with and without disabilities can enjoy together.

Occupational therapists (OTs) are concerned with a child's participation in activities, especially those that will be useful in self-help, employment, recreation, communication, and aspects of daily living (e.g., dressing, eating, personal hygiene). They may help a child learn (or relearn) diverse motor behaviors such as drinking from a modified cup, buttoning clothes, tying shoes, pouring liquids, cooking, and typing on a computer keyboard. These activities can enhance a child's physical development, independence, vocational potential, and self-concept. OTs conduct specialized assessments and make recommendations to parents and teachers regarding the effective use of appliances, materials, and activities at home and school. Many OTs also work with vocational rehabilitation specialists in helping students find opportunities for work and independent living after completing an educational program.

Figure 11.4 shows how a PT and an OT worked with a third-grade student with spastic cerebral palsy and other members of the student's IEP team to support five learning outcomes.

Other specialists who frequently provide related services to children with physical disabilities and health impairments include the following (Downing, 2004; Etzel-Wise & Mears, 2004; Neal, Bigby, & Nicholson, 2004):

- *Speech-language pathologists (SLPs),* who provide speech therapy, language interventions, oral motor coordination (e.g., chewing and swallowing), and augmentative and alternative communication (AAC) services
- *Adapted physical educators,* who provide physical education activities designed to meet the individual needs of students with disabilities
- *Recreation therapists,* who provide instruction in leisure activities and therapeutic recreation

To learn more about PTs and how they interact with students, go to the Homework & Exercises section in Chapter 11 of MyEducationLab and complete Homework Exercise 3.

A physical therapist leads Kavana through exercises to increase her muscular strength and postural control.

FIGURE 11.4	Direct and indirect physical therapy and occupational therapy supports for five IEP goals/learning outcomes for a third-grade student with spastic cerebral palsy

One	Two	Three	Four	Five
Learning Outcomes				
Maddie will independently complete her morning routine from exiting school bus to storing her belongings, and preparing for class.	Maddie will use computer at desk to complete 25% of her work independently.	Maddie will attend to educator and focus on task at hand 70% of the time during classroom activities, requiring only minimal assistance 25% of the time to refocus attention despite competing sounds, sights, or actions.	Maddie will participate with classmates in 50% of the physical education activities.	Maddie will participate at least 25% with basic self-care tasks during school.
Physical Therapy Direct Service				
Instruction in maneuvering wheel chair off bus, over school grounds, and into classroom.	Work on postural control and stabilization of upper body to improve use of hands and head control for desktop work.	Work on postural control to improve head, torso, and shoulder stability to allow eyes and hands to move yet still attend to class activity; work on coordination of breathing during activity to maintain focus on task.	Instruct in maneuvering and positioning self during activities; assist in teaching various gross-motor activities.	Work on increasing independence with transfers on/off toilet.
Physical Therapy Indirect Service				
Work with bus driver to assure safe exit from bus.	Instruct aide in techniques to facilitate proper posture at desk.	Consult with educator regarding strengths and limitations during class.	Work with educator to supplement activities with components appropriate for inclusion; train educator and aide to facilitate participation in group activities; work with administrators to ensure accessibility to both indoor and outdoor activity areas.	Teach aide toilet transfers; recommendations made for adaptive toilet and sink to be installed in bathroom.
Occupational Therapy Direct Service				
Work on organizational skills and efficiency during routine.	Introduce computer at desk with adaptations; work on fine motor coordination and equipment use.	Work during class on attention to task-refocusing techniques.	Work on upper extremity coordination to increase participation during group play.	Introduce and instruct in use of adaptive and modified equipment to facilitate independence in hygiene activities of daily living.
Occupational Therapy Indirect Service				
Work with teacher to set up achievable AM schedule; suggest reorganization of materials in classroom to make them more accessible; instruct classroom aide in routine and necessary cues to initially assist with completion of routine.	Instruct educators and aide in computer use, adaptations needed and current limitations; instruct aide and family in techniques to assist with use of device.	Instruct educators and aide in cues to assist with attention to task and identify appropriate reinforcers; make recommendations for environmental changes that will reduce distractions.	Instruct aide to assist with participation in activities. Work with educator to supplement activities with components appropriate for inclusion.	Teach aide use of adaptive equipment and how to assist with the activities of daily living.

Source: From Szabo, J. L. (2000). Maddie's story: Inclusion through physical and occupational therapy. *Teaching Exceptional Children, 33*(2), p. 15. Reprinted by permission.

- *School nurses,* who provide certain health care services to students, monitor students' health, and inform IEP teams about the effects of medical conditions on students' educational programs
- *Prosthetists,* who make and fit artificial limbs
- *Orthotists,* who design and fit braces and other assistive devices
- *Orientation and mobility specialists,* who teach students to navigate their environment as effectively and independently as possible
- *Biomedical engineers,* who develop or adapt technology to meet a student's specialized needs
- *Health aides,* who carry out medical procedures and health-care services in the classroom
- *Counselors and medical social workers,* who help students and families adjust to disabilities

PTs, OTs, and other related-services specialists

Content Standards for Beginning Teachers—P&HD: Roles and responsibilities of school and community-based medical and related-services personnel (PH10K3).

Environmental Modifications

Environmental modifications are frequently necessary to enable a student with physical and health impairments to participate more fully and independently in school. Environmental modifications include adaptations to provide increased access to a task or an activity, changing the way in which instruction is delivered, and changing the manner in which the task is done (Best, Heller, & Bigge, 2005; Heller, Dangel, & Sweatman, 1995). Although barrier-free architecture is the most publicly visible type of environmental modification for making community buildings and services more accessible, some of the most functional adaptations require little or no cost:

- Install paper-cup dispensers near water fountains so students in wheelchairs can use them.
- Move a class or an activity to an accessible part of a school building so that a student with a physical impairment can participate.
- Provide soft-tip pens that require less pressure for writing.
- Provide a head-mounted pointer stick and keyboard guard that enable a student with limited fine-motor control to strike one computer key at a time.
- Change desks and tabletops to appropriate heights for students who are very short or use wheelchairs.
- Provide a wooden pointer to enable a student to reach the upper buttons on an elevator control panel.
- Modify response requirements by allowing written responses instead of spoken ones, or vice versa.

Environmental modifications

Content Standards for Beginning Teachers—PH&D: Adaptations of educational environments necessary to accommodate individuals with P&HD (PH5K1) (also CC5K1).

Assistive Technology

Although the term *technology* often conjures up images of sophisticated computers and other hardware, technology includes any systematic method based on scientific principles for accomplishing a practical task or purpose. IDEA defines **assistive technology** as both assistive technology devices and the services needed to help a child obtain and effectively use the devices.

> *Assistive technology device* means any item, piece of equipment, or product system, whether acquired commercially off the shelf, modified, or customized, that is used to increase, maintain, or improve the functional capabilities of a child with a disability. The term does not include a medical device that is surgically implanted or the replacement of such device. (20 U.S.C. §1401 [2004], 20 C.F.R. §300.5)

> *Assistive technology service* means any service that directly assists a child with a disability in the selection, acquisition, or use of an assistive technology device. (20 U.S.C. §1401 [2004], 20 C.F.R. §300.6)

The types of assistive technology that persons with disabilities use are often the same as those that individuals without disabilities use, for example, a flexible drinking straw (Williams, 1991).

Assistive technology

Content Standards for Beginning Teachers—P&HD: Communication and social interaction alternatives for individuals who are nonspeaking (PH6K1).

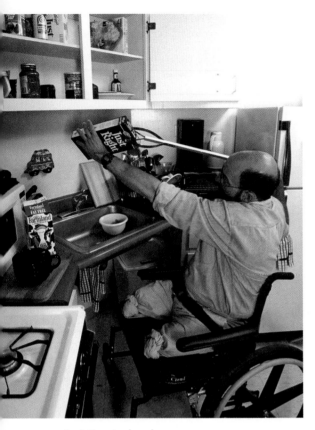

Assistive technology includes low-tech devices such as this simple "reacher."

Go to the Homework & Exercises section in Chapter 11 of MyEducationLab and complete Homework Exercise 4. As you watch the videos and answer the accompanying questions, think about the difference mobility has made in all three of these students' lives.

Individuals with physical disabilities use both low-tech assistive devices (e.g., adapted eating utensils, a "grabber" or "reacher" that enables a person in a wheelchair to reach items on a shelf) and high-tech assistive devices (e.g., computerized synthetic speech devices, electronic switches activated by eye movements) for a wide variety of purposes, including mobility, performance of daily life skills, improved environmental manipulation and control, better communication, access to computers, recreation and leisure, and enhanced learning (Dell, Newton, & Petroff, 2008; Parette, 1998). IEP team members should not view a student's acquisition and use of assistive technology as an educational outcome in itself but as a means of increasing the student's independence and access to various activities and opportunities.

Some students cannot move freely from place to place without the assistance of a mobility device. Many children as young as 3 to 5 years old can learn to explore their environment with freedom and independence in "energy efficient, creative, wheeled scooter boards and wheeled go-carts that provide mobility without restricting upper or lower extremity functions" (Evans & Smith, 1993, p. 1418). Adapted bicycles enable children with disabilities to enjoy the thrill of bicycle riding and reap the health benefits (Klein, McHugh, Harrington, Davis, & Lieberman, 2005).

Advances in wheelchair design have made manual chairs lighter and stronger, powered chairs have been adapted for use in rural areas, and new environmental controls have put the wheelchair user into contact with both immediate and distant parts of her world. Approved by the U.S. Food and Drug Administration in 2003, the iBot Mobility System is an extremely sophisticated wheelchair that can go up and down stairs, climb curbs up to 5 inches, and raise its user up to reach high shelves and countertops and interact with people at eye level (www.ibotnow.com).

Incidentally, a student should not be described as being "confined to a wheelchair." This expression suggests that the person is restrained or even imprisoned. Most students who use wheelchairs leave them from time to time to exercise, travel in an automobile, or lie down. The preferred language is "has a wheelchair" or "uses a wheelchair to get around."

New technological aids for communication are used increasingly by children whose physical impairments prevent them from speaking clearly. For students who can speak but have limited motor function, voice input/output products enable them to access computers (Dell et al., 2008). Such developments allow students with physical impairments to communicate expressively and receptively with others and take part in a wide range of instructional programs. Many individuals with physical disabilities use telecommunications technologies to expand their world, gain access to information and services, and meet new people. Many children and adults with disabilities use e-mail and instant messaging to communicate with others, make new friends, and build and maintain relationships.

Technology can seldom be pulled off the shelf and serve a student with disabilities with maximum effectiveness. Before purchasing and training a child to use any assistive technology device, the IEP team should carefully consider certain characteristics of the child and the potential technologies that might be selected as well as the impact of using those technologies on the child's family (Alper & Raharinirina, 2006; Parette & McMahan, 2002). An assessment of the child's academic skills, social skills, and physical capabilities should help identify the goals and objectives for the technology and narrow down the kinds of devices that may be effective. The team should also determine the child's preferences for certain types of technology. The IEP team should then consider the characteristics of potentially appropriate technologies, including availability, simplicity of operation, initial and ongoing cost, adaptability to meet the child's changing needs, and the device's reliability and repair record. Several excellent resources on designing, selecting, and using assistive technology are also available (e.g., Bryant & Bryant, 2003; Gray, Quartrano, & Liberman, 1998; Johnston, Beard, & Bowden Carpenter, 2007).

Animal Assistance

Animals can help children and adults with physical disabilities in many ways. Nearly everyone is familiar with guide dogs, which can help people who are blind travel independently. Some agencies now train hearing dogs to assist people who are deaf by alerting them to sounds. Another recent and promising approach to the use of animals by people with disabilities is the helper or service dog. Depending on a person's needs, dogs can be trained to carry books and other objects (in saddlebags), pick up telephone receivers, turn light switches on or off, and open doors. Dogs can also be used for balance and support—for example, to help a person propel a wheelchair up a steep ramp or stand up from a seated position. And dogs can be trained to contact family members or neighbors in an emergency.

Monkeys also have been trained to serve as personal care attendants for people with disabilities. See Current Issues and Future Trends, "Monkey Helpers: Personal Care Attendants and Companions for People With Disabilities."

In addition to providing practical assistance and enhancing the independence of people with disabilities, animals also have social value as companions. People frequently report that their helper animals serve as icebreakers in opening up conversations and contacts with people without disabilities in the school and community.

"Helper" or "service dogs" can be trained to assist with many daily living and work-related tasks.

Special Health Care Routines

Many students with physical disabilities have health care needs that require specialized procedures such as taking prescribed medication or self-administering insulin shots, CIC (described earlier in this chapter), tracheotomy care, ventilator/respirator care, and managing special nutrition and dietary needs (Heller, Bigge, & Allgood, 2005). These special health-related needs are prescribed in an **individualized health care plan (IHCP)**, which is included as part of the student's IEP. In addition to general information describing the history, diagnosis, and assessment data relevant to the condition, the IHCP "includes precise information about how to handle routine healthcare procedures, physical management techniques, and medical emergencies that may arise while the child is at school" (Getch et al., 2007, p. 48). Teachers and school personnel must be trained to safely administer the health care procedures they are expected to perform (Heller, Fredrick, Best, Dykes, & Cohen, 2000; Porter, Haynie, Bierle, Heintz Caldwell, & Palfrey, 1997).

Often, well-meaning teachers, classmates, and parents tend to do too much for a child with a physical or health impairment. It may be difficult, frustrating, and/or time-consuming for the child to learn to care for his own needs, but the confidence and skills gained from independent functioning are well worth the effort in the long run (Rues et al., 2006). Students who learn to perform all or part of their daily health care needs increase their ability to function independently in nonschool environments and lessen their dependence on caregivers (Bosner & Belfiore, 2001; Collins, 2007). Figure 11.5 shows IHCP objectives that might be included in a student's IEP.

IHCPs

 Council for Exceptional Children — Content Standards for Beginning Teachers—P&HD: Integrate an individual's health care plan into daily programming (PH7S5).

Importance of Positioning, Seating, and Movement   Proper positioning, seating, and regular movement are critically important for children with physical disabilities. Proper positioning and movement encourage the development of muscles and bones and help maintain healthy skin (Heller, Forney, Alberto, Schwartzman, & Goeckel, 2000). In addition to these health benefits, positioning can influence how a child with physical disabilities is perceived and accepted by others. Simple adjustments can contribute to improved appearance and greater comfort and increased health for the child with physical disabilities (Best, Reed, & Bigge, 2005; Cantu, 2004):

- Good positioning results in alignment and proximal support of the body.
- Stability positively affects use of the upper body.

Positioning, seating, and movement

Council for Exceptional Children — Content Standards for Beginning Teachers—P&HD: Use positioning techniques that decrease inappropriate tone and facilitate appropriate postural reactions to enhance participation (PH5S3) (also PH2K3).

CURRENT ISSUES AND FUTURE TRENDS

MONKEY HELPERS: PERSONAL CARE ATTENDANTS AND COMPANIONS FOR PEOPLE WITH DISABILITIES

The first edition of *Exceptional Children,* in 1980, included a description of an exciting research project by M. J. Willard at Tufts New England Medical Center exploring the possibility of capuchin monkeys as service animals for people with spinal cord injuries. Dr. Willard described her early work with Crystal, one of the first monkeys to participate in her noble experiment.

> One of the first things I taught Crystal was to feed me. I used a shaping procedure. If Crystal would just touch the spoon she was rewarded with a pellet of food and "Good girl!" Then she had to learn to grasp the spoon on the right end. Once Crystal got to holding the spoon, then any movement where she raised it was reinforced. . . . Once she could raise the spoon and put it into my mouth, I taught her to touch the bowl first and do scooping motions. Then we went to fake food, Styrofoam bits, because she had to learn not to touch the food. Finally we went to real food, applesauce, and about 95% of it would get into me—and that took about 3 months of 20-minute training sessions every day. But we learned a lot and we're getting much better now. Teaching new skills in a matter of days. (quoted in Heward, 1980, p. 265)

Crystal proved such a capable learner that she was eventually placed with Bill Powell, a computer engineer living in Boston. Dr. Willard's pioneering work laid the foundation for Helping Hands, a nonprofit organization that by 2006 had placed 122 monkeys with individuals with spinal cord injuries but now also serves those with muscular dystrophy, multiple sclerosis, Lou Gehrig's disease, and other mobility-limiting diseases.

WHY MONKEYS

Capuchin monkeys—species *Cebus* indigenous to South America—are especially well suited to be monkey helpers. Capuchins are natural tool users in the wild, and their small size (6 to 10 pounds) is well suited to a home environment. "These little monkeys tend to form wonderful relationships with people," says Judi Zazula, the director of Helping Hands. "They also are very curious and they love to manipulate objects."

Only positive reinforcement is needed to teach capuchins new tasks. Training is accomplished simply by rewarding the monkeys for doing activities that already come naturally to them.

Monkeys can do a wider range of tasks for a much longer time than other animals. It costs about $35,000 to

Dr. Willard uses a shaping procedure to teach Crystal to feed her with a spoon. Crystal's success is immediately reinforced with a bit of *her* favorite food.

support each monkey placement from breeding through lifelong care of 30 to 40 years. This compares favorably to $50,000 needed to train and support a service dog with a 10-year lifespan.

MONKEY CARE AND MONKEY COLLEGE

- Once it was decided that capuchins were capable of being effective helpers and wonderful companions, Helping Hands began a selective breeding program to influence the health and behavior characteristics of monkeys in the program, and to ensure that no monkeys would be taken from the wild for this purpose. Since 1995, monkeys that have been specially bred at Southwick's Zoo in Mendon, Massachusetts, enter the Helping Hands program.

- Monkeys are raised in volunteer foster homes until they move to the training center. The focus of the Foster Home Program is to raise happy and healthy monkeys, and to prepare them for their important roles as helpers and companions.

- Monkeys are educated at the Helping Hands Carvel Foundation Training Center in Boston (a.k.a., Monkey College). After learning a basic repertoire of helping tasks, each monkey is matched by personality to a particular recipient and then taught tasks specific to the needs of the selected recipient.

- Initial placement in the home of the recipient includes eight days of setup and on-site training by the Helping Hands placement team, which also furnishes customized equipment and adaptations to the recipient's living space.

- Each monkey is supported postplacement by a placement specialist (including lifelong health and behavioral support) and training for new tasks, when needed. Helping Hands provides continued support, such as training for new tasks when needed, to all established placement pairs, some of whom have been together for well over 20 years.

- Monkeys receive lifetime medical care by a specially selected network of veterinary doctors.

- Monkeys are given all necessary respite and retirement care, if needed.

Helping Hands has learned that although task assistance is fundamentally valuable to its recipients, the true magic of the program is the emotional benefit of companionship and the animal–human bond. Chris Watts, who has no feeling from the chest down and limited use of his arms and hands as the result of breaking his neck in a diving accident, describes what his capuchin monkey helper, Sadie, means to him:

> "If I dropped the phone on the floor, if I dropped my water on the floor, or I dropped my pills or any of those kinds of things, they stayed on the floor until someone came home."
>
> But since he got Sadie about a year ago, that has changed. Sadie is able to turn lights off and on, do the same thing with the television, pick up things like a phone or a remote and even get a water bottle out of a refrigerator, open it, insert a straw and give it to Watts. Watts uses a laser pointer to show Sadie what he wants and the monkey goes to work.
>
> "It's somewhere between having a daughter and a friend, and a pet and a personal care attendant all wrapped in one."
>
> "We give something to each other," says Watts. "She needs my affection just as much as I need hers. It just feels really good just to know there's something that loves you unconditionally like she does." (from television news report by Scott Wahle, CBS 4 Boston, January 17, 2006)

 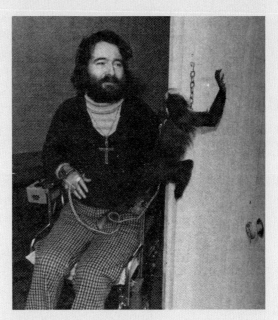

Crystal unlocks the door to Bill's apartment, pushes it open, and turns on the light.

Companionship and the emotional bond recipients form with their monkey helpers are just as important as task assistance. (Courtesy of Megan Talbert, Helping Hands.)

To learn more about Helping Hands and see videos of people and their helper monkeys, go the http://www.helpinghandsmonkeys.org/.

Portions of this essay adapted from *Helping Hands: Monkey Helpers for the Disabled, 2005 Annual Report* and other materials provided by Helping Hands.

What Do You Think?

1. How might having a monkey helper and companion contribute to the quality of life experienced by a person with disabilities?

2. What skills would a person need to be a responsible partner for a helper monkey?

3. How might animal species other than dogs and monkeys help people with disabilities?

FIGURE 11.5 Example of IHCP objectives included in an IEP for a student with special health care needs

Tube feeding:
- Student will explain (orally, in writing, or through other means) reasons for alternative eating method.
- Student will describe steps necessary in implementing the procedure.
- Student will indicate desire to eat.
- Student will measure feeding liquid to be placed in feeding bag or syringe.
- Student will pour food in feeding bag or syringe.
- Student will direct cleaning of feeding equipment.
- Student will clean equipment.
- Student will feed self.

Tracheostomy suctioning:
- Student will indicate need to be suctioned.
- Student will turn on suction machine.
- Student will hold suction tube while procedure is being implemented.
- Student will describe steps necessary to suction.
- Student will explain to others the indicators of need for suctioning.

Catheterization:
- Student will indicate time to be catheterized.
- Student will self-catheterize.
- Student will describe steps in implementing the process.
- Student will wash materials necessary.
- Student will assemble materials necessary.
- Student will hold catheter steady during procedure.
- Student will describe indicators of problems related to catheterization.

Source: From Lehr, D. H., & Macurdy, S. (1994). Meeting special health care needs of students. In M. Agran, N. E. Marchand-Martella, & R. C. Martella (Eds.), *Promoting health and safety: Skills for independent living* (p. 82). Baltimore, MD: Paul H. Brookes. Reprinted by permission.

- Stability promotes feelings of physical security and safety.
- Good positioning distributes pressure evenly and provides comfort for seating tolerance and long-term use.
- Good positioning can reduce deformity.
- Positions must be changed frequently.

Proper seating helps combat poor circulation, muscle tightness, and pressure sores and contributes to proper digestion, respiration, and physical development. Be attentive to the following (Heller, Forney, et al., 2000):

- Face should be forward, in midline position.
- Shoulders should be in midline position, not hunched over.
- Trunk should be in midline position; maintain normal curvature of spine.
- Seatbelt, pommel or leg separator, and/or shoulder and chest straps may be necessary for shoulder/upper trunk support and upright positions.
- Pelvic position: hips as far back in the chair as possible and weight distributed evenly on both sides of the buttocks.
- Foot support: both feet level and supported on the floor or wheelchair pedals.

Skin care is a major concern for many children with physical disabilities. Caregivers should check the skin underneath braces or splints daily to identify persistent red spots that indicate an improper fit. Someone should perform skin checks at least twice daily. Students who can conduct self-checks of their skin should be taught to do so. Use of a long-handled mirror can reduce the student's dependence on others for this self-care task (Ricci-Balich & Behm, 1996). A health care professional should be contacted if any spot does not fade within 20 minutes after the pressure is relieved (Campbell, 2006). Students who can use their arms should be taught to perform "chair pushups" in which they lift their buttocks off the seat for 5 to 10 seconds. Doing chair pushups every 30 to 60 minutes may prevent pressure sores. Children who cannot perform pushups can shift their weight by bending forward and sideways.

Lifting and Transferring Students   To prevent the development of pressure sores and help students maintain proper seating and positioning, teachers must know how to move and transfer students with physical disabilities. Teachers should follow routines for lifting and transferring children with physical disabilities for each child that entail standard procedures for (a) making contact with the child, (b) communicating what is going to happen in a manner the child can understand, (c) preparing the child physically for the transfer, and (d) requiring the child to participate in the routine as much as possible (Stremel et al., 1990). Figure 11.6 shows an example of an individualized routine for lifting and carrying a preschool child with cerebral palsy and spastic quadriplegia. Posting charts and photos of recommended positions for individual students can remind teachers and other staff to use proper transferring and positioning techniques. Parette and Hourcade (1986) provide guidelines for shifting the position of students in their wheelchairs and for moving students to and from a wheelchair to toilets and to the classroom floor.

Independence and Self-Esteem

All children, whether or not they face the challenges presented by a physical disability or a chronic health condition, need to develop respect for themselves and feel that they have a rightful place in their families, schools, and communities. Effective teachers accept and treat children with physical impairments and special health care needs as worthwhile and whole individuals rather than as disability cases. They encourage the children to develop a positive, realistic view of themselves and their physical conditions. They enable the children to experience success, accomplishment, and, at times, failure. They expect the children to meet reasonable standards of performance and behavior. They help the children cope with disabilities wherever possible and realize that, beyond their physical impairments, these children have many qualities that make them unique individuals.

Students with physical limitations should be encouraged to develop as much independence as possible (Enright, 2000; McGill & Vogle, 2001). Nevertheless, most persons with physical disabilities find it necessary to rely on others for assistance at certain times and in

Lifting and transferring students

 Content Standards for Beginning Teachers—P&HD: Demonstrate appropriate body mechanics to ensure student and teacher safety in teacher safety in transfer, lifting, positioning, and seating (PH5S3).

Developing independence and self-esteem

 Content Standards for Beginning Teachers—P&HD: Barriers to accessibility and acceptance of individuals with P&HD (PH5K3) (also CC5K4).

FIGURE 11.6	Example of a routine for lifting and carrying a child with physical disabilities

Name: Susan   **Date:** 5/12/2008
Lifting and Carrying Routine
Follow these steps each time you pick Susan up from the floor or move her from one piece of equipment to another or move her in the classroom from one location to another.

Step	Activity	Desired response
Contacting	Touch Susan on her arm or shoulder and tell her you are going to move her from _____ to _____	Wait for Susan to relax.
Communicating	Tell Susan where you are going and show her a picture or object that represents where she is going. For example, show her coat and say, "We are going outside now to play."	Wait for Susan to respond with facial expressions and vocalizations. (Try not to get her so hyped that she becomes more spastic.)
Preparing	Make sure Susan's muscle tone is not stiff before you move her. Use deep pressure touch with a flat hand on her chest area to help relax her.	Wait to make sure that Susan's body is relaxed and in alignment (as much as possible).
Lifting	Place Susan in a sitting position and lift her from sitting unless she is in the stander, where she will need to be lifted from standing. Tell her that you are going to lift her. Put your arms around Susan's back and under her knees and bend her knees to her chest so that you maintain her in a flexed position.	Wait for Susan to reach her arms forward toward you and facilitate at her shoulders if she does not initiate reach within 10 seconds.
Carrying	Turn Susan away from you so that she is facing away and can see where you are moving. Lean her back against your body to provide support and hold her with one arm under her hips with her legs in front. If her legs become stiff, Use you other arm to hold her legs apart by coming under one leg and between the two legs to hold them gently apart.	Susan will be able to see where she is going and can use her arms to indicate location (grossly).
Repositioning	Put Susan in the next position she is to use for the activity. Tell her what is happening; "Music is next, and you are going to sit one the floor so you can play the instruments with Jilly and Tommy."	Susan is ready to participate in the next activity.

Source: From Campbell, P. H. (2006). Addressing motor disabilities. In M. E. Snell & F. Brown (Eds.), *Instruction of students with severe disabilities* (6th ed., p. 313). © 2006 by Merrill/Prentice Hall. Reprinted by permission of Pearson Education, Inc., Upper Saddle River, NJ.

certain situations. Effective teachers can help students cope with their disabilities, set realistic expectations, and accept help gracefully when it is needed.

Many people with disabilities report that their hardware (wheelchairs, prosthetic limbs, communication devices, etc.) creates a great deal of curiosity and leads to frequent, repetitive questions from strangers. Learning how to explain their physical disabilities or health condition and to respond to questions can be an appropriate component of the educational programs for some children. They may also benefit from discussing concerns such as when to ask for help from others and when to decline offers of assistance.

Many self-help groups are available for people with disabilities. These groups can help provide information and support to children affected by similar disabilities. It is usually encouraging for a child and parent to meet and observe capable, independent adults who have disabilities; and worthwhile helping relationships can be established. Teachers can help promote self-knowledge and self-confidence in their students with physical disabilities by introducing them to such adults and groups. Some self-advocacy groups operate centers for independent living, which emphasize adaptive devices, financial benefits, access to jobs, and provision of personal care attendants.

EDUCATIONAL PLACEMENT ALTERNATIVES

For no group of exceptional children is the continuum of educational services and placement options more relevant than for students with physical impairments and special health needs. Most children with physical and health impairments today spend at least part of the school day in general education classrooms. During the 2005–2006 school year, about 47% of all students who received special education services under the disability category of orthopedic impairments and 56% of those with other health impairments were educated in general education classrooms (U.S. Department of Education, 2007b). The percentage of students in each disability category served in resource rooms was 18% and 28%, respectively.

Placement alternates

Content Standards for Beginning Teachers—Common Core: Demands of learning environments (CC5K1).

Many children with physical disabilities are also served in special classes in the public schools. During the 2005–2006 school year, about 25% of all students who received special education services under the disability category of orthopedic impairments and 12% of those with other health impairments were educated in separate classrooms (U.S. Department of Education, 2007b). Special classes usually provide smaller class size, more adapted equipment, and easier access to the services of professionals such as physicians, physical and occupational therapists, adapted physical educators, and specialists in communication disorders and therapeutic recreation. Some districts build or adapt school buildings especially for students with physical disabilities.

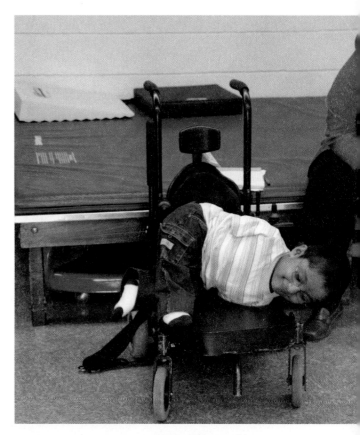

Some children with the most severe physical and health impairments are served in homebound or hospital education programs. If a child's medical condition necessitates hospitalization or treatment at home for a lengthy period (generally 30 days or more), the local school district is obligated to develop an IEP and provide appropriate educational services to the child through a qualified teacher. Some children need home- or hospital-based instruction because their life-support equipment cannot be made portable.

A **technology-dependent student** is "one who needs both a medical device to compensate for the loss of a vital body function and substantial and ongoing nursing care to avoid death or further disability" (Office of Technology Assessment, 1987, p. 3). Educators also use the term *medically fragile* to refer to students "who are in constant need of medical supervision to prevent life-threatening situations" (Katsiyannis & Yell, 2000, p. 317). As Lehr and McDaid (1993) pointed out, however, many of these children are "survivors of many adverse conditions, who in fact are not fragile at all, but remarkably strong to be able to rebound from periods of acute illness" (p. 7).

Jose has learned how to get in and out of his wheelchair, which helps him take part in his health care and increases his independence.

Home or hospital settings are usually regarded as the most restrictive placements because little or no interaction with students without disabilities is likely. Most large hospitals and medical centers employ educational specialists who cooperate with the hospitalized student's home school district in planning and delivering instruction. Homebound children are visited regularly by itinerant teachers or tutors hired by the school district. Some school programs use a closed-circuit TV system to enable children to see, hear, and participate in class discussions and demonstrations from their beds.

To learn more about students with orthopedic impairments and go on a guided tour of a neighborhood school designed for students with physical disabilities and health care needs, go to the Homework & Exercises Section in Chapter 11 on MyEducationLab and complete Homework Exercise 5.

One should not assume that a technology-dependent child cannot be educated in the public schools. After examining the experiences of 77 families of children who are ventilator-assisted, the authors of a study on the educational placements of such children concluded that "barriers to the integration of these children into school-based programs are attitudinal more than technological" (Jones, Clatterbuck, Marquis, Turnbull, & Moberly, 1996, p. 47).

Related Services in the Classroom

We will likely see a continuation of the trend to serve children with physical and health impairments in general education classrooms as much as possible. Therapists and other related service and support personnel will come into the classroom to assist the teacher, child, and classmates (Szabo, 2000). Wherever and by whomever needed health and other related services are carried out, we must heed Orelove and Sobsey's (1996) caution:

> The challenge for the team is to determine how to work with and around the student's medical and physical needs to provide an appropriate education, rather than turning the school day into an extended therapy session. Therapy and specialized health care procedures should facilitate, not replace, instruction. (pp. 3–4)

Including students with physical impairments and special health care needs in general education classrooms, however, has raised several controversial issues. Many questions center on the extent of responsibility properly assumed by teachers and schools for a child's physical health care needs. Some educators and school administrators believe that services such as catheterization, tracheotomy care, and tube feeding are more medical than educational and should not be the school's responsibility. The expense of such services, the training and supervision of personnel, and the availability of insurance pose potential problems for school districts. Similar questions have been raised with regard to the assistive devices and special therapeutic services that children with physical or health impairments may need to access and benefit from a public education. For example, who should bear the cost of an expensive computerized communication system for a child with cerebral palsy—the parents, the school, both, or some other agency?

Two landmark U.S. Supreme Court cases have made clear the government's position. In *Irving Independent School District v. Tatro* (1984), the Court decided that a school district was obligated to provide CIC to a young child with spina bifida. The Court considered catheterization to be a related service, necessary for the child to remain in the least restrictive educational setting and able to be performed by a trained layperson.

Cedar Rapids Community School District v. Garret F. (1999) involved nursing care for a middle school student who was paralyzed in a motorcycle accident at the age of 4 and could breathe only with an electric ventilator or by someone pumping an air bag attached to his tracheotomy tube. In addition to having someone monitor and check the settings on his ventilator, Garret required continuous assistance with his tracheotomy, positioning in his wheelchair, observations to determine if he was in respiratory distress, catheterization, assessments of his blood pressure, and assistance with food and drink. Garret's mother had used money from insurance and a settlement with the motorcycle company to hire a nurse to care for his medical needs. When Garret reached middle school, his mother asked the school district to assume the cost of his physical care during the school day. The school district refused, believing it was not responsible under IDEA for providing continuous nursing care. The Supreme Court agreed with lower courts that the nursing services were related services because Garret could not attend school without them and ruled that the school district had to pay for continuous one-on-one nursing care. These two rulings used what is known as a "bright-line test" for making decisions about related services (Katsiyannis & Yell, 2000). A bright-line test is clearly stated and easy to follow (Thomas & Hawke, 1999). The bright-line test established in the *Tatro* case and upheld by the *Garret* case is that if a licensed physician is required to perform a service, the school district is not responsible for paying for it. If a nurse or a health aide can perform the service, even if it is medical in nature, it is considered a related service that the school district must provide under IDEA to give the child access to a free appropriate public education.

You can find reviews and discussions of special education law and legal precedents concerning the schools' responsibility for providing assistive technology and special health care services in Heller, Fredrick, and colleagues (2000); Katsiyannis and Yell (2000); Murdick, Gartin, and Crabtree (2007); Wright and Wright (2006); and Yell (2006).

Inclusive Attitudes

After health care objectives, acceptance is the most basic need of children with physical disabilities and health impairments. How parents, teachers, classmates, and others react to a

---

Tatro and Garret cases

 Content Standards for Beginning Teachers—P&HD: Laws and policies related to specialized health care in the educational setting (PH1K3).

 Go to the Homework & Exercises section of MyEducationLab and complete Homework Exercise 6. As you watch the video, think about the importance of holding high expectations for all students and positive teacher attitudes in an inclusive school for students with physical disabilities and special health care needs.

child with physical disabilities is at least as important as the disability itself. Many children with physical disabilities suffer from excessive pity, sympathy, and overprotection; others are cruelly rejected, stared at, teased, and excluded from participating in activities with nondisabled children (Pivik, McComas, & LaFlamme, 2002). Turner-Henson, Holaday, Corser, Ogletree, and Swan (1994) conducted interviews with the parents of 365 children with chronic illnesses and reported that one third (34.5%) of the parents had experienced specific incidences of discrimination concerning their children. Although the study did not focus on the schools, more than half (55%) of the problems cited by the parents occurred at school (e.g., child not allowed to participate in play activities because of a brace or excluded from parties because of food limitations; teacher thinks child is faking low blood sugar). Peers were the second most common source of discrimination (36%).

The classroom can be a useful place to discuss disabilities and encourage understanding and acceptance of a child with a physical disability or health impairment. Some teachers find that simulation or role-playing activities are helpful. Classmates might, for example, have the opportunity to use wheelchairs, braces, or crutches to expand their awareness of some barriers a classmate with physical disabilities faces. Factual information can also help build a general understanding of impairment. Classmates should learn to use accurate terminology and offer the correct kind of assistance when needed.

Attitudes and practices that hinder or support inclusion of students with P&HD

Council for Exceptional Children — Content Standards for Beginning Teachers—P&HD: Barriers to accessibility and acceptance of individuals with P&HD (PH5K3) (also CC5K4).

To learn more about how some students perceive disabilities and inclusion, go to the Homework & Exercises section on MyEducationaLab and complete Homework Exercise 7.

TIPS for Beginning Teachers

PROMOTING THE SUCCESS OF STUDENTS WITH PHYSICAL DISABILITIES AND SPECIAL HEALTH CARE NEEDS
by Mary Kate Ryan-Griffith

If you become a teacher, you will have students with physical disabilities or special health care needs in your classroom at different times throughout your career. Here are some basic tips that will make your work with these students more effective and enjoyable for you and your students.

ENCOURAGE INDEPENDENT MOVEMENT

Sometimes our efforts to assist and be nice to a student with physical and health challenges can contribute to learned helplessness, which becomes increasingly difficult to overcome as the child grows older. Teachers should help children with physical and health challenges learn to be as motorically independent and self-sufficient as possible. Doing things for themselves develops and maintains children's muscular function and enhances their self-esteem.

- A child's independence can be sabotaged by inefficient room arrangement. Plan the layout of your classroom so that the child can access the water fountain, the blackboard, the reading area, the small-group-activities area, and the computer and can enter and exit the classroom for bathroom and emergency situations.

- If one of your students uses a wheelchair, obtain one (ask the school nurse or the PT), get in it, and navigate the classroom layout yourself. Looking at wheelchair access from this level is very sobering.

- Troubleshoot each situation in the classroom and around the school building and grounds that children should do themselves if they can: opening doors, turning pages in a book, feeding the class pet, holding up a test tube in science lab, going through the lunch line in the cafeteria. Look for ways to adapt the task and/or provide an assistive device that will enable the student to participate as independently as possible. A student who moves purposively throughout the day develops and maintains muscular function and interacts more naturally with classmates.

TEACH STUDENTS TO ASK FOR AND DECLINE HELP

As important as it is to build their independence, students with physical and special health needs must also learn to recognize and accept their limits.

- Teach children that it is okay to politely request assistance with tasks or situations that they cannot do independently. Manners should always be stressed! The pendulum can swing very quickly from a child who does not self-advocate to an imperious leader barking orders at one and all.

- A child who has politely requested and received assistance from others will likely experience an increase in unsolicited offers of help. Teach the student that it is also okay to say, "No, thanks, I don't need help now."

Ask Before You Push

My school is very large, so I will often enlist the aid of a student to help push me. You'd be surprised how many people start pushing my chair without asking. Why is it important to ask before pushing someone's wheelchair?

- Think of the chair as an extension of the person's body. You wouldn't touch someone, or want someone to touch you, without gaining permission.
- Pushing without the person's knowledge can be dangerous. For example, because my injury was high on the spinal cord, I don't have the balance needed to stay in my chair if I am suddenly pushed.
- Teach the target student's classmates how to ask, "Would you like some help pushing?"
- Ask the PT to co-teach a lesson with you and the target student on how to push the wheelchair in a safe and efficient manner. Too often, I've seen children pushing a chair one-handed or racing down

the hall with one. Pushers need to know how to take off the brakes and rebrake when they get to where they're going. Wheelchair brakes are very important!

Don't Be Afraid of the Equipment

The special equipment used by some children with physical disabilities and special health needs—braces, wheelchairs, ventilators, and voice boxes—can be intimidating to other children and to adults.

- If one of your students uses special equipment, get to know it. Ask the PT, the OT, the school nurse, or other health professionals on the child's IEP team to demonstrate and explain the equipment to you before the first week of school begins. If appropriate and possible, the student should participate in this demonstration and discussion. Ask what to look for to ensure that the equipment is in good working order and who to contact if you notice any problems.
- Ask the student with physical disabilities or special health care needs to do a show-and-tell of his equipment for the class. This not only helps classmates become comfortable with the equipment but also helps build friendships and quickly puts the equipment in the background where it should be so that children can see their classmate as just another kid.

Key Terms and Concepts

absence seizure, p. 415
acquired immune deficiency syndrome (AIDS), p. 419
acute condition, p. 408
assistive technology, p. 435
asthma, p. 418
ataxia, p. 410
athetosis, p. 410
attention-deficit/hyperactivity disorder (ADHD), p. 420
cerebral palsy, p. 409
chronic condition p. 408
clean intermittent catheterization (CIC), p. 413
complex partial seizure, p. 416
cystic fibrosis, p. 418
diabetes, p. 417
Duchenne muscular dystrophy (DMD), p. 413

epilepsy, p. 415
generalized tonic-clonic seizure, p. 415
human immunodeficiency virus (HIV), p. 419
hydrocephalus, p. 413
hypertonia, p. 410
hypotonia, p. 410
individualized health care plan (IHCP), p. 437
meningocele, p. 411
muscular dystrophy, p. 413
myelomeningocele, p. 411
neuromotor impairment, p. 408
occupational therapist (OT), p. 433
orthopedic impairment, p. 408
other health impairment, p. 408
paraplegia, p. 414
physical therapist (PT), p. 433
quadriplegia, p. 414

shunt, p. 413
simple partial seizure, p. 416
spina bifida, p. 411
spina bifida occulta, p. 411

technology-dependent student, p. 443
Type 1 diabetes, p. 417
Type 2 diabetes, p. 417
universal precautions, p. 420

SUMMARY

Definitions of Physical Disabilities and Health Impairments

- Children with physical disabilities and health impairments are eligible for special education under two disability categories of IDEA: orthopedic impairments and other health impairments.
- Orthopedic impairments involve the skeletal system; a neuromotor impairment involves the nervous system. Both are frequently described in terms of the affected parts of the body.
- Physical disabilities and health impairments may be congenital or acquired, chronic, or acute.

Prevalence

- In 2005–2006, 10.3% of all school-age children who received special education services were served under the disability categories of orthopedic impairments and other health impairments. This figure does not include all children with physical or health impairments because some are reported under other disability categories and some do not require special education services.

Types and Causes

- Cerebral palsy is a long-term condition arising from impairment to the brain and causing disturbances in voluntary motor functions.
- Spina bifida is a congenital condition that may cause loss of sensation and severe muscle weakness in the lower part of the body. Children with spina bifida can usually participate in most classroom activities but need assistance in toileting.
- Muscular dystrophy is a long-term condition; most children gradually lose the ability to walk independently.
- Spinal cord injuries are caused by a penetrating injury, stretching of the vertebral column, fracture of the vertebrae, or compression of the spinal cord and usually result in some form of paralysis below the site of the injury.
- Epilepsy produces disturbances of movement, sensation, behavior, and/or consciousness.
- Diabetes is a disorder of metabolism that can often be controlled with injections of insulin.
- Children with cystic fibrosis, asthma, HIV/AIDS, and other chronic health conditions may require special education and other related services, such as health care services and counseling.

Attention-Deficit/Hyperactivity Disorder

- To be diagnosed with attention-deficit/hyperactivity disorder (ADHD), a child must consistently display six or more symptoms listed in the DSM-IV of inattention or hyperactivity-impulsivity for a period of at least 6 months.
- Students with ADHD are eligible for special education under the other health impairment category if they have a heightened alertness to environmental stimuli that results in limited alertness with respect to the educational environment that adversely affects academic performance. Many children with ADHD who meet eligibility requirements for special education are served under other disability categories, most often emotional disturbance or learning disabilities. Some children with ADHD are eligible for services under Section 504 of the Rehabilitation Act.
- The prevalence of ADHD is estimated to be 3% to 5% of all school-age children.
- Boys are much more likely to be diagnosed with ADHD than are girls.
- Genetic factors may place individuals at a greater-than-normal risk of an ADHD diagnosis. ADHD is associated with a wide range of genetic disorders and diseases such as fragile X syndrome, Turner syndrome, Williams syndrome, fetal alcohol syndrome, prenatal exposure to cocaine, and lead poisoning.

- Some individuals with ADHD have structural or biochemical differences in their brains that may play a causal role in their behavioral deficits and excesses.
- Ritalin is the most frequently prescribed medication for children with ADHD. About 70% to 80% of children with ADHD respond positively to Ritalin, at least in the short term. Common but usually manageable side effects of Ritalin and other stimulant medications include insomnia, decreased appetite, headaches, weight loss, and irritability.
- The use of stimulant medications with children is controversial. Some professionals believe the benefits outweigh the liabilities and that drug therapy should be part of a comprehensive treatment program for children with ADHD. Other professionals are concerned that stimulant medications have few long-term benefits and that educators and parents rely too heavily on medical interventions.
- Behavioral interventions for students with ADHD include reinforcing on-task behavior, modifying assignments and instructional activities to promote success, and teaching self-control strategies.

Characteristics

- Perrin and colleagues' (1993) noncategorical system for classifying and understanding children's chronic physical and medical conditions includes 13 dimensions that are rated on a continuum from mild to profound.
- Many factors must be taken into consideration when assessing the effects of a physical impairment or health condition on a child's development and behavior. Two particularly important variables are the age of onset and the visibility of the impairment.

Educational Approaches

- Most children with physical disabilities and health impairments require services from an interdisciplinary team of professionals.
- Physical therapists (PTs) use specialized knowledge to plan and oversee a child's program for making correct and useful movements. Occupational therapists (OTs) are concerned with a child's participation in activities, especially those that will be useful in self-help, employment, recreation, communication, and other aspects of daily living.
- Modifications to the physical environment and to classroom activities can enable students with physical and health impairments to participate more fully in the school program.
- An assistive technology device is any piece of equipment used to increase, maintain, or improve the functional capabilities of a child with disabilities.
- Animals, particularly dogs and monkeys, can assist people with physical disabilities in various ways.
- Students can increase their independence by learning to take care of their personal health care routines such as clean intermittent catheterization and self-administration of medication.
- Proper positioning and seating are important for children with physical disabilities. All teachers and other staff should follow a standard routine for lifting and moving a child with physical disabilities.
- How parents, teachers, classmates, and others react to a child with physical disabilities is at least as important as the disability itself.
- Students with physical limitations should be encouraged to develop as much independence as possible. Effective teachers help students cope with their disabilities, set realistic expectations, and accept help gracefully when needed.
- Children with physical disabilities and health impairments can gain self-knowledge and self-confidence by meeting capable adults with disabilities and joining self-advocacy groups.

Educational Placement Alternatives

- About 50% of students with physical impairments and chronic health conditions are served in general education classrooms.
- The amount of support and accommodations required to enable a student with physical disabilities to function effectively in a general education class varies greatly according to each child's condition, needs, and level of functioning.

- Special classes usually provide smaller class size, more adapted equipment, and easier access to the services of professionals such as physicians, physical and occupational therapists, and specialists in communication disorders and therapeutic recreation.
- Some technology-dependent children require home- or hospital-based instruction because their life-support equipment cannot be made portable.
- The education of students with physical and health impairments in general education classrooms has raised several controversial issues, particularly with regard to the provision of medically related procedures in the classroom.
- Successful reentry of children who have missed extended periods of school because of illness or the contraction of a disease requires preparation of the child, parents, classmates, and school personnel.

 Now go to MyEducationLab at www.myeducationlab.com and take the pretest to assess your initial comprehension of chapter content. Once you have taken the pretest, use your individualized Study Plan for Chapter 11 to enhance your understanding of the concepts discussed in the chapter. Finally, take the posttest to assess your comprehension of Chapter 11 content.

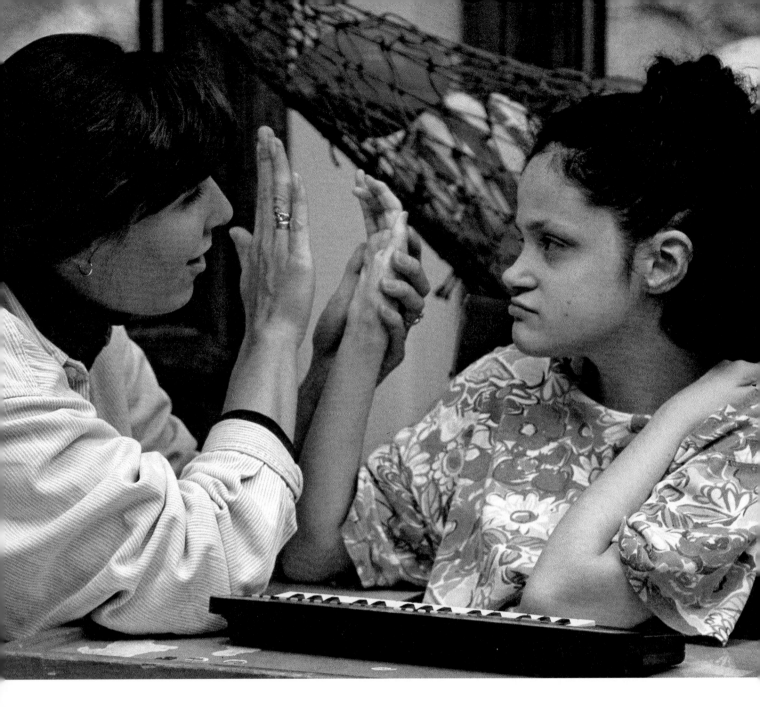

Low-Incidence Disabilities: Severe/Multiple Disabilities, Deaf-Blindness, and Traumatic Brain Injury

- Why is a curriculum based on typical developmental stages and milestones inappropriate for students with severe and multiple disabilities?
- How can a teacher increase the learning potential of students who exhibit significant and obvious deficits in multiple life-skill or developmental areas?
- How can a teacher assist a child who has been hospitalized with a traumatic brain injury return to school?
- Why is it so critical to select functional and age-appropriate curriculum objectives for students with severe and multiple disabilities?
- What are the most important skills for a teacher of students with severe and multiple disabilities? Why?
- How much time should a student with severe and multiple disabilities spend in the general education classroom?

FEATURED TEACHER

CAREY CREECH-GALLOWAY
Clark Middle School • Winchester, Kentucky

Carey Creech-Galloway

Education—Certification—Experience

- B.S., special education, University of Kentucky in 2004
- M.Ed. student in Special Education Moderate and Severe Disabilities, University of Kentucky
- Kentucky Moderate and Severe Disabilities, P–12

- 4 years as a special education teacher; 3 years as an instructional assistant for secondary students with moderate and severe disabilities

I became a special education teacher for several reasons. I enjoy the individual programming that occurs in special education and allows for a very student-centered approach to teaching. The combination of a functional curriculum and academic curriculum for students with severe disabilities keeps the job challenging and, with varying student ability levels, always exciting! With each new group of students, I must discover new and creative ways to deliver instruction, and I think that keeps me fresh and on my toes. To be an effective teacher of students with severe disabilities, you have to be organized, flexible, and knowledgeable about systematic instruction strategies.

Collaboration and Preparation for Meaningful Inclusion My classroom functions more like a resource room than a self-contained setting. Each of my students is included in a general education classroom for at least 40% of the school day. While I am not an advocate of full inclusion for every student with severe disabilities, when appropriate people supports and instructional supports are in place, meaningful and beneficial inclusion occurs. The staff at my school has been supportive in this effort, and I have found that if the general education teacher is committed to collaborating, then most people will support the inclusion process.

Inclusion has gone well for my students because we provide appropriate adaptations and modifications in the general education setting. I think it is important to look at the core content that the general education teacher is focusing on and obtain the essential information. Teachers can embed self-care, communication, and vocational goals into the general education setting in numerous ways. For example, one of my students, Liz, is learning to use a voice output switch for communication. She is included in a general education science class and works on using her switch to answer yes–no questions during group work with her peers. During the lecture portion of the class, Liz accesses her switch to give information to the class that corresponds with the teacher's lecture. If an experiment or seat work is planned for the class, Liz uses her switch to give instructions or rules for the activity. Sometimes she uses her yes–no side-by-side switch to answer questions when peers or adults talk to her. This is just one example of how a student with severe disabilities in my classroom has participated in the general education setting.

I want to note how important it is to have materials prepared for the student prior to class. If you are committed to the inclusion process and to making that student a true member of the class, then that student must be present and participate like those peers without disabilities.

Research-Based Instruction and Positive Behavior Support I am a dedicated user of research-based instructional methods proven to be effective in teaching students with moderate and severe disabilities. I use many different systematic instruction methods, but I rely on constant time delay, the system of least prompts, and simultaneous prompting for most instructional objectives. I strive to keep a balance of appropriate functional and academic goals for my students, and I have found that these methods are easiest to implement and apply to many different skills. In addition, constant time delay, the system of least prompts, and simultaneous prompting are easy to re-teach to paraprofessionals and general education teachers involved in the students, educational program. For example, Shari is working on self-feeding, and my using the system of least prompts has allowed her to move from feeding herself with physical prompts to feeding herself with gesture and verbal prompts. The goal is to continue using the system until the stimulus transfers from a teacher prompt to a naturally occurring stimulus such as setting the food in front of Shari.

The all-important question that many special educators always ask one another is, "How do you handle challenging behaviors?" Every teacher will have students whose frequent displays of inappropriate or defiant behavior challenge their ability to be effective. I use applied behavior analysis (ABA), which encompasses differential reinforcement. When faced with such behaviors, I begin by analyzing my daily log of the frequency of the behavior along with ABC (antecedent-behavior-consequence) observations. These data help me understand the function of the behavior for the student and whether I need to teach a replacement behavior, reduce the frequency of the behavior, or stop the behavior completely. I select a differential reinforcement method to lower the rate of the behavior. I always collect data continuously on severe behaviors, but for some behaviors, you may need to collect data only at certain times or in specific settings. Finally, I make sure I have positive reinforcement in place for the student that will promote the desired behaviors.

This year I have a student, Jacob, who often has a difficult time keeping his hands to himself and, when asked to perform a task that he doesn't like, exhibits some very aggressive behaviors. I began pairing some of his individualized education program (IEP) goals with an activity he really enjoys in order to reinforce good behavior during the instructional period. I observed Jacob's behavior while he worked on different activities with each of the two paraprofessionals in my classroom. After those observations, I had one of the paraprofessionals observe me working with Jacob. We used ABC observation forms during these observations and compiled them to try to find a function and pattern for the behavior. We developed a plan for a DRO (differential reinforcement of zero rates or other behaviors) that we implemented on a fixed-interval schedule. We realized very quickly after implementing the DRO that Jacob could anticipate when the interval was over and that he needed reinforcement on a variable schedule. We applied the DRO at 3 minutes, 5 minutes, or 8 minutes in a random order. At the end of each interval when he displayed no aggressive behavior and kept his hands and feet to himself, Jacob received pretzels or popcorn. His aggressive behavior increased during the first 3 days of this intervention, but then his behavior improved dramatically over the next 2 weeks. I gradually increased the duration of the intervals until Jacob was working for reinforcement each hour. Continuing to revisit the ABA components and evaluating your data are the best ways to plan and revise behavior intervention plans.

One of the most difficult parts of my job is managing my time efficiently between teaching, collaborating, and keeping up with paperwork. I collaborate with related service professionals as well as general education teachers. I never seem to have enough planning time, and in order to maintain open lines of communication, I must collaborate through e-mail or at the vending machine. The field of special education requires a lot of paperwork. I collect data on every instructional objective I teach, and I graph all of the data, so keeping up with progress data is very challenging. I have a minimum of 10 instructional objectives for each student, so on any given school day, I may collect data on as many as 50 or 60 IEP objectives. Whenever possible, I group students with similar objectives in small groups and collect data using that model, but some students have individual objectives that require 1:1 teaching in order to collect data. I cannot stress enough how important direct and frequent data collection is when teaching students with severe disabilities. It allows the teacher to make data-based decisions about instruction and gives information about the student's independence level. For example, I may have a student who is working on using a communication board to request items. That student may require all model or physical prompts at the beginning of the year, but by the end of the school year, he may need only verbal prompts to perform the skill. This is a huge amount of growth that may not be as evident without data collection. I have excellent paraprofessionals who can assist me in keeping up with records and data collection, which in my opinion is one of the most important aspects of my job.

If I shared only one idea with those who plan to become teachers of students with severe disabilities, it would be to get as much "hands-on experience" with this population of students as possible. I think working as an instructional assistant, working as an employment trainer, and being involved in local Special Olympics have been as valuable to me as the excellent education I received at the University of Kentucky.

Preschooler Zack shows a card with a symbol and picture that says, "I want toy," to a classmate, who responds, "Here's the toy, Zack." First-grader Emily is learning to feed herself with a spoon. A teacher shows 13-year-old Terrence that it is more appropriate to shake hands than to hug a person when first introduced. Manuela, who is 20, is learning to ride a city bus to her afternoon job at the cafeteria, where she clears tables and sorts silverware. Zack, Emily, Terrence, and Manuela have severe disabilities or multiple disabilities. Except for their general need for ongoing support from others and for instruction in skills that children without disabilities usually acquire naturally at a younger age, these students have little in common with each other.

Special educators sometimes use the term *low-incidence disabilities* to refer to disabilities that do not occur very often. Together, multiple disabilities, traumatic brain injury, and deaf-blindness (the three IDEA disability categories described in this chapter) represent less than 3% of all children who receive special education.

Students with severe disabilities are a highly diverse population. Each student often has a combination of obvious and not-so-obvious disabilities. Because of differences in their intellectual, physical, and behavioral abilities, each student requires different supports or adaptations in their education. Without direct and systematic instruction, many students with severe and multiple disabilities cannot perform the most basic, everyday activities that most of us take for granted, such as eating, toileting, and communicating our needs and feelings to others.

Having a severe disability does not preclude meaningful achievements. Despite the severity and multiplicity of their disabilities, these students can and do learn. An ever-growing body of evidence demonstrates that people with severe disabilities can learn and participate meaningfully in integrated school, work, and community settings.

DEFINING SEVERE, PROFOUND, AND MULTIPLE DISABILITIES

Severe Disabilities

As used by most special educators, the term **severe disabilities** generally includes students with significant disabilities in intellectual, physical, and/or social functioning. Students with multiple disabilities and deaf-blindness—two of the three IDEA disability categories described in this chapter—as well as those with severe mental retardation, severe emotional disturbance, and severe disabilities or health impairments are encompassed by the term.

No single widely accepted definition of severe disabilities exists. Most definitions are based on scores on tests of intellectual functioning, developmental progress compared to chronological age, or the extent of educational and other supports needed. According to the system of classifying levels of mental retardation previously used by the American Association on Intellectual and Developmental Disabilities, a person obtaining IQ scores of 35 to 40 and below was considered to have severe mental retardation; scores of 20 to 25 and below resulted in a classification of profound mental retardation. In practice, however, the term *severe disabilities* often includes many individuals who score in the moderate level of mental retardation (IQ scores of 40 to 55) (Collins, 2007).

Traditional methods of intelligence testing are virtually useless with children whose disabilities are profound. Imagine the difficulty, as well as the inappropriateness, of giving an IQ test to a student who cannot hold up his head or point, let alone talk. If tested, such

After reading this chapter, complete the pretest for Chapter 12 on MyEducationLab to assess your initial understanding of chapter content.

Definitions of severe disabilities, profound disabilities, and multiple disabilities

 Content Standards for Beginning Teachers—INDEP CURR: Definitions and issues related to the identification of individuals with disabilities (IC1K1) (also CC1K5).

Special education for students with severe disabilities includes systematic instruction in basic skills.

students tend to be assigned IQ scores at the extreme lower end of the continuum. Knowing that a particular student has an IQ of 25, however, is of no value in designing an appropriate educational program.

A developmental approach to defining severe disabilities was once common. For example, Justen (1976) proposed that individuals with severe disabilities are "those individuals age 21 and younger who are functioning at a general developmental level of half or less than the level which would be expected on the basis of chronological age" (p. 5). Most special educators today maintain that developmental levels have little relevance to this population and instead emphasize that a student with severe disabilities, regardless of age, is one who needs instruction in basic skills, such as getting from place to place independently, communicating with others, controlling bowel and bladder functions, and self-feeding. Most children without disabilities acquire these basic skills in the first 5 years of life, but the student with severe disabilities needs special instruction to do so. The basic-skills definition makes it clear that special education for students with severe disabilities must not focus on traditional academic instruction.

The organization TASH (formerly The Association for Persons with Severe Handicaps) describes the people for whom it advocates as individuals

> who require ongoing support in more than one major life activities in order to participate in an integrated community and enjoy a quality of life similar to that available to all citizens. Support may be required for life activities such as mobility, communication, self-care, and learning as necessary for community living, employment, and self-sufficiency. (TASH, 2000)

Compared with other areas of special education (intellectual disabilities, learning disabilities, and behavioral disorders, in particular), educators have shown much less concern and debate over the definition of *severe disabilities*. This does not indicate that professionals are uninterested in defining the population of students they serve but reflects two inherent features of severe disabilities. First, there is little need for a definition that precisely describes who is and is not to be identified by the term *severe disabilities*. Although the specific criteria used to define learning disabilities have a major impact on who will be eligible for special education services, whether or not special education is needed by any child who might be considered to have severe disabilities is never an issue. Second, because of the tremendous diversity of learning and physical challenges that these students experience, any single set of descriptors is inadequate. Statements that specify the particular educational goals and support needs of each individual student are more meaningful.

Profound Disabilities

Some professionals make a distinction between children with severe disabilities and those with profound disabilities. Sternberg (1994) believes that distinguishing between severe and profound disabilities is necessary because the "expectations and implications for each are different. These differences are related not only to one's capability for independent functioning but also to the utility of specific educational or training models and methods" (p. 7). According to Sternberg, an individual with **profound disabilities** is one who

> exhibits profound developmental disabilities in all five of the following behavioral-content areas: cognition, communication, social skills development, motor-mobility, and activities of daily living (self-help skills); and requires a service structure with continuous monitoring and observation. . . . This definition also posits a ceiling of 2 years of age for each area of

functioning (6 years of age for those classified as severely disabled). If the individual functions above that level, the individual cannot be classified as profoundly disabled. (p. 6)

Thus, a person with profound disabilities, according to Sternberg, functions at a level no higher than that of a typically developing 2-year-old in all five areas (whereas the functioning of a student with severe disabilities in one or more of these areas may be less delayed, up to the level of a typical 6-year-old). Mechling (2006) provided the following description of two students with profound disabilities:

Adam was a 6-year, 6-month-old boy diagnosed with cerebral palsy and significant development delay (age equivalent 11 months, *Bayley Scales of Infant Development II*). He was fed through a gastrostomy tube, was recently equipped with a power wheelchair, and was learning to hold his head upright in the midline position. He activated a switch using the top of his head by straightening and extending his body upright into a pillow switch (Enabling Devices, www.enablingdevices.com) mounted to his wheelchair. He smiled, cried, laughed, and vocalized with open vowel sounds to communicate displeasure, pain, and happiness. He enjoyed music, interaction with peers, movement toys, sensory toys, swimming, and interacting with peers and adults.

Kyle was an 18-year, 10-month-old young man diagnosed with cerebral palsy and functioning at a 13-month level (IQ 24, *Bayley Scales of Infant Development II*). He was able to extend his right arm, open his right hand, and activate a small 2.5-in.-round Jelly Bean® switch (AbleNet) placed on the table at midline. He smiled and was able to make some vocalizations and facial expressions to indicate wants and needs. He rejected activities by pushing away items or persons. He responded positively to swimming, listening to music, bowling, interacting with high school peers, and watching his instructors engaged in activities. He was able to walk short distances with a posterior walker. (pp. 95–96)

Some professionals use the term *profound multiple disabilities* to refer to children such as Adam and Kyle, who have severe cognitive impairments as well as severe motor disabilities (e.g., Nakken, 2002). "People with profound multiple disabilities have the same needs as others with regard to participation, relationships, choices, resources and physical and socio-emotional well-being" (Petry & Maes, 2007, p. 130).

IDEA mandates that *all* children are entitled to a free public education in the least restrictive environment no matter how complicated or challenging their learning, behavioral, or medical problems may be. However, some individuals have questioned whether children with profound disabilities can benefit from education. To read one viewpoint on whether children with the most severe disabilities are "educable," see Figure 12.1.

Multiple Disabilities

IDEA defines **multiple disabilities** as

concomitant impairments (such as mental retardation–blindness, mental retardation–orthopedic impairment), the combination of which causes such severe educational needs that they cannot be accommodated in special education programs solely for one of the impairments. Multiple disabilities does not include deaf-blindness. (20 U.S.C. §1401 [2004], 20 C.F.R. §300.8[c][7])

Deaf-Blindness

IDEA defines **deaf-blindness** as

concomitant hearing and visual impairments, the combination of which causes such severe communication and other developmental and educational needs that they cannot be accommodated in special education programs solely for children with deafness or children with blindness. (20 U.S.C. §1401 [2004], 20 C.F.R. §300.8[c][2])

Although 94% of individuals with deaf-blindness have some functional hearing and/or vision (Baldwin, 1995), the combined effects of the dual impairments severely impede learning communication and social skills. An educational program for children who are deaf is often inappropriate for a child who also has limited vision because many methods of instruction and communication rely heavily on the use of sight. On the other hand, programs for

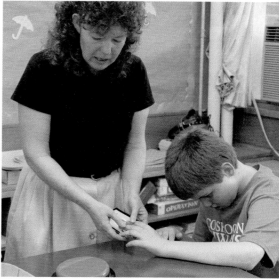

Teaching techniques involving the sense of touch are used to provide and supplement instructional stimuli for students with dual sensory impairments.

FIGURE 12.1   Are all children educable?

Some people question the wisdom of spending large amounts of money, time, and human resources attempting to educate children who have such profound disabilities that they may never be able to function independently. Some would prefer to see resources spent on children with higher apparent potential—especially when economic conditions limit the quality of educational services for all children in the public schools. "Why bother with children who fail to make meaningful progress?" they ask.

Our knowledge of the learning and developmental processes of individuals with severe and profound disabilities is still primitive and incomplete. We do know, however, that children with severe disabilities can benefit from intense and "customized" special education (Smith, Gast, Logan, & Jacobs, 2001). Even when a student shows little or no progress, it would be wrong to conclude that the student is incapable of learning. Instead, our teaching methods may be imperfect, and the future may bring improved methods and materials to enable that student to learn useful skills. No matter how severe their disabilities, all children have the right to the best possible public education society can offer them.

No one knows for certain the true learning potential of children whose disabilities are complex and pervasive. We do know that students with the most severe disabilities will go no farther than we let them; it is up to us to open doors and to raise our sights, not to create additional barriers.

The late Don Baer, a pioneer in the development of effective teaching methods for people with disabilities, offered this perspective on the debate over who may or may not be educable:

> Some of us have ignored both the thesis that all persons are educable and the thesis that some persons are uneducable, and instead have experimented with ways to teach some previously unteachable people. Over a few centuries, those experiments have steadily reduced the size of the apparently ineducable group relative to the obviously educable group. Clearly, we have not finished that adventure. Why predict its outcome, when we could simply pursue it, and just as well without a prediction? Why not pursue it to see if there comes a day when there is such a small class of apparently ineducable persons left that it consists of one elderly person who is put forward as ineducable. If that day comes, it will be a very nice day. And the next day will be even better.

(D. M. Baer, February 15, 2002, personal communication)

Definition of deaf-blindness

 Council for Exceptional Children Content Standards for Beginning Teachers—INDEP CURR: Definitions and issues related to the identification of individuals with disabilities (IC1K1) (also CC1K5).

Impact of deaf-blindness

 Council for Exceptional Children Content Standards for Beginning Teachers—INDEP CURR: Impact of sensory impairments, physical and health disabilities on individuals, families, and society (IC2K2) (also CC2K2, CC2K6).

students with visual impairments usually require good hearing because much instruction is auditory. The majority of children who have both visual and hearing impairments at birth experience major difficulties in acquiring communication skills, motor and mobility skills, and appropriate social behavior.

> Because these individuals do not receive clear and consistent information from either sensory modality, a tendency exists to turn inward to obtain the desired level of stimulation. The individual therefore may appear passive, nonresponsive, and/or noncompliant. Students with dual sensory impairments may not respond to or initiate appropriate interactions with others and often exhibit behavior that is considered socially inappropriate (e.g., hand flapping, finger flicking, head rocking). (Downing & Eichinger, 1990, pp. 98–99)

Pease (2000) describes how unresponsiveness by a child with deaf-blindness can lead parents and caregivers to unwittingly contribute to his communication difficulties:

> Parents are likely to find their deafblind baby's "signals" difficult to read and may become discouraged, especially if the child seems to reject them or show little interest. Parents and carers may find it easier to do things for the children without waiting for his responses so that activities which for the typical child are full of fun and communication become a quiet routine for the deafblind infant. With little encouragement to interact or to exert control with activities, the child may become a passive recipient of care as "learned helplessness" develops. (p. 39)

In addition to their sensory impairments, about 60% of students with deaf-blindness also have physical disabilities, 68% have cognitive impairments, and 40% have complex health care needs (National Technical Assistance Center, 2004). Educational programs for students with dual sensory impairments who require instruction in basic skills are generally similar to those for other students with severe disabilities. Although most students with dual sensory impairments can make use of information presented in visual and auditory modalities, when used in instruction, these stimuli must be enhanced and the students' attention directed toward them. Tactile teaching techniques involving the sense of touch are used to supplement the information obtained through visual and auditory modes (Chen & Downing 2001, 2006a; Downing & Chen, 2003). A wealth of information about educating children who are deaf-blind can be found at the National Information Clearinghouse on Children Who Are Deaf-Blind, www.tr.wou.edu/dblink.

A man who is deaf-blind vividly described the importance of supplementing information about the world with other sensory modes:

> The senses of sight and hearing are unquestionably the two primary avenues by which information and knowledge are absorbed by an individual, providing a direct access to the world in which he lives. . . . When these senses are lost or severely limited, the individual is drastically limited to a very small area of concepts, most of which must come to him through his secondary senses or through indirect information supplied by others. The world literally shrinks; it is only as large as he can reach with his fingertips or by using his severely limited sight and hearing, and it is only when he learns to use his remaining secondary senses of touch, taste, smell, and kinesthetic awareness that he can broaden his field of information and gain additional knowledge. (Smithdas, 1981, p. 38)

CHARACTERISTICS OF STUDENTS WITH SEVERE AND MULTIPLE DISABILITIES

Throughout this book, we have seen how definitions and lists of characteristics used to describe the children within a disability category have limited meaning at the level of the individual student. And, of course, it is at the level of the individual student where decisions about what and how to teach should be made. As various physical, behavioral, and learning characteristics associated with severe disabilities are described, keep in mind that students with severe disabilities constitute the most heterogeneous group of all exceptional children. As Westling and Fox (2004) point out, the differences among students with severe disabilities are greater than their similarities.

Most students with severe disabilities exhibit significant deficits in intellectual functioning. The majority of students with severe disabilities have more than one disability. Many need special services and supports because of motor impediments; communication, visual, and auditory impairments; and medical conditions such as seizure disorders (Petry & Maes, 2007). Many have medical and physical problems that require frequent attention (Rues, Ault, Graff, & Holvoet, 2006). Even with the best available methods of diagnosis and assessment, it is often difficult to identify the nature and intensity of a child's multiple disabilities or to determine how a combination of impairments affects a child's learning and behavior. Some children, for example, do not respond in any apparent way to visual stimuli, such as bright lights or moving objects. Is this because the child is blind as a result of eye damage, or is the child's unresponsiveness a feature of profound intellectual disability caused by brain damage? Such questions arise frequently in planning educational programs for students with severe disabilities.

The one defining characteristic of students with severe disabilities is that they exhibit significant and obvious deficits in multiple life-skill or developmental areas. No specific set of behaviors is common to all individuals with severe disabilities. Although each student presents a unique combination of physical, intellectual, and social characteristics, the following behaviors and skill deficits are frequently observed in students with severe disabilities (Collins, 2007; Kim & Arnold, 2006; McDonnell, Hardman, & McDonnell, 2003; Siegel & Wetherby, 2006; Westling & Fox, 2004):

- *Slow acquisition rates for learning new skills.* Compared to other students with disabilities, students with severe disabilities learn at a slower rate, require more instructional trials to learn a given skill, learn a fewer number of skills, and have extreme difficulty learning abstract concepts.

To learn more about tactile teaching techniques and how they can be used in classroom instruction, go to the Homework & Exercises section in MyEducationLab and complete Homework Exercise 1.

Characteristics of severe disabilities

 Content Standards for Beginning Teachers—INDEP CURR: Psychological and social-emotional characteristics of individuals with disabilities (IC2K4) (also CC2K2).

Every child with severe and multiple disabilities presents a unique combination of physical, intellectual, and social characteristics.

- *Poor generalization and maintenance of newly learned skills.* *Generalization* refers to the performance of a skill in settings or under conditions different from those in which the skill was learned initially. *Maintenance* refers to the continued use of a skill after instruction has been terminated. In the absence of instruction that has been meticulously planned and implemented to facilitate generalization and maintenance, students with severe disabilities seldom show such outcomes.

- *Limited communication skills.* Almost all students with severe and multiple disabilities are limited in their abilities to express themselves and to understand others. Some cannot talk or gesture meaningfully and might not respond when communication is attempted.

- *Impaired physical and motor development.* Many children with severe disabilities have limited physical mobility. Many cannot walk; some cannot stand or sit up without support. They are slow to perform such basic tasks as rolling over, grasping objects, and holding up their heads. Physical impairments and health conditions are common and may worsen without consistent physical therapy and medical treatment.

- *Deficits in self-help skills.* Some children with severe disabilities cannot independently care for their most basic needs, such as dressing, eating, exercising bowel and bladder control, and maintaining personal hygiene. They often require special training involving prosthetic devices and/or adapted skill sequences to learn these basic skills.

- *Infrequent constructive behavior and interaction.* Children without disabilities and those whose disabilities are less severe typically play with other children, interact with adults, and seek out information about their surroundings. Some children with severe disabilities do not. They may appear to be completely out of touch with reality and may not show normal human emotions. It may be difficult to capture the attention of or evoke any observable response from a child with profound disabilities.

- *Stereotypic and challenging behavior.* Some children with severe disabilities engage in behaviors that are ritualistic (e.g., rocking back and forth, waving fingers in front of the face, twirling the body); self-stimulatory (e.g., grinding the teeth, patting the body); self-injurious (e.g., head banging, hair pulling, eye poking, hitting or scratching or biting oneself); and/or aggressive (e.g., hitting or biting others). In addition to safety issues, the high frequency with which some children emit these challenging behaviors is a serious concern because they interfere with learning more adaptive behaviors and with acceptance and functioning in integrated settings.

Descriptions of behavioral characteristics such as those just mentioned can easily give an overly negative impression. Despite the intense challenges their disabilities impose on them, many students with severe disabilities also exhibit warmth, persistence, determination, cheerfulness, a sense of humor, sociability, and various other desirable traits (Collins, 2007; Forest & Lusthaus, 1990; Petry & Maes, 2007). Many teachers find great satisfaction in working with students who have severe disabilities and in observing their progress in school, home, and community settings.

PREVALENCE OF SEVERE AND MULTIPLE DISABILITIES

Because no definition of severe disabilities is universally accepted, no accurate and uniform figures on prevalence exist. Estimates of the prevalence of severe disabilities range from 0.1% to 1% of the population (Kim & Arnold, 2006). Brown (1990) considers students with severe disabilities to be those who function intellectually in the lowest functioning 1% of the school-age population.

Because the category of severe disabilities is not one of the disability categories under which the states make their annual report to the federal government, the number of students with severe disabilities who receive special education services under IDEA cannot be determined from data supplied by the U.S. Department of Education. Students who have severe disabilities are served and reported under several disability categories, including mental retardation, multiple disabilities, other health impairments, autism, traumatic brain injury, and deaf-blindness.

In the 2005–2006 school year, 132,595 school-age children received special education and related services under the IDEA disability category of multiple disabilities. Deaf-blindness is a very low-incidence disability. Before the passage of IDEA in 1975, fewer than 100 children with dual-sensory impairments were receiving specialized education services, virtually all of which were located at residential schools for children who are blind. Although just 1,539 school-age children received special education under the disability category of deaf-blindness in the 2005–2006 school year (U.S. Department of Education, 2007a), a national census counted 9,853 children with deaf-blindness from birth through age 18 (National Technical Assistance Center, 2004).

CAUSES OF SEVERE AND MULTIPLE DISABILITIES

Severe intellectual disabilities can be caused by a wide variety of conditions, largely biological, that may occur before (prenatal), during (perinatal), or after birth (postnatal). In almost every case, a brain disorder is involved. Brain disorders are the result of either *brain dysgenesis* (abnormal brain development) or *brain damage* (caused by influences that alter the structure or function of a brain that had been developing normally up to that point). From a review of 10 epidemiological studies, Coulter (1994) estimated that prenatal brain dysgenesis accounts for most cases of severe cognitive limitations and that perinatal and postnatal brain damage account for a minority of cases. Coulter states that a brain disorder is "the only condition that will account for the existence of profound disabilities" (p. 41).

A significant percentage of children with severe disabilities are born with chromosomal abnormalities, such as Down syndrome, or with genetic or metabolic disorders that can cause serious problems in physical or intellectual development. Complications of pregnancy—including prematurity, Rh incompatibility, and infectious diseases contracted by the mother—can cause or contribute to severe disabilities. A pregnant woman who uses drugs, drinks alcohol excessively, or is poorly nourished has a greater risk of giving birth to a child with severe disabilities. Because their disabilities tend to be more extreme and more readily observable, children with severe disabilities are more frequently identified at or shortly after birth than are children with mild disabilities.

Severe disabilities also may develop later in life from head trauma caused by automobile and bicycle accidents, falls, assaults, or abuse. Malnutrition, neglect, ingestion of poisonous substances, and certain diseases that affect the brain (e.g., meningitis, encephalitis) also can cause severe disabilities. Although hundreds of medically related causes of severe disabilities have been identified, in about one sixth of all cases, the cause cannot be clearly determined (Coulter, 1994).

TRAUMATIC BRAIN INJURY

Definition

When it was originally passed, IDEA did not specifically mention the needs of children who have experienced head trauma and/or coma. However, when Congress amended the law in 1990 (P.L. 101–476), it added traumatic brain injury to the list of disability categories under which children could be eligible for special education services. IDEA defines **traumatic brain injury** as

> an acquired injury to the brain caused by an external physical force, resulting in total or partial functional disability or psychosocial impairment, or both, that adversely affects a child's educational performance. Traumatic brain injury applies to open or closed head injuries resulting in impairments in one or more areas, such as cognition; language; memory; attention; reasoning; abstract thinking; judgment; problem-solving; sensory, perceptual, and motor abilities; psychosocial behavior; physical functions; information processing; and

Causes of severe disabilities

 Content Standards for Beginning Teachers—INDEP CURR: Etiologies and medical aspects of conditions affecting individuals with disabilities (IC2K3).

Definition of TBI

 Content Standards for Beginning Teachers—P&HD: Issues and educational definitions of individuals with P&HD (PH1K1).

speech. Traumatic brain injury does not apply to brain injuries that are congenital or degenerative, or to brain injuries induced by birth trauma. (20 U.S.C. §1401 [2004], 20 C.F.R. §300.8[c][12])

As with the IDEA definitions of other disabilities, the key phrase in the definition of traumatic brain injury is "that adversely affects a child's educational performance." It is also important to note that traumatic brain injury is an *acquired* condition. Although the effects of some types of traumatic brain injury on learning and behavior are similar to the effects of other disabilities, children whose learning or behavioral problems are caused by disease or congenital malformation to the brain (e.g., cerebral palsy, some causes of mental retardation) are not considered to have traumatic brain injury.

Prevalence of Traumatic Brain Injury

About 1.5 million people sustain a traumatic brain injury each year in the United States (National Center for Injury Prevention and Control, 2007). Of those, 50,000 will die of their injury and 235,000 will be hospitalized. The two age groups at highest risk for traumatic brain injury are birth to 4-year-olds and 15- to 19-year-olds (Langlois, Rutland-Brown, & Thomas, 2006). Traumatic brain injury—most often the result of motor vehicle accident—is the leading cause of death in children and the most common acquired disability in childhood (Brain Injury Association, 2007). It is estimated that 5.3 million Americans have long-term need for help in performing activities of daily living as a result of traumatic brain injury (Brain Injury Association, 2007).

In spite of the sobering statistics on head injuries, the number of children receiving special education under the category of traumatic brain injury is quite small. In 1991–1992, the first school year after traumatic brain injury was added to IDEA as a separate disability category, only 330 school-age children were served nationally. By 2005–2006 school year, the number had increased to 23,449 (U.S. Department of Education, 2007a).

While it is likely that greater numbers of children with traumatic brain injury will be identified and served in the future, as educators increase their understanding and recognition of head injuries, the gap between incidence and the number of children served is huge. What accounts for this significant difference? First, recovery is good following most brain injuries. The skull is very good at protecting the brain, and the human brain has a remarkable capacity to naturally compensate for injury. Second, the vast majority of head injuries sustained by children are mild and do not result in obvious adverse effects on educational performance. Third, many students with mild brain injuries are identified and served under another disability category, most likely learning disabilities or emotional or behavioral disorders. Fourth, students with severe head injuries are often served under other disability categories.

Types and Causes of Traumatic Brain Injury

Types and causes of TBI

 Council for Exceptional Children Content Standards for Beginning Teachers—P&HD: Etiology and characteristics of P&HD across the life span (PH2K2) (also PH2K1).

Head injuries are classified by the type of injury (open or closed), by the kind of the damage sustained by the brain, and by the location of the injury. An **open head injury** is the result of penetration of the skull, such as that caused by a bullet or a forceful blow to the head with a hard or sharp object. Open head injuries that are not fatal often result in specific deficits or problems with particular behavioral or sensory functions controlled by the part of the brain where the injury occurred (see Figure 12.2).

The most common type of head injury does not involve penetration of the skull. A **closed head injury** occurs when the head hits a stationary object with such force that the brain slams against the inside of the cranium. The stress of this rapid movement and impact pulls apart and tears nerve fibers, or axons, breaking connections between different parts of the brain. Car and bicycle accidents, falls, and accidents while playing sports are the primary causes of closed head injuries. *Shaken baby syndrome* is another unfortunate but common cause of traumatic brain injury in children. Violent shaking of a baby causes rapid acceleration and deceleration of the head, which in turn causes the baby's brain whip back and forth, bouncing off the inside of the skull.

FIGURE 12.2

Parts of the brain and
some of their functions

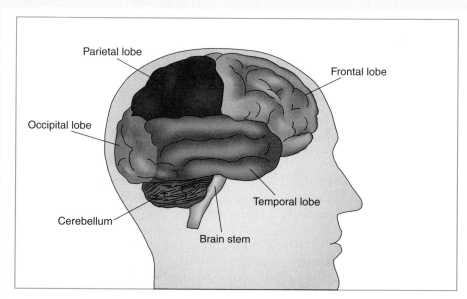

Frontal lobe

- Emotions
- Expressive language
- Word associations
- Memory for habits and motor activities
- Problem solving
- Reasoning

Parietal lobe

- Integration of different senses
- Location for visual attention
- Location for touch perception
- Manipulation of objects

Occipital lobe

- Vision

Cerebellum

- Balance and equilibrium
- Some memory for reflex motor acts

Brain stem

- Regulates body functions (e.g., breathing, heart rate, swallowing)
- Reflexes to seeing and hearing (e.g., startle response)
- Controls autonomic nervous system (e.g., sweating, blood pressure, digestion, internal temperature)
- Affects level of alertness

Temporal lobe

- Hearing
- Speech
- Memory acquisition
- Categorization of objects

The effects of traumatic brain injury on learning and behavior are determined by the severity of the injury and the part of the brain that sustained damage. A mild brain injury results in a *concussion,* a brief or momentary loss of consciousness (from seconds or minutes, up to 30 minutes) without any subsequent complications or damage. Even a mild concussion, however, is often followed by post-concussion syndrome, which can include temporary headaches, dizziness spells, and fatigue. Repeated mild traumatic brain injuries over a period of months or years can result in cumulative neurological and cognitive deficits. Repeated mild traumatic brain injuries occurring within a short period of time (i.e., hours, days, or weeks) can be catastrophic or fatal (Centers for Disease Control and Prevention, 1997).

Contusions (bruising, swelling, and bleeding) usually accompany a moderate brain injury. Blood vessels in the brain may also rupture, causing a *hematoma* (aggregation or clotting of blood) that may grow and put pressure on vital brain structures. A moderate brain injury usually results in a loss of consciousness lasting more than 30 minutes up to 24 hours followed by a few days or weeks of confusion. Individuals who sustain a moderate brain injury will experience significant cognitive and behavioral impairments for many months. Most, however, will make a complete or nearly complete recovery.

Severe head trauma almost always results in a *coma,* a state of prolonged unconsciousness lasting days, weeks, or even longer. A person in a coma cannot be awakened and makes no meaningful response to external stimulation. In addition to brain contusions and hematomas or damage to the nerve fibers, or axons, a person with severe brain injury may have suffered from **anoxia** (loss of oxygen to the brain for a period of time). Although many people with severe brain injuries make significant improvements during the first year after their injury and continue to improve at a more gradual pace for many years, most will have permanent physical, behavioral, and/or cognitive impairments.

Effects and Educational Implications of Traumatic Brain Injury

Though not always visible and sometimes seemingly minor or inconsequential, traumatic brain injury is complex. The symptoms vary widely depending on the severity of the injury, its extent and site, the age of the child at the time of the injury, and time passed since the injury (Semrud-Clikeman, 2001; von Hahn, 2004).

Impairments caused by brain injuries may be temporary or lasting and fall into three main categories: (1) physical and sensory changes (e.g., lack of coordination, spasticity of muscles); (2) cognitive impairments (e.g., short- and long-term memory deficits, difficulty maintaining attention and concentration); and (3) social, behavioral, and emotional problems (e.g., mood swings [emotional lability], self-centeredness, lack of motivation). Figure 12.3 provides additional examples of characteristics that may be signs of traumatic brain injury.

The educational and lifelong needs of students with head injuries are likely to require comprehensive programs of academic, psychological, and family support (Tyler & Mira, 1999). Recovery from a brain injury is often inconsistent. A student might make excellent progress, then regress to an earlier stage, and then make a rapid series of gains. Individuals with brain injuries sometimes reach plateaus in their recovery during which no improvements occur for some time. A plateau does not signal the end to functional improvement.

Students who have been hospitalized with head injuries reenter school with deficits from their injuries compounded by an extended absence from school. Ylvisaker (2005) recommends that the child return to school when she is physically capable, can respond to instructions, and can sustain attention for 10 to 15 minutes. School programs can assist reentry of the student with traumatic brain injury in several ways (Semrud-Clikeman, 2001; Tyler & Mira, 1999; von Hahn, 2004):

- A shortened school day, concentrating academic instruction during peak performance periods; frequent breaks; and a reduced class load may be necessitated by the chronic fatigue that some students with head injury experience for a year or more.
- Rehearse social situations in advance and provide explicit instructions and prompts about social interactions such as maintaining socially accepted body space and tone of voice.
- Provide clear, uncomplicated instructions; break multistep instructions into simplified steps.
- Pair auditory instructions with visual cues.
- A special resource period at the beginning and end of each school day may be required because of problems with loss of memory and organization. During this time, a teacher, counselor, or aide helps the student plan or review the day's schedule, keep track of assignments, and monitor progress.
- Modifications such as an extra set of textbooks at home, a peer to help the student move efficiently from class to class, and early dismissal from class to allow time to get to the next room can help the student who has difficulties with mobility, balance, or coordination. (Adaptive physical education is often indicated.)
- Behavior management and/or counseling interventions may be needed to help with problems such as poor judgment, impulsiveness, overactivity, aggression, destructiveness, and socially uninhibited behavior often experienced by students with head injury.
- Modifications of instruction and testing procedures such as tape-recording lectures, assigning a note taker, and allowing extra time to take tests may be needed.
- IEP goals and services may need to be reviewed and modified as often as every 30 days because of the dramatic changes in behavior and performance by some children during the early stages of recovery.

Signs and effects of TBI

 Content Standards for Beginning Teachers—Common Core: Educational implications of various exceptionalities (CC2K2) (also PH3K1).

Accommodations for students with TBI

 Content Standards for Beginning Teachers—P&HD: Adaptations of educational environments necessary to accommodate individuals with P&HD (PH5K1) (also CC5K1).

FIGURE 12.3   Possible signs and effects of traumatic brain injury

Physical and sensory changes

- Chronic headaches, dizziness, light-headedness, nausea
- Vision impairments (e.g., double vision, visual field defects, blurring, sensitivity to light)
- Hearing impairment (e.g., increased sensitivity to sound)
- Alterations in sense of taste, touch, and smell
- Sleep problems (e.g., insomnia, day/night confusion)
- Stress-related disorders (e.g., depression)
- Poor body temperature regulation
- Recurrent seizure activity
- Poor coordination and balance
- Reduced speed of motor performance and precision of movement

Cognitive changes and academic problems

- Difficulty keeping up with discussions, instructional presentations, note taking
- Difficulty concentrating or attending to task at hand (e.g., distractible, confused)
- Difficulty making transitions (e.g., home to school, class to class, switching from fractions to decimal problems on same math worksheet)
- Inability to organize work and environment (e.g., difficulty keeping track of books, assignments, lunch box)
- Problems in planning, organizing, pacing tasks and activities
- Extremely sensitive to distraction (e.g., unable to take a test in a room with other students)
- Tendency to perseverate; inflexible in thinking
- Impairments in receptive oral language (e.g., difficulty following directions; misunderstanding what is said by others)
- Inability to perceive voice inflections or nonverbal cues
- Impairments in reading comprehension
- Impairments in expressive oral or written language (e.g., aphasia, difficulty retrieving words, poor articulation, slow speech, difficulty in spelling or punctuation)

Social, emotional, and behavioral problems

- Chronically agitated, irritable, restless, or anxious
- Increased aggressiveness
- Impaired ability to self-manage; lowered impulse control; poor anger control
- Difficulty dealing with change (i.e., rigid); poor coping strategies
- May overestimate own ability (often evidenced as "bragging")
- Decreased insight into self and others; reduced judgment
- Decreased frustration tolerance; frequent temper outbursts and overreactions to events
- May talk compulsively and excessively
- Inability to take cues from the environment (often leading to socially inappropriate behavior)

Source: Adapted from Hill, J. L. (1999). *Meeting the needs of children with special physical and health care needs* (pp. 259–260). Upper Saddle River, NJ: Merrill/Prentice Hall. © 1999 by Merrill/Prentice Hall. Used by permission.

EDUCATIONAL APPROACHES

How does one go about teaching students with severe and multiple disabilities? To begin to answer this question, three fundamental and interrelated questions must be considered:

1. What skills should be taught?
2. What methods of instruction should be used?
3. Where should instruction take place?

Of course, each of these questions must be asked for all students; but when a student is challenged by severe disabilities, the answers take on enormous importance.

Curriculum: What Should Be Taught?

Not long ago, a student's "mental age" as determined by norm-referenced tests of development played a significant role in the selection of curriculum content and teaching activities. This practice led to an emphasis on activities thought to be essential prerequisites for higher-level skills because typically developing children of a given age demonstrated these skills. As a result, students with severe disabilities spent many hundreds of hours working on artificially contrived activities that had no immediate value and, because they were not age-appropriate (e.g., teenage students sorting blocks by color or clapping their hands to the rhythm of a song for preschoolers), may have contributed to the perception that students with severe disabilities are eternal children.

Today, most educators recognize that students with severe disabilities do not acquire skills in the same sequence that most students do and that developmental ages should not serve as the basis for determining curriculum content and instructional activities. For example, a 16-year-old student who is learning to feed herself should not be taught in the same way or with the same materials as a typically developing 2-year-old learning to feed herself. Even though both individuals need to learn the same skill, their past experiences, present environments, and future prospects differ significantly and demand different instructional activities and materials.

Contemporary curriculum content for students with severe disabilities is characterized by its focus on functional skills that can be used in immediate and future domestic, vocational, community, and recreational/leisure environments. Educational programs are future-oriented in their efforts to teach skills that will enable students with severe disabilities to participate in integrated settings as meaningfully and independently as possible after they leave school (Inge & Moon, 2006).

Functionality Functional skills are immediately useful to a student, frequently required in school and nonschool environments, result in less dependence on others, and allow the student to participate in less restrictive environments (Slaton, Schuster, Collins, & Carnine, 1994). Placing pegs into a pegboard and sorting wooden blocks by color do not meet any of these criteria (see Figure 12.4). Examples of functional skills for many students with severe disabilities include activities such as learning to dress oneself, prepare a snack, ride a public bus, purchase items from coin-operated vending machines, and recognize common sight words in community settings. Whenever possible, functional instructional activities should employ authentic materials (Westling & Fox, 2004). For example, students learning to make purchases should practice with real money instead of simulated bills and coins.

Age-Appropriateness Students with severe disabilities should participate in activities that are appropriate for their same-age peers without disabilities. Adolescents with severe disabilities should not use the same materials as younger children without disabilities. Having teenagers sit on the floor and play clap-your-hands games or cutting and pasting cardboard snowmen highlights their differences and discourages integration. It is more appropriate to teach recreation and leisure skills, such as bowling and iPod operation or to engage the students in holiday projects, such as printing greeting cards.

It is critically important to build an IEP for a student with severe disabilities around functional and age-appropriate skills. Because nonschool settings demand these skills and peers without disabilities exhibit them, functional and age-appropriate behaviors are more likely to be reinforced in the natural environment and, as a result, maintained in the student's repertoire.

Making Choices Imagine going through an entire day without being able to make a choice, any choice at all. Someone else—a teacher, a staff person, a parent—will decide what

Functional curriculum activities use authentic, age-appropriate materials with meaningful outcomes. Each school day, Kevin sorts, labels, and delivers the newspaper to "customers" in his school.

Functional and age-appropriate skills

Content Standards for Beginning Teachers—Common Core: Theories and research that form the basis of curriculum developments and instructional practice (CC7K1) (also CC4S4, CC7K2, IC5S2, IC5S12).

FIGURE 12.4 | **My brother Darryl: A case for teaching functional skills**

Eighteen years old, moderately/severely handicapped, Darryl has been in school for 12 years. He's never been served in any setting other than an elementary school. He has had a number of years of "individualized instruction." Darryl can now do lots of things he couldn't do before:

- He can put 100 pegs in a board in less than 10 minutes with 95% accuracy, but he can't put quarters into a vending machine.
- Upon command he can touch his nose, shoulder, leg, hair, ear. He is still working on wrist, ankle, hips, but he can't blow his nose when needed.
- He can do a 12-piece Big Bird puzzle with 100% accuracy and color an Easter bunny and stay in the lines. He prefers music but has never been taught to use a radio or record player.
- He can now fold primary paper in half and even quarters, but he can't sort clothes, white from colors, for washing.
- He can roll Play-Doh and make wonderful clay snakes, but he can't roll bread dough and cut out biscuits.
- He can string beads in alternating colors and match it to a pattern on a DLM card, but he can't lace his shoes.
- He can sing his ABCs and tell me the names of all the letters in the alphabet with 80% accuracy when they are presented on a card in upper case, but he can't tell "Men's" room from "Ladies'" when we go to McDonald's.
- He can be told it's cloudy/rainy and take a black felt cloud and put it on the day of the week on an enlarged calendar (with assistance), but he still goes out in the rain without a raincoat or hat.
- He can identify with 100% accuracy 100 different Peabody Picture Cards by pointing, but he can't order a hamburger by pointing to a picture or gesturing.
- He can walk on a balance beam forward, sideways, and backward, but he can't walk up the steps of the bleachers unassisted in the gym or go to basketball games.
- He can count to 100 by rote memory, but he doesn't know how many dollars to pay the waitress for a $2.59 McDonald coupon special.
- He can put a cube in the box, under the box, beside the box, and behind the box, but he can't find the trash bin in McDonald's and empty his trash into it.
- He can sit in a circle with appropriate behavior and sing songs and play "Duck Duck Goose," but nobody else in his neighborhood his age seems to want to do that.

I guess he's just not ready yet.

Written by Preston Lewis, a curriculum specialist in the Kentucky Department of Education.

---

you will wear, what you will do next, what you will eat for lunch, whom you will sit next to, and so on throughout the day, every day. In the past, students with severe disabilities had few opportunities to express preferences and make choices; the emphasis was on establishing instructional control over students. Traditionally, persons with severe disabilities were simply cared for and taught to be compliant. As Guess, Benson, and Siegel-Causey (1985) noted, some caregivers may have felt that completing tasks for persons with disabilities is easier and faster than allowing them to do it for themselves; while others may have believed that the person already has enough problems coping with his or her disability. "Regardless of the underlying intention, the result can be to overprotect, to encourage learned helplessness, and to deprive the individual of potentially valuable life experiences" (Guess et al., 1985, p. 83).

Special educators today recognize the importance of choice as a way of making activities meaningful and as an indicator of quality of life for students with severe disabilities (Agran & Hughes, 2006; Wehmeyer, 2006). Educators are increasing efforts to help these students express their preferences and make decisions about matters that will affect them. For example, a child might be presented with pictures of two activities and asked to point to the one she would rather engage in. Another might be asked, "Whom would you like for your partner?" Or the teacher might say, "Should we do this again?" Of course, in presenting such choices, the teacher must be prepared to accept whichever alternative the student selects and to follow through accordingly. Bambara and Koger (1996) describe procedures for providing increased opportunities for choice making throughout the day.

Teaching choice making

 Content Standards for Beginning Teachers—INDEP CURR: Teach individuals to give and receive meaningful feedback from peers and adults (IC5S5) (also IC4K3, CC4S5).

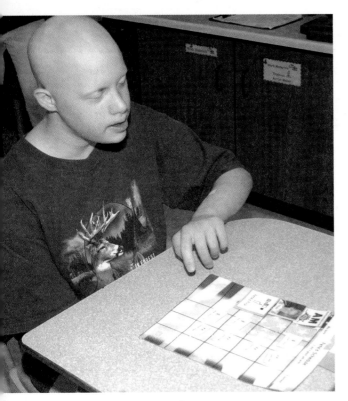

Learning to choose what he wants to do next is an important IEP goal for Daniel.

Several studies have found that nonverbal students with severe disabilities can learn to use picture activity schedules to indicate their preferences for learning and leisure-time activities (e.g., Bryan & Gast, 2000; Morrison, Sainato, BenChaaban, & Endo, 2002). Mithaug (2002) describes procedures for teaching students with multiple disabilities to choose and self-regulate their schedules and academic activities in the classroom. Other researchers have discovered ways to help people with severe disabilities express preferences for where they will live (Faw, Davis, & Peck, 1996), what foods they will purchase and eat (Cooper & Browder, 1998; Parsons, McCarn, & Reid, 1993), leisure activities (Browder, Cooper, & Lim, 1998), and whether or not they want to participate in daily routines and activities (Bambara & Ager, 1992; Lancioni et al., 2006). Stafford (2005) describes how to teach choice making to students with severe disabilities.

Communication Skills Effective communication is essential to our quality of life, enabling us to express our desires and choices, obtain and give information, and, most important, form and maintain relationships with others. Communication process does not develop naturally or easily for children with severe and multiple disabilities. Chen (1999) noted that the child's early communicative behaviors

may be subtle or unusual and therefore difficult to identify and interpret. For example, an infant (who is totally blind and hard of hearing) may become quiet when her mother speaks to her. This passivity may be misinterpreted as disinterest rather than attentiveness. Another infant (who has cerebral palsy and is deaf) may grimace his body when his father picks him up. These behaviors may be misinterpreted as rejection rather than excitement. At the same time, our usual responses, i.e., by talking to hearing infants or by signing to deaf infants, may not be understood or even perceived by infants with sensory impairments and multiple disabilities. (p.0)

Early research and training in communication for persons with severe disabilities focused on remediation of specific forms of communication, such as the production of speech sounds, words, and descriptive phrases (Kaiser & Goetz, 1993). However, the focus of and methods used to teach communication skills to these students have undergone significant changes during the past 20 years. Three changes in perspective regarding the nature of communication are shaping contemporary research and instructional practices (Ferguson, 1994; Kaiser & Goetz, 1993; Kaiser & Grim, 2006); these changes encompass shared meanings, modes of communication, and function, and are discussed next:

1. *Communication occurs when communication partners establish shared meanings.* The responsibility for successful communication rests with both partners. However, shared meaning is more likely when the partner who is relatively more skilled uses the principles of responsive interaction, such as following the lead of the less skilled speaker, balancing turns between conversation partners, and responding with interest and affect. "It is the responsibility of those who communicate with greater ease to do whatever they can to help the student understand what is being said and to find a way to give him or her a voice" (Downing, 2005, p. 14).

2. *Communication is independent of the specific form or mode that is used as a channel for communication.* Many students with severe disabilities can learn to understand and produce spoken language. Speech is always a desirable goal, of course, for those who can attain it. A student who can communicate verbally is likely to have a wider range of educational, employment, residential, and recreational opportunities than a student who cannot speak. But because of sensory, motor, cognitive, or behavioral limitations, some students with severe disabilities may not learn to speak intelligibly even after extensive instruction.

Many systems of augmentative and alternative communication (AAC) have proven useful—including gestures, various sign language systems, communication boards, picture exchange communication systems (PECSs), and electronic communication aids (Rowland & Schweigert, 2000; Siegel & Wetherby, 2006). (See Chapter 8 for a detailed description of AAC.)

Communication is achieved only with great difficulty by persons who are deaf-blind and requires greater effort on the part of communication partners. The use of dual-communication boards can help students who are deaf-blind discriminate the receptive or expressive functions of responses from a partner (Heller & Bigge, 2005). When a communication partner points to pictures or symbols on her board, a receptive message is provided to the student, requiring a response from the student on his board. The partner can point to the student's board and provide imitative prompts or corrective feedback to help the student make expressive messages.

The specialized forms of communication used by some individuals with severe disabilities limit the number of people with whom they can communicate because the contrived and idiosyncratic nature of their systems requires specialized knowledge from the communication partner (Heller & Bigge, 2005). However, they do enable many students with severe disabilities to receive and express basic information, feelings, needs, and wants (Peck, 2004). A student's teachers, peers, parents, and employers can learn sign language and other communication systems, thus encouraging use outside the classroom.

3. *Communication must "work"; that is, it must be functional for the child by influencing the behavior of others.* Examples of communication functions include the following:

- Name objects, people, activities
- Tell people what to do
- Secure help
- Convey social pleasantries ("Hi," "Bye")
- Convey interest in an activity
- Protest
- Convey emotional or physical state
- Make a choice
- Request and/or report information (Cascella & McNamara, 2005, p. 40)

Figure 12.5 compares examples of functional communication goals with developmental goals for an 11-year-old student with severe and multiple disabilities.

Recreation and Leisure Skills   Most children develop the ability to play and later to occupy themselves constructively and pleasurably during their free time. But children with

AAC

Council for Exceptional Children

Content Standards for Beginning Teachers—Common Core: Augmentative and assistive communication strategies (CC6K4) (also IC6K2).

FIGURE 12.5	Examples of developmental versus functional IEP communication goals for an 11-year-old student with severe and multiple disabilities
Receptive Vocabulary	
Developmental	Jessica will identify 5 common objects during speech therapy with 80% accuracy.
Functional	Jessica will get 5 objects that are needed to participate in art activities after a request by the teacher.
Articulation	
Developmental	Jessica will produce the consonants /f/, /t/, and /s/ with 80% accuracy in word-initial position (e.g., fun, ton, sun).
Functional	Jessica will repeat herself when teacher asks for clarification of misunderstood messages during free play activities outside.
Speech	
Developmental	Jessica will imitate consonant-vowel (CV) and vowel-consonant (VC) combinations in 8/10 trials.
Functional	Jessica will vocalize to indicate her presence during morning roll call.

Source: Cascella, P. W., & McNamara, K. M. (2005). Empowering students with severe disabilities to actualize communication skills. *Teaching Exceptional Children, 37*(3), p. 39. Reprinted with permission.

Modifying the equipment and rules of team games may enable a student with severe disabilities to participate while maintaining the integrity of the game for players without disabilities.

severe disabilities may not learn to enjoy recreation and leisure skills without explicit instruction and supports. Teaching appropriate leisure and recreational skills helps students with severe disabilities interact socially, maintain their physical health and motor skills, and become more involved in community activities. Many persons with severe disabilities do not use their unstructured time appropriately; rather than participate in enjoyable pursuits, they may spend excessive time sitting, wandering, or looking at television. A variety of programs to teach recreational and leisure skills have recently been developed; this area is now generally acknowledged as an important part of the curriculum for students with severe disabilities (Bambara, Browder, & Koger, 2006).

In one study, researchers used task analysis, picture prompts, and modified game materials to help young elementary children with moderate and severe disabilities learn to independently play a board game (Raschke, Dedrick, Heston, & Farris, 1996). Sometimes modifying the equipment and rules by which team games are played can provide enough supports to enable an individual with severe disabilities to participate while maintaining the integrity of the game for players without disabilities. Figure 12.6 shows how the equipment and rules of flag football and basketball could be modified to accommodate the specific physical abilities and skill limitations of two students with severe disabilities. Figure 12.7 describes how those game modifications meet five standards for appropriate inclusion of students with disabilities in team sports (Block, 2007; Ohtake, 2004).

For information and guidelines for selecting and teaching recreation, leisure, and sport activities, see Bambara and colleagues (2006); Best, Bigge, Musante, and Macias (2005); Block (2007); Kleinert, Miracle, and Sheppard-Jones (2007); and Schlein and Ray (1998).

Prioritizing and Selecting Instructional Targets Teachers must learn good choice-making skills, too. Students with severe disabilities present numerous skill deficits often compounded by the presence of challenging behaviors, and each of those deficits could (but not necessarily should) be targeted as an IEP goal or instructional objective. It is seldom, if ever, possible, however, to design and implement a teaching program to deal simultaneously with all of the learning needs presented by a student with severe disabilities. (Even if the resources were available, such an all-at-once approach would not be appropriate.) One of the greatest responsibilities a special educator undertakes in his role as a member of an IEP team is the selection of instructional objectives.

Increasingly, students with severe disabilities are contacting the general education curriculum (Cushing, Clark, Carter, & Kennedy, 2005). The authors of a study that investigated the procedures for conducting alternate assessments used in 16 states and the perspectives of administrators and teachers responsible for implementing the assessments reported that "teachers are finding that [students with the most significant cognitive disabilities] can do much more; some teachers never thought they could teach reading and math" (Kohl, McLaughlin, & Nagle, 2006, p. 120). These authors also reported that

> several representatives noted that their "more experienced and skilled teachers" understand how to integrate academic standards with traditional functional skills. However, these teachers are in the minority. State representatives felt that the issue of competing priorities, namely teaching academic versus functional life skills, is causing the most problems for teachers. (p. 120)

The expectation that all students show progress in the general education curriculum has caused many special educators to fear that teaching practical skills to students with severe disabilities is taking a back seat to the academic demands of No Child Left Behind (Kenning, 2007; Kohl et al., 2006). See Current Issues and Future Trends, "What Happened to Functional Curriculum?"

Accurate predictions of how much any particular skill—whether functional or academic—ultimately will contribute to a student's overall quality of life are difficult to make. In many

Prioritizing instructional targets

 Council for Exceptional Children Content Standards for Beginning Teachers—Common Core: Identify and prioritize areas of the general curriculum and accommodations for individuals with exceptional learning needs (CC7S1) (also CC7S2, CC7S3).

FIGURE 12.6 Examples of modifying equipment and rules to enable students with severe disabilities to participate meaningfully in team sports

Maki and Flag Football

Maki is a sixth grader with cerebral palsy and severe mental retardation. She moves using a walker, but does so in an unstable manner when the surface is rough, bumpy, or slanting. One of her IEP goals is to walk without falling with her walker regardless of the condition of the surface.

Maki shows interest in flag football. When blocking practice begins, she actively practices pushing a dummy.

Her preference and IEP skills can be infused into flag football games. For safety reasons, she plays out of bounds. On offense, she is positioned along the intersection between the sideline and the first-down marker. Her role is to start pushing a dummy toward the line of scrimmage each time her team players start playing. She continues pushing until her team stops playing.

As part of the modification, the first-down marker for her team is moved to the point she reached at the end of the play. Thus, the more she pushes the dummy, the closer her team is to a first down. This procedure is repeated each time the team on offense starts playing.

Maki's efforts to push a dummy are converted momentarily and proportionally into the position of the first-down marker and therefore allows her to help her team gain yardage.

David and Basketball

David is a tenth-grade student with cerebral palsy and severe mental retardation. He moves around in his wheelchair with full support from others. One of David's IEP objectives addresses participation in recreational activities that include a movement of picking up and throwing a ball.

In basketball games, two types of baskets are placed side by side: one has a higher rim, the other has a lower rim. To ensure David's essential involvement in the game, which basket his team can use depends totally on the degree of effort David makes. During a basketball game, David engages in picking up and throwing a basketball to make an adapted shot outside of the basket court. Each time he successfully makes an adapted shot, his team is allowed to use the lower basket.

Thus, David's efforts to throw a ball are converted momentarily and proportionally into the height of a basket. In this way, he can assist team players without disabilities, who are not good at shooting, in making more successful shots. Therefore, David is considered an active participant in an essential part of the basketball game.

Source: Ohtake, Y. (2004). Meaningful inclusion of *all* students in team sports. *Teaching Exceptional Children, 37*(2), p. 25. Reprinted with permission.

cases, we simply do not know how useful a behavior change will prove to be. Whichever skills are chosen for instruction, they ultimately must be meaningful for the learner and her family. A variety of person-centered planning methods have been devised to help IEP teams work with the individual and family members to identify and prioritize the relative significance of skills or learning activities (e.g., Browder, 2001; Giangreco, Cloninger, & Iverson, 1998; Keyes & Owens-Johnson, 2003). For example, Figure 12.8 shows a form on which an IEP team summarized the outcomes of various assessment and IEP goal recommendations for a student with severe disabilities in an inclusive classroom setting.

Instructional Methods: How Should Students With Severe and Multiple Disabilities Be Taught?

Care and concern for the well-being of students with severe disabilities and assurance that they have access to meaningful curricular content and extracurricular activities are important. By themselves, however, care and access are not enough. To learn effectively, students

FIGURE 12.7	How game modifications described in Figure 12.6 meet five standards of appropriateness for meaningful inclusion in team sports	

Standard	Maki: Flag Football	David: Basketball
Challenging	Maki needs to start pushing a dummy toward the line of scrimmage.	David engages in picking up and throwing a basketball to make an adapted shot out of the basketball court.
Safety	Maki plays out of bounds.	David is placed out of the court.
Integrity	Students without disabilities play as usual.	Students without disabilities play as usual with an exception that they need to change the target rim.
Implementation	The first down marker for her team is moved to the point Make reached at the end of the play.	Two types of baskets are placed side by side: one has a higher rim, the other has a lower rim.
Essential	Maki's efforts to push a dummy are converted momentarily and proportionally into the position of the first down marker and therefore allow . her to help her team gain yardage	Each time David successfully makes an adapted shot, his team is allowed to use a lower basket. In this way, he can assist team players without disabilities, who are not good at shooting, in making more successful shots.

Source: Ohtake, Y. (2004). Meaningful inclusion of *all* students in team sports. *Teaching Exceptional Children,* *37*(2), p. 25. Reprinted with permission.

with severe disabilities need more than love, care, and a supportive classroom and social environment. They seldom acquire complex skills through imitation and observation alone; they are not likely to blossom on their own.

The skills deficits and learning problems of students with severe disabilities are so extreme and significant that instruction must be carefully planned, systematically executed, and continuously monitored for effectiveness. The teacher must know what skill to teach, why it is important, how to teach it, and how to determine that the student has achieved or performed the skill at a sufficient level of mastery. Collectively, the authors of leading texts on teaching students with severe disabilities recommend that teachers should give attention to the following components of an instructional program (e.g., Browder, 2001; Collins, 2007; McDonnell et al., 2003; Snell & Brown, 2006a; Scheuermann & Webber, 2002; Westling & Fox, 2004):

- *Precisely assess the student's current level of performance.* Precise assessment of current performance is necessary to determine which skills to teach and at what level instruction should begin. Can Keeshia hold her head up without support? For how many seconds? Under what conditions? In response to what verbal or physical signals? Unlike traditional assessment procedures, which rely heavily on standardized scores and developmental levels, assessment of students with severe disabilities emphasizes each learner's ability to perform specific, observable behaviors. Assessment should not be a one-shot procedure but should take place at different times, in different settings, and with different persons. The fact that a student with severe disabilities does not demonstrate a skill at one particular time or place does not mean that she is incapable of demonstrating that skill.

- *Clearly define the skill to be taught.* "Carlos will feed himself" is too broad a goal for many students with severe disabilities. A more appropriate statement might be

Components of systematic instruction

 Council for Exceptional Children

Content Standards for Beginning Teachers—Common Core: Theories and research that form the basis of curriculum developments and instructional practice (CC7K1) (also CC4S4, CC7S5, CC7S13, IC1K7, IC4S6).

saying, *"I want . . ."* As Mark requests food (e.g., *"I want Jell-O"*), the peer buddy says, *"Good, you want the Jell-O"* (praise and expanded language). Mark receives the designated food item (natural reinforcement) and moves down the line.

Model When students can perform the behavior but hesitate to do so, teachers may dispense with mands and just model the correct behavior for students to imitate.

> *The peer buddy notices that Mark cannot reach the chocolate-milk carton in the lunch line. He gains Mark's attention and says, "Please help me," or "I want the milk, please" (model), then waits for a response. When Mark imitates the model, his buddy praises him, repeats the correct response, and helps him retrieve the milk. If two models result in incorrect responses, teachers should add a mand and/or a prompt or end the teaching interaction and use a mand and/or prompt procedure at the next opportunity. At the end of the line, the peer buddy again provides a model for Mark by handing the cashier his money and saying, "You're welcome," when the cashier says, "Thank you." When Mark imitates these responses, the peer praises him and leads him to his seat (natural reinforcement).*

HOW TO GET STARTED

Following are some pointers for successful implementation of naturalistic teaching:

- *Attend to the students.* Teachers should be good observers of student preferences, anticipating student needs and searching for communicative intent in all student behavior.

- *Teach functional skills at opportune moments.* Teach during lunchtime, free time, transition time, before and after class time, and on the bus if possible.
- *Establish a stimulating environment.* Provide many situations in which students will be motivated to produce communicative and social behaviors.
- *Refrain from providing too much assistance.* Require students to use functional behaviors to make requests or to protest. Provide only as much assistance as is necessary for successful responding.
- *Reinforce appropriate communicative and social behaviors.* Begin with frequent reinforcement and fade to less frequent reinforcement and natural consequences.
- *Assess results.* As with all teaching, collect data to determine if the student has learned spontaneous communication and social skills.

Jo Webber and Brenda Scheuermann are professors of special education at Southwest Texas State University in San Marcos, Texas. They are the authors of *Autism: Teaching DOES Make a Difference* (Wadsworth, 2002).

 To learn more about building communication skills in students with severe disabilities, go to the Homework & Exercises section in MyEducationLab and complete Homework Exercise 2.

Positive Behavioral Support Notable changes have occurred in how teachers respond to disruptive, aggressive, or socially unacceptable behaviors by students with disabilities. In the not-too-distant past, a student who engaged in stereotypic head weaving may have had his head restrained or perhaps have had a teacher manipulate his head up and down for several minutes. A student who tantrumed or screamed may have been "treated" with the application of aversive consequences (e.g., being sprayed with water mist) or extended time-out from instruction. These were "modes of intervention which most people would reject as absolutely unacceptable if they were used with a person who does not have disabilities" (Center on Human Policy, 1986, p. 4).

Today, a growing number of special education programs are responding to challenging, excessive, or unacceptable behaviors of students with a treatment approach called *positive behavioral support*. Elements of positive behavior support include (1) understanding the meaning that a behavior has for a student, (2) teaching the student a positive alternative behavior, (3) using environmental restructuring to make the undesired behaviors less likely, and (4) using strategies that are socially acceptable and intended for use in integrated school and community settings (Carr et al., 2002).

Positive behavioral support begins with a functional assessment of the problem behavior (Crone & Horner, 2003). (Functional behavioral assessment is described in Chapter 6.) Results of functional assessments guide the development of positive behavior support plans. For example, functional assessments conducted by Lalli and colleagues (1993) revealed that self-injury and aggressive outbursts by three nonvocal students with severe disabilities during instructional activities were maintained by teacher attention (in the form of reprimands) and/or escape (misbehavior often resulted in termination of the academic task).

Positive behavioral support

 Council for Exceptional Children — Content Standards for Beginning Teachers—Common Core: Laws, policies, and ethical principles regarding behavior management planning and implementation (CC1K2) (also CC5S5).

Functional assessment, functional analysis

Council for Exceptional Children — Content Standards for Beginning Teachers—Common Core: Use functional assessments to develop intervention plans (CC7S4) (also CC8K1, IC7S1, IC8S1).

TABLE 12.1

Using partial participation within each step of a task analysis for making a blender drink

TASK: MAKING A BLENDER DRINK   LEARNER: SAUNDRA

TEACHER'S ASSISTANCE	LEARNER'S PARTICIPATION	GOAL
1. Announces activity	Lifts her head to listen	Active
2. Wheels Saundra to the cabinet	—	—
3. Gets out the utensils	Grasps a spoon	Active
4. Wheels Saundra to the table	Releases the spoon on the table	Active
5. Shows fruits	Selects one fruit by grasping it and pushing it to the teacher	Choice
6. Shows beverages	Selects one beverage by grasping it and pushing it to the teacher	Choice
7. Puts the ingredients in the blender	Operates the blender with a switch when the chosen ingredients are in	Control
8. Spoons the blender drink into a glass	Indicates if ready to drink	Control
9. Holds out a straw	Places the straw in the glass and drinks	Active Control

Key: Partial participation may have the goal of encouraging the learner to be more active in the routine (Active), to make more choices (Choice), or to have more control of the routine (Control). These goals are shown for each step of the task analysis.

Source: Reprinted from Browder, D. M., & Snell, M. E. (1993). Daily living and community skills. In M. E. Snell (Ed.), *Instruction for students with severe disabilities* (4th ed.) (p. 494). Upper Saddle River, NJ: Pearson Education, Inc. Used by permission.

This information led to the design of successful interventions that included frequent positive comments for appropriate behaviors, withholding attention for problem behavior, and teaching the students a socially acceptable behavior for communicating their wishes (e.g., choosing the next activity by pointing to a picture schedule, tapping the teacher on the shoulder).

Compared to interventions that do not take the function of problem behavior into account, treatments informed by functional analyses are more likely to produce durable improvements in behavior, are less restrictive in nature, and are more likely to be viewed by consumers as acceptable (Hastings & None, 2005; Neef & Peterson, 2007; Pelios, Morren, Tesch, & Axelrod, 1999). Several authors provide detailed procedures and guidelines for developing positive behavioral support plans (e.g., Cipani & Schock, 2007; Horner, Albin, Todd, & Sprague, 2006; O'Neill, et al., 1997; Umbreit, Ferro, Liaupsin, & Lane, 2007).

Problem behaviors such as noncompliance, aggression, acting out, and self-injury can sometimes be reduced in frequency or prevented altogether through relatively simple modifications of curriculum or the way in which learning activities are presented (Cannella-Malone, O'Reilly, & Lancioni, 2006; Ferro, Foster-Johnson, & Dunlap, 1996; O'Reilly et al., 2006; Smith & Iwata, 1997). For example:

- Provide students with a choice of tasks or a task sequence (Kern, Mantegna, Vorndran, Bailin, & Hilt, 2001; Peterson, Neef, Van Norman, & Ferreri, 2005; Romaniuk et al., 2002).
- Intersperse easy or high-probability tasks or requests with more difficult items or low-probability requests (Ardoin, Martens, & Wolfe, 1999; Killu, Sainato, Davis, Ospelt, & Paul, 1998).
- Maintain a rapid pace of instruction (Dunlap, Dyer, & Koegel, 1983; Tincani, Ernsbarger, Harrison, & Heward, 2005).

To learn more about applying functional assessment and positive behavioral support in the classroom, go to the Homework & Exercises section in Chapter 12 of MyEducationLab and complete Homework Exercise 3.

- Use a response-prompting procedure that results in fewer errors (Axe, Murphy, Van Norman, & Heward, 2006; Ebanks & Fisher, 2003; Heckaman, Alber, Hooper, & Heward, 1998).
- Modify task difficulty (Carr & Durand, 1985; Friman & Poling, 1995; Piazza, Roane, Kenney, Boney, & Abt, 2002).
- Deliver reinforcement noncontingently on a fixed time schedule (Carr, Kellum, & Chong, 2001; Kodak, Miltenberger, & Romaniuk, 2003).
- Provide free access to leisure items and activities (Lindberg, Iwata, Roscoe, Worsdell, & Hanley, 2003).

Research-based methods of positive behavioral support should not be confused with relationship-based approaches that do not entail systematic environmental arrangements and differential consequences for behavior. For example, gentle teaching is a philosophy and approach for treating problem behaviors by people with disabilities that relies on "valuing" the person and "giving warm assistance and protection when necessary" (McGee & Gonzalez, 1990, p. 244). McGee (1992), the major proponent of gentle teaching, claims that "behavior problems will evaporate like the morning dew if we express unconditional valuing" (McGee & Menolascino, 1992, p. 109). Although gentle teaching and other relationship-based approaches such as holding therapy (Tinbergen & Tinbergen, 1983) may sound wonderful, little scientific evidence demonstrates their effectiveness (Bailey, 1992; Cullen & Mudford, 2005; Heflin & Simpson, 2002; Romanczyk, Weinter, Lockshin, & Ekdahl, 1999; Schreibman, 2005).

Small-Group Instruction   For many years, most professionals believed that one-to-one instruction was the only effective teaching arrangement for students with severe disabilities. The rationale was that one-to-one teaching minimized distractions and increased the likelihood that the student would respond only to the teacher. Although a one-to-one teaching format allows for the intensive, systematic instruction known to be effective with students who have severe disabilities, small-group instruction also has potential advantages (Collins, 2007; Kamps, Dugan, Leonard, & Daoust, 1994; Munk, Laarhoven, Goodman, & Repp, 1998; Snell & Brown, 2006b):

Small-group instruction

Council for Exceptional Children **Content Standards for Beginning Teachers—INDEP CURR:** Methods for ensuring individual academic success in one-to-one, small-group, and large-group settings (IC5K4) (also CC5K3).

- Skills learned in small-group instruction may be more likely to generalize to group situations and settings.
- Small-group instruction provides opportunities for social interaction and reinforcement from peers that are missed when a student is taught alone and isolated from other students.
- Small-group instruction provides opportunities for incidental or observation learning from other students.
- In some instances, small-group instruction may be a more cost-effective use of the teacher's time.

The effectiveness of group instruction for all students is enhanced when teachers (Collins, Gast, Ault, & Wolery, 1991; Kamps et al., 1994; Munk et al., 1998):

- Ensure that students possess basic prerequisite skills such as (a) sitting quietly for a period of time, (b) maintaining eye contact, and (c) following simple instructions or imitating simple responses.
- Encourage students to listen and watch other group members and then praise them for doing so.
- Make instruction interesting by keeping individual turns short, giving all members turns, giving turns contingent on attending, and using demonstrations and a variety of materials that can be handled.
- Use methods that produce high rates of active student response, such as choral responding and response cards (see Chapter 4), which enable every student in the group to respond to each instructional trial.
- Teach at a lively pace with very brief intertrial intervals.

Friendships and after-school relationships between students with disabilities and their nondisabled peers are more likely to develop when all students attend their home school.

Benefits of neighborhood schools

 Council for Exceptional Children
Content Standards for Beginning Teachers—INDEP CURR: Advantages and disadvantages of placement options and programs on the continuum of services for individuals with disabilities (IC5K5) (also IC1K6, CC5K1).

- Involve all members by using multilevel instruction individualized to each student's targeted skills and mode of response.
- Use partial participation and material adaptation to enable all students to respond.
- Keep waiting time to a minimum by controlling the group size and limiting the amount of teacher talk and the amount/length of student response in a single turn.
- Promote cooperation among group members.

Where Should Students With Severe Disabilities Be Taught?

What is the least restrictive and most appropriate educational setting for a student with severe disabilities? This important question continues to be the subject of much debate and discussion (Gallagher et al., 2000; Giangreco, 2006).

Benefits of Neighborhood Schools Lou Brown (who has long championed the inclusion of persons with severe disabilities in integrated school, vocational, and community settings) and his colleagues at the University of Wisconsin made a strong case 20 years ago for why students with severe disabilities should attend the same school they would attend if they were not disabled:

The environments in which students with severe intellectual disabilities receive instructional services have critical effects on where and how they spend their postschool lives. Segregation begets segregation. We believe that when children with intellectual disabilities attend separate schools, they are denied opportunities to demonstrate to the rest of the community that they can function in integrated environments and activities; their nondisabled peers do not know or understand them and too often think negatively of them; their parents become afraid to risk allowing them opportunities to learn to function in integrated environments later in life; and taxpayers assume they need to be sequestered in segregated group homes, enclaves, work crews, activity centers, sheltered workshops, institutions, and nursing homes. (Brown et al., 1989a, p. 1)

Brown and his colleagues offered four reasons why students with severe disabilities should be educated in neighborhood schools instead of segregated and clustered schools. Brown et al. define a clustered school as "a regular school attended by an unnaturally large proportion of students with intellectual disabilities, but it is not the one any or most would attend if they were not labeled disabled" (p. 1). Each rationale has received various levels of support in the literature (Ryndak & Fisher, 2007). First, when students without disabilities go to an integrated school with peers who have disabilities, they are more likely to develop a greater acceptance of diversity and are likely to function responsibly as adults in a pluralistic society (Downing, Spencer, & Cavallaro, 2004). Second, integrated schools are more meaningful instructional environments (Fisher & Meyer, 2002). Third, parents and families have greater access to school activities when children are attending their home schools. Fourth, attending one's home school provides greater opportunities to develop a wide range of social relationships with nondisabled peers (Kennedy, Shukla, & Fryxell, 1997). Table 12.2 presents examples of 11 kinds of social relationships that might develop between students with severe disabilities and their nondisabled peers when they attend the same school.

Social Relationships Establishing and maintaining a network of social relationships are among the desired outcomes of inclusive educational practices for students with severe disabilities (Schwartz, 2000; Schwartz, Staub, Peck, & Gallucci, 2006). Although research has shown that simply placing students with disabilities into neighborhood schools and classrooms does not necessarily lead to increased positive social interactions, participation

TABLE 12.2

Social relationships that can develop between students with severe disabilities and their peers without disabilities when they attend the same school

SOCIAL RELATIONSHIP	EXAMPLE
Peer tutor	Leigh role-plays social introductions with Margo, providing feedback and praise for Margo's performance.
Eating companion	Jennifer and Rick eat lunch with Linda in the cafeteria and talk about their favorite music groups.
Art, home economics, industrial arts, music, physical education companion	In art class, students were instructed to paint a sunset. Tom sat next to Dan and offered suggestions and guidance about the best colors to use and how to complete the task.
Regular class companion	A fifth-grade class is doing a "Know Your Town" lesson in social studies. Ben helps Karen plan a trip through their neighborhood.
During-school companion	"Hangs out" and interacts on social level: after lunch and before the bell for class rang, Molly and Phyllis went to the student lounge for a soda.
Friend	David, a member of the varsity basketball team, invites Ralph, a student with severe disabilities, to his house to watch a game on TV.
Extracurricular companion	Sarah and Winona prepare their articles for the school newspaper together and then work on the layout in the journalism lab.
After-school-project companion	The sophomore class decided to build a float for the homecoming parade. Joan worked on it with Maria, a nondisabled companion, after school and on weekends in Joan's garage.
After-school companion	On Saturday afternoon, Mike, who is not disabled, and Bill go to the shopping mall.
Travel companion	David walks with Ralph when he wheels from last-period class to the gym, where Ralph helps the basketball team as a student manager.
Neighbor	Interacts with student in everyday environments and activities. Parents of nondisabled students in the neighborhood regularly exchange greetings with Mary when they are at school, around the neighborhood, at local stores, at the mall, at the grocery.

Source: Adapted from Brown, L., Long, E., Udvari-Solner, A., Davis, L., VanDeventer, P., Ahlgren, C., Johnson, F., Gruenewald, L., & Jorgensen, J. (1989). The home school: Why students with severe disabilities must attend the schools of their brothers, sisters, friends, and neighbors. *Journal of The Association for Persons with Severe Handicaps, 14,* 4. Used by permission.

in a general education class can provide additional opportunities for positive social contacts and the development of friendships (e.g., Carter, Clark, Cushing, & Kennedy, 2005; Staub, Spaulding, Peck, Gallucci, & Schwartz, 1996). See Teaching & Learning, "Including Students in General Education: The Peer Buddy Program."

For example, Kennedy and Itkonen (1994) studied the effects of class participation on social contacts with peers without disabilities for three high school students with severe and multiple disabilities. Don was 18 years old and classified as having severe intellectual retardation, along with paraplegia, cerebral palsy, and visual impairments. He used a wheelchair to move himself for short distances and lived in a 50-person facility for people with multiple disabilities and intensive health care needs. Manny was also 18 years old and classified as having severe retardation. He communicated with two- or three-word sentences and had a 10-year history of hitting and pinching others. Ann was 19 years old with moderate mental retardation. Her communications ranged from a few words to elaborate sentences. She was receiving instruction regarding appropriate topics of conversation and maintaining physical distance when interacting with others. Ann received medication for

Inclusion and social relationships

 Content Standards for Beginning Teachers—INDEP CURR: Advantages and disadvantages of placement options and programs on the continuum of services for individuals with disabilities (IC5K5) (also IC5K2, CC5K1).

Including Students in General Education:
The Peer Buddy Program

BY CAROLYN HUGHES, ERIK CARTER, MARILEE DYE, AND CORIE BYERS

As inclusion of students with disabilities into general education classes and activities is sought in more and more schools, educators are seeking direction in how to actually accomplish this goal. Peer buddy programs—in which general education students interact with and support special education students—are an effective strategy for increasing inclusion and access to the general education environment and curriculum (Hughes & Carter, 2006).

At the secondary level, classroom teachers often find it especially difficult to get special and general education students together. Most high school schedules are broken into 50- to 60-minute class periods—often with no free periods—which makes it difficult to include students with disabilities in the mainstream of school life. In addition, many special education students are involved in community-based training, which require longer blocks of time. Scheduling constraints may be one reason why most inclusion projects and research take place at the preschool and elementary levels.

The Peer Buddy Program attempts to remove scheduling barriers to inclusion by providing daily class times in which general education and special education students may interact. The program was developed and is being implemented in all comprehensive high schools in Metropolitan Nashville Public Schools—an urban school district of 75,000 students. This program has become the prototype for peer interaction and inclusion programs adopted by many schools and school districts nationwide. An elective, one-credit course allows peer buddies to spend at least one period each day with their special education partners. Peer buddies serve as positive role models for social interaction and provide the support their partners need to be included within general education and career/technical classes and the extracurricular activities that make up a typical high school day. Peer buddies report an increase in disability awareness, communication skills, understanding of themselves and others, and appreciation of individual differences (Copeland et al., 2004). Many of the interactions have developed into friendships with shared experiences in the students' homes and the community.

A TEACHER'S PERSPECTIVE: MARILEE DYE, SPECIAL EDUCATION TEACHER AT MCGAVOCK HIGH SCHOOL

My classroom includes the entire spectrum of students with severe disabilities: students with intellectual disabilities, multiple disabilities, communication deficits, sensory impairments, and autism. Peer tutors from the peer buddy program have been effective with all of these students. In my classroom, peer buddies perform a wide variety of activities. But the main thing they do is develop a friendship with the student to whom they are assigned.

Social interaction skills are a deficit for all of my students, and they are the single most difficult set of skills for an adult to teach a teenager. Peer buddies are much more successful at teaching social skills. Often, they are not trying to work on social skills, but through the course of a regular conversation or interaction, it just seems to occur. My first peer buddy, Amy, worked with Melissa on reading skills every day. Also during the school year, the two often discussed personal hygiene issues. I had absolutely nothing to do with these conversations. In a period of 2 months, we saw positive changes in Melissa's cleanliness and appearance. I had been working with Melissa for 1 year on these same issues, as had teachers for the past several years. We had had no impact on her behavior either singly or collectively. It was amazing to me what a peer accomplished in such a short time and with very little effort. After 2 years, Melissa continues to use the skills she learned from Amy; with no prompting, she keeps her hair washed and combed, brushes her teeth, and wears clothes that match.

This year I have a student with autism in my class. When Kim first came into my room, she appeared to have no interest in others and initiated interactions only when she wanted to eat or go to the rest room. Then Kim developed a friendship with her peer buddy, Corie. Now she watches the door for Corie every day. When they are together, Kim makes eye contact with her buddy frequently, laughs often, and even initiates conversations. We never saw Kim do these behaviors before. Kim also has increased her verbal repertoire from 4 to 11 words. I have been truly amazed at the difference peer buddies have made in the lives of my students.

A STUDENT'S PERSPECTIVE: CORIE BYERS, SENIOR AT MCGAVOCK HIGH SCHOOL

I heard about the peer buddy program from my guidance counselor and because I didn't have another class for one of my class periods, I decided to take it. I was kind of interested in it anyway, because I had been a peer tutor in seventh and eighth grade, and I wondered if I could get into it again.

I learned a lot about different people and different aspects of handicaps. My second semester as a peer buddy I spent mostly with Kim in Ms. Dye's room. And that girl—whew! She was a handful. When I first got into the classroom, Kim would just sit there and either sleep all day or cry about something. Or kind of just wander around with her eyes and look and not do anything. After my first semester, I noticed how she wouldn't deal with anybody. She was just always by herself. So I would go over there and tickle her and, all of a sudden, she just livened up! It was like someone had to just talk to her one time, and she burst out with life. When I first started talking to her, she really didn't have many words that she could say. Mostly she just said, "Milk," if she wanted milk, or if she had to go to the bathroom, she would tell us. That was about it. Then I got to talking to her, and toward the end of the year, she developed more language and everything.

We played games like hand-slap games and tickled each other. The bean bag chair was the best because she just loved that thing. Kim would just lay on it and wallow all over the floor and just laugh. It was so cool!

Well, that's Kim! She's cool now.

HOW TO GET STARTED

Steps for implementing a peer buddy program are well established and can easily be adapted to your individual situation (Hughes, Guth, Hall, Presley, Dye, & Byers, 1999):

1. *Develop a one-credit course.*
   - Incorporate a peer-tutoring course into your school's curriculum that allows peer buddies to spend at least one period each day with their special education partners.
   - Follow the school district's established procedures when you apply for the new course offering.
   - Include the course description in your school's official class schedule.

2. *Recruit peer buddies.*
   - Present information about the new program at a faculty meeting.
   - Actively recruit peer buddies during the first year. After that, peer buddies will recruit for you.
   - Include announcements, posters, and articles in the school newspaper and parent–teacher organization newsletter and videos on the school's closed-circuit television. Have peer buddies speak in school clubs and classes.
   - Have guidance counselors refer students who have interest, good attendance, and adequate grades.

3. *Screen and match students.*
   - Allow students to observe in the special education classroom to learn about the role of a peer buddy and decide if they would be an appropriate match for the class.
   - Have students interview with the special education teachers and meet potential partners.
   - Have students provide information on past experiences with students with disabilities and

clubs or activities they are involved in that their special education partners could join.

4. *Teach instructional strategies to peer buddies.*
   - Conduct a peer buddy orientation that includes people-first language, disability awareness, communication strategies, and suggested activities.
   - Communicate teachers' expectations for the peer buddy course, including attendance and grading policies.
   - Model prompting and reinforcement techniques.
   - Provide suggestions for dealing with inappropriate behavior, setting limits, and modifying general education curricula.

5. *Provide feedback and evaluate the program.*
   - Schedule observations and feedback sessions with peer buddies to address their questions or concerns.
   - Give peer buddies feedback on their interaction skills, time management, use of positive reinforcement, and activities engaged in with their partners.
   - Have peer buddies keep a daily journal of their activities and reflections, which the classroom teacher should review weekly.
   - Establish a peer buddy club that allows students to share experiences and ideas.

6. *Hold a lunch bunch.*
   - Invite peer buddies to join special education students in the cafeteria for lunch.
   - Encourage buddies to invite their general education friends to join the group, increasing social contacts for special education partners.

7. *Establish an advisory board.*
   - Develop an advisory board that includes students (buddies and partners), their parents, participating general and special education teachers, administrators, and guidance counselors.
   - Include community representatives to expand the peer buddy program to community-based activities, such as work experiences.

Carolyn Hughes is a professor of Special Education and Human and Organizational Development at Vanderbilt University. Erik Carter is assistant professor of Rehabilitation Psychology and Special Education at the University of Wisconsin—Madison. Marilee Dye is a special education teacher, and Corie Byers was a senior at McGavock High School in Nashville.

To learn more about how a student with disabilities can benefit from a peer buddy, go to the Building Teaching Skills section in Chapter 12 on MyEducationLab and complete the activities.

In the end, the best inclusion facilitators are the students themselves.

generalized tonic-clonic seizures and would often yell, run away, and hit others during transitions from one class or activity to another. Contingency contracts were in effect for both Manny and Ann as a preventive behavior management procedure; they could earn privileges for not engaging in problem behaviors.

Kennedy and Itkonen define a social contact as the interaction of a student with disabilities with peers in the context of a meaningful activity (e.g., eating lunch, conducting a science project) for a minimum of 15 minutes. Each of the three students participated in a different regular classroom (average size: 25 students) for one period each school day, 5 days per week.

Several aspects of this study deserve special comment. First, general education class participation increased the number of social contacts for each student even though ongoing opportunities to contact peers without disabilities were provided through "friendship" and peer-tutoring programs during those weeks when the students were not in the general education classroom. Second, the increases in social contacts were the result of participation for only one class period per day. Additional participation (e.g., two or three periods per day) might result in even more frequent contacts. Third, social contacts increased without an elaborate training program or intensive intervention. Each student simply began participating in the general education classroom after a "circle of friends" introduction by the special education teacher to the general education class peers that stressed the similarities among all students, the need for students to support one another, and the importance of social relationships.

Educators have developed a wide variety of strategies for promoting desired social relationships. One strategy is to give the student with disabilities a skill for initiating and maintaining interaction (Hughes et al., 2000). For example, Jolly, Test, and Spooner (1993) taught two nonverbal boys with severe and profound mental retardation and multiple physical disabilities to initiate play activities with nondisabled peers by showing badges with photographs of activities. Other strategies focus on teaching classmates without disabilities to initiate social contacts during free time, cooperative learning, or peer tutoring and peer buddy activities (Copeland et al., 2002; Hughes et al., 2001; Putnam, 1998; Romer, White, & Haring, 1996). Still other approaches involve changes in the roles and responsibilities of instructional faculty, such as collaborative teaching teams (Dettmer, Thurston, & Dyck, 2005; Giangreco, Cloninger, Dennis, & Edelman, 2000; Hunt, Soto, Maier, & Doering, 2003; Kochar, West, & Taymans, 2000; Snell & Janney, 2005).

Many of these strategies for facilitating the inclusion of students with severe disabilities are compatible with one another; and typically programs incorporate multiple, concurrent methods for identifying and providing supports for students, their teachers, and their peers.

Experiences and Transformations of General Education Teachers   To find out how general education teachers reacted to having a student with severe disabilities placed in their classrooms, Giangreco, Dennis, Cloninger, Edelman, and Shattman (1993) interviewed 19 K–9 general education teachers. They found that regardless of how the child with severe disabilities was placed in the general education classroom, most teachers initially described the placement in cautious or negative terms (e.g., "reluctant," "nervous," "unqualified," "angry"). Despite their initial negative reactions, 17 of the teachers experienced "increased

Changing attitudes of general education teachers

Council for Exceptional Children

Content Standards for Beginning Teachers—Common Core: Teacher attitudes and behaviors that influence behavior of individuals with exceptional learning needs (CC5K4) (also IC5K2).

ownership and involvement" with the child with severe disabilities as the school year progressed. Giangreco et al. refer to this process of changing attitude and perspective as *transformation*.

> Transformations were gradual and progressive, rather than discrete and abrupt. . . . A number of teachers who had these experiences reportedly came to the realization they could be successful and that including the student was not as difficult as they had originally imagined. . . . The following quotes typify the comments of teachers who underwent significant transformation.
>
> "I started seeing him as a little boy. I started feeling that he's a person too. He's a student. Why should I not teach him? He's in my class. That's my responsibility. I'm a teacher!"
>
> "I made the full swing of fighting against having Bobbi Sue placed in my room to fighting for her to be in a mainstream classroom working with kids in the way that she had worked with them all year long. I'm a perfect example of how you have to have an open mind."
>
> "I started watching my own regular classroom students. They didn't treat him any differently. They went about their business like everything was normal. So I said, 'If they can do it, I can do it.' He's not getting in their way. They're treating him like everybody else.'"
>
> "They were always letting me know when I forgot something. 'You didn't remember to include Sarah.' So they were very good at letting me know."
>
> "The kids help you figure it out." (Giangreco et al., 1993, pp. 359–372)

You will find detailed information about administrative, curricular, and instructional strategies designed to support the education of students with severe disabilities in neighborhood schools and inclusive classrooms in Bauer and Brown (2001), Block (2007), Browder and Wilson (2001), Downing and Eichinger (2003), Ryndak and Fisher (2007), Giangreco and Doyle (2007), Kennedy and Horn (2004), Snell and Janney (2005), and Wolfe and Hall (2003).

How Much Time in the General Education Classroom? Although research has clearly shown the social benefits of general education class participation for students with disabilities, as well as for their peers without disabilities, the effects of full inclusion on the attainment of IEP goals are not yet known. The functional IEP goals and objectives for students with severe disabilities are seldom reflected in the academic curriculum of the general education classroom (especially at the secondary level). Making the most effective use of available instruction time is critical to students who by definition require direct, intensive, and "customized" instruction to acquire basic skills that students without disabilities learn without instruction (Smith et al., 2001). A major challenge for both special and general educators is to develop models and strategies for including students with severe disabilities in general education classroom activities without sacrificing their opportunities to acquire, practice, and generalize the functional skills they need most.

The question of how much time students with severe disabilities should spend in the general education classroom is an important one. Although a few full-inclusion advocates might argue that every student with disabilities should have a full-time general education-class placement regardless of the nature of her educational needs, most special educators probably would agree with Brown and colleagues (1991), whose position is that students with severe disabilities should be based in the same schools and classrooms they would attend if they were not disabled but that they should also spend some time elsewhere.

> There are substantial differences between being based in and confined to regular education classrooms. "Based in" refers to being a member of a real class, where and with whom you start the school day, you may not spend all your time with your class, but it is still your group and everyone knows it. . . . It is our position that it is unacceptable for students with severe disabilities to spend either 0% or 100% of their time in regular education classrooms. . . . How much time should be spent in regular classes? Enough to ensure that the student is a member, not a visitor. A lot, if the student is engaged in meaningful activities. Quite a bit if she is young, but less as she approaches 21. There is still a lot we do not know. (pp. 40, 46)

The Challenge and Rewards of Teaching Students With Severe and Multiple Disabilities

Virtually every parent of a child with severe disabilities has heard a host of negative predictions from educators, doctors, and concerned friends and family. Parents often are offered such discouraging forecasts as "Your child will never talk" or "Your child will never be toilet-trained." Yet in many instances those children make gains that far exceed the professionals' original predictions: They have learned to walk, talk, toilet themselves, and perform other "impossible" tasks.

Teachers—special as well as general educators—who are providing instruction to students with severe and multiple disabilities can rightfully be called pioneers on an exciting new frontier of education. More than 20 years ago, Orelove (1984) stated that professionals who were involved in educating students with severe disabilities could "look back with pride, and even awe, at the advances they have made. In a relatively brief period, educators, psychologists, and other professionals have advocated vigorously for additional legislation and funds, extended the service delivery model into the public schools and community, and developed a training technology" (p. 271).

Although significant progress has been made in the two decades since Orelove's positive assessment, a great deal more must be accomplished. Future research must increase our understanding of how students with severe disabilities acquire, maintain, and generalize functional skills. As we develop more effective techniques for changing behavior, they must be balanced with concern for the personal rights and dignity of individuals with severe disabilities. Current and future teachers of students with severe disabilities have the opportunity to be at the forefront of those developments.

Teaching students with severe disabilities is difficult and demanding. The teacher must be well organized, firm, and consistent. He must be able to manage a complex educational operation, which usually involves supervising paraprofessional aides, student teachers, peer tutors, and volunteers. The teacher must be knowledgeable about one-to-one and small-group instruction formats and be able to work cooperatively with other teachers and related-services professionals. He must maintain accurate records and constant planning for the future needs of his students. Effective communication with parents and families, school administrators, vocational rehabilitation personnel, and community agencies is also vital.

Students with the most severe disabilities sometimes give little or no apparent response, so their teachers must be very sensitive to small changes in behavior. The effective teacher is consistent and persistent in designing and implementing strategies to improve learning and behavior (even if some of the students' previous teachers were not). The effective teacher should not be too quick to remove difficult tasks or requests that result in noncompliance or misbehavior. It is better to teach students to request assistance and to intersperse tasks that are easy for the student to perform.

There is a difference between either expecting miracles or being passively patient and simply working each day at the job of designing, implementing, and evaluating systematic instruction and supports. It can be a mistake to expect a miracle:

> In the beginning, we were expecting a sudden step forward, that we might somehow turn a cognitive, emotional, or social key inside the child's mind that would produce a giant leap ahead. . . . Such a leap would have been so gratifying, and it would have made our work so much easier. But it never happened. Instead, progress followed a slow, step-by-step progression, with only a few and minor spurts ahead from time to time. We learned to settle in for hard work. (Lovaas, 1994, n.p.)

Some might consider it undesirable to work with students with severe and multiple disabilities because of the extent of their behavioral challenges and learning problems. Yet working with students who require instruction at its very best can offer many highly rewarding teaching experiences. Much satisfaction can be felt in teaching a child to feed and dress herself independently; helping a student make friends with nondisabled peers; and supporting a young adult's efforts to live, travel, and work as independently as possible in the community. Both the challenge and the potential rewards of teaching students with severe disabilities are great.

TIPS for Beginning Teachers

TIPS FOR TEACHING STUDENTS WITH SEVERE DISABILITIES
by Carey Creech-Galloway

DEVELOP A SCHEDULE FOR THE CLASSROOM AND STICK WITH IT

- Begin by listing all of the student's IEP objectives and related services first and other activities that have set times during the school day (e.g., lunch). Schedule the students, instructional assistants, and the teacher all on the same schedule so that everyone knows their responsibilities for that block of time. Don't forget to schedule breaks and lunch breaks as well as time for student restroom breaks.

- List the student(s) and instructor and the goal or activity for that time period on the schedule. You may even want to list the materials needed until your paraprofessionals become familiar with your expectations.

- You'll probably revise this schedule five or six times before it runs smoothly, but stick with it!

PAIR PICTURE CUES WITH PRINT AS MUCH AS POSSIBLE

- Pairing pictures with print is especially important when you are teaching at the elementary level. Students with severe disabilities acquire and generalize language quicker when the words are paired with text.

- Use this with schedules, labeling items, learning centers, and class rules.

GET ORGANIZED WITH YOUR INSTRUCTIONAL DATA

- Develop a system for keeping each student's instructional data organized. You could begin with a binder with each IEP objective on a tab with the data sheet and graph behind the tab. You can organize this per student or per IEP objective if that applies (e.g., all students working on brushing teeth in one binder).

- Take data on the IEP objective every time you provide instruction, because you need the data to make decisions on instruction. As one University of Kentucky professor told me, "If you aren't taking data on the skill, why teach it?"

KEY TERMS AND CONCEPTS

anoxia, p. 462
closed head injury, p. 460
deaf-blindness, p. 455
multiple disabilities, p. 455
open head injury, p. 460

partial participation, p. 475
profound disabilities, p. 454
severe disabilities, p. 453
traumatic brain injury, p. 459

SUMMARY

Defining Severe, Profound, and Multiple Disabilities

- Students with severe disabilities need instruction in many basic skills that most children without disabilities acquire without instruction in the first 5 years of life.

- TASH defines persons with severe disabilities as individuals "who require ongoing support in more than one major life activity in order to participate in an integrated community and enjoy a quality of life similar to that available to all citizens."

- Students with profound disabilities have pervasive delays in all domains of functioning at a developmental level no higher than 2 years.

- Students with severe disabilities frequently have multiple disabilities, including physical impairments and health conditions.
- Students with deaf-blindness cannot be accommodated in special education programs designed solely for students with hearing or visual impairments. Although the vast majority of children who are deaf-blind have some functional hearing and/or vision, the dual impairments severely impede learning.

Characteristics of Students With Severe and Multiple Disabilities

- Students with severe disabilities need instruction in many basic skills that most children without disabilities learn without help. Children with severe disabilities may show some or all of the following behaviors or skill deficits: slow acquisition rates for learning new skills, difficulty in generalizing and maintaining newly learned skills, severe deficits in communication skills, impaired physical and motor development, deficits in self-help skills, infrequent constructive behavior and interaction, and frequent inappropriate behavior.
- Despite their intense challenges, students with severe disabilities often exhibit many positive characteristics, such as warmth, humor, sociability, and persistence.
- Despite their limitations, children with severe disabilities can and do learn.

Prevalence of Severe and Multiple Disabilities

- Estimates of the prevalence of severe disabilities range from 0.1% to 1% of the population.
- Together, children served under the IDEA disability categories of multiple disabilities, traumatic brain injury, and deaf-blindness represent less than 3% of all children who receive special education.

Causes of Severe and Multiple Disabilities

- Brain disorders, which are involved in most cases of severe intellectual disabilities, are the result of either brain dysgenesis (abnormal brain development) or brain damage (caused by influences that alter the structure or function of a brain that had been developing normally up to that point).
- Severe and profound disabilities most often have biological causes, including chromosomal abnormalities, genetic and metabolic disorders, complications of pregnancy and prenatal care, birth trauma, and later brain damage.
- In about one sixth of all cases of severe disabilities, the cause cannot be clearly determined.

Traumatic Brain Injury

- IDEA defines traumatic brain injury (TBI) as an acquired injury to the brain caused by an external physical force, resulting in total or partial functional disability or psychosocial impairments, or both, that adversely affects a child's educational performance.
- Of the 1.5 million people who sustain a traumatic brain injury each year in the United States, 50,000 will die of their injury and 235,000 will be hospitalized.
- Traumatic brain injury is the leading cause of death in children and the most common cause of acquired disability in childhood.
- Causes of TBI are open head injuries, which are the result of penetration of the skull, and closed head injuries, which are more common and result from the head hitting a stationary object with such force that the brain slams against the inside of the cranium.
- Major causes of traumatic brain injury in children are car and bicycle accidents, falls, accidents during contact sports, and shaken baby syndrome.
- A mild brain injury results in a concussion (a brief or momentary loss of consciousness), usually without any subsequent complications.
- A moderate brain injury usually results in contusions (bruising, swelling, and bleeding), hematomas (aggregation or clotting of blood), loss of consciousness, and significant cognitive and behavioral impairments for many months.
- In addition to brain contusions, hematomas, and damage to the nerve fibers or axons, a severe brain injury results in a coma and often permanent impairments in functioning.
- Impairments caused by brain injuries fall into three main categories: (a) physical and sensory changes (e.g., lack of coordination, spasticity of muscles); (b) cognitive impairments (e.g., short- and long-term memory deficits, difficulty maintaining attention and

concentration); and (c) social, behavioral, and emotional problems (e.g., mood swings [emotional lability], self-centeredness, lack of motivation).

Educational Approaches

- A curriculum based on typical developmental milestones is inappropriate for most students with severe disabilities.
- Students with severe disabilities must be taught skills that are functional, age-appropriate, and directed toward current and future environments.
- Students with severe disabilities should be taught choice-making skills.
- The emphasis of research and training in communication for persons with severe disabilities has shifted from instruction of specific forms of communication to a focus on functional communication in any mode that enables communication partners to establish shared meanings.
- Some students with severe disabilities use augmentative and alternative systems of communication (AAC), such as gestures, various sign language systems, pictorial communication boards, picture exchange communication systems (PECSs), and electronic communication aids.
- Students with severe disabilities should be taught age-appropriate recreation and leisure skills.
- Because each student with severe disabilities has many learning needs, teachers must carefully prioritize and choose IEP objectives and learning activities that will be of most benefit to the student and his family.
- Effective instruction of students with severe disabilities is characterized by these elements:
  - The student's current level of performance is precisely assessed.
  - The skill to be taught is defined clearly.
  - The skills are ordered in an appropriate sequence.
  - The teacher provides clear prompts or cues to the student.
  - The student receives immediate feedback and reinforcement from the teacher.
  - Strategies that promote generalization of learning are used.
  - The student's performance is directly and frequently assessed.
- Partial participation is both a philosophy for selecting activities and a method for adapting activities and supports to enable students with severe disabilities to actively participate in meaningful tasks they cannot perform independently.
- The teacher of students with severe disabilities must be skilled in positive, instructionally relevant strategies for assessing and dealing with challenging and problem behaviors.
- Research has shown that integrated small-group instructional arrangements with students with severe disabilities can be effective.
- Students with severe disabilities are more likely to develop social relationships with students without disabilities if they attend their home school and are included in the general education classroom.
- Although the initial reactions of many general education teachers who have a student with severe disabilities placed in their classrooms are negative, those apprehensions and concerns often transform into positive experiences as the student becomes a regular member of their classroom.
- Teachers must be sensitive to small changes in behavior. The effective teacher is consistent and persistent in evaluating and changing instruction to improve learning and behavior.
- Working with students who require instruction at its very best can be highly rewarding to teachers.

Now go to MyEducationLab at www.myeducationlab.com, and take the pretest to assess your initial comprehension of chapter content. Once you have taken the pretest, use your individualized Study Plan for Chapter 12 to enhance your understanding of the concepts discussed in the chapter. Finally, take the posttest to assess your comprehension of Chapter 12 content.

Giftedness and Talent

BY JANE PIIRTO AND WILLIAM L. HEWARD

- How has the evolving definition of giftedness changed the ways in which students are identified and served?
- Why do students who are very bright need special education?
- How do estimates of the prevalence of giftedness in the school-age population compare to the number of students in K–12 gifted programs?
- What provisions should be made to accurately identify students with outstanding talents who are from diverse cultural groups or have disabilities?
- How can the general education classroom teacher provide instruction at the pace and depth needed by gifted and talented students while meeting the needs of other students in the classroom?
- Should gifted students be educated with their same-age peers or with older students who share the same intellectual and academic talents and interests?

FEATURED TEACHER

LINDA MICHAEL
Edison Elementary School • Ashland City Schools, Ashland, Ohio

Linda Michael

Education—Teaching Credentials—Experience

- B.A. in anthropology and history, Miami University
- M.S. in textiles and clothing, Ohio University
- Ohio teacher licenses: Middle Grades (4–9) Science and Language Arts and Reading, Gifted Intervention Specialist

I have been a teacher of the gifted for 3 years, having come to the field of teaching after many work and life experiences. Some refer to this as a second career. I disagree. I view all the choices I have made as preparation to my first career—teaching.

My Classroom My first 2 years I taught fourth to sixth graders in a pull-out program. This year I am teaching a self-contained class of fourth- and fifth-grade students who have been identified as superior cognitive. Superior cognitive is one of the four categories by which students in Ohio are identified as gifted. This means I am the teacher of record for 16 students. I feel that the self-contained classroom is the best way to meet the needs of the students who have superior cognitive abilities. Pull-out programs offer enrichment, but usually only for a few hours, once or twice a week. In our state, inclusion of a gifted intervention specialist in the regular classroom is replacing pull-out programs, or districts are offering inclusion along with pull-out programs. Most districts do not have enough teachers to meet the needs of all the identified gifted and talented students. Students aren't just gifted for part of the day or in increments throughout the week; they must have their needs met throughout the school day. I have found the self-contained classroom gives me the opportunity to do that.

The self-contained class option is often controversial. More than one teacher has told me she was against the idea because I would be taking away the best and brightest students, the "sparkplugs." I have several responses to this viewpoint. The first is if the "sparkplugs" are the only students that regularly participate in class, the rest of the students are not being adequately reached. My second response is those "sparkplugs" may be draining the other students who are too intimidated to respond or who have grown complacent to be in a nonresponsive role.

The third response I have is a question: What is more important, a student's education or a teacher's routine? Gifted students who must wait for others to catch up or who are used as tutors in the classroom are not having their needs met. My final response is "don't stereotype the gifted kid!" Gifted students are individuals and are not all "sparkplugs," constantly raising their hands in class. A gifted and talented student can just as often be the trouble maker, the quiet kid staring out the window, or the class clown who frequently forgets his assignments.

The birth of my self-contained class has not been without its problems, but it has been worth the struggle. Students and parents are excited and my day is never dull. Teachers are beginning to understand that gifted education is not a threat to the general classroom but another positive way to serve students.

Teaching Strategies   I've discovered how important it is to understand the learning strengths and challenges of your students. Sometimes it can be difficult getting students to step out of their comfort zones and to try new approaches in problem solving. For example, one of my students this year would rather read than do anything else. Once, during a math lesson, the students were creating isometric figures with cubes and then drawing their figures on grid paper. This activity was very difficult for my reader because she couldn't visualize the 3-D figure on a 2-D surface. But I didn't let her give up. When she finally saw the patterns, she got very excited about her accomplishment. Will she ever be an architect or engineer? Probably not, but that's not the point. She realized she has even more talents and abilities than she thought, and she realized the value of persistence when faced with a challenging activity.

Becoming involved in a cause one feels strongly about is an excellent way for students to feel their education has personal meaning. In my first year of teaching, two of my students approached me with a petition to save Mountain Gorillas. They had read about them and wanted to help in some way. The entire class began researching Mountain Gorillas, the causes of their dwindling population, and organizations that were helping alleviate the problems. The students discovered the Dian Fossey Foundation for Gorilla Research and decided to have a fund-raiser to adopt as many Mountain Gorillas as possible. They sold brownies, called Gorilla Bars, at the elementary schools. A parent who is a chef helped us bake the bars in one of the school kitchens. The experience brought the kids together for a cause they believed in and became a great lesson in math as the students estimated the quantity of the ingredients they needed and what the cost of the bars should be to make a profit. I must stress, I didn't initiate the idea. I guided and suggested, but the kids made it their own.

One of the best bits of teaching advice I have encountered comes from an article by Steven C. Reinhart in the journal *Mathematics Teaching in the Middle School* (April 2000, Vol. 5, No. 8). Reinhart simply stated, "Never say anything a kid can say" (p. 1). Instead of answering a question, ask good questions that require students to think. Believe that each student can contribute. This approach isn't easy. It demands that the teacher have a mastery of the academic content areas she is teaching. It also means the teacher must recognize her role is one of facilitator, and not of lecturer. This isn't to say lecturing does not have its place, but it should be a brief introduction to a lesson, not the beginning, middle, and end.

Teaching gifted and talented students is a daily challenge that I wouldn't trade for anything. My classroom always seems to have a buzz about it because the students are excited to be there. This can be exhausting, especially when I feel like I can't do it all. Most of the time, however, it is exhilarating because I believe so much in the students and their potential.

After reading this chapter, complete the pretest for Chapter 13 on MyEducationLab to assess your initial understanding of chapter content.

Our study of exceptional children thus far has focused on students with intellectual, behavioral, or physical disabilities—children who require individually designed programs of specialized instruction and related services to benefit from education. On the other end of the continuum of cognitive, academic, artistic, and social abilities are gifted and talented students who find that traditional curriculum and methods of instruction do not provide the advanced and unique challenges they require to learn most effectively. They, too, need special education to reach their potential.

Janie has just completed her report on the solar system for class tomorrow. She looks out her bedroom window and wonders what might be happening on the countless planets that circle all of those stars. And she thinks about the circumstances that made life possible on the third planet from the star called Sol. What Janie is doing may not seem special; after all, most students write school reports and wonder about extraterrestrial life—until we learn that she is just 6 years old. Janie is functioning years ahead of her peers. She writes in complete sentences, expresses herself exceptionally well, and has a powerful urge to know the answers to many and varied problems.

Toney Jojola saunters down a dusty back road near his home in the southwest. Toney is excited because today his mentor and great-aunt have promised to teach him the process of applying the rich charcoal slip to the pottery he is making. His people have been making pottery for hundreds of years, but somehow it seems to take on multiple meanings in his hands. He notices and uses small variations in color and texture to embed symbolism into his pieces. Perhaps this one will have the winged serpent that he favors so much, reminding everyone that an immense trade network existed in prehistoric America that reached from present-day Canada to South America. Toney sees much in his pottery, in his ancestors who have inspired him, in the beauty that is the earth made functional, and in a desire for continuity in his life. Toney does not say much in school or express himself very well in writing, but he understands everything that is being said and talked about. He is very patient and seems tentative in his behavior, not wanting to create a disturbance that would draw attention to himself. During class he dreams of the pottery designs he will someday create in the studio that he will inherit from his great-aunt.

Ninth grader Malcolm runs from school to the bus stop for the bus that will take him to the local university, where he is taking his second course on creative writing. He is excited about showing his latest short story to the professor. Malcolm's prose brings into focus all of the pain he sees around him, critically analyzing the leadership of his community and nation. He believes he has a message that must be heard; he is powerfully moved to reach out to the disaffected, the disenfranchised, as well as the ambivalent of all races. He has many ideas for changing what he believes is wrong with his government. He believes deeply in his vision and knows he can make a difference once he learns how to communicate his message as effectively as possible. Bursting with energy and desire, Malcolm struggles to sit still while the bus moves him ever closer to his training ground for the future.

Janie, Toney, and Malcolm need special education—in the form of curriculum modifications and specialized instructional activities—to enhance and develop their individual talents. These precocious youngsters, and others like them, will become the outstanding scientists, artists, writers, inventors, and leaders of the future. Understanding and working to develop the talents of these exceptional children is an important undertaking of special educators who work in the area of gifted and talented education.

DEFINITIONS

Intelligence, creativity, and talent have been central to the various definitions of giftedness that have been proposed over the years. Lewis Terman (1925), one of the pioneers of the field, defined the gifted as those who score in the top 2% on standardized tests of intelligence. Guilford (1967) called for the identification of people with creative potential. Witty (1951), recognizing the value of including special skills and talents, described gifted and talented children as those "whose performance is consistently remarkable in any potentially valuable area" (p. 62). These three concepts continue to be reflected in the current and still-evolving definitions of gifted and talented children.

Federal Definitions

The first federal definition of gifted and talented students was included in a 1972 report to Congress titled *Education of the Gifted,* by U.S. Commissioner of Education Sydney Marland.

> [T]he term "gifted and talented children" means children, and whenever applicable, youth, who are identified at the preschool, elementary, or secondary level as possessing demonstrated or potential high performance capabilities in areas such as intellectual, creative, specific academic, or leadership ability or in the performing and visual arts and who by reason thereof require services or activities not ordinarily provided by the school.... gifted and talented will encompass a minimum of 3 to 5 percent of the school population. (p. 5)

The Marland definition had the earliest and most influence on state definitions. Since its beginnings, the field of gifted education has sought to include multiple kinds of giftedness in its definitions, not just the high IQ or superior cognitive type of giftedness.

Early definitions of G&T and Marland Report

 Content Standards for Beginning Teachers—G&T: Historical foundations of gifted and talented education (GT1K1) (also CC1K5).

Federal definition of G&T

Council for Exceptional Children

Content Standards for Beginning Teachers—G&T: Issues in definition and identification of individuals with gifts and talents, including those from culturally and linguistically diverse backgrounds (GT1K5).

In 1992, a federal report titled *National Excellence: A Case for Developing America's Talent* featured a revised definition of gifted and talented children that was motivated by new cognitive research and concerns about inequity in participation in programs for the intellectually gifted. The word *gifted* was eliminated, and the terms *outstanding talent* and *exceptional talent* were embraced. The definition proposed that giftedness—or talent—occurs in all groups, across all cultures, and is not necessarily apparent in test scores but in a person's "high-performance capability" in intellectual, creative, and artistic realms. Giftedness is said to connote "a mature power rather than a developing ability." Talent is to be found by "observing students at work in rich and varied educational settings."

The current federal definition was first promulgated in the Jacob K. Javits Gifted and Talented Student Education Act of 1988 (P.L. 100-297) as part of the Elementary and Secondary Education Act and now included in the No Child Left Behind Act of 2001:

> Students, children, or youth who give evidence of high achievement capability in areas such as intellectual, creative, artistic, or leadership capacity, or in specific academic fields, and who need services and activities not ordinarily provided by the school in order to fully develop those capabilities. (Title IX, Part A, Section 9101 [22])

Many states have now incorporated aspects of the federal definition into their definitions of giftedness and talent. Although the general intelligence element of the definition prevails (39 states consider superior cognitive ability as giftedness), 33 states include specific academic ability, 30 include creative thinking, 20 include the visual and performing arts, and 18 include leadership in their definitions of giftedness and talent (Stephens & Karnes, 2000).

Other Contemporary and Complementary Definitions

Contemporary conceptions of giftedness represent a growing recognition of the importance of balancing theoretical with practical definitions of giftedness that emphasize situated problem solving (Sternberg, 1988; Sternberg & Grigorenko, 2000); talents that are context- and domain-related (Gagné, 2000, 2003; Gardner, 1983/1994, 1999; Piirto, 2004a, 2004b); and the influence of sustained, deliberate practice on the realization of exceptional talent (Ericsson, Charness, Feltovich, & Hoffman, 2006; Ericsson, Nadogapal, & Roring, 2005). The following definitions of gifted and talented students, offered by Joseph Renzulli, Jane Piirto, and June Maker, are examples of these contemporary views.

Many gifted and talented students display characteristics such as superior memory, observational powers, curiosity, creativity, and the ability to learn school-related subject matter with a minimum of drill and repetition.

Renzulli's Three-Trait Definition Renzulli's (2003) definition of giftedness is based on an interaction among three basic clusters of human traits: (a) above-average general intellectual abilities, (b) a high level of task commitment, and (c) creativity. Gifted and talented children are those

> possessing or capable of developing this composite set of traits and applying them to any potentially valuable area of human performance. Children who manifest or are capable of developing an interaction among the three clusters require a wide variety of educational opportunities and services that are not ordinarily provided through regular instructional programs. (p. 184)

Figure 13.1 illustrates how the three components of ability (actual or potential), task commitment, and creative expression are jointly applied to a valuable area of human endeavor. Like the federal definition, Renzulli's definition provides a great deal of freedom in determining who is considered gifted and talented, depending on the interpretation of "valuable area of human performance."

Piirto's Concept of Talent Development Piirto (2007) defines the gifted as

> those individuals who, by way of having certain learning characteristics such as superior memory, observational powers, curiosity, creativity, and the ability to learn school-related

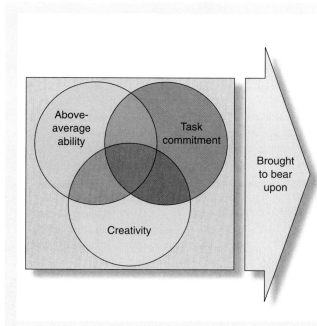

General Performance Areas

Mathematics • Visual Arts • Physical Sciences •
Philosophy • Social Sciences • Law • Religion •
Language Arts • Music • Life Sciences • Movement
Arts

Specific Performance Areas

Cartooning • Astronomy • Public Opinion Polling •
Jewelry Design • Map Making • Choreography •
Biography • Film Making • Statistics • Local
History • Electronics • Musical Composition •
Landscape Architecture • Chemistry •
Demography • Microphotography • City Planning •
Pollution Control • Poetry • Fashion Design •
Weaving • Play Writing • Advertising • Costume
Design • Meteorology • Puppetry • Marketing •
Game Design • Journalism • Electronic Music •
Child Care • Consumer Protection • Cooking •
Ornithology • Furniture Design • Navigation •
Genealogy • Sculpture • Wildlife Management • Set
Design • Agricultural Research • Animal Learning •
Film Criticism • etc.

FIGURE 13.1

Renzulli's three-component definition of giftedness

Source: From Renzulli, J. S. (2003). Conception of giftedness and its relationship to the development of social capital.
In N. Colangelo & G. A. Davis (Eds.), *Handbook of gifted education* (3rd ed., p. 76). Needham Heights, MA: Allyn &
Bacon. Used by permission.

subject matters rapidly and accurately with a minimum of drill and repetition, have a right
to an education that is differentiated according to those characteristics. (p. 37)

Such children become apparent early and should be served throughout their educational lives, from preschool through college. While they may or may not become producers
of knowledge or makers of novelty, their education should give them the background to
become adults who do produce knowledge or make new artistic and social products.

Piirto's pyramid model emphasizes (1) a foundation of genetic endowment; (2) personality attributes such as drive, resilience, intuition, perception, intensity, and the like; (3) the
minimum intelligence level necessary to function in the domain in which the talent is
demonstrated; (4) talent in a specific domain such as mathematics, writing, visual arts,
music, science, or athletics; and (5) the environmental influences of five "suns": (a) the sun
of home; (b) the sun of community and culture; (c) the sun of school; (d) the sun of chance;
and (e) the sun of gender (see Figure 13.2). Which talent is developed depends on the
"thorn" of passion, calling, or sense of vocation.

Maker's Problem-Solving Perspective   Maker's dynamic perspective incorporates the
three elements that appear most often within contemporary definitions of the gifted and
talented: high intelligence, high creativity, and excellent problem-solving skills. She
characterizes a gifted person as

a problem solver—one who enjoys the challenge of complexity and persists until the problem is solved in a satisfying way. Such an individual is capable of: a) creating a new or more
clear definition of an existing problem, b) devising new and more efficient or effective methods, and c) reaching solutions that may be different from the usual, but are recognized as being effective, perhaps more effective, than previous solutions. (Maker, 1993, p. 71)

Numerous other conceptions of giftedness and talent include Robert Sternberg's
(1988, 2003, 2007) triarchic theory of successful intelligence, Francoys Gagné's (2000,
2003) differentiated model of giftedness and talent, and Howard Gardner's (2000, 2006)

*Renzulli's, Piirto's, and
Maker's conceptions of G&T*

Council for
Exceptional
Children

Content
Standards for
Beginning
Teachers—G&T: Issues in
definition and identification
of individuals with gifts and
talents, including those
from culturally and linguistically diverse backgrounds
(GT1K5).

FIGURE 13.2

Piirto pyramid of talent development

Source: From Piirto, J. (2004). *Understanding creativity.* Scottsdale, AZ: Great Potential. Also in *"My teeming brain": Understanding creative writers.* Cresskill, NJ: Hampton. Original version in Piirto, J. (1994). *Talented children and adults: Their development and education.* Upper Saddle River, NJ: Merrill/Prentice Hall. Revised in Piirto, J. (1999). *Talented children and adults: Their development and education,* 2nd ed. Used with permission.

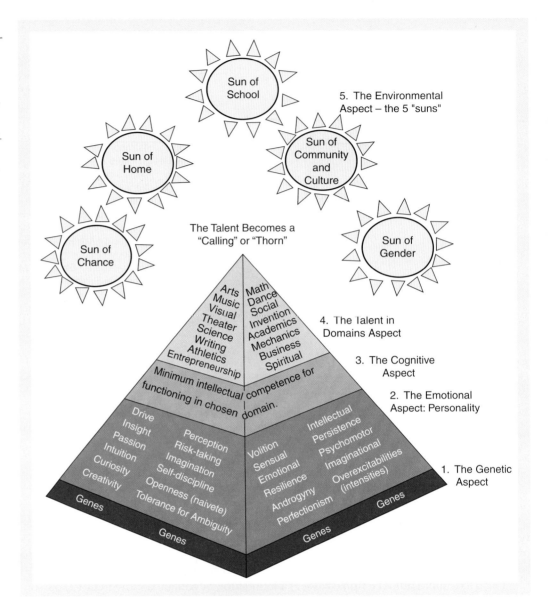

theory of multiple intelligences. To summarize, all these definitions present the new conception of intelligence and giftedness that radically departs from earlier definitions by broadening the understanding of talents, reducing the focus on IQ, and emphasizing certain environmental and personality areas as well as specific talents. In 1998, the two major associations for the gifted and talented, the Council for Exceptional Children Association for the Gifted (CEC-TAG) and the National Association for Gifted Children (NAGC), adopted a joint statement of core beliefs and goals incorporating the recent thinking (see Figure 13.3).

CHARACTERISTICS

Giftedness is a complex human condition covering a wide range of abilities and traits. While the definitions of giftedness are social constructions (i.e., they are not absolute but vary according to situation), without doubt, advanced students have special educational needs. Some students have special talents, but rarely do these match the stereotypes that many people have of giftedness. These students may not be outstanding in academics, but they may have special abilities in areas such as music, dance, art, or leadership. Gifted and highly talented individuals are found across gender, cultural, linguistic, and even disability groups.

| FIGURE 13.3 | Educating America's Gifted and Talented Children: A Joint Statement of Core Beliefs and Goals of the National Association for Gifted Children (NAGC) and The Association for the Gifted, The Council for Exceptional Children (CEC-TAG), 1998 |

We believe that:

- Talent comes in many forms and may be manifested in multiple domains.
- Children are individuals who bring to the classroom a diverse set of aptitudes, achievements, and potential.
- Gifts and talents may be developed over a period of time and may manifest themselves at different stages in a child's development.
- The full spectrum of talents is present in every cultural, racial, and socioeconomic group.
- The population diversity that characterizes our schools is a positive source of talent potential.
- The range of aptitudes, achievements, and potential among children suggests a need for varied educational experiences designed so that every child in the classroom is actively engaged in respectful, challenging, and meaningful learning.
- It is the responsibility of educators to design educational experiences to maximize the development of talents in all children.

Therefore, we as organizations join in a common commitment to the highest standards for educational practices in an effort to ensure that:

- Local educational agencies provide a continuum of educational opportunities to ensure that a sufficient variety of options is available to assist each child's development in one or more apparent or emergent areas of strength.
- Teachers have the opportunity to learn and are encouraged to implement methods necessary to develop the strength areas within every child, from the struggling learner to those who learn more quickly.
- Every student has access to opportunities to develop his or her full potential through strength-based learning and highly engaging learning activities.
- Educators and related-service personnel who work with children in our schools are trained and expected to recognize and develop exceptional gifts and talents in any domain such as the traditional academic areas, the arts, or leadership.
- Curriculum reflects a high level of challenge and is adapted in classrooms to the educational needs of students in that classroom.

To achieve these goals, we envision a partnership based on cooperation, collaboration, and commitment that will result in a common understanding that talent development and enhancement contribute positively to the goal of providing maximum learning for each and every child.

Learning and intellectual characteristics in those persons who are considered to be gifted and talented include the following (Clark, 2008; Maker, 1993; Piirto, 2007):

- The ability to rapidly acquire, retain, and use large amounts of information
- The ability to relate one idea to another
- The ability to make sound judgments
- The ability to perceive the operation of larger systems of knowledge that may not be recognized by the typical person
- The ability to acquire and manipulate abstract symbol systems
- The ability to solve problems by reframing the question and creating novel solutions

Cognitive and learning characteristics of G&T

 Content Standards for Beginning Teachers—G&T: Cognitive characteristics of individuals with gifts and talents in intellectual, academic, creative, leadership, and artistic domains (GT2K7).

Some children may have intellectual abilities found only in 1 child in 1,000 or 1 child in 10,000. Silverman (1995) identified the following characteristics for the highly gifted—children with IQ scores 3 standard deviations or greater above the mean (IQ > 145):

- Intense intellectual curiosity
- Fascination with words and ideas
- Perfectionism
- Need for precision
- Learning in great intuitive leaps
- Intense need for mental stimulation
- Difficulty conforming to the thinking of others
- Early moral and existential concern
- Tendency toward introversion (pp. 220–221)

We must also realize that many lists of gifted characteristics portray gifted children as having only virtues and no flaws. The very attributes by which we identify gifted children, however, can cause problems (Cross, 2006; Nugent, 2005). High verbal ability, for example, may prompt gifted students to talk themselves out of troublesome situations or allow them to dominate class discussions. High curiosity may give them the appearance of being aggressive or snoopy as they pursue anything that comes to their attention. Nevertheless, these children are born every day, and teachers and parents who are alert to such cues can notice their characteristics.

Individual Differences Among Gifted and Talented Students

Awareness of individual differences is also important in understanding gifted students. Like other children, gifted children show both inter- and intraindividual differences. For example, if two students are given the same reading achievement test and each obtains a different score, we can speak of *interindividual* differences in reading achievement. If a student who obtains a high reading achievement score obtains a much lower score on an arithmetic achievement test, we say the student has an *intraindividual* difference between the two areas of performance. A graph of any student's abilities would reveal some high points and some lower points; scores would not be the same across all dimensions. **Asynchrony** is a term used to describe disparate rates of intellectual, emotional, and physical growth or development often displayed by gifted children.

The gifted student's overall pattern of performance, however, may be well above the average for that grade and/or age, as we see in Figure 13.4. Lefki performs higher in

Go to the Homework & Exercises section in Chapter 13 of MyEducationLab and complete Homework Exercise 1. As you read the article and answer the accompanying questions, consider the heterogeneous nature of students who are gifted and the differences among these students.

Inter- and intraindividual differences

Content Standards for Beginning Teachers—G&T: Similarities and differences of individuals with and without gifts and talents and the general population of learners (GT2K2). Similarities and differences among individuals with and without gifts and talents (GT2K3).

FIGURE 13.4

Profiles of two gifted and talented students, both age 10 and in fifth grade

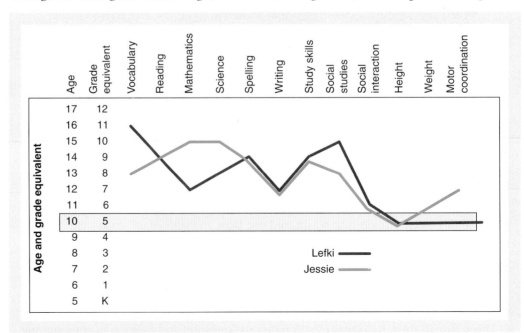

vocabulary and social studies than Jessie does, however, and Jessie shows higher performance in science and mathematics than Lefki does. These are interindividual differences. Each student also has intraindividual differences in scores. For example, Lefki has the vocabulary of an 11th grader but scores only at a 7th-grade equivalent in mathematics; Jessie earned grade equivalents of 10th grade in science and mathematics and 7th grade in writing.

Creativity

Many writers and teachers believe that creative ability is central to the definition of giftedness. Although we all profess to know creativity when we see it, no universally accepted definition of creativity exists. Guilford (1959, 1967, 1987), who studied the emergence of creativity as one aspect of his overall theory concerning human intelligence, describes these dimensions of cognitive creative behavior, which he called *divergent production,* in his Structure of Intellect model:

- *Fluency.* The creative person can produce many ideas per unit of time.
- *Flexibility.* The person offers a wide variety of ideas, unusual ideas, and alternative solutions.
- *Novelty/originality.* The person uses words in unique ways and uses low-probability words and responses; the creative person has novel ideas.
- *Elaboration.* The person demonstrates the ability to provide details.
- *Synthesizing ability.* The person can link unlikely ideas together.
- *Analyzing ability.* The person can organize ideas into larger, inclusive patterns. Symbolic structures must often be broken down before they can be reformed into new ones.
- *Ability to reorganize or redefine existing ideas.* The creative person shows the ability to transform an existing object into one of different design, function, or use.
- *Complexity.* The person shows the ability to manipulate many interrelated ideas at the same time.

Clark (2008) suggests that the purpose of creativity is "to recognize and bring forth that which is new, diverse, advanced, complex, and/or previously unknown so that human kind can experience life as fuller, richer, and/or more meaningful" (p. 158). Many gifted and talented students do become scientists, physicians, inventors, and great artists and performers. However, they have no obligation to do so, and providing them with the differentiated education they need should not be predicated on an expectation that they "owe society," any more than all children do.

Piirto (1998, 2004a, 2004b) studied creative individuals in a variety of areas and summarized the characteristics of highly creative individuals within their fields of creativity, thus linking their high abilities to particular areas of expertise. She reports that (a) each of these fields has specific predictive behaviors in childhood, (b) a developmental process in the emergence of talents occurs in various domains, and (c) IQ scores should be minimized in importance and subsumed into a more contextual view of children who are performing tasks within specific domains. Piirto maintains that all people are creative and that creativity is more an aspect of personality than a type of giftedness. Testing for creative potential is often invalid and not reliable (Piirto, 1998, 2004b; Gagné, 2003).

It is often difficult to differentiate between the concepts of talent and creativity, perhaps because they may exist on a continuum rather than as separate entities. If we examine the life of a highly talented individual, such as the famous dancer Martha Graham, we can see the relationship between creativity and talent. Her creativity was evident in her pioneering modern dance techniques and her innovative methods of expression in the choreography of the dance. However, her great talent as a dancer, seen in her elegant movements, was equally impressive and deserves notice. Creativity, talent, and/or extreme intellectual ability that is atypical for their age most often identify gifted and talented children. See Current Issues and Future Trends, "Precocity as a Hallmark of Giftedness."

Guilford's elements of creativity

Council for Exceptional Children — Content Standards for Beginning Teachers—G&T: Cognitive characteristics of individuals with gifts and talents in intellectual, academic, creative, leadership, and artistic domains (GT2K7) (also GT2K2, GT7K3).

Gifted and talented children are often identified by their precociousness. The unique abstract style of Alexandra Nechita, shown here at age 16, was evident when she was 4 years old.

CURRENT ISSUES AND FUTURE TRENDS

PRECOCITY AS A HALLMARK OF GIFTEDNESS

BY JANE PIIRTO

Four-year-old Maria has been waiting and waiting to go to school. She plays school all the time. She is the teacher, and her dolls are the students. At her day-care center, she is the one who always leads the other kids in games because she is the only one who can read. The other kids look up to her, except when she tries to make them do things they really don't want to do, such as count by twos. The day-care center teacher told Maria's mother that Maria was very bright. When Maria went for her preschool screening, the district recommended that the school psychologist test her. The school psychologist told Maria's mother that Maria had an IQ of 145 on the Stanford-Binet Intelligence Scale, a score that put her in the 99th percentile. This score would qualify her for the district's program for the academically talented, which started at the third grade, although they did have enrichment lessons in first and second grade.

Finally, it is the first day of school; Maria turned 5 in August. She has her new dress and new shoes on. Her mother braids her hair and fastens it with new barrettes. When she gets to school, she is anxious for her mother to leave, yet still she feels shy, with all of these children here. Half of them are crying as their parents leave them. Maria looks around the room and sees a shelf of books. She always reads when she doesn't know what else to do, so she goes over to the shelf and waits for things to calm down. After all of the parents have gone, the teacher tells the children to sit on a line painted on the floor. As the children have come into the room, they have been given large name tags. The teacher sits on a small chair with the children in a semicircle around her and says, "My name is Mrs. Miller, boys and girls. Welcome to kindergarten. In kindergarten, we will learn our letters and our numbers so that we can learn to read in first grade."

"I can read already," Maria says, jumping up.

"That's nice," says Mrs. Miller. "Maria, when we want to talk, first we must stand, and then we must wait until Mrs. Miller calls on us."

"But I can read already!" Maria's voice gets petulant, and tears form in the corners of her eyes.

"Maria, that's nice," said Mrs. Miller. "But in kindergarten, we will learn how to read right. Please sit down now."

Maria is chagrined. Feeling shame and embarrassment, she sits down. She has taken the first step to underachievement.

Underachievement is the prevailing situation in the education of academically talented young children in most schools today. By the time she has been socialized into the kindergarten milieu, Maria will have learned to keep quiet about her abilities and even to suppress that she can read. In first grade, she will comply with the reading tasks in order to fit in. By second grade, even though she will be getting all of her work right, she will have learned that she doesn't have to put forth any effort in school in order to be the best student. By third grade, she will have learned that boredom (as long as she's quietly bored) and waiting (as long as she's not disruptive while she's waiting) are what the school seems to expect of her. By fourth grade, when she gets into a pullout program for academically talented students, she will resent it when the teacher of the academically talented tries to challenge her and, in challenging her, stretches her capabilities. Maria's story, unfortunately, is typical of many young academically talented children who enter the public school system.

Maria's scenario indicates the types of precocious behavior talented students might display when their abilities are great. Like other young gifted and talented children, Maria can easily do things typically seen only in older children. Even without special testing, their talents can be spotted by teachers who are sensitive to the concept of precocity. In fact, I believe the main way to recognize talented students is by their precocity: achievements resembling those of older children. I call these behaviors *predictive behaviors*. These children are often difficult to locate because they might wish to fit in and not to create disturbances; but teachers, parents, and educators who look closely can find their talents.

What Do You Think?

1. How do you think Mrs. Miller should have responded to Maria's insisting that "I can read already!"?

2. As the parent of a highly precocious kindergartner, what would your hopes and expectations be for your child's academic and social opportunities in the classroom? How would you communicate those to her teacher and the school?

3. How should teachers' efforts to accommodate and build upon a child's precociousness differ depending upon the child's areas of advanced knowledge and skill, age, and grade level?

PREVALENCE

Using the normal curve, one would predict that 3% to 5% of students would be gifted in the category of superior cognitive ability, scoring 2 standard deviations above the mean on a standardized intelligence test. If we include those students regarded as highly talented, estimates for the prevalence of giftedness can range as high as 10% to 15% of the total school-age population (Gagné, 2003; Renzulli & Reis, 2003).

The number and percentage of students identified as gifted and talented vary widely from state to state; for instance, six states identified more than 10% of the student population as gifted and talented, and six states identified 3% or less. A biannual survey conducted by the National Association for Gifted Children (State of the States, 2004–2005) and the Council of State Directors of Gifted Education showed that the United States has approximately 3 million academically talented students from pre-K to grade 12. This discrepancy between need and the level of service may make gifted and talented children the most underserved group of exceptional children.

In fact, the No Child Left Behind Act, which emphasizes the measurement of educational progress for all students, especially those who may risk lack of academic success, may not serve the gifted and talented students adequately (Gallagher, 2004; Kaplan, 2004). DeLacy (2004) asked these questions: (a) "What group of students makes the lowest achievement gains in school?" (b) "What group of students has been harmed most by the No Child Left Behind Act?" The answer was "The brightest students" (p. 40). She explained that studies by various states had shown that the emphasis on bringing up the lowest-achieving students means that the highest-achieving students are neglected and ignored while teachers concentrate on the lowest-achieving students. DeLacy said that

> gifted students are truly our forgotten children. Neglected in our schools and ignored by our policymakers, they spend their days dozing through classes in which they aren't learning. Many suffer from depression. It is time to take them out of their holding pens and give them a chance to stretch and to grow. (p. 40)

IDENTIFICATION AND ASSESSMENT

A multifactored assessment approach that uses information from a variety of sources is considered to be more accurate and equitable in identification of the gifted and talented. This approach incorporates data from a variety of sources, including the following:

- Group and individual intelligence tests
- Achievement tests
- Portfolios of student work
- Teacher nomination based on reports of student behavior in the classroom
- Parent nomination
- Self-nomination
- Peer nomination
- Extracurricular or leisure activities

Professionals in gifted education recommend a comprehensive approach for identifying students who require specialized services for their talents (Johnsen, 2004; Karnes & Stephens, 2008). Clark (2008) describes an approach to identification based on a model first developed by the California Association for Gifted Children. The approach features a progressive filtering process that refines a large pool of potentially gifted students down to a smaller, formally identified group. The process is time-consuming and thorough, beginning with the development of a large pool of potentially gifted students in the initial stage (screening); testing, consulting, and analyzing data (development of profile and case study); identification decisions and placement (committee meeting for consideration; placement in gifted program); and finally the development of an appropriate educational program for the child.

Quantitative and qualitative approaches to assessment should be part of the identification process (Ryser, 2004). Types of qualitative assessment include portfolios, interviews, and

Prevalence of G&T

 Council for Exceptional Children
Content Standards for Beginning Teachers—G&T: Prevalence of individuals with gifts and talents (GT1K6).

Multidimensional screening for G&T students

Council for Exceptional Children
Content Standards for Beginning Teachers—G&T: Screening, prereferral, and identification procedures for individuals with gifts and talents (GT8K4).

observations. Educators can use observations to find students who are demonstrating characteristics that indicate giftedness. Observations can include checklists or rating scales (e.g., Renzulli et al., 2002) as well as simple "jot-down" procedures (p. 29). Interviews of peers and parents can also indicate potential talent.

Let's examine how this process would work with a student thought to have great potential, for example, the little girl Janie, described at the beginning of this chapter. First, Janie's highly refined intellectual behaviors would have to be noticed by a teacher, a parent, her peers, or another person, who would then forward a nomination for additional screening. Figure 13.5 shows questions that Janie's teacher might ask. The teacher's report would contribute to the multidimensional, or multifactored, screening approach that is gaining in popularity among educators of the gifted and talented.

FIGURE 13.5 Questions about classroom behavior that can guide a teacher's efforts to identify students who may be gifted and talented

Does the child
- Ask a lot of questions?
- Show a lot of interest in progress?
- Have in-depth information on many things?
- Often want to know why or how something is so?
- Become unusually upset at injustices?
- Seem interested in and concerned about social or political problems?
- Often have a better reason for not doing what you want done than you have asking them to do it?
- Refuse to drill on spelling, mathematics, facts, flash cards, or handwriting?
- Criticize others for dumb ideas?
- Become impatient if work is not "perfect"?
- Seem to be a loner?
- Seem bored and often have nothing to do?
- Complete only part of an assignment or project and then take off in a new direction?
- Stick to a subject long after the class has gone on to other things?
- Seem restless and leave his or her seat often?
- Daydream?
- Seem to understand easily?
- Like solving puzzles and problems?
- Have his or her own idea about how something should be done? And stay with it?
- Talk a lot?
- Love metaphors and abstract ideas?
- Love debating issues?

This child may be showing giftedness through cognitive ability.

Does the child
- Show unusual ability in some area—maybe reading or mathematics?
- Show fascination with one field of interest? And manage to include this interest in all discussion topics?
- Enjoy meeting or talking with experts in this field?
- Get mathematics answers correct, but find it difficult to tell you how?

- Enjoy graphing everything? Seem obsessed with probabilities?
- Invent new obscure systems and codes?

This child may be showing giftedness through academic ability.

Does the child
- Try to do things in different, unusual, imaginative ways?
- Have a really zany sense of humor?
- Enjoy new routines or spontaneous activities?
- Love variety and novelty?
- Create problems with no apparent solutions? And enjoy asking you to solve them?
- Love controversial and unusual questions?
- Have a vivid imagination?
- Seem never to proceed sequentially?

This child may be showing giftedness through creative ability.

Does the child
- Organize and lead group activities? Sometimes take over?
- Enjoy taking risks?
- Seem cocky, self-assured?
- Enjoy decision making? Stay with that decision?
- Synthesize ideas and information from a lot of different sources?

This child may be showing giftedness through leadership ability.

Does the child
- Seem to pick up skills in the arts—music, dance, drama, or painting, for example—without instruction?
- Invent new techniques? Experiment?
- See minute detail in products or performances?
- Have high sensory sensitivity?

This child may be showing giftedness through visual or performing arts ability.

Source: From Clark, Barbara, *Growing up gifted: Developing the potential of children at home and at school*, 7th ed., © 2007. Reproduced by permission of Pearson Education, Inc., Upper Saddle River, NJ.

Multidimensional screening also involves a rigorous examination of teacher reports, family history, student inventories, and work samples and perhaps the administration of group achievement or group or individual intelligence tests. In many states, the coordinator of gifted services at the school, district, or regional level reviews this information and determines whether the results indicate a potential for giftedness and justify referral to a placement committee. If the coordinator believes the evidence is sufficient to continue assessment, the parents are asked if they would like to refer Janie for more extensive testing to determine whether she qualifies for gifted services. The coordinator then manages the development of a case study that includes screening data, parent interviews, test protocols, an individual intelligence test, tests in specific content areas, and creativity tests. The committee compiles, organizes, and presents the data to the placement committee for consideration. The committee determines whether Janie qualifies for services and what type of program would best be suited for her particular pattern of giftedness. The parents are an integral part of this meeting and have to agree with the results and placement decisions that the committee develops. Janie is then placed in a gifted program, and the special education teacher or person in charge of the program initiates special services. This level of assessment is more focused and uses all of the previous case study materials and other assessment data to determine where Janie should start in the program and the overall focus of the special education services she will receive.

Assessment of young children's abilities to solve mathematical-spatial problems might include the time used to complete puzzles, the number of puzzles completed, and the particular problem-solving strategies used by the child.

Multicultural Assessment and Identification

"One of the most persistent and pervasive problems in education is the underrepresentation of African American, Hispanic American, and Native American students in gifted education programs and services" (Ford, 2007, p. 401). For decades, reports and census studies have shown that these three groups of culturally diverse students have always been underrepresented in gifted education (Artiles, Trent, & Palmer, 2004; Donovan & Cross, 2002; Ford, 1998). Biases inherent in the identification process are primarily to blame for the underrepresentation of students from diverse ethnic, cultural, and language groups (Castellano, 2004; Ford, 2004a; Grantham, 2003; Klug, 2004; Montgomery, 2001).

Frasier and her colleagues (1995) showed 10 core attributes of giftedness across socioeconomic, ethnic, and racial groups. Gifted and talented people across ethnic groups demonstrate (1) communication skills, (2) imagination/creativity, (3) humor, (4) inquiry, (5) insight, (6) interests, (7) memory, (8) motivation, (9) problem solving, and (10) reasoning. Many youth from special populations have not had the extensive opportunities to develop such a broad pattern of giftedness, but they have often developed special talent within a particular domain. The identification process should be designed to find the special talent. Subsequent educational service should focus on facilitating growth in this talent area. Current best practices for identifying gifted and talented students from diverse cultural groups involve a multifactored, or multidimensional, assessment process that meets these criteria (Castellano, 2003; Ford, 2007; Frasier, Garcia, & Passow, 1995; Frasier et al., 1995; Montgomery, 2001; Plummer, 1995):

- Identification should have a goal of inclusion rather than exclusion.
- Data should be gathered from multiple sources providing both objective and subjective data (e.g., parent interviews, individual intelligence testing, performance on group

Issues and procedures for identifying G&T children from diverse cultural groups

 Council for Exceptional Children Content Standards for Beginning Teachers—G&T: Issues in definition and identification of individuals with gifts and talents, including those from culturally and linguistically diverse backgrounds (GT1K5) (also GT3K7, GT8K5).

problem-solving tasks, motivational and behavioral factors, individual conferences with candidates).

- A combination of formal and informal testing techniques, including teacher referrals, the results of intelligence tests, and individual achievement tests, should be used.
- A generally greater sensitivity to aspects of acculturation and assimilation that allows for multiple perspectives to be identified and honored should be demonstrated.
- Identification procedures should begin as early as possible—before children are exposed to prejudice and stereotyping—and be continuous.
- Unconventional measures involving arts and aesthetic expression such as dance, music, creative writing, and crafts should be used.
- Information gathered during the identification process should be used to help determine the curriculum.

DISCOVER problem-solving activities

 Council for Exceptional Children   Content Standards for Beginning Teachers—G&T: Differing learning styles of individuals with gifts and talents, including those from culturally diverse backgrounds, and strategies for addressing these styles (GT3K7) (also GT8K4, GT8K5).

Maker (1996, 2005) developed a procedure called DISCOVER (Discovering Strengths and Capabilities while Observing Varied Ethnic Responses) that educators have used to identify gifted children from diverse cultural groups. The DISCOVER assessment process involves a series of five progressively more complex problems that provide children with various ways to demonstrate their problem-solving competence by interacting with the content and with one another.

> Problem Types I and II require convergent thinking and are most similar to the types of question found on standardized intelligence and achievement tests. Type I problems are highly structured. The solver knows the solution method and must recall or derive the correct answer and involve convergent thinking. Type II problems also are highly structured, but the solver must decide on the correct method to use. Type III problems are clearly structured, but a range of methods can be used to solve them and they have a range of acceptable answers. Type IV and V problems are more open ended, less structured, and require much more divergent thinking.…Type IV problems are commonly found in tests of creativity. Type V problems are extremely ill structured. The solver must explore the possibilities, identify the questions to be answered, and determine the criteria by which an effective solution will be recognized. (Maker, Nielson, & Rogers, 1994, p. 7)

Maker (2005) states that an assessment emphasis on problem solving instead of formal tests of acquired knowledge has the potential to "level the playing field," enabling students who solve problems on a daily basis to demonstrate their abilities.

> "Little Claudia," a 5-year-old Mexican American girl, who was responsible for dressing her 2-year-old brother and making sure he was taken to daycare before she went to kindergarten class, had extensive practice in problem solving. However, she was not exposed to advanced knowledge through visits to museums or a home environment with many sources of information, nor was she given opportunities to produce sophisticated products through special courses, lessons, or other opportunities afforded to children from middle and upper socio-economic status (SES) families. Many children from diverse economic, geographic, and cultural groups face challenges similar to Little Claudia's. (n.p.)

Maker (1994, 2001) and other researchers (Powers, 2003; Reid, Udall, Romanoff, & Algozzine, 1999; Sarouphim, 2001) report positive results from using the DISCOVER model to assess the problem-solving abilities of students from African American, Navajo, Tohono O'Odham, and Mexican American cultural groups: (a) The children identified by the process closely resemble the cultural characteristics of the communities from which they come; (b) equitable percentages of children from various ethnic, cultural, linguistic, and economic groups are identified; (c) the process is equally effective with boys and girls; and (d) students identified through the process make gains equal to or greater than those of students who were identified by traditional standardized tests when placed in special enrichment programs.

Other means of identifying culturally diverse gifted learners have been tried and found to have moderate success. Tests that do not require the use of verbal symbol systems have also been recommended and widely used, such as Raven's Standard Progressive Matrices Test (Raven, Court, & Raven, 1983) and the Naglieri Nonverbal Ability Test (Naglieri & Ford, 2003). Naglieri and Ford (2005) argue that traditional tests of intelligence and achievement penalize students from low-socioeconomic status backgrounds and culturally diverse groups who have not had the opportunity to learn the language or vocabulary required for success on such tests.

As noted in all the literature about culturally diverse students, the identification procedure must not contain merely an IQ score or any one score; rather, educators must use a multitude of methods (Joseph & Ford, 2006). Researchers and thinkers are now beginning to realize that test scores and checklists themselves can even be harmful to students, because they are scored in the aggregate (the total, the accumulation): A talented child may have only one of the characteristics and thus not be selected.

The talented child comes from a family with goals, a milieu, a history, and a background. For example, it is far more likely for a child to be identified as talented if she has books in the home and is read to regularly. This is as true for bilingual talented children as it is for monolingual talented children. Other promising alternative assessment methods are these: (a) the Frasier method (1991), which focuses on the 10 characteristics mentioned earlier; (b) the Renzulli Revolving Door method (1986), which identifies the top 25% of students; (c) the "quota" method (Mitchell, 1988b), which identifies a certain, representative quota of students; (d) the case study method (Borland & Wright, 1994), which conducts in-depth case studies of students; (e) the use of portfolios, which assess achievement without testing; (f) performance assessment (Van Tassel-Baska, Johnson, Avery, 2002), which assesses how students perform on certain universal tasks; (g) dynamic assessment (Chaffey, 2004), which gives the assessment, teaches the assessment, and then gives it again; and (h) Multiple Intelligence (MI) Assessment, which assesses according to Gardner's (2006) theory of multiple intelligences. All alternative assessments should be nondiscriminatory, taking into account the culture, language, and home life of the child being assessed.

Identifying gifted and talented children from diverse and underrepresented groups is, of course, just the beginning. In the absence of high-quality curriculum and instruction that are sensitive and responsive to their cultural heritage, gifted students from diverse backgrounds will not benefit (Foley & Seknandore, 2003; Ford, 2004b, 2007).

Gifted and Talented Girls

Cultural barriers; test and social biases; organizational reward systems; sex-role stereotyping; and conflicts among career, marriage, and family all act as external impediments to the advancement of gifted and talented women (Kerr, 1994). In reviewing the topic of gifted women, Silverman (1986) noted that the history of genius and women's roles has been contradictory (eminent contributions cannot be made from a subservient status) and that identification procedures reflect masculine (product-oriented) versus feminine (development-oriented) concepts of giftedness.

Thus, some of the key issues that appear in the literature concerning the identification and education of females who are gifted and talented involve conflicts concerning role definitions (Cross, 2006; Rimm, 2000, 2002), extreme stress related to a lack of self-esteem (Genshaft, Greenbaum, & Borovosky, 1995), poor course selection based on academic choices made in middle school and high school (Boothe, 2004; Clark, 2008), and a lack of parental and general community support for female achievements (Hollinger, 1995).

Gifted and Talented Boys

Recently, the problems and situations of gifted and talented boys have been highlighted as well (Kerr & Cohen, 2001; Neu & Weinfeld, 2006). Among these are negative stereotyping for boys who have talent in and want to enter the arts, a boy code (Pollack, 1998) that operates against the expression of feelings and emotions, and a reluctance on the part of parents and teachers to permit boys' creative behavior. However, despite the stereotyping and name calling ("nerds," "geeks," etc.) that is present in U.S. schools, boys continue to outscore girls at the highest levels on tests such as the Scholastic Aptitude Test, the American College Test, the Differential Aptitude Test, and most achievement tests (Boothe, 2004).

Gifted and Talented Students With Disabilities

It may be surprising to learn that the incidence of giftedness and talent among a large proportion of students with disabilities mirrors that of the larger general education population.

Identification of G&T girls and boys

 Council for Exceptional Children **Content Standards for Beginning Teachers—G&T:** Issues in definition and identification of individuals with gifts and talents, including those from culturally and linguistically diverse backgrounds (GT1K5).

Go to the Homework & Exercises section in Chapter 13 of MyEducationLab and complete Homework Exercise 2.

So we would expect to have almost as many gifted students within the subpopulation of all students with disabilities. However, the combination of a disability and giftedness brings with it an even more complicated set of behaviors and attitudes to challenge educators and parents (Nielsen & Higgins, 2005).

King (2005) recommended that teachers could support the social and emotional needs of twice-exceptional students by doing the following:

- Foster clear understanding of students' disabilities as well as their strengths to promote self-understanding and self-acceptance.
- Encourage students to succeed, and enlist support of parents and other teachers in this endeavor.
- Teach coping strategies to use when students become frustrated.
  - If needed, encourage counseling to monitor each student's emotions that accompany frustration and perceived failures.
  - Think of these children not only as having a disability or as being gifted but as having individual needs.
  - Provide support in establishing and maintaining social relationships.
  - Ensure parents' understanding of their child's giftedness and disabilities, emphasizing the child's potential.
  - Support students with future goals and career planning; make sure students are aware of their potential and encourage them not to sell themselves short.
  - Provide a mentorship with an adult who is also gifted/learning disabled.

Willard-Holt (1998) drew similar implications for practice and reported case study analyses of the academic and personality characteristics of gifted students with cerebral palsy and no speech.

An appropriate education for gifted students with disabilities requires the creation of what Neu (2003) terms a *dually differentiated* curriculum that recognizes and "meets the needs of students who exhibit two contradictory sets of learning characteristics by creating a balance between nurturing the students' strengths and compensating for their learning deficits" (p. 158).

Affective concerns for twice-exceptional and second-language learners prevail (Rance-Roney, 2004). These include issues of acculturation, including culture shock, loss of first language and second-language acquisition, and delayed identity formation.

The intellectual abilities and talents of children with disabilities are fostered by daily opportunities to practice superior abilities and enjoy the feelings of success.

EDUCATIONAL APPROACHES

Curricular Goals

The overall goal of educational programs for gifted and talented students should be the fullest possible development of every child's actual and potential abilities. In the broadest terms, the educational goals for these youngsters do not differ from those for all children. Feelings of self-worth, self-sufficiency, and civic responsibility and vocational and avocational competence are important for everyone. Some additional specific educational outcomes, however, are especially desirable for gifted and talented students.

Gifted students need both content knowledge and the abilities to develop and use that knowledge effectively. Most educators of gifted and talented students agree that the most important concern in developing appropriate curriculum is to match the students' specific needs with a qualitatively different curricular intervention. The need to *differentiate curriculum* for gifted students is "based on the recognized strengths of these learners and the acknowledged inadequacy of the regular or core curriculum to meet those needs" (Kaplan, 2005, p. 107).

Piirto (2007) recommends the following features for curriculum and instruction for gifted and talented students:

- *Based on learning characteristics of academically talented students in their area of strength:* These characteristics include "their ability to learn at a faster rate; their ability to think abstractly about content that is challenging; their ability to think productively, critically, creatively, and analytically; and their ability to constantly and rapidly increase their store of knowledge, both knowledge of facts and knowledge of processes and procedures" (p. 429).

- *Possessing academic rigor:* The widespread abuse of grading practices, the dumbing down of the curriculum, and the lowered expectations of teachers all have sapped curriculum of its strength and rigor. The curriculum should include systematic teaching of research skills, keyboarding and computer use, speed reading, at least one foreign language, and interpersonal and affective development. These students have a distinct need for increased relevance, discipline, and depth of current curriculum, primarily within the general education setting, where most gifted students are for most of the day.

- *Thematic and interdisciplinary:* Academically talented students should be exposed to the structures, terminologies, and methodologies of various disciplines. The skills of systematic investigation are fundamental abilities that gifted students use throughout a lifetime of learning. These skills include the use of references, the use of the library, the gathering of information (data), and the reporting of findings in a variety of ways. These skills may ultimately be used in diverse settings, such as law and medical libraries, museums, chemical and electrical laboratories, theatrical archives, and national parks.

Nine states have passed legislation that requires individualized education programs (IEPs) and some of the other provisions of Individuals with Disabilities Education Act (IDEA) for gifted and talented students similar to those developed for students with disabilities (Shaunessy, 2003). In other states, schools design an individualized growth plan for gifted and talented students. These plans differ from an IEP along several important dimensions: (a) It is not a requirement for services to be provided; (b) they are more flexible, having no time restrictions, reporting requirements, or physical boundaries; and (c) they are primarily collaboratively planned but essentially student-directed. The growth plan should include assessment information, student-generated goals (in consultation with others), and the recommended activities for accomplishing these goals. A key feature of this approach is that the student is guided toward the establishment of her own goals and is an active participant in all instructional and evaluative activities.

Differentiating Curriculum: Acceleration and Enrichment

Differentiation is an educational strategy. *Differentiation* is a broad term referring to the need to tailor teaching environments, curricula, and instructional practices to create appropriately different learning experiences for different students. The premise that learners differ in important ways is the guiding premise of differentiation. The point is to engage learners in instruction through different learning modalities, appeal to differing interests, use varied rates of instruction, and provide varied degrees of complexity within and across a challenging and conceptually rich curriculum (Roberts & Inman, 2007).

Because gifted students learn at a faster rate than most students and can absorb and reconfigure more concepts, they benefit from a differentiated curriculum that is modified in both its pace and depth. **Acceleration** is the general term for modifying the pace at which the student moves through the curriculum; **enrichment** means probing or studying a subject at a greater depth than would occur in the general education curriculum.

Acceleration *Acceleration* is permitting the student to move as swiftly as possible through required curriculum content. Silverman (1995) believes that acceleration is a

Functions and characteristics of differentiated curriculum

 Council for Exceptional Children

Content Standards for Beginning Teachers—G&T: Differential curriculum needs of individuals with gifts and talents (GT7K6) (also GT7K2, GT7K5).

Acceleration

 Content Standards for Beginning Teachers—G&T: Acceleration, enrichment, and counseling within a continuum of service options for individuals with gifts and talents (GT5K4) (also GT7K2).

"necessary response to a highly gifted student's faster pace of learning" (p. 229). What the classroom teacher decides to do to differentiate for the academically talented student depends on the subject matter. Curriculum material consists of essentially two types: (1) that which readily lends itself to enrichment, such as reading or social studies; and (2) that which readily lends itself to acceleration, such as mathematics or foreign languages. Subjects that are sequential are candidates for accelerative treatment. In mathematics, a child must learn to add before subtracting, must learn to multiply before dividing. By the time an academically talented child is in the fourth grade, he or she probably will have mastered the skills of reading; enrichment with more difficult reading matter is a way of differentiation. In mathematics, however, the child must be taught; and the sequence of mathematics proceeds from arithmetic to algebra to calculus, and so on. Often, one of the most difficult tasks for the teacher of the academically talented is to persuade the administration and fellow teachers that acceleration in mathematics is necessary for the academically talented student and that this acceleration must occur in the structure of more advanced course taking.

Academically talented students often need less explanation; they just need to know the next step. A young academically talented student interested in fractal geometry and attending the Johns Hopkins University summer program told how he had sat, bored, during a plane geometry class that was required at his school for intellectually academically talented students but where testing out of a course was not permitted. To this student, plane geometry consisted of nothing but "two points on a line, two points on a line." Even though the plane geometry class was being offered to eighth graders, whereas in most schools it is offered to sophomores, this student had already mastered the material and was interested in fractal geometry. The high point in his day was being able to ask the teacher one or two questions about fractal geometry at the end of the period when the students began their homework. Although the teacher kept him pointed in the right direction, and he experimented with fractal geometry on his home computer, an accelerated curriculum would have saved this student from having to sit through plane geometry day after day.

Likewise, the student who has a deep and abiding interest in and propensity for science will find the elementary school science curriculum nonchallenging and quite frustrating. Generally, elementary school science curricula do not offer the meat that challenged science aficionados need. A glance at the scope and sequence of the typical elementary school science curriculum shows that the motivated, academically talented science student could probably master all that information in a highly condensed year. Advanced study of science requires mastery of mathematics, for to scientists, mathematics is a necessary tool. Thus, the student who has a propensity for thinking in scientific terms (what Gardner, 2006, calls logical-mathematical intelligence) should also be accelerated in mathematics.

The National Association for Gifted Children (2004) states that "educational acceleration is one of the cornerstones of exemplary gifted education practices, with more research supporting this intervention than any other in the literature on gifted education" (p. 1). In 2004, the Templeton Foundation published a major report on the benefits of acceleration. With the somewhat hyperbolic title *A Nation Deceived* (Colangelo, Assouline, & Gross, 2004), it detailed cases where acceleration was the solution to the curriculum problems of bright children, showing that acceleration is not the social and emotional bugaboo it has been called by many in the schools. As a result of this report, which was featured on the front pages of many newspapers, many states and school districts have begun to formulate acceleration policies, whereby individual students can receive an education at their intellectual level, rather than their age level.

Southern and Jones (2004) listed 18 types of acceleration options:

1. Early admission to kindergarten
2. Early admission to first grade
3. Grade skipping
4. Continuous progress

5. Self-paced instruction
6. Subject-matter acceleration
7. Combined classes
8. Curriculum compacting
9. Telescoping curriculum
10. Mentoring
11. Extracurricular programs
12. Correspondence courses
13. Early graduation
14. Concurrent/dual enrollment
15. Advanced placement
16. Credit by examination
17. Acceleration in college
18. Early entrance into junior high, high school, or college (p. 6)

One commonly heard concern is that early admission and grade skipping will lead to social or emotional problems because the child will be in a classroom with older students who are more advanced physically and emotionally. School personnel and parents are usually concerned that talented students will suffer from the pressure to achieve at higher levels and will burn out or become social misfits. Although this concern is understandable, when acceleration is done properly, few, if any, socioemotional problems result (Colangelo et al., 2004; Van Tassel-Baska, 2004). After reviewing a decade of longitudinal research on the academic acceleration of mathematically precocious youths, Swiatek (1993) found no evidence that acceleration harms willing students either academically or socially.

Enrichment   Enriching the content of instruction to include more innovation, novelty, and sophistication is the most common method of differentiating curriculum for academically talented students. Enrichment generally involves adding new and different information from a variety of disciplines outside the traditional curriculum. This is the strategy of choice among most general education teachers who are attempting to provide additional opportunities for gifted and talented students in their classrooms. It is important to remember that enrichment is meant to be thoughtfully and systematically applied to the educational program of targeted students.

Enrichment experiences let students investigate topics of interest in greater detail than is ordinarily possible with the standard school curriculum. Topics of investigation may be based on the ongoing activities of the classroom but may permit students to go beyond the limits of the day-to-day instructional offerings. However, by allowing the students to help define the area of interest and independently access a variety of information and materials, the teacher can learn to facilitate the development of gifted and talented students' competencies and skills.

Enrichment is not a "do-your-own-thing" approach with no structure or guidance. Children involved in enrichment experiences should not be released to do a random, haphazard project. A basic framework that defines limits and sets outcomes is necessary. Projects should have purpose, direction, and specified outcomes. A teacher should provide guidance where necessary—and to the degree that is necessary—to keep students working efficiently. To learn about enrichment activities in language arts for gifted students, see Teaching & Learning, "Using the Literary Masters to Inspire Written Expression in Gifted Students."

Although acceleration and enrichment are often viewed as separate options for talented students, as Southern and Jones (1991) point out, the two strategies are intertwined: "advanced study in any discipline may entail the kind of activities normally associated with enrichment" (p. 22). Enrichment is supposed to broaden the curriculum and include material that is not in the general education course of study. However, acceleration often involves advanced material not contained in the general education course of study.

Enrichment

 Content Standards for Beginning Teachers—G&T: Acceleration, enrichment, and counseling within a continuum of service options for individuals with gifts and talents (GT5K4) (also GT7K2).

Using the Literary Masters to Inspire Written Expression in Gifted Students

BY SHEILA R. ALBER-MORGAN, CHRISTA M. MARTIN, AND DEIDRA M. GAMMILL

Gifted children's natural inclination to explore ideas and manipulate linguistic expressions endows them with the potential to become great writers (Fraser, 2003; Kauffman & Gentile, 2002). Exposing gifted students to important literature can inspire them to find their own voices and attain personal growth while making contributions to their culture.

HOW TO GET STARTED

We designed the instructional activities described here for students in grades 8 through 12, but you can easily adapt them for younger children.

Provide an Overview and Structural Framework

Provide an overview of the history and substance of great literature by showing how authors and their works can be categorized by period and culture, literary movements, and genres. Students can use a matrix classifying literature by genre, as shown in Figure A, as a structural framework for the following activities.

Encourage Independent Exploration

- *Biographical author study.* Each student selects one author from the matrix and researches the author's time period and culture and major events in the author's life and explores how those experiences may have influenced his or her work writing.
- *Compare and contrast.* The student compares and contrasts several authors from a given time period and culture. For example, how were the lives and works of Homer, Aesop, Sophocles, and Euripides similar and different? What aspects of 1st-century AD Greek culture influenced each author?
- *Literary evolution within a culture.* Each student researches the development of the literature of a selected culture evolved from its origins to the present. For example, what events in 17th-century North America set the stage for authors such as Cotton Mather and Anne Bradstreet?
- *Literary evolution within a time period.* The student researches literary masters from around the world who lived during a specific historical period and describes the relationship between those authors and the historical events that may have shaped their writing. For example, the 19th century produced writers such as Karl Marx in the Germanic culture and Victor Hugo in the French culture. What world events might have inspired or influenced these authors?

Encourage Cooperative Learning

- *Learn and teach.* Each student writes a critical analysis of a selected book in the context of its place in history. What events influenced this literature? What was the author trying to tell us? For example, Ernest Hemingway became involved with Spain's loyalist army during the Spanish civil war, and his novel *For Whom the Bell Tolls* tells the story of an American fighting the fascist forces in Spain. Students should elaborate on their analyses and provide references from the literature to support their viewpoints. After completing this writing assignment, each student teaches the other members of his cooperative learning group what he has learned about his selected work.
- *Common threads.* After the students have shared their literature with their cooperative learning groups, each group attempts to identify common threads across the selected works. Students can discuss how their selected readings are similar to one another in terms of theme, mood, characters, plot, setting, style, or any other aspect they wish to explore, and then create a cohesive class presentation.
- *Genre analysis.* Each cooperative learning group determines a genre to investigate, and each member selects a representative author. For example, a group of four students chooses Romanticism, and each team member selects one of the following works to read: Daniel Defoe's *Robinson Crusoe,* James Fenimore Cooper's *The Last of the Mohicans,* Edgar Allan Poe's *The Fall of the House of Usher,* and Mark Twain's *The Adventures of Tom Sawyer.* Based on their readings and discussion, the group then collaborates to develop a written definition of Romanticism and description of how each work illustrates the team's definition. The final product is a class presentation.
- *Panel discussion or debate.* Group members examine a single piece of literature and present their collective interpretations to the class in the form of a panel discussion or debate.

Help Students Discover Their Own Voices

In-depth study of a piece of literature provides students with many launching points for examining their own perspectives, making personal connections, and producing their own inspired work. The following example of Mary Shelley's work illustrates how to use a piece of literature to inspire written expression.

FIGURE A

Examples of literary genres

Allegory	Adventure	Comedy	Chronicle	Epic	Fantasy
Religious Dante Alighieri, *The Divine Comedy* (1320); Faulkner, *A Fable* (1954); John Bunyan, *The Pilgrim's Progress* (1684) **Symbolic** Melville, *Moby Dick* (1851) **Philosophical** Kafka, *The Castle* (1926): Goethe, *Faust* (1808/1831) **Moral** Henry James, *The Turn of the Screw* (1898)	**Heroic** *The Epic of Gilgamesh* (2000 B.C.); *Hercules and His Twelve Labors* (unknown); Homer, *Odyssey* (6th century B.C.)	Shakespeare, *Comedy of Errors* (1592); Moliere, *Tartuffe* (1664) **Social** Jane Austin, *Emma* (1816) **Romantic** Aristophanes, *Lysistrata* (411 B.C.) **Comedy of Manners** Oscar Wilde, *The Importance of Being Earnest* (1895); Moliere, *The Misanthrope* (1666); Jane Austin, *Pride and Prejudice* (1813)	**Historical** Willa Cather, *Death Comes for the Archbishop* (1927); Shakespeare, *Henry the Fourth* (1597) **Regional** John Steinbeck, *East of Eden* (1952); Willa Cather, *My Antonia* (1918) **Social Chronicle** Pearl S. Buck, *The Good Earth*; (1931) Victor Hugo, *Les Misérables* (1862) **Philosophical** Thomas Mann, *The Magic Mountain* (1924)	**Heroic** *Beowulf* (1000): Virgil, *Aeneid* (70–19 B.C.); Homer, *Iliad* (6th century B.C.); *Mahabharata* (5th century); *The Nibelungenlied* (1200) **Religious** Valmiki, *Ramayana* (350 B.C.)	Lewis Carroll, *Alice's Adventures in Wonderland* (1865); Anatole France, *Penguin Island* (1908); Robert Louis Stevenson, *The Strange Case of Dr. Jekyll and Mr. Hyde* (1886); H. G. Wells, *The Time Machine* (1895); Kafka, *The Trial* (1925); Kafka, *The Castle*; Samuel T. Coleridge, *The Rime of the Ancient Mariner* (1798)

Naturalism	Realism	Romance	Satire	Social Criticism	Tragedy
Honore de Balzac, *Eugenie Grandet* (1833); *Pere Goriot* (1835); Emile Zola, *Germinal* (1885); Strinberg, *Miss Julie* (1888); Arnold Bennett, *The Old Wives' Tale* (1908)	**Psychological** William Faulkner, *As I Lay Dying* (1930); Virginia Woolf, *Mrs. Dalloway* (1925); Henry James, *The Portrait of a Lady* (1881); Dostoevsky, *Crime and Punishment* (1888); George Eliot, *Middlemarch* (1872) **Philosophical** Jean-Paul Sartre, *Nausea* (1938); Thomas Hardy, *Tess of D'Urbervilles* (1891) **Impressionistic** Stephen Crane, *Red Badge of Courage* (1895); Dostoevsky, *The Brothers Karamazov* (1880)	**Adventure** Mark Twain, *The Adventures of Tom Sawyer* (1876); Rudyard Kipling, *Kim* (1901); Daniel Defoe, *Robinson Crusoe* (1719) **Psychological** Charlotte Bronte, *Jane Eyre* (1847); Nathaniel Hawthorne, *The Scarlet Letter* (1850) **Chivalric** Chaucer, *Canterbury Tales* (1390) **Historical** Victor Hugo, *The Hunchback of Notre Dame* (1831); James Fenimore Cooper, *Last of the Mohicans* (1826) **Gothic** Edgar Allan Poe, *The Fall of the House of Usher* (1839); Mary Shelley, *Frankenstein* (1818)	**Social** Johnathan Swift, *Gulliver's Travels* (1726); Sinclair Lewis, *Babbitt* (1922); Nikolai Gogol, *Dead Souls* (1855); Anthony Trollope, *Barchester Towers* (1857); Aristophanes, *The Birds* (414 B.C.); Voltaire, *Candide* (1759) **Political** George Orwell, *Nineteen Eighty-Four* (1949) **Humorous** Mark Twain, *Huckleberry Finn* (1884)	E. M. Forster, *A Passage to India* (1924); Nikolai Gogol, *The Overcoat* (1842); Leo Tolstoy, *Anna Karenina* (1877); Henrik Ibsen, *A Doll's House* (1879); John Steinbeck, *Grapes of Wrath* (1939); F. Scott Fitzgerald, *The Great Gatsby* (1925)	**Symbolic** Herman Melville, *Billy Budd* (1924) **Classical** Sophocles, *Antigone* (441 B.C.); Euripides, *The Bacchae* (405 B.C.); *Medea* (431 B.C.); Jean Racine, *Phaedra* (1677); Aeschylus, *Prometheus Bound* (5th century) **Romantic** Shakespeare, *Julius Caesar* (1601); *Romeo and Juliet* (1595); Christopher Marlowe, *Doctor Faustus* (1588); Thomas Hardy, *The Return of the Native* (1878); Strassburg, *Tristan and Isolde* (1210) **Domestic** Edith Wharton, *Ethan Fromme* (1911)

TEACHING & LEARNING

Since its publication in 1818, Mary Shelley's *Frankenstein* has been regarded as a novel of horror and science fiction. Many students are familiar with the novel's protagonist: the nameless monster. Immortalized by 1930's Hollywood, the monster has become an icon for the dangers and hubris of unchecked scientific research. But those who read the actual novel find that while Frankenstein's monster does commit terrible acts, so does his creator. Both give birth to evil through their irresponsibility and their isolation. Frankenstein's monster levels a terrible accusation at his maker: "How dare you thus sport with life? Do your duty towards me, and I will do mine towards you and the rest of mankind" (Shelley, 1818, p. 145). "Sporting with life" serves as a focal point for the tension that exists between maker and monster. Frankenstein sports with life by creating and then abandoning his creature; the creature sports with life as he attempts, unsuccessfully, to participate in his creator's world. This tension opens up a wealth of writing opportunities within the gifted classroom. Students can explore *Frankenstein* from several vantage points often overlooked in the traditional English classroom. The following activities are designed to enhance gifted students' understanding of the novel and to encourage creative, critical writing.

- *Role-play and debate.* Each student adopts the role of Victor Frankenstein or the monster and seeks to justify his character's desire to "sport with life." Each student writes a defense of her character's actions, either in creating life or in participating in it. Once the students are satisfied with their positions, ask them to break into pairs and debate each other.
- *Contemporary first-person short story.* Students imagine a modern counterpart for their character. Encourage students to move beyond obvious connections such as cloning and harvesting embryos for stem cells and to think of other parallels that impact them on a personal and emotional level (e.g., teen pregnancy/parenthood, plastic surgery). Once the students have decided on a parallel issue, have them write a short story in first-person narrative in which their character personifies the scientist/creator or the victim/monster. How does their character "sport with life," and what is the outcome? Does their story contain a moral or a warning? Or does it simply paint a vignette and allow the reader to decide?
- *Contemporary short story with narrator.* Mary Shelley tells Frankenstein's story through her narrator, Robert Walton, in his series of letters to his sister. This stylistic device allows Walton to serve as a go-between for Frankenstein and the reader. Had Frankenstein related his story directly, the reader would have questioned his objectivity and honesty. Have students consider adopting this same device by employing an outside narrator to convey their tale. What type of character is best suited to be objective yet involved enough to offer accurate insight? This activity should take approximately three to five class periods, if students work on their stories at home and bring them to class for peer editing and revision.

Source: Adapted from "Using the Literary Masters to Inspire Written Expression in Gifted Students," by S. R. Alber, C. M. Martin, and D. M. Cammill, 2005. *Gifted Child Today, 28*(2), 50–59. Copyright © 2005 by Prufrock Press. Adapted with permission.

 To learn more about how to inspire written expression in gifted students, go to the Building Teaching Skills section in Chapter 13 of MyEducationLab and complete the activities.

Lesson Differentiation in the General Education Classroom

Methods for differentiation within the general education classroom include curriculum compacting, tiered lessons, and using Bloom's taxonomy and multiple intelligences as frameworks for modifying questions and creating instructional activities.

Curriculum compacting

 Council for Exceptional Children Content Standards for Beginning Teachers—G&T: Acceleration, enrichment, and counseling within a continuum of service options for individuals with gifts and talents (GT5K4) (also GT7K2).

Curriculum Compacting Many gifted and talented students have already mastered much of the content of the general education curriculum when the school year begins. **Curriculum compacting** involves compressing the instructional content and materials so that academically able students have more time to work on more challenging materials (Reis & Renzulli, 2005). Reis and co-workers studied the effects of curriculum compacting on 336 students in grades two through six with demonstrated advanced content knowledge and superior academic ability. When teachers used curriculum compacting to eliminate 36% to 54% of content in mathematics or language arts curricula, no significant differences resulted in achievement test scores between gifted students whose curriculum had been compacted and those who had received the general education curriculum (Reis, Westberg, Kulikowich, & Purcell, 1998). Another study showed that when teachers compacted the curriculum, gifted and talented students scored significantly higher on tests of mathematics and science concepts after the content was altered (Reis, 1995).

Curriculum compacting entails three steps: (a) assess the target content areas, (b) determine the content to be eliminated, and (c) substitute the more appropriate content. Most teachers find the third step to be the most difficult as they "lack expertise in knowing what to substitute for high-ability students" (Renzulli & Reis, 2004, p. 98). When pretesting academically talented students to find out what they already know, the most difficult problems or content should be presented first. Students who can solve the most difficult problems do not need to do the other, easier problems (Winebrenner, 2001).

For curriculum compacting to be effective, teachers must have a substantial understanding of the curricular content and not only condense the material but also modify its presentation, create more meaningful instruction, and evaluate that instruction for individual students. For example, Juan's teacher, Mr. Dominguez, suspects that Juan has already mastered substantial amounts of the mathematics that students are doing in the fourth grade, perhaps by as much as two grade levels. To discover if Juan is a good candidate for curricular compacting, Mr. Dominguez first determines the scope and sequence of the mathematics problems that Juan should be able to do in the fifth and sixth grades. Then he constructs an evaluation process that will accurately determine at what level Juan can perform the mathematics problems. If Juan has mastered the content and strategies of the higher-level math, then Mr. Dominguez must design and provide replacement activities that are a more challenging and productive use of Juan's time.

Tiered Lessons A **tiered lesson** provides different extensions of the same basic lesson for groups of students of differing abilities. For example, after the whole class is exposed to a basic lesson on a poem, three groups of students might work on follow-up activities or assignments of basic, middle, and high difficulty. Figure 13.6 shows an example of a tiered lesson on riddles.

Using Bloom's Taxonomy for Phrasing Questions and Assigning Student Products
Bloom and his colleagues (Bloom, Englehart, Furst, Hill, & Krathwohl, 1956) formulated a taxonomy of educational objectives that has proven very useful for differentiating curriculum. The original **Bloom's taxonomy** contained six levels or types of cognitive understanding: knowledge, comprehension, application, analysis, synthesis, and evaluation. In 2001, the taxonomy was revised (Anderson et al.). Nouns have become active verbs in the revised taxonomy. Knowledge is called *remember,* comprehension is called *understand,* application is *apply,* analysis is *analyze,* evaluation is *evaluate,* and synthesis is called *create.* A contributor to both the original and the revised taxonomies, Krathwohl (2002) noted that the original hierarchy implied that activities become more complex as one moves from level to level, while the new hierarchy "gives much greater weight to teacher usage, the requirement of a strict hierarchy has been relaxed to allow the categories to overlap one another" (p. 215).

Teachers most often ask knowledge (remember) and comprehension (understand) questions. Figure 13.7 illustrates how Bloom's taxonomy could guide the types of questions asked and possible student products in a unit based on the Cinderella story. Although both average and high-ability students should have learning opportunities at all levels of Bloom's taxonomy, opportunities and expectations to work at the advanced levels of the taxonomy are especially important for academically talented students. As Clark (2008) points out, however, it is a mistake to think that gifted learners do not need instructional activities at the lower levels of the taxonomy. To analyze, evaluate, and create meaningful concepts and relationships, students must remember and understand basic information about the topic.

Why modify questioning as a means of differentiation? Student-centered instruction requires teachers to ask stimulating questions according to the ability of the student, and proper questioning is a sophisticated facet of teaching. Techniques such as increasing wait time are part of modifying questioning, as is making sure that the discussion "zigzags"—that is, the students get a chance to talk with each other, not just with the teacher. With practice, the general education classroom teacher can "think on her feet" during questioning; thus, all students, both slow and fast, precocious and delayed, can experience challenge and success during classroom activities.

Go to the Homework & Exercises section in Chapter 13 of MyEducationLab and complete Homework Exercise 3. As you read the article and answer the accompanying questions, consider the different methods for lesson differentiation that are available for students who are gifted.

Bloom's taxonomy

 Council for Exceptional Children Content Standards for Beginning Teachers—G&T: Theories and research that form the basis of curriculum development and instructional practice (GT7K3).

FIGURE 13.6 **A tiered lesson using riddles to promote thinking and problem-solving skills**

Author: Ms. Erin Morris Miller (National Research Center/Gifted and Talented)	**Author's e-mail:** HOTLINX@virginia.edu
Curriculum area(s): math, science, social studies	Grade Level: 3
Time required: 30 minutes	Instructional grouping: heterogeneous

Overview

This is a thinking skills lesson to help students practice thinking openly and flexibly. Use this lesson as a mental warm-up session before beginning a challenging lesson that requires the students to think flexibly or counterintuitively. Use this lesson to prepare the students for times when making assumptions would be bad. Examples: solving word problems in math, finding patterns in math, drawing conclusions from reading selections, and making decisions during a unit on economy. (Idea inspired by a high school advanced placement calculus teacher, Fred Pence, who began class with a puzzle to get students in the mood to problem-solve. The concept was adapted for younger students.) In this lesson students first solve a riddle as a whole class and then divide into small groups to solve additional riddles. Groups are formed according to the students' readiness to read and understand difficult vocabulary. Each group works independently as the teacher moves from group to group, facilitating discussions.

Standards

This lesson helps students develop the skills necessary to achieve any standard that involves problem solving. Examples include math and science problems as well as dilemmas in social studies and analysis of literature.

Materials

There are three levels of riddles. Level 1 consists of three simple riddles, level 2 consists of one medium-hard riddle, and level 3 consists of one difficult riddle.

As a result of this lesson, students should
> **know . . .**
>> Riddles are written puzzles.
> **understand . . .**
>> Riddles require people to think creatively.
>> Riddles require people to not make assumptions.
> **be able to do . . .**
>> Students should be able to solve riddles.

Preassessment

One main difference between the riddles is the difference in the vocabulary involved. Groups should be formed based on the students' verbal proficiency.

Basic riddles

What can go up a chimney down but can't go down a chimney up? (an umbrella)

If a rooster laid a brown egg and a white egg, what kind of chicks would hatch? (None. Roosters don't lay eggs!)

What needs an answer, but doesn't ask a question? (the phone)

Medium-hard riddle
I can sizzle like bacon,
I am made with an egg,
I have plenty of backbone but lack a good leg,
I peel layers like onions but still remain whole,
I can be long like a flagpole yet fit in a hole.
What am I?
(a snake)

Challenging riddle
This thing devours all,
Birds, beasts, trees, flowers,
Gnaws iron, bites steel,
Grinds hard stones to meal,
Slays kings, ruins towns,
And beats high mountains down.
(time) (by J. R. R. Tolkien)

FIGURE 13.7	Using Bloom's taxonomy as a guide for differentiating instruction based on the Cinderella story		
Level	**Common verbs to use to phrase questions**	**Example from Cinderella story**	**Possible student products**
Remember	know, collect, cite, repeat, recall, define, enumerate, list, name, label, tell, recount, relate, specify, memorize, identify	1. How many stepsisters did Cinderella have? 2. Do you recall what the slipper was made of?	Test, list, definition, fact, reproduction.
Understand	restate, recognize, locate, summarize, explain, report, convert, discuss, express, retell, describe, identify, translate, estimate	1. Discuss the events on the night of the ball. 2. Describe what happened to the pumpkin.	Same as for knowing level.
Apply	exhibit, apply, dramatize, solve, employ, practice, compute	1. Make an exhibit of the ball gowns Cinderella's two sisters and stepmother wore. 2. Dramatize what happened when the Prince came to Cinderella's house with the glass slipper.	Illustration, diagram, map, diary, model, collection, diorama, puzzle.
Analyze	interpret, categorize, dissect, analyze, classify, diagram, outline, compare, group, arrange, contrast, examine, inventory, subdivide	1. Compare and contrast Cinderella's treatment by her stepmother and by the Prince. 2. Examine why the stepmother was so cruel to Cinderella.	Questionnaire, survey, report, graph, chart, outline.
Evaluate	judge, criticize, prove, decide, assess, revise, appraise, estimate, rate, evaluate, determine, conclude	1. Prove that Cinderella deserves to go to the ball. 2. Determine what would have happened if Cinderella had run away but had not lost her slipper.	Panel discussion, evaluation scale, report, survey, editorial, verdict, recommendation.
Create	compose, propose, produce, invent, imagine, formulate, create, design, predict, construct, improve, develop, rearrange	1. Compose a song that Cinderella would sing while she did her work in the cinders. 2. Design Cinderella's ball gown; chariot; slipper.	Formula, invention, film, new game, story, poem, art product, machine, advertisement.

Source: Jane Piirto, © 2007. Used with permission.

Figure 13.8 shows how Bloom's taxonomy can be combined with Gardner's concept of multiple intelligences to provide a framework for designing instructional activities and student tasks for a unit on mammals.

Curriculum Differentiation Outside the Classroom

For some students with outstanding talents, what takes place outside the classroom may be more important and rewarding than many of the activities within it. The teacher should always attempt to connect classwork with human and physical resources available in the community.

Internships and Mentor Programs The value and power of a viable mentor to the realization of talent or creativity have been recognized since the Middle Ages.

Differentiating curriculum outside the classroom

 Content Standards for Beginning Teachers—G&T: Community-based and service learning opportunities for individuals with gifts and talents (GT7K7).

FIGURE 13.8 Example of combining Bloom's taxonomy (Revised) with Gardner's eight intelligences as a guide for assigning student products for a unit on mammals

The Eight Intelligences	Remember	Understand	Apply	Analyze	Evaluate	Create
Linguistic	Define the term "mammal" and create a word list for characteristics of mammals.	Find three examples of mammals and explain why each fits into that category.	Write a poem, word game, or report on a mammal of your choice.	Compare and contrast a mammal and another animal (not a mammal) of your choosing.	Write a review about a source that you had read to learn about mammals.	Create a new animal from a combination of others (or entirely original) that would be categorized as a mammal.
Logical-Mathematical	List at least five attributes that all mammals have in common.	Find average weights and heights for at least three different mammals.	Show, on a timeline, the evolution or growth pattern of a mammal of your choice.	Make a travel plan, including a budget, which will allow you to study or visit a mammal of your choice in another country.	Identify the "best" mammal, and explain what, in your opinion, makes that mammal the best. Or, suggest improvements on a mammal. Remember to explain why.	Create a math game centered on a mammal of your choice. Check with the teacher for approval BEFORE beginning.
Visual/Spatial	Draw a picture of a mammal of your choice. List its mammalian characteristics.	Make up a computer quiz about mammals. You may use diagrams from the Internet.	Make a brochure advertising a mammal of your choice. Be sure to explain why this animal would be a good pet.	Research a mammal of your choice. Present the information that you find to the class, using a chart, diorama, or other idea okayed by the teacher.	Critically evaluate websites on a given mammal. Explain which is the most/least useful and why.	Build your own art gallery, centered on a mammal or a group of mammals. Be prepared to share (and explain, if necessary) your work to the class.
Bodily/Kinesthetic	Build a model of a mammal of your choice.	List good and bad features of being a mammal. Act out at least one.	Perform a dance to represent a mammal or to call on a mammal for help or another reason.	Develop a rubric to assess the performance of a mammal in a fair, race, or other setting.	Evaluate the construction of a given mammal. Why is it made the way it is?	Make up a sport in which a mammal of your choice is a participant. Explain the rules and the mammal's role.

Musical	Imitate the sounds of a mammal of your choice or sing a song about that mammal.	Identify instruments that may be used to represent a horse, cow, pig, sheep, and another mammal of your choice.	Locate several songs about mammals and share your favorite with the class.	Choose a musical piece on a mammal of your choice and analyze its effects on your feelings/thoughts about that mammal.	Select the best music for a sound track representing a mammal of your choice.	Write a song or jingle promoting a mammal of your choice.
Naturalist	Write a list to show what makes a mammal a mammal.	Explain the role(s) of mammals in our world. Support your answer.	Write a "care for" booklet for a mammal of your choice.	Compare several mammals and the climates in which each lives.	Write a review on a nature film about mammals.	Plan and organize a nature excursion, which will allow you to come in contact with at least five different mammals in their original habitat.
Interpersonal	Describe how others fit into the category of "mammal."	Compare two people, focusing on how each has characteristics common to all mammals and other characteristics that are different.	Teach someone how to take care of a mammal. (The mammal may be domesticated or wild. If it is wild, you may want to include directions for taming it.)	Pretend that a group of people are mammals living in a forest. Develop social skills and rules for success (i.e., survival in the forest).	A group of mammals is upset because the group refuses to share its food with the others. Assess the situation and negotiate a solution. Support your decision.	Organize a community service activity that will result in better living conditions for a group of mammals.
Intrapersonal	Describe how you fit into the category of "mammal."	Explain what you have learned about mammals, and how.	Make a personal timeline regarding your interactions with mammals.	Analyze your strengths as a person. How might these characteristics benefit a different mammal?	Choose a mammal to represent you. Why did you choose this mammal? How is this mammal like you?	Develop a self-improvement program for yourself and a mammal of your choice. How do they differ? How are they the same?

Source: Created by Rebecca Elkevizth, Literacy*Americorps member. Ashland University/Literacy*Americorps.

A mentor provides opportunities for students with exceptional talents to develop their conceptual and performance skills in a real-world setting.

The importance of mentors cannot be overestimated in certain artistic and scientific fields, where the development of both conceptual and performance skills is critical to success. These opportunities allow students with exceptional talents to be exposed to one of the most powerful and proven educational strategies—modeling, practice, and direct feedback and reinforcement of important behaviors—within a real-world setting (Siegle & McCoach, 2005).

Special Courses Specialized courses and workshops are offered in many communities, arts and cultural venues, museums, and recreation centers. These courses, which may or may not award high school or college continuing education credits, form a rich variety of opportunities for students to encounter mentors, new friends, and expansive concepts that may not be available in the confines of the school curriculum.

Junior Great Books This is a highly structured educational program in which students read selections from a number of areas, including classics, philosophy, fiction, and poetry, and then discuss their meaning with teachers. The teachers must undergo special training and use specific questioning techniques designed to evoke high-quality responses from the students.

Summer Programs Many summer programs are available to gifted and talented students that offer educational experiences as diverse as environmental studies and space and aeronautical studies. A number of new program offerings have been aimed at gifted minority students at the state and local levels. Summer programs are usually relatively brief but intense learning experiences that concentrate on specific areas of intellectual, artistic, or cultural affairs.

International Experiences New Zealanders have a cultural rite of passage they refer to as "the trek," wherein they pack their bags and travel in modest fashion to the far reaches of the planet. It is an eye-opening experience for people from a tiny Pacific island and one that gives them an exceptional opportunity to see and touch the world in an intimate fashion. An international curricular experience can merge this act of exploration with the demands of a structured learning experience—for example, the International Baccalaureate Program. Numerous international programs offer academic credits for study at participating educational agencies around the world. They are excellent opportunities for students to develop global interactional skills with academically rigorous studies.

Instructional Models and Methods

Each of the four instructional models described in this section engages students in similar ways, focusing on independent exploration and inquiry, substantial modifications to the individual student's learning environment, and tangible products as an outcome of the learning activities. These models were selected because they offer the best examples of how special education for gifted and talented students can truly be differentiated from the general education curriculum. Although the Schoolwide Enrichment Model (SEM) (Renzulli & Reis, 2003) is the only model to attempt to provide activities for both typically developing and gifted students, each of the other models includes components that can be modified and applied to a broad range of student abilities and talents within inclusive classrooms.

The Schoolwide Enrichment Model The SEM not only attempts to meet the needs of gifted and talented students within the general education classroom setting but also is meant to be used with the other students in the class (Renzulli & Reis, 2003).

The Schoolwide Enrichment Model (SEM) focuses on applying the know-how of gifted education to a systematic plan for total school improvement. This plan is not intended to replace

Schoolwide Enrichment Model

 Council for Exceptional Children
Content Standards for Beginning Teachers—G&T: Models, theories, and philosophies that form the basis of gifted education (GT1K2) (also GT7K3).

existing services to students who are identified as gifted according to various state or local criteria. Rather, the model should be viewed as an umbrella under which many different types of enrichment and acceleration services are made available to targeted groups of students, as well as all students within a given school or grade level. (Renzulli, 1998, p. 1)

The first step of the SEM is identifying a talent pool of high-ability students (usually 15% to 25% of the school's enrollment) by using a multifactored assessment approach, including achievement tests, teacher and peer nominations, and creativity assessments. Once the students are identified, they can take part in specialized services, many of which are also available and appropriate for other learners in the same classroom. Reis (1995) discusses some of the relevant features of this instructional approach:

- Teachers use interest and learning styles assessments with talent pool students. Teachers also use informal and formal methods to create and/or identify individual students' interests and to encourage students to further develop and pursue their interests in various ways.
- Teachers offer curriculum compacting to all eligible students. The general education curriculum of the classroom is modified by eliminating redundant or repetitious information and materials.
- Teachers offer three types of enrichment activities to students: Type I, general exploratory experiences; Type II, purposefully designed instructional methods and materials; and Type III, advanced-level studies with greater depth and complexity.

Letting students choose the kinds of problems they wish to study and how they will go about their investigations is one method for differentiating curriculum for students with outstanding academic abilities.

All children in the talent pool participate in Type I and Type II enrichment activities. Only students who show serious interest in a specific topic evolve into Type III investigators. Students are never compelled to begin Type III projects; the level remains an open option for them. In 2005, the Renzulli group unveiled a web-based individualized program for students, which includes a profiler, a differentiation search engine, a total talent portfolio, and a wizard product maker. For details, see www.renzullilearning.com.

Maker's Active Problem Solver Model Maker proposes a process by which the key elements of content, process, products, and the environment of a child's learning situation can be modified (Maker, 2001; Maker & Nielson, 1996). Maker and co-workers have conducted extensive research on reliability and validity of the DISCOVER assessment and curriculum model, showing that teachers whose beliefs parallel the theory behind the model can help students raise their test scores. Arts infusion with this model also has been successful. The teachers use four kinds of modifications:

Maker's Problem-Solving Model

 Content Standards for Beginning Teachers—G&T: Models, theories, and philosophies that form the basis of gifted education (GT1K2) (also GT7K3).

- *Content modifications.* The content of a curriculum is the type of subject matter being taught. In general, the goal is to develop content that is more advanced, complex, innovative, and original than what is usually encountered in the classroom.
- *Process modifications.* The strategies and methods used in delivering the content to learners are key features of instruction. The goal is to provide students with many opportunities to actively respond to the content, including independent research, cooperative learning, peer coaching, simulations, and apprenticeships.
- *Product modifications.* The products of learning are the outcomes associated with instruction. The goal is to encourage a variety of ways that students can present their thoughts, ideas, and results.
- *Environment modifications.* The learning environment includes both the physical characteristics of the setting(s) and the ambiance created by the teachers or facilitators. The goal is first to establish a positive working environment and then to rearrange the layout. Ideas such as peer tutoring, learning centers, management

Problem-Based Learning Units

 Council for Exceptional Children Content Standards for Beginning Teachers—G&T: Models, theories, and philosophies that form the basis of gifted education (GT1K2) (also GT4K1).

sheets, and learning packets can help students take more active control over and interest in their learning.

Problem-Based Learning   Problem-based learning (PBL) challenges students to "learn to learn" while working cooperatively in groups to seek solutions to real-world problems. The problems are used to engage students' curiosity and initiate learning of subject matter. Since the mid-1990s, Joyce Van Tassel-Baska at the College of William and Mary has served as overall project director for a series of federally funded grants to develop a thematic, interdisciplinary, problem-based curriculum for gifted students. Gifted educators throughout the country created and field-tested units in science, language arts, and the social sciences. (Figure 13.9 describes several examples.)

FIGURE 13.9	Examples of College of William and Mary problem-based learning units in science, language arts, and social studies

SCIENCE

Acid, Acid Everywhere	This unit poses an ill-structured problem that leads the students into an interdisciplinary inquiry about the structures of and interaction between several systems, centering around the study of an acid spill on a local highway.
The Chesapeake Bay	This unit focuses on the various systems involved in the pollution of the Chesapeake Bay. The systems included in this unit are ecosystems, chemical reaction systems, government systems, and economic systems.
What a Find!	An exploration of the field of archaeology. Students are put in the role of junior archaeologists at a research museum and discover that construction work has been halted on a new school because of the discovery of historic artifacts.

For more information on problem-based units in science, go to www.wm.edu/education/gifted-ed/Curriculum/Science_materials.htm

LANGUAGE ARTS

Literary Reflections on Personal and Social Change (Grades 4–6)	This unit involves students' interacting with literature while enhancing reading comprehension and textual analysis skills. The literature selections, including Burnett's *The Secret Garden* and world-class short stories by such authors as Tolstoy and Singer, serve as a basis for discussion.
Literature of the 1940s: A Decade of Change (Grades 7–9)	This unit looks at the historical events and social issues of the 1940s through the literature of the decade. The unit is rich in materials that highlight the concept of change, including works such as Hersey's *Hiroshima, The Diary of Anne Frank,* and McCuller's *The Member of the Wedding.*
Change Through Choices: A Literature Unit for High School Students (Grades 10–12)	This unit focuses on catalytic choices that determine change in a variety of situations. This unit attempts to give the student a chance to question real world choices and problems and decide what valuable lessons can be learned through careful individual examination of options.

For more information on problem-based units in language arts, go to www.wm.edu/education/gifted-ed/Curriculum/Language_Arts_materials.htm

SOCIAL STUDIES

Ancient China: The Middle Kingdom (Grades 2–3)	Human civilizations develop and sustain themselves as a collection of interdependent systems. The unit provides opportunities for students to broaden their understanding by comparing ancient Chinese civilization with aspects of their own lives and communities.
A House Divided? The Civil War, Its Causes and Effects (Grades 5–6)	The concept of cause and effect serves as a central organizing theme of this unit, which explores the events and perspectives leading to the American Civil War and the chronology and context of the war itself, using primary-source documents.
The 1930s in America: Facing Depression (Grades 6–7)	The unit explores Depression-era America from the perspective of many different groups of people, using a variety of primary sources to illustrate events and the social-political context.

For more information on problem-based units in social studies, go to www.wm.edu/education/gifted-ed/Curriculum/Social_Studies_materials.htm

An ill-formed, real-world problem serves as the basis for each of the science units, and understanding and applying the concept of systems form the overarching theme. These units give students experience in collecting, organizing, analyzing, and evaluating scientific data and learning to communicate their understanding to others. The PBL language arts units feature change as the overarching theme; the social studies units focus on the concept of interdependence.

The PBL units have won many major curriculum awards from discipline-based subject matter groups as well as the National Association for Gifted Children's "red apple" award for excellence. In addition to wide use in the United States, PBL units are used by teachers in 18 countries and have been adopted by the American Embassy Schools and the Department of Defense schools. Although the PBL units were developed initially for gifted and talented students, they can be used with students of all ability levels by modifying the activities up or down depending on student ability.

Guidance and Counseling Needs

A pressing need exists for guidance and counseling services for gifted and talented students (Neihart, Robinson, & Moon, 2002). Piirto (2007) listed these guidance issues: academic planning, acceleration, career development, finding mentors, multipotentiality (being able to do many things at a very high level), learning styles, testing, program articulation, vocational guidance, volunteerism and service, and gender differences in all of these issues. In addition, these counseling issues are frequent with the gifted and talented: anger, attention disorders and other medical conditions, genuine boredom, bullying, creativity, delinquency, depression, dropping out of school, very high IQ, introversion, intuition, meeting the expectations of others, motivation, intensities, peer relations, perfectionism, overachievement, resilience, self-concept/self-esteem, stress, sexual identity, and underachievement (Piirto, 2007). Our track record of understanding and then facilitating the emotional growth of gifted and talented students is weak to nonexistent. As with all children and adults, a number of predictable and unpredictable crises will occur throughout their lives. With their heightened sense of social justice and greater awareness of the needs of others, students who are gifted and talented often experience confusion and estrangement more deeply than their peers. Teachers are not counselors, but they often become aware of issues specific to their individual students' needs.

EDUCATIONAL PLACEMENT ALTERNATIVES AND ABILITY GROUPING

Special Schools

Special schools for gifted and talented students have a long history. Special high schools for students of both genders began in the early 20th century with the establishment of Stuyvesant High School in New York City. The establishment of the Hunter College High School for Gifted Girls came even earlier. The Hunter College Elementary School for gifted students opened in 1941. Children are selected for admission to these schools on the basis of competitive examinations and scores on individual IQ tests. These arrangements for academically talented children became popular in the 1980s as mandates for desegregation caused urban school systems to change the concept of the neighborhood school to the concept of the magnet school. Even on the elementary school level in many urban areas, special magnet schools emphasize various themes: for example, Columbus, Ohio, has a French language school; most large cities have a special high school for the visual and performing arts and special schools for mathematics and science. Recently, many states have permitted special charter schools for gifted and talented students.

Self-Contained Classrooms

The primary advantage of the self-contained classroom is that all curriculum and instruction can be focused on needs of high-ability students. Other advantages of self-contained classrooms are that students are more likely to work at a pace commensurate with their abilities, and membership in a class of intellectual equals may challenge some gifted students to excel even further. The self-contained classroom model may also be more efficient because

Placement alternatives

 Content Standards for Beginning Teachers—G&T: Issues, assurances, and due process rights related to assessment, eligibility, and placement within a continuum of services (GT1K7).

gifted education teachers do not have to move from classroom to classroom or school to school to serve students.

In addition to sharing many of the disadvantages of self-contained classrooms for students with disabilities (e.g., limited opportunity to interact with peers in general education), self-contained classroom programs for gifted and talented students must often deal with the stigma of being viewed as elitist. Some districts may be too small to support the self-contained classroom option, even multiage or across-grade-level classes.

Resource Room or Pull-Out Programs

Some educators believe that the resource room, or pull-out model, is the best option for serving gifted and talented students. Although pull-out programs offer many of the advantages of a self-contained classroom without the disadvantages of complete segregation from the general education classroom, they pose a number of challenges and disadvantages as well (see Figure 13.10). Administrators and teachers in schools that provide resource room/pull-out services for gifted and talented students should recognize that these children do not stop being gifted when they leave the resource room and return to the general education classroom. Although the learning opportunities and instruction provided to talented students in the resource room may be of the highest quality, they do not eliminate the need to differentiate curriculum for these students when they are in the general education classroom during the rest of the school day.

FIGURE 13.10	Advantages and disadvantages of resource room and pull-out models for gifted and talented students

Advantages	Disadvantages
1. Pull-out programs are quite easy to set in motion.	1. Costs more as extra teachers have to be hired and special facilities provided.
2. The teacher in the regular classroom has more time to work with the other students.	2. The regular classroom teachers get frustrated and often feel that students leaving disrupts their instructional plan.
3. Students who are left in the classroom have a chance to shine.	3. Students in the regular classroom might feel resentful.
4. The teacher in the pull-out program can focus on critical and creative thinking since the teacher in the regular classroom focuses on the standard curriculum.	4. The academically talented students might have to make up work in the regular classroom while having more work in the pull-out classroom.
5. The differentiation of curriculum is separated from the classroom flow.	5. Curriculum may have no relationship to curriculum in the regular classroom.
6. Students receive special help in areas of strength.	6. Students are treated differently according to ability.
7. Teachers can feel as if they have "their" kids.	7. Teachers are isolated from the other teachers.
8. Students can have time with other students to discuss intellectual interests that may not be shared by students in the regular classroom.	8. Students may feel different from the rest of the students in their regular classroom.
9. Collaboration with other teachers is encouraged.	9. Students are academically talented all the time, and not just during pull-out time.
10. Small groups of students can do special projects that would not be possible in the regular classroom.	10. Small groups of students may receive special privileges other students don't receive (e.g., access to computers, field trips).
11. Teachers of the talented can provide intensive instruction in areas of expertise (e.g., the arts, foreign language).	11. Turf issues with regular classroom teacher may arise (e.g., homework, lessons and assemblies missed).

Source: From Piirto, J. (1999). *Talented children and adults: Their development and education* (2nd ed., p. 73). Upper Saddle River, NJ: Merrill/Prentice Hall. Used by permission.

General Education Classroom

For gifted and talented students, inclusion in the general education classroom has not been an issue as it is with other exceptional children. Most academically or otherwise talented students are served in general education classrooms. If the school district has a program for gifted and talented students, a teacher with special training in gifted education provides direct and indirect support for the general education classroom teacher. Working in consultation with the general education classroom teacher, this special educator—sometimes called a facilitator, a consulting teacher, or an intervention specialist for the gifted—might provide specialized instruction in science, math, the humanities, or other subjects to flexible groups of students. She may work with a high-ability reading or math group while the rest of the class works in these domains. She may mentor independent projects, design special learning centers, plan special field trips, and help students prepare for academic competitions.

An advantage of this model is that the gifted education teacher is no longer isolated and alone, working in her resource room or pull-out classroom without knowledge of what the students are doing in their home classrooms. She is in partnership with general education classroom teachers, collaborating on curriculum planning teams as they plan multilevel lessons. Another important advantage of the consultant teacher model is that students of all ability levels in the general education classroom can benefit from smaller student–teacher ratios, participating in multitiered lessons and learning activities on creativity, critical thinking, or study strategies that the gifted specialist may teach to the whole classroom.

Landrum (2002) has written extensively about the consultation/collaboration model. Possible activities can consist of (a) team or grade-level co-planning sessions, where the talent development specialist joins in the planning sessions with the general education team; (b) communicating about organizational needs such as grouping and scheduling; (c) identifying and placing students in groups; (d) gathering materials to supplement general education classroom activities; (e) facilitating differentiation activities; (f) administering and managing independent studies and student learning contracts; (g) monitoring the progress of student learning through rubrics and pre-assessment.

Many schools, however, do not have a gifted education specialist, and the general education classroom teacher is responsible for differentiating curriculum for students with advanced educational needs.

Ability Grouping

An issue involving considerable debate and strong opinions over the years is the extent to which academically talented students should be taught in groups composed of their intellectual equals or in heterogeneous groups of students encompassing a wide range of abilities. Social injustices and upheavals have resulted in increased calls for equity in all of society's institutions. For some, equity in education includes the idea that all students should be taught in heterogeneous groups so that no single group can progress faster than any other. But most educators and researchers in the field of gifted education believe that heterogeneous group instruction prevents talented students from reaching their full potential. (See the National Association for Gifted Children's policy on ability grouping in Figure 13.11.)

Ability grouping has been used in schools, both formally and informally, for more than 100 years. As soon as the number of students in any classroom or school became so large that the differences in their abilities to learn stood out, teachers automatically placed students in groups for subject matter instruction. These groups were often informal, consisting of two or more students who could keep pace with each other. When teachers began to group students according to chronological age and when developmental experts cautioned that students should remain in classes only with their age mates, ability grouping began to be the norm rather than the exception.

XYZ Grouping or Tracking *XYZ grouping* places students into different levels of curriculum requirements or offerings according to high, middle, and low ability based on test scores or other indicators or predictors of performance. Detroit had such a plan as early as 1919. Students had the same curricula and the same textbooks; the only differences were in pace of instruction and depth of enrichment. Students in the top 20% in achievement

Consulting teacher model

 Content Standards for Beginning Teachers—G&T: Models and strategies for consultation and collaboration (GT10K4).

Ability grouping issues and concerns

Content Standards for Beginning Teachers—G&T: Relationship of gifted education to the organization and function of educational agencies (GT1K4).

 Go to the Homework & Exercises section in Chapter 13 of MyEducationLab and complete Homework Exercise 4. As you watch the video, think about the pros and cons of ability grouping for students.

FIGURE 13.11 — National Association for Gifted Children's policy on ability grouping

Ability Grouping

The National Association for Gifted Children (NAGC) is fully committed to national goals that advocate both excellence and equity for all students, and we believe that the best way to achieve these goals is through *differentiated* educational opportunities, resources, and encouragement for all students.

The practice of grouping, enabling students with advanced abilities and/or performance to be grouped together to receive appropriately challenging instruction, has recently come under attack. NAGC wishes to reaffirm the importance of grouping for instruction of gifted students. Grouping allows for more appropriate, rapid, and advanced instruction, which matches the rapidly developing skills and capabilities of gifted students.

Special attention should be given to the identification of gifted and talented students who may not be identified through traditional assessment methods (including economically disadvantaged individuals, individuals of limited English proficiency, and individuals with handicaps), to help them participate effectively in special grouping programs.

Strong research evidence supports the effectiveness of ability grouping for gifted students in accelerated classes, enrichment programs, advanced placement programs, etc. Ability and performance grouping has been used extensively in programs for musically and artistically gifted students, and for athletically talented students with little argument. Grouping is a necessary component of every graduate and professional preparation program, such as law, medicine, and the sciences. It is an accepted practice that is used extensively in the education programs in almost every country in the western world.

NAGC does not endorse a tracking system that sorts all children into fixed layers in the school system with little attention to particular content, student motivation, past accomplishment, or present potential.

To abandon the proven instructional strategy of grouping students for instruction at a time of educational crisis in the U.S. will further damage our already poor competitive position with the rest of the world, and will renege on our promise to provide an appropriate education for all children. (Approved 11/91)

Source: National Association for Gifted Children, Washington, DC. Reprinted by permission.

were placed in the *X* classes, students in the next 60% were placed in the *Y* classes, and the lowest 20% were placed in the *Z* classes. Another name for XYZ grouping is *tracking*. Well-founded concern over the potential dangers (e.g., reduced expectations and limited learning opportunities for children in lower tracks, permanent placement in lower tracks at an early age) and abuses of tracking (e.g., as a procedure for de facto segregation of students by race, culture, and/or socioeconomic status) have caused some critics to call for an elimination of all forms of ability grouping for instruction (e.g., Oaks, 1985).

Within-class ability groupings

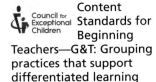

Content Standards for Beginning Teachers—G&T: Grouping practices that support differentiated learning environments (GT5K5).

Within-Class Grouping In contrast to tracking, a second type of ability grouping is *within-class grouping,* in which teachers group students within the same heterogeneous class for instruction according to their achievement. The most common form of within-class grouping is regrouping by subject; students are generally grouped into three or more levels, and they study material from different textbooks at different levels. Meta-analysis studies from the University of Michigan (Kulik, 1992a, 1992b, 2003; Kulik & Kulik, 1984a, 1984b, 1987, 1992) and from Johns Hopkins University (Slavin, 1987, 1991) found that this type of ability grouping had positive results, with gains for low-, middle-, and high-ability students averaging 1.2 years in a school year. Students should be grouped by ability for reading and mathematics. Kulik (2004) said, "Well-designed and well-controlled studies unequivocally show that homogeneous grouping helps children when it is used as a means of providing appropriate curricular material to them" (abstract).

Another form of within-class grouping is *cluster grouping,* in which several talented students receive specialized instruction from a teacher who treats them as talented. Four to six talented students should make up a cluster. Cluster grouping can be used effectively at all grade levels and in all subject areas. It can be especially effective when there are not enough students to form an advanced placement section for a particular subject. Cluster grouping is also a welcome option in rural settings or wherever small numbers of gifted students make appropriate accommodations difficult. The advantage of this type of grouping is that it fits philosophically with the special educational practice of inclusion yet still provides talented students with a peer group. Teachers have found that cluster grouping helps achievement of the other students as well.

Cross-Grade Grouping **Cross-grade grouping** was first tried in the Joplin Plan in Missouri in the 1950s. In this model, students in the fourth, fifth, and sixth grades were broken into nine reading groups, ranging from the second-grade to the ninth-grade levels. Students went to reading class at the same hour but to the level of instruction at which they were achieving. Other types of cross-grade grouping are (a) ability-grouped class assignments, (b) ability grouping for selected subjects, (c) nongraded plans, and (d) special classes. Cross-grade grouping is an effective means of delivering differentiated instruction, and researchers have found achievement gains similar to those of within-grade grouping (Lloyd, 1999). Still other types of grouping are peer-tutoring dyads, cooperative grouping for like-ability students, and mixed-ability cooperative grouping using the "default" option (Rogers, 2002). It is important to note that using a brighter student to tutor a child of lower ability "does not increase the bright child's achievement. Peer tutoring using mixed-ability dyads will only enhance the achievement and behavior of the lower ability student" (Rogers, 2002, p. 245). Webb, Nemer, and Zuniga (2002), studying heterogeneous and homogeneous grouping of high-ability eighth-grade science students, said that high-ability students could learn in heterogeneous groups if the group dynamics were suitable.

Grouping is not going to go away, but it should always be flexible. That is, students should be able to move into and out of groups depending on task and subject and even on whim. The days of a child's being put into the "redbird" reading group in first grade and remaining with the same students until high school graduation are over. Ability grouping, when used properly, produces academic gains for academically talented students when challenging materials are also used. If students are grouped across grades for high-level instruction, no lasting negative social or emotional effects result (Rogers, 2002).

Languages and mathematics seem most amenable for ability grouping. And if grouping occurs, the curriculum should be adapted as well. Although this may seem obvious, some teachers think that just putting children into different ability groups is enough, and they do not provide differentiated curriculum.

The National Research Center on the Gifted and Talented recommends the following guidelines for ability grouping:

Guideline 1: Although some school programs that group children by ability have only small effects, other grouping programs help children a great deal. Schools should therefore resist calls for the wholesale elimination of ability grouping.

Guideline 2: Highly talented youngsters profit greatly from work in accelerated classes. Schools should therefore try to maintain programs of accelerated work.

Guideline 3: Highly talented youngsters also profit greatly from an enriched curriculum designed to broaden and deepen their learning. Schools should therefore try to maintain programs of enrichment.

Guideline 4: Bright, average, and slow youngsters profit from grouping programs that adjust the curriculum to the aptitude levels of the groups. Schools should try to use ability grouping in this way.

Guideline 5: Benefits are slight from programs that group children by ability but prescribe common curricular experiences for all ability groups. Schools should not expect student achievement to change dramatically with either establishment or elimination of such programs.

Cross-grade ability grouping

 Council for Exceptional Children Content Standards for Beginning Teachers—G&T: Grouping practices that support differentiated learning environments (GT5K5).

Guidelines for ability grouping

Council for Exceptional Children Content Standards for Beginning Teachers—G&T: Grouping practices that support differentiated learning environments (GT5K5) (also GT1K4).

Advocacy

Use of the term "gifted"

Council for Exceptional Children

Content Standards for Beginning Teachers—G&T: Impact of labeling individuals with gifts and talents (GT1K8) (also GT1K12).

Some advocates and writers in the field are growing increasingly wary of the term *gifted,* realizing that in some ways it perpetuates the myth that talent is predetermined and not the result of extensive effort on the part of students, teachers, parents, and communities. It simply makes it too easy for society as a whole to ignore these students' needs and to ascribe their growth and development (or lack thereof) to uncontrollable, unseen forces beyond the reach of our instructional interventions. An unintended result is that both individuals and societal institutions can assert that because these students can easily make it on their own, they need no extra help from society. If only the misconception that all of these students make it were true! The available data indicate that large numbers of students who would qualify for gifted and talented services drop out of school and that many more students who are culturally different, disabled, or economically disadvantaged are never even identified. Estimates of this group of underachieving gifted students range from 10% to 20% of all high school dropouts (Davis & Rimm, 2004).

Gifted and talented students need special education; they need differentiated curriculum, instructional strategies, materials, and experiences that will enable them to realize their potential. There are new approaches and perspectives concerning the manner in which students are identified and services are delivered that reflect insights into the way humans learn and create. These innovations promise a brighter future for students with high ability and talents, a future that benefits the world in which they live.

TIPS for Beginning Teachers

TEACHING GIFTED AND TALENTED CHILDREN
by Linda Michael

If you become a general education teacher, you may never have a student who is blind, a student who is deaf, a student with autism, or a student with severe and multiple disabilities. You will, however, have students who are gifted and talented in your classroom. The general education classroom is where gifted and talented students spend most of their time in school.

Young, inexperienced teachers—sometimes armed only with the knowledge gained from the small portion of an introduction to special education course devoted to gifted education—are expected to teach gifted and talented students. This can be daunting, even frightening, at first. Here are some tips that may help:

DIFFERENTIATE

Curriculum for gifted students must be adapted. The content can be compacted and accelerated because the students move at a more rapid pace. Gifted children have academic behaviors similar to children who are 2, 3, or more years older. To provide learning experiences appropriate to their advanced abilities, you should be prepared to do the following:

- *Pretest before you teach.* You may find that a gifted and talented student already knows most or all of the material planned for a unit of study. Gifted students don't always move at the same accelerated pace. Pretesting for each unit of study is a must. The classroom must be flexible enough to adapt to a flow in and out of groups. For example, in math, a student may have no trouble with the abstract functions of algebra, yet she may struggle with geometry. Don't let your ideas about where students fall along an imaginary grouping line become stagnant.
- *Compact the curriculum.* Even after you have placed gifted and talented students ahead in the curriculum based on their pretest performances, you will probably find that those students can move through the advanced material faster than most students. You might give them an independent project, a more advanced lesson, or an assignment in the same area but based on their interests.
- *Accelerate.* Accelerating a gifted student one, two, or even three grade levels in certain subject areas is often easier and less costly than developing your own materials within the classroom.

DON'T BE AFRAID TO CREATE YOUR OWN CURRICULUM

Many schools do not have established curricular plans or preexisting menus of enriched learning opportunities for the education of gifted and talented students. This leaves classroom teachers with the responsibility, and the opportunity, to develop differentiated curriculum.

- *Administer an interest survey.* Find out what the students are studying and learning on their own. Young science students may have elaborate collections. Young math students might be interested in elaborate and complicated number games. Young writers may be reading several grade levels above what the other students are reading. Tailor your assignments to these interests.

- *Build a library of curriculum materials spanning several years above grade level, and keep those materials in your classroom.* These materials will provide ideas and content for developing tiered lessons.

- *Take advantage of curriculum guides and materials for gifted students.* Have advanced materials available in your classroom. District curriculum directors are used to supplying textbooks and materials designed for specific grade levels, and they may not be familiar with materials outside this realm. Gifted and talented students need to be exposed to materials from all levels. In my classroom I have 4th-, 5th-, and 6th-grade curriculum materials and a plethora of reference materials spanning from elementary to college level. I don't rely solely on textbooks. I prefer to develop units that cover a variety of academic standards and provide opportunities for my students to take an active role in projects. Some of the best problem-based units for gifted and talented students that I have used are Interact Simulations (www.interact-simulations.com), the GEMS Program (Great Explorations in Math and Science) from the Lawrence Hall of Science at the University of California at Berkeley (www.lhs.org), and the William and Mary Units developed by the Center for Gifted Education at the College of William and Mary.

- *Provide learning opportunities outside the classroom.* Take advantage of the opportunities in your region. Too often, field trips are taken as a reward, or a day off from the classroom. Field trips are much more meaningful if they have relevance and are connected to what is happening in the classroom. I live in a college town and am lucky to have professors willing to share their expertise with my students. This may be a geologist taking my students to a local site, or visiting the campus television and radio station to see a production in action. Our regional theater also has several offerings for schools throughout the year. This year I am planning to take my class to a production based on Jack London's *Call of the Wild.* We will have a literary study of the novel before attending the play and a post-production discussion. Children's theater groups often offer very good suggestions for lessons.

- *Involve your students in academic contests.* Gifted and talented students are often competitive. They like to participate in regional and national competitions to see how their abilities compare. Local and district-wide academic challenges are a great way for kids from other schools to meet and compete. *Power of the Pen, Odyssey of the Mind, Math Olympiad,* spelling bees, geography bees, and science fairs are just a few examples of competitions your students may choose to enter. Attending and observing these activities will show support for your students and give you additional ideas for curriculum content and instructional activities to bring back to the classroom.

TAILOR YOUR INSTRUCTIONAL ARRANGEMENTS AND TEACHING METHODS

Gifted and talented children do not need specialized methods of instruction as much as they need opportunities to explore challenging curriculum in a supportive environment. Differentiate lessons as much as possible according to students' abilities and interests. Tier, or layer, lessons so that the top students are always challenged.

- *Provide regular opportunities for gifted and talented students to share their ideas and talk about what they have learned.*

- *Challenge them to think, not just pass tests.* Many gifted students already can pass grade-level tests. Encourage and require them to explore the deeper meaning, extensions, and implications of concepts.

- *Use cooperative or collaborative groups that encourage pair sharing.* It is a mistake to make gifted and talented students responsible for the learning of the whole group.

- *Don't assume that because a gifted and talented student is advanced in some subject area that she has mastered the entire curriculum.* However, when you notice gaps in a student's learning, you will often find that she can quickly catch up with direct instruction in the skills that are missing and that a lot of drill and practice is not necessary.

KEY TERMS AND CONCEPTS

ability grouping, p. 523
acceleration, p. 507
asynchrony, p. 498
Bloom's taxonomy, p. 513

cross-grade grouping, p. 525
curriculum compacting, p. 512
enrichment, p. 507
tiered lesson, p. 513

SUMMARY

Definitions

- The federal government defines gifted and talented children as those who give evidence of high-achievement capability in areas such as intellectual, creative, artistic, or leadership capacity, or in specific academic fields, and who need services and activities not ordinarily provided by the school in order to fully develop those capabilities.

- Renzulli's definition of giftedness is based on the traits of above-average general abilities, high level of task commitment, and creativity.

- Piirto defines the gifted as having superior memory, observational powers, curiosity, creativity, and ability to learn.

- Maker defines the gifted and talented student as a problem solver who can (a) create a new or clearer definition of an existing problem, (b) devise new and more efficient or effective methods, and (c) reach solutions that may differ from the usual.

Characteristics

- Learning and intellectual characteristics of gifted and talented students include the ability to do the following:
  - Rapidly acquire, retain, and use large amounts of information.
  - Relate one idea to another.
  - Make sound judgments.
  - Perceive the operation of larger systems of knowledge that others may not recognize.
  - Acquire and manipulate abstract symbol systems.
  - Solve problems by reframing the question and creating novel solutions.

- *Asynchrony* is a term used to describe disparate rates of intellectual, emotional, and physical growth or development often displayed by gifted children.

- Many gifted children are creative. Although no universally accepted definition of creativity exists, we know that creative children have knowledge, examine it in a variety of ways, critically analyze the outcomes, and communicate their ideas.

- Guilford's definition of creativity includes dimensions of fluency, flexibility, originality, and elaboration.

Prevalence

- The most commonly cited prevalence estimate is that high-IQ gifted students make up 3% to 5% of the school-age population and that many forms of talents do not require a high IQ. Perhaps 10% to 15% of students possess such talents.

Identification and Assessment

- Multifactored identification of gifted and talented students includes a combination of intelligence tests; achievement measures; checklists; teacher, parent, community, and peer nominations; self-nomination; and leisure interests.

- Maker's DISCOVER procedure can be used to equitably identify gifted and talented students from diverse cultural groups and low-socioeconomic status backgrounds.

- Teachers of gifted students with disabilities must strive for a balance between nurturing the students' strengths and teaching and providing accommodations and supports as needed for their disabilities.

Educational Approaches

- Curriculum should consider the learning characteristics of gifted and talented students, preserve academic rigor, be thematic and interdisciplinary, consider various curriculum orientations, and be balanced and articulate.
- *Differentiation* is a broad term referring to a variety of strategies for providing gifted and talented students with a challenging and conceptually rich curriculum.
- *Acceleration* is the general term for modifying the pace at which the student moves through the curriculum.
- *Enrichment* means probing or studying a subject at a greater depth than would occur in the general education curriculum.
- Curriculum compacting involves compressing instructional content so students have time to work on more challenging materials.
- Tiered lessons provide extensions of the same basic lesson for groups of students of differing abilities.
- Bloom's taxonomy of educational objectives provides a framework for differentiating curriculum by asking questions and assigning activities that require students to demonstrate different types of knowledge.
- Options for learning outside of school include internships and mentorships, special courses and workshops in the community, Junior Great Books, summer programs, and international experiences.
- Three models for differentiating curriculum for gifted students are Renzulli's Schoolwide Enrichment Model, Maker's Active Problem Solver Model, and the Problem-Based Learning units.

Educational Placement Alternatives and Ability Grouping

- Special schools for gifted and talented students have a long history. Students are selected for admission based on competitive exams and IQ scores. Magnet schools emphasize themes such as foreign language, performing arts, or math and science.
- Curriculum and instruction in self-contained classrooms can focus on the needs of high-ability students. In addition to sharing many of the disadvantages of self-contained classrooms for students with disabilities, some may view self-contained classroom programs for gifted students as elitist.
- Some schools use a resource room or pull-out model for serving gifted and talented students. While resource room programs offer many advantages, they pose a number of challenges and disadvantages as well.
- Most gifted and talented students are served in general education classrooms. A consultant teacher trained in gifted education often helps the general education classroom teacher plan and deliver specialized instruction.
- Most educators and researchers in the field of gifted education believe that ability grouping is necessary if gifted and talented students are to reach their potential. Within-class grouping and cross-age grouping are two forms of ability grouping that offer effective means of delivering differentiated instruction to students according to their achievement and interests.
- As we have seen with other exceptional children, we must improve society's attitudes toward gifted and talented children if we are to improve their futures.

Now go to MyEducationLab at www.myeducationlab.com, and take the pretest to assess your initial comprehension of chapter content. Once you have taken the pretest, use your individualized Study Plan for Chapter 13 to enhance your understanding of the concepts discussed in the chapter. Finally, take the posttest to assess your comprehension of Chapter 13 content.

PART III

Special Education Across the Life Span

14 Early Childhood Special Education

15 Transitioning to Adulthood

Early Childhood Special Education

- Why is it so difficult to measure the impact of early intervention?
- How can we provide early intervention for a child whose disability is not yet present?
- How are the four different purposes of assessment and evaluation in early childhood special education related to one another?
- Which do you think are the most important goals of early childhood special education?
- How can a play activity or an everyday routine become a specially designed learning opportunity for a preschooler with disabilities?

FEATURED TEACHER

DONELLE TYLER
Phantom Lake Elementary School • Bellevue, Washington

Donelle Tyler

Education—Teaching Credentials—Experience
- B.A., American Ethnic Studies, University of Washington, 1999
- M.Ed., Early Childhood Special Education, University of Washington, 2001
- Washington State, Special Education K–12, endorsement P–3

- 6 years of teaching preschoolers with and without disabilities

Meet Some of My Students I teach morning and afternoon sessions of integrated preschool for children ages from 3 to 5. I have 14 students in the morning; 11 students have disabilities, and 3 are typically developing. Ten of the eleven children in my afternoon class have disabilities. Approximately two thirds of my students qualify for services under the Individuals with Disabilities Education Act (IDEA) eligibility category of developmental delay. The remainder of my students have received a diagnosis of autism, health impairment, or communication disorder. Some of my students come from very affluent families while others live in households at or near the poverty line. One third of my students come from homes that are bilingual or where English is not spoken regularly. The latter are from homes where the following languages are spoken: Cantonese, Mandarin, Polish, Spanish, Somali, Telugu, and Urdu. It is my pleasure to introduce you to two of my students.

Lucy: Lucy, a 5-year-old with a diagnosis of high-functioning autism, receives a full-day program provided by the school district. She participates in a social group in the morning and attends my class in the afternoon. Lucy is very bright and talkative. Her favorite color is pink, followed closely by orange. She is passionate about sea life and knows more about many sea creatures than many older children do. Lucy has worked very hard over the course of the school year to learn how to self-regulate. This can be difficult when her peers get too close or try to take her favorite toy. She is proud of the certificates that she earns at the end of the day if she successfully completed her star chart.

Matt: Matt is an adorable 4-year-old with Down syndrome. He loves the Wiggles and has seen them in concert several times. Matt loves to come to school, and he greets each of his friends by saying "hi" and their name. He uses a variety of communication strategies to meet his needs, including sign, pictures, and speech. Matt works very hard when he comes to school; he is very proud that he can count to 15, draw a self-portrait, and tell his mom all about his day at school.

A Day in Preschool My students spend 2 hours and 40 minutes, 4 days a week in an integrated preschool classroom. My classroom is run very much like a typical preschool classroom; however, we embed each child's IEP goals and objectives into every classroom activity. During a typical day, we have circle, small group, snack, recess, and choice time. Circle is a large-group instruction time when students participate in literacy activities (listening to age-appropriate text, answering recall questions, and choral reading), math activities (counting and pattern recognition), and music and movement activities. In circle, we also work on social skills, including greeting others, basic conversation skills, and learning school rules. One student with cerebral palsy uses his voice output device to make choices and answer questions during circle.

Small-group instruction occurs at the table and usually focuses on fine motor skills such as cutting, coloring, and writing. During small group, we also teach the children how to complete activities independently, follow directions, and respond to their peers when they request materials or comment on what others are doing. Lucy is learning to write her first and last name, and small group provides a great opportunity to practice.

During snack time, we teach children to feed themselves using their fingers and utensils, and the children learn about healthy eating. My students try a variety of different fruits and vegetables during snack time by taking "adventure bites." Matt is learning to take small bites, chew, and swallow before eating more food. He needs direct adult supervision during snack.

At recess we work on gross-motor skills and social skills. Children have access to a specially designed playground that enables all children to participate regardless of their motor skills. Children practice independent mobility, running, climbing, tricycle riding, and they participate in social games. We also teach problem solving, turn taking, and sharing during recess.

Choice time provides children with an opportunity to actively engage in a variety of age-appropriate activities with their peers. Activities include pretend play, building with blocks, working with manipulatives such as puzzles and games, reading books, exploring sensory materials, and participating in art activities. Choice time provides many opportunities for problem solving.

IEP Goals and Objectives Before writing a child's annual individualized education program (IEP), it is important to clearly understand the child's current functioning. Using the data you have collected on a child's previous goals and objectives will give you a starting place when developing a new IEP. These data will indicate which objectives have been successfully met and which should be continued. I also use the Assessment, Evaluation, and Programming System (AEPS) (Bricker, 2002) to determine a child's current functioning in the

adaptive, cognitive, and social domains. Finally, I ask parents to fill out a questionnaire on what they would like to see us work on in the year ahead. Once I have gathered all of this information, I am ready to write a child's IEP. Here is an example of social IEP goal and objectives:

Annual social goal. By 5/28/2009, Lucy will work cooperatively as a member of a group. This will be demonstrated by moving from her current level of initiating conversations, participating in chosen cooperative activities, and not yet reading social cues to independently maintaining conversations, participating in peer chosen activities, and reading social cues of others.

Objectives. By 5/28/2009, during a class session, Lucy will maintain topical conversations with peers for three exchanges during (a) topics of her choosing and (b) topics of a peer's choosing in 3/4 opportunities for 3 consecutive observations.

By 5/28/2009, during unstructured activities, Lucy will independently comply with a peer chosen activity and participate in that activity for 5 minutes in 3/4 opportunities for 3 consecutive observations as measured by monthly classroom data.

By 5/28/2009, during a class session, Lucy will attempt to read and appropriately respond to the social cues of others (a) in pictures or role plays and (b) in naturally occurring opportunities in 3/4 opportunities for 3 consecutive observations as measured by monthly classroom data.

Teaching Strategies My classroom is designed for hands-on learning. Children have access to a wide variety of materials including pretend-play materials, blocks, puzzles, games, books, sensory materials, and art materials. I try to limit the amount of any one item so that my students must work together and practice their social skills during all parts of the school day. Some materials are out of reach so that students have to request the item they want. This encourages students to use and expand on their communication skills.

Naturalistic strategies are extremely useful when teaching children communication skills. I find mand–model and incidental teaching procedures (see Chapter 12) especially effective because they allow the teacher to follow the child's lead and embed instruction into activities that interest the child. For example, Matt loves to build with blocks. As he builds, I'll ask him, "What are you building?", and he responds, "Tower." This is my opportunity to add a little more by saying, "It is a tall tower." Matt smiles and repeats "tall tower," expanding his language.

Collaboration I work with a great team of professionals at my school. Many of my students receive services from a speech and language pathologist (SLP), occupational therapist (OT), and physical therapists (PT). Therapists see my students for a varied amount of time each week depending on each child's IEP.

Therapists either see my students in the classroom or pull them out to a therapy room, depending on each child's objectives and ability to focus in the classroom. I also work with each therapist to ensure that I am providing daily practice on my students' motor and communication goals and supporting the skills that the therapists are teaching our students'. Working collaboratively with the therapists who serve my students is one of the most rewarding things that I do. By coordinating with these professionals, I know that my students have ample amounts of practice on all of their IEP goals and objectives. In addition, I learn new strategies.

Working With Families My preschoolers spend 2 hours and 40 minutes at school 4 days a week, which means that the majority of their time is spent at home or in child care. It is crucial that I understand not only my students' disabilities but also their families' lives and expectations for their child. I use a variety of strategies to communicate with families: weekly newsletters, phone calls, e-mails, and written notes—whatever method is most effective for them. Additionally, I have parent conferences in the fall, and I offer families home visits at any time throughout the school year. I find home visits incredibly beneficial because I learn about the child's home life.

Rewards and Lessons as a Special Educator I find it incredibly gratifying to teach a child with extremely challenging behaviors to express herself effectively and learn how to function appropriately in a classroom setting. It is amazing to watch a student who worried and frustrated me at the beginning of the school year transform into a child who will succeed on entering a general education kindergarten classroom. Lucy is one of those success stories. When she began preschool, Lucy had a very difficult time expressing her emotions appropriately. When other children got close to her or took a toy, she would frequently bite or hit. She seldom followed my directions or complied with school rules, which frequently led to tantrums and aggressive outbursts. Over the course of the school year, Lucy learned to self-regulate, express her emotions appropriately, play with her peers, and use words to solve problems. Next year, Lucy will transition to her neighborhood school for kindergarten, where she will attend a general education classroom with some support from a resource teacher.

Each and every student that I have worked with has had a special gift to share with me. My students have taught me about tenacity and true strength of character. I have learned what it means to be a good friend and how easy it is to see beyond differences. I have learned how to be silly, laugh hard, and have fun with my students. I hope that I have learned as much from my students as I have taught them.

Most children learn a phenomenal amount from the time they are born until they enter school. They grow and develop in orderly, predictable ways, learning to move about their world, communicate, and play. As their ability to manipulate their environment increases, so does their level of independence. Typical rates and patterns of child development contrast sharply with the progress experienced by many children with disabilities. If they are to master the basic skills that most children acquire naturally, many preschoolers with disabilities need carefully planned and implemented early childhood special education services.

Early childhood experts agree that the earlier intervention begins, the better. Child development expert Burton White, who has conducted years of research with typically developing infants and preschoolers at Harvard University's Preschool Project, believes that the period between 8 months and 3 years is critical to cognitive and social development: "to begin to look at a child's educational development when he is 2 years of age is already much too late" (White, 1995, p. 4). If the first years of life are the most important for children without disabilities, they are even more critical for the child with disabilities, who, with each passing month, risks falling even further behind her typically developing age mates. Yet parents concerned about deficits in their child's development used to be told, "Don't worry. Wait and see. She'll probably grow out of it."

It is clear that developmental delays do not just go away with time and that young children who are behind do not simply "catch up." In summarizing the findings of their 20-year follow-up of children with developmental delays who had been identified at age 3 years, Keogh, Bernheimer, and Guthrie (2004) noted:

> The majority of the children did not "outgrow" their delays. As young adults they continued to have problems. Most lived with their families or in group homes, were unemployed or underemployed, and had few friends. . . .
>
> In sum, our findings confirm that signs of developmental delay in the preschool years signal the probability of continuing problems in the early adult years. (pp. 227, 229)

After reading this chapter, complete the pretest for Chapter 14 on the MyEducationLab to assess your initial understanding of chapter content.

The first years of life are critical for children with disabilities, who, with each passing month, risk falling even further behind their typically developing age mates.

Over the past 25 years, the "extraordinary vulnerability of young children at risk for developmental problems . . . as well as those with established disabilities has been recognized" (Guralnick, 1998, p. 319). Today, early childhood special education has become one of the most prominent and growing components in education, and the creation of an effective system of early intervention services has become a national priority.

THE IMPORTANCE OF EARLY INTERVENTION

Defining Early Intervention

In the early childhood and special education literature, the term *early intervention* sometimes refers only to services provided to infants and toddlers from birth through age 2. *Early childhood special education* refers to educational and related services provided to preschoolers ages 3 to 5. **Early intervention** consists of a comprehensive system of therapies, educational, nutritional, child care, and family supports, all designed to reduce the effects of disabilities or prevent the occurrence of learning and developmental problems later in life for children presumed to be at risk for such problems (Smith & Guralnick, 2007). For example:

Carl is a 6-month-old who was born at a gestational age of 26 weeks. After a difficult 4-month hospitalization in the neonatal intensive care unit, he was discharged home. Neurodevelopmental assessment just prior to discharge showed that he had cognitive function at a newborn level and markedly increased tone in his legs. Carl was considered to have significant developmental delays and was referred to the local early intervention program. After a comprehensive, multidisciplinary assessment, he was found to be eligible for services, and a treatment plan (individualized family service plan, or IFSP) was developed. Because both Carl's parents worked outside the home, a physical therapist and early childhood educator came to Carl's child care center once a week to provide early intervention services. Carl's parents arrange their work schedules so that at least one of them could meet with the early intervention professional every other week at the child care center. Together, Carl's parents, educators, and child care workers have come up with creative activities that encourage Carl to develop his motor skills. As a result of these interactions, both parents are feeling increasingly comfortable in caring for Carl and in playing with him at home. (Guralnick & Conlon, 2007, p. 511)

Examining the Effectiveness of Early Intervention

Does early intervention work? If so, what kinds of interventions work best? Hundreds of studies have been conducted in an effort to answer these questions. We'll look at a few of those studies here. First, we'll consider two widely cited examples of what Guralnick (1997) calls first-generation research: studies that try to answer the question "Does early intervention make a difference for children and their families?" Then we'll look at three examples of second-generation research studies designed to find what factors make early intervention more or less effective for particular groups of children.

Skeels and Dye   The earliest and one of the most dramatic demonstrations of the critical importance and potential impact of early intervention was conducted by Skeels and Dye (1939). They found that intensive stimulation, one-to-one attention, and a half-morning kindergarten program with 1- to 2-year-old children who were classified as mentally retarded resulted in IQ gains and eventual independence and success as adults when compared to similar children in the institution who received adequate medical and health services but no individual attention. Although the Skeels and Dye study can be justly criticized for its lack of tight experimental methodology, it challenged the widespread belief at the time that intelligence was fixed and that little could be expected from intervention efforts. This study served as the catalyst for many subsequent investigations into the effects of early intervention.

The Milwaukee Project   The goal of the Milwaukee Project was to reduce the incidence of mental retardation through a program of parent education and infant stimulation for children considered at risk for retarded development because of their mothers' levels of intelligence (IQs below 70) and conditions of poverty (Garber & Heber, 1973; Heber & Garber, 1971; Strickland, 1971). The mothers received training in child care and were taught how to interact with and stimulate their children through play. Beginning before the age of 6 months, the children also participated in an infant stimulation program conducted by trained teachers. By the age of 3 1/2, the experimental children tested an average of 33 IQ points higher than did a control group of children who did not participate in the program. (Play is critically important to children's learning and development. See Teaching & Learning, "Selecting Toys for Young Children With Disabilities" later in this chapter.)

Although the Milwaukee Project was criticized for its research methods (e.g., Page, 1972), this study is sometimes offered as evidence that a program of maternal education and early infant stimulation can reduce the incidence of intellectual disabilities caused by psychosocial disadvantage. **Psychosocial disadvantage** is a combination of social and environmental deprivation early in a child's life, and it is believed to be a major cause of mild mental retardation.

The Abecedarian Project   The Abecedarian Project was designed as an experiment to test whether intellectual disabilities caused by psychosocial disadvantage could be prevented by intensive, early education preschool programs (in conjunction with medical and nutritional supports) beginning shortly after birth and continuing until children enter kindergarten (Martin, Ramey, & Ramey, 1990). Children in the Abecedarian Project received early intervention that was both intensive and long: a full-day preschool program, 5 days per week, 50 weeks per year. Compared with children in a control group who received supplemental medical, nutritional, and social services but no daily early educational intervention services, children in the early intervention group made positive gains in IQ scores by age 3, were 50% less likely to fail a grade, and scored higher on IQ and reading and mathematics achievement tests at age 12.

A related finding was that children of low-IQ mothers benefited most from early intervention. For the mothers with IQs below 70 who were in the control condition, all but one of their children had IQs in the mentally retarded or borderline intelligence range at age 3. In contrast, all of the children in the early intervention group tested within the normal range of intelligence (above 85) by age 3.

> This finding supports the concept of *targeted intervention*, which indicates that primary prevention of childhood disorders is more likely for certain subgroups than for others (Landesman & Ramey, 1989). Because the majority of children with mild and moderate mental retardation come from families with extremely low resources and with parents who have limited intellectual resources themselves, these families are the ones that are most in need of early intervention and are those that benefit the most in terms of outcomes valued by society. (Ramey & Ramey, 1992, p. 338)

Project CARE   Project CARE compared the effectiveness of home-based early intervention in which mothers learned how to provide developmental stimulation for their infants and toddlers with center-based early intervention such as that provided in the Abecedarian Project (Wasik, Ramey, Bryant, & Sparling, 1990). Children who received the full-day, center-based preschool program 5 days per week, supplemented by home visits, showed gains in intellectual functioning almost identical to those found in the Abecedarian Project. A disappointment was that the intellectual functioning of children in the home-based–only treatment group did not improve. Ramey and Ramey (1992) suggest, "One plausible interpretation of these results is that the home-based treatment was not sufficiently intensive, on a day-to-day basis, to produce the same benefits that occur when a more formally organized and monitored center-based program is provided year round" (p. 339).

The Infant Health and Development Program   The Infant Health and Development Program (IHDP) provided early intervention services to infants who were born prematurely and at low birth weight (less than 2,500 grams, or about 5 1/2 pounds), two conditions that place children at risk for developmental delays (Ramey et al., 1992). This large-scale study involved nearly 1,000 children and their families in eight locations throughout the United

Skeels and Dye study and Milwaukee Project

 Council for Exceptional Children   Content Standards for Beginning Teachers of Early Childhood Students: Historical and philosophical foundations of services for young children both with and without exceptional learning needs (EC1K1).

In 1916, John Dewey said, "Children learn by doing." He might just as well have said, "Children learn by playing." Play provides children with natural, repeated opportunities for critical learning. It is the way they explore the world and discover their own capabilities. An infant bats a mobile with her hand, repeats the action, and begins learning about her surroundings. As a toddler, her interactions with play materials teach her to discriminate and compare shapes and sizes and learn concepts such as *cause* and *effect* and *fast* and *slow* (Hughes, Elicker, & Veen, 1995; Malone & Langone, 1999). A preschooler's increasingly complex play develops gross- and fine-motor skills, requires her to communicate and negotiate plans with others, and exposes her to pre-academic math and literacy skills (DiCarlo & Reid, 2004; Morrison, Sainato, BenChaaban, & Endo, 2002; Nelson, McDonnell, Johnston, Crompton, & Nelson, 2007; Widerstrom, 2004).

If play is the work of childhood, then toys are the child's tools. Ideally, play materials, whether store-bought toys or everyday household items such as pots and pans, should provide meaningful, motivating activities that serve as a precursor to more complex learning (Brewer & Kieff, 1996; Carter, 2006; Hamm, Mistrett, & Goetz Ruffino, 2006; Mann, 1996). Not all toys, however, are accessible to children with disabilities.

HOW TO GET STARTED

The National Lekotek Center is a nationwide, non-profit network of play centers, toy lending libraries, and computer loan programs dedicated to making play accessible for children with disabilities and to those living in poverty. Diana Nielander, planning and information officer at Lekotek, recommends keeping the following 10 tips in mind when selecting toys for young children with disabilities:

1. *Multisensory appeal.* Does the toy respond with lights, sounds, or movements? Are there contrasting colors? Does it have scent? texture?

2. *Method of activation.* Will the toy provide a challenge without frustration? What force is required to activate it? What are the number and complexity of steps required?

3. *Adjustability.* Does the toy have adjustable height, sound, volume, speed, and level of difficulty?

4. *Opportunities for success.* Can play be open-ended with no definite right or wrong way?

5. *Child's individual characteristics.* Does the toy provide activities that reflect both developmental and chronological ages? Does it reflect the child's interests?

6. *Self-expression.* Does the toy allow for creativity and choice making? Will it give the child experience with a variety of media?

7. *Potential for interaction.* Will the child be an active participant during use? Will the toy encourage social and language engagement with others?

8. *Safety and durability.* Are the toy and its parts sized appropriately given the child's size and strength? Can it be washed and cleaned? Is it moisture resistant?

9. *Where the toy will be used.* Will the toy be easy to store? Is there space in the home? Can the toy be used in a variety of positions (e.g., by a child lying on his side) or on a wheelchair tray?

10. *Current popularity.* Is it a toy almost any child would like? Does it tie in with popular books, TV programs, or movies?

Information on specific toys can be found in Lekotek's Toy Guide for Differently-Abled Kids!, a free resource published in conjunction with Toys "R" Us®

Play provides children with natural, repeated opportunities for critical learning.

TEACHING & LEARNING

and endorsed by the National Parent Network on Disabilities. The catalog includes pictures and descriptions of more than 100 toys that have been tested with preschoolers with disabilities. Each toy is identified according to its likelihood of promoting growth in 10 developmental or skill areas: auditory, language, visual, tactile, gross motor, fine motor, social skills, self-esteem, creativity, and thinking.

Information about Lekotek and its services to families can be obtained at its website (http://www.lekotek.org). Lekotek also operates a toy resource helpline at (800)366-PLAY, a toll-free service that anyone can use to talk directly to trained play experts who will recommend appropriate toys and play activities for a particular child as well as make referrals to other disability-related resources for families.

Go to the Homework & Exercises section in Chapter 14 of MyEducationLab and complete Homework Exercise 1. As you read the article and answer the accompanying questions, consider how this "toy" helps preschoolers become more independent and prepares them for future academic challenges.

States. Early intervention specialists conducted home visits for newborns through age 3. Because of health problems associated with prematurity and low birth weight, the children did not begin attending the center-based early education program until 12 months of age and continued until age 3. Improvements in intellectual functioning were noted, with babies of comparatively higher birth weight showing increases similar in magnitude to those found in the Abecedarian Project and Project CARE.

The IHDP study found a positive correlation between how much children and their families participated in early intervention and the intellectual development of the children. The percentages of children whose IQ scores fell into the mental retardation range based on tests administered at age 3 for each of the groups were 17% for the control group, 13% for those with low participation, 4% for medium participation, and less than 2% for high participation. The most active participants had an almost ninefold reduction in the incidence of mental retardation compared to the control group.

Together, these three second-generation studies provide strong evidence that children at risk for developmental delays and poor school outcomes respond favorably to systematic early intervention. They also point to two factors that appear highly related to the outcome effectiveness of early intervention: the *intensity of the intervention* and the *level of participation* by the children and their families (Guralnick & Conlon, 2007; Hill, Brooks-Gunn, & Waldfogel, 2003).

Summarizing the Research Base Numerous methodological problems make it difficult to conduct early intervention research in a scientifically sound manner. Among the problems are difficulties in selecting meaningful and reliable outcome measures; the wide disparity among children in the developmental effects of their disabilities; the tremendous variation across early intervention programs in curriculum focus, teaching strategies, length, and intensity; and the ethical concerns of withholding early intervention from some children so that they may form a control group for comparison purposes (Guralnick, 1998, 2005; Hill et al., 2003; Smith, Groen, & Wynn, 2000).

In addition to enhancing the development of infants and toddlers with disabilities, early intervention can help reduce the need for special education and related services after those children reach school age.

Despite these problems, many educators agree with Guralnick's (2005) conclusion that

> the thoughtful implementation of systematic, comprehensive, experientially based early intervention programs ... will enhance the development of young children already exhibiting intellectual delays (of known or unknown etiology) both by altering their developmental trajectories and by preventing secondary complications from occurring. For children at risk of intellectual delays because of a variety of biological and/or environmental conditions, it is expected that these delays can be prevented entirely or their magnitude minimized. (p. 314)

Our national policy makers also believe that early intervention produces positive results for young children with disabilities, those who are at risk for developmental delays, and their families. Citing research and testimony from families, Congress identified the following outcomes for early intervention in the Individuals with Disabilities education Improvement Act of 2004:

(1) to enhance the development of infants and toddlers with disabilities, to minimize their potential for developmental delay, and to recognize the significant brain development that occurs during a child's first 3 years of life;

(2) to reduce the educational costs to our society, including our Nation's schools, by minimizing the need for special education and related services after infants and toddlers with disabilities reach school age;

(3) to maximize the potential for individuals with disabilities to live independently in society;

(4) to enhance the capacity of families to meet the special needs of their infants and toddlers with disabilities; and

(5) to enhance the capacity of State and local agencies and service providers to identify, evaluate, and meet the needs of all children, particularly minority, low-income, inner city, and rural children, and infants and toddlers in foster care. (P.L. 108-446, USC 1431, Sec. 631[a])

IDEA AND EARLY INTERVENTION/EARLY CHILDHOOD SPECIAL EDUCATION

Since 1975, Congress has enacted five bills reauthorizing and amending the original IDEA. The second of those bills, P.L. 99-457, has been called the most important legislation ever enacted for young children with developmental delays (Shonkoff & Meisels, 2000). Before passage of this law, Congress estimated that states served at most about 70% of preschool children with disabilities, and systematic early intervention services for infants and toddlers with disabilities from birth through age 2 were scarce or nonexistent in many states. P.L. 99-457 included a mandatory preschool component for children with disabilities ages 3 to 5 and a voluntary incentive grant program for early intervention services to infants and toddlers and their families.

Early Intervention for Infants and Toddlers

IDEA and early intervention

 Content Standards for Beginning Teachers of Early Childhood Students: Laws and policies that affect young children, families, and programs for young children (EC1K3).

If a state chooses to provide comprehensive early intervention services to infants and toddlers and their families, it can receive federal funds under IDEA's early intervention provisions. Currently, all states are participating; each state receives federal funds under this program based on the number of children birth through age 2 in the state's general population. In 2005–2006, approximately 293,816 infants and toddlers were served nationally.

IDEA mandates early intervention services for any child under 3 years of age who:

(i)   needs early intervention services because of developmental delays, as measured by appropriate diagnostic instruments or procedures, in 1 or more of the areas of cognitive development, physical development, communication development, social or emotional development, or adaptive development; or

(ii) has a diagnosed physical or medical condition that has a high probability of resulting in developmental delay. (P.L. 108-446, 20 USC 1432, Sec. 632[5])

Each state may also, at its discretion, serve at-risk infants and toddlers "who would be at risk of experiencing a substantial developmental delay if early intervention services were not provided" (P.L. 108-446, 20 USC 1432, Sec. 632[1]). Thus, states that receive IDEA funds for early intervention services must serve all infants and toddlers with developmental delays or established risk conditions. Although not required to do so, states may also use IDEA funds to provide early intervention services to infants and toddlers who fall under two types of *documented risk*, biological and environmental.

Definitions of developmental delays and risk conditions

 Content Standards for Beginning Teachers of Early Childhood Students: Laws and policies that affect young children, families, and programs for young children (EC1K3).

- *Developmental delays* are significant delays or atypical patterns of development that make children eligible for early intervention. Each state's definition of developmental delay must be broad enough to include all disability categories covered by IDEA, but children do not need to be classified or labeled according to those categories to receive early intervention services.

- *Established risk conditions* include diagnosed physical or medical conditions that almost always result in developmental delay or disability. Examples of established risk conditions are Down syndrome, fragile X syndrome, fetal alcohol spectrum disorder

(FASD), and other conditions associated with mental retardation, brain or spinal cord damage, sensory impairments, and maternal acquired immune deficiency syndrome (AIDS). (Down syndrome, fragile-X syndrome, and FASD are discussed in Chapter 4.)

- *Biological risk conditions* include pediatric histories or current biological conditions (e.g., significantly premature birth, low birth weight) that result in a greater-than-usual probability of developmental delay or disability.
- *Environmental risk conditions* include factors such as extreme poverty, parental substance abuse, homelessness, abuse or neglect, and parental intellectual impairment, which are associated with higher-than-normal probability of developmental delay.

Individualized Family Services Plan   IDEA requires that early intervention services for infants and toddlers be delivered according to an **individualized family services plan (IFSP)** developed by a multidisciplinary team that includes the child's parents and other family members and must include each of the following eight elements:

1. a statement of the infant's or toddler's present levels of physical development, cognitive development, communication development, social or emotional development, and adaptive development, based on objective criteria;
2. a statement of the family's resources, priorities, and concerns relating to enhancing the development of the family's infant or toddler with a disability;
3. a statement of the measurable results or outcomes expected to be achieved for the infant or toddler and the family, including pre-literacy and language skills, as developmentally appropriate for the child, and the criteria, procedures, and timelines used to determine the degree to which progress toward achieving the results or outcomes is being made and whether modifications or revisions of the outcomes or services are necessary;
4. a statement of the specific early intervention services based on peer-reviewed research, to the extent practicable, necessary to meet the unique needs of the infant or toddler and the family, including the frequency, intensity, and method of delivering services;
5. a statement of the natural environments in which early intervention services will appropriately be provided, including a justification of the extent, if any, to which the services will not be provided in a natural environment;
6. the projected dates for initiation of services and the anticipated length, duration, and frequency of services;
7. the identification of the service coordinator from the profession most immediately relevant to the infant's or toddler's or family's needs (or who is otherwise qualified to carry out all applicable responsibilities under this part) who will be responsible for the implementation of the plan and coordination with other agencies and persons, including transition services; and
8. the steps to be taken to support the transition of the toddler with a disability to preschool or other appropriate services. (P.L. 108-446, 20 USC 1436, Sec. 636[d])

IFSPs differ from IEPs in several important ways (Bruder, 2000). Unlike the IEP, an IFSP does the following:

- Revolves around the family system as the constant and most important factor in the child's life
- Defines the family as being the recipient of early intervention services rather than the child alone
- Focuses on the natural environments in which the child and family live, extending the settings in which services can be provided beyond formal, contrived settings such as preschools to everyday routines in home and community
- Includes interventions and services provided by a variety of health and human service agencies in addition to education

The IFSP must be evaluated once a year and reviewed with the family at 6-month intervals. Recognizing the critical importance of time for the infant with disabilities, IDEA allows for initiation of early intervention services before the IFSP is completed if the parents give their consent. Figure 14.1 shows portions of an IFSP developed with and for the family of a 26-month-old child with disabilities.

IFSP

 Content Standards for Beginning Teachers of Early Childhood Students: Laws and policies that affect young children, families, and programs for young children (EC1K3).

FIGURE 14.1 Portion of an IFSP written with the family of a 26-month-old child with disabilities

INDIVIDUALIZED FAMILY SERVICE PLAN (IFSP) for Children Birth to Three Years   SANTA CLARA COUNTY

Child's name: _Cathy Rae Wright_   Birth Date: _11-15-07_   Age: _26_ months   Sex: _F_

Parent(s)/Guardian(s): _Martha and Gary Wright_   Address: _1414 Coolidge Drive Cupertino_   Zip: _95014_

Home phone: ⁴⁰⁸_398-2461_   Work phone: ⁴⁰⁸_554-2490_ Primary language of the home: _English_   Other languages _____

Date of this IFSP _1/15/09_ Projected periodic review _7/15/09_ Projected annual review _1/15/10_ Tentative IFSP exit _11/15/11_
(at 6 months or before)

Service Coordinator Name	Agency	Phone	Date Appointed	Date Ended
Sandy Drohman	Regional Center	408-461-2192	12/10/08	/ /

Family's strengths and preferred resources (With the family, identify the family strengths and the resources they might find helpful in addressing family concerns and priorities.)   Mr. and Mrs. Wright are well-educated and constantly seek additional information about Cathy's condition. They are anxious to help Cathy in any way possible. Mrs. Wright's family is very supportive. They provide child care for Cathy's older brother.

Because of Cathy's tendency to be medically fragile, Mr. and Mrs. Wright prefer a home based early intervention program. They appreciate receiving written materials to help them understand how to work with Cathy. Mrs. Wright wants to be home when the home visitor comes so she can learn from her.

Family's concerns and priorities   (With the family, identify major areas of concerns for the child with special needs and the family as a whole.)   Mr. and Mrs. Wright are very concerned about Cathy's delays in walking, using her fingers to pick up things, and in talking with other children. They also worry about her small size. Cathy is their second child and was born at 24 weeks gestation. Mr. and Mrs. Wright would like to have more information on the issues of prematurity and they would like to find an appropriate support group for themselves.

CHILD'S STRENGTHS AND PRESENT LEVELS OF DEVELOPMENT

With the family, identify what the child can do and what the child is learning to do. Include family and professional observations in each of the following areas:

PHYSICAL *Based on parent report and HELP Strands

Health   _Cathy is said by her parents to be healthy but is very petite. Her parents are working with a nutritionist to help Cathy gain weight._

Vision   _Cathy has had corrective surgery for strabismus._

Hearing   _She has had numerous ear infections and currently has tubes in her ears._

Gross Motor (large movement)   _Cathy stands on tiptoes, runs on toes, makes sharp turns around corners when running, walks upstairs with one hand held_

Fine Motor (small movement)   _Cathy grasps crayon adaptively and points with index finger; imitates horizontal strokes, builds 6 block tower, turns pages one at a time; has trouble picking up small objects._

COGNITIVE (responsiveness to environments, problem-solving)   _Cathy finds hidden object; attempts and succeeds in activating mechanical toy; demonstrates use of objects appropriate for age_

COMMUNICATION (language and speech)

RECEPTIVE (understanding)   _Cathy points to body parts when asked; obeys two-part commands._

EXPRESSIVE (making sounds, talking)   _Cathy names 8 pictures, interacts with peers using only gestures; attempts to sing songs with words_

SOCIAL/EMOTIONAL (how relates to others)   _Cathy expresses affection, is beginning to obey and respect simple rules, tends to be physically aggressive_

ADAPTIVE/SELF-HELP (sleeping, eating, dressing, toileting, etc.)   _Cathy can put on socks and shoes, verbalizes need to use the toilet, but is not potty trained, feeds self_

DIAGNOSIS (if known) _____

FIGURE 14.1 *continued*

INDIVIDUALIZED FAMILY SERVICE PLAN (IFSP) for Children Birth to Three Years   SANTA CLARA COUNTY

Child's name: ___Cathy Rae Wright___

> ### IFSP OUTCOMES
> With the family, identify the goals they would like to work on in the next six months.
> These should be directly related to the family's priorities and concerns as stated on page one.

OUTCOME: __Cathy will increase her attempts to vocally communicate in order to make her needs known and to__
positively interact with others.

Strategy or activity	Service Type (Individual = I Group = G) Location	Frequency of sessions / Length of each session	Start Date	End Date (anticipated)	Responsible Agency/ Group Including payment arrangements (if any)
Strategy or activity to achieve the outcome (Who will do what and when will they do it?) AIM Infant Educator will model for Mr. and Mrs. Wright techniques to solicit Cathy's vocalization efforts. **Criteria** (How will we know if we are making progress?) Increased vocalization will be observed by parents and infant educator.	I — Home-based infant program	1 hour each week	1-23-09	11-10-09	AIM (funded by SARC) Family
Strategy or activity to achieve the outcome (Who will do what and when will they do it?) Mrs. Wright will take Cathy to play with neighborhood children and will invite children to her home. She will encourage play and vocalization. **Criteria** (How will we know if we are making progress?) Mrs. Wright will observe and note extent of interaction.	G — Home and in the neighborhood	once each week for at least 30 minutes	2-1-09	ongoing	Mrs. Wright
Strategy or activity to achieve the outcome (Who will do what and when will they do it?) Cathy will be assessed by a speech pathologist by 2-15-03 and followed on an as needed basis. **Criteria** (How will we know if we are making progress?) A follow-up report will be submitted.	I — Regional Center Speech and Language Clinic	1 hour play-based assessment	2-1-09	as needed	Sandy Drohman will make arrange-ments (funded by SARC)

OUTCOME: __Mr. and Mrs. Wright will join Parents Helping Parents in order to receive peer parent support and__
learn more about Cathy's condition.

Strategy or activity	Location	Frequency / Length	Start Date	End Date	Responsible Agency/Group
Strategy or activity to achieve the outcome (Who will do what and when will they do it?) Sandy Drohman will provide all referral information to Mr. and Mrs. Wright and will accompany them to their first meeting if they desire. **Criteria** (How will we know if we are making progress?) Mr. and Mrs. Wright will find satisfaction in increased support and knowledge.	G — Parents Helping Parents	(up to parents' discretion)			Sandy Drohman Mr. and Mrs. Wright Parents Helping Parents
Strategy or activity to achieve the outcome (Who will do what and when will they do it?) AIM Infant Educator will assist Mr. and Mrs. Wright in obtaining additional information about Cathy's condition. **Criteria** (How will we know if we are making progress?) Mr. and Mrs. Wright will express satisfaction over the assistance received in becoming more informed.	I — Home	ongoing	2-1-09	11-10-09	AIM Infant Educator

Source: Adapted from Cook, R. E., Klein, M. D., & Tessier, A. (2008). *Adapting early childhood curricula for children in inclusive settings* (7th ed, pp. 115–120). Reproduced by permission of Pearson Education Inc., Upper Saddle River, NJ.

IDEA requires states to provide special education to all children with disabilities ages 3 to 5.

Special Education for Preschoolers

IDEA requires states to provide special education services to all children with disabilities ages 3 to 5. The regulations governing these programs are similar to those for school-age children, with the following exceptions (Odom et al., 2000):

- Preschool children do not have to be diagnosed with and reported under one of the traditional disability categories (e.g., mental retardation, emotional disturbance, orthopedic impairments) to receive services. They may instead receive services under the eligibility category *developmental delay* (Division for Early Childhood, 2005). This provision of IDEA also allows, but does not require, states to serve at-risk students from ages 3 through 9.
- Each state, at its discretion, may also serve children (from ages 3 through 9) who are

  a. experiencing developmental delays as defined by the State and as measured by appropriate diagnostic instruments and procedures in 1 or more of the following areas: physical development, cognitive development, communication development, social or emotional development, or adaptive development; and

  b. who, by reason thereof, need special education and related services. (P.L. 108-446, 20 USC 1401, Sec. 602[3][B][I])

- IEPs must include a section with suggestions and information for parents.
- Local education agencies may elect to use a variety of service-delivery options (home-based, center-based, or combination programs), and the length of the school day and year may vary.
- Although preschool special education programs must be administered by the state education agency, services from other agencies may be contracted to meet the requirement of a full range of services. For example, many preschoolers with disabilities are served in community-based Head Start programs.

SCREENING, IDENTIFICATION, AND ASSESSMENT

Assessment and evaluation in early childhood education are conducted for at least four different purposes, with specific evaluation tools for each (Elliott, Huai, & Roach, 2007; Greenwood, Carta, & Walker, 2005; Jones, 2004; McLean, Wolery, & Bailey, 2004; Neisworth & Bagnato, 2005; Ostrosky & Horn, 2001):

Screening. Quick, easy-to-administer tests to identify children who may have a disability and who should receive further testing

Diagnosis. In-depth, comprehensive assessment of all major areas of development to determine a child's eligibility for early intervention or special education services

Program planning. Curriculum-based, criterion-referenced assessments to determine a child's current skill level, identify IFSP/IEP objectives, and plan intervention activities

Evaluation. Curriculum-based, criterion-referenced measures to determine progress on IFSP/IEP objectives and evaluate the program's effectiveness

Screening Tools

Before young children and their families can be served, they must be identified. Some children's disabilities are so significant that no test is needed. As a general rule, the more severe a disability, the earlier it is detected. In the delivery room, medical staff can identify certain physical disabilities and health impairments, such as microcephaly and cleft palate, as well as most instances of Down syndrome. Within the first few weeks, other physical conditions such as paralysis, seizures, or rapidly increasing head size can signal possible disabilities. But most children who experience developmental delays are not identifiable by obvious physical characteristics or behavioral patterns, especially at very young ages. That is where screening tools come into play.

The Apgar Scale The **Apgar scale**, which measures the degree of *asphyxia* (oxygen deprivation) an infant experiences during birth, is administered to virtually all babies born in U.S. hospitals. The test administrator—nurse, nurse anesthetist, or pediatrician—evaluates

FIGURE 14.2	The Apgar evaluation scale			60 sec.	5 min.
Heart rate	Absent	(0)			
	Less than 100	(1)			
	100 to 140	(2)		1	2
Respiratory effort	Apneic	(0)			
	Shallow, irregular	(1)			
	Lusty cry and breathing	(2)		1	1
Response to catheter stimulation	No response	(0)			
	Grimace	(1)			
	Cough or sneeze	(2)		1	2
Muscle tone	Flaccid	(0)			
	Some flexion of extremities	(1)			
	Flexion resisting extension	(2)		1	2
Color	Pale, blue	(0)			
	Body pink, extremities blue	(1)			
	Pink all over	(2)		0	1
	Total			4	8

the newborn twice on five physiological measures: heart rate, respiratory effort, response to stimulation, muscle tone, and skin color. The child is given a score of 0, 1, or 2 on each measure according to the criteria described on the scoring form (see Figure 14.2).

The first administration of the test, which is conducted 60 seconds after birth, measures how the baby fared during the birth process. If the newborn receives a low score on the first test, the delivery room staff takes immediate resuscitation action. The scale is given again 5 minutes after birth. At that point a total score of 0 to 3 (out of a possible 10) indicates severe asphyxia, 4 to 6 moderate asphyxia, and 7 to 10 mild asphyxia. Some stress is assumed on all births, and the 5-minute score measures the success of any resuscitation efforts. A 5-minute score of 6 or less indicates follow-up assessment to determine what is causing the problem and what interventions may be needed.

The Apgar has been shown to identify high-risk infants—those with a greater-than-normal chance of developing later problems. Research has shown that oxygen deprivation at birth contributes to neurological impairment, and the 5-minute Apgar score correlates well with eventual neurological outcomes.

Newborn Blood Test Screening Some form of newborn screening is mandated in all states, but the components of the newborn screen vary from state to state. Phenylketonuria (PKU) is screened in all states. It causes severe mental retardation, which can be easily prevented if the condition is detected before symptoms develop and the child is treated with a special diet. Testing is also done for *hypothyroidism*, which can likewise lead to mental retardation if not detected early. Affected individuals are treated with supplemental thyroid hormone.

The American College of Medical Genetics (2004) submitted a report to the federal Health Resources and Services Administration identifying national standards for state newborn screening programs. The report identified a core of 29 conditions that screening should target, plus an additional 24 "secondary" conditions for which test results should be reported. States may also screen for conditions beyond the 53. As of August 2007, 14 states and the District of Columbia had enacted and fully implemented laws or rules requiring the universal screening for the 29 core conditions of all newborns.

Screening tests

 Council for Exceptional Children

Content Standards for Beginning Teachers—Common Core: Screening, prereferral, referral, and classification procedures (CC8K3).

Screening tests require a few small drops of blood collected from each newborn, usually taken in the hospital 24 to 48 hours after birth. This is done by a heel stick and spotting a few small drops of blood on a paper card, which is then sent for laboratory analysis that can test for as many as 30 congenital conditions or diseases that can lead to physical and health problems, sensory impairments, and/or developmental delays. Other common testing includes (but is not limited to) biotinidase deficiency, congenital adrenal hyperplasia, congenital hypothyroidism, cystic fibrosis, sickle cell diseases, maple syrup urine disease, and galactosemia and hemoglobinopathy (diseases of the red blood cells). More information is available from the National Newborn Screening and Genetics Resource Center (http://genes-r-us.uthscsa.edu/).

Developmental Screening Tests One of the most widely used screening tools for developmental delays is the Denver II (Frankenburg & Dodds, 1990). It can be used with children from 2 weeks to 6 years of age, using both testing–observation and a parent report format. The Denver II assesses 125 skills arranged in four developmental areas: gross motor, fine motor–adaptive, language, and personal-social. Each test item is represented on the scoring form by a bar showing at what ages 25%, 50%, 75%, and 90% of typically developing children can perform that skill. The child is allowed up to three trials per item. A child's performance on each item is scored as "pass" or "fail" and then interpreted as representing "advanced," "OK," "caution," or "delayed" performance by comparing the child's performance with those of the same age in the standardized population. Physicians most often administer the Denver II, and the test form was designed to fit the schedule of well-baby visits recommended by the American Academy of Pediatrics.

No one observes a child more often, more closely, and with more interest than his parents. Mothers' estimates of their preschool children's levels of development often correlate highly with those that professionals produce by using standardized scales, and parental involvement in screening has been found to reduce the number of misclassifications (Henderson & Meisels, 1994). Recognizing this fact, early childhood specialists have developed numerous screening tools for parent use. One such tool is the Ages and Stages Questionnaire (ASQ) (Bricker & Squires, 1999; see also Squires, Bricker, & Twombly, 2002). The ASQ includes 11 questionnaires that the parents complete when the child is 4, 6, 8, 12, 16, 18, 20, 24, 30, 36, and 48 months old. Each questionnaire consists of 30 items covering 5 areas of development: gross motor, fine motor, communication, personal-social, and adaptive. Many of the items include illustrations to help the parents evaluate their child's behavior.

Diagnostic Tools

When the results of a screening test raise suspicion that a disability or developmental delay may be present, the child is referred for diagnostic testing. The specific diagnostic tests to be used depend on the suspected delay or disability (Bondurant-Utz, 2002; McLean et al., 2004). Tests that seek to determine if a child is experiencing a developmental delay usually measure performance in five major developmental areas or domains:

- *Motor development.* The ability to move one's body and manipulate objects within the environment provides a critical foundation for all types of learning. Motor development involves improvements in general strength, flexibility, endurance, and eye–hand coordination and includes gross-motor or large-muscle movement and mobility (e.g., walking, running, throwing) and small-muscle, fine-motor control (e.g., to pick up a toy, write, tie a shoe).
- *Cognitive development.* Children use cognitive skills when they attend to stimuli, perform pre-academic skills such as sorting or counting, remember things they have done in the past, plan and make decisions about what they will do in the future, integrate newly learned information with previously learned knowledge and skills, solve problems, and generate novel ideas.
- *Communication and language development.* Communication involves the transmission of messages; information about needs, feelings, knowledge, desires; and so forth. Children use communication and language skills when they receive information from others, share information with other individuals, and use language to mediate their actions and effectively control the environment. This domain encompasses all forms of communication

Assessment of developmental domains

 Council for Exceptional Children Content Standards for Beginning Teachers—Common Core: Use and limitations of assessment instruments (CC8K4).

development, including a child's ability to respond nonverbally with gestures, smiles, or actions and the acquisition of spoken language—sounds, words, phrases, sentences, and so on.

- *Social and emotional development.* Children who have developed competence in social skills share toys and take turns, cooperate with others, and resolve conflicts. Children should feel good about themselves and know how to express their emotions and feelings.
- *Adaptive development.* As young children develop self-care and adaptive skills such as dressing/undressing, eating, toileting, tooth brushing, and hand washing, their ability to function independently across multiple environments increases, which provides and enhances opportunities for additional kinds of learning.

Generally, these five areas are broken down into specific, observable tasks and sequenced developmentally—that is, in the order in which most children learn them. Sometimes each task is tied to a specific age at which the majority of typically developing children can perform it. This arrangement allows the examiner to note significant delays or gaps as well as other unusual patterns in a child's development. These developmental domains are not mutually exclusive; considerable overlap exists between domains as well as across skills within a specific domain. Most activities of children in everyday settings involve skills from multiple domains. For example, playing marbles typically requires a child to use skills from the motor, cognitive, communication, and social domains.

Two widely used tests for diagnosing developmental delays are the Battelle Developmental Inventory (BDI-2) (Newborg, 2006) and the Bayley Scales of Infant Development—III (Bayley, 2005). The Battelle can be administered to children with and without disabilities, from birth through age 7 years, 11 months; and it has adapted testing procedures for use with children with different disabilities. The Bayley III evaluates development in cognition, language, social-emotional motor, and adaptive behavior in infants and toddlers from 1 to 42 months.

The Bayley Scales can be used to diagnose developmental delays in children from 2 months to 30 months.

Program Planning and Evaluation Tools

A growing number of early intervention programs have moved away from assessments based entirely on developmental milestones to curriculum-based assessment (CBA). CBA tools enable early childhood teams to (a) identify a child's current levels of functioning, (b) select IFSP/IEP goals and objectives, (c) determine the most appropriate interventions, and (d) evaluate the child's progress. Each item in a CBA relates directly to a skill in the program's curriculum, thereby providing a direct link among testing, teaching, and progress evaluation (Bagnato, Neisworth, & Munson, 1997).

One thoroughly developed and empirically tested CBA tool is the Assessment, Evaluation, and Programming System: For Infants and Young Children (AEPS) (Bricker, 2002). The AEPS is divided into two levels: one for infants and toddlers from birth to 3 years, one for children from 3 to 6 years. The AEPS is divided into six domains: fine motor, gross motor, adaptive, cognitive, social-communication, and social. Each domain is divided into strands that group related behaviors and skills considered essential for infants and young children to function independently. The AEPS tests can be used in conjunction with the associated AEPS curricula (Bricker & Waddell, 2002a, 2002b) or with other similar early childhood curricula such as the Carolina Curriculum for Preschoolers with Special Needs (Johnson-Martin, Attermeier, & Hacker, 2004a, 2004b).

Curriculum-based assessment in ECSE

 Council for Exceptional Children

Content Standards for Beginning Teachers of Early Childhood Students: Select, adapt, and use specialized formal and informal assessment for infants, young children, and their families (EC8S2).

CURRICULUM AND INSTRUCTION IN EARLY CHILDHOOD SPECIAL EDUCATION

Curriculum and Program Goals

Most professionals in early childhood special education agree that programs should be designed and evaluated with respect to the following outcomes or goals (Noonan & McCormick,

2006; Odom & Wolery, 2003; Pretti-Frontczak & Bricker, 2004; Sandall, Hemmeter, Smith, & McLean, 2005; Wolery & Sainato, 1993, 1996):

1. *Support families in achieving their own goals.* Although the child with special needs is undoubtedly the focal point, a major function of early intervention is helping families achieve the goals most important to them. Professionals realize that families function as a system and that separating the child from the system results in limited and fragmented outcomes (Turnbull, Turnbull, Erwin, & Soodak, 2006).

2. *Promote child engagement, independence, and mastery.* The goal of early childhood special education is to minimize the extent to which children depend on others and differ from their age mates. Intervention strategies should "promote active engagement (participation), initiative (choice making, self-directed behavior), autonomy (individuality and self-sufficiency) and age-appropriate abilities in many normalized contexts and situations" (Wolery & Sainato, 1993, p. 53). In situations in which independence is not safe, possible, or practical, support and assistance should be provided to enable the child to participate as much as she can. "For example, in getting ready for a bath, a 3-year-old child should not be expected to adjust the water to the appropriate temperature, but could be expected to help get ready for the bath (e.g., getting bath toys, assisting in taking off clothing)" (p. 53).

3. *Promote development in all important domains.* Successful early intervention programs help children make progress in each of the key areas of development already described. Because young children with disabilities are already behind their typically developing age mates, early childhood special educators should use only instructional strategies that lead to rapid learning (Wolery & Sainato, 1993, 1996). Strategies that produce rapid learning help the child with disabilities by saving time for other goals and moving closer to typical developmental levels.

4. *Build and support social competence.* Social skills, such as learning to get along with others and making friends, are among the most important skills anyone can learn. Most children learn such skills naturally, but many children with disabilities do not learn to interact effectively and properly simply by playing with others (Nelson, 2007; Sainato, Jung, Salmon, & Axe, 2008).

5. *Facilitate the generalized use of skills.* Most typically developing children effortlessly generalize what they learn in one situation to another place and time. But many children with disabilities have extreme difficulty remembering and using previously learned skills in other situations. "Early interventionists should not be satisfied if children learn new skills; they should only be satisfied if children use those skills when and wherever they are appropriate" (Wolery & Sainato, 1993, p. 54).

6. *Prepare and assist children for normalized life experiences with their families, in school, and in their communities.* Early intervention should be characterized by the principle of normalization; that is, services should be provided in settings that are as much like the typical settings in which young children without disabilities play and learn as is possible (Cook, Klein, & Tessier, 2008). A large and growing body of published research literature demonstrates the benefits of integrated early intervention to children with disabilities and their families and suggests strategies for effective inclusion programs (Grisham-Brown, Hemmeter, & Pretti-Frontczak, 2005; Guralnick, 2001; Odom, 2000; Purcell, Horn, & Palmer, 2007; Sandall & Schwartz, 2002).

7. *Help children and their families make smooth transitions.* A transition occurs when a child and his family move from one early intervention program or service delivery mode to another. For example, program transitions typically occur at age 3 when a child with disabilities moves from a home-based program to an early childhood special

Early childhood preschool programs should promote children's development in all important domains.

education classroom and again at age 5 when the child moves from a preschool classroom to a general education kindergarten classroom. Preparing and assisting children and their families for smooth transitions ensures continuity of services, minimizes disruptions to the family system, and is another important way for promoting the success of young children with disabilities as they move into more normalized environments (Brandes, Ormsbee, & Haring, 2007; Hanson et al., 2000; La Paro, Pianta, & Cox, 2000). Cooperative planning and supports for transitions must come from professionals in both the sending and the receiving programs (Fowler, Donegan, Lueke, Hadden, & Phillips, 2000; Rous & Hallam, 2006).

8. *Prevent or minimize the development of future problems or disabilities.* Early intervention programs that serve at-risk infants and toddlers are designed with prevention as their primary goal.

Developmentally Appropriate Practice

Virtually all early childhood educators—whether they work with typically developing children or those with disabilities—believe that learning environments, teaching practices, and other components of programs that serve young children should be based on what is typically expected of and experienced by children of different ages and developmental stages (Cook et al., 2008; Jalongo & Isenberg, 2008; Morrison, 2007). This philosophy and the guidelines for practice based on it are called **developmentally appropriate practice (DAP)** and are described in widely disseminated materials published by the National Association for the Education of Young Children (NAEYC) (Bredekamp & Copple, 1997; Copple & Bredekamp, 2006). The DAP guidelines were created partially in response to concerns that too many early childhood programs were focusing on academic preparedness and not providing young children with enough opportunities to engage in the less structured play and other activities that typify early childhood. "For example, some people considered it developmentally appropriate for 4- and 5-year-olds to do an hour of seatwork, toddlers to sit in high chairs with dittos, or babies in infant seats to 'do' the calendar" (Bredekamp, 1993, p. 261). (To learn how puppets can help preschoolers with disabilities learn language skills, see Teaching & Learning, "Puppets as Teachers in the Early Childhood Classroom," later in this chapter.)

DAP recommends the following guidelines for early childhood education programs:

- Teachers should integrate activities across developmental domains.
- Teachers should identify children's interests and progress through teacher observation.
- Teachers should arrange the environment to facilitate children's active exploration and interaction.
- Learning activities and materials should be real, concrete, and relevant to the young child's life.
- Teachers should provide a wide range of interesting activities.
- The complexity and challenges of activities should increase as the children understand the skills involved.

While most early childhood special educators view the DAP guidelines as a foundation on which to provide early intervention for children with special needs, most also recognize that the guidelines alone may be inadequate to ensure the individualized, specially designed instruction that such children need (Cook et al., 2008; Noonan & McCormick, 2006; Odom & Wolery, 2003):

1. Many children with special needs have delays or disabilities that make them dependent on others.

2. Many children with special needs have delays or disabilities that keep them from learning well on their own.

3. Many children with special needs develop more slowly than their typically developing peers do.

4. Many children with special needs have disabilities that interfere with how they interact; as a result, they often acquire additional disabilities.

Developmentally appropriate practice

 Content Standards for Beginning Teachers of Early Childhood Students: Plan and implement developmentally and individually appropriate curriculum (EC7S2) (also CC7K2).

Although Bricker, Pretti-Frontczak, and McComas (1998) find "a basic congruence and compatibility" (p. 213) between DAP and the focused activity-based intervention used by many early childhood special educators, they note two significant differences. First, special educators must target specific goals and objectives to meet the unique developmental needs of individual children, while DAP is concerned with more general developmental goals (e.g., improve language skills or self-esteem) that apply to a broad range of children. Second, early childhood special educators use comprehensive and repeated assessments to determine learning objectives and monitor progress according to stated performance criteria. DAP, by contrast, does not require assessment or evaluation tools.

Selecting IFSP/IEP Goals and Objectives

The breadth of developmental domains and the activities that young children typically engage in provide an almost unlimited number of possibilities for instructional objectives. Consensus among many early childhood special educators is that potential IFSP/IEP goals and objectives for infants and young children should be evaluated according to five quality indicators (e.g., Notari-Syverson & Shuster, 1995; Pretti-Frontczak & Bricker, 2000):

1. *Functionality*. A functional skill (a) increases the child's ability to interact with people and objects in her daily environment and (b) may have to be performed by someone else if the child cannot do it.
2. *Generality*. In this context, a skill has generality if it (a) represents a general concept as opposed to a particular task; (b) can be adapted and modified to meet the child's disability; and (c) can be used across different settings, with various materials, and with different people.
3. *Instructional context*. The skill should be easily integrated into the child's daily routines and taught in a meaningful way that represents naturalistic use of the skill.
4. *Measurability*. A skill is measurable if its performance or a product produced by its performance can be seen, felt, and/or heard. Measurable skills can be counted or timed and enable objective determination of learning progress.
5. *Hierarchical relation between long-range goals and short-term objectives*. Short-term objectives should be hierarchically related; the achievement of short-term objectives should contribute directly to the attainment of long-term goals.

Figure 14.3 shows 11 questions that teachers can use to assess potential IFSP/IEP objectives according to those five criteria.

Instructional Adaptations and Modifications

Providing specialized instruction in an attempt to "remediate delays caused by the child's disabilities and prevent any secondary disabilities from developing" is the cornerstone of what early childhood special educators do (Sandall, Schwartz, & Joesph, 2000, p. 3). Like their colleagues who work with elementary and secondary students with disabilities, teachers who work with young children with disabilities must be skilled in using a wide range of instructional strategies and tactics.

Modifications and adaptations to the physical environment, materials, and activities themselves are often sufficient to support successful participation and learning. Such modifications range from subtle, virtually invisible supports (e.g., changing the duration or sequence of activities, using a child's preferences as a conversation topic while playing) to more obvious interventions and support (e.g., providing the child with an adaptive device, teaching peers to prompt and reward participation) (Sandall, Joseph, et al., 2000). The challenge is determining how much support a child needs for a given skill in a specific context.

> Too much support may result in children becoming over reliant on adult support. Too little support will result in children being unsuccessful, and may lead to decreasing rates of participation and increasing rates of challenging behaviors. (Sandall et al., 2000, p. 4)

Embedded Learning Opportunities   One effective method for incorporating specialized instruction into typical preschool activities for children with disabilities is called embedded learning opportunities. The concept of *embedded learning opportunities* is based on the

IFSP/IEP goals and objectives

 Council for Exceptional Children   Content Standards for Beginning Teachers of Early Childhood Students: Plan and implement developmentally and individually appropriate curriculum (EC7S2) (also CC7K1).

Modifying and adapting the physical environment

 Council for Exceptional Children   Content Standards for Beginning Teachers of Early Childhood Students: Design, implement, and evaluate environments to ensure developmental and functional appropriateness (EC5S3) (also CC5K1).

FUNCTIONALITY	GENERALITY	INSTRUCTIONAL CONTEXT	MEASURABILITY	HIERARCHICAL RELATION BETWEEN LONG-RANGE GOAL AND SHORT-TERM OBJECTIVE
1. Will the skill increase the child's ability to interact with people and objects within the daily environment? The child needs to perform the skill in all or most of the environments in which he or she interacts. *Skill:* Places object into container. *Opportunities: Home*—Places sweater in drawer, cookie in paper bag; *School*—Places lunch box in cubbyhole, trash in trash bin; *Community*—Places milk carton in grocery cart, rocks and soil in flower pot. 2. Will the skill have to be performed by someone else if the child cannot do it? The skill is a behavior or event that is critical for completion of daily routines. *Skill:* Looks for object in usual location. *Opportunities:* Finds coat on coat rack, gets food from cupboard.	3. Does the skill represent a general concept or class of responses? The skill emphasizes a generic process, rather than a particular instance. *Skill:* Fits objects into defined spaces. *Opportunities: Home*—Puts mail in mailbox, places crayon in box, puts cutlery into sorter. 4. Can the skill be adapted or modified for a variety of disabling conditions? The child's sensory impairment should interfere as little as possible with the performance. *Skill:* Correctly activates simple toy. *Opportunities: Motor impairments*—Activates light, easy-to-move toys (e.g., balls, rocking horse, toys on wheels, roly-poly toys). *Visual impairments:* Activates large, bright, noise-making toys (e.g., bells, drums, large rattles). 5. Can the skill be generalized across a variety of settings, materials, and/or people? The child can perform the skill with interesting materials and in meaningful situations. *Skill:* Manipulates two small objects simultaneously. *Opportunities: Home*—Builds with small interlocking blocks, threads laces on shoes. *School*—Sharpens pencil with pencil sharpener. *Community*—Takes coin out of small wallet.	6. Can the skill be taught in a way that reflects the manner in which the skill will be used in daily environments? The skill can occur in a naturalistic manner. *Skill:* Uses object to obtain another object. *Opportunities:* Uses fork to obtain food, broom to rake toy; steps on stool to reach toy on shelf. 7. Can the skill be elicited easily by the teacher/parent within classroom/home activities? The skill can be initiated easily by the child as part of daily routines. *Skill:* Stacks objects. *Opportunities:* Stacks books, cups/plates, wooden logs.	8. Can the skill be seen and/or heard? Different observers must be able to identify the same behavior. *Measurable skill:* Gains attention and refers to object, person, and/or event. *Nonmeasurable skill:* Experiences a sense of self-importance. 9. Can the skill be directly counted (e.g., by frequency, duration, distance measures)? The skill represents a well-defined behavior or activity. *Measurable skill:* Grasps pea-sized object. *Nonmeasurable skill:* Has mobility in all fingers. 10. Does the skill contain or lend itself to determina-tion of performance criteria? The extent and/or degree of accuracy of the skill can be evaluated. *Measurable skill:* Follows one-step directions with contextual cues. *Nonmeasurable skill:* Will increase receptive language skills.	11. Is the short-term objec-tive a developmental subskill or step thought to be critical to the achievement of the long-range goal? *Appropriate:* Short-Term Objective—Releases object with each hand. Long-Range Goal—Places and releases object balanced on top of another object. *Inappropriate:* 1. The Short-Term Objective is a restatement of the same skill as the Long-Range Goal, with the addition of an instructional prompt (e.g., Short-Term Objective—Activates mechanical toy with physical prompt. Long-Range Goal—Independently activates mechanical toy) or a quantitative limitation to the extent of the skill (e.g., Short-Term Objective—Stacks 5 1-inch blocks; Long-Range-Goal—Stacks 10 1-inch blocks). 2. The Short-Term Ob-jective is not conceptually or functionally related to the Long-Range Goal (e.g., Short-Term Objective—Releases object voluntarily; Long-Range Goal—Pokes with index finger).

Source: Adapted from Notari-Syverson, A. R., & Shuster, S. L. (1995). Putting real-life skills into IEP/IFSPs for infants and young children. *Teaching Exceptional Children, 272*(2), 31. Used by permission.

Using Puppets in the Early Childhood Classroom

BY MARY D. SALMON, STACIE MCCONNELL, DIANE M. SAINATO, AND REBECCA MORRISON

Early childhood educators promote active engagement, independence, and mastery across developmental domains for all children by providing a rich variety of experiences, materials, and ideas. Puppets can be effective tools for presenting activities that are engaging, interesting, and developmentally appropriate for the wide range of abilities of young children in early childhood settings (Salmon & Sainato, 2005).

Most young children are delighted by puppets. Their vivid colors, interesting textures, and larger-than-life expressions encourage curiosity and heighten attention levels among typically developing children as well as children with a range of developmental disabilities. A puppet's physical characteristics, overstated smiles or frowns, and motivational value make it a valuable prop for use with many young children. With this knowledge, we can put puppets to instructional use in inclusive early childhood classrooms.

USING PUPPETS DURING CIRCLE TIME

Circle time is important in the preschool day because it introduces activities and provides a time for review. Introducing new concepts and skills, while reinforcing previously learned material, requires upbeat, appropriately paced, and highly interactive instructional strategies. One way to incorporate these strategies and add dimension and excitement to circle time is by embedding the actions of a variety of puppets into songs, stories, or games.

Puppets can help children express their feelings and learn to empathize with others.

USING PUPPETS DURING TRANSITION TIMES

Like circle time, transition times in the preschool classroom can be chaotic, noisy, disruptive, or difficult for some young children. A puppet may help the teacher signal transitions between classroom activities, making them smoother and less stressful for students and teacher alike.

USING PUPPETS TO ENHANCE SOCIAL AND EMOTIONAL SKILLS

Young children frequently have difficulty expressing their emotions and interpreting the feelings of others. When paired with social stories and role-play activities, the exaggerated facial features of many character puppets make them especially well suited to modeling appropriate emotions. The actions of the puppets' large hands and feet may encourage an unwilling youngster to imitate their movement. Puppets can also help children match their own experiences with language, teach them to be an attentive audience, as well as help them develop more elaborate sociodramatic and symbolic play.

FINDING RESOURCES

A wide variety of puppets are available from many sources to stimulate the interest and active engagement of young students. Entertaining, engaging puppets such as glove or stick puppets, finger puppets, and sock puppets are quickly adapted for uncomplicated use by younger students or students with special needs.

HOW TO GET STARTED

Circle Time

- *Calendar helper.* The teacher or a child can be the puppeteer, leading the class during calendar time.
- *Weather helper.* Dress a large, full-bodied puppet in child-sized clothing to reinforce weather concepts. Spice up his wardrobe with a variety of hats, sunglasses, and mittens as well as attire appropriate for all types of weather.
- *Rule bunny.* Teaching classroom rules is an important and ongoing process. To increase impact, designate a puppet to teach these common procedures: "Rule Bunny says, 'Play nicely with your friends,' or 'Put materials away neatly.'"
- *Other activities.* Puppets can read stories, sing songs, play "Simon Says," and model a variety of motor skills.

Transition Time

- *Transition prompter.* To signal transition times, a puppet can shake a bell or ring a chime to indicate when it is time to clean up or move to the next activity.

- *Attention getter*. Capture the attention of a busy (and noisy) group of youngsters, using a puppet to lead the way to the next activity.
- *Transition helper*. Classroom helpers can take turns using a puppet to ready the class for special activities. Line leaders can guide the class to the library, gym, music, or art class, using a puppet to improve group attention.
- *Clean-up time*. Puppets can model appropriate clean-up behaviors such as placing blocks in a bin or putting away art materials.

Sociodramatic Play and Social Skills

- Assume different roles, such as police officer or firefighter, with simple hand puppets and a few accessories (e.g., hats, badges).
- Puppets representing familiar adults can be made by printing photos of faces onto transfer paper using a computer and an inkjet printer. Iron the pictures onto simple hand puppets made from durable fabric, and embellish the body with fabric markers or paint.
- Many characters from favorite books are available as puppets. Children can act out their favorite story and become any character they wish.
- Combine favorite stories with representative puppets to teach appropriate social behaviors. For example, use *Rainbow Fish* by Marcus Pfister to teach sharing.

Dealing With Emotions

- Puppets can make emotions "larger than life." Use them to demonstrate appropriate emotional responses while watching or acting out short skits.
- A child may be more inclined to express her feelings through a puppet. Teachers can also talk through a puppet to discuss appropriate classroom expectations and behavior.
- Help children solve simple problems by using puppets in role-play activities.

Mary Salmon coordinates the REACH program for children with autism spectrum disorders with the Columbus, Ohio, City Schools. An avid puppet collector, she was an early childhood special education teacher for more than 15 years. Stacie McConnell teaches in an early childhood special needs preschool classroom in Reynoldsberg, Ohio. Diane Sainato is a member of the special education faculty at The Ohio State University, where she directs the program in early childhood special education and conducts research on young children's independent engagement, social, and communicative behavior. Rebecca Morrison is the founder and director of Oakstone Academy and The Children's Center for Development Enrichment.

To learn more about this strategy, go to the Building Teaching Skills section in Chapter 14 of MyEducationLab. As you complete the activities, think about the benefits of using puppets with scripted stories to increase language skills.

premise that although quality early childhood programs offer opportunities for learning across the day, children with disabilities often need guidance and support to learn from those opportunities (Horn, Lieber, Li, Sandall, & Schwartz, 2000; McBride & Schwartz, 2003; Tate, Thompson, & McKerchar, 2005). Therefore, teachers should look and plan for ways to embed brief, systematic instructional interactions that focus on a child's IEP objectives in the context of naturally occurring classroom activities. Figure 14.4 shows a teacher's plan for embedding learning opportunities into four different activity centers to support an IEP objective in the fine-motor domain for a 4-year-old boy with cerebral palsy. For an annotated bibliography of research and teacher resources on naturalistic teaching methods featuring embedded learning opportunities and activities-based interventions for young children with and without disabilities, see Pretti-Frontczak, Barr, Macy, and Carter (2003).

Embedding learning opportunities to support young children's development of communication and language skills is an especially important teaching responsibility for an early childhood special educator. Most children learn to speak and communicate effectively with little or no formal teaching. But children with disabilities often do not acquire language in the spontaneous manner of their peers without disabilities. And as children with disabilities slip further and further behind their peers, their language deficits make social and academic development even more difficult. Preschoolers with disabilities need repeated opportunities for language use and development (Goldstein, 2002; Justice, 2004). In addition to providing systematic, explicit instruction of language skills to children in individual and small-group learning activities, teachers should embed meaningful opportunities for children to communicate throughout the day. Even transitions between activities can provide opportunities for learning (Wolery, Anthony, & Heckathorn, 1998).

Effective early childhood special educators are experts at embedding learning opportunities in the context of naturally occurring classroom activities.

FIGURE 14.4 Example of a plan for embedding learning opportunities into four different activity centers to support a child's IEP objective in the fine-motor domain

---

Embedded Learning Opportunities at a Glance for: <u>Alex</u>

Objective: <u>Will pour liquid or other fluid material (e.g., sand, beans) from one</u>
<u>container to another with no spillage.</u>

Date: <u>8/14</u>   Activity: <u>Center Time</u>
Material: <u>All centers available</u>

Modifications Needed:	What are you going to do?
—Water table: add a variety of containers with spouts (e.g., plastic measuring cups, teapot, play pitcher)	Move through center modeling use of these new activities/materials. Provide physical guidance for Alex
—Snack Center: Add to Alex's workjob pouring juice for other children	**What are you going to say?** Use natural cues— Let's see you do it. Can you do it and get all the beans in the pot?
—Art Center: Place tempera paint in small pitcher, have children pour into individual bowls	**How will you respond?** Praise, acknowledgment, feedback on accuracy Engagement in activity created
—Housekeeping: Add beans to kitchen cabinet in a small pitcher for pouring into pots, cups or plates	**What materials do you need?** Need to be prepared with clean-up supplies for spills—(see under modifications)

Source: "Supporting Young Children's IEP Goals in Inclusive Settings Through Embedded Learning Opportunities" by E. Horn, J. Lieber, S. Li, S. Sandall, & I. Schwartz, 2000. *Topics in Early Childhood Education, 20,* 208–223. Copyright 2000 by the Hammill Institute on Disability. Reprinted with permission.

---

*Embedded learning
opportunities*

Content Standards for Beginning Teachers—Common Core: Effective management of teaching and learning (CC5K3) (also EC7S2).

A creative and effective example of embedding language learning opportunities into mealtimes was reported by Robinson Spohn, Timko, and Sainato (1999). Each child was seated at the table in front of a placemat showing a picture of a food item, a cartoon character, an animal, and something silly (e.g., a cat wearing glasses and reading a book) (see Figure 14.5). There were 12 different placemats, and each child sat before a different one each day. At first, the teacher played "The Talking Game" with the children while they ate breakfast in the school lunchroom. The children took turns picking an index card from a shuffled set of cards. Each card had a photo of one of the children in the group. After a child selected a card, the teacher prompted him to say something to the child pictured on the card. If the children could not think of anything to say, they were prompted to talk about one of the pictures on their placemat. After several weeks, the teacher no longer used the index cards and stopped prompting the children's interactions. The children continued

FIGURE 14.5

A placemat used to encourage preschoolers with developmental disabilities to communicate with one another during mealtime

Source: Courtesy of Diane M. Sainato, The Ohio State University.

talking with one another during mealtimes at rates higher than they had before, often using the pictures on their placemats as conversation starters.

Preschool Activity Schedules

Teachers in preschool programs for children with disabilities face the challenge of organizing the program day into a schedule that meets each child's individual learning needs and provides children with many opportunities to explore the environment and communicate with others throughout the day. The schedule should include a balance of child-initiated and planned activities, large- and small-group activities, active and quiet times, and indoor and outdoor activities; it should allow easy transition from activity to activity (Cook et al., 2008). In short, the schedule should provide a framework for maximizing children's opportunities to develop new skills and practice what they have learned while remaining manageable and flexible. In addition, how activities are scheduled and organized has considerable effect on the frequency and type of interaction that occurs between children with and without disabilities (Harris & Handleman, 2000) and on the extent to which children with disabilities benefit from instructional activities.

Pretti-Frontczak and Bricker (2004) describe an activity-planning and scheduling process that combines children's individual IFSP/IEP objectives with group activity plans. Figure 14.6 shows how children's targeted learning goals can be integrated into daily classroom activities.

A Supportive Physical Environment

The physical arrangement of the classroom must support the planned activities. Designing an effective preschool classroom requires thoughtful planning to ensure that play areas and needed materials are accessible to and safe for all students, boundaries between areas minimize distractions, and, most important, the environment makes children want to explore and play. Suggestions for setting up a preschool classroom include the following (Cook et al., 2008; Johnson-Martin et al., 2004b; Morrison, 2008; Pretti-Frontczak & Bricker 2004):

- Organize the classroom into a number of different well-defined areas to accommodate different kinds of activities (e.g., quiet play, messy play, dramatic play, constructive play, active play).

- Locate quiet activities together, away from avenues of traffic, and loud activities together.

- Equip each area with abundant, appropriate materials that are desirable to children.

Preschool activity schedules

 Content Standards for Beginning Teachers—Common Core: Demands of learning environments (CC5K1) (also EC5S3).

Physical arrangement of preschool classroom

 Content Standards for Beginning Teachers of Early Childhood Students: Design, implement, and evaluate environments to ensure developmental and functional appropriateness (EC5S93).

FIGURE 14.6 — Example of embedding learning opportunities related to children's targeted goals and objectives into a schedule of daily classroom activities

Children's names: Serina, Tianna, and Patrice   Date schedule will be used: First quarter (Sept. to Nov.)

Team members: Classroom staff and therapists

Daily classroom activities

Children and target goals	Arrival	Free play	Circle activities	Snack	Centers
Serina 1. Manipulates objects	Ask Serina to unzip her coat.	Encourage Serina to play with blocks, puzzles, and art materials.		Provide a spoon or a fork to eat with, foods to prepare, and a knife for spreading or cutting.	Place objects to manipulate in writing center (pencils, scissors) and science center (tweezers, microscope with slides).
2. Uses one and two words to request, inform, and greet	Model saying "Good morning." Ask Serina to greet peers.		Sing the Good Morning song. Ask Serina to request a song. Ask Serina to tell the class what color shoes she has on (including black, pink, gray as targets).	Ask Serina what she is having for lunch. Label words related to snack/eating that end with target consonants (milk, nut, fruit, last).	Model greeting peers as they enter the different centers. Ask Serina what she is doing. Ask Serina where she wants to play or what toys she wants.
3. Uses one object to represent another		Model how to use different size blocks as food or a shoe for a doll's car.			Use a small dust pan or a ladle as a shovel in the discovery table. Use sticks as paintbrushes in the art area.
Tianna 1. Expresses likes and dislikes			Present song options for Tianna to choose.		Ask Tianna which activities she likes and does not like.
2. Sorts like objects		Ask Tianna to put all of the books together and all of the puppets together.		Encourage Tianna to put all cups on one table and all snack food on another.	
3. Uses spoon to feed self				Provide food requiring spoon use.	
Patrice 1. Uses toilet	Ask Patrice if she has to use the bathroom.			Ask Patrice if she has to use the bathroom.	
2. Follows routine directions	Remind Patrice to hang up her coat and put away her lunch.	Ask Patrice to put the blocks away.		Prompt Patrice to take one and pass to her friends.	

Source: Reprinted from Pretti-Frontczak, K., & Bricker, D. (2004). *An activity-based approach to early intervention* (3rd ed., p. 134). Baltimore: Brookes. Used by permission.

- Locate materials where children can easily retrieve them and do not depend on adults.
- Have an open area, perhaps a large rug, to conduct large-group activities such as circle time and story reading.
- Label or color code all storage areas so that aides and volunteers can easily find needed materials.
- Arrange equipment and group areas so that students can move easily from one activity to another. Apply pictures or color codes to various work areas.
- Provide lockers or cubbies for students so they know where to find their belongings. Again, add picture cues to help students identify their lockers.

SERVICE-DELIVERY ALTERNATIVES FOR EARLY INTERVENTION

IDEA requires that early intervention services be provided in natural environments to the greatest extent possible. Natural environments are the same home, school, and community settings that typically developing children inhabit (Noonan & McCormick, 2006). The setting for early intervention varies, depending on the age of the child and the special supports she and her family need.

Hospitals are frequently the setting for early intervention services for infants and newborns with significant disabilities. Most early childhood special education services, however, are provided in the child's home, in a center- or school-based facility, or in a combination of both settings. Young children with mild developmental delays are often served by itinerant special education teachers in general education preschool settings (Dinnebeil, McInerney, Roth, & Ramaswamy, 2001; Sadler, 2003).

Hospital-Based Programs

Increasingly, early intervention services are being provided to hospitalized newborns and their families. Low-birth-weight and other high-risk newborns who require specialized health care are placed in neonatal intensive care units (NICUs). Many NICUs include a variety of professionals, such as neonatologists who provide medical care for infants with special needs, nurses who provide ongoing medical assistance, social workers or psychologists who help parents and families with emotional and financial concerns, and infant education specialists who promote interactions between parents and infants.

Home-Based Programs

A home-based program depends heavily on the support of families. The parents typically assume primary responsibility as caregivers and teachers for their child with disabilities. They are usually supported by an early intervention specialist who visits the home regularly to model teaching procedures or other interventions, acts as a consultant, evaluates the success of intervention, and regularly assesses the child's progress. Home visitors (or home teachers or home advisors, as they are often called) in some programs are specially trained paraprofessionals. They may visit as frequently as several times a week but probably no less than a few times a month. They sometimes carry the results of their in-home evaluations back to other professionals, who may recommend changes in the program.

The Portage Project, one of the best known and most widely replicated home-based programs, was begun in 1969 by a consortium of 23 school districts in south-central Wisconsin (The Portage Project, 2007). A project teacher typically visits the home one day each week to review the child's progress during the previous week, describe activities for the upcoming week, demonstrate to the parents how to carry out activities with the child, observe parents and children interacting, offer suggestions and advice as needed, summarize where the program stands, and indicate what records parents should keep during the next week. The Portage Project has produced its own assessment materials, curriculum guides, and teaching activities. The original *The New Portage Guide to Early Education* was revised twice and translated by early childhood experts in over 30 countries. In 2003 a third revision, *The New Portage Guide: Birth to Six*, was published, based on 450 behaviors sequenced developmentally and classified into self-help, cognition, socialization, language, and motor skills. To learn more about The Portage Project, go to www.portageproject.org.

Differences between home-based, center-based, and combined programs

 Council for Exceptional Children   Content Standards for Beginning Teachers—Common Core: Family systems and the role of families in supporting development (CC2K4) (also CC5K1).

Home-based early intervention programs have several advantages:

- The home is the child's natural environment, and a parent can often give more time and attention to the child than even the most adequately staffed center or school.
- Other family members, such as siblings and grandparents, have more opportunity to interact with the child during instruction and socially. These significant others can play an important role in the child's growth and development.
- Home learning activities and materials are more likely to be natural and appropriate.
- Parents who are actively involved in helping their child learn and develop clearly have an advantage over parents who feel guilt, frustration, or defeat at their seeming inability to help their child.
- Home-based programs can be less costly to operate.

Home-based programs, however, can have disadvantages:

- Because home-based programs place so much responsibility on parents, they are not effective with all families. Not all parents are able or willing to spend the time required to teach their children, and some who try are not effective teachers.
- A large and growing number of young children do not reside in the traditional two-parent family—especially the many thousands of children with teenage mothers who are single, uneducated, and poor. Many of these infants and preschoolers are at risk for developmental delays because of the impoverished conditions in which they live. It is unlikely that a parent struggling with the realities of day-to-day survival will be able to meet the added demands of involvement in a home-based early intervention program (Turnbull et al., 2006).
- Because the parent—usually the mother—is the primary service provider, children in home-based programs may not receive as wide a range of services as they would in a center-based program, where they can be seen by a variety of professionals. (Note, however, that the services of professionals such as physical therapists, occupational therapists, and speech therapists are sometimes provided in the home.)
- The child may not receive sufficient opportunity for social interaction with peers.

Center-Based Programs

Center-based programs provide early intervention services in a special educational setting outside the home. The setting may be part of a hospital complex, a special day care center, or a preschool. Some children may attend a specially designed developmental center or training center that offers a wide range of services for children with varying types and degrees of disabilities. These centers offer the combined services of many professionals and paraprofessionals, often from several different fields.

Center-based programs encourage social interaction among children, and many integrate children with disabilities and typically developing children in day care or preschool classes (Winter, 2007). Some children attend a center each weekday for all or most of the day; others may come less frequently, although most centers expect to see each child at least once a week. Parents are sometimes given roles as classroom aides or encouraged to act as their child's primary teacher. A few programs allow parents to spend time with other professionals or take training while their child is somewhere else in the center. Virtually all effective programs for young children with disabilities recognize the critical need to involve parents, and they welcome parents in every aspect of the program.

Center-based programs generally offer three advantages that are difficult to build into home-based efforts:

- Increased opportunity exists for a team of specialists from different fields—education, physical and occupational therapy, speech and language pathology, medicine, and others—to observe each child and cooperate in intervention and continued assessment. The intensive instruction and related services that can be provided in a center-based program are especially important for children with severe disabilities.

To learn more about effectively promoting language skills and social interaction among preschoolers with and without disabilities, go to the Homework & Exercises section in Chapter 14 of MyEducationLab and complete Homework Exercise 3.

- The opportunity for interaction with typically developing peers makes center programs especially effective for some children.
- Most parents involved in center programs feel some relief at the support they get from the professionals who work with their child and from other parents with children at the same center.

Disadvantages of a center-based program include the expense of transportation, the cost and maintenance of the center itself, and the possibility of less parent involvement than in home-based programs.

Combined Home–Center Programs

Many early intervention programs combine center-based activities and home visitation. Few center programs take children for more than a few hours a day or more than 5 days per week. But because young children with disabilities require more intervention than a few hours a day, many programs combine the intensive help of a variety of professionals in a center with the continuous attention and sensitive care of parents at home. Intervention that carries over from center to home clearly offers many of the advantages of the two types of programs and negates some of their disadvantages.

LifeSpan Circle Schools in Charlotte, North Carolina, offer a combination home- and center-based early intervention program for infants and toddlers with severe/profound disabilities. The program is based on the social reciprocity model, which views the child's behavior as affecting the parent, whose behavior in turn affects the behavior of the child—hence the "circle" in the program's name. Nonresponsiveness, nonvocal behavior, irritability, lack of imitation responses, and the need for special health care routines (e.g., tube feeding, suctioning) all present special challenges to infant–parent interactions; behaviors associated with these problems are often viewed negatively. The program attempts to identify and increase the frequency of alternative positive behaviors that will cause parents to want to continue their interactions with their child (Calhoun & Kuczera, 1996; Calhoun, Rose, Hanft, & Sturkey, 1991). The center-based component of classroom instruction occurs from 9:00 A.M. to 1:00 P.M. throughout the year. The home-based/family-services component entails monthly home visits; the visits include family-focused assessment and planning, demonstrations of instructional techniques, and provision of information and other support. Between regularly scheduled home visits, ongoing individualized consultation and collaboration with parents and families are available as needed.

Families: Most Important of All

The success of efforts to prevent disabilities in children and to identify, assess, and intervene with children who have special needs as early as possible requires the training, experience, and cooperation of a wide range of professionals. Current best-practice guidelines for early childhood services call for a transdisciplinary approach to the delivery of related services in which parents and professionals work together in assessing needs, developing the IFSP or IEP, providing services, and evaluating outcomes (Horn, Ostrosky, & Jones, 2004; Kochhar-Bryant, 2008).

Of all the people needed to make early intervention work, parents and families are the most important. Given enough information and support, parents can help prevent many risks and causes of disabilities—before pregnancy, before birth, and certainly before a child has gone months or years without help. Given the chance, parents can take an active role in determining their children's educational needs and goals. And given some guidance, training, and support, many parents can teach their children at home and even at school.

LifeSpan Circle Schools in Charlotte, North Carolina, teach parents to identify and increase the frequency of positive behaviors by their infants such as smiling or imitating.

It is no wonder, then, that all successful intervention programs for young children with disabilities take great care to involve parents (Harris & Handleman, 2000; Howard et al., 2005). Parents are the most frequent and constant observers of their children's behavior. They usually know better than anyone else what their children need, and they can help educators set realistic goals. They can report on events in the home that outsiders might never see—for instance, how a child responds to other family members. They can monitor and report on their children's progress at home, beyond the more controlled environment of the early intervention center or preschool. In short, parents can contribute to their children's programs at every stage—assessment, planning, classroom activities, and evaluation. Many parents even work in preschool classrooms as teacher aides, volunteers, or other staff members.

But in our efforts to involve parents, we must recognize that while professionals come and go, parents and families are in it for the long haul. In their focus to help young children attain critical developmental gains, it is easy for early childhood professionals to overlook that parents are just beginning a lifetime of commitment and responsibility.

As Hutinger, Marshall, and McCarten (1983) aptly reminded us more than 25 years ago, we must not forget that early childhood is supposed to be a fun, happy time for children and for the adults who are fortunate enough to work with them.

> Part of our mission as professionals in the field of early childhood special education is to possess an art of enjoyment ourselves and to help instill it in the young children and families with whom we work.
>
> Early childhood comes but once in a lifetime. . . . Let's make it count!

TIPS for Beginning Teachers

EARLY CHILDHOOD SPECIAL EDUCATION
by Donelle Tyler

STRUCTURE, PREDICTABILITY, AND ROUTINES ARE CRUCIAL FOR PRESCHOOLERS

- *Create a consistent schedule, and post it so that children can predict what comes next.* Use a combination of words and pictures so that your schedule is easily understandable by all children.

- *Some children may need a smaller version of the classroom schedule to carry with them throughout the school day.* For children who struggle with transitions, this additional support can make them a lot easier. Practice makes perfect, and this is true about preschool routines too.

- *Teach, re-teach, and practice classroom expectations until they become routine for your students.* During the first couple of weeks, my students practice a variety of routines including how to walk in the hallways, how to sit at circle, and how to wash their hands.

COMMUNICATION IS EVERYWHERE

Young children communicate their wants and needs in a variety of ways—some more appropriate than others. As special educators, it is our job to teach children effective ways to communicate with their families, peers, and teachers:

- *Pick communication strategies that will be effective for the student and easily understood by others.* A student who has limited mobility may not be able pick up and exchange picture symbols but can be taught to touch a switch or use a voice-output device to communicate.

- *Expand on the language of your students who are just learning to talk.* Model simple language with age-appropriate concepts and vocabulary. Encourage and reinforce children for using longer utterances.

- *View challenging behaviors as communication.* Take time to identify why the challenging behavior is occurring. What happens right before the challenging behavior, and what happens after the behavior occurs? Once you understand the function of communication behind the behavior, you can teach your student a replacement behavior that serves the same communicative purpose.

LISTEN TO YOUR STUDENTS' FAMILIES

Families are the greatest source of information *about* the students you work with. They can provide you with valuable information about your student's abilities, likes and dislikes, and skills at home.

- *Actively listen to the families' concerns, hopes, and goals for their children.*
- *Ask questions* and take time to genuinely understand what skills are important for a student to learn to interact better at home and at school.
- *Make communication with your families as easy as possible.* Offer to communicate with families in a wide variety of ways (newsletters, phone calls, e-mail, home visits, and parent–teacher conferences).

DON'T BE AFRAID TO ASK FOR HELP

I am very lucky to work in a school with five other special education teachers and many speech language pathologists, occupational therapists, and physical therapists. I have found these professionals to be my greatest resource, especially when I am struggling to figure out an instructional or behavioral strategy.

- *Use the resources around you.* Never feel embarrassed because you aren't familiar with an acronym or a piece of special equipment that one of your students uses.
- *When you are struggling with a student, ask a colleague to come in to your classroom and observe.* Sometimes that second pair of eyes will see something that you have missed.
- *If you are the only special education teacher in your school, connect with a teacher from a different building and use that person as your resource.*

KEY TERMS AND CONCEPTS

Apgar scale, p. 544
developmentally appropriate practice (DAP), p. 549
early intervention, p. 536

individualized family services plan (IFSP), p. 541
psychosocial disadvantage, p. 537

SUMMARY

The Importance of Early Intervention

- Early intervention consists of educational, nutritional, child care, and family supports designed to reduce the effects of disabilities or prevent the occurrence of developmental problems later in life for children at risk for such problems.
- Research has documented that early intervention can provide both intermediate and long-term benefits for young children with disabilities and those at risk for developmental delay. Benefits of early intervention include
  - Gains in physical development, cognitive development, language and speech development, social competence, and self-help skills
  - Prevention of secondary disabilities
  - Reduction of family stress
  - Reduced need for special education services or placement during the school year
  - Savings to society of the costs of additional educational and social services that would be needed later without early intervention
  - Reduced likelihood of social dependence in adulthood
  - Increased effectiveness of early intervention when it begins as early in life as possible and is intensive and long-lasting

IDEA and Early Childhood Special Education

- States that receive IDEA funds for early intervention services must serve all infants and toddlers birth to age 3 with developmental delays or established risk conditions. At their discretion, states may serve infants and toddlers who are at risk for acquiring disabilities because of certain biological or environmental risk conditions.
- Early intervention services for infants and toddlers are family-centered, transdisciplinary, and described by IFSPs.
- IDEA requires states to provide special education services (via IEPs) to all preschool children with disabilities, ages 3 through 5.
- Preschool children do not have to be identified and reported under disability categories to receive services.

Screening, Identification, and Assessment

- Four major types of assessment purposes/tools are used in early childhood special education:
  - Screening involves quick, easy-to-administer tests to identify children who may have a disability and who should receive further testing.
  - Diagnosis requires in-depth, comprehensive assessment of all major areas of development to determine a child's eligibility for early intervention or special education services.
  - Program planning uses curriculum-based, criterion-referenced assessments to determine a child's current skill level, identify IFSP/IEP objectives, and plan intervention activities.
  - Evaluation uses curriculum-based, criterion-referenced measures to determine progress on IFSP/IEP objectives and evaluate a program's effects.
- Many early intervention programs are moving away from assessments based entirely on developmental milestones and are incorporating curriculum-based assessment, in which each item relates directly to a skill included in the program's curriculum. This provides a direct link among testing, teaching, and program evaluation.

Curriculum and Instruction in Early Childhood Special Education

- Early intervention and education programs for children with special needs should be designed and evaluated according to these outcomes or goals:
  - Support families in achieving their own goals
  - Promote child engagement, independence, and mastery
  - Promote development in all important domains
  - Build and support social competence
  - Facilitate the generalized use of skills
  - Prepare for and assist children with normalized life experiences in their families, schools, and communities
  - Help children and their families make smooth transitions
  - Prevent or minimize the development of future problems or disabilities
- Developmentally appropriate practices provide a foundation or context from which to build individualized programs of support and instruction for children with special needs.
- IEP/IFSP objectives for infants and young children should be evaluated according to their functionality, generality, instructional context, measurability, and relation between short- and long-range goals.
- Embedded learning opportunities are brief, systematic instructional interactions that focus on a child's IEP objectives in the context of naturally occurring classroom activities. They are an effective method for incorporating specialized instruction into typical preschool activities.
- A preschool activity schedule should maximize children's opportunities to develop new skills and practice what they have learned previously while remaining manageable and flexible.
- How activities are scheduled and organized affects the interaction between children with and without disabilities.

- Suggestions for setting up a preschool classroom include
  - Organize the classroom into different, well-defined areas to accommodate different kinds of activities.
  - Locate quiet activities together, away from avenues of traffic, and locate loud activities together.
  - Equip each area with appropriate and desirable materials.
  - Locate materials where children can retrieve them without help from adults.
  - Have an open area to conduct large-group activities.
  - Label or color code all storage areas.
  - Arrange equipment and group areas so that students can move easily from one activity to another.
  - Provide lockers or cubbies for students.

Service-Delivery Alternatives for Early Intervention

- In hospital-based programs, early intervention services are provided to low-birth-weight and other high-risk newborns in neonatal intensive care units (NICUs).
- In home-based programs, a child's parents act as the primary teachers, with regular training and guidance from a teacher or specially trained paraprofessional who visits the home.
- In center-based programs, a child comes to the center for instruction, although the parents are usually involved. Center programs allow a team of specialists to work with the child and enable the child to meet and interact with other children.
- Many programs offer the advantages of both models by combining home visits with center-based programming.
- Parents and families are the most important people in an early intervention program. They can act as advocates, participate in educational planning, observe their children's behavior, help set realistic goals, work in the classroom, and teach their children at home.

 Now go to MyEducationLab at www.myeducationlab.com, and take the pretest to assess your initial comprehension of chapter content. Once you have taken the pretest, use your individualized Study Plan for Chapter 14 to enhance your understanding of the concepts discussed in the chapter. Finally, take the posttest to assess your comprehension of Chapter 14 content.

Transitioning to Adulthood

- Why should postschool outcomes drive educational programming for secondary students with disabilities?
- What are the most important factors in determining the success of an individualized transition plan?
- How can teachers help elementary students with disabilities prepare for successful employment as adults?
- Why are self-determination skills so important for the success of students with disabilities in postsecondary education?
- How do the philosophy and principles of supported living differ from those associated with traditional residential placement services?
- How can teachers help school-age children with disabilities achieve satisfying recreation and leisure as adults?
- Should quality of life for adults with disabilities be the ultimate outcome measure for special education? Why or why not?

FEATURED TEACHER

DAN KILLIAN
Community-Based Transition Program • Metropolitan Nashville Public Schools • Nashville, Tennessee

Dan Killian

Education—Teaching Credentials—Experience
- B.A., accounting, St. Ambrose University, 1985
- M.Ed., special education, Vanderbilt University, 1993
- Tennessee teacher certification: special education, comprehensive K–12; administration
- 14 years' teaching experience, 7 years as a special education transition teacher

Current Teaching Position and Students I teach one of five community-based transition classes operated by the Metro Nashville Public Schools. My "classroom" is in an office building owned by a local university, given to us free of charge. This year I have nine students ranging in age from 19 to 21, all of whom have mild-to-moderate mental retardation. Additionally, one student has multiple disabilities and is in a wheelchair, and two others have cerebral palsy. All nine of the students have already attended 4 years of high school (a prerequisite for this program) and attend this optional program until

they "age out" of the school system at the age of 22. Our primary focus is to provide the students with a variety of job-training experiences in integrated settings, as well as taking concrete steps for what will happen when they must leave the program. The students spend about half of each school day involved in supervised job training in the community with me or with an educational assistant. We spend the rest of the school day in our community classroom, working on activities centered around each student's functional living individualized education program (IEP) goals.

Activities to Help Students Transition to Adult Life
Here is a general summary of the day-to-day activities we do with the students to help them in their transition from school to adult life:
- Daily job-training visits to community work sites to work on employability skills
- Friday outings into community to purchase own lunch
- Regular instruction in building the students' money skills
- Regular instruction in building their survival word vocabulary

- Strengthening students' computer skills through use of vocational and educational software, including basic word processing (typing) skills
- Regular planning meetings with the student, parents/caregivers, and adult service providers/agencies to discuss and plan for postschool desired outcomes

Transition/IEP Goals Each student's IEP includes a Transition Plan that details the postschool goals and outcomes and transition services that the student will need to help him reach his goals. For example, an important part of every Transition Plan is to identify the adult service providers who should be contacted. Transition-related IEP goals are generally written in the broad areas of employability skills, interpersonal-communication skills, and functional living skills. Here are examples of goals and instructional objectives in two of these areas:

Goal: By the end of the school year, Amy will have increased her employability skills (i.e., following directions, working cooperatively, and identifying unacceptable work performance) by exhibiting these behaviors at an 80% success rate or better.

Instructional Objectives:

1. At the job site, Amy will follow the verbal directions of the teacher or educational assistant on 8 of 10 requests.
2. When instructed to do an activity with a fellow student, Amy will work cooperatively with peer(s) by sharing materials, etc. on 8 of 10 requests.
3. At the job-training site, Amy will discriminate between acceptable and unacceptable work performance by verbally indicating the need to correct/redo unacceptable work.

Goal: By the end of the school year, Meg will exhibit socially appropriate and effective communication in a variety of speaking situations.

Instructional Objectives:

1. When working on the job site, Meg will ask necessary questions and/or state her needs at the appropriate times (e.g., to request more materials or restroom break or to clarify teacher instructions) on 8 of 10 observations.
2. At the job site, Meg will extend an appropriate greeting at least once during each job-training trip into the community.
3. Meg will maintain eye contact when talking to others, when observed on 9 of 10 occasions.

Importance of Communication With Families
Frequent communication with parents is important for all special education teachers, but it's absolutely critical for those who are helping prepare students for the transition to adult life. An important part of my job is to help parents and caregivers understand how important *their* role is in helping their child make the transition from high school. Adult service providers/agencies don't come looking for students with disabilities after they leave school—they, the parents/caregivers, must become active participants in understanding what options are available. I get much satisfaction in assisting them in any way I can to learn about their options. Regular communication with families via telephone, e-mail, and face-to-face meetings is a vital part of my job.

Two Success Stories Patti is a young adult with mental retardation who exited my program this past May. Throughout her 2 years in my classroom, Patti worked on goals such as consistently following directions on a job site, increasing her rate of production, and exhibiting appropriate social skills when around others. She was a real joy to work with but was somewhat challenging in the beginning. She worked hard at all of her IEP goals during her stay in our program, and I'm happy to say that life is looking good for her! She is living at home, but she has learned how to access public transportation. I recently learned that a local health club had hired her part time and was instructing her in how to use a time clock in preparation for her employment with them. Additionally, Patti continues to swim for the Special Olympics, a leisure activity that she has enjoyed for many years.

A few years ago, 21-year-old Hannah joined my transition class, having recently moved in from out of state. Hannah was set to age-out of the school system but had never "graduated" from high school. An important part of her Transition Plan was for her to officially graduate from high school. I was able to work with the school system to get her a special education diploma to give her at the end of the school year. In May, her parents had a big graduation party for her at their home, and in front of a houseful of her family and friends, I was there to present her with her official high school diploma. Seemingly everyone I met at her home that day said they had heard about me, and many complimented me on the work I'd done with Hannah. Before that day, I had no idea that I had such a positive impact on her. That will always be an unforgettable day!

Why I Like Being an Educator Some people, like me, become teachers after having pursued a career in an unrelated field. Before entering the education profession, I worked for 6 years as a Certified Public Accountant. Throughout that time, I felt something was missing; being a CPA wasn't completely fulfilling for me. Early experiences working with children with disabilities led me to make an abrupt change in career paths to pursue what would hopefully be a more fulfilling career in special education. I'm happy to say that I've never looked back! Special education provides me with a sense of fulfillment that could never have been matched in my former profession, so I always encourage and support anyone contemplating a career change into education. I like being around people who need my help; young adults with disabilities are such a great population to work with, always so open and willing to accept help. What a great fit it's been for me. Though the work is often exhausting, I head for home at the end of most days with what a colleague and I used to refer to as "a *good* tired."

What does it mean to become an adult? Ferguson and Ferguson (2006) suggest that adulthood is expressed through autonomy, membership, and change. Adults express autonomy by self-sufficiency (e.g., having the financial and emotional resources to take care of themselves), self-determination, and completeness (a sense of having "arrived"). Adults experience and enjoy membership in the form of connectedness with the community, citizenship activities, and affiliations. Adulthood is characterized by change rather than stasis (e.g., moving to a new community, going back to school, taking a new job, watching old friends move away, and making new friends). Becoming an adult can be tough work for anyone.

However it is conceptualized, transition from high school to adulthood, with its increased privileges and responsibilities, is especially challenging for youth with disabilities. Skill deficits, limited opportunities created by low expectations or discrimination, and the absence of needed supports are just some of the obstacles to successful transition for many youth with disabilities.

We begin our discussion of transition by looking at the results of several studies that focus on what is perhaps the most important question of all regarding "the ultimate outcome measure for the process of special education" (Ferguson & Ferguson, 2006, p. 621): What do students with disabilities do after they leave school?

After reading this chapter, complete the pretest for Chapter 15 on MyEducationLab to assess your initial understanding of chapter content.

HOW DO FORMER SPECIAL EDUCATION STUDENTS FARE AS ADULTS?

What happens to students with disabilities when they leave high school and enter the adult world? Do graduates of special education programs find work? Where do they live? How do the lives of adults with disabilities compare with the expectations and experiences of most citizens? How do adults with disabilities rate their quality of life? Are they happy?

Obtaining answers to such questions has become one of the highest priorities in special education today. More than 50 studies of graduates and leavers of secondary special education programs provide enlightening information on their experiences as young adults. The largest and most comprehensive studies of the adult adjustment of youth with disabilities after they leave secondary special education programs are the two National Longitudinal Transition Studies (NLTS1 and NLST2) funded by the U.S. Office of Special Education Programs. The NLTS1 assessed and monitored changes in the lives of 8,000 youths with disabilities who left U.S. secondary special education programs between 1985 and 1987 (Blackorby & Wagner, 1996). NLTS2 is a 10-year study of the experiences of a national sample of more than 11,000 students in special education who were 13 to 16 years of age in December 1, 2000, as they moved from secondary school into adult roles (Wagner, Newman, Cameto, Garza, & Levine, 2005).

Completing High School

Students who do not complete high school are likely to face more difficulties in adult adjustment than are those who do. Special education students who do not complete high school face lower levels of employment and wages, reduced access to postsecondary education and training opportunities, higher rates of problems with the criminal justice system, and less overall satisfaction with life in general (Holub & Rusch, 2008; Wagner et al., 2005). In 2001–2002, 51% of high school students with disabilities graduated from high school with a standard diploma (U.S. Department of Education, 2006). The overall dropout rate for secondary students with disabilities ranged from 28% (NLTS2) to "a staggering" 37.6% (Pacer Center, 2006). Dropout rates vary considerably by disability type, ranging from about 17% for students with autism and visual impairments to a

Judah's after-school job gives him a sense of autonomy and connectedness with the community.

high of 61% for students with emotional or behavioral disorders (U.S. Department of Education, 2006).

As Test, Aspel, and Everson (2006) point out, although completing high school is important to future success, even more critical is that students obtain not just a diploma but also the skills vital to adult living. Too many students with disabilities are focusing solely on achieving academic success at the expense of careful transition planning (Hasazi, Furney, & DeStefano, 1999).

Employment

Data from NLTS1 showed an unemployment rate of 46% for all youth with disabilities who had been out of school for less than 2 years. The unemployment rate for young adults with disabilities drops to 36.5% when they have been out of school for 3 to 5 years, but nearly 1 in 5 youth (19.6%) reported giving up looking for work (Blackorby & Wagner, 1996).

The employment outlook is much worse for students with physical, sensory, severe, and multiple disabilities. The NLTS1 found extremely low employment rates 3 to 5 years after secondary school for young adults with orthopedic impairments (22%), visual impairments (29%), and multiple disabilities (17%) (Blackorby & Wagner, 1996). NLTS2 reported that 43% of youth with disabilities were working for pay outside the home 2 years after leaving school, a rate well below the 63% employment rate among same-age youth in the general population.

Between one half and two thirds of young adults with disabilities who are employed work in part-time jobs (Frank & Sitlington, 2000). On average, youth with disabilities in the NLTS2 earned a median hourly wage of $7.30, and only about one third of working youth with disabilities receive any employment benefits such as health insurance, sick leave, paid vacation, or health benefits. A nationwide survey of Americans with disabilities aged 18 to 64 reported even more discouraging findings: only 35% of people with disabilities reported being employed full or part time, compared to 78% of those who do not have disabilities; further, three times as many people with disabilities live in poverty with annual household incomes below $15,000 (26% vs. 9%) compared with those who do not have disabilities (National Organization on Disability, 2004). Harris Poll Chairman Humphrey Taylor stated that "looking back four years, or ten years, to our earlier N.O.D./Harris surveys, we see Americans with disabilities heading in the right direction. But people with disabilities remain pervasively disadvantaged" (p. 1). Like other minority groups, persons with disabilities are often in the position of being the last hired and the first fired (Trupin, Sebesta, Yelin, & LaPlante, 1997).

Postsecondary Education

Attending college and postsecondary vocational programs greatly increases the likelihood of obtaining employment and generally experiencing success as an adult. NLTS2 found that 31% out-of-school youth with disabilities had been enrolled in some kind of postsecondary school in 2 years since leaving high school, a rate far below the 77% of those who had included postsecondary education goals as part of their transition plans in high school. At the time of the interview, 19% of the NLTS2 participants were currently enrolled in a postsecondary school program, a rate of current enrollment less than half that of their peers in the general population (41%).

Overall Adjustment and Success

Being a successful adult involves much more than holding a job; it means achieving status as an independent and active member of society. Independence for an adult includes the ability to participate in society, work, have a home, raise a family, and share the joys and responsibilities of community life (Ferguson & Ferguson, 2006). Adults with disabilities face numerous obstacles in day-to-day living that affect where and how they live, how well they can use community resources, and what opportunities they have for social interaction.

The NLTS includes a measure of adult adjustment that assesses independent functioning in three domains: (a) employment (competitively employed in a full-time job or engaged in job training or postsecondary education); (b) residential arrangements (living alone or with a spouse or a roommate); and (c) social activities (having friends, belonging to social groups). When assessed at a period less than 2 years out of school, only 6.4% of all youth with disabilities met these three criteria. When the same measures were assessed after individuals had been out of school for 3 to 5 years, 20% were judged to be independent in all three domains (Wagner et al., 1994). Even with this significant improvement after several years, four out of every five former special education students still had not achieved the status of independent adulthood after being out of high school for up to 5 years (NLTS1).

It is important to note that the very small percentage of young adults who met the criteria for successful transition to adult life in this study had graduated from secondary special education programs. Young adults who leave secondary programs by routes other than graduation do not fare as well as those who do complete school with a diploma or a certificate (Blackorby & Wagner et al., 1996; Malian & Love, 1998). Forthcoming reports from NLTS2 will reveal whether these outcome measures of transitioning to adulthood have improved. However, only about 60% of youth with disabilities ages 15–19 who participated in the NLTS2 reported that they thought of themselves as "nice, proud of themselves, able to handle challenges, feeling useful and important" (Wagner, Newman, Cameto, Levine, & Murder, 2007, p. x); this suggests that many secondary students and recent school leavers do not view themselves as ready for adulthood.

Such findings have focused attention on what has become a dominant issue in special education today—the transition from school to adult life in the community. Many youth who leave secondary special education programs discover to their dismay and discouragement that "the fiscal and logistical demands of daily life [are] far more complex than what they learned in functional math, home-economics, or life skills classes . . . [and that the] protective nature of their experiences in special education had left them ill-prepared for the real world" (Knoll & Wheeler, 2001, pp. 502–503). And it is not just students with major cognitive limitations or severe physical, sensory, or behavioral disabilities who have trouble adjusting to life after high school. Former special education students with mild disabilities face significant challenges in every aspect of adult life (Johnson, Mallard, & Lancaster, 2007; Tymchuk, Lakin, & Luckasson, 2001).

No longer can special educators be satisfied with students' improved performance on classroom-related tasks. We must work equally hard to ensure that the education students receive during their school years plays a direct and positive role in helping them deal successfully with the multifaceted demands of adulthood.

TRANSITION SERVICES AND MODELS

Will's Bridges Model of School-to-Work Transition

In response to growing concern over the failure of so many young adults with disabilities in the job market and community living, Congress authorized funding for secondary education and transitional services for youth with disabilities when it amended IDEA in 1983 (P.L. 98-199). In 1984, Madeline Will, director of the U.S. Office of Special Education and Rehabilitation Services, proposed a model of transition services that encompassed three levels of service, each conceptualized as a bridge between the secondary special education curriculum and adult employment (Will, 1986). Each level differs in terms of the nature and extent of the services an individual with disabilities needs to make a successful transition from school to work. At the first level are students who require no special transition services. On graduation from an appropriate secondary special education curriculum, these young adults, presumably those with mild disabilities, would make use of the generic employment services already available to people without disabilities in the community (e.g., job placement agencies). At the second level are persons with disabilities who require the time-limited transitional services offered by vocational rehabilitation or adult service agencies that are specially designed to help individuals with disabilities gain competitive, independent employment. The third level of transitional services consists of ongoing employment services that are necessary to enable persons with severe disabilities to enjoy the benefits of meaningful paid work.

Will's bridges model

 Council for Exceptional Children

Knowledge and Skill Base for Beginning Special Education Transition Specialists: Theoretical and applied models of transition (TS1K1) (also TS1K3).

FIGURE 15.1

Halpern's three-dimensional conceptualization of transition

Source: From "Transition: A Look at the Foundation" by A. S. Halpern. *Exceptional Children, 51*, 1985, p. 481. © 1985 by the Council for Exceptional Children. Reprinted with permission.

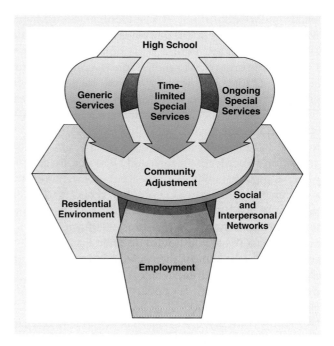

Halpern's Three-Dimensional Model

Because it showed the federal government's recognition of the need to improve employment outcomes for special education students, Will's bridges model for school-to-work transition was viewed as a move in the right direction. Many special educators, however, thought that its perspective on transition was too limited. Halpern (1985) wrote that it is a mistake to focus on adult employment as the sole purpose and outcome of transition services: "Living successfully in one's community should be the primary target of transitional services" (p. 480). Halpern proposed a transition model that directed Will's generic, time-limited, and ongoing support services toward helping students with disabilities adjust to adult life in the community in three domains: (1) quality of residential environment, (2) adequacy of social and interpersonal network, and (3) meaningful employment (see Figure 15.1).

Halpern's model influenced subsequent definitions of transition services in amendments to IDEA in 1990 and 1997. The view that transition must focus on all domains of adult functioning characterizes the field today.

Definition of Transition Services in IDEA

IDEA defines **transition services** as

> a coordinated set of activities for a child with a disability that—
>
> (A) is designed to be within a results-oriented process, that is focused on improving the academic and functional achievement of the child with a disability to facilitate the child's movement from school to post-school activities, including post-secondary education, vocational education, integrated employment (including supported employment), continuing and adult education, adult services, independent living, or community participation;
>
> (B) is based on the individual child's needs, taking into account the child's strengths, preferences, and interests; and
>
> (C) includes instruction, related services, community experiences, the development of employment and other post-school adult living objectives, and, when appropriate, acquisition of daily living skills and functional vocational evaluation. (P.L. 108-446, 20 USC 1401, Sec. 602[34])

Individualized Transition Plan

IDEA requires that IEPs for older students include information on how the child's transition from school to adult life will be supported:

> Beginning not later than the first IEP to be in effect when the child is 16, and updated annually thereafter—

a. appropriate measurable postsecondary goals based upon age appropriate transition assessments related to training, education, employment, and, where appropriate, independent living skills;

b. the transition services (including courses of study) needed to assist the child in reaching those goals; and

c. beginning not later than 1 year before the child reaches the age of majority under State law, a statement that the child has been informed of the child's rights under this title, if any, that will transfer to the child on reaching the age of majority under section 615(m). (P.L. 108-446, 20 USC 1401, Sec. 614 [d][1][A][8])

The intent of this provision is to focus the IEP team's attention on secondary curriculum and course planning related to postschool success. This portion of the student's IEP is called an **individualized transition plan (ITP)**. The ITP may be written at an earlier age if the IEP team determines it is appropriate for an individual student. It is important to begin coordinated transition planning early.

In contrast to IEP goals and objectives, which address 1 year at a time, transition planning requires the IEP team to think and plan several years ahead. Developed and included as part of the IEP process, a student's ITP outlines actions, events, and resources that will affect and support her move from school to adulthood. A well-written ITP details the types of curricular programming and supports that will prepare the student for a smooth and successful transition to adult life.

The student's IEP/ITP team designs transition plans within an outcome-oriented process based on the student's and family's vision of the future. The team specifies postschool outcomes and goals in four major areas: employment, postsecondary education/training, residential, and recreation/leisure. It then develops an individualized program of instruction, supports, and activities designed to help the student achieve those outcomes. Decisions about needed transition services should be guided by answers to questions such as the following (Brolin & Lloyd, 2004; Flexer, Simmons, Luft, & Baer, 2008; Lindstrom, Doren, Metheny, Johnson, & Zane, 2007; Rusch, 2008; Sitlington & Clark, 2006; Test et al., 2006; Wehman, 2006):

- What are the student's and family's dreams and visions of her life as a young adult?
- What are the student's strengths? How can she build on them to facilitate a successful transition?
- What skills does the student need to develop or improve to make progress toward her postschool goals?
- Will the student seek a regular high school diploma? If so, what course of study and proficiency tests will be required?
- Will she work toward a vocational certificate of completion instead of a regular diploma?
- Does she have an expressed career interest now? If not, what can the team do to help her explore career possibilities and discover her preferences?
- Is the student likely to remain in high school through the maximum age of eligibility for special education services? If so, what curriculum and work experiences will be needed after age 18?
- In what school and community activities will the student participate?
- What supports are necessary in the student's current and future environments that will enable the desired postschool goals and outcomes to become reality?

The purpose of transition planning is "to ensure that all of our students step into the adult life they desire. This doesn't mean locking a student into a life plan. It means that each student will leave high school recognizing her personal strengths, knowing where to turn for support, and looking toward adult life with confidence" (Horvath, 2006, p. 603). A well-written transition plan ensures that parents are aware of available adult services and employment options in the community, improves the chances that adult services will be available with few disruptions to the graduating student, and provides school and adult-service personnel with a set of procedures and timelines to follow. After graduation, service personnel can incorporate the ITP into an individual rehabilitation plan if the young adult is served by vocational rehabilitation or made part of an individualized habilitation plan if the young

Individualized transition plan (ITP)

Council for Exceptional Children **Knowledge and Skill Base for Beginning Special Education Transition Specialists: Transition-related laws and policies (TS1K2) (also CC1K4).**

adult is served by a community adult services agency (e.g., a county program for people with developmental disabilities).

Parents of students with disabilities can call the PACER Center at (952)838-9000 to speak with a trained advocate who will help them understand their rights and find resources to help with all aspects of transition. Transition resources for parents are available online at www.pacer.org/publications/transition.htm.

Like IEPs, transition plans can take many formats as long as they contain the necessary information (McPartland, 2005). Figure 15.2 shows the ITP developed for Jeff, a tenth grader with learning disabilities. Jeff and his parents share a vision for the future in which Jeff has a good job and lives as independently as possible. He is very interested in obtaining his driver's license; and based on some of his community-work experiences, he thinks he might like to work in the heating and air conditioning field. Jeff also sees himself getting married someday, but first he wants to live on his own for a while, probably in an apartment with a roommate or two. He has also expressed the desire to continue his education after high school; therefore, one of the activities on his ITP is to obtain information about community and technical colleges.

The goals and objectives numbers on the ITP refer to the goals and objectives on Jeff's IEP that support the transition plan (IEP objectives are at the bottom of the figure). Academic goals for Jeff, such as reading comprehension, use the content area from the transition plan, for example, a heating and air conditioning textbook and the driver's education manual. Jeff frequently relies on adults to assist him in decision making and to request information about days off at work, and he needs to better understand his disability. His self-advocacy goal relates to more self-reliance. Although specific skills will be taught, Jeff will practice his self-advocacy skills at his part-time job.

Transition Teaming

Transition planning requires a team that can help the student identify and reach her postschool goals. The team can include special education teachers, general education teachers, vocational education teachers, school counselors, related-services personnel, personnel from community and adult services agencies such as vocational rehabilitation, higher education, and/or developmental disabilities adult services agencies. All people involved must build and maintain communication links and supports among the team members.

Transition involves the coordination, delivery, and transfer of services from the secondary school program to receiving agencies (e.g., employers, postsecondary education and vocational training programs, and residential service providers). Although work-study and vocational training programs for special education students and vocational rehabilitation services for adults with disabilities have long existed in every state, systematic coordination of and communication between schools and community-based adult services have not typically occurred. Although interagency cooperation is critical to the success of transition, in the amendments to IDEA "special education is ultimately given the responsibility of implementing transition goals and activities" (Inge & Moon, 2006, p. 606).

Nowhere in special education are interdisciplinary teaming and interagency collaboration more important than when planning and delivering transition services for secondary students (Everson, Ivester, & Guillory, 2008; Kochhar-Bryant, 2008; Simmons, Flexer, & Bauder, 2008). The validity and likely effectiveness of the transition services described on a student's ITP depend on the student's involvement, family involvement, and the collaboration of professionals who are helping the student and family plan and implement transition services (Lindstrom et al., 2007; Parent et al., 2008). Cooperation and communication between and among professionals and families are keys to effective transition planning.

Beginning Transition Activities and Career Education Early

Numerous models for conceptualizing and guiding the delivery of transition services have been developed (e.g., Greene, 2003; Kohler, 1996; Martin, Woods, & Sylvester, 2008; Sitlington & Clark, 2006; Test et al., 2006; Wehman, 2006). Every transition model with research to support its effectiveness stresses the importance of providing career education at an early

---

Relating transition services to IEP goals and objectives

Council for Exceptional Children — Knowledge and Skill Base for Beginning Special Education Transition Specialists: Methods for linking academic content to transition goals (TS4K2) (also CC4S6).

Go to the Homework & Exercises section in Chapter 15 of MyEducationLab, and complete Homework Exercise 1. As you read the article, consider the types of communication breakdowns that could occur during transition planning meetings and how you might avoid them.

FIGURE 15.2 Example of an individualized transition plan (ITP)

STATEMENT OF NEEDED TRANSITION SERVICES

Name of Student ___Jeff Grace___ Date ___1-14-09___

Person Responsible for Coordinating Transition Services ___Nancy Long___

Title ___Work Study Coordinator___

INSTRUCTION: Goals and objectives for transition should be indicated below in the following areas and be incorporated into the body of the IEP (pages 2 and 3).

See IEP goals and objectives for curriculum modifications and adaptations

EMPLOYMENT & POSTSECONDARY OUTCOME(S): *Full-time job in heating/air conditioning*

ACTIVITIES AND SERVICES	Goal Number for Transition Goals and Objectives	Responsible Person/Provider	Initiation/Duration
Heating/air cond. voc. class	1.a, 1.b, 1.c	Voc Educ. Teacher	1/08 to 1/09
Explore Technical colleges	NA	Jeff, guidance coun.	1/08 to 6/09
Part-time job	2.a, 2.b, 2.c	Jeff, work study coord.	1/08 to 2/09

POSTSCHOOL/ADULT LIVING OUTCOME(S): *Live independently in apartment with roommate*

ACTIVITIES AND SERVICES	Goal Number for Transition Goals and Objectives	Responsible Person/Provider	Initiation/Duration
Family Planning Class	1.a, 1.b, 1.c	SPED Teacher/Reg. Teacher	1/08 to 6/09
Money management	3.a 3.b	SPED Teacher	1/08 to 1/09
Self-advocacy skills trn.	2.a, 2.b, 2.c	Jeff, SPED Teacher	1/08 to 2/09

COMMUNITY PARTICIPATION OUTCOME(S): *To participate in the community through social relationships and transportation.*

ACTIVITIES AND SERVICES	Goal Number for Transition Goals and Objectives	Responsible Person/Provider	Initiation/Duration
Drivers Ed.	1.a 1.b 1.c	Driver Ed Teacher / SPED Teacher	1/08 to 6/09
Register to vote	NA	Jeff and parents	1/08 to 6/09
Interact Club	NA	Jeff	1/08 to 6/09

Jeff's Transition-Related IEP Objectives

1. **Reading comprehension.** Goal: Jeff will increase his reading skills.
   a. When given a reading passage from the driver's education manual or heating and air conditioning textbook, Jeff will increase his reading comprehension skills by using the SQ3R study skills method.
   b. Given 10 functional vocabulary words from the course text, Jeff will identify and define each word.
   c. Given an unfamiliar/unknown word in the heating and air conditioning text (or other course texts), Jeff will decode the word using word attack skills.
2. **Self-advocacy.** Goal: Jeff will increase his self-advocacy skills.
   a. Jeff will increase his understanding of his disability by identifying and stating his strengths and areas of difficulty.
   b. When given various community and work situations, Jeff will identify and demonstrate appropriate decision-making skills.
   c. When given various community and work problem situations, Jeff will identify people who can assist him with difficult or unfamiliar situations.
3. **Money management.** Goal: Jeff will manage his personal finances.
   a. Jeff will construct and use a monthly personal budget for his present income.
   b. Jeff will record personal major income and expenses for three months.

Source: ITP form from Ohio Department of Education. (1998). *Model policies and procedures for the education of children with disabilities* (p. 608b). Columbus, OH: Author.

age, the student's choosing goals, a functional secondary school curriculum that offers work experiences in integrated community job sites, systematic coordination between the school and adult service providers, and parental involvement and support.

The Council for Exceptional Children's Division on Career Development and Transition (DCDT) recommends that career development and transition services begin in the

Council for Exceptional Children

Knowledge and Skill Base for Beginning Special Education Transition Specialists: Organizations and publications relevant to the field of transition (TS9K3).

Giving secondary students regular opportunities to participate in integrated work settings in the community builds career awareness and teaches valuable vocational skills.

Career awareness and transition-related curriculum activities

Council for Exceptional Children

Knowledge and Skill Base for Beginning Special Education Transition Specialists: Methods for linking academic content to transition goals (TS4K2) (also TS4K1, CC4S6).

elementary grades for all children with disabilities (Blalock et al., 2003). According to DCDT, three basic principles underlie the provision of career education and transition services:

1. *Education for career development and transition is for individuals with disabilities of all ages.*
2. *Career development is a process begun at birth and continues throughout life.*
3. *Early career development is essential for making satisfactory choices later.* A frequent criticism of secondary employment training programs is that there are too few choices and that professionals too often end up making those choices for students....The best way to prepare individuals for self-knowledge (interests, abilities, limiting barriers) and decision-making is to begin the process of self-awareness and choice-making as early as possible. (Clark, Carlson, Fisher, Cook, & D'Alonzo, 1991, pp. 115–116)

Developing career awareness and vocational skills during the elementary years does not mean that 8-year-old children should be placed on job sites for training. Appropriate transition-related objectives should be selected at each age level (Brolin, 2004; Cronin, Patton, & Wood, 2005, Wehman & Thoma, 2006). For example, elementary students might sample different types of jobs through classroom responsibilities such as watering plants, cleaning chalkboards, or taking messages to the office. Middle school students should begin to spend time at actual community job sites, with an increasing amount of in-school instruction devoted to the development of associated work skills, such as being on time, hygiene, dressing properly, staying on task, asking for help, and accepting direction (Beakley & Yoder, 1998).

Developing and operating a school-based business enterprise can help high school students learn functional academic, work, problem-solving, and social skills. Lindstrom, Benz, and Johnson (1997) describe four school-based businesses that students with disabilities in several high schools in Oregon helped develop and operate: an espresso and baked-goods bar, a take-out meals operation, a mail-order seed business, and a winter produce garden. Secondary students with moderate and severe disabilities should also spend an increasing amount of time experiencing and receiving instruction at actual community job sites (Inge & Moon, 2006). The remaining hours of in-school instruction should focus on acquisition of functional skills needed in the adult work, domestic, community, and recreational/leisure environments toward which the student is headed (Patton et al., 1997). Table 15.1 shows examples of transition-related curriculum activities in the domestic, community, leisure, and vocational domains that might be incorporated into a student's IEP.

Secondary special educators are becoming increasingly skilled in creating instructional materials and activities that simultaneously teach both transition skills and academic curriculum goals (Baer, Simmons, Bauder, & Flexer, 2008; Hughes, Wood, Konrad, & Test, 2006). For example, the EnvisionIT curricula integrate Internet research skills and transition planning with English academic standards (Izzo, Dillon, & Novak, 2007). Students complete online lessons that present information technology (IT) content and career activities using the Internet. In the process of creating a self-directed transition plan, students take assessment items that correlate to the high-stakes test that students must pass to earn a high school diploma. To learn about another example of combining transition and academic skill instruction, see Teaching & Learning, "Two for One: Teaching Self-Determination and Writing Together."

EMPLOYMENT

Work can be defined as using one's physical and/or mental energies to accomplish something productive. Our society is based on a work ethic; we place a high value on work and on people who contribute. Besides providing economic support, work offers opportunities for social interaction and a chance to use and enhance skills in a chosen area. Work generates the respect of others and provides a sense of pride and self-satisfaction. Individuals with disabilities who are employed report a higher-quality life (Kraemer, McIntyre, & Blacher, 2003).

TABLE 15.1

Examples of transition-related curriculum activities in four domains that might be included in a student's IEP

	Domestic	Community	Leisure	Vocational
Elementary	Picking up toys Washing dishes Making bed Dressing Grooming Eating skills Toileting skills Sorting clothes Vacuuming Setting the table at mealtime	Eating meals in a restaurant Using restroom in a local restaurant Putting trash into container Choosing correct change to ride city bus Giving the clerk money to purchase an item Responding appropriately to pedestrian safety signs Going to neighbor's house for lunch	Climbing on swing set Playing board games Playing tag with neighbors Coloring Playing kickball Croquet Riding bicycles Playing with age-appropriate toys Community soccer league	Returning toys to appropriate storage spaces Cleaning the room at the end of the day Working on a task for a designated period Wiping tables after meals Following 2- to 4-step instructions Answering the telephone Emptying trash Taking messages to people
Middle School	Washing clothes Preparing simple meals (soup, salad, and sandwich) Keeping bedroom clean Making snacks Mowing lawn Raking leaves Making grocery lists Purchasing items from a list Vacuuming and dusting Setting an alarm clock at night and turning it off when waking	Crossing streets safely Purchasing an item from a department store Purchasing a meal at a restaurant Using local transportation system to get to and from recreational facilities Participating in local scout troop Going to a neighbor's house for lunch on Saturday	Playing volleyball Taking aerobics classes Playing checkers with a friend Playing miniature golf Cycling Attending high school or local college basketball games Hanging out at local mall Swimming Attending crafts class at city recreation center	Mopping/waxing floors Cleaning windows Hanging and bagging clothes Busing tables Working for 1–2 hours Operating machinery (e.g., dishwasher, buffer) Cleaning sinks, bathtubs, and fixtures Internship with school janitor or office staff Following a job sequence
High School	Cleaning all rooms in place of residence Developing a weekly budget Cooking meals Operating thermostat to regulate heat or air Doing yard maintenance Maintaining personal needs Caring for and maintaining clothing	Using bus system to move about the community Depositing checks into bank account Using community department stores Using community grocery stores Using community health facilities (e.g., physician, pharmacist)	Jogging Boating Watching college basketball game Video games Card games YMCA swim class Gardening Going on a vacation Collecting tapes or CDs Reading magazines or comics Hanging out/sleeping over with friends	Janitorial duties (at J. C. Penney) Housekeeping duties (at Days Inn) Grounds keeping duties at local college campus Food service at mall cafeteria Laundry duties at local laundromat Performing job duties to company standards

Source: Adapted from Wehman, P., & Thoma, C. A. (2006). Teaching for transition. In P. Wehman, *Life beyond the classroom: Transition strategies for young people with disabilities* (4th ed., pp. 213–214). Baltimore: Brookes. Used by permission.

All young adults face important questions about what to do with their lives—attend college or technical school, work as a bricklayer or an accountant—but for the person without disabilities, answering those questions involves choosing from a number of options. By contrast, the young adult with disabilities typically has fewer options from which to choose. Occupational choices decrease if the person with disabilities has limited skills; they may decrease even more due to the nature of the disability and still further because of employers' (needless) prejudices and misconceptions about people with disabilities. For most adults with disabilities, obtaining and holding a job is a major life challenge and goal.

Two for One: Teaching Self-Determination and Writing Together

BY MOIRA KONRAD AND DAVID W. TEST

Research indicates that educators believe it is important to teach self-determination skills to students with disabilities. However, secondary special education teachers are already overwhelmed with a broad range of roles and responsibilities. Federal requirements have added to the burdens special educators carry. Teachers are now held accountable not only for documenting their students' progress in the general curriculum but also for preparing them to participate in standards-based, high-stakes assessments. In response, we developed the IEP Template and the GO 4 IT . . . NOW! strategies, which teachers can use to teach a self-determination skill (student involvement in the IEP process) and an academic skill (written expression) simultaneously.

THE IEP TEMPLATE

The IEP Template is essentially a "fill-in-the-blank" IEP that students can use to write a draft of a first-person IEP. The template serves as an organizer to help students understand the content and format of an IEP. It also helps students draft components of their IEPs in complete sentences.

GO 4 IT . . . NOW!

Once students have successfully used the IEP Template, they can move seamlessly to the GO 4 IT . . . NOW! learning strategy and apply their knowledge and skills. GO 4 IT . . . NOW! is a strategy that teaches students how to write paragraphs while simultaneously teaching them to write IEP goals and objectives (Konrad & Test, in press; Konrad, Trela, & Test, 2006). Specifically, students learn that each paragraph is about one particular goal. The goal itself serves as the topic sentence of the paragraph. The objectives are the supporting details in the paragraph, and a restatement of the goal with an indication of how long it will take to complete (a timeline) serves as a concluding sentence. The mnemonic GO 4 IT . . . NOW! helps students remember the structure of the paragraph, and, more specifically, what to include:

G—Goals
O—Objectives
4—4 objectives
IT—Identify timeline
N—Did I NAME my topic?
O—Did I ORDER my steps?
W—Did I WRAP it up and restate my topic?

HOW TO GET STARTED

1. *Help students identify their visions for the future.*
   - Use online interest, career inventories, and school guidance counselors to help students develop vision statements about what they want to do when they finish high school.
   - Work with students to help them identify their strengths and academic, functional, social, and behavioral needs.
   - Explicitly teach students how to turn a need into a goal.
   - Provide explicit instruction in how to complete the IEP template, using modeling and guided and independent practice.

Example of a vision statement <u>before</u> template instruction:

After high school I plan to . . .
Live _____ in New York _____
Learn _____
Work _____ as a lawyer _____
Play _____

Example of an academic strength <u>before</u> template instruction:

I can _____ math _____

Example of a goal <u>before</u> template instruction:

I will _____ writing _____

Example of a vision statement <u>after</u> template instruction:

After high school I plan to . . .
Live _____ in an apartment _____
Learn _____ how to be a lawyer _____
Work _____ in a restaurant _____
Play _____ basketball at the YMCA with my friends

Example of an academic strength <u>after</u> template instruction:

I can _____ say my multiplication facts quickly

Example of a goal <u>after</u> template instruction:

I will _____ write and edit paragraphs

---

2. *Teach students how to turn visions into goals and objectives.*
   - Help students identify their academic, functional, social, and behavioral needs and teach them how to turn a need into a goal using an "I will" statement.
   - Provide explicit instruction in how to write a goal paragraph, using modeling and guided and independent practice.
   - Emphasize the use of transition words to teach students how to put objectives into logical order.

3. *Build in writing and communication skills.*
   - Use the sentences students develop in their IEP Templates to teach capitalization, punctuation, and parts of speech.
   - Teach students how to use transition words and phrases to string sentences into paragraphs. For example, have students write sentences about a specific topic such as "My Strengths" or "My Services and Accommodations" and then use transition words to turn them into paragraphs.
   - Weave letter-writing skills into the curriculum by having students write letters to invite the IEP team members to attend annual review meetings.
   - Suggest that students prepare to participate in their IEP meetings by (1) bringing their completed templates and/or paragraphs to the meetings or (2) developing presentations about their templates.

4. *Take it a step further.*
   - Emphasize, teach, and model how GO 4 IT . . . NOW! can be used to write all kinds of paragraphs.

- Encourage students to create essays (once they can write effective paragraphs) by combining paragraphs.
- Suggest that students bring their paragraphs/essays to their IEP team meetings and share them with the team, or send out the essays with the IEP invitation letters as preparation for the meeting.

You can find detailed instructions and examples on using GO 4 IT in Konrad and Trela (2007).

Moira Konrad is a member of the special education faculty at The Ohio State University. Her research interests include self-determination and writing strategy instruction. David Test, a professor in the special education program at the University of North Carolina at Charlotte, is Co-Principal Investigator of the National Secondary Transition Technical Assistance Center (www.nsttac.org), co-editor of the journal *Career Development for Exceptional Individuals*, and senior author of the text *Transition Methods for Youth with Disabilities*.

To learn more about this strategy, go to the Building Teaching Skills section in Chapter 15 of MyEducationLab. As you complete the activities, think about the benefits of combining self-determination skill training with instruction in written expression.

Competitive Employment

A person who is competitively employed performs work valued by an employer, functions in an integrated setting with nondisabled co-workers, earns at or above the federal minimum wage, and is working without support from an outside human service agency. Virtually all special educators who have studied the transition of students with disabilities from school to adult life believe that only through significant revision of the public school curriculum and improved coordination of school and adult vocational habilitation services can the prospects of competitive employment be enhanced for young adults with disabilities (e.g., Flexer et al., 2008; Johnson & Wehman, 2001; Patton et al., 1997; Sitlington et al., 2006).

We have already identified some key characteristics of school programs that increase the likelihood of successful employment outcomes for students. First, the curriculum must stress functional skills; that is, students must learn vocational skills that they will actually need and use in local employment situations (Alwell & Cobb, 2007). Second, students with disabilities must receive ample opportunities to learn the interpersonal skills necessary to work effectively with colleagues in integrated work sites (Hughes, Washington, & Brown, 2008). Third, community-based work experience and employment skill instruction should ideally begin as early as ages 10–13 for students with severe disabilities and be used for progressively extended periods as students near graduation. While on community work sites, students should receive direct instruction in areas such as specific job skills, ways to increase production rates, and transportation to and from employment sites. Although students should train and work in the community whenever possible so they learn "the communication, behavior, dress

Characteristics of secondary school programs and competitive employment outcomes

 Knowledge and Skill Base for Beginning Special Education Transition Specialists: Research on relationships between individual outcomes and transition practices (TS1K4).

 To learn more about how students with disabilities can become gainfully employed after high school, go to the Homework & Exercises section in MyEducationLab and complete Homework Exercise 2.

and other codes critical for success in integrated environments ... [and] to get to and from important places on time or to produce consistently" (Brown, Farrington, Suomi, & Zeigler, 1999, p. 6), the effectiveness of job-site training can be increased when supplemented with simulation training in the classroom (Lattimore, Parsons, & Reid, 2006).

Research found a positive correlation between paid work experiences during the last 2 years of high school and postschool employment and total earnings (e.g., Baer et al., 2003; Benz, Lindstrom, Unruh, & Waintrup, 2004; Benz, Lindstrom, & Yavanoff, 2000; D'Amico, 1991; Kohler, 1994; Scuccimarra & Speece, 1990). Unpaid and volunteer work experience is also valuable for students with disabilities (Brown et al., 1999). Unfortunately, the NLTS1 found that only 39% of young adults with disabilities had been enrolled in work-experience programs during high school.

Whenever possible, students should experience community jobs that match their vocational interests. Martin, Woods, and Sylvester (2008) describe how Christopher, a 17-year-old student with moderate intellectual disabilities, used the *Choose and Take Action* vocational assessment software program (Martin et al., 2004) to select an entry-level job he would like to observe or try. The *Choose and Take Action* process includes four steps:

Step 1: *Choice Making*. During choice making, Christopher viewed pairs of randomly presented videos showing different employment settings, activities, and job characteristics (see Figure 15.3). From each pair, he selected the one he liked the best. After viewing all the videos once, the chosen videos were paired and Christopher chose again. This continued until he picked one final video.

Step 2: *Plan*. During the planning part of the program, Christopher determined if he wanted to *watch* someone do the activity at the selected setting or if he wanted to *do* the activity. A printed plan showed what Christopher chose. Evaluation questions regarding these choices are also printed on the plan.

Step 3: *Try It*. Based on the plan, Christopher went into the community to "try it" at the chosen setting.

Step 4: *Evaluate*. Christopher, with his teacher's guidance, evaluated the experience, and then entered that information into the computer. (adapted from Martin et al., 2008, pp. 95–96)

Supported Employment

Supported employment helps adults with severe disabilities, who have historically been unemployed or restricted to sheltered settings, earn real wages for real work (Wehman, Inge,

FIGURE 15.3

Example of screen shot from vocational assessment software program

Source: From Martin, J. E., Marshall, L. H., Wray, D., Wells, L., O'Brien, J., Olvey, G., et al. (2004). *Choose and take action: Finding the right job for you.* Longmont, CO: Sopris West. Used by permission.

Revell, & Brooke, 2007). The supported employment movement recognizes that many adults with severe disabilities require ongoing, often intensive support to obtain, learn, and hold a job.

Supported employment is defined in the 1998 Rehabilitation Act Amendments as

competitive work in an integrated work setting, or employment in integrated work settings in which individuals are working toward competitive employment, consistent with the strengths, resources, priorities, concerns, abilities, capabilities, interests, and informed choice of the individuals with ongoing support services for the individuals with the most significant disabilities

(A) for whom competitive employment has not traditionally occurred; or for whom competitive employment has been interrupted or intermittent as a result of a significant disability; and

(B) who, because of the severity of their disability, need intensive supported employment services . . . and extended services . . . to perform such work. (P.L. 102-569, Sec. 635[b][6][c][iii])

Supported employment has grown rapidly since its inception. In 1986, fewer than 10,000 individuals were working in federally assisted supported employment demonstration projects in 20 states. Just 2 years later, the supported employment movement had grown to a total of 32,342 participants nationally; and the cumulative wages these workers earned grew from $1.4 million to $12.4 million in the 15 states that reported earnings data (Wehman, Kregel, Shafer, & West, 1989). By 1995, it was estimated that almost 140,000 persons with disabilities were working through supported employment with an average hourly wage of $4.70 (Wehman, Revell, & Kregel, 1998). These employees earned more than $750 million in annual wages in 1995, many becoming taxpayers for the first time in their lives. Since 1995 the number of supported employees has grown nearly 30% (Braddock, Hemp, Parish, & Rizzolo, 2002). A statewide study in Maryland found that average weekly earnings of individuals placed in supported employment was 3.5 times greater than the earnings of individuals in sheltered work environments ($134.33 compared to weekly wages of $40.69) (Conley, 2003).

The success of supported employment depends in large part on job development—the identification and creation of community-based employment opportunities for individuals with disabilities (Griffin, Hammis, & Geary, 2007). Four distinct models of supported employment have evolved: small business enterprise, mobile work crew, work enclave, and individual placement.

Small Business Enterprise This model provides supported employment for persons with disabilities by establishing a business that takes advantage of existing commercial opportunities within a community. The business hires a small number of individuals with disabilities as well as several employees without disabilities.

Mobile Work Crew A mobile work crew involves a small group of supported employees organized around a small, single-purpose business, such as building or grounds maintenance, working in an integrated community-employment setting. A general manager may be responsible for finding and coordinating the work of several small crews of three to eight individuals, with each crew supervised by a supported employment specialist. Mobile work crews are organized as not-for-profit corporations; the extra costs the organizations incur because their employees do not work at full productivity levels are covered by public funds. Such costs are usually less than would be needed to support the work crew employees in activity centers, which provide little or no real work or reimbursement.

Enclave (or Clustered Placement) In this model of supported employment, a small group of people with disabilities performs work with special training or job supports within a typical business or industry. Work enclave employees typically receive wages commensurate with their productivity rates. The work enclave provides a useful alternative to traditional segregated sheltered employment, offering many of the benefits of

Definition of supported employment

Council for Exceptional Children **Knowledge and Skill Base for Beginning Special Education Transition Specialists: Transition-related laws and policies (TS1K2).**

Supported employment has enabled tens of thousands of people like Barry to experience, for the first time in their lives, the benefits of real work for real pay.

Supported employment models

Council for Exceptional Children **Knowledge and Skill Base for Beginning Special Education Transition Specialists: Theoretical and applied models of transition (TS1K1).**

community-based integrated employment as well as the ongoing supports necessary for long-term job success.

Individual Placement The individual placement model of supported employment consists of developing jobs with employers in the community, systematically assessing clients' job preferences, carefully placing employees in jobs they want, implementing intensive job-site training and advocacy, building systems of natural supports on the job site, monitoring client performance, and taking a systematic approach to long-term job retention (Wehman, Brooke, & Inge, 2006; Wehman et al., 2006).

An approach to individual placement, used increasingly in recent years, known as **customized employment** entails carving out or creating a job within an integrated competitive work environment based on the current skills of the employee (Luecking & Tilson, 2002; Office of Disability Employment Policy, 2004). Customized employment is a "value exchange between the employer and employee based on the unique needs and contributions of the individual and the discrete and emerging needs of the employer" (Parent et al., 2008, p. 114). *Supported self-employment* offers another possibility for meaningful employment by some persons with significant disabilities (Griffin & Hammis, 2001).

Roles of employment specialist

 Knowledge and Skill Base for Beginning Special Education Transition Specialists: Scope and role of agency personnel related to transition services (TS9K2) (also TS9K1).

Employment Specialist The supported employment specialist is the key to making a supported work program effective. The supported employment specialist, sometimes called a job coach or employment consultant, is a community-based professional who works in a nonprofit job placement program, a public vocational or adult services program, or a secondary special education program. Figure 15.4 identifies the major activities and responsibilities of a supported employment specialist in each component of the supported work model. "To successfully perform this vast array of functions, employment specialists must be skilled and successfully move in and out of a number of roles" in making supported employment work (Targett, 2007, p. 90).

In a typical supported employment program, the employment specialist provides direct, on-site job training to the employee with disabilities and serves as the primary source of support and assistance. Although the job coach gradually reduces the time spent in direct, on-site training and support, this model of outside assistance has several inherent drawbacks (Mank, Cioffi, & Yovanoff, 2000; Simmons & Flexer, 2008; Trach, 2008):

- The arrival and presence of the job coach can disrupt the natural work setting.
- The supported employee may perform differently in the presence of the job coach.
- The job coach's presence can reduce the frequency of interaction between the supported employee and co-workers without disabilities.
- It is difficult for the employment specialist to be sensitive to the changing demands of the job over time and provide continued support and training consistent with those changes.
- The cost for an employment specialist who must travel to the job site is higher and the efficiency of the approach is lower than one that takes advantage of the natural interactions of co-workers.
- The always-on-call job coach may prevent the employer and co-workers from figuring out and implementing natural solutions to problems.
- This approach may foster too much dependence on the job coach, working against the supported employee's success in learning how to solve problems and assuming responsibility for her own management.

Natural Supports The role of the employment specialist/job coach has evolved from one of primary supporter for the employee with disabilities to one of working with the employer and co-workers to help identify, develop, and facilitate the typical or indigenous supports of the workplace. Rogan, Hagner, and Murphy (1993) define natural supports as "any assistance, relationships or interactions that allow a person to secure or maintain a community job . . . in a way that corresponds to the typical work routines and social interactions of other employees" (p. 275). Figure 15.5 describes and gives examples of seven categories of natural supports identified by Rogan's SPANS model (1996).

FIGURE 15.4 Sample description of a supported employment specialist's responsibilities

Job Description: Employment Specialist

General Description

The employment specialist is involved in all aspects of community-based vocational training, placement, and follow-along for persons with an array of severe disabilities as part of the Excel Rehabilitation Program. The successful candidate will meet the employers to secure placements, provide one-on-one training for job and other related skills, and maintain systematic and regular contact with employers after job training has been completed. The employment specialist will work as part of a team and will interact frequently with other professionals related to specific cases.

Specific Duties/Responsibilities

1. *Job Development.* The employment specialist will complete job market screening activities and regularly present the employment program to prospective employers until adequate numbers of appropriate open positions have been identified. The specialist will analyze job duties and requirements of potential jobs.
2. *Consumer Assessment.* The employment specialist will complete and/or secure assessment and evaluation information as necessary to assist the consumer with informed decision making. This may include referral to other professionals/agencies and subsequent interpretation of reports, observations, and interviewing persons knowledgeable about the consumer.
3. *Job Placement.* The employment specialist will complete activities to secure placement of individuals with disabilities that include vocational guidance, assistance with application procedures, support during interview processes, advice regarding job offers and negotiation, and initial planning for work.
4. *Job Site Training.* The employment specialist will work with the consumer on and off the job site until the consumer can maintain employment without regular or frequent assistance from the specialist. These duties may include development and implementation of instructional and/or behavioral programming strategies, conferences with the employer, co-workers, and/or consumer, and collection of performance information such as measures of quality and rate of work.
5. *Follow-Along.* The employment specialist will establish and maintain periodic contact with consumers, employers, and others as necessary to facilitate continued successful placement of the employee with disabilities. The employment specialist will be on call to assist in the resolution of obstacles to continued employment.
6. *Other.* The employment specialist will perform other related duties including but not limited to participating in agency meetings, attending training and professional development meetings, developing materials, coordinating consumer services as necessary for continued placement, and maintaining accurate consumer case files.

Source: Reprinted from Wehman, P., & Revell, W. G., Jr. (1997). Transition from school to adulthood: Looking ahead. In P. Wehman (Ed.), *Exceptional individuals in school, community, and work* (p. 631). Austin, TX: PRO-ED. Used by permission.

Natural Cues and Self-Management   The belief that employees with disabilities should be taught independence in the workplace has gained widespread acceptance among supported employment professionals and has spawned exciting and promising research in the use of natural cues and self-management. Natural cues are features already existing in the work environment that the employee can see, hear, touch, or smell and use as a signal for what to do next (Inge & Moon, 2006). For example, clocks or whistles may signal that it is time to go to a job station, the sight of co-workers' stopping work and leaving the job station might be the prompt for break time, and a growing pile of dirty dishes should be the

FIGURE 15.5

Seven types of natural supports for assisting a person with disabilities to obtain and maintain a job

Organizational supports involve the preparation and organization of activities in the job setting, including, but not limited to, scheduling, order of tasks, and locations of materials. Supported employment professionals may be uneasy requesting such supports from employers, but the reality is that employers provide similar accommodations regularly to employees without disabilities. Examples include:

- All necessary supplies are moved to a storage area accessible to the supported employee.
- The supervisor adjusts the supported employee's schedule to accommodate the public bus schedule. For example, Brad needs wheelchair-accessible transportation to get to and from work. The paratransit system is unreliable on the weekends, so his supervisor excuses him from weekend shifts.
- The supervisor works with the employment consultant to carve out job responsibilities that will be most appropriate for the supported employee.

Physical supports involve the design and function of physical objects and equipment in a job setting, whether technical or nontechnical. These supports can range from the simplest jig to specialized computer equipment. Examples include:

- Greg's boss purchased mail pouches, which he attached to Greg's wheelchair every morning. Greg collects recyclables in the pouches.
- The supported employee purchases an augmentative communication device through vocational rehabilitation.

Social supports involve interactions with other individuals. Although social supports often include individuals in the work environment, they can involve individuals from any environment that affects the supported employee's outcomes at work. Examples include:

- With help from the supervisor, John's employment consultant identified a co-worker who has similar interests with John and requested that the co-worker take breaks with John occasionally.
- A neighbor gives the supported employee a ride to and from work.

Training supports involve the extension of personal competence and skill through direct training and instruction. The most common training support used in supported employment is direct training by a job coach. Examples of other training supports include:

- A co-worker receives consultation from an employment specialist on suggested training activities and then provides training to the supported employee.
- A supported employee shadows a co-worker performing the job that she is to perform.

Social service supports involve accessing professional and nonprofessional disability-related services. Examples include:

- The supported employee uses Social Security Plan for Achieving Self Sufficiency (PASS) to pay for transportation to and from work.
- A residential service provider assists the supported employee in finding an apartment near a bus line.

Community supports involve accessing community agencies and services that are available to all individuals. Examples include:

- The supported employee uses public transportation to get to and from work.
- The supported employee takes adult education courses to upgrade his skills.

Personal and family supports involve accessing family and personal resources. These supports often fall into another category, but the category itself is important as a reminder that a supported employee and his or her family or personal network often hold the answers to addressing many of the support needs that are identified. Examples include:

- The supported employee joins a self-advocacy group to learn to better advocate for herself at work.
- Family members provide employment referrals to the job seeker and the job developer.

Source: Adapted from Trach, J. S. (2008). Natural supports in the workplace and beyond. In F. R. Rusch (Ed.), *Beyond high school: Preparing adolescents for tomorrow's challenges* (2nd ed., pp. 259–261). Reproduced by permission of Pearson Education, Inc., Upper Saddle River, NJ.

cue to increase the rate of dishwashing. The employment specialist's role expands from training the employee how to perform various vocational and social skills to teaching him how to respond independently to the cues that occur naturally in the workplace. When those cues are insufficient to prompt the desired behavior, the supported employee can be taught to respond to contrived cues, such as picture prompts depicting individual steps in a multistep task (Wilson, Schepis, & Mason-Main, 1987) or prerecorded verbal prompts interspersed within favorite music that the employee might listen to on a Walkman-type cassette player (Grossi, 1998; Mechling, 2007).

Self-monitoring can also be effectively used in employment training. Research has shown that employees with disabilities can use self-monitoring (observing and recording one's performance) and self-evaluation (comparing self-monitored performance with a goal or production criterion) to increase their job productivity and independence (Ganz & Sigafoos, 2005; Grossi & Heward, 1998). For example, Allen, White, and Test (1992) developed a picture/symbol form that employees with disabilities can use to self-monitor their performance on the job (see Figure 15.6).

Natural and contrived cues, self-monitoring, and self-instruction in the workplace

 Content Standards for Beginning Teachers—Common Core: Use procedures to increase the individual's self-awareness, self-management, self-control, self-reliance, and self-esteem (CC4S5) (also CC4S6, TS5S1, TS8S5).

Task Sheet

Student:_____ Week of:_____ Observer:_____

		M	T	W	Th	Comments
	1.	Job needs (e.g., name tag, lunch).				
	2.	Get work assignment.				
	3.	Get cart.				
	4.	Find and enter room.				
	5.	Check drapes.				
	6.	Check TV.				
	7.	Make bed.				
	8.	Dust.				
	9.	Stock amenities.				
	10.	Empty wastebaskets.				
	11.	Clean bathroom.				
	12.	Vacuum.				
	13.	Fill out hotel checklist.				

FIGURE 15.6

A picture/symbol form that a student or employee with disabilities could use to self-monitor job performance

Source: From "Using a Picture/Symbol Form for Self-Monitoring within a Community-Based Training Program" by C. P. Allen, J. White, & D. W. Test. *Teaching Exceptional Children,* 24(2), 1992, p. 55. © 1992 by the Council for Exceptional Children. Reprinted with permission.

Employees with disabilities can also learn to self-manage their work performance by providing their own verbal prompts and self-instructions (Hughes, 1997). For example, Browder and Minarovic (2000) taught four adults with mental retardation to self-initiate job tasks in their community job settings (e.g., cafeteria, grocery store, garment factory). The employees were taught to complete and initiate the next job activity on their list of work tasks by verbalizing a "did-next-now" strategy (e.g., I did fill the bags, next I'm going to sweep the floor, now I'm sweeping the floor).

Sheltered Employment

Sheltered employment

 Knowledge and Skill Base for Beginning Special Education Transition Specialists: Range of postschool options within specific outcome areas (TS7K3).

Sheltered employment and work activities in segregated settings are the most common types of vocational activities for adults with severe disabilities. Sheltered workshops serve individuals with a wide variety of disabilities, although about half are persons with mental retardation. A national survey of employment programs funded by state agencies serving this population found that 365,165 individuals worked in sheltered and segregated employment settings in 2002, roughly 3 times the number of persons working in supported employment (Braddock, Rizzolo, & Hemp, 2004). **Sheltered workshops** provide one or more of three types of programs: (a) evaluation and training for community-based employment (commonly referred to as transitional workshops), (b) extended or long-term employment, and (c) work activities.

A **work activity center** offers programs of activities for individuals whose disabilities are viewed by local decision makers as too severe for productive work. Rehabilitation and training revolve around concentration and persistence at a task. Intervals of work may be short, perhaps only an hour long, interspersed with other activities—such as training in social skills, self-help skills, household skills, community skills, and recreation. There are approximately 5,000 sheltered work and day activity centers in the United States (Butterworth, Gilmore, Kiernan, & Schalock, 1999).

Many sheltered work programs offer both transitional and extended employment within the same building. Transitional workshops try to place their employees in community-based jobs. Extended employment workshops are operated to provide whatever training and support services are necessary to enable individuals with severe disabilities to work productively within the sheltered environment. The Wage and Hour Division of the U.S. Department of Labor allows sheltered workshops to pay employees hourly wages based on the employee's ability to produce in relation to a nondisabled standard. Workshops are required to determine prevailing wage rates for like-type work done by experienced workers in the surrounding community. Employees are evaluated in relation to a competitive standard at least once every 6 months. For example, if an employee is producing 50 units per hour and the competitive standard is 100 units, then his rate of pay is 50% of the prevailing wage rate for that job. If the prevailing wage rate is $9.00, the employee will receive $4.50 per hour. The workshop still pays the employee $9.00 for each 100 units produced, the same amount a nondisabled worker would make.

All sheltered workshops have at least two elements in common. First, they offer rehabilitation, training, and (in some instances) full employment. Second, to provide meaningful work for clients, a sheltered workshop must operate as a business. Sheltered workshops generally engage in one of three types of business ventures: contracting, prime manufacturing, or reclamation.

Contracting is the major source of work in most workshops. A contract is an agreement that a sheltered workshop will complete a specified job (e.g., assembling and packaging a company's product) within a specified time for a given price. Most sheltered workshops have one or more professional staff members, called contractors or contract procurement persons, whose sole job is to obtain and negotiate contracts with businesses and industries in the community.

Prime manufacturing involves the designing, producing, marketing, and shipping of a complete product. The advantage of prime manufacturing over contracting (assuming that a successful product is being manufactured) is that the workshops do not have problems with downtime when they are between contracts. They can plan their training and labor requirements more directly. Most sheltered workshops, however, are neither staffed nor equipped to handle the more sophisticated business venture of prime manufacturing.

In a *reclamation*, or salvage, operation, a workshop purchases or collects salvage-able material, performs the salvage or reclamation operation, and then sells the reclaimed product. Salvage and reclamation operations have proven successful for many sheltered workshops because they require a lot of labor, are low in overhead, and can usually continue indefinitely.

Problems are associated with sheltered employment, however, and most people no longer consider such sites to be appropriate transition outcomes for young people with disabilities (Simmons & Flexer, 2008). The theoretical purpose of sheltered workshops is to train individuals in specific job-related skills that will enable them to obtain competitive employment; however, few employees of sheltered workshops are ever placed in jobs in the community, and many who are placed do not keep their jobs for long (Gilmore & Butterworth, 1996; Rogan et al., 2002).

Many professionals believe that the poor competitive employment record of sheltered workshop graduates may indicate the limitations inherent in these sites rather than in the employment potential of persons with disabilities (Mank, Cioffi, & Yovanoff, 1998; Wehman et al., 2007). Because sheltered workshop employment is conducted in segregated settings, affords limited opportunities for job placement in the community, and provides extremely low pay, it has been called a dead-end street for individuals with mental retardation (Frank & Sitlington, 1993).

Poor prospects for sheltered employees

 Council for Exceptional Children

Knowledge and Skill Base for Beginning Special Education Transition Specialists: Research on relationships between individual outcomes and transition practices (TS1K4).

POSTSECONDARY EDUCATION

Postsecondary education is no longer a fantasy for individuals with disabilities; it is a reality occurring with greater frequency. As evidence of this increase in enrollment, using data from 2000, 9% of all undergraduates and 6% of all graduate students reported having a disability (National Center for Education Statistics, 2004), with learning disabilities the most prevalent type reported (29% to 35% of those reporting a disability). The rate of participation in postsecondary education programs by former high school special education students doubled from 15% in 1987 (NLTS1) to 31% in 2003 (NLTS2).

Many high school students look ahead to college. However, access to postsecondary education may be even more important for persons with disabilities than it is for individuals without them. Postsecondary education significantly improves chances of meaningful employment. Among adults with disabilities, only 15.6% of those who leave high school without a diploma are employed; participation in the labor force doubles to 30.2% for those who have completed high school and triples to 45.1% for those with some postsecondary education (Yelin & Katz, 1994). For individuals with disabilities who obtain a 4-year degree, the employment rate rises to 50.3%.

Relationship between postsecondary education and employment

 Council for Exceptional Children

Knowledge and Skill Base for Beginning Special Education Transition Specialists: Research on relationships between individual outcomes and transition practices (TS1K4).

Individuals with disabilities who obtain a postsecondary education—whether it be completing a technical training program, a community college's 2-year associate's degree, or a 4-year bachelor's degree—enjoy increased vocational options and greater lifetime earnings (Madaus, 2006; Stodden, 2005). A college degree does not guarantee full-time employment: fewer individuals with disabilities who hold bachelor's degrees work full time as compared to their counterparts without disabilities (National Center for the Study of Postsecondary Educational Supports, 2002). Nevertheless, a college degree is a factor in the salary that can be commanded once students are in the labor market. Overall, college graduates can expect to have better health, greater self-confidence, increased career options, higher-level problem-solving skills, improved interpersonal relationships, and a higher level of open-mindedness as well as more involvement in politics, community affairs, recreation, and leadership activities (Madaus, 2006). They will also be less dependent on parents and governmental benefits than will individuals who do not pursue postsecondary education (Turnbull, Turnbull, Wehmeyer, & Park, 2003).

Postsecondary education is increasingly becoming an option for students with significant disabilities such as mental retardation, autism, or multiple disabilities. Some school districts allow students who require special education services past the age of 18 to graduate with their nondisabled peers and continue educational programming on the campuses of community colleges, universities, or vocational-technical schools (Test et al., 2006). These programs enable youth with moderate and severe disabilities to continue their education in a more age-appropriate learning environment and to participate in some aspects of traditional college life, including auditing academic classes and enjoying recreation and physical education activities in an integrated setting with same-age peers (Casale-Giannola & Wilson Kamens, 2006; Goldrich Eskow & Fisher, 2004; Hamill, 2003). Most programs offer a combination of college classes, basic or functional skills classes, and job experiences (Grigal, Neubert, & Moon, 2002).

Although the range and availability of services offered by colleges and universities for students with disabilities have increased greatly in recent years, the success of students with disabilities as measured by graduation is well below that of students without disabilities. One study found that 80% of students with learning disabilities who had attended postsecondary education programs had not graduated 5 years after high school compared to 56% of students without disabilities (Murray, Goldstein, Nourse, & Edgar, 2000). Ten years after they had left high school, 56% of the students with learning disabilities had not graduated from postsecondary education compared to 32% of those without disabilities.

Becoming aware of the demands of postsecondary education environments is a necessary first step for high school teachers who want to help students acquire the skills, supports, and accommodations needed to succeed in those environments. Other key components and strategies for preparing and supporting secondary students with disabilities for successful transition to postsecondary education include the following (Cunningham, 2007; Hong, Ivey, Gonzalez, & Ehrensberger, 2007; Hurtubis Sahlen & Lehmann, 2006; Madaus, 2005; Mull, Sitlington, & Alper, 2001; Test et al., 2006; Thoma & Evans Getzel, 2005; Webster & Queen, 2008):

Individuals with disabilities are increasingly attending postsecondary education programs of all types.

- Students need exposure to increasingly rigorous curriculum content at the secondary level.
- Students need training in learning strategies for solving new content.
- Students need to be trained how to use assistive technology devices that will increase their access to and ability to manipulate curriculum content.
- Students need to learn self-determination skills that enable effective goal setting, planning, self-management, and advocacy skills to succeed in college.
- Students need to make early application to colleges.
- To be eligible for accommodations and support services at the postsecondary level, students must identify themselves as a student with a disability and provide documentation of the disability.
- Students must learn to identify the accommodations that supported their academic success at the secondary level and how to request these supports as needed at the postsecondary level.

RESIDENTIAL ALTERNATIVES

Where one lives determines a great deal about *how* one lives. It influences where a person can work, what community services and resources will be available, who her friends will be, what opportunities for recreation and leisure exist, and, to a great extent, what feelings of self and place in the community will develop. At one time, the only place someone with severe disabilities could live, if she did not live with family, was a large, state-operated institution. Although she had done no wrong to society, an institution was considered the best place for the person. There were no other options—no such thing as residential alternatives.

Today, however, most communities provide a continuum of residential options for adults with disabilities. Increased community-based residential services have meant a greater opportunity for adults with severe disabilities to live in more normalized settings.

Group Homes

Group homes provide family-style living for a small group of individuals, usually three to six persons. Most group homes serve adults with mental retardation, although some have residents with other disabilities. A national census found 263,415 persons with intellectual and developmental disabilities living in group homes in 2002, a 12-fold increase over the number of persons living there in 1977 (Lakin, Prouty, Polister, & Coucouvanis, 2003).

Some group homes are principally a permanent place to live for their residents. Staff in this type of home help the people who live there develop self-care and daily living skills, form interpersonal relationships, and participate in recreation and leisure skills. During the day, most residents work in the community or in a sheltered workshop.

Other group homes operate more as halfway houses. Their primary function is to prepare individuals with disabilities for a more independent living situation, such as a supervised apartment. These transitional group homes typically serve residents who have recently left institutions, bridging the gap between institutional and community living.

Compared to institutions, two aspects of group homes make them a much more normalized place to live: their size and their location. Most people grow up in a typical family-sized group with opportunity for personal attention, care, and privacy. The congregate-living arrangement of an institution cannot provide a normalized lifestyle, no matter how much effort a hardworking, caring staff makes. Because the number of people in a group home is small, there is a greater chance for a family-like atmosphere to develop. Size is also directly related to the neighborhood's ability to assimilate the members of the group home into typical activities within the community. Large groups tend to become self-sufficient, orienting inward and thereby resisting movement outward into the community. In groups of more than six or eight people, care providers can no longer relate properly to individuals. Large group homes tend to acquire the characteristics of a place of work for direct-care staff rather than a home where people live (Ferguson & Ferguson, 2006). Indeed, some evidence suggests that quality of life is better for persons residing in smaller rather than larger group homes (Burchard, Hasazi, Gordon, & Yoe, 1991; Conroy, 1996).

The location and physical characteristics of the group home itself are also vital determinants of its ability to provide a normalized lifestyle. A group home must be located within the community in a residential area, not a commercially zoned district. It must be in an area where the people who live there can conveniently access shopping, schools, churches, public transportation, and recreational facilities. In other words, a group home must be located in a typical residential area where any one of us might live. And it must look like a home not conspicuously different from other family dwellings on the same street.

Research has shown not only that the architectural features of the home influence the degree to which residents and others give it a high rating of homelikeness but also that some interior design features of a home correlate with the frequency of certain adaptive and maladaptive behaviors by residents (Thompson, Robinson, Dietrich, Farris, & Sinclair, 1996a, 1996b). For example, a laundry room located in the basement may present challenges for residents that create behavioral problems, and a cafeteria-style dining room table might not be conducive to conversations during meals.

Foster Homes

When a family opens its home to an unrelated person for an extended period, the term *foster home* applies. Although foster homes have provided temporary residential services and family care for children (usually wards of the court) for many years, more and more families have begun to share their homes with adults with disabilities. In return for providing room and board for their new family member, foster families receive a modest financial reimbursement.

Life in a foster family home can have numerous advantages for an adult with disabilities. Instead of interacting with paid group-home staff who may or may not actually live at the same address, the person with disabilities lives in a residence that is owned or rented by individuals or families as their primary domicile. The person can participate and share in day-to-day family activities, receive individual attention from people vitally interested in his continued growth and development, and develop close interpersonal relationships. As part

Residential options

Council for Exceptional Children

Knowledge and Skill Base for Beginning Special Education Transition Specialists: Range of postschool options within specific outcome areas (TS7K3).

Julian's transition plan includes learning housecleaning skills for independent apartment living.

Supported living

Council for Exceptional Children

Knowledge and Skill Base for Beginning Special Education Transition Specialists: Range of postschool options within specific outcome areas (TS7K3).

of a family unit, the adult with disabilities also has more opportunities to interact with and be accepted by the community at large.

Apartment Living

A rented apartment is one of the most common living arrangements for people without disabilities in our society. Today, an increasing number of adults with disabilities are enjoying the freedom and independence that apartment living offers. Apartment living offers them an even greater opportunity for integration into the community than do group homes. Whereas the resident of a group home interacts primarily with other persons with disabilities, in an apartment-living arrangement (assuming the apartment is in a regular apartment complex), the likelihood of interacting with persons without disabilities is greater. Burchard and colleagues (1991) found that people who lived in supervised apartments had about twice as many social and leisure activities in the community as did individuals who lived in small group homes or with their natural parents. They also found that persons living in supervised apartments were more likely to be accompanied in the community by peers who were not disabled than those living in group homes were.

Three types of apartment living for adults with disabilities are common: the apartment cluster, the co-residence apartment, and the maximum-independence apartment. An *apartment cluster* consists of a small number of apartments housing persons with disabilities and another nearby apartment for a support person or staff member. An apartment cluster allows for a great deal of flexibility in the amount and degree of support needed by residents in the various apartments. Whereas some people might require direct help with such things as shopping, cooking, or even getting dressed, others need only limited assistance or suggestions and prompts. To facilitate social integration, persons without disabilities may also occupy some apartments in an apartment cluster.

A *co-residence apartment* is shared by an individual with disabilities and a roommate without disabilities. Although this arrangement is sometimes permanent, most co-residence apartments are used as a step toward independent living. The live-in roommates are often unpaid volunteers.

Two to four adults with disabilities usually cohabit *maximum-independence apartments*. These adults have all of the self-care and daily living skills required to take care of themselves and their apartment on a day-to-day basis. A supervisory visit is made once or twice a week to help them deal with any special problems they may be having.

Supported Living

Several innovative models for residential services for adults with disabilities have been developed based on the belief that residential placements must be adapted to the needs of the person with disabilities, not vice versa (Baer & Daviso, 2008). **Supported living** is the term used to describe a growing movement toward helping people with disabilities live in the community as independently and normally as possible. Similar to the way in which supported employment provides ongoing, individualized supports to help a person with disabilities perform meaningful work in a community-based employment setting, supported living involves a personalized network of various kinds and levels of natural supports. Supported living is neither a place nor a single set of procedures to be provided for a person with disabilities.

Klein (1994) explains what supported living is by describing what it is not. Supported living does not revolve around a professional program. People should not live in a place referred to by an agency or provider name (e.g., UCP Group Home, New Life Center). There are no criteria for participation (e.g., persons in this program must be able to cook for themselves, have a physical disability, need more or less than 3 hours per day of attendant care, have visual impairments). Supported living is not based on readiness and movement through a continuum. Participation in traditional residential services is based on a professional's assessment of the person's readiness or ability to live in a particular program, and a person must perform well (learn new skills on her individual habilitation plan) in order to move ("earn" the right) to the next, less restrictive rung on the continuum.

Rather than a single approach or model, supported living is a philosophy about the kind of living experiences appropriate for citizens with disabilities and about commitment to figuring out how to best approximate the ideal for each individual. Supported living, according to Klein (1994), is guided by these nine principles:

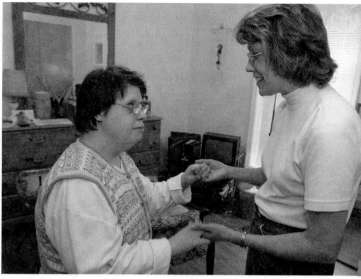

Supported living provides flexible supports when and as they are needed. Once or twice each week, Kay's neighbor stops by to see if she needs any help with her apartment.

1. *Individualization.* Supported living must focus on one person without exception. This does not mean that everyone must live alone. It does mean that if people want to live with someone else, they choose with whom they live.

2. *Everybody is ready.* There are no criteria for receiving support, because what occurs is individually designed. We must give up trying to make people ready by simulating life in a home and begin supporting people to have that home.

3. *Future planning.* People who are assisting others must get to know the individuals they are supporting. What are their desires and preferences? What would an ideal living situation look like for each person? After determining the answers to these questions, the people who care about the person get together regularly with the person to develop a plan for creating, as closely as possible, that ideal living situation.

4. *Use of connections.* Traditional residential services rely on system solutions to problems, referring to the procedures and policy manual to find out what rules and regulations suggest. Supported living relies on the assistance of all who want to and can help. This means that professional care providers and staff are replaced by friends, family members, and neighbors whenever possible. "Who do we know who can help?" becomes a key question for planning and arranging needed supports.

5. *Flexible supports.* Supports are based and provided on the individual's schedule and needs, not on a program's schedule. Persons receive support where, when, how, and with whom it is needed. Supports must be flexible enough to be adjusted to the individual's changing needs, preferences, and desires.

6. *Combining natural supports, learning, and technology.* As much as possible, supports are natural to the time, place, and person. Individuals are given opportunities to learn to provide their own support and use technology to gain control over their environment as much as possible.

7. *Focusing on what people can do.* Traditional residential programs often focus on what people cannot do and design treatment programs to remediate those skill deficiencies. Supportive living focuses on what people can do, provides support for things they cannot do, and provides opportunities for them to learn how to do the things they want to do.

8. *Using language that is natural to the setting.* The language of supported living is natural and promotes inclusion in the community. The places where people live are described as Joe's home or Mary's home. People clean their homes and do their laundry rather than learn programs; people live with roommates, not with staff or care providers; friends, not volunteers, come over to visit; and people with disabilities are referred to as neighbors, friends, and citizens rather than clients, consumers, and residents.

9. *Ownership and control.* Last and most important, the home is the person's, and that person controls the support that is received. Home ownership does not mean that individuals with disabilities who do not have many financial resources must hold the mortgage to a home. It does mean, however, that they sign the lease, that things in the home belong to them, and that the place is their home. Roommates sublet from the person;

support people are hired by the person; and support people respond to the need for assistance when, where, and how it is needed as determined by the person. (adapted from Klein, 1994, pp. 17–18)

Institutions

Most of the large, state-operated institutions in the United States were founded in the 19th or early 20th century, when it was generally believed that people with mental retardation could not be educated or trained. Large custodial institutions (many institutions once housed hundreds or even 1,000 or more people with intellectual and other disabilities) kept people with disabilities segregated from the rest of society; they were never designed to help people learn to live in the community. In the 1960s and 1970s, these institutions came under intense criticism for their inability to provide individualized residential services in a comfortable, humane, and normalized environment (Blatt, 1976; Blatt & Kaplan, 1966; Kugel & Wolfensberger, 1969; Wolfensberger, 1969). The complaints were not leveled against the concept of residential programs; there will probably always be persons whose disabilities are so severe that they require the kind of 24-hour support that residential facilities can offer. The problem lies with the inherent inability of an institutional environment to allow a person to experience a normal lifestyle.

Tremendous improvements have been made in the abysmal living conditions in institutions that Blatt and Kaplan (1966) exposed 40 years ago in their book *Christmas in Purgatory*. During the 1970s, the U.S. Department of Health, Education, and Welfare and the Joint Commission on the Accreditation of Hospitals developed extensive standards for residential facilities for individuals with mental retardation. A facility must meet these standards—which cover topics as diverse as building construction, staffing, and habilitative and educational programming—to qualify for federal and state Medicaid funding. Residential units that meet the standards are referred to as ICF-MR Medicaid facilities. Today, an ICF-MR facility serving 16 or more residents is considered an institution. Although the ICF-MR Medicaid system of rules and regulations has eliminated the inhumane and filthy conditions and the overcrowding that had been defining features of institutional life, the system has become the target of criticism because of residents' quality of life, the high operating costs, and the prevalence of lifetime placements for people in these transitional programs (e.g., Baer & Daviso, 2008; Knoll & Wheeler, 2005; Stancliffe & Hayden, 1998; Stancliffe & Lakin, 1998).

Deinstitutionalization is the movement of people with disabilities out of large institutions and into smaller, community-based living environments such as group homes or apartments. Deinstitutionalization has been an active reality over the past 4 decades. The number of persons with intellectual and developmental disabilities living in large state institutions has decreased steadily from a high of 194,650 in 1967 to 40,434 persons in 2005 (Coucouvanis, Lakin, Prouty, & Webster, 2006; Lakin, Smith, Prouty, & Polister, 2001). As part of this trend, 2004 and 2005 witnessed the closure of 11 state institutions.

Numerous studies have examined the outcomes of deinstitutionalization on people with intellectual disabilities. For a review of studies conducted between 1980 and 1999, see Kim, Larson, and Lakin (2001). The results of most of these studies indicate generally positive outcomes for residents transferred from institutions to group homes to smaller, community-based living arrangements (e.g., Conroy, Spreat, Yuskauskas, & Elks, 2003; Lerman, Hall Apgar, & Jordan, 2005). For example, a widely cited study by Conroy (1996) compared 35 quality-of-life measures over a 5-year period for individuals living in small institutions serving an average of eight people with outcomes for persons living in community-based living apartments or group homes of three people. Higher quality was found in the community living arrangements on 10 of the indicators (e.g., choice making, normalization, individualized treatment, family satisfaction). Higher quality was not found in the ICF-MR facilities on any of the indicators.

Although some studies reporting positive outcomes have been criticized for poor methodology and errors in interpreting the results (e.g., see Walsh & Kastner, 2006 for a critique of Conroy et al., 2003), most professionals and advocacy organizations today believe that large residential facilities are no longer an appropriate place. For example, the organization TASH (2000) has a resolution on deinstitutionalization calling for the termination of

Deinstitutionalization

Council for Exceptional Children

Knowledge and Skill Base for Beginning Special Education Transition Specialists: Range of postschool options within specific outcome areas (TS7K3).

FIGURE 15.7   TASH resolution on deinstitutionalization

Statement of Purpose

TASH calls for the termination of services, activities, and environments which:

- Remove individuals with disabilities from their homes, schools, neighborhoods, and communities;
- Require that persons with disabilities live under circumstances that would not be considered acceptable for persons within that same age range were they not labeled with a disability. These circumstances include institutions, large group homes, and ICFs/MR;
- Rely exclusively upon paid caregivers and other professionalized relationships to the detriment of social support networks, family systems, peer relationships, and friendships; and
- Stigmatize persons with disabilities by portraying them as individuals in need of help, care, and sympathy rather than dignity, respect, and mutual companionship.

TASH believes that both the commitment and the technology exist for people with disabilities to obtain needed and desired supports in communities and neighborhoods. THEREFORE BE IT RESOLVED, THAT TASH, an international advocacy association of people with disabilities, their family members, other advocates, and people who work in the disability field, calls upon the professional and advocacy community to work toward options for people with disabilities that reflect the full range of choices that are available to persons without disabilities.

FURTHER, TASH supports the spending of government funds in support of people with disabilities and families pursuing life in the community. (Revised March 2000)

---

residential facilities and programs (see Figure 15.7). It is important to recognize and respect, however, the fact that not all parents agree that leaving an institutional setting for community living is beneficial for their adult children with the most severe disabilities (e.g., McTernan & Ward, 2005; Swenson, 2005).

RECREATION AND LEISURE

Recreation and the enjoyable use of leisure time are important components of a self-satisfying adult life. Most of us take for granted our ability to pursue leisure and recreational activities. We benefit from a lifetime of learning how to play and how to enjoy personal hobbies or crafts.

Recreation and leisure activities do not come easily for many adults with disabilities, however. To use community recreational resources, one must have transportation, the physical ability or skills to play the game, and, usually, other willing and able friends with whom to play. These three variables, alone or in combination, often limit the recreation and leisure activities available to the adult with disabilities (Frey, Buchanan, & Rosser Sandt, 2005; Matheson, Olsen, & Weisner, 2007). Transportation is not available; the person's disability does not allow him to swim, bowl, or play tennis; and he has no friends with similar skills and interests. Because of these problems, the majority of recreation and leisure experiences for many adults with disabilities have consisted of segregated, disabled-only outings.

Sebine likes to dance. Choice is crucial to the enjoyment of leisure activities.

Too often, the so-called leisure activities for adults with disabilities consist of watching great amounts of television, listening to music in the solitude of their rooms, and spending discretionary time socially isolated (Strand & Kreiner, 2005). Choice is a crucial element for meaningful leisure activities.

> Without choice, activities become simply tasks rather than providing elements of control that lead to leisure satisfaction. If television is the only offering, choice is neglected. . . . Leisure education programs should focus on development of all of the knowledge, skills, and attitudes necessary to facilitate choice—not only traditional group activity skills, but also those individual skills that will have lifetime applications. (Best, Bigge, Musante, & Macias, 2005, p. 349)

Special educators must realize the importance of including training for recreation and leisure in curricula for school-age children with disabilities. Best and colleagues (2005) describe how numerous games, hobbies, crafts, and projects can be adapted to become enjoyable, worthwhile leisure-time pursuits for persons with disabilities. Areas they suggest include raising guinea pigs, music appreciation and study, photography, card games, and nature study. Suggestions are also available for adapting leisure activities for young adults who are deaf-blind, such as using permanent tactile prompts (e.g., attaching fabric to the flipper buttons of a pinball machine), adequately stabilizing materials, enhancing the visual or auditory input provided by the materials (e.g., using large-print, low-vision playing cards), and simplifying the requirements of the task (e.g., raising the front legs on a pinball machine, thereby reducing the speed with which the ball approaches the flippers).

Active recreation that includes physical exercise not only can increase life satisfaction for an adult with disabilities but also can help the person maintain a job by improving overall vitality and health condition (Ispen, 2006). Learning appropriate recreation and leisure skills is particularly important for adults with severe disabilities (Bambara, Browder, & Koger, 2006). Most persons with severe disabilities have ample free time, but many do not use it constructively and may instead engage in inappropriate behaviors such as body rocking, hand flapping, or bizarre vocalizations. A number of studies have been reported in which age-appropriate recreation and leisure skills have been taught to secondary students and adults with moderate and severe mental retardation (e.g., Bolton, Belfiore, Lalli, & Skinner, 1994; Collins, Hall, & Branson, 1997; Cooper & Browder, 1997; Zhang, Gast, Horvat, & Datillo, 1995). Vandercook (1991) taught five high school students with severe intellectual and physical disabilities to play pinball and bowl with partners without disabilities. In another study, four adults with moderate mental retardation learned to order drinks in an Irish pub (O'Reilly, Lancioni, & Kiernans, 2000).

Programs that encourage and support recreational and leisure activities among secondary students with disabilities and their classmates without disabilities are especially valuable for all parties involved (Hughes et al., in press). Participating in community recreation and leisure activities with an adult with disabilities is an excellent way for prospective teachers to appreciate the value of a functional curriculum for school-age students and in process perhaps make a good friend (Best Buddies, 2007; Dardig, 2006; Hardman & Clark, 2006). To read about one such program, see Teaching & Learning, "Next Chapter Book Club: Lifelong Learning and Community Inclusion."

Teaching recreation and leisure activities

Council for Exceptional Children

Knowledge and Skill Base for Beginning Special Education Transition Specialists: Arrange and evaluate instructional activities in relation to postschool goals (TS7S2) (also TS4S1).

Mike does not let anything get in the way of his quality of life. He enjoys an active lifestyle that includes softball and other fitness activities.

THE ULTIMATE TRANSITION GOAL: A BETTER LIFE
Quality of Life

Without question, significant strides have been made in the lives of many people with disabilities. Tens of thousands of people who previously were relegated to life in an institution now live in real homes in regular neighborhoods. Many thousands who never had an opportunity to learn meaningful job skills go to work each day and bring home a paycheck each week. But living in a community-based residence and having a job in an integrated setting do not translate automatically into a better life. Indeed, the Harris poll found that only 34% of adults with disabilities said they are very satisfied with life in general compared to 61% of those without disabilities (National Organization on Disability, 2004).

Most advocates and professionals now realize that the physical presence of people with disabilities in integrated residential, work, and community settings is an important first step but that the only truly meaningful outcome of human service programs must be an improved quality of life. How highly would we rate the quality of life for a woman who always sits alone during lunch and breaks at work because she has not developed a social relationship with her co-workers?

And what is the quality of life for a young man who lives in a group home in a residential neighborhood but seldom gets to choose what will be served for dinner or when he will go to bed and whose only "friends" are the paid staff responsible for supervising him on his weekly trip to the shopping mall? One measure of the quality of a person's life is the extent to which he can make choices. The choices we make play a significant role in defining our individual identities—from everyday matters, such as what to eat or wear, to the choices we make on larger matters, such as where to live or what kind of work to do (Ferguson & Ferguson, 2006).

There have been many different conceptions and definitions of quality of life, debates over how or even whether it can be measured, and recommendations about what should or must be done to improve it (e.g., Hagner, Snow, & Klein, 2006; Halpren, 1993; Hughes, Copeland, Fowler, & Church-Pupke, in press; Lachapelle et al., 2005; Schalock et al., 2002; Schalock, Gardner, & Bradley, 2007; Sheppard-Jones, Thompson Prout, & Kleinert, 2005; Szymanski, 2000).

One widely used measure of the quality of life of a person with intellectual disabilities is the Quality of Life Questionnaire (Schalock & Keith, 1993). The instrument consists of 40 items in four domains: (a) overall satisfaction (e.g., Does your job make you feel good?), (b) competence/productivity, (c) empowerment/independence (e.g., How much control do you have in when you go to bed and when you get up?), and (d) social belonging/community integration (e.g., How frequently do you spend time in recreational activities in town?). For individuals with sufficient language skills, the instrument is administered in an interview format. For people who lack the necessary language skills, the instrument is completed by two raters who know the individual well and who are familiar with the individual's current activities and living environment.

Misguided and Limiting Presumptions

A continuing problem for many adults with disabilities is lack of acceptance as full members of our society, with all the rights, privileges, and services granted to any citizen. Progress has been made in this regard (witness the litigation and legislation on behalf of persons with disabilities that have been discussed throughout this book), but we still have a long way to go. Courts can decree and laws can require, but neither can alter the way in which individuals treat people with disabilities.

Most adults with disabilities believe the biggest barriers to full integration into society are not inaccessible buildings or the actual restrictions imposed by their disabilities but the differential treatment afforded them by people without disabilities. Just as the terms *racism* and *sexism* indicate prejudiced, discriminatory treatment of racial groups and women, the term **handicapism** has been coined to describe biased reactions toward a person with a disability. Those reactions are not based on an individual's qualities or performance but on a presumption of what the person with a disability must feel or be like because of the disability (Bogdan & Taylor, 1994).

Only when a man or a woman with a disability is allowed to be simply an ordinary person—given the opportunity to strive and perhaps succeed but also allowed the freedom and dignity to strive and sometimes fail—can full membership and participation in society become a reality. Only then can people with disabilities enjoy a quality of life that citizens without disabilities take for granted.

> The truth is that every human being has some ordinary ways of being and some unusual ways. Everyone suffers sometimes and has burdens and sometimes burdens others. Everyone also has times of joy, sometimes gives something to someone else, and has the possibility of creating opportunity for others in the world. Paradoxically the most common thing about people is that everyone has unique ways of being himself or herself. (Snow, 2001, p. 8)

Handicapism

Council for Exceptional Children

Content Standards for Beginning Teachers—Common Core: Teacher attitudes and behaviors that influence behavior of individuals with exceptional learning needs (CC5K4).

Next Chapter Book Club: Lifelong Learning and Community Inclusion

BY TOM FISH, VICKI GRAFF, AND ANKE GROSS

Although many adults with intellectual disabilities are living independently in the community, they often experience loneliness, isolation, and lack of friendships. Too often people with intellectual disabilities live *in* the community but are not *part of* the community. There are those in our society who believe that people with special needs are not capable of lifelong learning and not interested in books. Beyond school, meaningful opportunities for literacy and ongoing learning are rare. Lower literacy skills usually result in a lower quality of life, with fewer employment and leisure opportunities.

The Next Chapter Book Club (NCBC) is a program of The Ohio State University's Nisonger Center, a University Center for Excellence in Developmental Disabilities (UCEDD). As the model below shows, the NCBC promotes literacy learning, community inclusion, and social connectedness for adolescents and adults with intellectual disabilities (Fish, Rabidoux, Ober, & Graff, 2006). Developed in 2002, the program has expanded from two clubs in Columbus, Ohio, to more than 80 clubs in 13 states and two cities in Germany.

THE NEXT CHAPTER BOOK CLUB MODEL

The premise is simple. A group of five to nine people with intellectual disabilities and two or three trained volunteer facilitators gather in a local bookstore or café to read and discuss a book for 1 hour a week. The members take turns reading aloud. Everyone has a copy of the same book, so they can follow along when it is not their turn to read. Much like members of other book clubs, NCBC members choose the book they want to read and how they want to structure their club. Books in the NCBC library include adapted classic novels such

as *The Secret Garden* and *Treasure Island* as well as current and sports-related literature. Let's take a closer look at the three model components.

Literacy Learning Although it isn't planned, each club is racially and ethnically diverse, and includes both readers and nonreaders. That's right—readers and nonreaders are in all clubs. In fact, 60% to 70% of members are not conventionally literate but demonstrate emerging literacy. At first we purchased tape players, thinking that members who couldn't read would want to listen to books on tape before coming to the club. The tape players remain unopened to date; it soon became clear that members wanted to read the books aloud together. That leads to a question often asked, What do we do about the emergent readers?

Our training program for volunteer facilitators includes a variety of strategies to help everyone join in. For example, facilitators often use "echo reading": After a brief pause, they say a word or phrase and let the member "echo" the words back. Over time, many members recognize more words. When any member is stuck on a word, facilitators encourage other members to help. Emergent readers can also participate by describing what's happening in the pictures.

The primary goal of the weekly meetings is to include everyone in the process of reading and talking about the story. It's not so much about reading as many pages as possible. The NCBC challenges as well as assists the members to read in a group setting with other adults who share their interests. It takes 12 to 16 weeks to complete one book in this way.

The NCBC provides people with intellectual disabilities a place where they can enjoy reading and don't feel obliged to do so. Scot, age 51, says, "I didn't like reading at school because I was teased by the other kids." Many members tell us that their motivation to read is to relax. Even though they often had bad experiences with learning to read and felt left out in school, they are still eager to participate in a book club.

The results of being a member are often amazing. Rob, age 49, says he wants to learn to drive, and the book club is helping him read the words on traffic signs. Angela, age 29, can see but is legally blind and can't read. Yet her mother, Kathy, says Angela's favorite place to go is the bookstore or library; she loves to be read to. Jessica, age 23, is an emergent reader who always loved books. Her mother, Minda, says since coming to the NCBC, Jessie pretends to read by imitating other beginning readers.

Community Inclusion Unlike book clubs that meet in private homes or libraries, NCBCs meet in

Next Chapter Book Club

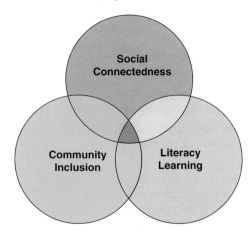

Social Connectedness

Community Inclusion

Literacy Learning

Volunteer facilitators use a variety of strategies to help Next Chapter Book Club members enjoy reading and discussing books.

busy, inviting community settings such as bookstores, coffee shops, and cafés. This follows the paradigm of normalization. Our host sites include Barnes and Noble, Borders, Panera Bread, Starbucks, and Target cafés, among others. These venues have become popular social gathering places for the larger society. Not only does meeting in such places provide the opportunity for people with intellectual disabilities to experience café culture; it also helps raise public awareness of exceptional people.

Tony, the night manager at a local Caribou Coffee, says he and his staff "usually have a good time" serving book club members each week. "It's an opportunity to see everybody socialize and participate like other people," he said. Because the store has no large table, the staff assembles several tables before the club arrives. Such things happen in our clubs spontaneously.

Community inclusion for exceptional people means more than simply living in the community. It should translate to going wherever and whenever one wants. Dependence on others for transportation and accessibility issues remain challenges. Phoebe says it's hard to get to her club, because the store has no ramp for her wheelchair. But somehow she gets there.

Ideally, people with disabilities hanging out with friends in cafés on their own will become commonplace. We recognize that the NCBC is merely a structured platform for people with intellectual disabilities to participate in mainstream society. But it's a start.

Social Connectedness Interpersonal connections, friendships, and belonging play important roles in a person's emotional and physical well-being. Over and over we hear from members, parents, and support staff how much members enjoy making friends and hanging out in the book club. Angela's mother, Kathy,

says Angela was shy at first but has improved her social skills and now greets other members and initiates conversations. "Angela's more outgoing and definitely happier. She has a more joyful attitude and . . . a brighter life!"

Reading in a group is an essential part of the book club that empowers the members. They have the chance to relate what is happening in the story to their own lives and learn from one another. Richard, age 32, says, "When I'm helping the others in the book club, I feel high-level."

CONCLUSION

People with intellectual disabilities have the right to participate as full and equal members of society. We encourage students, professionals in the field, and family members of people with intellectual disabilities to embrace activities such as the NCBC and seek similar opportunities for the people they support and advocate with.

HOW TO GET STARTED

Special education teachers can help promote adult literacy:

- Recognize that literacy experiences for adults with intellectual disabilities are severely lacking.
- Recognize that adults with intellectual disabilities enjoy reading, especially when the literacy experience is combined with hanging out with friends in a bookstore or café on a weekly basis.
- Find local groups or organizations (e.g., service providers, disability organizations, and advocacy or parent groups) that are interested in co-sponsoring an NCBC program in your community.
- Contact the NCBC staff to schedule a training workshop and help you take the next steps. Details are on the website: www.nextchapterbookclub.org.
- Introduce community literacy experiences as part of the classroom curriculum, e.g., visits to the library or reading books in a local bookstore or café.

Thomas R. Fish, Director of Social Work & Family Support Services, and Vicki L. W. Graff, Program Manager, both work at The Ohio State University's Nisonger Center. Anke Gross is Program Coordinator, University of Cologne, Germany.

Go to the Homework & Exercises section in Chapter 15 of MyEducationLab and complete Homework Exercise 3. As you watch the video, think about how the book club might use some of these strategies for their emergent readers.

Self-advocacy and self-determination

 Council for Exceptional Children

Knowledge and Skill Base for Beginning Special Education Transition Specialists: Use support systems to facilitate self-advocacy in transition planning (TS5S2) (also CC4S5).

Self-Advocacy and Self-Determination

Advocacy on behalf of children and adults with disabilities has had a tremendous impact, especially during the past 30 years. Indeed, most of the pervasive changes in education, employment opportunities, and residential services have occurred because of the efforts of advocates. Family members, friends, professionals, and attorneys have traditionally undertaken advocacy for persons with disabilities. Like a growing number of professionals and most individuals with disabilities, Bigge (1991) believes that

> the age of "doing for" a person with a disability is rapidly diminishing. Increasingly, our society is viewing individuals with disabilities as integral and contributing members of the community in which they are a part. Federal and state legislation have provided and supported equal access of individuals with disabilities into all walks of life. . . . Along with the acquisition of these equal rights has come the responsibility for the utilization and protection of these rights. It is now necessary for those with disabilities, as individuals and as groups, to assert themselves as self-advocates. (p. 493)

Persons with disabilities have begun to assert their legal rights, challenging the view that they are incapable of speaking for themselves. Perhaps most conspicuous has been the self-advocacy of individuals with physical disabilities, who have been highly effective in their lobbying as part of the independent living movement. Individuals with sensory impairments have also engaged in self-advocacy. A striking and successful example was Gallaudet University students' refusal in 1988 to accept the appointment of a hearing president who did not know American Sign Language. People with intellectual disabilities have engaged in little self-advocacy, perhaps because many have not learned to recognize when their rights are being violated and because they lack the verbal skills to advocate on their own behalf. Evidence indicates, however, that people with intellectual and developmental disabilities are beginning to use Internet resources and tools to further their civil rights (Zubal-Ruggieri, 2007).

Self-advocacy is a critical component of self-determination (see Chapter 4).

> Self-determined people know how to choose. They know what they want and how to get it. From an awareness of personal needs, self-determined individuals choose goals, then doggedly pursue them. This involves asserting an individual's presence, making his or her needs known, evaluating progress toward meeting goals, adjusting performance, and creating unique approaches to solve problems. (Martin & Marshall, 1995, p. 147)

This is a tall order for anyone, with or without disabilities. But acquiring the skills of self-determination enables freedom.

> Freedom to choose, what kind of job to have, where to live, to have relationships, to make all of the everyday decisions (big and small), and the freedom to make mistakes. Dignity of failure.

Tony Coehlo, chair of the President's Committee on Employment of People with Disabilities, opened the 1994 National Self-Advocacy Conference, "Voices for Choices'" with these remarks:

> We want everything we are entitled to as citizens, nothing more, but nothing less. We want the privileges of full citizenship, but we also welcome its responsibilities. We want the respect we deserve, and we demand the rights we have been denied. We now recognize that empowerment is not a gift to be given, but a right to be demanded. (Cone, 1994, p. 445)

Self-advocacy entails using and protecting one's rights.

Still a Long Way to Go

In general, the quality of life for most adults with disabilities is better today than it has ever been. Not only do more adults with disabilities live, work, and recreate in community-based, integrated environments, but more adults with disabilities have acquired or are acquiring the personal, social, work, and leisure skills that enable them to enjoy the benefits of those settings. But *more* people with disabilities is not the same as *all* people with disabilities. And individuals don't live life "in general"; they experience specific instances of joy and sadness, success and failure. There is still a long way to go.

True, the quality of life for someone who now has his own bedroom in a group home and works for wages in a sheltered workshop is appreciably better than it was before he left the institution where he ate and slept communally and his "work" consisted of an endless series of arts-and-crafts projects. But do the unacceptable standards of the past mean that a relatively better quality of life today is therefore good? Would it be good enough for you?

TIPS for Beginning Teachers

PREPARING STUDENTS FOR THE TRANSITION FROM SCHOOL TO ADULT LIFE
by Dan Killian

MANAGE THE PAPERWORK

Don't let the paperwork overwhelm you! Take some concrete steps to make it all more manageable, such as:

- *Develop a simple chart/spreadsheet to keep track of important dates.* Include each student's name, disability, IEP review date, and the review date for the psychological evaluation;
- *Make copies of all goal pages from your IEPs.* Use these as a master copy for the required 6-week update notations you must make and send home. Keep these IEP goal pages together in a binder in an accessible place.
- *Carry a clipboard wherever you go.* Keep on it your emergency contact information on the students, data collection sheets, and so on.

LEARN YOUR STUDENTS' BACKGROUNDS ASAP

- *At the beginning of the school year, make time to thoroughly review each student's cumulative file,* reviewing such things as the most recent psychological report, previous school and classroom placements, and any information about the nature of their disability.
- *Learn your students' present levels of functioning* (i.e., academic levels, adaptive/communication skills, and prevocational/vocational skills). If these are not documented in their current IEP, you must find them yourself through your own testing and screening.

THE VALUE OF COMMUNITY-BASED VOCATIONAL INSTRUCTION FOR STUDENTS

- *Community-based vocational instruction is most effective one-on-one or in small groups* (no more than four students per group). The teacher can then give personal attention to each individual's unique needs. Remember that frequent praise and encouragement should be interspersed throughout the instruction.
- *Hands-on instruction is the most effective!* For example, students learn best about money by doing activities involving *actual* coins and bills, not by completing worksheets.
- *Social skills are most effectively taught (and learned) in the environment where they actually are needed.* For example, just talking to students in a classroom about appropriate social skills/behaviors in the workplace has little impact if they don't get the opportunity to practice it in a real setting.

TEACH TO MAKE A DIFFERENCE

- *Before teaching a new skill, take some type of meaningful baseline data (keep it simple!) of where the student is with that skill.* Without it, it's very difficult to document if you're making progress.
- *Good transition planning requires a solid understanding of the postsecondary services that are available where the student lives,* such as vocational rehabilitation services, vocational training programs, and adult residential and employment agencies. Find an experienced teacher who can help you understand these postsecondary options for students. It can quickly seem overwhelming if you try to figure it all out by yourself.
- Unique challenges occur in special education that can sometimes seem overwhelming and frustrating. *Try not to forget why you went into special education, and take note of the good things you are doing for the students.*

Key Terms and Concepts

customized employment, p. 580
deinstitutionalization, p. 590
handicapism, p. 593
individualized transition plan (ITP), p. 571
sheltered workshop, p. 584

supported employment, p. 579
supported living, p. 588
transition services, p. 570
work activity center, p. 584

Summary

How Do Former Special Education Students Fare as Adults?

- About one half of students with disabilities who leave school graduate with a standard school diploma.
- Data from the National Longitudinal Transition Studies (NLTS1, NLSTS2) found an unemployment rate of 46% for all youth with disabilities who have been out of school for less than 2 years; most of the young adults who had found competitive employment were working in part-time, low-paying jobs.
- The unemployment rate for young adults with disabilities drops to 36.5% when they have been out of school for 3 to 5 years, but nearly one in five youth reported giving up looking for work (NLTS1).
- NTLS2 found that 31% of youth with disabilities had taken postsecondary education classes within 2 years of leaving high school, and that their rate of current enrollment (19%) was less than half that of their peers in the general population (41%).
- NLTS1 reported that four out of five former special education students had still not achieved the status of independent adulthood after being out of high school for up to 5 years.

Transition Services and Models

- Transition from school to life in the community has become perhaps the most challenging issue in special education today. Models for school-to-adult-life transition stress the importance of a functional secondary school curriculum that provides work experience in integrated community job sites, systematic coordination between school and adult service agencies, parental involvement and support, and a written individualized transition plan (ITP) to guide the entire process.
- Development of career awareness and vocational skills should begin in the elementary grades for children with severe disabilities.
- Middle school students should begin to spend time on actual community job sites.
- Secondary students should spend more time on actual community job sites, with in-school instruction focusing on the functional skills needed in the adult work, domestic, community, and recreational/leisure environments.

Employment

- Getting a job is the number one goal expectation of students and their parents.
- Secondary school programs can enhance the competitive employment prospects for young adults with disabilities by (a) stressing functional, vocational skills; (b) conducting school-based instruction in integrated settings as much as possible; and (c) beginning community-based instruction as early as age 12 for students with severe disabilities and for progressively extended periods as the student nears graduation.
- Supported employment recognizes that many adults with severe disabilities require ongoing support to obtain and hold a job. Supported employment is characterized by performance of real, paid work in regular, integrated work sites; it requires ongoing support from a supported work specialist.

- The role of the employment specialist has evolved from one of primary supporter for the employee with disabilities to one who works with the employer and co-workers to create innovative and natural support networks.
- Self-monitoring, self-evaluation, learning how to respond to naturally occurring cues, and self-instructions are four ways that employees with disabilities can increase their independence and productivity in the workplace.
- Many adults with severe disabilities work in sheltered workshops that provide one or a combination of three kinds of programs: training for competitive employment in the community, extended or long-term employment, and work activities.

Postsecondary Education

- Participation in postsecondary education significantly improves chances of meaningful employment for people with disabilities.
- Although the percentage of postsecondary students who indicate they have a disability has increased significantly in recent years, graduation rates of college students with disabilities remain far below those of students without disabilities.
- The difficulties reported by many college students with disabilities reveal the need for greater emphasis on postsecondary education goals and outcomes during high school transition planning.

Residential Alternatives

- Group homes provide family-style living for three to six persons. Most group homes serve adults with intellectual disabilities, although some have residents with other disabilities. Staff persons in this type of home help the people who live there develop self-care and daily living skills, form interpersonal relationships, and participate in recreation and leisure skills.
- Foster home placement allows an adult with disabilities to participate in day-to-day activities of family life, receive attention from people interested in his development, and experience close personal relationships.
- Apartment living offers the greatest opportunities for integration into the community and interaction with people without disabilities. Three common forms of apartment living for adults with disabilities are the apartment cluster, the co-residence apartment, and the maximum-independence apartment.
- Supported living is an approach toward helping people with disabilities live in the community as independently and normally as they can by providing a network of various kinds and levels of natural supports.
- Despite deinstitutionalization—the movement of persons with intellectual disabilities out of large public institutions and into smaller, community-based residences such as group homes—in 2005, more than 40,000 people, mostly adults with severe or profound mental retardation, still lived in large institutions.

Recreation and Leisure

- Learning to participate in age-appropriate recreation and leisure activities is necessary for a self-satisfying lifestyle.

The Ultimate Transition Goal: A Better Life

- Many adults with disabilities continue to face lack of acceptance as full members of society.
- Handicapism—discriminatory treatment and biased reactions toward someone with a disability—occurs on personal, professional, and societal levels. It must be eliminated before normalization can become a reality for every man and woman with a disability.
- Persons with disabilities have begun to assert their legal rights, challenging the view that they are incapable of speaking for themselves.

Now go to MyEducationLab at www.myeducationlab.com, and take the pretest to assess your initial comprehension of chapter content. Once you have taken the pretest, use your individualized Study Plan for Chapter 15 to enhance your understanding of the concepts discussed in the chapter. Finally, take the posttest to assess your comprehension of Chapter 15 content.

Postscript

Developing Your Own
Personal View of Special Education

All introductory textbooks contain a great deal of information. This book is no different from any other in that respect. I hope, however, that you have gained more than a collection of basic facts and information about learners with exceptional educational needs and special education, the profession dedicated to meeting those needs. I hope you have examined your own attitudes toward and relationships with children and adults with disabilities. At the beginning of the book, I shared 10 fundamental beliefs that underlie my personal, but by no means unique, view of special education. I repeat those beliefs here:

- *People with disabilities have a fundamental right to live and participate in the same settings and programs—in school, at home, in the workplace, and in the community—as do people without disabilities.* People with and without disabilities have a great deal to contribute to and learn from one another. We cannot do that without regular, meaningful interactions in shared environments.

- *People with disabilities have the right to as much self-determination as they can achieve.* Special educators have no more important teaching task than helping students with disabilities learn how to increase the level of autonomy over their own lives.

- *Special education must expand and improve the effectiveness of its early identification and prevention efforts.*

- *Special education must do a better job of helping students with disabilities transition from school to adult life.*

- *Special education must continue to improve its cultural competence.*

- *School and family partnerships enhance both the meaningfulness and the effectiveness of special education.*

- *The work of special educators is most effective when supplemented by the knowledge and services of all of the disciplines in the helping professions.*

- *All students have the right to an effective education.* The special educator's primary responsibility is designing, implementing, and evaluating instruction that helps students with disabilities acquire, generalize, and maintain knowledge and skills that improve the quality of their lives in school, at home, in the community, and in the workplace—now and in the future. To put it another way, the proof of the special education process is in the product. Therefore . . .

- *Teachers must demand effectiveness from the curriculum materials and instructional tools they use.* Although students with disabilities often need more instructional trials to master a skill than do their peers without disabilities (a reality that sometimes requires a heightened level of perseverance and energy by their teachers), the belief that special educators require unending patience is a disservice to students with special needs and to their educators—both special and general education teachers. Teachers should not wait patiently for exceptional children to learn but should modify the instructional program to improve its effectiveness.

- *The future for people with disabilities holds great promise.* We have only begun to discover ways to improve teaching, increase learning, prevent or minimize the effects of some of the conditions that cause and exacerbate the effects of disabilities, and use technology to compensate for disabilities. We have not come as far as we can in learning how to help exceptional children and adults build and enjoy fuller, more independent lives.

As a Member of the Profession If you consider yourself a prospective special educator, view special education as a profession and yourself as a professional. A professional is someone who has acquired a specific skill set and knowledge. Becoming a special educator will make you different from people without your professional training. This has nothing to do with arrogance but everything to do with recognizing that students with disabilities depend on their teachers' developing and responsibly using as much professional competence as they can muster.

Obtaining an objective understanding of the nature and scope of a special educator's responsibilities is the first step toward professional competence. Special education is serious business. The learning problems faced by students with disabilities are real, and they require intensive and systematic intervention. Be wary of the conceptions that disability is merely a socially constructed phenomenon: that all children who are diagnosed with a disability would be successful and happy learners if others simply viewed them more positively. This romantic ideology is seldom, if ever, promoted by people with disabilities or by their parents and families. Children with disabilities have skill deficits and difficulties in acquiring and generalizing new knowledge and skills—real disabilities that cannot be deconstructed away. Don't let the needs of exceptional children and their families become lost in such postmodern ideologies. They need and deserve systematic, effective special education.

It is commendable that you have the commitment and the desire to teach children with exceptional educational needs. You will probably hear often that you are "wonderful" or "patient" because of this. Good intentions are fine, but desire and commitment are only a first step. What learners with disabilities need more than anything are teachers who are in some ways *impatient*—impatient with curriculum, instructional methods, and policies that do not help their students learn and subsequently use new knowledge and skills required for successful functioning in the home, school, workplace, and community. So, my recommendation to you as a future teacher is this: Don't be patient; be effective.

You will increase your effectiveness as a teacher by using only those curriculum and instructional methods that are backed by sound, empirical research evidence. Special education research has produced a significant and reliable knowledge base about effective teaching practices. While no reasonable person believes that research has discovered all that we need to know about teaching exceptional students—many important questions remain to be answered—today's special educator can turn to a research base that includes many instructional strategies and tactics that did not exist when the Education of All Handicapped Children Act was signed into law in 1975.

When considering a new curriculum, program, or instructional method, teachers should ask questions such as the following:

- Has this program been tested in the classroom?
- What evidence shows that this program works?
- What measures of student performance were used to evaluate this program?
- Has any research on this program been published in peer-reviewed journals?
- Does any evidence suggest the program will succeed if modified to meet the skill levels and ages of my students?

Educating students with disabilities has always posed complex and difficult challenges. And today's special education teachers are expected to do more than ever before. For example, special educators must help ensure students' access to the general education curriculum while teaching them the functional skills needed for daily living and successful transition from school to adult life in the community and workplace. Prepare yourself for meeting this challenge as best you can. Demand relevant, up-to-date information and hands-on practical experiences from your teacher-education program. Continue your education and professional development throughout your career. Stay abreast of advances in special education by reading professional journals, actively participate in your school's in-service training opportunities, and attend professional conferences. Even better, experiment with instructional methods, and share the results of your research with colleagues through presentations and publications.

Special education is not a grim, thankless business. Quite the opposite: special education is an exciting, dynamic field that offers personal satisfaction and feelings of accomplishment unequaled in most areas of endeavor. Welcome aboard!

As a Member of the Community The degree of success and happiness that a person with disabilities enjoys in the normal routines of everyday life is not determined solely by his skills and abilities. In large measure, the integration of people with disabilities into contemporary society depends on the attitudes and actions of citizens with little knowledge of or experience with exceptional learners. How can people come to accept and support a group they do not know?

Society controls who enters and who is kept out, much as a gatekeeper lets some visitors pass but refuses others. For a particular individual, society's gatekeeper may have been a physician who urged parents to institutionalize their child or a teacher who resisted having difficult-to-teach students in her classroom. It may have been an employer who refused to hire workers with disabilities. It may have been a social worker, a school board member, or a voter. Saddest of all, it may even have been a parent whose low expectations kept the gate closed.

How society views people with disabilities influences how individual members of the community respond. Society's views are changing gradually for the better; they are being changed by people who believe that our past practices of exclusion and denial of opportunities were primitive, unfair, and ultimately detrimental to everyone. But to have maximum impact, the movement toward integration and opportunities described in this book must ultimately translate into personal terms for those of you who will not choose careers in special education. People with disabilities and people without disabilities do experience certain aspects of life differently, but we are more like one another than we are different. And the conclusion I hope you have reached is this: Every child and adult with disabilities must be treated as an individual, not as a member of a category or a labeled group.

In Sum Viewing every individual with disabilities first as a person and second as a person with a disability may be the most important step in integrating the individual into the mainstream of school and community life. But changing our attitudes will not diminish the disability. What it will do is give us a new outlook—a more objective and positive one—and allow us to see a disability as a set of special needs. Viewing exceptional people as individuals with special needs tells us much about how to respond to them—and how we respond is the essence of special education.

APPENDIX

Coverage of Content Areas for PRAXIS II Test Education of Exceptional Students: Core Content Knowledge (0353)

Many states require a passing score on one or more of the PRAXIS II™ tests for licensure or certification as a special education teacher. The PRAXIS II tests—the Subject Assessment/Specialty Area Tests of the PRAXIS Series of Professional Assessments for Beginning Teachers™—assess students' knowledge of critical content standards.

One of the most frequently required PRAXIS II tests in special education is Education of Exceptional Students: Core Content Knowledge (0353). This appendix enables you to locate the page numbers where each of the content areas covered by this test is explained in the text. A complete outline of the content areas covered by test 0353 is printed inside the back cover of this text.

The organization and format of this appendix, when used in conjunction with the CEC margin notes throughout the text and Subject Index at the end of the book, will also aid you in determining content areas covered by other PRAXIS II tests in special education.

A great deal of the basic content knowledge that a beginning special education teacher should possess is presented in this text, and learning this content will contribute to your obtaining a passing score on any of the PRAXIS II tests in special education. However, two important qualifiers must be recognized. First, each of the PRAXIS II tests in special education requires some knowledge beyond that included in an introductory text. That is why you will see a few of the PRAXIS II content areas without very much text coverage. Second, no matter how extensive and current the textbook, how well the instructor teaches the course, and how thoroughly you master the text content and course objectives, you will not be prepared to teach students with exceptional leaning needs as a result of this course alone. Successful completion of an introductory course in special education is but one step in a teacher preparation program.

I. Understanding Exceptionalities

PRAXIS Content Area	Relevant Textbook Content	
A. *Human development and behavior as related to students with disabilities, including* 1. Social and emotional development and behavior	• Intellectual disabilities (MR/DD), 141 • Learning disabilities, 185 • Emotional or behavioral disorders, 215, 219 • Autism spectrum disorders, 261, 264–265 • Communication disorders, 304–305, 307–308 • Hearing impairments, 337–338 • Visual impairments, 373–374	• Physical disabilities and health impairments, 427, 430–431 • ADHD, 420–422 • Severe/multiple disabilities, 453–455, 457–458 • Deaf-blindness, 455–457 • Traumatic brain injury, 462–463 • Infants and preschoolers with disabilities, 535–536
2. Language development and behavior	• Learning disabilities, 182, 184 • Autism spectrum disorders, 261–262 • Communication disorders, 300–305 • Hearing impairments, 343	• Visual impairments, 371 • Severe/multiple disabilities, 453–455, 457–458 • Deaf-blindness, 455–457 • Traumatic brain injury, 462–463
3. Cognition	• Intellectual disabilities (MR/DD), 139–140 • Learning disabilities, 174–179 • Emotional or behavioral disorders, 219–220 • Autism spectrum disorders, 262–263 • Hearing impairments, 333 • Visual impairments, 371	• Physical disabilities and health impairments, 409–411, 414–420 • Severe/multiple disabilities, 453–455, 457–458 • Deaf-blindness, 455–457 • Traumatic brain injury, 462–463

PRAXIS Content Area	Relevant Textbook Content	
4. Physical development, including motor and sensory	• Intellectual disabilities (MR/DD), 141 • Autism spectrum disorders, 263 • Visual impairments, 373–375	• Physical disabilities and health impairments, 409–411, 414–420 • Severe/multiple disabilities, 453–455, 457–458 • Traumatic brain injury, 462–463
B. *Characteristics of students with disabilities, including influence of* 1. Cognitive factors	• Intellectual disabilities (MR/DD), 139–140 • Learning disabilities, 174–179, 181–182 • Emotional or behavioral disorders, 219–220 • Autism spectrum disorders, 262–263 • Hearing impairments, 336–367 • Visual impairments, 373–374	• Physical disabilities and health impairments, 409–411, 414–420 • ADHD, 422 • Severe/multiple disabilities, 453–455, 457–458 • Deaf-blindness, 455–457 • Traumatic brain injury, 462–463
2. Affective and social-adaptive factors, including cultural, linguistic, gender, and socioeconomic factors	• Intellectual disabilities (MR/DD), 141 • Learning disabilities, 185 • Emotional or behavioral disorders, 214–215, 221, 224 • Autism spectrum disorders, 261 • Communication disorders, 304–305, 307–308 • Hearing impairments, 337–338	• Visual impairments, 375–376 • Physical disabilities and health impairments, 409–411, 414–420 • ADHD, 420–422 • Severe/multiple disabilities, 453–455, 457–458 • Deaf-blindness, 455–457 • Traumatic brain injury, 462–463
3. Genetic, medical, motor, sensory, and chronological-age factors	• Intellectual disabilities (MR/DD), 138–141 • Learning disabilities, 187–189 • Emotional or behavioral disorders, 224–225 • Autism spectrum disorders, 263 • Communication disorders, 306–309 • Hearing impairments, 337–338, 340 • Visual impairments, 373–375	• Physical disabilities and health impairments, 409–411, 414–420 • ADHD, 420–422 • Technology-dependent students, 443 • Severe/multiple disabilities, 453–455, 457–458 • Deaf-blindness, 455–457 • Traumatic brain injury, 462–463
C. *Basic concepts in special education, including* 1. Definitions of all major categories and specific disabilities, as well as the incidence and prevalence of various types of disabilities	*Definitions* • Exceptional children, impairment, disability, handicap, at risk, 9–10 • Intellectual disabilities (MR/DD), 132–136 • Learning disabilities, 173–174 • Dyslexia, 179 • Emotional or behavioral disorders, 213–215 • Anxiety, mood, and other emotional disorders, 217–219 • Autism spectrum disorders, 257–261	• Communication disorders, 297–305 • Hearing impairments, 334–336, 338–340 • Visual impairments, 371–373 • Physical disabilities and health impairments, 408–409 • ADHD, 420–422 • Severe/multiple disabilities, 453–455 • Deaf-blindness, 455–457 • Traumatic brain injury, 459–460 • Developmental delay, 544
	Incidence and prevalence • All disabilities, 10–12 • Intellectual disabilities (MR/DD), 142 • Learning disabilities, 186–187 • Emotional or behavioral disorders, 221–224 • Autism spectrum disorders, 268 • Communication disorders, 309	• Hearing impairments, 338 • Visual impairments, 376 • Physical disabilities and health impairments, 408–409 • ADHD, 422 • Severe/multiple disabilities, 458–459 • Deaf-blindness, 459 • Traumatic brain injury, 460
2. The causation and prevention of disability	• Preventive intervention, 35, 175–179 • Intellectual disabilities (MR/DD), 142–147 • Learning disabilities, 187–189 • Emotional or behavioral disorders, 224–227 • Autism spectrum disorders, 268–269 • Communication disorders, 309–311 • Hearing impairments, 340–341 • Visual impairments, 376–380	• Physical disabilities and health impairments, 409–411, 414–420 • ADHD, 423 • Severe/multiple disabilities, 459 • Traumatic brain injury, 460–462 • Early intervention as prevention, 536–537, 539–540

PRAXIS Content Area	Relevant Textbook Content	
3. The nature of behaviors, including frequency, duration, intensity, and degrees of severity	• Measurable dimensions of behavior, 230–231	
4. The classification of students with disabilities; labeling of students; ADHD; the implications of the classification process for persons classified, etc.	• Disability categories within IDEA, 11 • Emotional or behavioral disorders, 215–216, 219 • Intellectual disabilities (MR/DD), 132–138 • ILEP classification system, 134 • Pros and cons of labeling and classification, 12–16	• Alternatives to labeling, 14 • Disproportional representation of culturally diverse children in special education, 56–58 • ADHD, 422–423
5. The influence of level of severity and presence of multiple exceptionalities on students with disabilities	• Intellectual disabilities (MR/DD), 132–135, 147, 149–150 • Learning disabilities, 179, 181–182, 184–186 • Emotional or behavioral disorders, 215–221 • Autism spectrum disorders, 261–265 • Communication disorders, 306–309	• Hearing impairments, 334, 344–345 • Visual impairments, 371–373 • Physical disabilities and health impairments, 430–431 • Severe/multiple disabilities, 553–558 • Traumatic brain injury, 560–563
D. The influence of (an) exceptional condition(s) throughout an individual's life span	• Family life-cycle stages, 98–100 • Effects of early social and language deprivation on development, 145–146	• Early pattern of antisocial behavior for children with EBD, 227–228

II. Legal and Societal Issues

PRAXIS Content Area	Relevant Textbook Content	
A. *Federal laws and legal issues related to special education, including* 1. IDEA 2004	• Six major principles IDEA, 19, 22 • IDEA and early intervention for infants and toddlers, 22–23, 540–543 • IDEA and preschoolers, 22–23, 544 • Individuals with Disabilities Education Improvement Act of 2004, 18–19	• Definition of transition services, 570 • Individualized transition plan (ITP), 570–571, 573 • Definition of supported employment, 579
2. Section 504	• Basic provisions, 29 • ADHD and eligibility for special education services under IDEA or Section 504, 422–423	
3. Americans with Disabilities Act (ADA)	• Implications for educational agencies, 30	
4. Important legal issues, such as those raised in following cases: *Rowley* re: program appropriateness, *Taro* re: related services, *Honig* re: discipline, *Oberti* re: inclusion	• PARC case and equal protection, 17–18 • Rowley case, 26, 28 • Tatro case, 27	• Honig case, 27–28 • Garret case, 27 • Legal aspects of disciplining students with disabilities, 28
B. *The school's connections with the families, prospective and actual employers, and communities of students with disabilities, for example* 1. Teacher advocacy for students and families, developing student self-advocacy	• Respite care, 95–96 • Developing independence and self-esteem, 278–279, 596	• Promoting self-advocacy and self-determination, 150–155, 441–442, 596 • Teaching choice-making, 464–466, 478, 592

PRAXIS Content Area	Relevant Textbook Content	
2. Parent partnerships and roles	• IDEA and parent participation, 52–54, 63–71, 91–93 • Roles & responsibilities of exceptional parents, 95–98 • Effects of child's disability on family system, 93–95 • Barriers to effective communication and partnership with parents, 104–106	• Developing cultural reciprocity with parents & families from diverse backgrounds, 106–109 • Communicating with parents, 102–104 • Parent participation in transition planning, 571–572
3. Public attitudes toward individuals with disabilities	• Society's and education's past and changing attitudes toward individuals with disabilities, 16–18, 592–593, 596 • Handicapism, 593	• Normalization, 164 • Social role valorization, 164
4. Cultural and community influences on public attitudes toward individuals with disabilities	• Deaf culture and community, 334, 348–349, 359	
5. Interagency agreements	• Coordinating transition services with community agencies, 571–572	
6. Cooperative nature of the transition planning process	• Relationship between postsecondary education and employment, 585–586 • Transition team collaboration, 572	
C. *Historical movements/trends affecting the connections between special education and the larger society, for example* 1. Deinstitutionalization and community-based placements	• Residential options for adults with disabilities, 586–591 • Supported living, 588–590 • Deinstitutionalization, 590	

2. Inclusion	• Individuals with disabilities access to and placement in public education, 16–18
	• Components of inclusive education, 81
	• Perspectives on inclusion, overall,
	  • Intellectual disabilities (MR/DD), 161, 164
	  • Learning disabilities, 203, 205
	  • Emotional or behavioral disorders, 246–247
		• Autism spectrum disorders, 282–283
		• Hearing impairments, 364
		• Visual impairments, 395, 399–401
		• Physical disabilities and health impairments, 444–445
		• Severe/multiple disabilities, 480–485

3. Application of technology	• In general, 23 • Communication disorders, 321 • Hearing impairments, 347–349	• Visual impairments, 383–387, 392–393, 396–398 • Physical disabilities and health impairments, 431–432
4. Transition	• Will's Bridges model, 569 • Halpren's transition model, 570	• Competitive, supported, and sheltered employment, 568, 574–585 • Postsecondary education, 568, 585–586

5. Advocacy	• History of education of children with
	  • All disabilities, 16–18
	  • Intellectual disabilities (MR/DD), 147–149,
	  • Learning disabilities, 203, 205
	  • Autism spectrum disorders, 272–273
		• Hearing impairments, 351–354
		• Visual impairments, 380–381, 399
		• Physical disabilities and health impairments, 431–432
		• Severe/multiple disabilities, 16–17
		• Normalization and social role valorization, 164

6. Accountability and meeting educational standards	• IDEA, 18–19, 22–23, 541–543, 550–551	• No Child Left Behind Act, 30–32

III. Delivery of Services to Students with Disabilities

PRAXIS Content Area	Relevant Textbook Content	
A. *Background knowledge, including* 1. Conceptual approaches underlying service delivery to students with disabilities, including cognitive, constructivist, psychodynamic, behavioral, sociological, ecological, therapeutic (speech/language, physical, and occupational) and medical approaches	• Applied behavior analysis, 274–277 • Early intensive behavioral intervention, 273–274 • Oral/aural approach, 351–353 • Drug therapy for children with ADHD, 423–425 • Total communication, 355, 358	• ASL, 359 • Bicultural-bilingual approach, 359–360 • Goals for ECSE, 548–549 • Developmentally appropriate practice, 549–550 • Positive behavioral support, 235, 238, 477–479

2. Placement and program issues such as early intervention; least restrictive environment; inclusion; role of IEP team; due process guidelines; categorical, non-categorical, and cross-categorical programs; continuum of educational and related services; related services and their integration into the classroom; accommodations, including access to assistive technology; transition of students into and within special education placements; community-based training; post-school transitions	• Definitions of educational placements, 36–37, 40
	 • Placement alternatives for students with
	   • Intellectual disabilities (MR/DD), 161, 164–165
	   • Learning disabilities, 203–205
	   • Emotional or behavioral disorders, 246–247
	   • Autism spectrum disorders, 282–284
	   • Communication disorders, 325
	   • Hearing impairments, 361, 364
	   • Visual impairments, 394–395, 398–399
	   • Physical disabilities, health impairments, 443–445
	   • Severe/multiple disabilities, 480–485
		• Infants and preschoolers with disabilities, 557–559
		 • Least restrictive environment, 73–76
		 • Components of inclusive education, 76–77, 80–82
		 • Benefits of neighborhood schools, 480–481
		 • Role of IEP team, 63, 75–76
		 • Due process safeguards, 22
		 • Continuum of services—74–75, VI-
		 • Related services, 23, 28
		 • Promoting inclusion with buddy systems, 482–483
		 • Social relationships, 480–484

3. Integrating best practices from multidisciplinary research and professional literature into the education setting	• Asking for research evidence of effectiveness, 284–285, 288–289	• Closing research-to-practice gap, 42–44
B. *Curriculum and instruction and their implementation across the continuum of educational placements, including* 1. The Individualized Family Service Plan (IFSP)/Individualized Education Program (IEP) process	• IEP process, 63–71 • IEP team membership, 63 • IEP components, 63–64 • IEP goals and objectives, 68–70, 550 • IFSP definition, purpose, and content, 541–543, 550–551 • IHCP, 437, 440 • Considering communication needs of students who are deaf or hard of hearing, 360–363	• Transition plan component of IEP, 570–573 • Prioritizing instructional targets for students with severe/multiple disabilities, 468–469, 471

2. Instructional development and implementation; for example: instructional activities, curricular materials and resources, working with classroom and support personnel, tutoring options	• Programming and delivering instruction in inclusive settings for students with
	   • Intellectual disabilities (MR/DD), 147, 149–150, 152
	   • Learning disabilities, 192–194, 203
	   • Emotional or behavioral disorders, 233–235
	   • Autism spectrum disorders, 271–277, 280–282
	   • Communication disorders, 315–317, 319–325
		• Visual impairments, 394–395
		 • Physical disabilities, health impairments, 433–435, 441–442
		 • ADHD, 425–429
		 • Severe/multiple disabilities, 464–468, 472–474
		 • Traumatic brain injury, 462–463
		 • Preschoolers with special needs, 538, 544–551

PRAXIS Content Area	Relevant Textbook Content
3. Teaching strategies and methods; for example: modification of materials and equipments, learning centers, facilitated groups, study skills groups, self-management, cooperative learning, diagnostic-prescriptive method, modeling skill drill, guided practice, concept generalization, learning strategy instruction, and Direct Instruction	• Fluency building, 20–21 • Self-determination, 150, 152, 154–155 • Task analysis, 152–153 • Choral responding, 158–159 • Response cards, 162–163 • Systematic feedback, 156, 475 • Promoting generalization and maintenance, 157, 160, 475 • Content enhancements: guided notes, graphic organizers, and mnemonic strategies, 194–195, 198–202 • Active student response, 153, 156 • Direct Instruction, 195–198 • Explicit instruction, 196–198 • Learning strategies, 202–203 • Discrete trial training, 275 • Picture activity schedules, 277–279, 466 • Naturalistic teaching strategies, 319, 320–321, 322, 476–477 • Speech reading, 354–355 • Cued speech, 355 • Visual phonics, 355–357 • Elements of systematic instruction for students with severe disabilities, 470, 474–475 • Structure of learning environment, 226–227 • Embedding learning opportunities, 550, 553–555 • Partial participation, 475, 478
4. Instructional format and components; for example: small and large-group instruction, facilitated group strategies, functional academics, general academics with focus on special education, ESL and limited English proficiency, language and literacy acquisition, self-care and daily living skills, pre-vocational skills	• Functional curriculum goals, MR/DD–149–150, Severe/multiple disabilities, 464–465, 472–474 • Classwide peer tutoring, 78–80 • Integrating life skills into curriculum, MR/DD–150–152 • Phonemic awareness and alphabetic principle, 181–183 • Comprehension and beginning reading instruction, 182–183 • Response cards, 162–163 • Functional life skills for students, MR/DD–141, 149–150, 151, VI–394 • Small-group instruction, 479–480 • Orientation and mobility for students with VI, 389, 392–393 • Functional vision, 384–386 • Health care routines, 437–440 • Circle time for preschoolers, 552–553
5. Career development and transition issues as related to curriculum design and implementation according to the criteria of ultimate functioning	• Teaching functional and age-appropriate skills, 149–150 574–575 • Relating transition services to IEP goals and objectives, 572–573, 575–577 • Career awareness and transition related curriculum activities, 572–575 • Characteristics of secondary school programs and competitive employment outcomes, 574–575, 577–578 • Teaching recreation and leisure activities, 467–469, 591–592 • Residential alternatives for adults with disabilities, 586–591 • Quality of life for adults with disabilities, 592–593
6. Technology for teaching and learning in special education settings; for example: integrating assistive technology into the classroom; computer-assisted instruction; augmentative and alternative communication; adaptive access for microcomputers; positioning and power mobility for students with physical disabilities; accessing and using information technology; use of productivity tools; technology for sensory disabilities; and voice-activated, speech-synthesis, speech recognition and word-prediction software	• Assistive technology defined, 23 • Technology-enhanced activity schedules, 277–279 • Augmentative and alternative communication, 321–325, 466–467 • Hearing aids, 346–347 • Group listening devices, 347 • Speech-to-text translation and TV captioning, 350–351 • Auditory training/learning, 354 • Braille, brailler, slate and stylus, 382–383 • Tactile aids and manipulatives for students with VI, 383 • Adapting toys for children with physical impairment, 412–413 • Optical devices and technological aids for students with VI, 385–387 • Reading print, students with VI, 387–388 • Helping students with low vision, 390–391 • Listening skills for students with VI, 393–394 • Self-operated audio prompting systems, 396–398 • Assistive technology for students with physical disabilities, 412–413, 435–436 • Animal assistance for people with disabilities, 437–440

PRAXIS Content Area	Relevant Textbook Content
C. *Assessment, including* 1. Use of assessment for screening, diagnosis, placement, and the making of instructional decisions; for example: how to select and conduct nondiscriminatory assessments; how to interpret standardized and specialized assessment results; how to effectively use evaluation results in IFSP/IEP; how to prepare written reports and communicate findings	• Definitions of standardized tests, norm-referenced tests, the normal curve, and standard deviation, 136–138, 189–190 • IQ scores and diagnosis of Intellectual Disabilities (MR/DD), 136–138 • Projective tests, 230 • Issues to consider with IQ tests/scores, LD–189–190 • Criterion-referenced tests, LD–190 • Informal reading inventories, LD–190 • Purposes of screening assessment, and evaluation, 51–56, 229, 544 • Standardized achievement tests, 189–190 • Response to instruction for diagnosis of LD, 175–179 • Screening tools for Emotional or behavioral disorders, 229–230 • Screening and diagnostic tools for autism spectrum disorders, 269–271 • Screening, assessment and diagnosis of communication disorders, 311–315 • Audiometry and audiograms, 342–346 • Screening and assessment tools for early intervention, 544–547 • Functional behavior assessment, 230–233, 477–478 • Screening and assessment for hearing impairment, 342–346 • Determining communication needs for students with hearing impairment, 362–363
2. Procedures and test materials, both formal and informal, typically used for pre-referral, referral, eligibility, placement, and ongoing program monitoring	• Prereferral intervention, 21–55 • Responsiveness to intervention (RTI), 54–55, 175–179 • Multifactored evaluation, 55–56 • Monitoring student progress, 59–60, 190–192 • Precision teaching, 192 • Curriculum-based measurement, 190–192, 547 • Assessing adaptive behavior, 138 • Direct and frequent measurement, 192, 230–233 • Manifestation determination, 28–29
3. How to select, construct, and modify nondiscriminatory, developmentally and chronologically age-appropriate informal assessments, including teacher-made tests, curriculum-based assessment, and alternatives to norm-referenced testing (including observations, anecdotal records, error analysis, miscue analysis, self-evaluation questionnaire and interviews, journals and learning logs, portfolio assessment)	• See text content under, "Use of assessment for screening, diagnosis, placement, and the making of instructional decisions" • Assessing the communicative competence of culturally and linguistically diverse students, 314–315 • Nondiscriminatory assessment, 55–58. 314–315,
D. *Structuring and managing the learning environment, including* 1. Structuring the learning environment, for example: the physical-social environment for learning (e.g., expectations, rules, consequences, consistency, attitudes, lighting, acoustics, seating, access, safety provisions, strategies for positive interactions)	• Effects of teacher's reactions to noncompliance, 226–227 • Schoolwide positive behavior support, 235, 238 • Proactive classroom management strategies, 241–242 • Helping the child who stutters, 318 • Helping the student with low vision, 390–391 • Modifying and adapting physical environment for students with physical disabilities, 435 • Positioning, seating, and movement, 437, 441 • Lifting and transferring students, 441–442 • Positive behavioral support, 235, 238 • Structuring learning environment for students with TBI, 462 • Embedding learning opportunities for preschool children, 550, 553–555 • Preschool activity schedules, 555–556 • Physical arrangement of preschool classroom, 555, 557
2. Classroom management techniques, e.g., behavior analysis (identification and definitions of antecedents, target behavior, and consequent events); behavioral interventions; functional analysis; data gathering procedures (e.g., anecdotal data, frequency methods, and interval methods); self-management strategies and reinforcement; cognitive-behavioral interventions; social skills training	• Social stories, 280–282 • Social skills curricula and instruction, 234–235 • Contingent teacher praise and positive reinforcement, 236–237 • Signaling and recruiting teacher attention, 222–223 • Self-management, including self-monitoring and self-evaluation, 239–241, 428–429 • Peer-mediated support and interventions, 242 • Behavioral interventions for ADHD, 425–426, 428–429

PRAXIS Content Area	Relevant Textbook Content	
3. Behavior management strategies	• Positive behavioral support, 235, 238, 477–479 • Mystery Motivators, 244–245	• Teaching choice-making, 464–466, 478 • Manifestation determination, 28–29
E. *Professional roles, including* 1. Specific roles and responsibilities of teachers; for example: teacher as collaborator with other teachers, teacher educators, parents, community groups, and outside agencies; teacher as a multidisciplinary team member; maintaining effective and efficient documentation; selecting appropriate environments and service for students; critical evaluation and use of professional literature and organizations: reflecting on one's own teaching; teacher's role in a variety of teaching settings (e.g., self-contained classrooms, resource room, itinerant, co-teacher in inclusion setting, etc.); and maintaining student confidentiality	• Using research-based practices, 42–43, 72–73 • Teaming models, 60–63 • Co-teaching models, 62–63 • Wraparound services for students with EBD, 246 • Interpreters, 349–350 • Professional organizations AAIDD-131, ASAT-288, CCBD-214, LDA-173, NAGC-524, NJCLD-173 TASH-454 • Itinerant teachers for students with VI, 394–395	• Collaborating with PTs, OTs, SLPs, and other related-services specialists, 433–435 • Effective communication among transition team members, 572 • Employment specialist, 580–581
2. Influence of teacher attitudes, values and behaviors on the learning of exceptional students	• Differential acceptance and empathetic relationship, 243 • Focusing on alterable variables, 243 • Promoting self-determination, 150–155, 441–442, 596	• Changing attitudes of general education teachers toward students with severe disabilities, 484–485 • Expectation that all students can learn, 456, 486
3. Communicating with parents, guardians, and community collaborators; for example: directing parents and guardians to parent-educators or to other groups and resources; writing reports directly to parents; meeting with parents to discuss student concerns, progress, and IEPs; encouraging parent participation; reciprocal communication and training with other service providers	• Principles of effective communication, 102, 104 • Active listening, 103 • Roadblocks to communication, 104–105 • Dialoguing to resolve conflicts, 105–106 • Planning and conducting parent-teacher conferences, 109–112	• Home-school written communications, 112–115 • Guidelines for communicating with parents, 116 • Parents as tutors, 117–120 • Parent education and parent support groups, 120 • Mirror model for parent involvement, 122–123

GLOSSARY

ABC recording   A form of direct observation often used as a part of functional behavior assessment. The observer records a descriptive, temporally sequenced account of all behaviors of interest and the antecedent conditions and consequences for those behaviors as those events occur in the client's natural environment.

ability grouping   Placing students with similar levels of achievement and skill into the same classes or instructional groups.

absence seizure   A type of epileptic seizure in which the individual loses consciousness, usually for less than half a minute; can occur very frequently in some children.

acceleration   An educational approach that provides a child with learning experiences usually given to older children; most often used with gifted and talented children.

accommodation   The adjustment of the eye for seeing at different distances; accomplished by muscles that change the shape of the lens to bring an image into clear focus on the retina.

acquired (condition or disability)   A disability or condition that develops at any time after birth, from disease, trauma, or any other cause; contrast with *congenital*.

acquired immune deficiency syndrome (AIDS)   A fatal illness in which the body's immune system breaks down. At present there is no known cure for AIDS or a vaccine for the virus that causes it (see *human immunodeficiency virus*).

acquisition stage of learning   The initial phase of learning when the student is learning how to perform a new skill or use new knowledge; feedback should focus on the accuracy and topography of the student's response. Compare with *practice stage of learning*.

active student response (ASR)   A frequency-based measure of a student's active participation during instruction; measured by counting the number of observable responses made to an ongoing lesson or to curriculum materials.

acute condition   A serious state of illness or injury, but not permanent; contrast with *chronic*.

adaptive behavior   Conceptual, social, and practical skills that people have learned in order to function in their everyday lives; refers to typical performance of people without disabilities in meeting the expectations of everyday environments.

adaptive device   Any piece of equipment designed to improve the function of a body part. Examples include standing tables and special spoons for use by people with weak hands or poor muscle control.

adventitious   A disability that develops at any time after birth, from disease, trauma, or any other cause; most frequently used to describe sensory or physical impairments (also called *acquired*; contrast with *congenital*).

advocate   Someone who pleads the cause of a person with disabilities or group of people with disabilities, especially in legal or administrative proceedings or public forums.

albinism   A congenital condition marked by deficiency in, or total lack of, pigmentation. People with albinism have pale skin; white hair, eyebrows, and eyelashes; and eyes with pink or pale blue irises.

alphabetic principle   The understanding that words are composed of letters that represent sounds and the ability to pronounce and blend the sounds of letters into words (decoding) and to recode sounds into letters (spelling). See *phonics*.

amblyopia   Dimness of sight without apparent change in the eye's structures; can lead to blindness in the affected eye if not corrected.

American Sign Language (ASL)   A visual-gestural language with its own rules of syntax, semantics, and pragmatics; does not correspond to written or spoken English. ASL is the language of the Deaf culture in the United States and Canada.

amniocentesis   The insertion of a hollow needle through the abdomen into the uterus of a pregnant woman. Used to obtain amniotic fluid in order to determine the presence of genetic and chromosomal abnormalities. It also confirms the gender of the fetus.

anencephaly   Congenital malformation of the skull with absence of all or part of the brain.

anorexia nervosa   Refusal to maintain body weight at or above a minimally normal weight for age and height; obsessive concern with body weight or shape and intense anxiety about gaining weight, even though severely underweight. Two subtypes: restricting food intake by starving oneself down to an abnormal weight and binge eating/purging (see *bulimia nervosa*).

anoxia   A lack of oxygen severe enough to cause tissue damage; can cause permanent brain damage and mental retardation.

Apgar scale   A test that measures the degree of *asphyxia* (oxygen deprivation) an infant experiences during birth. Five physiological measures (heart rate, respiratory effort, response to stimulation, muscle tone, and skin color) are rated at 1 minute and 5 minutes after birth.

aphasia   Loss of speech functions; often, but not always, refers to inability to speak because of brain lesions.

applied behavior analysis (ABA)   "The science in which tactics derived from the principles of behavior are applied systematically to improve socially significant behavior and experimentation is used to identify the variables responsible for behavior change" (Cooper, Heron, & Heward, 2007, p. 20).

aqueous humor   Fluid that occupies the space between the lens and the cornea of the eye.

arena assessment   A group assessment procedure sometimes used with infants and preschoolers; professionals from different disciplines (e.g., early childhood specialist, speech-language pathologist, psychologist, physical therapist) seat themselves in a circle around the child and conduct simultaneous evaluations while the child interacts with parent or play materials.

articulation   The production of distinct language sounds by the vocal organs.

articulation disorder   Abnormal production of speech sounds.

Asperger syndrome   Developmental disorder characterized by normal cognitive and language development with impairments in all social areas, repetitive and stereotyped behaviors, preoccupation with atypical activities or items, pedantic speech patterns, and motor clumsiness; included in *autism spectrum disorders.*

assistive technology Any item, piece of equipment, or product system, whether acquired commercially off the shelf, modified, or customized, that is used to increase, maintain, or improve the functional capabilities of children with disabilities. (The Individuals with Disabilities Education Act [IDEA] regulations, 34 C.F.R. § 300.5)

asthma A respiratory condition characterized by recurrent episodes of wheezing, coughing, and difficulty breathing.

astigmatism A defect of vision usually caused by irregularities in the cornea; results in blurred vision and difficulties in focusing. Can usually be corrected by lenses.

asynchrony A term used to describe the disparate rates of intellectual, emotional, and physical growth or development characteristic of many gifted and talented children.

ataxia Poor sense of balance and body position and lack of coordination of the voluntary muscles; characteristic of one type of cerebral palsy.

at risk A term used to refer to children who are not currently identified as disabled but are considered to have a greater-than-usual chance of developing a disability. Physicians use the term *at risk* or *high risk* to refer to pregnancies with a greater-than-normal probability of producing a baby with disabilities.

athetosis A type of cerebral palsy characterized by large, irregular, uncontrollable twisting motions. The muscles may be tense and rigid or loose and flaccid. Often accompanied by difficulty with oral language.

attention deficit disorder (ADD) See *attention deficit/hyperactivity disorder (ADHD).*

attention-deficit/hyperactivity disorder (ADHD) Diagnostic category of the American Psychiatric Association for a condition in which a child exhibits developmentally inappropriate inattention, impulsivity, and hyperactivity.

audiogram A graph of the faintest level of sound a person can hear in each ear at least 50% of the time at each of several frequencies, including the entire frequency range of normal speech.

audiologist A professional who specializes in the evaluation of hearing ability and the treatment of impaired hearing.

audiology The science of hearing.

audiometer A device that generates sounds at specific frequencies and intensities; used to examine hearing.

audiometric zero The smallest sound a person with normal hearing can perceive; also called the zero hearing-threshold level (HTL).

audition The act or sense of hearing.

auditory canal (external acoustic meatus) The part of the ear that slightly amplifies and transports sound waves from the external ear to the middle ear.

auditory training A program that works on listening skills by teaching individuals with hearing impairments to make as much use as possible of their residual hearing.

augmentative and alternative communication (AAC) A diverse set of nonspeech communication strategies and methods to assist individuals who cannot meet their communication needs through speech; includes sign language, symbol systems, communication boards, and synthetic speech devices.

auricle External part of the ear; collects sound waves into the auditory canal.

autism See *autistic disorder; autism spectrum disorders.*

autism spectrum disorders Group of five related developmental disorders that share common core deficits or difficulties in social relationships, communication, and ritualistic behaviors; differentiated from one another primarily by the age of onset and severity of various symptoms; includes autistic disorder, Asperger syndrome, Rett syndrome, childhood disintegrative disorder, and pervasive developmental disorder not otherwise specified (PDD-NOS).

autistic disorder A pervasive developmental disorder marked by three defining features with onset before age 3: (a) impairment of social interaction; (b) impairment of communication; and (c) restricted, repetitive, and stereotyped patterns of behavior, interests, and activities.

autistic savant Individual who exhibits extraordinary ability in a specific area such as memorization, mathematical calculations, or musical ability while functioning at the mental retardation level in all other areas; very rare.

baseline A measure of the level or amount of a specific target behavior before implementation of an intervention designed to change the behavior. Baseline data are used as an objective measure against which to compare and evaluate the results obtained during intervention.

behavior observation audiometry A method of hearing assessment in which an infant's reactions to sounds are observed; a sound is presented at an increasing level of intensity until a response, such as head turning, eye blinking, or cessation of play, is reliably observed.

behavior trap An interrelated set of contingencies of reinforcement that can be especially powerful, producing substantial and long-lasting behavior changes. Effective behavior traps include four essential features: (a) They are "baited" with virtually irresistible reinforcers that "lure" the student to the trap; (b) only a low-effort response already in the student's repertoire is necessary to enter the trap; (c) once inside the trap, the student is motivated by interrelated contingencies of reinforcement to acquire, extend, and maintain targeted academic and/or social skills; and (d) they can remain effective for a long time because students show few, if any, satiation effects. (Cooper, Heron, & Heward, 2007, p. 691)

behavioral contract A written agreement between two parties in which one agrees to complete a specified task (e.g., a child agrees to complete a homework assignment by the next morning) and in return the other party agrees to provide a specific reward (e.g., the teacher allows the child to have 10 minutes of free time) upon completion of the task. Also called *contingency contract.*

behavioral disorder A disability characterized by behavior that differs markedly and chronically from current social or cultural norms and adversely affects educational performance.

behavioral intervention plan (BIP) Statement of specific strategies and procedures to prevent the occurrence of a child's problem behavior and intervene when necessary; based upon results of a *functional behavior assessment.* Required in the individualized education program (IEP) for all students with disabilities whose school performance is adversely affected by behavioral issues.

bilingual-bicultural (bi–bi) approach An approach to teaching students who are deaf in which American Sign Language (ASL) is used as the child's native language and English is taught as a second language; also stresses teaching of Deaf culture.

bilingual special education Uses the child's home language and home culture along with English in an individually designed program of special education.

binocular vision Vision using both eyes working together to perceive a single image.

bipolar disorder (formerly called *manic-depressive disorder*) Alternative episodes of depressive and manic states; during manic episodes, person is in an elevated mood of euphoria and exhibits three or more of the following symptoms: excessive egotism; very little sleep needed; incessant talkativeness; rapidly changing thoughts and ideas in uncontrolled order; easily distracted; agitated, "driven" activities; and participation in personally risky activities.

blind Having either no vision or only light perception; learning occurs through other senses.

blindness, legal See *legally blind.*

Bloom's taxonomy A hierarchy of educational objectives consisting of six types of cognitive understanding: (1) knowledge, (2) comprehension, (3) application, (4) analysis, (5) synthesis (create), and (6) evaluation. Can be used as a framework for differentiating curriculum by asking questions and assigning activities that require students to demonstrate different types of learning.

braille A system of writing letters, numbers, and other language symbols with a combination of six raised dots. A person who is blind reads the dots with his fingertips.

bulimia nervosa Recurrent episodes of binge eating and inappropriate compensatory behavior to prevent weight gain (e.g., self-induced vomiting, misuse of laxatives or other medications, fasting, excessive exercise).

cataract A reduction or loss of vision that occurs when the crystalline lens of the eye becomes cloudy or opaque.

catheter A tube inserted into the body to permit injections or withdrawal of fluids or to keep a passageway open; often refers to a tube inserted into the bladder to remove urine from a person who does not have effective bladder control.

cerebral palsy Motor impairment caused by brain damage, which is usually acquired during the prenatal period or during the birth process. Can involve a wide variety of symptoms (see *ataxia, athetosis, rigidity, spasticity,* and *tremor*) and range from mild to severe. Neither curable nor progressive.

childhood disintegrative disorder Shares behavioral characteristics with autistic disorder, but does not begin until after age 2 and sometimes not until age 10; medical complications are common; one type of autism spectrum disorder.

choral responding Each student in the class or group responds orally in unison to a question, problem, or item presented by the teacher.

chorionic villi sampling (CVS) A procedure for prenatal diagnosis of chromosomal abnormalities that can be conducted during the first 8 to 10 weeks of pregnancy; fetal cells are removed from the chorionic tissue, which surrounds the fetus, and directly analyzed.

chronic condition A long-lasting, often permanent condition; contrast with *acute.*

clean intermittent catheterization (CIC) A clean (not sterile) catheter (tube) is inserted into the urethra and advanced into the bladder; catheter remains in place until urine is released into a bag.

cleft palate A congenital split in the palate that results in an excessive nasal quality of the voice. Can often be repaired by surgery or a dental appliance.

closed head injury Caused by the head hitting a stationary object with such force that the brain slams against the inside of the cranium; stress of this rapid movement and impact pulls apart and tears nerve fibers, or axons, of the brain.

cluttering A type of fluency disorder in which speech is very rapid, with extra sounds or mispronounced sounds; speech may be garbled to the point of unintelligibility; compare to *stuttering.*

cochlea Main receptor organ for hearing located in the inner ear; tiny hairs within the cochlea transform mechanical energy into neural impulses that then travel through the auditory nerve to the brain.

cochlear implant A surgically implanted device that converts sound from the environment into electric impulses that are sent directly to the brain via the auditory nerve. Enables some people who are deaf to achieve a useful auditory understanding of the environment and to understand speech.

comorbidity Two or more conditions occurring in the same person (e.g., learning disabilities and ADHD).

communication An interactive process requiring at least two parties in which messages are encoded, transmitted, and decoded by any means, including sounds, symbols, and gestures.

communication disorder "An impairment in the ability to receive, send, process, and comprehend concepts or verbal, nonverbal, and graphic symbols systems. . . . disorder may be evident in the processes of hearing, language, and/or speech" (ASHA, 1993, p. 40).

complex partial seizure A type of seizure in which an individual goes through a brief period of inappropriate or purposeless activity (also called *psychomotor seizure*). Usually lasts from 2 to 5 minutes, after which the person has amnesia about the entire episode.

conduct disorder A group of behavior disorders including disobedience, disruptiveness, fighting, and tantrums, as identified by Quay (1975).

conductive hearing loss Hearing loss caused by obstructions in the outer or middle ear or malformations that interfere with the conduction of sound waves to the inner ear. Can often be corrected surgically or medically.

cones Light receptors that enable detection of color and detail; located in the center of the retina, and function best in good light.

congenital Any condition that is present at birth (contrasts with *adventitious*).

constant time delay A procedure for transferring stimulus control from teacher-provided response prompts to the instructional item itself. The teacher begins by simultaneously presenting the stimulus being taught and a controlling response prompt. After a number of zero-second-delay trials, the teacher waits for a fixed amount of time between presentation of the instructional stimulus and the response prompt. The teacher repeats practice trials with the constant delay until the student begins to respond correctly before the teacher's prompt.

contingency contract A document that specifies an if-then relationship between performance of a specified behavior(s) and access to, or delivery of, a specified reward. Also called *behaviorial contract*.

continuum of alternative placements A range of placement and instructional options for children with disabilities. Often depicted as a pyramid, with placements ranging from the general education classroom at the bottom to special schools, residential facilities, and homebound or hospital placements at the top. The Individuals with Disabilities Education Act (IDEA) requires schools to provide a continuum of alternative placements to meet the individual needs of students with disabilities.

convulsive disorder See *epilepsy*.

cornea The transparent part of the eyeball that admits light to the interior.

cortical visual impairments (CVI) Decreased vision or blindness due to known or suspected damage or malfunction of the parts of the brain that interpret visual information.

cri-du-chat syndrome A chromosomal abnormality resulting from deletion of material from the fifth pair of chromosomes. It usually results in severe retardation. Its name is French for "cat cry," named for the high-pitched crying of the child due to a related larynx dysfunction.

criterion-referenced test A test constructed so that a child's score can be compared with a predetermined criterion, or mastery level; contrast with *norm-referenced test*.

cross-grade grouping A form of ability grouping in which students at different grade levels attend classes at the level of instruction at which they are achieving.

cued speech A method of supplementing oral communication by adding cues in the form of eight different hand signals in four different locations near the chin.

cultural-familial mental retardation See *psychosocial disadvantage*.

cultural interpreter An individual who helps school personnel and family members from a diverse culture communicate effectively; may or may not speak the family's home language, but has sufficient understanding of both the home culture and school culture, policies, and practices to help the family and school understand one another.

cultural pluralism The value and practice of respecting, fostering, and encouraging the cultural and ethnic differences that make up society.

cultural reciprocity A two-way process between professionals and families of information sharing, understanding, and respecting how their differing values and belief systems may influence perspectives, wishes, and decisions. Requires careful examination of each party's own cultural background and belief system.

culture The established knowledge, ideas, values, and skills shared by a society; its program of survival and adaptation to its environment.

curriculum-based measurement A type of formative evaluation consisting of frequent measures of a student's progress in learning the objectives that comprise the curriculum in which the student is participating.

curriculum compacting Strategy for differentiating curriculum for gifted and talented students by replacing content that students have already mastered with more challenging material.

customized employment A form of supported employment in which a job is created within an integrated competitive work environment based on the current skills of the potential employee and needs of the employer.

cystic fibrosis An inherited disorder that causes a dysfunction of the pancreas, mucus, salivary, and sweat glands. Cystic fibrosis causes severe, long-term respiratory difficulties. No cure is currently available.

cytomegalovirus (CMV) A common virus that infects most people worldwide; can remain alive but dormant in the body for life; usually harmless, but in a very small percentage of children infected at birth, CMV may later develop and lead to various conditions, including mental retardation, visual impairment, and, most often, hearing impairment.

deaf The result of a hearing loss severe enough so that speech cannot be understood through the ears alone, even with a hearing aid; some sounds may still be perceived.

deaf-blindness Any combination of hearing and visual impairments that causes such severe communication, developmental, and educational needs that the individual cannot be accommodated in a special education program designed solely for children with hearing impairments or visual impairments.

Deaf culture Shared language (in the United States, American Sign Language [ASL]), social practices, literature, and beliefs of the Deaf community; members do not view deafness as a disability.

deafness See *deaf*.

decibel (dB) The unit of measure for the relative intensity of sound on a logarithmic scale beginning at zero. Zero decibels refers to the faintest sound a person with normal hearing can detect.

declassification If the individualized education program (IEP) team determines that a disability is no longer present or that the child's education is no longer adversely affected by the disability, the student is declassified and special education is discontinued.

deinstitutionalization The movement of individuals with disabilities, especially persons with mental retardation, from large institutions to smaller, community-based residences and work settings.

developmentally appropriate practice (DAP) A philosophy and guidelines for practice based on the belief that the learning environments, teaching practices, and other components of programs that serve young children should be based on educators' typical expectations and children's experiences for children of different ages and developmental stages.

diabetes Chronic disease in which the body does not produce or properly use insulin, a hormone needed to convert sugar, starches, and other food into energy (see *Type-1 diabetes*).

diabetic retinopathy Visual impairment caused by hemorrhages on the retina and other disorders of blood circulation in people with diabetes.

dialect A variety within a specific language; can involve variation in pronunciation, word choice, word order, and inflected forms.

differential reinforcement of other behavior (DRO) A procedure in which any behavior except the targeted inappropriate response is reinforced; results in a reduction of the inappropriate behavior.

diplegia Paralysis that affects the legs more often than the arms.

direct instruction Any systematic approach to teaching characterized by clear specification of learning objectives, explicit presentation of curriculum content, active engagement by students, systematic feedback for student performance, and evaluation by direct and frequent measures of student learning (aka, *little "d," little "i"*).

Direct Instruction (DI) Published curricula authored by Engelmann and colleagues for teaching reading, math, spelling, language, and thinking skills; DI programs are thoroughly field tested to ensure effectiveness and feature high rates of student engagement, immediate feedback and error correction, and scripted lessons to ensure consistent instruction.

disability Condition characterized by functional limitations that impede typical development as the result of a physical or sensory impairment or difficulty in learning or social adjustment.

discrete trial training Instructional format involving a series of three-part trials: (a) an antecedent stimulus (e.g., flashcard with "2 + 2 = ?"), (b) student response (e.g., "four"), and (c) feedback (reinforcement for a correct response; ignoring or correcting an incorrect response; and providing a response prompt or ignoring nonresponses).

double-blind, placebo-controlled study Procedure used to control for expectancy effects by subjects and bias by researchers in studies evaluating the effects of a treatment or intervention. Some subjects receive the actual treatment being tested; others receive a placebo (fake) designed to appear like the actual treatment; subjects do not know whether they are receiving the real treatment or a placebo (they are "blind"); the researchers do not know which subjects received the treatment (making it a "double-blind" experiment).

double hemiplegia Paralysis of the arms, with less severe involvement of the legs.

Down syndrome A chromosomal anomaly that often causes moderate-to-severe mental retardation, along with certain physical characteristics such as a large tongue, heart problems, poor muscle tone, and a broad, flat bridge of the nose.

dual discrepancy A criterion for identifying a student as unresponsive in a responsiveness to intervention (RTI) approach when the student (a) fails to make adequate growth in the presence of instruction and (b) completes tier-2 intervention(s) below the benchmark criteria (Fuchs & Fuchs, 2007).

dual sensory impairments See *deaf-blindness.*

Duchenne muscular dystrophy The most common form of muscular dystrophy, a group of long-term diseases that progressively weaken and waste away the body's muscles.

due process Set of legal steps and proceedings carried out according to established rules and principles; designed to protect an individual's constitutional and legal rights.

duration (of behavior) Measure of how long a person engages in a given activity.

dysarthria A group of speech disorders caused by neuromuscular impairments in respiration, phonation, resonation, and articulation.

dyslexia A specific language-based disorder of constitutional origin characterized by difficulties in single-word decoding, usually reflecting insufficient phonological processing. These difficulties, which are not the result of generalized developmental disability or sensory impairment, are often unexpected in relation to age and other cognitive and academic abilities and severely impair the individual's ability to read (Orton Dyslexia Society Research Committee, 1994).

early intervention Any form of therapy, treatment, educational program, nutritional intervention, or family support designed to reduce the effects of disabilities or prevent the occurrence of learning and developmental problems later in life for children from birth through age 5 presumed to be at risk for such problems.

echolalia The repetition of what other people have said as if echoing them; characteristic of some children with delayed development, autism, and communication disorders.

electroencephalograph (EEG) Device that detects and records brain wave patterns.

emotional disturbance A disability defined in the Individuals with Disabilities Education Act (IDEA) as a condition exhibiting one or more of the following characteristics over a long period of time and to a marked degree that adversely affects educational performance: inability to build or maintain satisfactory interpersonal relationships; inappropriate types of behavior or feelings under normal circumstances; a general pervasive mood of unhappiness or depression; or a tendency to develop physical symptoms or fears associated with personal or school problems. Many professionals prefer the term *emotional or behavioral disorders*.

emotional or behavioral disorders Defined by the Council for Children With Behavioral Disorders as a disability characterized by emotional or behavioral responses in school programs so different from appropriate age, cultural, or ethnic norms that the responses adversely affect educational performance; more than a temporary, expected response to stressful events in the environment; consistently exhibited in two different settings, at least one of which is school-related; and unresponsive to direct intervention in general education, or the condition of the child is such that general education interventions would be insufficient. Contrast with the Individuals with Disabilities Education Act (IDEA) definition of *emotional disturbance*.

encephalitis Inflammation of the brain; can cause permanent damage to the central nervous system and mental retardation.

endogenous Refers to an inherited cause of a disability or impairment.

enrichment Educational approach that provides a child with extra learning experiences that the standard curriculum would not normally include. Most often used with gifted and talented children.

epilepsy A condition marked by chronic and repeated seizures, disturbances of movement, sensation, behavior, and/or consciousness caused by abnormal electrical activity in the brain (see *generalized tonic-clonic seizure, complex partial seizure, simple partial seizure,* and *absence seizure*). Can usually be controlled with medication, although the drugs may have undesirable side effects. May be temporary or lifelong.

equal protection Legal concept included in the 14th Amendment to the Constitution of the United States stipulating that no state may deny any person equality or liberty because of that person's classification according to race, nationality, or religion. Several major court cases leading to the passage of P.L. 94-42, the

Individuals with Disabilities Education Act (IDEA), found that children with disabilities were not provided with equal protection if they were denied access to an appropriate education solely because of their disabilities.

ethnocentrism The view that the practices of one's own culture are natural and correct, while perceiving the practices of other cultures as odd, amusing, inferior, and/or immoral.

etiology The cause(s) of a disability, impairment, or disease. Includes genetic, physiological, environmental, and psychological factors.

evidence-based practice A policy, curriculum, or instructional technique with a sufficient number of high-quality research studies providing scientific evidence to support its effectiveness. Special education as a field is grappling with criteria defining *sufficient* and *high quality*.

evoked-response audiometry A method of testing hearing by measuring the electrical activity generated by the auditory nerve in response to auditory stimulation. Often used to measure the hearing of infants and children considered difficult to test.

exceptional children Children whose performance deviates from the norm, either below or above, to the extent that special education is needed.

exogenous Refers to a cause of a disability or impairment that stems from factors outside the body such as disease, toxicity, or injury.

expressive language disorder A language impairment that interferes with the production of language; contrast with *receptive disorder*.

externalizing behaviors Antisocial, disruptive behaviors (e.g., aggression, noncompliance, property destruction) characteristic of many children with emotional or behavioral disorders.

extinction A procedure in which reinforcement for a previously reinforced behavior is withheld. If the reinforcers that are maintaining the behavior are identified and withheld, the behavior will gradually decrease in frequency until it no longer, or seldom, occurs.

facilitated communication (FC) A type of augmentative communication in which a "facilitator" provides assistance to someone in typing or pointing to vocabulary symbols; typically involves an alphanumeric keyboard on which the user types out a message one letter at a time. To date, research designed to validate FC has repeatedly demonstrated either facilitator influence (correct or meaningful language is produced only when the facilitator "knows" what should be communicated) or no unexpected language competence compared to the participants' measured IQ or a standard language assessment.

fetal alcohol effects (FAE) Term used to identify the suspected etiology of developmental problems experienced by infants and toddlers who have some but not all of the diagnostic criteria for fetal alcohol syndrome (FAS) and have a history of prenatal alcohol exposure.

fetal alcohol spectrum disorder (FASD) A term referring to the related conditions of fetal alcohol syndrome (FAS), fetal alcohol effect (FAE), and alcohol-related neurodevelopmental disorder (ARND).

fetal alcohol syndrome (FAS) A condition sometimes found in the infants of alcoholic mothers; can involve low birth weight, developmental delay, and cardiac, limb, and other physical defects. Caused by excessive alcohol use during pregnancy; often produces serious physical defects and developmental delays; diagnosed when the child has two or more craniofacial malformations and growth is below the 10th percentile for height and weight. FAS is one of the leading known causes of mental retardation. In addition to physical problems, many children with FAS have neurological damage that contributes to cognitive and language delays.

field of vision The expanse of space visible with both eyes looking straight ahead, measured in degrees; 180 degrees is considered normal.

fingerspelling The manual alphabet used to spell out proper names for which no signs exist and to clarify meanings; an integral part of American Sign Language (ASL).

fluency A performance measure that includes both the accuracy and the rate with which a skill is performed; a fluent performer is both accurate and fast. In communication, the term refers to the rate and smoothness of speech; stuttering is the most common fluency disorder in speech.

fluency disorder A speech disorder characterized by atypical rate, rhythm, and repetitions in sounds, syllables, words, and phrases; see *stuttering, cluttering*.

formative evaluation Any type of ongoing evaluation of student performance or learning that occurs as instruction takes place over time; results can be used to modify instruction to make it more effective. See *curriculum-based measurement*.

foster home A living arrangement in which a family shares its home with a person who is not a relative. Long used with children who for some reason cannot live with their parents temporarily, foster homes are now being used with adults with disabilities as well.

fragile X syndrome A chromosomal abnormality associated with mild-to-severe mental retardation. Thought to be the most common known cause of inherited mental retardation. Affects males more often and more severely than females; behavioral characteristics are sometimes similar to individuals with autism. Diagnosis can be confirmed by studies of the X chromosome.

frequency (or rate of behavior) A measure of how often a particular response is emitted; usually reported as the number of responses per standard unit of time (e.g., 5 per minute).

functional analysis Experimental manipulation of antecedent or consequent events representing those observed in the child's natural environment to verify their function in either triggering or maintaining problem behavior.

functional behavior assessment (FBA) Systematic process of gathering information about the purposes (functions) a problem behavior serves for an individual; that information then guides the design of interventions. Three basic types of FBA are: indirect assessment (structured interviews with significant others), direct descriptive assessment (systematic observations), and functional analysis (see *functional analysis*).

functional vision A term that refers to how well a person uses whatever vision he has; cannot be determined or predicted by objective measurements of visual acuity or visual field. See also *visual efficiency*.

generalization Extent to which previously learned knowledge or skill either occurs under conditions different from those under which it was originally learned or is performed in a different but functionally equivalent manner. Situation or setting generalization occurs when a student performs a behavior in the presence of stimuli other than those that were present originally. Response generalization occurs when a person performs behaviors that were never directly trained but have the same effect on the environment as the original trained behavior.

generalized anxiety disorder Excessive, unrealistic worries, fears, tension that lasts 6 months or more; in addition to chronic anxiety, symptoms include restlessness, fatigue, difficulty concentrating, muscular aches, insomnia, nausea, excessive heart rate, dizziness, and irritability.

generalized tonic-clonic seizure The most severe type of seizure, in which the individual has violent convulsions, loses consciousness, and becomes rigid. Formerly called *grand mal seizure.*

genetic counseling A discussion between a specially trained medical counselor and persons who are considering having a baby about the chances of having a baby with a disability, based on the prospective parents' genetic backgrounds.

glaucoma An eye disease characterized by abnormally high pressure inside the eyeball. If left untreated, it can cause total blindness, but if detected early, most cases can be arrested.

grand mal seizure See *generalized tonic-clonic seizure.*

grapheme Smallest level of written language that corresponds to one phoneme; e.g., the grapheme *t* represents the phoneme /t/.

graphic organizers Visual-spatial arrangements of information containing words or concepts connected graphically that help students see meaningful hierarchical, comparative, and sequential relationships.

group contingencies A type of behavior management and motivation procedure in which consequences (rewards and/or penalties) are applied to the entire group or class of students contingent upon the behavior of selected students or the entire group.

group home A community-based residential alternative for adults with disabilities, most often persons with mental retardation, in which a small group of people live together in a house with one or more support staff.

guided notes Teacher-prepared handouts that provide background information and standard cues with specific spaces where students can write key facts, concepts, and/or relationships during a lecture.

handicap Refers to the problems a person with a disability or impairment encounters in interacting with the environment. A disability may pose a handicap in one environment but not in another.

handicapism Prejudice or discrimination based solely on a person's disability, without regard for individual characteristics.

hard of hearing A level of hearing loss that makes it difficult, although not impossible, to comprehend speech through the sense of hearing alone.

hearing aid An assistive listening device that amplifies sound.

hearing impairment A hearing loss significant enough to require special education, training, and/or adaptations; includes deafness as well as hard-of-hearing conditions.

hemiplegia Paralysis of both the arm and the leg on the same side of the body.

hemophilia An inherited deficiency in blood-clotting ability, which can cause serious internal bleeding.

hertz (Hz) A unit of sound frequency equal to one cycle per second; used to measure pitch.

human immunodeficiency virus (HIV) The virus that causes *acquired immune deficiency syndrome (AIDS).*

hydrocephalus An enlarged head caused by accumulation of cerebral spinal fluid in the cranial cavity; often causes brain damage and severe retardation. A condition present at birth or developing soon afterward. Can sometimes be treated successfully with a *shunt.*

hyperactive Excessive motor activity or restlessness.

hyperopia Farsightedness; condition in which the image comes to a focus behind the retina instead of on it, causing difficulty in seeing near objects.

hypertonia Muscle tone that is too high; tense, contracted muscles.

hypotonia Muscle tone that is too low; weak, floppy muscles.

immaturity Group of behavior disorders, including short attention span, extreme passivity, daydreaming, preference for younger playmates, and clumsiness, as identified by Quay (1975).

impairment Refers to the loss or reduced function of a particular body part or organ (e.g., a missing limb); compare to *disability* and *handicap.*

impedance audiometry Procedure for testing middle ear function by inserting a small probe and pump to detect sound reflected by the eardrum.

incidence The percentage of people who, at some time in their lives, will be identified as having a specific condition. Often reported as the number of cases of a given condition per 1,000 births or people of a given age.

inclusion Educating students with disabilities in general education classrooms.

individualized education program (IEP) Written document required by the Individuals with Disabilities Education Act (P.L. 94-142) for every child with a disability; includes statements of present performance, annual goals, short-term instructional objectives, specific educational services needed, extent of participation in the general education program, evaluation procedures and relevant dates; and must be signed by parents as well as educational personnel.

individualized education program (IEP) team Group of people who create the IEP for a student with a disability. The team must include (a) the parents of the child with a disability; (b) at least one regular education teacher of the child; (c) at least one special education teacher; (d) a representative of the local education agency who is qualified to provide, or supervise the provision of, specially designed instruction to meet the unique needs of children with disabilities; (e) an individual who is knowledgeable about the general curriculum and the availability of resources of the local education agency; (f) an individual who can interpret the instructional implications of evaluation results, who may be a member of the team described in clauses (b) through (f); (g) at the discretion of the parent or the agency, other individuals who have knowledge or special expertise regarding the child, including related service personnel as appropriate; and (h) whenever appropriate, the child with a disability.

individualized family services plan (IFSP) A requirement of the Individuals with Disabilities Education Act for the coordination of early intervention services for infants and toddlers with disabilities from birth to age 3. Similar to the individualized education program (IEP), which is required for all school-age children with disabilities.

individualized health care plan (IHCP) Individualized education program (IEP) component for students with special health-care needs; specifies health-care procedures and services administered by school personnel and a plan for emergencies.

individualized transition plan (ITP) Specifies desired postschool outcomes in four areas (employment, postsecondary education, residential, and recreation/leisure) and instructional programming and supports to help the student attain those outcomes; required part of each student's individualized education program (IEP) by age 16.

inflection Change in pitch or loudness of the voice to indicate mood or emphasis.

in service training Any educational program designed to provide practicing professionals (e.g., teachers, administrators, physical therapists) with additional knowledge and skills.

intellectual disabilities A disability characterized by significant limitations in both intellectual functioning and adaptive behavior as expressed in conceptual, social, and practical adaptive skills; the disability originates before age 18 (AAIDD, 2007). Refers to the same population of individuals who were diagnosed previously with mental retardation. (See *mental retardation.*)

interdisciplinary team Group of professionals from different disciplines (e.g., education, psychology, speech and language, medicine) who work together to plan and implement an individualized education program (IEP) for a child with disabilities.

interindividual differences Differences between two or more people in one skill or set of skills.

internalizing behaviors Immature and withdrawn behaviors (e.g., social withdrawal, irrational fears, depression) characteristic of some children with emotional or behavioral disorders.

interobserver agreement The degree to which two or more independent observers record the same results when observing and measuring the same target behavior(s); typically reported as a percentage of agreement.

interrater agreement See *interobserver agreement.*

intervention Any effort made on behalf of children and adults with disabilities; may be preventive (keeping possible problems from becoming a serious disability), remedial (overcoming disability through training or education), or compensatory (giving the individual new ways to deal with the disability).

intraindividual differences Differences within one individual on two or more measures of performance.

iris The opaque, colored portion of the eye that contracts and expands to change the size of the pupil and control light input.

joint attention A social communication skill in which two people interact with their shared environment in the same frame of reference. Joint attention is evident when a child looks where someone else is looking or turns head or eyes in the direction someone is pointing.

kinesics The study of bodily movement, particularly as it relates to and affects communication.

Klinefelter syndrome A chromosomal anomaly in which males receive an extra X chromosome; associated with frequent social retardation, sterility, underdevelopment of male sex organs, development of secondary female sex characteristics, and borderline or mild levels of mental retardation.

language A system used by a group of people for giving meaning to sounds, words, gestures, and other symbols to enable communication with one another. Languages can use vocal (speech sounds) or nonvocal symbols, such as American Sign Language, or use movements and physical symbols instead of sounds.

language disorder Impaired comprehension and/or use of spoken, written, and/or other symbol systems.

latency The time that elapses between the opportunity to respond and the beginning of the response.

learning channel A description of the modes with which a learner receives and sends information in performing a given learning task. Orally reading sight words, for example, uses the "see/say" learning channel; the "hear/write" learning channel is involved in taking a spelling test.

learning disabilities A general term that refers to a heterogeneous group of disorders manifested by significant difficulties in the acquisition and use of listening, speaking, reading, writing, reasoning, or mathematical abilities.

learning trial Consists of three major elements: (a) antecedent (i.e., curricular) stimuli, (b) the student's response to those stimuli, and (c) consequent stimuli (i.e., instructional feedback) following the response; serves as a basic unit of analysis for examining teaching and learning from both the teacher's perspective, as an opportunity to teach, and the student's perspective, as an opportunity to learn (Heward, 1994). Also called an *instructional trial, learn unit,* or *practice trial.*

least restrictive environment (LRE) The educational setting that most closely resembles a regular school program and also meets the child's special educational needs. For many students with disabilities, the general education classroom is the LRE; however, the LRE is a relative concept and must be determined for each individual student with disabilities.

legally blind Visual acuity of 20/200 or less in the better eye after the best possible correction with glasses or contact lenses, or vision restricted to a field of 20 degrees or less. Acuity of 20/200 means the eye can see clearly at 20 feet what the normal eye can see at 200 feet.

lens The clear part of the eye that focuses rays of light on the retina.

level system A behavior management system in which students access greater independence and more privileges as they demonstrate increased behavioral control; see also *token economy.*

longitudinal study A research study that follows one subject or group of subjects over an extended period of time, usually several years.

low-incidence disability A disability that occurs relatively infrequently in the general population; often used in reference to sensory impairments, severe and profound mental retardation, and multiple disabilities.

low vision Visual impairment severe enough so that special educational services are required. A child with low vision can learn through the visual channel and generally learns to read print.

macular degeneration A deterioration of the central part of the retina, which causes difficulty in seeing details clearly.

magnitude (of behavior) The force with which a response is emitted.

mainstreaming The process of integrating children with disabilities into regular schools and classes.

maintenance Extent to which a learner continues to exhibit a previously learned behavior after a portion or all of the instructional intervention originally used to teach the skill has been terminated.

manifestation determination A review of the relationship between a student's misconduct and his disability conducted by the individualized education program (IEP) team and other qualified personnel. Required by the Individuals with Disabilities Education Act (IDEA) amendments of 1997 when school officials seek to discipline a student with disabilities in a manner that would result in a change of placement, suspension, or expulsion in excess of 10 days.

mediated scaffolding Refers to a variety of instructional procedures that entail providing the learner with response prompts, cues, and other contrived supports and then gradually withdrawing those supports so the student can respond independently to naturally occurring stimuli.

meningitis An inflammation of the membranes covering the brain and spinal cord; can cause problems with sight and hearing and/or mental retardation.

meningocele Type of spina bifida in which the covering of the spinal cord protrudes through an opening in the vertebrae but the cord itself and the nerve roots are enclosed.

mental retardation A disability characterized by significant limitations in both intellectual functioning and adaptive behavior as expressed in conceptual, social, and practical adaptive skills; the disability originates before age 18 (AAIDD, 2007). Some professionals and organizations use the term *intellectual disabilities* instead of *mental retardation*.

meta-analysis A statistical analysis of a large collection of results from individual studies on the same topic; purpose is to integrate the findings and arrive at a description of the overall effects or outcomes.

microcephalus A condition characterized by an abnormally small skull with resulting brain damage and mental retardation.

milieu teaching strategies A variety of strategies used to teach speech and language that occur naturally during real or simulated activities in the home, school, or community environments in which a child normally functions; characterized by dispersed learning trials, following the child's attentional lead within the context of normal conversational interchanges, and teaching the form and content of language in the context of normal use.

minimal brain dysfunction A once-popular term used to describe the learning disabilities of children with no clinical (organic) evidence of brain damage.

mnemonic strategies Memory-enhancing strategies such as acronyms, acrostics, keywords, and peg words.

mobility The ability to move safely and efficiently from one point to another.

model program A program that implements and evaluates new procedures or techniques to serve as a basis for development of other similar programs.

monoplegia Paralysis affecting one limb.

morpheme The smallest element of a language that carries meaning.

morphology Refers to the basic units of meaning in a language and how those units are combined into words.

multicultural education An educational approach in which a school's curriculum and instructional methods are designed and implemented so that children acquire an awareness, acceptance, and appreciation of cultural diversity and recognize the contributions of many cultures.

multifactored evaluation (MFE) Assessment and evaluation of a child with a variety of test instruments and observation procedures. Required by the Individuals with Disabilities Education Act (IDEA) when assessment is for educational placement of a child who is to receive special education services. Prevents the misdiagnosis and misplacement of a student as the result of considering only one test score.

multiple disabilities Two or more disabilities in the same person; defined as a disability category in the Individuals with Disabilities Education Act as "concomitant impairments, the combination of which causes such severe educational needs that they cannot be accommodated in special education programs solely for one of the impairments."

multiple-gating screening A multistep process for screening children who may have disabilities. The initial step casts the broadest net (e.g., a multiple-gated screening for children who may have emotional or behavior problems might begin with teacher nominations); children identified in the first step are assessed more closely in a second step (e.g., a behavior checklist); children who have passed through the first two "gates" are screened further (e.g., direct observations in the classroom).

muscular dystrophy A group of diseases that gradually weakens muscle tissue; usually becomes evident by the age of 4 or 5.

myelomeningocele A protrusion on the back of a child with spina bifida, consisting of a sac of nerve tissue bulging through a cleft in the spine.

myopia Nearsightedness; results when light is focused on a point in front of the retina, resulting in a blurred image for distant objects.

neurologic impairment Any physical disability caused by damage to the central nervous system (brain, spinal cord, ganglia, and nerves).

neuromotor impairment Involves the central nervous system, affecting the ability to move, use, feel, or control certain parts of the body.

normal curve A mathematically derived curve depicting the theoretical probability or distribution of a given variable (e.g., as a physical trait or test score) in the general population. Indicates that approximately 68% of the population will fall within 1 standard deviation above or below the mean; approximately 27% will fall between 1 and 2 standard deviations either above or below the mean; and less than 3% will achieve more extreme scores of more than 2 standard deviations in either direction.

normalization As a philosophy and principle, the belief that individuals with disabilities should, to the maximum extent possible, be physically and socially integrated into the mainstream of society regardless of the degree or type of disability. As an approach to intervention, the use of progressively more normal settings and procedures "to establish and/or maintain personal behaviors which are as culturally normal as possible" (Wolfensberger, 1972, p. 28).

norm-referenced test A test constructed so that a person's score can be compared to others of same age or grade level; contrast with *criterion-referenced test*.

nystagmus A rapid, involuntary, rhythmic movement of the eyes that may cause difficulty in reading or fixating on an object.

obsessive/compulsive disorder (OCD) Persistent, recurring thoughts (obsessions) that reflect exaggerated anxiety or fears; typical obsessions include worry about being contaminated, behaving improperly, or acting violently. Obsessions may lead an individual to perform compulsive rituals or routines—such as washing hands, repeating phrases, or hoarding—to relieve the anxiety caused by the obsession.

occupational therapist (OT) A professional who programs and/or delivers instructional activities and materials to help children and adults with disabilities learn to participate in useful activities.

ocular motility The eye's ability to move.

open head injury Result of penetration of the skull, such as caused by a bullet or a forceful blow to the head with a hard or sharp object.

operant conditioning audiometry Method of measuring hearing by teaching the individual to make an observable response to sound. For example, a child may be taught to drop a block into a box each time a light and a loud tone are presented. Once this response is learned, the light is no longer presented and the volume and pitch of the tone are gradually decreased. When the child no longer drops the block into the box, the audiologist knows the child cannot hear the tone. Sometimes used to test the hearing of nonverbal children and adults.

ophthalmologist A physician who specializes in the diagnosis and treatment of diseases of the eye.

optic nerve The nerve that carries impulses from the eye to the brain.

optometrist A vision professional who specializes in the evaluation and optical correction of refractive errors.

oral/aural approach A philosophy and approach to educating deaf children that stresses learning to speak as the essential element for integration into the hearing world.

orientation The ability to establish one's position in relation to the environment.

orientation and mobility Two complementary sets of skills that are critical for people with visual impairments. *Orientation* is knowing where you are, where you are going, and how to get there by interpreting information from the environment; *mobility* involves moving safely and efficiently from one point to another.

orthopedic impairment Impairment of the skeletal system—bones, joints, limbs, and associated muscles.

ossicles Three small bones (hammer, anvil, and stirrup) that transmit sound energy from the middle ear to the inner ear.

osteogenesis imperfecta A hereditary condition in which the bones do not grow normally and break easily; sometimes called *brittle bones*.

other health impairment A disability category in the Individuals with Disabilities Education Act under which a child is eligible for special education; includes diseases and special health conditions that affect a child's educational activities and performance such as cancer, diabetes, and cystic fibrosis.

otitis media An infection or inflammation of the middle ear that can cause a conductive hearing loss.

otologist A physician who specializes in the diagnosis and treatment of diseases of the ear.

overcorrection A procedure in which the learner must make restitution for, or repair, the effects of his undesirable behavior and then put the environment in even better shape than it was before the misbehavior. Used to decrease the rate of undesirable behaviors.

paraplegia Paralysis of the lower part of the body, including both legs; usually results from injury to or disease of the spinal cord.

paraprofessionals (in education) Trained classroom aides who assist teachers; may include parents.

partial participation Teaching approach that acknowledges that even though an individual with severe disabilities may not be able to independently perform all the steps of a given task or activity, she can often be taught to do selected components or an adapted version of the task.

partially sighted Term used for legal and governmental purposes that means visual acuity of no better than 20/70 in the better eye after correction.

perceptual handicap A term formerly used to describe some conditions now included under the term *learning disabilities;* usually referred to problems with no known physical cause.

perinatal Occurring at or immediately after birth.

peripheral vision Vision at the outer limits of the field of vision.

personality disorder A group of behavior disorders, including social withdrawal, anxiety, depression, feelings of inferiority, guilt, shyness, and unhappiness, as identified by Quay (1975).

pervasive developmental disorders—not otherwise specified (PDD-NOS) Children who meet some but not all of the criteria for autistic disorder are often diagnosed as having PDD-NOS; included in the autism spectrum disorders.

petit mal seizure See *absence seizure.*

phenylketonuria (PKU) An inherited metabolic disease that can cause severe mental retardation; can now be detected at birth, and the detrimental effects can be prevented with a special diet.

phoneme The smallest unit of sound that can be identified in a spoken language. The English language has 45 phonemes, or sound families.

phonemic awareness The ability to hear and manipulate the sounds of spoken language; critical prerequisite for learning to read. A child with phonemic awareness can orally blend sounds to make a word; isolate beginning, middle, and ending sounds in words; segment words into component sounds; and manipulate sounds within words.

phonics   The relationship between the letters (graphemes) of written language and the sounds (phonemes) of spoken language. Although often misused, phonics does not refer to a method of teaching reading, but rather to curriculum content and a skill (decoding) that is critical to beginning reading instruction.

phonological awareness   The "conscious understanding and knowledge that language is made up of sounds" (Simmons, Kame'enui, Coyne, & Chard, 2007, p. 49). See *phonemic awareness.*

phonological disorder   A language disorder in which the child produces a given sound correctly in some instances but not at other times.

phonology   Refers to the linguistic rules governing a language's sound system.

photophobia   Extreme sensitivity of the eyes to light; occurs most notably in albino children.

physical therapist (PT)   A professional trained to help people with disabilities develop and maintain muscular and orthopedic capability and make correct and useful movements.

pica   A form of self-injurious behavior in which the person ingests nonnutritive substances (e.g., dirt, rocks, sticks, plastic, string, feces); exhibited by some persons with moderate and severe mental retardation.

play audiometry   A method for assessing a child's hearing ability by teaching the child to perform simple but distinct activities, such as picking up a toy or putting a ball into a cup whenever he hears the signal, either pure tones or speech.

positive reinforcement   Presentation of a stimulus or event immediately after a response has been emitted, which has the primary effect of increasing the occurrence of similar responses in the future.

postlingual hearing loss   Occurring after the development of language; usually used to classify hearing losses that begin after a person has learned to speak.

postnatal   Occurring after birth.

post-traumatic stress disorder   Prolonged and recurrent emotional reactions after exposure to a traumatic event (e.g., sexual or physical assault; unexpected death of a loved one; witnessing or being a victim of a natural disaster, acts of war, or terrorism). Symptoms: flashbacks and nightmares of the traumatic event; avoiding places or things related to the trauma; emotional detachment from others; difficulty sleeping, irritability, or poor concentration.

practice stage of learning   After a student has learned how to perform a new skill, she should work to develop fluency with the target skill. Feedback during the practice stage of learning should emphasize the rate or speed with which the student correctly performs the skill. Compare with *acquisition stage of learning.*

Prader-Willi syndrome   A condition linked to chromosomal abnormality that is characterized by delays in motor development, mild-to-moderate mental retardation, hypogenital development, insatiable appetite that often results in obesity, and small features and stature.

pragmatics   Refers to the rules that govern how language is used in a communication context.

precision teaching   An instructional approach that involves (a) pinpointing the skills to be learned; (b) measuring the initial frequency or rate per minute at which the student can perform those skills; (c) setting an aim, or goal, for the child's improvement; (d) using direct, daily measurement to monitor progress made under an instructional program; (e) charting the results of those measurements on a *standard celeration chart;* and (f) changing the program if progress is not adequate.

prelingual hearing loss   Describes a hearing impairment acquired before the development of speech and language.

prenatal   Occurring before birth.

prenatal asphyxia   A lack of oxygen during the birth process usually caused by interruption of respiration; can cause unconsciousness and/or brain damage.

prereferral intervention   Individualized intervention for a student experiencing academic or behavioral difficulties in the general education classroom before referring the student for formal testing and evaluation for special education eligibility. Usually coordinated by a building-based team that helps teachers devise and implement the additional academic or behavioral supports. See *responsiveness to intervention (RTI).*

prevalence   The number of people who have a certain condition at any given time.

primary prevention   Intervention designed to eliminate or counteract risk factors so that a disability is never acquired; aimed at all relevant persons.

profound disabilities   A person with profound disabilities functions at a level no higher than a typically developing 2-year-old in all behavioral and cognitive domains and requires intensive supports and continuous monitoring.

projective tests   Psychological tests that require a person to respond to a standardized task or set of stimuli (e.g., draw a picture or interpret an ink blot). Responses are thought to be a projection of the test taker's personality and are scored according to the given test's scoring manual to produce a personality profile.

prosthesis   Any device used to replace a missing or impaired body part.

psychomotor seizure   See *complex partial seizure.*

psychosocial disadvantage   Type of causation for mental retardation that requires evidence of subaverage intellectual functioning in at least one parent and one or more of any siblings. Typically associated with impoverished environments involving poor housing, inadequate diets, and inadequate medical care. Often used synonymously with *cultural-familial retardation;* suggests that mental retardation can be caused by a poor social and cultural environment.

pupil   The circular hole in the center of the iris of the eye, which contracts and expands to let light pass through.

quadriplegia   Paralysis of all four limbs.

randomized controlled trial   A research study in which participants are randomly assigned to the experimental group (which receives the intervention or treatment being evaluated) or to the control group (which does not receive the treatment). Also called *randomized experimental group design.*

randomized experimental group design   A research design in which participants are randomly assigned to the experimental group (which receives the intervention or treatment being evaluated) or to the control group (which does not receive the treatment). Studies using this design are also called *randomized controlled trials*.

rate (or frequency of behavior) A measure of how often a particular behavior is performed; usually reported as the number of responses per standard unit of time (e.g., 5 per minute).

receptive language disorder A language impairment characterized by difficulty in understanding language; contrast with *expressive language disorder*.

refraction The bending or deflection of light rays from a straight path as they pass from one medium (e.g., air) into another (e.g., the eye). Used by eye specialists in assessing and correcting vision.

regular education initiative (REI) A position advocated by some special educators that students with disabilities can and should be educated in regular classrooms under the primary responsibility of the general education program.

rehabilitation A social service program designed to teach a newly disabled person basic skills needed for independence.

reinforcement See *positive reinforcement*.

related services Developmental, corrective, and other supportive services required for a child with disabilities to benefit from special education. Includes special transportation services, speech and language pathology, audiology, psychological services, physical and occupational therapy, school health services, counseling and medical services for diagnostic and evaluation purposes, rehabilitation counseling, social work services, and parent counseling and training.

remediation A type of intervention designed to teach a person to overcome a disability through training and education.

repeated reading A technique for increasing reading fluency in which a student orally reads the same a passage, usually 3–5 times, during each session. With each successive reading, the student tries to increase the number of words read correctly per minute. When the student achieves a predetermined fluency criterion on a given passage, a new passage is introduced. The difficulty level of successive passages gradually increases over time.

residual hearing The remaining hearing, however slight, of a person who is deaf.

resource room Classroom in which special education students spend part of the school day and receive individualized special education services.

respite care The temporary care of an individual with disabilities by nonfamily members; provides much-needed support for many families of children with severe disabilities.

response cards Cards, signs, or items that are simultaneously held up by all students to display their response to a question or problem presented by the teacher; response cards enable every student in the class to respond to each question or item.

response cost A procedure for reducing the frequency of inappropriate behavior by withdrawing a specific amount of reinforcement contingent upon occurrence of the behavior.

responsiveness to intervention (RTI) A systematic prereferral and early intervention process that consists of universal screening and several tiers of increasingly intensive trials of research-based interventions before referral for assessment for special education eligibility. The Individuals with Disabilities Education Act (IDEA) of 2004 stipulates that schools can use RTI to determine a child's eligibility for special education under the specific learning disabilities category.

retina A sheet of nerve tissue at the back of the eye on which an image is focused.

retinitis pigmentosa (RP) An eye disease in which the retina gradually degenerates and atrophies, causing the field of vision to become progressively narrower.

retinopathy of prematurity (ROP) A condition characterized by an abnormally dense growth of blood vessels and scar tissue in the eye, often causing loss of visual field and retinal detachment. Usually caused by high levels of oxygen administered to premature infants in incubators. Also called *retrolental fibroplasia (RLF)*.

retrolental fibroplasia (RLF) See *retinopathy of prematurity*.

Rett syndrome Neurodevelopmental disorder of childhood characterized by normal early development followed by loss of purposeful use of the hands, distinctive hand movements, slowed brain and head growth, gait abnormalities, seizures, and mental retardation; affects females almost exclusively; included in *autism spectrum disorders*.

Reye's syndrome A relatively rare disease that appears to be related to a variety of viral infections; most common in children over the age of 6. About 30% of children who contract it die; survivors sometimes show signs of neurological damage and mental retardation. The cause is unknown, although some studies have found an increased risk after the use of aspirin during a viral illness.

rigidity A type of cerebral palsy characterized by increased muscle tone, minimal muscle elasticity, and little or no stretch reflex.

rods Light receptors for peripheral vision, detection of movement, and vision in dim light; located around the periphery of the retina.

rubella German measles; when contracted by a woman during the first trimester of pregnancy, may cause visual impairments, hearing impairments, mental retardation, and/or other congenital impairments in the child.

SAFMEDS (Say All Fast a Minute Each Day Shuffled) A deck of cards with a question, vocabulary term, or problem printed on one side of each card and the answer on the other side. A student answers as many items in the deck as he can during 1-minute practice trials by looking at the question or problem, stating an answer, flipping the card over to reveal the correct answer, and putting each card on a "correct" or "incorrect" pile.

schizophrenia A severe psychotic disorder characterized by delusions, hallucinations (hearing voices), unfounded fears of persecution, disorganized speech, catatonic behavior (stupor and muscular rigidity), restricted range and intensity of emotional expression (affective flattening), reduced thought and speech productivity, and decreased initiation of goal-directed behavior. Most persons with schizophrenia alternate between acute psychotic episodes and stable phases with few or no symptoms.

screening A procedure in which groups of children are examined and/or tested in an effort to identify children who are most likely to have a disability; identified children are then referred for more intensive examination and assessment.

secondary prevention   Intervention directed at reducing or eliminating the effects of existing risk factors; aimed at individuals exposed to or displaying specific risk factors.

selective mutism   Speaking normally in some settings or situations and not speaking in others.

self-contained class   A special classroom, usually located within a regular public school building, that includes only exceptional children.

self-determination   A combination of skills, knowledge, and beliefs that enable a person to engage in goal-directed, self-regulated, autonomous behavior; includes skills such as choice/decision making, goal setting, problem solving, self-evaluation, self-management, self-advocacy, and self-awareness.

self-evaluation   A procedure in which a person compares his performance of a target behavior with a predetermined goal or standard; often a component of self-management. Sometimes called *self-assessment*.

self-management   The personal application of behavior-change tactics that produces a desired change in behavior. This is an intentionally broad, functional definition in that the desired change in the target behavior must occur for self-management to be demonstrated (Cooper, Heron, & Heward, 2007, p. 578).

self-monitoring   A procedure whereby a person systematically observes his behavior and records the occurrence or nonoccurrence of a target behavior. (Also called *self-recording* or *self-observation*.)

semantics   Refers to the meaning in language.

sensorineural hearing loss   A hearing loss caused by damage to the auditory nerve or the inner ear.

severe disabilities   Term used to refer to challenges faced by individuals with severe and profound mental retardation, autism, and/or physical/sensory impairments combined with marked developmental delay. Persons with severe disabilities exhibit extreme deficits in intellectual functioning and need systematic instruction for basic skills such as self-care and communicating with others.

shaping   A process for teaching new behavior through differential reinforcement of successive approximations of targeted performance.

sheltered workshop   A structured work environment where persons with disabilities receive employment training and perform work for pay. May provide transitional services for some individuals (e.g., short-term training for competitive employment in the community) and permanent work settings for others.

shunt   Tube that diverts fluid from one part of the body to another; often implanted in people with hydrocephalus to remove extra cerebrospinal fluid from the head and send it directly into the heart or intestines.

sighted-guide technique   A method by which a sighted person can help a person with visual impairments travel. The person with visual impairment grasps the sighted person's arm just above the elbow and walks half a step behind in a natural manner.

simple partial seizure   A type of seizure characterized by sudden jerking motions with no loss of consciousness. Partial seizures may occur weekly, monthly, or only once or twice a year.

Snellen chart   A chart used to test visual acuity; developed by a Dutch ophthalmologist in 1862 and still used today. Consists of rows of letters, or Es facing up, down, left, or right; each row corresponds to the distance that a normally sighted person can discriminate the letters.

social stories   An intervention for teaching social skills that uses individualized stories usually constructed with one sentence per page accompanied by photographs or simple line drawings depicting a social situation from the viewpoint of the student. Often used with children with autism spectrum disorders to decrease anxiety about the situation, help the child learn relevant social cues and the expected behaviors, explain how to behave to achieve desired outcomes from the situation, and help understand the event from the perspective of others.

social validity   A desirable characteristic of the objectives, procedures, and results of intervention, indicating their appropriateness for the learner. For example, the goal of riding a bus independently would have social validity for students residing in most cities but not for those in small towns or rural areas.

socialized aggression   A group of behavior disorders, including truancy, gang membership, theft, and delinquency, as identified by Quay (1975).

spasticity   A type of cerebral palsy characterized by tense, contracted muscles.

special education   Individually planned, specialized, intensive, outcome-directed instruction. When practiced most effectively and ethically, special education is also characterized by the systematic use of research-based instructional methods, the application of which is guided by direct and frequent measures of student performance.

speech   Using breath and muscles to create the specific sounds of spoken language.

speech audiometry   Tests a person's detection and understanding of speech by presenting a list of two-syllable words at different decibel (sound-volume) levels.

speech impairment   Speech that "deviates so far from the speech of other people that it (1) calls attention to itself, (2) interferes with communication, or (3) provokes distress in the speaker or the listener" (Van Riper & Erickson, 1996, p. 110). The three basic types of speech impairments are articulation, fluency, and voice.

speech reception threshold (SRT)   The decibel (sound-volume) level at which an individual can understand half of the words during a speech audiometry test; the SRT is measured and recorded for each ear.

speechreading   Process of understanding a spoken message by observing the speaker's lips in combination with information gained from facial expressions, gestures, and the context or situation.

spina bifida   A congenital malformation of the spine in which the vertebrae that normally protect the spine do not develop fully; may involve loss of sensation and severe muscle weakness in the lower part of the body.

spina bifida occulta   A type of spina bifida that usually does not cause serious disability. Although the vertebrae do not close, no protrusion of the spinal cord and membranes is present.

standard celeration chart   A semilogarithmic chart with six log-base-10 (or x10) cycles on the vertical axis that can accommodate response rates as low as 1 per 24 hours (.000695 per minute) to as high as 1,000 per minute; enables the standardized charting of celeration, a factor by which frequency of behavior increases or decreases per unit of time; used in *precision teaching.*

standard deviation   A descriptive statistic that shows the average amount of variability among a set of scores. A small standard deviation indicates that the scores in the sample are distributed close to the mean; a larger standard deviation indicates that more scores in the sample fall farther from the mean.

stereotype   An overgeneralized or inaccurate attitude held toward all members of a particular group, on the basis of a common characteristic such as age, sex, race, or disability.

stereotypy   Repetitive, nonfunctional movements (e.g., hand flapping, rocking).

stimulus control   Occurs when a behavior is emitted more often in the presence of a particular stimulus than it is in the absence of that stimulus.

strabismus   A condition in which one eye cannot attain binocular vision with the other eye because of imbalanced muscles.

stuttering   Fluency disorder of speaking marked by rapid-fire repetitions of consonant or vowel sounds, especially at the beginning of words; prolongations; hesitations; interjections; and complete verbal blocks; compare to *cluttering.*

summative evaluation   Any type of evaluation of student performance or learning that occurs after instruction has been completed (e.g., a test given at the end of a grading period or school year).

supported employment   Providing ongoing, individualized supports to persons with disabilities to help them find, learn, and maintain paid employment at regular work sites in the community.

supported living   Personalized networks of natural supports to help people with disabilities live successfully in homes of their own in the community.

syntax   The system of rules governing the meaningful arrangement of words in a language.

systematic replication   A strategy for extending and determining the generality of research findings by changing one or more variables from a previous study to see if similar results can be obtained. For example, testing a particular instructional method with elementary students that a previous study found effective with secondary students.

task analysis   Breaking a complex skill or chain of behaviors into smaller, teachable units.

Tay-Sachs disease   A progressive nervous system disorder causing profound mental retardation, deafness, blindness, paralysis, and seizures. Usually fatal by age 5. Caused by a recessive gene; blood test can identify carrier; analysis of enzymes in fetal cells provides prenatal diagnosis.

technology-dependent student   A "student who needs both a medical device to compensate for the loss of a vital body function and substantial and ongoing nursing care to avoid death or further disability" (Office of Technology Assessment, 1987, p. 3).

temperament   A person's behavioral style or typical way of responding to situations.

tertiary prevention   Intervention designed to minimize the impact of a specific condition or disability; aimed at individuals with a disability.

tiered lesson   A lesson that entails different extensions of the same basic lesson for groups of students of differing abilities. For example, after the whole class is exposed to a basic lesson on a poem, three groups of students might work on follow-up activities or assignments of basic, medium, and high difficulty.

time out   A behavior management technique that involves removing the opportunity for reinforcement for a specific period of time following an inappropriate behavior; results in a reduction of the inappropriate behavior.

time trials   A fluency-building activity in which students correctly perform a particular skill (e.g., segmenting sounds, identifying animal species, writing answers to addition and subtraction problems) as many times as they can in a brief period, usually no longer than 1 minute.

token economy (token reinforcement system)   An instructional and behavior-management system in which students earn tokens (e.g., stars, points, poker chips) for performing specified behaviors. Students accumulate their tokens and exchange them at prearranged times for their choice of activities or items from a menu of backup rewards (e.g., stickers, hall monitor for a day).

topography (of behavior)   The physical shape or form of a response.

total communication   An approach to educating deaf students that combines oral speech, sign language, and fingerspelling.

Tourette syndrome   An inherited neurological disorder characterized by motor and vocal tics (repeated, involuntary movements) such as eye blinking, facial grimacing, throat clearing, arm thrusting, or kicking. About 15% of cases include *coprolalia* (repeated cursing, obscene language, and ethnic slurs). Symptoms typically appear before age 18; males affected 3 to 4 times more often than females.

transition services   A coordinated set of activities for a child with a disability designed to facilitate the child's movement from school to postschool activities, including postsecondary education, employment, independent living, and community participation; see *individualized transition plan.*

traumatic brain injury   An acquired injury to the brain caused by an external physical force, resulting in total or partial functional disability, psychosocial impairments, or both that adversely affect a child's educational performance.

tremor   A type of cerebral palsy characterized by regular, strong, uncontrolled movements. May cause less overall difficulty in movement than other types of cerebral palsy.

triplegia   Paralysis of any three limbs; relatively rare.

tunnel vision   Visual impairment in which a person has good central vision but poor peripheral vision.

Turner's syndrome   A sex chromosomal disorder in females, resulting from an absence of one of the X chromosomes. Lack of secondary sex characteristics, sterility, and short stature are common. Although not usually a cause of mental retardation, it is often associated with learning problems.

tympanic membrane (eardrum)   Located in the middle ear, the eardrum moves in and out to variations in sound pressure, changing acoustical energy to sound energy.

Type-1 diabetes   (formerly called *juvenile diabetes* or *early-onset diabetes*) A disease characterized by inadequate secretion or use of insulin and the resulting excessive sugar in the blood and urine. Managed with diet and/or medication but can be difficult to control. Can cause coma and eventually death if left untreated or treated improperly. Can also lead to visual impairments and limb amputation. Not curable at the present time.

Type-2 diabetes The most common form of diabetes; results from insulin resistance (the body's failure to properly use insulin), combined with relative insulin deficiency. Occurs most often in adults who are overweight, but the recent increase in childhood obesity has led to a rise in the incidence of Type-2 diabetes in children.

universal precautions A set of safety guidelines (e.g., wearing protective gloves) that interrupt the chain of infection spread by potential biohazards such as blood and bodily fluids.

Usher's syndrome An inherited combination of visual and hearing impairments. Usually, the person is born with a profound hearing loss and loses vision gradually in adulthood because of retinitis pigmentosa, which affects the visual field.

video modeling A teaching technique that entails making a videotape of someone (perhaps the student himself) successfully performing the targeted skill or task. The video is shown to the student at the beginning of each instructional session.

visual acuity The ability to clearly distinguish forms or discriminate details at a specified distance.

visual cortex Interprets electrical signals from the optic nerve into visual images; located in the occipital lobe at the back of the brain.

visual efficiency A term used to describe how effectively a person uses his vision. Includes such factors as control of eye movements, near and distant visual acuity, and speed and quality of visual processing. See also *functional vision*.

visual phonics A method for teaching phonemic awareness and phonics to students who are deaf and hard of hearing that uses hand cues and graphic symbols to visually depict the sounds of written words.

vitreous humor The jellylike fluid that fills most of the interior of the eyeball.

vocational rehabilitation A program designed to help adults with disabilities obtain and hold employment.

voice disorder "Abnormal production and/or absences of vocal quality, pitch, loudness, resonance, and/or duration, which is inappropriate for an individual's age and/or sex" (ASHA, 1993, p. 40).

work activity center A sheltered work and activity program for adults with severe disabilities; teaches concentration and persistence, along with basic life skills, for little or no pay.

Aaroe, L., & Nelson, J. R. (2000). A comparative analysis of teachers', Caucasian parents', and Hispanic parents' view of problematic school survival behaviors. *Education and Treatment of Children, 23,* 314-324.

Abikoff, H. (1991). Cognitive training in ADHD children: Less to it than meets the eye. *Journal of Learning Disabilities, 24,* 205-209.

Abrams, B. J. (2005). Becoming a therapeutic teacher for students with emotional and behavioral disorders. *Teaching Exceptional Children, 38*(2), 40-45.

Achenbach, T. M., & Edelbrock, C. S. (1991). *Manual for the child behavior checklist.* Burlington: University of Vermont, Department of Psychiatry.

Achenbach, T. M., & McConaughy, S. H. (2003). *The Achenbach System of Empirically Based Assessment.* In C. R. Reynolds & R. W. Kamphaus (Eds.), *Handbook of psychological and educational assessment of children: Personality, behavior, and context* (2nd ed.) (pp. 406-432). New York: Guilford.

Ad Hoc Committee on Terminology and Classification. (2001). Request for comment on proposed new edition of *Mental Retardation: Definition, classification, and systems of supports. AAMR News and Notes, 14*(5), 1, 9-12.

Adams, C. M., & Pierce, R. L. (2006). *Differentiating instruction: A practical guide for tiering lessons in the elementary grades.* Waco, TX: Prufrock Press.

Adams, G., & Carnine, D. (2003). Direct Instruction. In H. L. Swanson, K. R. Harris, & S. Graham (Eds.), *Handbook of learning disabilities* (pp. 403-416). New York: Guilford.

Adams, L., Gouvousis, A., VanLue, M., & Waldron, C. (2004). Social story intervention: Improving communication skills in a child with an autism spectrum disorder. *Focus on Autism and Other Developmental Disabilities, 19,* 87-94.

Adelman, H. S. (1994). Intervening to enhance home involvement in schooling. *Intervention in School and Clinic, 29*(5), 276-284.

Agran, M., Blanchard, C., Wehmeyer, M., & Hughes, C. (2002). Increasing problem-solving skills of students with developmental disabilities participating in general education. *Remedial and Special Education, 23,* 279-288.

Agran, M., Hong, S., & Blankenship, K. (2007). Promoting the self-determination of students with visual impairments: Reducing the gap between knowledge and practice. *Journal of Visual Impairment and Blindness, 101,* 453-464.

Agran, M., & Hughes, C. (2006). Introduction to special issue: Self-determination reexamined: How far have we come?

Research and Practice for Persons with Severe Disabilities, 30, 105-107.

Agran, M., King-Sears, M., Wehmeyer, M. L., & Copeland, S. R. (2003). *Teachers' guides to inclusive practices: Student-directed learning strategies.* Baltimore: Paul H. Brookes.

Agran, M., Sinclair, T., Alper, S., Cavin, M., Wehmeyer, M., & Hughes, C. (2005). Using self-monitoring to increase following-direction skills of students with moderate to severe disabilities in general education. *Education and Training in Developmental Disabilities, 40,* 3-13.

Agran, M., Snow, K., & Swaner, J. (1999). Teacher perceptions of self-determination: Benefits, characteristics, and strategies. *Education and Training in Mental Retardation and Developmental Disabilities, 34,* 293-301.

Aiello, B. (1976, April 25). Up from the basement: A teacher's story. *New York Times,* p. 14.

Akshoomoff, N. (2000). *Neurological underpinnings of autism* (Vol. 9). Baltimore: Brookes.

Al Otaiba, S. (2001). IRA outstanding dissertation award for 2001: Children who do not respond to early literacy instruction: A longitudinal study across kindergarten and first grade [Abstract]. *Reading Research Quarterly, 36,* 344-345.

Al Otaiba, S., & Hosp, M. K. (2004). Providing effective literacy instruction to students with Down syndrome. *Teaching Exceptional Children, 36*(4), 28-35.

Al Otaiba, S., & Smartt, S. M. (2003). Summer sound camp: Involving parents in early literacy intervention for children with speech and language delays. *Teaching Exceptional Children, 35*(3), 30-34.

Alber, S. R., & Heward, W. L. (1997). Recruit it or lose it! Training students to recruit positive teacher attention. *Intervention in School and Clinic, 32,* 275-282.

Alber, S. R., & Heward, W. L. (2000). Teaching students to recruit positive attention: A review and recommendations. *Journal of Behavioral Education, 10,* 177-204.

Alber, S. R., & Walshe, S. E. (2004). When to self-correct spelling words: A systematic replication. *Journal of Behavioral Education, 13,* 51-66.

Alber, S. R., Heward, W. L., & Hippler, B. J. (1999). Training middle school students with learning disabilities to recruit positive teacher attention. *Exceptional Children, 65,* 253-270.

Alber, S. R., Nelson, J. S., & Brennan, K. B. (2002). A comparative analysis of two homework study methods on elementary and secondary school students' acquisition and maintenance of social studies content. *Education and Treatment of Children, 26,* 172-196.

Alber Morgan, S. (2006). Introduction: Four classwide peer tutoring programs: Research, recommendations for implementation, and future directions. *Reading and Writing Quarterly, 22,* 1-4.

Alber-Morgan, S. R. (2007). Ten ways to enhance the effectiveness of repeated readings. *Journal of Early and Intensive Behavioral Intervention, 3,* 257-263.

Alber-Morgan, S. R., Ramp, E. M., Anderson, L. L. & Martin, C. M. (in press). The effects of repeated readings, error correction, and performance feedback on the fluency and comprehension of middle school students with behavior problems. *The Journal of Special Education.*

Alberto, P. A., & Fredrick, L. D. (2000). Teaching picture reading as an enabling skill. *Teaching Exceptional Children, 33*(6), 60-64.

Alberto, P. A., & Troutman, A. C. (2006). *Applied behavior analysis for teachers* (7th ed.). Upper Saddle River, NJ: Merrill/Prentice Hall.

Aldrich, F. K., & Parkin, A. J. (1989). Listening at speed. *British Journal of Visual Impairment, 7*(1), 16-18.

Algozzine, B., Audette, B., Ellis, E., Marr, M. B., & White, R. (2000). Supporting teacher, principals, and students, through unified discipline. *Teaching Exceptional Children, 33*(2), 42-47.

Algozzine, B., Browder, D., Karvonen, M., Test, D. W., & Wood, W. M. (2001). Effects of interventions to promote self-determination for individuals with disabilities. *Review of Educational Research, 71,* 219-277.

Algozzine, B., & Kay, P. (Eds.). (2002). *Preventing problem behaviors: A handbook of successful prevention strategies.* Thousand Oaks, CA: Corwin.

Allen, C. P., White, J., & Test, D. W. (1992). Using a picture/symbol form for self-monitoring within a community-based training program. *Teaching Exceptional Children, 24*(2), 54-56.

Allen, D. A., & Affleck, G. (1985). Are we stereotyping parents? A postscript to Blacher. *Mental Retardation, 23,* 200-202.

Allen, K. E., Hart, B. M., Buell, J. S., Harris, F. R., & Wolf, M. M. (1964). Effects of social reinforcement on isolate behavior of a nursery school child. *Child Development, 35,* 511-518.

Allen, N. J., Wood, C. L., Silvestri, S. M., Anderson, M. A., Murphy, C. M., & Heward, W. L. (2006). Getting involved in your child's education. In E. A. Boutot & M. Tincani (Eds.), *Autism spectrum disorders handouts: What parents need to know* (pp. 21-23). Austin, TX: PRO-ED.

Allen, T. (1986). Patterns of academic achievement among hearing impaired students: 1974 and 1983. In A. Schildroth & M. Karchmer (Eds.), *Deaf children in America* (pp. 161-206). San Diego: Little, Brown.

Allen, T. E. (1994). *Who are the deaf and hard-of-hearing students leaving high school and entering postsecondary education?* Unpublished manuscript, Gallaudet University, Center for Assessment and Demographic Studies, Washington, DC.

Allman, C. B., & Lewis, S. (2000). *Seeing eye to eye: An administrator's guide.* New York: AFB Press.

Alper, S., & Raharinirina, S. (2006). Assistive technology for individuals with disabilities: A review and synthesis of the literature. *Journal of Special Education Technology, 21,* 47.

Alwell, M., & Cobb, B. (2007). *A systematic review of the effects of curricular interventions on the acquisition of functional life skills by youth with disabilities.* National Secondary Transition Technical Assistance Center. [Retrieved September 27, 2007. http://www.nsttac.org/pdf/life_skills.pdf]

Al-Hassan, S., & Gardner, III, R. (2002). Involving immigrant parents of students with disabilities in the educational process. *Teaching Exceptional Children, 35*(2), 52–58.

American Academy of Pediatrics. (2001). *Clinical practice guideline: Treatment of the school-aged child with attention-deficit/hyperactivity disorder. Pediatrics, 105,* 1158–1170.

American Association on Mental Retardation. (2002). *Mental retardation: Definition, classification, and systems of supports* (10th ed.). Washington, DC: Author.

American Association on Mental Retardation. (1994). Policy on facilitated communication. *AAMR News & Notes, 7*(5), p. 1.

American College of Medical Genetics. (2004). *Newborn screening: Toward a uniform screening panel and system.* Report commissioned by the Health Resources and Services Administration. [Available: http://mchb.hrsa.gov/screening/]

American Council on Science and Health. (1979, May). *Diet and hyperactivity: Is there a relationship?* New York: Author.

American Diabetes Association. (2007). *Total prevalence of diabetes & pre-diabetes.* Alexandria, VA: Author. [Retrieved September 3, 2007. http://www.diabetes.org/diabetes-statistics/prevalence.jsp]

American Foundation for the Blind. (2007). *Glossary of eye conditions.* [Retrieved August 25, 2007. http://www.afb.org/Section.asp?SectionID=40&DocumentID=2139]

American Printing House for the Blind. (2006). *Distribution of eligible students based on the federal quota census of January 4, 2004 (Fiscal Year 2005).* Louisville, KY: Author. Retrieved February 7, 2007 at http://www.aph.org/fedquotpgm/dist05.html.

American Printing House for the Blind. (1992). *Annual report.* Louisville, KY: Author.

American Psychiatric Association. (1999). *Obsessive-compulsive disorder.* Washington, DC: Author. http://www.psych.org.

American Psychiatric Association. (2000a). *Diagnostic and statistical manual of mental disorders, text revision: DSM-IV-TR* (4th ed.). Washington, DC: Author.

American Psychiatric Association. (2000b). *Practice guideline for the treatment of patients with schizophrenia.* Washington, DC: Author. http://www.psych.org/clin_res/pg_schizo.cfm.

American Psychiatric Association. (2000c). *Practice guideline for the treatment of patients with bipolar disorder.* Washington, DC: Author. http://www.psych.org/clin_res/pg_bipolar.cfm.

American Psychiatric Association. (2002). *Practice guideline for the treatment of patients with bipolar disorder.* Washington, DC: Author. [Available online: http://www.psych.org/psych_pract/treatg/pg/Bipolar2ePG_05-15-06.pdf]

American Psychiatric Association. (2004). *Practice guideline for the treatment of patients with schizophrenia* (2nd ed.). Washington, DC: Author. [Available online: http://www.psych.org/psych_pract/treatg/pg/SchizPG-Complete-Feb04.pdf]

American Psychiatric Association. (2007). *Treating obsessive-compulsive disorder: A quick reference guide.* Washington, DC: Author. [Available online: http://www.psych.org/psych_pract/treatg/pg/FINALOCD_%20QRG_06-21-07.pdf]

American Psychological Association. (1994, August). *Resolution on facilitated communication by the American Psychological Association.* Washington, DC: Author.

American School for the Deaf. (2005). *History of deaf education in America.* [Retrieved August 23, 2007 from http://www.asd-1817.org/history/history-deafed.html]

American Speech-Language-Hearing Association. (1983). Position paper on social dialects. *ASHA, 25*(9), 23–27.

American Speech-Language-Hearing Association. (1995). Position paper and guidelines for acoustics in educational settings. *ASHA, 37*(Suppl. 14), 15–19.

American Speech-Language-Hearing Association. (1996, Spring). Inclusive practices for children and youths with communication disorders: Position statement and technical report). *ASHA, 38* (Suppl. 16), 33–44.

American Speech-Language-Hearing Association. (2000). *Guidelines for the roles and responsibilities of speech-language pathologists* [Guidelines]. Rockville, MD: Author. Available from www.asha.org/policy

American Speech-Language-Hearing Association. (2000). *Healthy people 2010—Health objectives for the nation and roles for speech-language pathologists and speech-language-hearing scientists.* Rockville, MD: Author.

American Speech-Language-Hearing Association. (2001a). *Effects of hearing loss.* http://www.asha.org.

American Speech-Language-Hearing Association. (2001b). *Language and literacy development.* Washington, DC: U.S. Department of Education and American Speech-Language-Hearing Association. http://www.asha.org/speech/development/languagedevelopment.cfm.

American Speech-Language-Hearing Association. (ASHA). (2001c). *Pragmatics, socially speaking.* www.asha.org.

American Speech-Language-Hearing Association. (ASHA). (2001d). Roles and responsibilities of speech-language pathologists with respect to reading and writing in children and adolescents. (Position statement, executive summary of guidelines, technical report). *ASHA Supplement 21,* 17–27. Rockville, MD: Author.

American Speech-Language-Hearing Association. (ASHA). (2001e). *Schools survey.* www.asha.org.

American Speech-Language-Hearing Association. (2004). *Pragmatics, socially speaking.* www.asha.org. Retrieved July 16, 2004.

American Speech-Language-Hearing Association. (2004b). *Social language use: Pragmatics.* Rockville, MD: Author. [Retrieved July 28, 2007. http://www.asha.org/public/speech/development/Pragmatics.htm]

American Speech-Language-Hearing Association. (2006). *2006 Schools Survey report: Caseload characteristics.* Rockville, MD: Author.

American Speech-Language-Hearing Association. (2007). *Typical speech and language development.* Rockville, MD: Author. [Retrieved July 28, 2007. http://asha.org/public/speech/development/]

American Speech-Language-Hearing Association. (2007a). *Effects of hearing loss on development.* Rockville, MD: Author. [Retrieved August 22, 2007 from http://www.asha.org/public/hearing/disorders/effects.htm]

American Speech-Language-Hearing Association. (2007b). *The prevalence and incidence of hearing loss in adults.* [Retrieved August 22, 2007 from http://asha.org/public/hearing/disorders/prevalence_adults.htm]

American Speech-Language-Hearing Association. (2007c). *Noise and hearing loss.* [Retrieved August 22, 2007 from http://www.asha.org/public/hearing/disorders/noise.htm]

American Speech-Language-Hearing Association. (2007d). *Status of state universal newborn and infant hearing screening legislation and laws.* Rockville, MD: Author. [Retrieved August 24, 2007 from http://www.asha.org/about/legislation-advocacy/state/issues/overview.htm]

American Speech-Language-Hearing Association. (2007e). *How does your child hear and talk?* Rockville, MD: Author. [Retrieved August 22, 2007 from http://asha.org/public/speech/development/chart.htm]

American Speech-Language-Hearing Association Ad-Hoc Committee on Service Delivery in the Schools. (1993). Definitions of communication disorders and variations. *Asha, 35* (Suppl. 100, 40–41.

Anderegg, M. L., Vergason, G. A., & Smith, M. C. (1992). A visual representation of the grief cycle for use by teachers with families of children with disabilities. *Remedial and Special Education, 13*(2), 17–23.

Anderson, C., & Katsiyannis, A. (1997). By what token economy: A classroom learning tool for inclusive settings. *Teaching Exceptional Children, 29*(4), 65-67.

Anderson, D. H., Fisher, A., Marchant, M., Young, K. R., & Smith, J. A. (2006). The cool card intervention: A positive support strategy for managing anger. *Beyond Behavior, 16*, 3-13.

Anderson, J. A., Kutash, K., & Duchnowski, A. J. (2001). A comparison of the academic progress of students with EBD and students with LD. *Journal of Emotional and Behavioral Disorders, 9*, 106-115.

Anderson, J. A., & Matthews, B. (2001). We CARE for students with emotional and behavioral disabilities and their families. *Teaching Exceptional Children, 33*(5), 34-39.

Anderson, L. W. (Ed.), Krathwohl, D. R. (Ed.), Airasian, P. W., Cruikshank, K. A., Mayer, R. E., Pintrich, P. R., Raths, J., & Wittrock, M. C. (2001). *A taxonomy for learning, teaching, and assessing: A revision of Bloom's Taxonomy of Educational Objectives* (Complete edition). New York: Longman.

Anderson, M. A., & Heward, W. L. (May 2006). *Effects of video-based self-recording of on-task behavior on the on-task behavior and academic productivity by elementary students with special education needs in inclusive classrooms.* Paper presented at the 32nd Annual Convention of the Association for Behavior Analysis, Atlanta.

Anderson, N. B., & Shames, G. H. (2006). *Human communication disorders: An introduction* (7th ed.). Boston: Allyn & Bacon.

Anderson, S. R., & Romanczyk, R. G. (1999). Early intervention for young children with autism: Continuum-based models. *Journal of The Association for Persons with Severe Handicaps, 24*, 162-173.

Anderson Downing, J. (2007). *Students with emotional and behavioral problems: Assessment, management, and intervention strategies.* Upper Saddle River, NJ: Merrill/Prentice Hall.

Andrews, J. F., Leigh, I. W., & Weiner, M. T. (2004). *Deaf people: Evolving perspectives from psychology, education, and sociology.* Boston: Allyn & Bacon.

Anthony, D. (1971). *Signing essential English.* Anaheim, CA: Anaheim School District.

Antle, B. J. (2004). Factors associated with self-worth in young people with physical disabilities. *Health and Social Work, 29*, 167-175.

Antunez, B. (2000). *When everyone is involved: Parents and communities in school reform.* National Council for Bilingual Education. http://www.ncbe. gwu.edu/ncbepubs/tasynthesis/framing/ 6parents.htm.

Anxiety Disorders Association of America. (2001). *Brief overview of anxiety disorders.* Rockville, MD: Author. [On-line]. Available: http://www.adaa.org/ AnxietyDisorderInfor/OverviewAnxDis. cfm.

Anxiety Disorders Association of America. (2007). *Brief overview of anxiety disorders.* Silver Spring, MD: Author. [On-line]. Available: http://www.adaa.org/ GettingHelp/Briefoverview.as

Apple, D. F., Anson, C. A., Hunter, J. D., & Bell, R. B. (1995). Spinal cord injury in youth. *Clinical Pediatrics, 34*, 90-95.

Ardoin, S. P., Martens, B. K., & Wolfe, L. A. (1999). Using high-probability instruction sequences with fading to increase student compliance during transitions. *Journal of Applied Behavior Analysis, 32*, 339-351.

Armbruster, B. B., Lehr, F., & Osborn, J. (2003). *Put reading first: The research building blocks for teaching children to read, kindergarten through grade 3.* Jessup, MD: National Institute for Literacy.

Armendariz, F., & Umbreit, J. (1999). Using active responding to reduce disruptive behavior in a general education classroom. *Journal of Positive Behavior Interventions, 1*, 152-158.

Armstrong v. Kline, 476 F. Supp. 583 (E.D. Pa. 1979), *modified and remanded sub nom.,* Battle vs. Commonwealth of Pennsylvania, 629 F.2d 259 (3rd Cr. 1980), on remand, 513 F. Supp. 425 (E.D. Ps. 1980), *cert. denied sub nom.,* Scanlon v. Battle 101 S.Ct. 3123 (1981).

Arndt, S. A., Konrad, M., & Test, D. W. (2006). Effects of the self-directed IEP on student participation in planning meetings. *Remedial and Special Education, 27*, 194-207.

Arnold, L. E., Christopher, J., Huestis, R. D., & Smeltzer, D. J. (1978). Megavitamins for minimal brain dysfunction: A placebo controlled study. *Journal of the American Medical Association, 240*, 2642-2643.

Arrasmith, D. (2003). *Definition of explicit instruction and systematic curriculum.* Retrieved April 19, 2004, from http://www. studydog.com/.

Arter, C. (1997). Listening skills. In H. Mason & S. McCall (Eds.), *Visual impairment: Access to education for children and young people* (pp. 143-148). London: Fulton.

Artiles, A. J., Aguirre-Munoz, Z., & Abedi, J. (1998). Predicting placement in learning disabilities programs: Do predictors vary by ethnic group? *Exceptional Children, 64*, 543-559.

Artiles, A., & Zamora-Durán, G. (1997). *Reducing disproportionate representation of culturally diverse students in special and gifted education.* Reston, VA: Council for Exceptional Children.

Artiles, A. J., Trent, S. C., & Palmer, J. D. (2004). *Culturally diverse students in special education Legacies and prospects.* In J. A. Banks & C. A. M. Banks (Eds.), *Handbook of research of multicultural education* (2nd ed.) (pp. 716-735). San Francisco: Jossey-Bass.

Aspiazu, G. G., Bauer, S. C., & Spillett, M. D. (1998). Improving the academic performance of Hispanic youth: A community education model. *Bilingual Research Journal, 22*(2), 1-20.

Association for Science in Autism Treatment. (2007). ASAT Online. http://www. asatonline.org/about_asat/about_asat.htm

Assouline, S., Colangelo, N., Lupkowski-Shoplik, A., Lipscomb, H., & Forstadt, L. (2003). *Iowa Acceleration Scale* (2nd ed.). Scottsdale, AZ: Great Potential Press.

Asthma and Allergy Foundation of America. (2001). *Facts and figures.* Washington, DC: Author. www.aafa.org.

Asthma and Allergy Foundation of America. (2007). *Asthma facts and figures.* Washington, DC: Author. [Retrieved August 26, 2007 http://www.aafa.org/ display.cfm?id=8&sub=42#_ftn12

Astley, S. J., & Clarren, S. K. (2000). Diagnosing the full spectrum of fetal alcohol-exposed individuals: Introducing the 4-digit diagnostic code. *Alcohol & Alcoholism, 35*, 400-410.

Attainment Company, Inc. (2007). *Talking Photo Album.* Verona, WI: Author.

Attwood, T. (2003). Understanding and managing circumscribed interests. In M. Prior (Ed.), *Learning and behavior problems in Asperger syndrome* (pp. 126-147). New York: Guilford Press.

Attwood, T. (2006). *The complete guide to Asperger's syndrome.* London: Jessica Kingsley.

Atwell, J. A., Conners, F. A., & Merrill, E. C. (2003). Implicit and explicit learning in young adults with mental retardation. *American Journal on Mental Retardation, 108*, 56-68.

Ault, M. M., Rues, J. P., Graff, J. C., & Holvoet, J. F. (2006). Special health care procedures. In M. E. Snell & F. Brown (Eds.), *Instruction of students with severe disabilities* (6th ed.). Upper Saddle River, NJ: Merrill/Prentice Hall.

Austin, J. L., Lee, M. G., Thibeault, M. D., Carr, J. E., & Bailey, J. S. (2002). Effects of guided notes on university students' responding and recall of information. *Journal of Behavioral Education, 11*, 243-254.

Autism Research Institute. (1998). Another genetic defect linked to autistic behavior, retardation. *Autism Research Review International, 12*(1), 4.

Autism Society of America. (2000). *Advocate, 33*(1), 3.

Autism Special Interest Group, Association for Behavior Analysis International. (2007). *Consumer guidelines for identifying, selecting, and evaluating behavior analysts working with individuals with autism spectrum disorders.* Available on-line: http://www.behavior.org/autism/ ABAAutismSIG_Gdlns_2007.pdf

Award-winning researchers raise questions about "inclusion." (2001). *DLD Times, 18*(2), 4.

Axe, J. B., Murphy, C. M., Van Norman, R. K., & Heward, W. L. (May 2006). *Antecedent-based interventions to reduce escape-maintained problem behavior and increase academic responding: A comparison of functional communication training and most-to-least prompting.* Poster presented at the 32nd Annual Convention of the Association for Behavior Analysis, Atlanta.

Ayres, K. M., & Langone, J. (2005). Intervention and instruction with video for students with autism: A review of the literature. *Education and Training in Developmental Disabilities, 40*, 183-196.

Ayres, K. M., Langone, J., Boon, R. T., & Norman, A. (2006). Computer-based instruction for purchasing skills. *Education and Training in Developmental Disabilities, 41,* 253-263.

Bacon, C. K., & Wilcox, M. J. (2006). Developmental language delay in infancy and early childhood. In N. B. Anderson & G. H. Shames (Eds.), *Human communication disorders: An introduction* (7th ed.) (pp. 325-351). Boston: Allyn & Bacon.

Baer, D. M. (1998). *How to plan for generalization* (2nd ed.). Austin, TX: PRO-ED.

Baer, D. M. (1999). *How to plan for generalization* (2nd ed.). Austin, TX: PRO-ED.

Baer, D. M. (2005). Letters to a lawyer. In W. L. Heward, T. E. Heron, N. A. Neef, S. M. Peterson, D. M. Sainato, G. Cartledge, R. Gardner III, L. D. Peterson, S. B. Hersh, & J. C. Dardig (Eds.), *Focus on behavior analysis in education: Achievements, challenges, and opportunities* (pp. 3-30). Upper Saddle River, NJ: Merrill/Prentice Hall.

Baer, R. M., & Daviso, A. W. III. (2008). Independent living and community participation. In R. W. Flexer, T. J. Simmons, P. Luft, & R. M. Baer (Eds.), *Transition planning for secondary students with disabilities* (3rd ed.) (pp. 290-316). Upper Saddle River, NJ: Merrill/Prentice Hall.

Baer, R. M., Flexer, R. W., Beck, S., Amstutz, N., Hoffman, L., Brothers, J., Stelzer, D., & Zechman, C. (2003). A collaborative follow-up study on transition service utilization and postschool outcomes. *Career Development for Exceptional Individuals, 26,* 7-25.

Baer, R. M., Simmons, T. J., Bauder, D., & Flexer, R. W. (2008). Standards based curriculum and transition. In R. W. Flexer, T. J. Simmons, P. Luft, & R. M. Baer (Eds.), *Transition planning for secondary students with disabilities* (3rd ed.) (pp. 134-160). Upper Saddle River, NJ: Merrill/Prentice Hall.

Baer, D. M., & Wolf, M. M. (1970). The entry into natural communities of reinforcement. In R. Ulrich, T. Stachnick, & J. Mabry (Eds.) *Control of human behavior* (pp. 319-324). Glenview, IL: Scott Foresman.

Bagnato, S. J., Neisworth, J. T., & Munson, S. M. (1997). *LINKing assessment and early intervention: An authentic curriculum-based approach.* Baltimore: Brookes.

Bailey, D., Skinner, D., Correa, V., Arcia, E., Reyes-Blanes, M., Rodriguez, P., Vazquez, E., & Skinner, M. (1999). Needs and supports reported by Latino families of young children with developmental disabilities. *American Journal on Mental Retardation, 104,* 437-451.

Bailey, D., Skinner, D., Correa, V., Blanes, M., Vasquez, E., & Rodriguez, P. (1999). Awareness, use, and satisfaction with services for Latino parents of young children with disabilities. *Exceptional Children, 65,* 367-381.

Bailey, D. B., & Simeonsson, R. J. (1988). *Family assessment in early intervention.* Upper Saddle River, NJ: Merrill/Prentice Hall.

Bailey, D. B., & Wolery, M. (1992). *Teaching infants and preschoolers with disabilities* (2nd ed.). Upper Saddle River, NJ: Merrill/Prentice Hall.

Bailey, J. S. (1992). Gentle teaching: Trying to win friends and influence people with euphemism, metaphor, smoke, and mirrors. *Journal of Applied Behavior Analysis, 25,* 879-883.

Bak, S. (1999). Relationships between inappropriate behaviors and other factors in young children with visual impairments. *RE:view, 31,* 84-91.

Baker, B. L. (1989). *Parent training and developmental disabilities.* Washington, DC: American Association on Mental Retardation.

Baker, C. (2000). *A parents' and teachers' guide to bilingualism* (2nd ed.). Tonawanda, NY: Multilingual Matters.

Baker, E., Wang, M., & Walberg, H. (1995). The effects of inclusion in learning. *Educational Leadership, 52*(4), 33-34.

Baker, J. M., & Zigmond, N. (1990). Are regular education classes equipped to accommodate students with learning disabilities? *Exceptional Children, 56,* 516-526.

Baker, J. M., & Zigmond, N. (1995). The meaning and practice of inclusions for students with learning disabilities: Themes and implications for the five cases. *Journal of Special Education, 29,* 163-180.

Baker, S., & Baker, K. (1997). Educating children who are deaf or hard of hearing: Bilingual-bicultural education. *ERIC Digest #553.* (ERIC Document Reproduction Service No. ED 416 671).

Baker, S., Gersten, R., & Scanlon, D. (2002). Procedural facilitators and cognitive strategies: Tools for unraveling the mysteries of comprehension and the writing process, and for providing meaningful access to the general curriculum. *Learning Disabilities Research & Practice, 17,* 65-77.

Baldwin, V. (1995). *Annual deaf-blind census.* Monmouth: Western Oregon State College, Teacher Research.

Bambara, L. M., & Ager, C. (1992). Using self-scheduling to promote self-directed leisure activity in home and community settings. *Journal of The Association for Persons with Severe Handicaps, 17,* 67-76.

Bambara, L., & Koger, F. (1996). *Innovations: Providing opportunities for choice throughout the day.* Washington, DC: American Association on Mental Retardation.

Bambara, L. M., Browder, D. M., & Koger, F. (2006). Home and community. In M. E. Snell & F. Brown (Eds.), *Instruction of students with severe disabilities* (6th ed.). Upper Saddle River, NJ: Merrill/Prentice Hall.

Banda, D. R., Matuszny, R. M., & Turkan, S. (2007). Video modeling strategies to enhance appropriate behaviors in children with autism spectrum disorders. *Teaching Exceptional Children, 36*(6), 47-52.

Banks, C. A. M. (2007). Communities, families, and educators working together for school improvement. In J. A. Banks & C. A. M. Banks (Eds.), *Multicultural education: Issues and perspectives* (6th ed.) (pp. 445-465). New York: John Wiley & Sons.

Banks, J. A., & Banks, C. A. M. (Eds.). (2007). *Multicultural education: Issues and perspectives* (6th ed.). Boston: Allyn & Bacon.

Bannerman, D. J., Sheldon, J. B., Sherman, J. A., & Harchik, A. E. (1990). Balancing the right to habilitation with the right to personal liberties: The rights of people with developmental disabilities to eat too many doughnuts and take a nap. *Journal of Applied Behavior Analysis, 23,* 79-89.

Barbera, M. L., with Rasmussen, T. (2007). *The verbal behavior approach: How to teach children with autism and related disorders.* Philadelphia: Jessica Kingsley.

Barbetta, P. M. (1990a). GOALS: A group-oriented adapted levels system for children with behavior disorders. *Academic Therapy, 25,* 645-656.

Barbetta, P. M. (1990b). Red light—green light: A classwide management system for students with behavior disorders in the primary grades. *Preventing School Failure, 34*(4), 14-19.

Barbetta, P. M. (2002, January). Personal communication.

Barbetta, P. M., & Heron, T. E. (1991). Project SHINE: Summer home instruction and evaluation. *Intervention in School and Clinic, 26,* 276-281.

Barbetta, P. M., Leong-Norona, K., & Bicard, D. (2002). Classroom management: A dozen mistakes and what to do instead. *Preventing School Failure, 45*(1), 1-8.

Barfels, M., Heward, W. L., & Al-Attrash, M. (1999). Using audio prompts to improve work performance by adults with developmental disabilities in an enclave supported employment setting. Manuscript submitted for publication.

Barkley, R. A. (2005). *Attention-deficit hyperactivity disorder: A handbook for diagnosis and treatment* (3rd ed.). New York: Guilford.

Barkley, R. A., Fischer, M., Edelbrock, C. S., & Smallish, L. (1990). The adolescent outcome of hyperactive children diagnosed by research criteria: I. An eight-year prospective follow-up study. *Journal of the American Academy of Children and Adolescent Psychiatry, 29,* 546-557.

Barlow, J. A. (2001). Prologue: Recent advances in phonological theory and treatment. *Language, Speech, and Hearing Services in Schools, 32,* 225-228.

Barnes, S. B., & Whinnery, K. W. (2002). Effects of functional mobility skills training for young students with physical disabilities. *Exceptional Children, 68,* 313-324.

Barnett, S. W., & Boyce, G. C. (1994). Effects of children with Down syndrome on parents' activities. *American Journal of Mental Retardation, 100,* 115-127.

Barnhill, G. P. (2007). Outcomes in adults with Asperger syndrome. *Focus on Autism and Other Developmental Disabilities, 22,* 116-126.

Barnhill, G. P., Hagiwara, T., Myles, B. S., Simpson, R. L., Brick, M. L., & Griswold, D. E. (2000). Parent, teacher, and self-report of problems and adaptive behaviors in children and adolescents with Asperger syndrome. *Diagnostique, 25*(2), 147-167.

Baron-Cohen, S., Allen, J., & Gillberg, C. (1992). Can autism be detected at 18 months? The needle, the haystack, and the CHAT. *British Journal of Psychiatry, 161*, 839-843.

Barraga, N. C., & Erin, J. N. (2001). *Visual impairments and learning* (4th ed.). Austin, TX: Exceptional Resources.

Barrera, I. (1995). To refer or not to refer: Untangling the web of diversity, "deficit," and disability. *New York State Association for Bilingual Education Journal, 10,* 54-66.

Barry, L. M., & Messer, J. J. (2003). A practical application of self-management for students diagnosed with attention-deficit/hyperactivity disorder. *Journal of Positive Behavior Interventions, 5,* 238-248.

Bartlett, L. D., Etscheidt, S., & Weisentstein, G. R. (2007). *Special education law and practice in public schools* (2nd ed.). Upper Saddle River, NJ: Merrill/Prentice Hall.

Bat-Chava, Y. (2000). Diversity of deaf identities. *American Annals of the Deaf, 145,* 420-428.

Bateman, B. (2005). The play's the thing. *Learning Disability Quarterly, 28,* 115-118.

Bateman, B. D., & Herr, C. M. (2006). *Writing measurable IEP goals and objectives.* Verona, WI: Attainment Company, Inc.

Bateman, B. D., & Linden, M. L. (2006). *Better IEPs: How to develop legally correct and educationally useful programs* (4th ed.). Verona, WI: Attainment Company, Inc.

Batshaw, M. L. (Ed.). (2002). *Children with disabilities* (5th ed.). Baltimore: Brookes.

Batshaw, M. L., Pellegrino, L, & Roizen, N. J. (Eds.). (2007). *Children with disabilities* (6th ed.). Baltimore: Brookes.

Battle, D. E. (Ed.). (1998). *Communication disorders in multicultural populations* (2nd ed.). Boston: Butterworth-Heinemann.

Bauer, A. M., & Brown, G. M. (2001). *Adolescents and inclusions: Transforming secondary schools.* Baltimore: Brookes.

Bauer, A. M., & Ulrich, M. E. (2002). "I've got a Palm in my pocket": Using handheld computers in an inclusive classroom. *Teaching Exceptional Children, 35*(2), 18-22.

Baum, D. D., Duffelmeyer, F., & Greenlan, M. (2001). Recourse teacher perceptions of the prevalence of social dysfunction among students with learning disabilities. *Journal of Learning Disabilities, 21,* 380-381.

Baumgart, D., & Giangreco, M. F. (1996). Key lessons learned about inclusion. In D. H. Lehr & F. Brown (Eds.), *People with disabilities who challenge the system* (pp. 79-97). Baltimore: Brookes.

Baumgart, D., Brown, L., Pumpian, I., Nisbet, J., Ford, A., Sweet, M., Messina, R., & Schroeder, J. (1982). Principle of partial participation and individualized adaptations in educational programs for severely handicapped students. *Journal of The Association for Persons with Severe Handicaps, 7,* 17-27.

Bayley, N. (2005). *Bayley Scales of Infant Development* (3rd ed.). San Antonio, TX: Harcourt Assessment.

Beadle-Brown, J., Murphy, G., & Wing, L. (2005). Long-term outcome for people with severe intellectual disabilities: Impact of social impairment. *American Journal on Mental Retardation, 110,* 1-12.

Beakley, B. A., & Yoder, S. L. (1998). Middle schoolers learn community skills. *Teaching Exceptional Children, 30*(3), 16-21.

Beard, K. Y, & Sugai, G. (2004). First step to success: An early intervention for elementary children at risk for antisocial behavior. *Behavioral Disorders, 29,* 396-409.

Beatty, L. S., Madden, R., Gardner, E. F., & Karlsen, B. (1995). *Stanford Diagnostic Mathematics Test—Fourth edition.* San Antonio, TX: Harcourt Brace Educational Measurement.

Bebko, J. M., & Luhaorg, H. (1998). The development of strategy use and metacognitive processing in mental retardation: Some source of difficulty. In J. A. Burack, R. M. Hodapp, & E. Zigler (Eds.), *Handbook of mental retardation and development* (pp. 382-407). Cambridge, UK: Cambridge University Press.

Beck, J., Broers, J., Hogue, E., Shipstead, J., & Knowlton, E. (1994). Strategies for functional community-based instruction and inclusion for children with mental retardation. *Teaching Exceptional Children, 26*(2), 44-48.

Beck, R., Conrad, A. D., & Anderson, P. (1999). *Basic skill builders handbook: One-minute fluency builders series.* Longmont, CO: Sopris West.

Becker, W. C., Engelmann, S., & Thomas, D. R. (1971). *Teaching: A course in applied psychology.* Chicago: Science Research Associates.

Becker-Cottrill, B., McFarland, J., & Anderson, V. (2003). A model of positive behavioral support for individuals with autism and their families: The family focus project. *Focus on Autism and Other Developmental Disabilities, 18,* 113-123.

Beckley, C. G., Al-Attrash, M., Heward, W. L., & Morrison, H. (2008). Using guided notes in an eighth-grade social studies class: Effects on next-day quiz scores and notetaking accuracy. Manuscript in preparation.

Behr, S. K., Murphy, D. L., & Summers, J. A. (1992). *User's manual: Kansas inventory of parental perceptions (KIPP).* Lawrence: University of Kansas, Beach Center on Families and Disability.

Beilke, J. R., & Yssel, N. (1999). The chilly climate for students with disabilities in higher education. *College Student Journal, 33*(3), 364-371.

Beirne-Smith, M., Patton, J. R., & Kim, S. H. (2006). *Mental retardation* (7th ed.). Upper Saddle River, NJ: Merrill/Prentice Hall.

Belcastro, F. (1993). Teaching addition and subtraction of whole numbers to blind students: A comparison of two methods. *Focus on Learning Problems in Mathematics, 15* (1), 14-22.

Belcastro, F. P .(1989). Use of Belcastro Rods to teach mathematical concepts to blind students. *RE:view, 21,* 71-79.

Belgrave, F. Z., & Mills, J. (1981). Effect upon desire for social interaction with a physically disabled person of mentioning the disability in different contexts. *Journal of Applied Social Psychology, 11,* 44-57.

Bellamy, G. T., & Wilcox, B. (1982). Secondary education for severely handicapped students: Guidelines for quality services. In K. P. Lynch, W. E. Kiernan, & J. A. Stark (Eds.), *Prevocational and vocational education for special needs youth: A blueprint for the 1980s.* Baltimore, Brookes.

Bellini, S., & Akullian, J. (2007). A meta-analysis of video modeling and video self-modeling interventions for children and adolescents with autism spectrum disorders. *Exceptional Children, 73,* 264-287.

Belmont, J. M. (1966). Long term memory in mental retardation. *International Review of Research in Mental Retardation, 1,* 219-255.

Belser, R. C., & Sudhalter, V. (2001). Conversational characteristics of children with Fragile X syndrome: Repetitive speech. *American Journal of Mental Retardation, 106,* 28-38.

Beninghof, A. M. (1998). *Ideas for inclusion: The classroom teacher's guide to integrating students with severe disabilities.* Longmont, CO: Sopris West.

Benner, G. J. (2007). The relative impact of remedial reading instruction on the basic reading skills of students with emotional disturbance and learning disabilities. *Journal of Direct Instruction, 7,* 1-15.

Bennett, D. (1997). Low vision devices for children and young people with a visual impairment. In H. Mason & S. McCall (Eds.), *Visual impairment: Access to education for children and young people* (pp. 64-75). London: Fulton.

Bennett, E. M. (2006). *Working with people who stutter.* Upper Saddle River, NJ: Merrill/Prentice Hall.

Bennett, K., & Cavanaugh, R. A. (1998). Effects of immediate self-correction, delayed self-correction, and no correction on the acquisition and maintenance of multiplication facts by a fourth-grade student with learning disabilities. *Journal of Applied Behavior Analysis, 31,* 303-306.

Benson, V., & Marano, M. A. (1998, October). Current estimates from the National Health Interview Survey, 1995. National Center for Health Statistics. *Vital Health Stat 10,* 199.

Benz, M. R., & Lindstrom, L. E. (1997). *Building school-to-work programs: Strategies for youth with special needs.* Austin, TX: PRO-ED.

Benz, M. R., Lindstrom, L., & Yavanoff, P. (2000). Improving graduation and employment outcomes of students with disabilities: Predictive factors and student perspectives. *Exceptional Children, 66,* 509-529.

Benz, M. R., Lindstrom, L., Unruh, B., & Waintrup, M. (2004). Sustaining secondary transition programs in local schools. *Remedial and Special Education, 25,* 39-50.

Bergeron, R., & Floyd, R. G. (2006). Broad cognitive abilities of children with mental retardation: An analysis of group and individual profiles. *American Journal on Mental Retardation, 111,* 417–432.

Berkson, G. (2004). Intellectual and physical disabilities in prehistory and early civilization. *Mental Retardation, 42,* 195–208.

Berney, T. P. (2000). Autism: An evolving concept. *British Journal of Psychiatry, 176,* 20–25.

Bernheimer, L. P., Keogh, B. K., & Guthrie, D. (2006). Young children with developmental delays as young adults: Predicting developmental and personal-social outcomes. *American Journal on Mental Retardation, 111,* 263–272.

Berquin, P. C., Giedd, J. N., Jacobson, L. K., Hamburger, S. D., Krain, A. L., Rappaport, J. L., & Castellanos, E. X. (1998). Cerebellum in attention-deficit/hyperactivity disorder: A Morphometric MRI study. *Neurology, 50,* 1087–1093.

Bérubé, R. L., & Achenbach, T. M. (2007). *Bibliography of published studies using the ASEBA.* Burlington, VT: University of Vermont, Research Center for Children, Youth, & Families.

Berument, S., Rutter, M., & Lord, C. (1999). Autism screening questionnaire: Diagnostic validity. *The British Journal of Psychiatry, 175,* 444–451.

Bess, F. (1999). School-aged children with minimal sensorineural hearing loss. *Hearing Journal, 52,* 10–16.

Best, A. B. (1992). *Teaching children with visual impairments.* Milton Keynes, England: Open University Press.

Best, S. J. (2005a). Physical disabilities. In S. J. Best, K. W. Heller, & J. L. Bigge, *Teaching individuals with physical or multiple disabilities* (5th ed.), (pp. 31–58). Upper Saddle River, NJ: Merrill/Prentice Hall.

Best, S. J. (2005b). Health impairments and infectious diseases. In S. J. Best, K. W. Heller, & J. L. Bigge, *Teaching individuals with physical or multiple disabilities* (5th ed.), (pp. 59–85). Upper Saddle River, NJ: Merrill/Prentice Hall.

Best, S. J., & Bigge, J. L. (2005). Cerebral palsy. In S. J. Best, K. W. Heller, & J. L. Bigge, *Teaching individuals with physical or multiple disabilities* (5th ed.), (pp. 87–109). Upper Saddle River, NJ: Merrill/Prentice Hall.

Best, S. J., Bigge, J. L., Musante, C. M., & Macias, C. M. (2005). Adaptations in physical education, leisure education, and recreation. In S. J. Best, K. W. Heller, & J. L. Bigge, (Eds.), *Teaching individuals with physical or multiple disabilities* (5th ed.), (pp. 337–366). Upper Saddle River, NJ: Merrill/Prentice Hall.

Best, S. J., Heller, K. W., & Bigge, J. L. (2005). *Teaching individuals with physical or multiple disabilities* (5th ed.). Upper Saddle River, NJ: Merrill/Prentice Hall.

Best, S. J., Reed, P., & Bigge, J. L. (2005). Assistive technology. In S. J. Best, K. W. Heller, & J. L. Bigge, *Teaching individuals with physical or multiple disabilities* (5th ed.), (pp. 179–226). Upper Saddle River, NJ: Merrill/Prentice Hall.

Best Buddies. (2007). *Best Buddies: About us.* Retrieved October 3, 2007, from www. bestbuddies.org.

Bettelheim, B. (1967). *The empty fortress: Infantile autism and the birth of the self.* London: Collier-Macmillan.

Beukelman, D. R., & Miranda, P. (1998). *Augmentative and alternative communication: Management of severe communication disorder in children and adults* (2nd ed.). Baltimore: Brookes.

Bevill, A. R., Gast, D. L., MaGuire, A. M., & Vail, C. O. (2001). Increasing engagement of preschoolers with disabilities through correspondence training and picture cues. *Journal of Early Intervention, 24,* 129–145.

Bhagwanji, Y., & McCollum, J. A. (1998). Parent involvement in preschool programs for children at risk for academic failure. *Infant-Toddler Intervention: The Transdisciplinary Journal, 8,* 53–66.

Bianco, M. (2005). The effects of disability labels on special education and general education teachers' referrals for gifted programs. *Learning Disability Quarterly, 28,* 285–293.

Bicard, D. F. (2000). Using classroom rules to construct behavior. *Middle School Journal, 31*(5), 37–45.

Bicard, D. F. (2002, September). *Behavior analysis in education: Research on attention deficit disorder.* Paper presented at The Ohio State University's Third Focus on Behavior Analysis in Education Conference, Columbus.

Bicard, D. F., & Neef, N. A. (2002). Effects of strategic versus tactical instructions on adaptation to changing contingencies in children with ADHD. *Journal of Applied Behavior Analysis, 35,* 375–389.

Bidabe, D. L., Barnes, S. B., & Whinnery, K. W. (2001). M.O.V.E: Raising expectations for individuals with severe disabilities. *Physical Disabilities: Education and Related Services, 19*(2), 31–48.

Bierman, K. L. (2005). *Peer rejection: Developmental processes and intervention strategies.* New York: Guilford.

Bigby, L. (2007). Legal, historical, and cultural perspectives. In J. Anderson Downing, *Students with emotional and behavioral problems: Assessment, management, and intervention strategies* (pp. 2–19). Upper Saddle River, NJ: Merrill/Prentice Hall.

Bigge, J. L. (1991). *Teaching individuals with physical and multiple disabilities* (3rd ed.). Upper Saddle River, NJ: Merrill/Prentice Hall.

Bigge, J. L., Stump, C. S., Spagna, M. E., & Silberman, R. K. (1999). *Curriculum, assessment, and instruction for students with disabilities.* Belmont, CA: Wadsworth.

Biglan, A. (1995). Translating what we know about the context of antisocial behavior into a lower prevalence of such behavior. *Journal of Applied Behavior Analysis, 28,* 479–492.

Biklen, D. (1990). Communication unbound: Autism and praxis. *Harvard Educational Review, 60,* 291–314.

Biklen, D. (1992). Typing to talk: Facilitated communication. *American Journal of Speech Language Pathology, 1*(2), 15–17.

Biklen, D. (2005). *Autism and the myth of the person alone.* New York: New York University Press.

Biklen, D., & Cardinal, D. N. (1997). *Contested words, contested science: Unraveling the facilitated communication controversy.* New York: Teachers College Press.

Billingsley, F. F. (1998). Behaving independently: Current practices and considerations in fading instructor assistance. In A. Hilton and R. P. Ringlaben (Eds.), Best and promising practices in developmental disabilities (pp. 157–168). Austin, TX: Pro-Ed.

Billingsley, F. F., Liberty, K. A., & White, O. R. (1994). The technology of instruction. In E. C. Cipani & F. Spooner (Eds.), *Curricular and instructional approaches for persons with severe disabilities* (pp. 81–116). Boston: Allyn & Bacon.

Binder, C. (1996). Behavioral fluency: Evolution of a new paradigm. *The Behavior Analyst, 19,* 163–197.

Bingham, M. A., Spooner, F., & Browder, D. (2007). Training paraeducators to promote the use of augmentative and alternative communication by students with significant disabilities. *Education and Training in Developmental Disabilities, 42,* 339–352.

Birkan, B. (2005). Using simultaneous prompting for teaching various discrete tasks to students with mental retardation. *Education and Training in Developmental Disabilities, 41,* 68–79.

Bishop, D. V. M., & Snowling, M. (2004). Developmental dyslexia and specific language impairment: Same or different? *Psychological Bulletin, 130,* 858–886.

Bishop, M., & Boag, E. M. (2006). Teachers' knowledge about epilepsy and attitudes toward students with epilepsy: Results of a national survey. *Epilepsy & Behavior, 8,* 397–405.

Bishop, V. E. (1986). Identifying the components of successful mainstreaming. *Journal of Visual Impairment and Blindness, 80,* 939–946.

Blacher, J. (1984). A dynamic perspective on the impact of a severely handicapped child on the family. In J. Blacher (Ed.), *Severely handicapped children and their families* (pp. 3–50). Orlando, FL: Academic Press.

Blacher, J. (2001). Transition to adulthood: Mental retardation, families, and culture. *American Journal of Mental Retardation, 106,* 173–188.

Blacher, J., & Baker, B. L. (2007). Positive impact of intellectual disability on families. *American Journal on Mental Retardation, 112,* 330–348.

Black, R., Smith, G., Chang, C., Harding, T., & Stodden, R. A. (2002). Provision of educational supports to students with disabilities in two-year postsecondary programs. *Journal for Vocational Special Needs Education, 24*(2/3), 3–17.

Blackorby, J., & Knokey, A. (2006). A national profile of students with hearing impairments in elementary and middle school: A special topic report from the Special Education Elementary Longitudinal Study. Menlo Park, CA: SRI International.

Blackorby, J., & Wagner, M. (1996). Longitudinal postschool outcomes of youth with disabilities: Findings from the National Longitudinal Transition Study. *Exceptional Children, 62,* 399–413.

Blackorby, J., & Wagner, M. (1997). The employment outcomes of youth with learning disabilities: A review of findings from the National Longitudinal Study of Special Education Students. In P. J. Gerber & D. S. Bowen (Eds.), *Learning disabilities and employment* (pp. 57-74). Austin, TX: PRO-ED.

Blackstone, S. W. (1991). Beyond public awareness: The road to involvement! *Augmentative Communication News, 4*(2), 6. Monterey, CA: Augmentative Communication, Inc.

Blackwell, A. J., & McLaughlin, T. F. (2005). Using guided notes, choral responding, and response cards to increase student performance. *The International Journal of Special Education, 20*(2), 1-5.

Blake, C., Wang, W., Cartledge, G., & Gardner, R. (2000). Middle school students with serious emotional disturbances serve as social skills trainers and reinforcers for peers with SED. *Behavioral Disorders, 25*, 280-298.

Blalock, G., Kochhar-Bryant, C., Test, D. W., Kohler, P., White, W., Lehmann, J., Bassett, D., & Patton, J. (2003). The need for comprehensive personnel preparation in transition and career development: DCDT position statement. *Career Development for Exceptional Individuals, 26*, 207-226.

Blatt, B. (1976). *Revolt of the idiots: A story*. Glen Ridge, NJ: Exceptional Press.

Blatt, B. (1987). *The conquest of mental retardation*. Austin, TX: PRO-ED.

Blatt, B. (1999). *In search of the promised land: The collected papers of Burton Blatt*. Washington, DC: American Association on Mental Retardation.

Blatt, B., & Kaplan, F. (1966). *Christmas in purgatory: A photographic essay on mental retardation*. Boston: Allyn & Bacon.

Bleck, E. E. (1987). *Orthopedic management of cerebral palsy—Clinics in developmental medicine No. 99/100*. Philadelphia: Lippincott.

Blick, D. W., & Test, D. W. (1987). Effects of self-recording on high school students' on-task behavior. *Learning Disability Quarterly, 10*, 203-213.

Block, M. E. (2007). *A teacher's guide to including students with disabilities in general physical education* (3rd ed.) Baltimore: Brookes.

Block, S. R. (1997). Closing the sheltered workshop: Toward competitive employment opportunities for persons with developmental disabilities. *Journal of Vocational Rehabilitation, 9*, 267-275.

Bloodstein, O. (1995). *A handbook on stuttering* (5th ed.). San Diego: Singular.

Bloom, B. S. (1980). The new direction in educational research: Alterable variables. *Phi Delta Kappan, 61*, 382-385.

Bloom, B. S., Englehart, M., Furst, E., Hill, W., & Krathwohl, D. (1956). *Taxonomy of educational objectives: The classification of educational goals. Handbook I: Cognitive domain*. New York: Longman's Green.

Blosser, J. L., & Kratcoski, A. (1997). PACs: A framework for determining appropriate service delivery options. *ASHA, 28*, 99-107.

Blue-Banning, M., Summers, J. A., Frankland, H. C., Nelson, L. L., & Beegle, G. (2004). Dimensions of family and professional partnerships: Constructive guidelines for collaboration. *Exceptional Children, 70*, 167-184.

Bluestone, C. D., & Klein, J. O. (2001). *Otitis media in infants and children* (3rd ed.). Philadelphia: Saunders.

Board of Education of the Hendrick Hudson Central School District v. Rowley, 102 S. Ct. 3034 (1982).

Boe, E. E., & Cook, L. H. (2006). The chronic and increasing shortage of fully certified teachers in special and general education. *Exceptional Children, 72*, 443-460.

Boekaerts, M. R., & Roeder, I. (1999). Stress, coping, and adjustment in children with a chronic disease: A review of the literature. *Disability and Rehabilitation, 21*, 311-327.

Bogdan, R., & Taylor, S. J. (1994). *The social meaning of mental retardation*. New York: Teachers College Press.

Bolt, S. E., & Thurlow, M. L. (2004). Five of the most frequently allowed testing accommodations in state policy. *Remedial and Special Education, 25*, 141-152.

Bolton, J. L., Belfiore, P. J., Lalli, J. S., & Skinner, C. H. (1994). The effects of stimulus modification on putting accuracy for adults with moderate and severe intellectual disabilities. *Education and Training in Mental Retardation and Developmental Disabilities, 29*, 236-242.

Bondurant-Utz, J. (2002). *Practical guide to assessing infants and preschoolers with special needs*. Upper Saddle River, NJ: Merrill/Prentice Hall.

Bondy, A., & Frost, L. (1994). PECS: The picture exchange communication system. *Focus on Autistic Behavior, 9*, 1-9.

Bondy, A., & Frost, L. (2002). *A picture's worth: PECS and other visual communication strategies in autism*. Bethesda, MD: Woodbine, House.

Book, D., Paul, T. L., Gwalla-Ogisi, N., & Test, D. W. (1990). No more bologna sandwiches. *Teaching Exceptional Children, 22*(2), 62-64.

Boothe, D. (2004). Gender differences in achievement and aptitude test results: Perspectives from the recent literature. In D. Boothe & J. Stanley (Eds.), *In the eyes of the beholder: Critical issues for diversity in gifted education* (pp. 179-189). Waco, TX: Prufrock.

Borland, J. H., & Wright, L. (1994). Identifying young, potentially gifted, economically disadvantaged students. *Gifted Child Quarterly, 44*, 33-42.

Bornstein, H. (1974). Signed English: A manual approach to English language development. *Journal of Speech and Hearing Disorders, 3*, 330-343.

Borsch, J., & Oaks, R. (1993). *The collaboration companion: Strategies and activities in and out of the classroom*. East Moline, IL: LinguiSystems.

Borthwick-Duffy, S. (1994). Review of mental retardation: Definition, causes, and systems of supports. *American Journal on Mental Retardation, 98*, 541-544.

Borthwick-Duffy, S. A., & Eyman, R. K. (1990). Who are the dually diagnosed? *American Journal on Mental Retardation, 94*, 586-595.

Bosch, S., & Fuqua, W. R. (2001). Behavioral cusps: A model for selecting target behaviors. *Journal of Applied Behavior Analysis, 34*, 123-125.

Bosner, S. M., & Belfiore, P. J. (2001). Strategies and considerations for teaching an adolescent with Down syndrome and type I diabetes to self-administer insulin. *Education and Treatment in Mental Retardation and Developmental Disabilities, 36*, 94-102.

Bouchard, D., & Tétreault, S. (2000). The motor development of sighted children and children with moderate low vision aged 8-13. *Journal of Visual Impairments and Blindness, 94*, 564-573.

Boudah, D. J., Schumaker, J. B., & Deshler, D. D. (1997). Collaborative instruction: Is it an effective option for inclusion in secondary classrooms? *Learning Disability Quarterly, 4*, 293-316.

Boulware, G. L., Schwartz, I. S., & McBride, B. M. (1999). Addressing challenging behavior at home: Working with families to find solutions. In S. R. Sandall & M. Ostrosky (Eds.), *Practical ideas for addressing challenging behaviors*. Monograph of *Young Exceptional Children* (pp. 29-40). Denver: Sopris West.

Boushey, A. (2001). The grief cycle—One parent's trip around. *Focus on Autism and Other Developmental Disabilities, 16*, 27-30.

Boutot, E. A., & Bryant, D. P. (2005). Social integration of students with autism. *Education and Training in Developmental Disabilities, 40*, 14-23.

Boutot, E. A., & Tincani, M. (Eds.). (2006). *Autism spectrum disorders handouts: What parents need to know*. Austin, TX: PRO-ED.

Bowe, F. (2000). *Teaching individuals with physical and multiple disabilities* (4th ed.). Upper Saddle River, NJ: Merrill/Prentice Hall.

Bowen, J., Olympia, D., & Jensen, W. (1996). *Study buddies: Parent tutoring tactics*. Longmont, CO: Sopris West.

Bower, E. M. (1960). *Early identification of emotionally handicapped children in the schools*. Springfield, IL: Thomas.

Bower, E. M. (1982). Defining emotional disturbance: Public policy and research. *Psychology in the Schools, 19*, 55-60.

Bowers, F. E., McGinnis, J. C., Ervin, R. A., & Friman, P. C. (1999). Merging research and practice: The example of positive peer reporting applied to social rejection. *Education and Treatment of Children, 22*, 218-226.

Boyd-Ball, A. (2007, June). *Native Americans with disabilities*. Eugene, OR: University of Oregon.

Boykin, A. W. (1983). The academic performance of Afro-American children. In J. Spence (Ed.), *Achievement and achievement motives* (pp. 324-371). San Francisco: Freeman.

Boyle, J. R. (2001). Enhancing the note-taking skills of students with mild disabilities.

Intervention in School and Clinic, 36, 221-224.

Boyle, J. R., & Weishaar, M. (2001). The effects of strategic notetaking on the recall and comprehension of lecture information for high school students with learning disabilities. *Learning Disabilities Research & Practice, 16,* 133-141.

Bozkurt, F., & Gursel, O. (2005). Effectiveness of constant time delay on teaching snack and drink preparation skills to children with mental retardation. *Education and Training in Developmental Disabilities, 40,* 390-400.

Braddock, D., Hemp, R., Parish, S., & Rizzolo, M. (2002). *The state of the states in developmental disabilities: 2002 study summary.* Boulder: University of Colorado at Boulder, Coleman Institute for Cognitive Disabilities.

Braddock, D., Rizzolo, M. C., & Hemp, R. (2004). Most employment services growth in developmental disabilities during 1988-2002 was in segregated settings. *Mental Retardation, 42,* 317-320.

Braden, J. P., Maller, S. J., & Paquin, M. M. (1993). The effects of residential versus day placement on the performance IQs of children with hearing impairment. *Journal of Special Education, 26,* 423-433.

Bradford, S., Shippen, M. E., Alberto, P., Houchins, D. E., & Flores, M. (2006). Using systematic instruction to teach decoding skills to middle school students with moderate intellectual disabilities. *Education and Training in Developmental Disabilities, 41,* 333-343.

Bradley, R., Danielson, L., & Doolitte, J. (2007). Responsiveness to intervention: 1997-2007. *Teaching Exceptional Children, 39*(5), 8-12.

Bradley, R., Danielson, L., & Hallahan, D. P. (Eds.). (2002). *Identification of learning disabilities: Research to practice.* Mahwah, NJ: Erlbaum.

Bradley, V. J., Knoll, J., & Agosta, J. M. (Eds.). (1992). *Emerging issues in family support.* Washington, DC: American Association on Mental Retardation.

Brain Injury Association. (2001). *Brain injury and you.* Alexandria, VA: Author. http://www.bia.org.

Brain Injury Association of America. (2007). *About brain injury.* Vienna, VA: Author. Retrieved September 9, 2007 from http://www.biausa.org/elements/aboutbi/factsheets/TBIincidence.pdf

Brambring, M. (2006). Divergent development of gross motor skills in children who are blind or sighted. *Journal of Visual Impairment and Blindness, 100,* 620-634.

Brambring, M. (2007). Divergent development of manual skills in children who are blind or sighted. *Journal of Visual Impairment and Blindness, 101,* 212-225.

Brame, P. (2000). Using picture storybooks to enhance the social skills training of special needs students. *Middle School Journal, 32*(1), 41.

Brandes, J. A., Ormsbee, C. K., & Haring, K. A. (2007). From early intervention to early childhood programs: Timeline for early successful transitions (TEST). *Intervention in School and Clinic, 42,* 204-211.

Brantlinger, E., Jimenez, R., Klingner, J., Pugach, M., & Richardson, V. (2005). Qualitative studies in special education. *Exceptional Children, 71,* 195-207.

Bray, N. W., Fletcher, K. L., & Turner, L. A. (1997). Cognitive competencies and strategy use in individuals with mental retardation. In W. W. MacLean, Jr. (Ed.), *Ellis' handbook of mental deficiency, psychological theory, and research* (3rd ed.), (pp. 197-217). Mahwah, NJ: Erlbaum.

Bredekamp, S. (1993). The relationship between early childhood education and early childhood special education: Healthy marriage or family feud? *Topics in Early Childhood Special Education, 13,* 258-273.

Bredekamp, S., & Copple, C. (Eds.). (1997). *Developmentally appropriate practice in early childhood programs.* Washington, DC: National Association for the Education of Young Children.

Brewer, J., & Kieff, J. (1996). Fostering mutual respect for play at home and school. *Childhood Education, 7,* 92-96.

Bricker, D. (1986). An analysis of early intervention programs: Attendant issues and future directions. In R. J. Morris & B. Blatt (Eds.), *Special education: Research and trends* (pp. 28-65). New York: Pergamon.

Bricker, D. (Ed.). (2002). *Assessment, evaluation, and programming system (AEP) for infants and children* (2nd ed.). Baltimore: Brookes.

Bricker, D., Pretti-Frontczak, K., & McComas, N. (1998). *An activity-based approach to early intervention* (2nd ed.). Baltimore: Brookes.

Bricker, D., & Squires, J. (1999). *Ages & Stages Questionnaires: A parent-completed, child-monitoring system* (2nd ed.). Baltimore: Brookes.

Bricker, D., & Waddell, M. (2002a). *AEPS curriculum for birth to three years* (2nd ed.). Baltimore: Brookes.

Bricker, D., & Waddell, M. (2002b). *AEPS curriculum for three to six years* (2nd ed.). Baltimore: Brookes.

Brickey, M. P., Campbell, K. M., & Browning, L. J. (1985). A five-year follow-up of sheltered workshop employees placed in competitive jobs. *Mental Retardation, 23,* 67-73.

Brigance, A. H. (1999). *Brigance Diagnostic Comprehensive Inventory of Basic Skills—Revised.* N. Billerica, MA: Curriculum Associates.

Briggs, A., Alberto, P., Sharpton, W., Berlin, K., McKinley, C., & Ritts, C. (1990). Generalized use of a self-operated audio prompt system. *Education and Training in Mental Retardation, 25,* 381-389.

Brigham, F. J., & Cole, J. E. (1999). Selective mutism: Developments in definition, etiology, assessment and treatment. In T. Scruggs & M. Mastropieri (Eds.), *Advances in learning and behavioral disabilities* (Vol. 13, pp. 183-216). Greenwich, CT: JAI.

Brigham, F. J., & Kauffman, J. M. (1998). Creating supportive environments for students with emotional or behavioral disorders. *Effective School Practices, 17*(2), 25-35.

Brigham, N., Morocco, C. C., Clay, K., & Zigmond, N. (2006). What makes a high school good for students with disabilities. *Learning Disabilities Research & Practice, 21,* 184-190.

Brigham, N., Parker, C. E., Morocco, C. C., & Zigmond, N. (2006). Apalachee high school: The last real high school in America—"You don't go to Apalachee, you belong to it." *Learning Disabilities Research & Practice, 21,* 172-183.

Brigham, R., & Brigham, M. (2001). *Current practice alerts: Mnemonic instruction.* Reston, VA: Division for Learning Disabilities and Division for Research of the Council for Exceptional Children.

Brilliant, R. L. (1999). *Essentials of low vision practice.* Boston: Butterworth-Heinemann.

Brinkerhoff, L. C., Shaw, S. F., & McGuire, J. M. (1993). *Promoting postsecondary education for students with learning disabilities.* Austin, TX: PRO-ED.

Bristol, M., Cohen, D., Costello, J., Denckla, M., Eckberg, T., Kallen, R., Kraemer, H., Lord, C. Maurer, R., McIlvane, W., Minshew, N. Sigman, M., & Spence, M. (1996). State of the science in autism: Report to the National Institute of Health. *Journal of Autism and Developmental Disorders, 26,* 121-154.

Brolin, D. E. (1991). *Life-centered career education: A competency-based approach* (3rd ed.). Reston, VA: Council for Exceptional Children.

Brolin, D. E. (2004). *Life-centered career education: A competency-based approach* (rev ed.). Arlington, VA: Council for Exceptional Children.

Brolin, D. E., & Loyd, R. J. (2004). *Career development and transition services* (4th ed.). Upper Saddle River, NJ: Merrill/Prentice Hall.

Bronicki, G. J., & Turnbull, A. P. (1987). Family-professional interactions. In M. E. Snell (Ed.), *Systematic instruction of persons with severe handicaps* (3rd ed.), (pp. 9-35). Upper Saddle River, NJ: Merrill/Prentice Hall.

Brookes, J., & Brookes, M. (1993). In search of understanding: The case for constructivist classrooms. Alexandria, VA: Association for Supervision and Curriculum Development.

Brophy, J. (1986). Teacher influences on student achievement. *American Psychologist, 41,* 1069-1077.

Browder, D. M. (2000). *Comments made as guest faculty for OSU teleconference seminar: Contemporary issues in special education.* Columbus, OH: The Ohio State University.

Browder, D. M. (2001). *Curriculum and assessment for students with moderate and severe disabilities.* New York: Guilford.

Browder, D. M., Ahlgrim-Delzell, L., Courtade Little, G., & Snell, M. E. (2006). General curriculum access. In M. E. Snell & F. Brown (Eds.), *Instruction of students with severe disabilities* (6th ed.), (pp. 489-525). Upper Saddle River, NJ: Merrill/Prentice Hall.

Browder, D. M., & Cooper, K. J. (2001). Community and leisure skills. In D. M. Browder, *Curriculum and assessment for students with moderate and severe disabilities* (pp. 244-278). New York: Guilford.

Browder, D. M., Cooper, K. J., & Lim, L. (1998). Teaching adults with severe disabilities to express their choice of settings for leisure activities. *Education and Training in Mental Retardation and Developmental Disabilities, 33,* 228-238.

Browder, D. M., & Cooper-Duffy, K. (2003). Evidence-based practices for students with severe disabilities and the requirements for accountability in "No Child Left Behind." *Journal of Special Education, 37,* 157-163.

Browder, D. M., Flowers, C., Ahlgrim-Delzell, L., Karvonen, M., Spooner, F., & Algozzine, B. (2004). The alignment of alternate assessment content with academic and functional curricula. *The Journal of Special Education, 37,* 211-223.

Browder, D. M., & Minarovic, T. J. (2000). Utilizing sight words in self-instruction training for employees with moderate mental retardation in competitive jobs. *Education and Training in Mental Retardation and Developmental Disabilities, 35,* 78-89.

Browder, D. M., & Snell, M. E. (2000). Functional academics. In M. E. Snell & F. Brown, *Instruction of students with severe disabilities* (5th ed.), (pp. 493-542). Upper Saddle River, NJ: Merrill/Prentice Hall.

Browder, D. M., & Wilson, B. (2001). Using ecological assessment in planning for inclusion. In D. M. Browder, *Curriculum and assessment for students with moderate and severe disabilities* (pp. 337-360). New York: Guilford.

Brown v. Board of Education of Topeka, 347 U.S. 483 (1954).

Brown, L. (1990). Who are they and what do they want? An essay on TASH. *TASH Newsletter, 16*(9), 1.

Brown, L., Farrington, K., Suomi, J., & Zeigler, M. (1999). Work-wage relationships and individuals with disabilities. *Journal of Vocational Rehabilitation, 13*(1), 5-13.

Brown, L., Ford, A., Nisbet, J., Sweet, M., Donnellan, A., & Gruenewald, L. (1983). Opportunities available when severely handicapped students attend chronological age appropriate regular schools. *Journal of the Association for Persons with Severe Handicaps, 8,* 16-24.

Brown, L., Long, E., Udvari-Solner, A., Davis, L., VanDeventer, P., Ahlgren, C., Johnson, F., Gruenewald, L., & Jorgensen, J. (1989a). The home school: Why students with severe disabilities must attend the schools of their brothers, sisters, friends, and neighbors. *Journal of The Association for Persons with Severe Handicaps, 14,* 1-7.

Brown, L., Long, E., Udvari-Solner, A., Davis, L., VanDeventer, P., Ahlgren, C., Johnson, F., Gruenewald, L., & Jorgensen, J. (1989b). Should students with severe intellectual disabilities be based in regular or in special education classrooms in home schools? *Journal of The Association for Persons with Severe Handicaps, 14,* 8-12.

Brown, L., Schwartz, P., Udvari-Solner, A., Kampschroer, E. F., Johnson, F., Jorgensen, J., & Gruenewald, L. (1991). How much time should students with severe intellectual disabilities spend in regular education classrooms and elsewhere? *Journal of The Association for Persons with Severe Handicaps, 16,* 39-47.

Brown, L. L., & Hammill, D. D. (1990). *Behavior rating profile: An ecological approach to behavioral assessment* (2nd ed.). Austin, TX: PRO-ED.

Brown, V. L., Cronin, M. E., & McEntire, E. (1994). *Test of Mathematical Abilities—2.* Austin, TX: PRO-ED.

Brown, V. L., Hammill, D. D., & Wiederholt, J. L. (1995). *Test of reading comprehension* (3rd ed.). Austin, TX: PRO-ED.

Brown, W., Thurman, S. K., & Pearl, L. W. (1993). *Family-centered intervention with infants and toddlers: Innovative cross-disciplinary approaches.* Baltimore: Brookes.

Brownell, W. E. (1999). How the ear works: Nature's solutions for listening. *Volta Review, 99*(5), 9-28.

Bruder, M. B. (2000, December). *The Individual Family Service Plan (IFSP).* Reston, VA: ERIC Clearinghouse on Disabilities and Gifted Education. (EDO-EC-00-14).

Brumback, R. A., Mathews, S., & Shenoy, S. R. (2001). Neurological disorders. In F. M. Kline, L. B. Silver, & S. C. Russell, (Eds.), *The educator's guide to medical issues in the classroom* (pp. 49-64). Baltimore: Brookes.

Bruninks, R. H., Woodcock, R. W., Weatherman, R. F., & Hill, B. K. (1996). *Scales of Independent Behavior—Revised.* Itasca, IL: Riverside.

Bryan, L. C., & Gast, D. L. (2000). Teaching on-task and on-schedule behaviors to high-functioning children with autism via picture activity schedules. *Journal of Autism and Developmental Disorders, 30,* 553-567.

Bryan, T. (1997). Assessing the personal and social status of students with learning disabilities. *Learning Disabilities, Research and Practice, 12,* 63-76.

Bryan, T. (2005). Science-based advances in the social domain of learning disabilities. *Learning Disability Quarterly, 28,* 119-121.

Bryan, T., & Ryan, A. (2001). Jacob's story: Amazing discoveries. In A. K. Ryan, *Strengthening the safety net: How school can help youth with emotional and behavioral needs complete their high school education and prepare for life after school* (p. 10). Burlington, VT: School Research Office, University of Vermont.

Bryant, D. P., & Bryant, B. R. (2003). *Assistive technology for people with disabilities.* Boston: Allyn & Bacon.

Buck, G. H., Polloway, E. A., Smith-Thomas, A., & Cook, K. W. (2003). Prereferral intervention processes: A survey of state practices. *Exceptional Children, 69,* 349-360.

Buck, S. M., Lees, R., & Cook, F. (2002). The influence of family history of stuttering on the onset of stuttering in young children. *Folia Phoniatrica et Logopaedica, 54,* 117-124.

Bui, Y. N., Schumaker, J. B., & Deshler, D. D. (2006). Effects of a strategies writing program for students with and without learning disabilities in inclusive fifth-grade classes. *Learning Disabilities Research & Practice, 22,* 129-136.

Bulgren, J. A. (2006). Integrated content enhancement routines: Responding to the needs of adolescents with disabilities in rigorous inclusive secondary content classes. *Teaching Exceptional Children, 38*(6), 54-58.

Bulgren, J. A., Deshler, D. D., Schumaker, J. B., & Lenz, B. K. (2000). The use and effectiveness of analogical instruction in diverse secondary content classrooms. *Journal of Educational Psychology, 16,* 426-441.

Bull, G. L., & Rushakoff, G. E. (1987). Computers and speech and language disordered individuals. In J. D. Lindsey (Ed.), *Computers and exceptional individuals* (pp. 83-104). Upper Saddle River, NJ: Merrill/Prentice Hall.

Bullis, M., & Otos, M. (1988). Characteristics of programs for children with deaf-blindness: Results of a national survey. *Journal of The Association for Persons with Severe Handicaps, 13,* 110-115.

Bullis, M., Yavonoff, P., Mueller, G., & Havel, F. (2002). Life on the "outs": Examination of facility-to-community transition of incarcerated youth. *Exceptional Children, 69,* 7-22.

Bullock, C., & Foegen, A. (2002). Constructive conflict resolution for students with behavioral disorders. *Behavioral Disorders, 27,* 289-295.

Burchard, S. N., Hasazi, J. S., Gordon, L. R., & Yoe, J. (1991). An examination of lifestyle and adjustment in three community residential alternatives. *Research in Developmental Disabilities, 12,* 127-142.

Bureau of Labor Statistics. (1999). *National industry—occupation employment matrix: Occupation report-teachers, special education.* Retrieved August 23, 2001, from http://www.bls.gov/opub/ooq/2000/spring/contents.htm.

Burkhardt, L. J. (1981). *Homemade battery powered toys and educational devices for severely disabled children.* Millville, PA: Burkhardt.

Burns, M. K., & Dean, V. J. (2005). Effect of acquisition rates on off-task behavior with children identified as having learning disabilities. *Learning Disability Quarterly, 28,* 273-281.

Bursuck, W., Polloway, E. A., Plante, L., Epstein, D. H., Jayanthi, M., & McConeghy, J. I. (1996). Report card grading and adaptations: A national survey of classroom practices. *Exceptional Children, 62,* 301-318.

Bursuck, W. D., & Damer, M. (2007). *Reading instruction for students who are at risk or have disabilities.* Boston: Allyn and Bacon.

Bushell, D., Jr., & Baer, D. M. (1994). Measurably superior instruction means close, continual contact with the relevant outcome data. Revolutionary! In R. Gardner III, D. M. Sainato, J. O. Cooper, T. E. Heron, W. L. Heward, J. Eshleman, & T. A. Grossi (Eds.), *Behavior analysis in education: Focus on measurably superior instruction* (pp. 3-10). Pacific Grove, CA: Brooks/Cole.

Butterworth, J., Gilmore, D., Kiernan, W. E., & Shalock, R. (1999). *Day and employment service in developmental disabilities: State and national trends.* Washington, DC: American Association on Mental Retardation.

Bybee, J., & Zigler, E. (1998). Outerdirectedness in individuals with and without mental retardation: A review. In J. A. Burack, R. M. Hodapp, & E. Zigler (Eds.), *Handbook of mental retardation* (pp. 434-460). Cambridge: Cambridge University Press.

Byford, J., & Veenstra, N. (2004). The importance of cultural factors in planning of rehabilitation services in a remote area of Papua, New Guinea. *Disability and Rehabilitation, 26*(3), 166-175.

Byzek, J. (February, 2001). Committed couples. *New Mobility: The Magazine for Active Wheelchair Users.* [Retrieved September 2, 2007: http://www.newmobility.com/articleView.cfm?id=333&action=browse]

Calculator, S. N., & Jorgensen, C. M. (1991). Integrating augmentative and alternative communication instruction into regular education settings: Expounding on best practices. *Augmentative and Alternative Communication, 7,* 204-214.

Calderon, R., & Naidu, S. (2000). Further support for the benefits of early identification and intervention for children with hearing loss. *Volta Review, 100*(5), 53-84.

Caldwell, B. (1997). Educating children who are deaf or hard of hearing: Cued speech. *ERIC Digest #555.* (ERIC Document Reproduction Service No. ED 414 673).

Calhoun, M. L., & Kuczera, M. (1996). Increasing social smiles of young children with disabilities. *Perceptual and Motor Skills, 82,* 1265-1266.

Calhoun, M. L., Rose, T. L., Hanft, B., & Sturkey, C. (1991). Social reciprocity interventions: Implications for developmental therapists. *Physical and Occupational Therapy in Pediatrics, 11,* 45-46.

California Department of Developmental Services (1999). *A report to the legislature: Changes in the populations of persons with autism and pervasive developmental disorders in California's Department of Developmental Services system: 1987 through 1998.* Sacramento, CA: California Health and Human Service Agency.

Callahan, K., Rademacher, J. A., & Hildreth, B. L. (1998). The effect of parent participation in strategies to improve the homework performance of students who are at risk. *Remedial and Special Education, 19*(3), 131-141.

Callister, J. P., Mitchell, L., & Talley, G. (1986). Profiling family preservation efforts in Utah. *Children Today, 15,* 23-25, 36-37.

Cameron, J. (2005). The detrimental effects of reward hypothesis: Persistence of a view in the face of disconfirming evidence. In W. L. Heward, T. E. Heron, N. A. Neef, S. M. Peterson, D. M. Sainato, G. Cartledge, R. Gardner, III, L. D. Peterson, S. B. Hersh, & J. C. Dardig (Eds.), *Focus on behavior analysis in education: Achievements,*

challenges, and opportunities (pp. 304-315). Upper Saddle River, NJ: Merrill/Prentice Hall.

Cameron, J., Banko, K. M., & Pierce, W. D. (2001). Pervasive negative effects of rewards on intrinsic motivation: The myth continues. *Behavior Analyst, 24,* 1-44.

Campbell, C., Campbell, S., Collicott, J., Perner, D., & Stone, J. (1988). Individualized instruction. *Education New Brunswick, 3,* 17-20.

Campbell, J. (2007). Understanding the emotional needs of children who are blind. *Journal of Visual Impairment and Blindness, 101,* 351-355.

Campbell, P. H. (2006). Addressing motor disabilities. In M. E. Snell & F. Brown (Eds.), *Instruction of students with severe disabilities* (6th ed.), (pp. 291-327). Upper Saddle River, NJ: Merrill/Prentice Hall.

Campbell, P. H. (2006). Promoting participation in natural environments by accommodating motor disabilities. In M. E. Snell & F. Brown (Eds.), *Instruction of students with severe disabilities* (6th ed.), (pp. 291-329). Upper Saddle River, NJ: Merrill/Prentice Hall.

Campbell Miller, M., Cooke, N. L., Test, D. W., & White, R. (2003). Effects of friendship circles on the social interactions of elementary age student with mild disabilities. *Journal of Behavioral Education, 12,* 167-184.

Cannella-Malone, H. I., O'Reilly, M. F., & Lancioni, G. (2005). Choice and preference assessment research with people with severe to profound developmental disabilities: A review of the literature. *Research in Developmental Disabilities, 26,* 1-15.

Cannella-Malone, H. I., O'Reilly, M. F., & Lancioni, G. E. (2006). Treatment of hand mouthing in individuals with severe to profound developmental disabilities: A review of the literature. *Research in Developmental Disabilities, 27,* 529-544.

Cantu, C. O. (2004). Wheelchair positioning: Foundation in wheelchair selection. *Exceptional Parent, 34*(5), 33-35.

Cardon, L. R., Smith, S. D., Fulker, D. W., Kimberling, B. F., Pennington, B. F., & DeFries, J. C. (1994). Quantitative trait locus for reading disability on chromosome 6. *Science, 226,* 276-279.

Carey, W. B. (1998). Temperament and behavior problems in the classroom. *School Psychology Review, 27,* 522-533.

Carlin, M., Chrysler, C., & Sullivan, K. (2007). Conjunctive search in individuals with and without mental retardation. *American Journal on Mental Retardation, 112,* 54-65.

Carlin, M. T., Soraci, S. A., & Strawbrige, C. P. (2005). Generative learning during visual search for scene changes: Enhancing free recall of individuals with and without mental retardation. *American Journal on Mental Retardation, 110,* 13-22.

Carlin, M. T., Soraci, S. A., Strawbrige, C. P., Dennis, N., Loiselle, R., & Chechile, N. A. (2003). Detection of changes in naturalistic scenes: Comparisons of individuals with and without mental retardation. *American Journal on Mental Retardation, 108,* 181-193.

Carnine, D. (1997). Bridging the research to practice gap. *Exceptional Children, 63,* 513-521.

Carnine, D., Jones, E., & Dixon, R. (1994). Mathematics: Educational tools for diverse learners. *School Psychology Review, 23,* 406-427.

Carnine, D. W., Silbert, J., Kame'enui, E. J., & Tarver, S. (2004). *Direct instruction reading* (4th ed.). Upper Saddle River, NJ: Merrill/Prentice Hall.

Carnine, D. W., Silbert, J., Kame'enui, E. J., Tarver, S. G., & Jongjohann, K. (2006). *Teaching struggling and at risk readers: A direct instruction approach.* Upper Saddle River, NJ: Merrill/Prentice Hall.

Caro, P., & Derevensky, J. L. (1997). An exploratory study using the sibling interaction scale: Observing interactions between siblings with and without disabilities. *Education and Treatment of Children, 20*(4), 383-403.

Carothers, D. E., & Taylor, R. L. (2004). How teachers and parents can work together to teach daily living skills to children with autism. *Focus on Autism and Other Developmental Disabilities, 19,* 102-104.

Carpenter, B. (2000). Sustaining the family: Meeting the needs of families of children with disabilities. *British Journal of Special Education, 27*(3), 135-144.

Carr, E. G., & Durand, V. M. (1985). Reducing behavior problems through functional communication training. *Journal of Applied Behavior Analysis, 18,* 111-126.

Carr, E. G., Dunlap, G., Horner, R. H., Koegel, R. L., Turnbull, A. P., Sailor, W., Anderson, J., Albin, R. W., Koegel, L. K., & Fox, L. (2002). Positive behavioral support: Evolution of an applied science. *Journal of Positive Behavior Interventions, 4,* 4-16.

Carr, E. G., Levin, L., McConnachie, G., Carlson, J. I., Kemp, D. C., & Smith, C. E. (1994). *Communication-based intervention for problem behavior: A user's guide for producing positive change.* Baltimore: Brookes.

Carr, J. (1988). Six-weeks to twenty-one years old: A longitudinal study of children with Down syndrome and their families. *Journal of Child Psychology and Psychiatry, 29*(4), 407-431.

Carr, J. E., Kellum, K. K., & Chong, I. M. (2001). The reductive effects of noncontingent reinforcement: Fixed-time versus variable-time schedules. *Journal of Applied Behavior Analysis, 34,* 505-509.

Carr, S. C., & Punzo, R. P. (1993). The effects of self-monitoring of academic accuracy and productivity on the performance of students with behavioral disorders. *Behavioral Disorders, 18,* 241-250.

Carroll, C. (1996). A look at parents, history, and deaf education in the United States. *Perspectives in Education and Deafness, 15*(2), 16-19.

Carta, J. J., Atwater, J. B., Greenwood, C. R., McConnell, S. R., McEvoy, M. A., & Williams, R. (2001). Effects of cumulative prenatal substance exposure and environmental risks on children's developmental trajectories. *Journal of Clinical Child Psychology, 30*(3), 327-337.

Carter, E. W., Clark, N. M., Cushing, L. S., & Kennedy, C. H. (2005). Number of peers in peer support programs for students with severe disabilities: Effects on social interactions and access to the general education curriculum. *Research and Practice for People with Severe Disabilities, 30*, 15–25.

Carter, E. W., Hughes, C., Guth, C. B., & Copeland, S. R. (2005). Factors influencing social interaction among high school students with intellectual disabilities and their general education peers. *American Journal on Mental Retardation, 110*, 366–377.

Carter, S. L. (2006). Everything you ever wanted to know in a bubble. *Teaching Exceptional Children, 39*(2), 40–43.

Cartledge, G., Gardner, III, R., & Ford, D. Y. (2008). *Teaching diverse learners in general education classrooms.* Upper Saddle River, NJ: Merrill/Prentice Hall.

Cartledge, G., Kea, C. D., & Ida, D. J. (2000). Anticipating differences—celebrating strengths: Providing culturally competent services for students with serious emotional disturbance. *Teaching Exceptional Children, 32*(3), 6–12.

Cartledge, G., & Kleefeld, J. (1991). *Taking part: Introducing social skills to children.* Circle Pines, MN: American Guidance Service.

Cartledge, G., & Milburn, J. F. (1995). *Teaching social skills to children and youth: Innovative approaches* (3rd ed.). Boston: Allyn & Bacon.

Casale-Giannola, D., & Wilson Kamens, M. (2006). Inclusion at a university: Experiences of a young woman with Down syndrome. *Mental Retardation, 44*, 344–352.

Cascella, P. W., & McNamara, K. M. (2005). Empowering students with severe disabilities to actualize communication skills. *Teaching Exceptional Children, 37*(3), 38–43.

Caspi, A., Henry, B., McGee, R. O., Moffitt, T. W., & Silva, P. A. (1995). Temperamental origins of child and adolescent behavior problems: From age three to age fifteen. *Child Development, 66*, 55–68.

Castellano, J. (2004). Empowering and serving Hispanic students in gifted education. In D. Boothe & J. Stanley (Eds.), *In the eyes of the beholder: Critical issues for diversity in gifted education* (pp. 1–14). Waco, TX: Prufrock.

Castellano, J. A. (2003). *Special populations in gifted education: Working with diverse gifted learners.* Boston: Allyn & Bacon.

Castellnos, F. X. (2001). Neural substrates of attention-deficit/hyperactivity disorder. *Clinical Pediatrics, 36*, 381–393.

Catts, H. W. (1993). The relationship between speech-language impairments and reading disabilities. *Journal of Speech and Hearing Research, 36*, 948–958.

Catts, H. W., Fey, M. E., Tomblin, J. B., & Zhang, Z. (2002). A longitudinal investigation of reading outcomes in children with language impairments. *Journal of Speech, language, and Hearing Research, 45*, 1142–1157.

Cavanaugh, R. A. (2003). *Embedding behaviorism in undergraduate teacher education: More than talking the talk.*

Paper presented at the 29th Annual Convention of the Association for Behavior Analysis, San Francisco.

Cavanaugh, R. A., Heward, W. L., & Donelson, F. (1996). Effects of response cards during lesson closure on the academic performance of secondary students in an earth science course. *Journal of Applied Behavior Analysis, 29*, 403–406.

Cavkaytar, A. (2007). Turkish parents as teachers: Teaching parents how to teach self-care and domestic skills to their children with mental retardation. *Education and Training in Mental Retardation and Developmental Disabilities, 42*, 85–93.

Cawley, J. F., Parmar, R. S., Foley, T. E., Salmon S., & Roy, S. (2001). Arithmetic performance of students: Implications for standards and programming. *Exceptional Children, 67*, 311–328.

Cawley, J. F., Parmar, R. S., Yan, W., & Miller, J. H. (1998). Arithmetic computation performance of students with learning disabilities: Implications for curriculum. *Learning Disabilities Research and Practice, 13*, 68–74.

Cawthon, S. W. (2001). Teaching strategies in inclusive classrooms with deaf students. *Journal of Deaf Studies and Deaf Education, 6*, 212–225.

Cazden, C. B. (1992). *Whole language plus: Essays on literacy in the United States and New Zealand.* New York: Teachers College Press.

CEC Today. (1998). Growing challenge for teachers—Providing medical procedures for students. 5(3), 1, 5, 15.

Cedar Rapids Community School District v. Garret F., 67 U.S. L. W. 4165 (1999).

Celeste, M. (2006). Play behaviors and social interactions of a child who is blind: In theory and practice. *Journal of Visual Impairment and Blindness, 100*, 75–90.

Center for Education Policy. (2006). *A public education primer: Basic (and sometimes surprising) facts about the U.S. education system.* Washington, DC: Author.

Center for Positive Behavioral Interventions & Supports. (2007). *School-wide behavioral support.* http://www.pbis.org/.

Center on Human Policy. (1986, December). Positive interventions for challenging behavior. *The Association for Persons with Severe Handicaps Newsletter, 12*(12), 4.

Centers for Disease Control and Prevention. (1997). Sports-related recurrent brain injuries—United States. *Morbidity and Mortality Weekly Reports, 46*(10), 224–227.

Centers for Disease Control and Prevention. (1998). HIV/AIDS prevention: Frequently asked questions. *CDC Update.* http://www.cdc.gov.hiv/pubs/facts/hivre/pfs/htm.

Centers for Disease Control and Prevention. (2001a). Divisions of HIV/AIDS prevention. *Surveillance Report, 12*(2). http://www.cdc.gov.hiv/stats/hasr1202.

Centers for Disease Control and Prevention. (2001b). *National health statistics.* Atlanta: Author.

Centers for Disease Control and Prevention. (2007a). *A glance at the HIV/AIDS epidemic.* [Retrieved August 31, 2007. http://www.cdc.gov/hiv/resources/factsheets/At-A-Glance.htm]

Centers for Disease Control and Prevention. (2007b). *Autism Information Center: Frequently Asked Questions-Prevalence.* Retrieved 7/15/07 from CDCP website, www.cdc.gov.

Centers for Disease Control and Prevention. (2007c). *Basic statistics.* [Retrieved August 31, 2007. http://www.cdc.gov/hiv/topics/surveillance/basic.htm#ddaids]

Centers for Disease Control and Prevention. (2007d). *HIV and its transmission.* [Retrieved August 31, 2007. http://www.cdc.gov/hiv/resources/factsheets/transmission.htm]

Centers for Disease Control and Prevention. (2007e). *Living with HIV/AIDS.* [Retrieved August 31, 2007. http://www.cdc.gov/hiv/resources/brochures/livingwithhiv.htm]

Cerney, J. (2007). *Deaf education in America: Voices of children from inclusion settings.* Washington, DC: Gallaudet University Press.

Chadsey, J. G., Linneman, D., Rusch, F. R., & Cimera, R. E. (1997). The impact of social integration interventions and job coaches in work settings. *Education and Training in Mental Retardation and Developmental Disabilities, 32*, 281–292.

Chaffey, G. (2004, August). *Coolabah Dynamic Assessment: A paradigm shift in the identification of giftedness?.* Paper presented at the Australian Association for the Gifted meeting, Melbourne, Australia.

Chafin Seal, B. (2004). *Best practices in educational interpreting* (2nd ed.). Boston: Allyn & Bacon.

Chaikind, S., Danielson, L. C., & Brauen, M. L. (1993). What do we know about the costs of special education? A selected review. *Journal of Special Education, 26*, 344–370.

Chakrabarti, S., & Fombonne, E. (2001). Pervasive developmental disorders in preschool children. *Journal of the American Medical Association, 285*, 3093–3099.

Chambers, C. R., Wehmeyer, M. L., Saito, Y., Lida, K. M., Lee, Y., & Singh, V. (2007). Self-determination: What do we know? Where do we go? *Exceptionality, 15*, 3–15.

Chambers, J. G., Parrish, T. B., & Harr, J. J. (2002, March). *What are we spending on special education in the United States, 1999–2000? Advance report #1,* Washington, DC: American Institutes for Research: Special Education Expenditure Project.

Chandler, L. K. (1993). Steps in preparing for transition: Preschool to kindergarten. *Teaching Exceptional Children, 25*(4), 52–55.

Chandler, L. K., & Dahlquist, C. M. (2006). *Functional assessment: Strategies to prevent and remediate challenging behavior in school settings* (2nd ed.). Upper Saddle River, NJ: Merrill/Prentice Hall.

Chard, D. J., & Kame'enui, E. J. (2000). Struggling first-grade readers: The frequency and progress of their reading. *Journal of Special Education, 34*, 28–38.

Charlop-Christy, M. H. (2007). *Social and interpersonal skills interventions for children with autism*. Presentation at: Progress and Challenges in the Behavioral Treatment of Autism Conference. Boston, MA. [Available on DVD from the Association for Behavior Analysis International.]

Charlop-Christy, M. H., Carpenter, M., Le, L., LeBlanc, L. A., & Kellet, K. (2002). Using the picture exchange communication system (PECS) with children with autism: Assessment of PECS acquisition, speech, social-communicative behavior, and problem behavior. *Journal of Applied Behavior Analysis, 35*, 213–231.

Charney, E. B. (1992). Neural tube defects: Spina bifida and myelomeningocele. In M. L. Batshaw & Y. M. Perret, *Children with disabilities: A medical primer* (3rd ed.) (pp. 471–488). Baltimore: Brookes.

Chen, D. (1999). Learning to communicate: Strategies for developing communication with infants whose multiple disabilities include visual impairment and hearing loss. *reSources, 10*(5), 1–6. [Published by California Deaf-Blind Services. Available: http://www.sfsu.edu/~cadbs/Summer99.pdf]

Chen, D., & Downing, J. E. (2001). Tactile learning strategies for children who are deaf-blind: Concerns and considerations from Project SALUTE. *Deaf-Blind Perspectives, 8*(2), 1–6.

Chen, D., & Downing, J. E. (2006a). *Tactile strategies for children who have visual impairments and multiple disabilities: Promoting communication and learning skills*. New York: AFB Press.

Chen, D., & Downing, J. E. (2006b). *Tactile learning strategies: Interacting with children who have visual impairments and multiple disabilities*. New York: AFB Press.

Cherry, K. E., Njardvok, U., & Dawson, J. E. (2000). Effects of verbal elaborations on memory for sentence in adults with mental retardation, *Research in Developmental Disabilities, 21*, 137–150.

Chesapeake Institute. (1994, September). *National agenda for achieving better results for children and youth with serious emotional disturbance*. Washington, DC: U.S. Department of Education.

Chesley, G. M., & Calaluce, P. D. (1997). The deception of inclusion. *Mental Retardation, 35*, 488–490.

Chiasson, K., & Reilly, A. (2008). Families and their children with disabilities. In G. Olsen & M. L. Fuller (Eds.), *Home-school relations: Working successfully with parents and families* (pp. 151–174). Boston: Allyn and Bacon.

Christensen, L., Young, K. R., & Marchant, M. (2004). The effects of a peer-mediated positive behavior support program on socially appropriate classroom behavior. *Education and Treatment of Children, 27*, 199–234.

Christle, C. A., & Schuster, J. W. (2003). The effects of using response cards on student participation, academic achievement, and on-task behavior during whole-class, math

instruction. *Journal of Behavioral Education, 12*, 147–165.

Chuch, G., & Glennen, S. (1992). *The handbook of assistive technology*. San Diego: Singular.

Cihak, D., Alberto, P. A., Taber-Doughty, T., & Gama, R. I. (2006). A comparison of static picture prompting and video prompting simulation strategies using group instructional procedures. *Focus on Autism and Other Developmental Disabilities, 21*, 89–99.

Cipani, E. (2004). *Classroom management for all teachers: 12 plans for evidence-based practice* (2nd ed.). Upper Saddle River, NJ: Merrill/Prentice Hall.

Cipani, E. (2008). *Classroom management for all teachers: Plans for evidence-based practice* (3rd ed.). Upper Saddle River, NJ: Merrill/Prentice Hall.

Cipani, E., & Schock, K. (2007). *Functional behavioral assessment, diagnosis, and treatment: A complete system for education and mental health settings*. New York: Springer.

Cipani, E. C., & Spooner, F. (Eds.). (1994). *Curricular and instructional approaches for persons with severe disabilities*. Boston: Allyn & Bacon.

Clark, B. (1997). *Growing up gifted: Developing the potential of children at home and at school* (5th ed.). Upper Saddle River, NJ: Merrill/Prentice Hall.

Clark, B. A. (2002). *Growing up gifted* (6th ed.). Upper Saddle River, NJ: Merrill/Prentice Hall.

Clark, B. A. (2008). *Growing up gifted* (7th ed.). Upper Saddle River, NJ: Merrill/Prentice Hall.

Clark, G. M. (1994). Is a functional curriculum approach compatible with an inclusive education model? *Teaching Exceptional Children, 26*(2), 36–39.

Clark, G. M., Carlson, B. C., Fisher, S., Cook, I. D., & D'Alonzo, B. J. (1991). Career development for students with disabilities in elementary schools: A position statement of the division on career development. *Career Development for Exceptional Individuals, 14*, 109–120.

Clark, S. G. (2000). The IEP process as a tool for collaboration. *Teaching Exceptional Children, 33*(2), 56–66.

Clarke-Klein, S., & Hodson, B. W. (1995). A phonologically based analysis of misspellings by third graders with disordered-phonology histories. *Journal of Speech and Hearing Research, 38*, 839–849.

Cleeland, L. K. (1984). The function of the auditory system in speech and language development. In R. K. Hull & K. I. Dilka (Eds.), *The hearing-impaired child in school* (pp. 15–16). Orlando, FL: Grune & Stratton.

Clements, S. D. (1966). *Minimal brain dysfunction in children* (NINDS Monograph No. 3, Public Health Service Bulletin No. 1415). Washington, DC: U.S. Department of Health, Education, and Welfare.

Cline, D. H. (1990). Interpretations of emotional disturbance and social maladjustment as policy problems: A legal

analysis of initiatives to exclude handicapped/disruptive students from special education. *Behavioral Disorders, 15*, 159–173.

Clinical Practice Guideline: Report of the Recommendations. (1999). Publication No. 4215. Albany: New York State Department of Health.

Cobb Morocco, C., Clay, K., Parker, C. E., & Zigmond, N. (2006). Walter Cronkite High School: A culture of freedom and responsibility. *Learning Disabilities Research & Practice, 21*, 146–158.

Cochran, L., Feng, H., Cartledge, G., & Hamilton, S. (1993). The effects of cross-age tutoring on the academic achievement, social behaviors, and self-perceptions of low-achieving African-American males with behavioral disorders. *Behavioral Disorders, 18*, 292–302.

Cohen, H., Amerine-Dickens, M., & Smith, T. (2006). Early intensive behavioral treatment: Replication of the UCLA Model in a community setting. *Journal of Developmental and Behavioral Pediatrics, 27*, S145–S155.

Cohen, M. J., & Sloan, D. L. (2007). *Visual supports for people with autism: A guide for parents & professionals*. Bethesda, MD: Woodbine House.

Cohen, S., Agosta, J., Cohen, J., & Warren, R. (1989). Supporting families of children with severe disabilities. *Journal of The Association for Persons with Severe Handicaps, 14*, 155–162.

Colangelo, N., Assouline, S. G., & Gross, M. U. M. (2004). *A nation deceived: How schools hold back America's brightest students*. Iowa City: University of Iowa Press.

Cole, C. M., Waldron, N., & Majd, M. (2004). Academic progress of students across inclusive and traditional settings. *Mental Retardation, 42*, 136–144.

Coleman, M., & Vaughn, S. R. (2000). Reading interventions with students with emotional/behavioral disorders. *Behavioral Disorders, 25*, 93–104.

Coleman, M., & Webber, J. (1988). Behavior problems? Try groups! *Academic Therapy, 23*, 265–274.

Colin, S., Magnan, A., & Ecalle, J. (2007). Relation between deaf children's phonological skills in kindergarten and word recognition performance in first grade. *The Journal of Child Psychology and Psychiatry and Allied Disciplines, 48*, 139–146.

Collicott, J. (1991). Implementing multi-level instruction: Strategies for classroom teachers. In G. Porter & D. Richler (Eds.), *Changing Canadian Schools: Perspectives on disability and inclusion* (pp. 191–218). Ottawa, Ontario, Canada: Roeher Institute.

Collins, B. C. (2007). *Moderate and severe disabilities: A foundational approach*. Upper Saddle River, NJ: Merrill/Prentice Hall.

Collins, B. C., Gast, D. L., Ault, M. J., & Wolery, M. (1991). Small group instruction: Guidelines for teachers of students with moderate to severe handicaps. *Education and Training in Mental Retardation, 26*, 18–32.

Collins, B. C., Hall, M., & Branson, T. A. (1997). Teaching leisure skills to adolescents with moderate disabilities. *Exceptional Children, 63,* 499-512.

Collins, D. W., & Rourke, B. (2003). Learning-disabled brains: A review of the literature. *Journal of Clinical and Experimental Neuropsychology, 25,* 1011-1034.

Colvin, G., Kame'enui, E., & Sugai, G. (1993). Reconceptualizing behavior management and school-wide discipline in general education. *Education and Treatment of Children, 16,* 361-381.

Comacho, M. R. (2007, April). *TENFEE: Spanish workshops for the needs of families in special education.* Poster presented at the 85th Annual Convention of the Council for Exceptional Children. Louisville, KY.

Commission on Education of the Deaf. (1988). *Toward equality: Education of the deaf.* Washington, DC: U.S. Government Printing Office.

Community Playthings. (1999). *Rifton equipment* [Catalog]. Rifton, NY: Community Products.

Compton, M. V., & Niemeyer, J. A. (1994). Expressions of affection in young children with sensory impairments: A research agenda. *Education and Treatment of Children, 17,* 68-85.

Cone, A. A. (1994). Reflections on "Self-advocacy: Voices for choices." *Mental Retardation, 32,* 444-445.

Coniglio, S. J., Lewis, J. D., Lang, C., Burns, T. G., Subhani-Siddique, R., Weintraub A., et al. (2001). A randomized, double-blind, placebo-controlled trial of a single-dose intravenous secretin as treatment for children with autism. *Journal of Pediatrics, 138*(5), 649-655.

Conley, R. W. (2003). Supported employment in Maryland: Successes and issues. *Mental Retardation, 41,* 237-249.

Connell, M. C., Carta, J. J., & Baer, D. M. (1993). Programming generalization of in-class transition skills: Teaching preschoolers with developmental delays to self-assess and recruit contingent teacher praise. *Journal of Applied Behavior Analysis, 26,* 3.

Connell, M. C., Randall, C., Wilson, J., Lutz, S., & Lamb, D. R. (1993). Building independence during in-class transitions: Teaching in-class transition skills to preschoolers with developmental delays through choral-response-based self-assessment and contingent praise. *Education and Treatment of Children, 16,* 160-174.

Conner, E. P., Scandary, J., & Tullock, D. (1988). Education of physically handicapped and health impaired individuals: A commitment to the future. *DPH Journal, 10*(1), 5-24.

Conners, C. K. (2000). Attention-deficit/hyperactivity disorder: Historical development and overview. *Journal of Attention Disorders, 3,* 173-191.

Connolly, A. J. (2007). *KeyMath—3: A Diagnostic Inventory of Essential Skills.* Minneapolis, MN: Pearson Assessments.

Connolly, C. M., Rose, J., & Austen, S. (2006). Identifying and assessing depression in prelingually deaf people: A literature review. *American Annals of the Deaf, 151,* 49-60.

Connor, L. E. (1986). Oralism in perspective. In D. M. Luterman (Ed.), *Deafness in perspective* (pp. 116-129). San Diego: College-Hill.

Conroy, J., Spreat, S., Yuskauskas, A., & Elks, M. (2003). The Hissom closure outcomes study: A report on six years of movement to supported living. *Mental Retardation, 41,* 263-275.

Conroy, J. W. (1996). The small ICF/MR program: Dimensions of quality and cost. *Mental Retardation, 34,* 13-26.

Conroy, J. W., & Bradley, V. J. (1985). *The Pennhurst longitudinal study: A report on five years of research and analysis.* Philadelphia: Temple University Developmental Disabilities Center.

Conroy, M. A., & Brown, W. H. (2006). Early identification, prevention, and early intervention with young children at risk for emotional and behavioral disorders: Issues, trends, and a call for action. *Behavioral Disorders, 29,* 224-236.

Conroy, M. A., & Davis, C. A. (2000). Early elementary-aged children with challenging behaviors: Legal and educational issues related to IDEA and assessment. *Preventing School Failure, 44,* 163-168.

Conte, R., & Andrews, J. (1993). Social skills in the context of learning disability definitions: A reply to Gresham and Elliott and directions for the future. *Journal of Learning Disabilities, 26,* 146-153.

Cook, A. M., & Hussey, S. M. (1995). *Assistive technologies: Principles and practice.* St. Louis: Mosby.

Cook, B. G. (2001). A comparison of teachers' attitudes toward their included students with mild and severe disabilities. *Journal of Special Education, 34,* 203-213.

Cook, B. G. (2004). Inclusive teachers' attitudes toward their students with disabilities: A replication and extension. *The Elementary School Journal, 104,* 307-320.

Cook, B. G., Cameron, D. L., & Tankersley, M. (2007). Inclusive teachers' attitudinal ratings of their students with disabilities. *The Journal of Special Education, 40,* 230-238.

Cook, B. G., & Semmel, M. I. (1999). Peer acceptance of included students with disabilities as a function of severity of disability and classroom composition. *Journal of Special Education, 33,* 50-61.

Cook, B. G., Tankersley, M., Cook, L., & Landrum, T. J. (2000). Teachers' attitudes toward their included students with disabilities. *Exceptional Children, 67,* 115-135.

Cook, R. E., Klein, M. D., & Tessier, A. (2008). *Adapting early childhood curricula for children with special needs* (7th ed.), (pp. 115-120). Upper Saddle River, NJ: Merrill/Prentice Hall.

Cooke, N. L., Heron, T. E., & Heward, W. L. (1983). *Peer tutoring: Implementing classwide programs in the primary grades.* Columbus, OH: Special Press.

Cooke, N. L., Heward, W. L., Test, D. W., Spooner, F., & Courson, F. H. (1991). Student performance data in the special education classroom: Measurement and evaluation of student progress. *Teacher Education and Special Education, 13,* 155-161.

Cooper, H. L., & Nichols, S. K. (2007). Technology and early braille literacy: Using the Mountbatten Pro Brailler in primary-grade classrooms. *Journal of Visual Impairment and Blindness, 101,* 22-31.

Cooper, J. O., Heron, T. E., & Heward, W. L. (2007). *Applied behavior analysis* (2nd ed.) Upper Saddle River, NJ: Merrill/Prentice Hall.

Cooper, J. O., Kubina, R., & Malanga, P. (1998). Six procedures for showing standard celebration charts. *Journal of Precision Teaching & Celebration, 15*(2), 58-76.

Cooper, K. J., & Browder, D. M. (1997). The use of a personal trainer to enhance participation of older adults with severe disabilities in community water exercise classes. *Journal of Behavioral Education, 7,* 421-434.

Cooper, K. J., & Browder, D. M. (1998). Enhancing choice and participation for adults with severe disabilities in community-based instruction. *Journal of The Association for Persons with Severe Handicaps, 23,* 252-260.

Copeland, S., & Hughes, C. (2000). Acquisition of a picture prompt strategy to increase independent performance. *Education and Training in Mental Retardation and Developmental Disabilities, 35,* 294-305.

Copeland, S. R., Hughes, C., Carter, W. W., Guth, C., Presley, J. A., Williams, C. R., & Fowler, S. E. (2004). Increasing access to general education: Perspectives of participants in a high school peer support program. *Remedial and Special Education, 25,* 342-352.

Copeland, S. R., McCall, J., Williams, C. R., Guth, C., Carter, E. W., Fowler, S. E., Presely, J. A., & Hughes, C. (2002). High school peer buddies: A win-win situation. *Teaching Exceptional Children, 35*(1), 16-21.

Coplan, J., Souders, M. C., Mulberg, A. E., et al. (2003). Children with autistic spectrum disorders. II: Parents are unable to distinguish secretin from placebo under double-blind conditions. *Archives of Disease in Childhood, 88,* 739.

Copple, C., & Bredekamp, S. (2006). *Basics of developmentally appropriate practice.* Washington, DC: National Association for the Education of Young Children.

Corn, A. L. (1989). Instruction in the use of vision for children and adults with low vision: A proposed program model. *RE:view, 21,* 26-38.

Corn, A. L. (2000). *Finding wheels: A curriculum for non-drivers with visual impairments for gaining control of transportation needs.* Austin: PRO-ED.

Corn, A. L., Erin, J. N., Ferrenkipf, C., Huebner, K. M., McNear, D., Spungin, S. J., & Torres, I. (Eds.). (2004). *When you have a visually impaired student in your classroom: A guide for teachers.* New York: AFB Press.

Corn, A. L., & Koenig, A. J. (1996). *Foundations of low vision: Clinical and functional perspectives.* New York: AFB Press.

Corn, A., & Ryser, G. (1989). Access to print for students with low vision. *Journal of Visual Impairment and Blindness, 83,* 340-349.

Cornett, R., & Daisey, M. (2001). *The cued speech resource book for parents of deaf children.* Cleveland, OH: National Cued Speech Association.

Cornett, R. O. (1974). What is cued speech? *Gallaudet Today, 5*(2), 3-5.

Correa, V., & Jones, H. (2000). Multicultural issues related to families of children with disabilities. In M. J. Fine (Ed.), *Collaboration with parents of exceptional children* (2nd ed.), (pp. 133–154). Austin, TX: PRO-ED.

Correa, V. I., Blanes-Reyes, M., & Rapport, M. J. (1995). Minority issues. In H. R. Turnbull & A. P. Turnbull (Eds.), *A compendium report to Congress.* Lawrence, KS: Beach Center.

Correa, V. I., Gollery, T., & Fradd, S. (1988). The handicapped undocumented alien student dilemma: Do we advocate or abdicate? *Journal of Educational Issues of Language Minority Students, 3,* 41–47.

Correa, V. I., & Heward, W. L. (2003). Special education in a culturally diverse society. In W. L. Heward, *Exceptional children: An introduction to special education* (7th ed.), (pp. 86–119). Upper Saddle River, NJ: Merrill/Prentice Hall.

Correa, V. I., Jones, H. A., Thomas, C. C., & Morsink, C. V. (2005). *Interactive teaming: Enhancing programs for students with special needs* (4th ed.). Upper Saddle River, NJ: Merrill/Prentice Hall.

Cortiella, C. (2006). *NCLB and IDEA: What parents of students with disabilities need to know and do.* Minneapolis, MN: University of Minnesota, National Center on Educational Outcomes.

Cosden, M., Brown, C., & Elliott, K. (2002). Development of self-understanding and self-esteem in children and adults with learning disabilities. In B. Wong & M. Donahue (Eds.), *The social dimensions of learning disabilities* (pp. 33–51). Hillsdale, NJ: Erlbaum.

Coster, W. J., & Haltiwanger, J. T. (2004). Social-behavioral skills of elementary students with physical disabilities included in general education classrooms. *Remedial and Special Education, 25,* 95–103.

Cott, A. (1972). Megavitamins: The orthomolecular approach to behavioral disorders and learning disabilities. *Academic Therapy, 7,* 245–258.

Coucouvanis, K., Lakin, K. C., Prouty, R., & Webster, A. (2006). Reductions continue in average daily populations of large state facilities; Nearly 70% decrease between 1980 and 2005. *Mental Retardation, 44,* 235–238.

Coulter, D. L. (1994). Biomedical conditions: Types, causes, and results. In L. Sternberg (Ed.), *Individuals with profound disabilities: Instructional and assistive strategies* (3rd ed.), (pp. 41–58). Austin, TX: PRO-ED.

Council for Children with Behavioral Disorders. (1989). Best assessment practices for students with behavioral disorders: Accommodation to cultural diversity and individual differences. *Behavioral Disorders, 14,* 263–278.

Council for Children with Behavioral Disorders. (1993, June). Staff position statement: Inclusion. CCBD *Newsletter,* p. 1.

Council for Children with Behavioral Disorders. (August, 2000). Draft Position Paper On Identification and Verification of Emotional or Behavioral Disorders. Reston, VA: Author, A Division of the Council for Exceptional Children, 1920 Association Drive, Reston, VA.

Council for Children with Behavioral Disorders. (October, 2000). *Draft position paper on terminology and definition of emotional or behavioral disorders.* Reston, VA: Author, A Division of the Council for Exceptional Children, 1920 Association Drive, Reston, VA.

Council for Exceptional Children. (2003). *What every special educator must know: The standards for the preparation and licensure of special educators* (5th ed.). Arlington, VA: Author.

Council for Exceptional Children. (2004). *The new IDEA: CEC's summary of significant issues.* Arlington, VA: Author.

Council for Exceptional Children. (2004, May 14). *CEC disappointed in lack of full funding in Senate IDEA bill: Once again, students with disabilities are let down* (Press release). Arlington, VA: Author.

Council for Exceptional Children. (2006a). *Evidence-based professional practices proposal.* Reston, VA: Professional Standard & Practice Committee, Council for Exceptional Children. Available online: http://www.cec.sped.org/Content/ NavigationMenu/ ProfessionalDevelopment/ ProfessionalStandards/ EVP_revised_03_2006.pdf

Council for Exceptional Children. (2006b). *Talking points on mandatory full funding of idea.* Reston, VA: Author. http://www.cec.sped.org/Content/ NavigationMenu/PolicyAdvocacy/ IDEAResources/default.htm [Retrieved March 24, 2007.]

Council for Exceptional Children (2006c). *Understanding IDEA 2004 regulations: CEC's side-by-side comparison and analysis.* Reston, VA: Author.

Council for Learning Disabilities. (1993). Concerns about the full inclusion of students with learning disabilities in regular education classrooms. *Journal of Learning Disabilities, 26,* 595.

Council of State Directors of Programs for the Gifted. (2000). *1998–99 state of the states gifted and talented education report.* Longmont, CO: Author.

Council of State Directors of Programs for the Gifted. (2003). *2001–2002 state of the states gifted and talented education report.* Longmont, CO: Author.

Council of State Directors of Programs for the Gifted. (2006). *2004–2005 state of the states gifted and talented education report.* Longmont, CO: Author.

Courson, F. H., & Hay, G. H. (1996). Parents as partners. *Beyond Behavior, 7*(3), 19–23.

Court, D., & Givon, S. (2003). Group intervention: Improving social skills of adolescents with learning disabilities. *Teaching Exceptional Children, 36*(2), 46–51.

Courtade-Little, G., & Browder, D. (2005). *Aligning IEPs to academic standards for students with moderate and severe disabilities.* Verona, WI: Attainment Company, Inc.

Coyne, M. D., Kame'enui, E. J., & Carnine, D. W. (Eds.). (2007). *Effective teaching strategies that accommodate diverse learners* (3rd ed.). Upper Saddle River, NJ: Merrill/Prentice Hall.

Craft, M. A., Alber, S. R., & Heward, W. L. (1998). Teaching elementary students with developmental disabilities to recruit teacher attention in a general education classroom: Effects on teacher praise and academic productivity. *Journal of Applied Behavior Analysis, 31,* 399–415.

Craig, S., Hall, K., Haggart, A. G., & Perez-Selles, M. (2000). Promoting cultural competence through teacher assistance teams. *Teaching Exceptional Children, 32*(3), 6–12.

Crandall, J., Jacobson, J., & Sloane, H. (Eds.). (1997). *What works in education.* Cambridge, MA: Cambridge Center for Behavioral Studies.

Crandell, C. C., & Smaldino, J. J. (2001a). Improving classroom acoustics: Utilizing hearing-assistive technology and communication strategies in the educational setting. *Volta Review, 101*(5), 47–64.

Crandell, C. C., & Smaldino, J. J. (2001b). Rehabilitative technologies for individuals with hearing loss and normal hearing. In J. Katz (Ed.), *Handbook of clinical audiology* (5th ed.), (pp. 607–630). New York: Lippincott, Williams, & Wilkins.

Crone, D. A., & Horner, R. H. (2003). *Building positive behavior support systems in schools: Functional behavioral assessment.* New York: Guildford Press.

Cronin, M. E., Patton, J. R., & Wood, S. J. (2005). *Life skills instruction: A practical guide for integrating real-life content into the curriculum at the elementary and secondary levels for students with special needs or who are placed at risk.* Austin: PRO-ED.

Cronin, M. E., Slade, D. L., Bechtel, C., & Anderson, P. (1992). Home-school partnerships: A cooperative approach to intervention. *Intervention in School and Clinic, 27,* 286–292.

Cronin, M. S., & Patton, J. R. (1993). *Life skills instruction for all students with special needs: A practical guide for integrating real-life content into the curriculum.* Austin, TX: PRO-ED.

Cross, T. L. (2006). *On the social and emotional lives of gifted kids: Understanding and guiding their development* (3rd ed.). Waco, TX: Prufrock Press.

Crossley, R. (1988). *Unexpected communication attainments by persons diagnosed as autistic and intellectually impaired.* Caulfield, Victoria: Deal Communication Centre.

Crossley, R., & Remington-Guerney, J. (1992). Getting the words out: Facilitated communication training. *Topics in Language Disorders, 12*(4), 29–45.

Crozier, S., & Sileo, N. M. (2005). Encouraging positive behavior with social stories: An intervention for children with autism spectrum disorders. *Teaching Exceptional Children, 37*(6), 26–31.

Crozier, S., & Tincani, M. J. (2005). Using a modified social story to decrease disruptive behavior of a child with autism. *Focus on Autism and Other Developmental Disabilities, 20,* 150–157.

Cruickshank, W. M. (1986). *Disputable decisions in special education.* Ann Arbor: University of Michigan Press.

Crundwell, R. M.A. (2006). Identifying and teaching children with selective mutism. *Teaching Exceptional Children, 38*(3), 48–54.

Crutchfield, M. D. (2003). What do CEC standards mean to me? Using the CEC standards to improve my practice. *Teaching Exceptional Children, 35*(6), 40–45.

Cruz, L., & Cullinan, D. (2001). Awarding points, using levels to help children improve behavior. *Teaching Exceptional Children, 33*(3), 16–23.

Culatta, B., & Wiig, E. H. (2006). Language disabilities in school-age children and youth. In N. B. Anderson & G. H. Shames (Eds.), *Human communication disorders: An introduction* (7th ed.) (pp. 352–385). Boston: Allyn & Bacon.

Cullen, C., & Mudford, O. (2005). Gentle teaching. In J. W. Jacobson, J. A. Mulick, & R. M. Foxx (Eds.). *Controversial therapies in developmental disabilities: Fads, fashion, and science in professional practice* (pp. 423–432). Hillsdale, NJ: Lawrence Erlbaum Associates.

Cullinan, D. (2002). *Students with emotional and behavioral disorders: An introduction for teachers and other helping professionals.* Upper Saddle River, NJ: Merrill/Prentice Hall.

Cullinan, D. (2007). *Students with emotional and behavioral disorders: An introduction for teachers and other helping professionals* (2nd ed.). Upper Saddle River, NJ: Merrill/Prentice Hall.

Cullinan, D., & Epstein, M. H. (1995). Behavior disorders. In N. G. Haring & L. McCormick (Eds.), *Exceptional children and youth* (6th ed.). Upper Saddle River, NJ: Merrill/Prentice Hall.

Cullinan, D., Epstein, M. H., & Sabornie, E. J. (1992). Selected characteristics of a national sample of seriously emotionally disturbed adolescents. *Behavioral Disorders, 17,* 273–280.

Cullinan, D., & Kauffman, J. M. (2005). Do race of student and race of teacher influence ratings of emotional and behavioral problem characteristics of students with emotional disorders? *Behavioral Disorders, 30,* 393–402.

Cullinan, D., & Sabornie, E. J. (2004). Characteristics of emotional disturbance in middle and high school students. *Journal of Emotional and Behavioral Disorders, 12,* 157–168.

Cummins, J. (1989). A theoretical framework for bilingual special education. *Exceptional Children, 56,* 111–119.

Cummins, J. (2002). Foreword. In P. Gibbons, *Scaffolding language, scaffolding learning: Teaching second language learners in the mainstream classroom.* Portsmouth, NH: Heinemann.

Cunningham, B. (2007). *Student transitional guide to college.* National Secondary Transition Technical Assistance Center. [Retrieved September 26, 2007. http://www.nsttac.org/?FileName= student_transitional_guide&type=1]

Curl, R. M. (1990). A demonstration project for teaching entry-level job skills: The Co-Worker Transition Model for Youths with Disabilities. *Exceptional News, 13*(3), 3–7.

Curl, R. M., Hall, S. M., Chisholm, L. A., & Rule, S. (1992). Co-workers as trainers for entry-level workers: A competitive employment model for individuals with developmental disabilities. *Rural Special Education Quarterly, 11,* 31–35.

Curl, R. M., Lignugaris/Kraft, B., Pawley, J. M., & Salzberg, C. L. (1988). "What's next?" A quantitative and qualitative analysis of the transition for trainee to valued worker. Unpublished manuscript.

Cushing, L. S., Clark, N. M., Carter, E. K., & Kennedy, C. H. (2005). Accessing the general education curriculum: An assessment and outcome based approach for students with severe disabilities. *Teaching Exceptional Children, 37,* 6–13.

Cushing, L. S., & Kennedy, C. H. (1997). Academic effects of providing peer support in general education classrooms on students without disabilities. *Journal of Applied Behavior Analysis, 30,* 139–152.

Cystic Fibrosis Foundation. (2001). *Facts about cystic fibrosis.* Bethesda, MD: Author. www.cff.org.

Cystic Fibrosis Foundation. (2003). *Facts about CF.* Bethesda, MD: Author. www.cff. org.

Cystic Fibrosis Foundation. (2007). *Cystic fibrosis: What you need to know.* Bethesda, MD: Author. [Retrieved August 26, 2007 http://www.cff.org:80/AboutCF/]

Daane, M. C., Campbell, J. R., Grigg, W. S., Goodman, M. J., & Oranje, A. (2005). *Fourth-grade students reading aloud: NAEP 2002 special study of oral reading* (NCES 2006–469). U.S. Department of Education. Institute of Education Sciences, National Center for Education Statistics. Washington, DC: Government Printing Office.

Daly, P. M., & Ranalli, P. (2003). Using countoons to teach self-monitoring skills. *Teaching Exceptional Children, 35*(5), 30–35.

D'Amico, R. (1991). The working world awaits. In M. Wagner, L. Newman, R. D'Amico, E. D. Jay, P. Butler-Nalin, C. Marder, & R. Cox (Eds.), *Youth with disabilities: How are they doing? A comprehensive report from Wave 1 of the National Longitudinal Transition Study of special education students.* Menlo Park, CA: SRI International.

Danforth, S., & Navarro, V. (1998). Speech acts: Sampling the social construction of mental retardation in everyday life. *Mental Retardation, 36,* 31–43.

Danforth, S., & Rhodes, W. C. (1997). On what basis hope? Modern progress and postmodern possibilities. *Remedial and Special Education, 18,* 357–366.

Dardig, J. C. (2005). The McClurg Monthly Magazine and 14 more practical ways to involve parents. *Teaching Exceptional Children, 38*(2), 46–51.

Dardig, J. C. (2006). A friendship program for future special education teachers. In W. L. Heward, *Exceptional children: An introduction to special education* (8th

ed) (pp. 624–626). Upper Saddle River, NJ: Merrill/Prentice Hall.

Dardig, J. C. (2008). *Teacher friendly and ready-to-use parent involvement strategies for teachers of students with special needs.* Thousand Oaks, CA: Corwin Press.

Daugherty, D. (2001). *IDEA '97 and disproportionate placement.* http://www. naspcenter.org/teachers/IDEA_disp.html.

Davern, L. (2004). School-to-home notebooks: What parents have to say. *Teaching Exceptional Children, 36*(5), 22–27.

Davis, C. A., Brady, M. P., Williams, R. E., & Burta, M. (1992). The effects of self-operated auditory prompting tapes on the performance fluency of persons with severe mental retardation. *Education and Training in Mental Retardation, 27,* 39–50.

Davis, G. A., & Rimm, S. B. (2004). *Education of the gifted and talented* (5th ed.). Boston: Allyn & Bacon.

Davis, J. M., Elfenbein, J., Schum, R., & Bentler, R. A. (1986). Effects of mild and moderate hearing impairments on language, educational, and psychological behavior of children. *Journal of Speech and Hearing Disorders, 51,* 53–62.

Davis, L. L., & O'Neill, R. E. (2004). Use of response cards with a group of students with learning disabilities including those for whom English is a second language. *Journal of Applied Behavior Analysis, 37,* 219–222.

Dawson, G., & Osterling, J. (1997). Early intervention in autism. In M. J. Guralnick (Ed.), *The effectiveness of early intervention* (pp. 307–326). Baltimore: Brookes.

Dean, P. (2006). Seizures and teens: When emergencies happen, what to do? *Exceptional Parent, 36*(8), 30–33.

DeAvila, E. (1976). Mainstreaming ethnically and linguistically different children: An exercise in paradox or a new approach? In R. I. Jones (Ed.), *Mainstreaming and the minority child* (pp. 93–108). Reston, VA: Council for Exceptional Children.

Deci, E. L., Koestner, R., & Ryan, R. M. (1999). A meta-analytic review of experiments examining the effects of extrinsic rewards on intrinsic motivation. *Psychological Bulletin, 125,* 627–668.

DeFilippo, C. L., Sims, D. G., & Gottermeier, L. (1995). Linking visual and kinesthetic imagery in lipreading instruction. *Journal of Speech and Hearing Research, 38,* 244–256.

deFur, S. (2000). Designing Individualized Education (IEP) Transition Plans. *ERIC Digest* (EDO-EC-00-7). Reston, VA: Council for Exceptional Children/ERIC Clearinghouse on Disabilities and Gifted Education.

Dekker, M., Koot, H., van der Ende, J., & Verhulst, F. (2002). Emotional and behavioral problems in children and adolescents with and without intellectual disability. *Journal of Child Psychology and Psychiatry, 43,* 1087–1098.

DeLacy, M. (2004, June 23). The "No Child" Law's biggest victims? An answer that may surprise. *Education Week, 23*(41), 40.

DeLana, M., Gentry, M.A., & Andrews, J. (2007). The efficacy of ASL/English bilingual education: Considering public schools. *American Annals of the Deaf, 152.*

Delaney, E. M., & Kaiser, A. P. (2001). The effects of teaching parents blended communication and behavior support strategies. *Behavior Disorders, 26,* 93–116.

Delano, M. E. (2007). Improving written language performance of adolescents with Asperger syndrome. *Journal of Applied Behavior Analysis, 40,* 345–351.

De La Paz, S., & Graham, S. (1997). Strategy instruction in planning: Effects on the writing performance and behavior of students with learning difficulties. *Exceptional Children, 63,* 167–181.

Dell, A. G., Newton, D., & Petroff, J. (2008). *Assistive technology in the classroom: Enhancing the school experiences of students with disabilities.* Upper Saddle River, NJ: Merrill/Prentice Hall.

De Martini-Scully, D., Bray, M.A., & Kehle, T. J. (2000). A packaged intervention to reduce disruptive behaviors in general education students. *Psychology in the Schools, 37,* 149–156.

Denham, A., & Lahm, E. A. (2001). Using technology to construct alternate portfolios of students with moderate and severe disabilities. *Teaching Exceptional Children, 33*(5), 10–17.

Denning, C. B., Chamberlain, J.A., & Polloway, E.A. (2000). An evaluation of state guidelines for mental retardation: Focus on definition and classification practices. *Education and Training in Mental Retardation and Developmental Disabilities, 35,* 226–232.

Dennis, R. E., & Giangreco, M. F. (1996). Creating conversation: Reflections on cultural sensitivity in family interviewing. *Exceptional Children, 53,* 103–116.

Dennis, R. E., Williams, W., Giangreco, M. F., & Cloninger, C. J. (1993). Quality of life as context for planning and evaluation of services for people with disabilities. *Exceptional Children, 53,* 499–512.

Deno, S. L. (1985). Curriculum-based measurement: The emerging alternative. *Exceptional Children, 52,* 219–232.

Deno, S. L. (1997). Whether thou goest . . . perspectives on progress monitoring. In J. W. Lloyd, E. J. Kame'enui, & D. Chard (Eds.), *Issues in educating students with disabilities* (pp. 77–99). Mahwah, NJ: Erlbaum.

Deno, S., Maruyama, G., Espin, C., & Cohen, C. (1990). Educating students with mild disabilities in general education classrooms: Minnesota alternatives. *Exceptional Children, 57,* 150–161.

Deshler, D. (2005). *Intervention research and bridging the gap between research and practice.* ERIC Clearinghouse on Disabilities and Gifted Education. Available online: www.ldonline.org/article/5596 [Retrieved June 25, 2007.]

Deshler, D. D., & Lenz, B. K. (1989). The strategies instructional approach. *International Journal of Disability, Development, and Education, 6*(3), 203–244.

Deshler, D. D., & Schumaker, J. B. (1993). Strategy mastery by at-risk students: Not a simple matter. *Elementary School Journal, 94,* 153–157.

Deshler, D. D., & Schumaker, J. B. (2006). *Teaching adolescents with disabilities: Accessing the general education curriculum.* Thousand Oaks, CA: Corwin Press.

Deshler, D. D., Schumaker, J. B., Bulgren, J.A., Lenz, B. K., Jantzen, J., Adams, G., Carnine, D., Grossen, B., Davis, B., & Marquis, J. (2001). Making things easier: Connecting new knowledge to things students already know. *Teaching Exceptional Children, 33*(4), 82–85.

Deshler, D. D., Schumaker, J. B., Lenz, B. K., Bulgren, J.A., Hock, M. F., Knight, J., & Ehren, B. J. (2001). Ensuring content-area learning by secondary students with learning disabilities. *Learning Disabilities Research and Practice, 16,* 96–108.

DeSimone, J. R., & Parmar, R. S. (2006). Middle school math teachers' beliefs about inclusion of students with learning disabilities. *Learning Disabilities Research & Practice, 21,* 98–110.

Detrich, R., Keyworth, R., & States, J. (2007). A roadmap to effective evidence-based education: Building an evidence-based culture. *Journal of Evidence-Based Practices for Schools, 8*(1).

Dettmer, P., Thurston, L. P., & Dyck, N. J. (2005). *Consultation, collaboration, and teamwork for students with special needs* (5th ed.). Boston: Allyn and Bacon.

De Valenzuela, J. S., Copeland, S. R., Huaqing Qi, C., & Park, M. (2006). Examining educational equity: Revisiting the disproportionate representation of minority students in special education. *Exceptional Children, 72,* 425–441.

Dever, R. B. (1988). *Community living skills: A taxonomy.* Washington, DC: American Association on Mental Retardation.

Dewey, J. (1916). *Democracy and education.* New York: Macmillan.

Dias, M. S. (2003). *Hydrocephalus and shunts in the person with spina bifida.* Washington, DC: Spina Bifida Association. [Available online: http://www.sbaa.org/atf/cf/{99DD789C-904D-467E-A2E4-DF1D36E381C0}/fs_hydrocephalus.pdf]

Díaz-Rico, L.T., & Weed, K. Z. (2005). *The cross-cultural, language, and academic development handbook: A complete K–12 reference guide* (3rd ed.). Boston: Allyn & Bacon.

Dib, N., & Sturmey, P. (2007). Reducing student stereotypy by improving teachers' implementation of discrete-trial teaching. *Journal of Applied Behavior Analysis, 40,* 339–343.

DiCarlo, C. F., & Reid, D. H. (2004). Increasing pretend toy play of toddlers with disabilities in an inclusive setting. *Journal of Applied Behavior Analysis, 37,* 197–207.

Dickson, C.A., Deutsch, C. K., Wang, S. S., & Dube, W. V. (2006). Matching-to-sample assessment of stimulus overselectivity in students with intellectual disabilities. *American Journal on Mental Retardation, 111,* 447–453.

Didden, R., Korzilius, H., van Oorsouw, W., & Sturmey, P. (2006). Behavioral treatment of challenging behaviors in individuals with mild mental retardation: Meta-analysis of single-subject research. *American Journal on Mental Retardation, 111,* 290–298.

Diefendorf, A. O. (1999). Screening for hearing loss in infants. *Volta Review, 99*(5), 43–61.

Dieker, L.A. (2002). *Co-teaching lesson plan book: Academic year version.* Arlington, VA: Council for Exceptional Children.

DiGangi, S.A., Maag, J.W., & Rutherford, R. B. (1991). Self-graphing of on-task behavior: Enhancing the reactive effects of self-monitoring on on-task behavior and academic performance. *Learning Disability Quarterly, 14,* 221–230.

Diller, L. H. (1998). *Running on Ritalin.* New York: Bantam.

Dimitropoulos, A., Feurer, I. D., Butler, M. G., & Thompson, T. (2001). Emergence of compulsive behavior and tantrums in children with Prader-Willi syndrome. *American Journal of Mental Retardation, 106,* 39–51.

Dinnebeil, L., & McInerney, W. (2000). Supporting inclusion in community-based settings: The role of the "Tuesday morning teacher." *Young Exceptional Children, 4*(1), 19–26.

Dinnebeil, L.A., McInerney, W., Roth, J., & Ramaswamy, V. (2001). Itinerant early childhood special education services. *Journal of Early Intervention, 21,* 35–44.

Dion, E., Fuchs, D., & Fuchs, L. S. (2005). Differential effects of Peer-Assisted Learning Strategies on students' social preference and friendship making. *Behavioral Disorders, 30,* 421–429.

Dion, E., Fuchs, D., & Fuchs, L. S. (2007). Peer-mediated programs to strengthen classroom instruction: Cooperative learning, reciprocal teaching, classwide peer tutoring, and peer-assisted learning strategies. In L. Flonan (Ed.), *Handbook of special education* (pp. 450–459). London: Sage.

Division for Early Childhood. (2005). *Developmental delay as an eligibility category* [Position statement approved by DEC Executive Board December 2005]. Missoula, MT: Author.

Division for Learning Disabilities. (1993). *Inclusion: What does it mean for students with learning disabilities?* Reston, VA: Author.

Division for Learning Disabilities. (2001). Award-winning researchers raise questions about "inclusion." *DLD Times, 18*(2), 4.

Division for Learning Disabilities. (2007). *Thinking about response to intervention and learning disabilities: A teacher's guide.* Arlington, VA: Author.

Dockrell, J. E., Lindsay, G., Connelly, V., & Mackie, C. (2007). Constraints in the production of written text in children with specific language impairments. *Exceptional Children, 73,* 147–164.

Dockrell, J. E., & Messer, D. (2004). Later vocabulary acquisition. In R. Berman (Ed.), *Language development across childhood and adolescence: Psycholinguistic and crosslinguistic perspectives* (pp. 35–52). Trends in Language Acquisition Research 3. Amsterdam: John Benjamins.

Dodd, A. W. (1996). Involving parents, avoiding gridlock. *Educational Leadership, 53*(7), 50-54.

Dodge, K. (1993). The future of research on conduct disorder. *Development and Psychopathology, 5*(1/2), 311-320.

Dohan, M., & Schulz, H. (1998). The speech-language pathologist's changing role: Collaboration with the classroom. *Journal of Children's Communication Development, 20*, 9-18.

Donley, C. R., & Williams, G. (1997). Parents exhibit children's progress at a poster session. *Teaching Exceptional Children, 29*(4), 46-51.

Donovan, M. S., & Cross, C. T. (Eds.). (2002). *Minority students in special education and gifted education.* Washington, DC: National Academy of Sciences.

Doren, B., Bullis, M., & Benz, M. R. (1996a). Predicting the arrest status of adolescents with disabilities in transition. *Journal of Special Education, 29*, 363-380.

Doren, B., Bullis, M., & Benz, M. R. (1996b). Predictors of victimization experiences of adolescents with disabilities in transition. *Exceptional Children, 63*, 7-18.

Dormans, J. P., & Pellegrino, L. (Eds.). (1998). *Caring for children with cerebral palsy: A team approach.* Baltimore: Brookes.

Dosen, A., & Day, K. (Eds.). (2001). *Treating mental illness and behavior disorders in children and adults with mental retardation.* Washington, DC: American Psychiatric Press.

Douma, J. C. H., Dekker, M. C., de Ruiter, K. P., Tick, N. T., & Koot, H. M. (2007). Antisocial and delinquent behaviors in youths with mild or borderline disabilities. *American Journal on Mental Retardation, 112*, 207-220.

Downing, J. (1999). *Teaching communication skills to students with severe disabilities.* Baltimore: Brookes.

Downing, J. (2000). Augmentative communication services: A critical aspect of assistive technology. *Journal of Special Education Technology, 15*(3), 35-38.

Downing, J. (2005). *Teaching communication skills to students with severe disabilities* (2nd ed.). Baltimore: Brookes.

Downing, J., & Eichinger, J. (1990). Instructional strategies for learners with dual sensory impairments in integrated settings. *Journal of The Association for Persons with Severe Handicaps, 15*, 98-105.

Downing, J. A. (2004). Related services for student with disabilities: Introduction to the special issue. *Intervention in School and Clinic, 39*, 195-208.

Downing, J. E., & Chen, D. (2003). Using tactile strategies with students who are blind and have severe disabilities. *Teaching Exceptional Children, 36*(2), 56-60.

Downing, J. E., & Eichinger, J. (2003). Creating learning opportunities for students with severe disabilities in inclusive classrooms. *Teaching Exceptional Children, 36*(1), 26-31.

Downing, J. E., Spencer, S., & Cavallaro, C. (2004). The development of an inclusive elementary school: Perceptions from stakeholders. *Research and Practice for People with Severe Disabilities, 29*, 11-24.

Doyle, P. M., Wolery, M., Ault, M. J., & Gast, D. L. (1988). System of least prompts: A literature review of procedural parameters. *Journal of The Association for Persons with Severe Handicaps, 13*, 28-40.

Drasgow, E. (1998). American Sign Language as a pathway to linguistic competence. *Exceptional Children, 64*, 329-342.

Drew, C. J., & Hardman, M. L. (2007). *Intellectual disabilities across the lifespan* (9th ed.). Upper Saddle River, NJ: Merrill/Prentice Hall.

Duckworth, S., Smith-Rex, S., Okey, S., Brookshire, M. A., Rawlinson, D., Rawlinson, R., Castillo, S., & Little, J. (2001). Wraparound services for young school children with emotional and behavior disorders. *Teaching Exceptional Children, 33*(4), 54-60.

Dugan, E., Kamps, D., Leonard, B., Watkins, N., Rheinberger, A., & Stackhaus, J. (1995). Effects of cooperative learning groups during social studies for students with autism and fourth-grade peers. *Journal of Applied Behavior Analysis, 28*, 175-188.

Dunlap, G., Clarke, S., Jackson, M., Wright, S., Ramos, E., & Brinson, S. (1995). Self-monitoring of classroom behaviors with students exhibiting emotional and behavioral challenges. *School Psychology Quarterly, 10*, 165-177.

Dunlap, G., Dyer, K., & Koegel, R. L. (1983). Autistic self-stimulation and intertrial interval duration. *American Journal of Mental Deficiency, 88*, 194-204.

Dunlap, G., & Fox, L. (1996). Early intervention and serious problem behavior: A comprehensive approach. In L. K. Koegel, R. L. Koegel, & G. Dunlap (Eds.), *Positive behavioral support: Including people with difficult behavior in the community* (pp. 31-50). Baltimore: Brookes.

Dunlap, G., Strain, P. S., Fox, L., Carta, J. J., Conroy, M., Smith, B. J., Kern, L., Hemmeter, M. L., Timm, M. A., McCart, A., Sailor, W., Markey, U., Markey, D. J., Lardieri, S., & Sowell, C. (2006). Prevention and intervention with young children's challenging behavior: Perspective regarding current knowledge: A review of reviews. *Behavioral Disorders, 32*, 29-45.

Dunn, L. M., & Dunn, L. M. (1997). *Peabody Picture Vocabulary Test—III.* Circle Pines, MN: American Guidance Services.

Dunn-Geier, J., Ho, H. H., Auersberg, E., Doyle, D., Eaves, L., Matsuba, C., et al. (2000). Effects of secretin on children with autism: A randomized controlled trial. *Developmental Medicine and Child Neurology, 42*(12), 796-802.

Dunst, C. (2001). Participation of young children with disabilities in community learning activities. In M. Guralnick (Ed.), *Early childhood inclusion: Focus on change* (pp. 307-333). Baltimore: Brookes.

Dunst, C. J., Trivette, C. M., & Deal, A. G. (1988). *Enabling and empowering families: Principles and guidelines for practice.* Cambridge, MA: Brookline.

DuPaul, G. J., & Stoner, G. (2003). *ADHD in the schools: Assessment and intervention strategies* (2nd ed.). New York: Guilford.

Durand, V. M., & Crimmins, D. (1992). *The Motivation Assessment Scale.* Topeka, KS: Monaco & Associates, Inc.

Dwyer, K. P., Osher, D., & Hoffman, C. C. (2000). Creating responsive schools: Contextualizing early warning, timely response. *Exceptional Children, 66*, 347-365.

Dye, G. A. (2000). Graphic organizers to the rescue! Helping student link—and remember—information. *Teaching Exceptional Children, 32*(3), 72-76.

Dyer, A., MacSweeney, M., Szczerbinksi, M., Green, L., & Campbell, R. (2003). Predictors of reading delay in deaf adolescents: The relative contributions of rapid automatic naming speed and phonological awareness and decoding. *Journal of Deaf Studies and Deaf Education, 8*, 215-229.

Dykens, E. M. (2000). Contaminated and unusual food combinations: What do people with Prader-Willi syndrome choose? *Mental Retardation, 38*, 163-171.

Dykens, E. M., Hodapp, R. M., & Finucane, B. M. (2000). *Genetics and mental retardation syndromes: A new look at behavior and interventions.* Baltimore: Brookes.

Dykens, E. M., & Rosner, B. A. (1999). Refining behavioral phenotypes: Personality-motivation in Williams and Prader-Willi syndromes. *American Journal of Mental Retardation, 104*, 158-169.

Dykes, J. (1992). Opinions of orientation and mobility instructors about using the long cane with preschool-age children. *RE:view, 24*, 85-92.

Dyson, L. (1996). The experiences of families of children with learning disabilities: Parental stress, family functioning, and sibling self-concept. *Journal of Learning Disabilities, 29*(3), 280-286.

Dyson, L., Edgar, E., & Crnic, K. (1989). Psychological predictors of adjustment by siblings of developmentally disabled children. *American Journal of Mental Retardation, 94*, 292-302.

Dzienkowski, R. C., Smith, K. K., Dillow, K. A., & Yucha, C. B. (1996). Cerebral palsy: A comprehensive review. *Nurse Practitioner, 21*(2), 45-59.

Easterbrooks, S. (1999). Improving practices for students with hearing impairments. *Exceptional Children, 65*, 537-554.

Easterbrooks, S. (2006). An examination of twenty literacy, science, and mathematics practices used to educate students who are deaf or hard of hearing. *American Annals of the Deaf, 151*, 385-397.

Easterbrooks, S. R., & Baker, S. K. (2001). Considering the communication needs of students who are deaf or hard of hearing. *Teaching Exceptional Children, 33*(3), 70-76.

Ebanks, M. E., & Fisher, W. W. (2003). Altering the timing of academic prompts to treat destructive behavior maintained by escape. *Journal of Applied Behavior Analysis, 36*, 355-359.

Eber, L., & Keenan, S. (2004). Collaboration with other agencies: Wraparound and systems of care for children and youths with emotional and behavioral disorders. In R. B. Rutherford, M. M. Quinn, &

R. Sathur (Eds.). *Handbook of research in emotional and behavioral disorders* (pp. 503–516). NY: Guilford Press.

Eber, L., Nelson, C. M., & Miles, P. (1997). School-based wraparound for students with emotional and behavioral challenges. *Exceptional Children, 63,* 539–555.

Eberle, L. (1922). The maimed, the halt and the race. Reprinted in R. H. Bremner (Ed.), *Children and youth in America: A documentary history. Vol. 2: 1866–1932* (pp. 1026–1028). Cambridge: Harvard University Press.

Edelbrock, C., Rende, R., Plomin, R., & Thompson, L.A. (1995). A twin study of competence and problem behavior in childhood and early adolescence. *Journal of Child Psychology and Psychiatry, 36,* 775–785.

Eden-Piercy, G. V. S., Blacher, J. B., & Eyman, R. K. (1986). Exploring parents' reactions to their young child with severe handicaps. *Mental Retardation, 24,* 285–291.

Edens, J. F. (1997). Home visitation programs with ethnic minority families: Cultural issues in parent consultation. *Journal of Educational and Psychological Consultation, 8*(4), 373–383.

Edens, R. M., Murdick, N. L., & Gartin, B. C. (2003). Preventing infection in the classroom: The use of universal precautions. *Teaching Exceptional Children, 35*(4), 62–66.

Edwards, L. C. (2007). Children with cochlear implants and complex needs: A review of outcome research and psychological practice. *The Journal of Deaf Studies and Deaf Education, 12,* 258–268.

Ehlers, S., Gillberg, C., & Wing, L. (1999). A screening questionnaire for Asperger syndrome and other high-functioning autism spectrum disorders in school age children. *Journal of Autism and Developmental Disorders, 29,* 129–141.

Ehren, B. J. (2000). Maintaining a therapeutic focus and sharing responsibility for student success: Keys to in-classroom speech-language services. *Language, Speech, and Hearing Services in Schools, 31,* 219–229.

Ehri, L. C. (2005). Learning to read words: Theory, findings, and issues. *Scientific Studies of Reading, 9,* 167–188.

Eikeseth, S., & Lovaas, O. I. (1992). The autistic label and its potentially detrimental effect on the child's treatment. *Journal of Behavioral Therapy and Experimental Psychiatry, 23*(3), 151–157.

Eikeseth, S., Smith, T., Jahr, E., & Eldevik, S. (2002). Intensive behavioral treatment at school for 4- to 7-year-old children with autism: A 1-year comparison controlled study. *Behavior Modification, 26,* 49–68.

Elbaum, B. (2002). The self-concept of students with learning disabilities: A meta-analysis of comparison across different placements. *Learning Disabilities Research and Practice, 17,* 216–226.

Eldredge, J. L. (2005). Foundations of fluency: An exploration. *Reading Psychology, 26,* 161–181.

Elksnin, L. K., & Elksnin, N. (2006). *Teaching social-emotional skills at school and home.* Denver: Love.

Elliot, L., Foster, S., & Stinson, M. (2002). Student study habits using notes from a speech-to-text support service. *Exceptional Children, 69,* 25–40.

Elliot, L., Stinson, M., Francis, P., Coyne, G., & Easton, D. (2003). *What's New with C-Print©?* Paper presented at the Instructional Technology and Education of the Deaf Symposium/National Technical Institute for the Deaf. Rochester, NY. [Available online: https://ritdml.rit.edu/dspace/bitstream/1850/987/32/LElliotPaper06-25-03.pdf]

Elliott, S. N., Huai, N., & Roach, R. T. (2007). Universal and early screening for educational difficulties: Current and future approaches. *Journal of School Psychology, 45,* 137–161.

Ellis, E. S., Deshler, D. D., Lenz, B. K., Schumaker, J. B., & Clark, F. L. (1991). An instructional model for teaching learning strategies. *Focus on Exceptional Children, 24*(1), 1–14.

Ellis, E. S., & Howard, P.W. (2007). Graphic organizers: Power tools for teaching students with learning disabilities. *Current Practice Alerts, Issue 13.* Reston, VA: Division for Learning Disabilities and Division for Research, Council for Exceptional Children. [Available online: www.teachingld.org/ld%5Fresources/alerts/]

Ellis, E. S., Worthington, L. A., & Larkin, M. J. (2002). *Executive summary of the research synthesis on effective teaching principles and the design of quality tools for educators.* [Available online: http://idea.uoregon.edu/-ncite/documents/techrep/tech06.html]

Ellis, N. R. (1963). The stimulus trace and behavior inadequacy. In N. R. Ellis (Ed.), *Handbook of mental deficiency* (pp. 134–158). New York: McGraw-Hill.

Emerson, E. (2003). Prevalence of psychiatric disorders in children and adolescents with and without intellectual disability. *Journal of Intellectual Disability Research, 47,* 51–58.

Emerson, R.W., & Corn, A. L. (2006). Orientation and mobility instructional content for children and youths: A Delphi study. *Journal of Visual Impairment and Blindness, 100,* 331–342.

Emlen, A. C. (1998). *AFS consumer survey: From parents receiving child care assistance.* Portland, OR: Portland State University, Regional Research Institute for Human Services.

Emmorey, K. (2002). *Language, cognition, and the brain: Insights from sign language research.* Mahwah, NJ: Erlbaum.

Engelman, M. D., Griffin, H. C., Griffin, L.W., & Maddox, J. I. (1999). A teacher's guide to communicating with students with deaf-blindness. *Teaching Exceptional Children, 31*(5), 64–70.

Engelmann, S. (1977). Sequencing cognitive and academic tasks. In R. D. Kneedler & S. G. Tarver (Eds.), *Changing perspectives in special education* (pp. 46–61). Upper Saddle River, NJ: Merrill/Prentice Hall.

Engelmann, S. (1997). Theory of mastery and acceleration. In J.W. Lloyd, E. J. Kame'enui,

& D. Chard (Eds.), *Issues in educating students with disabilities* (pp. 177–195). Mahwah, NJ: Erlbaum.

Engelmann, S. (2007). Student-program alignment and teaching to mastery. *Journal of Direct Instruction, 7,* 45–66.

Engelmann, S., & Bruner, E. C. (2008). *Reading mastery signature edition, Grade K.* Columbus, OH: SRA/McGraw-Hill.

Engelmann, S., & Colvin, G. (2006). *Rubric for identifying authentic Direct Instruction programs.* Eugene, OR: Stuff from the Computer of Zig Engelmann. [Available online at: http://www.zigsite.com/]

Engelmann, S., Osborn, J., Bruner, E. C., Engelmann, O., & Davis, K. L. (2002). *Reading mastery plus, level K.* Columbus, OH: SRA/McGraw-Hill.

Englert, C., Raphael, T., Anderson, L., Anthony, H., Stevens, D., & Fear, K. L. (1991). Making writing strategies and self-talk visible: Cognitive strategy instruction in writing in regular and special education classrooms. *American Educational Research Journal, 28,* 337–373.

Englert, C., Tarrant, K. L., Mariage, T. V., & Oxer, T. (1994). Lesson talk as the work of reading groups: The effectiveness of two interventions. *Journal of Learning Disabilities, 27,* 165–186.

Englert, C. S., Wu, X., & Zhao, Y. (2005). Cognitive tools for writing: Scaffolding the performance of students through technology. *Learning Disabilities Research & Practice, 20,* 184–198.

Enright, R. (2000). If life is a journey, make it a joyride: Some tips for young people. *Exceptional Parent, 31*(7), 50–51.

Epilepsy Foundation. (2007). *Treatment options: Medications.* Landover, MD: Author. [Retrieved September 3, 2007. http://www.epilepsyfoundation.org/about/treatment/medications/]

Epstein, M. H. (2004). *Behavioral and Emotional Rating Scale (BERS-2): A strength-based approach to assessment.* Austin, TX: PRO-ED.

Epstein, M. H., Hertzog, M.A., & Reid, R. (2001). The Behavioral and Emotional Rating Scale: Long term test-retest reliability. *Behavioral Disorders, 26,* 314–320.

Epstein, M. H., Kutash, K., & Duchnowski, A. (1998). *Outcomes for children and youth with emotional and behavioral disorders and their families: Programs and evaluation of best practices.* Austin, TX: PRO-ED.

Epstein, M. H., & Sharma, J. (1998). *Behavioral and Emotional Rating Scale.* Austin, TX: PRO-ED.

Erickson, K.A., & Koppenhaver, D.A. (1998). Using the "write talk-nology" with Patrick. *Teaching Exceptional Children, 31*(1), 58–64.

Ericsson, A. (2001). The acquired nature of expert performance: Implications for conceptions of giftedness and innate talent? In N. Colangelo & S. Assouline (Eds.), *Talent development IV: Proceedings from the 1998 Henry B. and Jocelyn Wallace National Research Symposium on Talent Development* (pp. 11–26). Scottsdale, AZ: Great Potential Press.

Ericsson, K. A., & Charness, N. (1994). Expert performance. Its structure and acquisition. *American Psychologist, 49*(8), 725-747.

Ericsson, K. A., Charness, N., Feltovich, P. J., & Hoffman, R. R. (Eds.). (2006). *The Cambridge handbook of expertise and expert performance.* New York: Cambridge University Press.

Ericsson, K. A., Nadogapal, K., & Roring, R. W. (2005). Giftedness from the expert-performance perspective. *Journal for the Education of the Gifted, 28,* 287-311.

Erin, J. N. (2004). *When you have a visually impaired student in your classroom: A guide for teachers.* New York: AFB Press.

Erin, J. N., Dignan, K., & Brown, P. A. (1991). Are social skills teachable? A review of the literature. *Journal of Visual Impairment and Blindness, 85,* 58-61.

Ernst, M., Cohen, R. M., Liebenauer, L. L., Jons, P. H., & Zametkin, A. J. (1997). Cerebral glucose metabolism in adolescent girls with attention-deficit/hyperactivity disorder. *Journal of Child Psychology and Psychiatry, 36,* 1399-1406.

Eshelman, J. W. (2004). *SAFMEDS on the Web: Guidelines and considerations for SAFMEDS.* [Available online: http://members.aol.com/standardcharter/safmeds.html] Retrieved March 24, 2007.

Etscheidt, S. (2006). Behavioral intervention plans: Pedagogical and legal analysis of issues. *Behavioral Disorders, 31,* 223-243.

Etzel-Wise, D., & Mears, B. (2004). Adapted physical education and therapeutic recreation in schools. *Intervention in School and Clinic, 39,* 223-232.

Evans, J. C., & Smith, J. (1993). Nursing planning, intervention, and evaluation for altered neurologic function. In D. B. Jackson & R. B. Saunders (Eds.), *Child health nursing: A comprehensive approach to the care of children and their health* (pp. 1353-1430). Philadelphia: Lippincott.

Everson, J. M., Ivester, J., & Guillory, J. D. (2008). Using interagency and interdisciplinary teams to enhance transition services. In F. R. Rusch (Ed.). *Beyond high school: Preparing adolescents for tomorrow's challenges* (2nd ed.) (pp. 136-159). Upper Saddle River, NJ: Merrill/Prentice Hall.

Ewolt, C. (1996). Deaf bilingualism: A holistic perspective. *Australian Journal of the Education of the Deaf, 2,* 5-9.

Fahsl, A. J. (2007). Mathematics accommodations for all students. *Intervention in School and Clinic, 42,* 198-203.

Fairbanks, S., Sugai, G., Guardino, D., & Lathrop, M. (2007). Response to intervention: Examining classroom behavior support in second grade. *Exceptional Children, 73,* 288-310.

Fairweather, J. S., & Shaver, D. M. (1991). Making the transition to postsecondary education and training. *Exceptional Children, 57,* 264-270.

Farlow, L. J., & Snell, M. E. (1994). *Making the most of student performance data.* Washington, DC: American Association on Mental Retardation.

Farlow, L. J., & Snell, M. E. (2006). Teaching self-care skills. In M. E. Snell & F. Brown (Eds.), *Instruction of students with severe disabilities* (6th ed.) (pp. 328-374). Upper Saddle River, NJ: Merrill/Prentice Hall.

Farrington, D. P. (1995). The development of offending and antisocial behavior from childhood: Key findings from the Cambridge Study in Delinquent Development. *Journal of Child Psychology and Psychiatry, 36,* 929-964.

Faw, G. D., Davis, P. K., & Peck, C. (1996). Increasing self-determination: Teaching people with mental retardation to evaluate residential options. *Journal of Applied Behavior Analysis, 29,* 173-188.

Feil, E. G, Small, J. W., Forness, S. R., Serna, L. A., Kaiser, A. P., Hancock, T. B., Brooks-Gunn, J., Bryant, D., Kuperschmidt, J., Burchinal M. R., Boyce, C. A., & Lopez, M. L. (2005). Using different measure, informants, and clinical cut-off points to estimate prevalence of emotional or behavior disorders in preschoolers: Effects on age, gender, and ethnicity. *Behavioral Disorders, 30,* 375-391.

Feinberg, E., & Vacca, J. (2000). The drama and trauma of creating public policies on autism: Critical issues to consider in the new millennium. *Focus on Autism and Other Developmental Disabilities, 15*(3), 130-137.

Feiner, S. K. (2002). Augmented reality: A new way of seeing. *Scientific American, 286*(4), 48-55.

Feingold, B. F. (1975). *Why your child is hyperactive.* New York: Random House.

Feingold, B. F. (1976). Hyperkinesis and learning disabilities linked to ingestion of artificial food colors and flavorings. *Journal of Learning Disabilities, 9,* 551-559.

Feldhusen, J. F. (1995). Talent development: The new direction in gifted education. *Roeper Review, 18,* 92.

Feldhusen, J. F. (2001). *Talent development in gifted education.* ERIC Digest E610. Arlington, VA: ERIC Clearinghouse on Disabilities and Gifted Education.

Feldhusen, J. F., & Moon, S. (1995). The educational continuum and delivery of services. In J. L. Genshaft, M. Bireley, & C. L. Hollinger (Eds.), *Serving gifted and talented students: A resource for school personnel* (pp. 103-121). Austin, TX: PRO-ED.

Feldman, D., Kinnison, L., Jay, R., & Harth, R. (1983). The effects of differential labeling on professional concepts and attitudes toward the emotionally disturbed/behaviorally disordered. *Behavioral Disorders, 8,* 191-198.

Ferguson, D. L. (1994). Is communication really the point? Some thoughts on interventions and membership. *Mental Retardation, 1,* 7-18.

Ferguson, D. L., & Baumgart, D. (1991). Partial participation revisited. *Journal of The Association for Persons with Severe Handicaps, 16,* 218-227.

Ferguson, H., Myles, B. S., & Hagiwara, T. (2005). Using a personal digital assistant to enhance the independence of an adolescent with Asperger syndrome. *Education and Training in Developmental Disabilities, 40,* 60-67.

Ferguson, P. M. (2003). A place in the family: An historical interpretation of research on parental reactions to having a child with a disability. *Journal of Special Education, 36,* 124-130.

Ferguson, P. M., & Ferguson, D. L. (2006). The promise of adulthood. In M. E. Snell & F. Brown (Eds.), *Instruction of students with severe disabilities* (6th ed.). Upper Saddle River, NJ: Merrill/Prentice Hall.

Ferrell, K. A. (1996). Your child's development. In M. C. Holbrook (Ed.), *Children with visual impairments: A parents' guide* (pp. 73-96). Bethesda, MD: Woodbine House.

Ferrell, K. A. (2007). *Range of estimates of severely visually impaired children.* New York: American Foundation for the Blind. Retrieved November 25, 2007 http://www.afb.org/Section.asp?SectionID=3&TopicID=138&DocumentID=3349

Ferrell, K. A., & Muir, D. W. (1996). A call to end vision stimulation training. *Journal of Visual Impairments and Blindness, 90,* 364-366.

Ferro, J., Foster-Johnson, L., & Dunlap, G. (1996). Relations between curricular activities and problem behaviors of students with mental retardation. *American Journal on Mental Retardation, 101,* 184-194.

Fiala, C. L., & Sheridan, S. M. (2003). Parent involvement and reading: Using curriculum-based measurement to assess the effects of paired reading. *Psychology in the Schools, 40,* 613-626.

Fidler, D. J., Hepburn, S. L., Mankin, G., & Rogers, S. J. (2005). Praxis skills in young children with Down syndrome, other developmental disabilities, and typically developing children. *American Journal on Occupational Therapy, 59,* 129-138.

Fidler, D. J., Hepburn, S. L., Most, D. E., Philofsky, A., & Rogers, S. J. (2007). Emotional responsivity in young children with Williams syndrome. *American Journal on Mental Retardation, 110,* 312-322.

Fidler, D. J., Philofsky, A., Hepburn, S. L., & Rogers, S. J. (2005). Nonverbal requesting and problem-solving by toddlers with Down syndrome. *American Journal on Mental Retardation, 110,* 312-322.

Fiedler, C. R., Simpson, R. L., & Clark, D. M. (2007). *Parents and families of children with disabilities: Effective school-based support services.* Upper Saddle River, NJ: Merrill/Prentice Hall.

Field, K. (2004, July 9). Battling the image of "a nerd's profession": Universities devise programs to lure more students to engineering. *Chronicle of Higher Education, 50*(44), A15.

Field, S., Martin, J., Miller, R., Ward, M., & Wehmeyer, M. L. (1998). *A practical guide for teaching self-determination.* Reston, VA: Council for Exceptional Children.

Figueroa, R. A. (1989). Psychological testing of linguistic-minority students: Knowledge gaps and regulations. *Exceptional Children, 56,* 145-152.

Filipek, P. A., Accardo, P., Ashwal, S., Baranek, G., Cook, E., Dawson, G., et al. (2000). Practice parameter: Screening and diagnosis of autism. *Neurology, 55,* 468-477.

Filipek, P. A., Semrud-Clikmann, M., Steingard, R. J., Renshaw, P. F., Kennedy, D. N., & Biederman, J. (1997). Volumetric MRI analysis comparing subject having attention-deficit/hyperactivity disorder with normal controls. *Neurology, 48,* 589-601.

Finn, C. E., Rotherham, A. J., & Hokanson, C. R., Jr. (Eds.). (2001). *Rethinking special education for a new century.* Washington, DC: Thomas B. Fordham Foundation and the Progressive Policy Institute.

Firth, U. (2003). *Autism: Explaining the enigma* (2nd ed.). Malden, MA: Blackwell Publishing.

Fish, T., Rabidoux, P., Ober, J., & Graff, V. L. W. (2006). Community literacy and friendship model for people with intellectual disabilities. *Mental Retardation, 44,* 443-446.

Fisher, C. S., Berliner, C. D., Filby, N. N., Marliave, R., Cahen, L. S., & Dishaw, M. M. (1980). Teaching behaviors, academic learning time, and student achievement. In C. Denham & A. Lieberman (Eds.), *Time to learn* (pp. 7-22). Washington, DC: National Institute of Education.

Fisher, C. W., & Berliner, D. C. (Eds.). (1985). *Perspectives on instructional time.* New York: Longman.

Fisher, D., & Ryndak, D. L. (Eds.). (2001). *The foundations of inclusive education: A compendium of articles on effective strategies to achieve inclusive education.* Baltimore: The Association for Persons with Severe Handicaps.

Fisher, M., & Meyer, L. H. (2002). Development and social competence after two years for students enrolled in inclusive and self-contained educational programs. *Research and Practice for People with Severe Disabilities, 27,* 165-174.

Fisher, W., Piazza, C. C., Bowman, L. G., Hagopian, L. P., Owens, J. C., & Slevin, I. (1992). A comparison of two approaches for identifying reinforcers for persons with severe and profound disabilities. *Journal of Applied Behavior Analysis, 25,* 491-498.

Fitzgerald, J. L., & Watkins, M. W. (2006). Parents' rights in special education: The readability of procedural safeguards. *Exceptional Children, 72,* 497-510.

FitzSimmons, S. C. (1993). The changing epidemiology of cystic fibrosis. *Journal of Pediatrics, 122,* 1-9.

Flaherty, E., & Glidden, L. M. (2000). Positive adjustment in parents rearing children with Down syndrome. *Early Education and Development, 11,* 407-422.

Flaute, A. J., Peterson, S. M., Van Norman, R. K., Riffle, T., & Eakins, A. (2005). Motivate me! 20 tips for using a MotivAider® for improving your classroom. *Teaching Exceptional Children Plus, 2*(2) Article 3. Retrieved July 3. 2006. http://escholarship.bc.edu/education/tecplus/vol2/iss2/art3<P

Fleischmann, A. (2004). Narratives published on the Internet by parents of children with autism: What do they reveal and why is it important? *Focus on Autism and Other Developmental Disabilities, 19,* 25-43.

Flener, B. S. (1993). The consultative-collaborative teacher for students with visual handicaps. *RE:view, 25,* 173-182.

Fletcher, J. M., Lyon, G. R., Barnes, M., Stuebing, K. K., Francis, D. J., Olson, R. K., Shaywitz, S. E., & Shaywitz, B. A. (2002). Classification of learning disabilities: An evidence-based evaluation. In R. Bradley, L. Danielson, & D. P. Hallahan (Eds.), *Identification of learning disabilities: Research to practice* (pp. 185-250). Mahwah, NJ: Erlbaum.

Fletcher, J. M., Shaywitz, S. E., Shankweiler, D. P., Katz, L., Liberman, I. Y., Fowler, A., Francis, D. J., Stuebing, K. K., & Shaywitz, B. A. (1994). Cognitive profiles of reading disability: Comparisons of discrepancy and low achievement definitions. *Journal of Educational Psychology, 86,* 1-18.

Flexer, R. W., Simmons, T. J., Luft, P., & Baer, R. M. (2008). *Transition planning for secondary students with disabilities* (3rd ed.). Upper Saddle River, NJ: Merrill/Prentice Hall.

Flick, G. L. (2000). *How to reach & teach teenagers with ADHD.* West Nyack, NY: Center for Applied Research in Education.

Flora, S. R. (2004). *The power of reinforcement.* Albany: State University of New York Press.

Flora, S. R. (2007). *Taking America off drugs: Why behavioral therapy is more effective for treating ADHD, OCD, depressions, and other psychological problems.* Ithaca, NY: SUNY Press.

Florian, L., Hollenweger, J., Simeonsson, R. J., Wedell, K., Riddell, S., Terzi, L., & Holland, A. (2006). Cross-cultural perspectives on the classification of children with disabilities: Part I. Issues in the classification of children with disabilities. *The Journal of Special Education, 40,* 36-45.

Florian, V., & Findler, L. (2001). Mental health and marital adaptation of mothers of children with cerebral palsy. *American Journal of Orthopsychiatry, 71,* 358-367.

Flynn, J. R. (1987). WAIS-III and WISC-III: IQ gains in the United States from 1972 to 1995: How to compensate for obsolete norms. *Perceptual & Motor Skills, 86,* 1231-1239.

Flynn, J. R. (1998). Massive IQ gains in 14 nations: What intelligence tests really measure. *Psychological Bulletin, 95,* 29-51.

Flynn, J. R. (2000). The hidden history of IQ and special education: Can the problems be solved? *Psychology, Public Policy, and Law, 6,* 191-198.

Foil, C. R., & Alber, S. R. (2002). Fun and effective ways to build your students' vocabulary. *Intervention in School and Clinic, 37,* 131-139.

Foley, K., & Seknandore, O. (2003). Gifted education for the Native American student. In J. A. Castellano (Ed.), *Special populations in gifted education: Working with diverse gifted learners* (pp. 117-118). Boston: Allyn & Bacon.

Fombonne, E. (1999). The epidemiology of autism: A review. *Psychological Medicine, 29,* 769-786.

Fombonne, E. (2003). The prevalence of autism. *Journal of the American Medical Association, 289*(1), 87-89.

Foorman, B., Francis, D., Fletcher, J., Schatschneider, C., & Mehta, P. (1998). Early interventions for children with reading problems: Study designs and preliminary findings. *Journal of Educational Psychology, 90*(1), 1-12.

Foorman, B. R. (2007). Primary prevention in classroom reading instruction. *Teaching Exceptional Children, 39*(5), 24-30.

Ford, B. A. (2000). *Multiple voices for ethnically diverse exceptional learners, 2000.* Reston, VA: Council for Exceptional Children.

Ford, D. Y. (1998). The underrepresentation of minority students in gifted education. *Journal of Special Education, 32*(1), 4-14.

Ford, D. Y. (2004a). *Intelligence testing and cultural diversity: Concerns, cautions, and considerations.* Storrs, CT: National Research Center on the Gifted and Talented.

Ford, D. Y. (2004b). A challenge for culturally diverse families of gifted children: Forced choices between achievement or affiliation. *Gifted Child Today, 27*(3), 26-27, 65.

Ford, D. Y. (2007). Recruiting and retaining gifted students from diverse ethnic, cultural, and language groups. In J. A. Banks & C. A. M. Banks (Eds.), *Multicultural education: Issues and perspectives* (6th ed.) (pp. 401-421). New York: John Wiley & Sons.

Ford-Harris, D., Alber, S. R., & Heward, W. L. (1998). Setting "motivation traps" for underachieving gifted students. *Gifted Child Today, 21*(2), 28-30, 32-33.

Forest, M., & Lusthaus, E. (1990). Everyone belongs with the MAPS Action Planning System. *Teaching Exceptional Children, 22*(2), 32-35.

Forgatch, M. S., & Paterson, G. R. (1998). Behavioral family therapy. In F. M. Dattilo (Ed.), *Case studies in couple and family therapy: Systematic and cognitive perspectives* (pp. 85-107). New York: Guilford.

Forness, S. R., & Kavale, K. A. (2000). Emotional or behavior disorders: Background and current status of the E/BD terminology and definition. *Behavioral Disorders, 25,* 264-269.

Forness, S. R., & Kavale, K. A. (in press). Impact of ADHD on school systems. In P. S. Jensen & J. R. Cooper (Eds.). Bethesda, MD: National Institutes of Health.

Forness, S. R., Kavale, K. A., Crenshaw, T. M., & Sweeney, D. P. (2000). Best practice in treating children with ADHD: Does not using medication in a comprehensive intervention program verge on malpractice? *Beyond Behavior, 10*(2), 4-7.

Forness, S., & Knitzer, J. (1992). A new proposed definition and terminology to replace "serious emotional disturbance" in the Individuals with Disabilities Education Act. *School Psychology Review, 21,* 12-20.

Foster, S., & Cue, K. (2007, April). *Roles and responsibilities of itinerant specialist teachers of deaf and hard of hearing students*. Paper presented at the annual conference of the American Educational Research Association, Chicago, IL.

Fowler, C. H., Konrad, M., Walker, A. R., Test, D. W., & Wood, W. M. (2007). Self-determination interventions' effects on the academic performance of students with developmental disabilities. *Education and Training in Developmental Disabilities, 42,* 270-285.

Fowler, S. A., Donegan, M., Lueke, B., Hadden, D. S., & Phillips, B. (2000). Evaluating community collaboration in writing interagency agreements on the age 3 transition. *Exceptional Children, 67,* 35-50.

Fowler, S. A., Dougherty, S. B., Kirby, K. C., & Kohler, F. W. (1986). Role reversals: An analysis of therapeutic effects achieved with disruptive boys during their appointments as peer monitors. *Journal of Applied Behavior Analysis, 19,* 437-444.

Fowler, S. A., Schwartz, I., & Atwater, J. (1991). Perspectives on the transition from preschool to kindergarten for children with disabilities and their families. *Exceptional Children, 58,* 136-145.

Fox, J., Shores, R., Lindeman, D., & Strain, P. (1986). Maintaining social initiations of withdrawn handicapped and nonhandicapped preschoolers through a response-dependent fading tactic. *Journal of Abnormal Child Psychology, 14,* 387-396.

Fox, L., Vaughn, B. J., Wyatte, M. L., & Dunlap, G. (2002). "We can't expect other people to understand": Family perspectives on problem behavior. *Exceptional Children, 68,* 437-450.

Fox, W., & Gay, G. (1995). Integrating multicultural and curriculum principles in teacher education. *Principles in Teacher Education, 70*(3), 64-82.

Foy, C. J., Von Scheden, M., & Waiculonis, J. (1992). The Connecticut pre-cane: Case study and curriculum. *Journal of Visual Impairment and Blindness, 86,* 178-181.

Frame, M. J. (2000). The relationship between visual impairment and gestures. *Journal of Visual Impairments and Blindness, 94,* 155-171.

Frank, A. R., & Sitlington, P. L. (1993). Graduates with mental disabilities: The story three years later. *Education and Training in Mental Retardation, 28,* 30-37.

Frank, A. R., & Sitlington, P. L. (2000). Young adults with mental disabilities—Does transition planning make a difference? *Education and Training in Mental Retardation and Developmental Disabilities, 35,* 119-134.

Frankenberger, W., & Cannon, C. (1999). Effects of Ritalin on academic achievement from first to fifth grade. *International Journal of Disability, Development, and Education, 46,* 199-221.

Frankenburg, W. K., & Dodds, J. B. (1990). *The Denver II training manual*. Denver: Denver Developmental Materials.

Frasier, M. (1991). Disadvantaged and culturally diverse gifted students. *Journal for the Education of the Gifted, 14,* 234-245.

Frasier, M., Garcia, J., & Passow, A. (1995). *A review of assessment issues in gifted education and their implications for identifying gifted minority students*. Storrs: University of Connecticut, National Research Center on the Gifted and Talented. (Research Monopoly RM95204).

Frasier, M., Hunsaker, S., Lee, J., Mitchell, S., Cramond, B., Krisel, S., Garcia, J., Martin, D., Frank, E., & Finley, S. (1995). *Core attributes of giftedness: A foundation for recognizing the gifted potential of minority and economically disadvantaged students*. Storrs: University of Connecticut, National Research Center on the Gifted and Talented.

Freeman, F., & Alkin, M. (2000). Academic and social attainments of children with mental retardation in general education and special education settings. *Remedial and Special Education, 21,* 3-18.

Frey, G. C., Buchanan, A. M., & Rosser Sandt, D. D. (2005). "I'd rather watch TV": An examination of physical activity in adults with mental retardation. *Mental Retardation, 43,* 241-254.

Frey, K. S., Fewell, R. R., & Vadasy, P. F. (1989). Parental adjustment and changes in child outcomes among families of young handicapped children. *Topics in Early Childhood Special Education, 8*(4), 38-57.

Friedman Narr, R. A. (2006). Teaching phonological awareness with deaf and hard-of-hearing students. *Teaching Exceptional Children, 38*(4), 53-58.

Friend, M., & Bursuck, W. D. (2006). *Including students with special needs: A practical guide for classroom teachers* (4th ed.). Needham Heights, MA: Allyn & Bacon.

Friend, M., & Cook, L. (2007). *Interactions: Collaboration skills for school professionals* (5th ed.). Boston: Allyn & Bacon.

Friend, M., & Hurley-Chamberlain, D. (2006, December 21). Is co-teaching effective? *CEC Today*. Downloaded April 6, 2007 at: http://www.cec.sped.org/AM/Template.cfm?Section=Home&TEMPLATE=/CM/ContentDisplay.cfm&CONTENTID=7504

Friman, P. C., & Poling, A. (1995). Making life easier with effort: Basic findings and applied research on response effort. *Journal of Applied Behavior Analysis, 28,* 538-590.

Frisk, D. (2006). Don't give up: Navigating the financial jungle of funding sources. *Exceptional Parent, 36*(11), 32-34.

Frost, L., & Bondy, A. (2002). *The Picture Exchange Communication System (PECS) training manual* (2nd ed.). Newark, DE: Pyramid Products.

Frostig, M., & Horne, D. (1973). *The Frostig program for the development of visual perception* (rev. ed.). Chicago: Follett.

Frostig, M., Lefever, D. W., & Whittlesey, J. R. B. (1964). *The Marianne Frostig development test of visual perception*. Palo Alto, CA: Consulting Psychologists Press.

Frueh, E. (2007). *Back to school: Creating a safe and supporting school environment for kids with epilepsy*. Landover, MD: Epilepsy Foundation. [Retrieved September 2, 2007. http://www.epilepsyfoundation.org/living/back-to-school-2007.cfm]

Fryxell, D., & Kennedy, C. H. (1995). Placement along the continuum of services and its impact on students' social relationships. *Journal of The Association for Persons with Severe Handicaps, 20,* 259-269.

Fuchs, D., & Deshler, D. D. (2007). What we need to know about responsiveness to intervention (and shouldn't be afraid to ask). *Learning Disabilities Research & Practice, 22,* 129-136.

Fuchs, D., & Fuchs, L. S. (1994). Inclusive schools movement and the radicalization of special education reform. *Exceptional Children, 60,* 294-309.

Fuchs, D., & Fuchs, L. S. (1998). Researchers and teachers working together to adapt instruction for diverse learners. *Learning Disabilities Research and Practice, 13,* 126-137.

Fuchs, D., Fuchs, L. S., Bahr, M. W., Fernstrom, P., & Stecker, P. (1990). Prereferral intervention: A prescriptive approach. *Exceptional Children, 56,* 493-513.

Fuchs, D., Fuchs, L. S., Fernstrom, P., & Hohn, M. (1991). Toward a responsible reintegration of behaviorally disordered students. *Behavioral Disorders, 16,* 133-147.

Fuchs, D., Fuchs, L. S., Mathes, P. G., & Simmons, D. C. (1996). *Peer-assisted learning strategies in reading: A manual*. (Available from Box 328 Peabody, Vanderbilt University, Nashville, TN 37203.)

Fuchs, D., Fuchs, L. S., Mathes, P. G., Lipsey, M. W., & Roberts, P. H. (2002). Is "learning disabilities" just a fancy term for low achievement?: A meta-analysis of reading differences between low achievers with and without the label. In R. Bradley, L. Danielson, & D. P. Hallahan (Eds.), *Identification of learning disabilities: Research to practice* (pp. 737-762). Mahwah, NJ: Erlbaum.

Fuchs, D., Fuchs, L. S., McMaster, K. N., & Al Otaiba, S. (2003). Identifying children at risk for reading failure: Curriculum-based measurement and the deal-discrepancy approach. In H. L. Swanson, K. R. Harris, & S. Graham (Eds.), *Handbook of learning disabilities* (pp. 431-449). New York: Guilford.

Fuchs, D., Fuchs, L. S., Thompson, A., Svenson, E., Yen, L., Al Otaiba, S., Yang, N., McMaster, K. N., Prentice, K., Kazdan, S., & Saenz, L. (2001). Peer-assisted learning strategies in reading: Extension for kindergarten, first grade, and high school. *Remedial and Special Education, 22,* 15-21.

Fuchs, D., & Young, C. L. (2006). On the irrelevance of intelligence in predicting responsiveness to reading instruction. *Exceptional Children, 73*(1), 8-30.

Fuchs, L. S., & Fuchs, D. (1996). Combining performance assessment and curriculum-based measurement to strengthen instructional planning. *Learning Disabilities Research and Practice, 11*(3), 183-192.

Fuchs, L. S., & Fuchs, D. (2001). Principles for the prevention and intervention of mathematics disabilities. *Learning Disabilities Research and Practice, 16,* 85-95.

Fuchs, L. S., & Fuchs, D. (2003). Enhancing the mathematical problem solving of students with mathematics disabilities. In H. L. Swanson, K. R. Harris, & S. Graham (Eds.), *Handbook of learning disabilities* (pp. 306-322). New York: Guilford.

Fuchs, L. S., & Fuchs, D. (2005). Responsiveness-to-intervention: A blueprint for practitioners, policymakers, and parents. *Teaching Exceptional Children, 38*(1), 57-61.

Fuchs, L. S., & Fuchs, D. (2007a). A model for implementing responsiveness to intervention. *Teaching Exceptional Children, 39*(5), 14-20.

Fuchs, L. S., & Fuchs, D. (2007b). *What is scientifically-based research on progress monitoring?* Washington, DC: National Center on Student Progress Monitoring. Available online: http://www. studentprogress.org/library/articles. asp#ann

Fuchs, L. S., Fuchs, D., Compton, D. L., Bryant, J. D., Hamlett, C. L., & Seethaler, P. M. (2007). Mathematics screening and progress monitoring at first grade: Implications for responsiveness to intervention. *Exceptional Children, 73,* 311-330.

Fuchs, L. S., Fuchs, D., Hamlett, C. L., & Steecker, P. M. (1991). Effects of curriculum-based measurement and consultation on teacher planning and student achievement in mathematics operations. *American Educational Research Journal, 28,* 617-641.

Fuchs, L. S., Fuchs, D., & Hollenbeck, K. N. (2007). Extending responsiveness to intervention to mathematics at first and third grade. *Learning Disabilities Research & Practice, 22,* 13-24.

Fuchs, L. S., Fuchs, D., & Kazdan, S. (1999). Effects of peer-assisted learning strategies on high school students with serious reading problems. *Remedial and Special Education, 20,* 309-318.

Fujiura, G. T. (2003). Continuum of intellectual disabilities: Demographic evidence for the "forgotten generation." *Mental Retardation, 41,* 420-429.

Fujiura, G. T., & Yamaki, K. (2000). Trends in demography of childhood poverty and disability. *Exceptional Children, 66,* 187-199.

Fujiura, J. E., & Yamaki, K. (1997). Analysis of ethnic variations in developmental disability prevalence and household economic status. *Mental Retardation, 35,* 286-294.

Fuller, M. L. (2008). Poverty: The enemy of children and families. In G. Olsen & M. L. Fuller (Eds.), *Home-school relations: Working successfully with parents and families* (pp. 271-285). Boston: Allyn and Bacon.

Furlong, M. J., Morrison, G. M., & Jimerson, S. (2004). Externalizing behaviors of aggression and violence in the school context. In R. B. Rutherford, M. M. Quinn, & S. R. Mathur (Eds.), *Handbook of research in emotional and behavioral disorders* (pp. 243-261). New York: Guilford.

Furth, H. G. (1973). *Deafness and learning: A psychosocial approach.* Belmont, CA: Wadsworth.

Gabel, S. (2004). South Asian Indian cultural orientations toward mental retardation. *Mental Retardation, 42,* 12-25.

Gadow, K. D., & Nolan, E. E. (1993). Practical considerations in conducting school-based medication evaluations for children with hyperactivity. *Journal of Emotional and Behavioral Disorders, 1,* 118-126.

Gagné, F. (2000). Understanding the complex choreography of talent development through DMGT-based analysis. In K. A. Heller, F. J. Monks, R. J. Sternberg, & R. Subotnik (Eds.), *International handbook for research on giftedness and talent* (2nd ed.), (pp. 67-79). Oxford: Paragon.

Gagné, F. (2003). Transforming gifts into talents: The DMGT as a developmental theory. In N. Colangelo & G. A. Davis (Eds.), *Handbook of gifted education* (3rd ed.), (pp. 60-74). Needham Heights, MA: Allyn & Bacon.

Gagnon, J. C., & Maccini, P. (2001). Preparing students with disabilities for algebra. *Teaching Exceptional Children, 34*(1), 8-15.

Gajar, A., Goodman, L., & McAfee, J. (1993). *Secondary schools and beyond: Transition of individuals with mild disabilities.* Upper Saddle River, NJ: Merrill/Prentice Hall.

Galaburda, A. M. (2005). Neurology of learning disabilities: What will the future bring? The answer comes from the successes of the recent past. *Learning Disability Quarterly, 28,* 107-109.

Gallagher, D. J., Heshusius, L., Iano, R. P., & Skrtic, T. M. (2004). *Challenging orthodoxy in special education: Dissenting voices.* Denver, CO: Love Publishing.

Gallagher, J. J. (1984). The evolution of special education concepts. In B. Blatt & R. J. Morris (Eds.), *Perspectives in special education: Personal orientations* (pp. 210-232). Glenview, IL: Scott, Foresman.

Gallagher, J. J., (2004). No Child Left Behind and gifted education. *Roeper Review, 26*(3), 121-123.

Gallagher, P. A., Floyd, J. H., Stafford, A. M., Taber, T. A., Brozovic, S. A., & Alberto, P. A. (2000). Inclusion of students with moderate and severe disabilities in educational and community settings: Perspectives from parents and siblings. *Education and Training in Mental Retardation and Developmental Disabilities, 35,* 135-147.

Gallagher, P. A., & Lambert, R. G., (2006). Classroom quality, concentration of children with special needs, and child outcomes in Head Start. *Exceptional Children, 73,* 31-52.

Gallaudet Research Institute. (December 2005). *Regional and national summary report of data from the 2004-2005 annual survey of deaf and hard of hearing children and youth.* Washington, DC: GRI, Gallaudet University.

Gallaudet University. (1998). *1996-1997 annual survey of deaf and hard-of-hearing children and youth.* Washington, DC: Gallaudet University, Center for Assessment and Demographic Studies.

Gallivan-Fenlon, A. (1994). Integrated transdisciplinary teams. *Teaching Exceptional Children, 26*(3), 16-20.

Ganz, J. B., & Sigafoos, J. (2005). Self-monitoring: Are young adults with MR and autism able to utilize cognitive strategies independently? *Education and Training in Developmental Disabilities, 40,* 24-33.

Garay, S. V. (2003). Listening to the voices of deaf students: Essential transition issues. *Teaching Exceptional Children, 35*(4), 44-48.

Garber, H., & Heber, R. (1973). *The Milwaukee Project: Early intervention as a technique to prevent mental retardation* [Technical paper]. Storrs: University of Connecticut.

Gardner, H. (1983/1994). *Frames of mind: The theory of multiple intelligences.* New York: Basic Books.

Gardner, H. (1999). *Intelligence reframed: Multiple intelligences for the 21st century.* New York: Basic Books.

Gardner, H. (2000). *Intelligence reframed: Multiple intelligences for the 21st century.* New York: Basic Books.

Gardner, H. (2006). *Multiple intelligences: New horizons in theory and practice.* New York: Basic Books.

Gardner, R., III, Cartledge, G., Seidl, B., Woolsey, M. L., Schley, G. S., & Utley, C. A. (2001). Mt. Olivet after-school program. *Remedial and Special Education, 22,* 22-33.

Gardner, R., III, Heward, W. L., & Grossi, T. A. (1994). Effects of response cards on student participation and academic achievement: A systematic replication with inner-city students during whole-class science instruction. *Journal of Applied Behavior Analysis, 27,* 63-71.

Gardner, R., III, Nobel, M. M., Hessler, T., Yawn, C. D., & Heron, T. E. (2007). Tutoring system innovations: Past practice to future prototypes. *Intervention in School and Clinic, 43*(2), 71-81.

Garrick Duhaney, L. M. (2003). A practical approach to managing the behaviors of students with ADD. *Intervention in School and Clinic, 38,* 267-279.

Garrick Duhaney, L. M., & Salend, S. (2000). Parental perceptions of inclusive educational placement. *Remedial and Special Education, 21,* 121-128.

Garten, B. C., Rumrill, P., & Serebreni, R. (1996). The higher education transition model: Guidelines for facilitating college transition among college-bound students with disabilities. *Teaching Exceptional Children, 29*(3), 30-33.

Gartland, D. (1993). Elementary teacher-parent partnerships: Effective communication strategies. *LD Forum, 18*(3), 40-42.

Garton, A., & Pratt, C. (1998). *Learning to be literate: The development of spoken and written language.* Oxford: Blackwell.

Geary, D. C. (2004). Mathematics and learning disabilities. *Journal of Learning Disabilities, 37,* 4-15.

Gelb, S. A. (1997). The problem of typological thinking in mental retardation. *Mental Retardation, 35,* 448-457.

Gena, A., Couloura, S., & Kymissis, E. (in press). Modifying the affective behavior of preschoolers with autism using in-vivo or video modeling and reinforcement contingencies. *Journal of Autism and Developmental Disorders*.

Genesee, R., Lindholm-Leary, K., Saunders, W., & Christian, D. (2006). English language learners in U. S. schools: An overview of research findings. *Journal of Education for Students Placed at Risk, 10*, 363-385.

Gense, M. H., & Gense, D. J. (1994). Identifying autism in children with blindness and visual impairments. *RE:view, 26*, 55-62.

Genshaft, J. L., Greenbaum, S., & Borovosky, S. (1995). Stress and the gifted. In J. L. Genshaft, M. Bireley, & C. L. Hollinger (Eds.), *Serving gifted and talented students: A resource for school personnel* (pp. 257-268). Austin, TX: PRO-ED.

Gentry, M. (2006). No Child Left Behind: Neglecting excellence. *Roeper Review, 29*(1), 24-27.

German, S. L., Martin, J. E., Huber Marshall, L., & Sale, R. P. (2000). Promoting self-determination: Using Take Action to teach goal attainment. *Career Development for Exceptional Individuals, 23*, 27-38.

Gersten, R. (1998). Recent advances in instructional research for students with learning disabilities: An overview. *Learning Disabilities Research and Practice, 13*, 162-170.

Gersten, R. (2001). Sorting out the roles of research in the improvement of practice. *Learning Disabilities Research and Practice, 16*, 45-50.

Gersten, R., Fuchs, L. S., Compton, D., Coyne, M., Greenwood, C., & Innocenti, M. S. (2005). Quality indicators for group experimental and quasi-experimental research in special education. *Exceptional Children, 71*, 149-164.

Geruschat, D. R. & Corn, A. L. (2006). A look back: 100 years of literature on low vision. *Journal of Visual Impairment and Blindness, 100*, 646-671.

Getch, Y., Bhukhanwala, F., & Neuharth-Pritchett, S. (2007). Strategies for helping children with diabetes in elementary and middle schools. *Teaching Exceptional Children, 39*(3), 46-51.

Getch, Y. Q., & Heuharth-Pritchett, S. (1999). Children with asthma: Strategies for educators. *Teaching Exceptional Children, 31*(3), 30-36.

Getty, L. A., & Summey, S. E. (2004). The course of due process. *Teaching Exceptional Children, 36*(3), 40-44.

Giangreco, M. F. (1992). Curriculum in inclusion-oriented schools: Trends, issues, challenges, and potential solutions. In S. Stainback & W. Stainback (Eds.), *Curriculum considerations in inclusive classrooms: Facilitating learning for all students* (pp. 239-263). Baltimore: Brookes.

Giangreco, M. F. (1996). "The stairs don't go anywhere!" A self-advocate's reflections on specialized services and their impact on people with disabilities [Invited interview]. *Physical Disabilities and Related Services, 14*(2), 1-12.

Giangreco, M. F. (2006). Foundational concepts and practices. In M. E. Snell & F. Brown (Eds.), *Instruction of students with severe disabilities* (6th ed., pp. 1-27). Upper Saddle River, NJ: Merrill/Prentice Hall.

Giangreco, M. F. (2007). *Absurdities and realities of special education: The complete digital set*. Minnetonka, MN: Peytral Publications.

Giangreco, M. F., Cloninger, C. J., Dennis, R. E., & Edelman, S. W. (2000). Problem-solving methods to facilitate inclusive education. In R. A. Villa & J. S. Thousand (Eds.), *Restructuring for caring and effective education: Piecing the puzzle together* (2nd ed.), (pp. 293-327). Baltimore: Brookes.

Giangreco, M. F., Cloninger, C. J., & Iverson, V. S. (1998). *Choosing options and accommodations for children: A guide to educational planning for students with disabilities* (2nd ed.). Baltimore: Brookes.

Giangreco, M. F., Dennis, R., Cloninger, C., Edelman, S., & Schattman, R. (1993). "I've counted Jon": Transformational experiences of teachers educating students with disabilities. *Exceptional Children, 59*, 359-372.

Giangreco, M. F., & Doyle, M. B. (2000). Curricular and instructional considerations for teaching students with disabilities in general education classrooms. In S. Wade (Ed.), *Inclusive education: A casebook of readings for prospective and practicing teachers* (Vol. 1), (pp. 51-69). Hillsdale, NJ: Erlbaum.

Giangreco, M. F., & Doyle, M. B. (2002). Students with disabilities and paraprofessional support: Benefits, balance, and Band-Aids. *Focus on Exceptional Children, 34*(7), 1-12.

Giangreco, M. F., & Doyle, M. B. (2007). Quick-guides to inclusion: Ideas for education students with disabilities (2nd ed.). Baltimore: Paul Brookes.

Giangreco, M. F., Edelman, S., & Dennis, R. (1991). Common professional practices that interfere with the integrated delivery of related services. *Remedial and Special Education, 12*(2), 16-24.

Giangreco, M. F., & Meyer, L. H. (1988). Expanding service delivery options in regular schools and classrooms for students with severe disabilities. In J. L. Graden, J. E. Zins, & M. J. Curtis (Eds.), *Alternative educational delivery systems: Enhancing instructional options for all students* (pp. 241-267). Washington, DC: National Association of School Psychologists.

Giangreco, M. F., & Putnam, J. W. (1991). Supporting the education of students with severe disabilities in regular education environments. In L. H. Meyer, C. A. Peck, & L. Brown (Eds.), *Critical issues in the lives of people with severe disabilities* (pp. 245-270). Baltimore: Brookes.

Giangreco, M. F., Yuan, S., McKenzie, B., Cameron, P., & Fialka, J. (2005). "Be careful what you wish for . . . ": Five reasons to be concerned about the assignment of individual paraprofessionals. *Teaching Exceptional Children, 37*(5), 28-34.

Gibb, G. S., & Dyches, T. T. (2007). *Guide to writing quality individualized education programs* (2nd ed.). Boston: Allyn & Bacon.

Giek, K. A. (1992). Monitoring student progress through efficient record keeping. *Teaching Exceptional Children, 24*(3), 22-26.

Gilchrist, E. (1916). The extent to which praise and reproof affect a pupil's work. *School and Society, 4*, 872-874.

Gilger, J. W., Pennington, B. F., & DeFries, J. C. (1992). A twin study of the etiology of comorbidity: Attention deficit-hyperactivity disorder and dyslexia. *Journal of the American Academy of Children and Adolescent Psychiatry, 31*, 343-348.

Gillberg, C. (1995). Clinical child neuropsychiatry, Cambridge: Cambridge University Press.

Gillberg, C., & Wing, L. (1999). Autism: Not an extremely rare disorder. *Acta Psychiatric Scand, 99*(6), 399-406.

Gilliam, J. E. (1995). *The Gilliam autism rating scale*. Austin: PRO-ED.

Gillies, R. M., & Ashman, A. F. (2000). The effects of cooperative learning on students with learning disabilities. *The Journal of Special Education, 34*, 19-27.

Gilmore, D., & Butterworth, J. (1996). *Work status trends for people with mental retardation*. Boston: Institute for Community Inclusion.

Gitlin, L. N., Mount, J., Lucas, W., Weirich, L. C., & Gramberg, L. (1997). The physical costs and psychosocial benefits of travel aids for persons who are visually impaired or blind. *Journal of Visual Impairment and Blindness, 91*, 347-359.

Glaeser, B. C., Pierson, M. R., & Fritschman, N. (2003). Comic strip conversation: A positive behavioral support strategy. *Teaching Exceptional Children, 36*(2), 14-19.

Glassberg, L. A., Hooper, S. R., & Mattison, R. E. (1999). Prevalence of learning disabilities at enrollment in special education students with behavioral disorders. *Behavioral Disorders, 26*, 164-172.

Gleason, J. B. (1999). *The development of language* (4th ed.). Boston: Allyn & Bacon.

Goddard, Y. I., & Heron, T. E. (1998). Please teacher: Help me learn to spell better, teach me self-correction. *Teaching Exceptional Children, 30*(6), 38-43.

Godfrey, S. A., Grisham-Brown, J., Schuster, J. W., & Hemmeter, M. L. (2003). The effects of three techniques on student participation with preschool children with attending problems. *Education and Treatment of Children, 26*, 255-272.

Goin, R. P., Myers, B. J., (2004). Characteristics of infantile autism: Moving toward earlier detection. *Focus on Autism and Other Developmental Disabilities, 19*, 5-12.

Goin-Kochel, R. P., Mackintosh, V. H., & Myers, B. J. (2006). How many doctors does it take to make an autism spectrum diagnosis? *Autism and Other Developmental Disabilities, 10*, 439-451.

Goldberg, D. (1997). *Educating children who are deaf/hard of hearing: Auditory/verbal option*. Reston, VA: ERIC Clearinghouse on Disabilities and Gifted Education. (ERIC Document Reproduction Service No. ED 414 670).

Goldin-Meadow, S. (2003). *The resilience of language: What gesture creation in deaf children can tell us about how all children learn language*. New York: Psychology Press.

Goldman, A. M. (2006). Genes, seizures, and epilepsy. *Exceptional Parent, 36*(9), 52, 54-59.

Goldman, R., Fristoe, M., & Woodcock, R. W. (1990). *Goldman-Fristoe-Woodcock Test of Auditory Discrimination.* Austin, TX: PRO-ED.

Goldman, R. M., & Fristoe, M. (2000). *Goldman-Fristoe Test of Articulation* (2nd ed.). Circle Pines, MN: American Guidance Service.

Goldrich Eskow, K., & Fisher, S. (2004). Getting together in college: An inclusion program for young adults with disabilities. *Teaching Exceptional Children, 36*(3), 26-32.

Goldstein, A. P. (1999). *The prepare curriculum: Teaching prosocial competencies* (2nd ed.). Champaign, IL: Research Press.

Goldstein, A. P. (2000). *The prepare curriculum: Teaching prosocial competencies* (rev. ed.). Champaign, IL: Research Press.

Goldstein, D. E., Murray, C., & Edgar, E. (1998). Employment earnings and hours of high school graduates with learning disabilities through the first decade after graduation. *Learning Disabilities Research and Practice, 13,* 53-64.

Goldstein, H. (2002). Communication intervention for children with autism: A review of treatment efficacy. *Journal of Autism and Developmental Disabilities, 32,* 373-396.

Goldstein, H., Kaczmarek, L. A., & English, K. M. (2001). *Promoting social communication: Children with developmental disabilities from birth to adolescence.* Baltimore: Brookes.

Goldstein, H., Kaczmarek, L., & Hepting, N. (1994). Communication interventions: The challenges of across-the-day implementation. In R. Gardner, III, D. M. Sainato, J. O. Cooper, T. E. Heron, W. L. Heward, J. Eshleman, & T. A. Grossi (Eds.), *Behavior analysis in education: Focus on measurably superior instruction* (pp. 101-113). Pacific Grove, CA: Brooks/Cole.

Goldstein, S., & Brooks, R. B. (2007). *Understanding and managing children's classroom behavior: Creating sustainable, resilient classrooms* (2nd ed.). New York: Wiley.

Goldstein, S., & Goldstein, M. (1998). *Managing attention-deficit hyperactivity disorder in children: A guide for practitioners* (2nd ed.). New York: Wiley.

Goleman, D. (1995). *Emotional intelligence: Why it can matter more than IQ.* New York: Bantam.

Gollnick, D. M., & Chinn, P. C. (2006). *Multicultural education in a pluralistic society* (7th ed.). Upper Saddle River, NJ: Merrill/Prentice Hall.

Gompel, M., van Bon, W. J. J., & Schreuder, R. (2004). Reading by children with low vision. *Journal of Visual Impairments and Blindness, 98,* 77-89.

Gomstyn, A. (2003, October 17). Minority enrollment in colleges more than doubled in past 20 years, study finds. *Chronicle of Higher Education, 50*(8), A25.

Gonzalez-Mena, J. (2006). *The young child in the family and the community* (4th ed.). Upper Saddle River, NJ: Merrill/Prentice Hall.

Good, R. H., & Kaminski, R. A. (2003). *DIBELS: Dynamic indicators of basic early literacy skills* (6th ed.). Longmont, CO: Sopris West.

Good, R. H., Kaminski, R. A., Smith, S., Simmons, D. S., Kame'enui, E. J., & Wallin, J. (2003). *Reviewing outcomes: Using DIBELS to evaluate a school's core curriculum and system of additional intervention in kindergarten.* In S. R. Vaughn & K. L. Briggs (Eds.), *Reading in the classroom: Systems for observing teaching and learning* (pp. 221-266). Baltimore: Paul H. Brookes.

Good, R. H., Simmons, D. C., & Kame'enui, E. J. (2001). The importance and decision-making utility of a continuum of fluency-based indicators of foundational reading skills for third-grade high-stakes outcomes. *Scientific Studies of Reading, 5*(3), 257-288.

Goodey, C. F. (2005). Blockheads, roundheads, pointed heads: Intellectual disability and the brain before modern medicine. *Journal of the History of the Behavioral Sciences, 41,* 165-183.

Goodman, G., & Poillion, M. J. (1992). ADD: Acronym for any dysfunction or difficulty. *Journal of Special Education, 26,* 37-56.

Goodman, G., & Williams, C. M. (2007). Interventions for increasing the academic engagement of students with autism spectrum disorders in inclusive classrooms. *Teaching Exceptional Children, 36*(6), 53-61.

Goodman, L. V. (1976). A bill of rights for the handicapped. *American Education, 12*(6), 6-8.

Goodrich, G. L., Kirby, J., Wagstaff, P., Oros, T., & McDevitt, B. (2004). A comparative study of reading performance with a head-mounted laser display and conventional low vision devices. *Journal of Visual Impairments and Blindness, 98,* 148-159.

Gordon, R. G., Jr. (Ed.). (2005). *Ethnologue: Languages of the world* (15th ed.). Dallas, TX: SIL International.

Gottesman, I. I. (1991). *Schizophrenia genesis: The origins of madness.* New York: Freeman.

Graf, S. A., & Lindsley, O. R. (2002). *Standard Celeration Charting 2002.* Poland, OH: Graf Implements.

Graham, S., & Harris, K. R. (1993). Self-regulated strategy development: Helping students with learning problems develop as writers. *Elementary School Journal, 94,* 169-181.

Graham, S., & Harris, K. R. (2003). Students with learning disabilities and the process of writing. In H. L. Swanson, K. R. Harris, & S. Graham (Eds.), *Handbook of learning disabilities* (pp. 323-344). New York: Guilford.

Graham, S., & Harris, K. R. (2005). *Writing better: Effective strategies for teaching students with learning difficulties.* Baltimore, MD: Brookes.

Grandin, T. (1995). *Thinking in pictures and other reports of my life with autism.* New York: Vintage Books.

Grandin, T. (2006, August 14). Seeing in beautiful, precise pictures. *On Morning Edition* [Radio program]. Washington, DC: National Public Radio. Retrieved July 24, 2007, from http://www.npr.org/templates/story/story.php?storyId=5628476

Grant, G., & McGrath, M. (1990). Need for respite-care services for caregivers of persons with mental retardation. *American Journal on Mental Retardation, 94,* 638-648.

Grantham, T. (2003). Increasing black student enrollment in gifted programs: An exploration of the Pulaski County Special School District's advocacy efforts. *Gifted Child Quarterly, 47,* 46-65.

Grass, D. (2001). *Making a switch adapted toy!* Petaluma, CA: The Alliance for Technology Access. [Retrieved September 2, 2007. http://www.ataccess.org/resources/wcp/enswitches/enadaptingtoy.pdf]

Graves, T. B., Collins, B. C., Shuster, J. W., & Kleinert, H. (2005). Using video prompting to teach cooking skills to students with moderate disabilities. *Education and Training in Developmental Disabilities, 40,* 34-46.

Gray, C., & Garand, J. (1993). Social stories: Improving responses of student with autism with accurate social information. *Focus on Autistic Behavior, 8,* 1-10.

Gray, C. A. (1994). The social story kit. In C. A. Gray (Ed.), *The new social story book* (pp 215-224). Arlington, TX: Future Horizons.

Gray, C. A. (1995). Teaching children with autism to read social stories. In K. A. Quill (Ed.), *Teaching children with autism* (pp. 219-241). New York: Delmar.

Gray, C. A. (2000). *The new social stories book (illustrated).* Arlington, TX: Future Horizons.

Gray, C. A. (2000). *Writing social stories with Carol Gray.* Arlington, TX: Future Horizons.

Gray, D. B., Quartrano, L. A., & Liberman, M. L. (1998). *Designing and using assistive technology.* Baltimore: Brookes.

Green, G. (1992, October). *Facilitated communication: Scientific and ethical issues: Research symposium for the E. K. Shriver Center University Affiliated Program.* Waltham, MA.

Green, G. (2001). Behavior analytic instruction for learners with autism: Advances in stimulus control technology. *Focus on Autism and Other Developmental Disabilities, 16,* 72-85.

Green, S. K., & Shinn, M. R. (1995). Parent attitudes about special education and reintegration: What is the role of student outcomes? *Exceptional Children, 61,* 269-281.

Greenbaum, P. E., Dedrick, R. F., Friedman, R. M., Kutash, K., Brown, E. C., Lardieri, S. P., & Pugh, A. M. (1996). National adolescent and children treatment study (NACTS): Outcomes for children with serious emotional and behavior disturbance. *Journal of Emotional and Behavioral Disorders, 4,* 130-146.

Greenberg, M. T., Weissberg, R. P., O'Brien, Zins, J. E., Fredericks, L., Resnik, H., & Elias, M. J. (2003). Enhancing school-based prevention and youth development through coordinated social, emotional, and academic learning. *American Psychologist, 58,* 466-474.

Greene, G. (2003). Best practices in transition. In G. Greene & C. A. Kochar-Bryant (Eds.), *Pathways to successful transition for youth with disabilities* (pp. 154-195). Upper Saddle River, NJ: Merrill/Prentice Hall.

Greenen, S., Powers, L. E., & Lopez-Vasquez, A. (2001). Multicultural aspects of parent involvement in transition planning. *Exceptional Children, 67,* 265-282.

Greenspan, S. (1992). Reconsidering the diagnosis and treatment of very young children with autistic spectrum or pervasive developmental disorder. *Zero to Three, 13*(2), 1-9.

Greenspan, S. (1997). Dead manual walking? Why the 1992 AAMR definition needs redoing. *Education and Training in Mental Retardation and Developmental Disabilities, 32,* 179-190.

Greenspan, S. (2006). Mental retardation in the real world: Why the AAMR definition is not there yet. In H. N. Switzky & S. Greenspan (Eds.), *What is mental retardation? Ideas for an evolving disability in the 21st century* (rev. ed.) (pp. 165-183). Washington, DC: American Association on Intellectual and Developmental Disabilities.

Greenspan, S., & Weider, S. W. (1997). Developmental patterns and outcomes in infants and children with disorders in relating and communicating: A chart review of 200 cases of children with autistic spectrum diagnoses. *Journal of Developmental and Learning Disorders, 1,* 87-141.

Greenwood, C. R., Carta, J. J., Hart, B., Kamps, D., Terry, D., Delquadri, J. C., Walker, D., & Risley, T. (1992). Out of the laboratory and into the community: Twenty-six years of applied behavior analysis at the Juniper Gardens Children's Center. *American Psychologist, 47,* 1464-1474.

Greenwood, C. R., Carta, J. J., & Walker, D. (2005). Individual growth and development indicators: Tools for assessing intervention results for infants and toddlers. In W. L. Heward, T. E. Heron, N. A. Neef, S. M. Peterson, D. M. Sainato, G. Cartledge, R. Gardner, III, L. D. Peterson, S. B. Hersh, & J. C. Dardig (Eds.), *Focus on behavior analysis in education: Achievements, challenges, and opportunities* (pp. 103-136). Upper Saddle River, NJ: Prentice Hall/Merrill.

Greenwood, C. R., & Delquadri, J. (1995). Classwide peer tutoring and the prevention of school failure. *Preventing School Failure, 39*(4), 21-25.

Greenwood, C. R., Delquadri, J., & Carta, J. J. (1997). *Together we can: Classwide peer tutoring to improve basic academic skills.* Longmont, CO: Sopris West.

Greenwood, C. R., Delquadri, J., & Hall, R. V. (1984). Opportunity to respond and student academic achievement. In W. L. Heward, T. E. Heron, D. S. Hill, & J. Trap-Porter (Eds.), *Focus on behavior analysis in education* (pp. 58-88). Upper Saddle River, NJ: Merrill/Prentice Hall.

Greenwood, C. R., Hart, B., Walker, D., & Risley, T. (1994). The opportunity to respond and academic performance revisited: A behavioral theory of developmental retardation and its prevention. In R. Gardner, III, D. M. Sainato, J. O. Cooper, T. E. Heron, W. L. Heward, J. Eshleman, & T. A. Grossi (Eds.), *Behavior analysis in education: Focus on measurably superior*

instruction (pp. 213-223). Pacific Grove, CA: Brooks/Cole.

Greenwood, C. R., & Maheady, L. (1997). Measurable change in student performance: Forgotten standard in teacher preparation? *Teacher Education and Special Education, 20,* 265-275.

Greenwood, C. R., Maheady, L., & Delquadri, J. C. (2002). Classwide peer tutoring. In G. Stoner, M. R. Shinn, & H. Walker (Eds.), *Interventions for achievement and behavior problems* (2nd ed.), (pp. 611-649). Washington, DC: National Association of School Psychologists.

Greer, R. D., & Ross, D. E. (2008). *Verbal behavior analysis: Inducing and expanding new verbal capabilities in children with language delays.* Boston: Pearson Allyn & Bacon.

Grenot-Scheyer, M., Fisher, M., & Staub, D. (2001). *Lessons learned in inclusive education at the end of the day.* Baltimore: Brookes.

Gresham, F. (2002). Responsiveness to intervention: An alternative approach to the identification of learning disabilities. In R. Bradley, L. Danielson, & D. P. Hallahan (Eds.), *Identification of learning disabilities: Research to practice* (pp. 467-519). Mahwah, NJ: Erlbaum.

Gresham, F. M. (2005). Response to intervention: An alternative means of identifying students as emotionally disturbed. *Education and Treatment of Children, 28,* 328-344.

Gresham, F. M., Cook, C. R., Crews, S. D., & Kern, L. (2004). Social skills training for children and youth with emotional and behavior disorders: Validity considerations and future directions. *Behavioral Disorders, 30,* 32-46.

Gresham, F. M., & Elliott, S. N. (1990). *Social skills rating system.* Circle Pines, MN: American Guidance Service, Inc.

Gresham, F. M., Lane, K. L., MacMillan, D.L., & Bocian, K. M. (1999). Social and academic profiles of externalizing and internalizing groups; Risk factors for emotional and behavioral disorders. *Behavioral Disorders, 24,* 231-245.

Gresham, F. M., & MacMillan, D. L. (1997a). Autistic recovery? An analysis and critique of the empirical evidence on the Early Intervention Project. *Behavioral Disorders, 22,* 185-201.

Gresham, F. M., & MacMillan, D. L. (1997b). Denial and defensiveness in the place of fact and reason: Rejoinder to Smith and Lovaas. *Behavioral Disorders, 22,* 219-230.

Griffin, C., & Hammis, D. (2001). Self-employment as the logical descendent of supported employment. In P. Wehman (Ed.), *Supported employment in business: Expanding the capacity of workers with disabilities* (pp. 251-268). St. Augustine, FL: Training Resource Network.

Griffin, C., Hammis, D., & Geary, T. (2007). *The job developer's handbook: Practical tactics for customized employment.* Baltimore: Brookes.

Griffin, H. C., Williams, S. C., Davis. M. L., & Engelman, M. (2002). Using technology to enhance cues for children with low vision.

Teaching Exceptional Children, 35(2), 36-42.

Griffin, K. L. (2001, October 7). Blind "see" via camera that tickles tongue. *Columbus Dispatch,* p. C6.

Grigal, M., Neubert, D. A., & Moon, M. S. (2002). Postsecondary options for students with significant disabilities. *Teaching Exceptional Children, 35*(2), 68-73.

Grigal, M., Test, D. W., Beattie, J., & Wood, W. (1997). An evaluation of transition components of individualized education programs. *Exceptional Children, 63,* 357-372.

Grigorenko, E. L. (2003). The first candidate gene for dyslexia: Turning the page of a new chapter of research. *Proc Natl Acad Sci U S A, 100*(20), 11190-11192.

Grindle, C. F., & Remington, B. (2002). Discrete-trial training for autistic children when reward is delayed: A comparison of conditioned cue-value and response-marking. *Journal of Applied Behavior Analysis, 32,* 187-190.

Grisham-Brown, J., Hemmeter, M. L., & Pretti-Frontczak, K. (2005). *Blended practices for teaching young children in inclusive settings.* Baltimore: Brookes.

Gross, B. H., & Hahn, H. (2004). Developing issues in the classification of mental and physical disabilities. *Journal of Disability Policy Studies, 15,* 130-134.

Grossi, T. A. (1998). Using a self-operated auditory prompting system to improve the work performance of two employees with severe disabilities. *Journal of The Association for Persons with Severe Handicaps, 23,* 149-154.

Grossi, T. A., & Heward, W. L. (1998). Using self-evaluation to improve the work productivity of trainees in a community-based restaurant training program. *Education and Training in Mental Retardation and Developmental Disabilities, 33,* 248-263.

Grossman, H. (Ed.) (1983). *Classification in mental retardation.* Washington, DC: American Association on Mental Deficiency.

Guess, D., Benson, H. A., & Siegel-Causey, E. (1985). Concepts and issues related to choice-making and autonomy among persons with severe disabilities. *Journal of The Association for Persons with Severe Handicaps, 10,* 79-86.

Guest, C. M., Collis, G. M., & McNicholas, J. (2006). Hearing dogs: A longitudinal study of social and psychological effects on deaf and hard-of-hearing recipients. *Journal of Deaf Studies and Deaf Education, 11,* 252-261.

Guilford, J. P. (1959). Traits of creativity. In H. H. Anderson (Ed.), *Creativity and its cultivation* (pp. 142-161). New York: Harper.

Guilford, J. P. (1967). *The nature of human intelligence.* New York: McGraw-Hill.

Guilford, J. P. (1987). Creativity research: Past, present and future. In S. Isaksen (Ed.), *Frontiers of creativity research* (pp. 33-66). Buffalo, NY: Bearly.

Gumpel, T. P., & Shlomit, D. (2000). Exploring the efficiency of self-regulation as a possible alternative to social skills training *Behavioral Disorders, 25,* 131-141.

Gunter, P. L., Denny, R. K., Jack, S. L., Shores, R. E., & Nelson, C. M. (1993). Aversive stimuli in academic interactions between students with serious emotional disturbance and their teachers. *Behavioral Disorders, 18,* 265-274.

Gunter, P. L., Miller, K. A., Venn, M. L., Thomas, K., & House, S. (2002). Self-graphing to success: Computerized data management. *Teaching Exceptional Children, 35*(2), 30-34.

Gupta, V. B. (2003). The history, definition and classification of pervasive developmental disorders. *Exceptional Parent, 33*(2), 58-62.

Gunter, P. L., Hummel, J. H., & Conroy, M. A. (1998). Increasing correct academic responding: An effective intervention strategy to decrease behavior problems. *Effective School Practices, 17*(2), 55-62.

Guralnick, M. J. (1997). *The effectiveness of early intervention.* Baltimore: Brookes.

Guralnick, M. J. (1998). Effectiveness of early intervention for vulnerable children: A developmental perspective. *American Journal of Mental Retardation, 102*(4), 319-345.

Guralnick, M. J. (2001). *Early childhood inclusion: Focus on change.* Baltimore: Brookes.

Guralnick, M. J. (2005). Early intervention for children with intellectual disabilities: Current knowledge and future prospects. *Journal of Applied Research in Intellectual Disabilities, 18,* 313-324.

Guralnick, M. J., & Conlon, C. (2007). Early intervention. In M. Batshaw, L. Pelligrino, & N. Roizen (Eds.), *Children with Disabilities* (6th ed., pp. 511-521). Baltimore: Paul H. Brookes.

Guralnick, M. J., Connor, R. T., Neville, B., & Hammond, M. A. (2006). Promoting the peer-related social development of young children with mild developmental delays: Effectiveness of a comprehensive intervention. *American Journal on Mental Retardation, 111,* 336-356.

Gurney, J. G., Fritz, M. S., Ness, K. K., Sievers, P., Newschaffer, C. J., & Shapiro, E. G. (2003). Analysis of prevalence trends of autism spectrum disorders in Minnesota. *Archives of Pediatric Adolescent Medicine, 157,* 622-627.

Gursel, O., Tekin-Iftar, E., & Boxkurt, F. (2006). Effectiveness of simultaneous prompting in small group: The opportunity of acquiring non-target skills through observational learning and instructive feedback. *Education and Training in Developmental Disabilities, 41,* 225-243.

Gustason, G. (1997). Educating children who are deaf or hard of hearing: English-based sign systems. *ERIC Digest #556.* (ERIC Document Reproduction Service No. ED 414 674).

Gustason, G., Pfetzing, D., & Zawolkow, E. (1980). *Signing exact English.* Los Alamitos, CA: Modern Signs.

Haager, D., & Vaughn, S. (1995). Parent, teacher, peer, and self-reports of the social competence of students with learning disabilities. *Journal of Learning Disabilities, 28,* 205-231.

Hadden, S., & Fowler, S. A. (1997). Preschool: A new beginning for children and parents. *Teaching Exceptional Children, 30*(1), 36-39.

Hadley, P. A. (1998). Language sampling protocols for eliciting text-level discourse. *Language, Speech, and Hearing Services in the Schools, 29,* 132-147.

Hadley, P. A., Simmerman, A., Long, M., & Luna, M. (2000). Facilitating language development for inner-city children: Experimental evaluation of a collaborative classroom-based intervention. *Language, Speech, and Hearing Services in Schools, 31,* 280-295.

Hage, C., & Leybaert, J. (2006). The effect of cued speech on the development of spoken language. In P. E. Spencer & M. Marschark (Eds.), *Advances in the spoken-language development of deaf and hard-of-hearing children* (pp. 193-211). New York: Oxford University Press.

Hagerman, R. J., & Cronsiter, A. (Eds.). (1996). *Fragile X syndrome: Diagnosis, treatment, and research* (2nd ed.). Baltimore: Johns Hopkins University Press.

Hagiwara, T., & Myles, B. (1999). A multi-media social story intervention: Teacher skills to children with autism. *Focus on Autism and Other Developmental Disabilities, 14,* 82-95.

Hagner, D., Snow, J., & Klein, J. (2006). Meaning of homeownership for individuals with developmental disabilities: A qualitative survey. *Mental Retardation, 44,* 295-303.

Hale, J. E. (2001). *Learning while black: Creating educational excellence for African American children.* Baltimore: Johns Hopkins University Press.

Hall, B. J., Oyer, H. J., & Haas, W. H. (2001). *Speech, language, and hearing disorders: A guide for the teacher* (3rd ed.). Boston: Allyn & Bacon.

Hall, M., Kleinert, H. L., & Kerns, J. F. (2000). Going to college! Postsecondary programs for students with moderate and severe disabilities. *Teaching Exceptional Children, 32*(2), 58-65.

Hall, R. V., Lund, D., & Jackson, D. (1968). Effects of teacher attention on study behavior. *Journal of Applied Behavior Analysis, 1,* 1-12.

Hall, T. E., Wolfe, P. S., & Bollig, A. A. (2003). The home-to-school notebook: An effective communication strategy for students with severe disabilities. *Teaching Exceptional Children, 36*(2), 68-73.

Hallahan, D. P. (1992). Some thoughts on why the prevalence of learning disabilities has increased. *Journal of Learning Disabilities, 25,* 523-528.

Hallahan, D. P. (1998). Teach. Don't flinch. *DLD Times, 16*(1), 1, 4.

Hallahan, D. P., & Mock, D. R. (2003). A brief history of the field of learning disabilities. In H. L. Swanson, K. R. Harris, & S. Graham (Eds.), *Handbook of learning disabilities* (pp. 16-29). New York: Guilford.

Hallenbeck, B. A., & Kauffman, J. M. (1995). How does observational learning affect the behavior of students with emotional or behavioral disorders? A review of research. *Journal of Special Education, 29,* 43-71.

Haller, A. K., & Montgomery, J. K. (2004). Noise-induced hearing loss in children: What educators need to know. *Teaching Exceptional Children, 36*(4), 22-27.

Halpern, A. S. (1985). Transition: A look at the foundations. *Exceptional Children, 51,* 479-486.

Halpern, A. S. (1993). Quality of life as a conceptual framework for evaluating transition outcomes. *Exceptional Children, 59,* 486-498.

Ham, R. (1986). *Techniques of stuttering therapy.* Upper Saddle River, NJ: Prentice Hall.

Hamill, L. B. (2003). Going to college: The experiences of a young woman with Down syndrome. *Mental Retardation, 41,* 340-353.

Hamilton, S. L., Seibert, M. A., Gardner, R., III, & Talbert-Johnson, C. (2000). Using guided notes to improve the academic achievement of incarcerated adolescents with learning and behavior problems. *Remedial and Special Education, 21,* 133-140.

Hamm, E. M., Mistrett, S. G., & Goetz Ruffino, A. (2006). Play outcomes and satisfaction with toys and technology of young children with special needs. *Journal of Special Education Technology, 21*(1), 29-35.

Hammer, M. R. (2004). Using the self-advocacy strategy to increase student participation in IEP conferences. *Intervention in School and Clinic, 39,* 295-300.

Hammill, D., & Larsen, S. (1978). The effectiveness of psycholinguistic training: A reaffirmation of position. *Exceptional Children, 44,* 402-417.

Hammill, D., & Newcomer, P. L. (1997). *Test of Language Development—3.* Austin, TX: PRO-ED.

Hancock, L. (1996, March 18). Mother's little helper. *Newsweek, 137*(12), 50-56.

Hancock, T. B., & Kaiser, A. P. (2006). Enhanced milieu teaching. In R. McCauley & M. Fey (Eds.), *Treatment of language disorders in children.* Baltimore: Paul Brookes.

Hanhan, S. F. (2008). Parent-teacher communication: Who's talking? In G. Olsen & M. L. Fuller (Eds.), *Home-school relations: Working successfully with parents and families* (pp. 104-126). Boston: Allyn and Bacon.

Hanline, M. F. (1993). Inclusion of preschoolers with profound disabilities: An analysis of children's interactions. *Journal of The Association for Persons with Severe Handicaps, 18,* 28-35.

Hannah, M. E., & Midlarsky, E. (2005). Helping by siblings of children with mental retardation. *American Journal on Mental Retardation, 110,* 87-99.

Hannon, T. S., Rao, G., & Arslanian, S. A. (2005). Childhood obesity and Type 2 diabetes mellitus. *Pediatrics, 116,* 473-480.

Hansen, D. A. (1989). Locating learning: Second language gains and language use in family, peer, and classroom contexts. *NABE Journal, 13,* 161-179.

Hansen, S. D., & Lignugaris/Kraft, B. (2005). Effects of a dependent group contingency on the verbal interactions of middle school students with emotional disturbance. *Behavioral Disorders, 30*, 170-184.

Hanson, M. J., Beckman, P. J., Horn, E., Marquart, J., Sandall, S., Greig, D., & Breenan, E. (2000). Entering preschool: Family and professional experiences in this transition process. *Journal of Early Intervention, 23*, 279-293.

Hanson, M. J., Horn, E., Sandall, S., Beckman, P., Morgan, M., Marquart, J., Barnwell, D. K., & Chou, H. (2001). After preschool inclusion: Children's educational pathways over the early school years. *Exceptional Children, 68*, 65-83.

Haptonstall-Nykaza, T. S., & Schick, B. (2007). The transition from fingerspelling to English print: Facilitating English decoding. *The Journal of Deaf Studies and Deaf Education, 12*, 172-183.

Harchik, A. E. (1994). Self-medication skills. In M. Agran, N. E. Marchand-Martella, & R. C. Martella (Eds.), *Promoting health and safety: Skills for independent living* (pp. 55-69). Pacific Grove, CA: Brooks/Cole.

Hardin, D. M., & Littlejohn, W. (1995). Family-school collaboration: Elements of effectiveness and program models. *Preventing School Failure, 39*(1), 4-8.

Hardman, M. L., & Clark, C. (2006). Promoting friendship through Best Buddies: A national survey of college program participants. *Mental Retardation, 44*, 56-63.

Hardman, M. L., McDonnell, J., & Welch, M. (1997). Perspectives on the future of IDEA. *Journal of The Association for Persons with Severe Handicaps, 22*, 61-77.

Harlacher, J. E., Roberts, N. E., & Merrell, K. W. (2006). Classwide interventions for students with ADHD. *Teaching Exceptional Children, 39*(2), 6-12.

Harland, V. T. (1997). *Youth street gangs: Breaking the gangs cycles in urban America.* San Francisco: Austin & Winfield.

Harmston, K. A., Strong, C. J., & Evans, D. D. (2001). International pen-pal correspondence for students with language-learning disabilities. *Teaching Exceptional Children, 33*(3), 46-51.

Harn, W., Bradshaw, M., & Ogletree, B. (1999). The speech-language pathologist in the schools: Changing roles. *Intervention in School and Clinic, 34*, 7.

Harris, F. R., Johnston, M. K., Kelly, C. S., & Wolf, M. M. (1964). Effects of positive social reinforcement on regressed crawling of a nursery school child. *Journal of Educational Psychology, 55*, 35-41.

Harris, H., & Harris, S. (1997). *The voice clinic handbook.* London: Whurr.

Harris, K. R., & Graham, S. (1996). Memo to constructivists: Skills count, too. *Educational Leadership, 53*(5), 26-29.

Harris, K. R., Graham, S., & Mason, L. (2006). Improving the writing, knowledge, and motivation of struggling young writers: Effects of self-regulated strategy development with and without peer support. *American Educational Research Journal, 43*, 295-340.

Harris, L., & Associates. (1986). *The ICD survey of disabled Americans: Bringing disabled Americans into the mainstream.* New York: Author.

Harris, M., & Moreno, C. (2004). Deaf children's use of phonological coding: Evidence from reading, spelling, and working memory. *Journal of Deaf Studies and Deaf Education, 9*, 253-268.

Harris, S. L., & Handleman, J. S. (Eds.). (2000). *Preschool programs for children with autism* (2nd ed.). Austin, TX: PRO-ED.

Harrop, A., & Swinson, J. (2000). Natural rates of approval and disapproval in British infant, junior, and secondary classrooms. *British Journal of Educational Psychology, 70*, 473-483.

Harry, B. (1992a). *Cultural diversity, families, and the special education system: Communication and empowerment.* New York: Teachers College Press.

Harry, B. (1992b). Making sense of disability: Low-income, Puerto Rican parents' theories of the problem. *Exceptional Children, 59*, 27-40.

Harry, B. (1994). *The disproportionate representation of minority students in special education: Theories and recommendations.* Alexandria, VA: National Association of State Directors of Special Education.

Harry, B. (2003). Trends and issues in serving culturally diverse families of children with disabilities. *Journal of Special Education, 36*, 131-138.

Harry, B., Kalyanpur, M., & Day, M. (1999). *Building cultural reciprocity with families: Case studies in special education.* Baltimore: Brookes.

Harry, B., & Klingner, J. K. (2006). *Why are so many minority students in special education? Understanding race and disability in schools.* New York: Teachers College Press.

Harry, B., & Klingner, J. (2007). Discarding the deficit model. *Educational Leadership, 64*(5), 16-21.

Harry, B., Rueda, R., & Kalyanpur, M. (1999). Cultural reciprocity in sociocultural perspective: Adapting the normalization principle for family collaboration. *Exceptional Children, 66*, 123-136.

Hart, B., & Risley, T. R. (1995). *Meaningful differences in the everyday experience of young American children.* Baltimore: Brookes.

Hart, B., & Risley, T. R. (1999). *The social world of children learning to talk.* Baltimore: Brookes.

Hart, B. M., Allen, K. E., Buell, J. S., Harris, F. R., & Wolf, M. M. (1964). Effects of social reinforcement on operant crying. *Journal of Experimental Child Psychology, 1*, 145-153.

Hasazi, S. B., Furney, K. S., & DeStefano, L. (1999). Implementing the IDEA transition mandates. *Exceptional Children, 65*(4), 555-566.

Haseltine, B., & Mittenburger, R. G. (1990). Teaching self-protection skills to persons with disabilities. *American Journal of Mental Retardation, 95*, 188-197.

Hastings, R. P., Beck, A., & Hill, C. (2005). Positive contributions made by children with an intellectual disability in the family: Mothers' and fathers' perceptions. *Journal of Intellectual Disabilities, 9*, 155-165.

Hastings, R. P., & Noone, S. J. (2005). Self-injurious behavior and functional analysis: Ethics and evidence. *Education and Training in Developmental Disabilities, 40*, 335-342.

Hatlen, P. (1996). *The core curriculum for blind and visually impaired students, including those with additional disabilities.* New York: American Foundation for the Blind.

Hatlen, P. (2004a). The core curriculum for blind and visually impaired students, including those with additional disabilities (rev. ed.). Retrieved April 14, 2006 from http://www.tsbvi.edu/Education/corecurric.htm.

Havey, J. M. (1999). School psychologists' involvement in special education due process hearings. *Psychology in the Schools, 36*(2), 117-121.

Hawkins, B. A., Eklund, S. J., James, D. R., & Foose, A. K. (2003). Adaptive behavior and cognitive function of adults with Down syndrome: Modeling change with age. *Mental Retardation, 41*, 7-28.

Hawkins, L., & Brawner, J. (1997). *Educating children who are deaf/hard of hearing: Total communication.* Reston, VA: ERIC Clearinghouse on Disabilities and Gifted Education. (ERIC Document Reproduction Service No. ED 414 677).

Haynes, W., & Pindzola, R. (2004). *Diagnosis and evaluation in speech pathology* (6th ed.). Needham Heights, MA: Allyn & Bacon.

Haywood, H. C. (2006). Broader perspectives on mental retardation. In H. N. Switzky & S. Greenspan (Eds.), *What is mental retardation? Ideas for an evolving disability in the 21st century* (rev. ed.) (pp. xv-xx). Washington, DC: American Association on Intellectual and Developmental Disabilities.

Healey, W. C. (2005). The learning disability phenomenon in pursuit of axioms. *Learning Disability Quarterly, 28*, 115-118.

Heber, R. F., & Garber, H. (1971). An experiment in prevention of cultural-familial mental retardation. In D. A. Primrose (Ed.), *Proceedings of the Second Congress of the International Association for the Scientific Study of Mental Deficiency.* Warsaw: Polish Medical Publishers.

Heckaman, K. A., Alber, S. R., Hooper, S., & Heward, W. L. (1998). A comparison of least-to-most prompts and progressive time delay on the disruptive behavior of students with autism. *Journal of Behavior Education, 8*, 171-201.

Heckaman, K., Conroy, M., Fox, J., & Chait, A. (2000). Functional assessment-based interventions research on students with or at risk for emotional and behavioral disorders in school settings. *Behavioral Disorders, 25*, 196-210.

Heering, P. W., & Wilder, D. A. (2006). The use of dependent group contingencies to increase on-task behavior in two general education classrooms. *Education & Treatment of Children, 29*, 459-468.

Heflin, L. J., & Alaimo, D. F. (2007). *Students with autism spectrum disorders: Effective instructional practices.* Upper Saddle River, NJ: Merrill/Prentice Hall.

Heflin, L. J., & Simpson, R. L. (2002). Understanding intervention controversies. In B. Scheuermann & J. Webber, *Autism: Teaching does make a difference* (pp. 248–277). Belmont, CA: Wadsworth.

Heikua, U. Linna, S-L., Olsén, P., Hartikaiinen, A-L., Taanila, A., & Järvelin, M-R. (2005). Etiological survey on intellectual disabilities in the Northern Finland birth cohort 1986. *American Journal on Mental Retardation, 110,* 171–180.

Heiman, T. (2002). Parents of children with disabilities: Resilience, coping, and future expectations. *Journal of Developmental and Physical Disabilities, 14,* 159–171.

Heimlich, S. G. (2005). *Effects of computer assisted guided notes and guided notes study cards on middle school special education students' note-taking completion and accuracy and next-day quiz scores.* Unpublished master's thesis, The Ohio State University.

Heinze, T. (1986). Communication skills. In G. T. Scholl (Ed.), *Foundations of education for blind and visually handicapped children and youth: Theory and practice* (pp. 301–314). New York: American Foundation for the Blind.

Heller, K. W., Alberto, P. A., Forney, P. E., & Schwartzman, M. N. (1996). *Understanding physical, sensory and health impairments.* Pacific Grove, CA: Brooks/Cole.

Heller, K. W., & Bigge, J. (2005). Augmentative and alternative communication. In S. J. Best, K. W. Heller, & J. L. Bigge, (Eds.), *Teaching individuals with physical or multiple disabilities* (5th ed.), (pp. 227–274). Upper Saddle River, NJ: Merrill/Prentice Hall.

Heller, K. W., Bigge, J. L., & Allgood, P. (2005). Adaptations for personal independence. In S. J. Best, K. W. Heller, & J. L. Bigge, (Eds.), *Teaching individuals with physical or multiple disabilities* (5th ed.), (pp. 309–335). Upper Saddle River, NJ: Merrill/Prentice Hall.

Heller, K. W., Dangel, H., & Sweatman, L. (1995). Systematic selection of adaptations for students with muscular dystrophy. *Journal of Developmental and Physical Disabilities, 7,* 253–265.

Heller, K. W., Forney, P. E., Alberto, P. A., Schwartzman, M. N., & Goeckel, T. M. (2000). *Meeting physical and health needs of children with disabilities: Teaching physician and health management skills.* Belmont, CA: Thompson.

Heller, K. W., Fredrick, L. D., Best, S., Dykes, M. K., & Cohen, E. T. (2000). Specialized health care procedures in the schools: Training and service delivery. *Exceptional Children, 66,* 173–186.

Henderson, C. (2001). *College freshmen with disabilities: A triennial statistical profile.* Washington, DC: American Council on Education/HEATH Resource Center.

Henderson, K., & Bradley, R. (2004). A national perspective on mental health and children with disabilities: Emotional disturbances in children. *Emotional and Behavioral Disorders in Youth, 4,* 67–74.

Henderson, L. W., & Meisels, S. J. (1994). Parental involvement in the developmental screening of their young children: A multiple-source perspective. *Journal of Early Intervention, 18,* 141–154.

Henggler, S. (1989). *Delinquency in adolescence.* Beverly Hills, CA: Sage.

Herer, G. R., Knightly, C. A., & Steinberg, A. G. (2007). Hearing: Sounds and silences. In M. L. Batshaw (Ed.), *Children with disabilities* (6th ed.). Baltimore: Brookes.

Hernandez, H. (2001). *Multicultural education: A teacher's guide to linking context, process, and content* (2nd ed.). Upper Saddle River, NJ: Merrill/Prentice Hall.

Heron, T. E., & Harris, K. C. (2001). *The educational consultant: Helping professionals, parents, and students in inclusive classrooms* (4th ed.). Austin, TX: PRO-ED.

Heron, T. E., Heward, W. L., Cooke, N. L., & Hill, D. S. (1983). Evaluation of a classwide peer tutoring system: First graders teach each other sight words. *Education & Treatment of Children, 6,* 137–152.

Heron, T. E., Villareal, D. M., Yo, M., Christianson, R. J., & Heron, K. M. (2006). Peer tutoring systems: Applications in classrooms and special environments. *Reading and Writing Quarterly, 22,* 27–45.

Heron, T. E., Welsch, R. G., & Goddard, Y. L. (2003). Applications of tutoring systems in specialized subject areas. *Remedial and Special Education, 24,* 288–300.

Hertzog, N. B. (1998). The changing role of the gifted education specialist. *Teaching Exceptional Children, 30*(3), 39–43.

Hetzner, A. (2007). Disparity shows in special ed: State deems 25 districts' minority enrollment disproportionate. *Milwaukee Journal Sentinel,* March 30.

Heumann, J. (1993). Building our own boats: A personal perspective on disability policy. In L. O. Gostin & H. A. Beyer (Eds.), *Implementing the Americans with Disabilities Act: Rights and responsibilities of all Americans.* Baltimore: Paul H. Brookes.

Heward, W. L. (1994). Three "low-tech" strategies for increasing the frequency of active student response during group instruction. In R. Gardner, III, D. M. Sainato, J. O. Cooper, T. E. Heron, W. L. Heward, J. Eshleman, & T. A. Grossi (Eds.), *Behavior analysis in education: Focus on measurably superior instruction* (pp. 283–320). Pacific Grove, CA: Brooks/Cole.

Heward, W. L. (2001). *Guided notes: Improving the effectiveness of your lectures.* Columbus, OH: The Ohio State University Partnership Grant for Improving the Quality of Education for Students with Disabilities.

Heward, W. L. (2003). Ten faulty notions about teaching and learning that hinder the effectiveness of special education. *Journal of Special Education, 36*(4), 186–205.

Heward, W. L. (2005). Reasons applied behavior analysis is good for education and why those reasons have been insufficient. In W. L. Heward, T. E. Heron, N. A. Neef, S. M. Peterson, D. M. Sainato, G. Cartledge, R. Gardner, III, L. D. Peterson, S. B. Hersh, & J. C. Dardig (Eds.), *Focus on behavior analysis in education: Achievements, challenges, and opportunities* (pp. 316–348). Upper Saddle River, NJ: Merrill/Prentice Hall.

Heward, W. L., & Dardig, J. C. (2001, Spring). What matters most in special education. *Education Connection, 41–44.*

Heward, W. L., Ernsbarger Bicard, S., & Cavanaugh, R. A. (2007). Educational equality for students with disabilities. In J. A. Banks & C. A. M. Banks (Eds.), *Multicultural education: Issues and perspectives* (6th ed.) (pp. 329–367). New York: John Wiley & Sons.

Heward, W. L., Gardner, R., III, Cavanaugh, R. A., Courson, F. H., Grossi, T. A., & Barbetta, P. M. (1996). Everyone participates in this class: Using response cards to increase active student response. *Teaching Exceptional Children, 28*(2), 4–10.

Heward, W. L., Heron, T. E., & Cooke, N. L. (1982). Tutor huddle: Key element in a classwide peer tutoring system. *Elementary School Journal, 83,* 115–123.

Heward, W. L., Heron, T. E., Gardner, R., III, & Prayzer, R. (1991). Two strategies for improving students' writing skills. In G. Stoner, M. R. Shinn, & H. M. Walker (Eds.), *A school psychologist's interventions for regular education* (pp. 379–398). Washington, DC: National Association of School Psychologists.

Heward, W. L., & Silvestri, S. M. (2005). The neutralization of special education. In J. W. Jacobson, J. A. Mulick, & R. M. Foxx, (Eds.), *Controversial therapies in developmental disabilities: Fads, fashion, and science in professional practice* (pp. 193–214). Hillsdale, NJ: Lawrence Erlbaum Associates.

Hill, B. K., Lakin, K. C., Bruininks, R. H., Amado, A. N., Anderson, D. J., & Copher, J. I. (1989). *Living in the community: A comparative study of foster homes and small group homes for people with mental retardation* (Report no. 28). Minneapolis: University of Minnesota, Center for Residential and Community Services.

Hill, E. W., & Snook-Hill, M. (1996). Orientation and mobility. In M. C. Holbrook (Ed.), *Children with visual impairments: A parents' guide* (pp. 259–286). Bethesda, MD: Woodbine House.

Hill, J. L. (1999). *Meeting the needs of students with special physical and health care needs.* Upper Saddle River, NJ: Merrill/Prentice Hall.

Hill, J. L., Brooks-Gunn, J., & Waldfogel, J. (2003). Sustained effects of high participation in an early intervention for low-birth-weight premature infants. *Developmental Psychology, 39,* 730–744.

Hintz, R., & Driscoll, A. (1988). Praise or encouragement? New insights into praise: Implications for early childhood teachers. *Young Children, 16,* 6–13.

Hitchings, W. E., Luzzo, D. A., Retish, P., Horvath, M., & Ristow, R. (1998). Identifying the needs of college students with disabilities.

Journal of College Student Development, 39(1), 23-32.

Hobbs, N. (1975). *The futures of children*. San Francisco: Jossey-Bass.

Hobbs, N. (Ed.). (1976a). *Issues in the classification of children (Vol. 1)*. San Francisco: Jossey-Bass.

Hobbs, N. (Ed.). (1976b). *Issues in the classification of children (Vol. 2)*. San Francisco: Jossey-Bass.

Hock, M. F., Schumaker, J. B., & Deshler, D. D. (1999). Closing the gap to success in secondary schools: A model for cognitive apprenticeship. In S. Graham, K. R. Harris, & M. Pressley (Series Eds.) & D. D. Deshler, K. R. Harris, & S. Graham (Vol. Eds.), *Advances in teaching and learning, teaching every child every day: Learning in diverse schools and classrooms* (pp. 1-52). Cambridge, MA: Brookline.

Hodapp, R. M., & Dykens, E. M. (2001). Strengthening behavioral research on genetic mental retardation syndromes. *American Journal of Mental Retardation, 106*, 4-15.

Hodapp, R. M., & Dykens, E. M. (in press). Behavioral effects of genetic intellectual disability syndromes. In J. W. Jacobson, J. A. Mulick, & J. Rojahn, (Eds.), *Handbook of intellectual and developmental disabilities*. New York: Kluwer Academic/Plenum Publishers.

Hodge, J., Riccomini, P. J., Buford, R., & Herbst, M. H. (2006). A review of instructional interventions in mathematics for students with emotional and behavioral disorders. *Behavioral Disorders, 31*, 297-311.

Hodges, D., Higbee Mandlebaum, L., Boff, C., & Miller, M. (2007). Instructional strategies online database (ISOD). *Intervention in School and Clinic, 42*, 219-224.

Hodson, B. W. (1994). Helping individuals become intelligible, literate, and articulate: The role of phonology. *Topics in Language Disorders, 14*(2), 1-16

Hoffman, C. D., Sweeney, D. P., Gilliam, J. E., & Lopez-Wagner, M. C. (2006). Sleep problems in children with autism and in typically developing children. *Focus on Autism and Other Developmental Disabilities, 21*, 146-152.

Holahan, A., & Costenbader, V. (2000). A comparison of developmental gain for preschool children with disabilities in inclusive and self-contained classrooms. *Topics in Early Childhood Special Education, 20*, 224-235.

Holden-Pitt, L., & Diaz, J. (1998). Thirty years of the annual survey of deaf and hard-of-hearing children and youth: A glance over the decades. *American Annals of the Deaf, 142*(2), 72-76.

Holland, K. D. (2006). Understanding the parent of the special needs child. *Exceptional Parent, 36*(8), 60-62.

Hollinger, C. L. (1995). Counseling gifted young women about educational and career choices. In J. L. Genshaft, M. Bireley, & C. L. Hollinger (Eds.), *Serving gifted and talented students: A resource for school personnel* (pp. 269-283). Austin, TX: PRO-ED.

Holsen, L., & Thompson, T. (2004). Compulsive behavior and eye blink in Prader-Willi syndrome: Neurochemical implications. *American Journal on Mental Retardation. 109*, 197-207.

Holt, J. (1993). Stanford Achievement Test—8th edition: Reading comprehension subgroup results. *American Annals of the Deaf, 138*, 172-175.

Holub, T., & Rusch, F. R. (2008). Dropout preventions: Using self-determination to achieve desired postschool outcomes. In F. R. Rusch (Ed.). *Beyond high school: Preparing adolescents for tomorrow's challenges* (2nd ed.) (pp. 288-303). Upper Saddle River, NJ: Merrill/Prentice Hall.

Hong, B. S. S., Ivey, W. F., Gonzalez, H. R., & Ehrensberger, W. (2007). Preparing students for postsecondary education. *Teaching Exceptional Children, 40*(1), 32-38.

Honig v. Doe, 485 U.S. 305, 108 S.Ct. 592, 98 L.Ed. 2d 686 (1988).

Hook, C. L., & DuPaul, G. J. (1999). Parent tutoring for students with attention-deficit/hyperactivity disorder: Effects on reading performance at home and school. *School Psychology review, 28*, 60-75.

Hoover, H. D., Hieronymus, A. N., Frisbie, D. A., & Dunbar, S. B. (1996). *Iowa Tests of Basic Skills*. Chicago: Riverside.

Hoover, H. D., Hieronymus, A. N., & Frisbie, D. A. (2007). *Iowa Tests of Basic Skills–Form C*. Rolling Meadows, IL: Riverside.

Hoover, J. J., Klinger, J. J., Baca, L. M., & Patton, M. M. (2008). *Methods for teaching culturally and linguistically diverse exceptional learners*. Upper Saddle River, NJ: Merrill/Prentice Hall.

Horn, C., Shuster, J. W., & Collins, B. C. (2006). Use of response cards to teach telling time to students with moderate and severe disabilities. *Education and Training in Developmental Disabilities, 41*, 382-391.

Horn, E., Lieber, J., Li, S., Sandall, S., & Schwartz, I. (2000). Supporting young children's IEP goals in inclusive settings through embedded learning opportunities. *Topics in Early Childhood Special Education, 20*, 208-223.

Horn, E., Ostrosky, M., & Jones, X. (2004). *Interdisciplinary teams* (Monograph series no. 6). Reston, VA: Council for Exceptional Children, Division for Early Childhood.

Horner, R. H., Albin, R. W., Todd, A. W., & Sprague, J. (2006). Positive behavior support for individuals with severe disabilities. In M. E. Snell & F. Brown (Eds.), *Instruction of students with severe disabilities* (6th ed.) (pp. 206-250). Upper Saddle River, NJ: Merrill/Prentice Hall.

Horner, R. H., & Carr, E. G. (1997). Behavioral support for students with severe disabilities: Functional assessment and comprehensive intervention. *Journal of Special Education, 31*, 84-104.

Horner, R. H., Carr, E. G., Halle, J., McGee, G., Odom, S., & Wolery, M. (2005). The use of single-subject research to identify evidence-based practices in special education. *Exceptional Children, 71*, 165-179.

Horner, R. H., Carr, E. G., Strain, P. S., Todd, A. W., & Reed, H. K. (2002). Problem behavior interventions for young children with autism: A research synthesis. *Journal of Autism and Developmental Disabilities, 32*, 423-441.

Horner, R. H., Dunlap, G., & Koegel, R. L. (1988). *Generalization and maintenance: Life-style changes in applied settings*. Baltimore: Brookes.

Horner, R. H., Sugai, G., Todd, A. W., & Lewis-Palmer, T. (2005). School-wide positive behavior support. In L. Bambara & L. Kern (Eds.), *Individualized supports for students with problem behaviors: Designing positive behavior support plans* (pp. 359-390). New York: Guilford Press.

Horstmeier, D. (2004). *Teaching math to people with Down syndrome and other hands-on learners*. Bethesda, MD: Woodbine House.

Horton, S. V., Lovitt, T. C., & Bergerud, D. (1990). The effectiveness of graphic organizers for three classifications of secondary students in content area classes. *Journal of Learning Disabilities, 23*, 12-22.

Horvath, B. (2006). Helping students step into adult life with confidence. In W. L. Heward, *Exceptional children: An introduction to special education* (8th ed) (pp. 602-603). Upper Saddle River, NJ: Merrill/Prentice Hall.

Horvath, K., Stefanatos, G., Sokolski, K. N., Wachtel, R., Nabors, L., & Tildon, J. T. (1998). Improved social and language skills after secretin administration in patients with autistic spectrum disorders. *Journal of the Association for Academic Minority Physicians, 9*(1), 9-15.

Hosp, J. L., & Reschly, D. J. (2003). Referral rates for intervention or assessment: A meta-analysis of racial differences. *Journal of Special Education, 37*, 67-80.

House, J. W. (1999). Hearing loss in adults. *Volta Review, 99*(5), 161-166.

Howard, J. S., Sparkman, C. R., Cohen, H. G., Green, G., & Stanislaw, H. (2005). A comparison of intensive behavior analytic and eclectic treatments for young children with autism. *Research in Developmental Disabilities, 26*, 359-383.

Howard, V. F., Williams, B. F., & McLaughlin, T. F. (1994). Children prenatally exposed to alcohol and cocaine: Behavioral solutions. In R. Gardner, III, D. M. Sainato, J. O. Cooper, T. E. Heron, W. L. Heward, J. Eshleman, & T. A. Grossi (Eds.), *Behavior analysis in education: Focus on measurably superior instruction* (pp. 131-146). Pacific Grove, CA: Brooks/Cole.

Howard, V. F., Williams, B. F., & Lepper, C. (2005). *Very young children with special needs: A formative approach for today's children* (3rd ed.). Upper Saddle River, NJ: Merrill/Prentice Hall.

Howe, J., Horner, R. H., & Newton, J. S. (1998). Comparison of supported living and traditional residential services in the state of Oregon. *Mental Retardation, 36*, 1-11.

Howell, K. W., Evans, D., & Gardiner, J. (1997). Medications in the classroom: A hard pill to swallow. *Teaching Exceptional Children, 29*(6), 58-61.

Howell, K. W., & Nolet, V. (2000). *Curriculum-based evaluation: Teaching and decision making* (3rd ed.). Belmont, CA: Wadsworth/Thompson Learning.

Howell, R. D. (2000). Grasping the future with robotic aids. In W. L. Heward, *Exceptional children: An introduction to special education* (6th ed.), (pp. 478–480). Upper Saddle River, NJ: Merrill/Prentice Hall.

Howlin, P. (2003). Outcome of high-functioning adults with autism with and without early language delays: Implications for the differentiating between autism and Asperger syndrome. *Journal of Autism and Developmental Disorders, 33,* 3–13.

Hoye, J. D. (1998, July). *Integrating school-to-work into preservice teacher education.* Paper presented at Conference for Professors of Education in Ohio, Kent, OH.

Hudson, P., Lignugaris/Kraft, B., & Miller, T. (1993). Using content enhancements to improve the performance of adolescents with learning disabilities in content classes. *Learning Disabilities Research and Practice, 8,* 106–126.

Hudson, P., & Miller, S. P. (1993). Home and school partnerships: Parent as teacher. *LD Forum, 18*(2), 31–33.

Huebner, K. M., Garber, M., & Wormsley, D. P. (2006). *Student-centered educational placement decisions: The meaning, interpretation, and application of least restrictive environment for students with visual impairments.* Arlington, VA: Division of Visual Impairments (DVI) of the Council for Exceptional Children. http://www.ed.arizona.edu/dvi/Position%20Papers/index_position_papers.htm

Huebner, M. K., Merk-Adam, B., Stryker, D., & Wolffe, K. E. (2004). *The national agenda for the education of children and youths with visual impairments, including those with multiple disabilities—Revised.* New York: AFB Press.

Huefner, D. S. (2000). The risks and opportunities of the IEP requirements under IDEA '97. *Exceptional Children, 63,* 195–204.

Huff, K. E., & DuPaul, G. J. (1998). Reducing disruptive behavior in general education classrooms: The use of self-management strategies. *School Psychology Review, 27,* 290–303.

Hughes, C. (1997). Self-instruction. In M. Agran (Ed.), *Student directed learning: Teaching self-determination skills* (pp. 144–170). Pacific Grove, CA: Brooks/Cole.

Hughes, C., & Carter, E. W. (2006). *Success for all students: Promoting inclusion in secondary schools through peer buddy programs.* Boston: Allyn and Bacon.

Hughes, C., Copeland, S. R., Fowler, S., & Church-Pupke, P. (in press). Quality of life. In K. Storey, P. Bates, & D. Hunter (Eds.), *The road ahead: Transition to adult life for persons with disabilities* (2nd ed.). St. Augustine, FL: Training Resource Network.

Hughes, C., Copeland, S. R., Guth, C., Rung, L. L., Hwang, B., Kleeb, G., & Strong, M. (2001). General education students' perspective on their involvement in a high school peer buddy program. *Education and Training in Mental Retardation and Developmental Disabilities, 36,* 343–356.

Hughes, C., Fowler, S. E., Copeland, S. R., Agran, M., Wehmeyer, M. L., & Church-Pupke, P. P. (in press). Supporting high school students to engage in recreational activities with peers. *Behavior Modification.*

Hughes, C., Guth, C., Hall, S., Presley, J., Dye, M., & Byers, C. (1999). "They are my best friends": Peer buddies promote inclusion in high school. *Teaching Exceptional Children, 31,* 32–37.

Hughes, C., Rung, L. L., Wehmeyer, M. L., Agran, M., Copland, S. R., & Hwang, B. (2000). Self-prompted communication book to increase social interaction among high school students. *Journal of The Association for Persons with Severe Handicaps, 25,* 153–166.

Hughes, C., & Rusch, F. R. (1989). Teaching supported employees with severe mental retardation to solve problems. *Journal of Applied Behavior Analysis, 22,* 365–372.

Hughes, C., Washington, B. H., & Brown, G. L. (2008). Supporting students in the transition from school to adult life. In F. R. Rusch (Ed.), *Beyond high school: Preparing adolescents for tomorrow's challenges* (2nd ed.) (pp. 266–287). Upper Saddle River, NJ: Merrill/Prentice Hall.

Hughes, C. A., & Suritsky, S. K. (1994). Note-taking skills of university students with and without learning disabilities. *Journal of Learning Disabilities, 27,* 20–24.

Hughes, F., Elicker, J., & Veen, L. (1995, January). A program of play for infants and their caregivers. *Young Children,* 52–58.

Hughes, W., Wood, W. M., Konrad, M., & Test, D. W. (2006). Get a life: Students practice being self-determined. *Teaching Exceptional Children, 38*(5), 57–63.

Huguenin, N. H. (2000). Reducing overselective attention to compound visual cues with extended training in adolescents with severe mental retardation. *American Journal on Mental Retardation, 111,* 447–453.

Hulit, L. M., & Howard, M. R. (2006). *Born to talk: An introduction to speech and language development* (4th ed.), Boston: Allyn & Bacon.

Hunt, P., Goetz, L., & Anderson, J. (1986). The quality of IEP objectives associated with placement on integrated versus segregated school sites. *Journal of The Association for Persons with Severe Handicaps, 11,* 125–130.

Hunt, P., Soto, G., Maier, J., & Doering, K. (2003). Collaborative teaming to support students at risk and students with severe disabilities in general education classrooms. *Exceptional Children, 69,* 315–332.

Hunt, P., Staub, D., Alwell, M., & Goetz, L. (1994). Achievement by all students within the context of cooperative learning groups. *Journal of The Association for Persons with Severe Handicaps, 19,* 290–301.

Huntze, S. L. (1985). A position paper of the Council for Children with Behavioral Disorders. *Behavioral Disorders, 10,* 167–174.

Hurtubis Sahlen, C. A., & Lehmann, J. P. (2006). Requesting accommodations in higher education. *Teaching Exceptional Children, 38*(3), 28–34.

Hutinger, P. L., Marshall, S., & McCarten, K. (1983). *Core curriculum: Macomb 0–3 regional project* (3rd ed.). Macomb: Western Illinois University.

Hutton, A. M., & Caron, S. L. (2005). Experience of families with children with autism in rural New England. *Focus on Autism and Other Developmental Disabilities, 20,* 180–189.

Hyde, M., & Power, D. (2006). Some ethical dimensions of cochlear implantation for Deaf children and their families. *The Journal of Deaf Studies and Deaf Education, 11,* 102–111.

Hyman, S. L., & Towbin, K. E. (2007). Autism spectrum disorders. In M. L. Batshaw, L. Pellegrino, & N. J. Roizen (Eds.), *Children with disabilities* (6th ed.). Baltimore: Brookes.

Inge, K. J., & Moon, M. S. (2006). Vocational preparation and transition. In M. E. Snell & F. Brown (Eds.), *Instruction of students with severe disabilities* (6th ed.) (pp. 328–374). Upper Saddle River, NJ: Merrill/Prentice Hall.

Inghram, J. (2003). Evidence-based treatment of stuttering: I. Definition and application. *Journal of Fluency Disorders, 28,* 197–206.

Ingram, A. L., Hathorn, L. G., and Evans, A. D. (2000). Beyond chat on the Internet. *Computers and Education, 35*(1), 21–35.

Institute of Medicine. (2004). *Immunization safety review: Vaccines and autism.* Washington, DC: National Academy of Sciences. Executive summary available online at: http://www.iom.edu/?ID=4705

Interactive Autism Network. (2007). Baltimore, MD. Kennedy Krieger Institute. http://www.ianproject.org/

International Classification of Functioning, Disability and Health Available on-line at http://www3.who.int/icf/intros/ICF-Eng-Intro.pdf. Retrieved March 25, 2007.

Ireland, J. C., Wray, D., & Flexer, C. (1988). Hearing for success in the classroom. *Teaching Exceptional Children, 20*(2), 15–17.

Irving Independent School District v. Tatro, 104 S. Ct. 3371, 82 L.Ed. 2d 664 (1984).

Iscoe, I., & Payne, S. (1972). Development of a revised scale for the functional classification of exceptional children. In E. P. Trapp & P. Himelstein (Eds.), *Readings on the exceptional child* (pp. 7–29). New York: Appleton-Century-Crofts.

Ispen, C. (2006). Health, secondary conditions, and employment outcomes for adults with disabilities. *Journal of Disability Policy Studies, 17,* 77–87.

Ita, C. M., & Friedman, H. A. (1999). The psychological development of children who are deaf or hard of hearing: A critical review. *Volta Review, 101,* 165–181.

Itard, J. M. G. (1806/1962). *The wild boy of Aveyron* (G. Humphrey & M. Humphrey, Eds. and Trans.). Englewood Cliffs, NJ: Prentice Hall. (Original work published in Paris by Guoyon).

Itoi, M. (2004). *Effects of guided notes study cards with post-lecture review on the note-completion and accuracy and next-day quiz scores by students in a 7th grade social studies classroom.* Unpublished master's thesis, The Ohio State University.

Ives, B. (2007). Graphic organizers applied to secondary algebra instruction for students with learning disorders. *Learning Disabilities Research & Practice, 22,* 110-118.

Ives, B., & Hoy, C. (2003). Graphic organizers applied to higher-level secondary mathematics. *Learning Disabilities Research & Practice, 18,* 36-51.

Ivey, M. L., Heflin, L. J., & Alberto, P. (2004). The use of social stories to promote independent behaviors in novel events for children with PDD-NOS. *Focus on Autism and Other Developmental Disabilities, 19,* 164-176.

Iwata, B. A., Dorsey, M., Slifer, K., Bauman, K., & Richman, G. (1994). Toward a functional analysis of self-injury. *Journal of Applied Behavior Analysis, 27,* 197-209.

Izzo, M., Dillon, K., & Novak, J. (2007, April). *Integrating transition into high school technology and English academic standards.* Poster presented at annual convention of the Council for Exceptional Children. Louisville, KY.

Jacobson, J. J., & Mulick, J. (1996). *Manual on diagnosis and professional practice in mental retardation.* Washington, DC: American Psychological Association.

Jacobson, J. W., Foxx, R. M., & Mulick, J. A. (Eds.). (2005a). *Controversial therapies for developmental disabilities: Fads, fashion, and science in professional practice.* Mahwah, NJ: Lawrence Erlbaum Associates.

Jacobson, J. W., Foxx, R. M., & Mulick, J. A. (2005b). Facilitated communication: The ultimate fad treatment. In J. W. Jacobson, R. M. Foxx, & J. A. Mulick (Eds.), *Controversial therapies for developmental disabilities: Fads, fashion, and science in professional practice* (pp. 363-383). Mahwah, NJ: Lawrence Erlbaum Associates.

Jacobson, J. W., Mulick, J. A., & Foxx, R. M. (Eds.). (2005). *Fads: Dubious and improbable treatments for developmental disabilities.* Hillsdale, NJ: Erlbaum.

Jacobson, J. W., Mulick, J. A., & Rojahn J. (Eds.). (2007). *Handbook of intellectual and developmental disabilities.* New York: Springer.

Jacobson, J. W., Mulick, J. A., & Green, G. (1998). Cost-benefit estimates for early intensive behavioral intervention for young children with autism: General model and single state case. *Behavioral Interventions, 13,* 201-226.

Jacobson, W. H. (1993). *The art and science of teaching orientation and mobility to persons with visual impairments.* New York: American Federation for the Blind.

Jalongo, M. R., & Isenberg, J. P. (2008). *Exploring your role: An introduction to early childhood education* (3rd ed.). Upper Saddle River, NJ: Merrill/Prentice Hall.

Janney, R. E., & Snell, M. E. (1996). Using peer interactions to include students with extensive disabilities in elementary general education classes. *Journal of The Association for Persons with Severe Handicaps, 21,* 72-80.

Janney, R. E., & Snell, M. E. (1997). How teachers include students with moderate and severe disabilities in elementary classes: The means and meaning of inclusion. *Journal of The Association for Persons with Severe Handicaps, 42*(3), 159-169.

Janney, R., & Snell, M. E. (2000). *Modifying schoolwork.* Baltimore: Brookes.

Janney, R., & Snell, M. E. (2000). *Teacher's guides to inclusive practices: Behavioral support.* Baltimore: Brookes.

Jenkins, J. R., & O'Conner, R. E. (2001). *Early identification and intervention for young children with reading/learning disabilities* (Executive Summary). Paper presented at the LD Summit, Washington, DC. http://ldsummit.air.org/download/Jenkins%20final%208-14-01.pdf

Jensen, P. S. (2000). Pediatric psychopharmacology in the United States: Issues and challenges in the diagnosis and treatment of attention-deficit/hyperactivity disorder. In L. L. Greenhill & B. B. Osman (Eds.). *Ritalin: Theory and practice* (2nd ed.) Larchmont, NY: Mary Ann Liebert, Inc.

Jensen, W. R., Sheridan, S. M., Olympia, D., & Andrews, D. (1994). Homework and students with learning disabilities and behavior disorders: A practical, parent-based approach. *Journal of Learning Disabilities, 27*(9), 538-548.

Jernigan, K. (1993, August). The pitfalls of political correctness: Euphemisms excoriated. *The Braille Monitor,* 865-867.

Jerome, J., Frantino, E. P., & Sturmey, P. (2007). The effects of errorless learning and backward chaining on the acquisition of Internet skills in adults with developmental disabilities. *Journal of Applied Behavior Analysis, 40,* 185-189.

Jimenez, R. T. (2002). Fostering the literacy development of Latino students. *Focus on Exceptional Children, 34*(6), 1-10.

Jitendra, A. K., Edwards, L. L., Sacks, G., & Jacobson, L. A. (2004). What research says about vocabulary instruction for students with learning disabilities. *Exceptional Children, 70,* 299-322.

Johnsen, S. K. (Ed.). (2004). *Identifying gifted students: A practical guide.* Waco, TX: Prufrock.

Johnson, B., & Cuvo, A. (1981). Teaching mentally retarded adults to cook. *Behavior Modification, 12,* 69-73.

Johnson, C. E., & Viramontez Anguiano, R. P. (2004). Latino parents in the rural Southeast: A study of family and school partnerships. *Journal of Family and Consumer Sciences, 96,* 4, 29-33.

Johnson, D. R., Mellard, D. F., & Lancaster, P. (2007). Road to success: Helping young adults with learning disabilities plan and prepare for employment. *Teaching Exceptional Children, 39*(6), 26-32.

Johnson, D. R., Stodden, R. A., Emanuel, E. J., Luecking, R., & Mack, M. (2002). Current challenges facing secondary education and transition services: What research tells us. *Exceptional Children, 68,* 519-531.

Johnson, D. W., & Johnson, R. T. (1987). *Learning together and alone: Cooperative, competitive, and individualistic learning* (2nd ed.). Englewood Cliffs, NJ: Prentice Hall.

Johnson, D. W., & Johnson, R. T. (1999). *Learning together and alone: Cooperative, competitive, and individualistic learning* (5th ed.). Boston: Allyn & Bacon.

Johnson, E., Mallard, D. F., Fuchs, D., & McKnight, M. A. (2006). *Responsiveness to intervention: How to do it.* Lawrence, KS: National Research Center on Learning Disabilities. [Available on-line at www.nrcld.org]

Johnson, H. A. (1997, June). *Internet use within deaf education: Current status, trends and applications.* Paper presented at the CAID/CEASD Conference, Hartford, CT.

Johnson, H. L. (1993). Stressful family experiences and young children: How the classroom teacher can help. *Intervention in School and Clinic, 28*(3), 165-171.

Johnson, K. R., & Layng, T. V. J. (1994). The Morningside Model of generative instruction. In R. Gardner, III, D. M. Sainato, J. O. Cooper, T. E. Heron, W. L. Heward, J. Eshleman, & T. A. Grossi (Eds.), *Behavior analysis in education: Focus on measurably superior instruction* (pp. 173-197). Monterey, CA: Brooks/Cole.

Johnson, R. (1985). *The picture communication symbols—Book II.* Solana Beach, CA: Mayer-Johnson.

Johnson, S., & Wehman, P. (2001). Teaching for transition. In P. Wehman (Ed.), *Life beyond the classroom: Transition strategies for young people with disabilities* (3rd ed.). Baltimore: Brookes.

Johnson, T. P. (1986). *The principal's guide to the educational rights of handicapped students.* Reston, VA: National Association of Secondary School Principals.

Johnson-Martin, N. M., Attermeier, S. M., & Hacker, B. (2004a). *The Carolina Curriculum for infants and toddlers with special needs* (3rd ed.). Baltimore: Brookes.

Johnson-Martin, N. M., Attermeier, S. M., & Hacker, B. (2004b). *The Carolina Curriculum for preschoolers with special needs* (2nd ed.). Baltimore: Brookes.

Johnston, D. (1994a). *Co:Writer* (Version 2.0) [Computer software]. Wauconda, IL: Don Johnston, Inc.

Johnston, D. (1994b). *Write:OutLoud* (Version 2.0) [Computer software]. Wauconda, IL: Don Johnston, Inc.

Johnston, L., Beard, L., & Bowden Carpenter, L. (2007). *Assistive technology: Access for all students.* Upper Saddle River, NJ: Merrill/Prentice Hall.

Johnston, M. K., Kelly, C. S., Harris, F. R., & Wolf, M. M. (1966). An application of reinforcement principles to the development of motor skills of a young child. *Child Development, 37,* 370-387.

Johnston, R., & Umberger, R. (1996). *The voice companion.* East Moline, IL: LinguiSystems.

Joint UN Programme on HIV/AIDS. (2006). *Global summary of the AIDS epidemic:*

December 2006. Geneva, Switzerland: Author. Retrieved August 24, 2007. http://data.unaids.org/pub/EpiReport/2006/02Global_Summary_2006_EpiUpdate_eng.pdf

Jolivette, K., Lingo, A. S., Houchins, D. E., Barton-Arwood, S. M. & Shippen, M. E. (2006). Building math fluency for students with developmental disabilities using *Great Leaps Math*. *Education and Training in Developmental Disabilities, 41*, 392-400.

Jolly, A. C., Test, D. W., & Spooner, F. (1993). Using badges to increase initiations of children with severe disabilities in a play setting. *Journal of The Association for Persons with Severe Handicaps, 18*, 46-51.

Jones, B. E., Clark, G. M., & Soltz, D. F. (1997). Characteristics and practices of sign language interpreters in inclusive education programs. *Exceptional Children, 63*, 257-268.

Jones, C. J. (2001). Teacher-friendly curriculum-based assessment in spelling. *Teaching Exceptional Children, 34*(3), 32-38.

Jones, D. E., Clatterbuck, C. C., Marquis, J., Turnbull, H. R., & Moberly, R. L. (1996). Educational placements for children who are ventilator assisted. *Exceptional Children, 63*, 47-57.

Jones, E. A., & Carr, E. G. (2004). Joint attention in children with autism: Theory and intervention. *Focus on Autism and Other Developmental Disabilities, 19*, 13-26.

Jones, J. (2004). Framing the assessment discussion. *Young Children, 10*(1), 14-18.

Jones, T. M., Garlow, J. A., Turnbull, H. R., & Barber, P. A. (1996). Family empowerment in a family support program. In G. H. S. Singer, L. E. Powers, & A. L. Olson (Eds.), *Redefining family support: Innovations in public-private partnerships* (p. 91). Baltimore: Brookes.

Jordan, L., Reyes-Blane, M. E., Peel, B. B., Peel, H. A., & Lane, H. B. (1998). Developing teacher-parent partnerships: Effective parent conferences. *Intervention in School and Clinic, 33*, 141-147.

Jordan, N. C., & Hanich, L. B. (2000). Mathematical thinking in second-grade children with different forms of LD. *Journal of Learning Disabilities, 33*, 567-578.

Jose, R. (1983). *Understanding low vision*. New York: American Foundation for the Blind.

Joseph, L., & Seery, M. E. (2004). Where is the phonics? A review of the literature on the use of phonetic analysis with students with mental retardation. *Remedial and Special Education, 25*, 88-94.

Joseph, L. M., & Konrad, M. (in press). Twenty ways to teach your students to self-manage their academic performance. *Intervention in School and Clinic*.

Jung, L. A. (2007). Writing SMART objectives and strategies that fit the routine. *Teaching Exceptional Children, 39*(4), 54-58.

Justen, J. E. (1976). Who are the severely handicapped? A problem in definition. *AAESPH Review, 1*(2), 1-12.

Justice, L. M. (2004). Creating language-rich preschool classroom environments.

Teaching Exceptional Children, 37(2), 36-44.

Justice, L. M. (2006). Communication sciences and disorders: An introduction. Boston: Allyn and Bacon.

Kadesjo, B., Gillberg, C., & Hagberg, B. (1999). The prevalence of autism and autism spectrum disorders. In F. C. Verhult & H. N. Koot (Eds.), *The epidemiology of child and adolescent psychopathology* (pp. 227-257). Oxford: Oxford University Press.

Kagan, J., & Snidman, N. (2004). *The long shadow of temperament*. Cambridge, MA: Harvard University Press.

Kagan, S. L., & Neuman, M. J. (1997, September). Highlights of the Quality 2000 Initiative: Not by chance. *Young Children*, pp. 54-62.

Kaiser, A. P., & Goetz, L. (1993). Enhancing communication with persons labeled severely disabled. *Journal of The Association for Persons with Severe Handicaps, 18*, 137-142.

Kaiser, A. P., & Grim, J. C. (2006). Teaching functional communication skills. In M. E. Snell & F. Brown (Eds.), *Instruction of students with severe disabilities* (6th ed.). Upper Saddle River, NJ: Merrill/Prentice Hall.

Kaiser, A. P., Hancock, T. B., Cai, X., Foster, E. M., & Hester, P. P. (2000). Parent-reported behavioral problems and language delays in boys and girls enrolled in head start classrooms. *Behavioral Disorders, 26*, 26-41.

Kame'enui, E. J. (1993). Diverse learners and the tyranny of time: Don't fix blame; fix the leaky roof. *The Reading Teacher, 46*, 376-383.

Kame'enui, E. J. (2007). A new paradigm: Responsiveness to intervention. *Teaching Exceptional Children, 39*(5), 6-7.

Kame'enui, E. J., Carnine, D. W., & Dixon, R. C. (2007). Introduction. In M. D. Coyne, E. J. Kame'enui, & D. W. Carnine (Eds.), *Effective teaching strategies that accommodate diverse learners* (3rd ed., p. 10). Upper Saddle River, NJ: Merrill/Prentice Hall. Reprinted by permission.

Kame'enui, E. J., Carnine, D. W., Dixon, R. C., Simmons, D. C., & Coyne, M. D. (Eds.), (2002). *Effective teaching strategies that accommodate diverse learners* (2nd ed.). Upper Saddle River, NJ: Merrill/Prentice Hall.

Kame'enui, E. J., Good R., III, & Harn, B. A. (2005). Beginning reading failure and the quantification of risk: Reading behavior as the supreme index. In W. L. Heward, T. E. Heron, N. A. Neef, S. M. Peterson, D. M. Sainato, G. Cartledge, R. Gardner, III, L. D. Peterson, S. B. Hersh, & J. C. Dardig (Eds.), *Focus on behavior analysis in education: Achievements, challenges, and opportunities* (pp. 69-89). Upper Saddle River, NJ: Merrill/Prentice Hall.

Kame'enui, E. J., & Simmons, D. C. (1990). *Designing instructional strategies: The prevention of academic learning problems*. Upper Saddle River, NJ: Merrill/Prentice Hall.

Kamps, D., Wendland, M., & Culpepper, M. (2006). Active teacher participation in functional behavior assessment for students

with emotional and behavioral disorders risks in general education classrooms. *Behavioral Disorders, 31*, 128-146.

Kamps, D. M., Dugan, E. P., Leonard, B. R., & Daoust, P. M. (1994). Enhanced small group instruction using choral responding and student interactions for children with autism and developmental disabilities. *American Journal on Mental Retardation, 99*, 60-73.

Kanaya, T., Scullin, M. H., & Ceci, S. J. (2003). The Flynn effect and U.S. policies: The impact of rising IQs on American society via mental retardation diagnoses. *American Psychologist, 58*, 778-790.

Kangas, K. A., & Lloyd, L. L. (2006). Augmentative and alternative communication. In N. B. Anderson & G. H. Shames (Eds.), *Human communication disorders: An introduction* (7th ed.), (pp. 436-470). Boston: Allyn & Bacon.

Kanner, A. M., & Schafer, P. O. (2006). Seizures and teens: When seizures aren't the only problem. *Exceptional Parent, 36*(11), 50, 52-55.

Kanner, L. (1943/1985). Autistic disturbance of affective contract. In A. M. Donnellan (Ed.), *Classic readings in autism* (pp. 11-53). New York: Teachers College Press.

Kaplan, D. E., Gayan, J., Ahn, J., Won, T. W., Pails, D. L., Olson, R. K., DeFries, C., Wood, F. B., Pennington, B. F., Page, G. P., Smith, S. D., & Gruen, J. R. (2002). Evidence for linkage and association with reading disability. *American Journal of Human Genetics, 70*, 1287-1298.

Kaplan, E., Fein, D., Kramer, J., Delis, D., & Morris, R. (2007). *Wechsler Intelligence Scale for Children-Fourth Edition Integrated*. San Antonio, TX: Harcourt Assessment.

Kaplan, S. (1988). Maintaining a gifted program. *Roeper Review, 11*(1), 35-37.

Kaplan, S. (2004). Where we stand determines the answers to the question: Can the No Child Left Behind legislation be beneficial to gifted students? *Roeper Review, 26*(3), 124-125.

Kaplan, S. (2004a). The concept of differentiation. *Tempo, 24*(1), 1, 18-19.

Kaplan, S. (2005). Layering differentiated curricula for the gifted and talented. In F. A. Karnes & S. M. Bean (Eds.), *Methods and materials for teaching the gifted* (2nd ed.) (pp. 107-132). Waco, TX: Prufrock Press.

Karchmer, M. A., & Allen, T. E. (1999). The functional assessment of deaf and hard of hearing students. *American Annals of the Deaf, 144*, 68-77.

Karchmer, M. A., & Mitchell, R. E. (2005). Demographic and achievement characteristics of deaf and hard-of-hearing students. In M. Marschark & P. E. Spencer (Eds.), *Oxford handbook of deaf studies, language, and education* (paperback ed.) (pp. 21-37). New York: Oxford University Press.

Karnes, F. A., & Stephens, K. R. (2008). *Achieving excellence: Educating the gifted and talented*. Upper Saddle River, NJ: Merrill/Prentice Hall.

Karnes, K. B., Beauchamp, K. D. F., & Pfaus, D. B. (1993). PEECH: A nationally validated early childhood special education model. *Topics in Early Childhood Special Education, 13,* 120-135.

Karnick, N. S. (2004). The social environment. In H. Steiner (Ed.), *Handbook of mental health interventions in children and adolescents* (pp. 51-72). San Francisco: Jossey-Bass.

Kasari, C., Freeman, S., & Paparella, T. (2006). Joint attention and symbolic play in young children with autism: A randomized controlled intervention study. *Journal of Child Psychology and Psychiatry, 47,* 611-620.

Kashara, M., & Turnbull, A. P. (2005). Meaning of family-professional partnerships: Japanese mothers' perspectives. *Exceptional Children, 71,* 249-265.

Kasper-Ferguson, S., & Moxley, A. (2002). Developing a writing package with student graphing of fluency. *Education and Treatment of Children, 25,* 249-267.

Katayama, A. D., & Robinson, D. H. (2000). Getting students "partially" involved in note-taking using graphic organizers. *The Journal of Experimental Education, 68,* 119-133.

Katsiyannis, A., & Maag, J. W. (2001). Manifestation determination as a golden fleece. *Exceptional Children, 68,* 85-96.

Katsiyannis, A., & Yell, M. L. (2000). The Supreme Court and school health services: Cedar Rapids v. Garret F. *Exceptional Children, 66,* 317-326.

Katsiyannis, A., & Yell, M. L. (2004). Critical issues and trends in the education of students with emotional or behavioral disorders [Introduction to special issue]. *Behavioral Disorders, 29,* 209-210.

Kauffman, J. M. (1999). How we prevent the prevention of emotional and behavioral disorders. *Exceptional Children, 65,* 448-468.

Kauffman, J. M. (2002). *Education deform: Bright people sometimes say stupid things about education.* Lanham, MD: The Scarecrow Press.

Kauffman, J. M. (2003). Appearance, stigma, and prevention. *Remedial and Special Education, 24,* 195-198.

Kauffman, J. M. (2005). *Characteristics of emotional and behavioral disorders of children and youth* (8th ed.). Upper Saddle River, NJ: Merrill/Prentice Hall.

Kauffman, J. M., & Hallahan, D. K. (2005). *The illusion of full inclusion: A comprehensive critique of a current special education bandwagon* (2nd ed.). Austin, TX: PRO-ED.

Kauffman, J. M., & Konold, T. R., (2007). Making sense in education: Pretense (including No Child Left Behind) and realities in rhetoric and policy about schools and schooling. *Exceptionality, 15,* 75-96.

Kauffman, J. M., & Krouse, J. (1981). The cult of educability: Searching for the substance of things hoped for; the evidence of things not seen. *Analysis and Intervention in Developmental Disabilities, 1*(1), 53-61.

Kauffman, J. M., Mock, D. R., Tankersley, M., & Landrum, T. J. (in press). Effective service delivery models. R. J. Morris & N. Mather (Eds.), *Evidence-based interventions for students with learning and behavioral challenges.* Mahwah, NJ: Lawrence Erlbaum Associates.

Kaufman, A. (2000). Clothing-selection habits of teenage girls who are sighted and blind. *Journal of Visual Impairments and Blindness, 94,* 527-531.

Kavale, K. A. (2002). Discrepancy models in the identification of learning disability. In R. Bradley, L. Danielson, & D. P. Hallahan (Eds.), *Identification of learning disabilities: Research to practice* (pp. 369-426). Mahwah, NJ: Erlbaum.

Kavale, K. A., & Forness, S. R. (1995). *Social skill deficits and training: A meta-analysis of the research in learning disabilities* (Vol. 9, pp. 119-160). Greenwich, CT: JAI Press.

Kavale, K. A., & Forness, S. R. (1996). Social skills deficits and learning disabilities: A meta-analysis. *Journal of Learning Disabilities, 29,* 226-237.

Kavale, K. A., & Forness, S. R. (2000). History, rhetoric and reality: Analysis of the inclusion debate. *Remedial and Special Education, 21,* 279-296.

Kavale, K. A., Holdnack, J. A., & Mostert, M. P. (2006). Responsiveness to intervention and the identification of learning disabilities: A critique and alternative proposal. *Learning Disability Quarterly, 29,* 113-127.

Kavale, K., & Mattson, P. D. (1983). One jumped off the balance beam: Meta-analysis of perceptual-motor training. *Journal of Learning Disabilities, 16,* 165-173.

Kavale, K. A., & Reese, J. H. (1992). The character of learning disabilities: An Iowa profile. *Learning Disability Quarterly, 15,* 74-94.

Kay, P. J., & Fitzgerald, M. (1997). Parents + teachers + action research = Real parent involvement. *Teaching Exceptional Children, 30*(1), 8-11.

Kazdin, A. (1987). *Conduct disorders in childhood.* Newbury Park, CA: Sage.

Kearsley, G. (2000). *Online education: Learning and teaching in cyberspace.* Belmont, CA: Wadsworth.

Keel, M. C., & Gast, D. L. (1992). Small-group instruction for students with learning disabilities: Observational and incidental learning. *Exceptional Children, 58,* 357-368.

Keenan, M., Kerr, K. P., & Dillenberger, K. (Eds.). (2000). *Parent's education as autism therapists: Applied behaviour analysis in context.* London: Jessica Kingsley.

Kehle, T. J., Bray, M. A., Theodore, L. A., Jenson, W. R., & Clark, E. (2000). A multi-component intervention designed to reduce disruptive classroom behavior. *Psychology in the Schools, 37,* 475-481.

Keith, T., Keith, P., Quirk, K., Sperduto, J., Santillo, S., & Killings, S. (1998). Longitudinal effects of parent involvement on high school grades: Similarities and differences across gender and ethnic groups. *Journal of School Psychology, 36,* 335-363.

Kelker, K., Hecimovic, A., & LeRoy, C. H. (1994). Designing a classroom and school environment for students with AIDS: A checklist for teachers. *Teaching Exceptional Children, 26*(4), 52-55.

Keller, C. L., Brady, M. P., & Taylor, R. L. (2005). Using self-evaluation to improve student teacher interns' use of specific praise. *Education and Training in Mental Retardation and Developmental Disabilities, 40,* 368-376.

Keller, C. L., & Duffy, M. L. (2005). "I said that?" How to improve our instructional behavior in just 5 minutes per day through data-based self-evaluation. *Teaching Exceptional Children, 37*(4), 36-39.

Kelly, D. J. (1998). A clinical synthesis of the "late talker" literature: Implications for service delivery. *Language, Speech and Hearing Services in the School, 29,* 76-84.

Kelly, M. L. (1990). *School-home notes.* New York: Guilford.

Kelly, S. J., Macaruso, P., & Sokol, S. M. (1997). Mental calculations in an autistic savant: A case study. *Journal of Clinical and Experimental Neuropsychology, 19*(2), 172-184.

Kennedy, C. H., & Fisher, D. (2001). *Inclusive middle schools.* Baltimore: Brookes.

Kennedy, C. H., & Horn, E. H. (2004). *Including students with severe disabilities.* Boston: Allyn and Bacon.

Kennedy, C. H., & Itkonen, T. (1994). Some effects of regular class participation on the social contacts and social network of high school students with disabilities. *Journal of The Association for Persons with Severe Handicaps, 19,* 1-10.

Kennedy, C. H., Shukla, S., & Fryxell, D. (1997). Comparing the effects of educational placement on the social relationships of intermediate school students with severe disabilities. *Exceptional Children, 64,* 31-47.

Kenning, C. (2007, March 4). Special educators find standards stifling: Some fear practical skills are taking a back seat to the new academic demands of No Child Left Behind. *The Courier-Journal,* Louisville, KY. Downloaded on-line http://www.courier-journal.com/apps/pbcs.dll/article?AID=2007703040504

Keogh, B. K., Bernheimer, L. P., & Guthrie, D. (2004). Children with developmental delays twenty years later: Where are they? How are they? *American Journal of Mental Retardation, 109,* 219-230.

Keogh, B. K. (2005a). Revisiting classification and identification. *Learning Disability Quarterly, 28,* 115-118.

Keogh, B. K. (2005b). Revisiting classification and identification. Labeling. *Learning Disability Quarterly, 28,* 100-102.

Kephart, N. C. (1971). *The slow learner in the classroom* (2nd ed.). Columbus, OH: Merrill.

Kern, J. K., Miller, V. S., Evans, P. A., & Trivedi, M. H. (2002). Efficacy of porcine secretin in children with autism and pervasive development disorder. *Journal of Autism and Developmental Disorders, 32,* 153-160.

Kern, L., Bambara, L., & Fogt, J. (2002). Class-wide curricular modifications to improve the behavior of students with emotional and behavioral disorders. *Behavioral Disorders, 27,* 317-326.

Kern, L., Dunlap, G., Clarke, S., & Childs, K. E. (1995). Student-assisted functional assessment interview. *Diagnostique, 19,* 29–39.

Kern, L., Mantegna, M. E., Vorndran, C. M., Bailin, D., & Hilt, A. (2001). Choice of task sequence to reduce problem behaviors. *Journal of Positive Behavior Interventions, 3,* 3–10.

Kerr, B. (1985). Smart girls, gifted women: Special guidance concerns. *Roeper Review, 8*(1), 30–33.

Kerr, B. (1994). Smart girls two: A new psychology of girls, women, and giftedness. Dayton, OH: Ohio Psychology Press.

Kerr, B., & Cohen, S. (2001). *Smart boys.* Tempe, AZ: Great Potential Press.

Kerr, M. M., & Nelson, C. M. (2002). *Strategies for addressing behavior problems in the classroom* (4th ed.). Upper Saddle River, NJ: Merrill/Prentice Hall.

Kerr, M. M., & Nelson, C. M. (2006). *Strategies for managing behavior problems in the classroom* (5th ed.). Upper Saddle River, NJ: Merrill/Prentice Hall.

Kershner, J., Hawks, W., & Grekin, R. (1977). Megavitamins and learning disorders: A controlled double-blind experiment. Unpublished manuscript, Ontario Institute for Studies in Education.

Keyes, M. W., & Owens-Johnson, L. (2003). Developing person-centered IEPs. *Intervention in School and Clinic, 38,* 145–152.

Kiewra, K. A. (2002). How classroom teachers can help students learn and teach them how to learn. *Theory and Practice, 41,* 71–80.

Killu, K., Sainato, D. M., Davis, C. A., Ospelt, H., & Paul, J. N. (1998). Effects of high-probability request sequences on preschoolers' compliance and disruptive behavior. *Journal of Behavioral Education, 8,* 347–368.

Kim, S., Larson, S., & Lakin, K. C. (2001). Behavioral outcomes of deinstitutionalization for people with intellectual disability. *Journal of Intellectual and Developmental Disability, 26,* 35–50.

Kim, S. H., & Arnold, M. B. (2006). Characteristics of persons with severe mental retardation. In M. Beirne-Smith, J. R. Patton, & S. H. Kim, (Eds.), *Mental retardation* (7th ed.). Upper Saddle River, NJ: Merrill/Prentice Hall.

Kimball, J., Kinney, E., Taylor, B., & Stromer R. (2004). Video enhanced activity schedules for children with autism: A promising package. *Education and Treatment of Children, 27,* 280–298.

King, E. W. (2005). Addressing the social and emotional needs of twice-exceptional learners. *Teaching Exceptional Children, 38*(1), 16–20.

King, N. J., Heyne, D., & Ollendick, T. H. (2005). Cognitive-behavioral interventions for anxiety and phobic disorders in children: A review. *Behavioral Disorders, 30,* 241–257.

King, S. J., DeCaro, J. J., Karchmer, M. A., & Cole, K. J. (2001). *College and career programs for deaf students* (11th ed.). Washington, DC, and Rochester, NY: Gallaudet University and National Technical Institute for the Deaf.

Kingsley, M. (1997). The effects of a visual loss. In H. Mason & S. McCall (Eds.), *Visual impairment: Access to education for children and young people* (pp. 23–29). London: Fulton.

Kirchner, C., & Diamont, S. (1999). Estimates of the number of visually impaired students, their teachers, and orientation and mobility specialists: Part 2. *Journal of Visual Impairment and Blindness, 93,* 738–744.

Kirk, S. A., McCarthy, J. J., & Kirk, W. D. (1968). *Illinois test of psycholinguistic abilities* (rev. ed.). Urbana, IL: University of Illinois Press.

Kirkwood, R. (1997). The adolescent. In H. Mason & S. McCall (Eds.), *Visual impairment: Access to education for children and young people* (pp. 110–123). London, Fulton.

Kirsten, I. (1981). *The Oakland picture dictionary.* Wauconda, IL: Johnston.

Kishi, G. S., & Meyer, L. H. (1994). What children report and remember: A six-year follow-up of the effects of social contact between peers with and without severe disabilities. *Journal of The Association for Persons with Severe Handicaps, 19,* 277–289.

Klein, J. (1994). Supported living: Not just another "rung" on the continuum. *TASH Newsletter, 20*(7), 16–18.

Klein, K. (2007, August 20). Pencils, pens, meds"As kids head to class, pharmaceutical companies ramp up their drug marketing–and it works. *Los Angeles Times.* [Retrieved September 3, 2007. http://www.latimes.com/news/opinion/laoeklein20aug20,0,6706516.story?coll= la-opinion-center]

Klein, R. E., McHugh, E., Harrington, S. L., Davis, T., & Lieberman, L. J. (2005). Adapted bicycles for teaching riding skills. *Teaching Exceptional Children, 37*(6), 50–56.

Kleinert, H. L., Miracle, S. A., & Sheppard-Jones, K. (2007). Including students with moderate and severe disabilities in extracurricular and community activities. *Teaching Exceptional Children, 39*(6), 33–38.

Kleinheksel, K. A., & Summy, S. E. (2003). Enhancing student learning and social behavior through mnemonic strategies. *Teaching Exceptional Children, 36*(2), 30–35.

Kleweno, C. P., Seibel, E. J., Viirre, E. S., Kelly, J. P., & Furness, T. A. (2001). The virtual-retinal display as a low-vision computer interface: Pilot study. *Journal of Rehabilitation Research and Development, 38,* 431–441.

Kliewer, C., & Biklen, D. (1996). Labeling: Who wants to be retarded? In W. Stainback & S. Stainback (Eds.), *Controversial issues confronting special education: Divergent perspectives* (pp. 83–95). Boston: Allyn & Bacon.

Klimes-Dougan, B., Lopez, J. A., Nelson, P., & Adelman, H. S. (1992). Two studies of low-income parents involvement in schooling. *The Urban Review, 24,* 185–202.

Kline, F. M., Silver, L. B., & Russell, S. C. (Eds.). (2001). *The educator's guide to medical issues in the classroom.* Baltimore: Brookes.

Klingner, J. K., & Vaughn, S. (1999). Students' perceptions of instruction in inclusion classrooms: Implications for students with learning disabilities. *Exceptional Children, 66,* 23–37.

Klingner, J. K., Vaughn, S., Hughes, M. T., Schumm, J. S., & Elbaum, B. (1998). Outcomes for students with and without learning disabilities in inclusive classrooms. *Learning Disabilities Research and Practice, 13,* 153–161.

Klug, B. J. (2004). Children of the starry cope: Gifted and talented Native American students. In D. Boothe & J. Stanley (Eds.), *In the eyes of the beholder: Critical issues for diversity in gifted education* (pp. 49–72). Waco, TX: Prufrock.

Kluth, P. (2004). Autism, autobiography, and adaptations. *Teaching Exceptional Children, 36*(4), 42–47.

Kluwin, T. N. (1985). Profiling the deaf student who is a problem in the classroom. *Adolescence, 20,* 863–875.

Kluwin, T. N. (1993). Cumulative effects of mainstreaming on the achievement of deaf adolescents. *Exceptional Children, 60,* 73–81.

Kluwin, T. N., & Moores, D. F. (1989). Mathematics achievement of hearing impaired adolescents in different placements. *Exceptional Children, 55,* 327–335.

Knecht, H. A., Whitelaw, G. M., & Nelson, P. B. (2000). *Structural variables and their relationship to background noise levels and reverberation times in unoccupied classrooms.* Unpublished manuscript.

Knoll, J. A., & Wheeler, C. B. (2005). My home and community: Developing supports for adult living. In R. W. Flexer, T. J. Simmons, P. Luft, & R. M. Baer (Eds.), *Transition planning for secondary students with disabilities* (2nd ed.), (pp. 499–539). Upper Saddle River, NJ: Merrill/Prentice Hall.

Knoors, H., & Vervloed, M. P. J. (2005). Educational programming for deaf children with multiple disabilities: Accommodating special needs. In M. Marschark & P. E. Spencer (Eds.), *Oxford handbook of deaf studies, language, and education* (paperback ed.) (pp. 82–96). New York: Oxford University Press.

Knotek, S. (2003). Bias in problem solving and the social process of student study teams. *Journal of Special Education, 37,* 2–14.

Knowlton, E. (1998). Considerations in the design of personalized curricula supports for students with developmental disabilities. *Education and Training in Mental Retardation and Developmental Disabilities, 33,* 95–107.

Kochhar, C. A., West, L. L., & Taymans, J. M. (2000). *Successful inclusion: Practical strategies for a shared responsibility.* Upper Saddle River, NJ: Merrill/Prentice Hall.

Kochhar-Bryant, C. A. (2008). *Collaboration and system coordination for student with special needs: From early childhood to the postsecondary years.* Upper Saddle River, NJ: Merrill/Prentice Hall.

Kochhar-Bryant, C.A., & Price, T. (2008). How does cultural and linguistic diversity affect school collaboration and system coordination? In C.A. Kochhar-Bryant, *Collaboration and system coordination for students with special needs: From early childhood to the postsecondary years* (pp. 228–253). Upper Saddle River, NJ: Merrill/Prentice Hall.

Kodak, T., Miltenberger, R. G., & Romaniuk, C. (2003). The effects of differential negative reinforcement of other behavior and noncontingent escape on compliance. *Journal of Applied Behavior Analysis, 36,* 379–382.

Koegel, L. K., Koegel, R. L., & Dunlap, G. (1996). *Positive behavioral support: Including people with difficult behavior in the community.* Baltimore: Brookes.

Koegel, L. K., Koegel, R. L., Harrower, J. K., & Carter, C. M. (1999). Pivotal response intervention I: Overview of approach. *Journal of The Association for Persons with Severe Handicaps, 24,* 174–185.

Koegel, R. L., & Koegel, L. (1995). *Teaching children with autism.* Baltimore: Brookes.

Koegel, R. L., & Koegel, L. K. (2006). *Pivotal response treatments for autism.* Baltimore: Brookes.

Koenig, A. J. (1996). Growing into literacy. In M. C. Holbrook (Ed.), *Children with visual impairments: A parents' guide* (pp. 227–257). Bethesda, MD: Woodbine House.

Koenig, A. J., & Holbrook, M. C. (2000a). Ensuring high-quality instruction for students in braille literacy programs. *Journal of Visual Impairments and Blindness, 94,* 677–694.

Koenig, A. J., & Holbrook, M. C. (Eds.). (2000b). *Foundations of education: Vol. 1: History and theory of teaching children and youths with visual impairments* (2nd ed.). New York: AFB Press.

Koestler, F.A. (2004). *The unseen minority: A social history of blindness in the United States.* New York: AFB Press.

Kohl, F. L., McLaughlin, M. J., & Nagle, K. (2006). Alternative achievement standards and assessments: A descriptive investigation of 16 states. *Exceptional Children, 73,* 107–123.

Kohler, P. (1996). *A taxonomy for transition programming: Linking research and practice.* Champaign: University of Illinois, Transition Research Institute.

Kohler, P. D. (1994). On-the-job training: A curricular approach to employment. *Career Development for Exceptional Individuals, 17,* 29–40.

Kohler, P. D. (1998). Implementing a transition perspective of education: A comprehensive approach to planning and delivering secondary education and transition service. In F. R. Rusch & J. G. Chadsey (Eds.), *Beyond high school: Transition from school to work* (pp. 179–205). New York: Wadsworth.

Kohler, P. D., & Field, S. (2003). Transition-focused education: Foundation for the future. *Journal of Special Education, 37,* 174–183.

Kohn, A. (1993a). *Punished by rewards.* Boston: Houghton Mifflin.

Kohn, A. (1993b). Why incentive plans cannot work. *Harvard Business Review, 71*(5), 54–63.

Kohn, A. (2001). Five reasons to stop saying "Good job!" *Young Children, 56*(5), 24–28.

Komesaroff, L. (2007). *Disabling pedagogy: Power, politics, and Deaf education.* Washington, DC: Gallaudet Press.

Konold, K. E., Miller, S. P., & Konold, K. B. (2004). Using teaching feedback to enhance student learning. *Teaching Exceptional Children, 36*(6), 64–69.

Konold, T. R., Walthall, J. C., & Pianta, R. C. (2004). The behavior of child behavior ratings: Measurement structure of the Child Behavior Checklist across time, informants, and child gender. *Behavioral Disorders, 29,* 372–383.

Konrad, M. (in press). Twenty ways to involve students in the IEP process. *Intervention in School and Clinic.*

Konrad, M., & Test, D. W. (in press). Effects of GO 4 IT . . . NOW! Strategy instruction on paragraph-writing and goal articulation of middle school students with disabilities. *Remedial and Special Education.*

Konrad, M., & Test, D. W. (2004). Teaching middle-school students with disabilities to use an IEP Template. *Career Development for Exceptional Individuals, 27,* 101–124.

Konrad, M., & Trela, K. (2007). Go 4 it . . . NOW! Extending writing strategies to support all students. *Teaching Exceptional Children, 39*(4), 42–51.

Konrad, M., Trela, K., & Test, D. W. (2006). The effects of Go 4 IT . . . NOW! instruction on paragraph-writing and goal-setting skills of students with orthopedic and cognitive disabilities. *Education and Training in Developmental Disabilities, 41,* 111–124.

Koyanagi, C., & Gaines, S. (1993). *All systems failure: An examination of the results of neglecting the needs of children with serious emotional disturbance.* Alexandria, VA: National Mental Health Association.

Kozloff, M.A., & Rice, J. (2000). Parent and family issues: Stress and knowledge. In P. Accardo (Ed.), *Autism: Clinical and research issues* (pp. 303–325). Timonium, MD: York.

Kraemer, B. R., McIntryre, L. L., & Blacher, J. (2003). Quality of life for young adults with mental retardation during transition. *Mental Retardation, 41,* 250–262.

Krajewski, J. J., & Flaherty, T. (2000). Attitudes of high school students toward individuals with mental retardation. *Mental Retardation, 38,* 154–162.

Krathwohl, D. R. (2002). A revision of Bloom's Taxonomy: An overview. *Theory Into Practice, 41,* 212–218.

Kratochwill, T. R., & Stoiber, K. C. (2000). Empirically supported interventions and school psychology. *School Psychology Quarterly, 15,* 233–253.

Krebs, P., & Coultier, G. (1992). Unified sports: I've seen the light. *Palaestra, 8*(2), 42–45.

Kreicbergs, U., Valdimarsdottir, U., Onelov, E., et al. (2004). Talking about death with children who have severe malignant disease. *New England Journal of Medicine, 351,* 1175–1186.

Kroth, R. L., & Edge, D. (2007). *Communicating with parents and families of exceptional children* (4th ed.). Denver: Love.

Kube, D.A., Peterson, M. C., & Palmer, F. B. (2002). Attention deficit hyperactivity disorder: Comorbidity and medication use. *Clinical Pediatrics, 41,* 461–469.

Kubina, R., & Cooper, J. O. (2001). Changing learning channels: An efficient strategy to facilitate instruction and learning. *Intervention in School and Clinic, 35,* 161–166.

Kubina, R. M., Jr. (2005). The relations among fluency, rate building, and practice: A response to Doughty, Chase, and O'Shields (2004). *The Behavior Analyst, 28,* 73–76.

Kubina, R. M., & Morrison, R. S. (2000). Fluency in education. *Behavior and Social Issues, 10,* 83–99.

Kugel, R. B., & Wolfensberger, W. (Eds.). (1969). *Changing patterns in residential services for the mentally retarded.* Washington, DC: Superintendent of Documents.

Kuhn, T. (1962). *The structure of scientific revolutions.* Chicago: University of Chicago Press.

Kulik, J.A. (1992a). Ability grouping and gifted students. In N. Colangelo, S. G. Assouline, & D. L. Ambroson (Eds.), *Talent development: Proceedings from the 1991 Henry B. and Jocelyn Wallace National Research Symposium on Talent Development* (pp. 261–266). Unionville, NY: Trillium.

Kulik, J.A. (1992b). An analysis of the research on ability grouping: Historical and contemporary perspectives. *Research-Based Decision Making Series.* Storrs: University of Connecticut, National Research Center on the Gifted and Talented.

Kulik, J.A. (2003). Grouping and tracking. In N. Colangelo & G.A. Davis (Eds.), *Handbook of gifted education* (3rd ed.), (pp. 268–281). Needham Heights, MA: Allyn & Bacon.

Kulik, J.A. (2004, May 25). *Grouping, tracking, and de-tracking.* Invited presentation. Seventh biennial Henry B. & Jocelyn Wallace National Research Symposium on Talent Development. Iowa City, Iowa: The University of Iowa.

Kulik, J.A., & Kulik, C. L. C. (1984a). Effects of accelerated instruction on students. *Review of Educational Research, 54,* 409–425.

Kulik, J.A., & Kulik, C. L. C. (1984b). Synthesis of research of effects of accelerated instruction. *Educational Leadership, 42,* 84–89.

Kulik, J.A., & Kulik, C. L. C. (1987). Effects of ability grouping on student achievement. *Equity and Excellence, 23,* 22–30.

Kulik, J.A., & Kulik, C. L. C. (1990). Ability grouping and gifted students. In N. Colangelo & G.A. Davis (Eds.), *Handbook of gifted education* (pp. 178–196). Boston, MA: Allyn & Bacon.

Kulik, J.A., & Kulik, C. L. C. (1992). Meta-analytic findings on grouping programs. *Gifted Child Quarterly, 36,* 73–77.

Kulman, L. (1999, April 26). What'd you say? *U.S. News & World Report,* 66–68, 71–74.

Kuna, J. (2001). The Human Genome Project and eugenics: Identifying the impact on individuals with mental retardation. *Mental Retardation, 39,* 158–160.

Kuntze, M. (1998). Literacy and deaf children: The language question. *Topics in Language Disorders, 18*(4), 1–15.

Kuoch, H., & Mirenda, P. (2003). Social story interventions for young children with autism spectrum disorders. *Focus on Autism and Other Developmental Disabilities, 18,* 219-227.

Kwasman, A., Tinsley, B. J., & Lepper, H. S. (1995). Pediatricians' knowledge and attitudes concerning diagnosis and treatment of attention deficit hyperactivity disorder. *Archives of Pediatric Adolescent Medicine, 149,* 1211-1216.

LaBlance, G. R., Steckol, K. F., & Smith, V. L. (1994). Stuttering: The role of the classroom teacher. *Teaching Exceptional Children, 26*(2), 10-12.

Laborit, E. (1998). *The cry of the gull.* Washington, DC: Gallaudet University Press.

Lachapelle, Y., Wehmeyer, M. L., Haelewyck, M. C., Courbois, Y., Keith, K. D., Schalock, R., Verdugo, M. A., & Walsh, P. N. (2005). The relationship between quality of life and self-determination: An international study. *Journal of Intellectual Disability Research, 49,* 740-744.

Lackaye, T., Margalit, M., Ziv, O., & Ziman, T. (2006). Comparison of self-efficacy, mood, effort, and hope between students with learning disabilities and their non-LD-matched peers. *Learning Disabilities Research & Practice, 21,* 111-112.

Lago-Delello, E. (1998). Classroom dynamics and the development of serious emotional disturbance. *Exceptional Children, 64,* 479-492.

Lahey, B. B., Applegate, B., McBurnett, K., Biederman, J., Greenhill, L., Hynd, G. W., Barkley, R. A., Newcorn, J., Jensen, P., Richters, J., Garfinkel, B., Kerdyk, L., Frick, P. J., Ollendick, T., Perez, D., Hart, E. L., Waldman, I., & Shaffer, D. (1994). DSM-IV field trials for attention deficit hyperactivity disorder in children and adolescents. *American Journal of Psychiatry, 151,* 1673-1685.

Lahm, E. A., & Everington, C. (2002). Communication and technology supports. In L. Hamill & C. Everington, *Teaching students with moderate to severe disabilities: An applied approach for inclusive environments* (pp. 51-79). Upper Saddle River, NJ: Merrill/Prentice Hall.

Lake, J. F., & Billingsley, B. S. (2000). An analysis of factors that contribute to parent-school conflict in special education. *Remedial and Special Education, 21,* 240-251.

Lakin, K. C., Prouty, R., Polister, B., & Coucouvanis, K. (2003). Selected changes in residential service systems over a quarter century, 1977-2002. *Mental Retardation, 41,* 303-306.

Lakin, K. C., Smith, J., Prouty, R., & Polister, B. (2001). State institutions during the 1990s: Changes in the number of facilities, average, daily populations, and expenditures between fiscal years 1991 and 2000. *Mental Retardation, 39,* 72-75.

Lalli, J. S., Browder, D. M., Mace, F. C., & Brown, D. K. (1993). Teacher use of descriptive analysis data to implement interventions to decrease students' problem behaviors. *Journal of Applied Behavior Analysis, 26,* 227-238.

Lambert, M. C., Cartledge, G., Lo, Y., & Heward, W. L. (2006). Effects of response cards on disruptive behavior and participation by fourth-grade students during math lessons in an urban school. *Journal of Positive Behavioral Interventions, 8,* 88-99.

Lambert, N., Nihira, K., & Leland, H. (1993). *Adaptive Behavior Scale—School* (2nd ed.). Austin, TX: PRO-ED.

Lambie, R. (2000). *Family systems within educational contexts: Understanding at-risk special needs students.* Denver: Love.

Lancaster, J. (1806). *Improvements in education.* London: Collins & Perkins.

Lancioni, G. E., O'Reilly, M. F., & Oliva, D. (2001). Self-operated verbal instruction for people with intellectual and visual disabilities: Using instructor cluster after task co acquisition. *International Journal of Disability, Development and Educator, 48,* 304-312.

Lancioni, G. E., O'Reilly, M. F., Singh, N. N., Sigafoos, J., Didden, R., Oliva, D., & Severini, L. (2006). A microswitch-based program to enable students with multiple disabilities to choose among environmental stimuli. *Journal of Visual Impairment and Blindness, 100,* 488-493.

Landa, R. (2003). Early identification of autism spectrum disorders. *Exceptional Parent, 33*(7), 60-63.

Landa, R. J. (2004). Early communication development and intervention for children with autism. *Mental Retardation Developmental Disability Research Reviews, 9*(1), 16-25.

Landa, R. J., & Garrett-Mayer, E. (2006). *Journal of Child Psychology and Psychiatry, 47*(6), 629-638.

Landa, R. J., Holman, K. C., & Garrett-Mayer, E. (2007). Social and communication development in toddlers with early and later diagnosis of autism spectrum disorders. *Archives of General Psychiatry, 64*(7), 853-864.

Landesman, S., & Ramey, C. T. (1989). Developmental psychology and mental retardation: Integrating scientific principles with treatment practices. *American Psychologist, 44,* 409-415.

Landrum, M. (2002). *Consultation in gifted education: Teachers working together to serve students.* Mansfield, CT: Creative Learning.

Landrum, T., Katsiyannis, A., & Archwamety, T. (2004). An analysis of placement and exit patterns of students with emotional and behavioral disorders. *Behavioral Disorders, 29,* 140-153.

Landrum, T., Tankersley, M., & Kauffman, J. M. (2003). What is special about special education for students with emotional or behavioral disorders? *Journal of Special Education, 37,* 148-156.

Landy, S. (2002). *Pathways to competence: Encouraging healthy social and emotional development in young children.* Baltimore: Brookes.

Lane, H. L. (1988). Is there a "psychology of the deaf"? *Exceptional Children, 55,* 7-19.

Lane, H. L., & Bahan, B. (1998). Ethics of cochlear implantation in young children: A review and reply from a Deaf-World perspective. *Otolaryngology Head and Neck Surgery, 119,* 297-308.

Lane, K. L., Carter, E. W., Pierson, M. R., & Glaeser, B. C. (2006). Academic, social, and behavioral characteristics of high school students with emotional disturbances and learning disabilities. *Journal of Emotional and Behavioral Disorders,* 108-117.

Lane, K. L., Falk, K., & Wehby, J. H. (2006). Classroom management in special education classrooms and resource rooms. In C. M. Evertson and C. S. Weinstein (Eds.). *Handbook of classroom management: Research, practice, and contemporary issues* (pp. 439-460). Mahwah, NJ: Lawrence Erlbaum.

Lane, K. L., Givner, C. C., & Pierson, M. R. (2004). Teacher expectations of student behavior: Social skills are necessary for success in elementary classrooms. *Journal of Special Education, 38,* 104-110.

Lane, K. L., Gresham, F. M., & O'Shaughnessy, T. E. (2002). *Interventions for children with or at risk for emotional and behavioral disorders.* Boston: Allyn & Bacon.

Lane, K. L., & Menzies, H. M. (2005). Teacher-identified students with and without academic and behavioral concerns: Characteristics and responsiveness. *Behavioral Disorders, 31,* 65-83.

Lane, K. L., Menzies, H., Barton-Arwood, S. M., Doukas, G. L., & Munton, S. M. (2005). Designing, implementing, and evaluating social skills interventions for elementary students: Step-by-step procedures based on actual school-based investigations. *Preventing School Failure, 49,* 18-26.

Lane, K. L., Pierson, M. R., & Givner, C. C. (2004). Teacher expectations of student behaviors: Which skills do elementary and secondary teachers deem necessary for success in the classroom? *Journal of Special Education, 38,* 174-186.

Lane, K. L., Wehby, J. H., & Cooley, C. (2006). Teacher expectations of student's classroom behavior across the grade span: Which social skills are necessary for success? *Exceptional Children, 72,* 153-167.

Lang, H. G. (2005). Perspectives on the history of deaf education. In M. Marschark & P. E. Spencer (Eds.), *Oxford handbook of deaf studies, language, and education* (paperback ed.) (pp. 9-20). New York: Oxford University Press.

Langdon, H. W., Novak, J. M., Quintanar, R. S. (2000). Setting the teaching-learning wheel in motion in assessing language minority students. *Multicultural Perspectives, 2*(2), 3-9.

Langlois, J. A., Rutland-Brown, W., & Thomas, K. E. (2006). *Traumatic brain injury in the United States: Emergency department visits, hospitalizations, and deaths.* Atlanta: Centers for Disease Control and Prevention, National Center for Injury Prevention and Control.

Lanigan, K. J., Audette, R. M. L., Dreier, A. E., & Kobersy, M. R. (2001). Nasty, brutish . . . and often not very short: The attorney perspective in due process. In C. E. Finn, A. J. Rotherham, & C. R. Hokanson, Jr. (Eds.), *Rethinking special education for a new century* (pp. 213-232). Washington, DC: Thomas B. Fordham Foundation and the Progressive Policy Institute.

Lannie, A. L., & McCurdy, B. L. (2007). Preventing disruptive behavior in the urban classroom: Effects of the Good Behavior Game on student and teacher behavior. *Education & Treatment of Children, 30*, 85-98.

La Paro, K. M., Pianta, R. C., & Cox, M. J. (2000). Teachers' reported transition practices for children transitioning into kindergarten and first grade. *Exceptional Children, 67*, 7-20.

Larrivee, L. S., & Catts, H. W. (1999). Early reading achievement in children with expressive phonological disorders. *American Journal of Speech-Language Pathology, 8*(2), 118-128.

Larson, S. A., & Lakin, K. C. (1989). Deinstitutionalization of persons with mental retardation. *Journal of The Association for Persons with Severe Handicaps, 14*, 324-332.

Larson, S. A., Lakin, K. C., Anderson, L., Kwak, N., Hak Lee, J., & Anderson, D. (2001). Prevalence of mental retardation and developmental disabilities: Estimates from the 1994/1995 National Health Interview Survey Disability Supplements. *American Journal of Mental Retardation, 105*, 231-252.

Lattimore, L. P., Parsons, M. B., & Reid, D. H. (2006). Enhancing job-site training of supported workers with autism: A reemphasis on simulation. *Journal of Applied Behavior Analysis, 39*, 91-102.

La Vor, M. L. (1976). Federal legislation for exceptional persons: A history. In F. J. Weintraub, A. Abeson, J. Ballard, & M. L. La Vor (Eds.), *Public policy and the education of exceptional children* (pp. 96-111). Reston, VA: Council for Exceptional Children.

Lazarus, B. D. (1993). Guided notes: Effects with secondary and postsecondary students with mild disabilities. *Education and Treatment of Children, 16*, 272-289.

Lazarus, B. D. (1996). Flexible skeletons: Guided notes for adolescents with mild disabilities. *Teaching Exceptional Children, 28*(3), 37-40.

Leach, D. J., & Siddall, S. W. (1992). Parental involvement in the teaching of reading: A comparison of Hearing Reading, Paired Reading, Pause, Prompt, Praise and Direct Instruction methods. *ADI News, 11*(2), 14-19.

Learning Disabilities of America Association. (1993, March/April). Position paper on full inclusion of all students with learning disabilities in the regular classroom. *LDA Newsbrief, 28*(2), 1.

Ledford, M. R., & Gast, D. L. (2006). Feeding problems in children with autism spectrum disorders: A review. *Focus on Autism and Other Developmental Disabilities, 21*, 153-166.

Lee, C., & Tindal, G. A. (1994). Self-recording and goal-setting: Task and math productivity of low-achieving Korean elementary school students. *Journal of Behavioral Education, 4*, 459-479.

Lee, M., Storey, K., Anderson, J. L., Goetz, L., & Zivolich, S. (1997). The effect of mentoring versus job coach instruction on integration in supported employment settings. *Journal of The Association for Persons with Severe Handicaps, 22*, 151-158.

Lee, S. H., Amos, B. A., Gragoudas, S., Lee, Y., Shogren, K. A., Theoharis, R., & Wehmeyer, M. L. (2006). Curriculum augmentation and adaptation strategies to promote access to the general curriculum for students with intellectual and developmental disabilities. *Education and Training in Developmental Disabilities, 41*, 199-212.

Lee, S. H., Wehmeyer, M. L., Palmer, S. B., Soukup, J. H., & Little, T. D. (in press). Promoting self-determination as a curriculum augmentation to promote access to the general education curriculum for students with disabilities. *The Journal of Special Education.*

Lee, S., Simpson, R. L., & Shogren, K. A. (2007). Effects and implications of self-management for students with autism: A meta-analysis. *Focus on Autism and Other Developmental Disabilities, 22*, 2-13.

Lehr, D. H., & Macurdy, S. (1994). Meeting special health care needs of students. In M. Agran, N. E. Marchand-Martella, & R. C. Martella (Eds.), *Promoting health and safety: Skills for independent living* (pp. 71-84). Pacific Grove, CA: Brooks/Cole.

Lehr, D. H., & McDaid, P. (1993). Opening the door further: Integrating students with complex health needs. *Focus on Exceptional Children, 25*(6), 1-7.

Leigh, S. A., & Barclay, L. A. (2000). High school braille readers: Achieving academic success. *RE:view, 32*, 123-131.

Lemay, R. (2006). Social role valorization insights into the social integration conundrum. *Mental Retardation, 44*, 1-12.

Lenz, B. K., & Bulgren, J. A. (1995). Promoting learning in content classes. In P. A. Cegelka & W. H. Berdine (Eds.), *Effective instruction for students with learning problems* (pp. 385-417). Needham Heights, MA: Allyn & Bacon.

Leonard, C. M. (2001). Imaging brain structure in children: Differentiating language disability and reading disability. *Learning Disability Quarterly, 24*, 158-176.

Leone, P. E., & Meisel, S. (1997). Improving education services for students in detention and confinement facilities. *Children's Legal Rights Journal, 17*(1), 2-12.

Leone, P. E., Rutherford, R. B., & Nelson, C. M. (1991). *Special education and juvenile corrections.* Reston, VA: Council for Exceptional Children.

Lepper, M. R., Keavney, M., & Drake, M. (1996). Intrinsic motivation and extrinsic rewards: A commentary on Cameron and Pierce's Meta-Analysis. *Review of Educational Research, 66*, 5-32.

Lerman, P., Hall Apgar, D., & Jordan, T. (2005). Longitudinal changes in adaptive behaviors of movers and stayers: Findings from a controlled research design. *Mental Retardation, 43*, 25-42.

Lerner, J. W., with Kline, F. (2006). *Learning disabilities and related disorders: Characteristics and teaching strategies* (10th ed.). Boston: Houghton Mifflin.

Lerro, M. (1994). Teaching adolescents about AIDS. *Teaching Exceptional Children, 26*(4), 49-51.

Levack, N. (1997). *Annotated bibliography of curricular materials related to the core curriculum for children and youths with visual impairment, including those with multiple disabilities.* Austin, TX: Texas School for the Blind and Visually Impaired. [Available online at: http://www.tsbvi.edu/bib/index.htm]

Levack, N., Stone, G., & Bishop, V. (1994). *Low vision: A resource guide with adaptations for students with visual impairments* (2nd ed.). Austin, TX: Texas School for the Blind and Visually Impaired.

Levendoski, L. S., & Cartledge, G. (2000). Self-monitoring for elementary school children with serious emotional disturbances: Classroom applications for increased academic responding. *Behavioral Disorders, 25*, 211-224.

Levine, K., & Wharton, R. (2000). Williams syndrome and happiness. *American Journal of Mental Retardation, 105*, 363-371.

Levy, F., Hay, D., & Bennett, K. (2006). Genetics of attention deficit hyperactivity disorder: A current review and future prospects. *International Journal of Disability, Development and Education, 53*, 5-20.

Lewis, M. S., & Jackson, D. W. (2001). Television literacy: Comprehension of program content using closed captions for the deaf. *Journal of Deaf Studies and Deaf Education, 5*, 43-53.

Lewis, R. B., & Doorlag, D. H. (2006). *Teaching special education in general education classrooms* (7th ed.). Upper Saddle River, NJ: Merrill/Prentice Hall.

Lewis, S., & Tolla, J. (2003). Creating and using tactile experience books for young children with visual impairments. *Teaching Exceptional Children, 35*(3), 22-28.

Lewis, T., Colvin, G., & Sugai, G. (2000). The effects of precorrection and active supervision on the recess behavior of elementary students means of identifying students as emotionally disturbed. *Education and Treatment of Children, 23*, 109-121.

Lewis, T., & Sugai, G. (1999). *Safe schools: School-wide discipline practices.* Reston, VA: Council for Exceptional Children.

Lewis, T. J., Hudson, S., Richter, M., & Johnson, N. (2004). Scientifically supported practices in emotional and behavioral disorders: A proposed approach and brief review of current practices. *Behavioral Disorders, 29*, 247-259.

Leybaert, J., & Alegria, J. (2005). The role of cued speech in language development of deaf children. In M. Marschark & P. E. Spencer (Eds.), *Oxford handbook of deaf studies, language, and education* (paperback ed.) (pp. 261-274). New York: Oxford University Press.

Li, A. (2003). A model for developing programs to improve the use of vision in students who are visually impaired with multiple disabilities. *RE:view, 35*(1), 31-45.

Li, A. (2004). Classroom strategies for improving and enhancing visual skills in students with disabilities. *Teaching Exceptional Children, 36*(6), 38-46.

Lian, M. G. J., & Fontánez-Phelan, S. M. (2001). Perceptions of Latino parents regarding cultural and linguistic issues and advocacy for children with disabilities. *Journal of The Association for Persons with Severe Handicaps, 26,* 189-194.

Liaupsin, C. J., Umbreit, J., Ferro, J. B., Urso, A., & Upreti, G. (2006). Improving academic engagement through systematic, function-based intervention. *Education & Treatment of Children, 29,* 573-591.

Lichtenstein, E. H. (1998). The relationships between reading processes and English skills of deaf college students. *Journal of Deaf Studies and Deaf Education, 3,* 80-134.

Lidoff, L., & Massof, R. W. (Eds.). (2000). *Issues in low vision rehabilitation: Service delivery, policy, and funding.* New York: AFB Press.

Lieberth, A. K. (1991). Use of scaffolded dialogue journals to teach writing to deaf students. *Teaching English to Deaf and Second-Language Students, 9*(1), 10-13.

Lienemann, T., Graham, S., Leader-Janssen, B., & Reid, R. (2006). Improving the writing performance of struggling writers in second grade. *Journal of Special Education, 40,* 66-78.

Lien-Thorne, S., & Kamps, D. (2005). Replication study of the First Step to Success intervention program. *Behavioral Disorders, 31,* 18-32.

Lifshitz, H., Irit H., & Weisse, I. (2007). Self-concept, adjustment to blindness, and quality of friendship among adolescents with visual impairments. *Journal of Visual Impairment and Blindness, 101,* 96-107.

Lighthouse International. (2007). *Eye disorders.* [Available online: http://www.lighthouse.org/medical/eye-disorders/]

Lignugaris/Kraft, B., Marchand-Martella, N., & Martella, R. C. (2001). Writing better goals and short-term objectives or benchmarks. *Teaching Exceptional Children, 34*(1), 52-58.

Lignugaris/Kraft, B., Rule, S., Salzberg, C. L., & Stowitschek, J. J. (1988). Social-vocational skills of handicapped and nonhandicapped adults at work. *Journal of Employment Counseling, 23,* 20-31.

Lim, S-Y. (2008). Parent involvement in education. In G. Olsen & M. L. Fuller (Eds.), *Home-school relations: Working successfully with parents and families* (pp. 127-150). Boston: Allyn and Bacon.

Lin, F. Y., & Kubina, R. M. (2005). The relationship between fluency and application for multiplication. *Journal of Behavioral Education, 14,* 73-87.

Lin, S. (2000). Coping and adaptations in families of children with cerebral palsy. *Exceptional Children, 66,* 201-218.

Lindberg, J. S., Iwata, B. A., Roscoe, E. M., Worsdell, A. S., & Hanley, G. P. (2003). Treatment efficacy of noncontingent reinforcement during brief and extended application. *Journal of Applied Behavior Analysis, 36,* 1-19.

Lindfors, J. W. (1987). *Children's language and learning* (2nd ed.). Upper Saddle River, NJ: Prentice Hall.

Lindley, L. (1990, August). Defining TASH: A mission statement. *TASH Newsletter, 16*(8), 1.

Lindsley, O. R. (1996). The four free-operant freedoms. *Behavior Analyst, 19,* 199-210.

Lindstrom, L., Doren, B., Metheny, J., Johnson, P., & Zane, C. (2007). Transition to employment: Role of the family in career development. *Exceptional Children, 73,* 348-366.

Lindstrom, L. E., Benz, M. R., & Johnson, M. D. (1997). From school grounds to coffee grounds: An introduction to school-based enterprises. *Teaching Exceptional Children, 29*(4), 20-24.

Ling, D. (1986). Devices and procedures for auditory learning. *Volta Review, 88*(5), 19-28.

Ling, D. (2002). *Speech and the hearing-impaired child: Theory and practice* (2nd ed.). San Diego: Plural Publishing.

Lingo, A. S., Bott Slaton, D., & Jolivette, K. (2006). Effects of Corrective Reading on the reading abilities and classroom behaviors of middle school students with reading deficits and challenging behavior. *Behavioral Disorders, 31,* 265-283.

Lippke, B. A., Dickey, S. E., Selmar, J. W., & Soder, A. L. (1997). *Photo articulation test* (3rd ed.). Austin, TX: PRO-ED.

Lipsey, M. W., & Derzon, J. H. (1998). Predictors of violent or serious delinquency in adolescence and early adulthood: A synthesis of longitudinal research. In R. Loeber & D. P. Farrington (Eds.), *Serious and violent juvenile offenders: Risk factors and successful interventions* (pp. 6-105). Thousand Oaks, CA: Sage.

Liptak, G. S. (2007). Neural tube defects. In M. L. Batshaw, L. Pellegrino, & N. J. Roizen, (Eds.), *Children with disabilities* (6th ed.). Baltimore: Brookes.

Livingston-White, D., Utter, C., & Woodard, Q. E. (1985). Follow-up study of visually impaired students of the Michigan School for the Blind. *Journal of Visual Impairment and Blindness, 79,* 150-153.

Llewellyn, G., Gething, L., Kendig, H., & Cant, R. (2004). Older parent caregiver's engagement with the service system. *American Journal of Mental Retardation, 109,* 379-396.

Lloyd, J. W., Kauffman, J. M., & Gansneder, B. (1987). Differential teacher response to descriptions of aberrant behavior. In R. B. Rutherford, C. M. Nelson, & S. R. Forness (Eds.), *Severe behavior disorders of children and youth* (pp. 41-52). Boston: College Hill Press.

Lloyd, L. (1999). Multi-age classes and high ability students. *Review of Educational Research, 69*(2), 187-212.

Lo, Y. (2003). *Functional assessment and individualized intervention plans: Increasing the behavioral adjustment of urban learners in general and special education settings.* Unpublished doctoral dissertation. Columbus, OH: The Ohio State University.

Lo, Y., & Cartledge, G. (2006). FBA and BIP: Increasing the behavior adjustment of African American boys in schools. *Behavioral Disorders, 31,* 147-161.

Lo, Y., Loe, S. A., & Cartledge, G. (2002). The effects of social skills instruction on the social behaviors of students at risk for emotional and behavioral disorders. *Behavioral Disorders, 27,* 371-385.

Lockshin, S. B., Gillis, J. M., & Romanczyk, R. G. (in press). *Defying autism: Keep your sanity and take control.* New York: DRL.

Logan, K. R., & Gast, D. L. (2001). Conducting preference assessments and reinforcer testing for individuals with profound multiple disabilities: Issues and procedures. *Exceptionality, 9*(3), 123-134.

Logan, K. R., Hansen, C. D., Nieminen, P. K., & Wright, E. H. (2001). Student support teams: Helping students succeed in general education classrooms or working to place students in special education? *Education and Training in Mental Retardation and Developmental Disabilities, 36,* 280-292.

Logan, K. R., Jacobs, H. A., Gast, D. L., Smith, P. D., Daniel, J., & Rawls, J. (2001). Preferences and reinforcers for students with profound multiple disabilities: Can we identify them? *Journal of Developmental and Physical Disabilities, 13,* 97-122.

Lohmeier, K. L. (2005). Implementing the expanded core curriculum in specialized schools for the blind. *RE:view: Rehabilitation Education for Blindness and Visual Impairment, 37.*

Lohrmann-O'Rouke, S., & Browder, D. M. (1998). Empirically based methods to assess the preferences of individuals with severe disabilities. *American Journal on Mental Retardation, 103,* 146-161.

Lord, C. (February 2007). *Autism in the twenty-first century.* Presentation at conference: Progress and Challenges in the Behavioral Treatment of Autism. Boston, MA. [Available on DVD from the Association for Behavior Analysis International.]

Lord, C., Risi, S., Lambrecht, L., Cook, E. H., Leventhal, B. L., DiLavore, P. C., et al. (2000). The autism diagnostic observation scale-generic: A standard measure of social and communication deficits associated with the spectrum of autism. *Journal of Autism and Developmental Disorders, 30,* 205-223.

Lord, C., Rutter, M., & Le Couteur, A. (1994). Autism diagnostic interview—revised: A revised version of a diagnostic interview for caregivers of individuals with possible pervasive developmental disabilities. *Journal of Autism and Developmental Disorders, 24,* 659-685.

Lorimer, P. A., Simpson, R. L., Myles, B. S., & Ganz, J. B. (2002). Effectiveness of facilitated communication with children and youth with autism. *Journal of Positive Behavior Interventions, 4,* 53-60.

Lovaas, O. I. (1987). Behavioral treatment and normal educational and intellectual functioning in young autistic children. *Journal of Consulting and Clinical Psychology, 55,* 3-9.

Lovaas, O. I. (1994, October). Comments made during Ohio State University teleconference on applied behavior analysis, The Ohio State University, Columbus.

Lovaas, O. I., Freitag, G., Gold, V. J., & Kassorla, I. C. (1965). Recording apparatus and procedure for observation of behaviors of children in free play settings. *Journal of Experimental Child Psychology, 2,* 108-120.

Lovaas, O. I., & Newsom, C. D. (1976). Behavior modification with psychotic children. In

H. Leitenberg (Ed.), *Handbook of behavior modification and behavior therapy* (pp. 303-360). Englewood Cliffs, NJ: Prentice-Hall.

Lovett, M. W., Steinbach, K. A., & Frijters, J. C. (2000). Remediating the core deficits of developmental reading disability: A double-deficit perspective. *Journal of Learning Disabilities, 33,* 334-358.

Lovitt, T. C. (1977). *In spite of my resistance ... I've learned from children.* Upper Saddle River, NJ: Merrill/Prentice Hall.

Lovitt, T. C. (2007). *Promoting school success: Tactics for teaching adolescents* (3rd ed.). Austin, TX: PRO-ED.

Lovitt, T. C., & Cushing, S. S. (1994). High school students rate their IEPs: Low opinions and lack of ownership. *Intervention in School and Clinic, 30,* 34-37.

Lowenthal, B. (2001). *Abuse and neglect: The educator's guide to the identification and prevention of child maltreatment.* Baltimore: Brookes.

Luchshyn, J. M., Dunlap, G., & Albin, R. W. (Eds.). (2002). *Families and positive behavioral support: Addressing the challenge of problem behavior in family contexts.* Baltimore: Brookes.

Luckasson, R., Coulter, D. L., Polloway, E. A., Reiss, S., Schalock, R. L., Snell, M. E., Spitalnik, D. M., & Stark, J. A. (2002). *Mental retardation: Definition, classification, and systems of supports* (10th ed.). Washington, DC: American Association on Mental Retardation.

Luckasson, R., & Reeve, A. (2001). Naming, defining, and classifying in mental retardation. *Mental Retardation, 39,* 47-52.

Luckner, J. (1994). Developing independent and responsible behaviors in students who are deaf or hard of hearing. *Teaching Exceptional Children, 26*(2), 13-17.

Lue, M. S. (2001). *A survey of communication disorders for the classroom teacher.* Boston: Allyn & Bacon.

Lueck, A. H. (2004). *Functional vision: A practitioner's guide to evaluation and intervention.* New York: AFB Press.

Luecking, R., & Tilson, G. (2002). *A practical introduction to customized employment.* Baltimore: TransCen, Inc.

Luker, C., & Lucker, T. (2007). A service is not a need. *Exceptional Parent, 37*(2), 31-32.

Lunsford, S. (2006). The debate within: Authority and the discourse of blindness. *Journal of Visual Impairment and Blindness, 100,* 26-35.

Lusk, K. E., & Corn, A. L. (2006a). Learning and using print and Braille: A study of dual-media learners Part 1. *Journal of Visual Impairment and Blindness, 100,* 606-619.

Lusk, K. E., & Corn, A. L. (2006b). An initial study of dual-media learning: Part 2. *Journal of Visual Impairment and Blindness, 100,* 653-665.

Luterman, D. (1999). Emotional aspects of hearing loss. *Volta Review, 99*(5), 75-83.

Lynch, E., & Hanson, M. (2004). *Developing cross-cultural competence: A guide for working with children and their families* (3rd ed.). Baltimore: Paul H. Brookes.

Lyon, G. R. (1995). Toward a definition of dyslexia. *Annals of Dyslexia, 45,* 3-27.

Lyon, G. R. (1999, December 12). Special education in state is failing on many fronts. *Los Angeles Times,* p. A1.

Lyon, G. R., Shaywitz, S. E., & Shaywitz, B. A. (2003). Defining dyslexia. *Annals of Dyslexia, 53,* 1-14.

Lyon, R., & Riccards, P. (2007). The continued need for Reading First. *EdNews.org.* (June 4, 2007).

Lytle, R. K., & Bordin, J. (2001). Enhancing the IEP team: Strategies for parents and professionals. *Teaching Exceptional Children, 33*(5), 28-33.

Maag, J. W. (2001). Rewarded by punishment: Reflections on the disuse of positive reinforcement in schools. *Exceptional Children, 67,* 173-186.

Maag, J. W. (2003). A contextually based approach for treating depression in school-age children. *Intervention in School and Clinic, 37,* 149-155.

Maag, J. W. (2006). Social skills training for students with emotional and behavioral disorder: A review of reviews. *Behavioral Disorders, 32,* 5-17.

Maag, J. W., & Reid, R. (1994). Attention-deficit hyperactivity disorder: A functional approach to assessment and treatment. *Behavioral Disorders, 20,* 5-23.

Maag, J. W., Reid, R., & DiGangi, S. A. (1993). Differential effects of self-monitoring attention, accuracy, and productivity. *Journal of Applied Behavior Analysis, 26,* 329-344.

Maag, J. W., & Swearer, S. M. (2005). Cognitive-behavioral interventions for depression: Review and implications for school personnel. *Behavioral Disorders, 30,* 259-276.

Maccini, P., & Hughes, C. A. (2000). Effects of problem-solving strategy on the algebraic subtraction of integers by secondary students with learning disabilities. *Learning Disabilities Research and Practice, 15,* 10-15.

Maccini, P., Mulcahy, C. A., & Wilson, M. G. (2007). A follow-up of mathematics interventions for secondary students with learning disabilities. *Learning Disabilities Research and Practice, 22,* 58-74.

MacGinitie, W. H., MacGinitie, R. K., Maria, K., & Dreyer, L. G. (2000). *Gates-MacGinitie Reading Tests—Fourth Edition.* Itasca, IL: Riverside.

Machek, G. R., & Nelson, J. M. (2007). How should reading disabilities be operationalized? A survey of practicing school psychologists. *Learning Disabilities Research & Practice, 22,* 147-157.

Macht, J. (1998). *Special education's failed system: A question of eligibility.* Westport, CT: Bergin & Garvey.

MacLean, K. (2003). The impact of institutionalization on child development. *Development and Psychopathology, 15,* 853-884.

MacMillan, D. L., Gresham, F. M., Bocian, K. M., & Lambros, K. M. (1998). Current plight of borderline students: Where do they belong? *Education and Training in Mental Retardation and Developmental Disabilities, 33,* 83-94.

MacMillan, D. L., Gresham, F. M., & Siperstein, G. N. (1993). Conceptual and psychometric concerns about the 1992 AAMR definition of mental retardation. *American Journal on Mental Retardation, 98,* 325-335.

MacMillan, D. L., Gresham, F. M., & Siperstein, G. N. (1996). Heightened concerns about the 1992 AAMR definition of mental retardation: Advocacy versus precision. *American Journal on Mental Retardation, 100,* 87-97.

MacMillan, D. L., Gresham, F. M., Siperstein, G. N., & Bocian, K. M. (1996). The labyrinth of IDEA: School decisions on referred students with subaverage general intelligence. *American Journal on Mental Retardation, 101,* 161-174.

MacMillan, D. L., & Reschly, D. J. (1998). Overrepresentation of minority students: The case for greater specificity or reconsideration of the variables examined. *Journal of Special Education, 32,* 15-24.

MacMillan, D. L., & Siperstein, G. N. (2002). Learning disabilities as operationally defined by schools. In R. Bradley, L. Danielson, & D. P. Hallahan (Eds.), *Identification of learning disabilities: Research to practice* (pp. 287-333). Mahwah, NJ: Erlbaum.

MacMillan, D. L., Siperstein, G. N., & Leffert, J. S. (2006). Children with mild mental retardation: A challenge for classification practices-revised. In H. N. Switzky & S. Greenspan (Eds.), *What is mental retardation? Ideas for an evolving disability in the 21st century* (rev. ed.) (pp. 197-220). Washington, DC: American Association on Intellectual and Developmental Disabilities.

Macy, M., & Hoyt-Gonzales, K. (2007). A linked system approach to early childhood special education eligibility assessment. *Teaching Exceptional Children, 39*(3), 40-44.

Madaus, J. W. (2005). Navigating the college transition maze: A guide for students with learning disabilities. *Teaching Exceptional Children, 37*(23), 32-37.

Madaus, J. W. (2006). Employment outcomes of university graduates with learning disabilities. *Learning Disability Quarterly, 29,* 19-31.

Madaus, M. M., Kehle, T. J., Madaus, J., & Bray, M. A., (2003). Mystery motivator as in intervention to promote homework completion and accuracy. *School Psychology International, 24,* 369-377.

Madsen, C. H., Jr., Becker, W. C., & Thomas, D. R. (1968). Rules, praise, and ignoring: Elements of elementary classroom control. *Journal of Applied Behavior Analysis, 1,* 343-353.

Maestas y Moores, J., & Moores, D. F. (1980). Language training with the young deaf child. In D. Bricker (Ed.), *Early language intervention with handicapped children.* San Francisco: Jossey-Bass.

Magiera, K., Smith, C., Zigmond, N., & Gebauer, K. (2005). Benefits of co-teaching in secondary mathematics classes. *Teaching Exceptional Children, 37*(3), 20-24.

Maheady, L., Harper, G. F., & Mallette, B. (2003). Classwide peer tutoring. *Current Practice Alerts, Issue 8.* Reston, VA: Division for

Learning Disabilities and Division for Research, Council for Exceptional Children. Available online: www.teachingld.org/ld%5Fresources/alerts/

Maheady, L., Harper, G. F., Sacca, M. K., & Mallette, B. (1991). *Classwide Student Tutoring Teams (CSTT): Instructor's manual and video package*. Fredonia, NY: SUNY College at Fredonia, School of Education.

Maheady, L., Mallette, B., & Harper, G. F. (2006). Four classwide peer tutoring models: Similarities, differences, and implications for research and practice. *Reading and Writing Quarterly, 22,* 65-89.

Maheady, L., Mallette, B., Harper, G. F., & Saca, K. (1991). Heads together: A peer-mediated option for improving the academic achievement of heterogeneous learning groups. *Remedial and Special Education, 12*(2), 25-33.

Maheady, L., Michielli-Pendl, J., Harper, G. F., & Mallette, B. (2006). The effects of numbered heads together with and without an incentive package on the science test performance of a diverse group of sixth graders. *Journal of Behavioral Education, 15,* 24-38.

Maheady, L., Michielli-Pendl, J., Mallette, B., & Harper, G. F. (2002). A collaborative research project to improve the academic performance of a diverse sixth grade science class. *Teacher Education and Special Education, 25,* 55-70.

Maheady, L., Sacca, M. K., & Harper, G. F. (1987). Classwide peer tutoring teams: Effects on the academic performance of secondary students. *Journal of Special Education, 21*(3), 107-121.

Mahr, G., & Leith, W. (1992). Psychogenic stuttering of adult onset. *Journal of Speech and Hearing Research, 35,* 283-286.

Mahshie, S. N. (1995). *Educating deaf children bilingually.* Washington, DC: Gallaudet University Press.

Maione, L., & Mirenda, P. (2006). Effects of video modeling and video feedback on peer-directed social language skills of a child with autism. *Journal of Positive Behavior Interventions, 8,* 106-118.

Maker, C. J. (1993). Creativity, intelligence, and problem solving: A definition and design for cross-cultural research and measurement related to giftedness. *Gifted Education International, 9*(2), 68-77.

Maker, C. J. (1996). Identification of gifted minority students: A national problem, needed changes, and a promising solution. *Gifted Child Quarterly, 40,* 41-50.

Maker, C. J. (1997). DISCOVER problem solving assessment. *Quest, 8*(1), 3, 4, 7.

Maker, C. J. (2001). DISCOVER: Assessing and developing problem solving. *Gifted Education International, 15,* 232-251.

Maker, C. J. (2005, Fall). The DISCOVER project: Improving assessment and curriculum for diverse gifted learners. *The National Research Center on the Gifted and Talented Newsletter.* [Retrieved September 18, 2007.]

Maker, C. J., & Nielson, A. B. (1996). *Curriculum development and teaching strategies for gifted learners* (2nd ed.). Austin: TX: PRO-ED.

Maker, C. J., Nielson, A. B., & Rogers, J. A. (1994). Giftedness, diversity, and problem-solving. *Teaching Exceptional Children, 27*(1), 4-19.

Malian, I. M., & Love, L. L. (1998). Leaving high school: An ongoing transition study. *Teaching Exceptional Children, 30*(3), 4-10.

Malone, D. M., & Langone, J. (1999). Teaching object-related play skills to preschool children with developmental concerns. *International Journal of Disability, Development and Education, 46*(3), 325-336.

Malott, R. W., & Harrison, H. (2002). *I'll stop procrastinating when I get around to it: Plus other cool ways to succeed in school and life using behavior analysis to get your act together.* Kalamazoo, MI: Department of Psychology, Western Michigan University.

Mancil, G. R. (2006). Functional communication training: A review of the literature related to children with autism. *Education and Training in Developmental Disabilities, 41,* 213-224.

Mangold, S. (Ed.) (1982). *A teacher's guide to the special educational needs of blind and visually handicapped children.* New York: American Foundation for the Blind.

Mank, D., Cioffi, A., & Yovanoff, P. (1998). Employment outcomes for people with severe disabilities: Opportunities for improvement. *Mental Retardation, 36,* 205-216.

Mank, D., Cioffi, A., & Yovanoff, P. (1999). The impact of coworker involvement with supported employees on wage and integrated outcomes. *Mental Retardation, 37,* 383-394.

Mank, D., Cioffi, A., & Yovanoff, P. (2000). Direct support in supported employment and its relation to job typicalness, coworker involvement, and employment outcomes. *Mental Retardation, 38,* 506-516.

Mank, D. M., & Horner, R. H. (1987). Self-recruited feedback: A cost-effective procedure for maintaining behavior. *Research in Developmental Disabilities, 8,* 91-112.

Mann, D. (1996). Serious play. *Teachers College Record, 97*(3), 447-469.

March, J., & Morris, T. L. (Eds.). (2004). *Anxiety disorders in children and adolescents* (2nd ed.). New York: Guilford.

Marchand-Martella, N. E., Slocum, T. A., & Martella, R. C. (Eds.). (2004). *Introduction to Direct Instruction.* Boston: Allyn & Bacon.

Marchisan, M. L., & Alber, S. R. (2001). The write way: Tips for teaching the writing process to resistant writers. *Intervention in School and Clinic, 36*(3), 154-162.

Marckel, J. M., Neef, N. A., & Ferreri, S. J. (2006). A preliminary analysis of teaching improvisation with the picture exchange communication system to children with autism. *Journal of Applied Behavior Analysis, 39,* 109-115.

Margolis, H., & Brannigan, G. (1990). Calming the storm. *Learning, 18,* 40-42.

Markwardt, F. C., Jr. (1998a). *Peabody Individual Achievement Test—Revised.* Circle Pines, MN: American Guidance Services.

Markwardt, F. C., Jr. (1998b). *Peabody Individual Achievement Test—Revised/Normative Update.* Minneapolis, MN: Pearson Assessments.

Marland, S. (1972). Education of the gifted and talented (Vol. 1). [Report to the U.S. Congress by the U.S. Commissioner of Education.] Office of Education (DHEW). Washington, DC (ERIC Document Reproduction Service No. ED 056 243)

Marmolejo, E. K., Wilder, D. A., & Bradley, L. (2004). A preliminary analysis of the effects of response cards on student performance and participation in an upper division university course. *Journal of Applied Behavior Analysis, 37,* 405-410.

Marschark, M. (2007). *Raising and educating a deaf child: A comprehensive guide to the choices, controversies, and decisions faced by parents and educators* (paperback ed.). New York: Oxford University Press.

Marschark, M., & Clark, M. D. (Eds.). (1998). *Psychological perspectives on deafness* (Vol. 2). Mahwah, NJ: Erlbaum.

Marschark, M., Rhoten, C., & Fabich, M. (2007). Effects of cochlear implants on children's reading and academic achievement. *The Journal of Deaf Studies and Deaf Education, 12,* 269-282.

Marsh, L. G., & Cooke, N. L. (1996). The effects of using manipulatives in teaching math problem solving to students with learning disabilities. *Learning Disabilities Research and Practice, 11*(1), 58-65.

Marston, J. R., Loomis, J. M., Klatzky, R. L., & Golledge, R. G. (2007). Nonvisual route following with guidance from a simple haptic or auditory display. *Journal of Visual Impairment and Blindness, 101,* 203-211.

Martella, R., Leonard, I. J., Marchand-Martella, N. E., & Agran, M. (1993). Self-monitoring negative statements. *Journal of Behavioral Education, 3,* 77-86.

Martella, R. C., Marchand-Martella, N. E., Young, K. R., & MacFarlane, C. A. (1995). Determining the collateral effects of peer tutoring on a student with severe disabilities. *Education and Treatment of Children, 19,* 170-191.

Martens, B. K., Lochner, D. G., & Kelly, S. Q. (1992). The effects of variable interval reinforcement on academic engagement: A demonstration of matching theory. *Journal of Applied Behavior Analysis, 25,* 143-151.

Martin, J. E., Huber Marshall, L., & Sale, P. (2004). A 3-year study of middle, junior high, and high school IEP meetings. *Exceptional Children, 70,* 285-297.

Martin, J. E., & Marshall, L. H. (1995). ChoiceMaker: A comprehensive self-determined transition program. *Intervention in School and Clinic, 30,* 147-156.

Martin, J. E., Marshall, L. H., Maxson, L. M., & Jerman, P. L. (1997). *The Self-Directed IEP.* Longmont, CO: Sopris West.

Martin, J. E., Marshall, L. H., Wray, D., Wells, L., O'Brien, J., Olvey, G., et al. (2004). *Choose and take action: Finding the right job for you.* Longmont, CO: Sopris West.

Martin, J. E., Van Dycke, J. L., Christensen, W. R., Greene, B. A., Gardner, J. E., & Lovett, D. L.

(2006). Increasing student participation in IEP meetings: Establishing the Self-Directed IEP as evidence-based practice. *Exceptional Children, 72*, 187–200.

Martin, J. E., Van Dycke, J. L., Greene, B. A., Gardner, J. E., Christensen, W. R., Woods, L. L., & Lovett, D. L. (2006). Direct observation of teacher-directed IEP meetings: Establishing the need for student IEP meeting instruction. *Exceptional Children, 72*, 187–200.

Martin, J. E., Woods, L. L., & Sylvester, L. (2008). Building an employment vision: Culturally attuning vocational interests, skills, and limits. In F. R. Rusch (Ed.). *Beyond high school: Preparing adolescents for tomorrow's challenges* (2nd ed.) (pp. 78–109). Upper Saddle River, NJ: Merrill/Prentice Hall.

Martin, J. R. (1985). *Reclaiming a conversation: The ideal of the educated woman.* New Haven, CT: Yale University Press.

Martin, S. L., Ramey, C. T., & Ramey, S. L. (1990). The prevention of intellectual impairment in children of impoverished families: Findings of a randomized trial of educational daycare. *American Journal of Public Health, 80*, 844–847.

Masataka, N. (1996). Perception of mothers in a signed language by 6-month-old deaf infants. *Developmental Psychology, 32*, 874–879.

Mason, C., Field, S., & Sawilowsky, S. (2004). Implementation of self-determination activities and student participation in IEPs. *Exceptional Children, 70*, 441–451.

Mason, C., McGahee-Kovac, M., Johnson, L., & Stillerman, S. (2002). Implementing student-led IEPs: Student participation and student and teacher reactions. *Career Development for Exceptional Individuals, 25*, 171–192.

Mason, C. Y., McGahee-Kovac, M., & Johnson, L. (2004). How to help students lead their IEP meetings. *Teaching Exceptional Children, 36*(3), 18–25.

Mason, H. (1997). Common eye defects and their educational implications. In H. Mason & S. McCall (Eds.), *Visual impairment: Access to education for children and young people* (pp. 38–50). London: Fulton.

Massey, N. G., & Wheeler, J. J. (2000). Acquisition and generalization of activity schedules and their effects on task engagement in a young child with autism in an inclusive preschool classroom. *Education and Training in Mental Retardation and Developmental Disabilities, 35*, 326–335.

Mastropieri, M. A., & Scruggs, T. E. (1993). *A practical guide for teaching science to students with special needs in inclusive settings.* Austin, TX: PRO-ED.

Mastropieri, M. A., & Scruggs, T. E. (2007). *The inclusive classroom: Strategies for effective instruction* (3rd ed.). Upper Saddle River, NJ: Merrill/Prentice Hall.

Mather, N., & Goldstein, S. (2001). *Learning disabilities and challenging behaviors.* Baltimore: Brookes.

Mathes, P. G., Clancy-Menchetti, J., & Torgesen, J. K. (2003). *K-PALS: Kindergarten peer-assisted literacy strategies.* Longmont, CO: Sopris West.

Mathes, P. G., Torgesen, J. K., Allen, S. H., & Howard-Allor, J. (2003). *First grade PALS: Peer-assisted literacy strategies.* Longmont, CO: Sopris West.

Matheson, C., Olsen, R. J., & Weisner, T. (2007). A good friend is hard to find: Friendship among adolescents with disabilities. *American Journal on Mental Retardation, 112*, 319–329.

Matheson, E., & Jahoda, A. (2005). Emotional understanding in aggressive and nonaggressive individuals with mild or moderate mental retardation. *American Journal on Mental Retardation, 110*, 57–67.

Matson, J. L. (Ed.). (1994). *Autism in children and adults: Etiology, assessment, and intervention.* Pacific Grove, CA: Brooks/Cole.

Matson, J. L., & Vollmer, T. R. (1995). *User's guide: Questions about behavioral function* (QABF). Baton Rouge, LA: Scientific Publishers, Inc.

Matuszny, R. M., Banda, D. R., & Coleman, T. J. (2007). A progressive plan for building collaborative relations with parents from diverse backgrounds. *Teaching Exceptional Children, 39*(4), 24–31.

Maughan, B., Pickles, A., Hagell, A., Rutter, M., & Yule, W. (1996). Reading problems and antisocial behavior: Developmental trends in comorbidity. *Journal of Child Psychology and Psychiatry, 37*, 405–418.

Mauk, J. E., Reber, M., & Batshaw, M. L. (1997). Autism. In M. L. Batshaw (Ed.), *Children with disabilities* (pp. 425–448). Baltimore: Brookes.

Maurice, C. (1993). *Let me hear your voice: A family's triumph over autism.* New York: Knopf.

Maurice, C. (2004, August). *Effective advocacy for children with autism.* Address given at Penn State National Autism Conference.

Maurice, C., Green, G., & Foxx, R. M. (2001). *Making a difference: Behavioral intervention for autism.* Austin, TX: PRO-ED.

Maurice, C., Green, G., & Luce, S. C. (1996). *Behavioral intervention for young children with autism: A manual for parents and professionals.* Austin, TX: PRO-ED.

Maurice, C., & Taylor, B. A. (2005). Early intensive behavioral intervention for autism. In W. L. Heward, T. E. Heron, N. A. Neef, S. M. Peterson, D. M. Sainato, G. Cartledge, R. Gardner, III, L. D. Peterson, S. B. Hersh, & J. C. Dardig (Eds.), *Focus on behavior analysis in education: Achievements, challenges, and opportunities* (pp. 31–52). Upper Saddle River, NJ: Merrill/Prentice Hall.

Mayer, C., & Akamatsu, C. T. (1999). Bilingual-bicultural models of literacy education for deaf students: Considering the claims. *Journal of Deaf Studies and Deaf Education, 4*, 1–8.

Mayer, G. R. (1995). Preventing antisocial behavior in schools. *Journal of Applied Behavior Analysis, 28*, 467–478.

Mayer-Johnson, R. (1986). *The picture communications symbols—Book 1.* Solana Beach, CA: Mayer-Johnson.

Mayes, S. D., Calhoun, S. L., & Crowell, E. W. (2000). Learning disabilities and ADHD: Overlapping spectrum disorders. *Journal of Learning Disabilities, 33*, 417–424.

McAdam, D. B., O'Cleirigh, C. M., & Cuvo, A. J. (1993). Self-monitoring and verbal feedback to reduce stereotypic body rocking in a congenitally blind adult. *RE:view, 24*, 163–172.

McBride, B. J., & Schwartz, I. (2003). Effects of teaching early interventionists to use discrete trials during ongoing classroom activities. *Topics in Early Childhood Special Education, 23*, 5–17.

McCabe, H. (2007). Parent advocacy in the face of adversity: Autism and families in the People's Republic of China. *Focus on Autism and Other Developmental Disabilities, 22*, 39–50.

McCauley, R. J. (2001). *Assessment of language disorders in children.* Mahwah, NJ: Erlbaum.

McClannahan, L. E., & Krantz, P. J. (1999). *Activity schedules for children with autism: Teaching independent behavior.* Woodbine House.

McConnell, M. E. (1999). Self-monitoring, cueing, recording, and managing: Teaching students to manage their own behavior. *Teaching Exceptional Children, 32*(2), 14–21.

McConnell, S. (2002). Interventions to facilitate social interactions for young children with autism: Review of available research and recommendations for education intervention and future research. *Journal of Autism and Developmental Disabilities, 32*, 351–372.

McConnell, S. R. (1994). Social context, social validity, and program outcome in early intervention. In R. Gardner, III, D. M. Sainato, J. O. Cooper, T. E. Heron, W. L. Heward, J. Eshleman, & T. A. Grossi (Eds.), *Behavior analysis in education: Focus on measurably superior instruction* (pp. 75–85). Pacific Grove, CA: Brooks/Cole.

McCormick, M. E., & Wolf, J. S. (1993). Intervention programs for gifted girls. *Roeper Review, 16*, 85–88.

McCuin, D., & Cooper, J. O. (1994). Teaching keyboarding and computer skills to persons with developmental disabilities. *Behaviorology, 2*(1), 63–78.

McDermott, S. (1994). Explanatory model to describe school district prevalence rates for mental retardation and learning disabilities. *American Journal on Mental Retardation, 99*, 175–185.

McDonnell, J., Thorson, N., Disher, S., Mathot-Buckner, C., Mendel, J., & Ray, L. (2003). The achievement of students with developmental disabilities and their peers without disabilities in inclusive settings: An exploratory study. *Education and Treatment of Children, 26*, 224–236.

McDonnell, J. J., Hardman, M. L., & McDonnell, A. P. (2003). *Introduction to persons with moderate and severe disabilities: Education and social issues* (2nd ed.). Boston: Allyn and Bacon.

McDonough, C. S., Covington, T., Endo, S., Meinberg, D., Spencer, T. D., & Bicard, D. F. (2005). The Hawthorne Country Day School: A behavioral approach to schooling. In W. L. Heward, T. E. Heron, N. A. Neef, S. M. Peterson, D. M. Sainato,

G. Cartledge, R. Gardner, III, L. D. Peterson, S. B. Hersh, & J. C. Dardig (Eds.), *Focus on behavior analysis in education: Achievements, challenges, and opportunities* (pp. 188-210). Upper Saddle River, NJ: Merrill/Prentice Hall.

McEachin, J. J., Smith, T., & Lovaas, I. O. (1993). Long-term outcome for children with autism who received early intensive behavioral treatment. *American Journal on Mental Retardation, 97,* 359-372.

McEvoy, A., & Welker, R. (2000). Antisocial behavior, academic failure, and school climate: A critical review. *Journal of Emotional and Behavioral Disorders, 8,* 130-140.

McEvoy, M. A., & Yoder, P. (1993). Interventions to promote social skills and emotional development. In *DEC Recommended Practices* (pp. 77-81). Reston, VA: Council for Exceptional Children, Division for Early Childhood.

McGahee, M., Mason, C., Wallace, T., & Jones, B. (2001). *Student-led IEPs: A guide for student involvement.* Arlington, VA: Council for Exceptional Children. Retrieved February 14, 2006, from http://www.cec.sped.org/bk/catalog2/student-led_ieps.pdf

McGee, G. G., Morrier, M. J., & Daly, T. (1999). An incidental teaching approach to early intervention for toddlers with autism. *Journal of The Association for the Severely Handicapped, 24,* 133-146.

McGee, J. J. (1992). Gentle teaching's assumptions and paradigm. *Journal of Applied Behavior Analysis, 25,* 869-872.

McGee, J. J., & Gonzalez, L. (1990). Gentle teaching and the practice of human interdependence: A preliminary group study of 15 persons with severe behavioral disorders and their caregivers. In A. C. Repp & N. N. Singh (Eds.), *Current perspectives on the use of nonaversive and aversive interventions for persons with developmental disabilities* (pp. 237-254). Sycamore, IL: Sycamore.

McGee, J. J., & Menolascino, F. J. (1991). *Beyond gentle teaching: A nonaversive approach to helping those in need.* New York: Plenum.

McGill, T., & Vogle, L. K. (2001). Driver's education for students with physical disabilities. *Exceptional Children, 67,* 455-466.

McGonigel, M. J., Woodruff, G., & Roszmann-Millican, M. (1994). The transdisciplinary team: A model for family-centered early intervention. In L. J. Johnson, R. J. Gallagher, M. J. LaMontagne, J. B. Jordan, J. J. Gallagher, P. L. Hutinger, & M. B. Karnes (Eds.). *Meeting early intervention challenges: Issues from birth to three* (pp. 95-131). Baltimore: Brookes.

McGuffin, P., & Rutter, M. (2002). Genetics of normal and abnormal development. In M. Rutter & E. Taylor (Eds.), *Child and adolescent psychiatry* (4th ed.) (pp. 185-204). Malden, MA: Blackwell Science.

McHale, S. M., & Gamble, W. W. (1989). Sibling relationships of children with disabled and nondisabled brothers and sisters. *Developmental Psychology, 25*(3), 421-429.

McHugh, M. (2003). *Special siblings: Growing up with someone with a disability.* Baltimore: Brookes.

McIntosh, R., Vaughn, S., & Zaragoza, N. (1991). A review of social interventions for students with learning disabilities. *Journal of Learning Disabilities, 24,* 451-458.

McIntyre, T. (1993a). Behaviorally disordered youth in correctional settings: Prevalence, programming, and teacher training. *Behavioral Disorders, 18,* 167-176.

McIntyre, T. (1993b). Reflections on the new definition for emotional or behavioral disorders: Who still falls through the cracks and why. *Behavioral Disorders, 18,* 148-160.

McIntyre, T., & Forness, S. R. (1996). Is there a new definition yet or are kids still seriously emotionally disturbed? *Beyond Behavior, 7*(3), 4-9.

McKee, B. G., Giles, P. G., Everhart, V. S., Stinson, M. S., & Henderson, J. B. (1998). C-Print: A computerized speech-to-print transcription system. *Captionist training manual.* Rochester, NY: Rochester Institute of Technology.

McKinley, A. M., & Warren, S. F. (2000). The effectiveness of cochlear implants for children with prelingual deafness. *Journal of Early Intervention, 23,* 252-263.

McLaren, J., & Bryson, S. E. (1987). Review of recent epidemiological studies of mental retardation: Prevalence, related disorders and etiology. *American Journal on Mental Retardation, 92,* 243-254.

McLoughlin, J. A., & Lewis, R. B. (2008). *Assessing students with special needs* (7th ed.). Upper Saddle River, NJ: Merrill/Prentice Hall.

McLaughlin, M. J., Dyson, A., Nagle, K., Thurlow, M., Rouse, M., Hardman, M., Norwich, B., Burke, P. J., & Perlin, M. (2006). Cross-cultural perspectives on the classification of children with disabilities: Part II. Implementing classification systems in schools. *The Journal of Special Education, 40,* 46-58.

McLaughlin, S. (1998). *Introduction to language development.* San Diego: Singular.

McLean, M., Wolery, M., & Bailey, D. B. (2004). *Assessing infants and preschoolers with special needs* (3rd ed.). Upper Saddle River, NJ: Merrill/Prentice Hall.

McLeskey, J. (1992). Students with learning disabilities at primary, intermediate, and secondary grade levels: Identification and characteristics. *Learning Disability Quarterly, 15,* 13-19.

McLeskey, J., Tyler, N. C., & Flippin, S. S. (2004). The supply and demand for special education teachers: A review of research regarding the chronic shortage of special education teachers. *Journal of Special Education, 38,* 5-21.

McLone, D. G., & Ito, J. (1998). *An introduction to spina bifida.* Chicago: Children's Memorial Hospital, Spina Bifida Team.

McLoone, J., Hudson, J. L., & Rapee, R. M. (2006). Treating anxiety disorders in a school setting. *Education & Treatment of Children, 29.*

McLoughlin, J. A., & Lewis, R. B. (2005). *Assessing students with special needs* (6th ed.). Upper Saddle River, NJ: Merrill/Prentice Hall.

McMaster, K. L., Fuchs, D., & Fuchs, L. S. (2006). Peer-assisted learning strategies: The promise and limitations of peer-mediated instruction. *Reading and Writing Quarterly, 22,* 5-25.

McNamara, B. E. (2007). Learning disabilities: Bridging the gap between research and classroom practice. Upper Saddle River, NJ: Merrill/Prentice Hall.

McNamara, K., & Hollinger, C. (2003). Intervention-based assessment: Evaluation rates and eligibility findings. *Exceptional Children, 69,* 181-193.

McPartland, P. (2005). *Implementing ongoing transition plans for the IEP: A student-driven approach to IDEA mandates.* Verona, WI: Attainment Company, Inc.

McReynolds, L. V. (1990). Articulation and phonological disorders. In G. H. Shames & E. H. Wiig (Eds.), *Human communication disorders* (3rd ed.), (pp. 30-73). Upper Saddle River, NJ: Merrill/Prentice Hall.

McTernan, M., & Ward, N. (2005). Outcomes that matter: Parents' perspectives. *Mental Retardation, 43,* 214-220.

Meadan, H., & Halle, J. W. (2004). Social perceptions of students with learning disabilities who differ in social status. *Learning Disabilities Research and Practice, 19,* 71-82.

Meadow-Orlans, K. P. (1985). Social and psychological effects of hearing loss in adulthood: A literature review. In H. Orlans (Ed.), *Adjustment to adult hearing loss* (pp. 35-57). San Diego: College-Hill.

Meadow-Orlans, K. P., Mertens, D. M., Sass-Lehrer, M. A., & Scott-Olson, K. (1997). Support services for parents and their children who are deaf or hard of hearing. *American Annals of the Deaf, 142,* 278-288.

Meadows, N. B., Neel, R. S., Scott, C. M., & Parker, G. (1994). Academic performance, social competence, and mainstream accommodations: A look at mainstreamed and nonmainstreamed students with serious behavioral disorders. *Behavioral Disorders, 19,* 170-180.

Meadows, N. B., & Stevens, K. B. (2004). Teaching alternative behaviors to students with emotional and behavioral disorders. In R. B. Rutherford, M. M. Quinn, & S. R. Mathur (Eds.), *Handbook of research in emotional and behaviors disorders* (pp. 385-395). New York: Guilford.

Mechling, L. (2007). Assistive technology as a self-management tool for prompting students with intellectual disabilities to initiate and complete daily tasks: A literature review. *Education and Training in Developmental Disabilities, 42,* 253-269.

Mechling, L. C. (2006). Comparison of the effects of three approaches on the frequency of stimulus activation, via a single switch, by students with profound intellectual disabilities. *Journal of Special Education, 40,* 94-102.

Mechling, L. C., & Gast, D. L. (1997). Combination audio/visual self-prompting system for teaching chained tasks to students with intellectual disabilities.

Education and Training in Mental Retardation and Developmental Disabilities, 32, 138-153.

Mechling, L. C., Pridgen, L. S., & Cronin, B. A. (2005). Computer-based video instruction to teach students with intellectual disabilities to verbally respond to questions and make purchases in fast food restaurants. *Education and Training in Developmental Disabilities, 40,* 47-59.

Mehler, J., Jusczyk, P. W., Lambertz, G., Halsted, N., Bettoncini, J., & Ameil-Tison, C. (1988). A precursor of language acquisition in young infants. *Cognition, 29,* 143-178.

Meier, C. R., DiPerna, J. C., & Oster, M. M. (2006). Importance of social skills in the elementary grades. *Education & Treatment of Children, 29,* 409-419.

Menard, C. (1999, September 2). Pica and the brain. Message posted to St. John's University Autism and Developmental Disabilities List, archived at http://maelstrom.stjohns.edu/archives/autism.html.

Menlove, R. R., Hudson, P. J., & Suter, D. (2001). A field of IEP dreams: Increasing general education teacher participation in the IEP development process. *Teaching Exceptional Children, 33*(5), 28-33.

Mercer, C. D., Jordan, L., Allsopp, D. H., & Mercer, A. R. (1995). Learning disabilities definitions and criteria used by state education departments. Unpublished manuscript.

Mercer, C. D., & Mercer, A. R. (2008). *Teaching students with learning problems* (8th ed.). Upper Saddle River, NJ: Merrill/Prentice Hall.

Mercer, C. D., & Pullen, P. C. (2008). *Students with learning disabilities* (7th ed.). Upper Saddle River, NJ: Merrill/Prentice Hall.

Merrill, E. C. (1990). Attentional resource allocation and mental retardation. In N. W. Bray (Ed.), *International review of research in mental retardation: Vol. 16* (pp. 51-88). San Diego: Academic Press.

Merrill, E. C. (2005). Preattentive orienting in adolescents with mental retardation. *American Journal on Mental Retardation, 110,* 28-35.

Merritt, D. D., & Culatta, B. (1998). *Language intervention in the classroom.* San Diego: Singular.

Mervis, C. B., Klein-Tasman, B. P., & Mastin, M. E. (2001). Adaptive behavior of 4- through 8-year-old children with Williams syndrome. *American Journal of Mental Retardation, 106,* 82-93.

Metz, B., Mulick, J. A., & Butter, E. M. (2005). Autism: A late 20th century fad magnet. In J. W. Jacobson, R. M. Foxx, & J. A. Mulick (Eds.), *Controversial therapies for developmental disabilities: Fads, fashion, and science in professional practice* (pp. 237-263). Mahwah, NJ: Lawrence Erlbaum Associates.

Meyer, D. (1995). *Uncommon fathers: Reflections on raising a child with a disability.* Bethesda, MD: Woodbine House.

Michael, J. (1993). *Principles and concepts of behavior analysis.* Kalamazoo, MI: Association for Behavior Analysis.

Miller, A. D., Barbetta, P. M., & Heron, T. E. (1994). START tutoring: Designing, training, implementing, adapting, and evaluating tutoring programs for school and home settings. In R. Gardner, III, D. M. Sainato, J. O. Cooper, T. E. Heron, W. L. Heward, J. Eshleman, & T. A. Grossi (Eds.), *Behavior analysis in education: Focus on measurably superior instruction* (pp. 75-85). Pacific Grove, CA: Brooks/Cole.

Miller, A. D., Hall, S. W., & Heward, W. L. (1995). Effects of sequential 1-minute time trials with and without intertrial feedback and self-correction on general and special education students' fluency with math facts. *Journal of Behavioral Education, 5,* 319-345.

Miller, C. J., Sanchez, J., & Hynd, G. W. (2003). Neurological correlates of reading disabilities. In H. L. Swanson, K. R. Harris, & S. Graham (Eds.), *Handbook of learning disabilities* (pp. 242-255). New York: Guilford.

Miller, G. (1993). Expanding vocational options. *RE:view, 25*(1), 27-31.

Miller, M. M. & Menacker, S. J. (2007). Vision: Our window to the world. In M. L. Batshaw, L. Pellegrino, & N. J. Roizen (Eds.), *Children with disabilities* (6th ed.). Baltimore: Brookes.

Miller, W. H. (1985). The role of residential schools for the blind in educating visually impaired students. *Journal of Visual Impairment and Blindness, 79,* 160.

Miltenberger, R. G. (2008). *Behavior modification: Principles and procedures* (4th ed.). Belmont, CA: Thompson.

Minner, S., Beane, A., & Prater, J. (1986). Try telephone answering machines. *Teaching Exceptional Children, 19*(1), 62-63.

Minor, R. J. (2001). The experience of living with and using a dog guide. *RE:view, 32,* 183-190.

Mirenda, P., & Erickson, K. (2000). Augmentative communication and literacy. In A. Wetherby & B. Prizant (Eds.), *Autism spectrum disorders: A transactional developmental perspective* (pp. 333-367). Baltimore: Brookes.

Mitchell, D. (Ed.). (2004a). *Contextualizing inclusive education: Evaluating old and new international paradigms.* London: Routledge Falmer.

Mitchell, D. (Ed.). (2004b). *Special educational needs and inclusive education: Major themes in education.* London: Routledge Falmer.

Mitchell, R. E. (2006). How Many Deaf People Are There in the United States? Estimates From the Survey of Income and Program Participation. *The Journal of Deaf Studies and Deaf Education, 11,* 112-119.

Mitchem, K. J., Young, K. R., West, R. P., & Benyo, J. (2001). CWPASM: A classwide peer-assisted self-management program for general education classrooms. *Education and Treatment of Children, 24,* 3-14.

Mithaug, D. K. (2002). "Yes" means success: Teaching students with multiple disabilities to self-regulate during independent work. *Teaching Exceptional Children, 35*(1), 22-27.

Moats, L. (2007). *Whole-language high jinks: How to tell when "scientifically-based reading instruction" isn't.* Washington, DC: Thomas B. Fordham Institute.

Mock, D. R., & Kauffman, J. M. (2005). *The delusion of full inclusion* In J. W. Jacobson, R. M. Foxx, & J. A. Mulick (Eds.). Controversial therapies in developmental disabilities: Fads, fashion, and science in professional practice (pp. 113-128). Hillsdale, NJ: Lawrence Erlbaum Associates.

Molloy, C. A., Manning-Courtney, P., Swayne, S., Bean, J., Brown, J. M., Murray, D. S., Kinsman, A. M., Brasington, M., & Ulrich II, C. D. (2002). Lack of benefit of intravenous synthetic human secretin in the treatment of autism. *Journal of Autism and Developmental Disorders, 32,* 545-551.

Monda-Amaya, L. E., Dieker, L., & Reed, F. (1998). Preparing students with learning disabilities to participate in inclusive classrooms. *Learning Disabilities Research and Practice, 13*(3), 171-182.

Monikowski, C., & Winston, E. A. (2005). Interpreters and interpreter education. In M. Marschark & P. E. Spencer (Eds.), *Oxford handbook of deaf studies, language, and education* (paperback ed.) (pp. 347-360). New York: Oxford University Press.

Montague, M., Enders, C., & Castro, M. (2005). Academic and behavioral outcomes for students with emotional and behavioral disorders. *Behavioral Disorders, 31,* 18-32.

Montgomery, D. (2001). Increasing Native American Indian enrollment in gifted programs in rural schools. *Psychology in the Schools, 38,* 467-475.

Montgomery, D. J. (2005). Communicating without harm: Strategies to enhance parent-teacher communication. *Teaching Exceptional Children, 37*(5), 50-55.

Montgomery, W. (2001). Creating culturally responsive, inclusive classroooms. *Teaching Exceptional Children, 33*(4), 4-9.

Moody, S. W., Vaughn, S., Hughes, M. T., & Fischer, M. (2000). Reading instruction in the resource room: Set up for failure. *Exceptional Children, 66,* 305-316.

Moon, M. S. (1994). *Making school and community recreation fun for everyone: Places and ways to integrate.* Baltimore: Brookes.

Moon, M. S., & Inge, K. (2000). Vocational preparation and transition. In M. E. Snell & F. Brown (Eds.), *Instruction of students with severe disabilities* (5th ed.), (pp. 591-628). Upper Saddle River, NJ: Merrill/Prentice Hall.

Mooney, P., Epstein, M. H., Reid, R., & Nelson, J. R. (2003). Status of and trends in academic intervention research for students with emotional disturbance. *Remedial and Special Education, 24,* 273-287.

Moore, J. E. (2006). 100 years of trends and issues in employment, rehabilitation, and legislation. *Journal of Visual Impairment and Blindness, 100,* 453-458.

Moores, D. F. (1993). Total inclusion/zero rejection models in general education: Implication for deaf children. *American Annals of the Deaf, 138,* 251.

Moores, D. F. (2001). *Educating the deaf: Psychology, principles, and practices* (5th ed.). Boston: Houghton Mifflin.

Moores, D. F. (2004). No Child Left Behind: The good, the bad, and the ugly. *American Annals of the Deaf, 148,* 347-348.

Morgan, C. D., & Murray, H. A. (1935). A method for investigating fantasies: The Thematic Apperception Test. *Archives of Neurology and Psychiatry, 34,* 289–306.

Morgan, D., Young, K. R., & Goldstein, S. (1983). Teaching behaviorally disordered students to increase teacher attention and praise in mainstreamed classrooms. *Behavioral Disorders, 8,* 265–273.

Morgan, P. L., Young, C., & Fuchs, D. (2006). Peer-Assisted Learning Strategies: An effective intervention for young readers. *Insights on Learning Disabilities, 3*(1), 23–41.

Morocco, C. C., Brigham, N., & Aguilar, C. M. (2006). *Visionary middle schools: Signature practices and the power of local innovation.* New York: Teachers College Press.

Morocco, C. C., Clay, K., Parker, C. E., & Zigmond, N. (2006). Walter Cronkite High School: A culture of freedom and responsibility. *Learning Disabilities Research & Practice, 21,* 146–158.

Morris, R. J., & Kratochwill, T. R. (1998). Childhood fears and phobias. In R. J. Morris & T. R. Kratochwill (Eds.), *The practice of child therapy* (3rd ed.). Boston: Allyn & Bacon.

Morris, R. J., Shah, K., & Morris, Y. P. (2002). Internalizing behavior disorders. In K. L. Lane, F. M. Gresham, & T. E. O'Shaughnessy (Eds.), *Children with or at risk for emotional and behavior disorders* (pp. 223–241). Boston: Allyn and Bacon.

Morris, T. L. (2004). Treatment of social phobia in children and adolescents. In P. M. Barrett & T. H. Ollendick (Eds.), *Handbook of interventions that work with children and adolescents: Prevention and treatment* (pp. 171–186). London: Wiley.

Morrison, G., & D'Incau, B. (2000). Developmental and service trajectories of students with disabilities recommended for expulsion from school. *Exceptional Children, 66,* 55–66.

Morrison, G. S. (2007). *Early childhood education today* (10th ed.). Upper Saddle River, NJ: Merrill/Prentice Hall.

Morrison, G. S. (2008). *Fundamentals of early childhood education* (5th ed.). Upper Saddle River, NJ: Merrill/Prentice Hall.

Morrison, R. S., Sainato, D. M., BenChaaban, D., & Endo, S. (2002). Increasing play skills of children with autism using activity schedules and correspondence training. *Journal of Early Intervention, 25,* 58–72.

Morse, T. E., & Schuster, J. W. (2000). Teaching elementary students with moderate intellectual disabilities how to shop for groceries. *Exceptional Children, 66,* 273–288.

Morse, W. C. (1976). Worksheet on life-space interviewing for teachers. In N. Long, W. Morse, & R. Newman (Eds.), *Conflict in the classroom* (pp. 337–341). Belmont, CA: Wadsworth.

Morse, W. C. (1985). *The education and treatment of socioemotionally impaired children and youth.* Syracuse, NY: Syracuse University Press.

Mortweet, S. L., Utley, C. A., Walker, D., Dawson, H. L., Delquadri, J. C., Reddy, S. S., Greenwood, C. R., Hamilton, S., & Ledford,

D. (1999). Classwide peer tutoring: Teaching students with mild mental retardation in inclusive classrooms. *Exceptional Children, 65,* 524–536.

Moser, H. W. (2000). Genetics and gene therapies. In M. L. Wehmeyer & J. R. Patton (Eds.), *Mental Retardation in the 21st century* (pp. 235–250). Austin, TX: PRO-ED.

Most, T., & Greenbank, A. (2000). Auditory, visual, and auditory-visual perception of emotions by adolescents with and without learning disabilities, and their relationship to social skills. *Learning Disabilities Research and Practice, 15,* 171–178.

Mostert, M. P., Kavale, K. A., & Kauffman, J. M. (2008). *Challenging the refusal of reason in special education.* Denver: Love.

Mottram, L., & Berger-Gross, P. (2004). An intervention to reduce disruptive behaviours in children with brain injury. *Pediatric Rehabilitation, 7,* 133–143.

Mow, S. (1989). How do you dance without music? In S. Wilcox (Ed.), *American Deaf Culture: An anthology.* Silver Spring, MD: Linstok Press.

Moxley, R. A. (1998). Treatment-only designs and student self-recording strategies for public school teachers. *Education and Treatment of Children, 21,* 37–61.

Mudford, O. C. (1995). Review of the gentle teaching data. *American Journal on Mental Retardation, 99,* 345–355.

Mueller, R. A., & Courchesne, E. (2000). Autism's home in the brain: Reply. *Neurology, 54*(1), 270.

Mulick, J. A., & Antonak, R. (Eds.). (1994). *Life styles: Transitions in mental retardation* (Vol. 5). Norwood, NJ: Ablex.

Mull, C., Sitlington, P. L., & Alper, S. (2001). Postsecondary education for students with learning disabilities: A synthesis of the literature. *Exceptional Children, 68,* 97–118.

Multimodal Treatment Study Group. (1999). A 14-month randomized clincial trial of treatment strategies for attention-deficit/hyperactivity disorder. *Archives of General Psychiatry, 56,* 1088–1096.

Munk, D. D., Van Laarhoven, T., Goodman, S., & Repp, A. C. (1998). Small-group Direct Instruction for students with moderate to severe disabilities. In A. Hilton & R. Ringlaben (Eds.), *Best and promising practices in developmental disabilities* (pp. 127–138). Austin, TX: PRO-ED.

Munson, L. J., & Hunt, N. (2005). Teachers grieve! What can we do for our colleagues and ourselves when a student dies? *Teaching Exceptional Children, 37*(4), 48–51.

Murdick, N. L., Gartin, B. C., & Crabtree, T. (2007). *Special education law* (2nd ed.). Upper Saddle River, NJ: Merrill/Prentice Hall.

Murphy, C. M. (2003). *Using functional assessment to determine the maintaining contingencies of non-contextual speech by children with autism.* Unpublished master's thesis, The Ohio State University, Columbus.

Murphy, K. A., Theodore, L. A., Danielle Aloiso, D., Alric-Edwards, J. M., & Hughes, T. L. (2006). Interdependent group contingency and mystery motivators to reduce

preschool disruptive behavior. *Psychology in the Schools, 44,* 53–63.

Murray, C., Goldstein, D. E., Nourse, S., & Edgar, E. (2000). The postsecondary school attendance and completion rates of high school graduates with learning disabilities. *Learning Disabilities Research and Practice, 15,* 119–127.

Musselman, C. (2000). How do children who can't hear learn to read an alphabetic script? A review of the literature on reading and deafness. *Journal of Deaf Studies and Deaf Education, 5,* 9–31.

Myers, A., & Eisenman, L. (2005). Student-led IEPs: Take the first step. *Teaching Exceptional Children, 34*(7), 52–58.

Myers, P. I., & Hammill, D. D. (1976). *Methods for learning disorders* (2nd ed.). New York: John Wiley.

Myers, P. I., & Hammill, D. D. (1990). *Learning disabilities: Basic concepts, assessment practices, and instructional strategies* (3rd ed.). Austin, TX: PRO-ED.

Myles, B. S., & Simpson, R. L. (2001). Effective practices for students with Asperger syndrome. *Focus on Exceptional Children, 34*(3) 1–14.

Myles, B. S., Bock, S. J., & Simpson, R. L. (2001). *Asperger syndrome diagnostic scale.* Austin: PRO-ED.

Naglieri, J. A., & Ford, D. Y. (2003). Addressing under representation of minority children using the Naglieri Nonverbal Ability Test. *Gifted Child Quarterly, 47,* 155–160.

Naglieri, J. A., & Ford, D. Y. (2005). Increasing minority children's participation in gifted classes using the NNAT: A response to Lohman. *Gifted Child Quarterly, 49,* 29–31.

Najdowski, A. C., Wallace, M. D., Doney, J. K., & Ghezzi, P. M. (2003). Parental assessment and treatment of food selectivity in natural settings. *Journal of Applied Behavior Analysis, 36,* 383–386.

Nakken, H. (2002). Individuals with profound multiple disabilities (PMD): Description, treatment and support, a discussion. *Journal of Intellectual Disability Research, 48,* 355–365.

Narayan, J. S., Heward, W. L., Gardner, R., III, Courson, F. H., & Omness, C. (1990). Using response cards to increase student participation in an elementary classroom. *Journal of Applied Behavior Analysis, 23,* 483–490.

Naseef, R. A. (2001). *Special children, challenged parents: The struggles and rewards of raising a child with a disability* (Rev. ed.). Baltimore: Brookes.

National Association for Gifted Children. (2004). *Position paper: Acceleration.* Washington, DC: Author. [Retrieved September 18, 2007. http://www.nagc.org/CMS400Min/index.aspx?id=383]

National Association for Gifted Children. (2004–2005). *State of the nation in gifted education.* Washington, DC: Author.

National Association for the Deaf. (2000). *Cochlear implants: NAD position statement* (Approved by NAD Board of Directors, October 6, 2000). Washington, DC: Author. Available online: http://www.nad.org/ciposition

National Association for the Deaf. (2007). *Cochlear implants: Frequently asked questions.* [Retrieved August 24, 2007 from http://www.nad.org/site/pp.asp?c= foINKQMBF&b=399061#14]

National Association of the Deaf. (2002). *Inclusion: NAD position statement.* [Approved by the NAD Board of Directors on January 26, 2002.] Silver Spring, MD: Author. Available online at http://www.nad.org/site/pp.asp?c=foINK QMBF&b=180362.

National Autism Center. (2007). *National standards project for evidence-based treatment approaches for autism.* Randolph, MA. Author. [www. nationalautismcenter.org]

National Center for Educational Statistics. (1998). *Postsecondary education quick information system: Survey of students with disabilities at postsecondary education institutions.* Washington, DC: U.S. Department of Education.

National Center for Education Statistics. (2004). *Postsecondary education quick information system: Survey of students with disabilities at postsecondary education institutions.* Washington, DC: U.S. Department of Education.

National Center for Injury Prevention and Control. (2007). *Traumatic brain injury.* Atlanta, GA: Author. [Retrieved September 9, 2007 from http://www.cdc.gov/ncipc/ factsheets/tbi.htm]

National Center for the Study of Postsecondary Educational Supports. (2002, July). *Preparation for and support of youth with disabilities in postsecondary education and employment: Implications for policy, priorities and practice.* Proceedings and briefing book for the National Summit on Postsecondary Education for People with Disabilities, presented in Washington, DC, on July 8, 2002. Retrieved January 7, 2004, from http://www.ncset.hawaii.edu/ summits/july2002/briefing/default.htm.

National Center on Student Progress Monitoring. (2007). www.studentprogress. org.

National Council on Disability. (2000, May 15). *National disability policy: A progress report: December 2001–December 2002.* http://www.ncd.gov/newsroom/ publications/progressreport2000.html.

National Dissemination Center for Children with Disabilities (NICHCY). (2004). *Cerebral palsy, Fact sheet 2.* Washington, DC: Author. [Retrieved September 2, 2007. http://www.nichcy.org/pubs/factshe/ fs2txt.htm#common]

National Education Association. (2003). *Status of the American public school teacher, 2001–2002.* Washington, DC: Author.

National excellence: A case for developing America's talent. (1993). Washington, DC: U.S. Department of Education, Office of Educational Research and Improvement.

National Institute of Allergy and Infectious Diseases. (2001). *Fact sheet: HIV infection and adolescents.* http://www.niaid.nih. gov/factsheets/hivadolescent.htm.

National Institute of Child Health and Human Development. (2000). *Report of the National Reading Panel. Teaching children to read: An evidence-based assessment of the scientific research literature on reading and its implications for reading instruction: Reports of the subgroups* (NIH Publication No. 00-4754). Washington, DC: U.S. Government Printing Office.

National Institute of Health Consensus Statement. (1998). Diagnosis and treatment of attention deficit/hyperactivity disorder. *NIH Consensus Statement, 16*(2), 1–37.

National Institute of Mental Health (NIH). (2004). *Congressional appropriations report on the state of autism research.* Bethesda, MD: Author.

National Institute of Mental Health (NIH). (2007). Tiny, spontaneous gene mutations may boost autism risk. Bethesda, MD: Author. [Report retrieved March 17, 2007 from *Science Daily*, March 16. http:// www.sciencedaily.com/releases/2007/03/ 070315161043.htm]

National Institute on Deafness and Other Communication Disorders. (2001). Cochlear implants. In *Health information: Hearing and balance.* http://www.nih. gov/nidcd/health/pubs_hb/coch.htm.

National Institute on Deafness and Other Communication Disorders. (2007a). *Statistics about hearing disorders, ear infections, and deafness.* [Retrieved August 24, 2007. http://www.nidcd.nih. gov/health/statistics/hearing.asp]

National Institute on Deafness and Other Communication Disorders. (2007b). *Noise-induced hearing loss.* [Retrieved August 22, 2007. http://www.nidcd.nih.gov/ health/hearing/noise.asp]

National Institutes of Health. (2007). *Muscular dystrophy information page.* Bethesda, MD: Author. [Retrieved September 2, 2007 from http://www.ninds.nih.gov/disorders/ md/md.htm]

National Joint Committee for the Communication Needs of Persons With Severe Disabilities. (2003). *Position statement on access to communication services and supports: Concerns regarding the application of restrictive "eligibility" policies* [Position Statement]. Available from www.asha.org/policy or www.asha.org/njc.

National Joint Committee on Learning Disabilities. (1989, September 18). Letter from NJCLD to member organizations. Topic: Modifications to the NJCLD definition of learning disabilities.

National Joint Committee on Learning Disabilities. (1990/2001). Learning disabilities: Issues on definition. In National Joint Committee on Learning Disabilities (Ed.), *Collective perspectives on issues affecting learning disabilities: Position papers, statements, and reports* (2nd ed., pp. 27–32). Austin, TX: Pro-Ed. Available from http://www.ldonline.org. (Original work published 1990)

National Joint Committee on Learning Disabilities. (1993, January). *A reaction to full inclusion: A reaffirmation of the right of students with learning disabilities to a continuum of services.* http://www. ldonline.org/njcld/react_inclu.html.

National Joint Committee on Learning Disabilities. (2005, June). *Responsiveness to intervention and learning disabilities.* [Available: www.ldonline.org/about/ partners/njcld#reports] Retrieved June 18, 2007.

National Joint Committee on Learning Disabilities. (2006, October). *Learning disabilities and young children: Identification and intervention.* [Available: www.ldonline.org/about/ partners/njcld#reports] Retrieved June 18, 2007.

National Organization on Disability. (2004). *Harris survey of Americans with disabilities.* New York: Author.

National Reading Panel. (2000). *Teaching children to read: An evidence-based assessment of the scientific research literature on reading and its implications for reading instruction. Reports of the subgroups.* http://www. nichd.nih.gov/publications/nrp/ smallbook.htm.

National Research Center on Learning Disabilities. (2005). *Responsiveness to intervention in the SLD determination process.* Lawrence, KS: Author. [Available on-line at www.nrcld.org]

National Research Council. (1998). *Preventing reading difficulties in young children.* Washington, DC: National Academy Press.

National Research Council. (2000). *Testing English-language learners in U.S. schools: Report and workshop summary.* http:// www.nap.edu.

National Research Council. (2001). *Educating children with autism.* Washington, DC: National Academy Press.

National Science Foundation. (2004). *Women, minorities, and persons with disabilities in science and engineering.* Washington, DC: Author.

National Spinal Cord Injury Association. (2007). *Facts and figures.* Rockville, MD: Author.

National Spinal Cord Injury Statistical Center. (2006a). *What are the leading causes of SCI?* Birmingham, AL: Author. [Retrieved September 3, 2007. http://www. spinalcord.uab.edu/show.asp?durki=20188 &site=1021&return=20183]

National Spinal Cord Injury Statistical Center. (2006b). *Facts and figures at a glance-June 2006.* Birmingham, AL: Author. [Retrieved September 3, 2007. http://www.spinalcord.uab.edu/show.asp? durki=21446]

National Symposium on Learning Disabilities in English Language Learners. (2004). *Symposium summary.* Washington, DC: U.S. Office of Special Education and Rehabilitation Services.

National Technical Assistance Center. (2004). *National deaf-blind child count summary: December 1, 2003.* Monmouth, OR: NTAC, Teaching Research Institute, Western Oregon University.

Neal, J., Bigby, L., & Nicholson, R. (2004). Occupational therapy, physical therapy, and orientation and mobility services in public schools. *Intervention in School and Clinic, 39,* 218–222.

Nechring, W. M., & Steele, S. (1996). Cerebral palsy. In P. L. Jackson & J. A. Vessey (Eds.), *Primary care of the child with a chronic condition* (2nd ed.), (pp. 232–254). St. Louis: Mosby.

Neef, N. A., Bicard, D. F., & Endo, S. (2001). Assessment of impulsivity and the development of self-control in students with attention-deficit hyperactivity disorder. *Journal of Applied Behavior Analysis, 34,* 397–407.

Neef, N. A., McCord, B. E., & Ferreri, S. J. (2006). Effects of guided notes versus completed notes during lecture on college students' quiz performance. *Journal of Applied Behavior Analysis, 39,* 123–130.

Neef, N. A., Parrish, J. M., Egel, A. L., & Sloan, M. E. (1986). Training respite care providers for families with handicapped children: Experimental analysis and validation of an instructional package. *Journal of Applied Behavior Analysis, 19,* 105–124.

Neef, N. A., & Peterson, S. M. (2007). Functional behavior assessment. In J. O. Cooper, T. E. Heron, & W. L. Heward, *Applied behavior analysis* (2nd ed.) (pp. 500–524). Upper Saddle River, NJ: Merrill/Prentice Hall.

Nehring, W. M. (2003). Newborn screening in the 21st century: Current status and considerations. *Exceptional Parent, 33*(4), 53–57.

Neihart, M., Robinson, N., & Moon, S. (2002). *The social and emotional development of gifted children: What do we know?* Waco, TX: Prufock.

Neilsen, M. E., & Higgins, L. D. (2005). The eye of the storm: Services and programs for twice-exceptional learners. *Teaching Exceptional Children, 38*(1), 8–15.

Neisworth, J. T., & Bagnato, S. J. (2005). Recommended practices: Assessment. In S. Sandall, M. L. Hemmeter, B. J. Smith, & M. E. McLean (Eds.), *DEC recommended practices: A comprehensive guide for practical application in early intervention/early childhood special education* (pp. 45–69). Arlington, VA: Council for Exceptional Children, Division for Early Childhood.

Neisworth, J. T., & Wolfe, P. S. (Eds.). (2005). *The autism dictionary.* Baltimore: Paul H. Brookes.

Nelson, C., & Huefner, D. S. (2003). Young children with autism: Judicial responses to the Lovaas and discrete trial training debates. *Journal of Early Intervention, 26,* 1–19.

Nelson, C., McDonnell, A. P., Johnston, S. S., Crompton, A., & Nelson, A. R. (2007). Keys to play: A strategy to increase the social interactions of young children with autism and their typically developing peers. *Education and Training in Developmental Disabilities, 42,* 165–181.

Nelson, C. M. (2000). Educating students with emotional and behavioral disabilities in the 21st century: Looking through windows, opening doors. *Education and Treatment of Children, 23,* 204–222.

Nelson, L. G. L., Summers, J. A., & Turnbull, A. P. (2004). Boundaries in family-professional relationships: Implications for special education. *Remedial and Special Education, 25,* 153–165.

Nelson, J. R., Benner, G. J., & Cheney, D. (2005). An investigation of the language skills of students with emotional disturbance served in public school settings. *Journal of Special Education, 39,* 97–105.

Nelson, J. R., Benner, G. J., Lane, K., & Smith, B. W. (2004). Academic achievement of K-12 students with emotional and behavioral disorders. *Exceptional Children, 71,* 59–73.

Nelson, J. R., Martella, R. M., & Marchand-Martella, N. (2002). Maximizing student learning: The effects of a comprehensive school-based program for preventing problems behaviors. *Journal of Emotional and Behavioral Disorders, 10,* 136–148.

Nelson, J. R., Stage, S., Duppong-Hurley, K. Synhorst, L., & Epstein, M. H. (2007). Risk factors predictive of the problem behavior of children at risk for emotional and behavioral disorders. *Exceptional Children, 73,* 367–379.

Nelson, P. (2001). The changing demand for improved acoustics in our schools. *Volta Review, 101*(5), 23–32.

Netzel, D. M., and Eber, L. (2003). Shifting from reactive to proactive discipline in an urban school district: A change of focus through PBIS implementation. *Journal of Positive Behavior Interventions, 5,* 71–79.

Neu, T. (2003). When the gifts are camouflaged by disability: Identifying and developing the talent in gifted students with disabilities. In J. A. Castellano (Ed.), *Special populations in gifted education: Working with diverse gifted learners* (pp. 151–162). Boston: Allyn & Bacon.

Neu, T., & Weinfeld, R. (2006). *Helping boys succeed in school.* Waco, TX: Prufrock Press.

Newbold, S. (2000). *Emergent literacy for young blind children.* Phoenix, AZ: FBC Publications.

Newborg, J. (2006). *Battelle developmental inventory* (2nd ed.). Chicago: Riverside.

Newcomer, J. R., & Zirkel, P. A. (1999). An analysis of judicial outcomes of special education cases. *Exceptional Children, 65,* 469–480.

Newcomer, P. L., & Barenbaum, E. M. (1991). The written composing ability of children with learning disabilities: A review of the literature from 1980 to 1990. *Journal of Learning Disabilities, 24,* 578–593.

Newman, B., Reinecke, D. R., & Meinberg, D. (2000). Self-management of varied responding in children with autism. *Behavioral Interventions, 15,* 145–151.

Newman, L. (2004). *Family involvement in the educational development of youth with disabilities. A Special Topic Report from the National Longitudinal Transition Study-2 (NLTS-2).* Menlo Park, CA: SRI International.

Newman, R. S., & Golding, L. (1990). Children's reluctance to seek help with school work. *Journal of Educational Psychology, 82,* 92–100.

Nieto, S. (2000). *Affirming diversity: The sociopolitical context of multicultural education* (3rd ed.). New York: Addison Wesley Longman.

Nietupski, J., & Svoboda, R. (1982). Teaching a cooperative leisure skill to severely handicapped adults. *Education and Training of the Mentally Retarded, 17,* 38–43.

Nihira, K., Leland, H., & Lambert, N. K. (1993). *Adaptive Behavior Scale—Residential and Community* (2nd ed.). Austin, TX: PRO-ED.

Nikopoulos, C. K., & Keenan, M. (2004). Effects of video modeling on social initiations by children with autism. *Journal of Applied Behavior Analysis, 37,* 93–96.

Nirje, B. (1969). The normalization principle and its human management implications. In R. Kugel & W. Wolfensberger (Eds.), *Changing patterns in residential services for the mentally retarded* (pp. 181–195). Washington, DC: President's Committee on Mental Retardation.

Noens, I. L. J., & van Berckelaer-Onnes, I. A. (2005). Captured by details: Sense-making, language and communication in autism. *Journal of Communication Disorders, 38,* 123–141.

Noonan, M. J., & McCormick, L. (2006). *Young children with disabilities in natural environments: Methods and procedures.* Baltimore: Brookes.

Northern, J. L., & Downs, M. P. (2002). *Hearing in children* (5th ed.). Baltimore: Lippincott, Williams & Wilkins.

Northup, J., Fusilier, I., Swanson, V., Roane, H., & Borrero, J. (1997). An evaluation of methylphenidate as a potential establishing operation for some common classroom reinforcers. *Journal of Applied Behavior Analysis, 30,* 615–625.

Northup, J., Galley, V., Edwards, S., & Fountain, L. (2001). The effects of methylphenidate in the classroom: What dosage, for which children, for what problems? *School Psychology Quarterly, 16,* 303–323.

Norton, L. S., & Hartley, J. (1986). What factors contribute to good examination marks? The role of notetaking in subsequent examination performance. *Higher Education, 15,* 355–371.

Notari-Syverson, A. R., & Shuster, S. L. (1995). Putting real-life skills into IEP/IFSPs for infants and young children. *Teaching Exceptional Children, 27*(2), 29–32.

Nowacek, E. J., McKinney, J. D., & Hallahan, D. P. (1990). Instructional behaviors of more and less effective beginning regular and special educators. *Exceptional Children, 57,* 140–149.

Nugent, S. A. (2005). Affective education: Addressing the social and emotional needs of gifted students in the classroom. In F. A. Karnes & S. M. Bean (Eds.), *Methods and materials for teaching the gifted* (2nd ed.) (pp. 409–438). Waco, TX: Prufrock Press.

Oakes, J. (1985). *Keeping track.* New Haven, CT: Yale University Press.

Obiakor, F. E. (2007). *Multicultural special education: Culturally response teaching.* Upper Saddle River, NJ: Merrill/Prentice Hall.

Ochoa, S. H., & Palmer, D. J. (1995). A meta-analysis of peer rating sociometric studies with learning disabled pupils. *Journal of Special Education, 29,* 1–9.

O'Connell-Ross, P. (1997). Federal policy on gifted and talented education. In N. Colangelo and G. Davis (Eds.), *Handbook of Gifted Education* (2nd ed.) (pp. 553–559). Boston: Allyn & Bacon.

O'Conner, R. E. (2000). Increasing the intensity of intervention in kindergarten and first grade. *Learning Disabilities Research and Practice, 15*, 44-54.

Odding, E., Roebroeck, M. E., & Stam, H. J. (2006). The epidemiology of cerebral palsy: Incidence, impairments and risk factors. *Disability Rehabilitation, 28*, 183-91.

Odom, S. L. (2000). Preschool inclusion: What we know and where we go from here. *Topics in Early Childhood Special Education, 20*, 20-27.

Odom, S. L., Brantlinger, E., Gersten, R., Horner, R. H., Thompson, B., & Harris, K. R. (2005). Research in special education: Scientific methods and evidence-based practices. *Exceptional Children, 71*, 137-148.

Odom, S. L., & Brown, W. H. (1993). Social interaction skills interventions for young children with disabilities in integrated settings. In C. A. Peck, S. L. Odom, & D. Bricker (Eds.), *Integrating young children with disabilities into community programs: Ecological perspectives on research and implementation* (pp. 39-64). Baltimore: Brookes.

Odom, S. L., Hanson, M. J., Lieber, J., Marquart, J., Sandall, S., Wolery, R., Horn, E., Wolfberg, P., Schwartz, I., Beckman, P., Hikido, C., & Chambers, J. (2001). The costs of preschool inclusion. *Topics in Early Childhood Special Education, 21*, 146-155.

Odom, S. L., & Wolery, M. (2003). A unified theory of practice in early intervention/early childhood special education: Evidence-based practices. *Journal of Special Education, 37*, 164-173.

Office of Disability Employment Policy. (2004). *Customized employment Q and A*. Washington, DC: Author.

Office of Juvenile Justice and Delinquency Prevention. (2007). *OJJDP statistical briefing book*. Washington, DC: Author. Available online: http://ojjdp.ncjrs.gov/ojstatbb/crime/qa05101.asp?qaDate=2005.

Office of Technology Assessment. (1987). *Technology-dependent children: Hospital v. home care—A technical memorandum*. OTA-TM-H-38. Washington, DC: Author.

Ohtake, Y. (2004). Meaningful inclusion of *all* students in team sports. *Teaching Exceptional Children, 37*(2), 22-27.

Olmstead, J. E. (2005) *Itinerant teaching: Tricks of the trade for teachers of students with visual impairments* (2nd ed.). New York: AFB Press.

Olsen, R., & Sutton, J. (1998). More hassle, more alone: Adolescents with diabetes and the role of formal and informal support. *Child: Care, Health, and Development, 24*(1), 31-39.

Olympia, D., Andrews, D., Valum, L., & Jenson, W. (1993). *Homework teams: Homework management strategies for the classroom*. Longmont, CO: Sopris West.

Olympia, D. W., Sheridan, S. M., Jenson, W. R., & Andrews, D. (1994). Using student-managed interventions to increase homework completion and accuracy. *Journal of Applied Behavior Analysis, 27*, 85-99.

O'Neill, R. E., Horner, R. H., Albin, R. W., Sprague, J. R., Storey, K., & Newton, J. S. (1997). *Functional assessment and program development for problem behavior: A practical handbook*. Pacific Grove, CA: Brooks/Cole.

Onslow, M., Packman, A., & Harrison, E. (2003). *The Lidcombe Program of early stuttering intervention: A clinician's guide*. Austin, TX: PRO-ED.

O'Reilly, M., Green, V., Sigafoos, J., Lancioni, G., O'Reilly, B., Cannella-Malone, H., & Edrisinha, C. (2006). Working with students with mental retardation who exhibit severe challenging behavior. In C. Franklin, M. Harris, and P. Allen-Meares (Eds.), *The school services sourcebook: A guide for school-based professionals* (pp. 193-200). Oxford, United Kingdom: Oxford University Press.

O'Reilly, M. F., Lancioni, G. E., & Kierans, I. (2000). Teaching leisure social skills to adults with moderate mental retardation: An analysis of acquisition, generalization, and maintenance. *Education and Training in Mental Retardation and Developmental Disabilities, 35*, 250-258.

Orelove, F. P. (1984). The educability debate: A review and a look ahead. In W. L. Heward, T. E. Heron, D. S. Hill, & J. Trap-Porter (Eds.), *Focus on behavior analysis in education* (pp. 271-281). Upper Saddle River, NJ: Merrill/Prentice Hall.

Orelove, F. P., & Sobsey, D. (1996). *Educating children with multiple disabilities: A transdisciplinary approach* (3rd ed.). Baltimore: Brookes.

Orlansky, M. D., & Bonvillian, J. D. (1985). Sign language acquisition: Language development in children of deaf parents and implications for other populations. *Merrill-Palmer Quarterly, 31*, 127-143.

Orr, A. L., & Rogers, P. A. (2003) *Self-advocacy skills training for older individuals*. New York: AFB Press.

Orsillo, S. M., McCaffrey, R. J., & Fisher, J. M. (1993). Siblings of head-injured individuals: A population at risk. *Journal of Head Trauma Rehabilitation, 8*(1), 102-115.

Ormond, G. I., & Seltzer, M. M. (2000). Brothers and sisters of adults with mental retardation: Gendered nature of the sibling relationship. *American Journal of Mental Retardation, 105*, 486-508.

Ortiz, A. (1997). Learning disabilities occurring concomitantly with linguistic differences. *Journal of Learning Disabilities, 30*, 321-333.

Ortiz, V., & Gonzales, A. (1991). Gifted Hispanic adolescents. In M. Bireley & J. Genshaft (Eds.), *Understanding the gifted adolescent* (pp. 240-247). New York: Teachers College Press.

Osher, D., Cartledge, G., Oswald, D., Sutherland, K. S., Artiles, A. J., & Coutinho, M. (2004). Issues of cultural and linguistic competency in disproportionate representation. In R. B. Rutherford, M. M. Quinn, & S. R. Mathur (Eds.), *Handbook of research in emotional and behavioral disorders* (pp. 54-77). New York: Guilford.

Ostad, S. A. (1998). Developmental differences in solving simple arithmetic word problems and simple number-fact problems: A comparison of mathematically normal and mathematically disabled children. *Mathematical Cognition, 4*, 1-20.

Ostrosky, M., & Horn, E. (2001). *Assessment: Gathering meaningful information* (Monograph series no. 4). Reston, VA: Council for Exceptional Children, Division for Early Childhood.

Oswald, D. P. (1994). Facilitator influence in facilitated communication. *Journal of Behavioral Education, 4*, 191-200.

Oswald, D. P., & Coutinho, M. J. (2001). Trends in disproportionate representation: Implications for multicultural education. In C. Utley & F. Obiakor (Eds.), *Special education, multicultural education, and school reform: Components of quality education for learners with mild disabilities* (pp. 53-73). Springfield: Thomas.

Oswald, D. P., Coutinho, M. J., Best, A. M., & Singh, N. N. (1999). Ethnic representation in special education: The influence of school-related economic and demographic variables. *Journal of Special Education, 32*, 194-206.

Ovando, C. J. (2004). Language diversity and education. In J. A. Banks & C. A. M. Banks (Eds.), *Multicultural education: Issues and perspectives* (5th ed.), (pp. 289-313). New York: Wiley.

Overton, T. (2006). *Assessing learners with special needs: An applied approach* (5th ed.). Upper Saddle River, NJ: Merrill/Prentice Hall.

Owen, R. L., & Fuchs, L. S. (2002). Mathematical problem-solving strategy instruction for third-grade student with learning disabilities. *Remedial and Special Education, 23*, 268-278.

Owens, R. E. (2004). *Language disorders: A functional approach to assessment and intervention* (4th ed.). Boston: Allyn and Bacon.

Owens, R. E. (2008). *Language development: An introduction* (7th ed.). Boston: Allyn & Bacon.

Owens, R. E., Metz, D. E., & Haas, A. (Eds.). (2007). *Introduction to communication disorders: A lifespan perspective* (3rd ed.). Boston: Allyn & Bacon.

Owens-Johnson, L., & Hamill, L. B. (2002). Community-based instruction. In L. Hamill & C. Everington, *Teaching students with moderate to severe disabilities: An applied approach for inclusive environments* (pp. 347-378). Upper Saddle River, NJ: Merrill/Prentice Hall.

Owley, T., Steele, M., Corsello, C., Risi, S., McKaig, K., Lord, C., et al. (1999). A double-blind, placebo-controlled trial of secretin for the treatment of autistic disorder. *Medscape General Medicine/journal/1999/v.01.n10*.

Pacer Center. (2006). *Drop-out prevention: Parents play a key role*. Minneapolis, MN: Author. [Available: http://www.pacer.org/parent/php/PHP-c114.pdf]

Padden, C., & Humphries, T. (2006). *Inside Deaf culture*. Cambridge, MA: Harvard University Press.

Page, E. B. (1972). Miracle in Milwaukee: Raising the IQ. *Educational Researcher, 15*, 8-16.

Pakulski, L. A., & Kaderavek, J. N. (2002). Children with minimal hearing loss:

Interventions in the classroom. *Intervention in School and Clinic, 38,* 96-103.

Palfrey, J. S. (1995). Amber, Katie, and Ryan: Lessons from children with complex medical conditions. *Journal of School Health, 65,* 265-267.

Palincsar, A. S., Collins, K. M., Marano, N. L., & Magnusson, S. J. (2000). Investigating the engagement and learning of students with learning disabilities in guided inquiry science teaching. *Language, Speech, and Hearing Services in Schools, 31.*

Palmer, D. S., Fuller, K., Arora, T., & Nelson, M. (2001). Taking sides: Parents' views on inclusion for their children with severe disabilities. *Exceptional Children, 67,* 467-484.

Panerai, S., Ferrante, L., Caputo, V., & Impellizzeri, C. (1998). Use of structured teaching for the treatment of children with autism and severe and profound mental retardation. *Education and Training in Mental Retardation and Developmental Disabilities, 33,* 367-374.

Paniagua, F. A. (1992). Verbal-nonverbal correspondence training with ADHD children. *Behavior Modification, 16,* 226-252.

Parent, W., Gossage, D., Jones, M., Turner, P., Walker, C., & Feldman, R. (2008). Working with parents: Using strategies to promote planning and preparation, placement, and support. In F. R. Rusch (Ed.). *Beyond high school: Preparing adolescents for tomorrow's challenges* (2nd ed.) (pp. 110-133). Upper Saddle River, NJ: Merrill/Prentice Hall.

Parette, H. P. (1998). Assistive technology effective practices for students with mental retardation and developmental disabilities. In A. Hilton and R. Ringlaben (Eds.), *Best and promising practices in developmental disabilities* (pp. 205-224). Austin, TX: PRO-ED.

Parette, H. P., & Brotherson, M. J. (1996). Family participation in assistive technology assessment for young children with mental retardation and developmental disabilities. *Education and Training in Mental Retardation and Developmental Disabilities, 31,* 29-43.

Parette, H. P., & Petch-Hogan, B. (2000). Approaching families: Facilitating culturally/linguistically diverse family involvement. *Teaching Exceptional Children, 33*(2), 4-10.

Parette, H. P., & Hourcade, J. J. (1986). Management strategies for orthopedically handicapped students. *Teaching Exceptional Children, 18*(4), 282-286.

Parette, P., & McMahan, G. A. (2002). What should we expect of assistive technology? Being sensitive to family goals. *Teaching Exceptional Children, 35*(1), 56-61.

Park, J., Turnbull, A. P., & Park, H. S. (2001). Quality of partnerships in service provision for Korean American parents of children with disabilities: A qualitative inquiry. *Journal of The Association for Persons with Severe Handicaps, 26,* 158-170.

Parrish, T. B. (2001, April). Who's paying the rising cost of special education? *Journal of Special Education Leadership, 14*(1), 4-12.

Parson, L. R., & Heward, W. L. (1979). Training peers to tutor: Evaluation of a tutor training package for primary learning disabled students. *Journal of Applied Behavior Analysis, 12,* 309-312.

Parsons, L. D. (2006). Using video to teach social skills to secondary students with autism. *Teaching Exceptional Children, 39*(2), 32-38.

Parsons, M. B., McCarn, J. E., & Reid, D. H. (1993). Evaluating and increasing meal-related choices throughout a service setting for people with severe disabilities. *Journal of The Association for Persons with Severe Handicaps, 18,* 253-260.

Pascarella, E., & Terenzini, P. (1991). *How college affects students: Findings and insights from twenty years of research.* San Francisco, CA: Jossey-Bass.

Passow, H. A., & Rudnitski, R. A. (1995). *State policies regarding education of the gifted as reflected in legislation and regulation.* Storrs, CT: The University of Connecticut. National Research Center on the Gifted and Talented. Research Monograph.

Patel, P., & Laud, L. (2007). Integrating a story writing strategy into a resource curriculum. *Teaching Exceptional Children, 39*(4), 34-41.

Patterson, G. R. (1982). *Coercive family process.* Eugene, OR: Castilia.

Patterson, G. R., Cipaldi, D., & Bank, L. (1991). An early starter model for predicting delinquency. In D. J. Pepler & K. H. Rubin (Eds.), *The development and treatment of childhood aggression* (pp. 139-168). Hillsdale, NJ: Erlbaum.

Patterson, G. R., Reid, J. B., & Dishion, T. J. (1992). *Antisocial boys.* Vol. 4: *A social interactional approach.* Eugene, OR: Castalia.

Patterson, J. M., & Leonard, B. J. (1994). Caregiving and children. In E. Kahan, D. Biegel, & M. Wykle (Eds.), *Family caregiving across the lifespan* (pp. 133-158). Beverly Hills, CA: Sage.

Patton, B., Jolivette, K., & Ramsey, M. (2006). Students with emotional and behavioral disorders *can* manage their own behavior. *Teaching Exceptional Children, 39*(2), 14-21.

Patton, J. M. (1998). The disproportionate representation of African Americans in special education: Looking behind the curtain for understanding and solutions. *Journal of Special Education, 32,* 25-31.

Patton, J. R., Cronin, M. E., & Jairrels, V. (1997). Curricular implications of transition: Life-skills instruction as an integral part of transition education. *Remedial and Special Education, 18,* 294-306.

Patton, J. R., Jayanthi, M., & Polloway, E. A. (2001). Home-school collaboration about homework: What do we know and what should we do? *Reading and Writing Quarterly: Overcoming Learning Difficulties, 17,* 227-242.

Paul, P. V., & Jackson, D. (1993). *Towards a psychology of deafness* (2nd ed.). San Diego: Singular.

Paul, P. V., & Quigley, S. P. (1990). *Education and deafness.* New York: Longman.

Pavri, S. (2001). Developmental delay or cultural differences? Developing effective child find practices for young children from culturally and linguistically diverse families. *Young Exceptional Children, 4,* 2-9.

Pavri, S., & Monda-Amaya, L. (2000). Loneliness and students with learning disabilities in inclusive classrooms: Self-perceptions, coping strategies, and preferred interventions. *Learning Disabilities Research and Practice, 15*(2), 22-33.

Payne, K. T., & Taylor, O. L. (2006). Multicultural differences in human communication disorders. In N. B. Anderson & G. H. Shames (Eds.), *Human communication disorders: An introduction* (7th ed.) (pp. 93-124). Boston: Allyn & Bacon.

Payne, L., Marks, L. J., & Bogan, B. L. (2007). Using curriculum-based assessment to address the academic and behavioral deficits of students with emotional and behavioral disorders. *Beyond Behavior, 16,* 3-6.

Peacock Hill Working Group. (1991). Problems and promises in special education and related services for children and youth with emotional or behavioral disorders. *Behavioral Disorders, 16,* 299-313.

Pearson Education. (2000). *Scott Foresman reading: Links to reading first, grade 1, unit 1.* Glenview, IL: Author.

Pease, L. (2000). Creating a communication environment. In S. Aitken, M. Buultjenns, C. Clark, J. T. Eyre, & L. Pease (Eds.), *Teaching children who are deafblind: Contact communication and learning* (pp. 35-82). London: Fulton.

Pease-Alvarez, L., & Winsler, A. (1994). Cuando el maestro no habla Español: Children's bilingual language practices in the classroom. *Teachers of English to Speakers of Other Languages Quarterly, 28,* 507-535.

Peck, S. (2004). Communication made easier: Facilitating transitions for students with multiple disabilities. *Teaching Exceptional Children, 36*(5), 60-63.

Peckham, V. C. (1993). Children with cancer in the classroom. *Teaching Exceptional Children, 26*(1), 27-32.

Pedley, T. A., Scheuer, M. L., & Walczak, T. S. (1995). Epilepsy. In L. P. Rowland (Ed.), *Merritt's textbook of neurology* (9th ed.), (pp. 845-868). Baltimore: Williams & Wilkins.

Pelham, W. E., Wheeler, T., & Chronis, A. (1998). Empirically supported psychosocial treatments for attention deficit hyperactivity disorder. *Journal of Clinical Child Psychology, 27,* 190-205.

Pelham, W. W. (1999). The NIMH multimodal treatment study for attention-deficit hyperactivity disorder: Just say yes to drugs? *Canadian Journal of Psychiatry, 44,* 981-990.

Pelios, L., Morren, J., Tesch, D., & Axelrod, S. (1999). The impact of functional analysis methodology on treatment choice for self-injurious and aggressive behavior. *Journal of Applied Behavior Analysis, 32,* 185-195.

Pellegrino, L. (2007). Cerebral palsy. In M. L. Batshaw, L. Pellegrino, L, & Roizen, N. J.

(Eds.), *Children with disabilities* (6th ed.). Baltimore: Brookes.

Pence, K. L., & Justice, L. M. (2008). *Language development from theory to practice.* Upper Saddle River, NJ: Merrill/Prentice Hall.

Pennington, B. F. (1995). Genetics of learning disabilities. *Journal of Child Neurology, 10,* 69-77.

Pennington, B. F. (2002). The development of psychopathology: Nature and nurture. New York: Guilford.

Pennsylvania Association for Retarded Children v. Commonwealth of Pennsylvania, 343 F. Supp. 279 (1972).

Perl, J. (1995). Improving relationship skills for parent conferences. *Teaching Exceptional Children 28*(1), 29-31.

Perla, F., & Ducret, W. D. (1999). Guidelines for teaching orientation and mobility to children with multiple disabilities. *RE:view, 31,* 113-119.

Perla, F., & O'Donnell, B. (2004). Encouraging problem solving in orientation and mobility. *Journal of Visual Impairments and Blindness, 98,* 47-52.

Perlmutter, J., & Burrell, L. (1995, January). Learning through play as well as work. *Young Children,* pp. 14-21.

Perrin, E. C., Newacheck, P., Pless, B., Drotar, D., Gortmaker, S. L., Leventhal, J., Perrin, J. M., Stein, R. E. K., Walker, D. K., & Weitzman, M. (1993). Issues involved in the definition and classification of chronic health conditions. *Pediatrics, 91,* 787-793.

Perrin, J. M., Bloom, S. R., & Gortmaker, S. L. (2007). The increase of childhood chronic conditions in the United States. *Journal of the American Medical Association, 297,* 2755-2759.

Perske, R. (2004). Nirje's eight planks. *Mental Retardation, 42,* 147-150.

Perske, R. (2005). Strange shift in the case of Daryl Atkins. *Mental Retardation, 43,* 454-455.

Peterson, L. D., & Lacy-Rismiller, L. (2005). Building behaviors versus suppressing behaviors: Perspectives and prescriptions for schoolwide positive behavior change. In W. L. Heward, T. E. Heron, N. A. Neef, S. M. Peterson, D. M. Sainato, G. Cartledge, R. Gardner, III, L. D. Peterson, S. B. Hersh, & J. C. Dardig (Eds.), *Focus on behavior analysis in education: Achievements, challenges, and opportunities* (pp. 252-266). Upper Saddle River, NJ: Prentice Hall/Merrill.

Peterson, L. D., Young, K. R., West, R. P., & Hill Peterson, M. (1999). Effects of student self-management on generalization of student performance to regular classrooms. *Education and Treatment of Children, 19,* 170.

Peterson, S. M., & Neef, N. A. (2006). Functional behavior assessment. In J. O. Cooper, T. E. Heron, & W. L. Heward, *Applied behavior analysis.* Upper Saddle River, NJ: Merrill/Prentice Hall.

Peterson, S. M., Neef, N. A., Van Norman, R., & Ferreri, S. J. (2005). Choice making in educational settings. In W. L. Heward, T. E. Heron, N. A. Neef, S. M. Peterson, D. M. Sainato, G. Cartledge, R. Gardner, III, L. D. Peterson, S. B. Hersh, & J. C. Dardig (Eds.),

Focus on behavior analysis in education: Achievements, challenges, and opportunities (pp. 125-136). Upper Saddle River, NJ: Merrill/Prentice Hall.

Petry, K. & Maes, B. (2007). Description of the support needs of people with profound multiple disabilities using the 2002 AAMR System: An overview of the literature. *Education and Training in Developmental Disabilities, 42,* 130-143.

Petursdottir, A., McComas, J., McMaster, K., & Horner, K. (2007). The effects of scripted peer tutoring and programming common stimuli on social interactions of a student with autism spectrum disorder. *Journal of Applied Behavior Analysis, 40,* 353-357.

Piazza, C. C., Roane, H. S., Kenney, K. M., Boney, B., & Abt, K. A. (2002). Varying response effort in the treatment of PICA maintained by automatic reinforcement. *Journal of Applied Behavior Analysis, 35,* 233-246.

Piché, L. (2007). Augmentative and alternative communication. In R. E. Owens, D. E. Metz, & A. Haas (Eds.), *Introduction to communication disorders: A lifespan perspective* (3rd ed.) (465-489). Boston: Allyn & Bacon.

Pieper, E. (1983). *The teacher and the child with spina bifida* (2nd ed.). Rockville, MD: Spina Bifida Association of America.

Pierce, C. D., Reid, R., & Epstein, M. H. (2004). Teacher mediated interventions for children with EBD and their academic outcomes. *Remedial and Special Education, 25,* 175-188.

Piirto, J. (1991). Why are there so few? (Creative women: mathematicians, visual artists, musicians). *Roeper Review, 13*(3), 142-147.

Piirto, J. (1998). *Understanding those who create* (2nd ed.). Scottsdale, AZ: Gifted Psychology Press.

Piirto, J. (1999). Implications of postmodern curriculum theory for the education of the talented. *Journal for the Education of the Gifted, 22*(4), 386-406.

Piirto, J. (2002). *My teeming brain: Understanding creative writers.* Cresskill, NJ: Hampton.

Piirto, J. (2004a). The creative process in poets. In J. Kaufman & J. Baer (Eds.), *Creativity in domains: Faces of the muse* (pp. 1-15). Mahwah, NJ: Erlbaum.

Piirto, J. (2004b). *Understanding creativity.* Scottsdale, AZ: Great Potential.

Piirto, J. (2007). *Talented children and adults: Their development and education.* Waco, TX: Prufrock Press.

Pittman, P., & Huefner, D. S. (2001). Will the courts go bi-bi? IDEA '97, the courts, and deaf education. *Exceptional Children, 67,* 187-198.

Pivik, J., McComas, J., & LaFlamme, M. (2002). Barriers and facilitators to inclusive education. *Exceptional Children, 67,* 97-102.

Plaxen, J. R. (2005). *Adapt my world: Homemade adaptations for people with disabilities.* Santa Ana, CA: Seven Locks Press.

Plomin, R. (1995). Genetics and children's experiences in the family. *Journal of Child Psychology and Psychiatry, 36,* 33-68.

Plummer, D. (1995). Serving the needs of gifted children from a multicultural

perspective. In J. L. Genshaft, M. Bireley, & C. L. Hollinger (Eds.), *Serving gifted and talented students: A resource for school personnel* (pp. 285-300). Austin, TX: PRO-ED.

Pogrund, R. L., Fazzi, D. L., & Schreier, E. M. (1993). Development of a preschool "kiddy cane." *Journal of Visual Impairment and Blindness, 87,* 52-54.

Pollack, W. (1998). *Real boys: Rescuing our sons from the myths of boyhood.* New York: Holt.

Polloway, E. A., Smith, J. D., Patton, J. R., & Smith, T. E. C. (1996). Historic changes in mental retardation and developmental disabilities. *Education and Training in Mental Retardation and Developmental Disabilities, 31,* 3-12.

Polsgrove, L., & Ochoa, T. (2004). Trends and issues in behavioral interventions. In A. McCray Sorrells, H. J. Rieth, & P. T. Sindelar (Eds.), *Critical issues in special education: Access, diversity, and accountability* (pp. 16-37). Boston: Allyn & Bacon.

Ponchillia, P. E., MacKenzie, N., Long, R. G., Denton-Smith, P., Hicks, T. L., & Miley, P. (2007). Finding a target with an accessible global positioning system. *Journal of Visual Impairment and Blindness, 101,* 479-488.

Ponchillia, P. E., Rak, E. C., Freeland, A. L., & LaGrow, S. J. (2007). Accessible GPS: Reorientation and target location among users with visual impairments. *Journal of Visual Impairment and Blindness, 101,* 389-401.

Popkin, J., & Skinner, C. H. (2003). Enhancing academic performance in a classroom serving students with serious emotional disturbance: Interdependent group contingences with randomly selected components. *School Psychology Review, 32,* 271-284.

Portage Project, The. (2003). *The New Portage Guide: Birth to six.* Portage, WI: Author.

Portage Project, The. (2007). About us. [Retrieved September 23, 2007. http://www.portageproject.org/ABOUTUS.HTM]

Porter, J. H., & Hodson, B. W. (2001). Collaborating to obtain phonological acquisition data for local schools. *Language, Speech, and Hearing Services in Schools, 32,* 165-171.

Porter, S., Haynie, M., Bierle, T., Heintz Caldwell, T., & Palfrey, J. S. (Eds.). (1997). *Children and youth assisted by medical technology in educational settings guidelines for care* (2nd ed.). Baltimore: Brookes.

Porterfield, K. (1998). British researchers identify genetic area affecting speech. *ASHA Leader, 3*(4), 1, 4.

Post, M., & Storey, K. (2000). Review of using auditory prompting systems with persons who have moderate to severe disabilities. *Education and Training in Mental Retardation and Developmental Disabilities, 37,* 317-327.

Post, M., Storey, K., & Karabin, M. (2002). Cool headphones for effective prompts: Supporting students and adults in work and community environments. *Teaching Exceptional Children, 34,* 60-65.

Poulson, C. L., & Kymissis, E. (1988). Generalized imitation in infants. *Journal of Experimental Child Psychology, 46,* 324–336.

Poulton, S. (1996). *Guidelines to writing individualized healthcare plans.* http://www.nursing.uiowa.edu/www/nursing/courses/96-22/students/sp1996/96-222WEguideline/htm.

Powell, D. S., Batsche, C. J., Ferro, J., Fox, L., & Dunlap, G. (1997). A strength-based approach in support of multi-risk families: Principles and issues. *Topics in Early Childhood Special Education, 17*(1), 1–26.

Powell, L., Houghton, S., & Douglas, J. (1997). Comparison of etiology-specific cognitive functioning profiles for individuals with fragile X and individuals with Down syndrome. *Journal of Special Education, 34,* 362–376.

Powers, S. (2003). *Evaluation report for Project LISTO: Paradise Valley Unified School District, Arizona.* Tucson, AZ: Creative Research Associates.

Poyadue, F. S. (1993). Cognitive coping at Parents Helping Parents. In A. P. Turnbull, J. M. Paterson, S. K. Behr, D. L. Murphy, J. G. Marquis, & M. J. Blue-Banning (Eds.), *Cognitive coping, families, and disability* (pp. 95–110). Baltimore: Brookes.

Prabhala, A. (2007). Mental retardation is no more-new name is intellectual and developmental disabilities. *AAIDD News,* February 10. www.aamr.org/About—AAIDD/MR_name_change.htm [Retrieved April 4, 2007.]

Pratton, J., & Hales, L. W. (1986). The effects of active participation on student learning. *Journal of Educational Research, 79,* 210–215.

Prelock, P. A. (2000a). Prologue: Multiple perspectives for determining the roles of speech-language pathologists in inclusionary classrooms. *Language, Speech, and Hearing Services in Schools, 31,* 213–218.

Prelock, P. A. (2000b). Epilogue: An intervention focus for inclusionary practice. *Language, Speech, and Hearing Services in Schools, 31,* 296–298.

Prestia, K. (2003). Tourette's syndrome: Characteristics and interventions. *Intervention in School & Clinic, 39,* 67.

Pretti-Frontczak, K., & Bricker, D. (2004). *An activity-based approach to early intervention* (3rd ed.). Baltimore: Brookes.

Pretti-Frontczak, K., Barr, D. M., Macy, M., & Carter, C. (2003). Research and resources related to activity-based intervention, embedded learning opportunities, and routines-based instruction. *Topics in Early Childhood Special Education, 23*(1), 29–39.

Pretti-Frontczak, K. L., & Bricker, D. (2000). Enhancing the quality of Individualized Education Plan (IEP) goals and objectives. *Journal of Early Intervention, 23,* 92–105.

Price, L., Field, S., & Patton, J. R. (Guest Eds.). (2003). Adults with learning disabilities (Special Issue). *Remedial and Special Education, 24,* 322–382.

Prinz, P. M., Strong, M., Kuntze, M., Vincent, J., Friedman, J., Moyers, P. P., & Helman, E. (1996). A path to literacy through ASL and English for deaf children. In C. E. Johnson & J. H. V. Gilbert (Eds.), *Children's language* (Vol. 9), (pp. 235–251). Mahwah, NJ: Erlbaum.

Prizant, B. M., & Rubin, E. (1999). Contemporary issues in interventions for autism spectrum disorders: A commentary. *Journal of the Association for Persons with Severe Handicaps, 24,* 199–208.

Professional Development in Autism Center, Personnel Development in Autism. (2004). Available at http://depts.washington.edu/pdacent/sites/uw.html.

Pugh, G. S., & Erin, J. (1999). (Eds.). *Blind and visually impaired students: Education service guidelines.* Watertown, MA: Perkins School for the Blind.

Purcell, C. (1978). *Gifted and talented children's education act of 1978, Congressional Record.* Washington, DC: U.S. Government Printing Office.

Purcell, M. L., Horn, E., & Palmer, S. (2007). A qualitative study of the initiation and continuation of preschool inclusion programs. *Exceptional Children, 74,* 85–99.

Putnam, J. W. (1998). *Cooperative learning and strategies for inclusion: Celebrating diversity in the classroom* (2nd ed.). Baltimore: Brookes.

Qi, C. H., & Kaiser, A. P. (2003). Behavior problems of preschool children from low-income families: Review of the literature. *Teaching Early Childhood Special Education, 23,* 188–216.

Quinn, M. M., Rutherford, R. B., Leone, P. E., Osher, D. M., & Poirier, J. M. (2005). Youth with disabilities in juvenile corrections: A national survey. *Exceptional Children, 71,* 339–345.

Raimondo, B., & Henderson, A. (2001). Unlocking parent potential. *Principal Leadership, 2*(1), 26–32.

Ramey, C.T., Bryant, D. M., Wasik, B. H., Sparling, J. J., Fendt, K. H., & LaVange, L. M. (1992). The Infant Health and Development Program for low birthweight, premature infants: Program elements, family participation, and child intelligence. *Pediatrics, 89,* 454–465.

Ramey, C.T., & Ramey, S. L. (1992). Effective early intervention. *Mental Retardation, 30,* 337–345.

Ramig, P. R., & Shames, G. H. (2006). Stuttering and other disorders of fluency. In N. B. Anderson & G. H. Shames (Eds.), *Human communication disorders: An introduction* (7th ed.) (pp. 183–221). Boston: Allyn & Bacon.

Ramirez, A. Y. (2003). Dismay and disappointment: Parental involvement of Latino immigrant parents. *Urban Review, 35,* 93–110.

Rance-Roney, J. A. (2004). The affective dimension of second culture/second language acquisition in gifted adolescents. In D. Boothe & J. Stanley (Eds.), *In the eyes of the beholder: Critical issues for diversity in gifted education* (pp. 73–85). Waco, TX: Prufrock Press.

Randolph, J. J. (2007). Meta-analysis of the research on response cards: Effects on test achievement, quiz achievement, participation, and off-task behavior. *Journal of Positive Behavioral Interventions, 9,* 113–128.

Rao, S. M., & Gagie, B. (2006). Learning through seeing and doing: Visual supports for children with autism. *Teaching Exceptional Children, 38*(6), 26–33.

Rao, S. S. (2000). Perspectives of an African American mother on parent-professional relationships in special education. *Mental Retardation, 38,* 475–488.

Rapport, M. J. K. (1996). Legal guidelines for the delivery of health care services in schools. *Exceptional Children, 62,* 537–549.

Raschke, D. B., Dedrick, C. V. L., Heston, M. L., & Farris, M. (1996). Everyone can play! Adapting the Candy Land board game. *Teaching Exceptional Children, 28*(4), 28–33.

Raskind, M. H., Margalit, M., & Higgins, E. L. (2006). "My LD": Children's voices on the Internet. *Learning Disability Quarterly, 29,* 253–268.

Raskind, W. H. (2001). Current understanding of the genetic basis of reading and spelling disability. *Learning Disability Quarterly, 24,* 141–157.

Ratner, N. B. (2004). Caregiver-child interactions and their impact on children's fluency: Implications for treatment. *Language, Speech, and Hearing Services in Schools, 35,* 46–56.

Raven, J. C., Court, J. H., & Raven, J. (1983). *Manual for Raven's Progressive Matrices and vocabulary scales: Advanced progressive matrices.* London: Lewis.

Raver, S. (1984). Modification of head droop during conversation in a 3-year-old visually impaired child: A case study. *Journal of Visual Impairment and Blindness, 78,* 307–310.

Rawlings, B. W., Karchmer, M. A., Allen, T. E., & DeCaro, J. J. (1999). *College and career programs for deaf students* (10th ed.). Washington, DC, and Rochester, NY: Gallaudet University and National Technical Institute for the Deaf.

Rea, P. J., McLaughlin, V. L., & Walther-Thomas, C. (2002). Outcomes for students with learning disabilities in inclusive and pullout programs. *Exceptional Children, 68,* 203–222.

Reagon, K. A., Higbee, T. S., & Endicott, K. (2006). Teaching pretend play skills to a student with autism using video modeling with a sibling as model and play partner. *Education & Treatment of Children, 29,* 517–528.

Reed, V. A. (2005). *An introduction to children with language disorders* (3rd ed.). Needham Heights, MA: Allyn & Bacon.

Reeve, S. A., Reeve, K. F., Townsend, D. B., & Poulson, C. L. (2007). Establishing a generalized repertoire of helping behavior in children with autism. *Journal of Applied Behavior Analysis, 40,* 123–136.

Regan, K. S., Mastropieri, M. A., & Scruggs, T. E. (2005). Promoting expressive writing among students with emotional and behavioral disturbance via dialogue journals. *Behavioral Disorders, 31,* 33-50.

Rehfeldt, R. A., Kinney, E. M., Root, S., & Stromer, R. (2004). Creating activity schedules using Microsoft PowerPoint. *Journal of Applied Behavior Analysis, 37,* 115-128.

Reid, C., Udall, A., Romanoff, B., & Algozzine, B. (1999). Comparison of traditional and problem-solving assessment criteria. *Gifted Child Quarterly, 43,* 244-251.

Reid, R., Gonzalez, J. E., Nordness, P. D., Trout, A., & Epstein, M. H. (2004). A meta-analysis of the academic status of students with emotional/behavioral disturbance. *Journal of Special Education, 38,* 130-143.

Reid, R., & Harris, K. R. (1993). Self-monitoring attention versus self-monitoring of performance: Effects on attention and academic performance. *Exceptional Children, 60,* 29-40.

Reid, R., & Maag, J. W. (1998). Functional assessment: A method for developing classroom-based accommodations and interventions. *Reading & Writing Quarterly, 14,* 7-15.

Reid, R., Maag, J. W., & Vasa, S. F. (1994). Attention deficit hyperactivity disorder as a disability category: A critique. *Exceptional Children, 60,* 198-214.

Reid, R., Trout, A. L., & Schartz, M. (2005). Self-regulation interventions for children with attention deficit/hyperactivity disorder. *Exceptional Children, 71,* 361-377.

Reilly, J. S., & Bellugi, U. (1996). Competition on the face: Affect and language in ASL mothers. *Journal of Child Language, 23,* 219-239.

Reis, S. (1995). What gifted education can offer the reform movement: Talent development. In J. L. Genshaft, M. Bireley, & C. L. Hollinger (Eds.), *Serving gifted and talented students: A resource for school personnel* (pp. 371-387). Austin, TX: PRO-ED.

Reis, S., & Cellerino, M. (1983). Guiding gifted students through independent study. *Teaching Exceptional Children, 15,* 136-139.

Reis, S., Neu, T. W., & McGuire, J. M. (1995). *Talents in two places: Case studies of high ability students with learning disabilities who have achieved* (Research monograph 95114). Storrs: University of Connecticut, National Research Center on the Gifted and Talented.

Reis, S. M., & Renzulli, J. S. (2005). Curriculum compacting: An easy start to differentiating for high-potential students. Waco, TX: Prufrock Press.

Reis, S. M., Westberg, K. L., Kulikowich, J. M., & Purcell, J. H. (1998). Curriculum compacting and achievement test scores: What does the research say? *Gifted Child Quarterly, 42,* 123-129.

Reiss, S., & Reiss, M. M. (2004). Curiosity and mental retardation: Beyond IQ. *Mental Retardation, 42,* 77-81.

Renzulli, J. (1998). *Relationship between gifted programs and total school improvement using the schoolwide enrichment model.* Storrs: University of Connecticut, National Resource Center on the Gifted and Talented.

Renzulli, J. S. (2003). Conception of giftedness and its relationship to the development of social capital. In N. Colangelo & G. A. Davis (Eds.), *Handbook of gifted education* (3rd ed.), (pp. 75-87). Needham Heights, MA: Allyn & Bacon.

Renzulli, J. S., & Reis, S. M. (2003). The schoolwide enrichment model: Developing creative and productive giftedness. In N. Colangelo & G. A. Davis (Eds.), *Handbook of gifted education* (3rd ed.), (pp. 184-203). Needham Heights, MA: Allyn & Bacon.

Renzulli, J., & Reis, S. (2004). Curriculum compacting. In D. Boothe & J. Stanley (Eds.), *In the eyes of the beholder: Critical issues for diversity in gifted education* (pp. 87-100). Waco, TX: Prufrock.

Report of the autism task force. (1999). Augusta: Maine Administrators of Services for Children with Disabilities. Available at http://www.madsec.org.

Reschly, D. J. (1996). Identification and assessment of students with disabilities. *Future of Children, 6*(1), 40-53.

Resetar, J. L., Noell, G. H., & Pellegrin, A. L. (2006). Teaching parents to use research supported systematic strategies to tutor their children in reading. *School Psychology Quarterly, 21,* 241-261.

Revell, W. G., Wehman, P., Kregel, J., West, M., & Rayfield, R. (1994). Supported employment for persons with severe disabilities: Positive trends in wages, models, and funding. *Education and Training in Mental Retardation, 29,* 256-264.

Rex, E. J., Koenig, A. J., Wormsley, D. P., & Baker, R. L. (1994). *Foundations of braille literacy.* New York: American Foundation for the Blind.

Reyes-Blanes, M., Rodriguez, P., Vázquez, E., & Skinner, M. (1999). Needs and supports reported by Latino families of young children with developmental disabilities. *American Journal on Mental Retardation, 104,* 437-451.

Reynolds, C. R., & Kamphaus, R. W. (2002). *The clinician's guide to The Behavior Assessment System for Children.* New York: Guilford.

Reynolds, M. C., & Heistad, D. (1997). 20/20 analysis: Estimating school effectiveness in serving students at the margins. *Exceptional Children, 63,* 439-449.

Reynolds, M. C., Zetlin, A. G., & Heistad, D. (1996). *A manual for 20/20 analysis.* Philadelphia: Temple University, Center for Research in Human Development and Education. (ERIC Document Reproduction Service No. ED 358 183).

Rhee, S. H., & Waldman, I. D. (2002). Genetic and environmental influences on antisocial behavior: A meta-analysis of twin and adoption studies. *Psychological Bulletin, 128,* 490-529.

Rhode, G., Jenson, W. R., & Morgan, D. P. (2003). *Tough kid new teacher kit.* Longmont, CO: Sopris West.

Rhode, G., Jenson, W. R., & Reavis, H. K. (1998). *The tough kid book: Practical classroom management strategies.* Longmont, CO: Sopris West.

Rhode, G., Morgan, D. P., & Young, K. R. (1983). Generalization and maintenance of

treatment gains of behaviorally handicapped students from resource rooms to regular classrooms using self-evaluation procedures. *Journal of Applied Behavior Analysis, 16,* 171-188.

Rhodes, R. L., Ochoa, S. H., & Ortiz, S. O. (2005). *Assessing culturally and linguistically diverse students: A practical guide.* Arlington, VA: Council for Exceptional Children.

Ricci-Balich, J., & Behm, J. A. (1996). Pediatric rehabilitation nursing. In S. P. Hoeman (Ed.), *Rehabilitation nursing: Process and application* (pp. 660-682). St. Louis: Mosby.

Richards, T. L. (2001). Functional magnetic resonance imaging and spectroscopic imaging of the brain: Application of fMRI and fMRS to reading disabilities and education. *Learning Disability Quarterly, 24,* 189-203.

Richardson, B. G., & Shupe, M. J. (2003). The importance of teacher self-awareness in working with students with emotional and behavior disorders. *Teaching Exceptional Children, 36*(2), 8-13.

Ricketts, T. A. (2007). *Digital hearing aids: Current "state-of-the-art."* [Retrieved August 24, 2007 http://www.asha.org/public/hearing/treatment/digital_aid.htm]

Rigby. (2004). *Rigby literacy teacher's guide, grade 1.* Barrington, IL: Author.

Riggs, C. G. (2001). Working effectively with paraeducators in inclusive settings. *Intervention in School and Clinic, 35,* 54-70.

Rimland, B. (1993). Beware the advozealots: Mindless good intentions injure the handicapped. *Autism Research Review International, 7*(4), 1.

Rimland, B. (1994). The modern history of autism: A personal perspective. In J. L. Matson (Ed.), *Autism in children and adults: Etiology, assessment, and intervention.* Pacific Grove, CA: Brooks/Cole.

Rimm, S. (2000). *See Jane win.* New York: Crown.

Rimm, S. (2002). *How Jane won.* New York: Crown.

Rimm-Kaufman, S. E., & Kagan, J. (2005). Infant predictors of kindergarten behavior: The contribution of inhibited and uninhibited temperament types. *Behavioral Disorders, 30,* 331-347.

Risley, T. (2005). Montrose M. Wolf (1935-2004). *Journal of Applied Behavior Analysis, 38,* 279-287.

Ritvo, E. R. (2006). *Understanding the nature of autism and Asperger's disorder.* London: Jessica Kingsley.

Roberts, C. D., Stough, L. M., & Parrish, L. H. (2002). The role of genetic counseling in the elective termination of pregnancies involving fetuses with disabilities. *Journal of Special Education, 36,* 48-55.

Roberts, J. (2000). Pediatric HIV/AIDS: A review of neurological and psychosocial implications of infection. *Canadian Journal of School Psychology, 15*(2), 19-34.

Roberts, J. E., Schaaf, J. M., Skinner, M., Wheeler, A., Hooper, S., Hatton, D. D., & Bailey, D. B. (2005). Academic skills of boys with

Fragile X syndrome: Profiles and predictors. *American Journal on Mental Retardation, 110,* 107-120.

Roberts, J. E., Wallace, I. F., & Henderson, F. W. (1997). *Otitis media in young children: Medical, developmental, and education considerations.* Baltimore: Brookes.

Roberts, J. L., & Inman, T. F. (2007). *Strategies for differentiating instruction: Best practices for the classroom.* Waco, TX: Prufrock Press.

Roberts, R. E., Attkisson, C. C., & Rosenblatt, A. (1998). Prevalence of psychopathology among children and adolescents. *American Journal of Psychiatry, 155,* 715-725.

Robins, D., Fein, D., Barton, M., & Green, J. (2001). The modified checklist for autism in toddlers: An initial study investigating the early detection of autism and pervasive developmental disorders. *Journal of Autism and Developmental Disorders, 31,* 131-144.

Robinson, A., Shore, B. M., & Enersen, D. L. (2007). *Best practices in gifted education: An evidence-based guide.* Waco, TX: Prufrock Press.

Robinson, K. E., & Sheridan, S. M. (2000). Using the mystery motivator to improve child bedtime compliance. *Child & Family Behavior Therapy, 22,* 29-49.

Robinson Spohn, J. R., Timko, T. C., & Sainato, D. M. (1999). Increasing the social interactions of preschool children with disabilities during mealtimes: The effects of an interactive placemat game. *Education and Treatment of Children, 22,* 1-18.

Rock, M. L. (2000). Parents as equal partners: Balancing the scales in IEP development. *Teaching Exceptional Children, 32*(6), 30-37.

Rockwell, S., & Guetzloe, E. (1996). Group development for students with emotional/behavioral disorders. *Teaching Exceptional Children, 29*(1), 38-43.

Roeser, R., & Yellin, W. (1987). Pure-tone tests with preschool children. In F. Martin (Ed.), *Hearing disorders in children: Pediatric audiology* (pp. 217-264). Austin, TX: PRO-ED.

Rogan, P. (1996). Natural supports in the workplace: No need for a trial. *Journal of the Association for Persons with Severe Handicaps, 21*(4), 178-180.

Rogan, P., Grossi, T. A., Mank, D., Haynes, D. Thomas, E., & Majd, C. (2002). What happens when people leave the workshop? Outcomes of workshop participants now in SE. *Supported Employment Infolines, 13*(4), 1, 3.

Rogan, P., Hagner, D., & Murphy, S. (1993). Natural supports: Reconceptualizing job coach roles. *Journal of The Association for Persons with Severe Handicaps, 18,* 275-281.

Rogers, K. (2002). *Re-forming gifted education.* Scottsdale, AZ: Great Potential.

Rogers, M. F., & Myles, B. S. (2001). Using social stories and comic strip conversations to interpret social situations for an adolescent with Asperger's Syndrome. *Intervention in School and Clinic, 36,* 310-313.

Roid, G. H. (2003). *Stanford-Binet Intelligence Scales* (5th ed.). Itasca, IL: Riverside Publishing.

Rolider, A., & Van Houten, R. (1993). The interpersonal treatment model. In R. Van Houten & S. Axelrod (Eds.), *Behavior analysis and treatment.* (pp. 127-168). NY: Plenum.

Romanczyk, R. G., Weinter, T., Lockshin, S., & Ekdahl, M. (1999). Research in autism: Myths, controversies, and perspectives. In D. B. Zager (Ed.), *Autism: Identification, education, and treatment* (2nd ed.), (pp. 23-61). Mahwah, NJ: Erlbaum.

Romaniuk, C., Miltenberger, R., Conyers, C., Jenner, N., Jurgens, M., & Ringenberg, C. (2002). The influence of activity choice on problem behavior maintained by escape versus attention. *Journal of Applied Behavior Analysis, 35,* 349-362.

Romer, L. T., White, J., & Haring, N. G. (1996). The effect of peer mediated social competency training on the type and frequency of social contacts with students with deaf-blindness. *Education and Training in Mental Retardation and Developmental Disabilities, 31,* 324-338.

Rorschach, H. (1942). *Rorschach psychodiagnostic plates.* New York: Psychological Corporation.

Rosales-Ruiz, J., & Baer, D. M. (1997). Behavioral cusps: A developmental and pragmatic concept for behavior analysis. *Journal of Applied Behavior Analysis, 30,* 533-544.

Rose, K. C., White, J. A., Conroy, J., & Smith, D. M. (1993). Following the course of change: A study of adaptive and maladaptive behaviors in young adults living in the community. *Education and Training in Mental Retardation, 28,* 149-154.

Rose, T. L., & Calhoun, M. L. (1990). The Charlotte Circle Project: A program for infants and toddlers with severe/profound disabilities. *Journal of Early Intervention, 14,* 175-185.

Roseberry-McKibbin, C. (2007). *Language disorders in children: A multicultural and case perspective.* Boston: Allyn & Bacon.

Roseberry-McKibbin, C. (2008). *Multicultural students with special language needs: Practical strategies for assessment and intervention* (3rd ed.). Oceanside, CA: Academic Communication Associates, Inc.

Rosenblum, L. P. (1998). Best friendships of adolescents with visual impairments: A descriptive study. *Journal of Visual Impairments and Blindness, 92,* 593-608.

Rosenblum, L. P. (2000). Perceptions of the impact of visual impairments on the lives of adolescents. *Journal of Visual Impairments and Blindness, 94,* 434-445.

Rosenshine, B., & Berliner, D. C. (1978). Academic engaged time. *British Journal of Teacher Education, 4,* 3-16.

Rosenshine, B. V. (1986). Synthesis of research on explicit teaching. *Educational Leadership, 43*(7), 60-69.

Rosenshine, B. V. (1987). Explicit teaching and teacher training. *Journal of Teacher Education, 38*(3), 34-36.

Rosenthal, B., & Williams, D. (2000). Devices primarily for people with low vision. In B. Silverstone, M. Lang, B. Rosenthal, & E. Faye (Eds.), *The lighthouse handbook on vision impairment and vision rehabilitation* (pp. 951-982). New York: Oxford University Press.

Ross, M., & Levitt, H. (2000). Developments in research and technology: Otoacoustic emissions. *Volta Voices, 7,* 30-31.

Rourke, B. (2005). Neuropsychology of learning disabilities: Past and future: *Learning Disability Quarterly, 28,* 111-114.

Rous, B. S., & Hallam, R. A. (2006). *Tools for transition in early childhood: A step-by-step guide for agencies, teachers, and families.* Baltimore: Brookes.

Rousch, W. (1995). Arguing over why Johnny can't read. *Science, 267,* 1896-1898.

Rowland, C., & Schweigert, P. (2000). *Tangible symbol systems: Making the right to communicate a reality for individuals with severe disabilities.* Portland, OR: Design to Learn Products.

Rueda, R., Monzo, L., Shapiro, J., Gomez, J., & Blacher, J. (2005). Cultural models of transition: Latina mothers of young adults with developmental disabilities. *Exceptional Children, 71,* 401-414.

Rues, J. P., Ault, M. M., Graff, J. C., & Holvoet, J. F. (2006). Special health care procedures. In M. E. Snell & F. Brown (Eds.), *Instruction of students with severe disabilities* (6th ed.). Upper Saddle River, NJ: Merrill/Prentice Hall.

Runnheim, V., Frankenberger, W. R., & Hazelkorn, M. N. (1996). Medicating students with emotional and behavioral disorders and ADHD: A state survey. *Behavioral Disorders, 21,* 306-314.

Rusch, F. R., (1990). *Supported employment: Models, methods, and issues.* Sycamore, IL: Sycamore.

Rusch, F. R. (Ed.). (2008). *Beyond high school: Preparing adolescents for tomorrow's challenges* (2nd ed.). Upper Saddle River, NJ: Merrill/Prentice Hall.

Rusch, F. R., Hughes, C., McNair, J., & Wilson, P. G. (1990). *Co-worker involvement scoring manual and instrument.* Champaign: University of Illinois, Board of Trustees.

Rusch, F. R., Johnson, J. R., & Hughes, C. (1990). Analysis of co-worker involvement in relations to level of disability versus placement approach among supported employees. *Journal of The Association for Persons with Severe Handicaps, 15,* 32-39.

Rusch, F. R., & Minch, K. E. (1988). Identification of co-worker involvement in supported employment: A review and analysis. *Research in Developmental Disabilities, 9,* 247-254.

Rush, A. J., & Francis, A. (Eds.). (2000). Expert consensus guideline series: Treatment of psychiatric and behavioral problems in mental retardation. *American Journal of Mental Retardation, 105,* 159-228.

Russell-Minda, E., Jutai, J. W., Graham Strong, J., Campbell, K. A., Gold, D., Pretty, L., & Wilmot, L. (2007). The legibility of typefaces for readers with low vision: A research review. *Journal of Visual Impairment and Blindness, 101,* 402-415.

Rutherford, R. B., Quinn, M. M., & Sathur, R. (Eds.). (2004). *Handbook of research in emotional and behavioral disorders.* NY: Guilford Press.

Rutter, M. (1976). *Helping troubled children.* New York: Plenum.

Rutter, M. (2005). Autism research: Lessons from the past and prospects for the future. *Journal of Autism and Developmental Disorders, 35,* 241-257.

Rutter, M., Bailey, A., & Lord, C. (2003). *Social communication questionnaire.* Los Angeles: Western Psychological Services.

Ryan, B. P. (2004). Contingency management and stuttering in children. *Behavior Analyst Today, 5,* 144-150.

Ryan, J. B., Saunders, S., Katsiyannis, A., & Yell, M. L. (2007). Using time-out effectively in the classroom. *Teaching Exceptional Children, 39*(4), 60-67.

Ryan, R. M., & Deci, E. L. (1996). When paradigms clash: Comments on Cameron and Pierce's claim that rewards do not undermine intrinsic motivation. *Review of Educational Research, 66,* 33-38.

Ryan, S., & Ferguson, D. L. (2006). On, yet under, the radar: Students with fetal alcohol syndrome disorder. *Exceptional Children, 72,* 363-379.

Ryles, R. (1996). The impact of braille reading skills on employment, income, education, and reading habits. *Journal of Visual Impairment and Blindness, 90,* 219-226.

Ryndak, D. L., & Alper, S. (1996). *Curriculum content for students with moderate and severe disabilities in inclusive settings.* Boston: Allyn & Bacon.

Ryndak, D. L., & Fisher, D. (Eds.). (2007). *The foundations of inclusive education: A compendium of articles on effective strategies to achieve inclusive education* (2nd ed.). Baltimore: The Association for Persons with Severe Handicaps.

Ryser, G. (2004). Qualitative and quantitative approaches to assessment. In S. Johnsen (Ed.), *Identifying gifted students: A practical guide* (pp. 23-40). Waco, TX: Prufrock.

Sabornie, E. J., & Kauffman, J. M. (1986). Social acceptance of learning disabled adolescents. *Learning Disabilities Quarterly, 9,* 55-60.

Sack-Min, J. (2007). The issues of IDEA. *American School Board Journal, 194*(3).

Sacks, S. Z., & Silberman, R. K. (Eds.). (1998). *Educating students who have visual impairments with other disabilities.* Baltimore: Brookes.

Sacks, S. Z., & Wolffe, K. E. (2006). *Teaching social skills to students with visual impairments: From theory to practice.* New York: AFB Press.

Sacks, S. Z., Wolffe, K. E., & Tierney, D. (1998). Lifestyles of students with visual impairments—adolescents. Preliminary studies of social networks. *Exceptional Children, 64,* 463-478.

Sadler, F. H. (2003). The itinerant special education teacher in the early childhood classroom. *Teaching Exceptional Children, 35*(3), 8-15.

Safer, D. J., Zito, J. M., & Fine, E. M. (1996). Increased methylphenidate usage for attention-deficit disorder in the 1990s. *Pediatrics, 98,* 1084-1088.

Safford, P. L., & Safford, E. J. (1996). *A history of childhood disability.* New York: Teachers College Press.

Safran, J. S. (2002). A practitioner's guide to resources on Asperger syndrome. *Intervention in School and Clinic, 37,* 283-291.

Safran, S. P. (2001). Asperger syndrome: The emerging challenge to special education. *Exceptional Children, 67,* 151-160.

Safran, S. P., & Oswald, K. (2003). Positive behavior supports: Can schools reshape disciplinary practices? *Exceptional Children, 69,* 361-373.

Sagan, C. (1995). *The demon-haunted world: Science as a candle in the dark.* New York: Random House.

Sainato, D. M., Jung, S., Salmon, M. D., & Axe. J. B. (2008). Classroom influences on young children's emerging social competence. In W. H. Brown, S. L. Odom, & S. R. McConnell (Eds.), *Social competence of young children: Risk, disability, and intervention* (pp. 99-116). Baltimore: Paul H. Brookes.

Sainato, D. M., & Strain, P. S. (1993). Increasing integration success for preschoolers with disabilities. *Teaching Exceptional Children, 25*(2), 36.

Sainato, D. M., Strain, P. S., & Lyon, S. L. (1987). Increasing academic responding of handicapped preschool children during group instruction. *Journal of the Division of Early Childhood Special Education, 12,* 23-30.

Salend, S. J. (2006). Explaining your inclusion program to families. *Teaching Exceptional Children, 38*(4), 6-11.

Salend, S. J. (2008). *Creating inclusive classrooms: Effective and reflective practices* (6th ed.). Upper Saddle River, NJ: Prentice Hall/Merrill.

Salend, S. J., Elhoweris, H., & van Garderen, D. (2003). Educational interventions for students with ADD. *Intervention in School and Clinic, 38,* 280-288.

Salend, S. J., Ellis, L. L., & Reynolds, C. J. (1989). Using self-instruction to teach vocational skills to individuals who are severely retarded. *Education and Training of the Mentally Retarded, 24,* 248-254.

Salend, S. J., & Garrick Duhaney, L. M. (2005). Understanding and addressing the disproportionate representation of students of color in special education. *Intervention in School and Clinic, 40,* 213-221.

Salend, S. J., Jantzen, N. R., & Giek, K. (1992). Using a peer confrontation system in a group setting. *Behavioral Disorders, 17,* 211-218.

Salend, S. J., & Salinas, A. (2003). Language differences or learning difficulties: The work of the multidisciplinary team. *Teaching Exceptional Children, 35*(4), 36-43.

Salmon, M. D., & Sainato, D. M. (2005). Beyond Pinocchio: Puppets as teaching tools in inclusive early childhood classrooms. *Young Exceptional Children, 8*(3), 12-19.

Salvia, J., & Ysseldyke, J. E. (2001). *Assessment in special and remedial education* (8th ed.). Boston: Houghton Mifflin.

Salvia, J., Ysseldyke, J. E., & Bolt, S. (2007). *Assessment in special and inclusive education* (10th ed.). Boston: Houghton Mifflin.

Sameroff, A. (2001). *Risk and resilience from infancy to adolescence: Is it better to change the child or the context?* Keynote address at Research Project Directors' Conference, U.S. Office of Special Education Programs, Washington, DC. (July 11).

Sandall, S., Hemmeter, M. L., Smith, B. J., & McLean, M. E. (Eds.). (2005). *DEC recommended practices: A comprehensive guide for practical application in early intervention/early childhood special education.* Arlington, VA: Council for Exceptional Children, Division for Early Childhood.

Sandall, S., Joseph, G., Chou, H. Y., Schwartz, I. S., Horn, E., Lieber, J., Odom, S. L., & Wolery, R. (2000). *Talking to practitioners: Focus group report on curriculum modifications in inclusive preschool classrooms.* Unpublished manuscript.

Sandall, S., McLean, M. E., & Smith, B. J. (Eds.). (2000). *DEC recommended practices in early intervention/early childhood special education.* Reston, VA: Council for Exceptional Children, Division for Early Childhood.

Sandall, S., & Ostrosky, M. (2000). *Natural environments and inclusion: Young exceptional children.* (Monograph series no. 2). Reston, VA: Council for Exceptional Children, Division for Early Childhood.

Sandall, S., & Schwartz, I. (2002). *Building blocks for teaching preschoolers with special needs.* Baltimore: Brookes.

Sandall, S., Schwartz, I., & Joseph, G. (2000). A building blocks model for effective instruction in inclusive early childhood settings. *Young Exceptional Children, 4*(3), 3-9.

Sandler, A. D, Sutton, K. A., DeWeese, J., Giradi, M. A., Sheppard, V., & Bodfish, J. W. (1999). Lack of benefit of a single-dose of synthetic human secretin in the treatment of autism and pervasive developmental disorders. *New England Journal of Medicine, 341*(24), 1801-1806.

Sandler, A. G., Arnold, L. B., Gable, R. A., & Strain, P. S. (1987). Effects of peer pressure on disruptive behavior of behaviorally disordered students. *Behavioral Disorders, 16,* 9-22.

Sandler, A. G., & Mistretta, L. A. (1998). Positive adaptation in parents of adults with disabilities. *Education and Training in Mental Retardation and Developmental Disabilities, 33,* 123-130.

Sands, D. J., & Kozleski, E. B. (1994). Quality of life differences between adults with and without disabilities. *Education and Training in Mental Retardation, 29,* 90-101.

Santelli, B., Poyadue, F. S., & Young, J. L. (2001). *The parent to parent handbook:*

Connecting families of children with special needs. Baltimore: Brookes.

Santelli, B., Turnbull, A., Marquis, J., & Lernet, E. (1997). Parent to parent programs: A resource for parents and professionals. *Journal of Early Intervention, 21*(1), 73-83.

Santelli, B., Poyadue, F. S., & Young, J. L. (2001). The parent to parent handbook: Connecting families of children with special needs. Baltimore: Brookes.

Santoro, L. E., Coyne, M. D., & Simmons, D. C. (2006). The reading-spelling connection: Developing and evaluating a beginning spelling intervention for children at risk of reading disability. *Learning Disabilities Research & Practice, 21*, 122-133.

Santosti, F. J., Powell-Smith, K. A., & Kincaid, D. (2004). A research synthesis of social story interventions for children with autism spectrum disorders. *Focus on Autism and Other Developmental Disabilities, 19*, 194-204.

Sapienza, C., & Hicks, D. M. (2006). Voice disorders. In N. B. Anderson & G. H. Shames (Eds.), *Human communication disorders: An introduction* (7th ed.), (pp. 222-253). Boston: Allyn & Bacon.

Sapon-Shevin, M. (2007). *Widening the circle: The power of inclusive classrooms.* Boston: Beacon Press.

Sarouphim, K. M. (2001). DISCOVER: Concurrent validity, gender differences, and identification of minority students. *Gifted Child Quarterly, 45*(2), 130-139.

Sasso, G. (2001). The retreat from inquiry and knowledge in special education. *Journal of Special Education, 34*, 178-193.

Savage, R. C., & Wolcott, G. F. (Eds.). (1994). *Educational dimensions of acquired brain injury.* Austin, TX: PRO-ED.

Sax, L., & Kautz, K. J. (2003). Who suggests the diagnosis of attention-deficit/hyperactivity disorder? *Annals of Family Medicine, 1*, 171-174.

Scattone, D., Wilczynski, S. M., Edwards, R. P., & Rabian, B. (2002). Decreasing disruptive behaviors of children with autism using social stories. *Journal of Autism and Developmental Disorders, 32*, 535-543.

Schaeffler, C. (1988, Spring). Making toys accessible for children with cerebral palsy. *Teaching Exceptional Children, 20*, 26-28.

Schafer, P. O., & DiLorio, C. (2006). Self-management in epilepsy care: Putting teen and families in the center. *Exceptional Parent, 36*(6), 46-48.

Schalock, R., Coutler, D., Polloway, E., Reiss, S., Snell, M., Spitalnik, D., & Stark, J. (1994). The changing conception of mental retardation: Implications for the field. *Mental Retardation, 32*, 181-193.

Schalock, R. L. (Ed.). (1999). *Adaptive behavior and its measurement: Implications for the field of mental retardation.* Washington, DC: American Association on Mental Retardation.

Schalock, R. L., Bonham, G. S., & Marchand, C. B. (2000). Consumer based quality of life assessment: A path model of perceived satisfaction. *Evaluator and Program Planning, 23*, 75-85.

Schalock, R. L., Brown, I., Brown, R., Cummins, R. A., Felce, D., Matikka, L., Keith, K. D., & Parmenter, T. (2002). Conceptualization, measurement, and application of quality of life for persons with intellectual disabilities: Report of an international panel of experts. *Mental Retardation, 40*, 457-470.

Schalock, R. L., Buntinx, W., Borthwick-Duffy, S., Luckasson, R., Snell, M. E., Tassé, M. J., & Wehmeyer, M. (2007). *User's guide: Mental retardation definition, classification, and systems of support—10th edition.* Washington, DC: American Association on Intellectual and Developmental Disabilities.

Schalock, R. L., Gardner, J. F., & Bradley, V. J. (2007). *Quality of life: Applications for people with intellectual and developmental disabilities.* Washington, DC: American Association on Intellectual and Developmental Disabilities.

Schalock, R. L., & Keith, K. D. (1993). *Quality of Life Questionnaire.* Worthington, OH: IDS Publishing Company.

Schalock, R. L., Keith, K. D., Hoffman, K., & Karan, O. C. (1989). Quality of life: Its measurement and use. *Mental Retardation, 27*, 25-31.

Schalock, R. L., Luckasson, R., & Shogren, K. A. (2007). The renaming of *mental retardation:* Understanding the change to the term *intellectual disability. Intellectual and Developmental Disabilities, 45*, 116-124.

Scheetz, N. A. (2004). *Psychosocial aspects of deafness.* Boston: Allyn & Bacon.

Schessel, D. A. (1999). Ménière's disease. *Volta Review, 99*(5), 177-183.

Scheuermann, B., & Webber, J. (2002). *Autism: Teaching does make a difference.* Belmont, CA: Wadsworth.

Scheurmann, B. K., & Hall, J. A. (2008). *Positive behavioral supports for the classroom.* Upper Saddle River, NJ: Merrill/Prentice Hall.

Schick, B., & Williams, K. (1994). The evaluation of educational interpreters. In B. Schick & M. P. Moeller (Eds.), *Sign language in the schools: Current issues and controversies.* Omaha, NE: Boys Town Press.

Schick, B., Williams, K., & Bolster, L. (1999). Skill levels of educational interpreters working in public schools. *Journal of Deaf Studies and Deaf Education, 4*, 144-155.

Schick, B., Williams, K., & Kupermintz, H. (2006). Look who's being left behind: Educational interpreters and access to education for deaf and hard-of-hearing students. *The Journal of Deaf Studies and Deaf Education, 11*, 3-20.

Schirmer, B. R. (1997). Boosting reading success: Language, literacy, and content area instruction for deaf and hard-of-hearing students. *Teaching Exceptional Children, 30*(1), 52-55.

Schirmer, B. R. (2000). *Language and literacy development in children who are deaf* (2nd ed.). Boston: Allyn & Bacon.

Schirmer, B. R. (2001). *Psychological, social, and educational dimensions of deafness.* Boston: Allyn & Bacon.

Schirmer, B. R. (2004). Hearing loss. In R. Turnbull, A. Turnbull, M. Shank, & S. J. Smith, *Exceptional lives: Special education in today's schools* (4th ed.), (pp. 424-454). Upper Saddle River, NJ: Merrill/Prentice Hall.

Schirmer, B. R., & McGough, S. M. (2005). Teaching reading to children who are deaf: Do the conclusions of the National Reading Panel apply? *Review of Educational Research, 75*, 83-117.

Schleien, S. J., Kiernan, J., & Wehman, P. (1981). Evaluation of an age-appropriate leisure skills program for moderately retarded adults. *Education and Training of the Mentally Retarded, 16*, 13-19.

Schleien, S. J., Meyer, L. H., Heyne, L. A., & Brandt, B. B. (1995). *Lifelong leisure skills and lifestyles for persons with developmental disabilities.* Baltimore: Brookes.

Schleien, S. J., & Ray, M. T. (1998). *Community recreation and persons with disabilities: Strategies for integration* (2nd ed.). Baltimore: Brookes.

Schleien, S. J., Wehman, P., & Kiernan, J. (1981). Teaching leisure skills to severely handicapped adults: An age-appropriate darts game. *Journal of Applied Behavior Analysis, 14*, 513-519.

Schneider, B. H., & Leroux, J. (1994). Educational environments for the pupil with behavioral disorders: A "best evidence" synthesis. *Behavioral Disorders, 19*, 192-204.

Schnoes, C., Reid, R., Wagner, M., & Marder, C. (2006). ADHD among students receiving special education services: A national survey. *Exceptional Children, 72*, 483-496.

Schonert-Reichl, K. A. (1993). Empathy and social relationships in adolescents with behavioral disorders. *Behavioral Disorders, 18*, 189-204.

Schopler, E., Reichler, R. J., & Renner, B. R. (1988). *The childhood autism rating scale.* Los Angeles: Western Psychological Services.

Schroeder, S. (Ed.). (1987). *Toxic substances and mental retardation: Neurobiological toxicology and teratology.* Washington, DC: American Association on Mental Retardation.

Schreibman, L. (2005). *The science and fiction of autism.* Cambridge, MA: Harvard University Press.

Schulz, J. B. (1985). The parent-professional conflict. In H. R. Turnbull & A. P. Turnbull (Eds.), *Parents speak out: Then and now* (pp. 3-11). Upper Saddle River, NJ: Merrill/Prentice Hall.

Schum, R. L. (2002, September 24). Selective mutism: An integrated treatment approach. *The ASHA Leader Online.* [http://www.asha.org/about/publications/leader-online/archives/2002/q3/020924ftr.htm]

Schumaker, J. B., & Deshler, D. D. (1992). Validation of learning strategy interventions for students with learning disabilities: Results of a programmatic research effort. In B. Y. L. Wong (Ed.), *Contemporary intervention research in learning disabilities* (pp. 22-46). New York: Springer-Verlag.

Schumm, J. S., Moody, S. W., & Vaughn, S. (2000). Grouping for reading instruction: Does one size fit all? *Journal of Learning Disabilities, 33,* 477-488.

Schumm, J. S., Vaughn, D., Haager, D., McDowell, J., Rothlein, L., & Saumell, L. (1995). General education teacher planning: What can students with learning disabilities expect? *Exceptional Children, 61,* 335-352.

Schwartz, C. E., Snidman, N., & Kagan, J. (1999). Adolescent social anxiety and outcome of inhibited temperament in childhood. *Journal of the American Academy of Child and Adolescent Psychiatry, 38,* 1008-1015.

Schwartz, I. (2000). Standing on the shoulders of giants: Looking ahead to facilitating membership and relationships for children with disabilities. *Topics in Early Childhood Special Education, 20,* 123-128.

Schwartz, I. S., & Baer, D. M. (1991). Social validity assessments: Is current practice state of the art? *Journal of Applied Behavior Analysis, 24,* 189-204.

Schwartz, I., Garfinkle, A. N., & Bauer, J. (1998). The Picture Exchange Communication System: Communicative outcomes for young children with disabilities. *Topics in Early Childhood Special Education, 18,* 144-159.

Schwartz, I., Sandall, S. R., Garfinkle, A. N., & Bauer, J. (1998). Outcomes for children with autism: Three case studies. *Topics in Early Childhood Special Education, 18,* 132-143.

Schwartz, I. S. (2005). Inclusion and applied behavior analysis: Mending fences and building bridges. In W. L. Heward, T. E. Heron, N. A. Neef, S. M. Peterson, D. M. Sainato, G. Cartledge, R. Gardner, III, L. D. Peterson, S. B. Hersh, & J. C. Dardig (Eds.), *Focus on behavior analysis in education: Achievements, challenges, and opportunities* (pp. 239-251). Upper Saddle River, NJ: Merrill/Prentice Hall.

Schwartz, I. S., Staub, D., Peck, C. A., & Gallucci, C. (2006). Peer relationships. In M. E. Snell & F. Brown (Eds.), *Instruction of students with severe disabilities* (6th ed.). Upper Saddle River, NJ: Merrill/Prentice Hall.

Schwartz, N. H., Wolf, J. N., & Cassar, R. (1997). Predicting teacher referrals of emotionally disturbed children. *Exceptionality, 3,* 81-98.

Scorgie, K., & Sobsey, D. (2000). Transformational outcomes associated with parenting children who have disabilities. *Mental Retardation, 38,* 195-206.

Scott, B. J., & Vitale, M. R. (2003). Teaching writing process to students with LD. *Intervention in School and Clinic, 38,* 220-224.

Scott, T. M., & Eber, L. (2003). Functional assessment and wraparound as systemic school processes: Primary, secondary, and tertiary systems examples. *Journal of Positive Behavior Interventions, 5,* 131-143.

Scuccimarra, D. J., & Speece, D. L. (1990). Employment outcomes and social integration of students with mild handicaps: The quality of life two years after high school. *Journal of Learning Disabilities, 23,* 213-219.

Scullin, M. H. (2006). Large state-level fluctuations in mental retardation classifications related to introduction of renormed intelligence test. *American Journal on Mental Retardation, 111,* 322-335.

Sebald, A., & Luckner, J. (2007). Successful partnerships with families of children who are deaf. *Teaching Exceptional Children, 39*(3), 54-60.

Seigel, E., & Wetherby, A. (2006). Nonsymbolic communication. In M. E. Snell & F. Brown (Eds.), *Instruction of students with severe disabilities* (6th ed.) (405-446). Upper Saddle River, NJ: Merrill/Prentice Hall.

Semel, E., Wiig, E. H., & Secord, W. (2003). *Clinical evaluation of language fundamentals* (4th ed.). San Antonio, TX: The Psychological Corporation.

Semrud-Clikeman, M. (2001). *Traumatic brain injury in children and adolescents: Assessment and intervention.* New York: Guilford.

Senechal, M., & LeFevre, J. (2002). Parental involvement in the development of children's reading skills: A five-year longitudinal study. *Child Development, 73,* 445-461.

Serna, L. A., Forness, S. R., & Nielson, M. E. (1998). Intervention versus affirmation: Proposed solutions to the problem of disproportionate minority representation in special education. *Journal of Special Education, 32,* 48-51.

Sexson, S. B., & Dingle, A. D. (2001). Medical disorders. In F. M. Kline, L. B. Silver, & S. C. Russell (Eds.), *The educator's guide to medical issues in the classroom* (pp. 29-48). Baltimore: Brookes.

Sexton, M., Harris, K. R., & Graham, S. (1998). Self-regulated strategy development and the writing process: Effects on essay writing and attributions. *Exceptional Children, 64,* 295-311.

Seymour, H. N., Bland-Stewart, L., & Green, L. J. (1998). Difference versus deficit in child African American English. *Language, Speech, and Hearing Services in the Schools, 29,* 96-108.

Shaklee, B., Whitmore, J., Barton, L., Barbour, N., Ambrose, R., & Viechnicki, K. (1989). *Early assessment for exceptional potential for young and/or economically disadvantaged students.* (Grant No. R206A00160). Washington, DC: U.S. Department of Education, Office of Educational Research and Improvement.

Shames, G. H., & Anderson, N. B. (2002). *Human communication disorders: An introduction* (6th ed.). Boston: Allyn & Bacon.

Shapiro, D. R., & Sayers, L. K. (2003). Who does what on the interdisciplinary team regarding physical education for students with disabilities? *Teaching Exceptional Children, 35*(6), 32-38.

Shapiro, E. S., DuPaul, G. J., & Bradley-King, K. L. (1998). Self-management as a strategy to improve the classroom behavior of adolescents with ADHD. *Journal of Learning Disabilities, 31,* 545-555.

Shapiro, E. S., Miller, D. N., Swaka, K., Gardill, M. C., & Handler, M. W. (1999). Facilitating the inclusion of students with EBD into general education classrooms. *Journal of Emotional and Behavioral Disorders, 7,* 83-93.

Shaunessy, E. (2003). State policies regarding gifted education. *Gifted Child Today, 26*(3), 16-21.

Shaywitz, B. A., Fletcher, J. M., & Shaywitz, S. E. (1995). Defining and classifying learning disabilities and attention-deficit/hyperactivity disorder. *Journal of Child Neurology, 10,* 50-57.

Shaywitz, B. A., Shaywitz, S. E., Blachman, B. A., Pugh, K. R., Fulbright, R. K., Skudlarski, P., Menci, W. E., Constable, R. T., Holahan, J. M., Marchione, K. E., Fletcher, J. M., Lyon, G. R., & Gore, J. C. (2004). Development of left occipitotemporal systems for skilled reading in children after a phonologically-based intervention. *Biological Psychiatry, 55,* 926-933.

Shearer, M. S., & Shearer, D. E. (1979). *The Portage Project: A model for early childhood education.* Portage, WI: Portage Project.

Sheppard-Jones, K., Thompson Prout, H., & Kleinert, H. (2005). Quality of life dimensions for adults with developmental disabilities: A comparative study. *Mental Retardation, 43,* 281-291.

Shildroth, A. N., & Hotto, S. A. (1994). Inclusion or exclusion? Deaf students and the inclusion movement. *American Annals of the Deaf, 139,* 239-242.

Shinn, M. R., Tindal, G. A., & Spira, D. A. (1987). Special education referrals as an index of teacher tolerance: Are teachers imperfect tests? *Exceptional Children, 54,* 32-40.

Shonkoff, J. P., & Meisels, S. J. (Eds.). (2000). *Handbook of early childhood intervention* (2nd ed.). New York: Cambridge University Press.

Shores, R. E., Gunter, P. L., & Jack, S. L. (1993). Classroom management strategies: Are they setting events for coercion? *Behavioral Disorders, 18,* 92-102.

Shores, R. E., Jack, S. L., Gunter, P. L., Ellis, D. N., DeBriere, T. J., & Wehby, J. H. (1993). Classroom interactions of children with disorders. *Journal of Emotional and Behavioral Disorders, 1,* 27-39.

Shukla, S., Kennedy, C. H., & Cushing, L. S. (1998). Adult influence on the participation of peers without disabilities in peer support programs. *Journal of Behavioral Education, 8,* 397-413.

Sickmund, M., Sladky, T. J., Kang, W., & Puzzanchera, C. (2007). *Easy access to the census of juveniles in residential placement.* Washington, DC: Office of Juvenile Justice and Delinquency Prevention. Available: http://ojjdp.ncjrs.gov/ojstatbb/ezacjrp/

Sicley, D. (1993). Effective methods of communication: Practical interventions for classroom teachers. *Intervention in School and Clinic, 29,* 105-108.

Sidman, M. (1989). *Coercion and its fallout.* Boston: Authors Group.

Sidman, M. (1994). *Equivalence relations and behavior: A research story.* Boston: Authors Cooperative.

Siegel, I. J., & Senna, J. J. (1994). *Juvenile delinquency: Theory, practice, and law* (5th ed.). St. Paul, MN: West.

Siegle, D., & McCoach, D. B. (2005). Expanding learning through mentorships. In F. A. Karnes & S. M. Bean (Eds.), *Methods and materials for teaching the gifted* (2nd ed.) (pp. 473–518). Waco, TX: Prufrock Press.

Sileo, N. M. (2005). Design HIV/AIDS prevention education: What are the roles and responsibilities of classroom teachers? *Intervention in School and Clinic, 40,* 177–181.

Silliman, E. R., Bahr, R., Beasman, J., & Wilkinson, L. C. (2000). Scaffolds for learning to read in an inclusion classroom. *Language, Speech, and Hearing Services in Schools, 31,* 265–269.

Silliman, E. R., & Diehl, S. F. (2002). Assessing children with language learning disabilities. In D. K. Berstein & E. Tiegerman-Farber (Eds.), *Language and communication disorders in children* (5th ed.). Needham Heights, MA: Allyn & Bacon.

Silliman, E. R., Ford, C. S., Beasman, J., & Evans, D. (1999). An inclusion model for children with language learning disabilities: Building classroom partnerships. *Topics in Language Disorders, 19*(3), 1–18.

Silliman, E. R., Mills, L. R., & Murphy, M. M. (1997). How to start? One story of change in a middle school. In N. W. Nelson & B. Hoskins (Eds.), *Strategies for supporting classroom success* (pp. 1–22). San Diego: Singular.

Silliman, E. R., & Scott, C. M. (2006). Language impairment and reading disability: Connections and complexities. *Learning Disabilities Research & Practice, 21,* 1–7.

Silverman, L. K. (1986). Parenting young gifted children. *Journal of Children in Contemporary Society, 18,* 73–87.

Silverman, L. K. (1995). Highly gifted children. In J. L. Genshaft, M. Bireley, & C. L. Hollinger (Eds.), *Serving gifted and talented students: A resource for school personnel* (pp. 124–160). Austin, TX: PRO-ED.

Silvestri, S. M., & Heward, W. L. (May 2005). *Effects of self-scoring on teachers' rates of positive and negative statements during instruction.* Paper presented at the 31st Annual Convention of the Association for Behavior Analysis, Chicago.

Silvestri, S. M., Wood, C. L., Allen, N. J., Anderson, M. A., Murphy, C. M., & Heward, W. L. (in press). What is ABA? In E. A. Boutot & M. Tincani (Eds.), *Autism articles: What parents need to know.* Austin, TX: PRO-ED.

Simeonsson, R. J. (1994). Promoting children's health, education, and well-being. In R. J. Simeonsson (Ed.), *Risk, resilience, and prevention* (pp. 3–11). Baltimore: Brookes.

Simmons, D. C., Kame'enui, E. J., & Chard, D. J. (1998). General education teachers' assumptions about learning and students with learning disabilities: Design-of-instruction analysis. *Learning Disability Quarterly, 21,* 6–21.

Simmons, D. C., Kame'enui, E. J., Coyne, M. D., & Chard, D. J. (2007). Effective strategies for teaching beginning reading. In M. D. Coyne, E. J. Kame'enui, & D. W. Carnine (Eds.), *Effective teaching strategies that accommodate diverse learners* (3rd ed.), (pp. 45–77). Upper Saddle River, NJ: Merrill/Prentice Hall.

Simmons, T. J., & Flexer, R. W. (2008). Transition to employment. In R. W. Flexer, T. J. Simmons, P. Luft, & R. M. Baer (Eds.), *Transition planning for secondary students with disabilities* (3rd ed.) (pp. 230–257). Upper Saddle River, NJ: Merrill/Prentice Hall.

Simmons, T. J., Flexer, R. W., & Bauder, D. (2008). Collaborative transition services. In R. W. Flexer, T. J. Simmons, P. Luft, & R. M. Baer (Eds.), *Transition planning for secondary students with disabilities* (3rd ed.) (pp. 203–229). Upper Saddle River, NJ: Merrill/Prentice Hall.

Simon, R. (1987). *After the tears: Parents talk about raising a child with a disability.* San Diego: Harcourt Brace Jovanovich.

Simos, P. G., Breier, J. I., Fletcher, J. M., Bergman, E., & Papanicolaou, A. C. (2000). Cerebral mechanisms involved in word reading in dyslexic children: A magnetic source imaging approach. *Cerebral Cortex, 10,* 809–816.

Simpson, C. G., Swicegood, P. R., & Gaus, M. D. (2006). Nutrition and fitness curriculum: Designing instructional interventions for children with developmental disabilities. *Teaching Exceptional Children, 38*(6), 50–53.

Simpson, R. L. (1996). *Working with families and parents of exceptional children and youth: Techniques for successful conferencing and collaboration* (3rd ed.). Austin, TX: PRO-ED.

Simpson, R. L. (2001). ABA and students with autism spectrum disorders: Issues and considerations for effective practice. *Focus on Autism and Other Developmental Disabilities, 16,* 68–71.

Simpson, R. L. (2004). Finding effective intervention and personnel preparation practices for students with autism spectrum disorders. *Exceptional Children, 70,* 135–144.

Simpson, R. L. (2004). Inclusion of students with behavior disorders in general education settings. *Behavioral Disorders, 30,* 19–31.

Simpson, R. L. (2005). Evidence-based practices and students with autism spectrum disorders. *Focus on Autism and Other Developmental Disabilities, 20,* 140–149.

Simpson, R. L. (February 2007). *Issues, trends, and scientifically-based practices for children and youth with Asperger syndrome.* Presentation at: Progress and Challenges in the Behavioral Treatment of Autism Conference. Boston, MA. [Available on DVD from the Association for Behavior Analysis International.]

Simpson, R. L., & Myles, B. S. (1995). Effectiveness of facilitated communication with children and youth with autism. *Journal of Special Education, 28,* 424–439.

Sims, D. G., & Gottermeier, L. (1995). Computer-assisted, interactive video methods for speechreading instruction: A review. In K. Erik-Spens & G. Plant (Eds.), *Speech, communication and profound deafness* (pp. 220–241). London: Whurr.

Singer, G. H. S., Powers, L. E., & Olson, A. (1996). *Redefining family support: Innovations in public/private partnerships.* Baltimore: Brookes.

Singer, M. T., & Lalich, J. (1996). *Crazy therapies: What are they? Do they work?* San Francisco: Jossey-Bass.

Siperstein, G. N., Parker, R. C., Norins Bardon, J., & Widaman, K. F. (2007). A national study of youth attitudes toward the inclusion of students with intellectual disabilities. *Exceptional Children, 73,* 435–455.

Sitlington, P. L., & Clark, G. M. (2006). *Comprehensive transition education and services for students with disabilities* (4th ed.). Needham Heights, MA: Allyn & Bacon.

Sitlington, P. L., Clark, G. M., & Kolstoe, O. P. (2000). *Comprehensive transition education and services for adolescents with disabilities* (3rd ed.). Needham Heights, MA: Allyn & Bacon.

Sitlington, P. L., Frank, A. R., & Carson, R. (1993). Adult adjustment among high school graduates with mild disabilities. *Exceptional Children, 59,* 221–233.

Sitlington, P. L., & Payne, E. M. (2004). Information needed by postsecondary education: Can we provide it as part of the transition assessment process? *Learning Disabilities, 2*(2), 1–14.

Sivberg, B. (2003). Parents' detection of early signs in their children having an autism spectrum disorder. *Journal of Pediatric Nursing, 18,* 433–439.

Skau, L., & Cascella, P. W. (2006). Using assistive technology to foster speech and language skills at home and in preschool. *Teaching Exceptional Children, 38*(6), 12–17.

Skeels, H. M., & Dye, H. B. (1939). A study of the effects of differential stimulation on mentally retarded children. *Convention Proceedings, American Association on Mental Deficiency, 44,* 114–136.

Skellenger, A., Hill, E., & Hill, M. (1992). The social functioning of children with visual impairments. In S. L. Odom, S. R. McConnell, & M. A. McEvoy (Eds.), *Social competence of young children with disabilities: Issues and strategies for intervention* (pp. 165–188). Baltimore: Brookes.

Skiba, R. (2002). Special education and school discipline: A precarious balance. *Behavioral Disorders, 27,* 81–97.

Skiba, R. J., Poloni-Staudinger, L., Galine, S., Simmons, A. B., & Feggins-Azziz, R. (2006). Disparate access: The disproportionality of African American students with disabilities across environments. *Exceptional Children, 72,* 411–424.

Skinner, B. F. (1989). *Recent issues in the analysis of behavior.* Columbus, OH: Merrill.

Skinner, C. H., Pappas, D. N., & Davis, K. A. (2005). Enhancing academic engagement: Providing opportunities for responding and influencing students to choose to respond. *Psychology in the Schools, 42,* 389–403

Skinner, C. H., Williams, R. L., & Neddenriep, C. E. (2004). Using interdependent group-oriented reinforcement to enhance academic performance in general education classrooms. *School Psychology Review, 33*, 384-397.

Skinner, D., Bailey, D. D., Jr., Correa, V. I., & Rodriguez, P. (1999). Narrating self and disabilities: Latino mothers' construction of identities vis-à-vis their children with special needs. *Exceptional Children, 65*, 481-495.

Skinner, D., Correa, V., Skinner, M., & Bailey, D. (2001). Role of religion in the lives of Latino families of young children with developmental delays. *American Journal on Mental Retardation, 106*, 297-313.

Skinner, M. (1998). Promoting self-advocacy among college students with learning disabilities. *Intervention in School and Clinic, 33*(5), 278-283.

Slaton, D. E., Schuster, J., Collins, B., & Carnine, D. (1994). A functional approach to academic instruction. In E. Cipani & F. Spooner (Eds.), *Curricular and instructional approaches for persons with severe disabilities* (pp. 149-183). Boston: Allyn & Bacon.

Slavin, R. (1987). Ability grouping and student achievement in elementary schools: A best-evidence synthesis. *Review of Educational Research, 57*, 293-336.

Slavin, R. (1991). Synthesis of research on cooperative learning. *Educational Leadership, 47*(4), 3.

Slavin, R. E. (1986). *Using student team learning* (3rd ed.). Baltimore: Johns Hopkins University, Center for Research on Elementary and Middle Schools.

Slavin, R. E. (1990). Research on cooperative learning. *Educational Leadership, 47*(4), 52-54.

Slavin, R. E. (1995). *Cooperative learning: Theory, research and practice* (2nd ed.). Boston: Allyn & Bacon.

Slike, S. B., & Hobbis, D. H. (1998, March). *The development of a CD-ROM to teach speechreading skills.* Paper presented at the Association of College Educators of the Deaf and Hard of Hearing, Lexington, KY.

Slike, S. B., Thornton, N. E., Hobbis, D. H., Kokoska, S. M., & Job, K. A. (1995). The development and analysis of interactive videodisc technology to teach speechreading. *American Annals of the Deaf, 140*(4), 346-351.

Smith, B. J., & Guralnick, M. J. (2007). Definition of early intervention. In R. S. New & M. Cochran (Eds.), *Early childhood education: An international encyclopedia* (pp. 329-332). Westport, CT: Greenwood Publishing Group.

Smith, B. W., & Sugai, G. (2000). A self-management functional assessment-based behavior support plan for a middle school student with EBD. *Journal of Positive Behavior Interventions, 2*, 208-217.

Smith, C. R. (1997). Advocacy for students with emotional and behavior disorders: One call for redefined efforts. *Behavioral Disorders, 22*, 96-105.

Smith, C. R. (2000). Behavioral and discipline provisions of IDEA '97: Implicit competencies yet to be confirmed. *Exceptional Children, 66*, 403-412.

Smith, G. J., McDougall, D., & Edelen-Smith, P. (2006). Behavioral cusps: A person-centered concept for establishing pivotal individual, family, and community behaviors and repertoires. *Focus on Autism and Other Developmental Disabilities, 21*, 223-229.

Smith, J. D. (1994). The revised AAMR definition of mental retardation: The MRDD position. *Education and Training in Mental Retardation, 29*, 179-183.

Smith, J. D. (2000). The power of mental retardation: Reflections on the value of people with disabilities. *Mental Retardation, 38*, 70-72.

Smith, J. D. (2004). In A. McCray Sorrells, H. J. Rieth, & P. T. Sindelar (Eds.), *Critical issues in special education: Access, diversity, and accountability* (pp. 1-15). Boston: Allyn & Bacon.

Smith, J. D. (2006). Mental retardation: Is it time to abandon the myth? In W. L. Heward, *Exceptional children: An introduction to special education* (8th ed.) (pp. 171-172). Upper Saddle River, NJ: Merrill/Prentice Hall.

Smith, J. D., & Hilton, A. (1997). The preparation and training of the educational community for the inclusion of students with developmental disabilities: The MRDD position. *Education and Training of Mental Retardation and Developmental Disabilities, 32*, 3-10.

Smith, J. D., & Mitchell, A. L. (2001a). Disney's Tarzan, Edgar Rice Burroughs' eugenics, and visions of utopian perfection. *Mental Retardation, 39*, 221-225.

Smith, J. D., & Mitchell, A. L. (2001b). "Me? I'm not a drooler. I'm the assistant": Is it time to abandon mental retardation as a classification? *Mental Retardation, 39*, 144-146.

Smith, J. D., & Prior, M. (1995). Temperament and stress resilience in school-age children: A within-families study. *Journal of the American Academy of Children and Adolescent Psychiatry, 34*, 168-179.

Smith, L., & Fowler, S. A. (1984). Positive peer pressure: The effects of peer monitoring on children's disruptive behavior. *Journal of Applied Behavior Analysis, 17*, 213-227.

Smith, P. D., Gast, D. L., Logan, K. R., & Jacobs, H. A. (2001). Customizing instruction to maximize functional outcomes for students with profound disabilities. *Exceptionality, 9*, 135-145.

Smith, R. G., & Iwata, B. A. (1997). Antecedent influences of behavior disorders. *Journal of Applied Behavior Analysis, 30*, 343-375.

Smith, S. B., Baker, S., & Oudeans, M. K., Sr. (2001). Making a difference in the classroom with early literacy instruction. *Teaching Exceptional Children, 33*(6), 8-14.

Smith, S. W. (1990a). Comparison of Individualized Education Programs (IEPs) of students with behavioral disorders and learning disabilities. *Journal of Special Education, 24*(1), 85-100.

Smith, S. W. (1990b). Individualized Education Programs (IEPs) in special education— From intent to acquiescence. *Exceptional Children, 57*, 6-14.

Smith, S. W., & Brownell, M. T. (1995). Individualized education programs: From intent to acquiescence. *Focus on Exceptional Children, 28*(1), 1-12.

Smith, S. W., & Simpson, R. L. (1989). An analysis of individualized education programs (IEPs) for students with behavioral disorders. *Behavioral Disorders, 14*, 107-116.

Smith, T., Eikeseth, S., Klevstrand, M., & Lovaas, O. I. (1997). Intensive behavioral treatment for preschoolers with severe mental retardation and pervasive developmental disorders. *American Journal on Mental Retardation, 102*, 238-249.

Smith, T., Groen, A. D., & Wynn, J. W. (2000). Randomized trial of intensive early intervention for children with pervasive developmental disorder. *American Journal on Mental Retardation, 105*, 269-285.

Smith, T., & Lovaas, O. I. (1998). Intensive and early behavioral intervention with autism: The UCLA young autism project. *Infants and Young Children, 10*(3), 67-78.

Smith, T. B., Oliver, M. N. I., & Innocenti, M. S. (2001). Parenting stress in families of children with disabilities. *American Journal of Orthopsychiatry, 71*, 257-261.

Smith, T. C., Gartin, B. C., Murdick, N. L., & Hilton, A. (2006). *Families and children with special needs: Professionals and family partnerships.* Upper Saddle River, NJ: Merrill/Prentice Hall.

Smith, T. E. C. (2002). Section 504: What teachers need to know. *Intervention in School and Clinic, 37*, 259-266.

Smith, T. E. C. (2005). IDEA 2004: Another round in the reauthorization process. *Remedial and Special Education, 26*, 314-319.

Smith, T. J., & Adams, G. (2006). The effect of comorbid AD/HD and learning disabilities on parent-reported behavioral and academic outcomes of children. *Learning Disability Quarterly, 29*, 101-112.

Smith, T. S. (February 2007). *What has behavior analysis contributed to the understanding and treatment of autism spectrum disorders?* Presentation at: Progress and Challenges in the Behavioral Treatment of Autism Conference. Boston, MA. [Available on DVD from the Association for Behavior Analysis International.]

Smithdas, R. (1981). Psychological aspects of deaf-blindness. In S. R. Walsh & R. Holzberg (Eds.), *Understanding and educating the deaf-blind/severely and profoundly handicapped: An international perspective.* Springfield, IL: Thomas.

Smyth, P., & Keenan, M. (2002). Compound performance: The role of free and controlled operant components. *Journal of Precision Teaching and Celeration, 18*(2), 3-15.

Snell, M. E. (2004). What if your child lacks needed communication services and supports? *Exceptional Parent, 34*(2), 41-44.

Snell, M. E., & Beckman-Brindley, S. (1984). Family involvement in intervention with children having severe handicaps. *Journal of The Association for Persons with Severe Handicaps, 9*, 213-230.

Snell, M. E., & Brown, F. (2006a). Designing and implementing instructional programs. In M. E. Snell & F. Brown (Eds.), *Instruction of students with severe disabilities* (6th ed.) (pp. 111–169). Upper Saddle River, NJ: Merrill/Prentice Hall.

Snell, M. E., & Brown, F. (Eds.). (2006). *Instruction of students with severe disabilities* (6th ed.). Upper Saddle River, NJ: Merrill/Prentice Hall.

Snell, M. E., & Janney, R. E. (2000). Teachers' problem-solving about children with moderate and severe disabilities in elementary classrooms. *Exceptional Children, 66,* 472–490.

Snell, M. E., & Janney, R. E. (2005). *Practices for inclusive schools: Collaborative teaming* (2nd ed.). Baltimore: Brookes.

Snider, V. E., Busch, T., & Arrowood, L. (2003). Teacher knowledge of stimulant medication and ADHD. *Remedial and Special Education, 24,* 46–56.

Snow, K. (2001). *Disability is natural.* Woodland Park, CO: Braveheart.

Snowling, M., Bishop, D. V. M., & Stothard, S. E. (2000). Is preschool language impairment a risk factor for dyslexia in adolescences? *Journal of Child Psychology and Psychiatry, 41,* 587–600.

Snyder, H. M., & Sickmund, M. (2006). *Juvenile offenders and victims: 2006 national report.* Washington, DC: Office of Juvenile Justice and Delinquency Prevention. Available: http://ojjdp.ncjrs.gov/ojstatbb/nr2006/downloads/NR2006.pdf

Snyder, H. M., & Sickmund, M. (2007). *Juvenile offenders and victims: 2007 national report.* Washington, DC: Office of Juvenile Justice and Delinquency Prevention.

Snyder, H. N. (2000). *Juvenile arrests 1999.* Washington, DC: Office of Juvenile Justice and Delinquency Prevention.

Sobsey, D. (1996). Review of assistive technologies: Principles and practice by A. M. Cook & S. M. Hussey. *Journal of The Association for Persons with Severe Handicaps, 21,* 207–209.

Social Security Administration. (2000). *Titles II and XVI: Basic disability.* www.ssa.gov/disability.

Soenksen, D., & Alper, S. (2006). Teaching a young child to appropriately gain attention of peers using a social story intervention. *Focus on Autism and Other Developmental Disabilities, 21,* 36–44.

Solomon, B. (2007). When all you need is rest. *Exceptional Parent, 37*(4), 38–39.

Sonnenschein, S. (1981). Parents and professionals: An uneasy relationship. *Teaching Exceptional Children, 14,* 62–65.

Sontag, E., Sailor, W., & Smith, J. (1977). The severely/profoundly handicapped: Who are they? Where are we? *Journal of Special Education, 11*(1), 5–11.

Sonuga-Barke, E. J. S. (2001). Parent-based therapies for preschool ADHD: A randomized controlled trial with a community sample. *Journal of the American Academy of Child and Adolescent Psychiatry, 40,* 402–408.

Sonuga-Bourke, E. J. S., Dalen, L., Daley, D., & Remington, B. (2002). Are planning, working, memory, and inhibition associated with individual differences in preschool ADHD symptoms? *Developmental Neuropsychlogy, 21,* 255–272.

Soukup, J. H., Wehmeyer, M. L., Bashinski, S. M., & Bovaird, J. A. (2007). Classroom variables and access to the general curriculum for students with disabilities. *Exceptional Children, 74,* 101–120.

Southern, W. T., & Jones, E. (1991). *The academic acceleration of gifted children.* New York: Teachers College Press.

Southern, W. T., & Jones, E D. (2004). Types of acceleration: Dimensions and issues. In N. Colangelo, S. Assouline, & M. Gross (Eds.), *A nation deceived: How schools hold back America's brightest students* (pp. 5–12). Iowa City, IA: The Connie Belin & Jacqueline N. Blank International Center for Gifted Education and Talent Development.

Sowers, J., Verdi, M., Bourbeau, P., & Sheehan, M. (1985). Teaching job independence to mentally retarded students through the use of a self-control package. *Journal of Applied Behavior Analysis, 18,* 81–85.

Sparrow, S. S., Balla, D. A., & Cicchetti, D. V. (2005). *Vineland Adaptive Behavior Scales: Second edition (Vineland-II).* Upper Saddle River, NJ: Pearson Assessments.

Sparrow, S. S., Balla, D. A., & Cicchetti, D. V. (1985). *Vineland Adaptive Behavior Scales: Classroom edition form.* Circle Pines, MN: American Guidance Service.

Spear-Swerling, L., & Sternberg, R. J. (2001). What science offers teachers of reading. *Learning Disabilities Research and Practice, 16,* 51–57.

Spencer, P. E. (2001, July). *Cochlear implants for children: Language, culture, and education.* Paper presented at Office of Special Education Program Project Director's Conference, Washington, DC.

Spencer, V. G. (2006). Peer tutoring and students with emotional or behavioral disorders: A review of the literature. *Behavioral Disorders, 31,* 204–222.

Spinelli, C. G. (2004). Dealing with cancer in the classroom: The teacher's role and responsibilities. *Teaching Exceptional Children, 36*(4), 14–21.

Spinelli, C. G. (2006). *Classroom assessment for students in special and general education* (2nd ed.). Upper Saddle River, NJ: Merrill/Prentice Hall.

Spooner, F., Dymond, S., Smith, A., & Kennedy, C. H. (in press). Accessing the general curriculum: More questions than answers? *Research and Practice for People with Severe Disabilities.*

Sprague, J., & Walker, H. (2000). Early identification and intervention for youth with antisocial and violent behavior. *Exceptional Children, 66,* 367–379.

Sprague, J. R., & Horner, R. H. (1990). Preventing challenging behaviors. *Teaching Exceptional Children, 23*(1), 13–15.

Spriggs, A. D., Gast, D. L., & Ayres, K. M. (2007). Using picture activity schedules to increase on-schedule and on-task behaviors. *Education and Training in Developmental Disabilities, 42,* 209–223.

Spring, C., & Sandoval, J. (1976). Food additives and hyperkinesis: A critical evaluation of the evidence. *Journal of Learning Disabilities, 9,* 560–569.

Squires, J., Bricker, D., & Twombly, E. (2002). *Ages and Stages Questionnaires: Social-Emotional (ASQ:SE).* Baltimore: Brookes.

SRI International. (2005). *Declassification—students who leave special education: A special topic report from the special education elementary longitudinal study.* Menlo Park, CA: Author.

Sridhar, D., & Vaughn, S. (2000). Bibliotherapy for all: Enhancing reading comprehension, self-concept, and behavior. *Teaching Exceptional Children, 33*(2), 74–82.

Ssasz, T. (1961). *The myth of mental illness: Foundations of a theory of personal conduct.* New York: Harper.

Stafford, A. M. (2005). Choice making: A strategy for students with severe disabilities. *Teaching Exceptional Children, 37*(6), 12–17.

Stahl, L., & Pry, R. (2002). Joint attention and set-shifting in young children with autism. *Autism, 6,* 383–396.

Stahr, B., Cushing, D., Lane, K., & Fox, J. (2006). Efficacy of a function-based intervention in decreasing off-task behavior exhibited by a student with ADHD. *Journal of Positive Behavioral Interventions, 8,* 201–211.

Stainback, S., & Stainback, W. (Eds.). (1991). *Teaching in the inclusive classroom: Curriculum design, adaptation and delivery.* Baltimore: Brookes.

Stainback, S., & Stainback, W. (Eds.). (1996). *Inclusion: A guide for educators* (2nd ed.). Baltimore: Brookes.

Stainback, S., Stainback, W., & Ayres, B. (1996). Schools as inclusive communities. In S. Stainback & W. Stainback (Eds.), *Controversial issues confronting special education: Divergent perspectives* (2nd ed.) (pp. 31–43). Boston: Allyn and Bacon.

Stainton, T., & Besser, H. (1998). The positive impact of children with an intellectual disability on the family. *Journal of Intellectual and Developmental Disability, 23,* 57–70.

Stancliffe, R. J., & Hayden, C. (1998). Longitudinal study of institutional downsizing: Effects on individuals who remain in the institution. *American Journal on Mental Retardation, 102,* 500–510.

Stancliffe, R. J., & Lakin, K. C. (1998). Analysis of expenditures and outcomes of residential alternatives for persons with developmental disabilities. *American Journal on Mental Retardation, 102,* 552–568.

Stanovich, K. E., & Siegel, L. S. (1994). The phenotypic performance profile of reading-disabled children: A regression-based test of the phonological-core variable-difference model. *Journal of Educational Psychology, 86,* 24–53.

Stark, K. D., Bronik, M. D., Wong, S., Wells, G., & Ostrander, R. (2000). Depressive disorders. In M. Hersen & R. T. Ammerman (Eds.), *Advanced abnormal child psychology* (2nd ed.), (pp. 291–326). Hillsdale, NJ: Erlbaum.

Staub, D., Spaulding, M., Peck, C. A., Gallucci, C., & Schwartz, I. S. (1996). Using nondisabled peers to support the inclusion of students with disabilities at the junior high school level. *Journal of The Association for Persons with Severe Handicaps, 21,* 194–205.

Staub, R. W. (1990). The effects of publicly posted feedback on middle school students' disruptive hallway behavior. *Education and Treatment Children, 13,* 249–257.

Stecker, P. M. (2007). Tertiary intervention: Using progress monitoring with intensive services. *Teaching Exceptional Children, 39*(5), 50–57.

Stecker, P. M., & Fuchs, L. S. (2000). Effecting superior achievement using curriculum-based measurement: The importance of individual progress monitoring. *Learning Disabilities Research and Practice, 15,* 128–134.

Steinweg, S. B., Griffin, H. C., Griffin, L. W., & Gingras, H. (2005). Retinopathy of Prematurity. *RE:view: Rehabilitation Education for Blindness and Visual Impairment, 37.*

Stephens, K. R., & Karnes, F. A. (2000). State definitions for the gifted and talented revisited. *Exceptional Children, 66*(2), 219–238.

Stephens, T. M., & Wolf, J. S. (1989). *Effective skills in parent/teacher conferencing* (2nd ed.). Columbus: The Ohio State University, College of Education, School Study Council of Ohio.

Sterling, R., Barbetta, P. M., Heward, W. L., & Heron, T. E. (1997). A comparison of active student response and on-task instruction on the acquisition and maintenance of health facts by fourth grade special education students. *Journal of Behavioral Education, 7,* 151–165.

Sternberg, L. (Ed.). (1994). *Individuals with profound disabilities: Instructional and assistive strategies.* Austin, TX: PRO-ED.

Sternberg, R. (1988). *The triarchic mind: A new theory of human intelligence.* New York: Viking.

Sternberg, R., & Grigorenko, E. (2000). *Teaching for successful intelligence.* Upper Saddle River, NJ: Prentice Hall.

Sternberg, R. J. (1985). *Beyond IQ: A triarchic theory of human intelligence.* New York: Cambridge University Press.

Sternberg, R. J. (2000). Patterns of giftedness: A triarchic analysis. *Roeper Review, 22*(4), 231–235.

Sternberg, R. J. (2003). Giftedness according to the theory of successful intelligence. In N. Colangelo & G. A. Davis (Eds.), *Handbook of gifted education* (3rd ed.), (pp. 88–99). Needham Heights, MA: Allyn & Bacon.

Sternberg, R. J. (2007). Who are the bright children? *Educational Researcher, 36*(3), 148–155.

Stevens, R., & Rosenshine, B. (1981). Advances in research on teaching. *Exceptional Education Quarterly, 2,* 1–9.

Stewart, D. A. (1992). Initiating reform in total communication programs. *Journal of Special Education, 26,* 68–84.

Stewart, J. L. (1977). Unique problems of handicapped Native Americans. In *The White House Conference on Handicapped Individuals* (vol. 1), (pp. 438–444).

Washington, DC: U.S. Government Printing Office.

Stiegler, L. N. (2005). Understanding pica behavior: A review for clinical and education professionals. *Focus on Autism and Other Developmental Disabilities, 20,* 27–38.

Stiles, S., & Knox, R. (1996). Medical issues, treatments, and professionals. In M. C. Holbrook (Ed.), *Children with visual impairments: A parents' guide* (pp. 21–48). Bethesda, MD: Woodbine House.

Stinson, M. S., Elliot, L. B., McKee, B. G., & Francis, P. G. (2001). Accessibility in the classroom: The pros and cons of C-Print. *Volta Voices, 8*(3), 16–19.

Stinson, M. S., & Liu, Y. (1999). Participation of deaf and hard-of-hearing students in classes with hearing students. *Journal of Deaf Studies and Deaf Education, 4,* 191–202.

Stodden, R. A. (2005). The status of persons with disabilities in postsecondary education. *TASH Connections, 31*(11/12), 4–7.

Stokes, T. F., Fowler, S. A., & Baer, D. M. (1978). Training preschool children to recruit natural communities of reinforcement. *Journal of Applied Behavior Analysis, 11,* 285–303.

Stokoe, W. (1960). *The calculus of structure.* Washington, DC: Gallaudet University Press.

Stokoe, W., Armstrong, D. F., & Wilcox, S. (1995). *Gesture and the nature of language.* New York: Cambridge University Press.

Stone, C. A. (2002). Promises and pitfalls of scaffolded instruction for students with language learning disabilities. In K. G. Butler & E. R. Silliman (Eds.), *Speaking, reading, and writing in children with language learning disabilities: New paradigms for research and practice* (pp. 175–198). Mahwah, NJ: Erlbaum.

Stone, J. (1997). The preschool child. In H. Mason & S. McCall (Eds.), *Visual impairment: Access to education for children and young people* (pp. 87–96). London: Fulton.

Stone, P. (1997). Educating children who are deaf or hard of hearing: Auditory-oral option. *ERIC Digest #551.* (ERIC Document Reproduction Service No. ED 414 669).

Stoneman, Z. (1998). Research on siblings of children with mental retardation: Contributions of developmental theory and etiology. In J. A. Burach, R. M. Hodapp, & E. Zigler (Eds.), *Handbook of mental retardation and development* (pp. 669–692). Cambridge: Cambridge University Press.

Stoneman, Z., & Gavidia-Payne, S. (2006). Marital adjustment in families of young children with disabilities: Associations with daily hassles and problem-focused coping. *American Journal on Mental Retardation, 111,* 1–14.

Stoner, G., Carey, S. P., Ikeda, M. J., & Shinn, M. R. (1994). The utility of curriculum-based measurement for evaluating the effects of methylphenidate on academic performance. *Journal of Applied Behavior Analysis, 27,* 101–113.

Stoner, J. B., & Angell, M. E. (2006). Parent perspectives on role engagement: An investigation of parents of children with ASD and their self-reported roles with education professionals. *Focus on Autism and Other Developmental Disabilities, 21,* 177–189.

Stoner, J. B., Jones Bock, S., Thompson, J. R., Angell, M. E., Heyl, B. S., & Crowley, E. P. (2005). Welcome to our world: Parent perceptions of interactions between parents of young children with ASD and education professionals. *Focus on Autism and Other Developmental Disabilities, 20,* 39–51.

Stowe, M. J., Turnbull, H. R., III, & Sublet, C. (2006). The Supreme Court, "our town," and disability policy: Boardroom and bedrooms, courts, and classrooms. *Mental Retardation, 44,* 83–99.

Strain, P. S., & Joseph, G. E. (2004). A not so good job with "Good job." *Journal of Positive Behavior Interventions, 6*(1), 55–59.

Strain, P. S., & Schwartz, I. (2001). ABA and the development of meaningful social relations for young children with autism. *Focus on Autism and Other Developmental Disabilities, 16,* 120–128.

Strain, P. S., & Smith, B. J. (1986). A counter-interpretation of early intervention effects: A response to Casto and Mastropieri. *Exceptional Children, 53,* 260–265.

Strain, P. S., & Timm, M. A. (2001). Remediation and prevention of aggression: An evaluation of the Regional Intervention Program over a quarter century. *Behavioral Disorders, 26,* 297–313.

Strand, J., & Kreiner, J. (2005). Recreation and leisure in the community. In R. W. Flexer, T. J. Simmons, P. Luft, & R. M. Baer (Eds.), *Transition planning for secondary students with disabilities* (2nd ed.), (pp. 460–482). Upper Saddle River, NJ: Merrill/Prentice Hall.

Stratton, K., Howe, C., & Battaglia, F. (1996). *Fetal alcohol syndrome: Diagnosis, epidemiology, prevention, and treatment.* Washington, DC: National Academy Press.

Strauss, A. A., & Lehtinen, L. E. (1947). *Psychopathology and education of the brain-injured child.* New York: Grune and Stratton.

Strauss, M. (1999). Hearing loss and cytomegalovirus. *Volta Review, 99*(5), 71–74.

Stremel, K., Molden, V., Leister, C., Matthews, J., Wilson, R., Goodall, D. V., & Hoston, J. (1990). *Communication systems and routines: A decision making process.* Washington, DC: U.S. Office of Special Education.

Strickland, B. B., & Turnbull, A. P. (1993). *Developing and implementing Individualized Education Programs* (3rd ed.). Upper Saddle River, NJ: Merrill/Prentice Hall.

Strickland, S. P. (1971). Can slum children learn? *American Education, 7*(6), 3–7.

Stromer, R., Kimball, J., Kinney, E., & Taylor, B. (2006). Activity schedules, computer technology, and teaching children with autism spectrum disorders. *Focus on Autism and Other Developmental Disabilities, 21,* 14–24.

Strong, C. J., & North, K. H. (1996). *The magic of stories: Literature-based language intervention.* Eau Claire, WI: Thinking Publications.

Strong, M. (1995). A review of bilingual/bicultural programs for deaf children in North America. *American Annals of the Deaf, 140*(2), 84-94.

Strong, M., & Prinz, P. M. (1997). A study of the relationship between American Sign Language and English literacy. *Journal of Deaf Studies and Deaf Education, 2,* 36-46.

Stroul, B. A., & Friedman, R. M. (1996). *A system of care for children and adolescents with severe emotional disturbance* (Rev. ed.). Washington, DC: Georgetown University Child Development Center, National Technical Assistance Center for Child Mental Health.

Stuart, M. E., Lieberman, L., & Hand, K. E. (2006). Beliefs about physical activity among children who are visually impaired and their parents. *Journal of Visual Impairment and Blindness, 100,* 223-234.

Stuart, S. K., Flis, L. D., & Rinaldi, C. (2006). Connecting with families: Parents speak up about preschool services for their children with autism spectrum disorders. *Teaching Exceptional Children, 39*(1), 46-51.

Stuart v. Nappi, 443 F. Supp. 1235 (D. Conn. 1978).

Stump, C. S., Lovitt, T. C., Fister, S., Kemp, K., Moore, R., & Schroeder, B. (1992). Vocabulary intervention for secondary-level youth. *Learning Disability Quarterly, 15,* 207-222.

Sturmey, P., & Fitzer, A. (2007). *Autism spectrum disorders: Applied behavior analysis, evidence and practice.* Austin, TX: Pro-Ed.

Stuttering Foundation of America. (2007). *Facts on stuttering.* Memphis, TN: Author. [Retrieved July 28, 2007. http://www. stutteringhelp.org/Default.aspx?tabid=17]

Sudhalter, V., & Belser, R. C. (2001). Conversational characteristics of children with fragile X syndrome: Tangential language. *American Journal of Mental Retardation, 106,* 389-400.

Sugai, G., & Horner, R. H. (2005). Schoolwide positive behavior supports: Achieving and sustaining effective learning environments for all students. In W. L. Heward, T. E. Heron, N. A. Neef, S. M. Peterson, D. M. Sainato, G. Cartledge, R. Gardner, III, L. D. Peterson, S. B. Hersh, & J. C. Dardig (Eds.), *Focus on behavior analysis in education: Achievements, challenges, and opportunities* (pp. 90-102). Upper Saddle River, NJ: Merrill/Prentice Hall.

Sugai, G., & Horner, R. H. (2006). A promising approach for expanding and sustaining the implementation of school-wide positive behavior support. *School Psychology Review, 35,* 245-259.

Sugai, G., Horner, R. H., & McIntosh, K. (in press). Best practices in developing a broad scale system of school-wide positive behavior support. In A. Thomas & J. Grimes (Eds.), *Best practices in school psychology* (5th ed.). Bethesda, MD: National Association of School Psychologists.

Sugai, G., Sprague, J. R., Horner, R. H., and Walker, H. M. (2000). Preventing school violence: The use of office discipline referrals to assess and monitor school-wide discipline interventions. *Journal of Emotional and Behavioral Disorders, 8,* 94-101.

Sulzer-Azaroff, B., & Associates. (2007). *Applying behavior analysis across the autism spectrum: A field guide for practitioners.* Cornwall-on-Hudson, NY: Sloan Publishing.

Summers, J. A., Hoffman, L., Marquis, J., Turnbull, A., Poston, D., & Lord Nelson, L. (2005). Measuring the quality of family-professional partnerships in special education services. *Exceptional Children, 72,* 65-81.

Sundberg, M. L., & Partington, J. W. (1998). *Teaching language to children with autism or other developmental disabilities.* Pleasant Hill, CA: Behavior Analysts.

Sunderland, L. C. (2004). Speech, language, and audiology services in public schools. *Intervention in School and Clinic, 39,* 209-217.

Sutherland, K. S., Alder, N., & Gunter, P. L. (2003). The effect of varying rates of opportunities to respond to academic requests on the classroom behavior of students with EBD. *Journal of Emotional and Behavioral Disorders, 11,* 239-248.

Sutherland, K. S., & Singh, N. N. (2004). Learned helplessness and students with emotional or behavioral disorders: Deprivation in the classroom. *Behavioral Disorders, 29,* 169-181.

Sutherland, K. S., & Wehby, J. H. (2001). Exploring the relationship between increased opportunities to respond to academic requests and the academic and behavioral outcomes of students with EBD: A review. *Remedial and Special Education, 22,* 113-121.

Sutherland, K. S., Wehby, J. H., & Copeland, S. R. (2000). Effects of varying rates of behavior specific praise on the on-task behavior of students with emotional and behavioral disorders. *Journal of Emotional and Behavioral Disorders, 8,* 2-8.

Sutherland, K. S., Wehby, J. H., & Yoder, P. J. (2002). An examination of the relation between teacher praise and students with emotional/behavioral disorders' opportunities to respond to academic requests. *Journal of Emotional and Behavioral Disorders, 10,* 5-13.

Swallow, R. M. (1978, May). *Cognitive development.* Paper presented at the North American Conference on Visually Handicapped Infants and Preschool Children, Minneapolis.

Swanson, H. L. (1999). *Interventions for students with learning disabilities: A meta-analysis of treatment outcomes.* New York: Guilford.

Swanson, H. L. (2000). Issues facing the field of learning disabilities. *Learning Disability Quarterly, 23,* 37-50.

Swanson, H. L. (2001). Searching for the best model for instructing students with learning disabilities. *Focus on Exceptional Children, 34*(2), 1-14.

Swanson, J., McBurnett, K., Christain, D., & Wigal, T. (1995). Stimulant medication and treatment of children with ADHD. In T. H. Ollendick & R. J. Prinz (Eds.), *Advances in clinical child psychology* (Vol. 17) (pp. 265-322). New York: Plenum.

Swanson, H. L., & Hoskin, M. (2001). Instructing adolescents with learning disabilities: A component and composite analysis. *Learning Disabilities Research and Practice, 16,* 109-119.

Swanson, J. M., McBurnett, K., Wigal, T., Pfiffner, L. J., Lerner, M. A., Williams, L., Christian, D. L., Tamm, L., Willcutt, E., Crowley, K., Clevenger, W., Khouzam, N., Woo, C., Crinella, F. M., & Fisher, T. D. (1993). Effect of stimulant medication on children with attention deficit disorder: A "review of reviews." *Exceptional Children, 60,* 154-161.

Sweeney, W. J., Ehrhardt, A. M., Gardner, R., Jones, L., Greenfield, R., & Fribley, S. (1999). Using guided notes with academically at-risk high school students during a remedial summer social studies class. *Psychology in the Schools, 36,* 305-318.

Swenson, S. (2005). Response to McTernan and Ward. *Mental Retardation, 43,* 220-226.

Swiatek, M. A. (1993). A decade of longitudinal research on academic acceleration through the study of mathematically precocious youth. *Roeper Review, 15,* 120-123.

Switzky, H. N. (1997). Mental retardation and the neglected construct of motivation. *Education and Training in Mental Retardation and Developmental Disabilities, 32,* 194-196.

Switzky, H. N., & Greenspan, S. (2006). *What is mental retardation? Ideas for an evolving disability in the 21st century* (rev. ed.). Washington, DC: American Association on Intellectual and Developmental Disabilities.

Symons, F. J., Butler, M. G., Sanders, Feurer, I. D., & Thompson, T. (1999). Self-injurious behavior in Prader-Willi syndrome: Behavioral forms and body location. *American Journal of Mental Retardation, 104,* 260-269.

Symons, F. J., Clark, R. D., Roberts, J. P., & Bailey, Jr., D. B. (2001). Classroom behavior of elementary school-age boys with fragile X syndrome. *Journal of Special Education, 34,* 194-202.

Szabo, J. L. (2000). Maddie's story: Inclusion through physical and occupational therapy. *Teaching Exceptional Children, 33*(2), 26-32.

Szymanski, L., & King, B. H. (1999). Practice parameters for the assessment and treatment of children, adolescents, and adults with mental retardation and co-morbid mental disorders. *Journal of the American Academy of Children and Adolescent Psychiatry, 38,*(12 Suppl.), 5S-31S.

Szymanski, L. S. (2000). Happiness as a treatment goal. *American Journal of Mental Retardation, 105,* 352-362.

Talbott, E., & Thiede, K. (1999). Pathways to antisocial behavior among adolescent girls. *Journal of Emotional and Behavioral Disorders, 7,* 31-39.

Tam, K. Y. B., & Heng M. A. (2005). A case involving culturally and linguistically diverse parents in prereferral intervention. *Intervention in School and Clinic, 40,* 222-230.

Tam, K. Y. B., Heward, W. L., & Heng, M. A. (2006). Effects of vocabulary instruction, error correction, and fluency-building on oral reading rate and comprehension of English-language learners who are struggling readers. *The Journal of Special Education, 40,* 79-93.

Tardáguila-Harth & Correa, V. I. (2007). *Supporting the language development of migrant children with language delays using story books.* Poster presented at the 85th Annual Convention of the Council for Exceptional Children. Louisville, KY.

Tarver, S. (1999). *Direct instruction. Current Practice Alerts, Issue 2.* Reston, VA: Division for Learning Disabilities and Division for Research, Council for Exceptional Children. Available online: www.teachingld.org/ld%5Fresources/alerts/

TASH. (2000a, March). *TASH resolution on deinstitutionalization.* Washington, DC: Author. [Retrieved October 8, 2007 www.tash.org/IRR/resolutions/res02deinstitut.htm]

TASH. (2000b, March). *TASH resolution on the people for whom TASH advocates.* [Retrieved September 9, 2007 from http://www.tash.org/IRR/resolutions/res02advocate.htm]

Tate, T. L., Thompson, R. H., & McKerchar, P. M. (2005). Training teachers in an infant classroom to use embedded teaching strategies. *Education and Treatment of Children, 28,* 206-221.

Taunt, H. M., & Hastings, R. P. (2002). Positive impact of children with disabilities on their families: A preliminary study. *Education and Training in Mental Retardation and Developmental Disabilities, 37,* 410-420.

Taylor, N. C., Wall, S. M., Liebow, H., Sabatino, C. A., Timberlake, E. M., & Farber, M. Z. (2005). Mother and soldier: Raising a child with a disability in a low-income military family. *Exceptional Children, 72,* 83-99.

Taylor, P. B., Gunter, P. L., & Slate, J. R. (2001). Teachers' perceptions of inappropriate student behaviors as a function of teachers' and students' gender and ethnic background. *Behavioral Disorders, 26,* 146-151.

Taylor, S. J. (2005). Caught in the continuum: A critical analysis of the principle of the least restrictive environment. *Research and Practice for Persons with Severe Disabilities, 30,* 218-230.

Taylor, S. J., & Blatt, S. D. (Eds.). (1999). *In search of the promised land: The collected papers of Burton Blatt.* Washington, DC: American Association on Mental Retardation.

Taylor, S. J., Bogdan, R., & Lutfiyya, Z. M. (1995). *The variety of community experience: Qualitative studies of family and community life.* Baltimore: Brookes.

Teglasi, H. (2006). Temperament. In G. G. Bear & K. M. Minke (Eds.), *Children's needs III: Development, prevention, and intervention* (pp. 391-403). Bethesda, MD: National Association of School Psychologists.

Tellefson, M. (2000). Suitcase mobility: A case study packed with opportunities for learning. *RE:view, 32,* 25-33.

Terman, L. (Ed.). (1925). *Genetic studies of genius* (Vol. 1). Stanford, CA: Stanford University Press.

Terzi, L. (2005a). Beyond the dilemma of difference: The capability approach to disability and special education needs. *Journal of Philosophy of Education, 39,* 443-459.

Terzi, L. (2005b). A capability perspective on impairment, disability and special needs: Towards social justice in education. *Theory and Research in Education, 3,* 197-223.

Test, D. W., Aspel, N., & Everson, J. M. (2006). *Transition methods for youth with disabilities.* Upper Saddle River, NJ: Merrill/Prentice Hall.

Test, D. W., Browder, D. M., Karvonen, M., Wood, W. M., & Algozzine, B. (2002). Writing lesson plans for promoting self-determination. *Teaching Exceptional Children, 35*(1), 8-14.

Test, D. W., Cooke, N. L., Weiss, A. B., Heward, W. L., & Heron, T. E. (1986). A home-school communication system for special education. *Pointer, 30,* 4-7.

Test, D. W., Fowler, C. H., Brewer, W. M., & Wood, W. (2005). A content and methodological review of self-advocacy intervention studies. *Exceptional Children, 72,* 101-125.

Test, D. W., Karvonen, M., Wood, W. M., Browder, D. M., & Algozzine, B. (2000). Choosing a self-determination curriculum. *Teaching Exceptional Children, 33*(2), 48-54.

Test, D. W., Mason, C., Hughes, C., Neale, M., Konrad, M., & Wood, W. M. (in press). Student involvement in Individualized Education Program meetings: A review of the literature. *Exceptional Children.*

Test, D. W., Spooner, F. H., Keul, P. K., & Grossi, T. A. (1990). Teaching adolescents with severe disabilities to use the public telephone. *Behavior Modification, 14,* 157-171.

Therrien, W. J. (2004). Fluency and comprehension gains as a result of repeated reading: A meta-analysis. *Remedial and Special Education, 25,* 252-261.

Thiemann, K. S., & Goldstein, H. (2001). Social stories, written text cures, and video feedback: Effects on social communication of children with autism. *Journal of Applied Behavior Analysis, 34,* 425-446.

Thies, K. M., & McAllister, J. W. (2001). The health and education leadership project: A school initiative for children and adolescents with chronic health conditions. *The Journal of School Health, 71,* 167-172.

Thoma, C. A., & Evans Getzel, E. (2005). "Self-determination is what it's all about": What post-secondary students with disabilities tell us are important considerations for success. *Education and Training in Developmental Disabilities, 40,* 234-242.

Thomas, C., Correa, V., & Morsink, C. (2001). *Interactive teaming: Enhancing programs for students with special needs* (3rd ed.). Upper Saddle River, NJ: Merrill/Prentice Hall.

Thomas, L. A. (2001). Living with Prader-Willi: The "starving syndrome." *Exceptional Parent, 31*(11), 66-72.

Thomas, S. B., & Hawke, C. (1999). Health care standards for children with disabilities: Emerging standards and implications. *Journal of Special Education, 32,* 226-237.

Thompson, B., Diamond, K. E., McWilliam, R., Snyder, P., & Snyder, S. W. (2005). Evaluating the quality of evidence from correlational research for evidence-based practice. *Exceptional Children, 71,* 181-194.

Thompson, J. R., Bryant, B., Campbell, E. M., Craig, E. M., Hughes, C., Rothholz, D., Schalock, R. L., Silverman, W., Tasse, M. J., & Wehmeyer, M. L. (2004). *Supports Intensity Scale: User's manual.* Washington, DC: American Association on Mental Retardation.

Thompson, T., Robinson, J., Dietrich, M., Farris, M., & Sinclair, V. (1996a). Architectural features and perceptions of community residences for people with mental retardation. *American Journal on Mental Retardation, 101,* 292-314.

Thompson, T., Robinson, J., Dietrich, M., Farris, M., & Sinclair, V. (1996b). Interdependence of architectural features and program variables in community residences for people with mental retardation. *American Journal on Mental Retardation, 101,* 315-327.

Thorndike, R. L., Hagen, E. P., & Sattler, J. M. (1986). *Technical manual, the Stanford-Binet Intelligence Scale: Fourth edition.* Chicago: Riverside.

Thornton, C., & Krajewski, J. (1993). Death education for teachers: A refocused concern relative to medically fragile children. *Intervention in School and Clinic, 29,* 31-35.

Thurston, L. P., & Dasta, K. (1990). An analysis of in-home parent tutoring in children's academic behavior at home and in school and on parents' tutoring behaviors. *Remedial and Special Education, 11*(4), 41-52.

Timothy W. v. Rochester, N. H., School District, 875 F.2d 954 (1st Cir. 1989), *cert. Denied* 493 U.S. 983, 110 S.Ct. 519 (1989).

Tinbergen, N., & Tinbergen, E. A. (1983). *"Autistic" children: New hope for a cure.* London: Allen & Unwin.

Tincani, M., Ernsbarger, S., Harrison, T. J., & Heward, W. L. (2005). Effects of two instructional paces on pre-K students' participation rate, accuracy, and off-task behavior in the *Language for Learning* program. *Journal of Direct Instruction, 5,* 97-109.

Todd, A. W., Horner, R. H., & Sugai, G. (1999). Self-monitoring and self-recruited praise: Effects on problem behavior, academic engagement, and work completion in a typical classroom. *Journal of Positive Behavior Interventions, 1,* 66-76.

Todis, B., Severson, H. H., & Walker, H. M. (1990). The critical events scale: Behavioral profiles of students with externalizing and internalizing behavior disorders. *Behavioral Disorders, 15,* 75-86.

Tolan, P. H., & Thomas, P. (1995). The implications of age of onset for delinquency risk II: Longitudinal data. *Journal of Abnormal Child Psychology, 23,* 157-181.

Tolla, J. (2000). Follow that bear! Encouraging mobility in a young child with visual impairment and multiple disabilities. *Teaching Exceptional Children, 32*(5), 72-77.

Tomlinson, C. A., Kaplan, S. N., Renzulli, J. S., Purcell, J., Leppien, J., & Burns, D. (2002). *The parallel curriculum: A design to develop high potential and challenge high-ability learners.* Thousand Oaks, CA: Corwin.

Tomporowski, P. D., & Hagler, L. D. (1992). Sustained attention in mentally retarded individuals. In N. W. Bray (Ed.), *International review of research on mental retardation* (Vol. 18, pp. 111-136). New York: Academic Press.

Tonemah, S. A. (1987). Assessing American Indian gifted and talented student's abilities. *Journal for the Education of the Gifted, 10,* 181-194.

Torgeson, J. K. (2001). Individual differences in response to early intervention in reading: The lingering problem of treatment resisters. *Learning Disabilities Research & Practice, 15,* 55-644.

Torgesen, J. K., & Bryant, B. (1994). *Test of Phonological Awareness.* Austin, TX: PRO-ED.

Torgesen, J. K., & Wagner, R. K. (1998). Alternative diagnostic approaches for specific developmental reading disabilities. *Learning Disabilities Research and Practice, 13,* 220-232.

Torgesen, J. K., Wagner, R. K., & Rashotte, C. A. (1997). Prevention and remediation of severe reading disabilities: Keeping the end in mind. *Scientific Studies of Reading, 1,* 217-234.

Tourette Syndrome Association. (2007). *What is Tourette syndrome?* Bayside, NY: Author. http://www.tsa-usa.org.

Townsend, B. L. (2000). The disproportionate discipline of African American learners: Reducing school suspensions and expulsions. *Exceptional Children, 66,* 381-391.

Trach, J. S. (2008). Natural supports in the workplace and beyond. In F. R. Rusch (Ed.), *Beyond high school: Preparing adolescents for tomorrow's challenges* (2nd ed.) (pp. 250- 265). Upper Saddle River, NJ: Merrill/Prentice Hall.

Trammel, D. L., Schloss, P. J., & Alper, S. (1994). Using self-recording, evaluation, and graphing to increase completion of homework assignments. *Journal of Learning Disabilities, 27,* 75-81.

Tran, L. P., & Grunfast, K. M. (1999). Hereditary hearing loss. *Volta Review, 99*(5), 63-69.

Trask-Tyler, S. A., Grossi, T. A., & Heward, W. L. (1994). Teaching young adults with developmental disabilities and visual impairments to use tape-recorded recipes: Acquisition, generalization, and maintenance of cooking skills. *Journal of Behavioral Education, 4,* 283-311.

Traxler, C. B. (2000). The Stanford Achievement Test, 9th edition: National norming and performance standards for deaf and hard-of-hearing students. *Journal of Deaf Studies and Deaf Education, 5,* 337-348.

Treanor, R. B. (1993). *We overcame: The story of civil rights for disabled people.* Falls Church, VA: Regal Direct.

Treffert, D. A. (1988). The idiot savant: A review of the syndrome. *American Journal of Psychiatry, 145,* 563-572.

Treffert, D. A. (1989). *Extraordinary people: Understanding "idiot savants."* New York: Harper & Row.

Trembley, R. E. (2000). The development of aggressive behavior during childhood: What have we learned in the past century? *International Journal of Behavioral Development, 24,* 129-141.

Trent, J. W. (1994). *Inventing the feeble-minded: A history of mental retardation in the United States.* Berkeley: University of California Press.

Trezek, B. J., & Malmgren, K. (2005). The efficacy of utilizing a phonics treatment package with middle school deaf and hard of hearing students. *Journal of Deaf Studies and Deaf Education, 10,* 256-271.

Trezek, B. J., & Wang, Y. (2006). Implications of utilizing a phonics-based reading curriculum with children who are deaf or hard of hearing. *Journal of Deaf Studies and Deaf Education, 11,* 202-213.

Trezek, B. J., Wang, Y., Woods, D. G., Gampp, T. L., & Paul, P. V. (2007). Using visual phonics to supplement beginning reading instruction for students who are deaf or hard of hearing. *Journal of Deaf Studies and Deaf Education, 12,* 373-384.

Troia, G. A. (2004). Phonological awareness acquisition and intervention. *Current Practice Alerts, Issue 9.* Reston, VA: Division for Learning Disabilities and Division for Research, Council for Exceptional Children. Available online: www.teachingld.org/1d%5Fresources/alerts/

Trout, A., Nordness, P. D., Pierce, C. D., & Epstein, M. H. (2003). Research on the academic status of children and youth with emotional and behavioral disorders: A review of the literature from 1961-2000. *Journal of Emotional and Behavioral Disorders, 11,* 198-210.

Trupin, L., Sebesta, D., Yelin, E., & LaPlante, M. (1997). *Trends in labor force participation among persons with disabilities, 1983-1994.* San Francisco: University of California, Disabilities Statistics Rehabilitation Research and Training Center, Institute for Health and Aging.

Tryon, P. A., Mayes, S. D., Rhodes, R. L., & Waldo, M. (2006). Can Asperger's disorder be differentiated from autism using DSM-IV criteria? *Focus on Autism and Other Developmental Disabilities, 21,* 2-6.

Tuba Tuncer, A., & Altunay, B. (2006). The effect of a summarization-based cumulative retelling strategy on listening comprehension of college students with visual impairments. *Journal of Visual Impairment and Blindness, 100,* 353-365.

Tucker, B. (1993). Deafness: 1993-2013—The dilemma. *The Volta Review, 95,* 105-108.

Turnbull, A., Turnbull, H., Erwin, E., & Soodak, L. (2006). *Families, professionals, and exceptionality: Positive outcomes through partnership and trust* (5th ed.). Upper Saddle River, NJ: Merrill/Prentice Hall.

Turnbull, A. P., & Ruef, M. (1996). Family perspectives on problem behavior. *Mental Retardation, 34,* 280-293.

Turnbull, A. P., & Turnbull, H. R. (2006). *Families and exceptionality* (5th ed.). Upper Saddle River, NJ: Merrill/Prentice Hall.

Turnbull, H., Turnbull, P., Wehmeyer, M., & Park, J. (2003). A quality of life framework for special education outcomes. *Remedial and Special Education, 24,* 67-74.

Turnbull, H. R., & Cilley, M. (1999). *Explanations and implications of the 1997 amendments to IDEA.* Upper Saddle River, NJ: Merrill/Prentice Hall.

Turnbull, H. R., Stowe, M. J., & Huerta, N. E. (2007). *Free appropriate public education: The law and children with disabilities* (7th ed.). Denver: Love.

Turnbull, H. R., Turnbull, A., Warren, S., Eidelman, S., & Marchand, P. (2002). Shakespeare redux, or *Romeo and Juliet* revisited: Embedding a terminology and name change in a new agenda for the field of mental retardation. *Mental Retardation, 40,* 65-70.

Turner-Henson, A., Holaday, B., Corser, N., Ogletree, G., & Swan, J. H. (1994). The experiences of discrimination: Challenges for chronically ill children. *Pediatric Nursing, 20,* 571-577.

Tyler, J. S., & Mira, M. P. (1993). Educational modifications for students with head injuries. *Teaching Exceptional Children, 25*(3), 24-27.

Tyler, J. S., & Mira, M. P. (1999). *Traumatic brain injury in children and adolescents: A sourcebook for teachers and other school personnel* (2nd ed.). Austin, TX: Pro-Ed.

Tymchuk, A. J., Lakin, K. C., & Luckasson, R. (2001). *The forgotten generation: The status and challenges of adults with mild cognitive limitations.* Baltimore: Brookes.

Udvari-Solner, A., Causton-Theoharis, J., & York-Barr, J. (2004). Developing adaptations to promote participation in inclusive environments. In F. P. Orelove, D. Sobsey, & R. K. Silberman (Eds.), *Education children with multiple disabilities: A collaborative approach* (4th ed.) (pp. 151-192) Baltimore: Brookes.

Uffen, E. (1997). Speech and language disorders: Nature or nurture? *ASHA Leader, 2*(14), 8.

Ulrey, P. (1994). When you meet a guide dog. *RE:view, 26,* 143-144.

Ulrich, M. E., & Bauer, A. M. (2003). Levels of awareness: A closer look at communication between parents and professionals. *Teaching Exceptional Children, 35*(6), 20-23.

Umbel, V. M., and Oller, D. K. (1994). Developmental changes in receptive vocabulary in Hispanic bilingual school children. *Language Learning, 44,* 221-242.

Umbreit, J., & Blair, K. C. (1996). The effects of preference, choice, and attention on problem behavior at school. *Education and Training in Mental Retardation and Developmental Disabilities, 31,* 151-161.

Umbreit, J., Ferro, J., Liaupsin, C., & Lane, K. (2007). *Functional behavioral assessment and function-based intervention: An effective, practical approach.* Upper Saddle River, NJ: Prentice-Hall.

Unger, D., & Simmons, T. J. (2005). Transition to employment. In R. W. Flexer, T. J. Simmons, P. Luft, & R. M. Baer (Eds.), *Transition planning for secondary students with disabilities* (2nd ed.), (pp. 360-387). Upper Saddle River, NJ: Merrill/Prentice Hall.

U. S. Centers for Disease Control and Prevention. (2007). *Autism Information Center: Frequently Asked Questions-Prevalence.* Retrieved 7/15/07 from CDCP website, www.cdc.gov.

U.S. Congress. (1987). *Promotion opportunities for blind and handicapped workers in sheltered workshops under the Javitz-Wagner-O'Day Act.* Washington, DC: U.S. Government Printing Office.

U.S. Department of Education. (1993). *National excellence: A case for developing America's youth.* Washington, DC: U.S. Government Printing Office.

U.S. Department of Education. (1998). *The schools and staffing survey (SASS) and teacher followup survey (TFS) CD-ROM: Electronic codebook and public-use data for three cycles of ASSASS and TFS.* Washington, DC: National Center for Educational Statistics. (NCES 98-312).

U.S. Department of Education. (1998). *Twenty-first annual report to Congress on the implementation of the Individuals with Disabilities Education Act.* Washington, DC: Author.

U.S. Department of Education. (1999). Assistance to states for the education of children with disabilities and the early intervention program for infants and toddlers with disabilities: Final regulations. *Federal Register, 64*(48), CFR Parts 300 and 303.

U.S. Department of Education. (2000a). *Guide to the individualized education program.* Washington, DC: Author.

U.S. Department of Education. (2000b). *Twenty-second annual report to Congress on the implementation of the Individuals with Disabilities Education Act.* Washington, DC: Author.

U.S. Department of Education. (2002). *No Child Left Behind: A desktop reference.* Washington, DC: Author.

U.S. Department of Education. (2002). *Twenty-fourth annual report to Congress on the implementation of the Individuals with Disabilities Education Act.* Washington, DC: Author.

U.S. Department of Education. (2003). *Twenty-fifth annual report to Congress on the implementation of the Individuals with Disabilities Education Act.* Washington, DC: Author.

U.S. Department of Education. (2006a). *Identifying and treating attention deficit hyperactivity disorder: A resource for school and home.* Washington, DC, Author.

U.S. Department of Education. (2006b). *26th annual report to Congress on the implementation of the Individuals with Disabilities Education Act, 2004.* Washington, DC: Author.

U.S. Department of Education. (2007). *Individuals with Disabilities Education Act (IDEA) data* (Table 1-3). Washington, DC: Author. [Available online: https://www.ideadata.org/PartBReport.asp]

U.S. Department of Education, National Center for Education Statistics (NCES). (2000). *Entry and Persistence of Women and Minorities in College Science and Engineering Education.* Washington, DC: Office of Educational Research and Improvement.

U.S. Department of Education, National Center for Education Statistics. (2001). *Teacher preparation and professional development: 2000* (NCES 2001-088, by B. Parsad, L. Lewis & E. Farris). Washington, DC: Author. (ERIC Document Reproduction Service No. ED 458 204)

U.S. Department of Education, Office of Civil Rights. (1990). *Elementary and secondary school civil rights compliance report.* Washington, DC: Author.

U.S. Department of Labor. (1979). *Study of handicapped clients in sheltered workshops* (Vol. 2). Washington, DC: Author.

U.S. Drug Enforcement Agency. (2002). *Yearly aggregate production quotas (1990-1999).* Washington, DC: Office of Public Affairs, U.S. Drug Enforcement Agency.

U.S. Office of Education. (1977a). Implementation of Part B of the Education of the Handicapped Act. *Federal Register, 42,* 42474-42518.

U.S. Office of Education. (1977b). Procedures for evaluating specific learning disabilities. *Federal Register, 42,* 65082-65085.

U.S. Office of Special Education. (2004). *Individuals with Disabilities Education Act (IDEA) data.* Washington, DC: Author. http://www.ideadata.org/.

U.S. Office of Special Education Programs. (2004). Individuals with Disabilities Education Act (IDEA) data. Washington, DC: Author. http://www.ideadata.org/PartBdata.asp.

U.S. Office of Special Education Programs. (2007a). *Individuals with Disabilities Education Act (IDEA) data.* Washington, DC: Author. Available at http://www.ideadata.org/PartBdata.asp

U.S. Office of Special Education Programs. (2007b). *Individuals with Disabilities Education Act* (IDEA) data (Table 2-2c). Washington, DC: Author. Available at http://www.ideadata.org/PartBdata.asp

U.S. Office of the Census. (2004, June). *Educational attainment in the U.S.: 2003.* Washington, DC: U.S. Government Printing Office.

U.S. Public Health Service. (1990). *Healthy people 2000.* Washington, DC: U.S. Government Printing Office.

Utley, B. L., Roman, C., & Nelson, G. L. (1998). Functional vision. In S. Z. Sacks & R. K. Silberman (Eds.), *Educating students who have visual impairments with other disabilities* (pp. 371-412). Baltimore: Brookes.

Utley, C. A., & Obiakor, F. E. (2001). Learning problems or learning disabilities of multicultural learners: Contemporary perspectives. In C. Utley & F. Obiakor (Eds.), *Special education, multicultural education, and school reform: Components of quality education for learners with mild disabilities* (pp. 90-117). Springfield, IL: Thomas.

Valdes, K. A., Williamson, C. L., & Wagner, M. (1990). *The national longitudinal transition study of special education students.* Vol. 3: *Youth categorized as emotionally disturbed.* Palo Alto, CA: SRI International.

Valli, C., Lucas, C., & Mulrooney, K. (2005). *The linguistics of American Sign Language: An introduction* (4th ed.). Washington, DC: Gallaudet University Press.

Van Acker, R., Grant, S. H., & Henry, D. (1996). Teacher and student behavior as a function of risk for aggression. *Education and Treatment of Children, 19,* 316-334.

Vance, J., Fernandez, G., & Biber, M. (1998). Educational progress in a population of youth with aggression and emotional disturbance: The role of risk and protective factors. *Journal of Emotional and Behavioral Disorders, 6,* 214-221.

Van Cleve, J. V. (Ed.). (2007). *The Deaf history reader.* Washington, DC: Gallaudet Press.

Vandercook, T. (1991). Leisure instruction outcomes: Criterion performance, positive interactions, and acceptance by typical high school peers. *Journal of Special Education, 25,* 320-339.

Vandercook, T., York, J., & Forest, M. (1989). The McGill Action Planning System (MAPS): A strategy for building the vision. *Journal of The Association for Persons with Severe Handicaps, 14,* 205-215.

Vanderheiden, G. C., & Lloyd, L. L. (1986). Non-speech modes and systems. In S. W. Blackstone (Ed.), *Augmentative communication* (pp. 49-161). Rockville, MD: American Speech-Language-Hearing Association.

van der Lee, J. H., Mokkink, L. B., Grootenhuis, M. A., Heymans, H. S., & Offringa, M. (2007). Definitions and measurement of chronic health conditions in childhood: A systematic review. *Journal of the American Medical Association, 297,* 2741-2751.

Van Dycke, J. L., Martin, J. E., & Lovett, D. L. (2006). Why is this cake on fire? Inviting student into the IEP process. *Teaching Exceptional Children, 38*(3), 42-47.

Van Gurp, S. (2001). Self-concept of deaf secondary school students in different educational settings. *Journal of Deaf Studies and Deaf Education, 6,* 54-69.

Van Houten, R. (1984). Setting up performance feedback systems in the classroom. In

W. L. Heward, T. E. Heron, D. S. Hill, & J. Trap-Porter (Eds.), *Focus on behavior analysis in education* (pp. 114–125). Upper Saddle River, NJ: Merrill/Prentice Hall.

van Karnebeek, C. D. M., Scheper, F. Y., Abeling, N. G., Alders, M. K., Barth, P. G., Hoovers, J. M. N., Koevoets, C., Wanders, R. J. A., & Hennekam, R. C. M. (2005). Etiology of mental retardation in children referred to a tertiary care center: A prospective study. *American Journal on Mental Retardation, 110,* 253–267.

Van Keulen, J. E., Weddington, G. T., & DeBose, C. E. (1998). *Speech, language, learning, and the African American child.* Boston: Allyn & Bacon.

Van Norman, R. K., & Wood, C. L. (2007). Innovations in peer tutoring: Introduction to the special issue. *Intervention in School and Clinic, 43*(2), 69–70.

Van Riper, C., & Erickson, R. L. (1996). *Speech correction: An introduction to speech pathology and audiology* (9th ed.). Boston: Allyn & Bacon.

Van Tassel-Baska, J. (2004). *The acceleration of gifted students' programs and curricula.* Waco, TX: Prufrock Press.

Van Tassel-Baska, J., Johnson, D., & Avery, L. D. (2002). Using performance tasks in the identification of economically disadvantaged and minority gifted learners: Findings from Project STAR. *Gifted Child Quarterly, 46,* 110–123.

Van Tassel-Baska, J., Patton, J. M., & Prillaman, D. (1991). *Gifted youth at risk: A report of a national study.* Reston, VA: Council for Exceptional Children.

Vaughn, B. J., Clarke, S., & Dunlap, G. (1997). Assessment-based intervention for severe behavior problems in a natural family context. *Journal of Applied Behavior Analysis, 30,* 713–716.

Vaughn, S., Elbaum, B. E., & Schumm, J. S. (1996). The effects of inclusion on the social functioning of students with learning disabilities. *Journal of Learning Disabilities, 29,* 598–608.

Vaughn, S., & Fuchs, L. S. (Guest Eds.) (2003a). Redefining learning disabilities as inadequate response to instruction (Special Issue). *Learning Disabilities Research and Practice, 18,* 137–211.

Vaughn, S., & Fuchs, L. S. (2003b). Redefining learning disabilities as inadequate response to instruction: The promise and potential problems. *Learning Disabilities Research & Practice, 18,* 137–146.

Vaughn, S., Gersten, R. L., & Chard, D. J. (2000). The underlying message in LD intervention research: Findings from research syntheses. *Exceptional Children, 67,* 99–114.

Vaughn, S., Klingner, J., & Hughes, M. (2000). Sustainability of research-based practices. *Exceptional Children, 66,* 163–171.

Vaughn, S., Klingner, J. K., & Bryant, D. P. (2001). Collaborative strategic reading as a means to enhance peer- mediated instruction for reading comprehension and content- area learning. *Remedial and Special Education, 22,* 66–74.

Vaughn, S., Linan-Thompson, S., & Hickman, P. (2003). Response to instruction as a means of identifying students with reading/learning disabilities. *Exceptional Children, 69,* 391–409.

Vaughn, S., McIntosh, R., Schumm, J. S., Haager, D., & Callwood, D. (1993). Social status, peer acceptance, and reciprocal friendships revisited. *Learning Disabilities Research and Practice, 8,* 82–88.

Vaughn, S., & Roberts, G. (2007). Secondary interventions in reading: Providing additional instruction for students at risk. *Teaching Exceptional Children, 39*(5), 40–46.

Vaughn, S., Schumm, J. S., & Arguelles, M. E. (1997). The ABCDEs of co-teaching. *Teaching Exceptional Children, 30*(2), 42–45.

Vaughn, S., Schumm, J. S., & Brick, J. B. (1998). Using a rating scale to design and evaluate inclusion programs. *Teaching Exceptional Children, 30*(4), 41–45.

Venn, J. (2004). *Assessment of students with special needs* (3rd ed.). Upper Saddle River, NJ: Merrill/Prentice Hall.

Venn, J. J. (2007). *Assessing students with special needs* (4th ed.). Upper Saddle River, NJ: Merrill/Prentice Hall.

Vermeulen, A. M., van Bon, W., Schreuder, R., Knoors, H., & Snik, A. (2007). Reading comprehension of deaf children with cochlear implants. *The Journal of Deaf Studies and Deaf Education, 12,* 283–302.

Vig, S., & Jedrysek, E. (1996). Application of the 1992 AAMR definition: Issues for preschool children. *Mental Retardation, 34,* 244–246.

Villa, R. A., Thousand, J. S., & Nevin, A. I. (2004). *A guide to co-teaching: Practical tips for facilitating student learning.* Arlington, VA: Council for Exceptional Children.

Volkmar, F., & Pauls, D. (2003). Autism. *Lancet, 362,* 1133–1144.

Voltz, D. L. (1994). Developing collaborative parent-teacher relationships with culturally diverse parents. *Intervention in School and Clinic, 29*(5), 288–291.

von Hahn, L. (2004). Bipolar disorder: An overview. *Exceptional Parent, 34*(5), 56, 58–61.

von Hahn, L. (2004). Traumatic brain injury: Medical considerations and educational implications. *Exceptional Parent, 33*(11), 40–42.

Voyager Expanded Learning. (2008). *Voyager passport.* Dallas: Author.

Waddy-Smith, B., & Wilson, V. (2003). See that sound! Visual phonics for deaf children. *Odyssey, 5,* 14–17.

Wagner, B. W. (2000). Presidential address 2000—Changing visions into reality. *Mental Retardation, 38,* 436–443.

Wagner, L., & Lane, L., (1998). Lane County Department of Youth Services: 1997 report: Juvenile justice services. Eugene, OR Department of Youth Services.

Wagner, M., & Blackorby, J. (2002). *Disability profiles of elementary and middle school students with disabilities.* Menlo Park, CA: SRI International.

Wagner, M., Blackorby, J., Cameto, R., & Newman, L. (1994). *What makes a difference? Influences on postschool outcomes of youth with disabilities.* Menlo Park, CA: SRI International.

Wagner, M., & Cameto, R. (2004). *The characteristics, experiences, and outcomes of youth with emotional disturbances.* Minneapolis: National Center on Secondary Education and Transition. [Available online at: www.ncset.org]

Wagner, M., Kutash, K., Duchnowski, A. J., Epstein, M. H., & Sumi, C. (2005). The children and youth we serve: A national picture of the characteristics of students with emotional disturbances receiving special education. *Journal of Emotional and Behavioral Disorders, 11,* 194–197.

Wagner, M., Marder, C., Blackorby, J., & Cardoso, D. (2002). *The children we serve: The demographic characteristics of elementary school students with disabilities households.* Menlo Park, CA: SRI International.

Wagner, M., Newman, L., Cameto, R., Garza, N., & Levine, P. (2005). *After high school: A first look at the post-school experiences of youth with disabilities. A report from the National Longitudinal Transition Study-2 (NLTS-2).* Menlo Park, CA: SRI International. Available at www.nlts2.org/reports/2005_04/nlts2_report_2005_04_complete.pdf

Wagner, M., Newman, L., Cameto, R., Levine, P., & Marder, C. (2007). Perceptions and expectations of youth with disabilities. A special topic report of findings from the National Longitudinal Transition Study-2 (NLTS2) (NCSER 2007-3006). Menlo Park, CA: SRI International.

Wagner, R. K., Torgeson, J. K., & Rahsotte, C. A. (1999). *Comprehensive Test of Phonological Processing.* Austin, TX: PRO-ED.

Wagner-Lampl, A., & Oliver, G. W. (1994). Folklore of blindness. *Journal of Visual Impairment and Blindness, 88,* 267–276.

Wahl, H., Kämmerer, A., Holz, F., Miller, D., Becker, S., Kaspar, R., & Himmelsbach, I. (2006). Psychosocial intervention for age-related macular degeneration: A pilot project. *Journal of Visual Impairment and Blindness, 101,* 533–544.

Wahler, R. G., & Dumas, J. E. (1986). "A chip off the old block": Some interpersonal characteristics of coercive children across generations. In P. S. Strain, M. J. Guralnick, & H. M. Walker (Eds.), *Children's social behavior: Development, assessment, and modification* (pp. 49–91). Orlando, FL: Academic Press.

Wainapel, S. F. (1989). Attitudes of visually impaired persons toward cane use. *Journal of Visual Impairment and Blindness, 83,* 446–448.

Waldman, H. B., & Perlman, S. P. (2006). Advocating for children with special needs, or the wheel that squeaks gets the oil. *Exceptional Parent, 36*(5), 52, 54–55.

Walker, B., Shippen, M. E., Alberto, P., Houchins, D. E., & Cihak, D. F. (2005). Using the *Expressive Writing* program to improve the writing skills of high school students with learning disabilities. *Learning Disabilities Research & Practice, 20,* 175–183.

Walker, D. K., & Jacobs, F. H. (1985). Where there is a way, there is not always a will:

Technology, public policy, and the school integration of children who are technology-assisted. *Children's Health Care, 20,* 68-74.

Walker, H. M. (1997). *The acting out child: Coping with classroom disruption* (2nd ed.). Longmont, CO: Sopris West.

Walker, H. M., Colvin, G., & Ramsey, E. (1995). *Antisocial behavior in schools: Strategies and best practices.* Pacific Grove, CA: Brooks/Cole.

Walker, H. M., McConnell, S., Holmes, D., Todis, B., Walker, J., & Golden, N. (1988). *The ACCEPTS program: A curriculum for children's effective peer and teacher skills.* Austin, TX: PRO-ED.

Walker, H. M., Ramsey, E., & Gresham, R. M. (2005). *Antisocial behavior in school: Evidence-based practices* (2nd ed.). Belmont, CA: Wadsworth/Thomson Learning.

Walker, H. M., & Severson, H. H. (1992). *Systematic screening for behavior disorders: User's guide and administration manual* (2nd ed.). Longmont, CO: Sopris West.

Walker, H. M., & Sprague, J. R. (1999). The path to school failure, delinquency, and violence: Causal factors and some potential solutions *Intervention in School and Clinic, 35,* 67-73.

Walker, H. M., Sprague, J. R., Close, D. W., & Starlin, C. M. (1999-2000). What is right with behavior disorders: Seminal achievements and contributions of the behavior disorders field. *Exceptionality, 8,* 13-28.

Walker, H. M., & Sylvester, R. (1998). Reducing student refusal and resistance. *Teaching Exceptional Children, 30*(6), 52-57.

Walker, H. M., Todis, B., Holmes, D., & Horton, G. (1988). *ACCESS: Adolescent curriculum for communication and effective social skills.* Austin, TX: PRO-ED.

Walker, L.A. (1986). *A loss for words: The story of deafness in a family.* New York: Harper & Row.

Wall Emerson, R. S., & Corn, A. L. (2006). Orientation and mobility content for children and youths: A Delphi approach pilot study. *Journal of Visual Impairment and Blindness, 100,* 331-342.

Wallace, G., & Hammill, D. (2002). *Comprehensive Receptive and Expressive Vocabulary Test* (2nd ed.). Austin, TX: PRO-ED.

Walsh, J. M. (2001). Getting the "big picture" of IEP goals and state standards. *Teaching Exceptional Children, 33*(5), 18-26.

Walsh, K. K., & Kastner, T. A. (2006). The Hissom closure in Oklahoma: Errors and interpretations problems in Conroy et al. (2003). *Mental Retardation, 44,* 353-369.

Walther-Thomas, C., Korinek, L., McLaughlin, V., & Williams, B. (2000). *Collaboration for inclusive education.* Boston: Allyn & Bacon.

Warfield, M. E., & Hauser-Cram, P. (1996). Child care needs, arrangements, and satisfaction of mothers of children with developmental disabilities. *Mental Retardation, 34,* 294-302.

Wasik, B. H., Ramey, C. T., Bryant, D. M., & Sparling, J. J. (1990). A longitudinal study of two early intervention strategies: Project CARE. *Child Development, 61,* 1682-1692.

Watson, G. S., & Gross, A. M. (2000). Familial determinants. In M. Hersen & R. T. Ammerman (Eds.), *Advanced abnormal psychology* (2nd ed.) (pp. 81-99) . Hillsdale, NJ: Lawrence Erlbaum.

Webb, N. M., Nemer, K. M., & Zuniga, S. (2002). Short circuits of superconductors? Effects of group composition on high-achieving students' science assessment performance. *American Educational Research Journal, 39*(4), 943-989.

Webber, J., & Plotts, C. A. (2008). *Emotional and behavioral disorders: Theory and practice* (5th ed.). Boston: Allyn and Bacon.

Webber, J., & Scheuermann, B. (1991). Managing behavior problems: Accentuate the positive . . . Eliminate the negative! *Teaching Exceptional Children, 24,* 13-19.

Webber, J., Scheuermann, B., McCall, C., & Coleman, M. (1993). Research on self-monitoring as a behavior management technique in special education classrooms: A descriptive review. *Remedial and Special Education, 14*(2), 38-56.

Webb-Johnson, G. C. (2003). Behaving while black: A hazardous reality for African American learners. *Beyond Behavior, 12*(2), 3-7.

Weber, C., Behl, D., & Summers, M. (1994). Watch them play—watch them learn. *Teaching Exceptional Children, 27*(1), 30-35.

Webster's New World Dictionary of the American Language (2nd ed.). (1986). New York: Simon & Schuster.

Webster, D. D., Clary, G., & Griffith, P. L. (2005). Postsecondary education and career paths. In R. W. Flexer, T. J. Simmons, P. Luft, & R. M. Baer. *Transition planning for secondary students with disabilities* (2nd ed.), (pp. 388-423). Upper Saddle River, NJ: Merrill/Prentice Hall.

Webster, D. D., & Queen, R. M. (2008). Transition to postsecondary education. In R. W. Flexer, T. J. Simmons, P. Luft, & R. M. Baer (Eds.), *Transition planning for secondary students with disabilities* (3rd ed.) (pp. 258-289). Upper Saddle River, NJ: Merrill/Prentice Hall.

Wechsler, D. (2003). *Wechsler intelligence scale for children* (4th ed.). San Antonio, TX: Psychological Corporation.

Wedel, J. W., & Fowler, S. A. (1984). "Read me a story, Mom": A home-tutoring program to teach prereading skills to language-delayed children. *Behavior Modification, 8,* 245-266.

Wedell, K. (2003). What's in a label? *British Journal of Special Education, 30*(2), 107.

Wehby, J. H., Lane, K. L., & Falk, K. B. (2003). Academic instruction for students with emotional and behavioral disorders. *Journal of Emotional and Behavioral Disorders, 11,* 194-197.

Wehby, J. H., Symons, F. J., Canale, J. A., & Go, F. J. (1998). Teaching practices in classrooms for students with emotional and behavioral disorders: Discrepancies between recommendations and observations. *Behavioral Disorders, 24,* 51-56.

Wehby, J. H., Symons, F. J., & Shores, R. E. (1995). A descriptive analysis of aggressive behaviors in classrooms for children with emotional and behavioral disorders. *Behavioral Disorders, 20,* 87-105.

Wehman, P. (Ed.). (2002). *Individual transition plans: The teacher's curriculum guide for helping youth with special needs* (2nd ed.). Austin, TX: PRO-ED.

Wehman, P. (Ed.). (2006). *Life beyond the classroom: Transition strategies for young people with disabilities* (4th ed.). Baltimore: Brookes.

Wehman, P., Brooke, V., & Inge, K. J. (2006). Vocational placements and careers. In P. Wehman (Ed.), *Life beyond the classroom: Transition strategies for young people with disabilities* (4th ed.). Baltimore: Brookes.

Wehman, P., Inge, K. J., Revell, W. G., Jr., & Brooke, V. A. (Eds.). (2006). *Real work for real pay: Inclusive employment for people with disabilities.* Baltimore: Brookes.

Wehman, P., & Kregel, J. (1998). *More than a job: Securing satisfying careers for people with disabilities.* Baltimore: Brookes.

Wehman, P., Kregel, J., Shafer, M., & West, M. (1989). *Emerging trends in supported employment: A preliminary analysis of 27 states.* Richmond: Virginia Commonwealth University, Rehabilitation Research and Training Center.

Wehman, P., & Revell, G. (1997). Transition from school to adulthood: Looking ahead. In P. Wehman (Ed.), *Exceptional individuals in school, community, and work* (pp. 597-648). Austin, TX: PRO-ED,

Wehman, P., Revell, G., & Kregel, J. (1998). Supported employment: A decade of rapid growth and impact. *American Rehabilitation, 24*(1), 31-43.

Wehman, P., & Targett, P. (2002). Supported employment: The challenges of new staff requirements, selection and retention. *Education and Training in Mental Retardation and Developmental Disabilities, 37,* 434-446.

Wehman, P., & Thoma, C. A. (2006). Teaching for transition. In P. Wehman, *Life beyond the classroom: Transition strategies for young people with disabilities* (4th ed.) (pp. 213-214) . Baltimore: Brookes.

Wehmeyer, M. L. (1994). Perceptions of self-determination and psychological empowerment of adolescents with mental retardation. *Education and Training in Mental Retardation, 29,* 9-21.

Wehmeyer, M. L. (2006). Self-determination and individuals with severe disabilities: Reexamining meanings and misinterpretations. *Research and Practice in Severe Disabilities, 30,* 113-120.

Wehmeyer, M. L. (2006). Universal design for learning, access to the general education curriculum, and students with mild mental retardation. *Exceptionality, 14,* 225-235.

Wehmeyer, M. L., Agran, M., Hughes, C., Martin, J., Mithaug, D. E., & Palmer, S. (2007). *Promoting self-determination in students with intellectual and developmental disabilities.* New York: Guilford Press.

Wehmeyer, M. L., Kelchner, K., & Richards, S. (1996). Essential characteristics of self-determined behavior of individuals with mental retardation. *American Journal on Mental Retardation, 100,* 632-642.

Wehmeyer, M. L., Martin, J. E., & Sands, D. J. (1998). Self-determination for children and youth with developmental disabilities. In A. Hilton & R. Ringlaben (Eds.), *Best and promising practices in developmental disabilities* (pp. 191-203). Austin, TX: PRO-ED.

Wehmeyer, M. L., Palmer, S. B., Agran, M., Mithaug, D. E., & Martin, J. E. (2000). Promoting causal agency: The self-determined learning model of instruction. *Exceptional Children, 66,* 273.

Wehmeyer, M. S., & Schalock, R. L. (2001). Self-determination and quality of life: Implications for special education services and supports. *Focus on Exceptional Children, 33*(8), 1-14.

Weiner, J. (1999). *Time, love, and memory: a great biologist and his quest for the origins of behavior.* New York: Knopf.

Weinstein, S. L., & Gaillard, W. D. (2007). Epilepsy. In M. L. Batshaw, L. Pellegrino, L., & Roizen, N. J. (Eds.), *Children with disabilities* (6th ed.). Baltimore: Brookes.

Weintraub, F. J., & Abeson, A. (1974). New education policies for the handicapped: The quiet revolution. *Phi Delta Kappan, 55,* 526-529, 569.

Weiserbs, B. (2000). Social and academic integration using e-mail between children with and without hearing impairments. *Computers in the Schools, 16*(2), 29-44.

Weishaar, M. K., & Boyle, J. R. (1999). Note-taking strategies for students with disabilities. *The Clearinghouse, 72*(6), 392-395.

Weiss, K. W., & Dykes, M. K. (1995). Legal issues in special education: Assistive technology and supportive services. *Physical Disabilities: Education and Related Services, 14*(1), 29-36.

Weisz, J. R., Bromfield, R., Vines, D. L., & Weiss, B. (1985). Cognitive development, helpless behavior, and labeling effects in the lives of the mentally retarded. *Applied Developmental Psychology, 2,* 129-167.

Werker, J. E., & Lalonde, C. E. (1988). Cross language speech perception: Initial capabilities and developmental change. *Developmental Psychology, 24,* 672-683.

Werts, M. G., Caldwell, N. K., & Wolery, M. (2003). Instructive feedback: Effects of a presentation variable. *Journal of Special Education, 37,* 124-133.

Werts, M. G., Wolery, M., Gast, D. L., & Holcomb, A. (1996). Sneak in some extra learning by using instructive feedback. *Teaching Exceptional Children, 28*(3), 70-71.

Wesson, C. (1991). Curriculum-based measurement and two models of follow-up consultation. *Exceptional Children, 77,* 246-256.

Wesson, C., Wilson, R., & Higbee Mandlebaum, L. (1988). Learning games for active student responding. *Teaching Exceptional Children, 20*(2), 12-14.

West, E. A., & Billingsley, F. (2005). Improving the system of least prompts: A comparison of procedural variations. *Education and Training in Developmental Disabilities, 40,* 131-144.

West, E., Leon-Guerrero, R., & Stevens, D. (2007). Establishing codes of acceptable schoolwide behavior in a multicultural society. *Beyond Behavior, 16*(2), 32-38.

West, M., Rayfield, R. G., Clements, C., Unger, D., & Thornton, T. (1994). An illustration of positive behavioral support in the workplace for individuals with severe mental retardation. *Journal of Vocational Rehabilitation, 4*(4), 265-271.

West, M., Revell, G., & Wehman, P. (1998). Conversion from segregated services to supported employment: A continuing challenge to the VR service system. *Education and Training in Mental Retardation and Developmental Disabilities, 33,* 239-247.

Westling, D. L., & Fox, L. (2004). *Teaching students with severe disabilities* (3rd ed.). Upper Saddle River, NJ: Merrill/Prentice Hall.

WETA. (2002). *Reading rockets family guide: Give a big boost to a child you love.* Washington, DC: Author. Available on-line: www.ReadingRockets.org

Wetzel, R., & Knowlton, M. (2006a). Studies of braille reading rates and implications for the unified English braille code. *Journal of Visual Impairment and Blindness, 100,* 275-284.

Whalen, C., & Schreibman, L. (2003). Joint attention training for children with autism using behavior modification procedures. *Journal of Child Psychology and Psychiatry and Allied Disciplines, 44,* 456-468.

Whaley, L. F., & Wong, D. L. (1995). *Nursing care of infants and children* (5th ed.). St. Louis: Mosby.

Wheeler, D. L., Jacobson, J. W., Paglieri, R. A., & Schwartz, A. A. (1993). An experimental assessment of facilitated communication. *Mental Retardation, 31,* 49-60.

Wheeler, J. J., Bates, P., Marshall, K. J., & Miller, S. R. (1988). Teaching appropriate social behaviors to a young man with moderate mental retardation in a supported competitive employment setting. *Education and Training in Mental Retardation, 23,* 105-116.

Whinnery, K. W., & Barnes, S. B. (2002). Mobility training using the MOVE® curriculum: A parent's view. *Teaching Exceptional Children, 34*(3), 44-50.

White, B. L. (1995). *The first three years of life* (rev. ed.). New York: Fireside.

White, D. M. (1991). *Use of guided notes to promote generalized note taking behavior of high school students with learning disabilities.* Unpublished masters thesis, The Ohio State University, Columbus.

White, M. A. (1975). Natural rates of teacher approval and disapproval in the classroom. *Journal of Applied Behavior Analysis, 8,* 367-372.

Whitmore, J. R., & Maker, C. J. (1985). *Intellectual giftedness in disabled persons.* Rockville, MD: Aspen.

Widerstrom, A. H. (2004). *Achieving learning goals through play: Teaching young children with special needs* (2nd ed.). Baltimore: Brookes.

Wiederholt, J. L., & Bryant, B. R. (2001). Gray oral reading tests (4th ed.). Austin, TX: PRO-ED.

Wiener, J. (2004). Do peer relationships foster behavioral adjustment in children with learning disabilities? *Learning Disability Quarterly, 27,* 21-30.

Wiener, J., & Tardif, C. Y. (2004). Social and emotional functioning of children with learning disabilities: Does special education placement make a difference? *Learning Disabilities Research and Practice, 19,* 20-32.

Wiggins, L. D., Baio, J., & Rice, C. (2006). Examination of the time between first evaluation and autism diagnosis in a population based sample. *Journal of Developmental and Behavioral Pediatrics, 27,* S79-S87.

Wiggins, L. D., Bakeman, R., Adamson, L. B., & Robins, D. L. (2007). The utility of the Social Communication Questionnaire in screening for autism in children referred for early intervention. *Focus on Autism and Other Developmental Disabilities, 22,* 33-38.

Wilens, T. E., Biederman, J., & Spencer, T. J. (2002). Attention deficit/hyperactivity disorder across the lifespan. *Annual Review of Medicine, 53,* 113-131.

Wilgosh, L., Scorgie, K., & Fleming, D. (2000). Effective life management in parents of children with disabilities: A survey replication and extension. *Developmental Disabilities Bulletin, 28,* 1-14.

Wilkinson, G. S. (1994). *Wide Range Achievement Test—3.* Austin, TX: PRO-ED.

Wilkinson, G. S., & Robertson, G. J. (2005). *Wide Range Achievement Test—4.* Austin, TX: PRO-ED.

Will, M. C. (1986). Educating children with learning problems: A shared responsibility. *Exceptional Children, 52,* 411-415.

Willard-Holt, C. (1998). Academic and personality characteristics of gifted students with cerebral palsy: A multiple case study. *Exceptional Children, 65,* 37-50.

Willcutt, E. G., Pennington, B. F., & DeFries, J. C. (2000). Etiology of inattention and hyperactivity/impulsivity in a community ample of twins. *Journal of Abnormal Child Psychiatry, 28,* 149-159.

Willey, L. H. (Ed.). (2003). *Asperger syndrome in adolescence: Living with the ups, the downs, and things in between.* Philadelphia: Jessica Kingsley.

Williams, C. B., & Finnegan, M. (2003). From myth to reality: Sound information for teachers about students who are deaf. *Teaching Exceptional Children, 35*(3), 40-45.

Williams, K. E., & Foxx, R. M. (2007). Treating eating problems of children with autism spectrum disorders and developmental disabilities. Austin, TX: PRO-ED.

Williams, K. R., Wishart, J. G., Pitcairn, T. K., & Willis, D. S. (2005). Emotion recognition by children with Down syndrome: Investigation of specific impairments and error patterns. *American Journal on Mental Retardation, 110,* 378-392.

Williams, R. R. (1991). Assistive technology and people with disabilities: Separating fact from fiction. *A. T. Quarterly, 2*(3), 6-7.

Williams, S. C. (2002). How speech-feedback and word-prediction software can help students write. *Teaching Exceptional Children, 34*(3), 72-78.

Williams, V. L., & Cartledge, G. (1997). Passing notes to parents. *Teaching Exceptional Children, 30*(1), 30-34.

Williamson, G. G. (1978). The individualized education program: An interdisciplinary endeavor. In B. Sirvis, J. W. Baken, & G. G. Williamson (Eds.), *Unique aspects of the IEP for the physically handicapped, homebound, and hospitalized.* Reston, VA: Council for Exceptional Children.

Williamson, P., McLesky, J., Hoppey, D., & Rentz, T. (2006). Educating students with mental retardation in general education classrooms. *Exceptional Children, 72,* 347-361.

Willoughby, D. M., & Duffy, S. (1989). *Handbook for itinerant and resource teachers of blind and visually impaired students.* Baltimore: National Federation of the Blind.

Willy, L. H. (2001). *Asperger syndrome in the family: Redefining normal.* Philadelphia: Kingsley.

Wilson, C. L. (1995). Parents and teachers: "Can we talk?" *LD Forum, 20*(2), 31-33.

Wilson, C. L., & Hughes, M. (1994). Involving linguistically diverse parents. *LD Forum, 19*(3), 25-27.

Wilson, P. G., Schepis, M. M., & Mason-Main, M. (1987). In vivo use of picture prompt training to increase independent work at a restaurant. *Journal of The Association for Persons with Severe Handicaps, 12,* 145-150.

Winebrenner, S. (2001). *Teaching gifted kids in the regular classroom* (2nd ed.). Minneapolis: Free Spirit.

Winett, R. A., & Winkler, R. C. (1972). Current behavior modification in the classroom: Be still, be quiet, be docile. *Journal of Applied Behavior Analysis, 5,* 499-504.

Wing, L. (1992). Manifestations of social problems in high-functioning autistic people. In E. Schopler & G. B. Mesibov (Eds.), *High-functioning individuals with autism* (pp. 129-142). New York: Plenum.

Wing, L. (1998). The history of Asperger syndrome. In E. Schopler, G. B. Mesibov, & L. J. Kunce (Eds.), *Asperger syndrome or high-functioning autism?* (pp. 11-28). New York: Plenum.

Winter, S. M. (2007). *Inclusive early childhood education: A collaborative approach.* Upper Saddle River, NJ: Merrill/Prentice Hall.

Winter-Messiers, M. A. (in press). Toilet brushes and tarantulas: Understanding the origin and development of special interest areas in children and youth with Asperger's syndrome. *Journal of Remedial and Special Education.*

Winter-Messiers, M. A., Herr, C. M., Wood, C. E., Brooks, A. P., Gates, M. A. M., Houston, T. L., & Tingstad, K. I. (2007). How far can Brian ride the Daylight 4449 Express? A strength-based model of Asperger syndrome based on special interest areas. *Focus on Autism and Other Developmental Disabilities, 22,* 67-79.

Witte, R. H., Phillips, L., & Kakela, M. (1998). Job satisfaction of college students with learning disabilities. *Journal of Learning Disabilities, 31,* 259-265.

Wittenstein, S. H. (1994). Braille literacy: Preservice training and teachers' attitudes. *Journal of Visual Impairment and Blindness, 88,* 516-524.

Witty, P. A. (Ed.). (1951). *The gifted child.* Boston: Heath.

Witzel, B. S., Mercer, C. D., & Miller, M. D. (2003). Teaching algebra to students with learning difficulties: An investigation of an explicit instruction model. *Learning Disabilities Research and Practice, 18,* 121-131.

Witzer, B. S., & Mercer, C. D. (2003). Using rewards to teach students with disabilities: Implications for motivation. *Remedial and Special Education, 24,* 88-96.

Wolery, M. (2000). Recommended practices in child-focused interventions. In S. Sandall, M. E. McLean, & B. J. Smith (Eds.), *DEC recommended practices* (pp. 34-38). Longmont, CO: Sopris West.

Wolery, M., Anthony, L., & Heckathorn, J. (1998). Transition-based teaching: Effects on transitions, teachers' behavior, and children's learning. *Journal of Early Intervention, 21,* 117-131.

Wolery, M., Ault, M. J., & Doyle, P. M. (1992). *Teaching students with moderate to severe disabilities.* New York: Longman.

Wolery, M., Barton, E. E., & Hine, J. F. (in press). Evolution of applied behavior analysis in the treatment of individuals with autism. *Exceptionality.*

Wolery, M., Cybriwski, C. A., Gast, D. L., & Boyle-Gast, K. (1991). Use of constant time delay and attentional responses with adolescents. *Exceptional Children, 57,* 462-474.

Wolery, M., & Haring, T. G. (1994). Moderate, severe, and profound disabilities. In N. G. Haring, L. McCormick, & T. G. Haring (Eds.), *Exceptional children and youth* (6th ed.) (pp. 258-299). Upper Saddle River, NJ: Merrill/Prentice Hall.

Wolery, M., & Sainato, D. M. (1993). General curriculum and intervention strategies. In *DEC Recommended Practices* (pp. 50-57). Reston, VA: Council for Exceptional Children, Division for Early Childhood.

Wolery, M., & Sainato, D. M. (1996). General curriculum and intervention strategies. In S. L. Odom & M. McClean (Eds.), *Recommended practices in early intervention* (pp. 125-158). Austin, TX: PRO-ED.

Wolery, M., & Wilbers, J. S. (1994). *Including young children with special needs in early childhood programs.* Washington, DC: National Association for the Education of Young Children.

Wolf, M., & Bowers, P. G. (2000). Naming-speed processes and developmental reading disabilities: An introduction to the special issue on the double-deficit hypothesis. *Journal of Learning Disabilities, 33,* 322-324.

Wolf, M., Bowers, P. G., & Biddle, K. (2000). Retrieval, automaticity, vocabulary elaboration, orthography (RAVE-O): A comprehensive, fluency-based reading intervention program. *Journal of Learning Disabilities, 33,* 375-386.

Wolfe, L. H., Heron, T. E., & Goddard, Y. I. (2000). Effects of self-monitoring on the on-task behavior and written language performance of elementary students with learning disabilities. *Journal of Behavioral Education, 10,* 49-73.

Wolfe, P. S., & Hall, T. E. (2003). Making inclusion a reality for students with severe disabilities. *Teaching Exceptional Children, 35*(4), 56-60.

Wolfensberger, W. (1969). The origin and nature of our institutional models. In R. B. Kugel & W. Wolfensberger (Eds.), *Changing patterns in residential services for the mentally retarded* (pp. 59-71). Washington, DC: President's Committee on Mental Retardation.

Wolfensberger, W. (1972). *Normalization: The principle of normalization in human services.* Toronto: National Institute on Mental Retardation.

Wolfensberger, W. (1983). Social role valorization: A proposed new term for the principle of normalization. *Mental Retardation, 21,* 234-239.

Wolfensberger, W. (2000). A brief overview of social role valorization. *Mental Retardation, 38,* 105-123.

Wolford, T., Alber, S. R., & Heward, W. L. (2001). Teaching middle school students with learning disabilities to recruit peer assistance during cooperative learning group activities. *Learning Disabilities and Research and Practice, 16,* 161-173.

Wolfram, W., & Ward, B. (Eds.). (2006). *American voices: How dialects differ from coast to coast.* Malden, MA: Blackwell Publishing.

Woliver, R., & Woliver, G. M. (1991). Gifted adolescents in the emerging minorities: Asians and Pacific Islanders. In M. Bireley & J. Genshaft (Eds.), *Understanding the gifted adolescent* (pp. 248-258). New York: Teachers College Press.

Woll, B., & Ladd, P. (2005). Deaf communities. In M. Marschark & P. E. Spencer (Eds.), *Oxford handbook of deaf studies, language, and education* (paperback ed.) (pp. 151-162). New York: Oxford University Press.

Wolraich, M. L., (1999). Attention-deficit hyperactivity disorder: The most studied yet most controversial diagnosis. *Mental Retardation and Development Disabilities Research Reviews, 5,* 163-168.

Wolraich, M. L., Lindgren, S., Stromquist, A., Milich, R., Davis, C., & Watson, D. (1990). Stimulant medications used by primary care physicians in the treatment of attention deficit hyperactivity disorder. *Pediatrics, 86,* 95-101.

Wolters, P., Brouwers, P., & Moss, H. (1995). Pediatric HIV disease: Effect on cognition, learning, and behavior. *School Psychology Quarterly, 10,* 305-328.

Wood, B. A., Frank, A. R., & Hamre-Nietupski, S. M. (1996). How do you work this lock? Adaptations for teaching combination lock use. *Teaching Exceptional Children, 28*(2), 35-39.

Wood, C. L., & Heward, W. L. (2007). *Good noise! Using choral responding to increase the effectiveness of group instruction.* Manuscript to be submitted for publication review.

Wood, C. L., Heward, W. L., Heimlich, S. G., & Itoi, M. (May 2006). *Effects of random study checks and guided notes study cards on middle school special education students' notetaking accuracy and science vocabulary quiz scores.* Paper presented at the 32nd Annual Convention of the Association for Behavior Analysis, Atlanta.

Wood, C. L., Mackiewicz, S. M., Van Norman, R. K., & Cooke, N. L. (2007). Tutoring with technology. *Intervention in School and Clinic, 43*(2), 108-115.

Wood, F. H., Cheney, C. O., Cline D. H., Sampson, K., Smith, C. R., & Guetzloe, E. C. (1997). *Conduct disorders and social maladjustments: Policies, politics, and programming.* Reston, VA: Council for Children with Behavioral Disorders.

Wood, J. G., & Zabel, R. H. (2001). Adderall: special education's new (?) fix-it drug. *Beyond Behavior, 11*(1), 39-41.

Wood, J. W. (2006). *Inclusion: Adapting instruction to accommodate students in inclusive settings* (5th ed.). Upper Saddle River, NJ: Merrill/Prentice Hall.

Wood, J. W. (2006b). *Teaching students in inclusive settings: Adapting accommodating instruction* (5th ed.). Upper Saddle River, NJ: Merrill/Prentice Hall.

Wood, S. J., Murdock, J. Y., Cronin, M. E., Dawson, N. M., & Kirby, P. C. (1998). Effects of self-monitoring on on-task behaviors of at-risk middle school students. *Journal of Behavioral Education, 8,* 263-279.

Wood, W. M., Karvonen, M., Test, D. W., Browder, D., & Algozzine, B. (2004). Promoting student self-determination skills in IEP planning. *Teaching Exceptional Children, 70,* 391-412.

Woodcock, R. W. (1998). *Woodcock Reading Mastery Tests—Revised.* Circle Pines, MN: American Guidance Services.

Woodcock, R. W., McGrew, K. S., & Mather, N. (2001). *Woodcock-Johnson III tests of achievement.* Itasaca, IL: Riverside.

Woods, D. W., & Miltenberger, R. G. (Eds.). (2006). *Tic disorders, trichotillomania, and other repetitive behavior disorders behavioral approaches to analysis and treatment.* Norwell, MA: Luker Academic Publishers.

Woolsey, M. L. (1999, January). Personal communication.

Woolsey, M. L. (2001, January). Personal communication.

Woolsey, M. L., Satterfield, S. T., & Roberson, L. (2006). Visual phonics: An English code buster?" *American Annals of the Deaf, 151,* 452-457.

World Health Organization. (2001). *International Classification of Functioning, Disability and Health-Revised.* [Retrieved March 25, 2007. http://www3.who.int/icf/intros/ICF-Eng-Intro.pdf]

Wormsley, D. P. (2004). *Braille literacy: A functional approach.* New York: AFB Press.

Wrenn, R. L. (1994). A death at school: Issues and interventions. *Counseling and Human Development, 26*(7), 1-7.

Wright, C., & Momari, M. (1985). *From toys to computers: Access for the physically disabled child.* San Jose, CA: Wright.

Wright, J. E., Cavanaugh, R. A., Sainato, D. M., & Heward, W. L. (1995). Somos todos ayudantes y estudiantes: Evaluation of a classwide peer tutoring program in a modified Spanish class for secondary students identified as learning disabled or academically at-risk. *Education and Treatment of Children, 18,* 33-52.

Wright, P. W. D., & Wright, P. D. (2006). *Wrightslaw: From Emotions to Advocacy: The special education survival guide* (2nd ed.). Hartfield, VA: Harbor House Law Press, Inc.

Wright, P. W. D., & Wright, P. D. (2006). *Wrightslaw: Special education law* (2nd ed.). Hartfield, VA: Harbor House Law Press, Inc.

Wright-Gallo, G. L., Higbee, T. S., Reagon, K. A., & Davey, B. J. (2006). Classroom-based functional analysis and intervention for students with emotional/behavioral disorders. *Education & Treatment of Children, 29,* 421-436.

Xin, Y. P, Grasso, E., Dipipi-Hoy, C. M., & Jitenda, A. (2005). The effects of purchasing skill instruction for individuals with developmental disabilities: A meta-analysis. *Exceptional Children, 71,* 379-400.

Yairi, E. (1998). Is the basis for stuttering genetic? *American Speech-Language-Hearing Association, 70*(1), 29-32.

Yairi, E. (2004). The formative years of stuttering: A changing portrait. *Contemporary Issues in Communication Science and Disorders, 31,* 92-104.

Yairi, E., & Ambrose, E. N. (1999). Early childhood stuttering. I: Persistence and recovery rates. *Journal of Speech and Hearing Research, 42,* 1097-1112.

Yelin, E., & Katz, P. (1994). Labor force trends of persons with and without disabilities. *Monthly Labor Review, 72,* 593-620.

Yell, M. L. (1995). Least restrictive environment, inclusion, and students with disabilities: A legal analysis. *Journal of Special Education, 28,* 389-404.

Yell, M. L. (2006). *The law and special education* (2nd ed.). Upper Saddle River, NJ: Merrill/Prentice Hall.

Yell, M. L., & Drasgow, E. (2000). Litigating a free appropriate public education: The Lovaas hearing and cases. *Journal of Special Education, 33,* 205-214.

Yell, M. L., & Drasgow, E. (2005). *No Child Left Behind: A guide for professionals.* Upper Saddle River, NJ: Merrill/Prentice Hall.

Yell, M. L., Rozalski, M. E., & Drasgow, E. (2001). Disciplining students with disabilities. *Focus on Exceptional Children, 30*(1), 1-19.

Yell, M. L., Shriner, J. G., & Katsiyannis, A. (2006). Individuals with disabilities education improvement act of 2004 and IDEA regulations of 2006: Implications for educators, administrators, and teacher trainers. *Focus on Exceptional Children, 39*(1), 1-24.

Yergin-Allsopp, M., Rice, C., Karapurkar, T., Doernberg, N., Boyle, C., & Murphy, C. (2003). Prevalence of autism in a U.S. metropolitan community. *Journal of the American Medical Association, 289,* 49-55.

Ylvisaker, M. (1986). Language and communication disorders following pediatric head injury. *Journal of Head Trauma Rehabilitation, 1,* 48-56.

Ylvisaker, M. (2005). Children with cognitive, behavioral, communication, and academic difficulties. In W. M. High, A. M. Sander, M. A. Struchen, K. A. Hart (Eds.), *Rehabilitation for traumatic brain injury* (pp. 205-234). New York: Oxford University Press.

Yopp, R. H., & Yopp, H. K. (2001). *Literature-based reading activities.* Boston: Allyn & Bacon.

Young, J. L. (1997). Positive experiences with dogs: An important addition to the curriculum for blind and visually impaired children. *RE:view, 29*(2), 55-61.

Young, R. K., West, R. P., Smith, D. J., & Morgan, D. P. (1991). *Teaching self-management strategies to adolescents.* Longmont, CO: Sopris West.

Yousef, J. M. S. (1995). Insulin-dependent diabetes mellitus: Education implications. *Physical Disabilities: Education and Related Services, 13*(2), 43-53.

Ysseldyke, J. (2001). Reflections on a research career: Generalizations from 25 years of research on assessment and instructional decision making. *Exceptional Children, 67,* 295-309.

Ysseldyke, J. (2005). Assessment and decision making for students with learning disabilities: What if this is as good as it gets? *Learning Disability Quarterly, 28,* 125-128.

Ysseldyke, J., Nelson, J. R., Christenson, S., Johnson, D. R., Dennison, A., Triezenberg, H., Sharpe, M., & Hawes, M. (2004). What we know and need to know about the consequences of high-stakes testing for students with disabilities. *Exceptional Children, 71,* 75-94.

Yurick, A. L., Robinson, P. D., Cartledge, G., Lo, Y., & Evans, T. L. (2006). Using peer-mediated repeated readings as a fluency-building activity for urban learners. *Education & Treatment of Children, 29,* 469-506.

Zabel, R. H., & Nigro, F. A. (1999). Juvenile offenders with behavioral disorders, learning disabilities, and no disabilities: Self-reports of personal, family, and school characteristics. *Behavioral Disorders, 25,* 22-40.

Zamora-Durán, G., & Reyes, E. (1977). From tests to talking in the classroom: Assessing communicative competence. In A. Artiles & Zamora-Durán (Eds.), *Reducing disproportionate representation of culturally diverse students in special and gifted education* (p. 51). Reston, VA: Council for Exceptional Children.

Zeaman, D., & House, B. J. (1979). A review of attention theory. In N. R. Ellis (Ed.), *Handbook of mental deficiency: Psychological theory and research* (2nd ed.), (pp. 63-120). Hillside, NJ: Erlbaum.

Zentall, S. S. (2006). *ADHD and education: Foundations, characteristics, methods, and collaboration.* Upper Saddle River, NJ: Merrill/Prentice Hall.

Zhang, J., Gast, D., Horvat, M., & Datillo, J. (1995). The effectiveness of a constant time delay procedure on teaching lifetime sports skills to adolescents with severe to profound intellectual disabilities. *Education and Training in Mental Retardation and Developmental Disabilities, 30*, 51-64.

Zhang, D., Katsiyannis, A., & Herbst, M. (2004). Disciplinary exclusions in special education: A 4-year analysis. *Behavioral Disorders, 29*, 337-347.

Ziegler, D. (2002). *Reauthorization of the Elementary and Secondary Education Act: No Child Left Behind Act of 2001.* Arlington, VA: Council for Exceptional Children.

Zigler, E. (1999). The retarded child as a whole person. In E. Zigler & D. Bennett-Gates (Eds.), *Personality development in individuals with mental retardation* (pp. 1-16), Cambridge, UK: Cambridge University Press.

Zigmond, N. (2003). Where should students with disabilities receive special education services? Is one place better than another? *Journal of Special Education, 37*, 193-199.

Zigmond, N. (2006). Where should students with disabilities receive special education? Is one place better than another? In B. Cook & B. Shermer (Eds.), *What is special about special education?* (pp. 127-136). Austin, TX: PRO-ED.

Zigmond, N. (2007). Delivering special education is a two-person job: A call for unconventional thinking. In J. B. Crockett, M. M. Gerber, & T. J. Landrum, (Eds.), *Radical reform of special education: Essays in honor of James M. Kauffman.* Mahwah, NJ: Lawrence Erlbaum.

Zigmond, N., & Baker, J. M. (1995). Concluding comments: Current and future practices in inclusive schooling. *The Journal of Special Education, 29*, 245-250.

Zigmond, N., & Magiera, K. (2001a). Co-teaching. *Current Practice Alerts, Issue 6.* Reston, VA: Division for Learning Disabilities and Division for Research, Council for Exceptional Children.

Zigmond, N., & Matta, D. (2005). Value added of the special education teacher in secondary school co-taught classes. In T. M. Scruggs & M. A. Mastropieri (Eds.), *Advances in learning and behavioral disabilities: Research in secondary schools* (pp. 55-76). Oxford, UK: Elsevier.

Zimmerman, E. H., & Zimmerman, T. (1962). The alteration of behavior in a special classroom situation. *Journal of the Experimental Analysis of Behavior, 5,* 59-60.

Zionts, P., Simpson, R., & Zionts, L. (2001). *Emotional and behavioral problems: A handbook for understanding and handling students.* Thousand Oaks, CA: Corwin.

Zirkel, P. A., & D'Angelo, A. (2002). Special trends education case law: An empirical trends analysis. *Education Law Reporter, 161*, 731-753.

Zirpoli, T. J. (2008). *Behavior management: Applications for teachers* (5th ed.). Upper Saddle River, NJ: Merrill/Prentice Hall.

Zubal-Ruggieri, R. (2007). Making links, making connections: Internet resources for self-advocates and people with developmental disabilities. *Intellectual and Developmental Disabilities, 45*, 209-215.

Zucker, A. (2004). Law and ethics. *Death Studies, 28*, 803-806.

Abeson, A., 82
Abikoff, H., 426
Abrams, B. J., 243
Abt, K. A., 479
Achenbach, T. M., 229
Adams, G., 185
Adams, L., 280
Adamson, L. B., 270
Adelman, H. S., 14, 118
Ager, C., 466
Agran, M., 150, 152, 155, 161, 399, 428, 429, 440, 465
Aguilar, C. M., 199
Ahlgren, C., 481
Ahlgrim-Delzell, L., 149
Aiello, B., 17
Akamatsu, C. T., 360
Akshoomoff, N., 268
Akullian, J., 72, 279
Alaimo, D. F., 272
Al-Attrash, M., 200
Alber, S. R., 150, 182, 184, 199, 222, 223, 266, 319, 479, 512
Alber-Morgan, S. R., 21, 78, 222, 510
Alberto, P. A., 147, 158, 184, 274, 280, 319, 437
Albin, R. W., 97, 478
Alder, N., 234
Aldrich, F. J., 393
Alegria, J., 355
Algozzine, B., 71, 504
Al-Hassan, S., 108, 112
Alkin, M., 77
Allaire-Gifford, M., 62, 63, 84
Allan, K. E., 236
Allan, N. J., 276
Allen, C. P., 583
Allen, J., 270
Allen, K. E., 236
Allen, S. H., 78
Allen-Williams, N. J., 244
Allgood, P., 437
Aloiso, D., 244
Al Otaiba, S., 147, 161, 309, 327
Alper, S., 280, 428, 436, 586
Alric-Edwards, J. M., 244
Altunay, A., 393
Alwell, M., 577
Ambrose, E. N., 307, 316
American Academy of Pediatrics, 425
American Association on Mental Retardation (AAMR), 133, 134, 143, 285
American College of Medical Genetics, 545
American Foundation for the Blind, 379, 399, 401
American Printing House for the Blind, 376
American Psychiatric Association, 132, 219, 258, 259, 260, 269, 421, 422
American Speech-Language-Hearing Association (ASHA), 299, 302, 303, 305, 307, 308, 309, 310, 315, 319, 325, 336, 337, 338, 341, 342, 343, 347
Amerine-Dickens, M., 274
Amos, B. A., 155
Anderegg, M. L., 93
Anderson, C., 241
Anderson, D. H., 240
Anderson, J. A., 219
Anderson, L. L., 21
Anderson, M. A., 262, 276
Anderson, N. B., 302
Anderson, P., 21
Anderson, S. R., 275
Anderson, V., 97
Anderson Downing, J., 219
Andrews, D., 112, 429
Andrews, J., 360
Andrews, J. S., 336

Angell, M. E., 96, 98
Anthony, D., 358
Anthony, L., 553
Antle, B. J., 427
Antunez, B., 106, 107
Anxiety Disorders Association of America, 219
Archwamety, T., 219, 246
Arcia, E., 107, 108, 109
Ardoin, S. P., 478
Arguelles, M. E., 62
Armbruster, B. B., 196
Armendariz, F., 163
Armstrong, D. F., 359
Arndt, S. A., 71
Arnold, L. E., 189
Arnold, M. B., 457, 458
Arora, T., 76
Arrasmith, D., 196
Arrowood, L., 425, 426
Arslanian, S. A., 417
Arter, C., 393, 394
Artiles, A. J., 503
Aspel, N., 42, 568
Association for Science in Autism Treatment, 13
Assouline, S. G., 508
Asthma and Allergy Foundation of America, 418
Astley, S. J., 145
Attermeier, S. M., 547
Attkisson, C. C., 221
Attwood, T., 259
Atwell, J. A., 140
Atwood, T., 266
Audette, R. M., 25
Ault, M. J., 475, 479
Ault, M. M., 413, 457
Austen, S., 338
Austin, J. L., 200
Autism Research Institute, 269
Autism Special Interest Group of the Association for Behavior and Analysis International, 277
Axe, J. B., 479, 548
Axelrod, S., 478
Ayres, B., 81
Ayres, K. M., 149, 277

Baca, L. M., 58
Bacon, C. K., 310
Baer, D. M., 157, 266, 274, 275, 283, 456, 475
Baer, R. M., 571, 574, 578, 588, 590
Bagnato, S. J., 544, 547
Bahan, B., 349
Bailey, A., 270
Bailey, D., Jr., 93, 107, 108, 109, 145, 544
Bailey, J. S., 200, 479
Bailin, D., 478
Baio, J., 269
Bak, S., 375
Bakeman, R., 270
Baker, B. L., 93
Baker, C., 298
Baker, E., 203
Baker, J. M., 41, 236
Baker, K., 359, 362
Baker, R. L., 382
Baker, S., 195, 359, 362
Baker, S. K., 362, 363
Baldwin, V., 455
Balla, D. A., 138
Bambara, L. M., 465, 466, 468, 592
Banda, D. R., 102, 122
Banko, K. M., 236
Banks, C. A. M., 16, 58, 107
Banks, J. A., 16, 58
Barbera, M. L., 277

Barbetta, P. M., 241
Barbetta, T. M., 158
Barclay, L. A., 375, 380
Barenbaum, E. M., 182
Barkley, R. A., 420, 422, 424, 426
Barlow, J. A., 316
Barnes, S. B., 411
Barnhill, G. P., 259
Baron-Cohen, S., 270
Barr, D. M., 553
Barraga, N. C., 381, 384, 387
Barrera, I., 58
Barry, L. M., 428
Barton, M., 270
Barton-Arwood, S. M., 140, 235
Bashinski, S. M., 147
Bat-Chava, Y., 361
Bateman, B. D., 63, 65, 67, 69, 70, 71, 192
Batshaw, M. L., 143, 409
Battaglia, F., 145
Battle, D. E., 305
Bauder, D., 572, 574
Bauer, A. M., 94, 161, 485
Bauer, J., 272, 277
Baum, D. D., 185
Bauman, K., 232
Baumgart, D., 161, 475
Bayley, N., 547
Beadle-Brown, J., 138
Beakley, B. A., 574
Beard, K. Y., 226
Beard, L., 436
Beattie, J., 69
Beatty, L. S., 190
Bebko, J. M., 139
Beck, A., 93
Beck, J., 150
Beck, R., 21
Becker-Cottrill, B., 97
Beckley, C. G., 200
Beegle, G., 98, 101
Behm, J. A., 441
Behr, S. K., 93
Beilke, J. R., 13
Beirne-Smith, J. R., 139, 146
Beirne-Smith, M., 133, 145
Belcastro, F., 383
Belfiore, P. J., 437, 592
Bell, T., 244
Bellini, S., 72, 279
Belmont, J. M., 139
Belser, R. C., 145
BenChaaban, D., 277, 466, 538
Benner, G. J., 219, 220, 234
Bennett, D., 387
Bennett, K., 423
Benson, H. A., 465
Benz, M. R., 221, 574, 578
Berger-Gross, P., 244
Bergeron, R., 139
Bergerud, D., 195
Bergman, E., 188
Berkson, G., 12
Berliner, D. C., 153
Berney, T. P., 269
Bernheimer, L. P., 138, 535
Berquin, P. C., 423
Bérubé, R. L., 229
Best, A. B., 393
Best, A. M., 56
Best, S. J., 408, 409, 410, 413, 427, 431, 435, 437, 468, 592
Best Buddies, 592

Bettelheim, B., 268
Beukelman, D. R., 321
Bevill, A. R., 277
Bhukhanwala, F., 417
Bianco, M., 13
Bicard, D. F., 241, 420, 426
Biederman, J., 422
Bierle, T., 437
Bierman, K. L., 221
Bigby, L., 224, 433
Bigge, J. L., 60, 61, 408, 409, 410, 435, 437, 467, 468, 592, 596
Biglan, A., 225
Biklen, D., 12, 284, 285
Billingsley, B. S., 105
Billingsley, F. F., 157
Bishop, D. V. M., 306, 309
Bishop, M., 415
Blacher, J., 93, 107, 574
Blackorby, J., 11, 12, 185, 338, 567, 568, 569
Blackstone, S. W., 324
Blake, C., 242
Blalock, G., 574
Blanchard, C., 150
Bland-Stewart, L., 305
Blanes, M., 107, 108
Blankenship, K., 399
Blatt, B., 590
Bleck, E. E., 411
Block, M. E., 468, 485
Bloodstein, O., 307
Bloom, B. S., 243, 513
Bloom, S. R., 408
Blue-Banning, M., 98, 101, 102
Bluestone, C. D., 341
Boag, E. M., 415
Bocian, K. M., 221
Bock, S. J., 271
Boe, E. E., 43
Boekaerts, M. R., 427
Bogan, B. L., 220
Bogdan, R., 593
Bollig, A. A., 112
Bolt, S. E., 31, 54, 137
Bolton, J. L., 592
Bondurant-Utz, J., 546
Bondy, A., 277
Boney, B., 479
Book, D., 396
Boon, R. T., 149
Boothe, D., 505
Bordin, J., 71
Borland, J. H., 505
Bornstein, H., 358
Borovosky, S., 505
Borrero, J., 425
Bosner, S. M., 437
Bott Slaton, D., 234
Bouchard, D., 375
Boulware, G. L., 97
Boushey, A., 93
Boutot, E. A., 276, 282, 284
Bovaird, J. A., 147
Bowden Carpenter, L., 436
Bowe, F., 431
Bower, E. M., 214
Bowers, F. E., 242
Bowers, P. G., 182
Boxkurt, F., 156
Boyd-Ball, A., 108
Boykin, A. W., 58
Boyle, J. R., 199, 200
Braddock, D., 583
Bradford, S., 147, 161
Bradley, L., 163
Bradley, R., 95, 177, 221
Bradley, V. J., 593
Bradley-King, K. L., 426
Bradshaw, M., 325
Brady, M. P., 237, 397
Brain Injury Association, 460
Brambring, M., 374
Brame, P., 235

Brandes, J. A., 549
Branson, T. A., 592
Brantlinger, E., 72
Brawner, J., 355
Bray, M. A., 244
Bray, N. W., 139
Bredekamp, S., 549
Breier, J. I., 188
Brennan, K. B., 199
Brewer, J., 538
Brewer, W. M., 152
Brick, J. D., 81
Bricker, D., 534, 546, 547, 548, 550, 555, 556
Brigance, A. H., 190
Brigham, M., 199
Brigham, N., 199
Brigham, R., 199
Bristol, M., 257
Broers, J., 150
Brolin, D. E., 150, 571, 574
Bronicki, G. J., 105
Brooke, V., 579, 580
Brooks, A. P., 265, 267
Brooks, R. B., 425
Brooks-Gunn, J., 539
Brophy, J., 153
Brotherson, M. J., 96
Browder, D. M., 31, 65, 71, 147, 149, 466, 468, 469, 470, 471, 478, 485, 583, 592
Brown, C., 186
Brown, F., 81, 322, 442, 470, 475
Brown, G. L., 577
Brown, G. M., 161, 485
Brown, L., 458, 480, 481, 485, 578
Brown, L. L., 229
Brown, P. A., 375
Brown, S., 152, 153, 479
Brown, V. L., 190
Brown, W. H., 227, 228
Brownell, M. T., 71
Brownell, W. E., 333
Bruder, M. B., 541
Brumback, R. A., 415
Bruner, E. C., 196
Bruninks, R. H., 138
Bryan, L. C., 277, 466
Bryan, T., 185, 235
Bryant, B., 313
Bryant, B. R., 190, 436
Bryant, D. M., 537
Bryant, D. P., 77, 282, 436
Buchanan, A. M., 591
Buck, S. M., 307
Buell, J. S., 236
Buford, R., 234
Bui, Y. N., 182, 203
Bulgren, J. A., 42, 192, 195, 198
Bull, G. L., 319
Bullis, M., 221
Bullock, C., 242
Buntinx, W., 133, 137
Burchard, S. N., 587, 588
Bursuck, W. D., 21, 77
Burta, M., 397
Busch, T., 425, 426
Butler, M. G., 141, 145
Butter, E. M., 284
Butterworth, J., 583, 585
Bybee, J., 140
Byers, C., 482, 483
Byzek, J., 415

Calaluce, P. D., 105
Calderon, R., 342
Caldwell, N. K., 156
Calhoun, M. L., 559
California Department of Developmental Services, 268
Callahan, K., 123
Callwood, D., 185
Cameron, D. L., 76
Cameron, J., 236
Cameron, P., 60

Cameto, R., 92, 220, 234, 567, 569
Cammill, D. M., 512
Campbell, J. R., 21, 375
Campbell, P. H., 441, 442
Campbell, R., 356
Campbell Miller, M., 161
Canale, J. A., 42, 222
Cannella-Malone, H. I., 475, 478
Cannon, C., 424
Cant, R., 98
Cantu, C. O., 437
Cardinal, D. N., 285
Cardoso, D., 11
Carey, S. P., 425
Carlin, M. T., 139, 140
Carlson, B. C., 574
Carnine, D. W., 42, 43, 120, 192, 464
Caron, S. L., 94, 95, 97, 258
Carothers, D. E., 117
Carpenter, B., 95
Carpenter, M., 277
Carr, E. G., 120, 231, 261, 477, 479
Carr, J. E., 200, 479
Carroll, C., 351
Carta, J. J., 78, 544
Carter, C., 553
Carter, E. W., 77, 141, 161, 219, 468, 481, 482
Carter, S. L., 538
Cartledge, G., 21, 58, 107, 112, 113, 163, 222, 231, 235, 240, 242, 425, 428, 429
Cascella, P. W., 319, 467
Caspi, A., 225
Cast, D. L., 277
Castellano, J. A., 503
Castellnos, F. X., 423
Castro, M., 229
Catts, H. W., 306, 309
Causton-Theoharis, J., 475
Cavallaro, C., 480
Cavanaugh, R. A., 78, 163
Cavkaytar, A., 117
Cawley, J. F., 184
Cawthon, S. W., 350, 361
Ceci, S. J., 137
Celeste, M., 375
Center for Education Policy, 56
Center for Positive Behavioral Interventions & Supports, 238
Center on Human Policy, 477
Centers for Disease Control and Prevention (CDC), 268, 419, 420, 461
Cerney, J., 361
Chaffey, G., 505
Chafin Seal, B., 350
Chait, A., 230
Chakrabarti, S., 262
Chamber, C. R., 155
Chamberlain, J. A., 142
Chambers, J. G., 23
Chard, D. J., 42, 181, 203
Charlop-Christy, M. H., 277, 280
Charness, N., 494
Chen, D., 374, 380, 383, 457, 466
Cheney, D., 220
Cherry, K. E., 139
Chesley, G. M., 105
Chiasson, K., 95
Childs, K. E., 231
Chinn, P. C., 107
Chong, I. M., 479
Christain, D., 424
Christensen, L., 242
Christensen, W. R., 71
Christie, C. A., 163
Christopher, J., 189
Chronis, A., 424
Chrysler, C., 140
Church-Pupke, P., 593
Cicchetti, D. V., 138
Cihak, D. F., 158, 184
Cilley, M., 76
Cioffi, A., 580, 585
Cipani, E., 241, 478

Clancy-Menchetti, J., 78
Clark, B. A., 497, 499, 501, 502, 505, 513
Clark, C., 592
Clark, D. M., 106
Clark, E., 244
Clark, F. L., 203
Clark, G. M., 149, 571, 574
Clark, M. D., 338
Clark, N. M., 468, 481
Clark, R. D., 145
Clark, S. G., 60
Clarke, S., 231
Clarren, S. K., 145
Clatterbuck, C. C., 443
Clay, K., 77
Clements, S. D., 179, 193
Cloninger, C. J., 71, 92, 469, 484
Cobb, B., 577
Cobb Morocco, C., 77
Cohen, C., 236
Cohen, E. T., 437
Cohen, H. G., 274, 275
Cohen, M. J., 277
Cohen, S., 505
Colangelo, N., 495, 508, 509
Cole, C. M., 77
Cole, K. J., 364
Coleman, T. J., 102, 122
Colin, S., 356
Collins, B. C., 149, 437, 453, 457, 458, 464, 470,
        472, 475, 479, 592
Collins, D. W., 188
Collis, G. M., 351
Colvin, G., 158, 241
Comacho, M. R., 107
Commission on Education of the Deaf, 364
Community Playthings, 411
Compton, D. L., 54
Compton, M. V., 375
Cone, A. A., 596
Coniglio, S. J., 285
Conley, R. W., 579
Conlon, C., 536, 539
Connell, M. C., 236
Connelly, V., 306
Conner, E. P., 432
Conners, C. K., 420
Conners, F. A., 140
Connolly, C. M., 338
Connor, R. T., 141
Conrad, A. D., 21
Conroy, J. W., 587, 590
Conroy, M., 230
Conroy, M. A., 227, 228, 241
Cook, B. G., 76, 77, 203
Cook, C. R., 234
Cook, F., 307
Cook, I. D., 574
Cook, L., 43, 60, 62, 203
Cook, R. E., 543, 548, 549, 555
Cooke, N. L., 78, 118, 119, 161
Cooley, C., 222
Cooper, H. L., 241, 383
Cooper, J. O., 21, 140, 157, 192, 230, 232, 233, 241,
        274, 428, 475
Cooper, K. J., 466, 592
Cooper-Duffy, K., 31
Copeland, S. R., 56, 141, 155, 161, 236, 482,
        484, 593
Coplan, J., 285
Copple, C., 549
Corn, A. L., 380, 384, 387, 389, 390, 394
Cornett, R., 355
Correa, V. I., 58, 60, 93, 107, 108, 109, 117
Corser, N., 445
Cortiella, C., 30, 32
Cosden, M., 186
Coster W. J., 427
Cott, A., 189
Coucouvanis, K., 587, 590
Coulter, D. L., 459
Council for Children with Behavioral Disorders
        (CCBD), 214, 215, 247

Council for Exceptional Children (CEC), 23, 43, 72,
        82, 570
Council for Learning Disabilities (CLD), 207
Council of State Directors of Programs for the
        Gifted, 12
Courchesne, E., 269
Court, D., 185
Court, J. H., 504
Courtade-Little, G., 71, 149
Coutinho, M. J., 56
Cox, M. J., 549
Coyne, G., 350
Coyne, M. D., 42, 181, 192
Crabtree, T., 16, 444
Craft, M. A., 150, 222
Craig, S., 58
Crandell, C. C., 347, 353
Crangle, C., 89, 124
Creech-Galloway, C., 451, 487
Crenshaw, T. M., 424
Crimmins, D., 231
Crompton, A., 538
Crone, D. A., 248, 477
Cronin, B. A., 149
Cronin, M. E., 150, 151, 190, 240, 428, 574
Cronsiter, A., 145
Cross, C. T., 503
Cross, T. L., 498, 505
Crossley, R., 284
Crozier, S., 281, 282
Cruickshank, W. M., 394
Cruz, L., 241
Cue, K., 351
Culatta, B., 319, 327
Cullen, C., 479
Cullinan, D., 56, 185, 214, 219, 221, 224, 226, 230,
        241
Culpepper, M., 230
Cummins, J., 314
Cunningham, B., 586
Cushing, L. S., 468, 481
Cuvo, A. J., 375
Cystic Fibrosis Foundation, 419

Daane, M. C., 21
Daisey, M., 355
Dalen, L., 426
Daley, D., 426
D'Alonzo, B. J., 574
Daly, P. M., 240, 241, 428, 429
Daly, T., 277
Damer, M., 21
D'Amico, R., 578
Danforth, S., 12, 131
Dangel, H., 435
D'Angelo, A., 22
Danielson, L., 177
Daoust, P. M., 479
Dardig, J. C., 42, 110, 111, 113, 115, 592
Datillo, J., 592
Davern, L., 112
Davey, B. J., 231
Davis, C. A., 397, 478
Davis, G. A., 495, 526
Davis, L. L., 163, 481
Davis, M. L., 387
Davis, P. K., 466
Davis, T., 436
Daviso, A. W., III, 588, 590
Dawson, G., 272
Dawson, J. E., 139
Dawson, N. M., 240, 428
Day, K., 141
Dean, P., 415
Dean Crews, S., 234
DeAvila, E., 314
DeBose, C. E., 305
DeCaro, J. J., 364
Deci, E. L., 236
Dedrick, C. V. L., 468
DeFilippo, C. L., 355
DeFries, J. C., 423
Dekker, M. C., 141

DeLacy, M., 501
DeLana, M., 360
Delaney E. M., 97
De La Paz, S., 182
Dell, A. G., 436
Delquadri, J., 78, 153
De Martini-Scully, D., 244
Denham, A., 475
Denning, C. B., 142
Dennis, R. E., 62, 484
Denny, R. K., 227
Deno, S. L., 190, 236
De Ruiter, K. P., 141
Derzon, J. H., 215
Deshler, D. D., 43, 77, 178, 182, 186, 194, 195, 203
DeSimone, J. R., 76, 203
DeStefano, L., 568
Detrich, R., 73
Dettmer, P., 60, 62, 484
Deutsch, C. K., 140
De Valenzuela, J. S., 56, 57
Dias, M. S., 413
Díaz-Rico, L. T., 314
Dib, N., 275
DiCarlo, C. F., 538
Dickey, S. E., 312
Dickson, C. A., 140
Didden, R., 141
Diehl, S. F., 310, 311
Dieker, L. A., 62, 204
Dietrich, M., 587
DiGangi, S. A., 428
Dignan, K., 375
Dillenberger, K., 277
Diller, L. H., 423
Dimitropoulos, A., 141, 145
D'Incau, B., 235
Dingle, A. D., 408, 419, 427
Dinnebeil, L. A., 557
Dion, E., 77, 242
DiPerna, J. C., 234, 247
Dipipi-Hoy, C. M., 42, 149
Dishion, T. J., 225
Division for Early Childhood, 544
Division for Learning Disabilities, 175, 207
Division for the Blind and Physically Handicapped,
        Library of Congress, 382
Dockrell, J. E., 306, 319
Dodds, J. B., 546
Dodge, K., 225
Doering, K., 60, 484
Dohan, M., 325
Donegan, M., 549
Donelson, F., 163
Donley, C. R., 117, 122
Donovan, M. S., 503
Doolittle, J., 177
Doorlag, D. H., 77
Doren, B., 98, 221, 571
Dormans, J. P., 411
Dorsey, M., 232
Dosen, A., 141
Douglas, J., 142
Doukas, G. L., 235
Douma, J. C. H., 141
Downing, J. A., 304, 325, 374, 380, 383, 433, 456,
        457, 466, 480, 485
Downs, M. P., 336, 340, 343
Dowse, J. M., 369, 401
Doyle, M. B., 77, 161, 485
Doyle, P. M., 475
Drake, M., 236
Drasgow, E., 31, 98, 275, 351, 359
Dreier, A. E., 25
Drew, C. J., 142, 145, 146
Dreyer, L. G., 190
Dube, W. V., 140
Duchnowski, A. J., 219, 220
Ducret, W. D., 389
Duffelmeyer, F., 185
Duffy, M. L., 237
Dugan, E. P., 479
Dunlap, G., 95, 97, 226, 231, 247, 478

Dunn, L. M., 313
Dunn-Geier, J., 285
Dunst, C., 92
DuPaul, G. J., 425, 426
Duppong-Hurley, K. A., 216
Durand, V. M., 231, 479
Dwyer, K. P., 227
Dyches, T. T., 71
Dyck, N. J., 60, 484
Dye, G. A., 195
Dye, H. B., 536
Dye, M., 482, 483
Dyer, A., 356
Dyer, K., 478
Dykens, E. M., 142, 145
Dykes, E. M., 392
Dykes, M. K., 437
Dylan, K., 574
Dyson, L., 102

Eakins, A., 240, 429
Easterbrooks, S. R., 337, 362, 363
Easton, D., 350
Ebanks, M. E., 479
Eber, L., 238, 249
Eberle, L., 431
Ecalle, J., 356
Edelman, S., 62, 484
Eden-Piercy, G. V. S., 93
Edens, R. M., 420
Edgar, E., 586
Edge, D., 110, 112, 120, 123
Edwards, L. C., 348
Edwards, L. L., 319
Edwards, R. P., 280, 281
Edwards, S., 424
Ehlers, S., 270
Ehren, B. J., 327
Ehrensberger, W., 586
Ehri, L. C., 356
Eichinger, J., 456, 485
Eidelman, S., 16
Eikeseth, S., 13, 274, 275
Eisenman, L., 71
Ekdahl, M., 262, 479
Eklund, S. J., 138
Elbaum, B. E., 185, 203
Eldevik, S., 275
Eldredge, J. L., 356
Elhoweris, H., 425
Elicker, J., 538
Elkevich, R., 517
Elks, M., 590
Elksnin, L. K., 235
Elksnin, N., 235
Ellet, L., 204
Elliot, L., 350
Elliott, K., 186
Elliott, S. N., 51, 229, 544
Ellis, E. S., 73, 153, 162, 203
Ellis, N. R., 139
Emerson, E., 141
Emmorey, K., 359
Enders, C., 229
Endo, S., 277, 426, 466, 538
Engelman, M., 387
Engelmann, S., 158, 189, 196
Englehart, M., 513
Englert, C. S., 182
Enright, R., 441
Epilepsy Foundation, 416, 417
Epstein, M. H., 216, 219–220, 229, 234
Erickson, K. A., 324
Erickson, R. L., 304
ERIC/OSEP Special Project, 109
Ericsson, K. A., 494
Erin, J. N., 375, 384, 387, 390, 394
Ernsbarger, S., 159, 478
Ervin, R. A., 242
Erwin, E., 98, 100, 548
Eshleman, J. W., 21, 157
Espin, C., 236
Etscheidt, S., 25, 230

Etzel-Wise, D., 433
Evans, D. D., 319
Evans, J. C., 436
Evans, P. A., 285
Evans, T. L., 21
Evans Getzel, E., 586
Everhart, V. S., 350
Everling, S., 295, 326
Everson, J. M., 42, 568, 572
Ewolt, C., 360
Eyman, R. K., 93

Fabich, M., 348
Fahsl, A. J., 184
Fairbanks, S., 54, 229
Falk, K., 241
Farlow, L. J., 475
Farrington, D. P., 221
Farrington, K., 578
Farris, M., 468, 587
Faulk, K. B., 234
Faw, G. D., 466
Fazzi, D. L., 392
Feggins-Azziz, R., 57
Feil, E. G., 221
Fein, D., 270
Feinberg, E., 268
Feiner, S. K., 387
Feingold, D. F., 188
Feltovich, P. J., 494
Ferguson, D. L., 145, 147, 466, 475, 567, 568, 587, 593
Ferguson, P. M., 93, 567, 568, 587, 593
Ferrell, K. A., 374, 376, 385
Ferreri, S. J., 200, 277, 478
Ferro, J. D., 230, 233, 478
Feurer, I. D., 141, 145
Fewell, R. R., 93
Fey, M. E., 306
Fialka, J., 60
Fidler, D. J., 140, 145
Fiedler, C. R., 106, 111, 117
Field, S., 150, 186
Filipek, P. A., 270, 271, 423
Findler, L., 94, 97
Fine, E. M., 423
Finn, C. E., 59, 83
Finnegan, M., 337
Finucane, B. M., 142
Firth, U., 272
Fischer, M., 42, 77, 207
Fish, T., 594
Fisher, A., 240
Fisher, C. S., 153
Fisher, D., 76, 77, 161, 480, 485
Fisher, J. M., 97
Fisher, M., 161, 480
Fisher, S., 574, 586
Fisher, W. W., 479
Fitzer, A., 277
Fitzgerald, J. L., 112
Flaherty, E., 94, 97
Flaherty, T., 161
Flaute, A. J., 240, 429
Fleischmann, A., 93, 258
Flener, B. S., 394
Fletcher, J. M., 174, 179, 188
Fletcher, K. L., 139
Flexer, C., 347
Flexer, R. W., 571, 572, 574, 577, 580, 585
Flick, G. L., 425
Flis, L. D., 109
Flora, S. R., 236, 424
Flores, M., 147
Florian, L., 12
Florian, V., 94, 97
Floyd, R. G., 139
Flynn, J. R., 137
Foegen, A., 242
Foil, C. R., 319
Foley, K., 505
Foley, T. E., 184
Fombonne, E., 262, 268

Fontánez-Phelan, S. M., 107
Foorman, B. R., 176, 182
Foose, A. K., 138
Ford, B. A., 58
Ford, D. Y., 58, 503, 504, 505
Forest, M., 458
Forgatch, M. S., 226
Forness, S. R., 56, 72, 76, 174, 179, 185, 214, 424
Forney, P. E., 437, 441
Foster, S., 350, 351
Foster-Johnson, L., 478
Fountain, L., 424
Fowler, C. H., 140, 152
Fowler, S. A., 549, 593
Fox, J., 230, 425
Fox, L., 95, 96, 457, 464, 470, 475
Foxx, R. M., 72, 134, 264, 277, 284, 285, 288
Foy, C. J., 392
Fradd, S., 107
Frame, M. J., 375
Francis, A., 141
Francis, P., 350
Frank, A. R., 157, 568, 585
Frankenburg, W. K., 424, 546
Frankland, H. C., 98, 101
Frantino, E. P., 277
Frasier, M., 503, 505
Fredrick, L. D., 319, 437, 444
Freeland, A. L., 393
Freeman, F., 77
Freeman, S., 274
Freitag, G., 264
Frey, G. C., 591
Frey, K. S., 93
Friedman, H. A., 338
Friedman Narr, R. A., 355, 356
Friend, M., 60, 62, 63, 77
Frijters, J. C., 182
Friman, P. C., 242, 479
Frisbie, D. A., 189
Frisk, D., 95
Fristoe, M., 312
Fritschman, N., 280
Frost, L., 277
Frostig, M., 193
Frueh, E., 427
Fryxell, D., 480
Fuchs, D., 13, 54, 77, 78, 174, 175, 176, 177, 178, 184, 190, 196, 205, 242
Fuchs, L. S., 13, 54, 77, 78, 174, 175, 176, 177, 184, 190, 196, 205, 242
Fujiura, G. T., 142, 146
Fuller, K., 76
Fuller, M. L., 107
Furlong, M. J., 224, 226
Furney, K. S., 568
Furness, T. A., 387
Furst, E., 513
Fusilier, I., 425

Gabel, S., 108
Gadow, K. D., 425
Gagie, B., 277
Gagné, F., 494, 495, 499, 501
Gaillard, W. D., 415
Galaburda, A. M., 188
Galine, S., 57
Gallagher, J. J., 69, 501
Gallagher, P. A., 76, 77, 480
Gallagher, D. J., 83
Gallaudet Research Institute, 338, 340, 348, 364
Galley, V., 424
Gallucci, C., 480, 481
Gama, R., 158
Gamble, W. W., 97
Gammill, D. M., 510
Gampp, T. L., 355, 356, 357
Ganz, J. B., 152, 280, 583
Garand, J., 280
Garay, S. V., 361
Garber, H., 537
Garber, M., 399
Garcia, J., 503

Gardill, M. C., 247
Gardner, E. F., 190
Gardner, H., 494, 495, 505, 508
Gardner, J. F., 593
Gardner, R., III, 58, 77, 108, 112, 113, 157, 163, 200, 242
Garfinkle, A. N., 272, 277
Garrick Duhaney, L. M., 58, 76, 425
Gartin, B. C., 16, 106, 420, 444
Garza, N., 92, 567
Gast, D. L., 264, 277, 456, 466, 475, 479, 592
Gates, M. A. M., 265, 267
Gaus, M. D., 149
Gavidia-Payne, S., 97
Geary, D. C., 184
Geary, T., 579
Gebauer, K., 62
Gelb, S. A., 13, 43
Gense, D. J., 375
Gense, M. H., 375
Genshaft, J. L., 505
Gentry, M. A., 360
German, S. L., 152
Gersten, R. L., 42, 43, 72, 192, 195
Geruschat, D. R., 380
Getch, Y. Q., 417, 418, 437
Gething, L., 98
Getty, L. A., 22, 25
Giangreco, M. F., 60, 62, 71, 76, 77, 81, 92, 161, 469, 480, 484, 485
Gibb, G. S., 71
Giek, K. A., 59
Gifford, M. A., 49
Giles, P. G., 350
Gillberg, C., 268, 270
Gilliam, J. E., 264
Gillis, J. M., 286
Gilmore, D., 583, 585
Gingras, H., 379
Gitlin, L. N., 389
Givner, C. C., 185, 204, 222
Givon, S., 185
Glaeser, B. C., 219, 280
Glassberg, L. A., 220
Glidden, L. M., 94, 97
Go, F. J., 42, 222
Goddard, Y. I., 428
Godfrey, S. A., 163, 241
Goeckel, T. M., 437
Goetz, L., 466
Goetz Ruffino, A., 538
Goin, R. P., 269
Goin-Kochel, R. P., 269
Gold, V. J., 264
Goldberg, D., 362
Goldin-Meadow, S., 359
Goldman, A. M., 415
Goldman, R. M., 312
Goldrich Eskow, K., 586
Goldstein, A. P., 235
Goldstein, D. E., 586
Goldstein, H., 277, 281, 320, 475, 553
Goldstein, M., 420, 423, 424, 425
Goldstein, S., 420, 421, 423, 424, 425
Golledge, R. G., 393
Gollery, T., 107
Gollnick, B. M., 107
Gomez, J., 107
Gompel, M., 387
Gonzalez, H. R., 586
Gonzalez, J. E., 219–220
Gonzalez, L., 479
Gonzalez-Mena, J., 102, 105, 106
Good, R. H., 42, 179, 191, 192
Goodey, C. F., 132
Goodman, G., 277
Goodman, L. V., 82
Goodman, M. J., 21
Goodman, S., 479
Goodrich, G. L., 387
Gordon, L. R., 587
Gordon, R. G., Jr., 298
Gortmaker, S. L., 408

Gottermeier, L., 355
Gouvousis, A., 280
Graf, S. A., 192
Graff, J. C., 413, 457
Graff, V. L. W., 594
Graham, S., 182, 184, 196
Gramberg, L., 389
Grandin, T., 263, 264
Grant, S. H., 236
Grantham, T., 503
Grass, D., 412
Grasso, E., 42, 149
Graves, T. B., 149
Gray, C. A., 280, 282
Gray, D. B., 436
Green, G., 272, 274, 275, 277, 288, 475
Green, J., 270
Green, L. J., 305, 356
Greenbank, A., 185
Greenbaum, S., 505
Greenberger, M. T., 248
Greene, B. A., 71
Greene, G., 571
Greenen, S., 106
Greenlan, M., 185
Greenspan, S., 134, 264, 270
Greenwood, C. R., 41, 59, 78, 145, 153, 544
Greer, R. D., 277
Grekin, R., 189
Grenot-Scheyer, M., 161
Gresham, F. M., 174, 221, 229, 234, 249, 274, 423, 425
Gresham, R. M., 214
Griffin, C., 579, 580
Griffin, H. C., 379, 387
Griffin, L. W., 379
Grigal, M., 69, 586
Grigg, W. S., 21
Grigorenko, E. L., 188, 494
Grim, J. C., 321, 322, 466, 475, 476
Grindle, C. F., 275
Grisham-Brown, J., 548
Groen, A. D., 274, 539
Grootenhuis, M. A., 408
Gross, A. M., 225, 594
Gross, B. H., 136
Gross, M. U. M., 508
Grossen, B., 183, 356
Grossi, T. A., 141, 152, 157, 163, 397, 398, 429, 583
Grossman, H., 132
Gruenewald, L., 481
Grunfast, K. M., 340
Guardino, D., 54, 229
Guess, D., 465
Guest, C. M., 351
Guetzloe, E., 242
Guilford, J. P., 493, 499
Guillory, J. D., 572
Gumpel, T. P., 240, 428
Gunter, P. L., 59, 214, 227, 234, 241
Gupta, V. B., 271, 272
Guralnick, M. J., 92, 141, 536, 539, 548
Gurney, J. G., 268
Gursel, O., 156
Gushing, D., 425
Gustason, G., 358, 362
Guth, C. B., 141, 483
Guthrie, D., 138, 535
Gwalla-Ogisi, N., 396

Haager, D., 185
Haas, W. H., 307
Hacker, B., 547
Hadden, D. S., 549
Hadley, P. A., 313
Hagberg, B., 268
Hage, C., 355
Hagerman, R. J., 145
Haggart, A. G., 58
Hagler, L. D., 140
Hagner, D., 580, 593
Hahn, H., 136
Hale, J. E., 58

Hales, L. W., 159
Hall, B. J., 307, 308, 309, 311, 313, 315, 316, 327
Hall, K., 58
Hall, M., 592
Hall, R. V., 153
Hall, S. W., 21, 140, 483
Hall, T. E., 112, 485
Hallahan, D. K., 76, 205
Hallahan, D. P., 186, 192, 236
Hallam, R. A., 549
Hall Apgar, D., 590
Halle, J. W., 185
Hallenbeck, B. A., 242
Haller, A. K., 341
Halpern, A. S., 570, 593
Haltiwanger, J. T., 427
Ham, R., 316
Hamill, L. B., 37, 160, 586
Hamilton, S. L., 200
Hamlett, C. L., 190
Hamm, E. M., 538
Hammer, M. R., 71
Hammill, D. D., 188, 190, 194, 229, 313
Hammis, D., 579, 580
Hammond, M. A., 141
Hamre-Nietupski, S. M., 157
Hancock, L., 424
Hand, K. E., 374
Handleman, J. S., 277, 555, 560
Handler, M. W., 247
Hanft, B., 559
Hanhan, S. F., 102, 111
Hanich, L. B., 184
Hanley, J. P., 479
Hannah, M. E., 97
Hanncock, T. B., 320
Hannon, T. S., 417
Hansen, D. A., 242
Hanson, M. J., 102, 107, 549
Haptonstall-Nykaza, T. S., 358
Hardman, M. L., 14, 142, 145, 146, 457, 592
Haring, K. A., 549
Haring, N. G., 484
Harlacher, J. E., 425
Harland, V. T., 227
Harmston, K. A., 319
Harn, B. A., 42, 179
Harn, W., 325
Harper, G. F., 73, 77, 78
Harr, J. J., 23
Harrington, S. L., 436
Harris, F. R., 236
Harris, H., 316
Harris, K. C., 106, 204
Harris, K. R., 182, 184, 196
Harris, M., 356
Harris, S. L., 277, 316, 555, 560
Harrison, E., 316
Harrison, T. J., 159, 478
Harrop, A., 236
Harry, B., 12, 13, 56, 109
Hart, B. M., 95, 145, 189, 236, 302, 303
Hasazi, J. S., 587
Hasazi, S. B., 568
Hastings, R. P., 93, 478
Hatlen, P., 381, 389, 399
Hauser-Cram, P., 96
Havey, J. M., 76
Hawke, C., 444
Hawkins, B. A., 138
Hawkins, L., 355
Hawks, W., 189
Hay, D., 423
Hayden, C., 590
Haynes, W., 304, 306
Haynie, M., 437
Haywood, H. C., 135, 142
Healey, W. C., 192
Heber, R. F., 148, 537
Hecimovic, A., 420
Heckaman, J., 230
Heckaman, K. A., 479
Heckathorn, J., 553

Heering, P. W., 242
Heflin, L. J., 272, 280, 284, 479
Heikua, U., 139, 142
Heimlich, S. G., 7, 44, 200
Heintz Caldwell, T., 437
Heinze, T., 393
Heironymus, A. N., 189
Heistad, D., 14
Heller, K. W., 408, 409, 435, 437, 441, 444, 467
Hemmeter, M. L., 548
Hemp, R., 583
Henderson, A., 92
Henderson, J. B., 350
Henderson, K., 221
Henderson, L. W., 546
Heng, M. A., 21, 54, 58, 106, 108
Henry, B., 225
Henry, D., 236
Hepburn, S. L., 140, 145
Hepting, N., 320
Herbst, M. H., 234
Herer, G. R., 341
Heron, G. E., 77, 230
Heron, T. E., 78, 79, 106, 113, 140, 157, 158, 204, 232, 233, 274, 428, 475
Herr, C. M., 63, 70, 71, 265, 267
Hertzog, M. A., 229
Heshusius, L., 83
Hessler, T., 77
Heston, M. L., 468
Hetzner, A., 56, 142
Heumann, J., 15
Heward, W. L., 21, 38, 42, 43, 59, 72, 73, 78, 79, 83, 113, 140, 141, 150, 152, 153, 157, 158, 159, 161, 163, 183, 192, 199, 200, 201, 222, 223, 230, 232, 233, 237, 244, 266, 274, 275, 276, 398, 428, 429, 475, 478, 479, 583
Heymans, H. S., 408
Heyne, D., 216
Hicks, D. M., 308, 316
Higbee, T. S., 231
Higbee Mandelbaum, L., 117
Higgins, L. D., 506
Hildreth, B. L., 123
Hill, B. K., 138
Hill, C., 93
Hill, D. S., 78
Hill, E. W., 375, 392
Hill, J. L., 409, 410, 413, 414, 415, 417, 418, 420, 463, 539
Hill, M., 375
Hill, W., 513
Hill Peterson, M., 240
Hilt, A., 478
Hilton, A., 81, 106, 164
Hippler, B. J., 222
Hobbis, D. H., 355
Hobbs, N., 13
Hock, M. F., 77, 186, 192, 195
Hodapp, R. M., 142
Hodge, J., 234
Hodson, B. W., 302
Hoffman, C. C., 227
Hoffman, C. D., 264
Hoffman, R. R., 494
Hogue, E., 150
Hokanson, C. R., Jr., 59
Holaday, B., 445
Holdnack, J. A., 186
Holland, K. D., 93
Hollbrook, M. C., 380
Hollenbeck, K. N., 54
Hollinger, C. L., 54, 505
Holmes, D., 235
Holsen, L., 141
Holub, T., 567
Holvoet, J. F., 413, 457
Hong, B. S. S., 586
Hong, S., 399
Hooper, S. R., 220, 479
Hoover, H. D., 189
Hoover, J. J., 58
Horn, C., 149, 163

Horn, E. H., 485, 544, 548, 553, 554, 559
Horne, D., 193
Horner, A., 277
Horner, R. H., 35, 72, 120, 222, 231, 238, 248, 249, 429, 477, 478
Horton, G., 235
Horton, S. V., 195
Horvat, M., 592
Horvath, B., 571
Horvath, K., 285
Hoskyn, M., 153
Hosp, M. K., 147, 161
Houchins, D. E., 140, 147, 184
Houghton, S., 142
Hourcade, J. J., 441
House, S., 59
Houston, T. L., 265, 267
Howard, J. S., 116, 275, 560
Howard, M. R., 298, 299, 302, 304, 305, 308, 317, 333
Howard, P. W., 73
Howard, V. F., 102, 103, 147
Howard-Allor, J., 78
Howe, C., 145
Howell K. W., 190
Howlin, P., 261
Hoyt-Gonzales, K., 54
Huai, N., 51, 544
Huaqing Qi, C., 56
Huber Marshall, L., 71, 152
Hudson, S., 72, 235
Huebner, K. M., 399
Huefher, D. S., 359
Huerta, N. E., 19, 419
Huestis, R. D., 189
Huff, K. E., 426
Hughes, C. A., 77, 141, 150, 161, 200, 203, 465, 482, 483, 484, 577, 583, 593
Hughes, M. T., 42, 43, 77, 207
Hughes, S., 538
Hughes, T. L., 244
Hughes, W., 574
Huguenin, N. H., 140
Hulit, L. M., 298, 299, 302, 304, 305, 308, 317, 333
Hummel, J. H., 241
Humphries, T., 351
Hunt, N., 414
Hunt, P., 60, 484
Hurley-Chamberlain, D., 63
Hurtubis Sahlen, C. A., 586
Hutinger, P. L., 560
Hutton, A. M., 94, 95, 97, 258
Hyde, M., 349
Hyman, S. L., 268
Hynd, G. W., 188

Iano, R. P., 83
Ida, D. J., 107
Ikeda, D. J., 425
Immunization Safety Review Committee, 269
Inge, K. J., 464, 572, 574, 579, 580, 581
Inghram, J., 316
Inman, T. F., 507
Innocenti, M. S., 95
Interactive Autism Network, 269
Ireland, J. C., 347
Irit, H., 375
Iscoe, I., 14
Isenberg, J. P., 549
Ispen, C., 592
Ita, C. M., 338
Itard, J. M. C., 147
Itkonen, T., 481, 484
Ito, J., 413
Itoi, M., 200
Iverson, V. S., 71, 92, 469
Ives, B., 195
Ivester, J., 572
Ivey, M. L., 280
Ivey, W. F., 586
Iwata, B. A., 232, 478, 479
Izzo, M., 574

Jack, S. L., 227
Jackson, D. W., 331, 337, 351, 365
Jacobs, F. H., 431
Jacobs, H. A., 456
Jacobson, J. W., 72, 134, 274, 284, 285
Jacobson, L. A., 319
Jahoda, A., 141
Jahr, E., 275
Jalongo, M. R., 549
James, D. R., 138
Janney, R. E., 60, 161, 484, 485
Jenkins, J. R., 182
Jensen, P. S., 423
Jensen, W. R., 112, 215, 241, 244, 429
Jernigan, K., 15
Jerome, J., 277
Jimenez, R., 72
Jimerson, S., 224
Jitendra, A. K., 42, 149, 319
Job, K. A., 355
Johnsen, S. K., 501
Johnson, C. E., 118
Johnson, D. R., 569
Johnson, D. W., 77
Johnson, E., 175, 177
Johnson, F., 481
Johnson, H. L., 93
Johnson, K. R., 21
Johnson, L., 71
Johnson, M. D., 574
Johnson, N., 72, 235
Johnson, P., 98, 571
Johnson, R. T., 77, 322
Johnson, S., 577
Johnson, T. P., 29
Johnson-Martin, N. M., 547, 555
Johnston, L., 436
Johnston, M. A., 236
Johnston, M. K., 236
Johnston, R., 316
Johnston, S. S., 538
Joint UN Programme on HIV/AIDS, 419
Jolivette, J., 234
Jolivette, K., 140, 147, 161, 239, 240, 241, 428
Jolly, A. C., 484
Jones, D. E., 443
Jones, E. A., 261
Jones, E. D., 508, 509
Jones, H. A., 107
Jones, J., 544
Jones, X., 559
Jordan, L., 111–112
Jordan, N. C., 184
Jordan, T., 590
Jorgensen, J., 481
Joseph, G. E., 77, 236, 550
Joseph, L. M., 147, 161, 241, 428
Jung, L. A., 71
Jung, S., 548
Justen, J. E., 454
Justice, L. M., 298, 311, 319, 320, 553

Kaczmarek, L., 320
Kaderavek, J. N., 346
Kadesjo, B., 268
Kagan, J., 225
Kaiser, A. P., 97, 221, 320, 321, 322, 466, 475, 476
Kalyanpur, M., 109
Kame'enui, E. J., 42, 153, 179, 180, 181, 182, 191, 192, 203, 248
Kaminski, R. A., 191
Kamphaus, R. W., 229
Kamps, D. M., 226, 230, 479
Kanaya, T., 137
Kang, W., 224
Kangas, K. A., 321, 323
Kanner, A. M., 415, 417, 427
Kanner, L., 257, 268
Kaplan, D. E., 188
Kaplan, F., 590
Kaplan, S., 501, 507
Karabin, M., 397
Karchmer, M. A., 336, 337, 364

Karlsen, B., 190
Karnes, F. A., 494, 501
Karnick, N. S., 227
Karvonen, M., 71
Kasari, C., 274
Kashara, M., 98
Kassorla, I. C., 264
Kastner, T. A., 590
Katayama, A. D., 200
Katsiyannis, A., 28, 219, 220, 241, 246, 247, 248, 443, 444
Katz, P., 585
Kauffman, J. M., 12, 14, 42, 56, 59, 76, 185, 205, 214, 219, 220, 221, 224, 225, 226, 242, 247, 248
Kaufman, A., 394
Kautz, K. J., 422
Kavale, K. A., 42, 72, 76, 174, 175, 178, 179, 184, 185, 186, 187, 189, 194, 214, 424
Kazdan, S., 78
Kea, C. D., 107
Keavney, M., 236
Keenan, M., 20, 277
Kehle, T. J., 244
Keith, K. D., 593
Keith, T., 92
Kelker, K., 420
Keller, C. L., 237
Kellet, K., 277
Kellum, K. K., 479
Kelly, C. S., 236
Kelly, D. J., 303
Kelly, J. P., 387
Kelly, M. L., 112
Kelly, S. J., 262
Kendig, H., 98
Kennedy, C. H., 76, 161, 468, 480, 481, 484, 485
Kenney, K. M., 479
Keogh, B. K., 12, 138, 192, 535
Kephart, N. C., 193
Kern, J. K., 285
Kern, L., 231, 234, 478
Kerr, B., 505
Kerr, K. P., 277
Kerr, M. M., 113, 241
Kershner, J., 189
Keul, P. A., 152
Keyes, M. W., 71, 469
Keyworth, R., 73
Kieff, J., 538
Kieman, W. E., 583
Kiernans, I., 592
Kiewra, K. A., 199, 200
Killian, D., 565, 597
Killu, K., 478
Kim, S. H., 133, 145, 457, 458, 590
Kimball, J. W., 277, 278, 279
Kincaid, D., 280
King, B. H., 142
King, E. W., 506
King, N. J., 216
King, S. J., 364
King-Sears, M., 155, 161
Kingsley, M., 374, 375
Kinney, E. M., 277, 279
Kirby, J., 387
Kirby, P. C., 240, 428
Kirk, S. A., 173, 193
Kirk, W. D., 193
Kito, K., 255, 289
Klatzky, R. L., 393
Kleefeld, J., 235
Klein, J. O., 341, 588, 589, 590, 593
Klein, K., 424
Klein, M. D., 543, 548
Klein, R. E., 436
Kleinert, H. L., 149, 468, 593
Kleinheksel, K. A., 199
Klein-Tasman, B. P., 145
Klevstrand, M., 274
Kleweno, C. P., 387
Kliewer, C., 12
Klimes-Dougan, B., 118

Kline, F. M., 192, 427
Klingner, J., 72
Klingner, J. J., 58
Klingner, J. K., 12, 13, 43, 56, 77
Klug, B. J., 503
Kluth, P., 264
Kluwin, T. N., 337, 364
Knecht, H. A., 347
Knightly, C. A., 341
Knokey, A., 338
Knoll, J. A., 569, 590
Knoors, H., 338, 348
Knowlton, E., 150
Knowlton, M., 382
Kobersy, M. R., 25
Kochhar, C. A., 484
Kochhar-Bryant, C. A., 60, 76, 81, 94, 107, 559, 572
Kodak, T., 479
Koegel, L. K., 277, 475
Koegel, R. L., 277, 475, 478
Koenig, A. J., 380, 382, 383, 384, 390, 393
Koestler, F. A., 399
Koestner, R., 236
Koger, F., 465, 468, 592
Kohl, F. L., 468
Kohler, P. D., 571, 578
Kohn, A., 236
Kokoska, S. M., 355
Komesaroff, L., 336, 349
Konold, K. B., 156
Konold, K. E., 156
Konold, T. R., 12, 59, 214, 229
Konrad, M., 71, 140, 184, 241, 428, 574, 576, 577
Koot, H. M., 141
Koppenhaver, D. A., 324
Korzilius, H., 141
Kraemer, B. R., 574
Krajewski, J. J., 161, 414
Krantz, P. J., 277, 279
Krathwohl, D., 513
Kratochwill, T. R., 236
Kregel, J., 579
Kreicbergs, U., 414
Kreiner, J., 592
Kretlow, A. G., 118
Kroth, R. L., 110, 112, 120, 123
Kube, D. A., 422
Kubina, R. M., Jr., 20, 192
Kuczera, M., 559
Kugel, R. B., 590
Kuhn, T., 180
Kulik, C. L. C., 524
Kulik, J. A., 524
Kulikowich, J. M., 512
Kulman, L., 341
Kuna, J., 146
Kuntze, M., 337
Kuoch, H., 280
Kupermintz, H., 361
Kutash, K., 219, 220
Kymissis, E., 236

LaBlance, G. R., 318
Lachapelle, Y., 593
Lackaye, T., 186
Lacy-Rismiller, L., 238
Ladd, P., 334
LaFlamme, M., 445
Lago-Delello, E., 226
LaGrow, S. J., 393
Lahm, E. A., 475
Lake, J. F., 105
Lakin, K. C., 569, 587, 590
Lalich, J., 287
Lalli, J. S., 477, 592
Lamb, D. R., 236
Lambert, M. C., 163
Lambert, N. K., 138
Lambert, R. G., 77
Lancaster, J., 78
Lancaster, P., 569
Lancioni, G. E., 397, 466, 475, 478, 592
Landa, R. J., 269, 270

Landesman, S., 537
Landrum, M., 523
Landrum, T. J., 14, 203, 219, 220, 246
Landy, S., 226
Lane, H. B., 111–112
Lane, H. L., 336, 349
Lane, K. L., 185, 204, 216, 219, 221, 222, 228, 233, 234, 235, 241, 425, 478
Lane, L., 221
Lang, H. G., 351
Langdon, H. W., 58
Langlois, J. A., 460
Langone, J., 149, 538
Lanigan, K. J., 25
Lannie, A. L., 242
La Paro, K. M., 549
LaPlante, M., 568
Larkin, M. J., 153
Larsen, S., 194
Larson, S. A., 142, 590
Lathrop, M., 54, 229
Lattimore, L. P., 578
Laud, L., 184
La Vor, M. L., 431
Layng, T. V. J., 21
Lazarus, B. D., 199, 200
Le, L., 277
Leader-Janssen, B., 184
Learning Disabilities Association of America, 207
LeBlanc, L. A., 277
Le Couteur, A., 271
Ledford, M. R., 264
Lee, C., 429
Lee, M. G., 200
Lee, S. H., 152, 155, 161, 277
Lees, R., 307
Lefever, D. W., 193
LeFevre, J., 92
Leffert, J. S., 134
Lehmann, J. P., 586
Lehr, D. H., 440, 443
Lehr, S., 196
Lehtinen, L., 193
Lehtinen, S., 193
Leigh, I. W., 336
Leigh, S. A., 375, 380
Leith, W., 307
Leland, H., 138
Lemay, R., 164
Lenz, B. K., 186, 194, 195, 203
Leonard, B. J., 93
Leonard, B. R., 479
Leonard, C. M., 188
Leonard, I. J., 428, 429
Leone, P. E., 224, 246
Leong-Norona, K., 241
Leon-Guerrero, R., 58
Lepper, C., 102, 103
Lepper, M. R., 236
Lerman, P., 590
Lerner, J. W., 192
LeRoy, C. H., 420
Levack, N., 380
Levendoski, L. S., 240
Levine, K., 145
Levine, P., 92, 567, 569
Levitt, H., 335, 342
Levy, F., 423
Lewis, M. S., 351
Lewis, P., 465
Lewis, R. B., 77, 314
Lewis, S., 383
Lewis, T. J., 72, 235, 241, 247
Lewis-Palmer T., 248
Leybaert, J., 355
Li, A., 385, 386
Li, S., 553, 554
Lian, M. G. J., 107
Liaupsin, C. J., 230, 233, 478
Liberman, M. L., 436
Lieber, J., 553, 554
Lieberman, L. J., 374, 436
Lienemann, T., 184

Lien-Thorne, S., 226
Lifshitz, H., 375
Lighthouse International, 379
Lignugaris/Kraft, B., 71, 242
Lim, L., 466
Lim, S. Y., 116
Lin, F. Y., 20
Lin, S., 94
Lindberg, J. S., 479
Linden, M. L., 65, 67, 69
Lindfoors, J. W., 297
Lindsay, G., 306
Lindsley, O. R., 192
Lindstrom, L. E., 98, 571, 574, 578
Ling, D., 354
Lingo, A. S., 140, 234
Lippke, B. A., 312
Lipsey, M. W., 174, 215
Liptak, G. S., 411
Liu, Y., 364
Llewellyn, G., 98
Lloyd, L. L., 321, 323, 525
Lloyd, R. J., 571
Lo, Y., 21, 163, 222, 231, 425, 428, 429
Lockshin, S., 262, 479
Lockshin, S. B., 286
Logan, K. R., 456, 475
Lohmeier, K. L., 394
Long, E., 481
Loomis, J. M., 393
Lopez, J. A., 118
Lopez-Vasquez, A., 106
Lopez-Wagner, M. C., 264
Lord, C., 269, 270, 271
Lorimer, P. A., 280
Lovaas, O. I., 13, 264, 273, 274, 486
Love, L. L., 569
Lovett, D. L., 71
Lovett, M. W., 182
Lovitt, T. C., 14, 15, 42, 187, 195
Lowenthal, B., 415
Lucas, C., 359
Lucas, W., 389
Luce, S. C., 288
Luchshyn, J. M., 97
Luckasson, R., 133, 135, 137, 138, 142, 143, 145, 569
Lucker, T., 98
Lue, M. S., 298
Lueck, A. H., 385
Luecking, R., 580
Lueke, B., 549
Luft, P., 571
Luhaorg, H., 139
Luker, C., 98
Lunsford, S., 399
Lusk, K. E., 387
Lusthaus, E., 458
Luterman, D., 349
Lutz, S., 236
Lynch, E., 102, 107
Lyon, G. R., 179, 186
Lyon, R., 31
Lyon, S. L., 158
Lytle, R. K., 71

Maag, J. W., 28, 216, 219, 227, 234, 235, 237, 241, 422, 423, 424, 428, 429
Macaruso, P., 262
Maccini, P., 184, 203
MacFarlane, C. A., 236
MacGinitie, R. K., 190
MacGinitie, W. H., 190
Machek, G. R., 178, 189
Macias, C. M., 468, 592
Macintosh, K., 249
Mackie, C., 306
Mackiewicz, S. M., 118, 119
Mackintosh, V. H., 269
MacLean, K., 145
MacMillan, D. L., 56, 134, 221, 274
MacSweeney, M., 356
Macurdy, S., 440

Macy, M. L., 54, 171, 206, 553
Madaus, J., 244
Madaus, J. W., 244, 585, 586
Madaus, M. M., 244
Madden, R., 190
Maes, B., 455, 457, 458
Magiera, K., 62, 63
Magnan, A., 356
MaGuire, A. M., 277
Maheady, B., 89, 124
Maheady, L., 41, 59, 73, 77, 78, 162
Mahr, G., 307
Mahshie, S. N., 359, 360
Maier, J., 60, 484
Majd, M., 77
Maker, C. J., 495, 497, 504, 519
Malanga, P., 192
Malian, I. M., 569
Mallard, D. F., 175
Mallette, B., 73, 77, 78
Malmgren, K., 355, 356, 357
Malone, D. M., 538
Mancil, G. R., 277
Mank, D., 580, 585
Mankin, G., 140
Mann, D., 538
Mantegna, M. E., 478
March, J., 219
Marchand, T., 16
Marchand-Martella, N. E., 71, 196, 236, 242, 428, 429, 440
Marchand-Martella, R. C., 196
Marchant, M., 240, 242
Marchisan, M. L., 184
Marckel, J. M., 277
Marder, C., 11, 422, 569
Margalit, M., 186
Maria, K., 190
Marks, L. J., 220
Markwardt, F. C., Jr., 189
Marland, S., 493
Marmolejo, E. K., 163
Marquis, J., 443
Marschark, M., 338, 348, 360
Marshall, L. H., 578, 596
Marshall, S., 560
Marston, J. R., 393
Martella, R. C., 71, 236, 428, 429, 440
Martella, R. M., 242
Martens, B. K., 478
Martin, C. M., 21, 510, 512
Martin, J. E., 71, 150, 152, 428, 571, 578, 596
Martin, S. L., 537
Maruyama, G., 236
Masataka, N., 359
Mason, C. Y., 71
Mason, H., 379
Mason, L., 184
Mason-Main, M., 583
Massey, N. G., 277
Mastin, M. E., 145
Mastropieri, M. A., 77, 199, 202
Mather, N., 189–190, 420, 421, 424
Mathes, P. G., 78, 174
Matheson, C., 591
Matheson, E., 141
Mathews, S., 415
Matson, J. L., 231, 257
Matta, D., 62
Mattison, R. E., 220
Mattson, P. D., 194
Matuszny, R. M., 102, 106, 108, 120, 122
Maurice, C., 272, 277, 285, 288
Mayer, C., 360
Mayer, G. R., 248
Mayer-Johnson, R., 322
Mayes, S. D., 261
McAdam, D. B., 375
McAllister, J. W., 433
McBride, B. J., 553
McBride, B. M., 97
McBurnett, K., 424
McCabe, H., 98

McCaffrey, R. J., 97
McCarn, J. E., 466
McCarten, K., 560
McCarthy, J. J., 193
McClannahan, L. E., 277, 279
McCoach, D. B., 518
McComas, J., 277, 445
McComas, N., 550
McConaughy, S. H., 229
McConnell, M. E., 241, 428
McConnell, S., 235, 277, 282, 550
McCord, B. E., 200
McCormick, L., 548, 549, 557
McCuin, D., 21
McCurdy, B. L., 242
McDaid, P., 443
McDermott, S., 146
McDevitt, B., 387
McDonnell, A. P., 457, 538
McDonnell, J. J., 14, 457, 470
McDonough, C. S., 59
McEachin, J. J., 274
McEntire, E., 190
McEvoy, A., 225
McFarland, J., 97
McGahee-Kovac, M., 71
McGee, G. G., 277
McGee, J. J., 479
McGee, R. O., 225
McGill, T., 441
McGinnis, J. C., 242
McGonigel, M. J., 61
McGough, S. M., 356
McGrew, K. S., 189–190
McGuffin, P., 225
McHale, S. M., 97
McHugh, E., 436
McHugh, M., 97
McInerney, W., 557
McIntosh, R., 72, 185
McIntyre, L. L., 574
McIntyre, T., 246
McKee, B. G., 350
McKenzie, B., 60
McKerchar, P. M., 553
McKinney, J. D., 236
McKnight, M. A., 175
McLaughlin, J. A., 314
McLaughlin, M. J., 12, 468
McLaughlin, T. F., 147
McLaughlin, V. L., 203
McLean, M. E., 544, 546, 548
McLeskey, J., 185
McLone, D. G., 413
McMahan, G. A., 436
McMaster, K. L., 78, 277
McNamara, B. E., 192
McNamara, K., 54
McNamara, K. M., 54, 467
McNicholas, J., 351
McPartland, P., 572
McReynolds, L. V., 306
McTernan, M., 591
Meadan, H., 185
Meadow-Orlans, K. P., 342, 351, 355
Meadows, N. B., 235, 246
Mears, B., 433
Mechling, L. C., 149, 397, 455, 583
Meier, C. R., 234, 247
Meinberg, D., 277
Meisel, S., 246
Meisels, S. J., 540, 546
Mellard, D. F., 569
Menacker, S. J., 379
Menard, C., 264
Menlove, R. R., 71
Menolascino, F. J., 479
Menzies, H. M., 216, 228, 235
Mercer, C. D., 179, 184, 192, 241
Merrell, K. W., 425
Merrill, E. C., 139, 140
Mervis, C. B., 145
Messer, D., 319

Messer, J. J., 428
Metheny, J., 98, 571
Metz, B., 284
Meyer, L. H., 480
Michael, J., 425
Michael, L., 491, 526
Michielli-Pendl, J., 49, 62, 63, 77, 84
Midlarsky, E., 97
Miller, A. D., 21, 140
Miller, C. J., 188
Miller, D. N., 247
Miller, J. H., 184
Miller, K. A., 59
Miller, M. D., 184
Miller, M. M., 379
Miller, R., 150
Miller, S. P., 156
Miller, V. S., 285
Miltenberger, R. G., 375, 479
Minarovic, T. J., 583
Minor, R. J., 392
Mira, M. P., 462
Mirabal, J. V., 118
Miracle, S. A., 468
Miranda, P., 321
Mirenda, P., 280
Mistrett, S. G., 538
Mitchell, A. I., 13, 142, 146
Mitchell, D., 76
Mitchell, R. E., 336, 337, 338
Mithaug, D. K., 466
Moberly, R. L., 443
Mock, D. R., 14, 192, 205
Moffitt, T. W., 225
Mokkink, L. B., 408
Molloy, C. A., 285
Monda-Amaya, L. E., 185, 204
Monikowski, C., 350
Montague, M., 229
Montgomery, D. J., 106, 503
Montgomery, J. K., 341
Monzo, L., 107
Moody, S. W., 42, 77, 203, 207
Moon, M. S., 464, 572, 574, 581, 586
Moon, S., 521
Mooney, P., 234
Moore, J. E., 380
Moores, D. F., 31, 336, 340, 364
Moreno, C., 356
Morgan, C. D., 230
Morgan, D. P., 241, 429
Morgan, P. L., 78
Morocco, C. C., 199
Morren, J., 478
Morrier, M. J., 277
Morris, R. J., 228
Morris, T. L., 216, 219
Morris, W., 243
Morris, Y. P., 228
Morrison, G. M., 224
Morrison, G. S., 235, 549, 555
Morrison, H., 200
Morrison, R., 550
Morrison, R. S., 20, 277, 466, 538
Morse, T. E., 160
Morsink, C. V., 107
Mortweet, S. L., 161
Moser, H. W., 142
Most, D. E., 145
Most, T., 185
Mostert, M. P., 42, 186
Mottram, L., 244
Mount, J., 389
Mow, S., 354
Moxley, R. A., 240
Mudford, O., 479
Mueller, R. A., 269
Mueninghoff, B., 255, 289
Muir, D. W., 385
Mukooney, K., 359
Mulcahy, C. A., 184
Mulick, J. A., 72, 284, 285
Mull, C., 586

Mullick, J. A., 274
Multimodal Treatment Study Group, 424
Munk, D. D., 479
Munson, L. J., 414
Munson, S. M., 547
Munton, S. M., 235
Murdick, N. L., 16, 25, 106, 420, 444
Murdock, J. Y., 240, 428
Murphy, C. M., 262, 276, 479
Murphy, D. L., 93
Murphy, G., 138
Murphy, K. A., 244
Murphy, S., 580
Murray, C., 586
Murray, H. A., 230
Musante, C. M., 468, 592
Musselman, C., 360
Myers, A., 71
Myers, B. J., 269
Myers, P. I., 188, 194
Myles, B. S., 259, 271, 280, 285

Nadogapal, K., 494
Nagle, K., 468
Naglieri, J. A., 504
Naidu, S., 342
Nakken, H., 455
Naseef, R. A., 93
National Alliance for Autism Research, 288
National Association for Gifted Children, 501, 508, 524
National Association for the Education of Young Children (NAEYC), 549
National Association of the Deaf, 348, 364
National Center for Education Statistics, 585
National Center for Injury Prevention and Control, 460
National Center for the Study of Postsecondary Educational Supports, 585
National Center on Student Progress Monitoring, 59
National Education Association, 58
National Institute of Child Health and Human Development, 196
National Institute of Health Consensus Statement, 423
National Institute of Mental Health, 274
National Institute on Deafness and Other Communication Disorders (NIDCD), 338, 341, 348
National Institutes of Health (NIH), 269, 414
National Joint Committee on Learning Disabilities (NJCLD), 173, 174, 177, 188, 207
National Organization on Disability, 568, 592
National Reading Panel, 21, 42, 182, 191, 356
National Research Center on Learning Disabilities, 177, 178
National Research Center on the Gifted and Talented, 525
National Research Council, 261, 269, 288
National Spinal Cord Injury Statistical Center, 414
National Symposium on Learning Disabilities in English Language Learners, 107
National Technical Assistance Center, 457, 459
Navarro, V., 131
Neal, J., 433
Nechring, W. M., 409
Neddenriep, C. E., 244
Neef, N. A., 200, 231, 232, 233, 277, 426, 478
Neel, R. S., 246
Nehring, W. M., 146
Neihart, M., 521
Neilsen, M. E., 506
Neisworth, J. T., 544, 547
Nelson, A. R., 538
Nelson, C. M., 113, 227, 241, 246, 247, 347, 538
Nelson, G. L., 384, 385
Nelson, J. M., 178, 189
Nelson, J. R., 216, 219, 220, 225, 234, 242
Nelson, J. S., 199
Nelson, L. G. L., 102
Nelson, L. L., 98, 101
Nelson, M., 76
Nelson, P. B., 118, 347

Nemer, K. M., 525
Netzel, D. M., 238
Neu, T., 505, 506
Neubert, D. A., 586
Neuharth-Pritchett, S., 417, 418
Neville, B., 141
Nevin, A. I., 62
Newborg, J., 547
Newcomer, J. R., 22
Newcomer, P. L., 182, 313
Newman, B., 277
Newman, L., 92, 567, 569
Newsom, C. D., 264
Newton, D., 436
New York State Department of Health, 288
NICHCY, 410
Nichols, S. K., 383
Nicholson, R., 433
Nielson, A. B., 504, 519
Nielson, M. E., 56
Niemeyer, J. A., 375
Nihira, K., 138
Nirje, B., 164
Njardvok, U., 139
Nobel, M. M., 77
Noell, G. H., 92, 117
Noens, I. L. J., 263
Nolan, E. E., 425
Nolet, V., 190
Noonan, M. J., 548, 549, 557
Noone, S. J., 478
Nordness, P. D., 219–220
Norins Bardon, J., 77, 161
Norman, A., 149
North, K. H., 296
Northern, J. L., 336, 340, 343
Northup, J., 424, 425
Notari-Syverson, A. R., 550
Nourse, S., 586
Novak, J. M., 58, 574
Nowacek, E. J., 236
Nugent, S. A., 498

Oaks, J., 524
Ober, J., 594
Obiakor, F. E., 58
O'Brien, J., 578
Ochoa, S. H., 185
Ochoa, T., 247
O'Cleirigh, C. M., 375
O'Conner, R. E., 175, 182
Odding, E., 409, 410
Odom, S. L., 43, 72, 544, 547, 548, 549
O'Donnell, B., 389
Office of Disability Employment Policy, 580
Office of Juvenile Justice and Delinquency Prevention, 221
Office of Technology Assessment, 443
Offringa, M., 408
Ogletree, B., 325
Ogletree, G., 445
Ohio Department of Education, 573
Ohtake, Y., 468, 469, 470
Oliva, D., 397
Oliver, G. W., 376
Oliver, M. N. I., 95
Ollendick, T. H., 216
Olmstead, J. E., 394
Olsen, R. J., 427, 591
Olvey, G., 578
Olympia, D. W., 112, 429
O'Neill, R. E., 163, 231, 478
Onslow, M., 316
Oranje, A., 21
O'Reilly, M. F., 397, 475, 478, 592
Orelove, F. P., 444, 486
Ormsbee, C. J., 549
Oros, T., 387
Orsillo, S. M., 97
Orsmond, G. I., 97
Ortiz, A., 58
Osborn, J., 196
Osher, D., 56, 224, 227

Ospelt, H., 478
Oster, M. M., 234, 247
Osterling, J., 272
Ostrosky, M., 544, 559
Oswald, D. P., 56, 285
Oswald, K., 248
Overton, T., 137
Owen, R. L., 184
Owens, R. E., Jr., 297, 298, 302, 305, 312
Owens-Johnson, L., 37, 71, 160, 469
Oyer, H. J., 307

Pacer Center, 567
Packman, A., 316
Padden, C., 351
Page, E. B., 537
Paglieri, R. A., 285
Pakulski, L. A., 346
Palfrey, J. S., 432, 437
Palmer, D. J., 185
Palmer, D. S., 76
Palmer, J. D., 503
Palmer, S., 548
Paniagua, F. A., 426
Papanicolaou, A. C., 188
Paparella, T., 274
Parent, W., 571
Parette, H. P., 96, 120, 123, 436, 441
Parette, P., 436
Park, J., 585
Park, M., 56
Parker, C. E., 77, 199
Parker, G., 246
Parker, R. C., 77, 161
Parkin, A. J., 393
Parmar, R. S., 76, 184, 203
Parrish, L. H., 146
Parrish, T. B., 23
Parsons, M. B., 466, 578
Partington, J. W., 275, 277
Passow, A., 503
Patel, P., 184
Patterson, G. R., 225, 226, 227
Patterson, J. M., 93
Patton, B., 239, 240, 241, 428
Patton, J. R., 133, 145, 150, 151, 164, 186, 574
Patton, M., 58
Paul, J. N., 478
Paul, P. V., 336, 337, 353, 355, 356, 357
Paul, T. L., 396
Pauls, D., 258
Pavri, S., 185
Payne, K. T., 305
Payne, L., 220
Payne, S., 14
Pease, L., 456
Peck, C. A., 466, 480, 481
Peck, S., 467
Peckham, V. C., 414
Peel, B. B., 111–112
Peel, H. A., 111–112
Pelham, W. E., 424
Pelham, W. W., 424
Pelios, L., 478
Pellegrin, A. L., 92, 117
Pellegrino, L., 143, 409, 410, 411
Pence, K. L., 298
Pennington, B. F., 225, 423
Perez-Selles, M., 58
Perla, F., 389
Perlman, S. P., 96
Perrin, E. C., 430, 448
Perrin, J. M., 408
Perske, R., 136, 164
Petch-Hogan, B., 120, 123
Peterson, L. D., 238, 240
Peterson, S. M., 231, 232, 233, 240, 277, 429, 478
Petroff, J., 436
Petry, K., 455, 457, 458
Petursdottir, A., 277
Pfetzing, D., 358
Phillips, B., 549
Philofsky, A., 140, 145

Pianta, R. C., 214, 229, 549
Piazza, C. C., 479
Piché, L., 321
Pierce, C. D., 220, 234
Pierce, W. D., 236
Pierson, M. R., 185, 204, 219, 222, 280
Piirto, J., 494, 496, 497, 499, 500, 507, 515, 521, 522
Pindzola, R., 304, 306
Pitcarin, T. K., 141
Pittman, P., 359
Pivik, J., 445
Plaxen, J. R., 412
Plomin, R., 225
Plotts, C. A., 219, 224
Plumber, D., 503
Pogrund, R. L., 392
Poirier, J. M., 224
Poling, A., 479
Pollack, W., 505
Polloway, E. A., 142, 164
Pollster, B., 587, 590
Poloni-Staudinger, L., 57
Polsgrove, L., 247
Ponchillia, P. E., 393
Popkin, J., 242
Porter, J. H., 302
Porter, S., 437
Porterfield, K., 311
Post, M., 397
Poulson, C. L., 236, 275
Powell, L., 142
Powell-Smith, K. A., 280
Power, D., 349
Powers, L. E., 106
Powers, S., 504
Poyadue, F. S., 93, 120
Prabhala, A., 15
Pratton, J., 159
Prayzer, R., 113
Prelock, P. A., 327
Presley, J., 483
Prestia, K., 422
Pretti-Frontczak, K., 548, 550, 553, 555, 556
Price, L., 186
Price, T., 107
Pridgen, L. S., 149
Prinz, P. M., 360
Prior, M., 225
Professional Development in Autism Center, 261, 262, 270, 274
Prouty, R., 587, 590
Pugach, M., 72
Pugh, G. S., 394
Pullen, P. C., 179, 192
Purcell, J. H., 512
Purcell, M. L., 548
Putnam, J. W., 484
Puzzanchera, C., 224

Qi, C. H., 221
Quartrano, L. A., 436
Queen, R. M., 586
Quigley, S. P., 336, 353
Quinn, M. M., 219, 224
Quintanar, R. S., 58

Rabian, B., 280, 281
Rabidoux, P., 594
Rademacher, J. A., 123
Raharinirina, S., 436
Rahsotte, C. A., 313
Raimondo, B., 92
Rak, E. C., 393
Ramaswamy, V., 557
Ramey, C. T., 537
Ramey, S. L., 537
Ramig, P. R., 307
Ramp, E. M., 21
Ramsey, E., 214
Ramsey, M., 239, 240, 241, 428
Ranalli, P., 240, 241, 428, 429
Rance-Roney, J. A., 506

Randall, C., 236
Randolph, J. J., 161, 163
Rao, G., 417
Rao, S. M., 277
Rao, S. S., 105
Raschke, D. B., 468
Raskind, W. H., 188
Ratner, N. B., 311
Raven, J. C., 504
Ray, M. T., 468
Rea, P. J., 203
Reagon, K. A., 231
Reavis, H. K., 215, 244
Reed, F., 204
Reed, P., 437
Reed, V. A., 305, 309, 321
Reese, J. H., 184
Reeve, K. F., 275
Reeve, S. A., 275
Rehfeldt, R. A., 279
Reichler, R. J., 271
Reid, C., 504
Reid, D. H., 466, 538, 578
Reid, J. D., 225
Reid, R., 184, 219–220, 229, 234, 422, 423, 424, 426, 428
Reilly, A., 95
Reinecke, D. R., 277
Reinhart, S. C., 492
Reis, S. M., 501, 512, 513, 518, 519
Reiss, M. M., 142
Reiss, S., 142
Remington, B., 275, 426
Remington-Guerney, J., 284
Renner, B. R., 271
Renzulli, J. S., 494, 495, 501, 502, 505, 512, 513, 518, 519
Repp, A. C., 479
Reschly, D. J., 12, 56
Resetar, J. L., 92, 117, 118
Revell, G., 579
Revell, W. G., Jr., 579, 581
Rex, E. J., 382
Reyes-Blane, M. E., 111–112
Reynolds, C. R., 229
Reynolds, M. C., 14
Rhee, S. H., 225
Rhode, G., 215, 220, 226, 227, 241, 244, 245, 429
Rhodes, R. L., 261
Rhodes, W. C., 12
Rhoten, C., 348
Riccards, P., 31
Ricci-Balich, J., 441
Riccomini, P. J., 234
Rice, C., 269
Rich, K., 211, 250
Richards, T. L., 188
Richardson, B. G., 243
Richardson, V., 72
Richman, G., 232
Richter, M., 72, 235
Ricketts, T. A., 346
Riffle, T., 240, 429
Rimland, B., 272, 285
Rimm, S. B., 505, 526
Rimm-Kaufman, S. E., 225
Rinaldi, C., 109
Risley, T., 145, 236
Risley, T. R., 95, 189, 302, 303
Ritvo, E. R., 259
Rizzolo, M. C., 583
Roach, R. T., 51, 544
Roane, R., 425
Roane, H. S., 479
Roberson, L., 355
Roberts, C. D., 146
Roberts, G., 176, 182
Roberts, J. E., 143, 145
Roberts, J. L., 507
Roberts, J. P., 145
Roberts, N. E., 425
Roberts, P. H., 174
Roberts, R. E., 221

Robertson, G. J., 190
Robins, D. L., 270
Robinson, D. H., 200
Robinson, J., 587
Robinson, K. E., 244
Robinson, N., 521
Robinson, P. D., 21
Robinson Spohn, J. R., 554
Rockwell, S., 242
Rodriguez, P., 93
Roebroeck, M. E., 409
Roeder, I., 427
Rogan, P., 580
Rogers, J. A., 504
Rogers, K., 525
Rogers, M. F., 280
Rogers, S. J., 140, 145
Roid, G. H., 137
Roizen, N. J., 143, 409
Rojahn, J., 134
Rolider, A., 231
Roman, C., 384, 385
Romanczyk, R. G., 262, 275, 284, 286, 479
Romaniuk, C., 478, 479
Romanoff, B., 504
Romer, L. T., 484
Root, S., 279
Roring, R. W., 494
Rorschach, H., 230
Roscoe, E. M., 479
Rose, J., 338
Rose, T. L., 559
Roseberry-McKibbin, C., 314, 315
Rosenblatt, A., 221
Rosenblum, L. P., 375, 394
Rosenshine, B. V., 153, 196
Rosenthal, B., 387
Rosner, B. A., 145
Ross, D. E., 277
Ross, M., 335, 342
Rosser Sandt, D. D., 591
Roszmann-Millican, M., 61
Roth, J., 557
Rotherham, A. J., 59
Rourke, B., 188
Rous, B. S., 549
Rowland, C., 467
Roy, S., 184
Rueda, R., 107, 109
Ruef, M., 96, 97
Rues, J. P., 413, 414, 437, 457
Rusch, F. R., 567, 571, 582
Rush, A. J., 141
Rushakoff, G. E., 319
Russell, S. C., 427
Russell-Minda, E., 387
Rutherford, R. B., 219, 224, 246
Rutland-Brown, W., 460
Rutter, M., 216, 225, 268, 270, 271
Ryan, A., 235
Ryan, B. P., 316
Ryan, J. B., 241
Ryan, R. M., 236
Ryan, S., 145, 147
Ryan-Griffith, M. K., 405, 445
Ryndak, D. L., 77, 161, 480, 485
Ryser, G., 387, 501

Sabornie, E. J., 185, 219
Sacca, M. K., 78
Sack-Min, J., 23
Sacks, G., 319
Sacks, S. Z., 375, 376, 379, 385, 394
Sadler, F. H., 557
Safer, D. J., 423
Safford, E. J., 42
Safford, P. L., 42
Safran, J. S., 259
Safran, S. P., 248
Sagan, C., 287
Sailor, W., 14
Sainato, D. M., 78, 157, 158, 277, 466, 478, 538, 548, 550, 554

Sale, P., 71
Sale, R. P., 152
Salend, S. J., 58, 62, 76, 77, 161, 305, 314, 425
Salinas, A., 305, 314
Salmon, M. D., 548, 550
Salmon, S., 184
Salvia, J., 54, 137
Sanchez, J., 188
Sandall, S., 77, 548, 550, 553, 554
Sandall, S. R., 272
Sandler, A. D., 285
Sandoval, J., 189
Santelli, B., 120
Santosti, F. J., 280, 281
Sapienza, C., 308, 316
Sapon-Shevin, M., 81
Sarouphim, K. M., 504
Sasso, G., 76
Sathur, R., 219
Satterfield, S. T., 355
Saunders, S., 241
Sax, L., 422
Sayers, L. K., 60
Scandary, J., 432
Scanlon, D., 195
Scattone, D., 280, 281
Schaeffler, C., 413
Schafer, P. O., 415, 417, 427
Schalock, R. L., 133, 135, 137, 138, 239, 428, 583, 593
Schartz, M., 426
Schepis, M. M., 583
Schessel, D. A., 341
Scheuermann, B., 241, 268, 277, 470, 476
Schick, B., 358, 361
Schirmer, B. R., 336, 346, 356, 360
Schlein, S. J., 468
Schloss, P. J., 428
Schnoes, C., 422
Schock, K., 478
Schonert-Reichl, K. A., 221
Schopler, E., 271
Schreibman, L., 189, 268, 272, 277, 284, 285, 479
Schreier, E. M., 392
Schreuder, R., 348, 387
Schulz, H., 325
Schulz, J. D., 98
Schum, R. L., 219
Schumaker, J. B., 77, 182, 186, 194, 195, 203
Schumm, J. S., 62, 81, 185, 203, 222
Schuster, J. W., 160, 163, 464
Schwartz, A. A., 285
Schwartz, I. S., 75, 81, 97, 161, 225, 272, 277, 480, 481, 548, 550, 553, 554
Schwartzman, M. N., 437
Schweigert, P., 467
Scorgie, K., 94, 97
Scott, C. M., 246
Scott, T. M., 249
Scruggs, T. E., 77, 199, 202
Scuccimarra, D. J., 578
Scullin, M. H., 136, 137, 142
Sebesta, D., 568
Secord, W., 313
Seery, M. E., 147, 161
Seibel, E. J., 387
Seibert, M. A., 200
Seigel, E., 457, 467
Seknandore, O., 505
Selmar, J. W., 312
Seltzer, M. M., 97
Semel, E., 313
Semmel, M. I., 77
Semrud-Clikeman, M., 462
Senechal, M., 92
Serna, L. A., 56
Severson, H. H., 229
Sexon, S. E., 408, 419, 427
Sexton, M., 182
Seymour, H. M., 305
Shafer, M., 579
Shah, K., 228
Shames, G. H., 302, 307

Shapiro, D. R., 60
Shapiro, E. S., 247, 426
Shapiro, J., 107
Shattman, R., 484
Shaunessy, E., 507
Shaywitz, B. A., 179, 188
Shaywitz, S. E., 179
Shelley, M., 512
Shenoy, S. R., 415
Sheppard-Jones, K., 468, 593
Sheridan, S. M., 244, 429
Shinn, M. R., 425
Shippen, M. E., 140, 147, 184
Shipstead, J., 150
Shlomit, D., 240, 428
Shogren, J. K., 135
Shogren, K. A., 277
Shonkoff, J. P., 540
Shores, R. E., 227, 236
Shriner, J. G., 248
Shukla, S., 480
Shupe, M. J., 243
Shuster, J. W., 149
Shuster, S. L., 550
Sickmund, M., 221, 224
Sidman, M., 242
Siegel, L. S., 179
Siegel-Causey, E., 465
Siegle, D., 518
Sigafoos, J., 152, 583
Silberman, R. K., 60, 61, 376, 379, 385
Sileo, N. M., 281, 282, 420
Silliman, E. R., 310, 311
Silva, P. A., 225
Silver, L. B., 427
Silverman, L. K., 498, 505, 507
Silvestri, S. M., 43, 83, 237, 276
Simeonsson, R. J., 181
Simmons, A. B., 57
Simmons, D. C., 78, 181, 191
Simmons, T. J., 571, 572, 574, 580, 585
Simos, P. G., 188
Simpson, R. L., 71, 76, 106, 149, 246, 247, 257, 259, 268, 271, 272, 277, 280, 281, 284, 285, 288, 479
Sims, D. G., 355
Sinclair, V., 587
Singer, M. T., 287
Singh, N. N., 56
Siperstein, G. N., 77, 134, 161
Sitlington, P. L., 568, 571, 577, 585, 586
Sivberg, B., 269
Skau, L., 319
Skeels, H. M., 536
Skellenger, A., 375
Skiba, R. J., 57, 235
Skinner, B. F., 236
Skinner, C. H., 242, 244, 592
Skinner, D., 93, 107, 108, 109
Skinner, M., 108
Skrtic, T. M., 83
Sladky, T. J., 224
Slate, J. R., 214
Slaton, D. E., 464
Slavin, R. E., 77, 78, 524
Slifer, K., 232
Slike, S. B., 355
Sloan, D. L., 277
Smaldino, J. J., 347, 353
Smartt, S. M., 327
Smeltzer, D. J., 189
Smith, B. J., 536, 548
Smith, B. W., 219, 222, 240
Smith, C., 62
Smith, J. D., 13, 16, 81, 135, 142, 146, 164, 225, 436, 590
Smith, M. C., 93
Smith, P. D., 456, 485
Smith, R. G., 478
Smith, S. W., 71
Smith, T. B., 95, 274, 275, 539
Smith, T. C., 106, 111–112
Smith, T. E. C., 19, 30, 164

Smith, T. J., 185
Smith, T. S., 274
Smith, V. L., 318
Smithdas, R., 457
Smyth, P., 20
Snell, M. E., 60, 81, 147, 149, 152, 153, 161, 322, 442, 470, 475, 478, 479, 484, 485
Snider, V. E., 425, 426
Snidman, N., 225
Snik, A., 348
Snook-Hill, M., 392
Snow, J., 593
Snow, K., 95, 593
Snowling, M., 306, 309
Snyder, H. M., 221
Sobsey, D., 94, 97, 444
Social Security Administration, 371
Soder, A. L., 312
Soenksen, D., 280
Sokol, S. M., 262
Solomon, B., 96
Sonnenschein, S., 105
Sontag, E., 14
Sonuga-Barke, E. J. S., 424, 426
Soodak, L., 98, 100, 548
Soraci, S. A., 139
Soto, G., 60, 484
Soukup, J. H., 147
Southern, W. T., 508, 509
Spagna, M. E., 60, 61
Sparkman, C. R., 275
Sparling, J. J., 537
Sparrow, S. S., 138
Spaulding, M., 481
Speece, D. L., 578
Spencer, S., 480
Spencer, T. J., 422
Spencer, V. G., 77, 242
Spinelli, C. G., 53, 414
Spooner, F. H., 152, 484
Sprague, J., 225, 226, 227, 228, 247, 478
Spreat, S., 590
Spriggs, A. D., 277
Spring, C., 189
Squires, J., 546
Sridhar, D., 235
SRI International, 12, 60
Stafford, A. M., 466
Stage, S., 216
Stahr, B., 425
Stainback, S., 81, 161
Stainback, W., 81, 161
Stam, H. J., 409
Stancliffe, R. J., 590
Stanislaw, H., 275
Stanovich, K. E., 179
States, J., 73
Staub, D., 161, 480, 481
Stecker, P. M., 176, 190
Steckol, K. E., 318
Steele, S., 409
Steinbach, K. A., 182
Steinberg, A. G., 341
Steinweg, S. B., 379
Stephens, K. R., 494, 501
Stephens, T. M., 111
Sterling, R., 158
Sternberg, L., 454, 455
Sternberg, R. J., 494, 495
Stevens, D., 58
Stevens, K. B., 235
Stevens, R., 196
Stiegler, L. N., 264
Stillerman, S., 71
Stinson, M., 350
Stinson, M. S., 350, 364
Stodden, R. A., 585
Stoiber, K. C., 236
Stokoe, W., 359
Stoneman, Z., 97
Stoner, G., 425
Stoner, J. B., 96, 98, 102
Storey, K., 397

Stothard, S. B., 309
Stough, L. M., 146
Stowe, M. J., 19, 136, 419
Strain, P. S., 158, 236, 247, 277
Strand, J., 592
Stratton, K., 145
Strauss, M., 341
Strawbrige, C. P., 139
Stremel, K., 441
Strickland, B. B., 65, 67
Strickland, S. P., 537
Stromer, R., 277, 278, 279
Strong, C. J., 296, 319
Strong, M., 359, 360
Stuart, M. B., 374
Stuart, S. K., 109, 113
Stump, C. S., 21, 60, 61
Sturkey, C., 559
Sturmey, P., 141, 275, 277
Stuttering Foundation of America, 307
Sublet, C., 136
Sudhalter, V., 145
Sugai, G., 35, 54, 222, 226, 229, 235, 238, 240, 241, 247, 248, 249, 429
Sullivan, K., 140
Sulzer-Azaroff, B., 277
Sumi, C., 220
Summers, J. A., 93, 98, 101, 102
Summy, S. E., 22, 25, 199
Sundberg, M. L., 275, 277
Sunderland, L. C., 307
Suomi, J., 578
Suritsky, S. K., 200
Sutherland, K. S., 234, 236, 241
Sutton, J., 427
Swaka, K., 247
Swan, J. H., 445
Swanson, H. L., 153, 186, 192, 205
Swanson, J. M., 424
Swanson, V., 425
Swearer, S. M., 216, 219
Sweatman, L., 435
Sweeney, D. P., 264, 424
Sweeney, W. J., 200
Swenson, S., 591
Swiatek, M. A., 509
Swicegood, P. R., 149
Swinson, J., 236
Switzky, H. N., 140
Sylvester, L., 571, 578
Sylvester, R., 241
Symons, F. J., 42, 145, 222, 236
Synhorst, L., 216
Szabo, J. L., 434, 444
Szcerbinski, M., 356
Szymanski, L. S., 142, 593

Taber-Doughty, T., 158
Talbert-Johnson, C., 200
Talbott, E., 224
Tam, K. Y. B., 21, 54, 58, 106, 108
Tankersley, M., 14, 76, 203
Tardif, C. Y., 203
Targett, P., 580
Tarver, S., 73
TASH, 454, 590
Tate, T. L., 553
Taunt, H. M., 93
Taylor, B., 277, 279
Taylor, B. A., 272, 277, 285
Taylor, O. L., 305
Taylor, P. B., 214
Taylor, R. L., 117, 237
Taylor, S. J., 80, 95, 161, 593
Taymans, J. M., 484
Teglasi, H., 225
Tekin-Iftar, E., 156
Tellefson, M., 389
Templeton Foundation, 508
Terman, L., 493
Terzi, L., 13, 14
Tesch, D., 478
Tessier, A., 543, 548

Test, D., 161
Test, D. W., 42, 69, 71, 140, 152, 396, 484, 568, 571, 572, 574, 576, 583, 586
Tétreault, S., 375
Theodore, L. A., 244
Therrien, W. J., 21
Thibeault, M. D., 200
Thiede, K., 224
Thiemann, K. S., 281
Thies, K. M., 433
Thoma, C. A., 574, 575, 586
Thomas, C. C., 107
Thomas, K., 59
Thomas, K. E., 460
Thomas, L. A., 145
Thomas, S. B., 444
Thompson, B., 72
Thompson, J. R., 134, 138
Thompson, R. H., 553
Thompson, T., 141, 145, 587
Thompson Prout, H., 593
Thornton, C., 414
Thornton, N. E., 355
Thousand, J. S., 62
Thurlow, M. L., 31
Thurston, L. P., 60, 484
Tick, N. T., 141
Tilson, G., 580
Timko, T. C., 554
Timm, M. A., 247
Tinbergen, E. A., 479
Tinbergen, N., 479
Tincani, M., 159, 276, 281, 284, 478
Tindal, G. A., 429
Tingstad, K. I., 265, 267
Todd, A. W., 222, 240, 429, 478
Todis, B., 235
Tolla, J., 383, 389
Tomblin, J. B., 306
Temporowski, P. D., 140
Torgesen, J. K., 78, 175, 179, 313
Tourette Syndrome Association, 219
Towbin, K. E., 268
Townsend, B. L., 58
Townsend, D. B., 275
Trach, J. S., 580, 582
Trammel, D. L., 428
Tran, L. P., 340
Trask-Tyler, S. A., 129, 398
Traxler, C. B., 337
Treffert, D. A., 262
Trela, K., 184, 576, 577
Trent, J. W., 132
Trent, S. C., 503
Trezek, B. J., 355, 356, 357
Trivedi, M. H., 285
Troia, G. A., 73
Trout, A., 219–220
Trout, A. L., 426
Troutman, A. C., 274
Trupin, L., 568
Tryon, P. A., 261
Tuba Tuncer, A., 393
Tucker, B., 348, 349
Tullock, D., 432
Turnbull, A. P., 16, 65, 67, 82, 96, 97, 98, 100, 102, 104, 105, 120, 123, 548, 558, 585
Turnbull, H. R., 16, 19, 76, 82, 98, 100, 136, 419, 443, 548, 585
Turner, L. A., 139
Turner-Henson, A., 445
Twombly, E., 546
Tyler, D., 533, 560
Tyler, J. S., 462
Tymchuk, A. J., 569

Udall, A., 504
Udvari-Solner, A., 475, 481
Uffen, E., 311
Ulrey, P., 392
Ulrich, M. E., 94
Umberger, R., 316
Umbreit, J., 163, 230, 233, 478

Unruh, B., 578
Upreti, G., 230
Urso, A., 230
U.S. Department of Education, 11, 37, 40, 220, 224, 246, 268, 282, 309, 325, 327, 361, 394, 395, 409, 422, 443, 459, 460, 567, 568
U.S. Department of Education, National Center for Education Statistics, 43
U.S. Drug Enforcement Agency, 424
U.S. Office of Education, 174
U.S. Office of Special Education, 57, 186, 203, 205, 376
U.S. Office of Special Education Programs, 40, 142, 161
Utley, B. L., 384, 385
Utley, C. A., 58

Vacca, J., 268
Vadasy, P. F., 93
Vail, C. O., 277
Valli, C., 359
Valum, L., 112
Van Acker, R., 236
Van Berckelaer-Onnes, I. A., 263
Van Bon, W., 348
Van Bon, W. J. J., 387
Van Cleve, J. V., 351
Vandercook, T., 592
Van der Ende, J., 141
Vanderheiden, G. C., 323
Van der Lee, J. H., 408
VanDeventer, P., 481
Van Dycke, J. L., 71
Van Garderen, D., 425
Van Gurp, S., 361
Van Houten, R., 231
Van Karnebeek, C. D. M., 142
VanKeulen, J. E., 305
Van Laarhoven, T., 479
VanLue, M., 280
Van Norman, R., 478
Van Norman, R. K., 77, 119, 240, 429, 479
Van Oorsouw, W., 141
Van Riper, C., 304
Van Tassel-Baska, J., 505, 509, 520
Vasa, S. F., 422
Vaughn, B. J., 95
Vaughn, S., 42, 43, 62, 72, 77, 81, 175, 176, 177, 182, 185, 196, 203, 207, 235
Veen, L., 538
Venn, J. J., 136, 137
Venn, M. L., 59
Vergason, G. A., 93
Verhulst, F., 141
Vermeulen, A. M., 348
Vervloed, M. P. J., 338
Viirre, E. S., 387
Villa, R. A., 62
Viramontez Anguiano, R. P., 118
Vogle, L. K., 441
Volkmar, F., 258
Vollmer, T. R., 231
Voltz, D. L., 102
Von Hahn, L., 219, 462
Von Scheden, M., 392
Vorndran, C. M., 478
Voyager Expanded Learning, 196

Waddell, M., 547
Waddy-Smith, B., 355
Wagner, B. W., 164
Wagner, L., 221
Wagner, M., 11, 12, 92, 185, 220, 224, 228, 234, 422, 567, 568, 569
Wagner, R. K., 179, 313
Wagner-Lampl, A., 376
Wagstaff, P., 387
Wahl, H., 373
Waiculonis, J., 392
Waintrup, M., 578
Walberg, H., 203
Waldfogel, J., 539
Waldman, H. B., 96

Waldman, I. D., 225
Waldo, M., 261
Waldron, C., 280
Waldron, N., 77
Walker, A. R., 140
Walker, B., 184
Walker, D. K., 145, 431, 544
Walker, H. M., 214, 215, 225, 226, 227, 228, 229, 235, 241, 247
Walker, L. A., 333, 354
Wallace, G., 313
Wall Emerson, R. S., 389
Walsh, K. K., 590
Walshe, S. E., 182
Walthall, J. C., 214, 229
Walther-Thomas, C., 203
Wang, M., 203
Wang, S. S., 140
Wang, W., 242
Wang, Y., 355, 356, 357
Ward, B., 305
Ward, M., 150
Ward, N., 591
Warfield, M. E., 96
Warren, S., 16
Washington, B. H., 577
Wasik, B. H., 537
Watkins, M. W., 112
Watson, G. S., 225
Weatherman, R. F., 138
Webb, N. M., 525
Webber, J., 219, 224, 241, 268, 277, 470, 476
Webb-Johnson, G. C., 58
Webster, A., 590
Webster, D. D., 586
Wechsler, D., 137
Weddington, G. T., 305
Weed, K. Z., 314
Wehby, J. H., 42, 222, 234, 236, 241
Wehman, P., 571, 574, 575, 577, 579, 580, 581, 585
Wehmeyer, M. L., 140, 147, 150, 154, 155, 161, 465, 585
Wehmeyer, M. S., 239, 428
Weider, S. W., 264
Weiner, M. T., 336
Weinfeld, R., 505
Weinstein, S. L., 415
Weinter, T., 262, 479
Weintraub, F. J., 82
Weirich, L. C., 389
Weisentstein, G. R., 25
Weishaar, M., 199
Weisner, T., 591
Weisse, I., 375
Welch, M., 14
Welker, R., 225
Wells, L., 578
Wendland, M., 230
Werts, M. G., 156
Wesson, C., 117, 190
West, E., 58
West, E. A., 157
West, L. L., 484
West, M., 579
West, R. P., 240
Westberg, K. L., 512
Westling, D. L., 457, 464, 470, 475
Wetherby, A., 457, 467
Wetzel, R., 382
Whale, S., 439
Whalen, C., 277
Wharton, R., 145
Wheeler, C. B., 569, 590
Wheeler, D. L., 285
Wheeler, J. J., 277
Wheeler, T., 424
Whinnery, K. W., 411
White, B. L., 535
White, D. M., 201
White, J., 484, 583
White, M. A., 236
White, R., 161
Whitelaw, G. M., 347

Whittlesey, J. R. B., 193
Widamon, F., 77, 161
Widerstrom, A. H., 538
Wiederholt, J. L., 190
Wiener, J., 185, 203
Wigal, T., 424
Wiggins, L. D., 269, 270
Wiig, E. H., 313, 319, 327
Wilcox, M. J., 310
Wilcox, S., 359
Wilczynski, S. M., 280, 281
Wilder, D. A., 163, 242
Wilens, T. E., 422
Wilkinson, G. S., 190
Will, M. C., 569
Willard-Holt, C., 409, 506
Willcutt, E. G., 423
Willey, L. H., 264, 265
Williams, B. F., 102, 103, 147
Williams, C. B., 337
Williams, C. M., 277
Williams, D., 387
Williams, G., 117, 122
Williams, K., 361
Williams, K. E., 264
Williams, K. R., 141
Williams, R. E., 397
Williams, R. L., 244
Williams, R. R., 435
Williams, S. C., 184, 387
Williams, V. L., 112, 113
Williamson, G. G., 62
Willis, D. S., 141
Wilson, B., 471, 485
Wilson, C. L., 102
Wilson, J., 236
Wilson, M. G., 184
Wilson, P. G., 583
Wilson, R., 117
Wilson, V., 355
Winebrenner, S., 513
Wing, L., 138, 261, 268, 270
Winston, E. A., 350
Winter, S. M., 558
Winter-Messiers, M. A., 259, 265, 266, 267
Wishart, J. G., 141
Witty, P. A., 493
Witzel, B. S., 184, 241
Wolery, M., 156, 236, 475, 479, 544, 547, 548, 549, 553
Wolf, J. S., 111
Wolf, M., 182, 236
Wolf, M. M., 236, 266
Wolfe, L. A., 478
Wolfe, L. H., 428
Wolfe, P. S., 112, 485
Wolfensberger, W., 164, 590
Wolffe, K. E., 375
Wolford, T., 222
Wolfram, W., 305
Woll, B., 334
Wolraich, M. L., 420, 422
Wood, B. A., 157
Wood, C. E., 265, 267
Wood, C. L., 77, 118, 119, 158, 159, 200, 202, 276
Wood, D. G., 355, 356, 357
Wood, F. H., 214
Wood, J. G., 424
Wood, J. W., 77
Wood, S. J., 150, 151, 240, 428, 574
Wood, W., 69, 152
Wood, W. M., 71, 140, 574
Woodcock, R. W., 138, 189–190, 312
Woodruff, G., 61
Woods, D. W., 375
Woods, L. L., 571, 578
Woolsey, M. L., 342, 355
World Health Organization, 430
Wormsley, D. P., 382, 399
Worsdell, A., 479
Worthington, L. A., 153
Wray, D., 347, 578
Wrenn, R. L., 414

Wright, J. E., 78
Wright, L., 505
Wright, P. D., 25, 65, 98, 444
Wright, P. W. D., 25, 65, 98, 444
Wright-Gallo, G. L., 231
Wu, X., 182
Wyatte, M. L., 95
Wynn, J. W., 274, 539

Xin, Y. P., 42, 149

Yairi, E., 307, 311, 316
Yamaki, K., 146
Yan, W., 184
Yavanoff, P., 578
Yawn, C. D., 77
Yelin, E., 568, 585
Yell, M., 241
Yell, M. L., 17, 25, 31, 52, 98, 247, 248, 275, 443, 444

Yergin-Allsopp, M., 268
Ylvisaker, M., 462
Yoder, P. J., 241
Yoder, S. L., 574
Yoe, J., 587
Yopp, H. K., 296
Yopp, R. H., 296
York-Barr, J., 475
Young, C. L., 78, 175
Young, J. L., 120, 392
Young, K. R., 236, 240, 242, 429
Yovanoff, P., 580, 585
Yssel, N., 13
Ysseldyke, J., 31, 54, 55, 137, 175, 178
Yuan, S., 60
Yurick, A. L., 21
Yuskauskas, A., 590

Zabel, R. H., 424
Zane, C., 98, 571

Zaragoza, N., 72
Zawolkow, E., 358
Zeigler, M., 578
Zentall, S. S., 422
Zetlin, A. G., 14
Zhang, J., 592
Zhang, Z., 306
Zhao, Y., 182
Zigler, E., 140
Zigmond, N., 36, 41, 42, 62, 63, 76, 77, 82, 199, 205, 236
Ziman, T., 186
Zirkel, P. A., 22
Zirpoli, T. J., 241
Zito, J. M., 423
Ziv, O., 186
Zubal-Ruggieri, R., 596
Zucker, A., 146
Zuniga, S., 525

AAC (augmentative and alternative communication), 321–325, 466–467
AAIDD (American Association on Intellectual and Developmental Disabilities), 15, 131, 133–135, 149
AAMR Adaptive Behavior Scale-School (ABS-S:2), 138
AAMR (American Association on Mental Retardation), 15, 131, 133, 137, 148–149
ABA (applied behavior analysis), 274–277, 287, 452
Abacus, 383
ABC recording, 232, 452
Abecedarian Project, 537
Ability grouping, 523–525
Abrahamson v. Hershman (1983), 26
Absence seizure, 415
Academic achievement
    ADHD and, 422
    deafness/hearing loss and, 337
    emotional/behavioral disorders and, 219–220, 234
    physical disabilities/health impairments and, 427
    traumatic brain injury and, 463
Acceleration, 507–509, 526
Acceptance, differential, 243
Accommodation, in vision, 377
Accountability, 31, 77
Achenbach System of Empirically Based Assessment (ASEBA), 229
Achievement tests, 189–190
Acquired hearing loss, 341
Acquired immune deficiency syndrome (AIDS), 419–420
Acquired visual impairment, 373
Acquisition stage of learning, 156, 157
Activation switches, 412
Active listening, 102, 103
Active student response (ASR), 79, 153, 156, 158–159
Activity schedules
    multimedia, 278–279
    notebook, 279
    picture, 256, 277–279
    preschool, 555, 556
Acute conditions, 408
ADA (Americans with Disabilities Act) (1990), 30, 34, 351, 432
Adapted physical educators, 433
Adaptive behavior, 138, 141
Adaptive development, 547
Adderall, 423, 424, 426
ADHD. *See* Attention-deficit/hyperactivity disorder (ADHD)
Adolescence, 100, 395. *See also* Transitioning to adulthood
Adulthood. *See* Transitioning to adulthood
Adventitious visual impairment, 373
Adventure (literary genre), 511
Advocacy
    emotional/behavioral disorders and, 247
    giftedness/talent and, 526
    parents and, 90, 91–92, 98
    self-advocacy, 596
African American students, 56, 57, 58, 503, 504. *See also* Diversity issues
Ages and Stages Questionnaire, 546
Aggression, 216, 452
Aided AAC techniques, 321
AIDS (acquired immune deficiency syndrome), 419–420
Albinism, 378
Alcohol-related neurodevelopmental disorder, 144

Alerting devices, 351
Allaire-Gifford, Mary, 49–51
Allegory, 511
Alphabetic principle, 188
Alphafetoprotein, 146
Alternative teaching, 62
Amblyopia, 378
Amendments to the Education of the Handicapped Act (1983), 33, 569
Amendments to the Elementary and Secondary Education Act (1966), 33
Amendment to Title I of the Elementary and Secondary Education Act (1966), 33
American Academy of Pediatrics, 546
American Association on Intellectual and Developmental Disabilities (AAIDD), 15, 131, 133–135, 149
American Association on Mental Retardation (AAMR), 15, 131, 133, 137, 148–149
American Asylum for the Education of the Deaf and Dumb, 352
American Federation for the Blind, 381
American Printing House for the Blind, 387, 393–394
American School for the Deaf, 352
American Sign Language, 352, 353, 359–361
American Speech-Language-Hearing Association (ASHA), 303, 305, 307
Americans with Disabilities Act (1990), 30, 34, 351, 432
Amniocentesis, 146
Analyzing ability, 499
Animal assistance, 351, 392, 437, 438–440
Annual review, 59
Anorexia nervosa, 217
Anoxia, 462
Antisocial behavior, 216
Anvil, 334
Anxiety disorders, 217–218
Apartment clusters, 588
Apartment living, 588
Apgar scale, 544–545
Aphasia, 311
Applied behavior analysis (ABA), 274–277, 287, 452
Approach magnification, 387
Aqueous humor, 376
Arc, The, 91, 148
Arizona State Department of Education, 369
Armstrong v. Kline (1979), 26, 28
Articulation, 299
Articulation disorders, 306, 307, 316, 326
Articulation tests, 312
ASA (Autism Society of America), 268, 272
ASAT (Association for Science in Autism Treatment), 91, 273
ASD. *See* Autism spectrum disorders (ASD)
ASEBA (Achenbach System of Empirically Based Assessment), 229
ASHA (American Speech-Language-Hearing Association), 303, 305, 307
Asian American students, 56, 57. *See also* Diversity issues
Asperger, Hans, 272
Asperger syndrome, 258–260, 265–267, 273, 422. *See also* Autism spectrum disorders (ASD)
Asperger Syndrome Diagnostic Scale, 271
ASR (active student response), 79, 153, 156, 158–159
Assessment. *See also* Identification and assessment
    adaptive behavior, 138
    closed needs, 120, 121–122
    curriculum-based, 547
    descriptive functional behavioral, 232

direct daily, 192
early childhood special education, 547
ecological assessment, 471
functional behavioral, 230–233
indirect functional behavioral, 231–232
intellectual disabilities, 160–161
intellectual functioning, 136–138
needs, 120, 121–122
open needs, 120, 121–122
program planning and evaluation tools, 547
Assessment, Evaluation, and Programming System, 547
Assistive listening devices, 347
Assistive technology, 23, 347, 432, 435–436. *See also specific technology types*
Assistive technology devices, 435
Assistive technology services, 435
Association for Children with Learning Disabilities, 173, 193
Association for Persons with Severe Handicaps, The, 454
Association for Science in Autism Treatment (ASAT), 91, 273
Asthma, 418
Astigmatism, 378
Asynchrony, 498–499
Ataxia, 410
Ataxic cerebral palsy, 410
Athetoid cerebral palsy, 410
Athetosis, 410
At-risk, defined, 10
Atrophy, 413
Attention, 152, 261, 263
Attention-deficit/hyperactivity disorder (ADHD). *See also* Physical disabilities/health impairments
    academic achievement and, 422
    behavioral intervention for, 425–426, 428–429
    causes of, 423
    comorbidity with other disabilities, 422
    definition and diagnosis of, 420–422
    drug therapy for, 423–425, 426
    learning disabilities and, 185
    prevalence of, 422
    self-monitoring and, 426, 428–429
    special education, eligibility for, 422–423
    treatment of, 423–426, 428–429
Auctions, class, 130
Audiograms, 342, 344–345
Audiology, 24
Audiometers, 342
Audiometric zero, 335
Audiometry, 342, 344–345
Audition (hearing), 334–335
Auditory brain stem response, 342
Auditory canal, 334
Auditory discrimination tests, 312
Auditory learning, 354
Auditory training, 354
Augmentative and alternative communication (AAC), 321–325, 466–467
Augmented reality systems, 386–387
Aura, 415
Auricle, 334
Autism
    definitions of, 257–261
    early infantile, 257, 272
    high-functioning, 262
    low-functioning, 262
    statistics, 11
Autism Diagnostic Interview—Revised, 271
Autism Diagnostic Observation Scale—Generic, 271
Autism Society of America (ASA), 268, 272

Autism Speaks, 269
Autism spectrum disorders (ASD), 255–293. *See also* Educational approaches to autism spectrum disorders
  causes of, 268–269
  characteristics of, 261–265
  definitions of, 257–261
  educational approaches to, 271–282
  educational placement alternatives for, 282–284
  fads *versus* evidence-based practices, 284–289
  featured teachers, 255–257
  identification and assessment of, 269–271
  issues and trends in, 286–288
  prevalence of, 268
  special interest areas and, 265–267
  tips for beginning teachers, 289–290
Autism Spectrum Screening Questionnaire, 270
Autistic disorder, 258, 259. *See also* Autism spectrum disorders (ASD)
Autistic savants, 262
Autosomal dominant hearing loss, 340
Autosomal recessive hearing loss, 340

Back and Forth Counting, 159
Barraga, Natalie, 381
Basic interpersonal communications skills (BICS), 314–315
Battelle Developmental Inventory (BDI-2), 547
Bayley Scales of Infant Development—III, 455
BDI-2 (Battelle Developmental Inventory), 547
Beach-Plus talking calculator, 383
Beginning teachers, tips for
  autism spectrum disorders, 289–290
  blindness/low vision, 401–402
  collaborating with parents and families, 124
  communication disorders, 326
  co-teaching, 84
  deafness/hearing loss, 365
  early childhood special education, 560–561
  emotional/behavioral disorders, 250
  giftedness/talent, 526–527
  learning disabilities, 206
  organization, 165
  physical disabilities/health impairments, 445–446
  severe disabilities, 487
  severe/multiple disabilities, 487
  success and survival fundamentals, 44–45
  transitioning to adulthood, 597
Behavioral and Emotional Rating Scale, 229
Behavioral disorders. *See* Emotional/behavioral disorders
Behavioral intervention, 425–426, 428–429
Behavioral intervention plan (BIP), 230
Behavioral problems, 185, 463
Behavior observation audiometry, 345
Behavior support specialists, parents as, 96–97
Behavior traps, 267
Bell, Alexander Graham, 352
Bell-shaped curve, 136
Bettleheim, Bruno, 272
Bi-bi approach, 352, 353, 359–361
BICS (basic interpersonal communications skills), 314–315
Bicycles, adapted, 436
Bilateral hearing loss, 339
Bilingual-bicultural approach, 352, 353, 359–361
Binet, Alfred, 148
Binocular vision, 376–377
Biochemical imbalance, 188–189
Biological factors, 143, 224–225, 541
Biomedical engineers, 435
BIP (behavioral intervention plan), 230
Bipolar disorder, 218
Black students, 56, 57, 58, 503, 504. *See also* Diversity issues
Blind, as term, 15
Blindisms, 375
Blindness/low vision, 369–403. *See also* Deaf-blindness; Educational approaches to blindness/low vision
  age at onset of, 373
  causes of, 377–380

characteristics of, 373–376
  curriculum priorities for, 389, 392–394, 396–398
  definitions of, 371–373
  educational approaches to, 380–394
  educational placement alternatives for, 394–395, 398–399, 400–401
  featured teacher, 369–370
  IEP goals and objectives, sample, 369–370
  issues and trends in, 400–401
  prevalence of, 376
  tips for beginning teachers, 401–402
  types of, 377–380
Blind persons, as term, 15
Blissymbolics, 323
Bloom's taxonomy, 513, 515, 516–517
Bluer, Eugen, 272
Board of Education of the Hendrik Hudson Central School District v. Rowley (1982), 26, 28
Bodily/kinesthetic intelligence, 516
Bound morphemes, 299
Braille, 380, 381, 382–383
Braille, Louis, 380
Braille'n Speak, 383
Braillers, 381, 383
Braille technological aids, 383
Brain damage, 188, 459
Brain damage syndrome, 420
Brain disorders, 224–225, 459
Brain dysgenesis, 224–225, 459
Brain injury, 224–225. *See also* Traumatic brain injury
Bribery, 276
Bridges model of school-to-work transition, 569
Brigance Diagnostic Comprehensive Inventory of Basic Skills, 190
Bright-line test, 444
Brown, Lou, 472, 480
Brown v. Board of Education of Topeka (1954), 17, 26
Bulimia nervosa, 217
Byers, Corie, 482–483

Calendar helper, 552
California Association for Gifted Children, 501
CALP (cognitive academic language proficiency), 314–315
Canadian National Institute for the Blind, 393
Cane skills, 389, 392
Care, systems of, 249
Caregivers, parents as, 95
Carlson, Earl, 431
CARS (Childhood Autism Rating Scale), 271
Cataract, 377, 378
Catheters, 413
Caucasian students, 56, 57
CBA (curriculum-based assessment), 547
CBM (curriculum-based measurement), 175, 190–192
CCBD (Council for Children with Behavioral Disorders), 214–215, 246–247
CEC. *See* Council for Exceptional Children (CEC)
Cedar Rapids v. Garret F. (1999), 27, 432, 444
Celeration chart, standard, 192
Center-based programs, 558–559
Cerebral palsy, 406, 409–411, 412–413, 434, 470
Charts, special accomplishment, 114–115
CHAT (Checklist for Autism in Toddlers), 270
Checklist for Autism in Toddlers (CHAT), 270
Child Behavior Checklist, 229
Child find system, 19, 29
Children with Learning Disabilities Act (1969), 194
Choose and Take Action, 578
Choosing Outcomes and Accommodations for Children (COACH), 71
Choral responding, 158–159
Chorionic villi sampling, 146
Chronic conditions, 408
Chronicle (literary genre), 511
Cilia, 335
Cinderella story, 515
Circle time, 552

Classification, 12–16
Classroom adaptations
  blindness/low vision, 388–389
  early childhood special education, 555, 557
  giftedness/talent, 519
  physical disabilities/health impairments, 435
Classroom management, 212
Classrooms, separate. *See* Separate classrooms
Classroom schedules, 487
Classwide peer tutoring (CWPT), 77, 78–80
Classwide Student Tutoring Teams (CSTT), 78
Clean intermittent catheterization, 413
Cleburne v. Cleburne Living Center (1985), 27
Cleft palate, 310
Clerc, Laurent, 352
Clinical Evaluation of Language Fundamentals, 313
Closed-circuit television systems, 386
Closed-ended questions, 102, 104
Closed head injury, 460
Closed needs assessment, 120, 121–122
Clustered placement model, 579–580
Clustered schools, 480
Cluster grouping, 525
Cluttering, 308. *See also* Fluency disorders
COACH (Choosing Outcomes and Accommodations for Children), 71
Cochlea, 334–335
Cochlear implants, 25, 347–349, 353
Coehlo, Tony, 596
Coercive pain control, 226–227
Cognition, 139–141, 373–374
Cognitive academic language proficiency (CALP), 314–315
Cognitive development, 546
Collaboration. *See also* Parent/family involvement
  blindness/low vision and, 370
  communication disorders and, 296
  in early childhood special education, 534–535
  on responsiveness to intervention team, 172
  severe/multiple disabilities and, 451, 452
  in special education, 60
Collaborative consultation, 325
College of William and Mary, 520
Color deficiency/color blindness, 378
Coma, 461
Combating Autism Act (2006), 273
Combined home-center programs, 559
Comedy (literary genre), 511
Commission on Education of the Deaf, 353
Commitment, in family-professional partnerships, 101
Communication. *See also* Parent-teacher communication
  augmentative and alternative, 321–325, 466–467
  autism spectrum disorders and, 261–262, 282
  blindness/low vision and, 401
  deaf-blindness and, 466, 467
  deafness/hearing loss and, 339, 353, 355, 358–359, 362–363
  defined, 297
  diagnostic tools, 546–547
  dialoguing in, 105–106
  in early childhood special education, 560–561
  facilitated, 284–285
  in family-professional partnerships, 101
  principles of, 102–104
  professional roadblocks to, 104–105
  severe/multiple disabilities and, 458, 466–467
  simultaneous, 353, 355, 358–359
  total, 353, 355, 358–359
Communication boards, 324, 467
Communication differences, 304, 305
Communication disorders, 295–329. *See also* Educational approaches to communication disorders; Language impairments; Speech impairments
  causes of, 309–311
  characteristics of, 306–309
  communication differences *versus,* 304, 305
  definitions of, 297–305
  educational approaches to, 315–325
  educational placement alternatives for, 325, 327
  featured teacher, 295–297

functional, 309-310
identification and assessment of, 311-315
IEP goals and objectives, sample, 296
language diversity and, 314-315
organic, 309
prevalence of, 309
tips for beginning teachers, 326
Communities of care, 249
Community-based instruction, 37, 160, 327
Community supports, 582
Comorbidity, 185
Compensatory intervention, 36
Competitive employment, 577-578
Complex partial seizure, 415
Comprehensive Receptive and Expressive
    Vocabulary Test, 313
Comprehensive Test of Phonological Processing,
    313
Computer access, 384
Concept-anchoring table/routine, 195
Concussion, 461
Conductive hearing loss, 338
Cones, 377
Conferences, parent-teacher, 109-112
Conflict resolution through dialoguing, 105-106
Congenital cytomegalovirus, 341
Congenital hearing loss, 340-341
Congenital visual impairment, 373
Consultation, 60, 61, 523
Contests, academic, 527
Contingencies, group, 242
Contingency contracting, 241
Continuum of alternative placements, 74-75
Contracting, 113, 241, 584
Contractions, in braille, 382
Contusions, 461
Cooking skills instruction, 396-398
Cooperative learning, 77, 78-80, 510
Coordination, 60, 61
Coprolalia, 219
Co-residence apartments, 588
Cornea, 376
Correctional institutions, 246
Correspondence training, 426
Cortical visual impairments, 378
Co-teaching, 49-51, 62-63, 84
Council for Children with Behavioral Disorders
    (CCBD), 214-215, 246-247
Council for Exceptional Children (CEC)
    Division for Children with Learning Disabilities,
        194
    Division on Career Development and Transition,
        573-574
    Division on Developmental Disabilities, 273
    Division on Visual Impairments, 399
    evidence-based practice, 72-73
    inclusion, 81, 82
    The Association for the Gifted (CEC-TAG), 496,
        497
Council for Learning Disabilities, 207
Counseling services, 24, 104-105, 435, 521
Counselors, 96, 435
Countoons, 240-241
C-Print, 350
Crangle, Carolyn, 89-90
Cranmer abacus, 383
Creativity, 499
Creech-Galloway, Carey, 451-453
Criterion, dual discrepancy, 176
Criterion-referenced tests, 190
Critical Events Index, 229
Cross-grade grouping, 525
Crystal (monkey helper), 438
CSTT (Classwide Student Tutoring Teams), 78
Cued speech, 355
Cues
    ADHD and, 429
    autism spectrum disorders and, 282
    natural, 581, 583
    nonlinguistic, 298
    picture, 487
    severe/multiple disabilities and, 474-475, 487
    supplementary, 429

Cultural diversity. See Diversity issues
Cultural interpreters, 108
Cultural reciprocity, 108-109
Current Issues and Future Trends feature
    autism, 286-288
    blindness/low vision, 400-401
    cochlear implants, 348-349
    emotional/behavioral disorders, 248-249
    evidence-based practice, 72-73
    functional curriculum, 472-474
    labels of special education, 14-16
    monkey helpers, 438-440
    precocity as a hallmark of giftedness, 500
    responsiveness to intervention, 180-181
    self-determination, 154-155
Curriculum. See also Differentiated curriculum;
        Functional curriculum
    blindness/low vision, 389, 392-394, 396-398
    dually differentiated, 506
    early childhood special education, 547-549
    emotional/behavioral disorders, 233-235
    intellectual disabilities, 147, 149-150, 152,
        154-155
    No Child Left Behind Act and, 472-473
    parallel, 431, 433
    severe/multiple disabilities, 464-469, 470, 471,
        472-474
Curriculum-based assessment (CBA), 547
Curriculum-based measurement (CBM), 175,
    190-192
Curriculum compacting, 512-513, 526
Customized employment, 580
CWPT (classwide peer tutoring), 77, 78-80
Cylert, 423
Cystic fibrosis, 418-419
Cytomegalovirus, 341

Daily living skills, 141
DAP (developmentally appropriate practice),
    549-550, 552-553
Deaf-blindness, 455-457, 459, 466, 467. See also
        Blindness/low vision; Deafness/hearing loss
Deaf culture, 334, 348-349, 353, 359-360
Deafness, defined, 334
Deafness/hearing loss, 331-367. See also Deaf-
        blindness; Educational approaches to
        deafness/hearing loss
    causes of, 340-341
    characteristics of, 336-338
    definitions of, 334-336
    educational approaches to, 351-363
    educational placement alternatives for, 361, 364
    featured teacher, 331-333
    identification and assessment of, 342-346
    issues and trends in, 348-349
    postsecondary education and, 364
    prevalence of, 338
    technologies and supports for, 346-351
    tips for beginning teachers, 365
    types and age of onset of, 338-340
Deaf parents, 338
Decibels, 335
Declassification, 59-60
Deinstitutionalization, 590-591
Denasality, 308
Denver II screening test, 546
Department of Education v. Katherine D. (1984), 27
Depression, 218
Descriptive functional behavioral assessment, 232
Desoxyn, 423
Determinism, 154
Detroit, ability grouping in, 523-524
Developmental delays, 540, 544
Developmental Disabilities Assistance and Bill of
        Rights Act (1975), 33
Developmental Disabilities Assistance and Bill of
        Rights Act (1984), 33
Developmentally appropriate practice (DAP),
    549-550, 552-553
Developmental retardation, 145-146
Developmental screening tests, 546
Dewey, John, 538
Dextroamphetamine (Dexedrine), 423, 424, 426

Dextroamphetamine sulfate (Adderall), 423, 424,
    426
Diabetes, 417
Diabetic coma, 417
Diabetic retinopathy, 378
Diabetic shock, 417
Diagnosis. See also Identification and assessment
    adaptive development, 547
    ADHD, 420-422
    autism spectrum disorders, 271
    cognitive development, 546
    communication and language development,
        546-547
    early childhood special education, 546-547
    social and emotional development, 547
Diagnostic and Statistical Manual of Mental
        Disorders, Fourth Edition (DSM-IV),
        258-261, 273, 421
Dialects, 305
Dialogue notebooks, 112-113
Dialoguing, conflict resolution through, 105-106
Diana v. State Board of Education (1970), 26
DIBELS (Dynamic Indicators of Basic Early Literacy
        Skills), 191-192
Differential acceptance, 243
Differential reinforcement, 241, 452
Differentiated curriculum
    acceleration, 507-509, 526
    developing, 527
    dually, 506
    enrichment, 509-512
    in general education classroom, 512-515,
        516-517
    outside classroom, 515, 518, 527
Dinosaurs-integrated assignments, 267
Diplegia, 410
Direct instruction, 196-198, 206, 429
Disability, defined, 10
Discipline, 28-29
DISCOVER (Discovering Strengths and Capabilities
        while Observing Varied Ethnic Responses)
        model, 504, 519
Discrepancy criterion, dual, 176
Discrete trial training (DTT), 275
Discrimination activities (articulation), 316
Discrimination (vision), 399
Distortions, as speech-sound error, 306
Divergent production, 499
Diversity issues
    culturally responsive services for families,
        108-109
    disproportionate representation, 56-58
    giftedness/talent, 503-505
    parent/family involvement and, 90, 106-109,
        116, 118-119, 124
    understanding and respecting cultural
        differences, 107-108
DMD (Duchenne muscular dystrophy), 413
Documented risk, 540-541
Dogs, assistance from, 351, 392, 437
Doll, Edgar, 148
Double-blind, placebo-controlled studies, 285
Double-deficit hypothesis, 182
Double hemiplegia, 410
Down syndrome, 143, 144, 146, 459
Dowse, Jeanna Mora, 369-370
Dropout rates, 567-568
Drug therapy, for ADHD, 423-425, 426
DSM-IV (Diagnostic and Statistical Manual of
        Mental Disorders, Fourth Edition),
        258-261, 273, 421
DTT (discrete trial training), 275
Dual discrepancy criterion, 176
Dually differentiated curriculum, 506
Duchenne muscular dystrophy (DMD), 413
Due process safeguards, 22
Duration (behavior dimension), 231
Dye, Marilee, 482
Dynamic Indicators of Basic Early Literacy Skills
        (DIBELS), 191-192
Dysarthria, 310
Dyslexia, 179
Dysphonia, 308

Ear, parts of, 334–335
Eardrum, 334
Early childhood special education, 533–561
  assessment in, 547
  center-based programs, 558–559
  classroom adaptations for, 555, 557
  combined home-center programs, 559
  curriculum and program goals, 547–549
  defined, 536
  developmentally appropriate practice, 549–550, 552–553
  diagnostic tools, 546–547
  early intervention, importance of, 536–540
  educational placement alternatives for, 557–560
  families and, 535, 559–560
  featured teacher, 533–535
  home-based programs, 557–558
  hospital-based programs, 557
  IDEA and, 540–544
  IFSP/IEP goals and objectives, 550, 551
  instructional adaptations and modifications, 550, 553–555
  preschool activity schedules, 555, 556
  screening tools, 544–546
  tips for beginning teachers, 560–561
Early infantile autism, 257, 272
Early intervening teams, 53
Early intervention
  autism spectrum disorders and, 273–274
  as challenge, 43
  defined, 536
  effectiveness of, 536–540
  in IDEA, 22–23, 540–543
  intellectual disabilities and, 536–537, 539
  statistics, 11
Early-onset diabetes, 417
Echolalia, 261–262
Eclecticism, 73
Ecological assessment form, 471
Edmark Functional Site Word Series, 130
Edmark Reading Milestones Series, 130
Educability, 133, 456
Educational approaches to autism spectrum disorders, 271–282
  applied behavior analysis, 274–277
  early intensive behavioral intervention, 273–274
  history of field, 272–273
  picture activity schedules, 256, 277–279
  social stories, 280–282
  visual supports, 256, 277–282
Educational approaches to blindness/low vision, 380–394
  adaptations for blindness, 380, 382–384
  adaptations for low vision, 384–389, 390–391
  braille, 380, 381, 382–383
  braille technological aids, 383
  cane skills, 389, 392
  classroom adaptations, 388–389
  computer access, 384
  curriculum priorities, expanded, 389, 392–394, 396–398
  functional life skills, 394, 396–398
  functional vision, 384–385, 386
  guide dogs, 392
  history of field, 380–381
  listening skills, 393–394
  optical devices, 385–387, 388, 390–391
  orientation and mobility, 381, 389, 392–393
  reading print, 387, 388
  reading print, technological aids for, 383–384
  sighted guides, 392
  tactile aids and manipulatives, 383
  travel aids, electronic, 392–393
Educational approaches to communication disorders, 315–325
  articulation errors, 316
  augmentative and alternative communication, 321–325
  fluency disorders, 316–317, 318
  language disorders, 319–321
  naturalistic strategies, 319–321, 322
  phonological errors, 316
  speech sound errors, 316

  vocabulary building, 319, 326
  voice disorders, 317, 319
Educational approaches to deafness/hearing loss, 351–363
  American Sign Language, 352, 353, 359–361
  auditory learning, 354
  bilingual-bicultural approach, 352, 353, 359–361
  cued speech, 355
  fingerspelling, 358–359
  history, 352–353
  manually coded English, 358
  oral/aural approaches, 351, 353–355, 356–357
  selecting approach, 360–361, 362–363
  speechreading, 354–355
  total communication, 353, 355, 358–359
  visual phonics, 355, 356–358
Educational approaches to emotional/behavioral disorders, 233–245
  academic skills, 234
  alterable variables, 243
  classroom management, 241–242
  curriculum goals, 233–235
  evidence-based instructional practices, 235–243
  Mystery Motivators, 244–245
  peer mediation and support, 242
  positive behavioral support, 235, 238, 248
  self-management, 239–241
  social skills, 221, 234–235
  teacher praise, 236–237
  teacher-student relationships, 243
Educational approaches to giftedness/talent, 506–521
  acceleration, 507–509, 526
  active problem solver model, 519–520
  Bloom's taxonomy, 513, 515, 516–517
  curricular goals, 506–507
  curriculum compacting, 512–513, 526
  curriculum differentiation outside the classroom, 515, 518, 527
  enrichment, 509–512
  guidance and counseling needs, 521
  instructional models and methods, 518–521
  international experiences, 518
  internships and mentor programs, 515, 518
  Junior Great Books, 518
  lesson differentiation in general education classroom, 512–515, 516–517
  problem-based learning, 520–521
  Schoolwide Enrichment Model, 518–519
  special courses, 518
  summer programs, 518
  tiered lessons, 513, 514
Educational approaches to intellectual disabilities, 147–161
  active student response, 153, 156, 158–159
  curriculum goals, 147, 149–150, 152, 154–155
  feedback, 156, 157
  generalization and maintenance, 140, 157, 160
  history of field, 148–149
  instructional methods, 152–153, 156–161
  measurement, 160–161
  task analysis, 152–153
  transfer of stimulus control, 156–157
Educational approaches to learning disabilities, 192–195, 199–203
  content enhancements, 194–195, 199–203
  history of field, 193–194
Educational approaches to physical disabilities/health impairments, 431–442
  animal assistance, 437, 438–440
  assistive technology, 435–436
  environmental modifications, 435
  history of field, 431–432
  independence and self-esteem, 441–442, 445
  lifting and transferring students, 441
  positioning, seating, and movement, 437, 441
  special health-care routines, 437, 440–441, 442
  teaming and related services, 433–435
Educational approaches to severe/multiple disabilities, 452, 463–481, 484–485
  curriculum, 464–469, 470, 471, 472–474
  instructional methods, 469–470, 474–481, 484–485
  positive behavioral support, 452, 477–479

Educational interpreters, 350
Educational placement alternatives
  autism spectrum disorders, 282–284
  blindness/low vision, 394–395, 398–399, 400–401
  communication disorders, 325, 327
  continuum of, 74–75
  deafness/hearing loss, 361, 364
  early childhood special education, 557–560
  emotional/behavioral disorders, 246–247
  giftedness/talent, 521–523
  intellectual disabilities, 161–165
  learning disabilities, 203–205, 207
  overview, 36–37, 59
  physical disabilities/health impairments, 443–445
  severe/multiple disabilities, 480–481, 484–485
  statistics, 40
Educational transliterators, 350
Education Amendments (1970), 33
Education Amendments (1974), 33
Education for All Handicapped Children Act (1975), 18, 29, 33, 92. *See also* Individuals with Disabilities Education Act (IDEA)
Education for the Handicapped Act Amendments (1986), 22, 33, 540
Education of the Deaf Act (1986), 353
Education of the Gifted (Marland), 493
Elaboration, 499
Elective mutism, 218
Electrodes, in cochlear implants, 347
Elementary, Secondary, and Other Educational Amendments (1969), 33
Elementary and Secondary Education Act (1965), 32
Eligibility determination, 55–56
ELL (English-language learners), 106–107
Embedded learning opportunities, 550, 553–555
Emotional/behavioral disorders, 211–253. *See also* Educational approaches to emotional/behavioral disorders
  causes of, 224–227, 228
  challenges, achievements, and advocacy, 247
  characteristics of, 215–221
  definitions of, 213–215
  educational approaches to, 233–245
  educational placement alternatives for, 246–247
  featured teacher, 211–213
  identification and assessment of, 227–233
  issues and trends in, 248–249
  prevalence of, 221, 224
  tips for beginning teachers, 250
Emotional development, 547
Emotional disturbance, 214
Emotional skills, 552, 553
Empathetic relationship, 243
Employment
  competitive, 577–578
  overview of, 574–575
  sheltered, 584–585
  statistics, 568
  supported, 578–584
Employment specialists, 580, 581
Empty Fortress, An (Bettleheim), 272
Enclave model, 579–580
Encoding, 323–324
English-language learners (ELL), 106–107
Enrichment, 509–512
Environmental factors
  communication disorders, 311
  emotional/behavioral disorders, 225–227, 228
  intellectual disabilities, 145–146
  learning disabilities, 189
Environmental risk conditions, 541
Epic (literary genre), 511
Epilepsy, 415–417, 427
Equality in family-professional partnerships, 101
Established risk conditions, 540–541
Evaluation
  eligibility determination and, 55–56
  formative, 190
  multifactored, 52, 55–56
  nondiscriminatory, 19
  reevaluation, 59–60

self-evaluation, 239
summative, 190
Evaluation teams, multidisciplinary, 56
Everling, Steven, 295-297
Evidence-based practice, 71-73, 235-243
Exceptional children
defined, 9-10
labeling and classifying, 12-16
prevalence of, 10-12
Exceptional talent, as term, 494
Executive function deficits, 426
Expectations, 13, 206
Explaining/informing (communication), 298
Explicit instruction, 196-198, 206, 429
Exploration, independent, 510
Expressing (communication), 298
Expressive language impairment, 308
Extended school year, 28
Extensive supports, 134
External acoustic meatus, 334
Externalizing behaviors, 215-216
Extinction, 241

Facilitated communication, 284-285
Families. See also Parent/family involvement; Parents
early childhood special education and, 535, 559-560
employment and, 582
impact of disabilities on, 93-95
life-cycle stages and, 98, 99-100
roles of exceptional parents, 95-98
Family-Professional Partnership Scale, 98, 102
Fantasy (literary genre), 511
FAPE (free appropriate public education), 19
Farsightedness, 377, 379
FAS (fetal alcohol syndrome), 144, 423
FBA (functional behavioral assessment), 230-233
Featured Teachers feature
autism spectrum disorders, 255-257
blindness/low vision, 369-370
communication disorders, 295-297
co-teaching, 49-51
deafness/hearing loss, 331-333
early childhood special education, 533-535
emotional/behavioral disorders, 211-213
giftedness/talent, 491-492
intellectual disabilities, 129-131
learning disabilities, 171-172
parent/family involvement, 89-90
physical disabilities, health impairments, and ADHD, 405-407
severe/multiple disabilities, 451-453
special education in general, 7-9
transitioning to adulthood, 565-566
Federal funding, 23
Feedback, 79, 156, 157, 475
Fetal alcohol effect, 144
Fetal alcohol spectrum disorder, 144
Fetal alcohol syndrome (FAS), 144, 423
Field of vision, 372
Fingerspelling, 358-359
First Signs, Inc., 270
Fixation, 385
Flexibility, 84, 499
Fluency
building, 21
defined, 20
giftedness/talent and, 499
importance of, 8, 20
letter-naming, 191
nonsense word, 191
oral reading, 191
phonemic segmentation, 191
retell, 191
Fluency disorders, 307-308, 316-317, 318
Flynn effect, 137
Focus on Autism and Other Disabilities, 273
Footplate, 334
Formative evaluation, 190
Forms
communication needs matrix, 363
ecological assessment, 471
home-school reporting, 112

individualized education program, 66-67
parent-teacher conference outline, 110
picture/symbol for self-monitoring, 583
self-monitoring, 239, 428
Foster homes, 587-588
Fragile X syndrome, 143, 144, 423
Frankenstein (Shelley), 512
Fred S. Keller School, 122
Free appropriate public education (FAPE), 19
Free morphemes, 299
Frequency (behavior dimension), 231
Functional analysis, 232-233, 256
Functional Assessment Interview, 231-232
Functional behavioral assessment (FBA), 230-233
Functional communication disorders, 309-310
Functional curriculum
inclusion and, 472
intellectual disabilities and, 130-131, 149-150
overview of, 36
severe/multiple disabilities and, 464, 465, 472-474
Functional life skills, 394, 396-398
Functionally blind, 373
Functional vision, 384-385, 386
Funding, 23

Gallaudet, Thomas, 352
Gallaudet University, 352, 353, 364, 596
Games, 159, 393, 554-555
Gates-MacGinitie Reading Tests, 190
Gaze shift, 385
General education classrooms
autism spectrum disorders in, 282-283
in continuum of alternative placements, 74, 75
differentiated curriculum in, 512-515, 516-517
giftedness/talent in, 523
learning disabilities in, 203-204, 205, 207
severe/multiple disabilities in, 484-485
as term, 37
General education classrooms with consultation, 75
General education classrooms with supplementary instruction and services, 75
General education teachers, 71, 76
Generalization and maintenance
autism spectrum disorders, 283
early childhood special education, 548
intellectual disabilities, 140, 157, 160
severe/multiple disabilities, 458, 475
Generalized anxiety disorder, 217
Generalized hypotonia, 411
Generalized tonic-clonic seizure, 415, 416
Genetic counseling, 146
Genetic factors
autism spectrum disorders, 268-269
communication disorders, 311
deafness/hearing loss, 340
emotional/behavioral disorders, 225
learning disabilities, 188
German measles, 146, 340, 352
Gifted and Talented Children's Education Act (1978), 33
Giftedness/talent, 491-529. See also Educational approaches to giftedness/talent
ability grouping and, 523-525
advocacy for, 526
characteristics of, 496-500
definitions of, 493-496, 497
educational approaches to, 506-521
educational placement alternatives for, 521-523
featured teacher, 491-492
identification and assessment of, 501-506
individual differences among students, 498-499
instructional models and methods, 518-521
issues and trends in, 500
legislation concerning, 29
prevalence of, 12, 501
tips for beginning teachers, 526-527
Glaucoma, 377, 379
Global positioning system (GPS), 393
Goals 2000: Educate America Act (1994), 34
GO 4 IT ... NOW!, 576-577
GPS (global positioning system), 393
Graduation statistics, 567-568
Graham, Martha, 499

Grand mal seizure, 415, 416
Graphemes, 300
Graphic organizers, 195
Grasping aids, 412
Gray Oral Reading Tests, 190
Grief, 406
Group assistive listening devices, 347
Group contingencies, 242
Group goals, 77
Group homes, 587
Group process model, 242
Guided notes, 199, 200-202
Guide dogs, 392, 437
Guides, sighted, 392

Halpern's three-dimensional model, 570
Hammer (ear), 334
Handicap, defined, 10
Handicapism, 593
Handicapped Children's Early Assistance Act (1968), 33
Handicapped Children's Protection Act (1986), 33
Happy grams, 112
Hard of hearing, 334
Hauy, Victor, 380
Head trauma, 459, 460-462. See also Traumatic brain injury
Health aides, 435
Health impairments. See Physical disabilities/health impairments
Hearing, sense of, 334-335
Hearing aids, 346-347
Hearing-ear dogs, 351, 437
Hearing impairment, defined, 334
Hearing loss. See Deafness/hearing loss
Hearing tests, 312
Heimlich, Shawn, 7-9
Help, asking for and declining, 445-446
Helping Hands, 438-440
Hematoma, 461
Hemiplegia, 410
Heredity. See Genetic factors
Hertz, 335
High-functioning autism, 262
High school graduation statistics, 567-568
Hispanic students. See also Diversity issues
assessment of communication disorders in, 314
disabilities in, 106
giftedness/talent in, 503, 504
parent/family involvement and, 106
in special education, 56, 57
HIV (human immunodeficiency virus), 419-420
Hobson v. Hansen (1967), 26
Home-based programs, 37, 75, 557-558
Home-school communication. See Parent-teacher communication
Honig v. Doe (1988), 27, 28
Hoover, Richard, 381
Hospital-based programs, 37, 75, 557
Howe, Samuel Gridley, 148, 380
Human immunodeficiency virus (HIV), 419-420
Hunter College Elementary School, 521
Hunter College High School for Gifted Girls, 521
Hydrocephalus, 413
Hyperglycemia, 417
Hyperkinetic impulse disorder of children, 420
Hyperlexia, 260
Hypernasality, 308
Hyperopia, 377, 379
Hypersensitivity, 263
Hypertonia, 410
Hypoglycemia, 417
Hyponasality, 308
Hyposensitivity, 263
Hypothesis, double-deficit, 182
Hypothyroidism, 545
Hypotonia, 411

iBot Mobility System, 436
ICF-MR Medicaid facilities, 590
Iconic signs, 298, 359
IDEA. See Individuals with Disabilities Education Act (IDEA)

Identification and assessment. *See also* Assessment
autism spectrum disorders, 269–271
communication disorders, 311–315
deafness/hearing loss, 342–346
early, 24
emotional/behavioral disorders, 227–233
giftedness/talent, 501–506
in IDEA, 24
intellectual disabilities, 136–138
learning disabilities, 189–192
multicultural, 503–505
nondiscriminatory, 19
severe/multiple disabilities, 475
IEPs. *See* Individualized education programs (IEPs)
IFSPs (individualized family services plans), 22–23,
541–543, 550, 551
IHCPs (individualized health care plans), 437, 440
Illinois Test of Psycholinguistic Abilities, 193
Imitation skills, 282
Immigrants, undocumented, 106
Improving Access to Assistive Technology Act
(2004), 432
Inclusion
arguments for and against, 77, 80–82
cooperative learning and, 77, 78–80
defined, 76
educational placement alternatives and, 444–445
functional curriculum and, 472
in IDEA, 76
least restrictive environment *versus*, 76, 80
Peer Buddy Program and, 482–483
severe/multiple disabilities and, 451–452
Incomplete quadriplegics, 406
Independence
autism spectrum disorders and, 282–283
blindness/low vision and, 401–402
early childhood special education and, 548
learning disabilities and, 186
maximum-independence apartments, 588
physical disabilities/health impairments and,
441–442, 445
Independent exploration, 510
Indirect functional behavioral assessment, 231–232
Individualized education programs (IEPs), 63–71
blindness/low vision, 369–370
communication disorders, 296
components of, 63–64
deafness/hearing loss, 362–363
early childhood special education, 534, 550, 551
example of, 68–69
form for, 66–67
functions and formats of, 65–69, 70
in IDEA, 19, 63–64, 71
preschool, 534
problems and solutions for, 69, 71
student participation in, 22
team members and, 63
template for, 576
transitioning to adulthood, 566
transition-related curriculum activities in, 575
Individualized family services plans (IFSPs), 22–23,
541–543, 550, 551
Individualized health care plans (IHCPs), 437, 440
Individualized transition plans (ITPs), 570–572, 573
Individual placement model, 580
Individuals with Disabilities Education Act (IDEA)
assistive technology, 435
autism, 258
communication disorders assessment, 314
deaf-blindness, 455
deafness and hearing impairment, 334
early childhood special education, 540–544
early intervention, 22–23, 540–543
effects of, 82–83
emotional disturbance, 214
identification and assessment, 24
inclusion, 76
individualized education program, 19, 63–64, 71
labeling and eligibility for special education, 12
language impairment, 304
learning disabilities, 173, 174–175, 194, 203, 205
least restrictive environment, 19, 22, 73, 74, 76
legal challenges based on, 23, 25–29

mental retardation, 132–133
multifactored evaluation, 55–56
multiple disabilities, 455
No Child Left Behind Act and, 32
orientation and mobility services, 381
other health impairment, 408, 422–423
overview, 18–19, 22–29
parent/family involvement, 22, 92, 98
physical disabilities/health impairments, 432
prereferral intervention, 52
preschoolers, 544
principles of, 19, 22
purposes of, 18–19
recreation and leisure, 24
severe orthopedic impairment, 407
special education process, 51, 52–54
speech impairment, 304
student involvement, 22
transition services, 570–571
traumatic brain injury, 459–460
visual impairment definitions, 373
Individuals with Disabilities Education Act (IDEA)
Amendments (1990), 34, 258, 272, 432,
459–460
Individuals with Disabilities Education Act (IDEA) of
1997, 22, 28, 34
Individuals with Disabilities Education (IDEA)
Improvement Act (2004)
assistive technology, 435
deafness and hearing impairment, 334
disciplining students with disabilities, 28–29
early intervention, 540, 541
emotional disturbance, 214
evidence-based practice, 71–72
individualized education programs, 63–64
learning disability, 173, 174–175
least restrictive environment, 73
multifactored evaluation, 55–56
overview, 18–19, 22, 23, 34
prereferral intervention, 52
responsiveness to intervention, 180
special education for preschoolers, 544
specific learning disabilities, 194
transition services, 570–571
Industrial School for Crippled and Deformed
Children, 431
Infant Health and Development Program, 537, 539
Infants, 22–23, 342, 343, 540–543, 545–546
Inner ear, 334–335
Institutions, as residential alternative for adults,
590–591
Instruction, special education as, 36–37, 40
Instructional assistants, 60
Instructional design principles, 195
Instructional support teams, 53
Instructive feedback, 156
Insulin reaction, 417
Intellectual disabilities, 129–168. *See also*
Educational approaches to intellectual
disabilities
autism spectrum disorders and, 262
causes of, 142–146
characteristics of, 138–142
cognitive functioning and, 139–141
definitions and classification systems, 132–136
early intervention and, 536–537, 539
educational approaches to, 147–161
educational placement alternatives for, 161–165
featured teacher, 129–131
functional curriculum and, 130–131, 149–150
identification and assessment of, 136–138
positive attributes of, 141–142
prevalence of, 142
preventing, 146–147
as term, 15–16, 131, 135, 149
Intellectual functioning, 136–138, 262–263
Intelligences, multiple, 505, 516–517
Intelligence tests. *See* IQ tests
Interdependence, positive, 77
Interdisciplinary teams, 62
Interest areas, special, 265–267
Interest surveys, 527
Intermittent catheterization, 432

Intermittent direct service, 325, 522
Intermittent supports, 134
Internalizing behaviors, 216–219
International Baccalaureate Program, 518
International Communication Learning Institute, 357
International Dyslexia Association, 179
International experiences, 518
Internship programs, 515, 518
Interpersonal intelligence, 517
Interpreters, 24, 28, 108, 349–350
Intervention, special education as, 35–36
Intervention assistance teams, 53
Intrapersonal intelligence, 517
Iowa Tests of Basic Skills, 189
IQ tests
cautions concerning, 137–138
giftedness/talent, 498
intellectual disabilities and, 132, 136–137, 142
learning disabilities assessment and, 189
severe disabilities and, 453–454
Iris, 376
Irving Independent School District v. Tatro (1984),
27, 432, 444
Issues. *See* Current Issues and Future Trends feature;
Diversity issues
Itard, Jean Marc Gaspard, 147, 148
Itinerant teacher-consultants, 394–395
ITPs (individualized transition plans), 570–572, 573

Jackson, Douglas, 331–333
Jacob K. Javits Gifted and Talented Students
Education Act (1988), 29, 34, 494
Joint attention, 261
Joint Commission on the Accreditation of Hospitals,
590
Joplin Plan, 525
Jordan, I. King, 353
Journals, 290
Judicious review, 172, 195
Junior Great Books, 518
Juniper Gardens Children's Project, 78, 145
Juvenile delinquency, 221
Juvenile detention facilities, 224, 246
Juvenile diabetes, 417

Kanner, Leo, 272
Keller, Helen, 380
Kennedy, John F., 148
Keyboarding, 384
KeyMath-3, 190
Keyword mnemonic method, 199, 202
KidSkills, 241, 429
KidTools, 241, 429
Killian, Dan, 565–566
Kirk, Samuel, 173, 193
Kito, Kazuko, 255–257, 289–290
Klinefelter syndrome, 144
Kurzweil Reading Machine, 381, 384

Labeling, 12–16, 105
Language
autism spectrum disorders and, 261–262
blindness/low vision and, 373–374
defined, 298
development of, 300–303, 546–547
dimensions of, 298–299
parent/family involvement and, 106
samples of, 313
Language arts, 130, 520
Language delay, 309
Language disorders, 309, 310–311, 319–321
Language diversity, 106–107, 118–119, 314–315. *See
also* Diversity issues
Language impairments, 304, 305, 308–309, 326. *See
also* Communication disorders
Language-learning disability, 308
Large-print materials, 387
Larry P. v. Riles (1979), 26
Latency (behavior dimension), 231
Latino students. *See* Hispanic students
Laws, 16–18, 32–34. *See also specific laws*
LDA (Learning Disabilities Association of America),
91, 173, 207

Lead poisoning, 423
Learned helplessness, 140
Learning
    accountability for, 31, 77
    acquisition stage of, 156, 157
    auditory, 354
    cooperative, 77, 78–80, 510
    embedded opportunities for, 550, 553–555
    learning disabilities and, 202–203
    practice stage of, 156, 157
    problem-based, 520–521
    rate of, 139–140
    service, 8–9, 130–131
Learning disabilities, 171–209. *See also* Educational
    approaches to learning disabilities
    causes of, 187–189
    characteristics of, 179, 181–186, 187
    definitions of, 173–175
    educational approaches to, 192–195, 199–203
    educational placement alternatives for, 203–205,
        207
    featured teacher, 171–172
    identification and assessment of, 189–192
    prevalence of, 11, 186–187
    responsiveness to intervention approach to,
        175–179, 180–181
    as term, 173, 193
    tips for beginning teachers, 206
Learning Disabilities Association of America (LDA),
    91, 173, 207
Learning Disabilities Summit, 194
Least restrictive environment (LRE), 19, 22, 73–76,
    80
Legally blind, 371, 372, 390
Legislation, 16–18, 32–34. *See also specific laws*
Legislators, 92–93
Leisure. *See* Recreation and leisure
Lenses, 376, 387
Let Me Hear Your Voice (Maurice), 273
Letter-naming fluency, 191
Letters mnemonic strategy, 199
Letters to parents, 112, 114–115
Level system, 241
Library of Congress, 372, 381, 393
Lidcombe Program, 317
Life-cycle stages, 99–100
Life skills, functional, 394, 396–398
Life Skills Instruction, 150, 151
LifeSpan Circle Schools, 559
Lifting, 441, 442
Lighting, 388, 390
Limited supports, 134
Linguistic diversity, 106–107, 118–119, 314–315. *See
    also* Diversity issues
Linguistic intelligence, 516
Listening
    active, 102, 103
    blindness/low vision and, 393–394
    life skills instruction and, 151
    passive, 103
Literature, 510–512
Logical-mathematical intelligence, 516
Long-term memory, 139
Lovaas, Ivar, 272, 273–274
Low-functioning autism, 262
Low-incidence disabilities. *See* Deaf-blindness;
    Severe/multiple disabilities; Traumatic brain
    injury
Low vision, defined, 373. *See also* Blindness/low
    vision
LRE (least restrictive environment), 19, 22, 73–76, 80

Macular degeneration, 379
Macy, Meghan L., 171–172
Magnetic resonance imaging (MRI), 188
Magnitude (behavior dimension), 231
Maheady, Bethany, 89–90
Maintenance. *See* Generalization and maintenance
Maker's active problem solver model, 519–520
Mands, 476–477
Manic-depressive disorder, 218
Manifestation determination, 28
Manipulatives, 383

Manually coded English, 358
Marianne Frostig Developmental Test of Visual
    Perception, 193
Marland, Sydney, 493
Marriage partners, parents as, 97
Math, 130, 151, 184
Mathematical aids, for blindness/low vision, 383
Maurice, Catherine, 273, 286–288
Maximum-independence apartments, 588
McGavock High School, 482–483
M-CHAT (Modified Checklist for Autism in
    Toddlers), 270
Mediated scaffolding, 152, 171–172, 195
Medically fragile students, 443
Medical social workers, 435
Megavitamin therapy, 189
Memory, 139
Ménière's disease, 341
Meningitis, 341
Meningocele, 411
Mental retardation. *See also* Intellectual disabilities
    adaptations for, 469, 470
    IDEA definition of, 132–133
    as term, 15–16, 131, 135
Mental Retardation Facility and Community Center
    Construction Act (1963), 32
Mentors, 515, 518
Meta-analysis, 203–204
Methamphetamine hydrochloride (Desoxyn), 423
Methylphenidate (Ritalin), 423–424, 426
Metropolitan Nashville Public Schools, 482–483
Mexican American students, 108, 314, 504. *See also*
    Diversity issues
MFE (multifactored evaluation), 52, 55–56
Michael, Linda, 491–492
Michielli-Pendl, Jean, 49–51
Microphones, in cochlear implants, 347
Middle ear, 334
Mild hearing loss, 344, 346
Mild mental retardation, 132
Milieu teaching strategies, 319–321, 322
*Mills v. Board of Education of the District of
    Columbia* (1972), 26
Milwaukee Project, 536–537
Minimal brain dysfunction, 188, 193
Missed participation, 475
Mixed cerebral palsy, 411
Mixed hearing loss, 339
Mnemonics, 199, 202
Mobile work crew model, 579
Mobility. *See* Orientation and mobility
Mobility devices, 436
Mobility Opportunities Via Education (MOVE), 411
Modeling
    autism spectrum disorders and, 256
    emotional/behavioral disorders and, 223
    severe/multiple disabilities and, 477
    stuttering and, 318, 326
Moderate hearing loss, 344, 346
Moderate mental retardation, 132
Modified Checklist for Autism in Toddlers (M-
    CHAT), 270
Monitoring, 325
Monkey helpers, 437, 438–440
Monoplegia, 410
Mood disorders, 218
Morphemes, 299
Morphology, 299
Mothers, low-IQ, 537
MotivAider, 240, 429
Motivation, 80, 140
Motor development, 374–375, 458, 546
Mountbatten Pro Brailler, 383
MOVE (Mobility Opportunities Via Education), 411
Mowat Sensor, 392–393
MRI (magnetic resonance imaging), 188
Mueninghoff, Beth, 255–257, 289–290
Multidisciplinary teams, 56, 61–62
Multifactored evaluation (MFE), 52, 55–56
Multimedia activity schedules, 278–279
Multiple disabilities, defined, 455. *See also*
    Severe/multiple disabilities
Multiple gating screening, 229

Multiple intelligences, 505, 516–517
Muscular dystrophy, 413
Musical intelligence, 517
Myelomeningocele, 411, 413
Myopia, 377, 379
Myopic participation, 475
Mystery Motivators, 244–245

NAAR (National Alliance for Autism Research), 273,
    287
NAGC (National Association for Gifted Children),
    496, 497, 524
Narrating, 297
National Advisory Committee on Handicapped
    Children, 193
National Alliance for Autism Research (NAAR), 273,
    287
National Association for Gifted Children (NAGC),
    496, 497, 524
National Association for Retarded Citizens, 91, 148
National Association of the Deaf, 348
National Autism Center, 273, 288–289
National Deaf-Mute College, 352. *See also* Gallaudet
    University
National Defense Education Act (1958), 32
National Excellence, 494
National Federation of the Blind, 15
National Joint Committee on Learning Disabilities
    (NJCLD), 173–174, 207
National Lekotek Center, 538–539
National Longitudinal Transition Studies, 567–569
National Mental Health and Special Education
    Coalition, 214–215
National Research Center on the Gifted and
    Talented, 525
National Self-Advocacy Conference, 596
National Self-Determination Synthesis Project, 152
National Society for Autistic Children, 268, 272
National Society for Crippled Children, 91
National Standards Project, 273, 288–289
National Technical Institute for the Deaf (NTID),
    350, 352, 364
Native American students, 56, 57, 106–107, 503,
    504. *See also* Diversity issues
Natural cues, 581, 583
Naturalism (literary genre), 511
Naturalistic strategies, 282, 319–321, 322,
    476–477
Naturalist intelligence, 517
Natural supports, 580, 582
Navajo students, 504. *See also* Diversity issues
Nearsightedness, 377, 379
Necklace business, class, 131
Needs assessment, 120, 121–122
Negotiating, 106
Neonatal intensive care units, 557
Neural tube defects, 411
Neuromotor impairment, 408
Newborn blood test screening, 545–546
Newsletters, class, 113
Next Chapter Book Club, 594–595
Nirje, Bengt, 148
NJCLD (National Joint Committee on Learning
    Disabilities), 173–174, 207
No Child Left Behind Act (2001)
    accountability for student learning, 31
    educational implications of, 34
    effects on curriculum, 472–473
    evidence-based practice and, 31, 72
    giftedness/talent and, 494, 501
    goal of, 30
    IDEA and, 32
    implications for students with disabilities, 31
Noise-induced hearing loss, 341
Nomad, 387
Noncompliance, 215–216
Nonlinguistic cues, 298
Nonsense word fluency, 191
Normal curve, 136
Normal hearing, 334
Normalization, 164–165, 548
Norm-referenced tests, 136, 189–190
Notebook activity schedules, 279

Notebooks, dialogue, 112–113
Note-taking strategies, 195, 199, 200–202
NTID (National Technical Institute for the Deaf), 350, 352, 364
Numbered heads together strategy, 50
Nurseries, therapeutic, 286
Nurses, school, 25, 435
Nystagmus, 378, 379

Obsessive attention, 263
Obsessive/compulsive disorder (OCD), 217
Occupational therapists (OTs), 370, 433, 434
Occupational therapy, 24
OCD (obsessive/compulsive disorder), 217
Ocular motility, 376
Ohio State University, 78–79, 594
Omissions, as speech-sound error, 306
One teaching/one helping arrangement, 62
Onomatopoeic words, 298
Open-ended questions, 102, 104
Open head injury, 460
Open needs assessment, 120, 121–122
Operant conditioning audiometry, 344–345
Optacon, 383–384
Optical devices, 385–387, 388, 390–391
Optic nerve, 377
Oral/aural approaches to deafness/hearing loss, 351, 353–355, 356–357
Oral reading fluency, 191
Organic communication disorders, 309
Organization, 45, 165
Organizational supports, 582
Orientation, defined, 389
Orientation and mobility, 24, 374–375, 381, 389, 392–393
Orientation and mobility specialists, 395, 435
Orthopedic impairment, 408
Orthotists, 435
Ossicles, 334
Other health impairment category, 408, 422–423
Otitis media, 341
Otoacoustic emissions, 335, 342
OTs (occupational therapists), 370, 433, 434
Outer ear, 334
Outlines, 110
Outstanding talent, as term, 494
Oval window, 334
Overcorrection, 241
Overlays, 406
Overresponsiveness, 263
Overselectivity, 262–263

PALS (Peer-Assisted Learning Strategies), 78
Paraeducators, 60
Paralinguistic behaviors, 298
Parallel curriculum, 431, 433
Parallel teaching, 62
Paraplegia, 410, 414
Paraprofessionals, 60
Parent appreciation letters, 112, 114–115
Parent counseling and training, 24
Parent education and support groups, 120, 121–122
Parent/family involvement, 89–126. See also Parent-teacher communication
    advocacy role, 90, 91–92, 98
    amount of, 122–123
    defined, 116
    diversity issues and, 90, 106–109, 116, 118–119, 124
    early childhood special education and, 561
    featured teachers, 89–90
    in IDEA, 22, 92, 98
    life-cycle stages and, 99–100
    parent education and support groups, 120, 121–122
    parents as research partners, 120, 122
    parents as tutors, 117–120
    parent-to-parent groups, 120
    partnerships, developing and maintaining, 98, 101–106
    support for, 91–93
    tips for beginning teachers, 124

Parents. See also Families
    deaf, 338
    labeling, 105
    letters to, 112, 114–115
    as research partners, 120, 122
    roles of, 95–98
    as tutors, 117–120
Parent-teacher communication, 102–106, 109–116. See also Parent/family involvement
    autism spectrum disorders and, 290
    conflict resolution through dialoguing, 105–106
    guidelines for, 116
    intellectual disabilities and, 131
    parent-teacher conferences, 109–112
    principles of, 102–104
    professional roadblocks to, 104–105
    telephone communication, 113
    written, 112–113, 114–115
Parent-teacher conferences, 109–112
Parent-to-Parent programs, 120
Parent-to-Parent—USA, 120
Partially sighted, 371–372
Partial participation, 475, 478
Partial seizure, 415
Participation, 475, 478
Participatory theater, 332
Partnerships, family-professional, 98, 101–106
Passive listening, 103
Passive participation, 475
PBL (problem-based learning), 520–521
PBS (positive behavioral support), 235, 238, 248, 452, 457–479
PDD-NOS (pervasive developmental disorder-not otherwise specified), 261. See also Autism spectrum disorders (ASD)
PDD (pervasive developmental disorder), 258
Peabody Individual Achievement Test, 189
Peabody Picture Vocabulary Test—III, 313
Peer-Assisted Learning Strategies (PALS), 78
Peer Buddy Program, 482–483
Peer reporting, positive, 242
Peer tutoring, 77, 78–80, 242
Pegword mnemonic method, 202
Pemoline (Cylert), 423
Pennsylvania Association for Retarded Children (PARC) v. Commonwealth of Pennsylvania (1972), 17–18, 26
Pennsylvania Training School, 148
People with blindness, as term, 15
Perinatal factors, 142, 143, 410, 459
Perkins School for the Blind, 380
Perseveration, 263
Personal and family supports, 582
Personal care attendants, 414
Pervasive developmental disorder-not otherwise specified (PDD-NOS), 261. See also Autism spectrum disorders (ASD)
Pervasive developmental disorder (PDD), 258
Pervasive supports, 134
Petit mal seizure, 415
Phelps, Winthrop, 431
Phenylketonuria (PKU), 144, 146, 545
Phobias, 217
Phonation, 299
Phonation disorder, 308
Phone logs, 45
Phonemes, 181, 183, 188, 298
Phonemic awareness, 181, 183, 356–357
Phonemic segmentation fluency, 191
Phonics instruction, 356–357
Phonological awareness, 181, 313
Phonological disorders, 306–307
Phonological errors, 316
Phonology, 298
Photo Articulation Test, 312
Physical disabilities/health impairments, 405–449. See also Attention-deficit/hyperactivity disorder (ADHD); Educational approaches to physical disabilities/health impairments
    characteristics of, 427, 430–431
    definitions of, 407–408
    educational approaches to, 431–442
    educational placement alternatives for, 443–445

featured teacher, 405–407
    prevalence of, 408–409
    tips for beginning teachers, 445–446
    types and causes of, 409–411, 413–420
Physical educators, adapted, 433
Physical supports, 582
Physical therapists (PTs), 370, 433, 434
Physical therapy, 24
Pica, 264
Picture activity schedules, 256, 277–279
Picture cards, 256
Picture cues, 487
Piecemeal participation, 475
Piirto, Jane, 494–495, 496
Pilot Parents, 120
Pinna, 334
PKU (phenylketonuria), 144, 146, 545
Placebo-controlled studies, 285
Placement alternatives. See Educational placement alternatives
Play, 537, 538–539, 553
Play audiometry, 344
Plegia, 410
Polio, 431
Ponce de Leon, Pedro, 352
Portage Project, 557
Positioning, 437, 441
Positive behavioral support (PBS), 235, 238, 248, 452, 457–479
Positive interdependence, 77
Positive peer reporting, 242
Positive reinforcement, 156
Postencephalitic disorder, 420
Postlingual hearing loss, 340
Postnatal factors, 142, 143, 410, 459
Postsecondary education, 364, 568, 585–586
Post-traumatic stress disorder (PTSD), 218
Poverty, 106
Practice stage of learning, 156, 157
Prader-Willi syndrome, 141, 145
Pragmatics, 299
Praise, 79, 236–237
Precautions, universal, 420
Precision teaching, 192
Precocity, 500
Prelingual hearing loss, 340
Prematurity, 341, 459
Prenatal factors
    ADHD, 423
    cerebral palsy, 410
    intellectual disabilities, 142, 143, 144–145
    severe/multiple disabilities, 459
Prepare Curriculum, The (Goldstein), 235
Preprinted response cards, 162–163
Prereferral process, 51–55
Preschool activity schedules, 555, 556
Preschoolers, 22–23, 320. See also Early childhood special education
President's Panel on Mental Retardation, 148
Prevention, 35, 43, 238, 248
Primary intervention, 176, 177
Primary prevention, 35, 238, 248
Prime manufacturing, 584
Problem-based learning (PBL), 520–521
Problem solving
    autism spectrum disorders and, 256
    giftedness/talent and, 495, 519–520
    life skills instruction and, 151
    riddles to promote, 514
Profound disabilities, 454–455
Profound hearing loss, 345, 346
Profound mental retardation, 132, 453
Profound multiple disabilities, 455
Program planning, 53, 59, 547
Project CARE, 537
Projective tests, 230
Prompts
    autism spectrum disorders and, 282, 283
    in employment, 584
    severe/multiple disabilities and, 452–453, 474–475, 476–477
Prosthetists, 435
Providers, parents as, 95–96

Psychogenesis, 268
Psychological services, 24
Psychomotor seizure, 415
Psychopathology and Education of the Brain-Injured Child (Strauss and Lehtinen), 193
Psychosocial disadvantage, 145, 537
PTSD (post-traumatic stress disorder), 218
PTs (physical therapists), 370, 433, 434
Public Law 85-926 (National Defense Education Act), 32
Public Law 87-276 (Special Education Act), 32
Public Law 88-164 (Mental Retardation Facility and Community Center Construction Act), 32
Public Law 89-10 (Elementary and Secondary Education Act), 32
Public Law 89-313 (Amendment to Title I of the Elementary and Secondary Education Act), 33
Public Law 89-750 (Amendments to the Elementary and Secondary Education Act), 33
Public Law 90-538 (Handicapped Children's Early Assistance Act), 33
Public Law 93-112 (Section 504 of the Rehabilitation Act), 29-30, 33, 423
Public Law 93-380 (Education Amendments of 1974), 33
Public Law 94-103 (Developmental Disabilities Assistance and Bill of Rights Act of 1975), 33
Public Law 94-142 (Education for All Handicapped Children Act), 18, 29, 33, 92
Public Law 95-561 (Gifted and Talented Children's Education Act), 33
Public Law 98-199 (Amendments to the Education of the Handicapped Act), 33, 569
Public Law 98-527 (Developmental Disabilities Assistance and Bill of Rights Act of 1984), 33
Public Law 99-372 (Handicapped Children's Protection Act), 33
Public Law 99-457 (Education for the Handicapped Act Amendments), 22, 33, 540
Public Law 99-506 (Rehabilitation Act Amendments of 1986), 33
Public Law 100-297 (Jacob K. Javits Gifted and Talented Students Education Act), 29, 34, 494
Public Law 100-407 (Technology-Related Assistance for Individuals with Disabilities Act), 34, 432
Public Law 101-336 (Americans with Disabilities Act), 30, 34, 351, 432
Public Law 101-476. *See* Individuals with Disabilities Education Act (IDEA) Amendments (1990)
Public Law 102-569 (Rehabilitation Act Amendments of 1998), 579
Public Law 103-227 (Goals 2000: Educate America Act), 34
Public Law 105-17 (Individuals with Disabilities Education Act of 1997), 22, 28, 34
Public Law 108-364 (Improving Access to Assistive Technology Act), 432
Public Law 108-446. *See* Individuals with Disabilities Education (IDEA) Improvement Act (2004)
Public Law 109-416 (Combating Autism Act), 273
Puerto Rican culture, 108. *See also* Diversity issues
Pull-out programs, 325, 522
Punishment, 276
Pupil (vision), 376
Puppets, 552-553
Pure-tone audiometry, 342, 344-345
Pyramid model of talent development, 494-495

Quadriplegia, 406, 410, 414
Quality of Life Questionnaire, 593
Questions, open- *versus* closed-ended, 102, 104

Randomized experimental group design, 72
Rate (behavior dimension), 231
Reading
    blindness/low vision and, 383-384, 387, 388
    instruction in, 183
    intellectual disabilities and, 130
    learning disabilities and, 179, 181-182, 183
    life skills instruction and, 151
    repeated, 21

responsiveness to intervention approach to, 175-177
    technological aids for, 383-384
    worksheets for, 199
Reading buddies, 130
Reading First programs, 31
Reading fluency, oral, 191
Reading inventories, informal, 190
Reading Mastery Signature Edition, Grade K (Engelmann & Bruner), 196, 197
Realism (literary genre), 511
Reasoning, 106
Receivers/stimulators, in cochlear implants, 347
Receptive language impairment, 305, 308
Recidivists, 221
Reclamation operation, 584
Recorded materials, 393-394
Recordings for the Blind, 393
Recreation and leisure
    in IDEA, 24
    severe/multiple disabilities and, 467-468, 469, 470
    transitioning to adulthood and, 591-592, 594-595
Recreation therapists, 433
Recruitment training, 152
Reevaluation, 59-60
Refraction, 377
Refractive errors, 377
Registry of Interpreters for the Deaf, 349
Regular classrooms, defined, 37
Rehabilitation Act Amendments (1986), 33
Rehabilitation Act Amendments (1998), 579
Rehabilitative counseling services, 24
Reinforcement, 156, 241, 276, 452, 475
Related services, 23, 24-25, 28, 444
Remedial intervention, 35
Renzulli, Joseph S., 494, 495
Repeated reading, 21
Reporting forms, 112
Requesting (communication), 298
RERUN approach, 105-106
Research partners, parents as, 120, 122
Research-to-practice gap, 42-43
Residential alternatives for adults, 586-591
    apartment living, 588
    foster homes, 587-588
    group homes, 587
    institutions, 590-591
    supported living, 588-590
Residential facility, defined, 37
Residential schools, 75, 395, 398-399
Residual hearing, 334
Resilience model, 93-94
Resonance disorder, 308
Resonation, 299
Resource room
    autism spectrum disorders and, 283-284
    in continuum of alternative placements, 74, 75
    federal government definition of, 37
    giftedness/talent and, 522
    learning disabilities and, 205
    signal flags in, 38-39
Respect, 101, 105, 401
Respiration, 299
Respite care, 95, 96
Response cards, 161, 162-163
Response cost, 241
Responsiveness to intervention (RTI), 54, 175-179, 180-181, 229, 248-249
Responsiveness to intervention teams, 172
Retell fluency, 191
Retina, 376
Retinitis pigmentosa, 379
Retinopathy of prematurity (ROP), 379, 381
Rett syndrome, 260, 269. *See also* Autism spectrum disorders (ASD)
Review, annual, 59
Rewards, 244-245, 276
Rich, Kimberly, 211-213, 250
Riddles, 514
Rifton Gait Trainer, 411
Rigby Literacy, 198

Rigidity type of cerebral palsy, 410
Risk conditions, 540-541
Ritalin, 423-424, 426
Roberts, Ed, 432
Rods, 377
Role playing, 223, 512
Role release, 62
Romance (literary genre), 511
Ronald McDonald House charities, 8-9
ROP (retinopathy of prematurity), 379, 381
Rorschach Test, 230
Rowley, Amy, 28
RTI (responsiveness to intervention), 54, 175-179, 180-181, 229, 248-249
Rubella, 146, 340, 352
Ryan-Griffith, Mary Kate, 405-407

SAFMEDS (Say All Fast a Minute Each Day Shuffled), 21
Salvage operation, 584
Satire (literary genre), 511
Say All Fast a Minute Each Day Shuffled (SAFMEDS), 21
Scaffolding, mediated, 152, 171-172, 195
Scale of Independent Behavior-Revised, 138
Scanning, 323, 385
Schaffer v. Weast (2005), 27
Schedules, classroom, 487
Schizophrenia, 219, 225
School for Idiotic and Feeble Minded Youth, 148
School health services, 25
School nurses, 25, 435
Schools
    clustered, 480
    residential, 75, 395, 398-399
    separate, 37, 75, 521
Schoolwide Enrichment Model (SEM), 518-519
School year, extended, 28
Science, 130, 520
Science in Autism Treatment, 273
Screening. *See also* Identification and assessment
    autism spectrum disorders, 269-270
    communication disorders, 311, 312
    developmental, 546
    early childhood special education, 544-546
    emotional/behavioral disorders, 229-230
    multiple gating, 229
    otoacoustic emission, 342
    tests for, 51, 229-230
Seating, 441
Secondary intervention, 176, 178
Secondary prevention, 35, 238, 248
Secretin therapy, 285
Section 504 of the Rehabilitation Act (1973), 29-30, 33, 423
Seguin, Edouard, 148
Seizure, 415
Seizure disorder, 415-417, 427
Selective mutism, 218
Self-advocacy, 596
Self-care, 141
Self-confidence, 106
Self-contained classrooms. *See* Separate classrooms
Self-determination
    blindness/low vision and, 399
    intellectual disabilities and, 150, 152, 154-155, 164-165
    social role valorization and, 164-165
    transitioning to adulthood and, 576-577, 596
    writing and, 576-577
Self-Determined Learning Model of Instruction, 155
Self-esteem, 318, 441, 442
Self-evaluation, 239. *See also* Self-management
Self-fulfilling prophecy, 13
Self-help groups, 442
Self-help skills, 458
Self-injury, 264
Self-management, 239-241, 583-584
Self-monitoring. *See also* Self-management
    ADHD and, 426, 428-429
    emotional/behavioral disorders and, 239-240
    in employment training, 583-584
    forms for, 239, 428

Self-operated audio prompting systems (SOAPs), 396-398
Semantics, 299
Semicircular canals, 334-335
SEM (Schoolwide Enrichment Model), 518-519
Sensorineural hearing loss, 338-339
Separate classrooms
    communication disorders and, 327
    in continuum of alternative placements, 74-75
    federal government definition of, 37
    giftedness/talent and, 491-492, 521-522
    learning disabilities and, 205
Separate schools, 37, 75, 521
Service learning, 8-9, 130-131
Severe disabilities, defined, 453-454. See also Severe/multiple disabilities
Severe discrepancy, 180
Severe hearing loss, 345, 346
Severe mental retardation, 132, 453
Severe/multiple disabilities. See also Educational approaches to severe/multiple disabilities
    causes of, 459
    challenges/rewards of, 486
    characteristics of, 457-458
    definitions of, 453-455
    educational approaches to, 452, 463-481, 484-485
    educational placement alternatives for, 480-481, 484-485
    featured teacher, 451-453
    prevalence of, 12, 458-459
    tips for beginning teachers, 487
Severe orthopedic impairment, 407
Shaken baby syndrome, 460
Shaping, 241
Shelley, Mary, 512
Sheltered employment, 584-585
Shopping game, 393
Short-term memory, 139
Shunts, 413
SIAs (special interest areas), 265-267
Siblings without disabilities, 97
Sighted guides, 392
Signal flags, 38-39
Signs, iconic, 298, 359
Simcom (simultaneous communication), 353, 355, 358-359
Simon, Theodore, 148
Simple partial seizure, 415
Simultaneous communication (simcom), 353, 355, 358-359
Skincare, 441
Slate-and-stylus braille method, 383
Slight hearing loss, 346
SLPs. See Speech-language pathologists (SLPs)
Small business enterprise model, 579
Small group instruction, 479-480
Smart Board, 332
Smith v. Robinson (1984), 27
Snellen Eye Chart, 371, 381
SOAPs (self-operated audio prompting systems), 396-398
Social Communication Questionnaire, 270
Social criticism (literary genre), 511
Social role valorization (SRV), 164-165
Social service supports, 582
Social skills
    autism spectrum disorders and, 261, 282
    blindness/low vision and, 375-376
    deafness/hearing loss and, 337-338, 339
    diagnostic tools, 547
    early childhood special education and, 548
    emotional/behavioral disorders and, 221, 234-235
    intellectual disabilities and, 141
    learning disabilities and, 185
    life skills instruction and, 151
    physical disabilities/health impairments and, 427
    puppets to enhance, 552, 553
    severe/multiple disabilities and, 480-481, 484
    transitioning to adulthood and, 597
Social skills training (SST), 234-235, 597
Social stories, 280-282

Social studies, 130, 520
Social supports, 582
Social work services, 25
Sociodramatic play, 553
SonicGuide, 393
Sound, 335-336
Spanish-speaking children, 314. See also Diversity issues; Hispanic students
Spastic cerebral palsy, 410, 434
Speaking. See Speech
Special education, 35-41
    challenges in, 42-44
    defining features of, 41-42
    federal funding of, 23
    future of, 82-84
    as instruction, 36-37, 40
    as intervention, 35-36
    process of, 51-60
    statistics, 11-12
Special Education Act (1961), 32
Special interest areas (SIAs), 265-267
Special schools, 37, 75, 521
Specific learning disability, 173, 187
Specific reading disability, 179
Speech
    cued, 355
    deafness/hearing loss and, 337
    defined, 299
    development of, 300-303
    production of, 299-300
    skills, 151
Speech audiometry, 342
Speech clinicians. See Speech-language pathologists (SLPs)
Speech impairments, 304, 310. See also Communication disorders
Speech-language pathologists (SLPs)
    blindness/low vision and, 370
    communication disorders and, 309
    educational approaches and, 315-316
    educational placement alternatives and, 325, 326, 327
    language disorders and, 319
    physical disabilities/health impairments and, 433
    screening for communication disorders and, 311, 313
    stuttering and, 317
    voice disorders and, 317
Speech-language pathology services, 25
Speech organs, 299-300
Speech phobia, 218
Speech processors, in cochlear implants, 347
Speechreading, 354-355
Speech reception threshold, 342
Speech-sound errors, 306-307, 316
Speech teachers. See Speech-language pathologists (SLPs)
Speech therapists. See Speech-language pathologists (SLPs)
Speech-to-text translation, 350
Spina bifida, 411, 413
Spina bifida occulta, 411
Spinal cord injuries, 414-415
Splinter skills, 262
Spratt, Ronni, 38-39
SRV (social role valorization), 164-165
SST (social skills training), 234-235, 597
Standard celeration chart, 192
Standard deviation, 136-137
Stanford-Binet Intelligence Scale, 137, 148
Stanford Diagnostic Mathematics Test, 190
Station teaching, 62
Stereotypy, 263, 279, 375, 458
Still's disease, 420
Stimulus control, 156-157
Stirrup, 334
Stokoe, William, 352, 359
Strabismus, 378, 379
Structure of Intellect model, 499
Stuart v. Nappi (1978), 28
Student participation in IEP process, 22
Student study teams, 56
Student support teams, 53

Students with disabilities, as term, 9-10
Stuttering, 307-308, 316-317, 318, 326
Stuyvesant High School, 521
Substitutions, as speech-sound error, 306
Sugai, G., 248-249
Sullivan, Anne, 380
Summative evaluation, 190
Summer programs, 518
SUNY Fredonia Classwide Student Tutoring Teams (CSTT), 78
Superior cognitive students, 491
Supported employment, 578-584
Supported living, 588-590
Supported self-employment, 580
Supports
    community, 582
    deafness/hearing loss, 346-351
    extensive, 134
    intermittent, 134
    limited, 134
    natural, 580, 582
    organizational, 582
    peer, 242
    personal and family, 582
    pervasive, 134
    physical, 582
    social, 582
    social service, 582
    training, 582
    visual, 256, 277-282
Surgically implanted devices, 25
Survival skills, 151
Symbol sets, 322-323
Symbol systems, 323
Syndrome, defined, 143
Syntax, 299
Synthesizing ability, 499
Systematic Screening for Behavioral Disorders, 229
Systems of care, 249

Tactile aids and manipulatives, 383
Taking Part (Cartledge & Kleefeld), 235
Talent. See Giftedness/talent
Talking Books, 372, 381
Talking Game, 554-555
Talking Photo Albums, 118-119
Tandem mass spectrometry, 146
TASH, 91, 454, 590-591
Task analysis, 152-153
Task cards, 78-79
Teachable moments, 289
Teacher aides, 60
Teacher assistance teams, 53
Teacher-parent communication. See Parent-teacher communication
Teachers. See also Beginning teachers, tips for; Featured Teachers feature
    general education, 71, 76
    parent/family involvement with, 92
    parents as, 96
    with physical disabilities/health impairments, 405-407
    recruiting attention of, 222-223
Teaching & Learning feature
    Asperger syndrome, 266-267
    cerebral palsy, 412-413
    choral responding, 158-159
    classwide peer tutoring, 78-80
    explicit instruction, 196-198
    fluency-building activities, 20-21
    gifted students, 510-512
    guided notes, 200-202
    multimedia activity schedules, 278-279
    Mystery Motivators, 244-245
    naturalistic teaching strategies, 476-477
    Next Chapter Book Club, 594-595
    parent appreciation letters, 114-115
    Peer Buddy Program, 482-483
    puppets in early childhood classroom, 552-553
    recruiting teacher attention, 222-223
    response cards, 162-163
    self-monitoring, 428-429
    severe disabilities, 476-477

signal flags, 38-39
Talking Photo Albums, 118-119
teacher praise, 236-237
toys, 412-413, 538-539
Teaming, 60-62, 433-435, 572
Teams, 53, 56, 61-62, 172
Team teaching, 62
Technology-dependent students, 443
Technology-Related Assistance for Individuals with
    Disabilities Act (1988), 34, 432
Television captioning, 350-351
Television systems, closed-circuit, 386
Temperament, 225
Temporal bone, 334
Terman, Lewis, 148
Tertiary intervention, 176-177
Tertiary prevention, 35, 238, 248
Test of Auditory Discrimination, 312
Test of Language Development, 313
Test of Mathematical Abilities, 190
Test of Phonological Awareness, 313
Test of Reading Comprehension, 190
Tests. *See also* IQ tests; *specific tests*
    achievement, 189-190
    articulation, 312
    auditory discrimination, 312
    classwide peer tutoring and, 79
    criterion-referenced, 190
    hearing, 312
    norm-referenced, 136, 189-190
    projective, 230
    screening, 51, 229-230
Tetraplegia, 410, 414
Text telephones, 351
Theater, participatory, 332
Thematic Apperception Test, 230
Therapeutic nurseries, 286
*Thinking in Pictures and Other Reports of My Life
    with Autism* (Grandin), 263
Think-pair-share, 50-51
Three-dimensional transition services model, 570
Tiered lessons, 513, 514
Time out, 241
Timers, digital, 250
Time trials, 21
Timothy W. v. Rochester School District (1989), 27, 29
Tinnitus, 341
Tips for beginning teachers. *See* Beginning teachers,
    tips for
Toddlers, 22-23, 540-543. *See also* Early childhood
    special education
To-Do lists, 45
Tohono O'Odham students, 504. *See also* Diversity
    issues
Token economy, 241
Topography (behavior dimension), 231
TORCHES, 341
Total communication, 353, 355, 358-359
Totally blind, 373
Tourette syndrome, 219, 422
Toys, 412-413, 538-539
Tracking, 385, 523-524
Tragedy (literary genre), 511
Trainable mentally retarded, as term, 133

Training supports, 582
Transdisciplinary teams, 62
Transferring, 441, 442
Transitional workshops, 584
Transitioning to adulthood, 565-597
    as challenge, 43
    employment, 568, 574-575, 577-585
    featured teacher, 565-566
    parent/family involvement during, 100
    postsecondary education, 568, 585-586
    recreation and leisure, 591-592, 594-595
    residential alternatives, 586-591
    statistics, 567-569
    tips for beginning teachers, 597
    transition services and models, 569-574,
        576-577
    ultimate transition goal, 592-593, 596
Transitions during school, 548-549, 552-553
Transition services and models
    beginning transition activities early, 572-574,
        576-577
    Halpern's three-dimensional model, 570
    in IDEA, 570-571
    individualized transition plans, 570-572, 573
    transition teaming, 572
    Will's bridges model of school-to-work
        transition, 569
Transition teaming, 572
Transmitters, in cochlear implants, 347
Transportation, 25
Trask-Tyler, Sandie, 129-131
Traumatic brain injury, 432, 459-463
Travel aids, electronic, 392-393
Tremor type of cerebral palsy, 410-411
Trends. *See* Current Issues and Future Trends feature
Trials to criterion measure, 139
Triplegia, 410
Tuberculosis, 431
Tunnel vision, 372
Turner syndrome, 423
Tutoring, 77, 78-80, 242
Tutors, parents as, 117-120
20/20 analysis, 14
Tyler, Donelle, 533-535
Tympanic membrane, 334
Type 1 diabetes, 417
Type 2 diabetes, 417

Unaided AAC techniques, 321
Underresponsiveness, 263
Unilateral hearing loss, 339
United Cerebral Palsy Association, 91, 432
Universal precautions, 420
University of California at Los Angeles, 273-274
University of Rochester, 350, 352, 364
U.S. Department of Education, 37
U.S. Department of Health, Education, and Welfare,
    590
U.S. Office of Special Education, 194

Vaccinations, 269
Van Tassel-Baska, Joyce, 520
Victor (Wild Boy of Aveyron), 147, 148

Video, 277-279
Vineland Adaptive Behavior Scales, 138
Vision, 376-377. *See also* Blindness/low vision
Vision specialists, 394-395
Visual acuity, 371-372
Visual and visual-motor skills, 384, 385
Visual cortex, 377
Visual efficiency, 384
Visual impairment, defined, 373. *See also*
    Blindness/low vision
Visually challenged, as term, 15
Visual naming speed, 181-182
Visual phonics, 355, 356-358
Visual/spatial intelligence, 516
Visual supports, 256, 277-282
Vitreous humor, 376
Vocabulary building, 319, 326
Vocational instruction, 130, 597
Voice disorders, 308, 317, 319. *See also* Speech
    impairments
Voice mail, 113
Voices for Choices, 596
Voyager Passport, Level A, 196, 197

Walker Social Skills Curriculum, The (Walker et
    al.), 235
Watts, Chris, 439
Wayne County Training School, 193
Websites, class, 113
Weschler Intelligence Scale for Children (WISC-IV),
    137
Wheelchairs, 436, 446
Wide Range Achievement Test-4, 190
Wild Boy of Aveyron, 147, 148
Willard, M. J., 438
Williams syndrome, 145, 423
Will's bridges model of school-to-work transition,
    569
Wing, Lorna, 272
WISC-IV (Weschler Intelligence Scale for Children),
    137
Within-class grouping, 524-525
Wolfensberger, Wolf, 148
Woodcock-Johnson III Tests of Achievement, 189
Woodcock Reading Mastery Test, 190
Work activity centers, 584
Work enclave model, 579-580
Working memory, 139
Workshops, sheltered, 584-585
World Institute on Disability, 432
Write-on response cards, 163
Writing, 130, 151, 510-512, 576-577
Written language deficits, 182, 184
Wyatt v. Stickney (1972), 26

X-linked hearing loss, 340
XYZ grouping, 523-524

Young Autism Project, 272

Zazula, Judi, 438
Zero hearing-threshold level, 335
Zero reject, 19, 29

CREDITS

Photo Credits

Katelyn Metzger/Merrill, pp. iv, 5, 6, 15, 19, 20, 23, 41, 59, 65, 127, 179, 192, 205, 235, 242, 368, 383, 387, 389, 391, 396, 426, 430, 433, 443, 455, 474, 588, 600; David Mager/Pearson Learning Photo Studio, p. 2; Laura Bolesta/Merrill, pp. 11, 55, 62, 74, 135, 150, 182, 254, 262, 264, 275, 288, 454, 464, 466; Masterfile Royalty Free Division, p. 30; Anthony Magnacca/Merrill, pp. 38, 43, 48, 83, 170, 519, 532; David Young-Wolff/PhotoEdit Inc., pp. 58, 480, 494; Scott Cunningham/Merrill, pp. 81, 111, 132, 156, 161, 162, 174, 222, 246, 299, 333, 346, 354, 359, 373, 404, 411, 412, 413, 450, 484, 503, 506, 536, 538, 564, 579, 591; Laura Dwight/PhotoEdit Inc., pp. 88, 117, 547; Amy Etra/PhotoEdit Inc., p. 91; Robin Nelson/PhotoEdit Inc., p. 97; Michael Newman/PhotoEdit Inc., pp. 104, 342, 360, 539; Paul Conklin/PhotoEdit Inc., pp. 108, 160; Charles Wood, p. 118; Jeff Greenberg/PhotoEdit Inc., p. 120; Mark Richards/PhotoEdit Inc., p. 128; Photolibrary.com/Index Stock, p. 139; Mika/Corbis/Zefa Collection, pp. 141, 154, 567; PunchStock, p. 184; Richard Hutchings/PhotoEdit Inc., p. 210; Tony Freeman/PhotoEdit Inc., p. 216; Mary Kate Denny/PhotoEdit Inc., pp. 227, 294; Natalie Allen-Williams, p. 245; Lori Whitley/Merrill, pp. 258, 271, 282, 372, 544, 548, 553; courtesy of Robert Stromer, p. 278; Silver Burdett Ginn, p. 303; Bill Bachmann Photography, p. 306; Patrick White/Merrill, pp. 313, 316; Gail Meese/Meese Photo Research, p. 324; Will & Deni McIntyre/Photo Researchers, Inc., p. 330; San Francisco SPCA Hearing Dog Program, p. 351; Rachel Friedmann Narr, pp. 356, 357; Elizabeth Young-Dove, p. 374; Janis Miglavs/Image Source, Inc., p. 390; Bob Daemmrich/The Image Works, p. 395; courtesy of Behavioral Dynamics, Inc., p. 429; Will Hart/PhotoEdit Inc., pp. 436, 592; photo provided by Canine Companions for Independence, p. 437; Daniel Bernstein, pp. 438, 439; courtesy of Helping Hands: Monkey Helpers for the Disabled, Inc., p. 440; Lauren Shear/Photo Researchers, Inc., p. 458; Ariel Skelley/Corbis/Bettmann, p. 468; Getty Images–Stockbyte, p. 490; Kevork Djansezian/AP Wide World Photos, p. 499; Susan Burger/www.naturephotohawaii.com, p. 518; AP Wide World Photos, p. 531; Carl Harris/Merrill, p. 552; Hattie Young/Photo Researchers, Inc., p. 559; Jorgen Schytte/Peter Arnold, Inc., p. 574; Doug Menuez/Getty Images, Inc.–Photodisc, p. 586; © Ellen B. Senisi/Ellen Senisi, p. 589; Next Chapter Book Club, The Ohio State University, p. 595; Kamenko Pajic/AP Wide World Photos, p. 596. The Featured Teacher photos were supplied by the teachers shown.

Text Credits

p. 12. Excerpt from Kauffman: From "Appearances, stigma, and prevention" by J. M. Kauffman, 2003. *Remedial and Special Education, 24,* 195-198. Copyright 2003 by the Hammill Institute on Disability. Reprinted by permission.

p. 82. Excerpt from Zigmond: From "Where should students with disabilities receive special education services? Is one place better than another?" By N. Zigmond, 2003. *Journal of Special Education, 37,* 193-199. Copyright 2003 by the Hammill Institute on Disability. Reprinted by permission.

p. 266. Excerpt about Carlos: From "'GOTCHA!' Twenty-five behavior traps guaranteed to extend your students' academic and social skills" by S. R. Alber and W. L. Heward, 1996, *Intervention in School and Clinic, 31,* 285-289. Copyright 1996 by the Hammill Institute on Disability. Reprinted by permission.

p. 424. Excerpt from Klein, K. "Pencils, pens, meds. As kids head to class, pharmaceutical companies ramp up their drug marketing—and it works." Copyright © 2007, *Los Angeles Times.* Reprinted by permission.

p. 425. Excerpt from "Teacher knowledge of stimulant medication and ADHD" by V. E. Snider, T. Busch, and L. Arrowood, 2003, *Remedial and Special Education, 24,* 46-56. Copyright 2003 by the Hammill Institute on Disability. Reprinted with permission.

p. 455. Excerpt from "Comparison of the effects of three approaches on the frequency of stimulus activations via a single switch by students with profound intellectual disabilities" by L. C. Mechling, 2006, *The Journal of Special Education, 40,* 94-102. Copyright 2006 by the Hammill Institute on Disability. Reprinted by permission.

p. 457. Excerpt from Smithdas, R., "Psychological aspects of deaf-blindness" in Sara R. Walsh and Robert Holzbert, *Understanding and educating the deaf-blind/severely and profoundly handicapped: An international perspective,* 1981. Courtesy of Charles C. Thomas Publisher, Ltd., Springfield, Illinois.

p. 506. Excerpt from "Addressing the social and emotional needs of twice-exceptional learners" by E. W. King, *Teaching Exceptional Children, 38*(1), 2005, p. 19. Copyright 2005 by The Council for Exceptional Children. Reprinted by permission.

pp. 589-590. Excerpt from Klein, J. (1994). Supported living: Not just another "rung" on the continuum. *TASH Newsletter, 20*(7), 16-18. Used by permission.